Cases on
Criminal Procedure
2013-2014

ASPEN COURSEBOOK SERIES

Cases on Criminal Procedure 2013-2014

ROBERT M. BLOOM

Professor of Law
Boston College Law School

Wolters Kluwer
Law & Business

Printed in the United States of America.

1 2 3 4 5 6 7 8 9 0

ISBN 978-1-4548-1068-1

Library of Congress Cataloging-in-Publication Data

Bloom, Robert M.
   Cases on criminal procedure : 2013-2014 / Robert M. Bloom, professor of law, Boston College Law School.
       pages cm. — (Aspen coursebook series)
   ISBN 978-1-4548-1068-1
   1. Criminal procedure—United States. 2. Criminal procedure—United States—Cases. I. Title.

   KF9619.85B584 2013
   345.73'05—dc23

                                                                    2012041509

About Wolters Kluwer Law & Business

Wolters Kluwer Law & Business is a leading global provider of intelligent information and digital solutions for legal and business professionals in key specialty areas, and respected educational resources for professors and law students. Wolters Kluwer Law & Business connects legal and business professionals as well as those in the education market with timely, specialized authoritative content and information-enabled solutions to support success through productivity, accuracy and mobility.

Serving customers worldwide, Wolters Kluwer Law & Business products include those under the Aspen Publishers, CCH, Kluwer Law International, Loislaw, Best Case, ftwilliam.com and MediRegs family of products.

CCH products have been a trusted resource since 1913, and are highly regarded resources for legal, securities, antitrust and trade regulation, government contracting, banking, pension, payroll, employment and labor, and healthcare reimbursement and compliance professionals.

Aspen Publishers products provide essential information to attorneys, business professionals and law students. Written by preeminent authorities, the product line offers analytical and practical information in a range of specialty practice areas from securities law and intellectual property to mergers and acquisitions and pension/benefits. Aspen's trusted legal education resources provide professors and students with high-quality, up-to-date and effective resources for successful instruction and study in all areas of the law.

Kluwer Law International products provide the global business community with reliable international legal information in English. Legal practitioners, corporate counsel and business executives around the world rely on Kluwer Law journals, looseleafs, books, and electronic products for comprehensive information in many areas of international legal practice.

Loislaw is a comprehensive online legal research product providing legal content to law firm practitioners of various specializations. Loislaw provides attorneys with the ability to quickly and efficiently find the necessary legal information they need, when and where they need it, by facilitating access to primary law as well as state-specific law, records, forms and treatises.

Best Case Solutions is the leading bankruptcy software product to the bankruptcy industry. It provides software and workflow tools to flawlessly streamline petition preparation and the electronic filing process, while timely incorporating ever-changing court requirements.

ftwilliam.com offers employee benefits professionals the highest quality plan documents (retirement, welfare and non-qualified) and government forms (5500/PBGC, 1099 and IRS) software at highly competitive prices.

MediRegs products provide integrated health care compliance content and software solutions for professionals in healthcare, higher education and life sciences, including professionals in accounting, law and consulting.

Wolters Kluwer Law & Business, a division of Wolters Kluwer, is headquartered in New York. Wolters Kluwer is a market-leading global information services company focused on professionals.

To my wife, Tina, my children, Martha, David, and Stephanie, my grandchildren, Liam and Matthew, and to the memory of my parents, Henry and Martha.

R.M.B.

Summary of Contents

Contents   xi
Table of Cases   xix
Preface   xxiii
Acknowledgments   xxv
Pertinent Amendments to the Constitution of the United States   xxvii
Justices of the Supreme Court from 1930 to the Present   xxix

CHAPTER 1
Exclusionary Rule   1

CHAPTER 2
Search and Seizure—Fourth Amendment   129

CHAPTER 3
Level of Justification   243

CHAPTER 4
Warrants   471

CHAPTER 5
Interrogation   649

CHAPTER 6
Eyewitness Identification   965

Contents

Table of Cases   *xix*

Preface   *xxiii*

Acknowledgments   *xxv*

Pertinent Amendments to the Constitution of the United States   *xxvii*

Justices of the Supreme Court from 1930 to the Present   *xxix*

CHAPTER 1
Exclusionary Rule   1

Introduction   1

A. Origin of the Exclusionary Rule   2
      Weeks v. United States   2
      Silverthorne Lumber Company v. United States   4

B. Applicability to States   6
      Wolf v. Colorado   6
      Mapp v. Ohio   11

C. Incorporation   20
      Adamson v. People of State of California   20

D. Early Criticism   29
      Bivens v. Six Unknown Named Agents of Federal Bureau of Narcotics   29

E. Direct Cutbacks   33
     1. Balancing   33
      United States v. Calandra   33
      Pennsylvania Board of Probation & Parole v. Scott   38
     2. Good-Faith Exception to the Exclusionary Rule   44
      United States v. Leon   44
      Massachusetts v. Sheppard   53
      Groh v. Ramirez   55
      Messerschmidt v. Millender   60
      Illinois v. Krull   60
      Arizona v. Evans   65

Herring v. United States	68
Davis v. United States	76
F. Exceptions to Fruits Doctrine	**88**
Wong Sun v. United States	88
Brown v. Illinois	92
Murray v. United States	95
Nix, Warden of the Iowa State Penitentiary v. Williams	100
Hudson v. Michigan	103
G. Standing	**116**
Jones v. United States	116
Rakas v. Illinois	119

CHAPTER 2

4 ✓

Search and Seizure—Fourth Amendment

	129
Introduction	**129**
A. Overview	**130**
New Jersey v. T.L.O.	130
B. Expectation of Privacy	**145**
1. Overview	145
Katz v. United States	145
United States v. Jones	152
2. Area Considerations	166
Oliver v. United States	166
3. Third Party	172
Hoffa v. United States	172
United States v. White	175
United States v. Miller	179
California v. Greenwood	183
4. Enhancement Devices	189
a. Public Places	189
United States v. Place	189
Illinois v. Caballes	192
United States v. Knotts	195
United States v. Jones	198
Bond v. United States	198
b. Home	201
Kyllo v. United States	201
c. Curtilage	208
United States v. Dunn	208
California v. Greenwood	214
Florida v. Riley	214

C. Standing
   1. Original   224
      Jones v. United States   224
   2. Merging of Expectation of Privacy with Standing   224
      Rakas v. Illinois   224
      Rawlings v. Kentucky   224
      Minnesota v. Olson   230
      Minnesota v. Carter   234
      Brendlin v. California   238

CHAPTER 3
Level of Justification   243

Introduction   243

A. Probable Cause   245
   1. Generally   245
      Aguilar v. Texas   245
      Spinelli v. United States   247
      Illinois v. Gates   253
      United States v. Grubbs   265
   2. Pretext and Scope of Probable Cause   270
      Maryland v. Pringle   270
      Whren v. United States   273
      Atwater v. City of Lago Vista   277
      Virginia v. Moore   289
      Florence v. Burlington   292

B. Reasonable Suspicion   300
   1. Overview   300
      Camara v. Municipal Court of San Francisco   300
      Terry v. Ohio   305
   2. When Does a Stop Implicate the Fourth Amendment?   318
      United States v. Mendenhall   318
      California v. Hodari D.   325
      United States v. Drayton   331
   3. Reasonable Suspicion Standard   337
      United States v. Arvizu   337
      Illinois v. Wardlow   341
      Florida v. J.L.   345
      Virginia v. Harris   347
   4. Scope of *Terry* Stop   349
      Hiibel v. Sixth Judicial District Court of Nevada,
      Humboldt County   349
      Michigan v. Long   354
      United States v. Place   358
      Minnesota v. Dickerson   362

Illinois v. Caballes	367
Arizona v. United States	370
Arizona v. Johnson	389
C. Administrative Searches	394
1. Housing	394
Camara v. Municipal Court of San Francisco	394
2. Schools	394
Safford Unified School District #1 v. Redding	394
Board of Education of Independent School District No. 92 of Pottawatomie County v. Earls	402
3. Roadways	415
Michigan Department of State Police v. Sitz	415
City of Indianapolis v. Edmond	423
Illinois v. Lidster	428
4. Workplace	433
Skinner v. Railway Labor	433
Chandler v. Miller	448
5. Probation	455
Samson v. California	455
6. Borders	461
United States v. Martinez-Fuerte	461
United States v. Flores-Montano	468

CHAPTER 4
Warrants

Warrants	**471**
Introduction	**471**
A. Arrest Warrants	472
Chimel v. California	472
Maryland v. Buie	480
Payton v. New York	485
Steagald v. United States	494
B. Search Warrants	499
Lo-Ji Sales, Inc. v. New York	499
Andresen v. Maryland	503
Messerschmidt v. Millender	507
United States v. Banks	522
Illinois v. McArthur	525
Hudson v. Michigan	528
C. Exceptions to Warrant Requirement	543
1. Consent	543
Schneckloth v. Bustamonte	543
Illinois v. Rodriguez	554

Georgia v. Randolph	
Florida v. Jimeno	569
2. Plain View	572
Arizona v. Hicks	572
Minnesota v. Dickerson	577
3. Search Incident to Arrest	579
Chimel v. California	579
United States v. Robinson	579
Florence v. Burlington	589
Maryland v. Buie	589
4. Automobile — Search Incident to Arrest	589
New York v. Belton	589
Thornton v. United States	595
Arizona v. Gant	602
5. Probable Cause to Search an Automobile	615
Carroll v. United States	615
Chambers v. Maroney	616
California v. Acevedo	620
6. Exigent Circumstances	631
Welsh v. Wisconsin	631
Brigham City, Utah v. Stuart	633
Michigan v. Fisher	635
Kentucky v. King	639

CHAPTER 5

Interrogation

Interrogation	**649**
Introduction	649
A. Voluntariness	651
1. Historical	651
Brown v. State of Mississippi	651
Rogers v. Richmond	655
2. Modern	660
Colorado v. Connelly	660
Arizona v. Fulminante	670
Torture: Extract from Israeli Supreme Court Ruling	683
B. Movement Away from Voluntariness Standard	684
Malloy v. Hogan	684
Massiah v. United States	686
Escobedo v. Illinois	690
C. *Miranda*	695
1. *Miranda v. Arizona*	695
Miranda v. Arizona	695
2. Warnings	716
Florida v. Powell	716

Contents

3. Custody	722
Berkemer v. McCarty	722
Yarborough v. Alvarado	726
J.D.B. v. North Carolina	737
Howes v. Fields	752
4. Interrogation	760
Rhode Island v. Innis	760
Arizona v. Mauro	768
Illinois v. Perkins	774
Pennsylvania v. Muniz	779
5. *Miranda* Waiver	787
a. Overview	787
North Carolina v. Butler	787
Colorado v. Spring	791
Connecticut v. Barrett	795
Davis v. United States	799
b. Silence	805
Michigan v. Mosley	805
Berghuis v. Thompkins	811
c. Request for Counsel	827
Edwards v. Arizona	827
Oregon v. Bradshaw	832
Maryland v. Shatzer	838
6. *Miranda* and the Exclusionary Rule	845
Oregon v. Elstad	845
New York v. Quarles	859
7. *Miranda* Reconsidered	869
Dickerson v. United States	869
Chavez v. Martinez	880
Missouri v. Seibert	889
United States v. Patane	898
D. Sixth Amendment	903
1. Mechanism to Analyze Interrogation	903
Massiah v. United States	903
Brewer v. Williams	903
United States v. Henry	917
Kuhlmann v. Wilson	921
Texas v. Cobb	926
2. Waiver	932
Michigan v. Jackson	932
Patterson v. Illinois	937
Montejo v. Louisiana	943
3. Fruits Analysis and Exclusionary Rule	957
Fellers v. United States	957
Kansas v. Ventris	959

CHAPTER 6
Eyewitness Identification

Introduction   965

A. Warren Court Approach   966
    United States v. Wade   966
    Stovall v. Denno   977
    Gilbert v. California   980

B. Sixth Amendment — Attachment of Right to Counsel   982
    Kirby v. Illinois   982
    Rothgery v. Gillespie County, Texas   987
    United States v. Ash   989

C. Due Process   998
    Manson v. Brathwaite   998
    Perry v. New Hampshire   1009

Table of Cases

Adamson v. People of State of California, 332 U.S. 46 (1947) — 1, 20
Aguilar v. Texas, 378 U.S. 108 (1964) — 243, 245
Andresen v. Maryland, 427 U.S. 463 (1976) — 471, 503
Arizona v. Evans, 514 U.S. 1 (1995) — 2, 65
Arizona v. Fulminante, 499 U.S. 279 (1991) — 649, 670
Arizona v. Gant, 556 U.S. 332 (2009) — 472, 602
Arizona v. Hicks, 480 U.S. 321 (1987) — 472, 572
Arizona v. Johnson, 555 U.S. 323 (2009) — 244, 389
Arizona v. Mauro, 481 U.S. 520 (1987) — 650, 768
Arizona v. United States, 132 S. Ct. 2492 (2012) — 370
Arvizu; United States v., 534 U.S. 266 (2002) — 244, 337
Ash; United States v., 413 U.S. 300 (1973) — 965, 989
Atwater v. City of Lago Vista, 532 U.S. 318 (2001) — 243, 277

Banks; United States v., 540 U.S. 31 (2003) — 471, 522
Berghuis v. Thompkins, 130 S. Ct. 2250 (2010) — 650, 811
Berkemer v. McCarty, 468 U.S. 420 (1984) — 650, 722
Bivens v. Six Unknown Named Agents of Federal Bureau
   of Narcotics, 403 U.S. 388 (1971) — 2, 29
Board of Education of Independent School District
   No. 92 of Pottawatomie County v. Earls, 536 U.S. 822 (2002) — 244, 402
Bond v. United States, 529 U.S. 334 (2000) — 130, 198
Brendlin v. California, 551 U.S. 249 (2007) — 130, 238
Brewer v. Williams, 430 U.S. 387 (1977) — 650, 903
Brigham City, Utah v. Stuart, 547 U.S. 398 (2006) — 472, 633
Brown v. Illinois, 422 U.S. 590 (1975) — 2, 649
Brown v. State of Mississippi, 297 U.S. 278 (1936) — 2, 651

Calandra; United States v., 414 U.S. 338 (1974) — 2, 33
California v. Acevedo, 500 U.S. 565 (1991) — 472, 620
California v. Greenwood, 486 U.S. 35 (1988) — 130, 183, 214
California v. Hodari D., 499 U.S. 621 (1991) — 325
Camara v. Municipal Court of San Francisco, 387 U.S. 523 (1967) — 243, 300, 394
Carroll v. United States, 267 U.S. 132 (1925) — 472, 615
Chambers v. Maroney, 399 U.S. 42 (1970) — 472, 616
Chandler v. Miller, 520 U.S. 305 (1997) — 448
Chavez v. Martinez, 538 U.S. 760 (2003) — 650, 880

Chimel v. California, 395 U.S. 752 (1969)   471, 472
City of Indianapolis. *See Indianapolis, City of.*
Colorado v. Connelly, 479 U.S. 157 (1986)   649, 660
Colorado v. Spring, 479 U.S. 564 (1987)   650, 791
Connecticut v. Barrett, 479 U.S. 523 (1987)   650, 795

Davis v. United States, 131 S. Ct. 2419 (2011)   2, 76
Davis v. United States, 512 U.S. 452 (1994)   650, 799
Dickerson v. United States, 530 U.S. 428 (2000)   244, 362, 472, 577, 650, 869
Drayton; United States v., 536 U.S. 194 (2002)   244, 331
Dunn; United States v., 480 U.S. 294 (1987)   130, 208

Edwards v. Arizona, 451 U.S. 477 (1981)   650, 827
Escobedo v. Illinois, 378 U.S. 478 (1964)   649, 690

Fellers v. United States, 540 U.S. 519 (2004)   650, 957
Florence v. Burlington, 132 S. Ct. 1510 (2012)   243, 292, 589
Flores-Montano; United States v., 541 U.S. 149 (2004)   244, 468
Florida v. J.L., 529 U.S. 266 (2000)   244, 345
Florida v. Jimeno, 500 U.S. 248 (1991)   471, 569
Florida v. Powell, 130 S. Ct. 1195 (2009)   650, 716
Florida v. Riley, 488 U.S. 445 (1985)   130, 214

Georgia v. Randolph, 547 U.S. 103 (2006)   471, 559
Gilbert v. California, 388 U.S. 263 (1967)   965, 980
Groh v. Ramirez, 540 U.S. 551 (2004)   55
Grubbs; United States v., 547 U.S. 90 (2006)   243, 265

Henry; United States v., 447 U.S. 264 (1980)   650, 917
Herring v. United States, 555 U.S. 135 (2009)   2, 68
Hiibel v. Sixth Judicial District Court of Nevada,
     Humboldt County, 542 U.S. 177 (2004)   244, 349
Hoffa v. United States, 385 U.S. 293 (1966)   130, 172
Howes v. Fields, 131 S. Ct. 1047 (2011)   650, 752
Hudson v. Michigan, 547 U.S. 586 (2006)   2, 103, 528

Illinois v. Caballes, 543 U.S. 405 (2005)   130, 192, 244, 367
Illinois v. Gates, 462 U.S. 213 (1983)   243, 253
Illinois v. Krull, 480 U.S. 340 (1987)   2, 60
Illinois v. Lidster, 540 U.S. 419 (2004)   428
Illinois v. McArthur, 531 U.S. 326 (2001)   471, 525
Illinois v. Perkins, 496 U.S. 292 (1990)   650, 774
Illinois v. Rodriguez, 497 U.S. 177 (1990)   471, 554
Illinois v. Wardlow, 528 U.S. 119 (2000)   341
Indianapolis, City of, v. Edmond, 531 U.S. 32 (2000)   244, 423
Israel, Supreme Court: Extract from Ruling on
     Torture, J.D.B. v. North Carolina, 131 S. Ct. 2394 (2011)   649, 683

Jones, United States v., 132 S. Ct. 945 (2012)   152, 198
Jones v. United States, 362 U.S. 257 (1960)   2, 116, 130, 224

Kansas v. Ventris, 556 U.S. 586 (2009)   650, 959
Katz v. United States, 389 U.S. 347 (1967)   130, 145
Kentucky v. King, 131 S. Ct. 1849 (2011)   472, 639
Kirby v. Illinois, 406 U.S. 682 (1972)   965, 982
Knotts, United States v., 460 U.S. 276 (1983)   130, 197
Kuhlmann v. Wilson, 477 U.S. 436 (1986)   650, 921
Kyllo v. United States, 533 U.S. 27 (2001)   130, 201

Leon; United States v., 468 U.S. 897 (1984)   2, 44
Lo-Ji Sales v. New York, 442 U.S.319 (1979)   471, 499

Malloy v. Hogan, 378 U.S. 1 (1964)   649, 684
Manson v. Brathwaite, 432 U.S. 98 (1977)   965, 998
Mapp v. Ohio, 367 U.S. 643 (1961)   1, 2, 11
Martinez-Fuerte; United States v., 428 U.S. 543 (1976)   244, 461
Maryland v. Buie, 494 U.S. 325 (1990)   471, 472, 480
Maryland v. Pringle, 540 U.S. 366 (2003)   270
Maryland v. Shatzer, 130 S. Ct. 1213 (2010)   650, 838
Massachusetts v. Sheppard, 468 U.S. 981 (1984)   51, 53
Massiah v. United States, 377 U.S. 201 (1964)   649, 650, 686
Mendenhall; United States v., 446 U.S. 544 (1980)   244, 318
Messerschmidt v. Millender, 132 S. Ct. 1235 (2012)   2, 60, 507
Michigan Department of State Police v. Sitz, 496 U.S. 444 (1990) 244, 415
Michigan v. Fisher, 130 S. Ct. 546 (2009)   472, 635
Michigan v. Jackson, 475 U.S. 625 (1986)   650, 932
Michigan v. Long, 463 U.S. 1032 (1983)   244, 354
Michigan v. Mosley, 423 U.S. 96 (1975)   650, 805
Miller; United States v., 425 U.S. 435 (1976)   130, 179
Minnesota v. Carter, 525 U.S. 83 (1998)   130, 234
Minnesota v. Dickerson, 508 U.S. 366 (1993)   244, 362, 472, 577, 869
Minnesota v. Olson, 495 U.S. 91 (1990)   130, 230
Miranda v. Arizona, 384 U.S. 436 (1966)   649, 650, 695
Missouri v. Seibert, 542 U.S. 600 (2004)   650, 889
Montejo v. Louisiana, 556 U.S. 778 (2009)   650, 943
Murray v. United States, 487 U.S. 533 (1988)   2, 95

New Jersey v. TLO, 469 U.S. 325 (1985)   129, 130
New York v. Belton, 453 U.S. 454 (1981)   589
New York v. Quarles, 467 U.S. 649 (1984)   650, 859
Nix, Warden of the Iowa State Penitentiary v. Williams,
     467 U.S. 431 (1984)   2, 100, 903
North Carolina v. Butler, 441 U.S. 369 (1979)   650, 787

Oliver v. United States, 466 U.S. 170 (1984)   130, 166
Oregon v. Bradshaw, 462 U.S. 1039 (1983)   832
Oregon v. Elstad, 470 U.S. 298 (1985)   650, 845

Patane; United States v., 542 U.S. 630 (2004)   650, 898
Patterson v. Illinois, 487 U.S. 285 (1988)   650, 937
Payton v. New York, 445 U.S. 573 (1980)   471, 485
Pennsylvania Board of Probation & Parole v.
    Scott, 524 U.S. 357 (1998)   2, 38
Pennsylvania v. Muniz, 496 U.S. 582 (1990)   650, 779
Perry v. New Hampshire, 132 S. Ct. 716 (2012)   965, 1009
Place; United States v., 462 U.S. 696 (1983)   130, 189, 358

Rakas v. Illinois, 439 U.S. 128 (1978)   2, 119, 130, 224
Rawlings v. Kentucky, 448 U.S. 98 (1980)   130, 224
Rhode Island v. Innis, 446 U.S. 291 (1980)   650, 760
Robinson; United States v., 414 U.S. 218 (1973)   472, 579
Rogers v. Richmond, 365 U.S. 534 (1961)   649, 655
Rothgery v. Gillespie County, 554 U.S. 191 (2008)   965, 987

Safford Unified School District #1 v. Redding,
    557 U.S. 364 (2009)   244, 394
Samson v. California, 547 U.S. 843 (2006)   244, 455
Schneckloth v. Bustamonte, 412 U.S. 218 (1973)   471, 543
Silverthorne Lumber Company v. United States,
    251 U.S. 385 (1920)   1, 2, 4
Skinner v. Railway Labor, 489 U.S. 602 (1989)   433
Spinelli v. United States, 393 U.S. 410 (1969)   243, 247
Steagald v. United States, 451 U.S. 204 (1981)   471, 494
Stovall v. Denno, 388 U.S. 293 (1967)   965, 977

Terry v. Ohio, 392 U.S. 1 (1968)   243, 244, 305, 349
Texas v. Cobb, 532 U.S. 162 (2001)   650, 926
Thornton v. United States, 541 U.S. 615 (2004)   472, 595

United States v. *See name of opposing party.*

Virginia v. Harris, 130 S. Ct. 10 (2009)   244, 347
Virginia v. Moore, 553 U.S. 164 (2008)   243, 289

Wade; United States v., 388 U.S. 218 (1967)   965, 966
Weeks v. United States, 232 U.S. 383 (1914)   1, 2
Welsh v. Wisconsin, 466 U.S. 740 (1984)   472, 631
White; United States v., 401 U.S. 745 (1971)   130, 175
Whren v. United States, 517 U.S. 806 (1996)   243, 273
Wolf v. Colorado, 338 U.S. 25 (1949)   1, 2, 6
Wong Sun v. United States, 371 U.S. 471 (1963)   2, 88

Yarborough v. Alvarado, 541 U.S. 652 (2004)   650, 726

Preface

Nowhere are differences in constitutional decision making by the United States Supreme Court in a confined period of time (the past 50 years) more graphic than in criminal procedure. Criminal procedure offers a rich opportunity to compare and contrast Supreme Court decisions on police practices involving the Fourth, Fifth, and Sixth Amendments to the United States Constitution. *Cases on Criminal Procedure* demonstrates the different approaches taken initially by the Warren Court and then later by the Burger, Rehnquist, and Roberts Courts as they sought to achieve a balance between individual rights and the ability of police to solve crime. So that students can graphically observe how the justices have undertaken to balance those issues in their decision making, the book sets forth the voting alignment for each case and also includes a chart of the makeup of the Court, allowing readers to monitor the individual justices involved in each decision.

The differences in approaches taken by the Supreme Court are considered not only for comparative purposes but also to identify approaches taken by many states as they interpret their own laws. In recent years, the present Supreme Court has interpreted the United States Constitution in a way that curtails individual rights. As a result, some states have turned to their own constitutions to provide greater individual rights, those that were previously provided by the Warren Court. Some characterize this approach as the "new federalism." In addition, societal challenges such as the war on drugs and the war on terror have influenced Court decisions and can explain the curtailment of individual rights since the Warren Court. The cases in this book have been arranged with such themes in mind.

Each chapter opens with a brief introduction describing the relevance of each case presented. Students will observe that the cases during the Warren Court often were more protective of the individual and restrictive of police power. Subsequent Supreme Courts have often somewhat limited individual rights and have been more permissive with regard to police power. I deliberately refrain from significant analysis of the cases presented so that teachers can have maximum range and authority in their pedagogical approach. The number of cases included is expansive, to provide teachers with the flexibility to select the particular cases that best fit their teaching.

The book can also be used as a reference tool for study and application of the Fourth, Fifth, and Sixth Amendments.

To introduce the different approaches taken by the Supreme Court, the cases in Chapter 1 deal with the exclusionary rule, the principal remedy for addressing constitutional violations. The chapter illustrates how the rule has evolved and outlines how its application has been cut back in recent years. The cases that are included present a road map to the Court's attitudes toward the power of law enforcement and the rights of individuals as well as to the differences between the Warren Court and subsequent Courts.

Because the book focuses on the Constitution and its effect on governmental practices, Chapters 2 through 6 address relevant police practices. Chapters 2 through 4 deal with searches and seizures and their Fourth Amendment implications. The subject of Chapter 5 is interrogation, which the Court analyzes using the Fifth Amendment protection against self-incrimination, the Sixth Amendment right to counsel, and the due process clause in the Fifth and Fourteenth Amendments. Chapter 6 deals with eyewitness identification, a process that raises potential Sixth Amendment and due process issues. Taken together, the chapters of this book open a key perspective on the range and variety of Supreme Court approaches to ensuring some of our most fundamental rights and goals as a society.

Robert M. Bloom
October 2012

Acknowledgments

I wish to thank my research assistants, Susan L. Harris, a 2012 graduate of Boston College Law School and Lindsey Tremaine, a member of the class of 2014 of Boston College Law School. I also acknowledge with gratitude the generous support provided by the R. Robert Popeo Fund of Boston College Law School.

Pertinent Amendments to the Constitution of the United States

AMENDMENT IV—Search and Seizure (1791)

The right of the people to be secure in their persons, houses, papers, and effects, against unreasonable searches and seizures, shall not be violated, and no Warrants shall issue, but upon probable cause, supported by Oath or affirmation, and particularly describing the place to be searched, and the persons or things to be seized.

AMENDMENT V—Trial and Punishment, Compensation for Takings (1791)

No person shall be held to answer for a capital, or otherwise infamous crime, unless on a presentment or indictment of a Grand Jury, except in cases arising in the land or naval forces, or in the Militia, when in actual service in time of War or public danger; nor shall any person be subject for the same offense to be twice put in jeopardy of life or limb; nor shall be compelled in any criminal case to be a witness against himself, nor be deprived of life, liberty, or property, without due process of law; nor shall private property be taken for public use, without just compensation.

AMENDMENT VI—Right to Speedy Trial, Confrontation of Witnesses (1791)

In all criminal prosecutions, the accused shall enjoy the right to a speedy and public trial, by an impartial jury of the State and district wherein the crime shall have been committed, which district shall have been previously ascertained by law, and to be informed of the nature and cause of the accusation; to be confronted with the witnesses against him; to have compulsory process for obtaining witnesses in his favor, and to have the Assistance of Counsel for his defence.

AMENDMENT XIV—Citizenship Rights (1868)

1. All persons born or naturalized in the United States, and subject to the jurisdiction thereof, are citizens of the United States and of the State wherein they reside. No State shall make or enforce any law which shall abridge the privileges or immunities of citizens of the United States; nor shall any State deprive any person of life, liberty, or property, without due process of law; nor deny to any person within its jurisdiction the equal protection of the laws.

Justices of the Supreme Court from 1930 to the Present

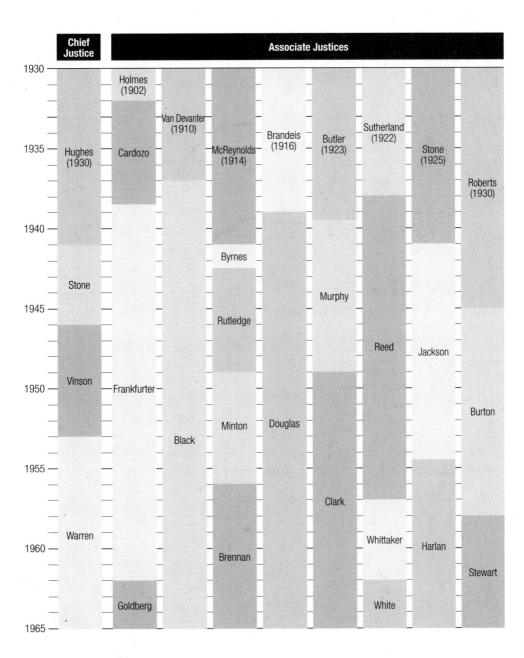

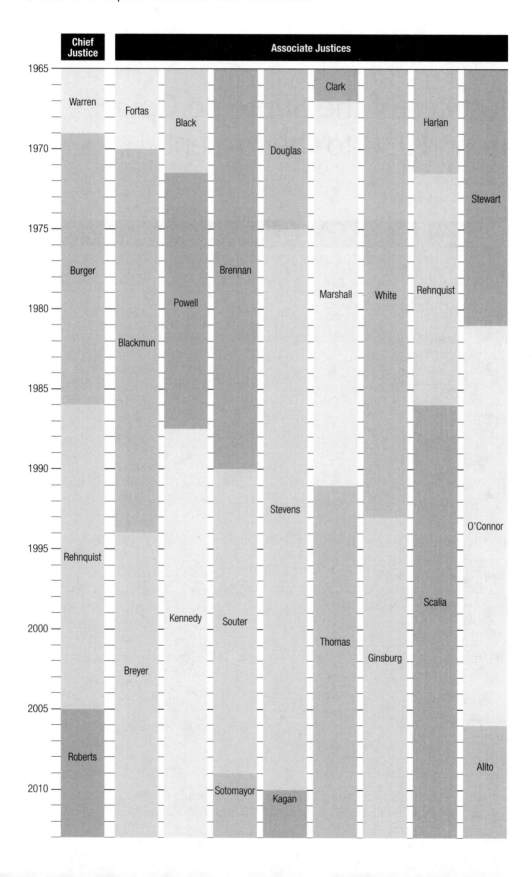

Cases on
Criminal Procedure
2013-2014

CHAPTER 1

Exclusionary Rule

Introduction

The book commences with the exclusionary rule, whereby evidence gained by unconstitutional police conduct is suppressed. The exclusion of evidence is the major remedy to redress a constitutional violation. Our study of criminal procedure begins with this subject because it presents a good road map of the Supreme Court's changing approach to balancing law enforcement needs and individuals' rights. The exclusionary remedy is utilized elsewhere in the world, albeit infrequently.

Weeks is the first case that introduces the exclusionary rule for Fourth Amendment violations. The remedy in *Weeks* is limited to federal officials. *Silverthorne* extends the exclusionary rule to include not only the direct result of the Fourth Amendment violations but also all the evidence that flowed from the violation. This is referred to as "the fruits of the poisonous tree doctrine." The trunk of the tree is the Fourth Amendment violation. The branch attached to the trunk is evidence found directly from the violation. The fruit grown on that branch is the derivative evidence found from the initial branch and would be barred under the exclusionary rule.

The next group of cases, *Wolf* and *Mapp*, traces the development of the Fourth Amendment exclusionary rule to the states. *Mapp* ultimately applies the exclusionary rule to the states. The applicability of the Fourth Amendment and the exclusionary rule to the states involved the issue of incorporation of the Bill of Rights (for purposes of this book, the Bill of Rights refers to the first eight amendments to the United States Constitution) to the states through the due process clause of the Fourteenth Amendment. The *Adamson* case presented the approaches to incorporation. Justice Frankfurter's concurrence talked about selective incorporation (those amendments that were "implicit in the concept of ordered liberty") so as to provide maximum flexibility to the due process clause of the Fourteenth Amendment. The Justice Black dissent in *Adamson* criticizes the uncertainty of selective incorporation and argues for total incorporation of the Bill of Rights to the states. At this point in our history, Justice Black's approach, although never adopted by a majority of the Court, has won the day, as most of the provisions of the Bill of Rights have been incorporated to the states. The reader should note the incorporation discussion in *Wolf* and *Mapp*.

Chief Justice Burger's dissenting opinion in *Bivens* criticizes the exclusionary rule. This is an important dissent as it highlights the problems with the exclusionary rule and the approaches taken by later courts.

The remainder of the chapter demonstrates various cutbacks to the exclusionary rule. *Calandra* introduces the "balancing test," which weighs the costs against the benefits of applying the exclusionary rule in a context other than a criminal trial. *Calandra* is a grand jury proceeding, and *Scott* is a parole revocation hearing. All implement the balancing approach to cut back the exclusionary rule. This balancing is also utilized in *Leon* and *Shepherd* to create the good-faith exception to the exclusionary rule when police have obtained a warrant. *Ramirez* and *Messerschmidt* provide a good example of the *Leon* Doctrine. *Krull, Evans, Herring,* and *Davis* represent expansions to this good-faith exception. Balancing and the good-faith exception represent direct cutbacks to the exclusionary rule.

Indirect cutbacks can be found in the next group of cases. The *Silverthorne* case, in extending the exclusionary rule, created an exception to the poisonous fruits doctrine called independent source. This exception is further discussed in *Wong Sun, Brown,* and *Murray* which deal with the "attenuation of the taint" exception to the fruits doctrine, when intervening events have the effect of dissipating the illegality. *Nix* introduces the inevitable discovery exception. Finally, *Hudson* represents the most recent exclusionary rule approach by the Court and is a good indication of the current Court's attitude.

The final two cases, *Jones* and *Rakas*, deal with the issue of who can raise a Fourth Amendment violation, often referred to as standing. *Jones*'s expansive approach to standing is substantially narrowed in *Rakas*. By limiting the people who can raise a Fourth Amendment violation, you are reducing the thrust of the exclusionary rule.

A. ORIGIN OF THE EXCLUSIONARY RULE

Weeks v. United States

232 U.S. 383 (1914)

DAY, J., delivered the opinion of a unanimous court.

An indictment was returned against the plaintiff in error, defendant below, and herein so designated, in the District Court of the United States for the Western District of Missouri, containing nine counts. The seventh count, upon which a conviction was had, charged the use of the mails for the purpose of transporting certain coupons or tickets representing chances or shares in a lottery or gift enterprise, in violation of §213 of the Criminal Code. Sentence of fine and imprisonment was imposed. This writ of error is to review that judgment.

The defendant was arrested by a police officer, so far as the record shows, without warrant, at the Union Station in Kansas City, Missouri, where he was employed by an express company. Other police officers had gone to the house of the defendant and being told by a neighbor where the key was kept, found it and entered the house. They searched the defendant's room and took possession of various papers and articles found there, which were afterwards turned over to the United States marshal. Later in the same day police officers returned with the marshal, who thought he might find additional evidence, and, being admitted by someone in the house, probably a boarder, . . . the marshal searched the defendant's room and carried away certain letters and envelopes found in the drawer of a chiffonier. Neither the marshal nor the police officers had a search warrant.

The defendant before trial filed "Petition to Return Private Papers, Books and Other Property."

After the jury had been sworn and before any evidence had been given, the defendant again urged his petition for the return of his property, which was denied by the court. Upon the introduction of such papers during the trial, the defendant objected on the ground that the papers had been obtained without a search warrant and by breaking open his home, in violation of the Fourth and Fifth Amendments to the Constitution of the United States, which objection was overruled by the court. Among the papers retained and put in evidence were a number of lottery tickets and statements with reference to the lottery, taken at the first visit of the police to the defendant's room, and a number of letters written to the defendant in respect to the lottery, taken by the Marshal upon his search of defendant's room.

The defendant assigns error, among other things, in the court's refusal to grant his petition for the return of his property and in permitting the papers to be used at the trial.

■ ■ ■

The effect of the Fourth Amendment is to put the courts of the United States and Federal officials, in the exercise of their power and authority, under limitations and restraints as to the exercise of such power and authority, and to forever secure the people, their persons, houses, papers and effects against all unreasonable searches and seizures under the guise of law. This protection reaches all alike, whether accused of crime or not, and the duty of giving to it force and effect is obligatory upon all entrusted under our Federal system with the enforcement of the laws. The tendency of those who execute the criminal laws of the country to obtain conviction by means of unlawful seizures and enforced confessions, the latter often obtained after subjecting accused persons to unwarranted practices destructive of rights secured by the Federal Constitution, should find no sanction in the judgments of the courts which are charged at all times with the support of the Constitution and to which people of all conditions have a right to appeal for the maintenance of such fundamental rights.

■ ■ ■

The United States Marshal could only have invaded the house of the accused when armed with a warrant issued as required by the Constitution, upon sworn information and describing with reasonable particularity the thing for which the search was to be made. Instead, he acted without sanction of law, doubtless prompted by the desire to bring further proof to the aid of the Government, and under color of his office undertook to make a seizure of private papers in direct violation of the constitutional prohibition against such action. Under such circumstances, without sworn information and particular description, not even an order of court would have justified such procedure, much less was it within the authority of the United States Marshal to thus invade the house and privacy of the accused. To sanction such proceedings would be to affirm by judicial decision a manifest neglect if not an open defiance of the prohibitions of the Constitution, intended for the protection of the people against such unauthorized action.

■ ■ ■

We therefore reach the conclusion that the letters in question were taken from the house of the accused by an official of the United States acting under color of his office in direct violation of the constitutional rights of the defendant; that having made a seasonable application for their return, which was heard and passed upon by the court, there was involved in the order refusing the application a denial of the constitutional rights of the accused, and that the court should have restored these letters to the accused. In holding them and permitting their use upon the trial, we think prejudicial error was committed. As to the papers and property seized by the policemen, it does not appear that they acted under any claim of Federal authority such as would make the Amendment applicable to such unauthorized seizures. The record shows that what they did by way of arrest and search and seizure was done before the finding of the indictment in the Federal court, under what supposed right or authority does not appear. What remedies the defendant may have against them we need not inquire, as the Fourth Amendment is not directed to individual misconduct of such officials. Its limitations reach the Federal Government and its agencies. . . .

It results that the judgment of the court below must be reversed, and the case remanded for further proceedings in accordance with this opinion.

Reversed.

Silverthorne Lumber Company v. United States

251 U.S. 385 (1920)

HOLMES, J., delivered the opinion of the Court, in which MCKENNA, DAY, VAN DEVANTER, REYNOLDS, BRANDEIS, and CLARKE, JJ., joined. WHITE, C.J., and PITNEY, J., dissented.

This is a writ of error brought to reverse a judgment of the District Court fining the Silverthorne Lumber Company two hundred and fifty dollars for contempt of court and ordering Frederick W. Silverthorne to be imprisoned until he should purge himself of a similar contempt. The contempt in question was a refusal to obey subpoenas and an order of Court to produce books and documents of the company before the grand jury to be used in regard to alleged violation of the statutes of the United States by the said Silverthorne and his father. One ground of the refusal was that the order of the Court infringed the rights of the parties under the Fourth Amendment of the Constitution of the United States.

The facts are simple. . . . [While the Silverthornes were being detained pursuant to a lawful arrest, representatives of the Department of Justice and the United States marshal without any authorization went to the office of their company and seized books, papers and documents found there.] . . . An application was made as soon as might be to the District Court for a return of what thus had been taken unlawfully. It was opposed by the District Attorney so far as he had found evidence against the plaintiffs in error, and it was stated that the evidence so obtained was before the grand jury. Color had been given by the District Attorney to the approach of those concerned in the act by an invalid subpoena for certain documents relating to the charge in the indictment then on file. . . . Photographs and copies of material papers were made and a new indictment was framed based upon the knowledge thus obtained. The District Court ordered a return of the originals but impounded the photographs and copies. Subpoenas to produce the originals then were served and on the refusal of the plaintiffs in error to produce them the Court made an order that the subpoenas should be complied with, although it had found that all the papers had been seized in violation of the parties' constitutional rights. The refusal to obey this order is the contempt alleged. The Government now, while in form repudiating and condemning the illegal seizure, seeks to maintain its right to avail itself of the knowledge obtained by that means which otherwise it would not have had.

The proposition could not be presented more nakedly. It is that although of course its seizure was an outrage which the Government now regrets, it may study the papers before it returns them, copy them, and then may use the knowledge that it has gained to call upon the owners in a more regular form to produce them; that the protection of the Constitution covers the physical possession but not any advantages that the Government can gain over the object of its pursuit by doing the forbidden act. *Weeks v. United States* (1914), to be sure, had established that laying the papers directly before the grand jury was unwarranted, but it is taken to mean only that two steps are required instead of one. In our opinion such is not the law. It reduces the Fourth Amendment to a form of words. The essence of a provision forbidding the acquisition of evidence in a certain way is that not merely evidence so acquired shall not be used before the Court but that it shall not be used at all. Of course this does not mean that the facts thus obtained become sacred and inaccessible. If knowledge of them is gained from an independent source they may be proved like any others, but the knowledge gained by the Government's own wrong cannot be used by it in the way proposed.

   Judgment reversed.

B. APPLICABILITY TO STATES

Wolf v. Colorado

338 U.S. 25 (1949)

FRANKFURTER, J., delivered the opinion of the Court, in which VINSON, C.J., REED, JACKSON and BURTON, JJ., joined. DOUGLAS, J., filed a dissenting opinion. MURPHY, J., filed a dissenting opinion, in which RUTLEDGE, J., joined. RUTLEDGE, J., filed a dissenting opinion, in which MURPHY, J., joined.

   The precise question for consideration is this: Does a conviction by a State court for a State offense deny the "due process of law" required by the Fourteenth Amendment, solely because evidence that was admitted at the trial was obtained under circumstances which would have rendered it inadmissible in a prosecution for violation of a federal law in a court of the United States because there deemed to be an infraction of the Fourth Amendment as applied in *Weeks v. United States* (1914). The Supreme Court of Colorado has sustained convictions in which such evidence was admitted and we brought the cases here.

   Unlike the specific requirements and restrictions placed by the Bill of Rights (Amendments I to VIII) upon the administration of criminal justice by federal authority, the Fourteenth Amendment did not subject criminal justice in the States to specific limitations. The notion that the "due process of law" guaranteed by the Fourteenth Amendment is shorthand for the first eight amendments of the Constitution and thereby incorporates them has been rejected by this Court again and again, after impressive consideration.

■ ■ ■

   For purposes of ascertaining the restrictions which the Due Process Clause imposed upon the States in the enforcement of their criminal law, we adhere to the views expressed in *Palko v. Connecticut* (1937). That decision speaks to us with the great weight of the authority, particularly in matters of civil liberty, of a court that included Mr. Chief Justice Hughes, Mr. Justice Brandeis, Mr. Justice Stone and Mr. Justice Cardozo, to name only the dead. In rejecting the suggestion that the Due Process Clause incorporated the original Bill of Rights, Mr. Justice Cardozo reaffirmed on behalf of that Court a different but deeper and more pervasive conception of the Due Process Clause. This Clause exacts from the States for the lowliest and the most outcast all that is "implicit in the concept of ordered liberty."

Due process of law thus conveys neither formal nor fixed nor narrow requirements. It is the compendious expression for all those rights which the courts must enforce because they are basic to our free society. But basic rights do not become petrified as of any one time, even though, as a matter of human experience, some may not too rhetorically be called eternal verities. It is of the very nature of a free society to advance in its standards of what is deemed reasonable and right. Representing as it does a living principle, due process is not confined within a permanent catalogue of what may at a given time be deemed the limits or the essentials of fundamental rights.

To rely on a tidy formula for the easy determination of what is a fundamental right for purposes of legal enforcement may satisfy a longing for certainty but ignores the movements of a free society. It belittles the scale of the conception of due process. The real clue to the problem confronting the judiciary in the application of the Due Process Clause is not to ask where the line is once and for all to be drawn but to recognize that it is for the Court to draw it by the gradual and empiric process of "inclusion and exclusion." *Davidson v. New Orleans* (1878).

■ ■ ■

The security of one's privacy against arbitrary intrusion by the police—which is at the core of the Fourth Amendment—is basic to a free society. It is therefore implicit in "the concept of ordered liberty," and as such enforceable against the States through the Due Process Clause. The knock at the door, whether by day or by night, as a prelude to a search, without authority of law but solely on the authority of the police, did not need the commentary of recent history to be condemned as inconsistent with the conception of human rights enshrined in the history and the basic constitutional documents of English-speaking peoples.

Accordingly, we have no hesitation in saying that were a State affirmatively to sanction such police incursion into privacy it would run counter to the guaranty of the Fourteenth Amendment. But the ways of enforcing such a basic right raise questions of a different order. How such arbitrary conduct should be checked, what remedies against it should be afforded, the means by which the right should be made effective, are all questions that are not to be so dogmatically answered as to preclude the varying solutions which spring from an allowable range of judgment on issues not susceptible of quantitative solution.

In *Weeks v. United States,* this Court held that in a federal prosecution the Fourth Amendment barred the use of evidence secured through an illegal search and seizure. This ruling was made for the first time in 1914. It was not derived from the explicit requirements of the Fourth Amendment; it was not based on legislation expressing Congressional policy in the enforcement of the Constitution. The decision was a matter of judicial implication. Since then it has been frequently applied and we stoutly adhere to it. But the immediate question is whether the basic right to protection against arbitrary intrusion by the police demands the exclusion of logically relevant evidence obtained by an unreasonable search and seizure because, in a federal prosecution for a federal crime, it would be excluded. As a matter of inherent reason, one would suppose this to be an issue as to which men with complete devotion to the protection of the right of privacy might give different answers. When we find that in fact most of the English-speaking world does not regard as vital to such protection the exclusion of evidence thus obtained, we must hesitate to treat this remedy as an essential ingredient of the right. The contrariety of views of the States is particularly impressive in view of the careful reconsideration which they have given the problem in the light of the *Weeks* decision.

■ ■ ■

As of today 31 States reject the *Weeks* doctrine, 16 States are in agreement with it. Of 10 jurisdictions within the United Kingdom and the British Commonwealth of Nations which have passed on the question, none has held evidence obtained by illegal search and seizure inadmissible.

■ ■ ■

Granting that in practice the exclusion of evidence may be an effective way of deterring unreasonable searches, it is not for this Court to condemn as falling below the minimal standards assured by the Due Process Clause a State's reliance upon other methods which, if consistently enforced, would be equally effective. . . . We cannot brush aside the experience of States which deem the incidence of such conduct by the police too slight to call for a deterrent remedy not by way of disciplinary measures but by overriding the relevant rules of evidence. There are, moreover, reasons for excluding evidence unreasonably obtained by the federal police which are less compelling in the case of police under State or local authority. The public opinion of a community can far more effectively be exerted against oppressive conduct on the part of police directly responsible to the community itself than can local opinion, sporadically aroused, be brought to bear upon remote authority pervasively exerted throughout the country.

We hold, therefore, that in a prosecution in a State court for a State crime the Fourteenth Amendment does not forbid the admission of evidence obtained by an unreasonable search and seizure. And though we have interpreted the Fourth Amendment to forbid the admission of such evidence, a different question would be presented if Congress under its legislative powers were to pass a statute purporting to negate the *Weeks* doctrine. We would then be faced with the problem of the respect to be accorded the legislative judgment on an issue as to which, in default of that judgment, we have been forced to depend upon our own. Problems of a converse character, also not before us, would be presented should Congress under §5 of the Fourteenth Amendment undertake to enforce the rights there guaranteed by attempting to make the *Weeks* doctrine binding upon the States.

Affirmed.

Justice Douglas, dissenting.

I believe for the reasons stated by Mr. Justice Black in his dissent in *Adamson v. California* (1947) that the Fourth Amendment is applicable to the States. I agree with Justice Murphy that the evidence obtained in violation of it *must* be excluded in state prosecutions as well as in federal prosecutions, since in absence of that rule of evidence the Amendment would have no effective sanction. I also agree with him that under that test this evidence was improperly admitted and that the judgments of conviction must be reversed.

Justice Murphy, with whom Justice Rutledge joins, dissenting.

It is disheartening to find so much that is right in an opinion which seems to me so fundamentally wrong. Of course I agree with the Court that the Fourteenth Amendment prohibits activities which are proscribed by the search and seizure clause of the Fourth Amendment. See my dissenting views, and those of Mr. Justice Black, in *Adamson v. California*. Quite apart from the blanket application of the Bill of Rights to the States, a devotee of democracy would ill suit his name were he to suggest that his home's protection against unlicensed governmental invasion was not "of the very essence of a scheme of ordered liberty." *Palko v. Connecticut*. It is difficult for me to understand how the Court can go this far and yet be unwilling to make the step which can give some meaning to the pronouncements it utters.

Imagination and zeal may invent a dozen methods to give content to the commands of the Fourth Amendment. But this Court is limited to the remedies currently available. It cannot legislate the ideal system. If we would attempt the enforcement of the search and seizure clause in the ordinary case today, we are limited to three devices: judicial exclusion of the illegally obtained evidence; criminal prosecution of violators; and civil action against violators in the action of trespass.

Alternatives are deceptive. Their very statement conveys the impression that one possibility is as effective as the next. In this case their statement is blinding. For there is but one alternative to the rule of exclusion. That is no sanction at all.

■ ■ ■

Little need be said concerning the possibilities of criminal prosecution. Self-scrutiny is a lofty ideal, but its exaltation reaches new heights if we expect a District Attorney to prosecute himself or his associates for well-meaning violations of the search and seizure clause during a raid the District Attorney or his associates have ordered. But there is an appealing ring in another alternative. A trespass action for damages is a venerable means of securing reparation for unauthorized invasion of the home. Why not put the old writ to a new use? When the Court cites cases permitting the action, the remedy seems complete.

But what an illusory remedy this is, if by "remedy" we mean a positive deterrent to police and prosecutors tempted to violate the Fourth Amendment. The appealing ring softens when we recall that in a trespass action the measure of damages is simply the extent of the injury to physical property. If the officer searches with care, he can avoid all but nominal damages—a penny, or a dollar. Are punitive damages possible? Perhaps. But a few states permit none, whatever the circumstances. In those that do, the plaintiff must show the real ill will malice of the defendant, and surely it is not unreasonable to assume that one in honest pursuit of crime bears no malice toward the search victim. If that burden is carried, recovery may yet be defeated by the rule that there must be physical damages before punitive damages may be awarded. In addition, some states limit punitive damages to the actual expenses of litigation.... Even assuming the ill will of the officer, his reasonable grounds for belief that the home he searched harbored evidence of crime is admissible in mitigation of punitive damages.... And even if the plaintiff hurdles all these obstacles, and gains a substantial verdict, the individual officer's finances may well make the judgment useless—for the municipality, of course, is not liable without its consent. Is it surprising that there is so little in the books concerning trespass actions for violation of the search and seizure clause?

The conclusion is inescapable that but one remedy exists to deter violations of the search and seizure clause. That is the rule which excludes illegally obtained evidence. Only by exclusion can we impress upon the zealous prosecutor that violation of the Constitution will do him no good. And only when that point is driven home can the prosecutor be expected to emphasize the importance of observing constitutional demands in his instructions to the police.

■ ■ ■

I cannot believe that we should decide due process questions by simply taking a poll of the rules in various jurisdictions, even if we follow the *Palko* "test." Today's decision will do inestimable harm to the cause of fair police methods in our cities and states. Even more important, perhaps, it must have tragic effect upon public respect for our judiciary. For the Court now allows what is indeed shabby business: lawlessness by officers of the law.

Since the evidence admitted was secured in violation of the Fourth Amendment, the judgment should be reversed.

Justice RUTLEDGE, with whom Justice MURPHY joins, dissenting.

> "Wisdom too often never comes, and so one ought not to reject it merely because it comes late." Similarly, one should not reject a piecemeal wisdom, merely because it hobbles toward the truth with backward glances. Accordingly, although I think that all "the specific guarantees of the Bill of Rights should be carried over intact into the first section of the Fourteenth Amendment," *Adamson v. California*, dissenting opinion at 124, I welcome the fact that the Court, in its slower progress toward this goal, today finds the substance of the Fourth Amendment "to be implicit in the concept of ordered liberty, and thus, through the Fourteenth Amendment, ... valid as against the states." *Palko v. Connecticut.*

But I reject the Court's simultaneous conclusion that the mandate embodied in the Fourth Amendment, although binding on the states, does not carry with it the one sanction—exclusion of evidence taken in violation of the Amendment's terms—failure to observe which means that "the protection of the Fourth Amendment . . . might as well be stricken from the Constitution." *Weeks v. United States*. For I agree with my brother Murphy's demonstration that the Amendment without the sanction is a dead letter. Twenty-nine years ago this Court, speaking through Justice Holmes, refused to permit the Government to subpoena documentary evidence which it had stolen, copied and then returned, for the reason that such a procedure "reduces the Fourth Amendment to a form of words." *Silverthorne Lumber Co. v. United States* (1920). But the version of the Fourth Amendment today held applicable to the states hardly rises to the dignity of a form of words; at best it is a pale and frayed carbon copy of the original, bearing little resemblance to the Amendment the fulfillment of whose command I had heretofore thought to be "an indispensable need for a democratic society." *Harris v. United States* (1947), dissenting opinion at 161.

■ ■ ■

The Court makes the illegality of this search and seizure its inarticulate premise of decision. I acquiesce in that premise and think the convictions should be reversed.

Mapp v. Ohio

367 U.S. 643 (1961)

CLARK, J., delivered the opinion of the Court, in which WARREN, C.J., BLACK, DOUGLAS, and BRENNAN, JJ., joined. BLACK, J. filed a concurring opinion. . . . STEWART, J., filed a memorandum. HARLAN, J., filed a dissenting opinion, in which FRANKFURTER and WHITTAKER, JJ., joined.

Appellant stands convicted of knowingly having had in her possession and under her control certain lewd and lascivious books, pictures, and photographs in violation of § 2905.34 of Ohio's Revised Code.

■ ■ ■

On May 23, 1957, three Cleveland police officers arrived at appellant's residence in that city pursuant to information that "a person [was] hiding out in the home, who was wanted for questioning in connection with a recent bombing, and that there was a large amount of policy paraphernalia being hidden in the home." Miss Mapp and her daughter by a former marriage lived on the top floor of the two-family dwelling. Upon their arrival at that house, the officers knocked on the door and demanded entrance but appellant, after telephoning her attorney, refused to admit them without a search warrant. They advised their headquarters of the situation and undertook a surveillance of the house.

The officers again sought entrance some three hours later when four or more additional officers arrived on the scene. When Miss Mapp did not come to the door immediately, at least one of the several doors to the house was forcibly opened[2] and the policemen gained admittance. Meanwhile Miss Mapp's attorney arrived, but the officers, having secured their own entry, and continuing in their defiance of the law, would permit him neither to see Miss Mapp nor to enter the house. It appears that Miss Mapp was halfway down the stairs from the upper floor to the front door when the officers, in this highhanded manner, broke into the hall. She demanded to see the search warrant. A paper, claimed to be a warrant, was held up by one of the officers. She grabbed the "warrant" and placed it in her bosom. A struggle ensued in which the officers recovered the piece of paper and as a result of which they handcuffed appellant because she had been "belligerent" in resisting their official rescue of the "warrant" from her person. Running roughshod over appellant, a policeman "grabbed" her, "twisted [her] hand," and she "yelled [and] pleaded with him" because "it was hurting." Appellant, in handcuffs, was then forcibly taken upstairs to her bedroom where the officers searched a dresser, a chest of drawers, a closet and some suitcases. They also looked into a photo album and through personal papers belonging to the appellant. The search spread to the rest of the second floor including the child's bedroom, the living room, the kitchen and a dinette. The basement of the building and a trunk found therein were also searched. The obscene materials for possession of which she was ultimately convicted were discovered in the course of that widespread search.

At the trial no search warrant was produced by the prosecution, nor was the failure to produce one explained or accounted for.

■ ■ ■

The State says that even if the search were made without authority, or otherwise unreasonably, it is not prevented from using the unconstitutionally seized evidence at trial, citing *Wolf v. Colorado* (1949), in which this Court did indeed hold "that in a prosecution in a State court for a State crime the Fourteenth Amendment does not forbid the admission of evidence obtained by an unreasonable search and seizure." On this appeal, of which we have noted probable jurisdiction, it is urged once again that we review that holding.[3]

■ ■ ■

Less than 30 years after *Boyd [v. United States* (1886)], this Court, in *Weeks v. United States* (1914), clearly stated that use of the seized evidence involved "a denial of the constitutional rights of the accused." Thus, in the year 1914, in the *Weeks* case, this Court "for the first time" held that "in a federal prosecution the

---

2. A police officer testified that "we did pry the screen door to gain entrance"; the attorney on the scene testified that a policeman "tried . . . to kick in the door" and then "broke the glass in the door and somebody reached in and opened the door and let them in"; the appellant testified that "The back door was broken."

3. Other issues have been raised on this appeal but, in the view we have taken of the case, they need not be decided. Although appellant chose to urge what may have appeared to be the surer ground for favorable disposition and did not insist that *Wolf* be overruled, the *amicus curiae*, who was also permitted to participate in the oral argument, did urge the Court to overrule *Wolf*.

Fourth Amendment barred the use of evidence secured through an illegal search and seizure." *Wolf v. Colorado*. This Court has ever since required of federal law officers a strict adherence to that command which this Court has held to be a clear, specific, and constitutionally required—even if judicially implied—deterrent safeguard without insistence upon which the Fourth Amendment would have been reduced to "a form of words." *Silverthorne Lumber Co. v. United States* (1920). It meant, quite simply, that "conviction by means of unlawful seizures and enforced confessions . . . should find no sanction in the judgments of the courts . . . ," *Weeks v. United States,* and that such evidence "shall not be used at all." *Silverthorne Lumber Co. v. United States.*

There are in the cases of this Court some passing references to the *Weeks* rule as being one of evidence. But the plain and unequivocal language of *Weeks*—and its later paraphrase in *Wolf*—to the effect that the *Weeks* rule is of constitutional origin, remains entirely undisturbed. . . . "The striking outcome of the *Weeks* case and those which followed it was the sweeping declaration that the Fourth Amendment, although not referring to or limiting the use of evidence in courts, really forbade its introduction if obtained by government officers through a violation of the Amendment." [*Olmstead v. United States* (1928).]

■ ■ ■

In 1949, 35 years after *Weeks* was announced, this Court, in *Wolf v. Colorado*, again for the first time, discussed the effect of the Fourth Amendment upon the States through the operation of the Due Process Clause of the Fourteenth Amendment. It said:

> "We have no hesitation in saying that were a State affirmatively to sanction such police incursion into privacy it would run counter to the guaranty of the Fourteenth Amendment."

Nevertheless, after declaring that the "security of one's privacy against arbitrary intrusion by the police" is "implicit in 'the concept of ordered liberty' and as such enforceable against the States through the Due Process Clause," and announcing that it "stoutly adhere[d]" to the *Weeks* decision, the Court decided that the *Weeks* exclusionary rule would not then be imposed upon the States as "an essential ingredient of the right."

■ ■ ■

While they are not basically relevant to a decision that the exclusionary rule is an essential ingredient of the Fourth Amendment as the right it embodies is vouchsafed against the States by the Due Process Clause, we will consider the current validity of the factual grounds upon which *Wolf* was based.

■ ■ ■

While in 1949, prior to the *Wolf* case, almost two-thirds of the States were opposed to the use of the exclusionary rule, now, despite the *Wolf* case, more than half of those since passing upon it, by their own legislative or judicial decision, have wholly or partly adopted or adhered to the *Weeks* rule. Significantly, among those now following the rule is California, which, according to

its highest court, was "compelled to reach that conclusion because other remedies have completely failed to secure compliance with the constitutional
provisions...." *People v. Cahan* (1955). In connection with this California
case, we note that the second basis elaborated in *Wolf* in support of its failure
to enforce the exclusionary doctrine against the States was that "other means of
protection" have been afforded "the right to privacy." The experience of
California that such other remedies have been worthless and futile is buttressed by the experience of other States. The obvious futility of relegating
the Fourth Amendment to the protection of other remedies has, moreover,
been recognized by this Court since *Wolf*. See *Irvine v. California* (1954).

Likewise, time has set its face against what *Wolf* called the "weighty testimony" of *People v. Defore* (1926). There Justice (then Judge) Cardozo, rejecting
adoption of the *Weeks* exclusionary rule in New York, had said that "the Federal rule as it stands is either too strict or too lax." However, the force of that
reasoning has been largely vitiated by later decisions of this Court. These
include the recent discarding of the "silver platter" doctrine which allowed
federal judicial use of evidence seized in violation of the Constitution by state
agents, *Elkins v. United States* [(1960)]; the relaxation of the formerly strict
requirements as to standing to challenge the use of evidence thus seized, so
that now the procedure of exclusion, "ultimately referable to constitutional
safeguards," is available to anyone even "legitimately on [the] premises"
unlawfully searched, *Jones v. United States* (1960); and, finally, the formulation
of a method to prevent state use of evidence unconstitutionally seized by
federal agents, *Rea v. United States* (1956). Because there can be no fixed formula, we are admittedly met with "recurring questions of the reasonableness
of searches," but less is not to be expected when dealing with a Constitution,
and, at any rate, "reasonableness is in the first instance for the [trial court] ... to
determine." *United States v. Rabinowitz* (1950).

It, therefore, plainly appears that the factual considerations supporting the
failure of the *Wolf* Court to include the *Weeks* exclusionary rule when it recognized the enforceability of the right to privacy against the States in 1949, while
not basically relevant to the constitutional consideration, could not, in any
analysis, now be deemed controlling.

Since the Fourth Amendment's right of privacy has been declared enforceable against the States through the Due Process Clause of the Fourteenth, it is
enforceable against them by the same sanction of exclusion as is used against
the Federal Government. Were it otherwise, then just as without the *Weeks* rule
the assurance against unreasonable federal searches and seizures would be "a
form of words," valueless and undeserving of mention in a perpetual charter of
inestimable human liberties, so too, without that rule the freedom from state
invasions of privacy would be so ephemeral and so neatly severed from its
conceptual nexus with the freedom from all brutish means of coercing evidence as not to merit this Court's high regard as a freedom "implicit in the
concept of ordered liberty." At the time that the Court held in *Wolf* that
the Amendment was applicable to the States through the Due Process Clause,

the cases of this Court, as we have seen, had steadfastly held that as to federal officers the Fourth Amendment included the exclusion of the evidence seized in violation of its provisions. Even *Wolf* "stoutly adhered" to that proposition. The right to privacy, when conceded operatively enforceable against the States, was not susceptible of destruction by avulsion of the sanction upon which its protection and enjoyment had always been deemed dependent under the *Boyd*, *Weeks* and *Silverthorne* cases. Therefore, in extending the substantive protections of due process to all constitutionally unreasonable searches—state or federal—it was logically and constitutionally necessary that the exclusion doctrine—an essential part of the right to privacy—be also insisted upon as an essential ingredient of the right newly recognized by the *Wolf* case. In short, the admission of the new constitutional right by *Wolf* could not consistently tolerate denial of its most important constitutional privilege, namely, the exclusion of the evidence which an accused had been forced to give by reason of the unlawful seizure. To hold otherwise is to grant the right but in reality to withhold its privilege and enjoyment. Only last year the Court itself recognized that the purpose of the exclusionary rule "is to deter—to compel respect for the constitutional guaranty in the only effectively available way—by removing the incentive to disregard it." *Elkins v. United States*.

Indeed, we are aware of no restraint, similar to that rejected today, conditioning the enforcement of any other basic constitutional right. The right to privacy, no less important than any other right carefully and particularly reserved to the people, would stand in marked contrast to all other rights declared as "basic to a free society." *Wolf v. Colorado*. This Court has not hesitated to enforce as strictly against the States as it does against the Federal Government the rights of free speech and of a free press, the rights to notice and to a fair, public trial, including, as it does, the right not to be convicted by use of a coerced confession, however logically relevant it be, and without regard to its reliability. *Rogers v. Richmond* (1961). And nothing could be more certain than that when a coerced confession is involved, "the relevant rules of evidence" are overridden without regard to "the incidence of such conduct by the police," slight or frequent. Why should not the same rule apply to what is tantamount to coerced testimony by way of unconstitutional seizure of goods, papers, effects, documents, etc.? We find that, as to the Federal Government, the Fourth and Fifth Amendments and, as to the States, the freedom from unconscionable invasions of privacy and the freedom from convictions based upon coerced confessions do enjoy an "intimate relation" in their perpetuation of "principles of humanity and civil liberty [secured]...only after years of struggle," *Bram v. United States* (1897). They express "supplementing phases of the same constitutional purpose—to maintain inviolate large areas of personal privacy." *Feldman v. United States* (1944). The philosophy of each Amendment and of each freedom is complementary to, although not dependent upon, that of the other in its sphere of influence—the very least that together they assure in either sphere is that no man is to be convicted on unconstitutional evidence. *Rochin v. California* (1952).

Moreover, our holding that the exclusionary rule is an essential part of both the Fourth and Fourteenth Amendments is not only the logical dictate of prior cases, but it also makes very good sense. There is no war between the Constitution and common sense. Presently, a federal prosecutor may make no use of evidence illegally seized, but a State's attorney across the street may, although he supposedly is operating under the enforceable prohibitions of the same Amendment. Thus the State, by admitting evidence unlawfully seized, serves to encourage disobedience to the Federal Constitution which it is bound to uphold. Moreover, as was said in *Elkins*, "the very essence of a healthy federalism depends upon the avoidance of needless conflict between state and federal courts." Such a conflict, hereafter needless, arose this very term, in *Wilson v. Schnettler* (1961), in which . . . we gave full recognition to our practice in this regard by refusing to restrain a federal officer from testifying in a state court as to evidence unconstitutionally seized by him in the performance of his duties. Yet the double standard recognized until today hardly put such a thesis into practice. In nonexclusionary States, federal officers, being human, were by it invited to and did, as our cases indicate, step across the street to the State's attorney with their unconstitutionally seized evidence. Prosecution on the basis of that evidence was then had in a state court in utter disregard of the enforceable Fourth Amendment. If the fruits of an unconstitutional search had been inadmissible in both state and federal courts, this inducement to evasion would have been sooner eliminated.

Federal-state cooperation in the solution of crime under constitutional standards will be promoted, if only by recognition of their now mutual obligation to respect the same fundamental criteria in their approaches. "However much in a particular case insistence upon such rules may appear as a technicality that inures to the benefit of a guilty person, the history of the criminal law proves that tolerance of shortcut methods in law enforcement impairs its enduring effectiveness." *Miller v. United States* (1958). Denying shortcuts to only one of two cooperating law enforcement agencies tends naturally to breed legitimate suspicion of "working arrangements" whose results are equally tainted. *Byars v. United States* (1927); *Lustig v. United States* (1949).

There are those who say, as did Justice (then Judge) Cardozo, that under our constitutional exclusionary doctrine "the criminal is to go free because the constable has blundered." *People v. Defore*. In some cases this will undoubtedly be the result. But, as was said in *Elkins*, "there is another consideration—the imperative of judicial integrity." The criminal goes free, if he must, but it is the law that sets him free. Nothing can destroy a government more quickly than its failure to observe its own laws, or worse, its disregard of the charter of its own existence. As Mr. Justice Brandeis, dissenting, said in *Olmstead v. United States*: "Our Government is the potent, the omnipresent teacher. For good or for ill, it teaches the whole people by its example. . . . If the Government becomes a lawbreaker, it breeds contempt for law; it invites every man to become a law unto himself; it invites anarchy." Nor can it lightly be assumed that, as a practical matter, adoption of the exclusionary rule fetters law enforcement. Only last year this Court expressly considered that contention and found that "pragmatic evidence of a sort" to the contrary was not wanting. *Elkins v. United States.* The Court noted that

> "The federal courts themselves have operated under the exclusionary rule of *Weeks* for almost half a century; yet it has not been suggested either that the Federal Bureau of Investigation has thereby been rendered ineffective, or that the administration of criminal justice in the federal courts has thereby been disrupted. Moreover, the experience of the states is impressive. . . . The movement towards the rule of exclusion has been halting but seemingly inexorable."

The ignoble shortcut to conviction left open to the State tends to destroy the entire system of constitutional restraints on which the liberties of the people rest. Having once recognized that the right to privacy embodied in the Fourth Amendment is enforceable against the States, and that the right to be secure against rude invasions of privacy by state officers is, therefore, constitutional in origin, we can no longer permit that right to remain an empty promise. Because it is enforceable in the same manner and to like effect as other basic rights secured by the Due Process Clause, we can no longer permit it to be revocable at the whim of any police officer who, in the name of law enforcement itself, chooses to suspend its enjoyment. Our decision, founded on reason and truth, gives to the individual no more than that which the Constitution guarantees him, to the police officer no less than that to which honest law enforcement is entitled, and, to the courts, that judicial integrity so necessary in the true administration of justice.

The judgment of the Supreme Court of Ohio is reversed and the cause remanded for further proceedings not inconsistent with this opinion.

Reversed and remanded.

Justice BLACK, concurring.

■ ■ ■

I am still not persuaded that the Fourth Amendment, standing alone, would be enough to bar the introduction into evidence against an accused of papers and effects seized from him in violation of its commands. For the Fourth Amendment does not itself contain any provision expressly precluding the use of such evidence, and I am extremely doubtful that such a provision could properly be inferred from nothing more than the basic command against unreasonable searches and seizures. Reflection on the problem, however, in the light of cases coming before the Court since *Wolf*, has led me to conclude that when the Fourth Amendment's ban against unreasonable searches and seizures is considered together with the Fifth Amendment's ban against compelled self-incrimination, a constitutional basis emerges which not only justifies but actually requires the exclusionary rule.

Comb of
4ᵗʰ + 5ᵗʰ
compels
conclusion

The close interrelationship between the Fourth and Fifth Amendments, as they apply to this problem, has long been recognized and, indeed, was expressly made the ground for this Court's holding in *Boyd v. United States.* There the Court fully discussed this relationship and declared itself "unable to perceive that the seizure of a man's private books and papers to be used in evidence against him is substantially different from compelling him to be a witness against himself." It was upon this ground that Mr. Justice Rutledge largely relied in his dissenting opinion in the *Wolf* case. And, although I rejected the argument at that time, its force has, for me at least, become compelling with the more thorough understanding of the problem brought on by recent cases. In the final analysis, it seems to me that the *Boyd* doctrine, though perhaps not required by the express language of the Constitution strictly construed, is amply justified from an historical standpoint, soundly based in reason, and entirely consistent with what I regard to be the proper approach to interpretation of our Bill of Rights—. . . .

■ ■ ■

Memorandum of Justice STEWART.

Agreeing fully with Part I of Mr. Justice Harlan's dissenting opinion, I express no view as to the merits of the constitutional issue which the Court today decides. I would, however, reverse the judgment in this case, because I am persuaded that the provision of § 2905.34 of the Ohio Revised Code, upon which the petitioner's conviction was based, is, in the words of Mr. Justice Harlan, not "consistent with the rights of free thought and expression assured against state action by the Fourteenth Amendment."

Justice HARLAN, with whom Justice FRANKFURTER and Justice WHITTAKER join, dissenting.

In overruling the *Wolf* case the Court, in my opinion, has forgotten the sense of judicial restraint which, with due regard for *stare decisis,* is one element that should enter into deciding whether a past decision of this Court should be overruled. Apart from that I also believe that the *Wolf* rule represents sounder Constitutional doctrine than the new rule which now replaces it.

I

From the Court's statement of the case one would gather that the central, if not controlling, issue on this appeal is whether illegally state-seized evidence is Constitutionally admissible in a state prosecution, an issue which would of course face us with the need for re-examining *Wolf.* However, such is not the situation. For, although that question was indeed raised here and below among appellant's subordinate points, the new and pivotal issue brought to the Court by this appeal is whether § 2905.34 of the Ohio Revised Code making criminal the *mere* knowing possession or control of obscene material, and under which appellant has been convicted, is consistent with the rights of free thought and expression assured against state action by the Fourteenth Amendment. That was the principal issue which was decided by the Ohio Supreme Court, which was tendered by appellant's Jurisdictional Statement, and which was briefed[5] and argued[6] in this Court.

In this posture of things, I think it fair to say that five members of this Court have simply "reached out" to overrule *Wolf*. With all respect for the views of the majority, and recognizing that *stare decisis* carries different weight in Constitutional adjudication than it does in nonconstitutional decision, I can perceive no justification for regarding this case as an appropriate occasion for re-examining *Wolf*.

■ ■ ■

Since the demands of the case before us do not require us to reach the question of the validity of *Wolf*, I think this case furnishes a singularly inappropriate occasion for reconsideration of that decision, if reconsideration is indeed warranted. Even the most cursory examination will reveal that the doctrine of the *Wolf* case has been of continuing importance in the administration of state criminal law. Indeed, certainly as regards its "nonexclusionary" aspect, *Wolf* did no more than articulate the then existing assumption among the States that the federal cases enforcing the exclusionary rule "do not bind [the States], for they construe provisions of the Federal Constitution, the Fourth and Fifth Amendments, not applicable to the States." *People v. Defore.*

■ ■ ■

The occasion which the Court has taken here is in the context of a case where the question was briefed not at all and argued only extremely tangentially. The unwisdom of overruling *Wolf* without full-dress argument is aggravated by the circumstance that that decision is a comparatively recent one (1949) to which three members of the present majority have at one time or other expressly subscribed, one to be sure with explicit misgivings.

■ ■ ■

II

■ ■ ■

---

5. The appellant's brief did not urge the overruling of *Wolf*. Indeed it did not even cite the case. The brief of the appellee merely relied on *Wolf* in support of the State's contention that appellant's conviction was not vitiated by the admission in evidence of the fruits of the alleged unlawful search and seizure by the police. The brief of the American and Ohio Civil Liberties Unions, as *amici*, did in one short concluding paragraph of its argument "request" the Court to re-examine and overrule *Wolf*, but without argumentation. I quote in full this part of their brief:

"This case presents the issue of whether evidence obtained in an illegal search and seizure can constitutionally be used in a State criminal proceeding. We are aware of the view that this Court has taken on this issue in *Wolf v. Colorado*. It is our purpose by this paragraph to respectfully request that this Court re-examine this issue and conclude that the ordered liberty concept guaranteed to persons by the due process clause of the Fourteenth Amendment necessarily requires that evidence illegally obtained in violation thereof, not be admissible in state criminal proceedings."

6. Counsel for appellant on oral argument, as in his brief, did not urge that *Wolf* be overruled. Indeed, when pressed by questioning from the bench whether he was not in fact urging us to overrule *Wolf*, counsel expressly disavowed any such purpose.

The preservation of a proper balance between state and federal responsibility in the administration of criminal justice demands patience on the part of those who might like to see things move faster among the States in this respect. Problems of criminal law enforcement vary widely from State to State. One State, in considering the totality of its legal picture, may conclude that the need for embracing the *Weeks* rule is pressing because other remedies are unavailable or inadequate to secure compliance with the substantive Constitutional principle involved. Another, though equally solicitous of Constitutional rights, may choose to pursue one purpose at a time, allowing all evidence relevant to guilt to be brought into a criminal trial, and dealing with Constitutional infractions by other means. Still another may consider the exclusionary rule too rough-and-ready a remedy, in that it reaches only unconstitutional intrusions which eventuate in criminal prosecution of the victims. Further, a State after experimenting with the *Weeks* rule for a time may, because of unsatisfactory experience with it, decide to revert to a non-exclusionary rule. And so on. From the standpoint of Constitutional permissibility in pointing a State in one direction or another, I do not see at all why "time has set its face against" the considerations which led Mr. Justice Cardozo, then chief judge of the New York Court of Appeals, to reject for New York in *People v. Defore* the *Weeks* exclusionary rule. For us the question remains, as it has always been, one of state power, not one of passing judgment on the wisdom of one state course or another. In my view this Court should continue to forbear from fettering the States with an adamant rule which may embarrass them in coping with their own peculiar problems in criminal law enforcement.

■ ■ ■

In conclusion, it should be noted that the majority opinion in this case is in fact an opinion only for the *judgment* overruling *Wolf*, and not for the basic rationale by which four members of the majority have reached that result. For my Brother Black is unwilling to subscribe to their view that the *Weeks* exclusionary rule derives from the Fourth Amendment itself but joins the majority opinion on the premise that its end result can be achieved by bringing the Fifth Amendment to the aid of the Fourth.

■ ■ ■

C. INCORPORATION

Adamson v. People of State of California

332 U.S. 46 (1947)

REED, J., delivered the opinion of the Court, in which VINSON, C.J., JACKSON and BURTON, JJ., joined. FRANKFURTER, J., filed a concurring opinion. MURPHY, J., wrote a dissenting opinion, in which RUTLEDGE, J., joined. BLACK, J., wrote a dissenting opinion, in which DOUGLAS, J., joined.

The appellant, Adamson, a citizen of the United States, was convicted, without recommendation for mercy, by a jury in a Superior Court of the State of California of murder in the first degree. After considering the same objections to the conviction that are pressed here, the sentence of death was affirmed by the Supreme Court of the state. . . . The provisions of California law which were challenged in the state proceedings as invalid under the Fourteenth Amendment to the Federal Constitution are those of the state constitution and penal code in the margin. They permit the failure of a defendant to explain or to deny evidence against him to be commented upon by court and by counsel and to be considered by court and jury. The defendant did not testify. As the trial court gave its instructions and the District Attorney argued the case in accordance with the constitutional and statutory provisions just referred to, we have for decision the question of their constitutionality in these circumstances under the limitations of § 1 of the Fourteenth Amendment.

■ ■ ■

Appellant secondly contends that if the privilege against self-incrimination is not a right protected by the privileges and immunities clause of the Fourteenth Amendment against state action, this privilege, to its full scope under the Fifth Amendment, inheres in the right to a fair trial. A right to a fair trial is a right admittedly protected by the due process clause of the Fourteenth Amendment. Therefore, appellant argues, the due process clause of the Fourteenth Amendment protects his privilege against self-incrimination. The due process clause of the Fourteenth Amendment, however, does not draw all the rights of the federal Bill of Rights under its protection. That contention was made and rejected in *Palko v. Connecticut* (1937). It was rejected with citation of the cases excluding several of the rights, protected by the Bill of Rights, against infringement by the National Government. Nothing has been called to our attention that either the framers of the Fourteenth Amendment or the states that adopted intended its due process clause to draw within its scope the earlier amendments to the Constitution. *Palko* held that such provisions of the Bill of Rights as were "implicit in the concept of ordered liberty" became secure from state interference by the clause. But it held nothing more.

Specifically, the due process clause does not protect, by virtue of its mere existence the accused's freedom from giving testimony by compulsion in state trials that is secured to him against federal interference by the Fifth Amendment. For a state to require testimony from an accused is not necessarily a breach of a state's obligation to give a fair trial. Therefore, we must examine the effect of the California law applied in this trial to see whether the comment on failure to testify violates the protection against state action that the due process clause does grant to an accused. The due process clause forbids compulsion to testify by fear of hurt, torture or exhaustion. It forbids any other type of coercion that falls within the scope of due process. California follows Anglo-American legal tradition in excusing defendants in criminal prosecutions from compulsory testimony. That is a matter of legal policy and not because of the requirements of due process under the Fourteenth Amendment. So our inquiry is directed, not at the broad question of the constitutionality of compulsory testimony from the accused under the due process clause, but to the constitutionality of the provision of the California law that permits comment upon his failure to testify. It is, of course, logically possible that while an accused might be required, under appropriate penalties, to submit himself as a witness without a violation of due process, comment by judge or jury on inferences to be drawn from his failure to testify, in jurisdictions where an accused's privilege against self-incrimination is protected, might deny due process. For example, a statute might declare that a permitted refusal to testify would compel an acceptance of the truth of the prosecution's evidence.

■ ■ ■

It is true that if comment were forbidden, an accused in this situation could remain silent and avoid evidence of former crimes and comment upon his failure to testify. We are of the view, however, that a state may control such a situation in accordance with its own ideas of the most efficient administration of criminal justice. The purpose of due process is not to protect an accused against a proper conviction but against an unfair conviction. When evidence is before a jury that threatens conviction, it does not seem unfair to require him to choose between leaving the adverse evidence unexplained and subjecting himself to impeachment through disclosure of former crimes. Indeed, this is a dilemma with which any defendant may be faced. If facts, adverse to the defendant, are proven by the prosecution, there may be no way to explain them favorably to the accused except by a witness who may be vulnerable to impeachment on cross-examination. The defendant must then decide whether or not to use such a witness. The fact that the witness may also be the defendant makes the choice more difficult but a denial of due process does not emerge from the circumstances. . . .

We find no other error that gives ground for our intervention in California's administration of criminal justice.

Affirmed.

Justice FRANKFURTER, concurring.

Less than ten years ago, Mr. Justice Cardozo announced as settled constitutional law that while the Fifth Amendment, "which is not directed to the states, but solely to the federal government," provides that no person shall be compelled in any criminal case to be a witness against himself, the process of law assured by the Fourteenth Amendment does not require such immunity from self-crimination: "in prosecutions by a state, the exemption will fail if the state elects to end it." *Palko v. Connecticut.* . . .

For historical reasons a limited immunity from the common duty to testify was written into the Federal Bill of Rights, and I am prepared to agree that, as part of that immunity, comment on the failure of an accused to take the witness stand is forbidden in federal prosecutions. . . . But to suggest that such a limitation can be drawn out of "due process" in its protection of ultimate decency in a civilized society is to suggest that the Due Process Clause fastened fetters of unreason upon the States. . . .

Between the incorporation of the Fourteenth Amendment into the Constitution and the beginning of the present membership of the Court—a period of seventy years—the scope of that Amendment was passed upon by forty-three judges. Of all these judges, only one, who may respectfully be called an eccentric exception, ever indicated the belief that the Fourteenth Amendment was a shorthand summary of the first eight Amendments theretofore limiting only the Federal Government, and that due process incorporated those eight Amendments as restrictions upon the powers of the States. Among these judges were not only those who would have to be included among the greatest in the history of the Court, but—it is especially relevant to note—they included those whose services in the cause of human rights and the spirit of freedom are the most conspicuous in our history. It is not invidious to single out Miller, Davis, Bradley, Waite, Matthews, Gray, Fuller, Holmes, Brandeis, Stone and Cardozo (to speak only of the dead) as judges who were alert in safeguarding and promoting the interests of liberty and human dignity through law. But they were also judges mindful of the relation of our federal system to a progressively democratic society and therefore duly regardful of the scope of authority that was left to the States even after the Civil War. And so they did not find that the Fourteenth Amendment, concerned as it was with matters fundamental to the pursuit of justice, fastened upon the States procedural arrangements which, in the language of Mr. Justice Cardozo, only those who are "narrow or provincial" would deem essential to "a fair and enlightened system of justice." *Palko v. Connecticut.* . . .

The short answer to the suggestion that the provision of the Fourteenth Amendment, which ordains "nor shall any State deprive any person of life, liberty, or property, without due process of law," was a way of saying that every State must thereafter initiate prosecutions through indictment by a grand jury, must have a trial by a jury of twelve in criminal cases, and must have trial by such a jury in common law suits where the amount in controversy exceeds twenty dollars, is that it is a strange way of saying it. It would be extraordinarily strange for a Constitution to convey such specific commands in such a roundabout and inexplicit way. After all, an amendment to the Constitution should be read in a "sense most obvious to the common understanding at the time of its adoption." See Mr. Justice Holmes in *Eisner v. Macomber* (1920). . . . Those reading the English language with the meaning which it ordinarily conveys, those conversant with the political and legal history of the concept of due process, those sensitive to the relations of the States to the central government as well as the relation of some of the provisions of the Bill of Rights to the process of justice, would hardly recognize the Fourteenth Amendment as a cover for the various explicit provisions of the first eight Amendments. Some of these are enduring reflections of experience with human nature, while some express the restricted views of Eighteenth-Century England regarding the best methods for the ascertainment of facts. The notion that the Fourteenth Amendment was a covert way of imposing upon the States all the rules which it seemed important to Eighteenth Century statesmen to write into the Federal Amendments, was rejected by judges who were themselves witnesses of the process by which the Fourteenth Amendment became part of the Constitution. Arguments that may now be adduced to prove that the first eight Amendments were concealed within the historic phrasing of the Fourteenth Amendment were not unknown at the time of its adoption. A surer estimate of their bearing was possible for judges at the time than distorting distance is likely to vouchsafe. Any evidence of design or purpose not contemporaneously known could hardly have influenced those who ratified the Amendment. Remarks of a particular proponent of the Amendment, no matter how influential, are not to be deemed part of the Amendment. What was submitted for ratification was his proposal, not his speech. Thus, at the time of the ratification of the Fourteenth Amendment the constitutions of nearly half of the ratifying States did not have the rigorous requirements of the Fifth Amendment for instituting criminal proceedings through a grand jury. It could hardly have occurred to these States that by ratifying the Amendment they uprooted their established methods for prosecuting crime and fastened upon themselves a new prosecutorial system.

Indeed, the suggestion that the Fourteenth Amendment incorporates the first eight Amendments as such is not unambiguously urged. Even the boldest innovator would shrink from suggesting to more than half the States that they may no longer initiate prosecutions without indictment by grand jury, or that thereafter all the States of the Union must furnish a jury of twelve for every case involving a claim above twenty dollars. There is suggested merely a selective incorporation of the first eight Amendments into the Fourteenth Amendment. Some are in and some are out, but we are left in the dark as to which are in and which are out. Nor are we given the calculus for determining which go in and which stay out. If the basis of selection is merely that those provisions of the first eight Amendments are incorporated which commend themselves to individual justices as indispensable to the dignity and happiness of a free man, we are thrown back to a merely subjective test. The protection against unreasonable search and seizure might have primacy for one judge, while trial by a jury of twelve for every claim above twenty dollars might appear to another as an ultimate need in a free society. In the history of thought "natural law" has a much longer and much better founded meaning and justification than such subjective selection of the first eight Amendments for incorporation into the Fourteenth. If all that is meant is that due process contains within itself certain minimal standards which are "of the very essence of a scheme of ordered liberty," *Palko v. Connecticut* . . . then we have merely arrived at the insight which our predecessors long ago expressed. The Amendment neither comprehends the specific provisions by which the founders deemed it appropriate to restrict the federal government nor is it confined to them. The Due Process Clause of the Fourteenth Amendment has an independent potency, precisely as does the Due Process Clause of the Fifth Amendment in relation to the Federal Government. . . . To consider "due process of law" as merely a short-hand statement of other specific clauses in the same amendment is to attribute to the authors and proponents of this Amendment ignorance of, or indifference to, a historic conception which was one of the great instruments in the arsenal of constitutional freedom which the Bill of Rights was to protect and strengthen.

A construction which gives to due process no independent function but turns it into a summary of the specific provisions of the Bill of Rights would, as has been noted, tear up by the roots much of the fabric of law in the several States, and would deprive the States of opportunity for reforms in legal process designed for extending the area of freedom. It would assume that no other abuses would reveal themselves in the course of time than those which had become manifest in 1791. Such a view not only disregards the historic meaning of "due process." It leads inevitably to a warped construction of specific provisions of the Bill of Rights to bring within their scope conduct clearly condemned by due process but not easily fitting into the pigeon-holes of the specific provisions. It seems pretty late in the day to suggest that a phrase so laden with historic meaning should be given an improvised content consisting of some but not all of the provisions of the first eight Amendments, selected on an undefined basis, with improvisation of content for the provisions so selected.

And so, when, as in a case like the present, a conviction in a State court is here for review under a claim that a right protected by the Due Process Clause of the Fourteenth Amendment has been denied, the issue is not whether an infraction of one of the specific provisions of the first eight Amendments is disclosed by the record. The relevant question is whether the criminal proceedings which resulted in conviction deprived the accused of the due process of law to which the United States Constitution entitled him. Judicial review of that guaranty of the Fourteenth Amendment inescapably imposes upon this Court an exercise of judgment upon the whole course of the proceedings in order to ascertain whether they offend those canons of decency and fairness which express the notions of justice of English-speaking peoples even toward those charged with the most heinous offenses. These standards of justice are not authoritatively formulated anywhere as though they were prescriptions in a pharmacopoeia. But neither does the application of the Due Process Clause imply that judges are wholly at large. The judicial judgment in applying the Due Process Clause must move within the limits of accepted notions of justice and is not to be based upon the idiosyncrasies of a merely personal judgment. The fact that judges among themselves may differ whether in a particular case a trial offends accepted notions of justice is not disproof that general rather than idiosyncratic standards are applied. An important safeguard against such merely individual judgment is an alert deference to the judgment of the State court under review.

Justice BLACK, with whom Justice DOUGLAS joins, dissenting.

■ ■ ■

The first 10 amendments were proposed and adopted largely because of fear that Government might unduly interfere with prized individual liberties. The people wanted and demanded a Bill of Rights written into their Constitution. The amendments embodying the Bill of Rights were intended to curb all branches of the Federal Government in the fields touched by the amendments—Legislative, Executive, and Judicial. The Fifth, Sixth, and Eighth Amendments were pointedly aimed at confining exercise of power by courts and judges within precise boundaries, particularly in the procedure used for the trial of criminal cases. Past history provided strong reasons for the apprehensions which brought these procedural amendments into being and attest the wisdom of their adoption. For the fears of arbitrary court action sprang largely from the past use of courts in the imposition of criminal punishments to suppress speech, press, and religion. Hence the constitutional limitations of courts' powers were, in the view of the Founders, essential supplements to the First Amendment, which was itself designed to protect the widest scope for all people to believe and to express the most divergent political, religious, and other views.

But these limitations were not expressly imposed upon state court action. In 1833, *Barron v. Baltimore* was decided by this Court. It specifically held inapplicable to the states that provision of the Fifth Amendment which declares: "nor shall private property be taken for public use, without just compensation." In deciding the particular point raised, the Court there said that it could not hold that the first eight amendments applied to the states. This was the controlling constitutional rule when the Fourteenth Amendment was proposed in 1866.

My study of the historical events that culminated in the Fourteenth Amendment, and the expressions of those who sponsored and favored, as well as those who opposed its submission and passage, persuades me that one of the chief objects that the provisions of the Amendment's first section, separately, and as a whole, were intended to accomplish was to make the Bill of Rights, applicable to the states. With full knowledge of the import of the *Barron* decision, the framers and backers of the Fourteenth Amendment proclaimed its purpose to be to overturn the constitutional rule that case had announced. This historical purpose has never received full consideration or exposition in any opinion of this Court interpreting the Amendment.

■ ■ ■

In *Palko v. Connecticut*, a case which involved former jeopardy only, this Court re-examined the path it had traveled in interpreting the Fourteenth Amendment since the *Twining* opinion was written. In *Twining* [*v. New Jersey* (1908)] the Court had declared that none of the rights enumerated in the first eight amendments were protected against state invasion because they were incorporated in the Bill of Rights. But the Court in *Palko* answered a contention that all eight applied with the more guarded statement, similar to that the Court had used in *Maxwell v. Dow* (1900) that "there is no such general rule." Implicit in this statement, and in the cases decided in the interim between *Twining* and *Palko* and since, is the understanding that some of the eight amendments do apply by their very terms. Thus the Court said in the *Palko* case that the Fourteenth Amendment may make it unlawful for a state to abridge by its statutes the "freedom of speech which the First Amendment safeguards against encroachment by the Congress or the like freedom of the press or the free exercise of religion, or the right of peaceable assembly or the right of one accused of crime to the benefit of counsel. In these and other situations immunities that are valid as against the federal government by force of the specific pledges of particular amendments have been found to be implicit in the concept of ordered liberty, and thus, through the Fourteenth Amendment, become valid as against the states." The Court went on to describe the Amendments made applicable to the States as "the privileges and immunities that have been taken over from the earlier articles of the Federal Bill of Rights and brought within the Fourteenth Amendment by a process of absorption." In the *Twining* case fundamental liberties were things apart from the Bill of Rights. Now it appears that at least some of the provisions of the Bill of Rights in their very terms satisfy the Court as sound and meaningful expressions of fundamental liberty. If the Fifth Amendment's protection against self-incrimination be such an expression of fundamental liberty, I ask, and have not found a satisfactory answer, why the Court today should consider that it should be "absorbed" in part but not in full? Cf. Warren, The New Liberty under the Fourteenth Amendment. Nothing in the *Palko* opinion requires that when the Court decides that a Bill of Rights' provision is to be applied to the States, it is to be applied piecemeal. Nothing in the *Palko* opinion recommends that the Court apply part of an amendment's established meaning and discard that part which does not suit the current style of fundamentals.

■ ■ ■

I cannot consider the Bill of Rights to be an outworn 18th Century "strait jacket" as the *Twining* opinion did. Its provisions may be thought outdated abstractions by some. And it is true that they were designed to meet ancient evils. But they are the same kind of human evils that have emerged from century to century wherever excessive power is sought by the few at the expense of the many. In my judgment the people of no nation can lose their liberty so long as a Bill of Rights like ours survives and its basic purposes are conscientiously interpreted, enforced and respected so as to afford continuous protection against old, as well as new, devices and practices which might thwart those purposes. I fear to see the consequences of the Court's practice of substituting its own concepts of decency and fundamental justice for the language of the Bill of Rights as its point of departure in interpreting and enforcing that Bill of Rights. If the choice must be between the selective process of the *Palko* decision applying some of the Bill of Rights to the States, or the *Twining* rule applying none of them, I would choose the *Palko* selective process. But rather than accept either of these choices, I would follow what I believe was the original purpose of the Fourteenth Amendment—to extend to all the people of the nation the complete protection of the Bill of Rights. To hold that this Court can determine what, if any, provisions of the Bill of Rights will be enforced, and if so to what degree, is to frustrate the great design of a written Constitution.

Conceding the possibility that this Court is now wise enough to improve on the Bill of Rights by substituting natural law concepts for the Bill of Rights. I think the possibility is entirely too speculative to agree to take that course. I would therefore hold in this case that the full protection of the Fifth Amendment's proscription against compelled testimony must be afforded by California. This I would do because of reliance upon the original purpose of the Fourteenth Amendment.

It is an illusory apprehension that literal application of some or all of the provisions of the Bill of Rights to the States would unwisely increase the sum total of the powers of this Court to invalidate state legislation. The Federal Government has not been harmfully burdened by the requirement that enforcement of federal laws affecting civil liberty conform literally to the Bill of Rights. Who would advocate its repeal? It must be conceded, of course, that the natural-law–due-process formula, which the Court today reaffirms, has been interpreted to limit substantially this Court's power to prevent state violations of the individual civil liberties guaranteed by the Bill of Rights. But this formula also has been used in the past and can be used in the future, to license this Court, in considering regulatory legislation, to roam at large in the broad expanses of policy and morals and to trespass, all too freely, on the legislative domain of the States as well as the Federal Government.

Since *Marbury v. Madison* (1803) was decided, the practice has been firmly established for better or worse, that courts can strike down legislative enactments which violate the Constitution. This process, of course, involves interpretation, and since words can have many meanings, interpretation obviously may result in contraction or extension of the original purpose of a constitutional provision thereby affecting policy. But to pass upon the constitutionality of statutes by looking to the particular standards enumerated in the Bill of Rights and other parts of the Constitution is one thing; to invalidate statutes because of application of "natural law" deemed to be above and undefined by the Constitution is another. "In the one instance, courts proceeding within clearly marked constitutional boundaries seek to execute policies written into the Constitution; in the other they roam at will in the limitless area of their own beliefs as to reasonableness and actually select policies, a responsibility which the Constitution entrusts to the legislative representatives of the people." *Federal Power Commission v. Natural Gas Pipeline Co. of America* (1942).

■ ■ ■

D. EARLY CRITICISM

Bivens v. Six Unknown Named Agents of Federal Bureau of Narcotics

403 U.S. 388 (1971)

BRENNAN, J., delivered the opinion of the Court, in which DOUGLAS, STEWART, WHITE and MARSHALL, JJ., joined.... BURGER, C.J., wrote a dissenting opinion....

■ ■ ■

This case has its origin in an arrest and search carried out on the morning of November 26, 1965. Petitioner's complaint alleged that on that day respondents, agents of the Federal Bureau of Narcotics acting under claim of federal authority, entered his apartment and arrested him for alleged narcotics violations. The agents manacled petitioner in front of his wife and children, and threatened to arrest the entire family. They searched the apartment from stem to stern. Thereafter, petitioner was taken to the federal courthouse in Brooklyn, where he was interrogated, booked, and subjected to a visual strip search.

> *Bivens brought lawsuit in Federal District Court claiming that the arrest and search were effected without a warrant and that unreasonable force was employed in making the arrest; fairly read, it alleges as well that the arrest was made without probable cause. He claimed to have suffered great humiliation, embarrassment, and mental suffering as a result of the agents' unlawful conduct, and sought $15,000 in damages. After dismissal in the lower federal courts, the Supreme Court created a civil claim for violation of the Fourth Amendment.*

Chief Justice BURGER, dissenting.

I dissent from today's holding which judicially creates a damage remedy not provided for by the Constitution and not enacted by Congress. We would more surely preserve the important values of the doctrine of separation of powers—and perhaps get a better result—by recommending a solution to the Congress as the branch of government in which the Constitution has vested the legislative power. Legislation is the business of the Congress, and it has the facilities and competence for that task—as we do not.

■ ■ ■

This case has significance far beyond its facts and its holding. For more than 55 years this Court has enforced a rule under which evidence of undoubted reliability and probative value has been suppressed and excluded from criminal cases whenever it was obtained in violation of the Fourth Amendment. *Weeks v. United States* (1914); *Boyd v. United States* (1886) (dictum). This rule was extended to the States in *Mapp v. Ohio* (1961). The rule has rested on a theory that suppression of evidence in these circumstances was imperative to deter law enforcement authorities from using improper methods to obtain evidence.

The deterrence theory underlying the suppression doctrine, or exclusionary rule, has a certain appeal in spite of the high price society pays for such a drastic remedy. Notwithstanding its plausibility, many judges and lawyers and some of our most distinguished legal scholars have never quite been able to escape the force of Cardozo's statement of the doctrine's anomalous result: "The criminal is to go free because the constable has blundered.... A room is searched against the law, and the body of a murdered man is found.... The privacy of the home has been infringed, and the murderer goes free." *People v. Defore* (1926).

■ ■ ■

"Rejection of the evidence does nothing to punish the wrong-doing official, while it may, and likely will, release the wrong-doing defendant. It deprives society of its remedy against one lawbreaker because he has been pursued by another. It protects one against whom incriminating evidence is discovered, but does nothing to protect innocent persons who are the victims of illegal but fruitless searches." *Irvine v. California* (1954).

From time to time members of the Court, recognizing the validity of these protests, have articulated varying alternative justifications for the suppression of important evidence in a criminal trial. Under one of these alternative theories the rule's foundation is shifted to the "sporting contest" thesis that the government must "play the game fairly" and cannot be allowed to profit from its own illegal acts. *Olmstead v. United States* (1928) (dissenting opinions); see *Terry v. Ohio* (1968). But the exclusionary rule does not ineluctably flow from a desire to ensure that government plays the "game" according to the rules. If an effective alternative remedy is available, concern for official observance of the law does not require adherence to the exclusionary rule. Nor is it easy to understand how a court can be thought to endorse a violation of the Fourth Amendment by allowing illegally seized evidence to be introduced against a defendant if an effective remedy is provided against the government.

■ ■ ■

Rather the exclusionary rule has rested on the deterrent rationale—the hope that law enforcement officials would be deterred from unlawful searches and seizures if the illegally seized, albeit trustworthy, evidence was suppressed often enough and the courts persistently enough deprived them of any benefits they might have gained from their illegal conduct.

This evidentiary rule is unique to American jurisprudence. Although the English and Canadian legal systems are highly regarded, neither has adopted our rule.

I do not question the need for some remedy to give meaning and teeth to the constitutional guarantees against unlawful conduct by government officials. Without some effective sanction, these protections would constitute little more than rhetoric. Beyond doubt the conduct of some officials requires sanctions as cases like *Irvine* indicate. But the hope that this objective could be accomplished by the exclusion of reliable evidence from criminal trials was hardly more than a wistful dream. Although I would hesitate to abandon it until some meaningful substitute is developed, the history of the suppression doctrine demonstrates that it is both conceptually sterile and practically ineffective in accomplishing its stated objective. This is illustrated by the paradox that an unlawful act against a totally innocent person—such as petitioner claims to be—has been left without an effective remedy, and hence the Court finds it necessary now—55 years later—to construct a remedy of its own.

■ ■ ■

There are several reasons for this failure. The rule does not apply any direct sanction to the individual official whose illegal conduct results in the exclusion of evidence in a criminal trial. With rare exceptions law enforcement agencies do not impose direct sanctions on the individual officer responsible for a particular judicial application of the suppression doctrine. Thus there is virtually nothing done to bring about a change in his practices. The immediate sanction triggered by the application of the rule is visited upon the prosecutor whose case against a criminal is either weakened or destroyed. The doctrine deprives the police in no real sense; except that apprehending wrongdoers is their business, police have no more stake in successful prosecutions than prosecutors or the public.

The suppression doctrine vaguely assumes that law enforcement is a monolithic governmental enterprise. For example, the dissenters in *Wolf v. Colorado* [(1949)], argued that:

> "Only by exclusion can we impress upon the zealous *prosecutor* that violation of the Constitution will do him no good. And only when that point is driven home can the *prosecutor* be expected to emphasize the importance of observing the constitutional demands in *his instructions to the police*." (Emphasis added.)

But the prosecutor who loses his case because of police misconduct is not an official in the police department; he can rarely set in motion any corrective action or administrative penalties. Moreover, he does not have control or direction over police procedures or police actions that lead to the exclusion of evidence. It is the rare exception when a prosecutor takes part in arrests, searches, or seizures so that he can guide police action.

Whatever educational effect the rule conceivably might have in theory is greatly diminished in fact by the realities of law enforcement work. Policemen do not have the time, inclination, or training to read and grasp the nuances of the appellate opinions that ultimately define the standards of conduct they are to follow. The issues that these decisions resolve often admit of neither easy nor obvious answers, as sharply divided courts on what is or is not "reasonable" amply demonstrate. Nor can judges, in all candor, forget that opinions sometimes lack helpful clarity.

The presumed educational effect of judicial opinions is also reduced by the long time lapse—often several years—between the original police action and its final judicial evaluation. Given a policeman's pressing responsibilities, it would be surprising if he ever becomes aware of the final result after such a delay. Finally, the exclusionary rule's deterrent impact is diluted by the fact that there are large areas of police activity that do not result in criminal prosecutions—hence the rule has virtually no applicability and no effect in such situations.

Today's holding seeks to fill one of the gaps of the suppression doctrine—at the price of impinging on the legislative and policy functions that the Constitution vests in Congress. Nevertheless, the holding serves the useful purpose of exposing the fundamental weaknesses of the suppression doctrine. Suppressing unchallenged truth has set guilty criminals free but demonstrably has neither deterred deliberate violations of the Fourth Amendment nor decreased those errors in judgment that will inevitably occur given the pressures inherent in police work having to do with serious crimes.

Although unfortunately ineffective, the exclusionary rule has increasingly been characterized by a single, monolithic, and drastic judicial response to all official violations of legal norms. . . .

■ ■ ■

Freeing either a tiger or a mouse in a schoolroom is an illegal act, but no rational person would suggest that these two acts should be punished in the same way. From time to time judges have occasion to pass on regulations governing police procedures. I wonder what would be the judicial response to a police order authorizing "shoot to kill" with respect to every fugitive. It is easy to predict our collective wrath and outrage. We, in common with all rational minds, would say that the police response must relate to the gravity and need; that a "shoot" order might conceivably be tolerable to prevent the escape of a convicted killer but surely not for a car thief, a pickpocket or a shoplifter.

I submit that society has at least as much right to expect rationally graded responses from judges in place of the universal "capital punishment" we inflict on all evidence when police error is shown in its acquisition. See ALI, Model Code of Pre-Arraignment Procedure § SS 8.02 (2), p. 23 (Tent. Draft No. 4, 1971), reprinted in the Appendix to this opinion. Yet for over 55 years, and with increasing scope and intensity . . . our legal system has treated vastly dissimilar cases as if they were the same. Our adherence to the exclusionary rule, our resistance to change, and our refusal even to acknowledge the need for effective enforcement mechanisms bring to mind Holmes' well-known statement:

> "It is revolting to have no better reason for a rule of law than that so it was laid down in the time of Henry IV. It is still more revolting if the grounds upon which it was laid down have vanished long since, and the rule simply persists from blind imitation of the past." The Path of the Law, 10 Harv. L. Rev. 457, 469 (1897).

■ ■ ■

I do not propose, however, that we abandon the suppression doctrine until some meaningful alternative can be developed. In a sense our legal system has become the captive of its own creation. To overrule *Weeks* and *Mapp*, even assuming the Court was now prepared to take that step, could raise yet new problems. Obviously the public interest would be poorly served if law enforcement officials were suddenly to gain the impression, however erroneous, that all constitutional restraints on police had somehow been removed—that an open season on "criminals" had been declared. I am concerned lest some such mistaken impression might be fostered by a flat overruling of the suppression doctrine cases.

■　■　■

I dissent.

E. DIRECT CUTBACKS

1. Balancing

United States v. Calandra

414 U.S. 338 (1974)

Powell, J., delivered the opinion of the Court, in which Burger, C.J., Blackmun, White, Rehnquist and Stewart, JJ., joined. Brennan, J., filed a dissenting opinion, in which Douglas and Marshall, JJ., joined.

This case presents the question whether a witness summoned to appear and testify before a grand jury may refuse to answer questions on the ground that they are based on evidence obtained from an unlawful search and seizure. The issue is of considerable importance to the administration of criminal justice.

■　■　■

The institution of the grand jury is deeply rooted in Anglo-American history. In England, the grand jury served for centuries both as a body of accusers sworn to discover and present for trial persons suspected of criminal wrongdoing and as a protector of citizens against arbitrary and oppressive governmental action. In this country the Founders thought the grand jury so essential to basic liberties that they provided in the Fifth Amendment that federal prosecution for serious crimes can only be instituted by "a presentment or indictment of a Grand Jury."

■　■　■

Traditionally the grand jury has been accorded wide latitude to inquire into violations of criminal law. No judge presides to monitor its proceedings. It deliberates in secret and may determine alone the course of its inquiry.

■　■　■

The scope of the grand jury's powers reflects its special role in insuring fair and effective law enforcement. A grand jury proceeding is not an adversary hearing in which the guilt or innocence of the accused is adjudicated. Rather, it is an *ex parte* investigation to determine whether a crime has been committed and whether criminal proceedings should be instituted against any person. The grand jury's investigative power must be broad if its public responsibility is adequately to be discharged.

■ ■ ■

In the instant case, the Court of Appeals held that the exclusionary rule of the Fourth Amendment limits the grand jury's power to compel a witness to answer questions based on evidence obtained from a prior unlawful search and seizure. The exclusionary rule was adopted to effectuate the Fourth Amendment right of all citizens "to be secure in their persons, houses, papers, and effects, against unreasonable searches and seizures. . . ." Under this rule, evidence obtained in violation of the Fourth Amendment cannot be used in a criminal proceeding against the victim of the illegal search and seizure. *Weeks v. United States* (1914); *Mapp v. Ohio* (1961). This prohibition applies as well to the fruits of the illegally seized evidence. *Wong Sun v. United States* (1963); *Silverthorne Lumber Co. v. United States* (1920).

■ ■ ■

Instead, the rule's prime purpose is to deter future unlawful police conduct and thereby effectuate the guarantee of the Fourth Amendment against unreasonable searches and seizures:

> "The rule is calculated to prevent, not to repair. Its purpose is to deter—to compel respect for the constitutional guaranty in the only effectively available way—by removing the incentive to disregard it." *Elkins v. United States* (1960).

In sum, the rule is a judicially created remedy designed to safeguard Fourth Amendment rights generally through its deterrent effect, rather than a personal constitutional right of the party aggrieved.

Despite its broad deterrent purpose, the exclusionary rule has never been interpreted to proscribe the use of illegally seized evidence in all proceedings or against all persons. As with any remedial device, the application of the rule has been restricted to those areas where its remedial objectives are thought most efficaciously served. The balancing process implicit in this approach is expressed in the contours of the standing requirement. Thus, standing to invoke the exclusionary rule has been confined to situations where the Government seeks to use such evidence to incriminate the victim of the unlawful search.

■ ■ ■

In deciding whether to extend the exclusionary rule to grand jury proceedings, we must weigh the potential injury to the historic role and functions of the grand jury against the potential benefits of the rule as applied in this context. It is evident that this extension of the exclusionary rule would seriously impede the grand jury. Because the grand jury does not finally adjudicate guilt or innocence, it has traditionally been allowed to pursue its investigative and accusatorial functions unimpeded by the evidentiary and procedural restrictions applicable to a criminal trial. Permitting witnesses to invoke the exclusionary rule before a grand jury would precipitate adjudication of issues hitherto reserved for the trial on the merits and would delay and disrupt grand jury proceedings. Suppression hearings would halt the orderly progress of an investigation and might necessitate extended litigation of issues only tangentially related to the grand jury's primary objective.

■ ■ ■

Against this potential damage to the role and functions of the grand jury, we must weigh the benefits to be derived from this proposed extension of the exclusionary rule. Suppression of the use of illegally seized evidence against the search victim in a criminal trial is thought to be an important method of effectuating the Fourth Amendment. But it does not follow that the Fourth Amendment requires adoption of every proposal that might deter police misconduct. In *Alderman v. United States* (1969), for example, this Court declined to extend the exclusionary rule to one who was not the victim of the unlawful search:

> "The deterrent values of preventing the incrimination of those whose rights the police have violated have been considered sufficient to justify the suppression of probative evidence even though the case against the defendant is weakened or destroyed. We adhere to that judgment. But we are not convinced that the additional benefits of extending the exclusionary rule to other defendants would justify further encroachment upon the public interest in prosecuting those accused of crime and having them acquitted or convicted on the basis of all the evidence which exposes the truth."

We think this observation equally applicable in the present context.

Any incremental deterrent effect which might be achieved by extending the rule to grand jury proceedings is uncertain at best. Whatever deterrence of police misconduct may result from the exclusion of illegally seized evidence from criminal trials, it is unrealistic to assume that application of the rule to grand jury proceedings would significantly further that goal. Such an extension would deter only police investigation consciously directed toward the discovery of evidence solely for use in a grand jury investigation. The incentive to disregard the requirement of the Fourth Amendment solely to obtain an indictment from a grand jury is substantially negated by the inadmissibility of the illegally seized evidence in a subsequent criminal prosecution of the search victim. For the most part, a prosecutor would be unlikely to request an indictment where a conviction could not be obtained. We therefore decline to embrace a view that would achieve a speculative and undoubtedly minimal advance in the deterrence of police misconduct at the expense of substantially impeding the role of the grand jury.

■ ■ ■

Reversed.

Justice BRENNAN, with whom Justice DOUGLAS and Justice MARSHALL join, dissenting.

The Court holds that the exclusionary rule in search-and-seizure cases does not apply to grand jury proceedings because the principal objective of the rule is "to deter future unlawful police conduct," and "it is unrealistic to assume that application of the rule to grand jury proceedings would significantly further that goal." This downgrading of the exclusionary rule to a determination whether its application in a particular type of proceeding furthers deterrence of future police misconduct reflects a startling misconception, unless it is a purposeful rejection, of the historical objective and purpose of the rule.

The commands of the Fourth Amendment are, of course, directed solely to public officials. Necessarily, therefore, only official violations of those commands could have created the evil that threatened to make the Amendment a dead letter. But curtailment of the evil, if a consideration at all, was at best only a hoped-for effect of the exclusionary rule, not its ultimate objective. Indeed, there is no evidence that the possible deterrent effect of the rule was given any attention by the judges chiefly responsible for its formulation. Their concern as guardians of the Bill of Rights was to fashion an enforcement tool to give content and meaning to the Fourth Amendment's guarantees. They thus bore out James Madison's prediction in his address to the First Congress on June 8, 1789:

> "If they [the rights] are incorporated into the Constitution, independent tribunals of justice will consider themselves in a peculiar manner the guardians of those rights; they will be an impenetrable bulwark against every assumption of power in the Legislative or Executive; they will be naturally led to resist every encroachment upon rights expressly stipulated for in the Constitution by the declaration of rights." 1 Annals of Cong. 439 (1789).

Since, however, those judges were without power to direct or control the conduct of law enforcement officers, the enforcement tool had necessarily to be one capable of administration by judges. The exclusionary rule, if not perfect, accomplished the twin goals of enabling the judiciary to avoid the taint of partnership in official lawlessness and of assuring the people—all potential victims of unlawful government conduct—that the government would not profit from its lawless behavior, thus minimizing the risk of seriously undermining popular trust in government.

That these considerations, not the rule's possible deterrent effect, were uppermost in the minds of the framers of the rule clearly emerges from the decision which fashioned it:

> "The effect of the Fourth Amendment is to put the courts of the United States and Federal officials, in the exercise of their power and authority, under limitations and restraints as to the exercise of such power and authority, and to forever secure the people, their persons, houses, papers and effects

against all unreasonable searches and seizures under the guise of law.... The tendency of those who execute the criminal laws of the country to obtain conviction by means of unlawful seizures ... *should find no sanction in the judgments of the courts which are charged at all times with the support of the Constitution and to which people of all conditions have a right to appeal for the maintenance of such fundamental rights....*

This protection is equally extended to the action of the Government and officers of the law acting under it.... To sanction such proceedings would be to affirm by judicial decision a manifest neglect if not an open defiance of the prohibitions of the Constitution, intended for the protection of the people against such unauthorized action." *Weeks v. United States* (emphasis added).

Mr. Justice Brandeis and Mr. Justice Holmes added their enormous influence to these precepts in their notable dissents in *Olmstead v. United States* (1928). Mr. Justice Brandeis said:

"In a government of laws, existence of the government will be imperilled if it fails to observe the law scrupulously. Our Government is the potent, the omnipresent teacher. For good or for ill, it teaches the whole people by its example. Crime is contagious. If the Government becomes a lawbreaker, it breeds contempt for law; it invites every man to become a law unto himself; it invites anarchy."

And Mr. Justice Holmes said:

"We must consider the two objects of desire, both of which we cannot have, and make up our minds which to choose. It is desirable that criminals should be detected, and to that end that all available evidence should be used. It also is desirable that the Government should not itself foster and pay for other crimes, when they are the means by which the evidence is to be obtained.... We have to choose, and for my part I think it a less evil that some criminals should escape than that the Government should play an ignoble part.

... If the existing code does not permit district attorneys to have a hand in such dirty business it does not permit the judge to allow such iniquities to succeed."

■ ■ ■

It is true that deterrence was a prominent consideration in the determination whether *Mapp v. Ohio*, which applied the exclusionary rule to the States, should be given retrospective effect. But that lends no support to today's holding that the application of the exclusionary rule depends solely upon whether its invocation in a particular type of proceeding will significantly further the goal of deterrence.

■ ■ ■

Thus, the Court seriously errs in describing the exclusionary rule as merely "a judicially created remedy designed to safeguard Fourth Amendment rights generally through its deterrent effect...." Rather, the exclusionary rule is "part and parcel of the Fourth Amendment's limitation upon [governmental] encroachment of individual privacy," and "an essential part of both the Fourth and Fourteenth Amendments," that "gives to the individual no more than that which the Constitution guarantees him, to the police officer no less than that to which honest law enforcement is entitled, and, to the courts, that judicial integrity so necessary in the true administration of justice." *Mapp v. Ohio.*

■ ■ ■

Pennsylvania Board of Probation & Parole v. Scott

524 U.S. 357 (1998)

THOMAS, J., delivered the opinion of the Court, in which REHNQUIST, C.J., and O'CONNOR, SCALIA, and KENNEDY, JJ., joined. STEVENS, J., filed a dissenting opinion. SOUTER, J., filed a dissenting opinion, in which GINSBURG and BREYER, JJ., joined.

This case presents the question whether the exclusionary rule, which generally prohibits the introduction at criminal trial of evidence obtained in violation of a defendant's Fourth Amendment rights, applies in parole revocation hearings. We hold that it does not.

■ ■ ■

We have emphasized repeatedly that the government's use of evidence obtained in violation of the Fourth Amendment does not itself violate the Constitution. *United States v. Leon* (1984); *Stone v. Powell* (1976). Rather, a Fourth Amendment violation is "fully accomplished" by the illegal search or seizure, and no exclusion of evidence from a judicial or administrative proceeding can cure the invasion of the defendant's rights which he has already suffered. The exclusionary rule is instead a judicially created means of deterring illegal searches and seizures. As such, the rule does not "proscribe the introduction of illegally seized evidence in all proceedings or against all persons," *Stone v. Powell*, but applies only in contexts "where its remedial objectives are thought most efficaciously served," *United States v. Calandra* (1974); see also *United States v. Janis* (1976) ("If... the exclusionary rule does not result in appreciable deterrence, then, clearly, its use in the instant situation is unwarranted"). Moreover, because the rule is prudential rather than constitutionally mandated, we have held it to be applicable only where its deterrence benefits outweigh its "substantial social costs." *United States v. Leon.*

Recognizing these costs, we have repeatedly declined to extend the exclusionary rule to proceedings other than criminal trials. *United States v. Janis.* For example, in *United States v. Calandra*, we held that the exclusionary rule does not apply to grand jury proceedings; in so doing, we emphasized that such proceedings play a special role in the law enforcement process and that the traditionally flexible, nonadversarial nature of those proceedings would be jeopardized by application of the rule. Likewise, in *United States v. Janis*, we held that the exclusionary rule did not bar the introduction of unconstitutionally obtained evidence in a civil tax proceeding because the costs of excluding relevant and reliable evidence would outweigh the marginal deterrence benefits, which, we noted, would be minimal because the use of the exclusionary rule in criminal trials already deterred illegal searches. Finally, in *INS v. Lopez-Mendoza* (1984), we refused to extend the exclusionary rule to civil deportation proceedings, citing the high social costs of allowing an immigrant to remain illegally in this country and noting the incompatibility of the rule with the civil, administrative nature of those proceedings.

As in *Calandra, Janis,* and *Lopez-Mendoza,* we are asked to extend the operation of the exclusionary rule beyond the criminal trial context. We again decline to do so. Application of the exclusionary rule would both hinder the functioning of state parole systems and alter the traditionally flexible, administrative nature of parole revocation proceedings. The rule would provide only minimal deterrence benefits in this context, because application of the rule in the criminal trial context already provides significant deterrence of unconstitutional searches. We therefore hold that the federal exclusionary rule does not bar the introduction at parole revocation hearings of evidence seized in violation of parolees' Fourth Amendment rights.

Because the exclusionary rule precludes consideration of reliable, probative evidence, it imposes significant costs: It undeniably detracts from the truthfinding process and allows many who would otherwise be incarcerated to escape the consequences of their actions. Although we have held these costs to be worth bearing in certain circumstances, our cases have repeatedly emphasized that the rule's "costly toll" upon truth-seeking and law enforcement objectives presents a high obstacle for those urging application of the rule.

The costs of excluding reliable, probative evidence are particularly high in the context of parole revocation proceedings. Parole is a "variation on imprisonment of convicted criminals," *Morrissey v. Brewer* (1972). . . . In most cases, the State is willing to extend parole only because it is able to condition it upon compliance with certain requirements. The State thus has an "overwhelming interest" in ensuring that a parolee complies with those requirements and is returned to prison if he fails to do so. The exclusion of evidence establishing a parole violation, however, hampers the State's ability to ensure compliance with these conditions by permitting the parolee to avoid the consequences of his noncompliance. The costs of allowing a parolee to avoid the consequences of his violation are compounded by the fact that parolees (particularly those who have already committed parole violations) are more likely to commit future criminal offenses than are average citizens. . . .

The exclusionary rule, moreover, is incompatible with the traditionally flexible, administrative procedures of parole revocation. Because parole revocation deprives the parolee not "of the absolute liberty to which every citizen is entitled, but only of the conditional liberty properly dependent on observance of special parole restrictions," *Morrissey v. Brewer*, States have wide latitude under the Constitution to structure parole revocation proceedings.

■ ■ ■

The deterrence benefits of the exclusionary rule would not outweigh these costs. As the Supreme Court of Pennsylvania recognized, application of the exclusionary rule to parole revocation proceedings would have little deterrent effect upon an officer who is unaware that the subject of his search is a parolee. In that situation, the officer will likely be searching for evidence of criminal conduct with an eye toward the introduction of the evidence at a criminal trial. The likelihood that illegally obtained evidence will be excluded from trial provides deterrence against Fourth Amendment violations, and the remote possibility that the subject is a parolee and that the evidence may be admitted at a parole revocation proceeding surely has little, if any, effect on the officer's incentives.

■ ■ ■

Even when the officer performing the search is a parole officer, the deterrence benefits of the exclusionary rule remain limited. Parole agents, in contrast to police officers, are not "engaged in the often competitive enterprise of ferreting out crime," *United States v. Leon*; instead, their primary concern is whether their parolees should remain free on parole. Thus, their relationship with parolees is more supervisory than adversarial. . . .

We have long been averse to imposing federal requirements upon the parole systems of the States. A federal requirement that parole boards apply the exclusionary rule, which is itself a "'grud[g]ingly taken medicament,'" *United States v. Janis*, would severely disrupt the traditionally informal, administrative process of parole revocation. The marginal deterrence of unreasonable searches and seizures is insufficient to justify such an intrusion. We therefore hold that parole boards are not required by federal law to exclude evidence obtained in violation of the Fourth Amendment. Accordingly, the judgment below is reversed, and the case is remanded to the Pennsylvania Supreme Court.

It is so ordered.

■ ■ ■

Justice SOUTER, with whom Justice GINSBURG and Justice BREYER join, dissenting.

The Court's holding that the exclusionary rule of *Mapp v. Ohio* (1961) has no application to parole revocation proceedings rests upon mistaken conceptions of the actual function of revocation, of the objectives of those who gather evidence in support of petitions to revoke, and, consequently, of the need to deter violations of the Fourth Amendment that would tend to occur in administering the parole laws. In reality a revocation proceeding often serves the same function as a criminal trial, and the revocation hearing may very well present the only forum in which the State will seek to use evidence of a parole violation, even when that evidence would support an independent criminal charge. The deterrent function of the exclusionary rule is therefore implicated as much by a revocation proceeding as by a conventional trial, and the exclusionary rule should be applied accordingly. From the Court's conclusion to the contrary, I respectfully dissent.

This Court has said that the primary purpose of the exclusionary rule "is to deter future unlawful police conduct and thereby effectuate the guarantee of the Fourth Amendment against unreasonable searches and seizures." *United States v. Calandra.* Because the exclusionary rule thus "operates as a judicially created remedy designed to safeguard Fourth Amendment rights generally through its deterrent effect, rather than a personal constitutional right of the party aggrieved," *United States v. Leon,* "[w]hether the exclusionary sanction is appropriately imposed in a particular case . . . is 'an issue separate from the question whether the Fourth Amendment rights of the party seeking to invoke the rule were violated by police conduct.'" The exclusionary rule does not, therefore, mandate the exclusion of illegally acquired evidence from all proceedings or against all persons, *United States v. Calandra,* and we have made clear that the rule applies only in "those instances where its remedial objectives are thought most efficaciously served," *Arizona v. Evans* (1995). Only then can the deterrent value of applying the rule to a given class of proceedings be seen to outweigh its price, including "the loss of often probative evidence and all of the secondary costs that flow from the less accurate or more cumbersome adjudication that therefore occurs." *INS v. Lopez-Mendoza;* see also *United States v. Janis; United States v. Calandra.*

Because we have found the requisite efficacy when the rule is applied in criminal trials, see *Elkins v. United States* (1960); *Mapp v. Ohio; Weeks v. United States* (1914), the deterrent effect of the evidentiary limitation upon prosecution is a baseline for evaluating the degree (or incremental degree) of deterrence that could be expected from extending the exclusionary rule to other sorts of cases, see *INS v. Lopez-Mendoza.* Thus, we have thought that any additional deterrent value obtainable from applying the rule in civil tax proceedings, see *United States v. Janis,* habeas proceedings, see *Stone v. Powell,* and grand jury proceedings, see *United States v. Calandra,* would be so marginal as to be outweighed by the incremental costs.

■ ■ ■

In a formal sense, such is the reasoning of the Court's majority in deciding today that application of the exclusionary rule in parole revocation proceedings would have only an insignificant marginal deterrent value, "because application of the rule in the criminal trial context already provides significant deterrence of unconstitutional searches." In substance, however, the Court's conclusion will not jibe with the examples just cited, for it rests on erroneous views of the roles of regular police and parole officers in relation to revocation proceedings, and of the practical significance of the proceedings themselves.

As to the police, the majority says that regular officers investigating crimes almost always act with the prospect of a criminal prosecution before them. Their fear of evidentiary suppression in the criminal trial will have as much deterrent effect as can be expected, therefore, while any risk of suppression in parole administration is too unlikely to be on their minds to influence their conduct.

The majority's assumption will only sometimes be true, however, and in many, or even most cases, it will quite likely be false. To be sure, if a police officer acts on the spur of the moment to seize evidence or thwart crime, he may have no idea of a perpetrator's parole status. But the contrary will almost certainly be the case when he has first identified the person he has his eye on: the local police know the local felons, criminal history information is instantly available nationally, and police and parole officers routinely cooperate....

As these cases show, the police very likely do know a parolee's status when they go after him, and (contrary to the majority's assumption) this fact is significant for three reasons. First, and most obviously, the police have reason for concern with the outcome of a parole revocation proceeding, which is just as foreseeable as the criminal trial and at least as likely to be held. Police officers, especially those employed by the same sovereign that runs the parole system, therefore have every incentive not to jeopardize a recommitment by rendering evidence inadmissible. Second, as I will explain below, the actual likelihood of trial is often far less than the probability of a petition for parole revocation, with the consequence that the revocation hearing will be the only forum in which the evidence will ever be offered. Often, therefore, there will be nothing incremental about the significance of evidence offered in the administrative tribunal, and nothing "marginal" about the deterrence provided by an exclusionary rule operating there. Finally, the cooperation between parole and police officers, as in the instances shown in the cases cited above, casts serious doubt upon the aptness of treating police officers differently from parole officers, doubt that is confirmed by the following attention to the Court's characterization of the position of the parole officer.

The Court recalls our description of the police as "engaged in the often competitive enterprise of ferreting out crime," which raises the temptation to cut constitutional corners (which in turn requires the countervailing influence of the exclusionary rule). *United States v. Leon.* As against this picture of the police, the Court paints the parole officer as a figure more nearly immune to such competitive zeal. As the Court describes him, the parole officer is interested less in catching a parole violator than in making sure that the parolee continues to go straight, since "'realistically the failure of the parolee is in a sense a failure for his supervising officer.'" This view of the parole officer suffers, however, from its selectiveness. Parole officers wear several hats; while they are indeed the parolees' counselors and social workers, they also "often serve as both prosecutors and law enforcement officials in their relationship with probationers and parolees." ...

Once, in fact, the officer has turned from counselor to adversary, there is every reason to expect at least as much competitive zeal from him as from a regular police officer. See *Gagnon v. Scarpelli* (1973) ("[A]n exclusive focus on the benevolent attitudes of those who administer the probation/parole system when it is working successfully obscures the modification in attitude which is likely to take place once the officer has decided to recommend revocation"). If he fails to respond to his parolee's further criminality he will be neglecting the public safety, and if he brings a revocation petition without enough evidence to sustain it he can hardly look forward to professional advancement. And as for competitiveness, one need only ask whether a parole officer would rather leave the credit to state or local police when a parolee has to be brought to book.

The Court, of course, does not mean to deny that parole officers are subject to some temptation to skirt the limits on search and seizure, but it believes that deterrents other than the evidentiary exclusion will suffice. The Court contends that parole agents will be kept within bounds by "departmental training and discipline and the threat of damages actions." The same, of course, might be said of the police, and yet as to them such arguments are not heard, perhaps for the same reason that the Court's suggestion sounds hollow as to parole officers. The Court points to no specific departmental training regulation; it cites no instance of discipline imposed on a Pennsylvania parole officer for conducting an illegal search of a parolee's residence; and, least surprisingly of all, the majority mentions not a single lawsuit brought by a parolee against a parole officer seeking damages for an illegal search. In sum, if the police need the deterrence of an exclusionary rule to offset the temptations to forget the Fourth Amendment, parole officers need it quite as much.

Just as the Court has underestimated the competitive influences tending to induce police and parole officers to stint on Fourth Amendment obligations, so I think it has misunderstood the significance of admitting illegally seized evidence at the revocation hearing. On the one hand, the majority magnifies the cost of an exclusionary rule for parole cases by overemphasizing the differences between a revocation hearing and a trial, and on the other hand it has minimized the benefits by failing to recognize the significant likelihood that the revocation hearing will be the principal, not the secondary, forum, in which evidence of a parolee's criminal conduct will be offered.

The Court is, of course, correct that the revocation hearing has not only an adversarial side in factfinding, but a predictive and discretionary aspect in addressing the proper disposition when a violation has been found. And I agree that open-mindedness at the discretionary, dispositional stage is promoted by the relative informality of the proceeding even at its factfinding stage. That informality is fostered by limiting issues so that lawyers are not always necessary, and by appointing lay members to parole boards. There is no question, either, that application of an exclusionary rule, if there is no waiver of Fourth Amendment rights, will tend to underscore the adversary character of the factfinding process. This cannot, however, be a dispositive objection to an exclusionary rule. Any revocation hearing is adversary to a degree: counsel must now be provided whenever the complexity of fact issues so warrant, and lay board members are just as capable of passing upon Fourth Amendment issues as the police, who are necessarily charged with responsibility for the legality of warrantless arrests, investigatory stops, and searches.

As to the benefit of an exclusionary rule in revocation proceedings, the majority does not see that in the investigation of criminal conduct by someone known to be on parole, Fourth Amendment standards will have very little deterrent sanction unless evidence offered for parole revocation is subject to suppression for unconstitutional conduct. It is not merely that parole revocation is the government's consolation prize when, for whatever reason, it cannot obtain a further criminal conviction, though that will sometimes be true.

benefits of ER in proceedings

■   ■   ■

The reasons for this tendency to skip any new prosecution are obvious. If the conduct in question is a crime in its own right, the odds of revocation are very high. Since time on the street before revocation is not subtracted from the balance of the sentence to be served on revocation, the balance may well be long enough to render recommitment the practical equivalent of a new sentence for a separate crime. And all of this may be accomplished without shouldering the burden of proof beyond a reasonable doubt; hence the obvious popularity of revocation in place of new prosecution.

The upshot is that without a suppression remedy in revocation proceedings, there will often be no influence capable of deterring Fourth Amendment violations when parole revocation is a possible response to new crime. Suppression in the revocation proceeding cannot be looked upon, then, as furnishing merely incremental or marginal deterrence over and above the effect of exclusion in criminal prosecution. Instead, it will commonly provide the only deterrence to unconstitutional conduct when the incarceration of parolees is sought, and the reasons that support the suppression remedy in prosecution therefore support it in parole revocation.

Because I would apply the exclusionary rule to evidence offered in revocation hearings, I would affirm the judgment in this case. Scott gave written consent to warrantless searches; the form he signed provided that he consented "to the search of my person, property and residence, without a warrant by agents of the Pennsylvania Board of Probation and Parole." The Supreme Court of Pennsylvania held the consent insufficient to waive any requirement that searches be supported by reasonable suspicion, and in the absence of any such waiver, the State was bound to justify its search by what the Court has described as information indicating the likelihood of facts justifying the search. The State makes no claim here to have satisfied this standard. It describes the parole agent's knowledge as rising no further than "the possibility of the presence of weapons in Scott's home," and rests on the argument that not even reasonable suspicion was required.

Because the search violated the Fourth Amendment, and because I conclude that the exclusionary rule ought to apply to parole revocation proceedings, I would affirm the decision of the Supreme Court of Pennsylvania.

2. Good-Faith Exception to the Exclusionary Rule

United States v. Leon

468 U.S. 897 (1984)

WHITE, J., delivered the opinion of the Court, in which BURGER, C.J., BLACKMUN, POWELL, REHNQUIST and O'CONNOR, JJ., joined. BRENNAN, J., filed a dissenting opinion, in which MARSHALL, J., joined. STEVENS, J., also filed a dissenting opinion.

Q

This case presents the question whether the Fourth Amendment exclusionary rule should be modified so as not to bar the use in the prosecution's case in chief of evidence obtained by officers acting in reasonable reliance on a search warrant issued by a detached and neutral magistrate but ultimately found to be unsupported by probable cause. To resolve this question, we must consider once again the tension between the sometimes competing goals of, on the one hand, deterring official misconduct and removing inducements to unreasonable invasions of privacy and, on the other, establishing procedures under which criminal defendants are "acquitted or convicted on the basis of all the evidence which exposes the truth." *Alderman v. United States* (1969).

In August 1981, a confidential informant of unproven reliability informed an officer of the Burbank Police Department that two persons known to him as "Armando" and "Patsy" were selling large quantities of cocaine and methaqualone from their residence at 620 Price Drive in Burbank, Cal. The informant also indicated that he had witnessed a sale of methaqualone by "Patsy" at the residence approximately five months earlier and had observed at that time a shoebox containing a large amount of cash that belonged to "Patsy." He further declared that "Armando" and "Patsy" generally kept only small quantities of drugs at their residence and stored the remainder at another location in Burbank.

facts

On the basis of this information, the Burbank police initiated an extensive investigation focusing first on the Price Drive residence and later on two other residences as well. Cars parked at the Price Drive residence were determined to belong to respondents Armando Sanchez, who had previously been arrested for possession of marihuana, and Patsy Stewart, who had no criminal record. During the course of the investigation, officers observed an automobile belonging to respondent Ricardo Del Castillo, who had previously been arrested for possession of 50 pounds of marihuana, arrive at the Price Drive residence. The driver of that car entered the house, exited shortly thereafter carrying a small paper sack, and drove away. A check of Del Castillo's probation records led the officers to respondent Alberto Leon, whose telephone number Del Castillo had listed as his employer's. Leon had been arrested in 1980 on drug charges, and a companion had informed the police at that time that Leon was heavily involved in the importation of drugs into this country. Before the current investigation began, the Burbank officers had learned that an informant had told a Glendale police officer that Leon stored a large quantity of methaqualone at his residence in Glendale. During the course of this investigation, the Burbank officers learned that Leon was living at 716 South Sunset Canyon in Burbank.

Subsequently, the officers observed several persons, at least one of whom had prior drug involvement, arriving at the Price Drive residence and leaving with small packages; observed a variety of other material activity at the two residences as well as at a condominium at 7902 Via Magdalena; and witnessed a variety of relevant activity involving respondents' automobiles. The officers also observed respondents Sanchez and Stewart board separate flights for

Miami. The pair later returned to Los Angeles together, consented to a search of their luggage that revealed only a small amount of marihuana, and left the airport. Based on these and other observations summarized in the affidavit, App. 34, Officer Cyril Rombach of the Burbank Police Department, an experienced and well-trained narcotics investigator, prepared an application for a warrant to search 620 Price Drive, 716 South Sunset Canyon, 7902 Via Magdalena, and automobiles registered to each of the respondents for an extensive list of items believed to be related to respondents' drug-trafficking activities. Officer Rombach's extensive application was reviewed by several Deputy District Attorneys.

A facially valid search warrant was issued in September 1981 by a State Superior Court Judge. The ensuing searches produced large quantities of drugs at the Via Magdalena and Sunset Canyon addresses and a small quantity at the Price Drive residence. Other evidence was discovered at each of the residences and in Stewart's and Del Castillo's automobiles. Respondents were indicted by a grand jury in the District Court for the Central District of California and charged with conspiracy to possess and distribute cocaine and a variety of substantive counts.

The respondents then filed motions to suppress the evidence seized pursuant to the warrant. The District Court held an evidentiary hearing and, while recognizing that the case was a close one, granted the motions to suppress in part. It concluded that the affidavit was insufficient to establish probable cause, but did not suppress all of the evidence as to all of the respondents because none of the respondents had standing to challenge all of the searches. In response to a request from the Government, the court made clear that Officer Rombach had acted in good faith, but it rejected the Government's suggestion that the Fourth Amendment exclusionary rule should not apply where evidence is seized in reasonable, good-faith reliance on a search warrant.

The District Court denied the Government's motion for reconsideration, and a divided panel of the Court of Appeals for the Ninth Circuit affirmed.... The Court of Appeals refused the Government's invitation to recognize a good-faith exception to the Fourth Amendment exclusionary rule.

The Government's petition for certiorari expressly declined to seek review of the lower courts' determinations that the search warrant was unsupported by probable cause and presented only the question "[whether] the Fourth Amendment exclusionary rule should be modified so as not to bar the admission of evidence seized in reasonable, good-faith reliance on a search warrant that is subsequently held to be defective." We granted certiorari to consider the propriety of such a modification....

We have concluded that, in the Fourth Amendment context, the exclusionary rule can be modified somewhat without jeopardizing its ability to perform its intended functions. Accordingly, we reverse the judgment of the Court of Appeals.

■ ■ ■

4th Amendment wrong proscribe

The Fourth Amendment contains no provision expressly precluding the use of evidence obtained in violation of its commands, and an examination of its origin and purposes makes clear that the use of fruits of a past unlawful search or seizure "[works] no new Fourth Amendment wrong." *United States v. Calandra* (1974). The wrong condemned by the Amendment is "fully accomplished" by the unlawful search or seizure itself, the exclusionary rule is neither intended nor able to "cure the invasion of the defendant's rights which he has already suffered." The rule thus operates as "a judicially created remedy designed to safeguard Fourth Amendment rights generally through its deterrent effect, rather than a personal constitutional right of the party aggrieved."

■ ■ ■

The substantial social costs exacted by the exclusionary rule for the vindication of Fourth Amendment rights have long been a source of concern. "Our cases have consistently recognized that unbending application of the exclusionary sanction to enforce ideals of governmental rectitude would impede unacceptably the truth-finding functions of judge and jury." *United States v. Payner* (1980). An objectionable collateral consequence of this interference with the criminal justice system's truth-finding function is that some guilty defendants may go free or receive reduced sentences as a result of favorable plea bargains.[6] Particularly when law enforcement officers have acted in objective good faith or their transgressions have been minor, the magnitude of the benefit conferred on such guilty defendants offends basic concepts of the criminal justice system. *Stone v. Powell* (1976). Indiscriminate application of the exclusionary rule, therefore, may well "[generate] disrespect for the law and administration of justice." Accordingly, "[as] with any remedial device, the application of the rule has been restricted to those areas where its remedial objectives are thought most efficaciously served." *United States v. Calandra*; see *Stone v. Powell*; *United States v. Janis* (1976).   *limits of ER*

---

6. Researchers have only recently begun to study extensively the effects of the exclusionary rule on the disposition of felony arrests. One study suggests that the rule results in the nonprosecution or nonconviction of between 0.6% and 2.35% of individuals arrested for felonies. Davies, A Hard Look at What We Know (and Still Need to Learn) About the "Costs" of the Exclusionary Rule: The NIJ Study and Other Studies of "Lost" Arrests, 1983 ABF. Res. J. 611, 621. The estimates are higher for particular crimes the prosecution of which depends heavily on physical evidence. Thus, the cumulative loss due to nonprosecution or nonconviction of individuals arrested on felony drug charges is probably in the range of 2.8% to 7.1%. *Id.*, at 680. Davies' analysis of California data suggests that screening by police and prosecutors results in the release because of illegal searches or seizures of as many as 1.4% of all felony arrestees, *id.*, at 650, that 0.9% of felony arrestees are released, because of illegal searches or seizures, at the preliminary hearing or after trial, *id.*, at 653, and that roughly 0.05% of all felony arrestees benefit from reversals on appeal because of illegal searches. *Id.*, at 654. See also K. Brosi, A Cross-City Comparison of Felony Case Processing 16, 18-19 (1979); U.S. General Accounting Office, Report of the Comptroller General of the United States, Impact of the Exclusionary Rule on Federal Criminal Prosecutions 10-11, 14 (1979); F. Feeney, F. Dill, & A. Weir, Arrests Without Convictions: How Often They Occur and Why 203-206 (National Institute of Justice 1983); National Institute of Justice, The Effects of the Exclusionary Rule: A Study in California 1-2 (1982); Nardulli, The Societal Cost of the Exclusionary Rule: An Empirical Assessment, 1983 ABF. Res. J. 585, 600. The exclusionary rule also has been found to affect the plea-bargaining process. S. Schlesinger, Exclusionary Injustice: The Problem of Illegally Obtained Evidence 63 (1977). But see Davies, *supra*, at 668-669; Nardulli, *supra*, at 604-606.

costs of exclusion

Many of these researchers have concluded that the impact of the exclusionary rule is insubstantial, but the small percentages with which they deal mask a large absolute number of felons who are released because the cases against them were based in part on illegal searches or seizures. "[Any] rule of evidence that denies the jury access to clearly probative and reliable evidence must bear a heavy burden of justification, and must be carefully limited to the circumstances in which it will pay its way by deterring official unlawlessness." *Illinois v. Gates* (1983) (White, J., concurring in judgment). Because we find that the rule can have no substantial deterrent effect in the sorts of situations under consideration in this case, we conclude that it cannot pay its way in those situations.

Close attention to those remedial objectives has characterized our recent decisions concerning the scope of the Fourth Amendment exclusionary rule. The Court has, to be sure, not seriously questioned, "in the absence of a more efficacious sanction, the continued application of the rule to suppress evidence from the [prosecution's] case where a Fourth Amendment violation has been substantial and deliberate. . . ." *Franks v. Delaware* (1978); *Stone v. Powell*. Nevertheless, the balancing approach that has evolved in various contexts— including criminal trials—"forcefully [suggests] that the exclusionary rule be more generally modified to permit the introduction of evidence obtained in the reasonable good-faith belief that a search or seizure was in accord with the Fourth Amendment." *Illinois v. Gates* (White, J., concurring in judgment).

■ ■ ■

As yet, we have not recognized any form of good-faith exception to the Fourth Amendment exclusionary rule. But the balancing approach that has evolved during the years of experience with the rule provides strong support for the modification currently urged upon us. As we discuss below, our evaluation of the costs and benefits of suppressing reliable physical evidence seized by officers reasonably relying on a warrant issued by a detached and neutral magistrate leads to the conclusion that such evidence should be admissible in the prosecution's case in chief.

Because a search warrant "provides the detached scrutiny of a neutral magistrate, which is a more reliable safeguard against improper searches than the hurried judgment of a law enforcement officer 'engaged in the often competitive enterprise of ferreting out crime,'" United *States v. Chadwick* (1977), quoting *Johnson v. United States* (1948), we have expressed a strong preference for warrants and declared that "in a doubtful or marginal case a search under a warrant may be sustainable where without one it would fall." *United States v. Ventresca* (1965). Reasonable minds frequently may differ on the question whether a particular affidavit establishes probable cause, and we have thus concluded that the preference for warrants is most appropriately effectuated by according "great deference" to a magistrate's determination.

Deference to the magistrate, however, is not boundless. It is clear, first, that the deference accorded to a magistrate's finding of probable cause does not preclude inquiry into the knowing or reckless falsity of the affidavit on which that determination was based. *Franks v. Delaware*. Second, the courts must also insist that the magistrate purport to "perform his 'neutral and detached' function and not serve merely as a rubber stamp for the police." *Aguilar v. Texas* (1964). See *Illinois v. Gates*. A magistrate failing to "manifest that neutrality and detachment demanded of a judicial officer when presented with a warrant application" and who acts instead as "an adjunct law enforcement officer" cannot provide valid authorization for an otherwise unconstitutional search. *Lo-Ji Sales, Inc. v. New York* (1979).

Third, reviewing courts will not defer to a warrant based on an affidavit that does not "provide the magistrate with a substantial basis for determining the existence of probable cause." *Illinois v. Gates*. "Sufficient information must be presented to the magistrate to allow that official to determine probable cause; his action cannot be a mere ratification of the bare conclusions of others."

■ ■ ■

Only in the first of these three situations, however, has the Court set forth a rationale for suppressing evidence obtained pursuant to a search warrant; in the other areas, it has simply excluded such evidence without considering whether Fourth Amendment interests will be advanced. To the extent that proponents of exclusion rely on its behavioral effects on judges and magistrates in these areas, their reliance is misplaced. First, the exclusionary rule is designed to deter police misconduct rather than to punish the errors of judges and magistrates. Second, there exists no evidence suggesting that judges and magistrates are inclined to ignore or subvert the Fourth Amendment or that lawlessness among these actors requires application of the extreme sanction of exclusion.[14]

Third, and most important, we discern no basis, and are offered none, for believing that exclusion of evidence seized pursuant to a warrant will have a significant deterrent effect on the issuing judge or magistrate. Many of the factors that indicate that the exclusionary rule cannot provide an effective "special" or "general" deterrent for individual offending law enforcement officers apply as well to judges or magistrates. And, to the extent that the rule is thought to operate as a "systemic" deterrent on a wider audience, it

---

14. Although there are assertions that some magistrates become rubber stamps for the police and others may be unable effectively to screen police conduct, see, *e.g.*, 2 W. LaFave, Search and Seizure § 4.1 (1978); Kamisar, Does (Did) (Should) the Exclusionary Rule Rest on a "Principled Basis" Rather than an "Empirical Proposition"?, 16 Creighton L. Rev. 565, 569-571 (1983); Schroeder, Deterring Fourth Amendment Violations: Alternatives to the Exclusionary Rule, 69 Geo. L.J. 1361, 1412 (1981), we are not convinced that this is a problem of major proportions. See L. Tiffany, D. McIntyre, & D. Rotenberg, Detection of Crime 119 (1967); Israel, Criminal Procedure, the Burger Court, and the Legacy of the Warren Court, 75 Mich. L. Rev. 1319, 1414, n. 396 (1977); P. Johnson, New Approaches to Enforcing the Fourth Amendment 8-10 (Working Paper, Sept. 1978), quoted in Y. Kamisar, W. LaFave, & J. Israel, Modern Criminal Procedure 229-230 (5th ed. 1980); R. Van Duizend, L. Sutton, & C. Carter, The Search Warrant Process, ch. 7 (Review Draft, National Center for State Courts, 1983).

clearly can have no such effect on individuals empowered to issue search warrants. Judges and magistrates are not adjuncts to the law enforcement team; as neutral judicial officers, they have no stake in the outcome of particular criminal prosecutions. The threat of exclusion thus cannot be expected significantly to deter them. Imposition of the exclusionary sanction is not necessary meaningfully to inform judicial officers of their errors, and we cannot conclude that admitting evidence obtained pursuant to a warrant while at the same time declaring that the warrant was somehow defective will in any way reduce judicial officers' professional incentives to comply with the Fourth Amendment, encourage them to repeat their mistakes, or lead to the granting of all colorable warrant requests.

■ ■ ■

We have frequently questioned whether the exclusionary rule can have any deterrent effect when the offending officers acted in the objectively reasonable belief that their conduct did not violate the Fourth Amendment. "No empirical researcher, proponent or opponent of the rule, has yet been able to establish with any assurance whether the rule has a deterrent effect...." *United States v. Janis*. But even assuming that the rule effectively deters some police misconduct and provides incentives for the law enforcement profession as a whole to conduct itself in accord with the Fourth Amendment, it cannot be expected, and should not be applied, to deter objectively reasonable law enforcement activity.

■ ■ ■

This is particularly true, we believe, when an officer acting with objective good faith has obtained a search warrant from a judge or magistrate and acted within its scope. In most such cases, there is no police illegality and thus nothing to deter. It is the magistrate's responsibility to determine whether the officer's allegations establish probable cause and, if so, to issue a warrant comporting in form with the requirements of the Fourth Amendment. In the ordinary case, an officer cannot be expected to question the magistrate's probable-cause determination or his judgment that the form of the warrant is technically sufficient.

■ ■ ■

We conclude that the marginal or nonexistent benefits produced by suppressing evidence obtained in objectively reasonable reliance on a subsequently invalidated search warrant cannot justify the substantial costs of exclusion. We do not suggest, however, that exclusion is always inappropriate in cases where an officer has obtained a warrant and abided by its terms. "[Searches] pursuant to a warrant will rarely require any deep inquiry into reasonableness," *Illinois v. Gates* (White, J., concurring in judgment), for "a warrant issued by a magistrate normally suffices to establish" that a law enforcement officer has "acted in good faith in conducting the search." *United States v. Ross* (1982). Nevertheless, the officer's reliance on the magistrate's probable-cause determination and on the technical sufficiency of the warrant he issues must be objectively reasonable....

Suppression therefore remains an appropriate remedy if the magistrate or judge in issuing a warrant was misled by information in an affidavit that the affiant knew was false or would have known was false except for his reckless disregard of the truth. *Franks v. Delaware.* The exception we recognize today will also not apply in cases where the issuing magistrate wholly abandoned his judicial role in the manner condemned in *Lo-Ji Sales, Inc. v. New York*; in such circumstances, no reasonably well trained officer should rely on the warrant. Nor would an officer manifest objective good faith in relying on a warrant based on an affidavit "so lacking in indicia of probable cause as to render official belief in its existence entirely unreasonable." *Brown v. Illinois* (1975) (Powell, J., concurring in part); see *Illinois v. Gates* (White, J., concurring in judgment). Finally, depending on the circumstances of the particular case, a warrant may be so facially deficient—*i.e.*, in failing to particularize the place to be searched or the things to be seized—that the executing officers cannot reasonably presume it to be valid. Cf. *Massachusetts v. Sheppard* (1984).

■ ■ ■

Accordingly, the judgment of the Court of Appeals is
Reversed.

Justice BRENNAN, with whom Justice MARSHALL joins, dissenting.

This opinion applies also to Massachusetts v. Sheppard.

Ten years ago in *United States v. Calandra*, I expressed the fear that the Court's decision "may signal that a majority of my colleagues have positioned themselves to reopen the door [to evidence secured by official lawlessness] still further and abandon altogether the exclusionary rule in search-and-seizure cases." . . . That today's decisions represent the *piece de resistance* of the Court's past efforts cannot be doubted, for today the Court sanctions the use in the prosecution's case in chief of illegally obtained evidence against the individual whose rights have been violated—a result that had previously been thought to be foreclosed.

The Court seeks to justify this result on the ground that the "costs" of adhering to the exclusionary rule in cases like those before us exceed the "benefits." But the language of deterrence and of cost/benefit analysis, if used indiscriminately, can have a narcotic effect. It creates an illusion of technical precision and ineluctability. It suggests that not only constitutional principle but also empirical data support the majority's result. When the Court's analysis is examined carefully, however, it is clear that we have not been treated to an honest assessment of the merits of the exclusionary rule, but have instead been drawn into a curious world where the "costs" of excluding illegally obtained evidence loom to exaggerated heights and where the "benefits" of such exclusion are made to disappear with a mere wave of the hand.

■ ■ ■

... [S]ome criminals will go free not, in Justice (then Judge) Cardozo's misleading epigram, "because the constable has blundered," *People v. Defore* (1926), but rather because official compliance with Fourth Amendment requirements makes it more difficult to catch criminals. Understood in this way, the Amendment directly contemplates that some reliable and incriminating evidence will be lost to the government; therefore, it is not the exclusionary rule, but the Amendment itself that has imposed this cost.[8]

In addition, the Court's decisions over the past decade have made plain that the entire enterprise of attempting to assess the benefits and costs of the exclusionary rule in various contexts is a virtually impossible task for the judiciary to perform honestly or accurately. Although the Court's language in those cases suggests that some specific empirical basis may support its analyses, the reality is that the Court's opinions represent inherently unstable compounds of intuition, hunches, and occasional pieces of partial and often inconclusive data. In *Calandra*, for example, the Court, in considering whether the exclusionary rule should apply in grand jury proceedings, had before it no concrete evidence whatever concerning the impact that application of the rule in such proceedings would have either in terms of the long-term costs or the expected benefits. To the extent empirical data are available regarding the general costs and benefits of the exclusionary rule, such data have shown, on the one hand, as the Court acknowledges today, that the costs are not as substantial as critics have asserted in the past, and, on the other hand, that while the exclusionary rule may well have certain deterrent effects, it is extremely difficult to determine with any degree of precision whether the incidence of unlawful conduct by police is now lower than it was prior to *Mapp* (1961). See *United States v. Janis*; *Stone v. Powell*. The Court has sought to turn this uncertainty to its advantage by casting the burden of proof upon proponents of the rule, see, *e.g., United States v. Janis*. "Obviously," however, "the assignment of the burden of proof on an issue where evidence does not exist and cannot be obtained is outcome determinative. [The] assignment of the burden is merely a way of announcing a predetermined conclusion." Dworkin, Fact Style Adjudication and the Fourth Amendment: The Limits of Lawyering, 48 Ind. L.J. 329, 332-333 (1973).

■ ■ ■

---

8. Justice Stewart has explained this point in detail in a recent article: "Much of the criticism leveled at the exclusionary rule is misdirected; it is more properly directed at the Fourth Amendment itself. It is true that, as many observers have charged, the effect of the rule is to deprive the courts of extremely relevant, often direct evidence of the guilt of the defendant. But these same critics fail to acknowledge that, in many instances, the same extremely relevant evidence would not have been obtained had the police officer complied with the commands of the Fourth Amendment in the first place.... The exclusionary rule places no limitations on the actions of the police. The Fourth Amendment does. The inevitable result of the Constitution's prohibition against unreasonable searches and seizures and its requirement that no warrant shall issue but upon probable cause is that police officers who obey its strictures will catch fewer criminals.... [T]hat is the price the framers anticipated and were willing to pay to ensure the sanctity of the person, the home, and property against unrestrained governmental power." Stewart, 83 Colum. L. Rev., at 1392-1393.

By remaining within its redoubt of empiricism and by basing the rule solely on the deterrence rationale, the Court has robbed the rule of legitimacy. A doctrine that is explained as if it were an empirical proposition but for which there is only limited empirical support is both inherently unstable and an easy mark for critics. The extent of this Court's fidelity to Fourth Amendment requirements, however, should not turn on such statistical uncertainties.

■ ■ ■

Even if I were to accept the Court's general approach to the exclusionary rule, I could not agree with today's result. There is no question that in the hands of the present Court the deterrence rationale has proved to be a powerful tool for confining the scope of the rule. In *Calandra*, for example, the Court concluded that the "speculative and undoubtedly minimal advance in the deterrence of police misconduct," was insufficient to outweigh the "expense of substantially impeding the role of the grand jury." . . . Thus, in this bit of judicial stagecraft, while the sets sometimes change, the actors always have the same lines. Given this well-rehearsed pattern, one might have predicted with some assurance how the present case would unfold. First there is the ritual incantation of the "substantial social costs" exacted by the exclusionary rule, followed by the virtually foreordained conclusion that, given the marginal benefits, application of the rule in the circumstances of these cases is not warranted. Upon analysis, however, such a result cannot be justified even on the Court's own terms.

Massachusetts v. Sheppard

468 U.S. 981 (1984)

Massachusetts v. Sheppard *was a companion case to* Leon, *which involves the particularity requirement of the Fourth Amendment.*

WHITE, J., delivered the opinion of the Court, in which BURGER, C.J., BLACKMUN, POWELL, REHNQUIST, and O'CONNOR, JJ., joined. STEVENS, J., filed a concurring opinion. BRENNAN, J., filed a dissenting opinion, in which MARSHALL, J., joined.

The badly burned body of Sandra Boulware was discovered in a vacant lot in the Roxbury section of Boston at approximately 5 a.m., Saturday, May 5, 1979. An autopsy revealed that Boulware had died of multiple compound skull fractures caused by blows to the head. After a brief investigation, the police decided to question one of the victim's boyfriends, Osborne Sheppard. Sheppard told the police that he had last seen the victim on Tuesday night and that he had been at a local gaming house (where card games were played) from 9 p.m. Friday until 5 a.m. Saturday. He identified several people who would be willing to substantiate the latter claim.

■ ■ ■

On the basis of the evidence gathered thus far in the investigation, Detective Peter O'Malley drafted an affidavit designed to support an application for an arrest warrant and a search warrant authorizing a search of Sheppard's residence.

■ ■ ■

Detective O'Malley showed the affidavit to the District Attorney, the District Attorney's first assistant, and a sergeant, who all concluded that it set forth probable cause for the search and the arrest.

Because it was Sunday, the local court was closed, and the police had a difficult time finding a warrant application form. Detective O'Malley finally found a warrant form previously in use in the Dorchester District. The form was entitled "Search Warrant—Controlled Substance." Realizing that some changes had to be made before the form could be used to authorize the search requested in the affidavit, Detective O'Malley deleted the subtitle "controlled substance" with a typewriter. He also substituted "Roxbury" for the printed "Dorchester" and typed Sheppard's name and address into blank spaces provided for that information. However, the reference to "controlled substance" was not deleted in the portion of the form that constituted the warrant application and that, when signed, would constitute the warrant itself.

Detective O'Malley then took the affidavit and the warrant form to the residence of a judge who had consented to consider the warrant application. The judge examined the affidavit and stated that he would authorize the search as requested. Detective O'Malley offered the warrant form and stated that he knew the form as presented dealt with controlled substances. He showed the judge where he had crossed out the subtitles. After unsuccessfully searching for a more suitable form, the judge informed O'Malley that he would make the necessary changes so as to provide a proper search warrant. The judge then took the form, made some changes on it, and dated and signed the warrant. However, he did not change the substantive portion of the warrant, which continued to authorize a search for controlled substances; nor did he alter the form so as to incorporate the affidavit.[2] The judge returned the affidavit and the warrant to O'Malley, informing him that the warrant was sufficient authority in form and content to carry out the search as requested. O'Malley took the two documents and, accompanied by other officers, proceeded to Sheppard's residence. The scope of the ensuing search was limited to the items listed in the affidavit, and several incriminating pieces of evidence were discovered. Sheppard was then charged with first-degree murder.

At a pretrial suppression hearing, the trial judge concluded that the warrant failed to conform to the commands of the Fourth Amendment because it did not particularly describe the items to be seized. The judge ruled, however, that the evidence could be admitted notwithstanding the defect in the warrant

---

2. The warrant directed the officers to "search for any controlled substance, article, implement or other paraphernalia used in, for, or in connection with the unlawful possession or use of any controlled substance, and to seize and securely keep the same until final action...."

because the police had acted in good faith in executing what they reasonably thought was a valid warrant. At the subsequent trial, Sheppard was convicted.

On appeal, Sheppard argued that the evidence obtained pursuant to the defective warrant should have been suppressed. The Supreme Judicial Court of Massachusetts agreed.

■ ■ ■

Having already decided that the exclusionary rule should not be applied when the officer conducting the search acted in objectively reasonable reliance on a warrant issued by a detached and neutral magistrate that subsequently is determined to be invalid, the sole issue before us in this case is whether the officers reasonably believed that the search they conducted was authorized by a valid warrant. There is no dispute that the officers believed that the warrant authorized the search that they conducted. Thus, the only question is whether there was an objectively reasonable basis for the officers' mistaken belief. Both the trial court, and a majority of the Supreme Judicial Court concluded that there was. We agree.

■ ■ ■

The officers in this case took every step that could reasonably be expected of them. Detective O'Malley prepared an affidavit which was reviewed and approved by the District Attorney. He presented that affidavit to a neutral judge. The judge concluded that the affidavit established probable cause to search Sheppard's residence and informed O'Malley that he would authorize the search as requested. O'Malley then produced the warrant form and informed the judge that it might need to be changed. He was told by the judge that the necessary changes would be made. He then observed the judge make some changes and received the warrant and the affidavit. At this point, a reasonable police officer would have concluded, as O'Malley did, that the warrant authorized a search for the materials outlined in the affidavit.

In sum, the police conduct in this case clearly was objectively reasonable and largely error-free. An error of constitutional dimensions may have been committed with respect to the issuance of the warrant, but it was the judge, not the police officers, who made the critical mistake. Accordingly, federal law does not require the exclusion of the disputed evidence in this case. The judgment of the Supreme Judicial Court is therefore reversed, and the case is remanded for further proceedings not inconsistent with this opinion.

Groh v. Ramirez

540 U.S. 551 (2004)

STEVENS, J., delivered the opinion of the Court, in which O'CONNOR, SOUTER, GINSBURG, and BREYER, JJ., joined. KENNEDY, J., filed a dissenting opinion, in which REHNQUIST, C.J., joined. THOMAS, J., filed a dissenting opinion, in which SCALIA, J., joined, and in which REHNQUIST, C.J., joined [in part].

Petitioner conducted a search of respondents' home pursuant to a warrant that failed to describe the "persons or things to be seized." The questions presented are (1) whether the search violated the Fourth Amendment, and (2) if so, whether petitioner nevertheless is entitled to qualified immunity, given that a Magistrate Judge, relying on an affidavit that particularly described the items in question, found probable cause to conduct the search.

Respondents, Joseph Ramirez and members of his family, live on a large ranch in Butte-Silver Bow County, Montana. Petitioner, Jeff Groh, has been a Special Agent for the Bureau of Alcohol, Tobacco and Firearms (ATF) since 1989. In February 1997, a concerned citizen informed petitioner that on a number of visits to respondents' ranch the visitor had seen a large stock of weaponry, including an automatic rifle, grenades, a grenade launcher, and a rocket launcher. Based on that information, petitioner prepared and signed an application for a warrant to search the ranch. The application stated that the search was for "any automatic firearms or parts to automatic weapons, destructive devices to include but not limited to grenades, grenade launchers, rocket launchers, and any and all receipts pertaining to the purchase or manufacture of automatic weapons or explosive devices or launchers." Petitioner supported the application with a detailed affidavit, which he also prepared and executed, that set forth the basis for his belief that the listed items were concealed on the ranch. Petitioner then presented these documents to a Magistrate, along with a warrant form that petitioner also had completed. The Magistrate signed the warrant form.

Although the application particularly described the place to be searched and the contraband petitioner expected to find, the warrant itself was less specific; it failed to identify any of the items that petitioner intended to seize. In the portion of the form that called for a description of the "person or property" to be seized, petitioner typed a description of respondents' two-story blue house rather than the alleged stockpile of firearms. The warrant did not incorporate by reference the itemized list contained in the application. It did, however, recite that the Magistrate was satisfied the affidavit established probable cause to believe that contraband was concealed on the premises, and that sufficient grounds existed for the warrant's issuance.

■ ■ ■

The warrant was plainly invalid. The Fourth Amendment states unambiguously that "no Warrants shall issue, but upon probable cause, supported by Oath or affirmation, and *particularly describing* the place to be searched, and *the persons or things to be seized.*" The warrant in this case complied with the first three of these requirements: It was based on probable cause and supported by a sworn affidavit, and it described particularly the place of the search. On the fourth requirement, however, the warrant failed altogether. Indeed, petitioner concedes that "the warrant . . . was deficient in particularity because it provided no description of the type of evidence sought."

The fact that the *application* adequately described the "things to be seized" does not save the *warrant* from its facial invalidity. The Fourth Amendment by its terms requires particularity in the warrant, not in the supporting documents. See *Massachusetts v. Sheppard* (1984). And for good reason: "The presence of a search warrant serves a high function," *McDonald v. United States* (1948), and that high function is not necessarily vindicated when some other document, somewhere, says something about the objects of the search, but the contents of that document are neither known to the person whose home is being searched nor available for her inspection. We do not say that the Fourth Amendment prohibits a warrant from cross-referencing other documents. Indeed, most Courts of Appeals have held that a court may construe a warrant with reference to a supporting application or affidavit if the warrant uses appropriate words of incorporation, and if the supporting document accompanies the warrant. But in this case the warrant did not incorporate other documents by reference, nor did either the affidavit or the application (which had been placed under seal) accompany the warrant. Hence, we need not further explore the matter of incorporation.

Petitioner argues that even though the warrant was invalid, the search nevertheless was "reasonable" within the meaning of the Fourth Amendment. He notes that a Magistrate authorized the search on the basis of adequate evidence of probable cause, that petitioner orally described to respondents the items to be seized, and that the search did not exceed the limits intended by the Magistrate and described by petitioner. Thus, petitioner maintains, his search of respondents' ranch was functionally equivalent to a search authorized by a valid warrant.

We disagree. This warrant did not simply omit a few items from a list of many to be seized, or misdescribe a few of several items. Nor did it make what fairly could be characterized as a mere technical mistake or typographical error. Rather, in the space set aside for a description of the items to be seized, the warrant stated that the items consisted of a "single dwelling residence . . . blue in color." In other words, the warrant did not describe the items to be seized *at all.* In this respect the warrant was so obviously deficient that we must regard the search as "warrantless" within the meaning of our case law.

■ ■ ■

Petitioner asks us to hold that a search conducted pursuant to a warrant lacking particularity should be exempt from the presumption of unreasonableness if the goals served by the particularity requirement are otherwise satisfied. He maintains that the search in this case satisfied those goals—which he says are "to prevent general searches, to prevent the seizure of one thing under a warrant describing another, and to prevent warrants from being issued on vague or dubious information." But unless the particular items described in the affidavit are also set forth in the warrant itself (or at least incorporated by reference, and the affidavit present at the search), there can be no written assurance that the Magistrate actually found probable cause to search for, and to seize, every item mentioned in the affidavit. . . .

We have long held, moreover, that the purpose of the particularity requirement is not limited to the prevention of general searches. A particular warrant also "assures the individual whose property is searched or seized of the lawful authority of the executing officer, his need to search, and the limits of his power to search."

■ ■ ■

It is incumbent on the officer executing a search warrant to ensure the search is lawfully authorized and lawfully conducted. Because petitioner did not have in his possession a warrant particularly describing the things he intended to seize, proceeding with the search was clearly "unreasonable" under the Fourth Amendment. The Court of Appeals correctly held that the search was unconstitutional.

■ ■ ■

Accordingly, the judgment of the Court of Appeals is affirmed.
It is so ordered.

■ ■ ■

Justice THOMAS, with whom Justice SCALIA joins, and with whom THE CHIEF JUSTICE joins [in part], dissenting.

■ ■ ■

The precise relationship between the Amendment's *Warrant Clause* and Unreasonableness Clause is unclear. But neither Clause explicitly requires a warrant. While "it is of course textually possible to consider [a warrant require-ment] implicit within the requirement of reasonableness," the text of the *Fourth Amendment* certainly does not mandate this result. Nor does the Amendment's history, which is clear as to the Amendment's principal target (general war-rants), but not as clear with respect to when warrants were required, if ever. Indeed, because of the very different nature and scope of federal authority and ability to conduct searches and arrests at the founding, it is possible that neither the history of the *Fourth Amendment* nor the common law provides much guidance.

As a result, the Court has vacillated between imposing a categorical warrant requirement and applying a general reasonableness standard. The Court has most frequently held that warrantless searches are presumptively unreasonable but has also found a plethora of exceptions to presumptive unreasonableness, that is, our cases stand for the illuminating proposition that warrantless searches are *per se* unreasonable, except, of course, when they are not.

Today the Court holds that the warrant in this case was "so obviously deficient" that the ensuing search must be regarded as a warrantless search and thus presumptively unreasonable. However, the text of the Fourth Amendment, its history, and the sheer number of exceptions to the Court's categorical warrant requirement seriously undermine the bases upon which the Court today rests its holding. Instead of adding to this confusing jurispru-dence, as the Court has done, I would turn to first principles in order to deter-mine the relationship between the Warrant Clause and the Unreasonableness Clause. But even within the Court's current framework, a search conducted pursuant to a defective warrant is constitutionally different from a "warrant-less search." Consequently, despite the defective warrant, I would still ask whether this search was unreasonable and would conclude that it was not.

Furthermore, even if the Court were correct that this search violated the Constitution (and in particular, respondents' Fourth Amendment rights), given the confused state of our Fourth Amendment jurisprudence and the reasonableness of petitioner's actions, I cannot agree with the Court's conclusion that petitioner is not entitled to qualified immunity. For these reasons, I respectfully dissent.

■ ■ ■

The Court bases its holding that a defect in the particularity of the warrant by itself renders a search "warrantless" on a citation of a single footnote in *Massachusetts v. Sheppard*. In *Sheppard*, the Court, after noting that "the sole issue . . . in th[e] case is whether the officers reasonably believed that the search they conducted was authorized by a valid warrant," rejected the petitioner's argument that despite the invalid warrant, the otherwise reasonable search was constitutional. The Court recognized that under its case law a reasonableness inquiry would be appropriate if one of the exceptions to the warrant requirement applied. But the Court declined to consider whether such an exception applied and whether the search actually violated the Fourth Amendment because that question presented merely a "fact-bound issue of little importance." Because the Court in *Sheppard* did not conduct any sort of inquiry into whether a Fourth Amendment violation actually occurred, it is clear that the Court assumed a violation for the purposes of its analysis. Rather than rely on dicta buried in a footnote in *Sheppard*, the Court should actually analyze the arguably dispositive issue in this case.

The Court also rejects the argument that the details of the warrant application and affidavit save the warrant, because "'[t]he presence of a search warrant serves a high function.'" But it is not only the physical existence of the warrant and its typewritten contents that serve this high function. The Warrant Clause's principal protection lies in the fact that the "'Fourth Amendment has interposed a magistrate between the citizen and the police . . . so that an objective mind might weigh the need to invade [the searchee's] privacy in order to enforce the law.'" *Massachusetts v. Sheppard*, quoting *McDonald v. United States*.

■ ■ ■

But the actual contents of the warrant are simply manifestations of this protection. Hence, in contrast to the case of a truly warrantless search, where a warrant (due to a mistake) does not specify on its face the particular items to be seized but the warrant application passed on by the magistrate judge contains such details, a searchee still has the benefit of a determination by a neutral magistrate that there is probable cause to search a particular place and to seize particular items. In such a circumstance, the principal justification for applying a rule of presumptive unreasonableness falls away.

In the instant case, the items to be seized were clearly specified in the warrant application and set forth in the affidavit, both of which were given to the Judge (Magistrate). The Magistrate reviewed all of the documents and signed the warrant application and made no adjustment or correction to this application. It is clear that respondents here received the protection of the

Warrant Clause. Under these circumstances, I would not hold that any ensuing search constitutes a presumptively unreasonable warrantless search. Instead, I would determine whether, despite the invalid warrant, the resulting search was reasonable and hence constitutional.

■ ■ ■

For the foregoing reasons, I respectfully dissent.

Messerschmidt v. Millender

132 S. Ct. 1235 (2012)

See Chapter 4B.

Illinois v. Krull

480 U.S. 340 (1987)

BLACKMUN, J., delivered the opinion of the Court, in which REHNQUIST, C.J., and WHITE, POWELL, and SCALIA, JJ., joined. MARSHALL, J., filed a dissenting opinion. O'CONNOR, J., filed a dissenting opinion, in which BRENNAN, MARSHALL, and STEVENS, JJ., joined.

 In *United States v. Leon* (1984), this Court ruled that the Fourth Amendment exclusionary rule does not apply to evidence obtained by police officers who acted in objectively reasonable reliance upon a search warrant issued by a neutral magistrate, but where the warrant was ultimately found to be unsupported by probable cause. See also *Massachusetts v. Sheppard* (1984). The present case presents the question whether a similar exception to the exclusionary rule should be recognized when officers act in objectively reasonable reliance upon a *statute* authorizing warrantless administrative searches, but where the statute is ultimately found to violate the Fourth Amendment.

The State of Illinois, as part of its Vehicle Code, has a comprehensive statutory scheme regulating the sale of motor vehicles and vehicular parts. A person who sells motor vehicles, or deals in automotive parts, or processes automotive scrap metal, or engages in a similar business must obtain a license from the Illinois Secretary of State. A licensee is required to maintain a detailed record of all motor vehicles and parts that he purchases or sells, including the identification numbers of such vehicles and parts, and the dates of acquisition and disposition. In 1981, the statute in its then form required a licensee to permit state officials to inspect these records "at any reasonable time during the night or day" and to allow "examination of the premises of the licensee's established place of business for the purpose of determining the accuracy of required records."

 Respondents in 1981 operated Action Iron & Metal, Inc., an automobile wrecking yard located in the city of Chicago. Detective Leilan K. McNally of the Chicago Police Department regularly inspected the records of wrecking yards pursuant to the state statute. On the morning of July 5, 1981, he entered respondents' yard. He identified himself as a police officer to respondent Lucas, who was working at the yard, and asked to see the license and records of vehicle purchases. Lucas could not locate the license or records, but he did produce a paper pad on which approximately five vehicle purchases were listed. McNally then requested and received permission from Lucas to look at the cars in the yard. Upon checking with his mobile computer the serial numbers of several of the vehicles, McNally ascertained that three of them were stolen. Also, the identification number of a fourth had been removed. McNally seized the four vehicles and placed Lucas under arrest. Respondent Krull, the holder of the license, and respondent Mucerino, who was present at the yard the day of the search, were arrested later. Respondents were charged with various criminal violations of the Illinois motor vehicle statutes.

■ ■ ■

The court rejected the State's argument that the evidence seized from respondents' wrecking yard should nevertheless be admitted because the police officer had acted in good-faith reliance on the statute authorizing such searches. . . .

We granted certiorari to consider whether a good-faith exception to the Fourth Amendment exclusionary rule applies when an officer's reliance on the constitutionality of a statute is objectively reasonable, but the statute is subsequently declared unconstitutional.

In *Leon*, the Court held that the exclusionary rule should not be applied to evidence obtained by a police officer whose reliance on a search warrant issued by a neutral magistrate was objectively reasonable, even though the warrant was ultimately found to be defective. On the basis of three factors, the Court concluded that there was no sound reason to apply the exclusionary rule as a means of deterring misconduct on the part of judicial officers who are responsible for issuing warrants. First, the exclusionary rule was historically designed "to deter police misconduct rather than to punish the errors of judges and magistrates." Second, there was "no evidence suggesting that judges and magistrates are inclined to ignore or subvert the Fourth Amendment or that lawlessness among these actors requires application of the extreme sanction of exclusion." Third, and of greatest importance to the Court, there was no basis "for believing that exclusion of evidence seized pursuant to a warrant will have a significant deterrent effect on the issuing judge or magistrate." The Court explained: "Judges and magistrates are not adjuncts to the law enforcement team; as neutral judicial officers, they have no stake in the outcome of particular criminal prosecutions." Thus, the threat of exclusion of evidence could not be expected to deter such individuals from improperly issuing warrants, and a judicial ruling that a warrant was defective was sufficient to inform the judicial officer of the error made.

The Court then considered whether application of the exclusionary rule in that context could be expected to alter the behavior of law enforcement officers. In prior cases, the Court had observed that, because the purpose of the exclusionary rule is to deter police officers from violating the Fourth Amendment, evidence should be suppressed "only if it can be said that the law enforcement officer had knowledge, or may properly be charged with knowledge, that the search was unconstitutional under the Fourth Amendment." . . .

The Court in *Leon* concluded that a deterrent effect was particularly absent when an officer, acting in objective good faith, obtained a search warrant from a magistrate and acted within its scope. "In most such cases, there is no police illegality and thus nothing to deter." It is the judicial officer's responsibility to determine whether probable cause exists to issue a warrant, and, in the ordinary case, police officers cannot be expected to question that determination. Because the officer's sole responsibility after obtaining a warrant is to carry out the search pursuant to it, applying the exclusionary rule in these circumstances could have no deterrent effect on a future Fourth Amendment violation by the officer.

■ ■ ■

The approach used in *Leon* is equally applicable to the present case. The application of the exclusionary rule to suppress evidence obtained by an officer acting in objectively reasonable reliance on a statute would have as little deterrent effect on the officer's actions as would the exclusion of evidence when an officer acts in objectively reasonable reliance on a warrant. Unless a statute is clearly unconstitutional, an officer cannot be expected to question the judgment of the legislature that passed the law. If the statute is subsequently declared unconstitutional, excluding evidence obtained pursuant to it prior to such a judicial declaration will not deter future Fourth Amendment violations by an officer who has simply fulfilled his responsibility to enforce the statute as written. To paraphrase the Court's comment in *Leon*: "Penalizing the officer for the [legislature's] error, rather than his own, cannot logically contribute to the deterrence of Fourth Amendment violations."

Any difference between our holding in *Leon* and our holding in the instant case, therefore, must rest on a difference between the effect of the exclusion of evidence on judicial officers and the effect of the exclusion of evidence on legislators. Although these two groups clearly serve different functions in the criminal justice system, those differences are not controlling for purposes of this case. We noted in *Leon* as an initial matter that the exclusionary rule was aimed at deterring police misconduct. Thus, legislators, like judicial officers, are not the focus of the rule. Moreover, to the extent we consider the rule's effect on legislators, our initial inquiry, as set out in *Leon*, is whether there is evidence to suggest that legislators "are inclined to ignore or subvert the Fourth Amendment." Although legislators are not "neutral judicial officers," as are judges and magistrates, neither are they "adjuncts to the law enforcement team." The role of legislators in the criminal justice system is to enact laws for the purpose of establishing and perpetuating that system. In order to fulfill this responsibility, legislators' deliberations of necessity are significantly different from the hurried judgment of a law enforcement officer "engaged in the often competitive enterprise of ferreting out crime." . . .

There is no evidence suggesting that Congress or state legislatures have enacted a significant number of statutes permitting warrantless administrative searches violative of the Fourth Amendment. Legislatures generally have confined their efforts to authorizing administrative searches of specific categories of businesses that require regulation, and the resulting statutes usually have been held to be constitutional. . . .

Even if we were to conclude that legislators are different in certain relevant respects from magistrates, because legislators are not officers of the judicial system, the next inquiry necessitated by *Leon* is whether exclusion of evidence seized pursuant to a statute subsequently declared unconstitutional will "have a significant deterrent effect" on legislators enacting such statutes. Respondents have offered us no reason to believe that applying the exclusionary rule will have such an effect. Legislators enact statutes for broad, programmatic purposes, not for the purpose of procuring evidence in particular criminal investigations. Thus, it is logical to assume that the greatest deterrent to the enactment of unconstitutional statutes by a legislature is the power of the courts to invalidate such statutes. Invalidating a statute informs the legislature of its constitutional error, affects the admissibility of all evidence obtained subsequent to the constitutional ruling, and often results in the legislature's enacting a modified and constitutional version of the statute, as happened in this very case. There is nothing to indicate that applying the exclusionary rule to evidence seized pursuant to the statute prior to the declaration of its invalidity will act as a significant, additional deterrent. Moreover, to the extent that application of the exclusionary rule could provide some incremental deterrent, that possible benefit must be weighed against the "substantial social costs exacted by the exclusionary rule." When we indulge in such weighing, we are convinced that applying the exclusionary rule in this context is unjustified.

Respondents argue that the result in this case should be different from that in *Leon* because a statute authorizing warrantless administrative searches affects an entire industry and a large number of citizens, while the issuance of a defective warrant affects only one person. This distinction is not persuasive. In determining whether to apply the exclusionary rule, a court should examine whether such application will advance the deterrent objective of the rule. Although the number of individuals affected may be considered when "weighing the costs and benefits" of applying the exclusionary rule, the simple fact that many are affected by a statute is not sufficient to tip the balance if the deterrence of Fourth Amendment violations would not be advanced in any meaningful way. . . .

Accordingly, the judgment of the Supreme Court of Illinois is reversed, and the case is remanded to that court for further proceedings not inconsistent with this opinion.

It is so ordered.

Justice O'CONNOR, with whom Justice BRENNAN, Justice MARSHALL, and Justice STEVENS join, dissenting. . . .

Unlike the Court, I see a powerful historical basis for the exclusion of evidence gathered pursuant to a search authorized by an unconstitutional statute. Statutes authorizing unreasonable searches were the core concern of the Framers of the Fourth Amendment. This Court has repeatedly noted that reaction against the ancient Act of Parliament authorizing indiscriminate general searches by writ of assistance.... James Otis' argument to the royal Superior Court in Boston against such overreaching laws is as powerful today as it was in 1761:

> "...I will to my dying day oppose with all the powers and faculties God has given me, all such instruments of slavery on the one hand, and villany on the other, as this writ of assistance is....
>
> ...It is a power, that places the liberty of every man in the hands of every petty officer....
>
> ...No Acts of Parliament can establish such a writ; though it should be made in the very words of the petition, it would be void. An act against the constitution is void." 2 Works of John Adams 523-525 (C. Adams ed. 1850).

See *Paxton's Case,* Quincy 51 (Mass. 1761). James Otis lost the case he argued; and, even had he won it, no exclusionary rule existed to prevent the admission of evidence gathered pursuant to a writ of assistance in a later trial. But, history's court has vindicated Otis. The principle that no legislative Act can authorize an unreasonable search became embodied in the Fourth Amendment.

Almost 150 years after Otis' argument, this Court determined that evidence gathered in violation of the Fourth Amendment would be excluded in federal court. *Weeks v. United States* (1914). In *Mapp v. Ohio* (1961), the rule was further extended to state criminal trials. This exclusionary rule has, of course, been regularly applied to evidence gathered under statutes that authorized unreasonable searches.

■ ■ ■

This history also supplies the evidence that *Leon* demanded for the proposition that the relevant state actors, here legislators, might pose a threat to the values embodied in the Fourth Amendment. Legislatures have, upon occasion, failed to adhere to the requirements of the Fourth Amendment, as the cited cases illustrate. Indeed, as noted, the history of the Amendment suggests that legislative abuse was precisely the evil the Fourth Amendment was intended to eliminate. In stark contrast, the Framers did not fear that judicial officers, the state actors at issue in *Leon,* posed a serious threat to Fourth Amendment values. James Otis is as clear on this point as he was in denouncing the unconstitutional Act of Parliament....

The distinction drawn between the legislator and the judicial officer is sound. The judicial role is particularized, fact specific, and nonpolitical. Judicial authorization of a particular search does not threaten the liberty of everyone, but rather authorizes a single search under particular circumstances. The legislative Act, on the other hand, sweeps broadly, authorizing whole classes of searches, without any particularized showing. A judicial officer's unreasonable authorization of a search affects one person at a time; a legislature's unreasonable authorization of searches may affect thousands or millions and will almost always affect more than one. Certainly the latter poses a greater threat to liberty.

Moreover, the *Leon* Court relied explicitly on the tradition of judicial independence in concluding that, until it was presented with evidence to the contrary, there was relatively little cause for concern that judicial officers might take the opportunity presented by the good-faith exception to authorize unconstitutional searches. "Judges and magistrates are not adjuncts to the law enforcement team; as neutral judicial officers, they have no stake in the outcome of particular criminal prosecutions." ...

Finally, I disagree with the Court that there is "no reason to believe that applying the exclusionary rule" will deter legislation authorizing unconstitutional searches. "The inevitable result of the Constitution's prohibition against unreasonable searches and seizures and its requirement that no warrant shall issue but upon probable cause is that police officers who obey its strictures will catch fewer criminals." Stewart, 83 Colum. L. Rev. 1365, 1393 (1983). Providing legislatures a grace period during which the police may freely perform unreasonable searches in order to convict those who might have otherwise escaped creates a positive incentive to promulgate unconstitutional laws. While I heartily agree with the Court that legislators ordinarily do take seriously their oaths to uphold the Constitution and that it is proper to presume that legislative Acts are constitutional, it cannot be said that there is no reason to fear that a particular legislature might yield to the temptation offered by the Court's good-faith exception.

Accordingly, I find that none of *Leon*'s stated rationales supports the Court's decision in this case. History suggests that the exclusionary rule ought to apply to the unconstitutional legislatively authorized search, and this historical experience provides a basis for concluding that legislatures may threaten Fourth Amendment values. Even conceding that the deterrent value of the exclusionary rule in this context is arguable, I am unwilling to abandon both history and precedent weighing in favor of suppression. And if I were willing, I still could not join the Court's opinion because the rule it adopts is both difficult to administer and anomalous. ...

For all these reasons, I respectfully dissent.

Arizona v. Evans

514 U.S. 1 (1995)

REHNQUIST, C.J., delivered the opinion of the Court, in which O'CONNOR, SCALIA, KENNEDY, SOUTER, THOMAS, and BREYER, JJ., joined. O'CONNOR, J., wrote a concurring opinion, in which SOUTER and BREYER, JJ., joined. STEVENS, J., wrote a dissenting opinion. ...

This case presents the question whether evidence seized in violation of the Fourth Amendment by an officer who acted in reliance on a police record indicating the existence of an outstanding arrest warrant—a record that is later determined to be erroneous—must be suppressed by virtue of the exclusionary rule regardless of the source of the error. The Supreme Court of Arizona held that the exclusionary rule required suppression of evidence even if the erroneous information resulted from an error committed by an employee of the office of the Clerk of Court. We disagree.

In January 1991, Phoenix police officer Bryan Sargent observed respondent Isaac Evans driving the wrong way on a one-way street in front of the police station. The officer stopped respondent and asked to see his driver's license. After respondent told him that his license had been suspended, the officer entered respondent's name into a computer data terminal located in his patrol car. The computer inquiry confirmed that respondent's license had been suspended and also indicated that there was an outstanding misdemeanor warrant for his arrest. Based upon the outstanding warrant, Officer Sargent placed respondent under arrest. While being handcuffed, respondent dropped a hand-rolled cigarette that the officers determined smelled of marijuana. Officers proceeded to search his car and discovered a bag of marijuana under the passenger's seat.

The State charged respondent with possession of marijuana. When the police notified the Justice Court that they had arrested him, the Justice Court discovered that the arrest warrant previously had been quashed and so advised the police. Respondent argued that because his arrest was based on a warrant that had been quashed 17 days prior to his arrest, the marijuana seized incident to the arrest should be suppressed as the fruit of an unlawful arrest. Respondent also argued that "the 'good faith' exception to the exclusionary rule [was] inapplicable . . . because it was police error, not judicial error, which caused the invalid arrest."

At the suppression hearing, the Chief Clerk of the Justice Court testified that a Justice of the Peace had issued the arrest warrant on December 13, 1990, because respondent had failed to appear to answer for several traffic violations. On December 19, 1990, respondent appeared before a *pro tem* Justice of the Peace who entered a notation in respondent's file to "quash warrant."

The Chief Clerk also testified regarding the standard court procedure for quashing a warrant. Under that procedure a justice court clerk calls and informs the warrant section of the Sheriff's Office when a warrant has been quashed. The Sheriff's Office then removes the warrant from its computer records. After calling the Sheriff's Office, the clerk makes a note in the individual's file indicating the clerk who made the phone call and the person at the Sheriff's Office to whom the clerk spoke. The Chief Clerk testified that there was no indication in respondent's file that a clerk had called and notified the Sheriff's Office that his arrest warrant had been quashed. A records clerk from the Sheriff's Office also testified that the Sheriff's Office had no record of a telephone call informing it that respondent's arrest warrant had been quashed.

At the close of testimony, respondent argued that the evidence obtained as a result of the arrest should be suppressed because "the purposes of the exclusionary rule would be served here by making the clerks for the court, or the clerk for the Sheriff's office, whoever is responsible for this mistake, to be more careful about making sure that warrants are removed from the records." The trial court granted the motion to suppress because it concluded that the State had been at fault for failing to quash the warrant. Presumably because it could find no "distinction between State action, whether it happens to be the police department or not," the trial court made no factual finding as to whether the Justice Court Sheriff's Office was responsible for the continued presence of the quashed warrant in the police records.

A divided panel of the Arizona Court of Appeals reversed because it "believed that the exclusionary rule [was] not intended to deter justice court employees or Sheriff's Office employees who are not directly associated with the arresting officers or the arresting officers' police department." Therefore, it concluded, "the purpose of the exclusionary rule would not be served by excluding the evidence obtained in this case."

The Arizona Supreme Court reversed. The court rejected the "distinction drawn by the court of appeals . . . between clerical errors committed by law enforcement personnel and similar mistakes by court employees." The court predicted that application of the exclusionary rule would "hopefully serve to improve the efficiency of those who keep records in our criminal justice system." Finally, the court concluded that "even assuming that deterrence is the principal reason for application of the exclusionary rule, we disagree with the court of appeals that such a purpose would not be served where carelessness by a court clerk results in an unlawful arrest."

We granted certiorari to determine whether the exclusionary rule requires suppression of evidence seized incident to an arrest resulting from an inaccurate computer record, regardless of whether police personnel or court personnel were responsible for the record's continued presence in the police computer. We now reverse.

■ ■ ■

Applying the reasoning of [*United States v.*] *Leon* [(1984)] to the facts of this case, we conclude that the decision of the Arizona Supreme Court must be reversed. The Arizona Supreme Court determined that it could not "support the distinction drawn . . . between clerical errors committed by law enforcement personnel and similar mistakes by court employees," and that "even assuming . . . that responsibility for the error rested with the justice court, it does not follow that the exclusionary rule should be inapplicable to these facts,"

This holding is contrary to the reasoning of *Leon; Massachusetts v. Sheppard* (1984); and *Krull* (1983). If court employees were responsible for the erroneous computer record, the exclusion of evidence at trial would not sufficiently deter future errors so as to warrant such a severe sanction. First, as we noted in *Leon*, the exclusionary rule was historically designed as a means of deterring police misconduct, not mistakes by court employees. Second, respondent offers no evidence that court employees are inclined to ignore or subvert the Fourth Amendment or that lawlessness among these actors requires application of the extreme sanction of exclusion. To the contrary, the Chief Clerk of the Justice Court testified at the suppression hearing that this type of error occurred once every three or four years.

Finally, and most important, there is no basis for believing that application of the exclusionary rule in these circumstances will have a significant effect on court employees responsible for informing the police that a warrant has been quashed.... The judgment of the Supreme Court of Arizona is therefore reversed, and the case is remanded to that court for proceedings not inconsistent with this opinion.

It is so ordered.

Justice O'CONNOR, with whom Justice SOUTER and Justice BREYER join, concurring.

The evidence in this case strongly suggests that it was a court employee's departure from established recordkeeping procedures that caused the record of respondent's arrest warrant to remain in the computer system after the warrant had been quashed. Prudently, then, the Court limits itself to the question whether a court employee's departure from such established procedures is the kind of error to which the exclusionary rule should apply. The Court holds that it is not such an error, and I agree with that conclusion and join the Court's opinion. The Court's holding reaffirms that the exclusionary rule imposes significant costs on society's law enforcement interests and thus should apply only where its deterrence purposes are "most efficaciously served." *Leon.* ...

Justice STEVENS, dissenting.

■ ■ ■

The Court seems to assume that the Fourth Amendment—and particularly the exclusionary rule, which effectuates the Amendment's commands—has the limited purpose of deterring police misconduct. Both the constitutional text and the history of its adoption and interpretation identify a more majestic conception. The Amendment protects the fundamental "right of the people to be secure in their persons, houses, papers, and effects," against *all* official searches and seizures that are unreasonable. The Amendment is a constraint on the power of the sovereign, not merely on some of its agents.

Herring v. United States

555 U.S. 135 (2009)

ROBERTS, C.J., delivered the opinion of the Court, in which SCALIA, KENNEDY, THOMAS, and ALITO, JJ., joined. GINSBURG, J., filed a dissenting opinion, in which STEVENS, SOUTER, and BREYER, JJ., joined. BREYER, J., filed a dissenting opinion, in which SOUTER, J., joined.

The Fourth Amendment forbids "unreasonable searches and seizures," and this usually requires the police to have probable cause or a warrant before making an arrest. What if an officer reasonably believes there is an outstanding arrest warrant, but that belief turns out to be wrong because of a negligent bookkeeping error by another police employee? The parties here agree that the ensuing arrest is still a violation of the Fourth Amendment, but dispute whether contraband found during a search incident to that arrest must be excluded in a later prosecution.

Our cases establish that such suppression is not an automatic consequence of a Fourth Amendment violation. Instead, the question turns on the culpability of the police and the potential of exclusion to deter wrongful police conduct. Here the error was the result of isolated negligence attenuated from the arrest. We hold that in these circumstances the jury should not be barred from considering all the evidence.

On July 7, 2004, Investigator Mark Anderson learned that Bennie Dean Herring had driven to the Coffee County Sheriff's Department to retrieve something from his impounded truck. Herring was no stranger to law enforcement, and Anderson asked the county's warrant clerk, Sandy Pope, to check for any outstanding warrants for Herring's arrest. When she found none, Anderson asked Pope to check with Sharon Morgan, her counterpart in neighboring Dale County. After checking Dale County's computer database, Morgan replied that there was an active arrest warrant for Herring's failure to appear on a felony charge. Pope relayed the information to Anderson and asked Morgan to fax over a copy of the warrant as confirmation. Anderson and a deputy followed Herring as he left the impound lot, pulled him over, and arrested him. A search incident to the arrest revealed methamphetamine in Herring's pocket, and a pistol (which as a felon he could not possess) in his vehicle.

There had, however, been a mistake about the warrant. The Dale County sheriff's computer records are supposed to correspond to actual arrest warrants, which the office also maintains. But when Morgan went to the files to retrieve the actual warrant to fax to Pope, Morgan was unable to find it. She called a court clerk and learned that the warrant had been recalled five months earlier. Normally when a warrant is recalled the court clerk's office or a judge's chambers calls Morgan, who enters the information in the sheriff's computer database and disposes of the physical copy. For whatever reason, the information about the recall of the warrant for Herring did not appear in the database. Morgan immediately called Pope to alert her to the mixup, and Pope contacted Anderson over a secure radio. This all unfolded in 10 to 15 minutes, but Herring had already been arrested and found with the gun and drugs, just a few hundred yards from the sheriff's office.

■ ■ ■

When a probable-cause determination was based on reasonable but mistaken assumptions, the person subjected to a search or seizure has not necessarily been the victim of a constitutional violation. The very phrase "probable cause" confirms that the Fourth Amendment does not demand all possible precision. And whether the error can be traced to a mistake by a state actor or some other source may bear on the analysis. For purposes of deciding this case, however, we accept the parties' assumption that there was a Fourth Amendment violation. The issue is whether the exclusionary rule should be applied.

The Fourth Amendment protects "[t]he right of the people to be secure in their persons, houses, papers, and effects, against unreasonable searches and seizures," but "contains no provision expressly precluding the use of evidence obtained in violation of its commands," *Arizona v. Evans* (1995). Nonetheless, our decisions establish an exclusionary rule that, when applicable, forbids the use of improperly obtained evidence at trial. See, *e.g.*, *Weeks v. United States* (1914). We have stated that this judicially created rule is "designed to safeguard Fourth Amendment rights generally through its deterrent effect."

In analyzing the applicability of the rule, [*United States v.*] *Leon* [(1984)] admonished that we must consider the actions of all the police officers involved. ("It is necessary to consider the objective reasonableness, not only of the officers who eventually executed a warrant, but also of the officers who originally obtained it or who provided information material to the probable-cause determination.") The Coffee County officers did nothing improper. Indeed, the error was noticed so quickly because Coffee County requested a faxed confirmation of the warrant.

The Eleventh Circuit concluded, however, that somebody in Dale County should have updated the computer database to reflect the recall of the arrest warrant. The court also concluded that this error was negligent, but did not find it to be reckless or deliberate. That fact is crucial to our holding that this error is not enough by itself to require "the extreme sanction of exclusion."

The fact that a Fourth Amendment violation occurred—*i.e.*, that a search or arrest was unreasonable—does not necessarily mean that the exclusionary rule applies. Indeed, exclusion "has always been our last resort, not our first impulse," *Hudson v. Michigan* (2006), and our precedents establish important principles that constrain application of the exclusionary rule.

... [T]he exclusionary rule is not an individual right and applies only where it "'result[s] in appreciable deterrence.'" *Leon*, quoting *United States v. Janis* (1976).

■ ■ ■

In addition, the benefits of deterrence must outweigh the costs. "We have never suggested that the exclusionary rule must apply in every circumstance in which it might provide marginal deterrence." *Pennsylvania Board of Probation & Parole v. Scott* (1998)....

These principles are reflected in the holding of *Leon*. When police act under a warrant that is invalid for lack of probable cause, the exclusionary rule does

Leon holding

not apply if the police acted "in objectively reasonable reliance" on the subsequently invalidated search warrant. We (perhaps confusingly) called this objectively reasonable reliance "good faith." In a companion case, *Massachusetts v. Sheppard* (1984), we held that the exclusionary rule did not apply when a warrant was invalid because a judge forgot to make "clerical corrections" to it.

Shortly thereafter we extended these holdings to warrantless administrative searches performed in good-faith reliance on a statute later declared unconstitutional. . . .

The extent to which the exclusionary rule is justified by these deterrence principles varies with the culpability of the law enforcement conduct. As we said in *Leon*, "an assessment of the flagrancy of the police misconduct constitutes an important step in the calculus" of applying the exclusionary rule.

■ ■ ■

ER test

To trigger the exclusionary rule, police conduct must be sufficiently deliberate that exclusion can meaningfully deter it, and sufficiently culpable that such deterrence is worth the price paid by the justice system. As laid out in our cases, the exclusionary rule serves to deter deliberate, reckless, or grossly negligent conduct, or in some circumstances recurring or systemic negligence. The error in this case does not rise to that level.

■ ■ ■

The pertinent analysis of deterrence and culpability is objective, not an "inquiry into the subjective awareness of arresting officers." We have already held that "our good-faith inquiry is confined to the objectively ascertainable question whether a reasonably well trained officer would have known that the search was illegal" in light of "all of the circumstances." These circumstances frequently include a particular officer's knowledge and experience, but that does not make the test any more subjective than the one for probable cause, which looks to an officer's knowledge and experience, but not his subjective intent, *Whren v. United States* (1996).

We do not suggest that all recordkeeping errors by the police are immune from the exclusionary rule. In this case, however, the conduct at issue was not so objectively culpable as to require exclusion. In *Leon* we held that "the marginal or nonexistent benefits produced by suppressing evidence obtained in objectively reasonable reliance on a subsequently invalidated search warrant cannot justify the substantial costs of exclusion." The same is true when evidence is obtained in objectively reasonable reliance on a subsequently recalled warrant.

If the police have been shown to be reckless in maintaining a warrant system, or to have knowingly made false entries to lay the groundwork for future false arrests, exclusion would certainly be justified under our cases should such misconduct cause a Fourth Amendment violation. We said as much in *Leon*, explaining that an officer could not "obtain a warrant on the basis of a 'bare bones' affidavit and then rely on colleagues who are ignorant of the circumstances under which the warrant was obtained to conduct the search." . . .

■ ■ ■

Petitioner's claim that police negligence automatically triggers suppression cannot be squared with the principles underlying the exclusionary rule, as they have been explained in our cases. In light of our repeated holdings that the deterrent effect of suppression must be substantial and outweigh any harm to the justice system . . . we conclude that when police mistakes are the result of negligence such as that described here, rather than systemic error or reckless disregard of constitutional requirements, any marginal deterrence does not "pay its way." . . .

The judgment of the Court of Appeals for the Eleventh Circuit is affirmed.

It is so ordered.

Justice GINSBURG, with whom Justice STEVENS, Justice SOUTER, and Justice BREYER join, dissenting.

Petitioner Bennie Dean Herring was arrested, and subjected to a search incident to his arrest, although no warrant was outstanding against him, and the police lacked probable cause to believe he was engaged in criminal activity. The arrest and ensuing search therefore violated Herring's Fourth Amendment right "to be secure . . . against unreasonable searches and seizures." The Court of Appeals so determined, and the Government does not contend otherwise. The exclusionary rule provides redress for Fourth Amendment violations by placing the government in the position it would have been in had there been no unconstitutional arrest and search. The rule thus strongly encourages police compliance with the Fourth Amendment in the future. The Court, however, holds the rule inapplicable because careless recordkeeping by the police—not flagrant or deliberate misconduct—accounts for Herring's arrest.

I would not so constrict the domain of the exclusionary rule and would hold the rule dispositive of this case: "[I]f courts are to have any power to discourage [police] error of [the kind here at issue], it must be through the application of the exclusionary rule." *Arizona v. Evans* (Stevens, J., dissenting). The unlawful search in this case was contested in court because the police found methamphetamine in Herring's pocket and a pistol in his truck. But the "most serious impact" of the Court's holding will be on innocent persons "wrongfully arrested based on erroneous information [carelessly maintained] in a computer data base."

■ ■ ■

The Court states that the exclusionary rule is not a defendant's right; rather, it is simply a remedy applicable only when suppression would result in appreciable deterrence that outweighs the cost to the justice system.

The Court's discussion invokes a view of the exclusionary rule famously held by renowned jurists Henry J. Friendly and Benjamin Nathan Cardozo. Over 80 years ago, Cardozo, then seated on the New York Court of Appeals, commented critically on the federal exclusionary rule, which had not yet been applied to the States. He suggested that in at least some cases the rule exacted too high a price from the criminal justice system. In words often quoted, Cardozo questioned whether the criminal should "go free because the constable has blundered." *People v. Defore* (1926).

Judge Friendly later elaborated on Cardozo's query. "The sole reason for exclusion," Friendly wrote, "is that experience has demonstrated this to be the only effective method for deterring the police from violating the Constitution." The Bill of Rights as a Code of Criminal Procedure, 53 Calif. L. Rev. 929, 951 (1965). He thought it excessive, in light of the rule's aim to deter police conduct, to require exclusion when the constable had merely "blundered"—when a police officer committed a technical error in an on-the-spot judgment. . . . As the Court recounts, Judge Friendly suggested that deterrence of police improprieties could be "sufficiently accomplished" by confining the rule to "evidence obtained by flagrant or deliberate violation of rights."

Others have described "a more majestic conception" of the Fourth Amendment and its adjunct, the exclusionary rule. *Evans* (Stevens, J., dissenting). Protective of the fundamental "right of the people to be secure in their persons, houses, papers, and effects," the Amendment "is a constraint on the power of the sovereign, not merely on some of its agents." I share that vision of the Amendment.

The exclusionary rule is "a remedy necessary to ensure that" the Fourth Amendment's prohibitions "are observed in fact." Stewart, The Road to *Mapp v. Ohio* and Beyond: The Origins, Development and Future of the Exclusionary Rule in Search-and-Seizure Cases, 83 Colum. L. Rev. 1365, 1389 (1983). The rule's service as an essential auxiliary to the Amendment earlier inclined the Court to hold the two inseparable.

Beyond doubt, a main objective of the rule "is to deter—to compel respect for the constitutional guaranty in the only effectively available way—by removing the incentive to disregard it." *Elkins v. United States* (1960). But the rule also serves other important purposes: It "enabl[es] the judiciary to avoid the taint of partnership in official lawlessness," and it "assur[es] the people— all potential victims of unlawful government conduct—that the government would not profit from its lawless behavior, thus minimizing the risk of seriously undermining popular trust in government." *United States v. Calandra* (1974) (Brennan, J., dissenting). See also *Terry v. Ohio* (1968) ("A rule admitting evidence in a criminal trial, we recognize, has the necessary effect of legitimizing the conduct which produced the evidence, while an application of the exclusionary rule withholds the constitutional imprimatur.").

The exclusionary rule, it bears emphasis, is often the only remedy effective to redress a Fourth Amendment violation. . . .

The Court maintains that Herring's case is one in which the exclusionary rule could have scant deterrent effect and therefore would not "pay its way."

The exclusionary rule, the Court suggests, is capable of only marginal deterrence when the misconduct at issue is merely careless, not intentional or reckless. The suggestion runs counter to a foundational premise of tort law—that liability for negligence, *i.e.*, lack of due care, creates an incentive to act with greater care. The Government so acknowledges.

That the mistake here involved the failure to make a computer entry hardly means that application of the exclusionary rule would have minimal value. "Just as the risk of *respondeat superior* liability encourages employers to supervise . . . their employees' conduct [more carefully], so the risk of exclusion of evidence encourages policymakers and systems managers to monitor the performance of the systems they install and the personnel employed to operate those systems." *Evans* (Ginsburg, J., dissenting).

Consider the potential impact of a decision applying the exclusionary rule in this case. As earlier observed, the record indicates that there is no electronic connection between the warrant database of the Dale County Sheriff's Department and that of the County Circuit Clerk's office, which is located in the basement of the same building. When a warrant is recalled, one of the "many different people that have access to th[e] warrants" must find the hard copy of the warrant in the "two or three different places" where the department houses warrants, return it to the Clerk's office, and manually update the Department's database. The record reflects no routine practice of checking the database for accuracy, and the failure to remove the entry for Herring's warrant was not discovered until Investigator Anderson sought to pursue Herring five months later. Is it not altogether obvious that the Department could take further precautions to ensure the integrity of its database? The Sheriff's Department "is in a position to remedy the situation and might well do so if the exclusionary rule is there to remove the incentive to do otherwise."

Is the potential deterrence here worth the costs it imposes? In light of the paramount importance of accurate recordkeeping in law enforcement, I would answer yes, and next explain why, as I see it, Herring's motion presents a particularly strong case for suppression.

Electronic databases form the nervous system of contemporary criminal justice operations. In recent years, their breadth and influence have dramatically expanded. Police today can access databases that include not only the updated National Crime Information Center (NCIC), but also terrorist watchlists, the Federal Government's employee eligibility system, and various commercial databases.

■ ■ ■

The Court assures that "exclusion would certainly be justified" if "the police have been shown to be reckless in maintaining a warrant system, or to have knowingly made false entries to lay the groundwork for future false arrests." This concession provides little comfort.

First, by restricting suppression to bookkeeping errors that are deliberate or reckless, the majority leaves Herring, and others like him, with no remedy for violations of their constitutional rights. There can be no serious assertion that relief is available under 42 U.S.C. § 1983. The arresting officer would be sheltered by qualified immunity. Moreover, identifying the department employee who committed the error may be impossible.

Second, I doubt that police forces already possess sufficient incentives to maintain up-to-date records. The Government argues that police have no desire to send officers out on arrests unnecessarily, because arrests consume resources and place officers in danger. The facts of this case do not fit that description of police motivation. Here the officer wanted to arrest Herring and consulted the Department's records to legitimate his predisposition.

Third, even when deliberate or reckless conduct is afoot, the Court's assurance will often be an empty promise: How is an impecunious defendant to make the required showing? . . .

Negligent recordkeeping errors by law enforcement threaten individual liberty, are susceptible to deterrence by the exclusionary rule, and cannot be remedied effectively through other means. Such errors present no occasion to further erode the exclusionary rule. The rule "is needed to make the Fourth Amendment something real; a guarantee that does not carry with it the exclusion of evidence obtained by its violation is a chimera." . . .

For the reasons stated, I would reverse the judgment of the Eleventh Circuit.

Justice BREYER, with whom Justice SOUTER joins, dissenting.

I agree with Justice Ginsburg and join her dissent. I write separately to note one additional supporting factor that I believe important. In *Arizona v. Evans*, we held that recordkeeping errors made by a court clerk do not trigger the exclusionary rule, so long as the police reasonably relied upon the court clerk's recordkeeping. The rationale for our decision was premised on a distinction between judicial errors and police errors, and we gave several reasons for recognizing that distinction.

First, we noted that "the exclusionary rule was historically designed as a means of deterring *police* misconduct, not mistakes by court employees." *Second*, we found "no evidence that court employees are inclined to ignore or subvert the Fourth Amendment or that lawlessness among these actors requires application of the extreme sanction of exclusion." *Third*, we recognized that there was "no basis for believing that application of the exclusionary rule . . . [would] have a significant effect on court employees responsible for informing the police that a warrant has been quashed. Because court clerks are not adjuncts to the law enforcement team engaged in the often competitive enterprise of ferreting out crime, they have no stake in the outcome of particular criminal prosecutions." Taken together, these reasons explain why police recordkeeping errors should be treated differently than judicial ones.

Other cases applying the "good faith" exception to the exclusionary rule have similarly recognized the distinction between police errors and errors made by others, such as judicial officers or legislatures. See *United States v. Leon* (police reasonably relied on magistrate's issuance of warrant); *Massachusetts v. Sheppard* (same); *Illinois v. Krull* (1987) (police reasonably relied on statute's constitutionality).

Distinguishing between police recordkeeping errors and judicial ones not only is consistent with our precedent, but also is far easier for courts to administer than The Chief Justice's case-by-case, multifactored inquiry into the degree of police culpability. I therefore would apply the exclusionary rule when police personnel are responsible for a recordkeeping error that results in a Fourth Amendment violation.

The need for a clear line, and the recognition of such a line in our precedent, are further reasons in support of the outcome that Justice Ginsburg's dissent would reach.

Davis v. United States

131 S. Ct. 2419 (2011)

ALITO, J. delivered the opinion of the Court, in which ROBERTS, C.J., and SCALIA, KENNEDY, THOMAS, and KAGAN, JJ., joined. SOTOMAYOR, J., filed an opinion concurring in the judgment. BREYER, J., filed a dissenting opinion, in which GINSBURG, J., joined.

The Fourth Amendment protects the right to be free from "unreasonable searches and seizures," but it is silent about how this right is to be enforced. To supplement the bare text, this Court created the exclusionary rule, a deterrent sanction that bars the prosecution from introducing evidence obtained by way of a Fourth Amendment violation. The question here is whether to apply this sanction when the police conduct a search in compliance with binding precedent that is later overruled. Because suppression would do nothing to deter police misconduct in these circumstances, and because it would come at a high cost to both the truth and the public safety, we hold that searches conducted in objectively reasonable reliance on binding appellate precedent are not subject to the exclusionary rule.

I

The question presented arises in this case as a result of a shift in our Fourth Amendment jurisprudence on searches of automobiles incident to arrests of recent occupants.

A

Under this Court's decision in *Chimel v. California* (1969), a police officer who makes a lawful arrest may conduct a warrantless search of the arrestee's person and the area "within his immediate control." This rule "may be stated clearly enough," but in the early going after *Chimel* it proved difficult to apply, particularly in cases that involved searches "inside of automobiles after the arrestees were no longer in them." See *New York v. Belton* (1981). A number of courts upheld the constitutionality of vehicle searches that were "substantially contemporaneous" with occupants' arrests. Other courts disapproved of automobile searches incident to arrests, at least absent some continuing threat that the arrestee might gain access to the vehicle and "destroy evidence or grab a weapon." In *New York v. Belton*, this Court granted certiorari to resolve the conflict. . . .

In *Belton*, a police officer conducting a traffic stop lawfully arrested four occupants of a vehicle and ordered the arrestees to line up, un-handcuffed, along the side of the thruway. The officer then searched the vehicle's passenger compartment and found cocaine inside a jacket that lay on the backseat. This Court upheld the search as reasonable incident to the occupants' arrests. In an opinion that repeatedly stressed the need for a "straightforward," "workable rule" to guide police conduct, the Court announced "that when a policeman has made a lawful custodial arrest of the occupant of an automobile, he may, as a contemporaneous incident of that arrest, search the passenger compartment of that automobile."

For years, *Belton* was widely understood to have set down a simple, bright-line rule. Numerous courts read the decision to authorize automobile searches incident to arrests of recent occupants, regardless of whether the arrestee in any particular case was within reaching distance of the vehicle at the time of the search. See *Thornton v. United States* (2004) (Scalia, J., concurring in judgment) (collecting cases). Even after the arrestee had stepped out of the vehicle and had been subdued by police, the prevailing understanding was that *Belton* still authorized a substantially contemporaneous search of the automobile's passenger compartment.

Not every court, however, agreed with this reading of *Belton*. In *State v. Gant* (2007), the Arizona Supreme Court considered an automobile search conducted after the vehicle's occupant had been arrested, handcuffed, and locked in a patrol car. The court distinguished *Belton* as a case in which "four unsecured" arrestees "presented an immediate risk of loss of evidence and an obvious threat to [a] lone officer's safety." The court held that where no such "exigencies exist"—where the arrestee has been subdued and the scene secured—the rule of *Belton* does not apply.

This Court granted certiorari in *Gant*, and affirmed in a 5-to-4 decision. *Arizona v. Gant* (2009). Four of the Justices in the majority agreed with the Arizona Supreme Court that *Belton*'s holding applies only where "the arrestee is unsecured and within reaching distance of the passenger compartment at the time of the search." The four dissenting Justices, by contrast, understood *Belton* to have explicitly adopted the simple, bright-line rule stated in the *Belton* Court's opinion. See *Belton* ("We hold that when a policeman has made a lawful custodial arrest of the occupant of an automobile, he may, as a contemporaneous incident of that arrest, search the passenger compartment of that automobile"). To limit *Belton* to cases involving unsecured arrestees, the dissenters thought, was to overrule the decision's clear holding. Justice Scalia, who provided the fifth vote to affirm in *Gant*, agreed with the dissenters' understanding of *Belton*'s holding. Justice Scalia favored a more explicit and complete overruling of *Belton*, but he joined what became the majority opinion to avoid "a 4-to-1-to-4" disposition. As a result, the Court adopted a new, two-part rule under which an automobile search incident to a recent occupant's arrest is constitutional (1) if the arrestee is within reaching distance of the vehicle during the search, or (2) if the police have reason to believe that the vehicle contains "evidence relevant to the crime of arrest."

B

The search at issue in this case took place a full two years before this Court announced its new rule in *Gant*. On an April evening in 2007, police officers in Greenville, Alabama, conducted a routine traffic stop that eventually resulted in the arrests of driver Stella Owens (for driving while intoxicated) and passenger Willie Davis (for giving a false name to police). The police handcuffed both Owens and Davis, and they placed the arrestees in the back of separate patrol cars. The police then searched the passenger compartment of Owens's vehicle and found a revolver inside Davis's jacket pocket.

Davis was indicted in the Middle District of Alabama on one count of possession of a firearm by a convicted felon. In his motion to suppress the revolver, Davis acknowledged that the officers' search fully complied with "existing Eleventh Circuit precedent." Like most courts, the Eleventh Circuit had long read *Belton* to establish a bright-line rule authorizing substantially contemporaneous vehicle searches incident to arrests of recent occupants. Davis recognized that the District Court was obligated to follow this precedent, but he raised a Fourth Amendment challenge to preserve "the issue for review" on appeal. The District Court denied the motion, and Davis was convicted on the firearms charge.

While Davis's appeal was pending, this Court decided *Gant*. The Eleventh Circuit, in the opinion below, applied *Gant*'s new rule and held that the vehicle search incident to Davis's arrest "violated his Fourth Amendment rights." As for whether this constitutional violation warranted suppression, the Eleventh Circuit viewed that as a separate issue that turned on "the potential of exclusion to deter wrongful police conduct." The court concluded that "penalizing the arresting officer" for following binding appellate precedent would do nothing to "deter Fourth Amendment violations." It therefore declined to apply the exclusionary rule and affirmed Davis's conviction. We granted certiorari.

II

The Fourth Amendment protects the "right of the people to be secure in their persons, houses, papers, and effects, against unreasonable searches and seizures." The Amendment says nothing about suppressing evidence obtained in violation of this command. That rule—the exclusionary rule—is a "prudential" doctrine, created by this Court to "compel respect for the constitutional guaranty." *Elkins v. United States* (1960). Exclusion is "not a personal constitutional right," nor is it designed to "redress the injury" occasioned by an unconstitutional search. The rule's sole purpose, we have repeatedly held, is to deter future Fourth Amendment violations. *E.g., United States v. Leon* (1984). Our cases have thus limited the rule's operation to situations in which this purpose is "thought most efficaciously served." Where suppression fails to yield "appreciable deterrence," exclusion is "clearly unwarranted."

■ ■ ■

The basic insight of the *Leon* line of cases is that the deterrence benefits of exclusion "vary with the culpability of the law enforcement conduct" at issue. When the police exhibit "deliberate," "reckless," or "grossly negligent" disregard for Fourth Amendment rights, the deterrent value of exclusion is strong and tends to outweigh the resulting costs. But when the police act with an objectively "reasonable good-faith belief" that their conduct is lawful, or when their conduct involves only simple, "isolated" negligence, the "deterrence rationale loses much of its force, "and exclusion cannot "pay its way."

The Court has over time applied this "good-faith" exception across a range of cases. *Leon* itself, for example, held that the exclusionary rule does not apply when the police conduct a search in "objectively reasonable reliance" on a warrant later held invalid. The error in such a case rests with the issuing magistrate, not the police officer, and "punishing the errors of judges" is not the office of the exclusionary rule.

Other good-faith cases have sounded a similar theme. *Illinois v. Krull* (1987) extended the good-faith exception to searches conducted in reasonable reliance on subsequently invalidated statutes. ("[L]egislators, like judicial officers, are not the focus of the rule"). In *Arizona v. Evans*, the Court applied the good-faith exception in a case where the police reasonably relied on erroneous information concerning an arrest warrant in a database maintained by judicial employees. . . . Most recently, in *Herring v. United States* (2009), we extended *Evans* in a case where *police* employees erred in maintaining records in a warrant database. "Isolated," "nonrecurring" police negligence, we determined, lacks the culpability required to justify the harsh sanction of exclusion.

III

The question in this case is whether to apply the exclusionary rule when the police conduct a search in objectively reasonable reliance on binding judicial precedent. At the time of the search at issue here, we had not yet decided *Arizona v. Gant*, and the Eleventh Circuit had interpreted our decision in *New York v. Belton* to establish a bright-line rule authorizing the search of a vehicle's passenger compartment incident to a recent occupant's arrest. *United States v. Gonzalez* (1996). The search incident to Davis's arrest in this case followed the Eleventh Circuit's *Gonzalez* precedent to the letter. Although the search turned out to be unconstitutional under *Gant*, all agree that the officers' conduct was in strict compliance with then-binding Circuit law and was not culpable in any way.

Under our exclusionary-rule precedents, this acknowledged absence of police culpability dooms Davis's claim. Police practices trigger the harsh sanction of exclusion only when they are deliberate enough to yield "meaningful" deterrence, and culpable enough to be "worth the price paid by the justice system." *Herring*. The conduct of the officers here was neither of these things. The officers who conducted the search did not violate Davis's Fourth Amendment rights deliberately, recklessly, or with gross negligence. Nor does this case involve any "recurring or systemic negligence" on the part of law enforcement. The police acted in strict compliance with binding precedent, and their behavior was not wrongful. Unless the exclusionary rule is to become a strict-liability regime, it can have no application in this case.

Indeed, in 27 years of practice under *Leon*'s good-faith exception, we have "never applied" the exclusionary rule to suppress evidence obtained as a result of nonculpable, innocent police conduct. If the police in this case had reasonably relied on a warrant in conducting their search, or on an erroneous warrant record in a government database, the exclusionary rule would not apply. And if Congress or the Alabama Legislature had enacted a statute codifying the precise holding of the Eleventh Circuit's decision in *Gonzalez*, we would swiftly conclude that "penalizing the officer for the legislature's error cannot logically contribute to the deterrence of Fourth Amendment violations." The same should be true of Davis's attempt here to "penalize the officer for the appellate judges' error."

About all that exclusion would deter in this case is conscientious police work. Responsible law-enforcement officers will take care to learn "what is required of them" under Fourth Amendment precedent and will conform their conduct to these rules. But by the same token, when binding appellate precedent specifically *authorizes* a particular police practice, well-trained officers will and should use that tool to fulfill their crime-detection and public-safety responsibilities. An officer who conducts a search in reliance on binding appellate precedent does no more than "'act as a reasonable officer would and should act'" under the circumstances. The deterrent effect of exclusion in such a case can only be to discourage the officer from "doing his duty."

That is not the kind of deterrence the exclusionary rule seeks to foster. We have stated before, and we reaffirm today, that the harsh sanction of exclusion "should not be applied to deter objectively reasonable law enforcement activity." Evidence obtained during a search conducted in reasonable reliance on binding precedent is not subject to the exclusionary rule.

IV

Justice Breyer's dissent and Davis argue that, although the police conduct in this case was in no way culpable, other considerations should prevent the good-faith exception from applying. We are not persuaded.

A

1

The principal argument of both the dissent and Davis is that the exclusionary rule's availability to enforce new Fourth Amendment precedent is a retroactivity issue, see *Griffith v. Kentucky* (1987), not a good-faith issue. They contend that applying the good-faith exception where police have relied on overruled precedent effectively revives the discarded retroactivity regime of *Linkletter v. Walker* (1965).

In *Linkletter,* we held that the retroactive effect of a new constitutional rule of criminal procedure should be determined on a case-by-case weighing of interests. For each new rule, *Linkletter* required courts to consider a three-factor balancing test that looked to the "purpose" of the new rule, "reliance" on the old rule by law enforcement and others, and the effect retroactivity would have "on the administration of justice." After "weighing the merits and demerits in each case," courts decided whether and to what extent a new rule should be given retroactive effect. In *Linkletter* itself, the balance of interests prompted this Court to conclude that *Mapp v. Ohio* (1961)—which incorporated the exclusionary rule against the States—should not apply retroactively to cases already final on direct review. The next year, we extended *Linkletter* to retroactivity determinations in cases on direct review.

Over time, *Linkletter* proved difficult to apply in a consistent, coherent way. Individual applications of the standard "produced strikingly divergent results," that many saw as "incompatible" and "inconsistent." *Desist v. United States* (1969) (Harlan, J., dissenting). Justice Harlan in particular, who had endorsed the *Linkletter* standard early on, offered a strong critique in which he argued that "basic judicial" norms required full retroactive application of new rules to all cases still subject to direct review. Eventually, and after more than 20 years of toil under *Linkletter,* the Court adopted Justice Harlan's view and held that newly announced rules of constitutional criminal procedure must apply "retroactively to all cases, state or federal, pending on direct review or not yet final, with no exception." *Griffith.*

2

The dissent and Davis argue that applying the good-faith exception in this case is "incompatible" with our retroactivity precedent under *Griffith.* We think this argument conflates what are two distinct doctrines.

Our retroactivity jurisprudence is concerned with whether, as a categorical matter, a new rule is available on direct review as a *potential* ground for relief. Retroactive application under *Griffith* lifts what would otherwise be a categorical bar to obtaining redress for the government's violation of a newly announced constitutional rule. Retroactive application does not, however, determine what "appropriate remedy" (if any) the defendant should obtain. Remedy is a separate, analytically distinct issue. As a result, the retroactive application of a new rule of substantive Fourth Amendment law *raises* the question whether a suppression remedy applies; it does not answer that question. See *Leon* ("Whether the exclusionary sanction is appropriately imposed in a particular case is an issue separate from the question whether the Fourth Amendment rights of the party seeking to invoke the rule were violated by police conduct").

When this Court announced its decision in *Gant,* Davis's conviction had not yet become final on direct review. *Gant* therefore applies retroactively to this case. Davis may invoke its newly announced rule of substantive Fourth

Amendment law as a basis for seeking relief. See *Griffith.* The question, then, becomes one of remedy, and on that issue Davis seeks application of the exclusionary rule. But exclusion of evidence does not automatically follow from the fact that a Fourth Amendment violation occurred. The remedy is subject to exceptions and applies only where its "purpose is effectively advanced."

The dissent and Davis recognize that at least some of the established exceptions to the exclusionary rule limit its availability in cases involving new Fourth Amendment rules. Suppression would thus be inappropriate, the dissent and Davis acknowledge, if the inevitable-discovery exception were applicable in this case. The good-faith exception, however, is no less an established limit on the *remedy* of exclusion than is inevitable discovery. Its application here neither contravenes *Griffith* nor denies retroactive effect to *Gant.*[5]

It is true that, under the old retroactivity regime of *Linkletter,* the Court's decisions on the "retroactivity problem in the context of the exclusionary rule" did take into account whether "law enforcement officers reasonably believed in good faith" that their conduct was in compliance with governing law. *United States v. Peltier* (1975). As a matter of retroactivity analysis, that approach is no longer applicable. It does not follow, however, that reliance on binding precedent is irrelevant in applying the good-faith exception to the exclusionary rule. When this Court adopted the good-faith exception in *Leon,* the Court's opinion explicitly relied on *Peltier* and imported its reasoning into the good-faith inquiry. That reasonable reliance by police was once a factor in our retroactivity cases does not make it any less relevant under our *Leon* line of cases.

B

Davis also contends that applying the good-faith exception to searches conducted in reliance on binding precedent will stunt the development of Fourth Amendment law. With no possibility of suppression, criminal defendants will have no incentive, Davis maintains, to request that courts overrule precedent.[7]

1

This argument is difficult to reconcile with our modern understanding of the role of the exclusionary rule. We have never held that facilitating the

---

5. The dissent argues that the good-faith exception is "unlike . . . inevitable discovery" because the former applies in all cases where the police reasonably rely on binding precedent, while the latter "applies only upon occasion." We fail to see how this distinction makes any difference. The same could be said—indeed, the same *was* said—of searches conducted in reasonable reliance on statutes. See *Krull,* 480 U.S., at 368-369 (O'Connor, J., dissenting) (arguing that result in *Krull* was inconsistent with *Griffith*). When this Court strikes down a statute on Fourth Amendment grounds, the good-faith exception may prevent the exclusionary rule from applying "in *every* case pending when the statute is overturned." This result does not make the Court's newly announced rule of Fourth Amendment law any less retroactive. It simply limits the applicability of a suppression remedy.

7. Davis also asserts that a good-faith rule would permit "new Fourth Amendment decisions to be applied only prospectively," thus amounting to "a regime of rule-creation by advisory opinion." For reasons discussed in connection with Davis's argument that application of the good-faith exception here would revive the *Linkletter* regime, this argument conflates the question of retroactivity with the question of remedy.

overruling of precedent is a relevant consideration in an exclusionary-rule case. Rather, we have said time and again that the *sole* purpose of the exclusionary rule is to deter misconduct by law enforcement.

We have also repeatedly rejected efforts to expand the focus of the exclusionary rule beyond deterrence of culpable police conduct. In *Leon,* for example, we made clear that "the exclusionary rule is designed to deter police misconduct rather than to punish the errors of judges." And in *Evans* (1995), we said that the exclusionary rule was aimed at deterring "police misconduct, not mistakes by court employees." These cases do not suggest that the exclusionary rule should be modified to serve a purpose other than deterrence of culpable law-enforcement conduct.

2

And in any event, applying the good-faith exception in this context will not prevent judicial reconsideration of prior Fourth Amendment precedents. In most instances, as in this case, the precedent sought to be challenged will be a decision of a Federal Court of Appeals or State Supreme Court. But a good-faith exception for objectively reasonable reliance on binding precedent will not prevent review and correction of such decisions. This Court reviews criminal convictions from 12 Federal Courts of Appeals, 50 state courts of last resort, and the District of Columbia Court of Appeals. If one or even many of these courts uphold a particular type of search or seizure, defendants in jurisdictions in which the question remains open will still have an undiminished incentive to litigate the issue. This Court can then grant certiorari, and the development of Fourth Amendment law will in no way be stunted.

■ ■ ■

At most, Davis's argument might suggest that—to prevent Fourth Amendment law from becoming ossified—the petitioner in a case that results in the overruling of one of this Court's Fourth Amendment precedents should be given the benefit of the victory by permitting the suppression of evidence in that one case. Such a result would undoubtedly be a windfall to this one random litigant. But the exclusionary rule is "not a personal constitutional right." It is a "judicially created" sanction, specifically designed as a "windfall" remedy to deter future Fourth Amendment violations. The good-faith exception is a judicially created exception to this judicially created rule. Therefore, in a future case, we could, if necessary, recognize a limited exception to the good-faith exception for a defendant who obtains a judgment overruling one of our Fourth Amendment precedents.[10]

But this is not such a case. Davis did not secure a decision overturning a Supreme Court precedent; the police in his case reasonably relied on binding

---

10. In any event, even if some criminal defendants will be unable to challenge some precedents for the reason that Davis suggests, that provides no good reason for refusing to apply the good-faith exception. As noted, the exclusionary rule is not a personal right, and therefore the rights of these defendants will not be impaired. And because (at least in almost all instances) the precedent can be challenged by others, Fourth Amendment case law will not be insulated from reconsideration.

Circuit precedent. That sort of blameless police conduct, we hold, comes within the good-faith exception and is not properly subject to the exclusionary rule.

It is one thing for the criminal "to go free because the constable has blundered." *People v. Defore* (1926) (Cardozo, J.). It is quite another to set the criminal free because the constable has scrupulously adhered to governing law. Excluding evidence in such cases deters no police misconduct and imposes substantial social costs. We therefore hold that when the police conduct a search in objectively reasonable reliance on binding appellate precedent, the exclusionary rule does not apply. The judgment of the Court of Appeals for the Eleventh Circuit is

Affirmed.

Justice SOTOMAYOR, concurring in the judgment.

■ ■ ■

This case does not present the markedly different question whether the exclusionary rule applies when the law governing the constitutionality of a particular search is unsettled. As we previously recognized in deciding whether to apply a Fourth Amendment holding retroactively, when police decide to conduct a search or seizure in the absence of case law (or other authority) specifically sanctioning such action, exclusion of the evidence obtained may deter Fourth Amendment violations:

■ ■ ■

The dissent suggests that today's decision essentially answers those questions, noting that an officer who conducts a search in the face of unsettled precedent "is no more culpable than an officer who follows erroneous 'binding precedent.'" The Court does not address this issue. In my view, whether an officer's conduct can be characterized as "culpable" is not itself dispositive. We have never refused to apply the exclusionary rule where its application would appreciably deter Fourth Amendment violations on the mere ground that the officer's conduct could be characterized as nonculpable. Rather, an officer's culpability is relevant because it may inform the overarching inquiry whether exclusion would result in appreciable deterrence.... Whatever we have said about culpability, the ultimate questions have always been, one, whether exclusion would result in appreciable deterrence and, two, whether the benefits of exclusion outweigh its costs.

... [W]hether exclusion would result in appreciable deterrence in the circumstances of this case is a different question from whether exclusion would appreciably deter Fourth Amendment violations when the governing law is unsettled. The Court's answer to the former question in this case thus does not resolve the latter one.

Justice BREYER, with whom Justice GINSBURG joins, dissenting.

In 2009, in *Arizona v. Gant*, this Court held that a police search of an automobile without a warrant violates the Fourth Amendment if the police have previously removed the automobile's occupants and placed them securely in a squad car. The present case involves these same circumstances, and it was pending on appeal when this Court decided *Gant*. Because *Gant* represents a "shift" in the Court's Fourth Amendment jurisprudence, we must decide *whether* and *how Gant'* s new rule applies here.

I

I agree with the Court about *whether Gant's* new rule applies. It does apply. Between 1965, when the Court decided *Linkletter v. Walker,* and 1987, when it decided *Griffith v. Kentucky,* that conclusion would have been more difficult to reach. Under *Linkletter,* the Court determined a new rule's retroactivity by looking to several different factors, including whether the new rule represented a "clear break" with the past and the degree of "reliance by law enforcement authorities on the old standards." And the Court would often not apply the new rule to identical cases still pending on appeal.

After 22 years of struggling with its *Linkletter* approach, however, the Court decided in *Griffith* that *Linkletter* had proved unfair and unworkable. It then substituted a clearer approach, stating that "a new rule for the conduct of criminal prosecutions is to be applied retroactively to all cases, state or federal, pending on direct review or not yet final, with no exception for cases in which the new rule constitutes a 'clear break' with the past." The Court today, following *Griffith,* concludes that *Gant'* s new rule applies here. And to that extent I agree with its decision.

II

The Court goes on, however, to decide *how Gant's* new rule will apply. And here it adds a fatal twist. While conceding that, like the search in *Gant,* this search violated the Fourth Amendment, it holds that, unlike Gant, this defendant is not entitled to a remedy. That is because the Court finds a new "good faith" exception which prevents application of the normal remedy for a Fourth Amendment violation, namely, suppression of the illegally seized evidence. Leaving Davis with a right but not a remedy, the Court "keeps the word of promise to our ear" but "breaks it to our hope."

A

At this point I can no longer agree with the Court. A new "good faith" exception and this Court's retroactivity decisions are incompatible. For one thing, the Court's distinction between (1) retroactive application of a new rule and (2) availability of a remedy is highly artificial and runs counter to precedent. To determine that a new rule is retroactive *is* to determine that, at least in the normal case, there is a remedy. As we have previously said, the "source of a 'new rule' is the Constitution itself, not any judicial power to create new rules of law"; hence, "what we are actually determining when we assess the 'retroactivity' of a new rule is not the temporal scope of a newly announced right, but whether a violation of the right that occurred prior to the announcement of the new rule will entitle a criminal defendant to the relief sought."

The Court's "good faith" exception (unlike, say, inevitable discovery, a remedial doctrine that applies only upon occasion) creates "a categorical bar to obtaining redress" in *every* case pending when a precedent is overturned.

For another thing, the Court's holding re-creates the very problems that led the Court to abandon *Linkletter*'s approach to retroactivity in favor of *Griffith*'s. One such problem concerns workability. The Court says that its exception applies where there is "objectively reasonable" police "reliance on binding appellate precedent." But to apply the term "binding appellate precedent" often requires resolution of complex questions of degree. Davis conceded that he faced binding anti-*Gant* precedent in the Eleventh Circuit. But future litigants will be less forthcoming. Indeed, those litigants will now have to create distinctions to show that previous Circuit precedent was not "binding" lest they find relief foreclosed even if they win their constitutional claim.

At the same time, Fourth Amendment precedents frequently require courts to "slosh" their "way through the factbound morass of 'reasonableness.'" Suppose an officer's conduct is consistent with the language of a Fourth Amendment rule that a court of appeals announced in a case with clearly distinguishable facts? Suppose the case creating the relevant precedent did not directly announce any general rule but involved highly analogous facts? What about a rule that all other jurisdictions, but not the defendant's jurisdiction, had previously accepted? What rules can be developed for determining when, where, and how these different kinds of precedents do, or do not, count as relevant "binding precedent"? The *Linkletter*-like result is likely complex legal argument and police force confusion.

Another such problem concerns fairness. Today's holding, like that in *Linkletter*, "violates basic norms of constitutional adjudication." *Griffith*. It treats the defendant in a case announcing a new rule one way while treating similarly situated defendants whose cases are pending on appeal in a different way. Justice Harlan explained why this approach is wrong when he said:

> "We cannot release criminals from jail merely because we think one case is a particularly appropriate one to announce a constitutional doctrine. Simply fishing one case from the stream of appellate review, using it as a vehicle for pronouncing new constitutional standards, and then permitting a stream of similar cases subsequently to flow by unaffected by that new rule constitute an indefensible departure from our ordinary model of judicial review." *Williams.*

And in *Griffith*, the Court "embraced to a significant extent the comprehensive analysis presented by Justice Harlan."

Of course, the Court may, as it suggests, avoid this unfairness by refusing to apply the exclusionary rule even to the defendant in the very case in which it announces a "new rule." But that approach would make matters worse. What would then happen in the lower courts? How would courts of appeals, for example, come to reconsider their prior decisions when other circuits' cases lead them to believe those decisions may be wrong? Why would a defendant seek to overturn any such decision? After all, if the (incorrect) circuit precedent is clear, then even if the defendant wins (on the constitutional question), he loses (on relief). To what extent then could this Court rely upon lower courts to work out Fourth Amendment differences among themselves—through circuit reconsideration of a precedent that other circuits have criticized?

B

Perhaps more important, the Court's rationale for creating its new "good faith" exception threatens to undermine well-settled Fourth Amendment law. The Court correctly says that pre-*Gant* Eleventh Circuit precedent had held that a *Gant*-type search was constitutional; hence the police conduct in this case, consistent with that precedent, was "innocent." But the Court then finds this fact sufficient to create a new "good faith" exception to the exclusionary rule. It reasons that the "sole purpose" of the exclusionary rule "is to deter future Fourth Amendment violations". The "deterrence benefits of exclusion vary with the culpability of the law enforcement conduct at issue," Those benefits are sufficient to justify exclusion where "police exhibit deliberate, reckless, or grossly negligent disregard for Fourth Amendment rights." But those benefits do not justify exclusion where, as here, the police act with "simple, isolated negligence" or an "objectively reasonable good-faith belief that their conduct is lawful."

If the Court means what it says, what will happen to the exclusionary rule, a rule that the Court adopted nearly a century ago for federal courts, and made applicable to state courts a half century ago through the Fourteenth Amendment, *Mapp v. Ohio*? The Court has thought of that rule not as punishment for the individual officer or as reparation for the individual defendant but more generally as an effective way to secure enforcement of the Fourth Amendment's commands. This Court has deviated from the "suppression" norm in the name of "good faith" only a handful of times and in limited, atypical circumstances: where a magistrate has erroneously issued a warrant, *United States v. Leon*; where a database has erroneously informed police that they have a warrant, *Arizona v. Evans, Herring v. United States*; and where an unconstitutional statute purported to authorize the search, *Illinois v. Krull*.

The fact that such exceptions are few and far between is understandable. Defendants frequently move to suppress evidence on Fourth Amendment grounds. In many, perhaps most, of these instances the police, uncertain of how the Fourth Amendment applied to the particular factual circumstances they faced, will have acted in objective good faith. Yet, in a significant percentage of these instances, courts will find that the police were wrong. And, unless the police conduct falls into one of the exceptions previously noted, courts have required the suppression of the evidence seized. See Valdes, Frequency and Success: An Empirical Study of Criminal Law Defenses, Federal Constitutional Evidentiary Claims, and Plea Negotiations, 153 U. Pa. L. Rev. 1709, 1728 (2005) (suppression motions are filed in approximately 7% of criminal cases; approximately 12% of suppression motions are successful).

But an officer who conducts a search that he believes complies with the Constitution but which, it ultimately turns out, falls just outside the Fourth Amendment's bounds is no more culpable than an officer who follows erroneous "binding precedent." Nor is an officer more culpable where circuit precedent is simply suggestive rather than "binding," where it only describes how to treat roughly analogous instances, or where it just does not exist. Thus, if the Court means what it now says, if it would place determinative weight upon the culpability of an individual officer's conduct, and if it would apply the exclusionary rule only where a Fourth Amendment violation was "deliberate, reckless, or grossly negligent," then the "good faith" exception will swallow the exclusionary rule. Indeed, our broad dicta in *Herring*—dicta the Court repeats and expands upon today—may already be leading lower courts in this direction. Today's decision will doubtless accelerate this trend.

Any such change (which may already be underway) would affect not "an exceedingly small set of cases," but a very large number of cases, potentially many thousands each year. And since the exclusionary rule is often the only sanction available for a Fourth Amendment violation, the Fourth Amendment would no longer protect ordinary Americans from "unreasonable searches and seizures." It would become a watered-down Fourth Amendment, offering its protection against only those searches and seizures that are *egregiously* unreasonable.

III

In sum, I fear that the Court's opinion will undermine the exclusionary rule. And I believe that the Court wrongly departs from *Griffith* regardless. Instead I would follow *Griffith,* apply *Gant*'s rule retroactively to this case, and require suppression of the evidence. Such an approach is consistent with our precedent, and it would indeed affect no more than "an exceedingly small set of cases."

For these reasons, with respect, I dissent.

F. EXCEPTIONS TO FRUITS DOCTRINE

Wong Sun v. United States

371 U.S. 471 (1963)

Brennan, J., delivered the opinion of the Court, in which Warren, C.J., Black, Goldberg and Douglas, JJ., joined. Clark, J., filed a dissenting opinion in which Harlan, Stewart, and White, JJ., joined.

■ ■ ■

About 2 a.m. on the morning of June 4, 1959, federal narcotics agents in San Francisco, after having had one Hom Way under surveillance for six weeks, arrested him and found heroin in his possession. Hom Way, who had not before been an informant, stated after his arrest that he had bought an ounce of heroin the night before from one known to him only as "Blackie Toy," proprietor of a laundry on Leavenworth Street.

About 6 a.m. that morning six or seven federal agents went to a laundry at 1733 Leavenworth Street. The sign above the door of this establishment said "Oye's Laundry." It was operated by the petitioner James Wah Toy. There is, however, nothing in the record which identifies James Wah Toy and "Blackie Toy" as the same person. The other federal officers remained nearby out of sight while Agent Alton Wong, who was of Chinese ancestry, rang the bell. When petitioner Toy appeared and opened the door, Agent Wong told him that he was calling for laundry and dry cleaning. Toy replied that he didn't open until 8 o'clock and told the agent to come back at that time. Toy started to close the door. Agent Wong thereupon took his badge from his pocket and said, "I am a federal narcotics agent." Toy immediately "slammed the door and started running" down the hallway through the laundry to his living quarters at the back where his wife and child were sleeping in a bedroom. Agent Wong and the other federal officers broke open the door and followed Toy down the hallway to the living quarters and into the bedroom. Toy reached into a night-stand drawer. Agent Wong thereupon drew his pistol, pulled Toy's hand out of the drawer, placed him under arrest and handcuffed him. There was nothing in the drawer and a search of the premises uncovered no narcotics.

One of the agents said to Toy ". . . [Hom Way] says he got narcotics from you." Toy responded, "No, I haven't been selling any narcotics at all. However, I do know somebody who has." When asked who that was, Toy said, "I only know him as Johnny. I don't know his last name." However, Toy described a house on Eleventh Avenue where he said Johnny lived; he also described a bedroom in the house where he said "Johnny kept about a piece" of heroin, and where he and Johnny had smoked some of the drug the night before. The agents left immediately for Eleventh Avenue and located the house. They entered and found one Johnny Yee in the bedroom. After a discussion with the agents, Yee took from a bureau drawer several tubes containing in all just less than one ounce of heroin, and surrendered them. Within the hour Yee and Toy were taken to the Office of the Bureau of Narcotics. Yee there stated that the heroin had been brought to him some four days earlier by petitioner Toy and another Chinese known to him only as "Sea Dog."

Toy was questioned as to the identity of "Sea Dog" and said that "Sea Dog" was Wong Sun. Some agents, including Agent Alton Wong, took Toy to Wong Sun's neighborhood where Toy pointed out a multifamily dwelling where he said Wong Sun lived. Agent Wong rang a downstairs doorbell and a buzzer sounded, opening the door. The officer identified himself as a narcotics agent to a woman on the landing and asked "for Mr. Wong." The woman was the wife of petitioner Wong Sun. She said that Wong Sun was "in the back room sleeping." Alton Wong and some six other officers climbed the stairs and entered the apartment. One of the officers went into the back room and brought petitioner Wong Sun from the bedroom in handcuffs. A thorough search of the apartment followed, but no narcotics were discovered.

Petitioner Toy and Johnny Yee were arraigned before a United States Commissioner on June 4 on a complaint charging a violation. Later that day, each was released on his own recognizance. Petitioner Wong Sun was arraigned on a similar complaint filed the next day and was also released on his own recognizance. Within a few days, both petitioners and Yee were interrogated at the office of the Narcotics Bureau by Agent William Wong, also of Chinese ancestry. The agent advised each of the three of his right to withhold information which might be used against him, and stated to each that he was entitled to the advice of counsel, though it does not appear that any attorney was present during the questioning of any of the three. The officer also explained to each that no promises or offers of immunity or leniency were being or could be made.

■ ■ ■

The statute expressly provides that proof of the accused's possession of the drug will support a conviction under the statute unless the accused satisfactorily explains the possession. The Government's evidence tending to prove the petitioners' possession (the petitioners offered no exculpatory testimony) consisted of four items which the trial court admitted over timely objections that they were inadmissible as "fruits" of unlawful arrests or of attendant searches: (1) the statements made orally by petitioner Toy in his bedroom at the time of his arrest; (2) the heroin surrendered to the agents by Johnny Yee; (3) petitioner Toy's pretrial unsigned statement; and (4) petitioner Wong Sun's similar statement. The dispute below and here has centered around the correctness of the rulings of the trial judge allowing these items in evidence.

■ ■ ■

In order to make effective the fundamental constitutional guarantees of sanctity of the home and inviolability of the person, *Boyd v. United States* (1886), this Court held nearly half a century ago that evidence seized during an unlawful search could not constitute proof against the victim of the search. *Weeks v. United States* (1914). The exclusionary prohibition extends as well to the indirect as the direct products of such invasions. *Silverthorne Lumber Co. v. United States* (1920). Mr. Justice Holmes, speaking for the Court in that case, in holding that the Government might not make use of information obtained during an unlawful search to subpoena from the victims the very documents illegally viewed, expressed succinctly the policy of the broad exclusionary rule:

> "The essence of a provision forbidding the acquisition of evidence in a certain way is that not merely evidence so acquired shall not be used before the Court but that it shall not be used at all. Of course this does not mean that the facts thus obtained become sacred and inaccessible. If knowledge of them is gained from an independent source they may be proved like any others, but the knowledge gained by the Government's own wrong cannot be used by it in the way proposed."

The exclusionary rule has traditionally barred from trial physical, tangible materials obtained either during or as a direct result of an unlawful invasion. It follows from our holding in *Silverman v. United States* (1928) that the Fourth Amendment may protect against the overhearing of verbal statements as well as against the more traditional seizure of "papers and effects." Nor do the policies underlying the exclusionary rule invite any logical distinction between physical and verbal evidence.

■ ■ ■

The Government argues that Toy's statements to the officers in his bedroom, although closely consequent upon the invasion which we hold unlawful, were nevertheless admissible because they resulted from "an intervening independent act of a free will." This contention, however, takes insufficient account of the circumstances. Six or seven officers had broken the door and followed on Toy's heels into the bedroom where his wife and child were sleeping. He had been almost immediately handcuffed and arrested. Under such circumstances it is unreasonable to infer that Toy's response was sufficiently an act of free will to purge the primary taint of the unlawful invasion.

■ ■ ■

We now consider whether the exclusion of Toy's declarations requires also the exclusion of the narcotics taken from Yee, to which those declarations led the police. The prosecutor candidly told the trial court that "we wouldn't have found those drugs except that Mr. Toy helped us to." Hence this is not the case envisioned by this Court where the exclusionary rule has no application because the Government learned of the evidence "from an independent source," *Silverthorne Lumber Co. v. United States*; nor is this a case in which the connection between the lawless conduct of the police and the discovery of the challenged evidence has "become so attenuated as to dissipate the taint." *Nardone v. United States* (1939). We need not hold that all evidence is "fruit of the poisonous tree" simply because it would not have come to light but for the illegal actions of the police. Rather, the more apt question in such a case is "whether, granting establishment of the primary illegality, the evidence to which instant objection is made has been come at by exploitation of that illegality or instead by means sufficiently distinguishable to be purged of the primary taint." Maguire, Evidence of Guilt, 221 (1959). We think it clear that the narcotics were "come at by the exploitation of that illegality" and hence that they may not be used against Toy.

■ ■ ■

We turn now to the case of the other petitioner, Wong Sun. We have no occasion to disagree with the finding of the Court of Appeals that his arrest, also, was without probable cause or reasonable grounds. At all events no evidentiary consequences turn upon that question. For Wong Sun's unsigned confession was not the fruit of that arrest, and was therefore properly admitted at trial. On the evidence that Wong Sun had been released on his own recognizance after a lawful arraignment, and had returned voluntarily several days later to make the statement, we hold that the connection between the arrest and the statement had "become so attenuated as to dissipate the taint." *Nardone v. United States.* The fact that the statement was unsigned, whatever bearing this may have upon its weight and credibility, does not render it inadmissible; Wong Sun understood and adopted its substance, though he could not comprehend the English words. The petitioner has never suggested any impropriety in the interrogation itself which would require the exclusion of this statement.

■ ■ ■

The judgment of the Court of Appeals is reversed and the case is remanded to the District Court for further proceedings consistent with this opinion.

It is so ordered.

Brown v. Illinois

422 U.S. 590 (1975)

BLACKMUN, J., delivered the opinion of the Court, in which BURGER, C.J., BRENNAN, STEVENS, MARSHALL, and STEWART, JJ., joined. . . . POWELL concurred in part and filed an opinion in which REHNQUIST, J., joined.

This case lies at the crossroads of the Fourth and the Fifth Amendments. Petitioner was arrested without probable cause and without a warrant. He was given, in full, the warnings prescribed by *Miranda v. Arizona* (1966). Thereafter, while in custody, he made two inculpatory statements. The issue is whether evidence of those statements was properly admitted, or should have been excluded, in petitioner's subsequent trial for murder in state court. Expressed another way, the issue is whether the statements were to be excluded as the fruit of the illegal arrest, or were admissible because the giving of the *Miranda* warnings sufficiently attenuated the taint of the arrest. See *Wong Sun v. United States* (1963). . . .

In *Wong Sun*, the Court pronounced the principles to be applied where the issue is whether statements and other evidence obtained after an illegal arrest or search should be excluded. In that case, federal agents elicited an oral statement from defendant Toy after forcing entry at 6 a.m. into his laundry, at the back of which he had his living quarters. The agents had followed Toy down the hall to the bedroom and there had placed him under arrest. The Court of Appeals found that there was no probable cause for the arrest. This Court concluded that that finding was "amply justified by the facts clearly shown on this record." Toy's statement, which bore upon his participation in the sale of narcotics, led the agents to question another person, Johnny Yee, who actually possessed narcotics. Yee stated that heroin had been brought to him earlier by Toy and another Chinese known to him only as "Sea Dog." Under questioning, Toy said that "Sea Dog" was Wong Sun. Toy led agents to a multifamily dwelling where, he said, Wong Sun lived. Gaining admittance to the building through a bell and buzzer, the agents climbed the stairs and entered the apartment. One went into the back room and brought Wong Sun out in handcuffs. After arraignment, Wong Sun was released on his own recognizance. Several days later, he returned voluntarily to give an unsigned confession.

This Court ruled that Toy's declarations and the contraband taken from Yee were the fruits of the agents' illegal action and should not have been admitted as evidence against Toy. It held that the statement did not result from "an intervening independent act of a free will," and that it was not "sufficiently an act of free will to purge the primary taint of the unlawful invasion" With respect to Wong Sun's confession, however, the Court held that in the light of his lawful arraignment and release on his own recognizance, and of his return voluntarily several days later to make the statement, the connection between his unlawful arrest and the statement "had 'become so attenuated as to dissipate the taint.'"

The exclusionary rule thus was applied in *Wong Sun* primarily to protect Fourth Amendment rights. Protection of the Fifth Amendment right against self-incrimination was not the Court's paramount concern there. To the extent that the question whether Toy's statement was voluntary was considered, it was only to judge whether it "was sufficiently an act of free will to purge the primary taint of the unlawful invasion." . . .

The Illinois courts refrained from resolving the question, as apt here as it was in Wong Sun, whether Brown's statements were obtained by exploitation of the illegality of his arrest. They assumed that the *Miranda* warnings, by themselves, assured that the statements (verbal acts, as contrasted with physical evidence) were of sufficient free will as to purge the primary taint of the unlawful arrest. *Wong Sun*, of course, preceded *Miranda*.

This Court has described the *Miranda* warnings as a "prophylactic rule," and as a "procedural safeguard," *Miranda v. Arizona*, employed to protect Fifth Amendment rights against "the compulsion inherent in custodial surroundings." The function of the warnings relates to the Fifth Amendment's guarantee against coerced self-incrimination, and the exclusion of a statement made in the absence of the warnings, it is said, serves to deter the taking of an incriminating statement without first informing the individual of his Fifth Amendment rights.

Although, almost 90 years ago, the Court observed that the Fifth Amendment is in "intimate relation" with the Fourth, the *Miranda* warnings thus far have not been regarded as a means either of remedying or deterring violations of Fourth Amendment rights. Frequently, as here, rights under the two Amendments may appear to coalesce since "the 'unreasonable searches and seizures' condemned in the Fourth Amendment are almost always made for the purpose of compelling a man to give evidence against himself, which in criminal cases is condemned in the Fifth Amendment." The exclusionary rule, however, when utilized to effectuate the Fourth Amendment, serves interests and policies that are distinct from those it serves under the Fifth. It is directed at all unlawful searches and seizures, and not merely those that happen to produce incriminating material or testimony as fruits. In short, exclusion of a confession made without *Miranda* warnings might be regarded as necessary to effectuate the Fifth Amendment, but it would not be sufficient fully to protect the Fourth. *Miranda* warnings, and the exclusion of a confession made without them, do not alone sufficiently deter a Fourth Amendment violation.

Thus, even if the statements in this case were found to be voluntary under the Fifth Amendment, the Fourth Amendment issue remains. In order for the causal chain, between the illegal arrest and the statements made subsequent thereto, to be broken, *Wong Sun* requires not merely that the statement meet the Fifth Amendment standard of voluntariness but that it be "sufficiently an act of free will to purge the primary taint." *Wong Sun* thus mandates consideration of a statement's admissibility in light of the distinct policies and interests of the Fourth Amendment.

If *Miranda* warnings, by themselves, were held to attenuate the taint of an unconstitutional arrest, regardless of how wanton and purposeful the Fourth Amendment violation, the effect of the exclusionary rule would be substantially diluted. Arrests made without warrant or without probable cause, for questioning or "investigation," would be encouraged by the knowledge that evidence derived therefrom could well be made admissible at trial by the simple expedient of giving *Miranda* warnings. Any incentive to avoid Fourth Amendment violations would be eviscerated by making the warnings, in effect, a "cure-all," and the constitutional guarantee against unlawful searches and seizures could be said to be reduced to "a form of words."

It is entirely possible, of course, as the State here argues, that persons arrested illegally frequently may decide to confess, as an act of free will unaffected by the initial illegality. But the *Miranda* warnings, alone and per se, cannot always make the act sufficiently a product of free will to break, for Fourth Amendment purposes, the causal connection between the illegality and the confession. They cannot assure in every case that the Fourth Amendment violation has not been unduly exploited.

While we therefore reject the per se rule which the Illinois courts appear to have accepted, we also decline to adopt any alternative per se or "but for" rule.... The question whether a confession is the product of a free will under *Wong Sun* must be answered on the facts of each case. No single fact is dispositive. The workings of the human mind are too complex, and the possibilities of misconduct too diverse, to permit protection of the Fourth Amendment to turn on such a talismanic test. The *Miranda* warnings are an important factor, to be sure, in determining whether the confession is obtained by exploitation of an illegal arrest. But they are not the only factor to be considered. The temporal proximity of the arrest and the confession, the presence of intervening circumstances, and, particularly, the purpose and flagrancy of the official misconduct are all relevant....

Although the Illinois courts failed to undertake the inquiry mandated by *Wong Sun* to evaluate the circumstances of this case in the light of the policy served by the exclusionary rule, the trial resulted in a record of amply sufficient detail and depth from which the determination may be made. We therefore decline the suggestion of the United States as to remand the case for further factual findings. We conclude that the State failed to sustain the burden of showing that the evidence in question was admissible under *Wong Sun*. . . .

The illegality here, moreover, had a quality of purposefulness. The impropriety of the arrest was obvious; awareness of that fact was virtually conceded by the two detectives when they repeatedly acknowledged in their testimony that the purpose of their action was "for investigation" or for "questioning." The arrest, both in design and in execution, was investigatory. The detectives embarked upon this expedition for evidence in the hope that something might turn up. The manner in which Brown's arrest was effected gives the appearance of having been calculated to cause surprise, fright, and confusion.

We emphasize that our holding is a limited one. We decide only that the Illinois courts were in error in assuming that the *Miranda* warnings, by themselves, under *Wong Sun* always purge the taint of an illegal arrest.

The judgment of the Supreme Court of Illinois is reversed and the case is remanded for further proceedings not inconsistent with this opinion.

It is so ordered.

Murray v. United States

487 U.S. 533 (1988)

SCALIA, J., delivered the opinion of the Court, in which REHNQUIST, C.J., and WHITE and BLACKMUN, JJ., joined. MARSHALL, J., filed a dissenting opinion, in which STEVENS and O'CONNOR, JJ., joined. STEVENS, J., filed a dissenting opinion. BRENNAN and KENNEDY, JJ., took no part in the consideration or decision of the cases.

In *Segura v. United States* (1984), we held that police officers' illegal entry upon private premises did not require suppression of evidence subsequently discovered at those premises when executing a search warrant obtained on the basis of information wholly unconnected with the initial entry. In these consolidated cases we are faced with the question whether, again assuming evidence obtained pursuant to an independently obtained search warrant, the portion of such evidence that had been observed in plain view at the time of a prior illegal entry must be suppressed. . . .

. . . Based on information received from informants, federal law enforcement agents had been surveilling petitioner Murray and several of his co-conspirators. At about 1:45 p.m. on April 6, 1983, they observed Murray drive a truck and Carter drive a green camper, into a warehouse in South Boston. When the petitioners drove the vehicles out about 20 minutes later, the surveilling agents saw within the warehouse two individuals and a tractor-trailer rig bearing a long, dark container. Murray and Carter later turned over the truck and camper to other drivers, who were in turn followed and ultimately arrested, and the vehicles lawfully seized. Both vehicles were found to contain marijuana.

After receiving this information, several of the agents converged on the South Boston warehouse and forced entry. They found the warehouse unoccupied, but observed in plain view numerous burlap-wrapped bales that were later found to contain marijuana. They left without disturbing the bales, kept the warehouse under surveillance, and did not reenter it until they had a search warrant. In applying for the warrant, the agents did not mention the prior entry, and did not rely on any observations made during that entry. When the warrant was issued—at 10:40 p.m., approximately eight hours after the initial entry—the agents immediately reentered the warehouse and seized 270 bales of marijuana and notebooks listing customers for whom the bales were destined.

Before trial, petitioners moved to suppress the evidence found in the warehouse. The District Court denied the motion, rejecting petitioners' arguments that the warrant was invalid because the agents did not inform the Magistrate about their prior warrantless entry, and that the warrant was tainted by that entry.

■ ■ ■

Almost simultaneously with our development of the exclusionary rule, in the first quarter of this century, we also announced what has come to be known as the "independent source" doctrine. See *Silverthorne Lumber Co. v. United States* (1920). That doctrine, which has been applied to evidence acquired not only through Fourth Amendment violations but also through Fifth and Sixth Amendment violations, has recently been described as follows:

> "[T]he interest of society in deterring unlawful police conduct and the public interest in having juries receive all probative evidence of a crime are properly balanced by putting the police in the same, not a *worse,* position than they would have been in if no police error or misconduct had occurred.... When the challenged evidence has an independent source, exclusion of such evidence would put the police in a worse position than they would have been in absent any error or violation." *Nix v. Williams* (1984).

The dispute here is over the scope of this doctrine. Petitioners contend that it applies only to evidence obtained for the first time during an independent lawful search. The Government argues that it applies also to evidence initially discovered during, or as a consequence of, an unlawful search, but later obtained independently from activities untainted by the initial illegality. We think the Government's view has better support in both precedent and policy....

Petitioners' asserted policy basis for excluding evidence which is initially discovered during an illegal search, but is subsequently acquired through an independent and lawful source, is that a contrary rule will remove all deterrence to, and indeed positively encourage, unlawful police searches. As petitioners see the incentives, law enforcement officers will routinely enter without a warrant to make sure that what they expect to be on the premises is in fact there. If it is not, they will have spared themselves the time and trouble of getting a warrant; if it is, they can get the warrant and use the evidence despite the unlawful entry. We see the incentives differently. An officer with probable cause sufficient to obtain a search warrant would be foolish to enter the premises first in an unlawful manner. By doing so, he would risk suppression of all evidence on the premises, both seen and unseen, since his action would add to the normal burden of convincing a magistrate that there is probable cause the much more onerous burden of convincing a trial court that no information gained from the illegal entry affected either the law enforcement officers' decision to seek a warrant or the magistrate's decision to grant it. Nor would the officer *without* sufficient probable cause to obtain a search warrant have any added incentive to conduct an unlawful entry, since whatever he finds cannot be used to establish probable cause before a magistrate.

It is possible to read petitioners' briefs as asserting the more narrow position that the "independent source" doctrine does apply to independent acquisition of evidence previously derived *indirectly* from the unlawful search, but does not apply to what they call "primary evidence," that is, evidence acquired during the course of the search itself. In addition to finding no support in our precedent, see *Silverthorne Lumber* (referring specifically to evidence seized during an unlawful search), this strange distinction would produce results bearing no relation to the policies of the exclusionary rule. It would mean, for example, that the government's knowledge of the existence and condition of a dead body, knowledge lawfully acquired through independent sources, would have to be excluded if government agents had previously observed the body during an unlawful search of the defendant's apartment; but not if they had observed a notation that the body was buried in a certain location, producing consequential discovery of the corpse.

■ ■ ■

To apply what we have said to the present cases: Knowledge that the marijuana was in the warehouse was assuredly acquired at the time of the unlawful entry. But it was also acquired at the time of entry pursuant to the warrant, and if that later acquisition was not the result of the earlier entry there is no reason why the independent source doctrine should not apply. Invoking the exclusionary rule would put the police (and society) not in the *same* position they would have occupied if no violation occurred, but in a *worse* one. . . .

The ultimate question, therefore, is whether the search pursuant to warrant was in fact a genuinely independent source of the information and tangible evidence at issue here. This would not have been the case if the agents' decision to seek the warrant was prompted by what they had seen during the initial entry, or if information obtained during that entry was presented to the Magistrate and affected his decision to issue the warrant. On this point the Court of Appeals said the following:

> "[W]e can be absolutely certain that the warrantless entry in no way contributed in the slightest either to the issuance of a warrant or to the

discovery of the evidence during the lawful search that occurred pursuant to the warrant.

This is as clear a case as can be imagined where the discovery of the contraband in plain view was totally irrelevant to the later securing of a warrant and the successful search that ensued. As there was no causal link whatever between the illegal entry and the discovery of the challenged evidence, we find no error in the court's refusal to suppress. . . ."

Accordingly, we vacate the judgment and remand these cases to the Court of Appeals with instructions that it remand to the District Court for determination whether the warrant-authorized search of the warehouse was an independent source of the challenged evidence in the sense we have described.

It is so ordered.

Justice MARSHALL, with whom Justice STEVENS and Justice O'CONNOR join, dissenting.

The Court today holds that the "independent source" exception to the exclusionary rule may justify admitting evidence discovered during an illegal warrantless search that is later "rediscovered" by the same team of investigators during a search pursuant to a warrant obtained immediately after the illegal search. I believe the Court's decision, by failing to provide sufficient guarantees that the subsequent search was, in fact, independent of the illegal search, emasculates the Warrant Clause and undermines the deterrence function of the exclusionary rule. I therefore dissent. . . .

Given the underlying justification for the independent source exception, any inquiry into the exception's application must keep sight of the practical effect admission will have on the incentives facing law enforcement officers to engage in unlawful conduct. The proper scope of the independent source exception, and guidelines for its application, cannot be divined in a factual vacuum; instead, they must be informed by the nature of the constitutional violation and the deterrent effect of exclusion in particular circumstances. In holding that the independent source exception may apply to the facts of these cases, I believe the Court loses sight of the practical moorings of the independent source exception and creates an affirmative incentive for unconstitutional searches. This holding can find no justification in the purposes underlying both the exclusionary rule and the independent source exception. . . .

Under the circumstances of these cases, the admission of the evidence "reseized" during the second search severely undermines the deterrence function of the exclusionary rule. Indeed, admission in these cases affirmatively encourages illegal searches. The incentives for such illegal conduct are clear. Obtaining a warrant is inconvenient and time consuming. Even when officers have probable cause to support a warrant application, therefore, they have an incentive first to determine whether it is worthwhile to obtain a warrant. Probable cause is much less than certainty, and many "confirmatory" searches will result in the discovery that no evidence is present, thus saving the police the time and trouble of getting a warrant. If contraband is discovered, however, the officers may later seek a warrant to shield the evidence from the taint of the illegal search. The police thus know in advance that they have little to lose and much to gain by forgoing the bother of obtaining a warrant and undertaking an illegal search.

The Court, however, "see[s] the incentives differently." Under the Court's view, today's decision does not provide an incentive for unlawful searches, because the officer undertaking the search would know that "his action would add to the normal burden of convincing a magistrate that there is probable cause the much more onerous burden of convincing a trial court that no information gained from the illegal entry affected either the law enforcement officers' decision to seek a warrant or the magistrate's decision to grant it." The Court, however, provides no hint of why this risk would actually seem significant to the officers. Under the circumstances of these cases, the officers committing the illegal search have both knowledge and control of the factors central to the trial court's determination. First, it is a simple matter, as was done in these cases, to exclude from the warrant application any information gained from the initial entry so that the magistrate's determination of probable cause is not influenced by the prior illegal search. Second, today's decision makes the application of the independent source exception turn entirely on an evaluation of the officers' intent. It normally will be difficult for the trial court to verify, or the defendant to rebut, an assertion by officers that they always intended to obtain a warrant, regardless of the results of the illegal search. The testimony of the officers conducting the illegal search is the only direct evidence of intent, and the defendant will be relegated simply to arguing that the officers should not be believed. Under these circumstances, the litigation risk described by the Court seems hardly a risk at all; it does not significantly dampen the incentive to conduct the initial illegal search.

The strong Fourth Amendment interest in eliminating these incentives for illegal entry should cause this Court to scrutinize closely the application of the independent source exception to evidence obtained under the circumstances of the instant cases; respect for the constitutional guarantee requires a rule that does not undermine the deterrence function of the exclusionary rule. When, as here, the same team of investigators is involved in both the first and second search, there is a significant danger that the "independence" of the source will in fact be illusory, and that the initial search will have affected the decision to obtain a warrant notwithstanding the officers' subsequent assertions to the contrary. It is therefore crucial that the factual premise of the exception—complete independence—be clearly established before the exception can justify admission of the evidence. I believe the Court's reliance on the intent of the law enforcement officers who conducted the warrantless search provides insufficient guarantees that the subsequent legal search was unaffected by the prior illegal search.

To ensure that the source of the evidence is genuinely independent, the basis for a finding that a search was untainted by a prior illegal search must focus, as with the inevitable discovery doctrine, on "demonstrated historical facts capable of ready verification or impeachment." *Nix v. Williams*. In the instant cases, there are no "demonstrated historical facts" capable of supporting a finding that the subsequent warrant search was wholly unaffected by the prior illegal search. The same team of investigators was involved in both searches. The warrant was obtained immediately after the illegal search, and no effort was made to obtain a warrant prior to the discovery of the marijuana during the illegal search. The only evidence available that the warrant search was wholly independent is the testimony of the agents who conducted the illegal search. Under these circumstances, the threat that the subsequent search was tainted by the illegal search is too great to allow for the application of the independent source exception. The Court's contrary holding lends itself to easy abuse, and offers an incentive to bypass the constitutional requirement that probable cause be assessed by a neutral and detached magistrate before the police invade an individual's privacy....

In sum, under circumstances as are presented in these cases, when the very law enforcement officers who participate in an illegal search immediately thereafter obtain a warrant to search the same premises, I believe the evidence discovered during the initial illegal entry must be suppressed. Any other result emasculates the Warrant Clause and provides an intolerable incentive for warrantless searches. I respectfully dissent....

Nix, Warden of the Iowa State Penitentiary v. Williams

467 U.S. 431 (1984)

BURGER, C.J., delivered the opinion of the Court, in which BLACKMUN, POWELL, REHNQUIST, and O'CONNOR, JJ., joined. WHITE, J., filed a concurring opinion. STEVENS, J., filed an opinion concurring in the judgment. BRENNAN, J., filed a dissenting opinion, in which MARSHALL, J., joined.

■ ■ ■

On December 24, 1968, 10-year-old Pamela Powers disappeared from a YMCA building in Des Moines, Iowa, where she had accompanied her parents to watch an athletic contest. Shortly after she disappeared, Williams was seen leaving the YMCA carrying a large bundle wrapped in a blanket; a 14-year-old boy who had helped Williams open his car door reported that he had seen "two legs in it and they were skinny and white."

Williams' car was found the next day 160 miles east of Des Moines in Davenport, Iowa. Later several items of clothing belonging to the child, some of Williams' clothing, and an army blanket like the one used to wrap the bundle that Williams carried out of the YMCA were found at a rest stop on Interstate 80 near Grinnell, between Des Moines and Davenport. A warrant was issued for Williams' arrest.

Police surmised that Williams had left Pamela Powers or her body somewhere between Des Moines and the Grinnell rest stop where some of the young girl's clothing had been found. On December 26, the Iowa Bureau of Criminal Investigation initiated a large-scale search. Two hundred volunteers divided into teams began the search 21 miles east of Grinnell, covering an area several miles to the north and south of Interstate 80. They moved westward from Poweshiek County, in which Grinnell was located, into Jasper County. Searchers were instructed to check all roads, abandoned farm buildings, ditches, culverts, and any other place in which the body of a small child could be hidden.

Meanwhile, Williams surrendered to local police in Davenport, where he was promptly arraigned. Williams contacted a Des Moines attorney who arranged for an attorney in Davenport to meet Williams at the Davenport police station. Des Moines police informed counsel they would pick Williams up in Davenport and return him to Des Moines without questioning him. Two Des Moines detectives then drove to Davenport, took Williams into custody, and proceeded to drive him back to Des Moines.

During the return trip, one of the policemen, Detective Leaming, began a conversation with Williams, saying:

> "I want to give you something to think about while we're traveling down the road.... They are predicting several inches of snow for tonight, and I feel that you yourself are the only person that knows where this little girl's body is...and if you get a snow on top of it you yourself may be unable to find it. And since we will be going right past the area [where the body is] on the way into Des Moines, I feel that we could stop and locate the body, that the parents of this little girl should be entitled to a Christian burial for the little girl who was snatched away from them on Christmas [Eve] and murdered.... [After] a snow storm [we may not be] able to find it at all."

Leaming told Williams he knew the body was in the area of Mitchellville—a town they would be passing on the way to Des Moines. He concluded the conversation by saying: "I do not want you to answer me.... Just think about it...."

Later, as the police car approached Grinnell, Williams asked Leaming whether the police had found the young girl's shoes. After Leaming replied that he was unsure, Williams directed the police to a point near a service station where he said he had left the shoes; they were not found. As they continued the drive to Des Moines, Williams asked whether the blanket had been found and then directed the officers to a rest area in Grinnell where he said he had disposed of the blanket; they did not find the blanket. At this point Leaming and his party were joined by the officers in charge of the search. As they approached Mitchellville, Williams, without any further conversation, agreed to direct the officers to the child's body.

The officers directing the search had called off the search at 3 p.m., when they left the Grinnell Police Department to join Leaming at the rest area. At that time, one search team near the Jasper County-Polk County line was only two and one-half miles from where Williams soon guided Leaming and his party to the body. The child's body was found next to a culvert in a ditch beside a gravel road in Polk County, about two miles south of Interstate 80, and essentially within the area to be searched.

■ ■ ■

The doctrine requiring courts to suppress evidence as the tainted "fruit" of unlawful governmental conduct had its genesis in *Silverthorne Lumber Co. v. United States* (1920); there, the Court held that the exclusionary rule applies not only to the illegally obtained evidence itself, but also to other incriminating evidence derived from the primary evidence. The holding of *Silverthorne* was carefully limited, however, for the Court emphasized that such information does not automatically become "sacred and inaccessible."

> "If knowledge of [such facts] is gained from an *independent source*, they may be proved like any others. . . ." *Ibid.* (emphasis added).

Wong Sun v. United States (1963), extended the exclusionary rule to evidence that was the indirect product or "fruit" of unlawful police conduct, but there again the Court emphasized that evidence that has been illegally obtained need not always be suppressed, stating:

> "We need not hold that all evidence is 'fruit of the poisonous tree' simply because it would not have come to light *but for the illegal actions* of the police. Rather, the more apt question in such a case is 'whether, granting establishment of the primary illegality, the evidence to which instant objection is made has been come at by exploitation of that illegality or instead by means sufficiently distinguishable to be purged of the primary taint.'" (emphasis added) (quoting J. Maguire, Evidence of Guilt 221 (1959)).

■ ■ ■

Although *Silverthorne* and *Wong Sun* involved violations of the Fourth Amendment, the "fruit of the poisonous tree" doctrine has not been limited to cases in which there has been a Fourth Amendment violation. The Court has applied the doctrine where the violations were of the Sixth Amendment, see *United States v. Wade* (1967), as well as of the Fifth Amendment.

The core rationale consistently advanced by this Court for extending the exclusionary rule to evidence that is the fruit of unlawful police conduct has been that this admittedly drastic and socially costly course is needed to deter police from violations of constitutional and statutory protections. This Court has accepted the argument that the way to ensure such protections is to exclude evidence seized as a result of such violations notwithstanding the high social cost of letting persons obviously guilty go unpunished for their crimes. On this rationale, the prosecution is not to be put in a better position than it would have been in if no illegality had transpired.

By contrast, the derivative evidence analysis ensures that the prosecution is not put in a *worse* position simply because of some earlier police error or misconduct. The independent source doctrine allows admission of evidence that has been discovered by means wholly independent of any constitutional violation. That doctrine, although closely related to the inevitable discovery doctrine, does not apply here; Williams' statements to Leaming indeed led police to the child's body, but that is not the whole story. The independent source doctrine teaches us that the interest of society in deterring unlawful police conduct and the public interest in having juries receive all probative evidence of a crime are properly balanced by putting the police in the same, not a *worse*, position that they would have been in if no police error or misconduct had occurred. When the challenged evidence has an independent source, exclusion of such evidence would put the police in a worse position than they would have been in absent any error or violation. There is a functional similarity between these two doctrines in that exclusion of evidence that would inevitably have been discovered would also put the government in a worse position, because the police would have obtained that evidence if no misconduct had taken place. Thus, while the independent source exception would not justify admission of evidence in this case, its rationale is wholly consistent with and justifies our adoption of the ultimate or inevitable discovery exception to the exclusionary rule.

■ ■ ■

If the prosecution can establish by a preponderance of the evidence that the information ultimately or inevitably would have been discovered by lawful means—here the volunteers' search—then the deterrence rationale has so little basis that the evidence should be received. Anything less would reject logic, experience, and common sense.

■ ■ ■

The judgment of the Court of Appeals is reversed, and the case is remanded for further proceedings consistent with this opinion.

It is so ordered.

Hudson v. Michigan

547 U.S. 586 (2006)

SCALIA, J., delivered the opinion of the Court, in which ROBERTS, C.J., THOMAS, ALITO, and KENNEDY, JJ., joined except as to Part IV [not included in this excerpt]. KENNEDY, J., filed an opinion concurring in part and in the judgment. BREYER, J., filed an opinion dissenting, in which STEVENS, SOUTER, and GINSBURG, JJ., joined.

We decide whether violation of the "knock-and-announce" rule requires the suppression of all evidence found in the search.

■ ■ ■

The common-law principle that law enforcement officers must announce their presence and provide residents an opportunity to open the door is an ancient one. See *Wilson v. Arkansas* (1995).

■ ■ ■

We recognized that the new constitutional rule we had announced is not easily applied. *Wilson* and cases following it have noted the many situations in which it is not necessary to knock and announce. It is not necessary when "circumstances presen[t] a threat of physical violence," or if there is "reason to believe that evidence would likely be destroyed if advance notice were given," or if knocking and announcing would be "futile," *Richards v. Wisconsin* (1997). We require only that police "have a reasonable suspicion . . . under the particular circumstances" that one of these grounds for failing to knock and announce exists, and we have acknowledged that "[t]his showing is not high."

■ ■ ■

Happily, these issues do not confront us here. From the trial level onward, Michigan has conceded that the entry was a knock-and-announce violation. The issue here is remedy. *Wilson* specifically declined to decide whether the exclusionary rule is appropriate for violation of the knock-and-announce requirement. That question is squarely before us now.

Note this excellent summary of the exclusionary rule's history.

■ ■ ■

In *Weeks v. United States* (1914), we adopted the federal exclusionary rule for evidence that was unlawfully seized from a home without a warrant in violation of the Fourth Amendment. We began applying the same rule to the States, through the Fourteenth Amendment, in *Mapp v. Ohio* (1961).

Suppression of evidence, however, has always been our last resort, not our first impulse. The exclusionary rule generates "substantial social costs," *United States v. Leon* (1984), which sometimes include setting the guilty free and the dangerous at large. We have therefore been "cautio[us] against expanding" it and "have repeatedly emphasized that the rule's 'costly toll' upon truth-seeking and law enforcement objectives presents a high obstacle for those urging [its] application."

■ ■ ■

Expansive dicta in *Mapp,* for example, suggested wide scope for the exclusionary rule. See, *e.g.,* [*Mapp*] ("[A]ll evidence obtained by searches and seizures in violation of the Constitution is, by that same authority, inadmissible in a state court"). But we have long since rejected that approach. As explained in *Arizona v. Evans* (1995): "In *Whiteley*, the Court treated identification of a Fourth Amendment violation as synonymous with application of the exclusionary rule to evidence secured incident to that violation. Subsequent case law has rejected this reflexive application of the exclusionary rule." (Citation omitted.) We had said as much in *Leon*, a decade earlier, when we explained that "[w]hether the exclusionary sanction is appropriately imposed in a particular case . . . is 'an issue separate from the question whether the Fourth Amendment rights of the party seeking to invoke the rule were violated by police conduct.'"

In other words, exclusion may not be premised on the mere fact that a constitutional violation was a "but-for" cause of obtaining evidence. Our cases show that but-for causality is only a necessary, not a sufficient, condition for suppression. In this case, of course, the constitutional violation of an illegal *manner* of entry was *not* a but-for cause of obtaining the evidence. Whether that preliminary misstep had occurred *or not*, the police would have executed the warrant they had obtained, and would have discovered the gun and drugs inside the house. But even if the illegal entry here could be characterized as a but-for cause of discovering what was inside, we have "never held that evidence is 'fruit of the poisonous tree' simply because 'it would not have come to light but for the illegal actions of the police.'" *Segura v. United States* (1984). See also *id.* (Stevens, J., dissenting) ("We have not . . . mechanically applied the [exclusionary] rule to every item of evidence that has a causal connection with police misconduct"). Rather, but-for cause, or "causation in the logical sense alone," *United States v. Ceccolini* (1978), can be too attenuated to justify exclusion.

■ ■ ■

Attenuation can occur, of course, when the causal connection is remote. See, *e.g.*, *Nardone v. United States* (1939). Attenuation also occurs when, even given a direct causal connection, the interest protected by the constitutional guarantee that has been violated would not be served by suppression of the evidence obtained. "The penalties visited upon the Government, and in turn upon the public, because its officers have violated the law must bear some relation to the purposes which the law is to serve." *Ceccolini* (1978). Thus, in *New York v. Harris* (1990), where an illegal warrantless arrest was made in Harris' house, we held that:

> "suppressing [Harris'] statement taken outside the house would not serve the purpose of the rule that made Harris' in-house arrest illegal. The warrant requirement for an arrest in the home is imposed to protect the home, and anything incriminating the police gathered from arresting Harris in his home, rather than elsewhere, has been excluded, as it should have been; the purpose of the rule has thereby been vindicated."

Mapp . . . say[s] nothing about the appropriateness of exclusion to vindicate the interests protected by the knock-and-announce requirement. Until a valid warrant has issued, citizens are entitled to shield "their persons, houses, papers, and effects," U.S. Const., Amdt. 4, from the government's scrutiny. Exclusion of the evidence obtained by a warrantless search vindicates that entitlement. The interests protected by the knock-and-announce requirement are quite different—and do not include the shielding of potential evidence from the government's eyes.

■ ■ ■

What the knock-and-announce rule has never protected, however, is one's interest in preventing the government from seeing or taking evidence described in a warrant. Since the interests that *were* violated in this case

ER is inapplicable (handwritten)

have nothing to do with the seizure of the evidence, the exclusionary rule is inapplicable.

Costs (handwritten)

Quite apart from the requirement of unattenuated causation, the exclusionary rule has never been applied except "where its deterrence benefits outweigh its 'substantial social costs,'" *Pennsylvania Board of Probation & Parole v. Scott* (1998) (quoting *Leon*). The costs here are considerable. In addition to the grave adverse consequence that exclusion of relevant incriminating evidence always entails (viz., the risk of releasing dangerous criminals into society), imposing that massive remedy for a knock-and-announce violation would generate a constant flood of alleged failures to observe the rule, and claims that any asserted *Richards* justification for a no-knock entry had inadequate support. The cost of entering this lottery would be small, but the jackpot enormous: suppression of all evidence, amounting in many cases to a get-out-of-jail-free card. Courts would experience as never before the reality that "[t]he exclusionary rule frequently requires extensive litigation to determine whether particular evidence must be excluded." *Scott*.

Another consequence of the incongruent remedy Hudson proposes would be police officers' refraining from timely entry after knocking and announcing. As we have observed, the amount of time they must wait is necessarily uncertain. If the consequences of running afoul of the rule were so massive, officers would be inclined to wait longer than the law requires—producing preventable violence against officers in some cases, and the destruction of evidence in many others.

■ ■ ■

deterrence benefits (handwritten)

Next to these "substantial social costs" we must consider the deterrence benefits, existence of which is a necessary condition for exclusion. (It is not, of course, a sufficient condition: "[I]t does not follow that the Fourth Amendment requires adoption of every proposal that might deter police misconduct." *Calandra* (1974); see also *Leon*.) To begin with, the value of deterrence depends upon the strength of the incentive to commit the forbidden act. Viewed from this perspective, deterrence of knock-and-announce violations is not worth a lot. Violation of the warrant requirement sometimes produces incriminating evidence that could not otherwise be obtained. But ignoring knock-and-announce can realistically be expected to achieve absolutely nothing except the prevention of destruction of evidence and the avoidance of life-threatening resistance by occupants of the premises—dangers which, if there is even "reasonable suspicion" of their existence, *suspend the knock-and-announce requirement anyway*. Massive deterrence is hardly required.

It seems to us not even true, as Hudson contends, that without suppression there will be no deterrence of knock-and-announce violations at all. Of course even if this assertion were accurate, it would not necessarily justify suppression. Assuming (as the assertion must) that civil suit is not an effective deterrent, one can think of many forms of police misconduct that are similarly "undeterred." When, for example, a confessed suspect in the killing of a police officer, arrested (along with incriminating evidence) in a lawful warranted search, is subjected to physical abuse at the station house, would it seriously be suggested that the evidence must be excluded, since that is the only "effective deterrent"? And what, other than civil suit, is the "effective deterrent" of police violation of an already-confessed suspect's Sixth Amendment rights by denying him prompt access to counsel? Many would regard these violated rights as more significant than the right not to be intruded upon in one's nightclothes—and yet nothing but "ineffective" civil suit is available as a deterrent. And the police incentive for those violations is arguably greater than the incentive for disregarding the knock-and-announce rule.

We cannot assume that exclusion in this context is necessary deterrence simply because we found that it was necessary deterrence in different contexts and long ago. That would be forcing the public today to pay for the sins and inadequacies of a legal regime that existed almost half a century ago. Dollree Mapp could not turn to 42 U.S.C. § 1983 for meaningful relief; *Monroe v. Pape* (1961), which began the slow but steady expansion of that remedy, was decided the same Term as *Mapp*. It would be another 17 years before the § 1983 remedy was extended to reach the deep pocket of municipalities, *Monell v. Dep't of Soc. Servs.* (1978). Citizens whose Fourth Amendment rights were violated by federal officers could not bring suit until 10 years after *Mapp*, with this Court's decision in *Bivens v. Six Unknown Fed. Narcotics Agents* (1971).

Hudson complains that "it would be very hard to find a lawyer to take a case such as this," Tr. of Oral Arg. 7, but 42 U.S.C. § 1988(b) answers this objection. Since some civil-rights violations would yield damages too small to justify the expense of litigation, Congress has authorized attorney's fees for civil-rights plaintiffs. This remedy was unavailable in the heydays of our exclusionary-rule jurisprudence, because it is tied to the availability of a cause of action. For years after *Mapp*, "very few lawyers would even consider representation of persons who had civil rights claims against the police," but now "much has changed. Citizens and lawyers are much more willing to seek relief in the courts for police misconduct." M. Avery, D. Rudovsky, & K. Blum, Police Misconduct: Law and Litigation, p.v (3d ed. 2005); see generally N. Aron, Liberty and Justice for All: Public Interest Law in the 1980s and Beyond (1989) (describing the growth of public-interest law). The number of public-interest law firms and lawyers who specialize in civil-rights grievances has greatly expanded.

Hudson points out that few published decisions to date announce huge awards for knock-and-announce violations. But this is an unhelpful statistic. Even if we thought that only large damages would deter police misconduct (and that police somehow are deterred by "damages" but indifferent to the prospect of large § 1988 attorney's fees), we do not know how many claims have been settled, or indeed how many violations have occurred that produced anything more than nominal injury. It is clear, at least, that the lower courts are allowing colorable knock-and-announce suits to go forward, unimpeded by assertions of qualified immunity.

■ ■ ■

Another development over the past half-century that deters civil-rights violations is the increasing professionalism of police forces, including a new emphasis on internal police discipline. Even as long ago as 1980 we felt it proper to "assume" that unlawful police behavior would "be dealt with appropriately" by the authorities, *United States v. Payner* (1980), but we now have increasing evidence that police forces across the United States take the constitutional rights of citizens seriously. There have been "wide-ranging reforms in the education, training, and supervision of police officers." S. Walker, Taming the System: The Control of Discretion in Criminal Justice 1950-1990, p.51 (1993). Numerous sources are now available to teach officers and their supervisors what is required of them under this Court's cases, how to respect constitutional guarantees in various situations, and how to craft an effective regime for internal discipline. See, *e.g.*, D. Waksman & D. Goodman, The Search and Seizure Handbook (2d ed. 2006); A. Stone & S. DeLuca, Police Administration: An Introduction (2d ed. 1994); E. Thibault, L. Lynch, & R. McBridge, Proactive Police Management (4th ed. 1998). Failure to teach and enforce constitutional requirements exposes municipalities to financial liability. See *Canton v. Harris* (1989). Moreover, modern police forces are staffed with professionals; it is not credible to assert that internal discipline, which can limit successful careers, will not have a deterrent effect. There is also evidence that the increasing use of various forms of citizen review can enhance police accountability.

In sum, the social costs of applying the exclusionary rule to knock-and-announce violations are considerable; the incentive to such violations is minimal to begin with, and the extant deterrences against them are substantial—incomparably greater than the factors deterring warrantless entries when *Mapp* was decided. Resort to the massive remedy of suppressing evidence of guilt is unjustified.

■ ■ ■

For the foregoing reasons we affirm the judgment of the Michigan Court of Appeals.

It is so ordered.

Justice KENNEDY, concurring in part and concurring in the judgment.

Two points should be underscored with respect to today's decision. First, the knock-and-announce requirement protects rights and expectations linked to ancient principles in our constitutional order. See *Wilson v. Arkansas.* The Court's decision should not be interpreted as suggesting that violations of the requirement are trivial or beyond the law's concern. Second, the continued operation of the exclusionary rule, as settled and defined by our precedents, is not in doubt. Today's decision determines only that in the specific context of the knock-and-announce requirement, a violation is not sufficiently related to the later discovery of evidence to justify suppression.

As to the basic right in question, privacy and security in the home are central to the Fourth Amendment's guarantees as explained in our decisions and as understood since the beginnings of the Republic. This common understanding ensures respect for the law and allegiance to our institutions, and it is an instrument for transmitting our Constitution to later generations undiminished in meaning and force. It bears repeating that it is a serious matter if law enforcement officers violate the sanctity of the home by ignoring the requisites of lawful entry. Security must not be subject to erosion by indifference or contempt.

Our system, as the Court explains, has developed procedures for training police officers and imposing discipline for failures to act competently and lawfully. If those measures prove ineffective, they can be fortified with more detailed regulations or legislation. Supplementing these safeguards are civil remedies, such as those available under 42 U.S.C. § 1983, Rev. Stat. § 1979, that provide restitution for discrete harms. These remedies apply to all violations, including, of course, exceptional cases in which unannounced entries cause severe fright and humiliation.

Suppression is another matter. Under our precedents the causal link between a violation of the knock-and-announce requirement and a later search is too attenuated to allow suppression. Cf. *United States v. Ramirez* (1998) (application of the exclusionary rule depends on the existence of a "sufficient causal relationship" between the unlawful conduct and the discovery of evidence). When, for example, a violation results from want of a 20-second pause but an ensuing, lawful search lasting five hours discloses evidence of criminality, the failure to wait at the door cannot properly be described as having caused the discovery of evidence.

Today's decision does not address any demonstrated pattern of knock-and-announce violations. If a widespread pattern of violations were shown, and particularly if those violations were committed against persons who lacked the means or voice to mount an effective protest, there would be reason for grave concern. Even then, however, the Court would have to acknowledge that extending the remedy of exclusion to all the evidence seized following a knock-and-announce violation would mean revising the requirement of causation that limits our discretion in applying the exclusionary rule. That type of extension also would have significant practical implications, adding to the list of issues requiring resolution at the criminal trial questions such as whether police officers entered a home after waiting 10 seconds or 20.

■ ■ ■

I concur in the judgment.

Justice BREYER, with whom Justice STEVENS, Justice SOUTER, and Justice GINSBURG join, dissenting.

■ ■ ■

Today's opinion is . . . doubly troubling. It represents a significant departure from the Court's precedents. And it weakens, perhaps destroys, much of the practical value of the Constitution's knock-and-announce protection.

■ ■ ■

Why is application of the exclusionary rule any the less necessary here? Without such a rule, as in *Mapp*, police know that they can ignore the Constitution's requirements without risking suppression of evidence discovered after an unreasonable entry. As in *Mapp*, some government officers will find it easier, or believe it less risky, to proceed with what they consider a necessary search immediately and without the requisite constitutional (say, warrant or knock-and-announce) compliance. Cf. Mercli, The Apprehension of Peril Exception to the Knock and Announce Rule—Part I, 16 Search and Seizure L. Rep. 129, 130 (1989) (hereinafter Mericili) (noting that some "[d]rug enforcement authorities believe that safety for the police lies in a swift, surprising entry with overwhelming force—not in announcing their official authority").

Of course, the State or the Federal Government may provide alternative remedies for knock-and-announce violations. But that circumstance was true of *Mapp* as well. What reason is there to believe that those remedies (such as private damages actions under 42 U.S.C. § 1983), Rev. Stat. § 1979, which the Court found inadequate in *Mapp*, can adequately deter unconstitutional police behavior here? See Kamisar, In Defense of the Search and Seizure Exclusionary Rule, 26 Harv. J.L. & Pub. Pol'y 119, 126-129 (2003) (arguing that "five decades of post-*Weeks* 'freedom' from the inhibiting effect of the federal exclusionary rule failed to produce any meaningful alternative to the exclusionary rule in any jurisdiction" and that there is no evidence that "times have changed" post-*Mapp*).

The cases reporting knock-and-announce violations are legion. See, *e.g.*, 34 Geo. L.J. Ann. Rev. Crim. Proc. 31-35 (2005) (collecting Court of Appeals cases); Bremer, 85 A.L.R. 5th 1 (2001) (collecting state-court cases); Brief for Petitioner 16-17 (collecting federal and state cases). Indeed, these cases of reported violations seem sufficiently frequent and serious as to indicate "a widespread pattern." (Kennedy, J., concurring in part and concurring in judgment.) Yet the majority, like Michigan and the United States, has failed to cite a single reported case in which a plaintiff has collected more than nominal damages solely as a result of a knock-and-announce violation. Even Michigan concedes that, "in cases like the present one, . . . damages may be virtually nonexistent." And Michigan's *amici* further concede that civil immunities prevent tort law from being an effective substitute for the exclusionary rule at this time. Brief for Criminal Justice Legal Foundation 10; see also *Hope v. Pelzer* (2002) (difficulties of overcoming qualified immunity defenses).

As Justice Stewart, the author of a number of significant Fourth Amendment opinions, explained, the deterrent effect of damage actions "can hardly be said to be great," as such actions are "expensive, time-consuming, not readily available, and rarely successful." The Road to *Mapp v. Ohio* and Beyond: The Origins, Development and Future of the Exclusionary Rule in Search-and-Seizure Cases, 83 Colum. L. Rev. 1365, 1388 (1983). The upshot is that the need for deterrence—the critical factor driving this Court's Fourth Amendment cases for close to a century—argues with at least comparable strength for evidentiary exclusion here.

other remedies do not make suppression unnecessary

To argue, as the majority does, that new remedies, such as 42 U.S.C. § 1983 actions or better trained police, make suppression unnecessary is to argue that *Wolf* [*v. Colorado* (1949)], not *Mapp*, is now the law. (The Court recently rejected a similar argument in *Dickerson v. United States* (2000).) To argue that there may be few civil suits because violations may produce nothing "more than nominal injury" is to confirm, not to deny, the inability of civil suits to deter violations. And to argue without evidence (and despite myriad reported cases of violations, no reported case of civil damages, and Michigan's concession of their nonexistence) that civil suits may provide deterrence because claims *may* "have been settled" is, perhaps, to search in desperation for an argument. Rather, the majority, as it candidly admits, has simply "assumed" that, "[a]s far as [it] know[s], civil liability is an effective deterrent," a support-free assumption that *Mapp* and subsequent cases make clear does not embody the Court's normal approach to difficult questions of Fourth Amendment law.

It is not surprising, then, that after looking at virtually every pertinent Supreme Court case decided since *Weeks*, I can find no precedent that might offer the majority support for its contrary conclusion. The Court has, of course, recognized that not every Fourth Amendment violation necessarily triggers the exclusionary rule. *Illinois v. Gates* (1983) (application of the exclusionary rule is a separate question from whether the Fourth Amendment has been violated). But the class of Fourth Amendment violations that do not result in suppression of the evidence seized, however, is limited.

■ ■ ■

I can find nothing persuasive in the majority's opinion that could justify its refusal to apply the rule. It certainly is not a justification for an exception here (as the majority finds) to find odd instances in *other* areas of law that do not automatically demand suppression.

■ ■ ■

cost not great enough

Neither can the majority justify its failure to respect the need for deterrence, as set forth consistently in the Court's prior case law, through its claim of "'substantial social costs'"—at least if it means that those "'social costs'" are somehow special here. The only costs it mentions are those that typically accompany *any* use of the Fourth Amendment's exclusionary principle: (1) that where the constable blunders, a guilty defendant may be set free (consider *Mapp* itself); (2) that defendants may assert claims where Fourth Amendment rights are uncertain (consider the Court's qualified immunity jurisprudence), and (3) that sometimes it is difficult to decide the merits of those uncertain claims. In fact, the "no-knock" warrants that are provided by many States, by diminishing uncertainty, may make application of the knock-and-announce principle less "'cost[ly]'" on the whole than application of comparable Fourth Amendment principles, such as determining whether a particular warrantless search was justified by exigency. The majority's "substantial social costs" argument is an argument against the Fourth Amendment's exclusionary principle itself. And it is an argument that this Court, until now, has consistently rejected.

The majority, Michigan, and the United States make several additional arguments. In my view, those arguments rest upon misunderstandings of the principles underlying this Court's precedents.

The majority first argues that "the constitutional violation of an illegal *manner* of entry was *not* a but-for cause of obtaining the evidence." But taking causation as it is commonly understood in the law, I do not see how that can be so. See W. Keeton, D. Dobbs, R. Keeton, & D. Owen, Prosser and Keeton on Law of Torts 266 (5th ed. 1984). Although the police might have entered Hudson's home lawfully, they did not in fact do so. Their unlawful behavior inseparably characterizes their actual entry; that entry was a necessary condition of their presence in Hudson's home; and their presence in Hudson's home was a necessary condition of their finding and seizing the evidence. At the same time, their discovery of evidence in Hudson's home was a readily foreseeable consequence of their entry and their unlawful presence within the home. Cf. 2 Restatement (Second) of Torts § 435 (1963-1964).

Moreover, separating the "manner of entry" from the related search slices the violation too finely. As noted, we have described a failure to comply with the knock-and-announce rule, not as an independently unlawful event, but as a factor that renders the *search* "constitutionally defective."

■ ■ ■

The Court nonetheless accepts Michigan's argument that the requisite but-for-causation is not satisfied in this case because, whether or not the constitutional violation occurred (what the Court refers to as a "preliminary misstep"), "the police would have executed the warrant they had obtained, and would have discovered the gun and drugs inside the house." As support for this proposition, Michigan rests on this Court's inevitable discovery cases.

This claim, however, misunderstands the inevitable discovery doctrine. Justice Holmes in *Silverthorne* (1920), in discussing an "independent source" exception, set forth the principles underlying the inevitable discovery rule. That rule does not refer to discovery that would have taken place if the police behavior in question had (contrary to fact) been lawful. The doctrine does not treat as critical what *hypothetically could* have happened had the police acted lawfully in the first place. Rather, "independent" or "inevitable" discovery refers to discovery that did occur or that would have occurred (1) *despite* (not simply *in the absence of*) the unlawful behavior and (2) *independently* of that unlawful behavior. The government cannot, for example, avoid suppression of evidence seized without a warrant (or pursuant to a defective warrant) simply by showing that it could have obtained a valid warrant had it sought one. See, *e.g., Coolidge v. New Hampshire* (1971). Instead, it must show that the same evidence "inevitably *would* have been discovered *by lawful means.*" *Nix v. Williams* (1984). "What a man *could* do is not at all the same as what he *would* do." Austin, Ifs And Cans, 42 Proceedings of the British Academy 109, 111-112 (1956).

The inevitable discovery exception rests upon the principle that the remedial purposes of the exclusionary rule are not served by suppressing evidence discovered through a "later, *lawful* seizure" that is "*genuinely independent* of an earlier, tainted one." *Murray v. United States* (1988) (emphasis added); see also *id.* (Marshall, J., joined by Stevens and O'Connor, JJ., dissenting) ("When the seizure of the evidence at issue is 'wholly independent of' the constitutional violation, then exclusion arguably will have no effect on a law enforcement officer's incentive to commit an unlawful search").

Case law well illustrates the meaning of this principle. In *Nix*, police officers violated a defendant's Sixth Amendment right by eliciting incriminating statements from him after he invoked his right to counsel. Those statements led to the discovery of the victim's body. The Court concluded that evidence obtained from the victim's body was admissible because it would ultimately or inevitably have been discovered by a volunteer search party effort that was ongoing—whether or not the Sixth Amendment violation had taken place In other words, the evidence would have been found *despite*, and *independent of*, the Sixth Amendment violation.

In *Segura v. United States* (1984), one of the "trio of cases" Justice Scalia says "confirms [the Court's] conclusion," the Court held that an earlier illegal entry into an apartment did not require suppression of evidence that police later seized when executing a search warrant obtained on the basis of information unconnected to the initial entry. The Court reasoned that the "evidence was discovered the day following the entry, *during the search conducted under a valid warrant*"—i.e., a warrant obtained independently without use of any information found during the illegal entry—and that "it was the product of *that* search, wholly unrelated to the prior [unlawful] entry." *Segura.*

In *Murray,* the Court upheld the admissibility of seized evidence where agents entered a warehouse without a warrant, and then later returned with a valid warrant that was not obtained on the basis of evidence observed during the first (illegal) entry. The Court reasoned that while the agents' "[k]nowledge that the marijuana was in the warehouse was assuredly acquired at the time of the unlawful entry . . . it was *also* acquired at the time of entry pursuant to the warrant, and *if that later acquisition was not the result of the earlier entry* there is no reason why the independent source doctrine should not apply."

Thus, the Court's opinion reflects a misunderstanding of what "inevitable discovery" means when it says, "[i]n this case, of course, the constitutional violation of an illegal *manner* of entry was *not* a but-for cause of obtaining the evidence." The majority rests this conclusion on its next statement: "Whether that preliminary misstep has occurred *or not*, the police . . . would have discovered the gun and the drugs inside the house." Despite the phrase "of course," neither of these statements is correct. It is not true that, had the illegal entry not occurred, "police . . . would have discovered the guns and drugs inside the house." Without that unlawful entry they would not have been inside the house; so there would have been no discovery.

Of course, had the police entered the house lawfully, they would have found the gun and drugs. But that fact is beside the point. The question is not what police might have done had they not behaved unlawfully.

The question is what they did do. Was there set in motion an independent chain of events that would have inevitably led to the discovery and seizure of the evidence despite, and independent of, that behavior? The answer here is "no."

■ ■ ■

The majority and the United States set forth a policy-related variant of the causal connection theme: The United States argues that the law should suppress evidence only insofar as a Fourth Amendment violation causes the kind of harm that the particular Fourth Amendment rule seeks to protect against. It adds that the constitutional purpose of the knock-and-announce rule is to prevent needless destruction of property (such as breaking down a door) and to avoid unpleasant surprise. And it concludes that the exclusionary rule should suppress evidence of, say, damage to property, the discovery of a defendant in an "intimate or compromising moment," or an excited utterance from the occupant caught by surprise, but nothing more.

The majority makes a similar argument. It says that evidence should not be suppressed once the causal connection between unlawful behavior and discovery of the evidence becomes too "attenuated." But the majority then makes clear that it is not using the word "attenuated" to mean what this Court's precedents have typically used that word to mean, namely, that the discovery of the evidence has come about long after the unlawful behavior took place or in an independent way, *i.e.*, through "'means sufficiently distinguishable to be purged of the primary taint.'" *Wong Sun v. United States* (1963); see *Brown v. Illinois* (1975).

Rather, the majority gives the word "attenuation" a new meaning (thereby, in effect, making the same argument as the United States). "Attenuation," it says, "also occurs when, even given a direct causal connection, the interest protected by the constitutional guarantee that has been violated would not be served by suppression of the evidence obtained." The interests the knock-and-announce rule seeks to protect, the Court adds, are "human life" (at stake when a householder is "surprised"), "property" (such as the front door), and "those elements of privacy and dignity that can be destroyed by a sudden entrance," namely, "the opportunity to collect oneself before answering the door." Since none of those interests led to the discovery of the evidence seized here, there is no reason to suppress it.

There are three serious problems with this argument. First, it does not fully describe the constitutional values, purposes, and objectives underlying the knock-and-announce requirement. That rule does help to protect homeowners from damaged doors; it does help to protect occupants from surprise. But it does more than that. It protects the occupants' privacy by assuring them that government agents will not enter their home without complying with those requirements (among others) that diminish the offensive nature of any such intrusion. Many years ago, Justice Frankfurter wrote for the Court that the "knock at the door, . . . as a prelude to a search, without authority of law . . . [is]

inconsistent with the conception of human rights enshrined in [our] history" and Constitution.

■ ■ ■

Over a century ago this Court wrote that "it is not the breaking of his doors" that is the "essence of the offence," but the "invasions on the part of the government . . . of the sanctity of a man's home and the privacies of life." *Boyd* (1886). And just this Term we have reiterated that "'it is beyond dispute that the home is entitled to special protection as the center of the private lives of our people.'" *Georgia v. Randolph* (2006) (quoting *Minnesota v. Carter* (1998) (Kennedy, J., concurring)). The knock-and-announce requirement is no less a part of the "centuries-old principle" of special protection for the privacy of the home than the warrant requirement.

■ ■ ■

Second, whether the interests underlying the knock-and-announce rule are implicated in any given case is, in a sense, beside the point. As we have explained, failure to comply with the knock-and-announce rule renders the related search unlawful. *Wilson.* And where a search is unlawful, the law insists upon suppression of the evidence consequently discovered, even if that evidence or its possession has little or nothing to do with the reasons underlying the unconstitutionality of a search. The Fourth Amendment does not seek to protect contraband, yet we have required suppression of contraband seized in an unlawful search. See, *e.g., Kyllo v. United States* (2001). That is because the exclusionary rule protects more general "privacy values through deterrence of future police misconduct." *James v. Illinois* (1990). The same is true here.

Third, the majority's interest-based approach departs from prior law. Ordinarily a court will simply look to see if the unconstitutional search produced the evidence. The majority does not refer to any relevant case in which, beyond that, suppression turned on the far more detailed relation between, say, (1) a particular materially false statement made to the magistrate who issued a (consequently) invalid warrant and (2) evidence found after a search with that warrant. And the majority's failure does not surprise me, for such efforts to trace causal connections at retail could well complicate Fourth Amendment suppression law, threatening its workability.

■ ■ ■

There may be instances in the law where text or history or tradition leaves room for a judicial decision that rests upon little more than an unvarnished judicial instinct. But this is not one of them. Rather, our Fourth Amendment traditions place high value upon protecting privacy in the home. They emphasize the need to assure that its constitutional protections are effective, lest the Amendment "sound the word of promise to the ear but break it to the hope." They include an exclusionary principle, which since *Weeks* has formed the centerpiece of the criminal law's effort to ensure the practical reality of those promises. That is why the Court should assure itself that any departure from that principle is firmly grounded in logic, in history, in precedent, and in empirical fact. It has not done so. That is why, with respect, I dissent.

G. STANDING

Jones v. United States

362 U.S. 257 (1960)

FRANKFURTER, J., delivered the opinion of the Court, in which WARREN, C.J., BLACK, BRENNAN, CLARK, WHITAKER, HARLAN, and STEWART, JJ., joined. DOUGLAS, J., dissented in part.

Prior to trial petitioner duly moved to suppress the evidence obtained through the execution of the search warrant on the ground that the warrant had been issued without a showing of probable cause. The Government challenged petitioner's standing to make this motion because petitioner alleged neither ownership of the seized articles nor an interest in the apartment greater than that of an "invitee or guest." The District Court agreed to take evidence on the issue of petitioner's standing. Only petitioner gave evidence. On direct examination he testified that the apartment belonged to a friend, Evans, who had given him the use of it, and a key, with which petitioner had admitted himself on the day of the arrest. On cross-examination petitioner testified that he had a suit and shirt at the apartment, that his home was elsewhere, that he paid nothing for the use of the apartment, that Evans had let him use it "as a friend," that he had slept there "maybe a night," and that at the time of the search Evans had been away in Philadelphia for about five days.

Solely on the basis of petitioner's lack of standing to make it, the district judge denied petitioner's motion to suppress. When the case came on for trial before a different judge, the motion to suppress was renewed and was denied on the basis of the prior ruling. An unsuccessful objection was made when the seized items were offered in evidence at the trial.

In affirming petitioner's conviction the Court of Appeals agreed with the District Court that petitioner lacked standing, but proceeded to rule that even if it were to find that petitioner had standing, it would hold the evidence to have been lawfully received. . . .

The issue of petitioner's standing is to be decided with reference to Rule 41(e) of the Federal Rules of Criminal Procedure, 18 U.S.C.A. This is a statutory direction governing the suppression of evidence acquired in violation of the conditions validating a search. It is desirable to set forth the Rule.

> "A person aggrieved by an unlawful search and seizure may move the district court for the district in which the property was seized for the return of the property and to suppress for use as evidence anything so obtained on the ground that (1) the property was illegally seized without warrant, or (2) the warrant is insufficient on its face, or (3) property seized is not that described in the warrant, or (4) there was not probable cause for believing the existence of the grounds on which the warrant was issued, or (5) the warrant was illegally executed. The judge shall receive evidence on any issue of fact necessary to the decision of the motion. If the motion is

granted the property shall be restored unless otherwise subject to lawful detention and it shall not be admissible in evidence at any hearing or trial. The motion to suppress evidence may also be made in the district where the trial is to be had. The motion shall be made before trial or hearing unless opportunity therefor did not exist or the defendant was not aware of the grounds for the motion, but the court in its discretion may entertain the motion at the trial or hearing."

In order to qualify as a "person aggrieved by an unlawful search and seizure" one must have been a victim of a search or seizure, one against whom the search was directed, as distinguished from one who claims prejudice only through the use of evidence gathered as a consequence of a search or seizure directed at someone else. Rule 41(e) applies the general principle that a party will not be heard to claim a constitutional protection unless he "belongs to the class for whose sake the constitutional protection is given." The restrictions upon searches and seizures were obviously designed for protection against official invasion of privacy and the security of property. They are not exclusionary provisions against the admission of kinds of evidence deemed inherently unreliable or prejudicial. The exclusion in federal trials of evidence otherwise competent but gathered by federal officials in violation of the Fourth Amendment is a means for making effective the protection of privacy.

Ordinarily, then, it is entirely proper to require of one who seeks to challenge the legality of a search as the basis for suppressing relevant evidence that he allege, and if the allegation be disputed that he establish, that he himself was the victim of an invasion of privacy. But prosecutions like this one have presented a special problem. To establish "standing," Courts of Appeals have generally required that the movant claim either to have owned or possessed the seized property or to have had a substantial possessory interest in the premises searched. Since narcotics charges like those in the present indictment may be established through proof solely of possession of narcotics, a defendant seeking to comply with what has been the conventional standing requirement has been forced to allege facts the proof of which would tend, if indeed not be sufficient, to convict him. At the least, such a defendant has been placed in the criminally tendentious position of explaining his possession of the premises. He has been faced, not only with the chance that the allegations made on the motion to suppress may be used against him at the trial, although that they may is by no means an inevitable holding, but also with the encouragement that he perjure himself if he seeks to establish "standing" while maintaining a defense to the charge of possession.

The dilemma that has thus been created for defendants in cases like this has been pointedly put by Judge Learned Hand:

"Men may wince at admitting that they were the owners, or in possession, of contraband property; may wish at once to secure the remedies of a possessor, and avoid the perils of the part; but equivocation will not serve. If they come as victims, they must take on that role, with enough detail to cast them without question. The petitioners at bar shrank from that predicament; but they were obliged to choose one horn of the dilemma." *Connolly v. Medalie* (1932).

■ ■ ■

Judge Hand's dilemma is not inescapable. It presupposes requirements of "standing" which we do not find compelling. Two separate lines of thought effectively sustain defendant's standing in this case. (1) The same element in this prosecution which has caused a dilemma, i.e., that possession both convicts and confers standing, eliminates any necessity for a preliminary showing of an interest in the premises searched or the property seized, which ordinarily is required when standing is challenged. (2) Even were this not a prosecution turning on illicit possession, the legally requisite interest in the premises was here satisfied, for it need not be as extensive a property interest as was required by the courts below.

As to the first ground, we are persuaded by this consideration: to hold to the contrary, that is, to hold that petitioner's failure to acknowledge interest in the narcotics or the premises prevented his attack upon the search, would be to permit the Government to have the advantage of contradictory positions as a basis for conviction. Petitioner's conviction flows from his possession of the narcotics at the time of the search. Yet the fruits of that search, upon which the conviction depends, were admitted into evidence on the ground that petitioner did not have possession of the narcotics at that time. The prosecution here thus subjected the defendant to the penalties meted out to one in lawless possession while refusing him the remedies designed for one in that situation. It is not consonant with the amenities, to put it mildly, of the administration of criminal justice to sanction such squarely contradictory assertions of power by the Government. The possession on the basis of which petitioner is to be and was convicted suffices to give him standing under any fair and rational conception of the requirements of Rule 41(e).

■ ■ ■

As a second ground sustaining "standing" here we hold that petitioner's testimony on the motion to suppress made out a sufficient interest in the premises to establish him as a "person aggrieved" by their search. That testimony established that at the time of the search petitioner was present in the apartment with the permission of Evans, whose apartment it was. The Government asserts that such an interest is insufficient to give standing. The Government does not contend that only ownership of the premises may confer standing. It would draw distinctions among various classes of possessors, deeming some, such as "guests" and "invitees" with only the "use" of the premises, to have too "tenuous" an interest although concededly having "some measure of control" through their "temporary presence," while conceding that others, who in a "realistic sense, have dominion of the apartment" or who are "domiciled" there, have standing. Petitioner, it is insisted, by his own testimony falls in the former class.

While this Court has never passed upon the interest in the searched premises necessary to maintain a motion to suppress, the Government's argument closely follows the prevailing view in the lower courts. They have denied standing to "guests" and "invitees." We do not lightly depart from this course of decisions by the lower courts. We are persuaded, however, that it is unnecessary and ill-advised to import into the law surrounding the constitutional right to be free from unreasonable searches and seizures subtle distinctions, developed and refined by the common law in evolving the body of private property law which, more than almost any other branch of law, has been shaped by distinctions whose validity is largely historical. Even in the area from which they derive, due consideration has led to the discarding of these distinctions in the homeland of the common law.

■ ■ ■

We rejected such distinctions as inappropriate to the law of maritime torts.... We found there to be a duty of ordinary care to one rightfully on the ship, regardless of whether he was a "licensee" rather than an "invitee." "For the admiralty law at this late date to import such conceptual distinctions would be foreign to its traditions of simplicity and practicality." A fortiori we ought not to bow to them in the fair administration of the criminal law. To do so would not comport with our justly proud claim of the procedural protections accorded to those charged with crime. No just interest of the Government in the effective and rigorous enforcement of the criminal law will be hampered by recognizing that anyone legitimately on premises where a search occurs may challenge its legality by way of a motion to suppress, when its fruits are proposed to be used against him. This would of course not avail those who, by virtue of their wrongful presence, cannot invoke the privacy of the premises searched. As petitioner's testimony established Evans' consent to his presence in the apartment, he was entitled to have the merits of his motion to suppress adjudicated.

Rakas v. Illinois

439 U.S. 128 (1978)

REHNQUIST, J., delivered the opinion of the Court, in which BURGER, C.J., STEWART, POWELL, and BLACKMUN, JJ., joined. POWELL, J., filed a concurring opinion, in which BURGER, C.J., joined. WHITE, J., filed a dissenting opinion, in which BRENNAN, MARSHALL, and STEVENS, JJ., joined.

Petitioners were convicted of armed robbery in the Circuit Court of Kankakee County, Ill., and their convictions were affirmed on appeal. At their trial, the prosecution offered into evidence a sawed-off rifle and rifle shells that had been seized by police during a search of an automobile in which petitioners had been passengers. Neither petitioner is the owner of the automobile and neither has ever asserted that he owned the rifle or shells seized. The Illinois

Appellate Court held that petitioners lacked standing to object to the allegedly unlawful search and seizure and denied their motion to suppress the evidence. We granted certiorari in light of the obvious importance of the issues raised to the administration of criminal justice, and now affirm.

Because we are not here concerned with the issue of probable cause, a brief description of the events leading to the search of the automobile will suffice. A police officer on a routine patrol received a radio call notifying him of a robbery of a clothing store in Bourbonnais, Ill., and describing the getaway car. Shortly thereafter, the officer spotted an automobile which he thought might be the getaway car. After following the car for some time and after the arrival of assistance, he and several other officers stopped the vehicle. The occupants of the automobile, petitioners and two female companions, were ordered out of the car and, after the occupants had left the car, two officers searched the interior of the vehicle. They discovered a box of rifle shells in the glove compartment, which had been locked, and a sawed-off rifle under the front passenger seat. After discovering the rifle and the shells, the officers took petitioners to the station and placed them under arrest.

Before trial petitioners moved to suppress the rifle and shells seized from the car on the ground that the search violated the Fourth and Fourteenth Amendments. They conceded that they did not own the automobile and were simply passengers; the owner of the car had been the driver of the vehicle at the time of the search. Nor did they assert that they owned the rifle or the shells seized. The prosecutor challenged petitioners' standing to object to the lawfulness of the search of the car because neither the car, the shells nor the rifle belonged to them. The trial court agreed that petitioners lacked standing and denied the motion to suppress the evidence. In view of this holding, the court did not determine whether there was probable cause for the search and seizure. On appeal after petitioners' conviction, the Appellate Court of Illinois, Third Judicial District, affirmed the trial court's denial of petitioners' motion to suppress because it held that "without a proprietary or other similar interest in an automobile, a mere passenger therein lacks standing to challenge the legality of the search of the vehicle."

■ ■ ■

We believe that defendants failed to establish any prejudice to their own constitutional rights because they were not persons aggrieved by the unlawful search and seizure.... They wrongly seek to establish prejudice only through the use of evidence gathered as a consequence of a search and seizure directed at someone else and fail to prove an invasion of their own privacy....

Petitioners first urge us to relax or broaden the rule of standing enunciated in *Jones v. United States* (1960), so that any criminal defendant at whom a search was "directed" would have standing to contest the legality of that search and object to the admission at trial of evidence obtained as a result of the search. Alternatively, petitioners argue that they have standing to object to the search under *Jones* because they were "legitimately on [the] premises" at the time of the search.

The concept of standing discussed in *Jones* focuses on whether the person seeking to challenge the legality of a search as a basis for suppressing evidence was himself the "victim" of the search or seizure. Adoption of the so-called "target" theory advanced by petitioners would in effect permit a defendant to assert that a violation of the Fourth Amendment rights of a third party entitled him to have evidence suppressed at his trial. If we reject petitioners' request for a broadened rule of standing such as this, and reaffirm the holding of *Jones* and other cases that Fourth Amendment rights are personal rights that may not be asserted vicariously, we will have occasion to re-examine the "standing" terminology emphasized in *Jones*. For we are not at all sure that the determination of a motion to suppress is materially aided by labeling the inquiry identified in *Jones* as one of standing, rather than simply recognizing it as one involving the substantive question of whether or not the proponent of the motion to suppress has had his own Fourth Amendment rights infringed by the search and seizure which he seeks to challenge. We shall therefore consider in turn petitioners' target theory, the necessity for continued adherence to the notion of standing discussed in *Jones* as a concept that is theoretically distinct from the merits of a defendant's Fourth Amendment claim, and, finally, the proper disposition of petitioners' ultimate claim in this case.

■ ■ ■

We decline to extend the rule of standing in Fourth Amendment cases in the manner suggested by petitioners. As we stated in *Alderman v. United States* (1969), "Fourth Amendment rights are personal rights which, like some other constitutional rights, may not be vicariously asserted." A person who is aggrieved by an illegal search and seizure only through the introduction of damaging evidence secured by a search of a third person's premises or property has not had any of his Fourth Amendment rights infringed. And since the exclusionary rule is an attempt to effectuate the guarantees of the Fourth Amendment, it is proper to permit only defendants whose Fourth Amendment rights have been violated to benefit from the rule's protections.

■ ■ ■

"[T]he [target] rule would entail very substantial administrative difficulties. In the majority of cases, I would imagine that the police plant a bug with the expectation that it may well produce leads to a large number of crimes. A lengthy hearing would, then, appear to be necessary in order to determine whether the police knew of an accused's criminal activity at the time the bug was planted and whether the police decision to plant a bug was motivated by an effort to obtain information against the accused or some other individual. I do not believe that this administrative burden is justified in any substantial degree by the hypothesized marginal increase in Fourth Amendment protection. . . .

The deterrent values of preventing the incrimination of those whose rights the police have violated have been considered sufficient to justify the suppression of probative evidence even though the case against the defendant is weakened or destroyed. We adhere to that judgment. But we are not convinced that the additional benefits of extending the exclusionary rule to other defendants would justify further encroachment upon the public interest in prosecuting those accused of crime and having them acquitted or convicted on the basis of all the evidence which exposes the truth." *Alderman v. United States.*

Each time the exclusionary rule is applied it exacts a substantial social cost for the vindication of Fourth Amendment rights. Relevant and reliable evidence is kept from the trier of fact and the search for truth at trial is deflected. Since our cases generally have held that one whose Fourth Amendment rights are violated may successfully suppress evidence obtained in the course of an illegal search and seizure, misgivings as to the benefit of enlarging the class of persons who may invoke that rule are properly considered when deciding whether to expand standing to assert Fourth Amendment violations.

Had we accepted petitioners' request to allow persons other than those whose own Fourth Amendment rights were violated by a challenged search and seizure to suppress evidence obtained in the course of such police activity, it would be appropriate to retain *Jones'* use of standing in Fourth Amendment analysis. Under petitioners' target theory, a court could determine that a defendant had standing to invoke the exclusionary rule without having to inquire into the substantive question of whether the challenged search or seizure violated the Fourth Amendment rights of that particular defendant. However, having rejected petitioners' target theory and reaffirmed the principle that the "rights assured by the Fourth Amendment are personal rights, [which] . . . may be enforced by exclusion of evidence only at the instance of one whose own protection was infringed by the search and seizure," the question necessarily arises whether it serves any useful analytical purpose to consider this principle a matter of standing, distinct from the merits of a defendant's Fourth Amendment claim. We can think of no decided cases of this Court that would have come out differently had we concluded, as we do now, that the type of standing requirement discussed in *Jones* and reaffirmed today is more properly subsumed under substantive Fourth Amendment doctrine. Rigorous application of the principle that the rights secured by this Amendment are personal, in place of a notion of "standing," will produce no additional situations in which evidence must be excluded. The inquiry under either approach is the same. But we think the better analysis forthrightly focuses on the extent of a particular defendant's rights under the Fourth Amendment, rather than on any theoretically separate, but invariably intertwined concept of standing. The Court in *Jones* also may have been aware that there was a certain artificiality in analyzing this question in terms of standing because in at least three separate places in its opinion the Court placed that term within quotation marks.

It should be emphasized that nothing we say here casts the least doubt on cases which recognize that, as a general proposition, the issue of standing involves two inquiries: first, whether the proponent of a particular legal right has alleged "injury in fact," and, second, whether the proponent is asserting his own legal rights and interests rather than basing his claim for relief upon the rights of third parties.

■   ■   ■

Analyzed in these terms, the question is whether the challenged search or seizure violated the Fourth Amendment rights of a criminal defendant who seeks to exclude the evidence obtained during it. That inquiry in turn requires a determination of whether the disputed search and seizure has infringed an interest of the defendant which the Fourth Amendment was designed to protect. We are under no illusion that by dispensing with the rubric of standing used in *Jones* we have rendered any simpler the determination of whether the proponent of a motion to suppress is entitled to contest the legality of a search and seizure. But by frankly recognizing that this aspect of the analysis belongs more properly under the heading of substantive Fourth Amendment doctrine than under the heading of standing, we think the decision of this issue will rest on sounder logical footing.

■   ■   ■

Here petitioners, who were passengers occupying a car which they neither owned nor leased, seek to analogize their position to that of the defendant in *Jones v. United States.* In *Jones,* petitioner was present at the time of the search of an apartment which was owned by a friend. The friend had given Jones permission to use the apartment and a key to it, with which Jones had admitted himself on the day of the search. He had a suit and shirt at the apartment and had slept there "maybe a night," but his home was elsewhere. At the time of the search, Jones was the only occupant of the apartment because the lessee was away for a period of several days. Under these circumstances, this Court stated that while one wrongfully on the premises could not move to suppress evidence obtained as a result of searching them, "anyone legitimately on premises where a search occurs may challenge its legality." Petitioners argue that their occupancy of the automobile in question was comparable to that of Jones in the apartment and that they therefore have standing to contest the legality of the search—or as we have rephrased the inquiry, that they, like Jones, had their Fourth Amendment rights violated by the search.

We do not question the conclusion in *Jones* that the defendant in that case suffered a violation of his personal Fourth Amendment rights if the search in question was unlawful. Nonetheless, we believe that the phrase "legitimately on premises" coined in *Jones* creates too broad a gauge for measurement of Fourth Amendment rights. For example, applied literally, this statement would permit a casual visitor who has never seen, or been permitted to visit, the basement of another's house to object to a search of the basement if the visitor happened to be in the kitchen of the house at the time of the search. Likewise, a casual visitor who walks into a house one minute before a search of the house commences and leaves one minute after the search ends would be able to contest the legality of the search. The first visitor would have absolutely no interest or legitimate expectation of privacy in the basement, the second would have none in the house, and it advances no purpose served by the

Fourth Amendment to permit either of them to object to the lawfulness of the search.

We think that *Jones* on its facts merely stands for the unremarkable proposition that a person can have a legally sufficient interest in a place other than his own home so that the Fourth Amendment protects him from unreasonable governmental intrusion into that place. . . . But the *Jones* statement that a person need only be "legitimately on premises" in order to challenge the validity of the search of a dwelling place cannot be taken in its full sweep beyond the facts of that case.

Our Brother White in dissent expresses the view that by rejecting the phrase "legitimately on [the] premises" as the appropriate measure of Fourth Amendment rights, we are abandoning a thoroughly workable, "bright line" test in favor of a less certain analysis of whether the facts of a particular case give rise to a legitimate expectation of privacy. If "legitimately on premises" were the successful litmus test of Fourth Amendment rights that he assumes it is, his approach would have at least the merit of easy application, whatever it lacked in fidelity to the history and purposes of the Fourth Amendment. But a reading of lower court cases that have applied the phrase "legitimately on premises," and of the dissent itself, reveals that this expression is not a shorthand summary for a bright-line rule which somehow encapsulates the "core" of the Fourth Amendment's protections.

■ ■ ■

Judged by the foregoing analysis, petitioners' claims must fail. They asserted neither a property nor a possessory interest in the automobile, nor an interest in the property seized. And as we have previously indicated, the fact that they were "legitimately on [the] premises" in the sense that they were in the car with the permission of its owner is not determinative of whether they had a legitimate expectation of privacy in the particular areas of the automobile searched. It is unnecessary for us to decide here whether the same expectations of privacy are warranted in a car as would be justified in a dwelling place in analogous circumstances. We have on numerous occasions pointed out that cars are not to be treated identically with houses or apartments for Fourth Amendment purposes. But here petitioners' claim is one which would fail even in an analogous situation in a dwelling place, since they made no showing that they had any legitimate expectation of privacy in the glove compartment or area under the seat of the car in which they were merely passengers. Like the trunk of an automobile, these are areas in which a passenger *qua* passenger simply would not normally have a legitimate expectation of privacy.

Jones v. United States and *Katz v. United States* (1967) involved significantly different factual circumstances. Jones not only had permission to use the apartment of his friend, but also had a key to the apartment with which he admitted himself on the day of the search and kept possessions in the apartment. Except with respect to his friend, Jones had complete dominion and control over the apartment and could exclude others from it. Likewise in *Katz*, the defendant occupied the telephone booth, shut the door behind him to exclude all others and paid the toll, which "entitled [him] to assume that the words he utter[ed] into the mouthpiece [would] not be broadcast to the world." Katz and Jones could legitimately expect privacy in the areas which were the subject of the search and seizure each sought to contest. No such showing was made by these petitioners with respect to those portions of the automobile which were searched and from which incriminating evidence was seized. . . .

The Illinois courts were therefore correct in concluding that it was unnecessary to decide whether the search of the car might have violated the rights secured to someone else by the Fourth and Fourteenth Amendments to the United States Constitution. Since it did not violate any rights of these petitioners, their judgment of conviction is

Affirmed.

Justice POWELL, with whom Chief Justice BURGER joins, concurring.

I concur in the opinion of the Court, and add these thoughts. I do not believe my dissenting Brethren correctly characterize the rationale of the Court's opinion when they assert that it ties "the application of the Fourth Amendment . . . to property law concepts." On the contrary, I read the Court's opinion as focusing on whether there was a *legitimate* expectation of privacy protected by the Fourth Amendment.

The petitioners do not challenge the constitutionality of the police action in stopping the automobile in which they were riding; nor do they complain of being made to get out of the vehicle. Rather, petitioners assert that their constitutionally protected interest in privacy was violated when the police, after stopping the automobile and making them get out, searched the vehicle's interior, where they discovered a sawed-off rifle under the front seat and rifle shells in the locked glove compartment. The question before the Court, therefore, is a narrow one: Did the search of their friend's automobile after they had left it violate any Fourth Amendment right of the petitioners?

The dissenting opinion urges the Court to answer this question by considering only the talisman of legitimate presence on the premises. To be sure, one of the two alternative reasons given by the Court for its ruling in *Jones* was that the defendant had been legitimately on the premises searched. Since *Jones*, however, the view that mere legitimate presence is enough to create a Fourth Amendment right has been questioned. There also has been a signal absence of uniformity in the application of this theory. This Court's decisions since *Jones* have emphasized a sounder standard for determining the scope of a person's Fourth Amendment rights: Only legitimate expectations of privacy are protected by the Constitution. . . .

The ultimate question, therefore, is whether one's claim to privacy from government intrusion is reasonable in light of all the surrounding circumstances. As the dissenting opinion states, this standard "will not provide law enforcement officials with a bright line between the protected and the unprotected." Whatever the application of this standard may lack in ready administration, it is more faithful to the purposes of the Fourth Amendment than a test focusing solely or primarily on whether the defendant was legitimately present during the search.

■ ■ ■

This is not an area of the law in which any "bright line" rule would safeguard both Fourth Amendment rights and the public interest in a fair and effective criminal justice system. The range of variables in the fact situations of search and seizure is almost infinite. Rather than seek facile solutions, it is best to apply principles broadly faithful to Fourth Amendment purposes. I believe the Court has identified these principles.

Justice WHITE, with whom Justice BRENNAN, Justice MARSHALL, and Justice STEVENS join, dissenting.

The Court today holds that the Fourth Amendment protects property, not people, and specifically that a legitimate occupant of an automobile may not invoke the exclusionary rule and challenge a search of that vehicle unless he happens to own or have a possessory interest in it. Though professing to acknowledge that the primary purpose of the Fourth Amendment's prohibition of unreasonable searches is the protection of privacy—not property—the Court nonetheless effectively ties the application of the Fourth Amendment and the exclusionary rule in this situation to property law concepts. Insofar as passengers are concerned, the Court's opinion today declares an "open season" on automobiles. However unlawful stopping and searching a car may be, absent a possessory or ownership interest, no "mere" passenger may object, regardless of his relationship to the owner. Because the majority's conclusion has no support in the Court's controlling decisions, in the logic of the Fourth Amendment, or in common sense, I must respectfully dissent. If the Court is troubled by the practical impact of the exclusionary rule, it should face the issue of that rule's continued validity squarely instead of distorting other doctrines in an attempt to reach what are perceived as the correct results in specific cases.

■ ■ ■

It is true that the Court asserts that it is not limiting the Fourth Amendment bar against unreasonable searches to the protection of property rights, but in reality it is doing exactly that. Petitioners were in a private place with the permission of the owner, but the Court states that that is not sufficient to establish entitlement to a legitimate expectation of privacy. But if that is not sufficient, what would be? We are not told, and it is hard to imagine anything short of a property interest that would satisfy the majority. Insofar as the Court's rationale is concerned, no passenger in an automobile, without an ownership or possessory interest and regardless of his relationship to the owner, may claim Fourth Amendment protection against illegal stops and searches of the automobile in which he is rightfully present. The Court approves the result in *Jones*, but it fails to give any explanation why the facts in *Jones* differ, in a fashion material to the Fourth Amendment, from the facts here. More importantly, how is the Court able to avoid answering the question why presence in a private place with the owner's permission is insufficient? If it is "tautological to fall back on the notion that those expectations of privacy which are legitimate depend primarily on cases deciding exclusionary rule issues in criminal cases," then it surely must be tautological to decide that issue simply by unadorned fiat.

As a control on governmental power, the Fourth Amendment assures that some expectations of privacy are justified and will be protected from official intrusion. That should be true in this instance, for if protected zones of privacy can only be purchased or obtained by possession of property, then much of our daily lives will be unshielded from unreasonable governmental prying, and the reach of the Fourth Amendment will have been narrowed to protect chiefly those with possessory interests in real or personal property. I had thought that *Katz* firmly established that the Fourth Amendment was intended as more than simply a trespass law applicable to the government. Katz had no possessory interest in the public telephone booth, at least no more than petitioners had in their friend's car; Katz was simply legitimately present. And the decision in *Katz* was based not on property rights, but on the theory that it was essential to securing "conditions favorable to the pursuit of happiness" that the expectation of privacy in question be recognized.

At most, one could say that perhaps the Constitution provides some degree less protection for the personal freedom from unreasonable governmental intrusion when one does not have a possessory interest in the invaded private place. But that would only change the extent of the protection; it would not free police to do the unreasonable, as does the decision today. And since the accused should be entitled to litigate the application of the Fourth Amendment where his privacy interest is merely arguable, the failure to allow such litigation here is the more incomprehensible.

The Court's holding is contrary not only to our past decisions and the logic of the Fourth Amendment but also to the everyday expectations of privacy that we all share. Because of that, it is unworkable in all the various situations that arise in real life. If the owner of the car had not only invited petitioners to join her but had said to them, "I give you a temporary possessory interest in my vehicle so that you will share the right to privacy that the Supreme Court says that I own," then apparently the majority would reverse. But people seldom say such things, though they may mean their invitation to encompass them if only they had thought of the problem. If the nonowner were the spouse or child of the owner, would the Court recognize a sufficient interest? If so, would distant relatives somehow have more of an expectation of privacy than close friends? What if the nonowner were driving with the owner's permission? Would nonowning drivers have more of an expectation of privacy than mere passengers? What about a passenger in a taxicab? *Katz* expressly recognized protection for such passengers. Why should Fourth Amendment rights be present when one pays a cabdriver for a ride but be absent when one is given a ride by a friend?

The distinctions the Court would draw are based on relationships between private parties, but the Fourth Amendment is concerned with the relationship of one of those parties to the government. Divorced as it is from the purpose of the Fourth Amendment, the Court's essentially property-based rationale can satisfactorily answer none of the questions posed above. That is reason enough to reject it. The *Jones* rule is relatively easily applied by police and courts; the rule announced today will not provide law enforcement officials with a bright line between the protected and the unprotected. Only rarely will police know whether one private party has or has not been granted a sufficient possessory or other interest by another private party. Surely in this case the officers had no such knowledge. The Court's rule will ensnare defendants and police in needless litigation over factors that should not be determinative of Fourth Amendment rights.

More importantly, the ruling today undercuts the force of the exclusionary rule in the one area in which its use is most certainly justified—the deterrence of bad-faith violations of the Fourth Amendment. This decision invites police to engage in patently unreasonable searches every time an automobile contains more than one occupant. Should something be found, only the owner of the vehicle, or of the item, will have standing to seek suppression, and the evidence will presumably be usable against the other occupants. The danger of such bad faith is especially high in cases such as this one where the officers are only after the passengers and can usually infer accurately that the driver is the owner. The suppression remedy for those owners in whose vehicles something is found and who are charged with crime is small consolation for all those owners *and* occupants whose privacy will be needlessly invaded by officers following mistaken hunches not rising to the level of probable cause but operated on in the knowledge that someone in a crowded car will probably be unprotected if contraband or incriminating evidence happens to be found. After this decision, police will have little to lose by unreasonably searching vehicles occupied by more than one person.

Of course, most police officers will decline the Court's invitation and will continue to do their jobs as best they can in accord with the Fourth Amendment. But the very purpose of the Bill of Rights was to answer the justified fear that governmental agents cannot be left totally to their own devices, and the Bill of Rights is enforceable in the courts because human experience teaches that not all such officials will otherwise adhere to the stated precepts. Some policemen simply do act in bad faith, even if for understandable ends, and some deterrent is needed. In the rush to limit the applicability of the exclusionary rule somewhere, anywhere, the Court ignores precedent, logic, and common sense to exclude the rule's operation from situations in which, paradoxically, it is justified and needed.

CHAPTER 2

Search and Seizure— Fourth Amendment

Introduction

New Jersey v. T.L.O. provides a useful overview of Fourth Amendment violations. First, the Fourth Amendment must be applicable, which requires that there be government action and an expectation of privacy. If the Fourth Amendment is applicable, any justification for the search and seizure (Chapter 3) and the necessity for a warrant, as well as its scope or particularity (Chapter 4) must be examined to determine whether there has been a Fourth Amendment violation.

This case also highlights the debate among the justices as to how to read the two clauses of the Fourth Amendment. The first clause of the Fourth Amendment mentions the term *unreasonable,* and the second clause requires probable cause and particularity when obtaining a warrant. Some of the justices read the two clauses together. In this way, they rely on the second clause to give more meaning to the term *unreasonable* in the first clause. Some justices, now in the majority, read the two clauses separately, such that a warrant is but one of the factors in determining reasonableness.

The following chart highlights the overview analysis in *T.L.O.*

Overview Chart
Is the Fourth Amendment Applicable?
- Is there government involvement?
- Is there an expectation of privacy in the above government involvement?

If the Fourth Amendment Is Applicable:
Justification
- Reasonable Clause
  - Balancing
  - Reasonable Suspicion
- Probable Cause
Warrant
- Arrest
- Search
- Administrative

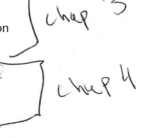

Particularity
- Warrant
- Scope

The remainder of the chapter deals with expectation of privacy. Fourth Amendment violations were originally based on trespass, a property law concept. With the advent of modern technology trespass did not adequately protect individual privacy. *Katz* presented a different way to analyze Fourth Amendment violations. Not all government activity implicates the Fourth Amendment, only that activity in which there is an expectation of privacy. This concept has its roots in the *Katz* case, where the court talked about an expectation of privacy that society would deem reasonable. The most recent case of *Jones,* which deals with the modern technology of a GPS device, reintroduces property law concepts. The application of *Katz* is then analyzed in a variety of settings and open fields (*Oliver*). It is further analyzed in various dealings involving third parties, including persons (*Hoffa* and *White*), banks (*Miller*), and trash collectors (*Greenwood*). The chapter then deals with types of enhancement devices and their use in various settings. The type of devices include dogs (*Place* and *Caballes*), GPS location finders (*Knotts* and *United States v. Jones*), thermal imaging (*Kyllo*), and helicopters (*Riley*). *Jones,* the last statement by the Court on expectation of privacy, emphasizes that property concepts are still applicable when considering the Fourth Amendment. The settings include airport (*Place*), highway (*Caballes* and *Knotts*), bus (*Bond*), home (*Kyllo*), and curtilage (*Dunn, Greenwood,* and *Riley*) and analysis of tactile (touching) enhancements (*Bond*). Finally, we look at how an expectation of privacy is utilized to determine who has standing to raise Fourth Amendment issues. The original concept of standing is explored in *Jones v. United States*. Then we look at *Rakas,* which introduces the expectation of privacy to the standing analysis. The remaining cases apply *Rakas* to third parties (*Rawlings*), overnight guests (*Olson*), commercial activity (*Carter*), and automobile passengers (*Brendlin*).

A. OVERVIEW

New Jersey v. T.L.O.

469 U.S. 325 (1985)

WHITE, J., delivered the opinion of the Court, in which BURGER, C.J., POWELL, REHNQUIST, O'CONNOR, JJ., joined. POWELL, J., filed a concurring opinion in which O'CONNOR, J., joined. BLACKMUN, J., filed an opinion concurring in the judgment. BRENNAN, J., filed an opinion concurring in part and dissenting in part, in which MARSHALL, J., joined. STEVENS, J., filed an opinion concurring in part and dissenting in part, in which Marshall, J., joined and Brennan, J., joined in Part I.

We granted certiorari in this case to examine the appropriateness of the exclusionary rule as a remedy for searches carried out in violation of the Fourth Amendment by public school authorities. Our consideration of the proper application of the Fourth Amendment to the public schools, however, has led us to conclude that the search that gave rise to the case now before us did not violate the Fourth Amendment. Accordingly, we here address only the questions of the proper standard for assessing the legality of searches conducted by public school officials and the application of that standard to the facts of this case.

I

On March 7, 1980, a teacher at Piscataway High School in Middlesex County, N.J., discovered two girls smoking in a lavatory. One of the two girls was the respondent T.L.O., who at that time was a 14-year-old high school freshman. Because smoking in the lavatory was a violation of a school rule, the teacher took the two girls to the Principal's office, where they met with Assistant Vice Principal Theodore Choplick. In response to questioning by Mr. Choplick, T.L.O.'s companion admitted that she had violated the rule. T.L.O., however, denied that she had been smoking in the lavatory and claimed that she did not smoke at all.

Mr. Choplick asked T.L.O. to come into his private office and demanded to see her purse. Opening the purse, he found a pack of cigarettes, which he removed from the purse and held before T.L.O. as he accused her of having lied to him. As he reached into the purse for the cigarettes, Mr. Choplick also noticed a package of cigarette rolling papers. In his experience, possession of rolling papers by high school students was closely associated with the use of marihuana. Suspecting that a closer examination of the purse might yield further evidence of drug use, Mr. Choplick proceeded to search the purse thoroughly. The search revealed a small amount of marihuana, a pipe, a number of empty plastic bags, a substantial quantity of money in one-dollar bills, an index card that appeared to be a list of students who owed T.L.O. money, and two letters that implicated T.L.O. in marihuana dealing.

Mr. Choplick notified T.L.O.'s mother and the police, and turned the evidence of drug dealing over to the police. At the request of the police, T.L.O.'s mother took her daughter to police headquarters, where T.L.O. confessed that she had been selling marihuana at the high school. On the basis of the confession and the evidence seized by Mr. Choplick, the State brought delinquency charges against T.L.O. in the Juvenile and Domestic Relations Court of Middlesex County. Contending that Mr. Choplick's search of her purse violated the Fourth Amendment, T.L.O. moved to suppress the evidence found in her purse as well as her confession, which, she argued, was tainted by the allegedly unlawful search.

The juvenile court held that school searches are subject to Fourth Amendment requirements, but that the search in this case was reasonable because Mr. Choplick had a well-founded suspicion that T.L.O. had violated the smoking rule. Once the purse was open, evidence of drug violation was in plain view, and Mr. Choplick was entitled to conduct a thorough search to determine the nature and extent of T.L.O.'s drug-related activity. Denying the motion to suppress, the juvenile court found T.L.O. to be delinquent and sentenced her to a year's probation.

The New Jersey Supreme Court held that the search was unreasonable because mere possession of cigarettes did not violate a school rule, because Mr. Choplick had no specific information that there were cigarettes in the purse, and because the slight evidence of drug use that he initially saw did not justify the extensive rummaging through T.L.O.'s papers and effects that followed.

Although we originally granted certiorari to decide the issue of the appropriate remedy in juvenile court proceedings for unlawful school searches, our doubts regarding the wisdom of deciding that question in isolation from the broader question of what limits, if any, the Fourth Amendment places on the activities of school authorities prompted us to order reargument on that question. Having heard argument on the legality of the search of T.L.O.'s purse, we are satisfied that the search did not violate the Fourth Amendment.

II

In determining whether the search at issue in this case violated the Fourth Amendment, we are faced initially with the question whether that Amendment's prohibition on unreasonable searches and seizures applies to searches conducted by public school officials. We hold that it does. . . . It may well be true that the evil toward which the Fourth Amendment was primarily directed was the resurrection of the pre-Revolutionary practice of using general warrants or "writs of assistance" to authorize searches for contraband by officers of the Crown. But this Court has never limited the Amendment's prohibition on unreasonable searches and seizures to operations conducted by the police. Accordingly, we have held the Fourth Amendment applicable to the activities of civil as well as criminal authorities: building inspectors, see *Camara v. Municipal Court* (1967), Occupational Safety and Health Act inspectors, see *Marshall v. Barlow's, Inc.* (1978), and even firemen entering privately owned premises to battle a fire, see *Michigan v. Tyler* (1978), are all subject to the restraints imposed by the Fourth Amendment. As we observed in *Camara v. Municipal Court*, "[the] basic purpose of this Amendment, as recognized in countless decisions of this Court, is to safeguard the privacy and security of individuals against arbitrary invasions by governmental officials." Because the individual's interest in privacy and personal security "suffers whether the government's motivation is to investigate violations of criminal laws or breaches of other statutory or regulatory standards," *Marshall v. Barlow's, Inc.*, it would be "anomalous to say that the individual and his private property are fully protected by the Fourth Amendment only when the individual is suspected of criminal behavior." *Camara v. Municipal Court*.

Notwithstanding the general applicability of the Fourth Amendment to the activities of civil authorities, a few courts have concluded that school officials are exempt from the dictates of the Fourth Amendment by virtue of the special nature of their authority over schoolchildren. See, e. g., *R.C.M. v. State* (1983). Teachers and school administrators, it is said, act in loco parentis in their dealings with students: their authority is that of the parent, not the State, and is therefore not subject to the limits of the Fourth Amendment.

Such reasoning is in tension with contemporary reality and the teachings of this Court. We have held school officials subject to the commands of the First Amendment, see *Tinker v. Des Moines Independent Community School District* (1969), and the Due Process Clause of the Fourteenth Amendment, see *Goss v. Lopez* (1975). If school authorities are state actors for purposes of the constitutional guarantees of freedom of expression and due process, it is difficult to understand why they should be deemed to be exercising parental rather than public authority when conducting searches of their students. More generally, the Court has recognized that "the concept of parental delegation" as a source of school authority is not entirely "consonant with compulsory education laws." *Ingraham v. Wright* (1977). Today's public school officials do not merely exercise authority voluntarily conferred on them by individual parents; rather, they act in furtherance of publicly mandated educational and disciplinary policies. . . . In carrying out searches and other disciplinary functions pursuant to such policies, school officials act as representatives of the State, not merely as surrogates for the parents, and they cannot claim the parents' immunity from the strictures of the Fourth Amendment.

III

To hold that the Fourth Amendment applies to searches conducted by school authorities is only to begin the inquiry into the standards governing such searches. Although the underlying command of the Fourth Amendment is always that searches and seizures be reasonable, what is reasonable depends on the context within which a search takes place. The determination of the standard of reasonableness governing any specific class of searches requires "balancing the need to search against the invasion which the search entails." *Camara v. Municipal Court*. On one side of the balance are arrayed the individual's legitimate expectations of privacy and personal security; on the other, the government's need for effective methods to deal with breaches of public order.

We have recognized that even a limited search of the person is a substantial invasion of privacy. *Terry v. Ohio* (1967). We have also recognized that searches of closed items of personal luggage are intrusions on protected privacy interests, for "the Fourth Amendment provides protection to the owner of every container that conceals its contents from plain view." *United States v. Ross* (1982). A search of a child's person or of a closed purse or other bag carried on her person,[5] no less than a similar search carried out on an adult, is undoubtedly a severe violation of subjective expectations of privacy.

Of course, the Fourth Amendment does not protect subjective expectations of privacy that are unreasonable or otherwise "illegitimate." See, e.g., *Hudson v. Palmer* (1984); *Rawlings v. Kentucky* (1980). To receive the protection of the Fourth Amendment, an expectation of privacy must be one that society is "prepared to recognize as legitimate." *Hudson v. Palmer*. The State of New Jersey has argued that because of the pervasive supervision to which children in the schools are necessarily subject, a child has virtually no legitimate expectation of privacy in articles of personal property "unnecessarily" carried into a school. This argument has two factual premises: (1) the fundamental incompatibility of expectations of privacy with the maintenance of a sound educational environment; and (2) the minimal interest of the child in bringing any items of personal property into the school. Both premises are severely flawed.

Although this Court may take notice of the difficulty of maintaining discipline in the public schools today, the situation is not so dire that students in the schools may claim no legitimate expectations of privacy. We have recently recognized that the need to maintain order in a prison is such that prisoners retain no legitimate expectations of privacy in their cells, but it goes almost without saying that "[the] prisoner and the schoolchild stand in wholly different circumstances, separated by the harsh facts of criminal conviction and incarceration." *Ingraham v. Wright* (1977). We are not yet ready to hold that the schools and the prisons need be equated for purposes of the Fourth Amendment.

Nor does the State's suggestion that children have no legitimate need to bring personal property into the schools seem well anchored in reality. Students at a minimum must bring to school not only the supplies needed for their studies, but also keys, money, and the necessaries of personal hygiene and grooming. In addition, students may carry on their persons or in purses or wallets such nondisruptive yet highly personal items as photographs, letters, and diaries. Finally, students may have perfectly legitimate reasons to carry with them articles of property needed in connection with extracurricular or recreational activities. In short, schoolchildren may find it necessary to carry with them a variety of legitimate, noncontraband items, and there is no reason to conclude that they have necessarily waived all rights to privacy in such items merely by bringing them onto school grounds.

Against the child's interest in privacy must be set the substantial interest of teachers and administrators in maintaining discipline in the classroom and on

---

5. We do not address the question, not presented by this case, whether a schoolchild has a legitimate expectation of privacy in lockers, desks, or other school property provided for the storage of school supplies. Nor do we express any opinion on the standards (if any) governing searches of such areas by school officials or by other public authorities acting at the request of school officials.

school grounds. Maintaining order in the classroom has never been easy, but in recent years, school disorder has often taken particularly ugly forms: drug use and violent crime in the schools have become major social problems. See generally 1 NIE, U.S. Dept. of Health, Education and Welfare, Violent Schools—Safe Schools: The Safe School Study Report to the Congress (1978). Even in schools that have been spared the most severe disciplinary problems, the preservation of order and a proper educational environment requires close supervision of schoolchildren, as well as the enforcement of rules against conduct that would be perfectly permissible if undertaken by an adult. "Events calling for discipline are frequent occurrences and sometimes require immediate, effective action." *Goss v. Lopez* (1975). Accordingly, we have recognized that maintaining security and order in the schools requires a certain degree of flexibility in school disciplinary procedures, and we have respected the value of preserving the informality of the student-teacher relationship. *Ingraham v. Wright.*

■ ■ ■

How, then, should we strike the balance between the schoolchild's legitimate expectations of privacy and the school's equally legitimate need to maintain an environment in which learning can take place? It is evident that the school setting requires some easing of the restrictions to which searches by public authorities are ordinarily subject. The warrant requirement, in particular, is unsuited to the school environment: requiring a teacher to obtain a warrant before searching a child suspected of an infraction of school rules (or of the criminal law) would unduly interfere with the maintenance of the swift and informal disciplinary procedures needed in the schools. Just as we have in other cases dispensed with the warrant requirement when "the burden of obtaining a warrant is likely to frustrate the governmental purpose behind the search," *Camara v. Municipal Court*, we hold today that school officials need not obtain a warrant before searching a student who is under their authority.

The school setting also requires some modification of the level of suspicion of illicit activity needed to justify a search. Ordinarily, a search—even one that may permissibly be carried out without a warrant—must be based upon "probable cause" to believe that a violation of the law has occurred. See, e.g., *Almeida-Sanchez v. United States* (1973); *Sibron v. New York* (1968). However, "probable cause" is not an irreducible requirement of a valid search. The fundamental command of the Fourth Amendment is that searches and seizures be reasonable, and although "both the concept of probable cause and the requirement of a warrant bear on the reasonableness of a search, . . . in certain limited circumstances neither is required." *Almeida-Sanchez v. United States* (Powell, J., concurring).

Thus, we have in a number of cases recognized the legality of searches and seizures based on suspicions that, although "reasonable," do not rise to the level of probable cause. See, e.g., *Terry v. Ohio*; *United States v. Brignoni-Ponce* (1975); *Delaware v. Prouse* (1979); *United States v. Martinez-Fuerte* (1976); cf. *Camara v. Municipal Court.* Where a careful balancing of governmental and private interests suggests that the public interest is best served by a Fourth

Amendment standard of reasonableness that stops short of probable cause, we have not hesitated to adopt such a standard.

We join the majority of courts that have examined this issue in concluding that the accommodation of the privacy interests of schoolchildren with the substantial need of teachers and administrators for freedom to maintain order in the schools does not require strict adherence to the requirement that searches be based on probable cause to believe that the subject of the search has violated or is violating the law. Rather, the legality of a search of a student should depend simply on the reasonableness, under all the circumstances, of the search. Determining the reasonableness of any search involves a twofold inquiry: first, one must consider "whether the . . . action was justified at its inception," *Terry v. Ohio*; second, one must determine whether the search as actually conducted "was reasonably related in scope to the circumstances which justified the interference in the first place." Under ordinary circumstances, a search of a student by a teacher or other school official will be "justified at its inception" when there are reasonable grounds for suspecting that the search will turn up evidence that the student has violated or is violating either the law or the rules of the school. Such a search will be permissible in its scope when the measures adopted are reasonably related to the objectives of the search and not excessively intrusive in light of the age and sex of the student and the nature of the infraction.

This standard will, we trust, neither unduly burden the efforts of school authorities to maintain order in their schools nor authorize unrestrained intrusions upon the privacy of schoolchildren. By focusing attention on the question of reasonableness, the standard will spare teachers and school administrators the necessity of schooling themselves in the niceties of probable cause and permit them to regulate their conduct according to the dictates of reason and common sense. At the same time, the reasonableness standard should ensure that the interests of students will be invaded no more than is necessary to achieve the legitimate end of preserving order in the schools.

There remains the question of the legality of the search in this case. We recognize that the "reasonable grounds" standard applied by the New Jersey Supreme Court in its consideration of this question is not substantially different from the standard that we have adopted today. Nonetheless, we believe that the New Jersey court's application of that standard to strike down the search of T.L.O.'s purse reflects a somewhat crabbed notion of reasonableness. Our review of the facts surrounding the search leads us to conclude that the search was in no sense unreasonable for Fourth Amendment purposes.[10]

---

10. Of course, New Jersey may insist on a more demanding standard under its own Constitution or statutes. In that case, its courts would not purport to be applying the Fourth Amendment when they invalidate a search.

The incident that gave rise to this case actually involved two separate searches, with the first—the search for cigarettes—providing the suspicion that gave rise to the second—the search for marihuana. Although it is the fruits of the second search that are at issue here, the validity of the search for marihuana must depend on the reasonableness of the initial search for cigarettes, as there would have been no reason to suspect that T.L.O. possessed marihuana had the first search not taken place. Accordingly, it is to the search for cigarettes that we first turn our attention.

The New Jersey Supreme Court pointed to two grounds for its holding that the search for cigarettes was unreasonable. First, the court observed that possession of cigarettes was not in itself illegal or a violation of school rules. Because the contents of T.L.O.'s purse would therefore have "no direct bearing on the infraction" of which she was accused (smoking in a lavatory where smoking was prohibited), there was no reason to search her purse. Second, even assuming that a search of T.L.O.'s purse might under some circumstances be reasonable in light of the accusation made against T.L.O., the New Jersey court concluded that Mr. Choplick in this particular case had no reasonable grounds to suspect that T.L.O. had cigarettes in her purse. At best, according to the court, Mr. Choplick had "a good hunch."

Both these conclusions are implausible. T.L.O. had been accused of smoking, and had denied the accusation in the strongest possible terms when she stated that she did not smoke at all. Surely it cannot be said that under these circumstances, T.L.O.'s possession of cigarettes would be irrelevant to the charges against her or to her response to those charges. T.L.O.'s possession of cigarettes, once it was discovered, would both corroborate the report that she had been smoking and undermine the credibility of her defense to the charge of smoking.

Of course, the New Jersey Supreme Court also held that Mr. Choplick had no reasonable suspicion that the purse would contain cigarettes. This conclusion is puzzling. A teacher had reported that T.L.O. was smoking in the lavatory. Certainly this report gave Mr. Choplick reason to suspect that T.L.O. was carrying cigarettes with her; and if she did have cigarettes, her purse was the obvious place in which to find them. Mr. Choplick's suspicion that there were cigarettes in the purse was not an "inchoate and unparticularized suspicion or 'hunch,'" *Terry v. Ohio*; rather, it was the sort of "common-sense [conclusion] about human behavior" upon which "practical people"—including government officials—are entitled to rely. *United States v. Cortez* (1981). Of course, even if the teacher's report were true, T.L.O. might not have had a pack of cigarettes with her; she might have borrowed a cigarette from someone else or have been sharing a cigarette with another student. But the requirement of reasonable suspicion is not a requirement of absolute certainty: "sufficient probability, not certainty, is the touchstone of reasonableness under the Fourth Amendment. . . ." *Hill v. California* (1971). Because the hypothesis that T.L.O. was carrying cigarettes in her purse was not itself not unreasonable, it is irrelevant that other hypotheses were also consistent with the teacher's accusation.

Accordingly, it cannot be said that Mr. Choplick acted unreasonably when he examined T.L.O.'s purse to see if it contained cigarettes.

Our conclusion that Mr. Choplick's decision to open T.L.O.'s purse was reasonable brings us to the question of the further search for marihuana once the pack of cigarettes was located. The suspicion upon which the search for marihuana was founded was provided when Mr. Choplick observed a package of rolling papers in the purse as he removed the pack of cigarettes. Although T.L.O. does not dispute the reasonableness of Mr. Choplick's belief that the rolling papers indicated the presence of marihuana, she does contend that the scope of the search Mr. Choplick conducted exceeded permissible bounds when he seized and read certain letters that implicated T.L.O. in drug dealing. This argument, too, is unpersuasive. The discovery of the rolling papers concededly gave rise to a reasonable suspicion that T.L.O. was carrying marihuana as well as cigarettes in her purse. This suspicion justified further exploration of T.L.O.'s purse, which turned up more evidence of drug-related activities: a pipe, a number of plastic bags of the type commonly used to store marihuana, a small quantity of marihuana, and a fairly substantial amount of money. Under these circumstances, it was not unreasonable to extend the search to a separate zippered compartment of the purse; and when a search of that compartment revealed an index card containing a list of "people who owe me money" as well as two letters, the inference that T.L.O. was involved in marihuana trafficking was substantial enough to justify Mr. Choplick in examining the letters to determine whether they contained any further evidence. In short, we cannot conclude that the search for marihuana was unreasonable in any respect.

Because the search resulting in the discovery of the evidence of marihuana dealing by T.L.O. was reasonable, the New Jersey Supreme Court's decision to exclude that evidence from T.L.O.'s juvenile delinquency proceedings on Fourth Amendment grounds was erroneous. Accordingly, the judgment of the Supreme Court of New Jersey is

Reversed.

Justice POWELL, with whom Justice O'CONNOR joins, concurring.

I agree with the Court's decision, and generally with its opinion. I would place greater emphasis, however, on the special characteristics of elementary and secondary schools that make it unnecessary to afford students the same constitutional protections granted adults and juveniles in a nonschool setting.

In any realistic sense, students within the school environment have a lesser expectation of privacy than members of the population generally. They spend the school hours in close association with each other, both in the classroom and during recreation periods. The students in a particular class often know each other and their teachers quite well. Of necessity, teachers have a degree of familiarity with, and authority over, their students that is unparalleled except perhaps in the relationship between parent and child. It is simply unrealistic to think that students have the same subjective expectation of privacy as the population generally....

■ ■ ■

The special relationship between teacher and student also distinguishes the setting within which schoolchildren operate. Law enforcement officers function as adversaries of criminal suspects. These officers have the responsibility to investigate criminal activity, to locate and arrest those who violate our laws, and to facilitate the charging and bringing of such persons to trial. Rarely does this type of adversarial relationship exist between school authorities and pupils. Instead, there is a commonality of interests between teachers and their pupils. The attitude of the typical teacher is one of personal responsibility for the student's welfare as well as for his education.

The primary duty of school officials and teachers, as the Court states, is the education and training of young people. A State has a compelling interest in assuring that the schools meet this responsibility. Without first establishing discipline and maintaining order, teachers cannot begin to educate their students. And apart from education, the school has the obligation to protect pupils from mistreatment by other children, and also to protect teachers themselves from violence by the few students whose conduct in recent years has prompted national concern. For me, it would be unreasonable and at odds with history to argue that the full panoply of constitutional rules applies with the same force and effect in the schoolhouse as it does in the enforcement of criminal laws.

In sum, although I join the Court's opinion and its holding, my emphasis is somewhat different.

Justice BLACKMUN, concurring in the judgment.

I join the judgment of the Court and agree with much that is said in its opinion. I write separately, however, because I believe the Court omits a crucial step in its analysis of whether a school search must be based upon probable cause. The Court correctly states that we have recognized limited exceptions to the probable-cause requirement "[where] a careful balancing of governmental and private interests suggests that the public interest is best served" by a lesser standard. I believe that we have used such a balancing test, rather than strictly applying the Fourth Amendment's Warrant and Probable-Cause Clause, only when we were confronted with "a special law enforcement need for greater flexibility." . . .

■ ■ ■

The Court's implication that the balancing test is the rule rather than the exception is troubling for me because it is unnecessary in this case. The elementary and secondary school setting presents a special need for flexibility justifying a departure from the balance struck by the Framers. The special need for an immediate response to behavior that threatens either the safety of schoolchildren and teachers or the educational process itself justifies the Court in excepting school searches from the warrant and probable-cause requirement, and in applying a standard determined by balancing the relevant interests. I agree with the standard the Court has announced, and with its application of the standard to the facts of this case. I therefore concur in its judgment.

Justice BRENNAN, with whom Justice MARSHALL joins, concurring in part and dissenting in part.

I fully agree with Part II of the Court's opinion. Teachers, like all other government officials, must conform their conduct to the Fourth Amendment's protections of personal privacy and personal security. As Justice Stevens points out, this principle is of particular importance when applied to school-teachers, for children learn as much by example as by exposition. It would be incongruous and futile to charge teachers with the task of [i]mbuing their students with an understanding of our system of constitutional democracy, while at the same time immunizing those same teachers from the need to respect constitutional protections.

I do not, however, otherwise join the Court's opinion. Today's decision sanctions school officials to conduct full-scale searches on a "reasonableness" standard whose only definite content is that it is not the same test as the "probable cause" standard found in the text of the Fourth Amendment. In adopting this unclear, unprecedented, and unnecessary departure from generally applicable Fourth Amendment standards, the Court carves out a broad exception to standards that this Court has developed over years of considering Fourth Amendment problems. Its decision is supported neither by precedent nor even by a fair application of the "balancing test" it proclaims in this very opinion.

Three basic principles underly this Court's Fourth Amendment jurisprudence. First, warrantless searches are per se unreasonable, subject only to a few specifically delineated and well-recognized exceptions. See, e.g., *Katz v. United States* (1967); accord, *Welsh v. Wisconsin* (1984); *United States v. Place* (1983); *Steagald v. United States* (1981); *Mincey v. Arizona* (1978); *Terry v. Ohio*; *Johnson v. United States* (1948). Second, full-scale searches—whether conducted in accordance with the warrant requirement or pursuant to one of its exceptions—are "reasonable" in Fourth Amendment terms only on a showing of probable cause to believe that a crime has been committed and that evidence of the crime will be found in the place to be searched. Third, categories of intrusions that are substantially less intrusive than full-scale searches or seizures may be justifiable in accordance with a balancing test even absent a warrant or probable cause, provided that the balancing test used gives sufficient weight to the privacy interests that will be infringed.

Assistant Vice Principal Choplick's thorough excavation of T.L.O.'s purse was undoubtedly a serious intrusion on her privacy. Unlike the searches in *Terry v. Ohio* or *Adams v. Williams* (1972), the search at issue here encompassed a detailed and minute examination of respondent's pocketbook, in which the contents of private papers and letters were thoroughly scrutinized. Wisely, neither petitioner nor the Court today attempts to justify the search of T.L.O.'s pocketbook as a minimally intrusive search in the *Terry* line. To be faithful to the Court's settled doctrine, the inquiry therefore must focus on the warrant and probable-cause requirements.

I agree that schoolteachers or principals, when not acting as agents of law enforcement authorities, generally may conduct a search of their students' belongings without first obtaining a warrant. To agree with the Court on this point is to say that school searches may justifiably be held to that extent to constitute an exception to the Fourth Amendment's warrant requirement. Such an exception, however, is not to be justified, as the Court apparently holds, by assessing net social value through application of an unguided "balancing test" in which "the individual's legitimate expectations of privacy and personal security" are weighed against "the government's need for effective methods to deal with breaches of public order." The Warrant Clause is something more than an exhortation to this Court to maximize social welfare as we see fit. It requires that the authorities must obtain a warrant before conducting a full-scale search. The undifferentiated governmental interest in law enforcement is insufficient to justify an exception to the warrant requirement.

In this case, such extraordinary governmental interests do exist and are sufficient to justify an exception to the warrant requirement. Students are necessarily confined for most of the schoolday in close proximity to each other and to the school staff. I agree with the Court that we can take judicial notice of the serious problems of drugs and violence that plague our schools. As Justice Blackmun notes, teachers must not merely "maintain an environment conducive to learning" among children who "are inclined to test the outer boundaries of acceptable conduct," but must also "protect the very safety of students and school personnel." A teacher or principal could neither carry out essential teaching functions nor adequately protect students' safety if required to wait for a warrant before conducting a necessary search.

I emphatically disagree with the Court's decision to cast aside the constitutional probable-cause standard when assessing the constitutional validity of a schoolhouse search. The Court's decision jettisons the probable-cause standard—the only standard that finds support in the text of the Fourth Amendment—on the basis of its Rohrschach-like "balancing test." Use of such a "balancing test" to determine the standard for evaluating the validity of a full-scale search represents a sizable innovation in Fourth Amendment analysis. This innovation finds support neither in precedent nor policy and portends a dangerous weakening of the purpose of the Fourth Amendment to protect the privacy and security of our citizens. Moreover, even if this Court's historic understanding of the Fourth Amendment were mistaken and a balancing test of some kind were appropriate, any such test that gave adequate weight to the privacy and security interests protected by the Fourth Amendment would not reach the preordained result the Court's conclusory analysis reaches today. Therefore, because I believe that the balancing test used by the Court today is flawed both in its inception and in its execution, I respectfully dissent.

An unbroken line of cases in this Court have held that probable cause is a prerequisite for a full-scale search. . . .

Our holdings that probable cause is a prerequisite to a full-scale search are based on the relationship between the two Clauses of the Fourth Amendment. The first Clause ("The right of the people to be secure in their persons, houses, papers and effects, against unreasonable searches and seizures, shall not be violated...") states the purpose of the Amendment and its coverage. The second Clause ("...and no Warrants shall issue but upon probable cause...") gives content to the word "unreasonable" in the first Clause. "For all but...narrowly defined intrusions, the requisite 'balancing' has been performed in centuries of precedent and is embodied in the principle that seizures are 'reasonable' only if supported by probable cause." *Dunaway v. New York* (1979).

I therefore fully agree with the Court that "the underlying command of the Fourth Amendment is always that searches and seizures be reasonable." But this "underlying command" is not directly interpreted in each category of cases by some amorphous "balancing test." Rather, the provisions of the Warrant Clause—a warrant and probable cause—provide the yardstick against which official searches and seizures are to be measured. The Fourth Amendment neither requires nor authorizes the conceptual free-for-all that ensues when an unguided balancing test is used to assess specific categories of searches. If the search in question is more than a minimally intrusive *Terry* stop, the constitutional probable-cause standard determines its validity.

■ ■ ■

I thus do not accept the majority's premise that "[to] hold that the Fourth Amendment applies to searches conducted by school authorities is only to begin the inquiry into the standards governing such searches." For me, the finding that the Fourth Amendment applies, coupled with the observation that what is at issue is a full-scale search, is the end of the inquiry. But even if I believed that a "balancing test" appropriately replaces the judgment of the Framers of the Fourth Amendment, I would nonetheless object to the cursory and shortsighted "test" that the Court employs to justify its predictable weakening of Fourth Amendment protections. In particular, the test employed by the Court vastly overstates the social costs that a probable-cause standard entails and, though it plausibly articulates the serious privacy interests at stake, inexplicably fails to accord them adequate weight in striking the balance.

The Court begins to articulate its "balancing test" by observing that "the government's need for effective methods to deal with breaches of public order" is to be weighed on one side of the balance. Of course, this is not correct. It is not the government's need for effective enforcement methods that should weigh in the balance, for ordinary Fourth Amendment standards—including probable cause—may well permit methods for maintaining the public order that are perfectly effective. If that were the case, the governmental interest in having effective standards would carry no weight at all as a justification for departing from the probable-cause standard. Rather, it is the costs of applying probable cause as opposed to applying some lesser standard that should be weighed on the government's side.

In order to tote up the costs of applying the probable-cause standard, it is thus necessary first to take into account the nature and content of that standard, and the likelihood that it would hamper achievement of the goal—vital not just to "teachers and administrators," see ante, at 339—of maintaining an effective educational setting in the public schools. The seminal statement concerning the nature of the probable-cause standard is found in *Carroll v. United States* (1925). *Carroll* held that law enforcement authorities have probable cause to search where "the facts and circumstances within their knowledge and of which they had reasonably trustworthy information [are] sufficient in themselves to warrant a man of reasonable caution in the belief" that a criminal offense had occurred. In *Brinegar v. United States* (1949), the Court amplified this requirement, holding that probable cause depends upon "the factual and practical considerations of everyday life on which reasonable and prudent men, not legal technicians, act."

Two Terms ago, in *Illinois v. Gates* (1983), this Court expounded at some length its view of the probable-cause standard. Among the adjectives used to describe the standard were "practical," "fluid," "flexible," "easily applied," and "nontechnical." The probable-cause standard was to be seen as a "common-sense" test whose application depended on an evaluation of the "totality of the circumstances."

Ignoring what *Gates* took such great pains to emphasize, the Court today holds that a new "reasonableness" standard is appropriate because it "will spare teachers and school administrators the necessity of schooling themselves in the niceties of probable cause and permit them to regulate their conduct according to the dictates of reason and common sense." I had never thought that our pre-*Gates* understanding of probable cause defied either reason or common sense. But after *Gates*, I would have thought that there could be no doubt that this "nontechnical," "practical," and "easily applied" concept was eminently serviceable in a context like a school, where teachers require the flexibility to respond quickly and decisively to emergencies.

A consideration of the likely operation of the probable-cause standard reinforces this conclusion. Discussing the issue of school searches, Professor LaFave has noted that the cases that have reached the appellate courts "strongly suggest that in most instances the evidence of wrongdoing prompting teachers or principals to conduct searches is sufficiently detailed and specific to meet the traditional probable cause test." 3 W. LaFave, Search and Seizure § 10.11, pp. 459-460 (1978).

As compared with the relative ease with which teachers can apply the probable-cause standard, the amorphous "reasonableness under all the circumstances" standard freshly coined by the Court today will likely spawn increased litigation and greater uncertainty among teachers and administrators. Of course, as this Court should know, an essential purpose of developing and articulating legal norms is to enable individuals to conform their conduct to those norms. A school system conscientiously attempting to obey the Fourth Amendment's dictates under a probable-cause standard could, for example, consult decisions and other legal materials and prepare a booklet expounding the rough outlines of the concept. Such a booklet could be distributed to teachers to provide them with guidance as to when a search may be lawfully conducted. I cannot but believe that the same school system faced with interpreting what is permitted under the Court's new "reasonableness" standard would be hopelessly adrift as to when a search may be permissible. The sad result of this uncertainty may well be that some teachers will be reluctant to conduct searches that are fully permissible and even necessary under the constitutional probable-cause standard, while others may intrude arbitrarily and unjustifiably on the privacy of students.

Applying the constitutional probable-cause standard to the facts of this case, I would find that Mr. Choplick's search violated T.L.O.'s Fourth Amendment rights. After escorting T.L.O. into his private office, Mr. Choplick demanded to see her purse. He then opened the purse to find evidence of whether she had been smoking in the bathroom. When he opened the purse, he discovered the pack of cigarettes. At this point, his search for evidence of the smoking violation was complete.

Mr. Choplick then noticed, below the cigarettes, a pack of cigarette rolling papers. Believing that such papers were "associated," with the use of marihuana, he proceeded to conduct a detailed examination of the contents of her purse, in which he found some marihuana, a pipe, some money, an index card, and some private letters indicating that T.L.O. had sold marihuana to other students. The State sought to introduce this latter material in evidence at a criminal proceeding, and the issue before the Court is whether it should have been suppressed.

On my view of the case, we need not decide whether the initial search conducted by Mr. Choplick—the search for evidence of the smoking violation that was completed when Mr. Choplick found the pack of cigarettes—was valid. For Mr. Choplick at that point did not have probable cause to continue to rummage through T.L.O.'s purse. Mr. Choplick's suspicion of marihuana possession at this time was based solely on the presence of the package of cigarette papers. The mere presence without more of such a staple item of commerce is insufficient to warrant a person of reasonable caution in inferring both that T.L.O. had violated the law by possessing marihuana and that evidence of that violation would be found in her purse. Just as a police officer could not obtain a warrant to search a home based solely on his claim that he had seen a package of cigarette papers in that home, Mr. Choplick was not entitled to search possibly the most private possessions of T.L.O. based on the mere presence of a package of cigarette papers. Therefore, the fruits of this illegal search must be excluded and the judgment of the New Jersey Supreme Court affirmed.

Justice STEVENS, with whom Justice MARSHALL joins, and with whom Justice BRENNAN joins as to Part I, concurring in part and dissenting in part.

■ ■ ■

IV

The schoolroom is the first opportunity most citizens have to experience the power of government. Through it passes every citizen and public official, from schoolteachers to policemen and prison guards. The values they learn there, they take with them in life. One of our most cherished ideals is the one contained in the Fourth Amendment: that the government may not intrude on the personal privacy of its citizens without a warrant or compelling circumstance. The Court's decision today is a curious moral for the Nation's youth. Although the search of T.L.O.'s purse does not trouble today's majority, I submit that we are not dealing with "matters relatively trivial to the welfare of the Nation. There are village tyrants as well as village Hampdens, but none who acts under color of law is beyond reach of the Constitution." *West Virginia State Board of Education v. Barnette* (1943).

I respectfully dissent.

B. EXPECTATION OF PRIVACY

1. Overview

Katz v. United States

389 U.S. 347 (1967)

STEWART, J., delivered the opinion of the Court, in which WARREN, C.J., BRENNAN, DOUGLAS, GORTAS, HARLAN, and WHITE, JJ., joined. DOUGLAS, J., filed a concurring opinion, in which BRENNAN, J., joined. HARLAN and WHITE, JJ., filed concurring opinions. BLACK, J., filed a dissenting opinion. MARSHALL, J., took no part in the consideration or decision of this case.

The petitioner was convicted in the District Court for the Southern District of California under an eight-count indictment charging him with transmitting wagering information by telephone from Los Angeles to Miami and Boston in violation of a federal statute. At trial the Government was permitted, over the petitioner's objection, to introduce evidence of the petitioner's end of telephone conversations, overheard by FBI agents who had attached an electronic listening and recording device to the outside of the public telephone booth from which he had placed his calls. In affirming his conviction, the Court of Appeals rejected the contention that the recordings had been obtained in violation of the Fourth Amendment, because "[t]here was no physical entrance into the area occupied by [the petitioner].

■ ■ ■

The petitioner had phrased those questions as follows:

"A. Whether a public telephone booth is a constitutionally protected area so that evidence obtained by attaching an electronic listening recording device to the top of such a booth is obtained in violation of the right to privacy of the user of the booth.

B. Whether physical penetration of a constitutionally protected area is necessary before a search and seizure can be said to be violative of the Fourth Amendment to the United States Constitution."

We decline to adopt this formulation of the issues. In the first place the correct solution of Fourth Amendment problems is not necessarily promoted by incantation of the phrase "constitutionally protected area." Secondly, the Fourth Amendment cannot be translated into a general constitutional "right to privacy." That Amendment protects individual privacy against certain kinds of governmental intrusion, but its protections go further, and often have nothing to do with privacy at all.[4] Other provisions of the Constitution protect personal privacy from other forms of governmental invasion. But the protection of a person's *general* right to privacy—his right to be let alone by other people—is, like the protection of his property and of his very life, left largely to the law of the individual States.

Because of the misleading way the issues have been formulated, the parties have attached great significance to the characterization of the telephone booth from which the petitioner placed his calls. The petitioner has strenuously argued that the booth was a "constitutionally protected area." The Government has maintained with equal vigor that it was not. But this effort to decide whether or not a given "area," viewed in the abstract, is "constitutionally protected" deflects attention from the problem presented by this case. For the Fourth Amendment protects people, not places. What a person knowingly exposes to the public, even in his own home or office, is not a subject of Fourth Amendment protection.

The Government stresses the fact that the telephone booth from which the petitioner made his calls was constructed partly of glass, so that he was as visible after he entered it as he would have been if he had remained outside. But what he sought to exclude when he entered the booth was not the intruding eye—it was the uninvited ear. He did not shed his right to do so simply because he made his calls from a place where he might be seen. No less than an individual in a business office, in a friend's apartment, or in a taxicab, a person in a telephone booth may rely upon the protection of the Fourth Amendment. One who occupies it, shuts the door behind him, and pays the toll that permits him to place a call is surely entitled to assume that the words he utters into the mouthpiece will not be broadcast to the world. To read the Constitution more narrowly is to ignore the vital role that the public telephone has come to play in private communication.

---

4. "The average man would very likely not have his feelings soothed any more by having his property seized openly than by having it seized privately and by stealth.... And a person can be just as much, if not more, irritated, annoyed and injured by an unceremonious public arrest by a policeman as he is by a seizure in the privacy of his office or home." *Griswold v. State of Connecticut* (1965) (dissenting opinion of Justice Black).

The Government contends, however, that the activities of its agents in this case should not be tested by Fourth Amendment requirements, for the surveillance technique they employed involved no physical penetration of the telephone booth from which the petitioner placed his calls. It is true that the absence of such penetration was at one time thought to foreclose further Fourth Amendment inquiry, *Olmstead v. United States* (1928), for that Amendment was thought to limit only searches and seizures of tangible property. But "[t]he premise that property interests control the right of the Government to search and seize has been discredited." Thus, although a closely divided Court supposed in *Olmstead* that surveillance without any trespass and without the seizure of any material object fell outside the ambit of the Constitution, we have since departed from the narrow view on which that decision rested. Indeed, we have expressly held that the Fourth Amendment governs not only the seizure of tangible items, but extends as well to the recording of oral statements overheard without any "technical trespass under local property law." Once this much is acknowledged, and once it is recognized that the Fourth Amendment protects people—and not simply "areas"—against unreasonable searches and seizures it becomes clear that the reach of that Amendment cannot turn upon the presence or absence of a physical intrusion into any given enclosure.

We conclude that the underpinnings of *Olmstead* ... have been so eroded by our subsequent decisions that the "trespass" doctrine there enunciated can no longer be regarded as controlling. The Government's activities in electronically listening to and recording the petitioner's words violated the privacy upon which he justifiably relied while using the telephone booth and thus constituted a "search and seizure" within the meaning of the Fourth Amendment. The fact that the electronic device employed to achieve that end did not happen to penetrate the wall of the booth can have no constitutional significance.

 The question remaining for decision, then, is whether the search and seizure conducted in this case complied with constitutional standards. In that regard, the Government's position is that its agents acted in an entirely defensible manner: They did not begin their electronic surveillance until investigation of the petitioner's activities had established a strong probability that he was using the telephone in question to transmit gambling information to persons in other States, in violation of federal law. Moreover, the surveillance was limited, both in scope and in duration, to the specific purpose of establishing the contents of the petitioner's unlawful telephonic communications. The agents confined their surveillance to the brief periods during which he used the telephone booth, and they took great care to overhear only the conversations of the petitioner himself.

Accepting this account of the Government's actions as accurate, it is clear that this surveillance was so narrowly circumscribed that a duly authorized magistrate, properly notified of the need for such investigation, specifically informed of the basis on which it was to proceed, and clearly apprised of the precise intrusion it would entail, could constitutionally have authorized, with appropriate safeguards, the very limited search and seizure that the Government asserts in fact took place. . . . Here, too, a similar judicial order could have accommodated "the legitimate needs of law enforcement" by authorizing the carefully limited use of electronic surveillance.

The Government urges that, because its agents relied upon the decisions in *Olmstead* and *Goldman* [*v. United States* (1942)], and because they did no more here than they might properly have done with prior judicial sanction, we should retroactively validate their conduct. That we cannot do. It is apparent that the agents in this case acted with restraint. Yet the inescapable fact is that this restraint was imposed by the agents themselves, not by a judicial officer. They were not required, before commencing the search, to present their estimate of probable cause for detached scrutiny by a neutral magistrate. They were not compelled, during the conduct of the search itself, to observe precise limits established in advance by a specific court order. Nor were they directed, after the search had been completed, to notify the authorizing magistrate in detail of all that had been seized. In the absence of such safeguards, this Court has never sustained a search upon the sole ground that officers reasonably expected to find evidence of a particular crime and voluntarily confined their activities to the least intrusive means consistent with that end. Searches conducted without warrants have been held unlawful "notwithstanding facts unquestionably showing probable cause," for the Constitution requires "that the deliberate, impartial judgment of a judicial officer . . . be interposed between the citizen and the police." *Wong Sun v. United States* (1963). "Over and again this Court has emphasized that the mandate of the [Fourth] Amendment requires adherence to judicial processes," *United States v. Jeffers* (1951), and that searches conducted outside the judicial process, without prior approval by judge or magistrate, are per se unreasonable under the Fourth Amendment—subject only to a few specifically established and well-delineated exceptions.

It is difficult to imagine how any of those exceptions could ever apply to the sort of search and seizure involved in this case. Even electronic surveillance substantially contemporaneous with an individual's arrest could hardly be deemed an "incident" of that arrest. Nor could the use of electronic surveillance without prior authorization be justified on grounds of "hot pursuit." And, of course, the very nature of electronic surveillance precludes its use pursuant to the suspect's consent.

The Government does not question these basic principles. Rather, it urges the creation of a new exception to cover this case. It argues that surveillance of a telephone booth should be exempted from the usual requirement of advance authorization by a magistrate upon a showing of probable cause. We cannot agree. Omission of such authorization "bypasses the safeguards provided by an objective predetermination of probable cause, and substitutes instead the far less reliable procedure of an after-the-event justification for the search, too likely to be subtly influenced by the familiar shortcomings of hindsight judgment." *Beck v. State of Ohio* (1964).

And bypassing a neutral predetermination of the *scope* of a search leaves individuals secure from Fourth Amendment violations "only in the discretion of the police."

These considerations do not vanish when the search in question is transferred from the setting of a home, an office, or a hotel room to that of a telephone booth. Wherever a man may be, he is entitled to know that he will remain free from unreasonable searches and seizures. The government agents here ignored "the procedure of antecedent justification that is central to the Fourth Amendment," a procedure that we hold to be a constitutional precondition of the kind of electronic surveillance involved in this case. Because the surveillance here failed to meet that condition, and because it led to the petitioner's conviction, the judgment must be reversed.

It is so ordered.

Judgment reversed.

Justice Douglas, with whom Justice Brennan joins, concurring.

While I join the opinion of the Court, I feel compelled to reply to the separate concurring opinion of my Brother White, which I view as a wholly unwarranted green light for the Executive Branch to resort to electronic eavesdropping without a warrant in cases which the Executive Branch itself labels "national security" matters.

Neither the President nor the Attorney General is a magistrate. In matters where they believe national security may be involved they are not detached, disinterested, and neutral as a court or magistrate must be. Under the separation of powers created by the Constitution, the Executive Branch is not supposed to be neutral and disinterested. Rather it should vigorously investigate and prevent breaches of national security and prosecute those who violate the pertinent federal laws. The President and Attorney General are properly interested parties, cast in the role of adversary, in national security cases. They may even be the intended victims of subversive action. Since spies and saboteurs are as entitled to the protection of the Fourth Amendment as suspected gamblers like petitioner, I cannot agree that where spies and saboteurs are involved adequate protection of Fourth Amendment rights is assured when the President and Attorney General assume both the position of adversary-and-prosecutor and disinterested, neutral magistrate. . . .

Justice Harlan, concurring.

I join the opinion of the Court, which I read to hold only (a) that an enclosed telephone booth is an area where, like a home, and unlike a field, *Hester v. United States*, a person has a constitutionally protected reasonable expectation of privacy; (b) that electronic as well as physical intrusion into a place that is in this sense private may constitute a violation of the Fourth Amendment; and (c) that the invasion of a constitutionally protected area by federal authorities is, as the Court has long held, presumptively unreasonable in the absence of a search warrant.

As the Court's opinion states, "the Fourth Amendment protects people, not places." The question, however, is what protection it affords to those people.

Generally, as here, the answer to that question requires reference to a "place." My understanding of the rule that has emerged from prior decisions is that there is a twofold requirement, first that a person have exhibited an actual (subjective) expectation of privacy and, second, that the expectation be one that society is prepared to recognize as "reasonable." Thus a man's home is, for most purposes, a place where he expects privacy, but objects, activities, or statements that he exposes to the "plain view" of outsiders are not "protected" because no intention to keep them to himself has been exhibited. On the other hand, conversations in the open would not be protected against being overheard, for the expectation of privacy under the circumstances would be unreasonable. Cf. *Hester v. United States* (1924).

The critical fact in this case is that "[o]ne who occupies it, [a telephone booth] shuts the door behind him, and pays the toll that permits him to place a call is surely entitled to assume" that his conversation is not being intercepted. The point is not that the booth is "accessible to the public" at other times, but that it is a temporarily private place whose momentary occupants' expectations of freedom from intrusion are recognized as reasonable. . . .

Justice WHITE, concurring.

I agree that the official surveillance of petitioner's telephone conversations in a public booth must be subjected to the test of reasonableness under the Fourth Amendment and that on the record now before us the particular surveillance undertaken was unreasonable absent a warrant properly authorizing it. This application of the Fourth Amendment need not interfere with legitimate needs of law enforcement.

In joining the Court's opinion, I note the Court's acknowledgment that there are circumstance in which it is reasonable to search without a warrant. In this connection, the Court points out that today's decision does not reach national security cases. Wiretapping to protect the security of the Nation has been authorized by successive Presidents. The present Administration would apparently save national security cases from restrictions against wiretapping. We should not require the warrant procedure and the magistrate's judgment if the President of the United States or his chief legal officer, the Attorney General, has considered the requirements of national security and authorized electronic surveillance as reasonable.

Justice BLACK, dissenting.

If I could agree with the Court that eavesdropping carried on by electronic means (equivalent to wiretapping) constitutes a "search" or "seizure," I would be happy to join the Court's opinion. For on that premise my Brother Stewart sets out methods in accord with the Fourth Amendment to guide States in the enactment and enforcement of laws passed to regulate wiretapping by government. In this respect today's opinion differs sharply from *Berger v. State of New York* (1967) decided last Term, which held void on its face a New York statute authorizing wiretapping on warrants issued by magistrates on showings of probable cause. The *Berger* case also set up what appeared to be insuperable obstacles to the valid passage of such wiretapping laws by States. The Court's opinion in this case, however, removes the doubts about state power in this field and abates to a large extent the confusion and near-paralyzing effect of the *Berger* holding. Notwithstanding these good efforts of the Court, I am still unable to agree with its interpretation of the Fourth Amendment.

My basic objection is twofold: (1) I do not believe that the words of the Amendment will bear the meaning given them by today's decision, and (2) I do not believe that it is the proper role of this Court to rewrite the Amendment in order "to bring it into harmony with the times" and thus reach a result that many people believe to be desirable.

While I realize that an argument based on the meaning of words lacks the scope, and no doubt the appeal, of broad policy discussions and philosophical discourses on such nebulous subjects as privacy, for me the language of the Amendment is the crucial place to look in construing a written document such as our Constitution. The Fourth Amendment says that

> "The right of the people to be secure in their persons, houses, papers, and effects, against unreasonable searches and seizures, shall not be violated, and no Warrants shall issue, but upon probable cause, supported by Oath or affirmation, and particularly describing the place to be searched, and the persons or things to be seized."

The first clause protects "persons, houses, papers, and effects, against unreasonable searches and seizures." These words connote the idea of tangible things with size, form, and weight, things capable of being searched, seized, or both. The second clause of the Amendment still further establishes its Framers' purpose to limit its protection to tangible things by providing that no warrants shall issue but those "particularly describing the place to be searched, and the persons or things to be seized." A conversation overheard by eavesdropping, whether by plain snooping or wiretapping, is not tangible and, under the normally accepted meanings of the words, can neither be searched nor seized. In addition the language of the second clause indicates that the Amendment refers not only to something tangible so it can be seized but to something already in existence so it can be described. Yet the Court's interpretation would have the Amendment apply to overhearing future conversations which by their very nature are nonexistent until they take place. How can one "describe" a future conversation, and, if one cannot, how can a magistrate issue a warrant to eavesdrop one in the future? It is argued that information showing what is expected to be said is sufficient to limit the boundaries of what later can be admitted into evidence; but does such general information really meet the specific language of the Amendment which says "particularly describing"? Rather than using language in a completely artificial way, I must conclude that the Fourth Amendment simply does not apply to eavesdropping.

Tapping telephone wires, of course, was an unknown possibility at the time the Fourth Amendment was adopted. But eavesdropping (and wiretapping is nothing more than eavesdropping by telephone) was, as even the majority opinion in *Berger*, recognized, "an ancient practice which at common law was condemned as a nuisance. In those days the eavesdropper listened by naked ear under the eaves of houses or their windows, or beyond their walls seeking out private discourse." There can be no doubt that the Framers were aware of this practice, and if they had desired to outlaw or restrict the use of evidence obtained by eavesdropping, I believe that they would have used the appropriate language to do so in the Fourth Amendment. They certainly would not have left such a task to the ingenuity of language-stretching judges. No one, it seems to me, can read the debates on the Bill of Rights without reaching the conclusion that its Framers and critics well knew the meaning of the words they used, what they would be understood to mean by others, their scope and their limitations. Under these circumstances it strikes me as a charge against their scholarship, their common sense and their candor to give to the Fourth Amendment's language the eavesdropping meaning the Court imputes to it today.

I do not deny that common sense requires and that this Court often has said that the Bill of Rights' safeguards should be given a liberal construction. This principle, however, does not justify construing the search and seizure amendment as applying to eavesdropping or the "seizure" of conversations. The Fourth Amendment was aimed directly at the abhorred practice of breaking in, ransacking and searching homes and other buildings and seizing people's personal belongings without warrants issued by magistrates. The Amendment deserves, and this Court has given it, a liberal construction in order to protect against warrantless searches of buildings and seizures of tangible personal effects. But until today this Court has refused to say that eavesdropping comes within the ambit of Fourth Amendment restrictions.

■ ■ ■

The Fourth Amendment protects privacy only to the extent that it prohibits unreasonable searches and seizures of "persons, houses, papers, and effects." No general right is created by the Amendment so as to give this Court the unlimited power to hold unconstitutional everything which affects privacy. Certainly the Framers, well acquainted as they were with the excesses of governmental power, did not intend to grant this Court such omnipotent lawmaking authority as that. The history of governments proves that it is dangerous to freedom to repose such powers in courts.

For these reasons I respectfully dissent.

United States v. Jones

132 S. Ct. 945 (2012)

SCALIA, J., delivered the opinion of the Court, in which ROBERTS, C.J., and KENNEDY, THOMAS, and SOTOMAYOR, JJ., joined. SOTOMAYOR, J., filed a concurring opinion. ALITO, J., filed an opinion concurring in the judgment, in which GINSBURG, BREYER, and KAGAN, JJ., joined.

We decide whether the attachment of a Global-Positioning-System (GPS) tracking device to an individual's vehicle, and subsequent use of that device to monitor the vehicle's movements on public streets, constitutes a search or seizure within the meaning of the Fourth Amendment.

I

In 2004 respondent Antoine Jones, owner and operator of a nightclub in the District of Columbia, came under suspicion of trafficking in narcotics and was made the target of an investigation by a joint FBI and Metropolitan Police Department task force. Officers employed various investigative techniques, including visual surveillance of the nightclub, installation of a camera focused on the front door of the club, and a pen register and wiretap covering Jones's cellular phone.

Based in part on information gathered from these sources, in 2005 the Government applied to the United States District Court for the District of Columbia for a warrant authorizing the use of an electronic tracking device on the Jeep Grand Cherokee registered to Jones's wife. A warrant issued, authorizing installation of the device in the District of Columbia and within 10 days.

On the 11th day, and not in the District of Columbia but in Maryland,[6] agents installed a GPS tracking device on the undercarriage of the Jeep while it was parked in a public parking lot. Over the next 28 days, the Government used the device to track the vehicle's movements, and once had to replace the device's battery when the vehicle was parked in a different public lot in Maryland. By means of signals from multiple satellites, the device established the vehicle's location within 50 to 100 feet, and communicated that location by cellular phone to a Government computer. It relayed more than 2,000 pages of data over the 4-week period.

The Government ultimately obtained a multiple-count indictment charging Jones with conspiracy to distribute and possess with intent to distribute five kilograms or more of cocaine and 50 grams or more of cocaine. . . . Before trial, Jones filed a motion to suppress evidence obtained through the GPS device. The District Court granted the motion only in part, suppressing the data obtained while the vehicle was parked in the garage adjoining Jones's residence. It held the remaining data admissible, because "'[a] person traveling in an automobile on public thoroughfares has no reasonable expectation of privacy in his movements from one place to another.'" (quoting *United States v. Knotts* (1983)).

. . . The Government introduced at trial the GPS-derived locational data which connected Jones to the alleged conspirators' stash house that contained $850,000 in cash, 97 kilograms of cocaine, and 1 kilogram of cocaine base.

---

6. In this litigation, the Government has conceded noncompliance with the warrant and has argued only that a warrant was not required. *United States v. Maynard* (C.A.D.C. 2010).

The jury returned a guilty verdict, and the District Court sentenced Jones to life imprisonment.

The United States Court of Appeals for the District of Columbia Circuit reversed the conviction because of admission of the evidence obtained by warrantless use of the GPS device which, it said, violated the Fourth Amendment. The D.C. Circuit denied the Government's petition for rehearing en banc. We granted certiorari.

II

A

The Fourth Amendment provides in relevant part that "[t]he right of the people to be secure in their persons, houses, papers, and effects, against unreasonable searches and seizures, shall not be violated." It is beyond dispute that a vehicle is an "effect" as that term is used in the Amendment. *United States v. Chadwick* (1977). We hold that the Government's installation of a GPS device on a target's vehicle, and its use of that device to monitor the vehicle's movements, constitutes a "search."

It is important to be clear about what occurred in this case: The Government physically occupied private property for the purpose of obtaining information. We have no doubt that such a physical intrusion would have been considered a "search" within the meaning of the Fourth Amendment when it was adopted. . . .

"[O]ur law holds the property of every man so sacred, that no man can set his foot upon his neighbour's close without his leave; if he does he is a trespasser, though he does no damage at all; if he will tread upon his neighbour's ground, he must justify it by law." *Entick* [*v. Carrington*, 95 Eng. Rep. 807 (C.P. 1765)], at 817.

The text of the Fourth Amendment reflects its close connection to property, since otherwise it would have referred simply to "the right of the people to be secure against unreasonable searches and seizures"; the phrase "in their persons, houses, papers, and effects" would have been superfluous.

Consistent with this understanding, our Fourth Amendment jurisprudence was tied to common-law trespass, at least until the latter half of the 20th century. *Kyllo v. United States* (2001). Thus, in *Olmstead v. United States* (1928), we held that wiretaps attached to telephone wires on the public streets did not constitute a Fourth Amendment search because "[t]here was no entry of the houses or offices of the defendants."

Our later cases, of course, have deviated from that exclusively property-based approach. In *Katz v. United States* (1967), we said that "the Fourth Amendment protects people, not places," and found a violation in attachment of an eavesdropping device to a public telephone booth. Our later cases have applied the analysis of Justice Harlan's concurrence in that case, which said that a violation occurs when government officers violate a person's "reasonable expectation of privacy."

The Government contends that the Harlan standard shows that no search occurred here, since Jones had no "reasonable expectation of privacy" in the area of the Jeep accessed by Government agents (its underbody) and in the locations of the Jeep on the public roads, which were visible to all. But we need not address the Government's contentions, because Jones's Fourth Amendment rights do not rise or fall with the *Katz* formulation. At bottom, we must "assur[e] preservation of that degree of privacy against government that existed when the Fourth Amendment was adopted." *Kyllo.* As explained, for most of our history the Fourth Amendment was understood to embody a particular concern for government trespass upon the areas ("persons, houses, papers, and effects") it enumerates. *Katz* did not repudiate that understanding. Less than two years later the Court upheld defendants' contention that the Government could not introduce against them conversations between *other* people obtained by warrantless placement of electronic surveillance devices in their homes. The opinion rejected the dissent's contention that there was no Fourth Amendment deviolation "unless the conversational privacy of the homeowner himself is invaded." *Alderman v. United States* (1969). "[W]e [do not] believe that *Katz*, by holding that the Fourth Amendment protects persons and their private conversations, was intended to withdraw any of the protection which the Amendment extends to the home...."

... As Justice Brennan explained in his concurrence in *Knotts, Katz* did not erode the principle "that, when the Government *does* engage in physical intrusion of a constitutionally protected area in order to obtain information, that intrusion may constitute a violation of the Fourth Amendment." (opinion concurring in judgment). We have embodied that preservation of past rights in our very definition of "reasonable expectation of privacy" which we have said to be an expectation "that has a source outside of the Fourth Amendment, either by reference to concepts of real or personal property law or to understandings that are recognized and permitted by society." *Minnesota v. Carter* (1998). *Katz* did not narrow the Fourth Amendment's scope.[5]

The Government contends that several of our post-*Katz* cases foreclose the conclusion that what occurred here constituted a search. It relies principally on two cases in which we rejected Fourth Amendment challenges to "beepers," electronic tracking devices that represent another form of electronic monitoring. The first case, *Knotts*, upheld against Fourth Amendment challenge the use of a "beeper" that had been placed in a container of chloroform, allowing law

---

5. The concurrence notes that post-*Katz* we have explained that "'an actual trespass is neither necessary *nor sufficient* to establish a constitutional violation.'" (quoting *United States v. Karo* (1984)). That is undoubtedly true, and undoubtedly irrelevant. *Karo* was considering whether a seizure occurred, and as the concurrence explains, a seizure of property occurs, not when there is a trespass, but "when there is some meaningful interference with an individual's possessory interests in that property." Likewise with a search. Trespass alone does not qualify, but there must be conjoined with that what was present here: an attempt to find something or to obtain information. Related to this, and similarly irrelevant, is the concurrence's point that, if analyzed separately, neither the installation of the device nor its use would constitute a Fourth Amendment search. Of course not. A trespass on "houses" or "effects," or a *Katz* invasion of privacy, is not alone a search unless it is done to obtain information; and the obtaining of information is not alone a search unless it is achieved by such a trespass or invasion of privacy.

enforcement to monitor the location of the container. We said that there had been no infringement of Knotts' reasonable expectation of privacy since the information obtained—the location of the automobile carrying the container on public roads, and the location of the off-loaded container in open fields near Knotts' cabin—had been voluntarily conveyed to the public. But as we have discussed, the Katz reasonable-expectation-of-privacy test has been *added to*, not *substituted for*, the common-law trespassory test. The holding in *Knotts* addressed only the former, since the latter was not at issue. The beeper had been placed in the container before it came into Knotts' possession, with the consent of the then-owner. Knotts did not challenge that installation, and we specifically declined to consider its effect on the Fourth Amendment analysis. *Knotts* would be relevant, perhaps, if the Government were making the argument that what would otherwise be an unconstitutional search is not such where it produces only public information. The Government does not make that argument, and we know of no case that would support it.

The second "beeper" case, *United States v. Karo* (1984), does not suggest a different conclusion. There we addressed the question left open by *Knotts*, whether the installation of a beeper in a container amounted to a search or seizure. As in *Knotts*, at the time the beeper was installed the container belonged to a third party, and it did not come into possession of the defendant until later. Thus, the specific question we considered was whether the installation *"with the consent of the original owner* constitute[d] a search or seizure . . . when the container is delivered to a buyer having no knowledge of the presence of the beeper."). We held not. The Government, we said, came into physical contact with the container only before it belonged to the defendant Karo; and the transfer of the container with the unmonitored beeper inside did not convey any information and thus did not invade Karo's privacy. That conclusion is perfectly consistent with the one we reach here. Karo accepted the container as it came to him, beeper and all, and was therefore not entitled to object to the beeper's presence, even though it was used to monitor the container's location. . . .

The Government also points to our exposition in *New York v. Class* (1986), that "[t]he exterior of a car . . . is thrust into the public eye, and thus to examine it does not constitute a 'search.'" That statement is of marginal relevance here since, as the Government acknowledges, "the officers in this case did *more* than conduct a visual inspection of respondent's vehicle" (emphasis added). By attaching the device to the Jeep, officers encroached on a protected area. In *Class* itself we suggested that this would make a difference, for we concluded that an officer's momentary reaching into the interior of a vehicle did constitute a search.

Finally, the Government's position gains little support from our conclusion in *Oliver v. United States* (1984), that officers' information-gathering intrusion on an "open field" did not constitute a Fourth Amendment search even though it was a trespass at common law. . . . Quite simply, an open field, unlike the curtilage of a home, see *United States v. Dunn* (1987), is not one of those protected areas enumerated in the Fourth Amendment. . . .

response to concurrence

B

The concurrence begins by accusing us of applying "18th-century tort law." That is a distortion. What we apply is an 18th-century guarantee against unreasonable searches, which we believe must provide at *a minimum* the degree of protection it afforded when it was adopted. The concurrence does not share that belief. It would apply *exclusively Katz's* reasonable-expectation-of-privacy test, even when that eliminates rights that previously existed.

The concurrence faults our approach for "present[ing] particularly vexing problems" in cases that do not involve physical contact, such as those that involve the transmission of electronic signals. . . . We entirely fail to understand that point. For unlike the concurrence, which would make *Katz* the *exclusive* test, we do not make trespass the exclusive test. Situations involving merely the transmission of electronic signals without trespass would *remain* subject to *Katz* analysis.

In fact, it is the concurrence's insistence on the exclusivity of the *Katz* test that needlessly leads us into "particularly vexing problems" in the present case. This Court has to date not deviated from the understanding that mere visual observation does not constitute a search. See *Kyllo.* We accordingly held in *Knotts* that "[a] person traveling in an automobile on public thoroughfares has no reasonable expectation of privacy in his movements from one place to another." Thus, even assuming that the concurrence is correct to say that "[t]raditional surveillance" of Jones for a 4-week period "would have required a large team of agents, multiple vehicles, and perhaps aerial assistance," our cases suggest that such visual observation is constitutionally permissible. It may be that achieving the same result through electronic means, without an accompanying trespass, is an unconstitutional invasion of privacy, but the present case does not require us to answer that question.

And answering it affirmatively leads us needlessly into additional thorny problems. The concurrence posits that "relatively short-term monitoring of a person's movements on public streets" is okay, but that "the use of longer term GPS monitoring in investigations *of most offenses*" is no good. That introduces yet another novelty into our jurisprudence. There is no precedent for the proposition that whether a search has occurred depends on the nature of the crime being investigated. And even accepting that novelty, it remains unexplained why a 4-week investigation is "surely" too long and why a drug-trafficking conspiracy involving substantial amounts of cash and narcotics is not an "extraordinary offens[e]" which may permit longer observation. What of a 2-day monitoring of a suspected purveyor of stolen electronics? Or of a 6-month monitoring of a suspected terrorist? We may have to grapple with these "vexing problems" in some future case where a classic trespassory search is not involved and resort must be had to *Katz* analysis; but there is no reason for rushing forward to resolve them here.

■ ■ ■

The judgment of the Court of Appeals for the D.C. Circuit is affirmed. *It is so ordered.*

Justice Sotomayor, concurring.

I join the Court's opinion because I agree that a search within the meaning of the Fourth Amendment occurs, at a minimum, "[w]here, as here, the Government obtains information by physically intruding on a constitutionally protected area." In this case, the Government installed a Global Positioning System (GPS) tracking device on respondent Antoine Jones' Jeep without a valid warrant and without Jones' consent, then used that device to monitor the Jeep's movements over the course of four weeks. The Government usurped Jones' property for the purpose of conducting surveillance on him, thereby invading privacy interests long afforded, and undoubtedly entitled to, Fourth Amendment protection

Of course, the Fourth Amendment is not concerned only with trespassory intrusions on property. See, *e.g., Kyllo v. United States.* Rather, even in the absence of a trespass, "a Fourth Amendment search occurs when the government violates a subjective expectation of privacy that society recognizes as reasonable." *Katz v. United States* (Harlan, J., concurring). In *Katz,* this Court enlarged its then-prevailing focus on property rights by announcing that the reach of the Fourth Amendment does not "turn upon the presence or absence of a physical intrusion." As the majority's opinion makes clear, however, *Katz's* reasonable-expectation-of-privacy test augmented, but did not displace or diminish, the common-law trespassory test that preceded it. . . . Thus, "when the Government *does* engage in physical intrusion of a constitutionally protected area in order to obtain information, that intrusion may constitute a violation of the Fourth Amendment." *United States v. Knotts* (Brennan, J., concurring in judgment); Justice Alito's approach, which discounts altogether the constitutional relevance of the Government's physical intrusion on Jones' Jeep, erodes that longstanding protection for privacy expectations inherent in items of property that people possess or control. By contrast, the trespassory test applied in the majority's opinion reflects an irreducible constitutional minimum: When the Government physically invades personal property to gather information, a search occurs. The reaffirmation of that principle suffices to decide this case.

Nonetheless, as Justice Alito notes, physical intrusion is now unnecessary to many forms of surveillance. With increasing regularity, the Government will be capable of duplicating the monitoring undertaken in this case by enlisting factory- or owner-installed vehicle tracking devices or GPS-enabled smartphones. See *United States v. Pineda-Moreno* (CA9 2010) (Kozinski, C.J., dissenting from denial of rehearing en banc). In cases of electronic or other novel modes of surveillance that do not depend upon a physical invasion on property, the majority opinion's trespassory test may provide little guidance. But "[s]ituations involving merely the transmission of electronic signals without trespass would *remain* subject to *Katz* analysis." As Justice Alito incisively observes, the same technological advances that have made possible nontrespassory surveillance techniques will also affect the *Katz* test by shaping the evolution of societal privacy expectations. Under that rubric, I agree with Justice Alito that, at the very least, "longer term GPS monitoring in investigations of most offenses impinges on expectations of privacy."

In cases involving even short-term monitoring, some unique attributes of GPS surveillance relevant to the *Katz* analysis will require particular attention. GPS monitoring generates a precise, comprehensive record of a person's public movements that reflects a wealth of detail about her familial, political, professional, religious, and sexual associations. . . .

Awareness that the Government may be watching chills associational and expressive freedoms. And the Government's unrestrained power to assemble data that reveal private aspects of identity is susceptible to abuse. The net result is that GPS monitoring—by making available at a relatively low cost such a substantial quantum of intimate information about any person whom the Government, in its unfettered discretion, chooses to track—may "alter the relationship between citizen and government in a way that is inimical to democratic society." *United States v. Cuevas-Perez* (CA7 2011) (Flaum, J., concurring).

I would take these attributes of GPS monitoring into account when considering the existence of a reasonable societal expectation of privacy in the sum of one's public movements. I would ask whether people reasonably expect that their movements will be recorded and aggregated in a manner that enables the Government to ascertain, more or less at will, their political and religious beliefs, sexual habits, and so on. I do not regard as dispositive the fact that the Government might obtain the fruits of GPS monitoring through lawful conventional surveillance techniques. . . .

More fundamentally, it may be necessary to reconsider the premise that an individual has no reasonable expectation of privacy in information voluntarily disclosed to third parties. *E.g.*, *Smith* [*v. Maryland* (1979)]; *United States v. Miller* (1976). This approach is ill suited to the digital age, in which people reveal a great deal of information about themselves to third parties in the course of carrying out mundane tasks. People disclose the phone numbers that they dial or text to their cellular providers; the URLs that they visit and the e-mail addresses with which they correspond to their Internet service providers; and the books, groceries, and medications they purchase to online retailers. Perhaps, as Justice Alito notes, some people may find the "tradeoff" of privacy for convenience "worthwhile," or come to accept this "diminution of privacy" as "inevitable," and perhaps not. I for one doubt that people would accept without complaint the warrantless disclosure to the Government of a list of every Web site they had visited in the last week, or month, or year. But whatever the societal expectations, they can attain constitutionally protected status only if our Fourth Amendment jurisprudence ceases to treat secrecy as a prerequisite for privacy. I would not assume that all information voluntarily disclosed to some member of the public for a limited purpose is, for that reason alone, disentitled to Fourth Amendment protection. See *Smith* (Marshall, J., dissenting) ("Privacy is not a discrete commodity, possessed absolutely or not at all. Those who disclose certain facts to a bank or phone company for a limited business purpose need not assume that this information will be released to other persons for other purposes"); see also *Katz* ("[W]hat [a person] seeks to preserve as private, even in an area accessible to the public, may be constitutionally protected").

Resolution of these difficult questions in this case is unnecessary, however, because the Government's physical intrusion on Jones' Jeep supplies a narrower basis for decision. I therefore join the majority's opinion.

Justice ALITO, with whom Justice GINSBURG, Justice BREYER, and Justice KAGAN join, concurring in the judgment.

This case requires us to apply the Fourth Amendment's prohibition of unreasonable searches and seizures to a 21st-century surveillance technique, the use of a Global Positioning System (GPS) device to monitor a vehicle's movements for an extended period of time. Ironically, the Court has chosen to decide this case based on 18th-century tort law. By attaching a small GPS device[1] to the underside of the vehicle that respondent drove, the law enforcement officers in this case engaged in conduct that might have provided grounds in 1791 for a suit for trespass to chattels.[2] And for this reason, the Court concludes, the installation and use of the GPS device constituted a search. . . .

This holding, in my judgment, is unwise. It strains the language of the Fourth Amendment; it has little if any support in current Fourth Amendment case law; and it is highly artificial.

I would analyze the question presented in this case by asking whether respondent's reasonable expectations of privacy were violated by the long-term monitoring of the movements of the vehicle he drove.

I

A

The Fourth Amendment prohibits "unreasonable searches and seizures," and the Court makes very little effort to explain how the attachment or use of the GPS device fits within these terms. The Court does not contend that there was a seizure. A seizure of property occurs when there is "some meaningful interference with an individual's possessory interests in that property," *United States v. Jacobsen* (1984), and here there was none. Indeed, the success of the surveillance technique that the officers employed was dependent on the fact that the GPS did not interfere in any way with the operation of the vehicle, for if

---

1. Although the record does not reveal the size or weight of the device used in this case, there is now a device in use that weighs two ounces and is the size of a credit card. . . .

2. At common law, a suit for trespass to chattels could be maintained if there was a violation of "the dignitary interest in the inviolability of chattels," but today there must be "some actual damage to the chattel before the action can be maintained." W. Keeton, D. Dobbs, R. Keeton, & D. Owen, Prosser & Keeton on Law of Torts 87 (5th ed. 1984). Here, there was no actual damage to the vehicle to which the GPS device was attached.

any such interference had been detected, the device might have been discovered.

The Court does claim that the installation and use of the GPS constituted a search, but this conclusion is dependent on the questionable proposition that these two procedures cannot be separated for purposes of Fourth Amendment analysis. If these two procedures are analyzed separately, it is not at all clear from the Court's opinion why either should be regarded as a search. It is clear that the attachment of the GPS device was not itself a search; if the device had not functioned or if the officers had not used it, no information would have been obtained. And the Court does not contend that the use of the device constituted a search either. On the contrary, the Court accepts the holding in *United States v. Knotts* that the use of a surreptitiously planted electronic device to monitor a vehicle's movements on public roads did not amount to a search.

The Court argues—and I agree—that "we must assur[e] preservation of that degree of privacy against government that existed when the Fourth Amendment was adopted." But it is almost impossible to think of late-18th-century situations that are analogous to what took place in this case. (Is it possible to imagine a case in which a constable secreted himself somewhere in a coach and remained there for a period of time in order to monitor the movements of the coach's owner?[3]) The Court's theory seems to be that the concept of a search, as originally understood, comprehended any technical trespass that led to the gathering of evidence, but we know that this is incorrect. At common law, any unauthorized intrusion on private property was actionable, but a trespass on open fields, as opposed to the "curtilage" of a home, does not fall within the scope of the Fourth Amendment because private property outside the curtilage is not part of a "hous[e]" within the meaning of the Fourth Amendment. See *Oliver v. United States*.

B

The Court's reasoning in this case is very similar to that in the Court's early decisions involving wiretapping and electronic eavesdropping, namely, that a technical trespass followed by the gathering of evidence constitutes a search. In the early electronic surveillance cases, the Court concluded that a Fourth Amendment search occurred when private conversations were monitored as a result of an "unauthorized physical penetration into the premises occupied" by the defendant. *Silverman v. United States (1961)*. In *Silverman*, police officers listened to conversations in an attached home by inserting a "spike mike" through the wall that this house shared with the vacant house next door. This procedure was held to be a search because the mike made contact with a heating duct on the other side of the wall and thus "usurp[ed] . . . an integral part of the premises."

---

3. The Court suggests that something like this might have occurred in 1791, but this would have required either a gigantic coach, a very tiny constable, or both—not to mention a constable with incredible fortitude and patience.

By contrast, in cases in which there was no trespass, it was held that there was no search. Thus, in *Olmstead v. United States*, the Court found that the Fourth Amendment did not apply because "[t]he taps from house lines were made in the streets near the houses." Similarly, the Court concluded that no search occurred in *Goldman v. United States* (1942), where a "detecta-phone" was placed on the outer wall of defendant's office for the purpose of overhearing conversations held within the room.

This trespass-based rule was repeatedly criticized. In *Olmstead*, Justice Brandeis wrote that it was "immaterial where the physical connection with the telephone wires was made." (dissenting opinion). Although a private conversation transmitted by wire did not fall within the literal words of the Fourth Amendment, he argued, the Amendment should be understood as prohibiting "every unjustifiable intrusion by the government upon the privacy of the individual." . . .

Katz v. United States finally did away with the old approach, holding that a trespass was not required for a Fourth Amendment violation. *Katz* involved the use of a listening device that was attached to the outside of a public telephone booth and that allowed police officers to eavesdrop on one end of the target's phone conversation. This procedure did not physically intrude on the area occupied by the target, but the *Katz* Court, "repudiate[ed]" the old doctrine, *Rakas v. Illinois* (1978), and held that "[t]he fact that the electronic device employed . . . did not happen to penetrate the wall of the booth can have no constitutional significance," ("[T]he reach of th[e] [Fourth] Amendment cannot turn upon the presence or absence of a physical intrusion into any given enclosure"); see *Rakas*, (describing *Katz* as holding that the "capacity to claim the protection for the Fourth Amendment depends not upon a property right in the invaded place but upon whether the person who claims the protection of the Amendment has a legitimate expectation of privacy in the invaded place"); *Kyllo* ("We have since decoupled violation of a person's Fourth Amendment rights from trespassory violation of his property"). What mattered, the Court now held, was whether the conduct at issue "violated the privacy upon which [the defendant] justifiably relied while using the telephone booth." *Katz*.

Under this approach, as the Court later put it when addressing the relevance of a technical trespass, "an actual trespass is neither necessary *nor sufficient* to establish a constitutional violation." *United States v. Karo.* . . .

II

The majority suggests that two post-*Katz* decisions—*Soldal v. Cook County* (1992) and *Alderman v. United States*—show that a technical trespass is sufficient to establish the existence of a search, but they provide little support.

In *Soldal*, the Court held that towing away a trailer home without the owner's consent constituted a seizure even if this did not invade the occupants' personal privacy. But in the present case, the Court does not find that there was a seizure, and it is clear that none occurred.

In *Alderman*, the Court held that the Fourth Amendment rights of home-owners were implicated by the use of a surreptitiously planted listening device to monitor third-party conversations that occurred within their home. *Alderman* is best understood to mean that the homeowners had a legitimate expectation of privacy in all conversations that took place under their roof. . . .

In sum, the majority is hard pressed to find support in post-*Katz* cases for its trespass-based theory.

III

Disharmony with a substantial body of existing case law is only one of the problems with the Court's approach in this case.

I will briefly note four others. First, the Court's reasoning largely disre-gards what is really important (the *use* of a GPS for the purpose of long-term tracking) and instead attaches great significance to something that most would view as relatively minor (attaching to the bottom of a car a small, light object that does not interfere in any way with the car's operation). Attaching such an object is generally regarded as so trivial that it does not provide a basis for recovery under modern tort law. See Prosser & Keeton. But under the Court's reasoning, this conduct may violate the Fourth Amendment. By contrast, if long-term monitoring can be accomplished without committing a technical trespass—suppose, for example, that the Federal Government required or per-suaded auto manufacturers to include a GPS tracking device in every car—the Court's theory would provide no protection.

Second, the Court's approach leads to incongruous results. If the police attach a GPS device to a car and use the device to follow the car for even a brief time, under the Court's theory, the Fourth Amendment applies. But if the police follow the same car for a much longer period using unmarked cars and aerial assistance, this tracking is not subject to any Fourth Amendment constraints.

In the present case, the Fourth Amendment applies, the Court concludes, because the officers installed the GPS device after respondent's wife, to whom the car was registered, turned it over to respondent for his exclusive use. But if the GPS had been attached prior to that time, the Court's theory would lead to a different result. The Court proceeds on the assumption that respondent "had at least the property rights of a bailee," but a bailee may sue for a trespass to chattel only if the injury occurs during the term of the bailment. So if the GPS device had been installed before respondent's wife gave him the keys, respondent would have no claim for trespass—and, presumably, no Fourth Amendment claim either.

Third, under the Court's theory, the coverage of the Fourth Amendment may vary from State to State. If the events at issue here had occurred in a community property State or a State that has adopted the Uniform Marital Property Act, respondent would likely be an owner of the vehicle, and it would not matter whether the GPS was installed before or after his wife turned over the keys. In non-community-property States, on the other hand, the regis-tration of the vehicle in the name of respondent's wife would generally be regarded as presumptive evidence that she was the sole owner

Fourth, the Court's reliance on the law of trespass will present particularly vexing problems in cases involving surveillance that is carried out by making electronic, as opposed to physical, contact with the item to be tracked. For example, suppose that the officers in the present case had followed respondent by surreptitiously activating a stolen vehicle detection system that came with the car when it was purchased. Would the sending of a radio signal to activate this system constitute a trespass to chattels? Trespass to chattels has traditionally required a physical touching of the property. See Restatement (Second) of Torts § 217 and Comment *e* (1963 and 1964). In recent years, courts have wrestled with the application of this old tort in cases involving unwanted electronic contact with computer systems, and some have held that even the transmission of electrons that occurs when a communication is sent from one computer to another is enough. But may such decisions be followed in applying the Court's trespass theory? Assuming that what matters under the Court's theory is the law of trespass as it existed at the time of the adoption of the Fourth Amendment, do these recent decisions represent a change in the law or simply the application of the old tort to new situations?

IV

A

The *Katz* expectation-of-privacy test avoids the problems and complications noted above, but it is not without its own difficulties. It involves a degree of circularity, see *Kyllo*, and judges are apt to confuse their own expectations of privacy with those of the hypothetical reasonable person to which the *Katz* test looks. See *Minnesota v. Carter* (Scalia, J., concurring). In addition, the *Katz* test rests on the assumption that this hypothetical reasonable person has a well-developed and stable set of privacy expectations. But technology can change those expectations. Dramatic technological change may lead to periods in which popular expectations are in flux and may ultimately produce significant changes in popular attitudes. New technology may provide increased convenience or security at the expense of privacy, and many people may find the tradeoff worthwhile. And even if the public does not welcome the diminution of privacy that new technology entails, they may eventually reconcile themselves to this development as inevitable.

On the other hand, concern about new intrusions on privacy may spur the enactment of legislation to protect against these intrusions. This is what ultimately happened with respect to wiretapping. After *Katz*, Congress did not leave it to the courts to develop a body of Fourth Amendment case law governing that complex subject. Instead, Congress promptly enacted a comprehensive statute, see 18 U.S.C. §§ 2510-2522 (2006 ed. and Supp. IV), and since that time, the regulation of wiretapping has been governed primarily by statute and not by case law.[7] In an ironic sense, although *Katz* overruled *Olmstead*,

---

7. See Kerr, The Fourth Amendment and New Technologies: Constitutional Myths and the Case for Caution, 102 Mich. L. Rev. 801, 850-851 (2004) (hereinafter Kerr).

Chief Justice Taft's suggestion in the latter case that the regulation of wiretapping was a matter better left for Congress has been borne out.

B

Recent years have seen the emergence of many new devices that permit the monitoring of a person's movements. In some locales, closed-circuit television video monitoring is becoming ubiquitous. On toll roads, automatic toll collection systems create a precise record of the movements of motorists who choose to make use of that convenience. Many motorists purchase cars that are equipped with devices that permit a central station to ascertain the car's location at any time so that roadside assistance may be provided if needed and the car may be found if it is stolen.

Perhaps most significant, cell phones and other wireless devices now permit wireless carriers to track and record the location of users—and as of June 2011, it has been reported, there were more than 322 million wireless devices in use in the United States. For older phones, the accuracy of the location information depends on the density of the tower network, but new "smart phones," which are equipped with a GPS device, permit more precise tracking. For example, when a user activates the GPS on such a phone, a provider is able to monitor the phone's location and speed of movement and can then report back real-time traffic conditions after combining ("crowdsourcing") the speed of all such phones on any particular road. Similarly, phone-location-tracking services are offered as "social" tools, allowing consumers to find (or to avoid) others who enroll in these services. The availability and use of these and other new devices will continue to shape the average person's expectations about the privacy of his or her daily movements.

V

In the pre-computer age, the greatest protections of privacy were neither constitutional nor statutory, but practical. Traditional surveillance for any extended period of time was difficult and costly and therefore rarely undertaken. The surveillance at issue in this case—constant monitoring of the location of a vehicle for four weeks—would have required a large team of agents, multiple vehicles, and perhaps aerial assistance.[10] Only an investigation of unusual importance could have justified such an expenditure of law enforcement resources. Devices like the one used in the present case, however, make long-term monitoring relatively easy and cheap. In circumstances involving dramatic technological change, the best solution to privacy concerns may be legislative. See, *e.g.*, Kerr, 102 Mich. L. Rev., at 805-806. A legislative body is

---

10. Even with a radio transmitter like those used in *United States v. Knotts* or *United States v. Karo*, such long-term surveillance would have been exceptionally demanding. The beepers used in those cases merely "emit[ted] periodic signals that [could] be picked up by a radio receiver." The signal had a limited range and could be lost if the police did not stay close enough. Indeed, in *Knotts* itself, officers lost the signal from the beeper, and only "with the assistance of a monitoring device located in a helicopter [was] the approximate location of the signal . . . picked up again about one hour later."

well situated to gauge changing public attitudes, to draw detailed lines, and to balance privacy and public safety in a comprehensive way.

To date, however, Congress and most States have not enacted statutes regulating the use of GPS tracking technology for law enforcement purposes. The best that we can do in this case is to apply existing Fourth Amendment doctrine and to ask whether the use of GPS tracking in a particular case involved a degree of intrusion that a reasonable person would not have anticipated.

Under this approach, relatively short-term monitoring of a person's movements on public streets accords with expectations of privacy that our society has recognized as reasonable. See *Knotts*. But the use of longer term GPS monitoring in investigations of most offenses impinges on expectations of privacy. For such offenses, society's expectation has been that law enforcement agents and others would not—and indeed, in the main, simply could not secretly monitor and catalogue every single movement of an individual's car for a very long period. In this case, for four weeks, law enforcement agents tracked every movement that respondent made in the vehicle he was driving. We need not identify with precision the point at which the tracking of this vehicle became a search, for the line was surely crossed before the 4-week mark. Other cases may present more difficult questions. But where uncertainty exists with respect to whether a certain period of GPS surveillance is long enough to constitute a Fourth Amendment search, the police may always seek a warrant. We also need not consider whether prolonged GPS monitoring in the context of investigations involving extraordinary offenses would similarly intrude on a constitutionally protected sphere of privacy. In such cases, long-term tracking might have been mounted using previously available techniques.

For these reasons, I conclude that the lengthy monitoring that occurred in this case constituted a search under the Fourth Amendment. I therefore agree with the majority that the decision of the Court of Appeals must be affirmed.

2. Area Considerations

Oliver v. United States

466 U.S. 170 (1984)

POWELL, J., delivered the opinion of the Court, in which BURGER, C.J., BLACKMUN, REHNQUIST, and O'CONNOR, JJ., joined. WHITE, J., filed an opinion concurring in part and concurring in the judgment. MARSHALL, J., filed a dissenting opinion, in which BRENNAN and STEVENS, JJ., joined.

The "open fields" doctrine, first enunciated by this Court in *Hester v. United States* (1924), permits police officers to enter and search a field without a warrant. We granted certiorari in these cases to clarify confusion that has arisen as to the continued vitality of the doctrine....

Acting on reports that marihuana was being raised on the farm of petitioner Oliver, two narcotics agents of the Kentucky State Police went to the farm to investigate. Arriving at the farm, they drove past petitioner's house to a locked gate with a "No Trespassing" sign. A footpath led around one side of the gate. The agents walked around the gate and along the road for several hundred yards, passing a barn and a parked camper. At that point, someone standing in front of the camper shouted: "No hunting is allowed, come back up here." The officers shouted back that they were Kentucky State Police officers, but found no one when they returned to the camper. The officers resumed their investigation of the farm and found a field of marihuana over a mile from petitioner's home.

Petitioner was arrested and indicted for "manufactur[ing]" a "controlled substance." After a pretrial hearing, the District Court suppressed evidence of the discovery of the marihuana field. Applying *Katz v. United States* (1967), the court found that petitioner had a reasonable expectation that the field would remain private because petitioner "had done all that could be expected of him to assert his privacy in the area of farm that was searched." He had posted "No Trespassing" signs at regular intervals and had locked the gate at the entrance to the center of the farm. Further, the court noted that the field itself is highly secluded: it is bounded on all sides by woods, fences, and embankments and cannot be seen from any point of public access. The court concluded that this was not an "open" field that invited casual intrusion.

The Court of Appeals for the Sixth Circuit, sitting en banc, reversed the District Court. The court concluded that *Katz*, upon which the District Court relied, had not impaired the vitality of the open fields doctrine of *Hester*. Rather, the open fields doctrine was entirely compatible with *Katz'* emphasis on privacy. The court reasoned that the "human relations that create the need for privacy do not ordinarily take place" in open fields, and that the property owner's common-law right to exclude trespassers is insufficiently linked to privacy to warrant the Fourth Amendment's protection. . . .

The rule announced in *Hester v. United States* was founded upon the explicit language of the Fourth Amendment. That Amendment indicates with some precision the places and things encompassed by its protections. As Justice Holmes explained for the Court in his characteristically laconic style: "[T]he special protection accorded by the Fourth Amendment to the people in their 'persons, houses, papers, and effects,' is not extended to the open fields. The distinction between the latter and the house is as old as the common law."

Nor are the open fields "effects" within the meaning of the Fourth Amendment. In this respect, it is suggestive that James Madison's proposed draft of what became the Fourth Amendment preserves "[t]he rights of the people to be secured in their persons, their houses, their papers, and their other property, from all unreasonable searches and seizures. . . ." See N. Lasson, The History and Development of the Fourth Amendment to the United States Constitution 100, n.77 (1937). Although Congress' revisions of Madison's proposal broadened the scope of the Amendment in some respects, the term "effects" is less inclusive than "property" and cannot be said to encompass open fields. We conclude, as did the Court in deciding *Hester v. United States*, that the government's intrusion upon the open fields is not one of those "unreasonable searches" proscribed by the text of the Fourth Amendment.

This interpretation of the Fourth Amendment's language is consistent with the understanding of the right to privacy expressed in our Fourth Amendment jurisprudence. Since *Katz*, the touchstone of Amendment analysis has been the question whether a person has a "constitutionally protected reasonable expectation of privacy." The Amendment does not protect the merely subjective expectation of privacy, but only those "expectation[s] that society is prepared to recognize as 'reasonable.'" . . .

No single factor determines whether an individual legitimately may claim under the Fourth Amendment that a place should be free of government intrusion not authorized by warrant. In assessing the degree to which a search infringes upon individual privacy, the Court has given weight to such factors as the intention of the Framers of the Fourth Amendment, e.g., the uses to which the individual has put a location . . . and our societal understanding that certain areas deserve the most scrupulous protection from government invasion. These factors are equally relevant to determining whether the government's intrusion upon open fields without a warrant or probable cause violates reasonable expectations of privacy and is therefore a search proscribed by the Amendment.

In this light, the rule of *Hester v. United States*, supra, that we reaffirm today, may be understood as providing that an individual may not legitimately demand privacy for activities conducted out of doors in fields, except in the area immediately surrounding the home. This rule is true to the conception of the right to privacy embodied in the Fourth Amendment. The Amendment reflects the recognition of the Framers that certain enclaves should be free from arbitrary government interference. For example, the Court since the enactment of the Fourth Amendment has stressed "the overriding respect for the sanctity of the home that has been embedded in our traditions since the origins of the Republic." *Payton v. New York* (1980).

In contrast, open fields do not provide the setting for those intimate activities that the Amendment is intended to shelter from government interference or surveillance. There is no societal interest in protecting the privacy of those activities, such as the cultivation of crops, that occur in open fields. Moreover, as a practical matter these lands usually are accessible to the public and the police in ways that a home, an office, or commercial structure would not be. It is not generally true that fences or "No Trespassing" signs effectively bar the public from viewing open fields in rural areas. And both petitioner Oliver and respondent Thornton concede that the public and police lawfully may survey lands from the air. For these reasons, the asserted expectation of privacy in open fields is not an expectation that "society recognizes as reasonable." . . .

We conclude, from the text of the Fourth Amendment and from the historical and contemporary understanding of its purposes, that an individual has no legitimate expectation that open fields will remain free from warrantless intrusion by government officers.

■ ■ ■

Nor is the government's intrusion upon an open field a "search" in the constitutional sense because that intrusion is a trespass at common law. The existence of a property right is but one element in determining whether expectations of privacy are legitimate. "'The premise that property interests control the right of the Government to search and seize has been discredited.'" *Katz.* "[E]ven a property interest in premises may not be sufficient to establish a legitimate expectation of privacy with respect to particular items located on the premises or activity conducted thereon." *Rakas v. Illinois* (1978).

The common law may guide consideration of what areas are protected by the Fourth Amendment by defining areas whose invasion by others is wrongful. The law of trespass, however, forbids intrusions upon land that the Fourth Amendment would not proscribe. For trespass law extends to instances where the exercise of the right to exclude vindicates no legitimate privacy interest. Thus, in the case of open fields, the general rights of property protected by the common law of trespass have little or no relevance to the applicability of the Fourth Amendment.

We conclude that the open fields doctrine, as enunciated in *Hester*, is consistent with the plain language of the Fourth Amendment and its historical purposes. Moreover, Justice Holmes' interpretation of the Amendment in *Hester* accords with the "reasonable expectation of privacy" analysis developed in subsequent decisions of this Court. We therefore affirm. . . .

It is so ordered.

Justice MARSHALL, with whom Justice BRENNAN and Justice STEVENS join, dissenting.

In each of these consolidated cases, police officers, ignoring clearly visible "No Trespassing" signs, entered upon private land in search of evidence of a crime. At a spot that could not be seen from any vantage point accessible to the public, the police discovered contraband, which was subsequently used to incriminate the owner of the land. In neither case did the police have a warrant authorizing their activities.

The Court holds that police conduct of this sort does not constitute an "unreasonable search" within the meaning of the Fourth Amendment. The Court reaches that startling conclusion by two independent analytical routes. First, the Court argues that, because the Fourth Amendment by its terms renders people secure in their "persons, houses, papers, and effects," it is inapplicable to trespasses upon land not lying within the curtilage of a dwelling. Second, the Court contends that "an individual may not legitimately demand privacy for activities conducted out of doors in fields, except in the area immediately surrounding the home." Because I cannot agree with either of these propositions, I dissent. . . .

Indeed, the Court's reading of the plain language of the Fourth Amendment is incapable of explaining even its own holding in this case. The Court rules that the curtilage, a zone of real property surrounding a dwelling, is entitled to constitutional protection. We are not told, however, whether the curtilage is a "house" or an "effect"—or why, if the curtilage can be incorporated into the list of things and spaces shielded by the Amendment, a field cannot.

The Court's inability to reconcile its parsimonious reading of the phrase "persons, houses, papers, and effects" with our prior decisions or even its own holding is a symptom of a more fundamental infirmity in the Court's reasoning. The Fourth Amendment, like the other central provisions of the Bill of Rights that loom large in our modern jurisprudence, was designed, not to prescribe with "precision" permissible and impermissible activities, but to identify a fundamental human liberty that should be shielded forever from government intrusion. We do not construe constitutional provisions of this sort the way we do statutes, whose drafters can be expected to indicate with some comprehensiveness and exactitude the conduct they wish to forbid or control and to change those prescriptions when they become obsolete. Rather, we strive, when interpreting these seminal constitutional provisions, to effectuate their purposes—to lend them meanings that ensure that the liberties the Framers sought to protect are not undermined by the changing activities of government officials. . . .

The second ground for the Court's decision is its contention that any interest a landowner might have in the privacy of his woods and fields is not one that "society is prepared to recognize as 'reasonable.'" The mode of analysis that underlies this assertion is certainly more consistent with our prior decisions than that discussed above. But the Court's conclusion cannot withstand scrutiny.

As the Court acknowledges, we have traditionally looked to a variety of factors in determining whether an expectation of privacy asserted in a physical space is "reasonable." Though those factors do not lend themselves to precise taxonomy, they may be roughly grouped into three categories. First, we consider whether the expectation at issue is rooted in entitlements defined by positive law. Second, we consider the nature of the uses to which spaces of the sort in question can be put. Third, we consider whether the person claiming a privacy interest manifested that interest to the public in a way that most people would understand and respect. When the expectations of privacy asserted by petitioner Oliver and respondent Thornton are examined through these lenses, it becomes clear that those expectations are entitled to constitutional protection. . . .

It is undisputed that Oliver and Thornton each owned the land into which the police intruded. That fact alone provides considerable support for their assertion of legitimate privacy interests in their woods and fields. But even more telling is the nature of the sanctions that Oliver and Thornton could invoke, under local law, for violation of their property rights. In Kentucky, a knowing entry upon fenced or otherwise enclosed land, or upon unenclosed land conspicuously posted with signs excluding the public, constitutes criminal trespass. . . .

Privately owned woods and fields that are not exposed to public view regularly are employed in a variety of ways that society acknowledges deserve privacy. Many landowners like to take solitary walks on their property, confident that they will not be confronted in their rambles by strangers or policemen. Others conduct agricultural businesses on their property. Some landowners use their secluded spaces to meet lovers, others to gather together with fellow worshippers, still others to engage in sustained creative endeavor. Private land is sometimes used as a refuge for wildlife, where flora and fauna are protected from human intervention of any kind. Our respect for the freedom of landowners to use their posted "open fields" in ways such as these partially explains the seriousness with which the positive law regards deliberate invasions of such spaces, see supra, and substantially reinforces the landowners' contention that their expectations of privacy are "reasonable."

Whether a person "took normal precautions to maintain his privacy" in a given space affects whether his interest is one protected by the Fourth Amendment. The reason why such precautions are relevant is that we do not insist that a person who has a right to exclude others exercise that right. A claim to privacy is therefore strengthened by the fact that the claimant somehow manifested to other people his desire that they keep their distance.

Certain spaces are so presumptively private that signals of this sort are unnecessary; a homeowner need not post a "Do Not Enter" sign on his door in order to deny entrance to uninvited guests. Privacy interests in other spaces are more ambiguous, and the taking of precautions is consequently more important; placing a lock on one's footlocker strengthens one's claim that an examination of its contents is impermissible. Still other spaces are, by positive law and social convention, presumed accessible to members of the public unless the owner manifests his intention to exclude them.

Undeveloped land falls into the last-mentioned category. If a person has not marked the boundaries of his fields or woods in a way that informs passersby that they are not welcome, he cannot object if members of the public enter onto the property. There is no reason why he should have any greater rights as against government officials. Accordingly, we have held that an official may, without a warrant, enter private land from which the public is not excluded and make observations from that vantage point. . . .

A very different case is presented when the owner of undeveloped land has taken precautions to exclude the public. As indicated above, a deliberate entry by a private citizen onto private property marked with "No Trespassing" signs will expose him to criminal liability. I see no reason why a government official should not be obliged to respect such unequivocal and universally understood manifestations of a landowner's desire for privacy. . . .

A clear, easily administrable rule emerges from the analysis set forth above: Private land marked in a fashion sufficient to render entry thereon a criminal trespass under the law of the State in which the land lies is protected by the Fourth Amendment's proscription of unreasonable searches and seizures. One of the advantages of the foregoing rule is that it draws upon a doctrine already familiar to both citizens and government officials. In each jurisdiction, a substantial body of statutory and case law defines the precautions a landowner must take in order to avail himself of the sanctions of the criminal law. The police know that body of law, because they are entrusted with responsibility for enforcing it against the public; it therefore would not be difficult for the police to abide by it themselves.

By contrast, the doctrine announced by the Court today is incapable of determinate application. Police officers, making warrantless entries upon private land, will be obliged in the future to make on-the-spot judgments as to how far the curtilage extends, and to stay outside that zone. In addition, we may expect to see a spate of litigation over the question of how much improvement is necessary to remove private land from the category of "unoccupied or undeveloped area" to which the "open fields exception" is now deemed applicable. . . .

The Fourth Amendment, properly construed, embodies and gives effect to our collective sense of the degree to which men and women, in civilized society, are entitled "to be let alone" by their governments. The Court's opinion bespeaks and will help to promote an impoverished vision of that fundamental right.

I dissent.

3. Third Party

Hoffa v. United States

385 U.S. 293 (1966)

STEWART, J. delivered the opinion of the Court, in which BLACK, BRENNAN, CLARK, WHITE, FORTAS, and HARLAN, JJ., joined. DOUGLAS filed a concurring opinion (found in *Osborn v. United States*). WARREN, C.J., filed a dissenting opinion.

Over a period of several weeks in the late autumn of 1962 there took place in a federal court in Nashville, Tennessee, a trial by jury in which James Hoffa was charged with violating a provision of the Taft-Hartley Act. That trial, known in the present record as the Test Fleet trial, ended with a hung jury. The petitioners now before us—James Hoffa, Thomas Parks, Larry Campbell, and Ewing King—were tried and convicted in 1964 for endeavoring to bribe members of that jury. The convictions were affirmed by the Court of Appeals. A substantial element in the Government's proof that led to the convictions of these four petitioners was contributed by a witness named Edward Partin, who testified to several incriminating statements which he said petitioners Hoffa and King had made in his presence during the course of the Test Fleet trial. Our grant of certiorari was limited to the single issue of whether the Government's use in this case of evidence supplied by Partin operated to invalidate these convictions.

The specific question before us, as framed by counsel for the petitioners, is this:

> "Whether evidence obtained by the Government by means of deceptively placing a secret informer in the quarters and councils of a defendant during one criminal trial so violates the defendant's Fourth, Fifth and Sixth Amendment rights that suppression of such evidence is required in a subsequent trial of the same defendant on a different charge." . . .

The controlling facts can be briefly stated. The Test Fleet trial, in which James Hoffa was the sole individual defendant, was in progress between October 22 and December 23, 1962, in Nashville, Tennessee. James Hoffa was president of the International Brotherhood of Teamsters. During the course of the trial he occupied a three-room suite in the Andrew Jackson Hotel in Nashville. One of his constant companions throughout the trial was the petitioner King, president of the Nashville local of the Teamsters Union. Edward Partin, a resident of Baton Rouge, Louisiana, and a local Teamsters Union official there, made repeated visits to Nashville during the period of the trial. On these visits he frequented the Hoffa hotel suite, and was continually in the company of Hoffa and his associates, including King, in and around the hotel suite, the hotel lobby, the courthouse, and elsewhere in Nashville. During this period Partin made frequent reports to a federal agent named Sheridan concerning conversations he said Hoffa and King had had with him and with each other, disclosing endeavors to bribe members of the Test Fleet jury. Partin's reports and his subsequent testimony at the petitioners' trial unquestionably contributed, directly or indirectly, to the convictions of all four of the petitioners.

The chain of circumstances which led Partin to be in Nashville during the Test Fleet trial extended back at least to September of 1962. At that time Partin was in jail in Baton Rouge on a state criminal charge. He was also under a federal indictment for embezzling union funds, and other indictments for state offenses were pending against him. Between that time and Partin's initial visit to Nashville on October 22 he was released on bail on the state criminal charge, and proceedings under the federal indictment were postponed. On October 8, Partin telephoned Hoffa in Washington, D.C., to discuss local union matters and Partin's difficulties with the authorities. In the course of this conversation Partin asked if he could see Hoffa to confer about these problems, and Hoffa acquiesced. Partin again called Hoffa on October 18 and arranged to meet him in Nashville. During this period Partin also consulted on several occasions with federal law enforcement agents, who told him that Hoffa might attempt to tamper with the Test Fleet jury, and asked him to be on the lookout in Nashville for such attempts and to report to the federal authorities any evidence of wrongdoing that he discovered. Partin agreed to do so.

After the Test Fleet trial was completed, Partin's wife received four monthly installment payments of $300 from government funds, and the state and federal charges against Partin were either dropped or not actively pursued. . . .

■ ■ ■

It is contended that only by violating the petitioner's rights under the Fourth Amendment was Partin able to hear the petitioner's incriminating statements in the hotel suite, and that Partin's testimony was therefore inadmissible under the exclusionary rule. . . . The argument is that Partin's failure to disclose his role as a government informer vitiated the consent that the petitioner gave to Partin's repeated entries into the suite, and that by listening to the petitioner's statements Partin conducted an illegal "search" for verbal evidence.

The preliminary steps of this argument are on solid ground. A hotel room can clearly be the object of Fourth Amendment protection as much as a home or an office. The Fourth Amendment can certainly be violated by guileful as well as by forcible intrusions into a constitutionally protected area. And the protections of the Fourth Amendment are surely not limited to tangibles, but can extend as well to oral statements.

Where the argument falls is in its misapprehension of the fundamental nature and scope of Fourth Amendment protection. What the Fourth Amendment protects is the security a man relies upon when he places himself or his property within a constitutionally protected area, be it his home or his office, his hotel room or his automobile. There he is protected from unwarranted governmental intrusion. And when he puts something in his filing cabinet, in his desk drawer, or in his pocket, he has the right to know it will be secure from an unreasonable search or an unreasonable seizure. So it was that the Fourth Amendment could not tolerate the warrantless search of the hotel room in *Jeffers* (1951), the purloining of the petitioner's private papers in *Gouled* (1921), or the surreptitious electronic surveillance in *Silverman* (1961). Countless other cases which have come to this Court over the years have involved a myriad of differing factual contexts in which the protections of the Fourth Amendment have been appropriately invoked. No doubt the future will bring countless others. By nothing we say here do we either foresee or foreclose factual situations to which the Fourth Amendment may be applicable.

In the present case, however, it is evident that no interest legitimately protected by the Fourth Amendment is involved. It is obvious that the petitioner was not relying on the security of his hotel suite when he made the incriminating statements to Partin or in Partin's presence. Partin did not enter the suite by force or by stealth. He was not a surreptitious eavesdropper. Partin was in the suite by invitation, and every conversation which he heard was either directed to him or knowingly carried on in his presence. The petitioner, in a word, was not relying on the security of the hotel room; he was relying upon his misplaced confidence that Partin would not reveal his wrongdoing. As counsel for the petitioner himself points out, some of the communications with Partin did not take place in the suite at all, but in the "hall of the hotel," in the "Andrew Jackson Hotel lobby," and "at the courthouse."

Neither this Court nor any member of it has ever expressed the view that the Fourth Amendment protects a wrongdoer's misplaced belief that a person to whom he voluntarily confides his wrongdoing will not reveal it. Indeed, the Court unanimously rejected that very contention less than four years ago. . . .

Affirmed.

Chief Justice WARREN, dissenting.

■ ■ ■

This type of informer and the uses to which he was put in this case evidence a serious potential for undermining the integrity of the truth-finding process in the federal courts. Given the incentives and background of Partin, no conviction should be allowed to stand when based heavily on his testimony. And that is exactly the quicksand upon which these convictions rest, because without Partin, who was the principal government witness, there would probably have been no convictions here. Thus, although petitioners make their main arguments on constitutional grounds and raise serious Fourth and Sixth Amendment questions, it should not even be necessary for the Court to reach those questions. For the affront to the quality and fairness of federal law enforcement which this case presents is sufficient to require an exercise of our supervisory powers. . . .

United States v. White

401 U.S. 745 (1971)

WHITE, J., announced the judgment of the Court and an opinion in which BURGER, C.J., STEWART and BLACKMUN, JJ., joined. BLACK, J. filed a statement concurring in the judgment. BRENNAN, J. filed an opinion concurring in the result. DOUGLAS, HARLAN, and MARSHALL, JJ., filed dissenting opinions.

In 1966, respondent James A. White was tried and convicted under two consolidated indictments charging various illegal transactions in narcotics. . . . He was fined and sentenced as a second offender to 25-year concurrent sentences. The issue before us is whether the Fourth Amendment bars from evidence the testimony of governmental agents who related certain conversations which had occurred between defendant White and a government informant, Harvey Jackson, and which the agents overheard by monitoring the frequency of a radio transmitter carried by Jackson and concealed on his person. On four occasions the conversations took place in Jackson's home; each of these conversations was overheard by an agent concealed in a kitchen closet with Jackson's consent and by a second agent outside the house using a radio receiver. Four other conversations—one in respondent's home, one in a restaurant, and two in Jackson's car—were overheard by the use of radio equipment. The prosecution was unable to locate and produce Jackson at the trial and the trial court overruled objections to the testimony of the agents who conducted the electronic surveillance. The jury returned a guilty verdict and defendant appealed. . . .

Until *Katz v. United States* [(1967)], neither wiretapping nor electronic eavesdropping violated a defendant's Fourth Amendment rights "unless there has been an official search and seizure of his person, or such a seizure of his papers or his tangible material effects, or an actual physical invasion of his house 'or curtilage' for the purpose of making a seizure." But where "eavesdropping was accomplished by means of an unauthorized physical penetration into the premises occupied" by the defendant, although falling short of a "technical trespass under the local property law," the Fourth Amendment was violated and any evidence of what was seen and heard, as well as tangible objects seized, was considered the inadmissible fruit of an unlawful invasion.

Katz v. United States, however, finally swept away doctrines that electronic eavesdropping is permissible under the Fourth Amendment unless physical invasion of a constitutionally protected area produced the challenged evidence. In that case government agents, without petitioner's consent or knowledge, attached a listening device to the outside of a public telephone booth and recorded the defendant's end of his telephone conversations. In declaring the recordings inadmissible in evidence in the absence of a warrant authorizing the surveillance, the Court overruled *Olmstead* [*v. United States* (1928)] and *Goldman* [*v. United States* (1942)] and held that the absence of physical intrusion into the telephone booth did not justify using electronic devices in listening to and recording Katz' words, thereby violating the privacy on which he justifiably relied while using the telephone in those circumstances.

The Court of Appeals understood *Katz* to render inadmissible against White the agents' testimony concerning conversations that Jackson broadcast to them. We cannot agree. *Katz* involved no revelation to the Government by a party to conversations with the defendant nor did the Court indicate in any way that a defendant has a justifiable and constitutionally protected expectation that a person with whom he is conversing will not then or later reveal the conversation to the police.

Hoffa v. United States (1966), which was left undisturbed by *Katz*, held that however strongly a defendant may trust an apparent colleague, his expectations in this respect are not protected by the Fourth Amendment when it turns out that the colleague is a government agent regularly communicating with the authorities. In these circumstances, "no interest legitimately protected by the Fourth Amendment is involved," for that amendment affords no protection to "a wrongdoer's misplaced belief that a person to whom he voluntarily confides his wrongdoing will not reveal it." No warrant to "search and seize" is required in such circumstances, nor is it when the Government sends to defendant's home a secret agent who conceals his identity and makes a purchase of narcotics from the accused, or when the same agent, unbeknown to the defendant, carries electronic equipment to record the defendant's words and the evidence so gathered is later offered in evidence. . . .

Our problem is not what the privacy expectations of particular defendants in particular situations may be or the extent to which they may in fact have relied on the discretion of their companions. Very probably, individual defendants neither know nor suspect that their colleagues have gone or will go to the police or are carrying recorders or transmitters. Otherwise, conversation would cease and our problem with these encounters would be nonexistent or far different from those now before us. Our problem, in terms of the principles announced in *Katz*, is what expectations of privacy are constitutionally "justifiable"—what expectations the Fourth Amendment will protect in the absence of a warrant. So far, the law permits the frustration of actual expectations of privacy by permitting authorities to use the testimony of those associates who for one reason or another have determined to turn to the police, as well as by authorizing the use of informants in the manner exemplified by *Hoffa*. If the law gives no protection to the wrongdoer whose trusted accomplice is or becomes a police agent, neither should it protect him when that same agent has recorded or transmitted the conversations which are later offered in evidence to prove the State's case.

Inescapably, one contemplating illegal activities must realize and risk that his companions may be reporting to the police. If he sufficiently doubts their trustworthiness, the association will very probably end or never materialize. But if he has no doubts, or allays them, or risks what doubt he has, the risk is his. In terms of what his course will be, what he will or will not do or say, we are unpersuaded that he would distinguish between probable informers on the one hand and probable informers with transmitters on the other. Given the possibility or probability that one of his colleagues is cooperating with the police, it is only speculation to assert that the defendant's utterances would be substantially different or his sense of security any less if he also thought it possible that the suspected colleague is wired for sound. At least there is no persuasive evidence that the difference in this respect between the electronically equipped and the unequipped agent is substantial enough to require discrete constitutional recognition, particularly under the Fourth Amendment which is ruled by fluid concepts of "reasonableness."

Nor should we be too ready to erect constitutional barriers to relevant and probative evidence which is also accurate and reliable. An electronic recording will many times produce a more reliable rendition of what a defendant has said than will the unaided memory of a police agent. It may also be that with the recording in existence it is less likely that the informant will change his mind, less chance that threat or injury will suppress unfavorable evidence and less chance that cross-examination will confound the testimony. Considerations like these obviously do not favor the defendant, but we are not prepared to hold that a defendant who has no constitutional right to exclude the informer's unaided testimony nevertheless has a Fourth Amendment privilege against a more accurate version of the events in question.

It is thus untenable to consider the activities and reports of the police agent himself, though acting without a warrant, to be a "reasonable" investigative effort and lawful under the Fourth Amendment but to view the same agent with a recorder or transmitter as conducting an "unreasonable" and unconstitutional search and seizure. . . .

The judgment of the Court of Appeals is reversed.

It is so ordered.

Justice HARLAN, dissenting. . . .

Before turning to matters of precedent and policy, several preliminary observations should be made. We deal here with the constitutional validity of instantaneous third-party electronic eavesdropping, conducted by federal law enforcement officers, without any prior judicial approval of the technique utilized, but with the consent and cooperation of a participant in the conversation, and where the substance of the matter electronically overheard is related in a federal criminal trial by those who eavesdropped as direct, not merely corroborative, evidence of the guilt of the nonconsenting party. The magnitude of the issue at hand is evidenced not simply by the obvious doctrinal difficulty of weighing such activity in the Fourth Amendment balance, but also, and more importantly, by the prevalence of police utilization of this technique. Professor Westin has documented in careful detail the numerous devices that make technologically feasible the Orwellian Big Brother. Of immediate relevance is his observation that "'participant recording,' in which one participant in a conversation or meeting, either a police officer or a co-operating party, wears a concealed device that records the conversation or broadcasts it to others nearby is used tens of thousands of times each year throughout the country, particularly in cases involving extortion, conspiracy, narcotics, gambling, prostitution, corruption by police officials and similar crimes." . . .

The impact of the practice of third-party bugging, must, I think, be considered such as to undermine that confidence and sense of security in dealing with one another that is characteristic of individual relationships between citizens in a free society. It goes beyond the impact on privacy occasioned by the ordinary type of "informer" investigation upheld in *Lewis* [*v. United States* (1966)] and *Hoffa*. The argument of the plurality opinion, to the effect that it is irrelevant whether secrets are revealed by the mere tattletale or the transistor, ignores the differences occasioned by third-party monitoring and recording which insures full and accurate disclosure of all that is said, free of the possibility of error and oversight that inheres in human reporting.

Authority is hardly required to support the proposition that words would be measured a good deal more carefully and communication inhibited if one suspected his conversations were being transmitted and transcribed. Were third-party bugging a prevalent practice, it might well smother that spontaneity—reflected in frivolous, impetuous, sacrilegious, and defiant discourse—that liberates daily life. Much offhand exchange is easily forgotten and one may count on the obscurity of his remarks, protected by the very fact of a limited audience, and the likelihood that the listener will either overlook or forget what is said, as well as the listener's inability to reformulate a conversation without having to contend with a documented record. All these values are sacrificed by a rule of law that permits official monitoring of private discourse limited only by the need to locate a willing assistant.

■ ■ ■

Finally, it is too easy to forget—and, hence, too often forgotten—that the issue here is whether to interpose a search warrant procedure between law enforcement agencies engaging in electronic eavesdropping and the public generally. By casting its "risk analysis" solely in terms of the expectations and risks that "wrongdoers" or "one contemplating illegal activities" ought to bear, the plurality opinion, I think, misses the mark entirely. *On Lee* [*v. United States* (1952)] does not simply mandate that criminals must daily run the risk of unknown eavesdroppers prying into their private affairs; it subjects each and every law-abiding member of society to that risk. The very purpose of interposing the Fourth Amendment warrant requirement is to redistribute the privacy risks throughout society in a way that produces the results the plurality opinion ascribes to the *On Lee* rule. Abolition of *On Lee* would not end electronic eavesdropping. It would prevent public officials from engaging in that practice unless they first had probable cause to suspect an individual of involvement in illegal activities and had tested their version of the facts before a detached judicial officer. The interest *On Lee* fails to protect is the expectation of the ordinary citizen, who has never engaged in illegal conduct in his life, that he may carry on his private discourse freely, openly, and spontaneously without measuring his every word against the connotations it might carry when instantaneously heard by others unknown to him and unfamiliar with his situation or analyzed in a cold, formal record played days, months, or years after the conversation. Interposition of a warrant requirement is designed not to shield "wrongdoers," but to secure a measure of privacy and a sense of personal security throughout our society.

The Fourth Amendment does, of course, leave room for the employment of modern technology in criminal law enforcement, but in the stream of current developments in Fourth Amendment law I think it must be held that third-party electronic monitoring, subject only to the self-restraint of law enforcement officials, has no place in our society. . . .

United States v. Miller

425 U.S. 435 (1976)

POWELL, J., delivered the opinion of the Court, in which BURGER, C.J., BLACKMUN, STEVENS, WHITE, REHNQUIST, and STEWART, JJ., joined. BRENNAN and MARSHALL, JJ., filed dissenting opinions.

Respondent was convicted of possessing an unregistered still, carrying on the business of a distiller without giving bond and with intent to defraud the Government of whiskey tax, possessing 175 gallons of whiskey upon which no taxes had been paid, and conspiring to defraud the United States of tax revenues. Prior to trial respondent moved to suppress copies of checks and other bank records obtained by means of allegedly defective subpoenas duces tecum served upon two banks at which he had accounts. The records had been maintained by the banks in compliance with the requirements of the Bank Secrecy Act, 12 U.S.C. § 1829b(d).

The District Court overruled respondent's motion to suppress, and the evidence was admitted. The Court of Appeals for the Fifth Circuit reversed on the ground that a depositor's Fourth Amendment rights are violated when bank records maintained pursuant to the Bank Secrecy Act are obtained by means of a defective subpoena. It held that any evidence so obtained must be suppressed. Since we find that respondent had no protectable Fourth Amendment interest in the subpoenaed documents, we reverse the decision below. . . .

On December 18, 1972, in response to an informant's tip, a deputy sheriff from Houston County, Ga., stopped a van-type truck occupied by two of respondent's alleged co-conspirators. The truck contained distillery apparatus and raw material. On January 9, 1973, a fire broke out in a Kathleen, Ga., warehouse rented to respondent. During the blaze firemen and sheriff department officials discovered a 7,500-gallon-capacity distillery, 175 gallons of nontax-paid whiskey, and related paraphernalia.

Two weeks later agents from the Treasury Department's Alcohol, Tobacco and Firearms Bureau presented grand jury subpoenas issued in blank by the clerk of the District Court, and completed by the United States Attorney's office, to the presidents of the Citizens & Southern National Bank of Warner Robins and the Bank of Byron, where respondent maintained accounts. The subpoenas required the two presidents to appear on January 24, 1973, and to produce

> "all records of accounts, *i.e.*, savings, checking, loan or otherwise, in the name of Mr. Mitch Miller (respondent), 3859 Mathis Street, Macon, Ga. and/or Mitch Miller Associates, 100 Executive Terrace, Warner Robins, Ga., from October, 1972, through the present date (January 22, 1973, in the case of the Bank of Byron, and January 23, 1973, in the case of the Citizens & Southern National Bank of Warner Robins)."

The banks did not advise respondent that the subpoenas had been served but ordered their employees to make the records available and to provide copies of any documents the agents desired. At the Bank of Byron, an agent was shown microfilm records of the relevant account and provided with copies of one deposit slip and one or two checks. At the Citizens & Southern National Bank microfilm records also were shown to the agent, and he was given copies of the records of respondent's account during the applicable period. These included all checks, deposit slips, two financial statements, and three monthly statements. The bank presidents were then told that it would not be necessary to appear in person before the grand jury. . . .

We find that there was no intrusion into any area in which respondent had a protected Fourth Amendment interest and that the District Court therefore correctly denied respondent's motion to suppress. Because we reverse the decision of the Court of Appeals on that ground alone, we do not reach the Government's latter two contentions. . . .

On their face, the documents subpoenaed here are not respondent's "private papers." Unlike the claimant in *Boyd* [*v. United States* (1886)], respondent can assert neither ownership nor possession. Instead, these are the business records of the banks. . . .

Respondent argues, however, that the Bank Secrecy Act introduces a factor that makes the subpoena in this case the functional equivalent of a search and seizure of the depositor's "private papers." We have held, in *California Bankers Assn. v. Shultz* (1974), that the mere maintenance of records pursuant to the requirements of the Act "invade[s] no Fourth Amendment right of any depositor." But respondent contends that the combination of the recordkeeping requirements of the Act and the issuance of a subpoena to obtain those records permits the Government to circumvent the requirements of the Fourth Amendment by allowing it to obtain a depositor's private records without complying with the legal requirements that would be applicable had it proceeded against him directly. Therefore, we must address the question whether the compulsion embodied in the Bank Secrecy Act as exercised in this case creates a Fourth Amendment interest in the depositor where none existed before. . . .

Respondent urges that he has a Fourth Amendment interest in the records kept by the banks because they are merely copies of personal records that were made available to the banks for a limited purpose and in which he has a reasonable expectation of privacy. He relies on this Court's statement in *Katz v. United States* (1967) . . . that "we have . . . departed from the narrow view" that "'property interests control the right of the Government to search and seize,'" and that a "search and seizure" become unreasonable when the Government's activities violate "the privacy upon which [a person] justifiably relie[s]." But in *Katz* the Court also stressed that "[w]hat a person knowingly exposes to the public . . . is not a subject of Fourth Amendment protection." We must examine the nature of the particular documents sought to be protected in order to determine whether there is a legitimate "expectation of privacy" concerning their contents.

Even if we direct our attention to the original checks and deposit slips, rather than to the microfilm copies actually viewed and obtained by means of the subpoena, we perceive no legitimate "expectation of privacy" in their contents. The checks are not confidential communications but negotiable instruments to be used in commercial transactions. All of the documents obtained, including financial statements and deposit slips, contain only information voluntarily conveyed to the banks and exposed to their employees in the ordinary course of business. The lack of any legitimate expectation of privacy concerning the information kept in bank records was assumed by Congress in enacting the Bank Secrecy Act, the expressed purpose of which is to require records to be maintained because they "have a high degree of usefulness in criminal tax, and regulatory investigations and proceedings."

The depositor takes the risk, in revealing his affairs to another, that the information will be conveyed by that person to the Government. *United States v. White* (1971). This Court has held repeatedly that the Fourth Amendment does not prohibit the obtaining of information revealed to a third party and conveyed by him to Government authorities, even if the information is revealed on the assumption that it will be used only for a limited purpose and the confidence placed in the third party will not be betrayed....

Since no Fourth Amendment interests of the depositor are implicated here, this case is governed by the general rule that the issuance of a subpoena to a third party to obtain the records of that party does not violate the rights of a defendant, even if a criminal prosecution is contemplated at the time the subpoena is issued....

The judgment of the Court of Appeals is reversed. The court deferred decision on whether the trial court had improperly overruled respondent's motion to suppress distillery apparatus and raw material seized from a rented truck. We remand for disposition of that issue.

So ordered.

Justice BRENNAN, dissenting.

The pertinent phrasing of the Fourth Amendment "The right of the people to be secure in their persons, houses, papers, and effects, against unreasonable searches and seizures, shall not be violated" is virtually in haec verba as Art. I, § 19, of the California Constitution "The right of the people to be secure in their persons, houses, papers, and effects, against unreasonable seizures and searches, shall not be violated." The California Supreme Court has reached a conclusion under Art. I, § 13, in the same factual situation, contrary to that reached by the Court today under the Fourth Amendment. I dissent because in my view the California Supreme Court correctly interpreted the relevant constitutional language....

> "The underlying dilemma in this and related cases is that the bank, a detached and disinterested entity, relinquished the records voluntarily. But that circumstance should not be crucial. For all practical purposes, the disclosure by individuals or business firms of their financial affairs to a bank is not entirely volitional, since it is impossible to participate in the economic life of contemporary society without maintaining a bank account. In the course of such dealings, a depositor reveals many aspects of his personal affairs, opinions, habits and associations. Indeed, the totality of bank records provides a virtual current biography. While we are concerned in the present case only with bank statements, the logical extension of the contention that the bank's ownership of records permits free access to them by any police officer extends far beyond such statements to checks, savings, bonds, loan applications, loan guarantees, and all papers which the customer has supplied to the bank to facilitate the conduct of his financial affairs upon the reasonable assumption that the information would remain confidential. To permit a police officer access to these records merely upon his request, without any judicial control as to relevancy or other traditional requirements

of legal process, and to allow the evidence to be used in any subsequent criminal prosecution against a defendant, opens the door to a vast and unlimited range of very real abuses of police power...."

I would therefore affirm the judgment of the Court of Appeals. I add only that *Burrows [v. Superior Court* (1974)] strikingly illustrates the emerging trend among high state courts of relying upon state constitutional protections of individual liberties—protections pervading counterpart provisions of the United States Constitution, but increasingly being ignored by decisions of this Court....

California v. Greenwood

486 U.S. 35 (1988)

WHITE, J., delivered the opinion of the Court, in which REHNQUIST, C.J., and BLACKMUN, STEVENS, O'CONNOR, and SCALIA, JJ., joined. BRENNAN, J., filed a dissenting opinion, in which MARSHALL, J., joined. Justice KENNEDY took no part in the consideration or decision of this case.

The issue here is whether the Fourth Amendment prohibits the warrantless search and seizure of garbage left for collection outside the curtilage of a home. We conclude, in accordance with the vast majority of lower courts that have addressed the issue, that it does not....

In early 1984, Investigator Jenny Stracner of the Laguna Beach Police Department received information indicating that respondent Greenwood might be engaged in narcotics trafficking. Stracner learned that a criminal suspect had informed a federal drug enforcement agent in February 1984 that a truck filled with illegal drugs was en route to the Laguna Beach address at which Greenwood resided. In addition, a neighbor complained of heavy vehicular traffic late at night in front of Greenwood's single-family home. The neighbor reported that the vehicles remained at Greenwood's house for only a few minutes.

Stracner sought to investigate this information by conducting a surveillance of Greenwood's home. She observed several vehicles make brief stops at the house during the late-night and early morning hours, and she followed a truck from the house to a residence that had previously been under investigation as a narcotics-trafficking location.

On April 6, 1984, Stracner asked the neighborhood's regular trash collector to pick up the plastic garbage bags that Greenwood had left on the curb in front of his house and to turn the bags over to her without mixing their contents with garbage from other houses. The trash collector cleaned his truck bin of other refuse, collected the garbage bags from the street in front of Greenwood's house, and turned the bags over to Stracner. The officer searched through the rubbish and found items indicative of narcotics use. She recited the information that she had gleaned from the trash search in an affidavit in support of a warrant to search Greenwood's home.

Police officers encountered both respondents at the house later that day when they arrived to execute the warrant. The police discovered quantities of cocaine and hashish during their search of the house. Respondents were arrested on felony narcotics charges. They subsequently posted bail.

The police continued to receive reports of many late-night visitors to the Greenwood house. On May 4, Investigator Robert Rahaeuser obtained Greenwood's garbage from the regular trash collector in the same manner as had Stracner. The garbage again contained evidence of narcotics use.

Rahaeuser secured another search warrant for Greenwood's home based on the information from the second trash search. The police found more narcotics and evidence of narcotics trafficking when they executed the warrant. Greenwood was again arrested.

The Superior Court dismissed the charges against respondents on the authority of *People v. Krivda* (1971), which held that warrantless trash searches violate the Fourth Amendment and the California Constitution. The court found that the police would not have had probable cause to search the Greenwood home without the evidence obtained from the trash searches.

The California Supreme Court denied the State's petition for review of the Court of Appeal's decision. We granted certiorari . . . and now reverse.

The warrantless search and seizure of the garbage bags left at the curb outside the Greenwood house would violate the Fourth Amendment only if respondents manifested a subjective expectation of privacy in their garbage that society accepts as objectively reasonable. . . .

They assert, however, that they had, and exhibited, an expectation of privacy with respect to the trash that was searched by the police: The trash, which was placed on the street for collection at a fixed time, was contained in opaque plastic bags, which the garbage collector was expected to pick up, mingle with the trash of others, and deposit at the garbage dump. The trash was only temporarily on the street, and there was little likelihood that it would be inspected by anyone.

It may well be that respondents did not expect that the contents of their garbage bags would become known to the police or other members of the public. An expectation of privacy does not give rise to Fourth Amendment protection, however, unless society is prepared to accept that expectation as objectively reasonable.

Here, we conclude that respondents exposed their garbage to the public sufficiently to defeat their claim to Fourth Amendment protection. It is common knowledge that plastic garbage bags left on or at the side of a public street are readily accessible to animals, children, scavengers, snoops, and other members of the public. Moreover, respondents placed their refuse at the curb for the express purpose of conveying it to a third party, the trash collector, who might himself have sorted through respondents' trash or permitted others, such as the police, to do so. Accordingly, having deposited their garbage "in an area particularly suited for public inspection and, in a manner of speaking, public consumption, for the express purpose of having strangers take it," respondents could have had no reasonable expectation of privacy in the inculpatory items that they discarded.

Furthermore, as we have held, the police cannot reasonably be expected to avert their eyes from evidence of criminal activity that could have been observed by any member of the public. Hence, "[w]hat a person knowingly exposes to the public, even in his own home or office, is not a subject of Fourth Amendment protection." *Katz v. United States* (1967). We held in *Smith v. Maryland* (1979), for example, that the police did not violate the Fourth Amendment by causing a pen register to be installed at the telephone company's offices to record the telephone numbers dialed by a criminal suspect. An individual has no legitimate expectation of privacy in the numbers dialed on his telephone, we reasoned, because he voluntarily conveys those numbers to the telephone company when he uses the telephone. Again, we observed that "a person has no legitimate expectation of privacy in information he voluntarily turns over to third parties."

Similarly, we held in *California v. Ciraolo* (1986), that the police were not required by the Fourth Amendment to obtain a warrant before conducting surveillance of the respondent's fenced backyard from a private plane flying at an altitude of 1,000 feet. We concluded that the respondent's expectation that his yard was protected from such surveillance was unreasonable because "[a]ny member of the public flying in this airspace who glanced down could have seen everything that these officers observed." . . .

We reject respondent Greenwood's alternative argument for affirmance: that his expectation of privacy in his garbage should be deemed reasonable as a matter of federal constitutional law because the warrantless search and seizure of his garbage was impermissible as a matter of California law. He urges that the state-law right of Californians to privacy in their garbage, announced by the California Supreme Court in *Krivda* . . . , survived the subsequent state constitutional amendment eliminating the suppression remedy as a means of enforcing that right. Hence, he argues that the Fourth Amendment should itself vindicate that right.

Individual States may surely construe their own constitutions as imposing more stringent constraints on police conduct than does the Federal Constitution. We have never intimated, however, that whether or not a search is reasonable within the meaning of the Fourth Amendment depends on the law of the particular State in which the search occurs. We have emphasized instead that the Fourth Amendment analysis must turn on such factors as "our *societal* understanding that certain areas deserve the most scrupulous protection from government invasion." We have already concluded that society as a whole possesses no such understanding with regard to garbage left for collection at the side of a public street. Respondent's argument is no less than a suggestion that concepts of privacy under the laws of each State are to determine the reach of the Fourth Amendment. We do not accept this submission. . . .

The judgment of the California Court of Appeal is therefore reversed, and this case is remanded for further proceedings not inconsistent with this opinion.

It is so ordered.

Justice BRENNAN, with whom Justice MARSHALL joins, dissenting.

Every week for two months, and at least once more a month later, the Laguna Beach police clawed through the trash that respondent Greenwood left in opaque, sealed bags on the curb outside his home. Complete strangers minutely scrutinized their bounty, undoubtedly dredging up intimate details of Greenwood's private life and habits. The intrusions proceeded without a warrant, and no court before or since has concluded that the police acted on probable cause to believe Greenwood was engaged in any criminal activity.

Scrutiny of another's trash is contrary to commonly accepted notions of civilized behavior. I suspect, therefore, that members of our society will be shocked to learn that the Court, the ultimate guarantor of liberty, deems unreasonable our expectation that the aspects of our private lives that are concealed safely in a trash bag will not become public.

■ ■ ■

"A container which can support a reasonable expectation of privacy may not be searched, even on probable cause, without a warrant." *United States v. Jacobsen* (1984). Thus, as the Court observes, if Greenwood had a reasonable expectation that the contents of the bags that he placed on the curb would remain private, the warrantless search of those bags violated the Fourth Amendment.

The Framers of the Fourth Amendment understood that "unreasonable searches" of "paper[s] and effects"—no less than "unreasonable searches" of "person[s] and houses"—infringe privacy. As early as 1878, this Court acknowledged that the contents of "[l]etters and sealed packages . . . in the mail are as fully guarded from examination and inspection . . . as if they were retained by the parties forwarding them in their own domiciles."

■ ■ ■

Respondents deserve no less protection just because Greenwood used the bags to discard rather than to transport his personal effects. Their contents are not inherently any less private, and Greenwood's decision to discard them, at least in the manner in which he did, does not diminish his expectation of privacy.

A trash bag, like any of the above-mentioned containers, "is a common repository for one's personal effects" and, even more than many of them, is "therefore . . . inevitably associated with the expectation of privacy." *Arkansas v. Sanders* (1979). . . . A single bag of trash testifies eloquently to the eating, reading, and recreational habits of the person who produced it. A search of trash, like a search of the bedroom, can relate intimate details about sexual practices, health, and personal hygiene. Like rifling through desk drawers or intercepting phone calls, rummaging through trash can divulge the target's financial and professional status, political affiliations and inclinations, private thoughts, personal relationships, and romantic interests. It cannot be doubted that a sealed trash bag harbors telling evidence of the "intimate activity associated with the 'sanctity of a man's home and the privacies of life,'" which the Fourth Amendment is designed to protect. *Oliver v. United States* (1984), quoting *Boyd v. United States* (1886).

■ ■ ■

When a tabloid reporter examined then-Secretary of State Henry Kissinger's trash and published his findings, Kissinger was "really revolted" by the intrusion and his wife suffered "grave anguish." The public response roundly condemning the reporter demonstrates that society not only recognized those reactions as reasonable, but shared them as well. Commentators variously characterized his conduct as "a disgusting invasion of personal privacy."

■ ■ ■

That is not to deny that isolated intrusions into opaque, sealed trash containers occur. When, acting on their own, "animals, children, scavengers, snoops, [or] other members of the public," *actually* rummage through a bag of trash and expose its contents to plain view, "police cannot reasonably be expected to avert their eyes from evidence of criminal activity that could have been observed by any member of the public." That much follows from cases like *Jacobsen*, which held that police may constitutionally inspect a package whose "integrity" a private carrier has *already* "compromised," because "[t]he Fourth Amendment is implicated only if the authorities use information with respect to which the expectation of privacy has not *already* been frustrated"; and *California v. Ciraolo*, which held that the Fourth Amendment does not prohibit police from observing what "[a]ny member of the public flying in this airspace who glanced down *could* have seen."

Had Greenwood flaunted his intimate activity by strewing his trash all over the curb for all to see, or had some nongovernmental intruder invaded his privacy and done the same, I could accept the Court's conclusion that an expectation of privacy would have been unreasonable. Similarly, had police searching the city dump run across incriminating evidence that, despite commingling with the trash of others, still retained its identity as Greenwood's, we would have a different case. But all that Greenwood "exposed . . . to the public," were the exteriors of several opaque, sealed containers. Until the bags were opened by police, they hid their contents from the public's view every bit as much as did Chadwick's double-locked footlocker and Robbins' green, plastic wrapping. Faithful application of the warrant requirement does not require police to "avert their eyes from evidence of criminal activity that could have been observed by any member of the public." Rather, it only requires them to adhere to norms of privacy that members of the public plainly acknowledge.

The mere *possibility* that unwelcome meddlers *might* open and rummage through the containers does not negate the expectation of privacy in their contents any more than the possibility of a burglary negates an expectation of privacy in the home; or the possibility of a private intrusion negates an expectation of privacy in an unopened package; or the possibility that an operator will listen in on a telephone conversation negates an expectation of privacy in the words spoken on the telephone. . . . Nor is it dispositive that "respondents placed their refuse at the curb for the express purpose of conveying it to a third party, . . . who might himself have sorted through respondents' trash or permitted others, such as the police, to do so." In the first place, Greenwood can hardly be faulted for leaving trash on his curb when a county ordinance commanded him to do so (must "remov[e] from the premises at least once each week" all "solid waste created, produced or accumulated in or about [his] dwelling house"), and prohibited him from disposing of it in any other way, see Orange County Code § 3-3-85 (1988) (burning trash is unlawful). Unlike in other circumstances where privacy is compromised, Greenwood could not "avoid exposing personal belongings . . . by simply leaving them at home." *O'Connor v. Ortega* (1987). More importantly, even the voluntary relinquishment of possession or control over an effect does not necessarily amount to a relinquishment of a privacy expectation in it. Were it otherwise, a letter or package would lose all Fourth Amendment protection when placed in a mailbox or other depository with the "express purpose" of entrusting it to the postal officer or a private carrier; those bailees are just as likely as trash collectors (and certainly have greater incentive) to "sor[t] through" the personal effects entrusted to them, "or permi[t] others, such as police to do so." Yet, it has been clear for at least 110 years that the possibility of such an intrusion does not justify a warrantless search by police in the first instance.

In holding that the warrantless search of Greenwood's trash was consistent with the Fourth Amendment, the Court paints a grim picture of our society. It depicts a society in which local authorities may command their citizens to dispose of their personal effects in the manner least protective of the "sanctity of [the] home and the privacies of life," *Boyd v. United States,* and then monitor them arbitrarily and without judicial oversight—a society that is not prepared to recognize as reasonable an individual's expectation of privacy in the most private of personal effects sealed in an opaque container and disposed of in a manner designed to commingle it imminently and inextricably with the trash of others. The American society with which I am familiar "chooses to dwell in reasonable security and freedom from surveillance," *Johnson v. United States* (1948), and is more dedicated to individual liberty and more sensitive to intrusions on the sanctity of the home than the Court is willing to acknowledge.

I dissent.

4. Enhancement Devices

a. Public Places

United States v. Place

462 U.S. 696 (1983)

O'CONNOR, J., delivered the opinion of the Court, in which BURGER, C.J., REHNQUIST, POWELL, STEVENS, and WHITE, JJ., joined. BRENNAN, J., filed an opinion concurring in the result, in which MARSHALL, J., joined. BLACKMUN, J. filed an opinion concurring in the judgment, in which MARSHALL, J., joined.

This case presents the issue whether the Fourth Amendment prohibits law enforcement authorities from temporarily detaining personal luggage for exposure to a trained narcotics detection dog on the basis of reasonable suspicion that the luggage contains narcotics. Given the enforcement problems associated with the detection of narcotics trafficking and the minimal intrusion that a properly limited detention would entail, we conclude that the Fourth Amendment does not prohibit such a detention. On the facts of this case, however, we hold that the police conduct exceeded the bounds of a permissible investigative detention of the luggage. . . .

Respondent Raymond J. Place's behavior aroused the suspicions of law enforcement officers as he waited in line at the Miami International Airport to purchase a ticket to New York's LaGuardia Airport. As Place proceeded to the gate for his flight, the agents approached him and requested his airline ticket and some identification. Place complied with the request and consented to a search of the two suitcases he had checked. Because his flight was about to depart, however, the agents decided not to search the luggage.

Prompted by Place's parting remark that he had recognized that they were police, the agents inspected the address tags on the checked luggage and noted discrepancies in the two street addresses. Further investigation revealed that neither address existed and that the telephone number Place had given the airline belonged to a third address on the same street. On the basis of their encounter with Place and this information, the Miami agents called Drug Enforcement Administration (DEA) authorities in New York to relay their information about Place.

Two DEA agents waited for Place at the arrival gate at LaGuardia Airport in New York. There again, his behavior aroused the suspicion of the agents. After he had claimed his two bags and called a limousine, the agents decided to approach him. They identified themselves as federal narcotics agents, to which Place responded that he knew they were "cops" and had spotted them as soon as he had deplaned. One of the agents informed Place that, based on their own observations and information obtained from the Miami authorities, they believed that he might be carrying narcotics. After identifying the bags as belonging to him, Place stated that a number of police at the Miami Airport had surrounded him and searched his baggage. The agents responded that their information was to the contrary. The agents requested and received identification from Place—a New Jersey driver's license, on which the agents later ran a computer check that disclosed no offenses, and his airline ticket receipt. When Place refused to consent to a search of his luggage, one of the agents told him that they were going to take the luggage to a federal judge to try to obtain a search warrant and that Place was free to accompany them. Place declined, but obtained from one of the agents telephone numbers at which the agents could be reached.

The agents then took the bags to Kennedy Airport, where they subjected the bags to a "sniff test" by a trained narcotics detection dog. The dog reacted positively to the smaller of the two bags but ambiguously to the larger bag. Approximately 90 minutes had elapsed since the seizure of respondent's luggage. Because it was late on a Friday afternoon, the agents retained the luggage until Monday morning, when they secured a search warrant from a magistrate for the smaller bag. Upon opening that bag, the agents discovered 1,125 grams of cocaine.

Place was indicted for possession of cocaine with intent to distribute in violation of 21 U.S.C. § 841(a)(1). In the District Court, Place moved to suppress the contents of the luggage seized from him at LaGuardia Airport, claiming that the warrantless seizure of the luggage violated his Fourth Amendment rights.

■ ■ ■

We granted certiorari . . . and now affirm.

The Fourth Amendment "protects people from unreasonable government intrusions into their legitimate expectations of privacy." We have affirmed that a person possesses a privacy interest in the contents of personal luggage that is protected by the Fourth Amendment. A "canine sniff" by a well-trained narcotics detection dog, however, does not require opening the luggage. It does not expose noncontraband items that otherwise would remain hidden from public view, as does, for example, an officer's rummaging through the contents of the luggage. Thus, the manner in which information is obtained through this investigative technique is much less intrusive than a typical search. Moreover, the sniff discloses only the presence or absence of narcotics, a contraband item. Thus, despite the fact that the sniff tells the authorities something about the contents of the luggage, the information obtained is limited. This limited disclosure also ensures that the owner of the property is not subjected to the embarrassment and inconvenience entailed in less discriminate and more intrusive investigative methods.

In these respects, the canine sniff is *sui generis*. We are aware of no other investigative procedure that is so limited both in the manner in which the information is obtained and in the content of the information revealed by the procedure. Therefore, we conclude that the particular course of investigation that the agents intended to pursue here—exposure of respondent's

no search, but seizure

luggage, which was located in a public place, to a trained canine—did not constitute a "search" within the meaning of the Fourth Amendment.

■ ■ ■

We conclude that, under all of the circumstances of this case (detention of luggage for an extended period), the seizure of respondent's luggage was unreasonable under the Fourth Amendment. Consequently, the evidence obtained from the subsequent search of his luggage was inadmissible, and Place's conviction must be reversed. The judgment of the Court of Appeals, accordingly, is affirmed.

It is so ordered.

Justice BRENNAN, with whom Justice MARSHALL joins, concurring in the result. . . .

The Court also suggests today, in a discussion unnecessary to the judgment, that exposure of respondent's luggage to a narcotics detection dog "did not constitute a 'search' within the meaning of the Fourth Amendment." In the District Court, respondent did "not contest the validity of sniff searches *per se.* . . ." The Court of Appeals did not reach or discuss the issue. It was not briefed or argued in this Court. In short, I agree with Justice Blackmun that the Court should not address the issue.

I also agree with Justice Blackmun's suggestion, that the issue is more complex than the Court's discussion would lead one to believe. As Justice Stevens suggested in objecting to "unnecessarily broad dicta" in *United States v. Knotts* (1983), the use of electronic detection techniques that enhance human perception implicates "especially sensitive concerns." Obviously, a narcotics detection dog is not an electronic detection device. Unlike the electronic "beeper" in *Knotts,* however, a dog does more than merely allow the police to do more efficiently what they could do using only their own senses. A dog adds a new and previously unobtainable dimension to human perception. The use of dogs, therefore, represents a greater intrusion into an individual's privacy. Such use implicates concerns that are at least as sensitive as those implicated by the use of certain electronic detection devices. Cf. *Katz v. United States* (1967).

I have expressed the view that dog sniffs of people constitute searches. . . . I suggested that sniffs of inanimate objects might present a different case. In any event, I would leave the determination of whether dog sniffs of luggage amount to searches, and the subsidiary question of what standards should govern such intrusions, to a future case providing an appropriate, and more informed, basis for deciding these questions.

■ ■ ■

The Court's resolution of the status of dog sniffs under the Fourth Amendment is troubling for a different reason. The District Court expressly observed that Place "does not contest the validity of sniff searches *per se.*" While Place may have possessed such a claim, he chose not to raise it in that court. The issue also was not presented to or decided by the Court of Appeals. Moreover, contrary to the Court's apparent intimation, an answer to the question is not necessary to the decision. For the purposes of this case, the precise nature of the legitimate investigative activity is irrelevant. Regardless of the validity of a dog sniff under the Fourth Amendment, the seizure was too intrusive. The Court has no need to decide the issue here.

As a matter of prudence, decision of the issue is also unwise. While the Court has adopted one plausible analysis of the issue, there are others. For example, a dog sniff may be a search, but a minimally intrusive one that could be justified in this situation under *Terry* [*v. Ohio* (1968)] upon mere reasonable suspicion. Neither party has had an opportunity to brief the issue, and the Court grasps for the appropriate analysis of the problem. Although it is not essential that the Court ever adopt the views of one of the parties, it should not decide an issue on which neither party has expressed any opinion at all. The Court is certainly in no position to consider all the ramifications of this important issue. Certiorari is currently pending in two cases that present the issue directly. There is no reason to avoid a full airing of the issue in a proper case.

For the foregoing reasons, I concur only in the judgment of the Court.

Illinois v. Caballes

543 U.S. 405 (2005)

STEVENS, J., delivered the opinion of the Court, in which O'CONNOR, SCALIA, KENNEDY, THOMAS, and BREYER, JJ., joined. SOUTER, J., filed a dissenting opinion. GINSBURG, J., filed a dissenting opinion, in which SOUTER, J., joined. REHNQUIST, C.J., took no part in the decision of the case.

Illinois State Trooper Daniel Gillette stopped respondent for speeding on an interstate highway. When Gillette radioed the police dispatcher to report the stop, a second trooper, Craig Graham, a member of the Illinois State Police Drug Interdiction Team, overheard the transmission and immediately headed for the scene with his narcotics-detection dog. When they arrived, respondent's car was on the shoulder of the road and respondent was in Gillette's vehicle. While Gillette was in the process of writing a warning ticket, Graham walked his dog around respondent's car. The dog alerted at the trunk. Based on that alert, the officers searched the trunk, found marijuana, and arrested respondent. The entire incident lasted less than 10 minutes.

Respondent was convicted of a narcotics offense and sentenced to 12 years' imprisonment and a $256,136 fine. The trial judge denied his motion to suppress the seized evidence and to quash his arrest. He held that the officers had not unnecessarily prolonged the stop and that the dog alert was sufficiently reliable to provide probable cause to conduct the search. Although the Appellate Court affirmed, the Illinois Supreme Court reversed, concluding that because the canine sniff was performed without any "'specific and articulable facts'" to suggest drug activity, the use of the dog "unjustifiably enlarg[ed] the scope of a routine traffic stop into a drug investigation."

The question on which we granted certiorari . . . is narrow: "Whether the Fourth Amendment requires reasonable, articulable suspicion to justify using a drug-detection dog to sniff a vehicle during a legitimate traffic stop." Thus, we proceed on the assumption that the officer conducting the dog sniff had no information about respondent except that he had been stopped for speeding; accordingly, we have omitted any reference to facts about respondent that might have triggered a modicum of suspicion. . . .

Despite this conclusion, the Illinois Supreme Court held that the initially lawful traffic stop became an unlawful seizure solely as a result of the canine sniff that occurred outside respondent's stopped car. That is, the court characterized the dog sniff as the cause rather than the consequence of a constitutional violation. In its view, the use of the dog converted the citizen-police encounter from a lawful traffic stop into a drug investigation, and because the shift in purpose was not supported by any reasonable suspicion that respondent possessed narcotics, it was unlawful. In our view, conducting a dog sniff would not change the character of a traffic stop that is lawful at its inception and otherwise executed in a reasonable manner, unless the dog sniff itself infringed respondent's constitutionally protected interest in privacy. Our cases hold that it did not.

Official conduct that does not "compromise any legitimate interest in privacy" is not a search subject to the Fourth Amendment. We have held that any interest in possessing contraband cannot be deemed "legitimate," and thus, governmental conduct that *only* reveals the possession of contraband "compromises no legitimate privacy interest." This is because the expectation "that certain facts will not come to the attention of the authorities" is not the same as an interest in "privacy that society is prepared to consider reasonable." In *United States v. Place* (1983), we treated a canine sniff by a well-trained narcotics-detection dog as "*sui generis*" because it "discloses only the presence or absence of narcotics, a contraband item." Respondent likewise concedes that "drug sniffs are designed, and if properly conducted are generally likely, to reveal only the presence of contraband."

■ ■ ■

Accordingly, the use of a well-trained narcotics-detection dog—one that "does not expose noncontraband items that otherwise would remain hidden from public view," . . . —during a lawful traffic stop, generally does not implicate legitimate privacy interests. In this case, the dog sniff was performed on the exterior of respondent's car while he was lawfully seized for a traffic violation. Any intrusion on respondent's privacy expectations does not rise to the level of a constitutionally cognizable infringement.

This conclusion is entirely consistent with our recent decision that the use of a thermal-imaging device to detect the growth of marijuana in a home constituted an unlawful search. *Kyllo v. United States* (2001). Critical to that decision was the fact that the device was capable of detecting lawful activity—in that case, intimate details in a home, such as "at what hour each night the lady of the house takes her daily sauna and bath." The legitimate expectation that information about perfectly lawful activity will remain private is categorically distinguishable from respondent's hopes or expectations concerning the non-detection of contraband in the trunk of his car. A dog sniff conducted during a concededly lawful traffic stop that reveals no information other than the location of a substance that no individual has any right to possess does not violate the Fourth Amendment.

The judgment of the Illinois Supreme Court is vacated, and the case is remanded for further proceedings not inconsistent with this opinion.

It is so ordered.

Justice SOUTER, dissenting.

I would hold that using the dog for the purposes of determining the presence of marijuana in the car's trunk was a search unauthorized as an incident of the speeding stop and unjustified on any other ground. I would accordingly affirm the judgment of the Supreme Court of Illinois, and I respectfully dissent.

In *United States v. Place*, we categorized the sniff of the narcotics-seeking dog as "*sui generis*" under the Fourth Amendment and held it was not a search. The classification rests not only upon the limited nature of the intrusion, but on a further premise that experience has shown to be untenable, the assumption that trained sniffing dogs do not err. What we have learned about the fallibility of dogs in the years since *Place* was decided would itself be reason to call for reconsidering *Place*'s decision against treating the intentional use of a trained dog as a search. The portent of this very case, however, adds insistence to the call, for an uncritical adherence to *Place* would render the Fourth Amendment indifferent to suspicionless and indiscriminate sweeps of cars in parking garages and pedestrians on sidewalks; if a sniff is not preceded by a seizure subject to Fourth Amendment notice, it escapes Fourth Amendment review entirely unless it is treated as a search. We should not wait for these developments to occur before rethinking *Place*'s analysis, which invites such untoward consequences.

At the heart both of *Place* and the Court's opinion today is the proposition that sniffs by a trained dog are *sui generis* because a reaction by the dog in going alert is a response to nothing but the presence of contraband. . . .

The infallible dog, however, is a creature of legal fiction. Although the Supreme Court of Illinois did not get into the sniffing averages of drug dogs, their supposed infallibility is belied by judicial opinions describing well-trained animals sniffing and alerting with less than perfect accuracy, whether owing to errors by their handlers, the limitations of the dogs themselves, or even the pervasive contamination of currency by cocaine. . . . Indeed, a study cited by Illinois in this case for the proposition that dog sniffs are "generally reliable" shows that dogs in artificial testing situations return false positives anywhere from 12.5% to 60% of the time, depending on the length of the search.

■ ■ ■

Once the dog's fallibility is recognized, however, that ends the justification claimed in *Place* for treating the sniff as *sui generis* under the Fourth Amendment: the sniff alert does not necessarily signal hidden contraband, and opening the container or enclosed space whose emanations the dog has sensed will not necessarily reveal contraband or any other evidence of crime. This is not, of course, to deny that a dog's reaction may provide reasonable suspicion, or probable cause, to search the container or enclosure; the Fourth Amendment does not demand certainty of success to justify a search for evidence or contraband. The point is simply that the sniff and alert cannot claim the certainty that *Place* assumed, both in treating the deliberate use of sniffing dogs as *sui generis* and then taking that characterization as a reason to say they are not searches subject to Fourth Amendment scrutiny. And when that aura of uniqueness disappears, there is no basis in *Place*'s reasoning, and no good reason otherwise, to ignore the actual function that dog sniffs perform.

It makes sense, then, to treat a sniff as the search that it amounts to in practice, and to rely on the body of our Fourth Amendment cases, including *Kyllo,* in deciding whether such a search is reasonable. As a general proposition, using a dog to sniff for drugs is subject to the rule that the object of enforcing criminal laws does not, without more, justify suspicionless Fourth Amendment intrusions. Since the police claim to have had no particular suspicion that Caballes was violating any drug law, this sniff search must stand or fall on its being ancillary to the traffic stop that led up to it. It is true that the police had probable cause to stop the car for an offense committed in the officer's presence, which Caballes concedes could have justified his arrest. . . .

The Court today does not go so far as to say explicitly that sniff searches by dogs trained to sense contraband always get a free pass under the Fourth Amendment, since it reserves judgment on the constitutional significance of sniffs assumed to be more intrusive than a dog's walk around a stopped car. For this reason, I do not take the Court's reliance on *Jacobsen* (1984) as actually signaling recognition of a broad authority to conduct suspicionless sniffs for drugs in any parked car, about which Justice Ginsburg is rightly concerned, or on the person of any pedestrian minding his own business on a sidewalk. But the Court's stated reasoning provides no apparent stopping point short of such excesses. For the sake of providing a workable framework to analyze cases on facts like these, which are certain to come along, I would treat the dog sniff as the familiar search it is in fact, subject to scrutiny under the Fourth Amendment.

United States v. Knotts

460 U.S. 276 (1983)

REHNQUIST, J., delivered the opinion of the Court, in which BURGER, C.J., BLACKMUN, O'CONNOR, POWELL, and WHITE, JJ., joined. STEVENS, J., filed an opinion concurring in the judgment, in which BRENNAN and MARSHALL, JJ., joined.

A beeper is a radio transmitter, usually battery operated, which emits periodic signals that can be picked up by a radio receiver. In this case, a beeper was placed in a five-gallon drum containing chloroform purchased by one of respondent's codefendants. By monitoring the progress of a car carrying the chloroform Minnesota law enforcement agents were able to trace the can of chloroform from its place of purchase in Minneapolis, Minnesota to respondent's secluded cabin near Shell Lake, Wisconsin. The issue presented by the case is whether such use of a beeper violated respondent's rights secured by the Fourth Amendment to the United States Constitution.

Respondent and two codefendants were charged in the United States District Court for the District of Minnesota with conspiracy to manufacture controlled substances, including but not limited to methamphetamine.

■ ■ ■

Suspicion attached to this trio when the 3M Company, which manufactures chemicals in St. Paul, notified a narcotics investigator for the Minnesota Bureau of Criminal Apprehension that Armstrong, a former 3M employee, had been stealing chemicals which could be used in manufacturing illicit drugs. Visual surveillance of Armstrong revealed that after leaving the employ of 3M Company, he had been purchasing similar chemicals from the Hawkins Chemical Company in Minneapolis. The Minnesota narcotics officers observed that after Armstrong had made a purchase, he would deliver the chemicals to codefendant Petschen.

With the consent of the Hawkins Chemical Company, officers installed a beeper inside a five-gallon container of chloroform, one of the so-called "precursor" chemicals used to manufacture illicit drugs. Hawkins agreed that when Armstrong next purchased chloroform, the chloroform would be placed in this particular container. When Armstrong made the purchase, officers followed the car in which the chloroform had been placed, maintaining contact by using both visual surveillance and a monitor which received the signals sent from the beeper.

Armstrong proceeded to Petschen's house, where the container was transferred to Petschen's automobile. Officers then followed that vehicle eastward towards the state line, across the St. Croix River, and into Wisconsin. During the latter part of this journey, Petschen began making evasive maneuvers, and the pursuing agents ended their visual surveillance. At about the same time officers lost the signal from the beeper, but with the assistance of a monitoring device located in a helicopter the approximate location of the signal was picked up again about one hour later. The signal now was stationary and the location identified was a cabin occupied by respondent near Shell Lake, Wisconsin. The record before us does not reveal that the beeper was used after the location in the area of the cabin had been initially determined.

Relying on the location of the chloroform derived through the use of the beeper and additional information obtained during three days of intermittent visual surveillance of respondent's cabin, officers secured a search warrant. During execution of the warrant, officers discovered a fully operable, clandestine drug laboratory in the cabin. In the laboratory area officers found formulas for amphetamine and methamphetamine, over $10,000 worth of laboratory equipment, and chemicals in quantities sufficient to produce 14 pounds of pure amphetamine. Under a barrel outside the cabin, officers located the five-gallon container of chloroform.

After his motion to suppress evidence based on the warrantless monitoring of the beeper was denied, respondent was convicted for conspiring to manufacture controlled substances. . . . A divided panel of the United States Court of Appeals for the Eighth Circuit reversed the conviction, finding that the monitoring of the beeper was prohibited by the Fourth Amendment because its use had violated respondent's reasonable expectation of privacy, and that all information derived after the location of the cabin was a fruit of the illegal beeper monitoring. . . .

The governmental surveillance conducted by means of the beeper in this case amounted principally to the following of an automobile on public streets and highways. We have commented more than once on the diminished expectation of privacy in an automobile:

> "One has a lesser expectation of privacy in a motor vehicle because its function is transportation and it seldom serves as one's residence or as the repository of personal effects. A car has little capacity for escaping public scrutiny. It travels public thoroughfares where both its occupants and its contents are in plain view."

A person travelling in an automobile on public thoroughfares has no reasonable expectation of privacy in his movements from one place to another. When Petschen travelled over the public streets he voluntarily conveyed to anyone who wanted to look the fact that he was travelling over particular roads in a particular direction, the fact of whatever stops he made, and the fact of his final destination when he exited from public roads onto private property. . . .

Visual surveillance from public places along Petschen's route or adjoining Knotts' premises would have sufficed to reveal all of these facts to the police. The fact that the officers in this case relied not only on visual surveillance, but on the use of the beeper to signal the presence of Petschen's automobile to the police receiver, does not alter the situation. Nothing in the Fourth Amendment prohibited the police from augmenting the sensory faculties bestowed upon them at birth with such enhancement as science and technology afforded them in this case. . . .

Respondent specifically attacks the use of the beeper insofar as it was used to determine that the can of chloroform had come to rest on his property at Shell Lake, Wisconsin. He repeatedly challenges the "use of the beeper to determine the location of the chemical drum at Respondent's premises," . . . he states that "[t]he government thus overlooks the fact that this case involves the sanctity of Respondent's residence, which is accorded the greatest protection available under the Fourth Amendment." The Court of Appeals appears to have rested its decision on this ground:

> "As noted above, a principal rationale for allowing warrantless tracking of beepers, particularly beepers in or on an auto, is that beepers are merely a more effective means of observing what is already public. But people pass daily

from public to private spheres. When police agents track bugged personal property without first obtaining a warrant, they must do so at the risk that this enhanced surveillance, intrusive at best, might push fortuitously and unreasonably into the private sphere protected by the Fourth Amendment."

We think that respondent's contentions, and the above quoted language from the opinion of the Court of Appeals, to some extent lose sight of the limited use which the government made of the signals from this particular beeper. As we have noted, nothing in this record indicates that the beeper signal was received or relied upon after it had indicated that the drum containing the chloroform had ended its automotive journey at rest on respondent's premises in rural Wisconsin. Admittedly, because of the failure of the visual surveillance, the beeper enabled the law enforcement officials in this case to ascertain the ultimate resting place of the chloroform when they would not have been able to do so had they relied solely on their naked eyes. But scientific enhancement of this sort raises no constitutional issues which visual surveillance would not also raise. A police car following Petschen at a distance throughout his journey could have observed him leaving the public highway and arriving at the cabin owned by respondent, with the drum of chloroform still in the car. This fact, along with others, was used by the government in obtaining a search warrant which led to the discovery of the clandestine drug laboratory. But there is no indication that the beeper was used in any way to reveal information as to the movement of the drum within the cabin, or in any way that would not have been visible to the naked eye from outside the cabin.

■ ■ ■

We thus return to the question posed at the beginning of our inquiry . . . did monitoring the beeper signals complained of by respondent invade any legitimate expectation of privacy on his part? For the reasons previously stated, we hold they did not. Since they did not, there was neither a "search" nor a "seizure" within the contemplation of the Fourth Amendment. The judgment of the Court of Appeals is therefore

Reversed.

United States v. Jones

132 S. Ct. 945 (2012)

See Chapter 2.B.1.

Bond v. United States

529 U.S. 334 (2000)

REHNQUIST, C.J., delivered the opinion of the Court, in which STEVENS, O'CONNOR, KENNEDY, SOUTER, THOMAS, and GINSBURG, JJ., joined. BREYER, J., filed a dissenting opinion, in which SCALIA, J., joined.

" physical manipulation"

This case presents the question whether a law enforcement officer's physical manipulation of a bus passenger's carry-on luggage violated the Fourth Amendment's proscription against unreasonable searches. We hold that it did.

Petitioner Steven Dewayne Bond was a passenger on a Greyhound bus that left California bound for Little Rock, Arkansas. The bus stopped, as it was required to do, at the permanent Border Patrol checkpoint in Sierra Blanca, Texas. Border Patrol Agent Cesar Cantu boarded the bus to check the immigration status of its passengers. After reaching the back of the bus, having satisfied himself that the passengers were lawfully in the United States, Agent Cantu began walking toward the front. Along the way, he squeezed the soft luggage which passengers had placed in the overhead storage space above the seats.

Petitioner was seated four or five rows from the back of the bus. As Agent Cantu inspected the luggage in the compartment above petitioner's seat, he squeezed a green canvas bag and noticed that it contained a "brick-like" object. Petitioner admitted that the bag was his and agreed to allow Agent Cantu to open it. Upon opening the bag, Agent Cantu discovered a "brick" of methamphetamine. The brick had been wrapped in duct tape until it was oval-shaped and then rolled in a pair of pants.

Petitioner was indicted for conspiracy to possess, and possession with intent to distribute, methamphetamine. . . . He moved to suppress the drugs, arguing that Agent Cantu conducted an illegal search of his bag. Petitioner's motion was denied, and the District Court found him guilty on both counts and sentenced him to 57 months in prison. On appeal, he conceded that other passengers had access to his bag, but contended that Agent Cantu manipulated the bag in a way that other passengers would not. The Court of Appeals rejected this argument, stating that the fact that Agent Cantu's manipulation of petitioner's bag was calculated to detect contraband is irrelevant for Fourth Amendment purposes.

■ ■ ■

. . . *Ciraolo* (1986) and *Riley* (1985) are different from this case because they involved only visual, as opposed to tactile, observation. Physically invasive inspection is simply more intrusive than purely visual inspection. For example, in *Terry v. Ohio* (1968), we stated that a "careful [tactile] exploration of the outer surfaces of a person's clothing all over his or her body" is a "serious intrusion upon the sanctity of the person, which may inflict great indignity and arouse strong resentment, and it is not to be undertaken lightly." Although Agent Cantu did not "frisk" petitioner's person, he did conduct a probing tactile examination of petitioner's carry-on luggage. Obviously, petitioner's bag was not part of his person. But travelers are particularly concerned about their carry-on luggage; they generally use it to transport personal items that, for whatever reason, they prefer to keep close at hand.

Here, petitioner concedes that, by placing his bag in the overhead compartment, he could expect that it would be exposed to certain kinds of touching and handling. But petitioner argues that Agent Cantu's physical manipulation of his luggage "far exceeded the casual contact [petitioner] could have expected from other passengers." . . .

Our Fourth Amendment analysis embraces two questions. First, we ask whether the individual, by his conduct, has exhibited an actual expectation of privacy; that is, whether he has shown that "he [sought] to preserve [something] as private." Here, petitioner sought to preserve privacy by using an opaque bag and placing that bag directly above his seat. Second, we inquire whether the individual's expectation of privacy is "one that society is prepared to recognize as reasonable." When a bus passenger places a bag in an overhead bin, he expects that other passengers or bus employees may move it for one reason or another. Thus, a bus passenger clearly expects that his bag may be handled. He does not expect that other passengers or bus employees will, as a matter of course, feel the bag in an exploratory manner. But this is exactly what the agent did here. We therefore hold that the agent's physical manipulation of petitioner's bag violated the Fourth Amendment.

The judgment of the Court of Appeals is
Reversed.

Justice BREYER, with whom Justice SCALIA joins, dissenting.

Does a traveler who places a soft-sided bag in the shared overhead storage compartment of a bus have a "reasonable expectation" that strangers will not push, pull, prod, squeeze, or otherwise manipulate his luggage? Unlike the majority, I believe that he does not.

Petitioner argues—and the majority points out—that, even if bags in overhead bins are subject to general "touching" and "handling," this case is special because "Agent Cantu's physical manipulation of [petitioner's] luggage 'far exceeded the casual contact [he] could have expected from other passengers.'" But the record shows the contrary. Agent Cantu testified that border patrol officers (who routinely enter buses at designated checkpoints to run immigration checks) "conduct an inspection of the overhead luggage by squeezing the bags as we're going out." On the occasion at issue here, Agent Cantu "felt a green bag" which had "a brick-like object in it." He explained that he felt "the edges of the brick in the bag," and that it was a "[b]rick-like object . . . that, when squeezed, you could feel an outline of something of [a] different mass inside of it." Although the agent acknowledged that his practice was to "squeeze [bags] very hard," he testified that his touch ordinarily was not "[h]ard enough to break something inside that might be fragile."

■ ■ ■

The record and these factual findings are sufficient to resolve this case. The law is clear that the Fourth Amendment protects against government intrusion that upsets an "'actual (subjective) expectation of privacy'" that is objectively "'reasonable.'" Privacy itself implies the exclusion of uninvited strangers, not just strangers who work for the Government. Hence, an individual cannot reasonably expect privacy in respect to objects or activities that he "knowingly exposes to the public."

■ ■ ■

If we are to depart from established legal principles, we should not begin here. At best, this decision will lead to a constitutional jurisprudence of "squeezes," thereby complicating further already complex Fourth Amendment law, increasing the difficulty of deciding ordinary criminal matters, and hindering the administrative guidance.... At worst, this case will deter law enforcement officers searching for drugs near borders from using even the most nonintrusive touch to help investigate publicly exposed bags. At the same time, the ubiquity of *non*-governmental pushes, prods, and squeezes (delivered by driver, attendant, passenger, or some other stranger) means that this decision cannot do much to protect true privacy. Rather, the traveler who wants to place a bag in a shared overhead bin and yet safeguard its contents from public touch should plan to pack those contents in a suitcase with hard sides, irrespective of the Court's decision today.

For these reasons, I dissent.

b. Home

Kyllo v. United States

533 U.S. 27 (2001)

SCALIA, J., delivered the opinion of the Court, in which SOUTER, THOMAS, GINSBURG, and BREYER, JJ., joined. STEVENS, J., filed a dissenting opinion, in which REHNQUIST, C.J., and O'CONNOR and KENNEDY, JJ., joined.

This case presents the question whether the use of a thermal-imaging device aimed at a private home from a public street to detect relative amounts of heat within the home constitutes a "search" within the meaning of the Fourth Amendment.

In 1991 Agent William Elliott of the United States Department of the Interior came to suspect that marijuana was being grown in the home belonging to petitioner Danny Kyllo, part of a triplex on Rhododendron Drive in Florence, Oregon. Indoor marijuana growth typically requires high-intensity lamps. In order to determine whether an amount of heat was emanating from petitioner's home consistent with the use of such lamps, at 3:20 a.m. on January 16, 1992, Agent Elliott and Dan Haas used an Agema Thermovision 210 thermal imager to scan the triplex. Thermal imagers detect infrared radiation, which virtually all objects emit but which is not visible to the naked eye. The imager converts radiation into images based on relative warmth—black is cool, white is hot, shades of gray connote relative differences; in that respect, it operates somewhat like a video camera showing heat images. The scan of Kyllo's home took only a few minutes and was performed from the passenger seat of Agent Elliott's vehicle across the street from the front of the house and also from the street in back of the house. The scan showed that the roof over the garage and a side wall of petitioner's home were relatively hot compared to the rest of the home and substantially warmer than neighboring homes in the triplex. Agent Elliott concluded that petitioner was using halide lights to grow marijuana in his house, which indeed he was. Based on tips from informants, utility bills, and the thermal imaging, a Federal Magistrate Judge issued a warrant authorizing a search of petitioner's home, and the agents found an indoor growing operation involving more than 100 plants. Petitioner was indicted on one count of manufacturing marijuana. . . . He unsuccessfully moved to suppress the evidence seized from his home and then entered a conditional guilty plea.

The Court of Appeals for the Ninth Circuit remanded the case for an evidentiary hearing regarding the intrusiveness of thermal imaging. On remand the District Court found that the Agema 210 "is a non-intrusive device which emits no rays or beams and shows a crude visual image of the heat being radiated from the outside of the house"; it "did not show any people or activity within the walls of the structure"; "[t]he device used cannot penetrate walls or windows to reveal conversations or human activities"; and "[n]o intimate details of the home were observed." Based on these findings, the District Court upheld the validity of the warrant that relied in part upon the thermal imaging, and reaffirmed its denial of the motion to suppress. A divided Court of Appeals initially reversed, but that opinion was withdrawn and the panel (after a change in composition) affirmed, with Judge Noonan dissenting. The court held that petitioner had shown no subjective expectation of privacy because he had made no attempt to conceal the heat escaping from his home, and even if he had, there was no objectively reasonable expectation of privacy because the imager "did not expose any intimate details of Kyllo's life," only "amorphous 'hot spots' on the roof and exterior wall."

■ ■ ■

The Fourth Amendment provides that "[t]he right of the people to be secure in their persons, houses, papers, and effects, against unreasonable searches and seizures, shall not be violated." "At the very core" of the Fourth Amendment "stands the right of a man to retreat into his own home and there be free from unreasonable governmental intrusion." *Silverman v. United States* (1961).

■ ■ ■

On the other hand, the antecedent question whether or not a Fourth Amendment "search" has occurred is not so simple under our precedent. The permissibility of ordinary visual surveillance of a home used to be clear because, well into the 20th century, our Fourth Amendment jurisprudence was tied to common-law trespass . . . (technical trespass not necessary for Fourth Amendment violation; it suffices if there is "actual intrusion into a constitutionally protected area"). Visual surveillance was unquestionably lawful because "'the eye cannot by the laws of England be guilty of a trespass.'" *Boyd v. United States* (1886). We have since decoupled violation of a person's Fourth Amendment rights from trespassory violation of his property, but the lawfulness of warrantless visual surveillance of a home has still been preserved. As we observed in *California v. Ciraolo* (1986), "[t]he Fourth

Amendment protection of the home has never been extended to require law enforcement officers to shield their eyes when passing by a home on public thoroughfares."...

The present case involves officers on a public street engaged in more than naked-eye surveillance of a home. We have previously reserved judgment as to how much technological enhancement of ordinary perception from such a vantage point, if any, is too much. While we upheld enhanced aerial photography of an industrial complex in *Dow Chemical* (1986), we noted that we found "it important that this is *not* an area immediately adjacent to a private home, where privacy expectations are most heightened."...

It would be foolish to contend that the degree of privacy secured to citizens by the Fourth Amendment has been entirely unaffected by the advance of technology. For example, as the cases discussed above make clear, the technology enabling human flight has exposed to public view (and hence, we have said, to official observation) uncovered portions of the house and its curtilage that once were private. The question we confront today is what limits there are upon this power of technology to shrink the realm of guaranteed privacy....

The Government maintains, however, that the thermal imaging must be upheld because it detected "only heat radiating from the external surface of the house." The dissent makes this its leading point, contending that there is a fundamental difference between what it calls "off-the-wall" observations and "through-the-wall surveillance." But just as a thermal imager captures only heat emanating from a house, so also a powerful directional microphone picks up only sound emanating from a house—and a satellite capable of scanning from many miles away would pick up only visible light emanating from a house. We rejected such a mechanical interpretation of the Fourth Amendment in [*United States v.*] *Katz* [(1967)], where the eavesdropping device picked up only sound waves that reached the exterior of the phone booth. Reversing that approach would leave the homeowner at the mercy of advancing technology—including imaging technology that could discern all human activity in the home. While the technology used in the present case was relatively crude, the rule we adopt must take account of more sophisticated systems that are already in use or in development. The dissent's reliance on the distinction between "off-the-wall" and "through-the-wall" observation is entirely incompatible with the dissent's belief, which we discuss below, that thermal-imaging observations of the intimate details of a home are impermissible. The most sophisticated thermal-imaging devices continue to measure heat "off-the-wall" rather than "through-the-wall"; the dissent's disapproval of those more sophisticated thermal-imaging devices is an acknowledgement that there is no substance to this distinction. As for the dissent's extraordinary assertion that anything learned through "an inference" cannot be a search, that would validate even the "through-the-wall" technologies that the dissent purports to disapprove. Surely the dissent does not believe that the through-the-wall radar or ultrasound technology produces an 8-by-10 Kodak glossy that needs no analysis (*i.e.*, the making of inferences). And, of course, the novel proposition that inference insulates a search is blatantly contrary to *United States v. Karo* (1984), where the police "inferred" from the activation of a beeper that a certain can of ether was in the home. The police activity was held to be a search, and the search was held unlawful.

The Government also contends that the thermal imaging was constitutional because it did not "detect private activities occurring in private areas." It points out that in *Dow Chemical* we observed that the enhanced aerial photography did not reveal any "intimate details." *Dow Chemical,* however, involved enhanced aerial photography of an industrial complex, which does not share the Fourth Amendment sanctity of the home.

■ ■ ■

Limiting the prohibition of thermal imaging to "intimate details" would not only be wrong in principle; it would be impractical in application, failing to provide "a workable accommodation between the needs of law enforcement and the interests protected by the Fourth Amendment." To begin with, there is no necessary connection between the sophistication of the surveillance equipment and the "intimacy" of the details that it observes—which means that one cannot say (and the police cannot be assured) that use of the relatively crude equipment at issue here will always be lawful. The Agema Thermovision 210 might disclose, for example, at what hour each night the lady of the house takes her daily sauna and bath—a detail that many would consider "intimate"; and a much more sophisticated system might detect nothing more intimate than the fact that someone left a closet light on. We could not, in other words, develop a rule approving only that through-the-wall surveillance which identifies objects no smaller than 36 by 36 inches, but would have to develop a jurisprudence specifying which home activities are "intimate" and which are not. And even when (if ever) that jurisprudence were fully developed, no police officer would be able to know *in advance* whether his through-the-wall surveillance picks up "intimate" details—and thus would be unable to know in advance whether it is constitutional.

■ ■ ■

We have said that the Fourth Amendment draws "a firm line at the entrance to the house." *Payton v. New York* (1979). That line, we think, must be not only firm but also bright—which requires clear specification of those methods of surveillance that require a warrant. While it is certainly possible to conclude from the videotape of the thermal imaging that occurred in this case that no "significant" compromise of the homeowner's privacy has occurred, we must take the long view, from the original meaning of the Fourth Amendment forward.

■ ■ ■

Where, as here, the Government uses a device that is not in general public use, to explore details of the home that would previously have been unknowable without physical intrusion, the surveillance is a "search" and is presumptively unreasonable without a warrant.

Since we hold the Thermovision imaging to have been an unlawful search, it will remain for the District Court to determine whether, without the evidence it provided, the search warrant issued in this case was supported by probable cause—and if not, whether there is any other basis for supporting admission of the evidence that the search pursuant to the warrant produced.

The judgment of the Court of Appeals is reversed; the case is remanded for further proceedings consistent with this opinion.

It is so ordered.

Justice STEVENS, with whom THE CHIEF JUSTICE, Justice O'CONNOR, and Justice KENNEDY join, dissenting.

There is, in my judgment, a distinction of constitutional magnitude between "through-the-wall surveillance" that gives the observer or listener direct access to information in a private area, on the one hand, and the thought processes used to draw inferences from information in the public domain, on the other hand. The Court has crafted a rule that purports to deal with direct observations of the inside of the home, but the case before us merely involves indirect deductions from "off-the-wall" surveillance, that is, observations of the exterior of the home. Those observations were made with a fairly primitive thermal imager that gathered data exposed on the outside of petitioner's home but did not invade any constitutionally protected interest in privacy. More-over, I believe that the supposedly "bright-line" rule the Court has created in response to its concerns about future technological developments is unneces-sary, unwise, and inconsistent with the Fourth Amendment.

■ ■ ■

There is no need for the Court to craft a new rule to decide this case, as it is controlled by established principles from our Fourth Amendment jurispru-dence. One of those core principles, of course, is that "searches and seizures *inside a home* without a warrant are presumptively unreasonable." *Payton v. New York.* But it is equally well settled that searches and seizures of property in plain view are presumptively reasonable. Whether that property is residential or commercial, the basic principle is the same: "'What a person knowingly exposes to the public, even in his own home or office, is not a subject of Fourth Amendment protection.'" *California v. Ciraolo,* quoting *Katz v. United States....* While the Court "take[s] the long view" and decides this case based largely on the potential of yet-to-be-developed technology that might allow "through-the-wall surveillance," this case involves nothing more than off-the-wall sur-veillance by law enforcement officers to gather information exposed to the general public from the outside of petitioner's home. All that the infrared camera did in this case was passively measure heat emitted from the exterior surfaces of petitioner's home; all that those measurements showed were rela-tive differences in emission levels, vaguely indicating that some areas of the roof and outside walls were warmer than others. As still images from the infrared scans show, no details regarding the interior of petitioner's home were revealed. Unlike an x-ray scan, or other possible "through-the-wall" techniques, the detection of infrared radiation emanating from the home did not accomplish "an unauthorized physical penetration into the premises," nor did it "obtain information that it could not have obtained by observation from outside the curtilage of the house."

■ ■ ■

To be sure, the homeowner has a reasonable expectation of privacy concerning what takes place within the home, and the Fourth Amendment's protection against physical invasions of the home should apply to their functional equivalent. But the equipment in this case did not penetrate the walls of petitioner's home, and while it did pick up "details of the home" that were exposed to the public, it did not obtain "any information regarding the *interior* of the home." . . .

Instead of trying to answer the question whether the use of the thermal imager in this case was even arguably unreasonable, the Court has fashioned a rule that is intended to provide essential guidance for the day when "more sophisticated systems" gain the "ability to 'see' through walls and other opaque barriers." The newly minted rule encompasses "obtaining [1] by sense-enhancing technology [2] any information regarding the interior of the home [3] that could not otherwise have been obtained without physical intrusion into a constitutionally protected area . . . [4] at least where (as here) the technology in question is not in general public use." In my judgment, the Court's new rule is at once too broad and too narrow, and is not justified by the Court's explanation for its adoption. As I have suggested, I would not erect a constitutional impediment to the use of sense-enhancing technology unless it provides its user with the functional equivalent of actual presence in the area being searched.

Despite the Court's attempt to draw a line that is "not only firm but also bright," the contours of its new rule are uncertain because its protection apparently dissipates as soon as the relevant technology is "in general public use." Yet how much use is general public use is not even hinted at by the Court's opinion, which makes the somewhat doubtful assumption that the thermal imager used in this case does not satisfy that criterion. In any event, putting aside its lack of clarity, this criterion is somewhat perverse because it seems likely that the threat to privacy will grow, rather than recede, as the use of intrusive equipment becomes more readily available.

■ ■ ■

The application of the Court's new rule to "any information regarding the interior of the home" is also unnecessarily broad. If it takes sensitive equipment to detect an odor that identifies criminal conduct and nothing else, the fact that the odor emanates from the interior of a home should not provide it with constitutional protection. The criterion, moreover, is too sweeping in that information "regarding" the interior of a home apparently is not just information obtained through its walls, but also information concerning the outside of the building that could lead to (however many) inferences "regarding" what might be inside. Under that expansive view, I suppose, an officer using an infrared camera to observe a man silently entering the side door of a house at night carrying a pizza might conclude that its interior is now occupied by someone who likes pizza, and by doing so the officer would be guilty of conducting an unconstitutional "search" of the home.

■ ■ ■

The two reasons advanced by the Court as justifications for the adoption of its new rule are both unpersuasive. First, the Court suggests that its rule is compelled by our holding in *Katz,* because in that case, as in this, the surveillance consisted of nothing more than the monitoring of waves emanating from a private area into the public domain. Yet there are critical differences between the cases. In *Katz,* the electronic listening device attached to the outside of the phone booth allowed the officers to pick up the content of the conversation inside the booth, making them the functional equivalent of intruders because they gathered information that was otherwise available only to someone inside the private area; it would be as if, in this case, the thermal imager presented a view of the heat-generating activity inside petitioner's home. By contrast, the thermal imager here disclosed only the relative amounts of heat radiating from the house; it would be as if, in *Katz,* the listening device disclosed only the relative volume of sound leaving the booth, which presumably was discernible in the public domain. Surely, there is a significant difference between the general and well-settled expectation that strangers will not have direct access to the contents of private communications, on the one hand, and the rather theoretical expectation that an occasional homeowner would even care if anybody noticed the relative amounts of heat emanating from the walls of his house, on the other. It is pure hyperbole for the Court to suggest that refusing to extend the holding of *Katz* to this case would leave the homeowner at the mercy of "technology that could discern all human activity in the home."

Second, the Court argues that the permissibility of "through-the-wall surveillance" cannot depend on a distinction between observing "intimate details" such as "the lady of the house [taking] her daily sauna and bath," and noticing only "the nonintimate rug on the vestibule floor" or "objects no smaller than 36 by 36 inches." This entire argument assumes, of course, that the thermal imager in this case could or did perform "through-the-wall surveillance" that could identify any detail "that would previously have been unknowable without physical intrusion." In fact, the device could not enable its user to identify either the lady of the house, the rug on the vestibule floor, or anything else inside the house, whether smaller or larger than 36 by 36 inches. Indeed, the vague thermal images of petitioner's home that are reproduced in the Appendix were submitted by him to the District Court as part of an expert report raising the question whether the device could even take "accurate, consistent infrared images" of the *outside* of his house. But even if the device could reliably show extraordinary differences in the amounts of heat leaving his home, drawing the inference that there was something suspicious occurring inside the residence—a conclusion that officers far less gifted than Sherlock Holmes would readily draw—does not qualify as "through-the-wall surveillance," much less a Fourth Amendment violation.

■ ■ ■

Although the Court is properly and commendably concerned about the threats to privacy that may flow from advances in the technology available to the law enforcement profession, it has unfortunately failed to heed the tried and true counsel of judicial restraint. Instead of concentrating on the rather mundane issue that is actually presented by the case before it, the Court has endeavored to craft an all-encompassing rule for the future. It would be far wiser to give legislators an unimpeded opportunity to grapple with these emerging issues rather than to shackle them with prematurely devised constitutional constraints.

I respectfully dissent.

c. Curtilage

United States v. Dunn

480 U.S. 294 (1987)

WHITE, J., delivered the opinion of the Court, in which, REHNQUIST, C.J., BLACKMUN, POWELL, STEVENS, and O'CONNOR, JJ., joined. SCALIA, J., filed a concurring opinion. BRENNAN, J., filed a dissenting opinion, in which MARSHALL, J., joined.

We granted the Government's petition for certiorari to decide whether the area near a barn, located approximately 50 yards from a fence surrounding a ranch house, is, for Fourth Amendment purposes, within the curtilage of the house. The Court of Appeals for the Fifth Circuit held that the barn lay within the house's curtilage, and that the District Court should have suppressed certain evidence obtained as a result of law enforcement officials' intrusion onto the area immediately surrounding the barn. We conclude that the barn and the area around it lay outside the curtilage of the house, and accordingly reverse the judgment of the Court of Appeals.

Respondent Ronald Dale Dunn and a codefendant, Robert Lyle Carpenter, were convicted by a jury of conspiring to manufacture phenylacetone and amphetamine, and to possess amphetamine with intent to distribute.... Respondent was also convicted of manufacturing these two controlled substances and possessing amphetamine with intent to distribute. The events giving rise to respondent's apprehension and conviction began in 1980 when agents from the Drug Enforcement Administration (DEA) discovered that Carpenter had purchased large quantities of chemicals and equipment used in the manufacture of amphetamine and phenylacetone. DEA agents obtained warrants from a Texas state judge authorizing installation of miniature electronic transmitter tracking devices, or "beepers," in an electric hot plate stirrer, a drum of acetic anhydride, and a container holding phenylacetic acid, a precursor to phenylacetone. All of these items had been ordered by Carpenter. On September 3, 1980, Carpenter took possession of the electric hot plate stirrer, but the agents lost the signal from the "beeper" a few days later. The agents were able to track the "beeper" in the container of chemicals, however, from October 27, 1980, until November 5, 1980, on which date Carpenter's pickup truck, which was carrying the container, arrived at respondent's ranch. Aerial photographs of the ranch property showed Carpenter's truck backed up to a barn behind the ranch house. The agents also began receiving transmission signals from the "beeper" in the hot plate stirrer that they had lost in early September and determined that the stirrer was on respondent's ranch property.

Respondent's ranch comprised approximately 198 acres and was completely encircled by a perimeter fence. The property also contained several interior fences, constructed mainly of posts and multiple strands of barbed wire. The ranch residence was situated ½ mile from a public road. A fence encircled the residence and a nearby small greenhouse. Two barns were located approximately 50 yards from this fence. The front of the larger of the two barns was enclosed by a wooden fence and had an open overhang. Locked, waist-high gates barred entry into the barn proper, and netting material stretched from the ceiling to the top of the wooden gates.

On the evening of November 5, 1980, law enforcement officials made a warrantless entry onto respondent's ranch property. A DEA agent accompanied by an officer from the Houston Police Department crossed over the perimeter fence and one interior fence. Standing approximately midway between the residence and the barns, the DEA agent smelled what he believed to be phenylacetic acid, the odor coming from the direction of the barns. The officers approached the smaller of the barns—crossing over a barbed wire fence—and, looking into the barn, observed only empty boxes. The officers then proceeded to the larger barn, crossing another barbed wire fence as well as a wooden fence that enclosed the front portion of the barn. The officers walked under the barn's overhang to the locked wooden gates and, shining a flashlight through the netting on top of the gates, peered into the barn. They observed what the DEA agent thought to be a phenylacetone laboratory. The officers did not enter the barn. At this point the officers departed from respondent's property, but entered it twice more on November 6 to confirm the presence of the phenylacetone laboratory.

On November 6, 1980, at 8:30 p.m., a Federal Magistrate issued a warrant authorizing a search of respondent's ranch. DEA agents and state law enforcement officials executed the warrant on November 8, 1980. The officers arrested respondent and seized chemicals and equipment, as well as bags of amphetamines they discovered in a closet in the ranch house. . . .

The curtilage concept originated at common law to extend to the area immediately surrounding a dwelling house the same protection under the law of burglary as was afforded the house itself. The concept plays a part, however, in interpreting the reach of the Fourth Amendment. . . . *Hester v. United States* (1924) held that the Fourth Amendment's protection accorded "persons, houses, papers, and effects" did not extend to the open fields, the Court observing that the distinction between a person's house and open fields "is as old as the common law."

We reaffirmed the holding of *Hester* (1924) in *Oliver* (1984). There, we recognized that the Fourth Amendment protects the curtilage of a house and that the extent of the curtilage is determined by factors that bear upon whether an individual reasonably may expect that the area in question should be treated as the home itself. We identified the central component of this inquiry as whether the area harbors the "intimate activity associated with the 'sanctity of a man's home and the privacies of life.'"

Drawing upon the Court's own cases and the cumulative experience of the lower courts that have grappled with the task of defining the extent of a home's curtilage, we believe that curtilage questions should be resolved with particular reference to four factors: the proximity of the area claimed to be curtilage to the home, whether the area is included within an enclosure surrounding the home, the nature of the uses to which the area is put, and the steps taken by the resident to protect the area from observation by people passing by. We do not suggest that combining these factors produces a finely tuned formula that, when mechanically applied, yields a "correct" answer to all extent-of-curtilage questions. Rather, these factors are useful analytical tools only to the degree that, in any given case, they bear upon the centrally relevant consideration—whether the area in question is so intimately tied to the home itself that it should be placed under the home's "umbrella" of Fourth Amendment protection. Applying these factors to respondent's barn and to the area immediately surrounding it, we have little difficulty in concluding that this area lay outside the curtilage of the ranch house.

First. The record discloses that the barn was located 50 yards from the fence surrounding the house and 60 yards from the house itself. Standing in isolation, this substantial distance supports no inference that the barn should be treated as an adjunct of the house.

Second. It is also significant that respondent's barn did not lie within the area surrounding the house that was enclosed by a fence. We noted in *Oliver* that "for most homes, the boundaries of the curtilage will be clearly marked; and the conception defining the curtilage—as the area around the home to which the activity of home life extends—is a familiar one easily understood from our daily experience." Viewing the physical layout of respondent's ranch in its entirety, it is plain that the fence surrounding the residence serves to demark a specific area of land immediately adjacent to the house that is readily identifiable as part and parcel of the house. Conversely, the barn—the front portion itself enclosed by a fence—and the area immediately surrounding it, stands out as a distinct portion of respondent's ranch, quite separate from the residence.

Third. It is especially significant that the law enforcement officials possessed objective data indicating that the barn was not being used for intimate activities of the home. The aerial photographs showed that the truck Carpenter had been driving that contained the container of phenylacetic acid was backed up to the barn, "apparently," in the words of the Court of Appeals, "for the unloading of its contents." When on respondent's property, the officers' suspicion was further directed toward the barn because of "a very strong odor" of phenylacetic acid. . . .

Fourth. Respondent did little to protect the barn area from observation by those standing in the open fields. Nothing in the record suggests that the various interior fences on respondent's property had any function other than that of the typical ranch fence; the fences were designed and constructed to corral livestock, not to prevent persons from observing what lay inside the enclosed areas. . . .

Justice SCALIA, concurring in part.

I join Justice White's opinion with the exception of "*Third.*" It does not seem to me "especially significant that the law enforcement officials possessed objective data indicating that the barn was not being used for intimate activities of the home." What is significant is that the barn was not being so used, whether or not the law enforcement officials knew it. The officers' perceptions might be relevant to whether intrusion upon curtilage was nevertheless reasonable, but they are no more relevant to whether the barn was curtilage than to whether the house was a house.

Justice BRENNAN, with whom Justice MARSHALL joins, dissenting.

The Government agents' intrusions upon Ronald Dunn's privacy and property violated the Fourth Amendment for two reasons. First, the barnyard invaded by the agents lay within the protected curtilage of Dunn's farmhouse. Second, the agents infringed upon Dunn's reasonable expectation of privacy in the barn and its contents. Our society is not so exclusively urban that it is unable to perceive or unwilling to preserve the expectation of farmers and ranchers that barns and their contents are protected from (literally) unwarranted government intrusion.

I briefly recount the relevant facts.

Respondent's ranch of 198 acres is encircled by a perimeter fence. The residence and its outbuildings are located in a clearing surrounded by woods, ½ mile from a road, down a chained, locked driveway. Neither the farmhouse nor its outbuildings are visible from the public road or from the fence that encircles the entire property. Once inside this perimeter fence, it is necessary to cross at least one more "substantial" fence before approaching Dunn's farmhouse or either of his two barns.

The front of the barn involved here is enclosed by a wooden fence. Its back and sides

> "were composed of brick, metal siding, and large metal sliding doors and were completely enclosed. The front of the barn was partially composed of a wooden wall with windows. The remainder was enclosed by waist-high wood slatting and wooden gates. At the time of [the] agent['s] visits . . . the top half of the front of the barn was covered by a fishnet type material from the ceiling down to the top of the locked wooden gates. To see inside the barn it was necessary to stand immediately next to the netting [under the barn's overhang]. From as little as a few feet distant, visibility into the barn was obscured by the netting and slatting."

The issues are whether the barn was within the protected curtilage of the house, and whether the conduct of the Drug Enforcement Agency (DEA) agents—"circling the large barn, being unable to see inside through the back or sides, climbing a wooden fence at its front, entering its overhang and going into the immediate proximity of the fishnet and wooden gate front enclosure"—infringed upon Dunn's reasonable expectation of privacy in the barn or its contents. . . .

The Court states that curtilage questions are often resolved through evaluation of four factors: "the proximity of the area claimed to be curtilage to the home, whether the area is included within an enclosure surrounding the home, the nature of the uses to which the area is put, and the steps taken by the resident to protect the area from observation by people passing by." The Court applies this test and concludes that Dunn's barn and barnyard were not within the curtilage of his dwelling. This conclusion overlooks the role a barn plays in rural life and ignores extensive authority holding that a barn, when clustered with other outbuildings near the residence, is part of the curtilage.

State and federal courts have long recognized that a barn, like many other outbuildings, is "a domestic building constituting an integral part of that group of structures making up the farm home." Consequently, the general rule is that the "[c]urtilage includes all outbuildings used in connection with a residence, such as garages, sheds, [and] *barns* . . . connected with and in close vicinity of the residence." . . .

Federal courts, too, have held that barns, like other rural outbuildings, lie within the curtilage of the farmhouse. . . .

Thus, case law demonstrates that a barn is an integral part of a farm home and therefore lies within the curtilage. The Court's opinion provides no justification for its indifference to the weight of state and federal precedent.

The above-cited authority also reveals the infirmities in the Court's application of its four-part test. First, the distance between the house and the barn does not militate against the barn or barnyard's presence in the curtilage. Many of the cases cited involve a barn separated from a residence by a distance in excess of 60 yards. Second, the cases make evident that the configuration of fences is not determinative of the status of an outbuilding. Here, where the barn was connected to the house by a "well walked" and a "well driven" path, and was clustered with the farmhouse and other outbuildings in a clearing surrounded by woods, the presence of intervening fences fades into irrelevance.

The third factor in the test—the nature of the uses to which the area is put— has been badly misunderstood and misapplied by the Court. The Court reasons that, because the barn and barnyard were not actually in domestic use, they were not within the curtilage. This reveals a misunderstanding of the level of generality at which the constitutional inquiry must proceed and is flatly inconsistent with the Court's analysis in *Oliver.* . . .

Moreover, the discovery that Dunn's barn was actually used as a drug laboratory is irrelevant to the question whether the area is typically in domestic use. No one would contend that, absent exigent circumstances, the police could intrude upon a home without a warrant to search for a drug manufacturing operation. The Fourth Amendment extends that same protection to outbuildings in the curtilage of the home.

Even accepting that courts should do a case-by-case inquiry regarding the use of buildings within the curtilage, the Court's analysis is faulty. The Court finds it significant that, because of the strong odor and the noise of a motor emanating from the barn, the officers knew that the barn was not in domestic use. But these Government agents *were already within the curtilage* when they detected the odor of phenylacetic acid. They were wandering about in the area between the barns and the farmhouse, an area that is itself part of the curtilage. The Court cannot abrogate the general rule that a barn is in the curtilage with evidence gathered after the intrusion has occurred.

Finally, neither the smell of the chemicals nor the sound of the motor running would remove the protection of the Fourth Amendment from an otherwise protected structure. A barn, like a home, may simultaneously be put to domestic and nondomestic uses, even the manufacture of drugs. Dual use does not strip a home or any building within the curtilage of Fourth Amendment protection. . . .

■ ■ ■

With regard to the fourth factor of the curtilage test, I find astounding the Court's conclusion that "[r]espondent did little to protect the barn area from observation by those standing in the open fields." Initially, I note that the fenced area immediately adjacent to the barn in this case is not part of the open fields, but is instead part of the curtilage and an area in which Dunn had a reasonable expectation of privacy. Second, Dunn in fact took elaborate measures to ensure his privacy. He locked his driveway, fenced in his barn, and covered its open end with a locked gate and fishnetting.

■ ■ ■

Today's decision has an unforeseen consequence. In narrowing the meaning given to the concept of curtilage, the Court also narrows the scope of searches permissible under a warrant authorizing a search of building premises. Police officers often proceed as if a warrant that authorizes a search of the premises or the dwelling also authorizes a search of any outbuildings (such as garages, barns, sheds, smokehouses) because such buildings are commonly deemed within the curtilage.

■ ■ ■

The Fourth Amendment prohibits police activity which, if left unrestricted, would jeopardize individuals' sense of security or would too heavily burden those who wished to guard their privacy. In this case, in order to look inside respondent's barn, the DEA agents traveled one-half mile off a public road over respondent's fenced-in property, crossed over three additional wooden and barbed wire fences, stepped under the eaves of the barn, and then used a flashlight to peer through otherwise opaque fishnetting. For the police habitually to engage in such surveillance—without a warrant—is constitutionally intolerable. Because I believe that farmers' and ranchers' expectations of privacy in their barns and other outbuildings are expectations society would regard as reasonable, and because I believe that sanctioning the police behavior at issue here does violence to the purpose and promise of the Fourth Amendment, I dissent.

California v. Greenwood

486 U.S. 35 (1988)

See Chapter 2.B.3.

Florida v. Riley

488 U.S. 445 (1989)

WHITE, J., announced the judgment of the Court and delivered an opinion in which REHNQUIST, C.J., and SCALIA and KENNEDY, JJ., joined. O'CONNOR, J., filed an opinion concurring in the judgment. BRENNAN, J., filed a dissenting opinion, in which MARSHALL and STEVENS, JJ., joined. BLACKMUN, J., filed a dissenting opinion.

On certification to it by a lower state court, the Florida Supreme Court addressed the following question: "Whether surveillance of the interior of a partially covered greenhouse in a residential backyard from the vantage point of a helicopter located 400 feet above the greenhouse constitutes a 'search' for which a warrant is required under the Fourth Amendment and Article I, § 12 of the Florida Constitution." The court answered the question in the affirmative, and we granted the State's petition for certiorari challenging that conclusion.

Respondent Riley lived in a mobile home located on five acres of rural property. A greenhouse was located 10 to 20 feet behind the mobile home. Two sides of the greenhouse were enclosed. The other two sides were not enclosed but the contents of the greenhouse were obscured from view from surrounding property by trees, shrubs, and the mobile home. The greenhouse was covered by corrugated roofing panels, some translucent and some opaque. At the time relevant to this case, two of the panels, amounting to approximately 10% of the roof area, were missing. A wire fence surrounded the mobile home and the greenhouse, and the property was posted with a "DO NOT ENTER" sign.

This case originated with an anonymous tip to the Pasco County Sheriff's office that marijuana was being grown on respondent's property. When an investigating officer discovered that he could not see the contents of the greenhouse from the road, he circled twice over respondent's property in a helicopter at the height of 400 feet. With his naked eye, he was able to see through the openings in the roof and one or more of the open sides of the greenhouse and to identify what he thought was marijuana growing in the structure. A warrant was obtained based on these observations, and the ensuing search revealed marijuana growing in the greenhouse. Respondent was charged with possession of marijuana under Florida law. The trial court granted his motion to suppress; the Florida Court of Appeals reversed but certified the case to the Florida Supreme Court, which quashed the decision of the Court of Appeals and reinstated the trial court's suppression order.

Ciraolo controls

We agree with the State's submission that our decision in *California v. Ciraolo* (1986) controls this case. There, acting on a tip, the police inspected the backyard of a particular house while flying in a fixed-wing aircraft at 1,000 feet. With the naked eye the officers saw what they concluded was marijuana growing in the yard. A search warrant was obtained on the strength of this airborne inspection, and marijuana plants were found. The trial court refused to suppress this evidence, but a state appellate court held that the inspection violated the Fourth and Fourteenth Amendments to the United States Constitution, and that the warrant was therefore invalid. We in turn reversed, holding that the inspection was not a search subject to the Fourth Amendment. We recognized that the yard was within the curtilage of the house, that a fence shielded the yard from observation from the street, and that the occupant had a subjective expectation of privacy. We held, however, that such an expectation was not reasonable and not one "that society is prepared to honor." Our reasoning was that the home and its curtilage are not necessarily protected from inspection that involves no physical invasion. "'What a person knowingly exposes to the public, even in his own home or office, is not a subject of Fourth Amendment protection.'" quoting *Katz* (1967). As a general proposition, the police may see what may be seen "from a public vantage point where [they have] a right to be." Thus the police, like the public, would have been free to inspect the backyard garden from the street if their view had been unobstructed. They were likewise free to inspect the yard from the vantage point of an aircraft flying in the navigable airspace as this plane was. "In an age where private and commercial flight in the public airways is routine, it is unreasonable for respondent to expect that his marijuana plants were constitutionally protected from being observed with the naked eye from an altitude of 1,000 feet. The Fourth Amendment simply does not require the police traveling in the public airways at this altitude to obtain a warrant in order to observe what is visible to the naked eye."

We arrive at the same conclusion in the present case. In this case, as in *Ciraolo*, the property surveyed was within the curtilage of respondent's home. Riley no doubt intended and expected that his greenhouse would not be open to public inspection, and the precautions he took protected against ground-level observation. Because the sides and roof of his greenhouse were left partially open, however, what was growing in the greenhouse was subject to viewing from the air. Under the holding in *Ciraolo*, Riley could not reasonably have expected the contents of his greenhouse to be immune from examination by an officer seated in a fixed-wing aircraft flying in navigable airspace at an altitude of 1,000 feet or, as the Florida Supreme Court seemed to recognize, at an altitude of 500 feet, the lower limit of the navigable airspace for such an aircraft. Here, the inspection was made from a helicopter, but as is the case with fixed-wing planes, "private and commercial flight [by helicopter] in the public airways is routine" in this country, *Ciraolo*, and there is no indication that such flights are unheard of in Pasco County, Florida. Riley could not reasonably have expected that his greenhouse was protected from public or official observation from a helicopter had it been flying within the navigable airspace for fixed-wing aircraft.

Nor on the facts before us, does it make a difference for Fourth Amendment purposes that the helicopter was flying at 400 feet when the officer saw what was growing in the greenhouse through the partially open roof and sides of the structure. We would have a different case if flying at that altitude had been contrary to law or regulation. But helicopters are not bound by the lower limits of the navigable airspace allowed to other aircraft. Any member of the public could legally have been flying over Riley's property in a helicopter at the altitude of 400 feet and could have observed Riley's greenhouse. The police officer did no more. This is not to say that an inspection of the curtilage of a house from an aircraft will always pass muster under the Fourth Amendment simply because the plane is within the navigable airspace specified by law. But it is of obvious importance that the helicopter in this case was *not* violating the law, and there is nothing in the record or before us to suggest that helicopters flying at 400 feet are sufficiently rare in this country to lend substance to respondent's claim that he reasonably anticipated that his greenhouse would not be subject to observation from that altitude. Neither is there any intimation here that the helicopter interfered with respondent's normal use of the greenhouse or of other parts of the curtilage. As far as this record reveals, no intimate details connected with the use of the home or curtilage were observed, and there was no undue noise, and no wind, dust, or threat of injury. In these circumstances, there was no violation of the Fourth Amendment.

The judgment of the Florida Supreme Court is accordingly reversed.

So ordered.

Justice O'CONNOR, concurring in the judgment.

I concur in the judgment reversing the Supreme Court of Florida because I agree that police observation of the greenhouse in Riley's curtilage from a helicopter passing at an altitude of 400 feet did not violate an expectation of privacy "that society is prepared to recognize as 'reasonable.'" *Katz v. United States*. I write separately, however, to clarify the standard I believe follows from *California v. Ciraolo*. In my view, the plurality's approach rests the scope of Fourth Amendment protection too heavily on compliance with FAA regulations whose purpose is to promote air safety, not to protect "[t]he right of the people to be secure in their persons, houses, papers, and effects, against unreasonable searches and seizures."

Ciraolo involved observation of curtilage by officers flying in an airplane at an altitude of 1,000 feet. In evaluating whether this observation constituted a search for which a warrant was required, we acknowledged the importance of curtilage in Fourth Amendment doctrine: "The protection afforded the curtilage is essentially a protection of families and personal privacy in an area intimately linked to the home, both physically and psychologically, where privacy expectations are most heightened." Although the curtilage is an area to which the private activities of the home extend, all police observation of the curtilage is not necessarily barred by the Fourth Amendment. As we observed: "The Fourth Amendment protection of the home has never been extended to require law enforcement officers to shield their eyes when passing by a home on public thoroughfares." In *Ciraolo*, we likened observation from a plane traveling in "public navigable airspace" at 1,000 feet to observation by police "passing by a home on public thoroughfares." We held that "[i]n an age where private and commercial flight in the public airways is routine," it is unreasonable to expect the curtilage to be constitutionally protected from aerial observation with the naked eye from an altitude of 1,000 feet.

■ ■ ■

Observations of curtilage from helicopters at very low altitudes are not perfectly analogous to ground-level observations from public roads or sidewalks. While in both cases the police may have a legal right to occupy the physical space from which their observations are made, the two situations are not necessarily comparable in terms of whether expectations of privacy from such vantage points should be considered reasonable. Public roads, even those less traveled by, are clearly demarked public thoroughfares. Individuals who seek privacy can take precautions, tailored to the location of the road, to avoid disclosing private activities to those who pass by. They can build a tall fence, for example, and thus ensure private enjoyment of the curtilage without risking public observation from the road or sidewalk. If they do not take such precautions, they cannot reasonably expect privacy from public observation. In contrast, even individuals who have taken effective precautions to ensure against ground-level observations cannot block off all conceivable aerial views of their outdoor patios and yards without entirely giving up their enjoyment of those areas. To require individuals to completely cover and enclose their curtilage is to demand more than the "precautions customarily taken by those seeking privacy." The fact that a helicopter could conceivably observe the curtilage at virtually any altitude or angle, without violating FAA regulations, does not in itself mean that an individual has no reasonable expectation of privacy from such observation.

In determining whether Riley had a reasonable expectation of privacy from aerial observation, the relevant inquiry after *Ciraolo* is not whether the helicopter was where it had a right to be under FAA regulations. Rather, consistent with *Katz*, we must ask whether the helicopter was in the public airways at an altitude at which members of the public travel with sufficient regularity that Riley's expectation of privacy from aerial observation was not "one that society is prepared to recognize as 'reasonable.'" Thus, in determining "'whether the government's intrusion infringes upon the personal and societal values protected by the Fourth Amendment,'" it is not conclusive to observe, as the plurality does, that "[a]ny member of the public could legally have been flying over Riley's property in a helicopter at the altitude of 400 feet and could have observed Riley's greenhouse." Nor is it conclusive that police helicopters may often fly at 400 feet. If the public rarely, if ever, travels overhead at such altitudes, the observation cannot be said to be from a vantage point generally used by the public and Riley cannot be said to have "knowingly expose[d]" his greenhouse to public view. However, if the public can generally be expected to travel over residential backyards at an altitude of 400 feet, Riley cannot reasonably expect his curtilage to be free from such aerial observation.

In my view, the defendant must bear the burden of proving that his expectation of privacy was a reasonable one, and thus that a "search" within the meaning of the Fourth Amendment even took place. Cf. *Jones v. United States* (1960) ("Ordinarily, then, it is entirely proper to require of one who seeks to challenge the legality of a search as the basis for suppressing relevant evidence that he allege, and if the allegation be disputed that he establish, that he himself was the victim of an invasion of privacy.")

■ ■ ■

Because there is reason to believe that there is considerable public use of airspace at altitudes of 400 feet and above, and because Riley introduced no evidence to the contrary before the Florida courts, I conclude that Riley's expectation that his curtilage was protected from naked-eye aerial observation from that altitude was not a reasonable one. However, public use of altitudes lower than that—particularly public observations from helicopters circling over the curtilage of a home—may be sufficiently rare that police surveillance from such altitudes would violate reasonable expectations of privacy, despite compliance with FAA air safety regulations.

Justice BRENNAN, with whom Justice MARSHALL and Justice STEVENS join, dissenting.

The Court holds today that police officers need not obtain a warrant based on probable cause before circling in a helicopter 400 feet above a home in order to investigate what is taking place behind the walls of the curtilage. I cannot agree that the Fourth Amendment to the Constitution, which safeguards "[t]he right of the people to be secure in their persons, houses, papers, and effects, against unreasonable searches and seizures," tolerates such an intrusion on privacy and personal security.

The opinion for a plurality of the Court reads almost as if *Katz* had never been decided. Notwithstanding the disclaimers of its final paragraph, the opinion relies almost exclusively on the fact that the police officer conducted his surveillance from a vantage point where, under applicable Federal Aviation Administration regulations, he had a legal right to be. *Katz* teaches, however, that the relevant inquiry is whether the police surveillance "violated the privacy upon which [the defendant] justifiably relied,"—or, as Justice Harlan put it, whether the police violated an "expectation of privacy . . . that society is prepared to recognize as 'reasonable.'" The result of that inquiry in any given case

depends ultimately on the judgment "whether, if the particular form of surveillance practiced by the police is permitted to go unregulated by constitutional restraints, the amount of privacy and freedom remaining to citizens
would be diminished to a compass inconsistent with the aims of a free and
open society."

The plurality undertakes no inquiry into whether low-level helicopter surveillance by the police of activities in an enclosed backyard is consistent with
the "aims of a free and open society." Instead, it summarily concludes that
Riley's expectation of privacy was unreasonable because "[a]ny member of the
public could legally have been flying over Riley's property in a helicopter at the
altitude of 400 feet and could have observed Riley's greenhouse." This observation is, in turn, based solely on the fact that the police helicopter was within
the airspace within which such craft are allowed by federal safety regulations
to fly.

I agree, of course, that "[w]hat a person knowingly exposes to the public . . .
is not a subject of Fourth Amendment protection." But I cannot agree that one
"knowingly exposes [an area] to the public" solely because a helicopter may
legally fly above it. Under the plurality's exceedingly grudging Fourth
Amendment theory, the expectation of privacy is defeated if a single member
of the public could conceivably position herself to see into the area in question
without doing anything illegal. It is defeated whatever the difficulty a person
would have in so positioning herself, and however infrequently anyone would
in fact do so. In taking this view the plurality ignores the very essence of *Katz*.
The reason why there is no reasonable expectation of privacy in an area that is
exposed to the public is that little diminution in "the amount of privacy and
freedom remaining to citizens" will result from police surveillance of something that any passerby readily sees. To pretend, as the plurality opinion does,
that the same is true when the police use a helicopter to peer over high fences is,
at best, disingenuous. Notwithstanding the plurality's statistics about the
number of helicopters registered in this country, can it seriously be questioned
that Riley enjoyed virtually complete privacy in his backyard greenhouse, and
that that privacy was invaded solely by police helicopter surveillance? Is the
theoretical possibility that any member of the public (with sufficient means)
could also have hired a helicopter and looked over Riley's fence of any relevance at all in determining whether Riley suffered a serious loss of privacy and
personal security through the police action?

In *California v. Ciraolo*, we held that whatever might be observed from the
window of an airplane flying at 1,000 feet could be deemed unprotected by any
reasonable expectation of privacy. That decision was based on the belief that
airplane traffic at that altitude was sufficiently common that no expectation of
privacy could inure in anything on the ground observable with the naked eye
from so high. Indeed, we compared those airways to "public thoroughfares,"
and made the obvious point that police officers passing by a home on such
thoroughfares were not required by the Fourth Amendment to "shield their
eyes." Seizing on a reference in *Ciraolo* to the fact that the police officer was in a

position "where he ha[d] a right to be," today's plurality professes to find this case indistinguishable because FAA regulations do not impose a minimum altitude requirement on helicopter traffic; thus, the officer in this case too made his observations from a vantage point where he had a right to be.

It is a curious notion that the reach of the Fourth Amendment can be so largely defined by administrative regulations issued for purposes of flight safety. It is more curious still that the plurality relies to such an extent on the legality of the officer's act, when we have consistently refused to equate police violation of the law with infringement of the Fourth Amendment. But the plurality's willingness to end its inquiry when it finds that the officer was in a position he had a right to be in is misguided for an even more fundamental reason. Finding determinative the fact that the officer was where he had a right to be is, at bottom, an attempt to analogize surveillance from a helicopter to surveillance by a police officer standing on a public road and viewing evidence of crime through an open window or a gap in a fence. In such a situation, the occupant of the home may be said to lack any reasonable expectation of privacy in what can be seen from that road—even if, in fact, people rarely pass that way.

The police officer positioned 400 feet above Riley's backyard was not, however, standing on a public road. The vantage point he enjoyed was not one any citizen could readily share. His ability to see over Riley's fence depended on his use of a very expensive and sophisticated piece of machinery to which few ordinary citizens have access. In such circumstances it makes no more sense to rely on the legality of the officer's position in the skies than it would to judge the constitutionality of the wiretap in *Katz* by the legality of the officer's position outside the telephone booth. The simple inquiry whether the police officer had the legal right to be in the position from which he made his observations cannot suffice, for we cannot assume that Riley's curtilage was so open to the observations of passersby in the skies that he retained little privacy or personal security to be lost to police surveillance. The question before us must be not whether the police were where they had a right to be, but whether public observation of Riley's curtilage was so commonplace that Riley's expectation of privacy in his backyard could not be considered reasonable. To say that an invasion of Riley's privacy from the skies was not impossible is most emphatically not the same as saying that his expectation of privacy within his enclosed curtilage was not "one that society is prepared to recognize as 'reasonable.'" While, as we held in *Ciraolo*, air traffic at elevations of 1,000 feet or more may be so common that whatever could be seen with the naked eye from that elevation is unprotected by the Fourth Amendment, it is a large step from there to say that the Amendment offers no protection against low-level helicopter surveillance of enclosed curtilage areas. To take this step is error enough. That the plurality does so with little analysis beyond its determination that the police complied with FAA regulations is particularly unfortunate.

■ ■ ■

Equally disconcerting is the lack of any meaningful limit to the plurality's holding. It is worth reiterating that the FAA regulations the plurality relies on as establishing that the officer was where he had a right to be set no minimum flight altitude for helicopters. It is difficult, therefore, to see what, if any, helicopter surveillance would run afoul of the plurality's rule that there exists no reasonable expectation of privacy as long as the helicopter is where it has a right to be.

■ ■ ■

I will deal with the "intimate details" below. For the rest, one wonders what the plurality believes the purpose of the Fourth Amendment to be. If through noise, wind, dust, and threat of injury from helicopters the State "interfered with respondent's normal use of the greenhouse or of other parts of the curtilage," Riley might have a cause of action in inverse condemnation, but that is not what the Fourth Amendment is all about. Nowhere is this better stated than in Justice White's opinion for the Court in *Camara v. Municipal Court* (1967): "The basic purpose of this Amendment, as recognized in countless decisions of this Court, is to safeguard the privacy and security of individuals against arbitrary invasions by governmental officials."

■ ■ ■

If indeed the purpose of the restraints imposed by the Fourth Amendment is to "safeguard the privacy and security of individuals," then it is puzzling why it should be the helicopter's noise, wind, and dust that provides the measure of whether this constitutional safeguard has been infringed. Imagine a helicopter capable of hovering just above an enclosed courtyard or patio without generating any noise, wind, or dust at all—and, for good measure, without posing any threat of injury. Suppose the police employed this miraculous tool to discover not only what crops people were growing in their greenhouses, but also what books they were reading and who their dinner guests were. Suppose, finally, that the FAA regulations remained unchanged, so that the police were undeniably "where they had a right to be." Would today's plurality continue to assert that "[t]he right of the people to be secure in their persons, houses, papers, and effects, against unreasonable searches and seizures" was not infringed by such surveillance? Yet that is the logical consequence of the plurality's rule that, so long as the police are where they have a right to be under air traffic regulations, the Fourth Amendment is offended only if the aerial surveillance interferes with the use of the backyard as a garden spot. Nor is there anything in the plurality's opinion to suggest that any different rule would apply were the police looking from their helicopter, not into the open curtilage, but through an open window into a room viewable only from the air.

Perhaps the most remarkable passage in the plurality opinion is its suggestion that the case might be a different one had any "intimate details connected with the use of the home or curtilage [been] observed." What, one wonders, is meant by "intimate details"? If the police had observed Riley embracing his wife in the backyard greenhouse, would we then say that his reasonable expectation of privacy had been infringed? Where in the Fourth Amendment or in our cases is there any warrant for imposing a requirement that the activity observed must be "intimate" in order to be protected by the Constitution?

It is difficult to avoid the conclusion that the plurality has allowed its analysis of Riley's expectation of privacy to be colored by its distaste for the activity in which he was engaged. It is indeed easy to forget, especially in view of current concern over drug trafficking, that the scope of the Fourth Amendment's protection does not turn on whether the activity disclosed by a search is illegal or innocuous. But we dismiss this as a "drug case" only at the peril of our own liberties. Justice Frankfurter once noted that "[i]t is a fair summary of history to say that the safeguards of liberty have frequently been forged in controversies involving not very nice people," and nowhere is this observation more apt than in the area of the Fourth Amendment, whose words have necessarily been given meaning largely through decisions suppressing evidence of criminal activity. The principle enunciated in this case determines what limits the Fourth Amendment imposes on aerial surveillance of any person, for any reason. If the Constitution does not protect Riley's marijuana garden against such surveillance, it is hard to see how it will prohibit the government from aerial spying on the activities of a law-abiding citizen on her fully enclosed outdoor patio. As Professor Amsterdam has eloquently written: "The question is not whether you or I must draw the blinds before we commit a crime. It is whether you and I must discipline ourselves to draw the blinds every time we enter a room, under pain of surveillance if we do not." 58 Minn. L. Rev., at 403.

■ ■ ■

I find little to disagree with Justice O'Connor's concurrence, apart from its closing paragraphs. A majority of the Court thus agrees that the fundamental inquiry is not whether the police were where they had a right to be under FAA regulations, but rather whether Riley's expectation of privacy was rendered illusory by the extent of public observation of his backyard from aerial traffic at 400 feet.

What separates me from Justice O'Connor is essentially an empirical matter concerning the extent of public use of the airspace at that altitude, together with the question of how to resolve that issue. I do not think the constitutional claim should fail simply because "there is reason to believe" that there is "considerable" public flying this close to earth or because Riley "introduced no evidence to the contrary before the Florida courts." . . . I think we could take judicial notice that, while there may be an occasional privately owned helicopter that flies over populated areas at an altitude of 400 feet, such flights are a rarity and are almost entirely limited to approaching or leaving airports or to reporting traffic congestion near major roadways. And, as the concurrence agrees, the extent of police surveillance traffic cannot serve as a bootstrap to demonstrate public use of the airspace.

If, however, we are to resolve the issue by considering whether the appropriate party carried its burden of proof, I again think that Riley must prevail. Because the State has greater access to information concerning customary flight patterns and because the coercive power of the State ought not be brought to bear in cases in which it is unclear whether the prosecution is a product of an unconstitutional, warrantless search, the burden of proof properly rests with the State and not with the individual defendant. The State quite clearly has not carried this burden.

■ ■ ■

The issue in this case is, ultimately, "how tightly the Fourth Amendment permits people to be driven back into the recesses of their lives by the risk of surveillance." The Court today approves warrantless helicopter surveillance from an altitude of 400 feet. While Justice O'Connor's opinion gives reason to hope that this altitude may constitute a lower limit, I find considerable cause for concern in the fact that a plurality of four Justices would remove virtually all constitutional barriers to police surveillance from the vantage point of helicopters. The Fourth Amendment demands that we temper our efforts to apprehend criminals with a concern for the impact on our fundamental liberties of the methods we use. I hope it will be a matter of concern to my colleagues that the police surveillance methods they would sanction were among those described 40 years ago in George Orwell's dread vision of life in the 1980's:

> "The black-mustachio'd face gazed down from every commanding corner. There was one on the house front immediately opposite. BIG BROTHER IS WATCHING YOU, the caption said. . . . In the far distance a helicopter skimmed down between the roofs, hovered for an instant like a bluebottle, and darted away again with a curving flight. It was the Police Patrol, snooping into people's windows."

Who can read this passage without a shudder, and without the instinctive reaction that it depicts life in some country other than ours? I respectfully dissent.

Justice BLACKMUN, dissenting.

The question before the Court is whether the helicopter surveillance over Riley's property constituted a "search" within the meaning of the Fourth Amendment. Like Justice Brennan, Justice Marshall, Justice Stevens, and Justice O'Connor, I believe that answering this question depends upon whether Riley has a "reasonable expectation of privacy" that no such surveillance would occur, and does not depend upon the fact that the helicopter was flying at a lawful altitude under FAA regulations. A majority of this Court thus agrees to at least this much. . . .

Thus, because I believe that private helicopters rarely fly over curtilages at an altitude of 400 feet, I would impose upon the prosecution the burden of proving contrary facts necessary to show that Riley lacked a reasonable expectation of privacy. Indeed, I would establish this burden of proof for any helicopter surveillance case in which the flight occurred below 1,000 feet—in other words, for any aerial surveillance case not governed by the Court's decision in *California v. Ciraolo*.

In this case, the prosecution did not meet this burden of proof, as Justice Brennan notes. This failure should compel a finding that a Fourth Amendment search occurred. But because our prior cases gave the parties little guidance on the burden of proof issue, I would remand this case to allow the prosecution an opportunity to meet this burden. . . .

C. STANDING

1. Original

Jones v. United States

362 U.S. 257 (1960)

See Chapter 1.G.

2. Merging of Expectation of Privacy with Standing

Rakas v. Illinois

439 U.S. 128 (1978)

See Chapter 1.G.

Rawlings v. Kentucky

448 U.S. 98 (1980)

REHNQUIST, J., delivered the opinion of the Court, in which BURGER, C.J., BLACKMUN, and POWELL, JJ., joined. BLACKMUN, J., filed a concurring opinion. WHITE, J., filed an opinion concurring in part and dissenting in part, in which STEWART, J., joined. MARSHALL, J., filed a dissenting opinion, in which BRENNAN, J., joined.

Justice REHNQUIST delivered the opinion of the Court.

Petitioner David Rawlings was convicted by the Commonwealth of Kentucky on charges of trafficking in, and possession of, various controlled substances. Throughout the proceedings below, Rawlings challenged the admissibility of certain evidence and statements on the ground that they were the fruits of an illegal detention and illegal searches. The trial court, the Kentucky Court of Appeals, and the Supreme Court of Kentucky all rejected Rawlings' challenges. We granted certiorari and now affirm.

■ ■ ■

In the middle of the afternoon on October 18, 1976, six police officers armed with a warrant for the arrest of one Lawrence Marquess on charges of drug distribution arrived at Marquess' house in Bowling Green, Ky. In the house at the time the police arrived were one of Marquess' housemates, Dennis Saddler, and four visitors, Keith Northern, Linda Braden, Vanessa Cox, and petitioner David Rawlings. While searching unsuccessfully in the house for Marquess, several police officers smelled marihuana smoke and saw marihuana seeds on the mantel in one of the bedrooms. After conferring briefly, Officers Eddie Railey and John Bruce left to obtain a search warrant. While Railey and Bruce were gone, the other four officers detained the occupants of the house in the living room, allowing them to leave only if they consented to a body search. Northern and Braden did consent to such a search and were permitted to depart. Saddler, Cox, and petitioner remained seated in the living room.

Approximately 45 minutes later, Railey and Bruce returned with a warrant authorizing them to search the house. Railey read the warrant to Saddler, Cox, and petitioner, and also read "*Miranda*" warnings from a card he carried in his pocket. At that time, Cox was seated on a couch with petitioner seated to her left. In the space between them was Cox's handbag.

After Railey finished his recitation, he approached petitioner and told him to stand. Officer Don Bivens simultaneously approached Cox and ordered her to empty the contents of her purse onto a coffee table in front of the couch. Among those contents were a jar containing 1,800 tablets of LSD and a number of smaller vials containing benzphetamine, methamphetamine, methyprylan, and pentobarbital, all of which are controlled substances under Kentucky law.

Upon pouring these objects out onto the coffee table, Cox turned to petitioner and told him "to take what was his." Petitioner, who was standing in response to Officer Railey's command, immediately claimed ownership of controlled substances. At that time, Railey searched petitioner's person and found $4,500 in cash in petitioner's shirt pocket and a knife in a sheath at petitioner's side. Railey then placed petitioner under formal arrest.

Petitioner was indicted for possession with intent to sell the various controlled substances recovered from Cox's purse. At the suppression hearing, he testified that he had flown into Bowling Green about a week before his arrest to look for a job and perhaps to attend the local university. He brought with him at that time the drugs later found in Cox's purse. Initially, petitioner stayed in the house where the arrest took place as the guest of Michael Swank, who shared the house with Marquess and Saddler. While at a party at that house, he met Cox and spent at least two nights of the next week on a couch at Cox's house.

On the morning of petitioner's arrest, Cox had dropped him off at Swank's house where he waited for her to return from class. At that time, he was carrying the drugs in a green bank bag. When Cox returned to the house to meet him, petitioner dumped the contents of the bank bag into Cox's purse. Although there is dispute over the discussion that took place, petitioner testified that he "asked her if she would carry this for me, and she said, 'yes'. . . ."

Petitioner then left the room to use the bathroom and, by the time he returned, discovered that the police had arrived to arrest Marquess.

The trial court denied petitioner's motion to suppress the drugs and the money and to exclude the statements made by petitioner when the police discovered the drugs. According to the trial court, the warrant obtained by the police authorized them to search Cox's purse. Moreover, even if the search of the purse was illegal, the trial court believed that petitioner lacked "standing" to contest that search. Finally, the trial court believed that the search that revealed the money and the knife was permissible "under the exigencies of the situation." After a bench trial, petitioner was found guilty of possession with intent to sell LSD and of possession of benzphetamine, methamphetamine, methyprylan, and pentobarbital.

The Kentucky Court of Appeals affirmed. Disagreeing with the trial court, the appellate court held that petitioner did have "standing" to dispute the legality of the search of Cox's purse but that the detention of the five persons present in the house and the subsequent searches were legitimate because the police had probable cause to arrest all five people in the house when they smelled the marihuana smoke and saw the marihuana seeds.

The Supreme Court of Kentucky in turn affirmed, but again on a somewhat different rationale. According to the Supreme Court, petitioner had no "standing" because he had no "legitimate or reasonable expectation of freedom from governmental intrusion" into Cox's purse. *Rakas v. Illinois* (1978). Moreover, according to the Supreme Court, the search uncovering the money in petitioner's pocket, which search followed petitioner's admission that he owned the drugs in Cox's purse, was justifiable as incident to a lawful arrest based on probable cause.

■ ■ ■

In holding that petitioner could not challenge the legality of the search of Cox's purse, the Supreme Court of Kentucky looked primarily to our then recent decision in *Rakas v. Illinois* . . . where we abandoned a separate inquiry into a defendant's "standing" to contest an allegedly illegal search in favor of an inquiry that focused directly on the substance of the defendant's claim that he or she possessed a "legitimate expectation of privacy" in the area searched. In the present case, the Supreme Court of Kentucky looked to the "totality of the circumstances," including petitioner's own admission at the suppression hearing that he did not believe that Cox's purse would be free from governmental intrusion, and held that petitioner "[had] not made a sufficient showing that his legitimate or reasonable expectations of privacy were violated" by the search of the purse.

We believe that the record in this case supports that conclusion. Petitioner, of course, bears the burden of proving not only that the search of Cox's purse was illegal, but also that he had a legitimate expectation of privacy in that purse. At the time petitioner dumped thousands of dollars worth of illegal drugs into Cox's purse, he had known her for only a few days. According to Cox's uncontested testimony, petitioner had never sought or received access to her purse prior to that sudden bailment. Nor did petitioner have any right to exclude other persons from access to Cox's purse. In fact, Cox testified that Bob Stallons, a longtime acquaintance and frequent companion of Cox's, had free access to her purse and on the very morning of the arrest had rummaged through its contents in search of a hairbrush. Moreover, even assuming that petitioner's version of the bailment is correct and that Cox did consent to the transfer of possession, the precipitous nature of the transaction hardly supports a reasonable inference that petitioner took normal precautions to maintain his privacy. In addition to all the foregoing facts, the record also contains a frank admission by petitioner that he had no subjective expectation that Cox's purse would remain free from governmental intrusion, an admission credited by both the trial court and the Supreme Court of Kentucky.

Petitioner contends nevertheless that, because he claimed ownership of the drugs in Cox's purse, he should be entitled to challenge the search regardless of his expectation of privacy. We disagree. While petitioner's ownership of the drugs is undoubtedly one fact to be considered in this case, *Rakas* emphatically rejected the notion that "arcane" concepts of property law ought to control the ability to claim the protections of the Fourth Amendment. Had petitioner placed his drugs in plain view, he would still have owned them, but he could not claim any legitimate expectation of privacy. Prior to *Rakas*, petitioner might have been given "standing" in such a case to challenge a "search" that netted those drugs but probably would have lost his claim on the merits. After *Rakas*, the two inquiries merge into one: whether governmental officials violated any legitimate expectation of privacy held by petitioner.

In sum, we find no reason to overturn the lower court's conclusion that petitioner had no legitimate expectation of privacy in Cox's purse at the time of the search.

■ ■ ■

Having found no error in the lower courts' refusal to suppress the evidence challenged by petitioner, we believe that the judgment of the Supreme Court of Kentucky should be, and the same hereby is,

Affirmed.

Justice BLACKMUN, concurring.

I join the Court's opinion, but I write separately to explain my somewhat different approach to the issues addressed. . . .

In my view, *Rakas v. Illinois* recognized two analytically distinct but "invariably intertwined" issues of substantive Fourth Amendment jurisprudence. The first is "whether [a] disputed search or seizure has infringed an interest of the defendant which the Fourth Amendment was designed to protect," the second is whether "the challenged search or seizure violated [that] Fourth Amendment righ[t]," *ibid*. The first of these questions is answered by determining whether the defendant has a "legitimate expectation of privacy" that has been invaded by a governmental search or seizure. The second is answered by determining whether applicable cause and warrant requirements have been properly observed.

I agree with the Court that these two inquiries "merge into one," in the sense that both are to be addressed under the principles of Fourth Amendment analysis developed in *Katz v. United States* (1967), and its progeny. But I do not read today's decision, or *Rakas*, as holding that it is improper for lower courts to treat these inquiries as distinct components of a Fourth Amendment claim. Indeed, I am convinced that it would invite confusion to hold otherwise. It remains possible for a defendant to prove that his legitimate interest of privacy was invaded, and yet fail to prove that the police acted illegally in doing so. And it is equally possible for a defendant to prove that the police acted illegally, and yet fail to prove that his own privacy interest was affected.

Nor do I read this Court's decisions to hold that property interests cannot be, in some circumstances at least, weighty factors in establishing the existence of Fourth Amendment rights. Not every concept of ownership or possession is "arcane." Not every interest in property exists only in the desiccated atmosphere of ancient maxims and dusty books. Earlier this Term the Court recognized that "the right to exclude" is an essential element of modern property rights. . . .

■ ■ ■

Mr. Justice MARSHALL, with whom Mr. Justice BRENNAN joins, dissenting. . . .

The Court holds first that petitioner may not object to the introduction of the pills into evidence because the unconstitutional actions of the police officers did not violate his personal Fourth Amendment rights. To reach this result, the Court holds that the Constitution protects an individual against unreasonable searches and seizures only if he has "a 'legitimate expectation of privacy' in the area searched." This holding cavalierly rejects the fundamental principle, unquestioned until today, that an interest in either the place searched or the property seized is sufficient to invoke the Constitution's protections against unreasonable searches and seizures.

The Court's examination of previous Fourth Amendment cases begins and ends—as it must if it is to reach its desired conclusion—with *Rakas v. Illinois*. Contrary to the Court's assertion, however, *Rakas* did not establish that the Fourth Amendment protects individuals against unreasonable searches and seizures only if they have a privacy interest in the place searched. The question before the Court in *Rakas* was whether the defendants could establish their right to Fourth Amendment protection simply by showing that they were "legitimately on [the] premises" searched. Overruling that portion of *Jones* (1960), the Court held that when a Fourth Amendment objection is based on an interest in the place searched, the defendant must show an actual invasion of his personal privacy interest. The petitioners in *Rakas* did not claim that they had standing either under the *Jones* automatic standing rule for persons charged with possessory offenses, which the Court overrules today, or because their possessory interest in the items seized gave them "actual standing." No Fourth Amendment claim based on an interest in the property seized was before the Court, and, consequently, the Court did not and could not have decided whether such a claim could be maintained. In fact, the Court expressly disavowed any intention to foreclose such a claim ("This is not to say that such [casual] visitors could not contest the lawfulness of the seizure of evidence or the search if their own property were seized during the search)," and suggested its continuing validity ("[P]etitioners' claims must fail. . . .").

The Court's decision today is not wrong, however, simply because it is contrary to our previous cases. It is wrong because it is contrary to the Fourth Amendment, which guarantees that "[t]he right of the people to be secure in their persons, houses, papers, and effects, against unreasonable searches and seizures, shall not be violated." The Court's reading of the Amendment is far too narrow. The Court misreads the guarantee of security "*in* their persons, houses, papers, and effects, *against* unreasonable searches and seizures" to afford protection only against unreasonable searches and seizures *of* persons and places.

The Fourth Amendment, it seems to me, provides in plain language that if one's security in one's "effects" is disturbed by an unreasonable search and seizure, one has been the victim of a constitutional violation; and so it has always been understood. Therefore the Court's insistence that in order to challenge the legality of the search one must also assert a protected interest in the premises is misplaced. The interest in the item seized is quite enough to establish that the defendant's personal Fourth Amendment rights have been invaded by the government's conduct.

■ ■ ■

When the government seizes a person's property, it interferes with his constitutionally protected right to be secure in his effects. That interference gives him the right to challenge the reasonableness of the government's conduct, including the seizure. If the defendant's property was seized as the result of an unreasonable search, the seizure cannot be other than unreasonable.

In holding that the Fourth Amendment protects only those with a privacy interest in the place searched, and not those with an ownership or possessory interest in the things seized, the Court has turned the development of the law of search and seizure on its head. The history of the Fourth Amendment shows that it was designed to protect property interests as well as privacy interests; in fact, until *Jones* the question whether a person's Fourth Amendment rights had been violated turned on whether he had a property interest in the place searched or the items seized. *Jones* and *Katz* expanded our view of the protections afforded by the Fourth Amendment by recognizing that privacy interests are protected even if they do not arise from property rights. But that recognition was never intended to exclude interests that had historically been sheltered by the Fourth Amendment from its protection. Neither *Jones* nor *Katz* purported to provide an exclusive definition of the interests protected by the Fourth Amendment. Indeed, as *Katz* recognized: "That Amendment protects individual privacy against certain kinds of governmental intrusion, but its protections go further, and often have nothing to do with privacy at all." Those decisions freed Fourth Amendment jurisprudence from the constraints of "subtle distinctions, developed and refined by the common law in evolving the body of private property law which, more than almost any other branch of law, has been shaped by distinctions whose validity is largely historical." Rejection of those finely drawn distinctions as irrelevant to the concerns of the Fourth Amendment did not render property rights wholly outside its protection, however. Not every concept involving property rights, we should remember, is "arcane."

In fact, the Court rather inconsistently denies that property rights may, by themselves, entitle one to the protection of the Fourth Amendment, but simultaneously suggests that a person may claim such protection only if his expectation of privacy in the premises searched is so strong that he may exclude all others from that place.

■ ■ ■

In the words of Mr. Justice Frankfurter: "A decision [of a Fourth Amendment claim] may turn on whether one gives that Amendment a place second to none in the Bill of Rights, or considers it on the whole a kind of nuisance, a serious impediment in the war against crime." *Harris v. United States* (1947). Today a majority of the Court has substantially cut back the protection afforded by the Fourth Amendment and the ability of the people to claim that protection, apparently out of concern lest the government's ability to obtain criminal convictions be impeded. A slow and steady erosion of the ability of victims of unconstitutional searches and seizures to obtain a remedy for the invasion of their rights saps the constitutional guarantee of its life just as surely as would a substantive limitation. Because we are called on to decide whether evidence should be excluded only when a search has been "successful," it is easy to forget that the standards we announce determine what government conduct is reasonable in searches and seizures directed at persons who turn out to be innocent as well as those who are guilty. I continue to believe that ungrudging application of the Fourth Amendment is indispensable to preserving the liberties of a democratic society. Accordingly, I dissent.

Minnesota v. Olson

495 U.S. 91 (1990)

WHITE, J., delivered the opinion of the Court, in which BRENNAN, MARSHALL, STEVENS, O'CONNOR, SCALIA, and KENNEDY, JJ., joined. STEVENS, J., and KENNEDY, J., filed concurring opinions. REHNQUIST, C.J., and BLACKMUN, J., dissented.

The police in this case made a warrantless, nonconsensual entry into a house where respondent Robert Olson was an overnight guest and arrested him. The issue is whether the arrest violated Olson's Fourth Amendment rights. We hold that it did.

Shortly before 6 a.m. on Saturday, July 18, 1987, a lone gunman robbed an Amoco gasoline station in Minneapolis, Minnesota, and fatally shot the station manager. A police officer heard the police dispatcher report and suspected Joseph Ecker. The officer and his partner drove immediately to Ecker's home, arriving at about the same time that an Oldsmobile arrived. The driver of the Oldsmobile took evasive action, and the car spun out of control and came to a stop. Two men fled the car on foot. Ecker, who was later identified as the gunman, was captured shortly thereafter inside his home. The second man escaped.

Inside the abandoned Oldsmobile, police found a sack of money and the murder weapon. They also found a title certificate with the name Rob Olson crossed out as a secured party, a letter addressed to a Roger R. Olson of 3151 Johnson Street, and a videotape rental receipt made out to Rob Olson and dated two days earlier. The police verified that a Robert Olson lived at 3151 Johnson Street.

The next morning, Sunday, July 19, a woman identifying herself as Dianna Murphy called the police and said that a man by the name of Rob drove the car in which the gas station killer left the scene and that Rob was planning to leave town by bus. About noon, the same woman called again, gave her address and phone number, and said that a man named Rob had told a Maria and two other women, Louanne and Julie, that he was the driver in the Amoco robbery. The caller stated that Louanne was Julie's mother and that the two women lived at 2406 Fillmore Northeast. The detective-in-charge who took the second phone call sent police officers to 2406 Fillmore to check out Louanne and Julie. When police arrived they determined that the dwelling was a duplex and that Louanne Bergstrom and her daughter Julie lived in the upper unit but were not home. Police spoke to Louanne's mother, Helen Niederhoffer, who lived in the lower unit. She confirmed that a Rob Olson had been staying upstairs but was not then in the unit. She promised to call the police when Olson returned. At 2 p.m., a pickup order, or "probable cause arrest bulletin," was issued for Olson's arrest. The police were instructed to stay away from the duplex.

At approximately 2:45 p.m., Niederhoffer called police and said Olson had returned. The detective-in-charge instructed police officers to go to the house and surround it. He then telephoned Julie from headquarters and told her Rob should come out of the house. The detective heard a male voice say, "tell them I left." Julie stated that Rob had left, whereupon at 3 p.m. the detective ordered the police to enter the house. Without seeking permission and with weapons drawn, the police entered the upper unit and found respondent hiding in a closet. Less than an hour after his arrest, respondent made an inculpatory statement at police headquarters.

The Hennepin County trial court held a hearing and denied respondent's motion to suppress his statement. The statement was admitted into evidence at Olson's trial, and he was convicted on one count of first-degree murder, three counts of armed robbery, and three counts of second-degree assault. On appeal, the Minnesota Supreme Court reversed. The court ruled that respondent had a sufficient interest in the Bergstrom home to challenge the legality of his warrantless arrest there, that the arrest was illegal because there were no exigent circumstances to justify a warrantless entry, and that respondent's statement was tainted by that illegality and should have been suppressed. Because the admission of the statement was not harmless beyond reasonable doubt, the court reversed Olson's conviction and remanded for a new trial. . . .

It was held in *Payton v. New York* (1980) that a suspect should not be arrested in his house without an arrest warrant, even though there is probable cause to arrest him. The purpose of the decision was not to protect the person of the suspect but to protect his home from entry in the absence of a magistrate's finding of probable cause. In this case, the court below held that Olson's warrantless arrest was illegal because he had a sufficient connection with the premises to be treated like a householder. The State challenges that conclusion. . . .

The State argues that Olson's relationship to the premises does not satisfy the 12 factors which in its view determine whether a dwelling is a "home." Aside from the fact that it is based on the mistaken premise that a place must be one's "home" in order for one to have a legitimate expectation of privacy there, the State's proposed test is needlessly complex. We need go no further than to conclude, as we do, that Olson's status as an overnight guest is alone enough to show that he had an expectation of privacy in the home that society is prepared to recognize as reasonable.

As recognized by the Minnesota Supreme Court, the facts of this case are similar to those in *Jones v. United States* (1960). In *Jones*, the defendant was arrested in a friend's apartment during the execution of a search warrant and sought to challenge the warrant as not supported by probable cause. . . .

The Court ruled that Jones could challenge the search of the apartment because he was "legitimately on [the] premises," Although the "legitimately on [the] premises" standard was rejected in *Rakas* (1978) as too broad, the *Rakas* Court explicitly reaffirmed the factual holding in *Jones:*

> "We do not question the conclusion in *Jones* that the defendant in that case suffered a violation of his personal Fourth Amendment rights if the search in question was unlawful. . . .
>
> We think that *Jones* on its facts merely stands for the unremarkable proposition that a person can have a legally sufficient interest in a place other than his own home so that the Fourth Amendment protects him from unreasonable governmental intrusion into that place."

Rakas thus recognized that, as an overnight guest, Jones was much more than just legitimately on the premises. The distinctions relied on by the State between this case and *Jones* are not legally determinative. The State emphasizes that in this case Olson was never left alone in the duplex or given a key, whereas in *Jones* the owner of the apartment was away and Jones had a key with which he could come and go and admit and exclude others. These differences are crucial, it is argued, because in not disturbing the holding in *Jones*, the Court pointed out that while his host was away, Jones had complete dominion and control over the apartment and could exclude others from it. We do not understand *Rakas,* however, to hold that an overnight guest can never have a legitimate expectation of privacy except when his host is away and he has a key, or that only when those facts are present may an overnight guest assert the "unremarkable proposition" that a person may have a sufficient interest in a place other than his home to enable him to be free in that place from unreasonable searches and seizures.

To hold that an overnight guest has a legitimate expectation of privacy in his host's home merely recognizes the everyday expectations of privacy that we all share. Staying overnight in another's home is a longstanding social custom that serves functions recognized as valuable by society. We stay in others' homes when we travel to a strange city for business or pleasure, when we visit our parents, children, or more distant relatives out of town, when we are in between jobs or homes, or when we house-sit for a friend. We will all be hosts and we will all be guests many times in our lives. From either perspective, we think that society recognizes that a houseguest has a legitimate expectation of privacy in his host's home.

From the overnight guest's perspective, he seeks shelter in another's home precisely because it provides him with privacy, a place where he and his possessions will not be disturbed by anyone but his host and those his host allows inside. We are at our most vulnerable when we are asleep because we cannot monitor our own safety or the security of our belongings. It is for this reason that, although we may spend all day in public places, when we cannot sleep in our own home we seek out another private place to sleep, whether it be a hotel room, or the home of a friend. Society expects at least as much privacy in these places as in a telephone booth—"a temporarily private place whose momentary occupants' expectations of freedom from intrusion are recognized as reasonable."

That the guest has a host who has ultimate control of the house is not inconsistent with the guest having a legitimate expectation of privacy. The houseguest is there with the permission of his host, who is willing to share his house and his privacy with his guest. It is unlikely that the guest will be confined to a restricted area of the house; and when the host is away or asleep, the guest will have a measure of control over the premises. The host may admit or exclude from the house as he prefers, but it is unlikely that he will admit someone who wants to see or meet with the guest over the objection of the guest. On the other hand, few houseguests will invite others to visit them while they are guests without consulting their hosts; but the latter, who have the authority to exclude despite the wishes of the guest, will often be accommodating. The point is that hosts will more likely than not respect the privacy interests of their guests, who are entitled to a legitimate expectation of privacy despite the fact that they have no legal interest in the premises and do not have the legal authority to determine who may or may not enter the household. If the untrammeled power to admit and exclude were essential to Fourth Amendment protection, an adult daughter temporarily living in the home of her parents would have no legitimate expectation of privacy because her right to admit or exclude would be subject to her parents' veto.

Because respondent's expectation of privacy in the Bergstrom home was rooted in "understandings that are recognized and permitted by society," *Rakas*, it was legitimate, and respondent can claim the protection of the Fourth Amendment.

■ ■ ■

We therefore affirm the judgment of the Minnesota Supreme Court.
It is so ordered.

Minnesota v. Carter

525 U.S. 83 (1998)

REHNQUIST, C.J., delivered the opinion of the Court, in which O'CONNOR, SCALIA, KENNEDY, and THOMAS, JJ., joined. SCALIA, J., filed a concurring opinion, in which THOMAS, J., joined. KENNEDY, J., filed a concurring opinion. BREYER, J., filed an opinion concurring in the judgment. GINSBURG, J., filed a dissenting opinion, in which STEVENS and SOUTER, JJ., joined.

Respondents and the lessee of an apartment were sitting in one of its rooms, bagging cocaine. While so engaged they were observed by a police officer, who looked through a drawn window blind. The Supreme Court of Minnesota held that the officer's viewing was a search that violated respondents' Fourth Amendment rights. We hold that no such violation occurred.

James Thielen, a police officer in the Twin Cities' suburb of Eagan, Minnesota, went to an apartment building to investigate a tip from a confidential informant. The informant said that he had walked by the window of a ground-floor apartment and had seen people putting a white powder into bags. The officer looked in the same window through a gap in the closed blind and observed the bagging operation for several minutes. He then notified headquarters, which began preparing affidavits for a search warrant while he returned to the apartment building. When two men left the building in a previously identified Cadillac, the police stopped the car. Inside were respondents Carter and Johns. As the police opened the door of the car to let Johns out, they observed a black, zippered pouch and a handgun, later determined to be loaded, on the vehicle's floor. Carter and Johns were arrested, and a later police search of the vehicle the next day discovered pagers, a scale, and 47 grams of cocaine in plastic sandwich bags.

After seizing the car, the police returned to Apartment 103 and arrested the occupant, Kimberly Thompson, who is not a party to this appeal. A search of the apartment pursuant to a warrant revealed cocaine residue on the kitchen table and plastic baggies similar to those found in the Cadillac. Thielen identified Carter, Johns, and Thompson as the three people he had observed placing the powder into baggies. The police later learned that while Thompson was the lessee of the apartment, Carter and Johns lived in Chicago and had come to the apartment for the sole purpose of packaging the cocaine. Carter and Johns had never been to the apartment before and were only in the apartment for approximately 2½ hours. In return for the use of the apartment, Carter and Johns had given Thompson one-eighth of an ounce of the cocaine.

Carter and Johns were charged with conspiracy to commit a controlled substance crime in the first degree and aiding and abetting in a controlled substance crime in the first degree.... They moved to suppress all evidence obtained from the apartment and the Cadillac, as well as to suppress several postarrest incriminating statements they had made. They argued that Thielen's initial observation of their drug packaging activities was an unreasonable search in violation of the Fourth Amendment and that all evidence obtained as a result of this unreasonable search was inadmissible as fruit of the poisonous tree. The Minnesota trial court held that since, unlike the defendant in *Minnesota v. Olson* (1990), Carter and Johns were not overnight social guests but temporary out-of-state visitors, they were not entitled to claim the protection of the Fourth Amendment against the government intrusion into the apartment. The trial court also concluded that Thielen's observation was not a search within the meaning of the Fourth Amendment. After a trial, Carter and Johns were each convicted of both offenses. The Minnesota Court of Appeals held that respondent Carter did not have "standing" to object to Thielen's actions because his claim that he was predominantly a social guest was "inconsistent with the only evidence concerning his stay in the apartment, which indicates that he used it for a business purpose—to package drugs."...

A divided Minnesota Supreme Court reversed, holding that respondents had "standing" to claim the protection of the Fourth Amendment because they had "'a legitimate expectation of privacy in the invaded place.'"

■ ■ ■

The text of the Amendment suggests that its protections extend only to people in "their" houses. But we have held that in some circumstances a person may have a legitimate expectation of privacy in the house of someone else. In *Minnesota v. Olson*, for example, we decided that an overnight guest in a house had the sort of expectation of privacy that the Fourth Amendment protects.

■ ■ ■

Respondents here were obviously not overnight guests, but were essentially present for a business transaction and were only in the home a matter of hours. There is no suggestion that they had a previous relationship with Thompson, or that there was any other purpose to their visit. Nor was there anything similar to the overnight guest relationship in *Olson* to suggest a degree of acceptance into the household. While the apartment was a dwelling place for Thompson, it was for these respondents simply a place to do business.

Property used for commercial purposes is treated differently for Fourth Amendment purposes from residential property. "An expectation of privacy in commercial premises, however, is different from, and indeed less than, a similar expectation in an individual's home." And while it was a "home" in which respondents were present, it was not their home. Similarly, the Court has held that in some circumstances a worker can claim Fourth Amendment protection over his own workplace....

If we regard the overnight guest in *Minnesota v. Olson* as typifying those who may claim the protection of the Fourth Amendment in the home of another, and one merely "legitimately on the premises" as typifying those who may not do so, the present case is obviously somewhere in between. But the purely commercial nature of the transaction engaged in here, the relatively short period of time on the premises, and the lack of any previous connection between respondents and the householder, all lead us to conclude that respondents' situation is closer to that of one simply permitted on the premises. We therefore hold that any search which may have occurred did not violate their Fourth Amendment rights.

Because we conclude that respondents had no legitimate expectation of privacy in the apartment, we need not decide whether the police officer's observation constituted a "search." The judgments of the Supreme Court of Minnesota are accordingly reversed, and the cause is remanded for proceedings not inconsistent with this opinion.

It is so ordered.

Justice SCALIA, with whom Justice THOMAS joins, concurring.

I join the opinion of the Court because I believe it accurately applies our recent case law, including *Minnesota v. Olson*. I write separately to express my view that that case law—like the submissions of the parties in this case—gives short shrift to the text of the Fourth Amendment, and to the well and long understood meaning of that text. Specifically, it leaps to apply the fuzzy standard of "legitimate expectation of privacy"—a consideration that is often relevant to whether a search or seizure covered by the Fourth Amendment is "unreasonable"—to the threshold question whether a search or seizure covered by the Fourth Amendment *has occurred*. If that latter question is addressed first and analyzed under the text of the Constitution as traditionally understood, the present case is not remotely difficult.

The Fourth Amendment protects "[t]he right of the people to be secure in *their* persons, houses, papers, and effects, against unreasonable searches and seizures...." U.S. Const., Amdt. 4 (emphasis added). It must be acknowledged that the phrase "their... houses" in this provision is, in isolation, ambiguous. It could mean "their respective houses," so that the protection extends to each person only in his *own* house. But it could also mean "their respective and each other's houses," so that each person would be protected even when visiting the house of someone else. As today's opinion for the Court suggests, however, it is not linguistically possible to give the provision the latter, expansive interpretation with respect to "houses" without giving it the same interpretation with respect to the nouns that are parallel to "houses"—"persons,... papers, and effects"—which would give me a constitutional right not to have your person unreasonably searched. This is so absurd that it has to my knowledge never been contemplated. The obvious meaning of the provision is that *each* person has the right to be secure against unreasonable searches and seizures in *his own* person, house, papers, and effects.

■ ■ ■

That "their . . . houses" was understood to mean "their respective houses" would have been clear to anyone who knew the English and early American law of arrest and trespass that underlay the Fourth Amendment. The people's protection against unreasonable search and seizure in their "houses" was drawn from the English common-law maxim, "A man's home is *his* castle." As far back as *Semayne's Case* of 1604, the leading English case for that proposition (and a case cited by Coke in his discussion of the proposition that Magna Carta outlawed general warrants based on mere surmise), the King's Bench proclaimed that "the house of any one is not a castle or privilege but for himself, and shall not extend to protect any person who flies to his house."

■ ■ ■

Justice GINSBURG, with whom Justice STEVENS and Justice SOUTER join, dissenting.

The Court's decision undermines not only the security of short-term guests, but also the security of the home resident herself. In my view, when a homeowner or lessee personally invites a guest into her home to share in a common endeavor, whether it be for conversation, to engage in leisure activities, or for business purposes licit or illicit, that guest should share his host's shelter against unreasonable searches and seizures.

I do not here propose restoration of the "legitimately on the premises" criterion stated in *Jones v. United States* (1960), for the Court rejected that formulation in *Rakas v. Illinois* (1978), as it did the "automatic standing rule" in *United States v. Salvucci* (1980). . . . Further, I would here decide only the case of the homeowner who chooses to share the privacy of her home and her company with a guest, and would not reach classroom hypotheticals like the milkman or pizza deliverer.

My concern centers on an individual's choice to share her home and her associations there with persons she selects. Our decisions indicate that people have a reasonable expectation of privacy in their homes in part because they have the prerogative to exclude others. The power to exclude implies the power to include. . . .

A homedweller places her own privacy at risk, the Court's approach indicates, when she opens her home to others, uncertain whether the duration of their stay, their purpose, and their "acceptance into the household" will earn protection. It remains textbook law that "[s]earches and seizures inside a home without a warrant are presumptively unreasonable absent exigent circumstances." The law in practice is less secure. Human frailty suggests that today's decision will tempt police to pry into private dwellings without warrant, to find evidence incriminating guests who do not rest there through the night. . . .

Through the host's invitation, the guest gains a reasonable expectation of privacy in the home. *Minnesota v. Olson* so held with respect to an overnight guest. The logic of that decision extends to shorter term guests as well. Visiting the home of a friend, relative, or business associate, whatever the time of day, "serves functions recognized as valuable by society." One need not remain overnight to anticipate privacy in another's home, "a place where [the guest] and his possessions will not be disturbed by anyone but his host and those his host allows inside." In sum, when a homeowner chooses to share the privacy of her home and her company with a short-term guest, the twofold requirement "emerg[ing] from prior decisions" has been satisfied: Both host and guest "have exhibited an actual (subjective) expectation of privacy"; that "expectation [is] one [our] society is prepared to recognize as 'reasonable.'"

As the Solicitor General acknowledged, the illegality of the host-guest conduct, the fact that they were partners in crime, would not alter the analysis. In *Olson*, for example, the guest whose security this Court's decision shielded stayed overnight while the police searched for him. The Court held that the guest had Fourth Amendment protection against a warrantless arrest in his host's home despite the guest's involvement in grave crimes (first-degree murder, armed robbery, and assault). Other decisions have similarly sustained Fourth Amendment pleas despite the criminality of the defendants' activities. Indeed, it must be this way. If the illegality of the activity made constitutional an otherwise unconstitutional search, such Fourth Amendment protection, reserved for the innocent only, would have little force in regulating police behavior toward either the innocent or the guilty.

Our leading decision in [*United States v.*] *Katz* [(1967)] is key to my view of this case. There, we ruled that the Government violated the petitioner's Fourth Amendment rights when it electronically recorded him transmitting wagering information while he was inside a public telephone booth. We were mindful that "the Fourth Amendment protects people, not places," and held that this electronic monitoring of a business call "violated the privacy upon which [the caller] justifiably relied while using the telephone booth." Our obligation to produce coherent results in this often visited area of the law requires us to inform our current expositions by benchmarks already established. . . .

The Court's decision in this case veers sharply from the path marked in *Katz*. I do not agree that we have a more reasonable expectation of privacy when we place a business call to a person's home from a public telephone booth on the side of the street, than when we actually enter that person's premises to engage in a common endeavor.

For the reasons stated, I dissent from the Court's judgment, and would retain judicial surveillance over the warrantless searches today's decision allows.

Brendlin v. California

551 U.S. 249 (2007)

SOUTER, J., delivered the opinion for a unanimous Court.

When a police officer makes a traffic stop, the driver of the car is seized within the meaning of the Fourth Amendment. The question in this case is whether the same is true of a passenger. We hold that a passenger is seized as well and so may challenge the constitutionality of the stop.

Early in the morning of November 27, 2001, Deputy Sheriff Robert Brokenbrough and his partner saw a parked Buick with expired registration tags. In his ensuing conversation with the police dispatcher, Brokenbrough learned that an application for renewal of registration was being processed. The officers saw the car again on the road, and this time Brokenbrough noticed its display of a temporary operating permit with the number "11," indicating it was legal to drive the car through November. The officers decided to pull the Buick over to verify that the permit matched the vehicle, even though, as Brokenbrough admitted later, there was nothing unusual about the permit or the way it was affixed. Brokenbrough asked the driver, Karen Simeroth, for her license and saw a passenger in the front seat, petitioner Bruce Brendlin, whom he recognized as "one of the Brendlin brothers." He recalled that either Scott or Bruce Brendlin had dropped out of parole supervision and asked Brendlin to identify himself. Brokenbrough returned to his cruiser, called for backup, and verified that Brendlin was a parole violator with an outstanding no-bail warrant for his arrest. While he was in the patrol car, Brokenbrough saw Brendlin briefly open and then close the passenger door of the Buick. Once reinforcements arrived, Brokenbrough went to the passenger side of the Buick, ordered him out of the car at gunpoint, and declared him under arrest. When the police searched Brendlin incident to arrest, they found an orange syringe cap on his person. A patdown search of Simeroth revealed syringes and a plastic bag of a green leafy substance, and she was also formally arrested. Officers then searched the car and found tubing, a scale, and other things used to produce methamphetamine.

Brendlin was charged with possession and manufacture of methamphetamine, and he moved to suppress the evidence obtained in the searches of his person and the car as fruits of an unconstitutional seizure, arguing that the officers lacked probable cause or reasonable suspicion to make the traffic stop. He did not assert that his Fourth Amendment rights were violated by the search of Simeroth's vehicle, but claimed only that the traffic stop was an unlawful seizure of his person. The trial court denied the suppression motion after finding that the stop was lawful and Brendlin was not seized until Brokenbrough ordered him out of the car and formally arrested him. Brendlin pleaded guilty, subject to appeal on the suppression issue, and was sentenced to four years in prison.

The California Court of Appeal reversed the denial of the suppression motion, holding that Brendlin was seized by the traffic stop, which they held unlawful. By a narrow majority, the Supreme Court of California reversed. The State Supreme Court noted California's concession that the officers had no reasonable basis to suspect unlawful operation of the car, but still held suppression unwarranted because a passenger "is not seized as a constitutional matter in the absence of additional circumstances that would indicate to a reasonable person that he or she was the subject of the peace officer's investigation or show of authority." . . .

■ ■ ■

A person is seized by the police and thus entitled to challenge the government's action under the Fourth Amendment when the officer, "'by means of physical force or show of authority,'" terminates or restrains his freedom of movement, *Florida v. Bostick* (1991) (quoting *Terry v. Ohio* (1968))....

When the actions of the police do not show an unambiguous intent to restrain or when an individual's submission to a show of governmental authority takes the form of passive acquiescence, there needs to be some test for telling when a seizure occurs in response to authority, and when it does not. The test was devised by Justice Stewart in *United States v. Mendenhall* (1980), who wrote that a seizure occurs if "in view of all of the circumstances surrounding the incident, a reasonable person would have believed that he was not free to leave." ...

The law is settled that in Fourth Amendment terms a traffic stop entails a seizure of the driver "even though the purpose of the stop is limited and the resulting detention quite brief." And although we have not, until today, squarely answered the question whether a passenger is also seized, we have said over and over in dicta that during a traffic stop an officer seizes everyone in the vehicle, not just the driver. See, *e.g.*, *Delaware v. Prouse* (1979) ("[S]topping an automobile and detaining its occupants constitute a 'seizure' within the meaning of [the Fourth and Fourteenth] Amendments")....

■ ■ ■

A traffic stop necessarily curtails the travel a passenger has chosen just as much as it halts the driver, diverting both from the stream of traffic to the side of the road, and the police activity that normally amounts to intrusion on "privacy and personal security" does not normally (and did not here) distinguish between passenger and driver. An officer who orders one particular car to pull over acts with an implicit claim of right based on fault of some sort, and a sensible person would not expect a police officer to allow people to come and go freely from the physical focal point of an investigation into faulty behavior or wrongdoing. If the likely wrongdoing is not the driving, the passenger will reasonably feel subject to suspicion owing to close association; but even when the wrongdoing is only bad driving, the passenger will expect to be subject to some scrutiny, and his attempt to leave the scene would be so obviously likely to prompt an objection from the officer that no passenger would feel free to leave in the first place.

It is also reasonable for passengers to expect that a police officer at the scene of a crime, arrest, or investigation will not let people move around in ways that could jeopardize his safety. In *Maryland v. Wilson* (1997), we held that during a lawful traffic stop an officer may order a passenger out of the car as a precautionary measure, without reasonable suspicion that the passenger poses a safety risk....

Our conclusion comports with the views of all nine Federal Courts of Appeals, and nearly every state court, to have ruled on the question....

■ ■ ■

Brendlin was seized from the moment Simeroth's car came to a halt on the side of the road, and it was error to deny his suppression motion on the ground that seizure occurred only at the formal arrest. It will be for the state courts to consider in the first instance whether suppression turns on any other issue. The judgment of the Supreme Court of California is vacated, and the case is remanded for further proceedings not inconsistent with this opinion.

It is so ordered.

CHAPTER 3

Level of Justification

Introduction

This chapter looks at three categories of justification for Fourth Amendment activity: (1) probable cause for criminal arrests and searches, (2) "stop and frisk" searches where the intrusion is less than arrest or a full-scale search for criminal activity, and (3) administrative searches, or non-criminal searches, where balancing the government interest and the amount of intrusion determines the justification.

Part A deals with probable cause, mostly in the context of information emanating from unnamed informants. *Aguilar* creates the so-called two-pronged test for evidence from informants. The first prong examines the underlying facts that show why the informant is reliable, and the second prong involves facts that demonstrate how the informant got the information. *Spinelli* presents methods to meet the two-pronged test through independent police corroboration of the information. *Gates* modifies the two-pronged test with the objective of making it more flexible. *Grubbs* deals with the issue of anticipatory warrants, where evidence will be found at a location in the future if certain events occur. *Whren* analyzes the issue of police pretext (a ploy to act) and its relationship to probable cause. *Atwater* and *Moore* deal with allowable police action when there is probable cause with regard to minor traffic violations. These cases should be considered with *Florence*, which allows for an extensive search regardless of the offense if one is about to be incarcerated.

Part B explores the stop and frisk of a suspect, or the *Terry* doctrine, where the level of justification is reasonable suspicion. This particular activity, which results in a lesser level of police intrusion, was designed to allow police to investigate suspicious activity. As the search becomes more intrusive, a parallel increase in level of justification occurs. Thus a frisk for weapons is allowed if the police officer has reason to believe the suspect is armed. *Camara*, an administrative search case involving the public health inspection of a residence, formulated justification by balancing government interest with the scope of the intrusion. In the *Terry*-context, the next step would be to balance the resultant justification with the scope of the intrusion. For instance, if the intrusion is less than an arrest or full-scale search, then the justification is less than probable cause.

Not all interactions between the police and citizens requires justification, as illustrated by the expectation-of-privacy cases discussed in Chapter 2. In this chapter, *Mendenhall* requires justification when there is a seizure for Fourth Amendment purposes. *Hodari* and *Drayton* deal with the seizure issue when a police chase is involved and when an individual is a passenger on a bus, respectively.

The reasonable suspicion standard is defined generally in *Arvizu* and then more specifically, when dealing with a furtive movement by a suspect (*Wardlow*) or with an informant tip (*J.L.*). The *Harris* case deals with the amount of information required for a drunken driving stop.

The scope of the allowable intrusion is examined with regard to identification information (*Hiibel*), automobile searches (*Long*), pat-down searches for weapons (*Dickerson*), dog searches at an airport or automobile stop (*Place* and *Caballes*), and police searches during an automobile stop (*Johnson*).

Part C pertains to administrative searches in a variety of contexts. The justification is evaluated by the balancing approach or the weighing of the government interest with the intrusion. These searches are primarily motivated by objectives other than investigating crime (*Edmond* and *Lidster*). Other administrative contexts include highway safety or drunk driving road-blocks (*Sitz*), school searches for drugs (*Redding* and *Earls*), workplace or occupational searches (*Skinner* and *Miller*), searches of people on probation (*Samson*), border searches (*Martinez-Fuerte* and *Flores-Montano*), and jail searches (*Florence*).

Because government interest can override an intrusion in administrative searches, weighty terrorism issues present themselves. For example, in *Edmond* (a vehicle checkpoint case) the Court stated,

> "Of course, there are circumstances that may justify a law enforcement checkpoint where the primary purpose would otherwise, but for some emergency, relate to ordinary crime control. For example, as the Court of Appeals noted, the Fourth Amendment would almost certainly permit an appropriately tailored roadblock set up to thwart an imminent terrorist attack or to catch a dangerous criminal who is likely to flee by way of a particular route."

Note also that in *Flores-Montano* the Court seems very concerned about terrorism issues in the border context.

A. PROBABLE CAUSE

1. Generally

Aguilar v. Texas

378 U.S. 108 (1964)

GOLDBERG, J., delivered the opinion of the Court, in which WARREN, C.J., DOUGLAS, BRENNAN, HARLAN, and WHITE, JJ., joined. CLARK, J., filed a dissenting opinion, in which BLACK and STEWART, JJ., joined.

This case presents questions concerning the constitutional requirements for obtaining a state search warrant.

Two Houston police officers applied to a local Justice of the Peace for a warrant to search for narcotics in petitioner's home. In support of their application, the officers submitted an affidavit which, in relevant part, recited that:

> "Affiants have received reliable information from a credible person and do believe that heroin, marijuana, barbiturates and other narcotics and narcotic paraphernalia are being kept at the above described premises for the purpose of sale and use contrary to the provisions of the law."

The search warrant was issued.

In executing the warrant, the local police, along with federal officers, announced at petitioner's door that they were police with a warrant. Upon hearing a commotion within the house, the officers forced their way into the house and seized petitioner in the act of attempting to dispose of a packet of narcotics.

At his trial in the state court, petitioner, through his attorney, objected to the introduction of evidence obtained as a result of the execution of the warrant. The objections were overruled and the evidence admitted. Petitioner was convicted of illegal possession of heroin and sentenced to serve 20 years in the state penitentiary. On appeal to the Texas Court of Criminal Appeals, the conviction was affirmed, . . . affirmance upheld on rehearing.

■ ■ ■

An evaluation of the constitutionality of a search warrant should begin with the rule that "the informed and deliberate determinations of magistrates empowered to issue warrants are to be preferred over the hurried action of officers who may happen to make arrests." . . . The reasons for this rule go to the foundations of the Fourth Amendment. A contrary rule "that evidence sufficient to support a magistrate's disinterested determination to issue a search warrant will justify the officers in making a search without a warrant would reduce the Amendment to a nullity and leave the people's homes secure only in the discretion of police officers." *Johnson v. United States* (1948). Under such a rule "resort to [warrants] would ultimately be discouraged." Thus, when a search is based upon a magistrate's, rather than a police officer's, determination of probable cause, the reviewing courts will accept evidence of a less "judicially competent or persuasive character than would have justified an officer in acting on his own without a warrant," and will sustain the judicial determination so long as "there was substantial basis for [the magistrate] to conclude that narcotics were probably present." As so well stated by Mr. Justice Jackson:

> "The point of the Fourth Amendment, which often is not grasped by zealous officers, is not that it denies law enforcement the support of the usual inferences which reasonable men draw from evidence. Its protection consists in requiring that those inferences be drawn by a neutral and detached magistrate instead of being judged by the officer engaged in the often competitive enterprise of ferreting out crime."

Johnson v. United States.

Although the reviewing court will pay substantial deference to judicial determinations of probable cause, the court must still insist that the magistrate perform his "neutral and detached" function and not serve merely as a rubber stamp for the police. . . . The Court, in *Giordenello v. United States* (1958), applied this rule to an affidavit similar to that relied upon here. . . . The Court announced the guiding principles to be:

> "that the inferences from the facts which lead to the complaint '[must] be drawn by a neutral and detached magistrate instead of being judged by the officer engaged in the often competitive enterprise of ferreting out crime.' The purpose of the complaint, then, is to enable the appropriate magistrate to determine whether the 'probable cause' required to support a warrant exists. The Commissioner must judge for himself the persuasiveness of the facts relied on by a complaining officer to show probable cause. He should not accept without question the complainant's mere conclusion."

The Court, applying these principles to the complaint in that case, stated that:

> "it is clear that it does not pass muster because it does not provide any basis for the Commissioner's determination that probable cause existed. The complaint contains no affirmative allegation that the affiant spoke with personal knowledge of the matters contained therein; it does not indicate any sources for the complainant's belief; and it does not set forth any other sufficient basis upon which a finding of probable cause could be made."

The vice in the present affidavit is at least as great as in . . . *Giordenello.* Here the "mere conclusion" that petitioner possessed narcotics was not even that of the affiant himself; it was that of an unidentified informant. The affidavit here not only "contains no affirmative allegation that the affiant spoke with personal knowledge of the matters contained therein," it does not even contain an "affirmative allegation" that the affiant's unidentified source "spoke with personal knowledge." For all that appears, the source here merely suspected, believed or concluded that there were narcotics in petitioner's possession. The magistrate here certainly could not "judge for himself the persuasiveness of the facts relied on to show probable cause." He necessarily accepted "without question" the informant's "suspicion," "belief" or "mere conclusion."

Although an affidavit may be based on hearsay information and need not reflect the direct personal observations of the affiant, the magistrate must be informed of some of the underlying circumstances from which the informant concluded that the narcotics were where he claimed they were, and some of the underlying circumstances from which the officer concluded that the informant, whose identity need not be disclosed was "credible" or his information "reliable." Otherwise, "the inferences from the facts which lead to the complaint" will be drawn not "by a neutral and detached magistrate," as the Constitution requires, but instead, by a police officer "engaged in the often competitive enterprise of ferreting out crime," or, as in this case, by an unidentified informant.

We conclude, therefore, that the search warrant should not have been issued because the affidavit did not provide a sufficient basis for a finding of probable cause and that the evidence obtained as a result of the search warrant was inadmissible in petitioner's trial.

The judgment of the Texas Court of Criminal Appeals is reversed and the case remanded for proceedings not inconsistent with this opinion.

Reversed and remanded.

Spinelli v. United States

393 U.S. 410 (1969)

HARLAN, J., delivered the opinion of the Court, in which WARREN, C.J., BRENNAN, DOUGLAS, MARSHALL, and WHITE, JJ., joined. BLACK, FORTAS, and STEWART, JJ., dissented.

William Spinelli was convicted of traveling to St. Louis, Missouri, from a nearby Illinois suburb with the intention of conducting gambling activities proscribed by Missouri law. At every appropriate stage in the proceedings in the lower courts, the petitioner challenged the constitutionality of the warrant which authorized the FBI search that uncovered the evidence necessary for his conviction. At each stage, Spinelli's challenge was treated in a different way. At a pretrial suppression hearing, the United States District Court for the Eastern District of Missouri held that Spinelli lacked standing to raise a Fourth Amendment objection. A unanimous panel of the Court of Appeals for the Eighth Circuit rejected the District Court's ground, a majority holding further that the warrant was issued without probable cause. After an en banc rehearing, the Court for Appeals sustained the warrant and affirmed the conviction by a vote of six to two.

■ ■ ■

In *Aguilar v. Texas* (1964), a search warrant had issued upon an affidavit of police officers who swore only that they had "received reliable information from a credible person and do believe" that narcotics were being illegally stored on the described premises. While recognizing that the constitutional requirement of probable cause can be satisfied by hearsay information, this Court held the affidavit inadequate for two reasons. First, the application failed to set forth any of the "underlying circumstances" necessary to enable the magistrate independently to judge of the validity of the informant's conclusion that the narcotics were where he said they were. Second, the affiant-officers did not attempt to support their claim that their informant was "credible" or his information "reliable." The Government is, however, quite right in saying that the FBI affidavit in the present case is more ample than that in *Aguilar*. Not only does it contain a report from an anonymous informant, but it also contains a report of an independent FBI investigation which is said to corroborate the informant's tip. We are, then, required to delineate the manner in which *Aguilar*'s two-pronged test should be applied in these circumstances.

In essence, the affidavit, reproduced in full in the Appendix to this opinion, contained the following allegations:

1. The FBI had kept track of Spinelli's movements on five days during the month of August 1965. On four of these occasions, Spinelli was seen crossing one of two bridges leading from Illinois into St. Louis, Missouri, between 11 a.m. and 12:15 p.m. On four of the five days, Spinelli was also seen parking his car in a lot used by residents of an apartment house at 1108 Indian Circle Drive in St. Louis, between 3:30 p.m. and 4:45 p.m. On one day, Spinelli was followed further and seen to enter a particular apartment in the building.

2. An FBI check with the telephone company revealed that this apartment contained two telephones listed under the name of Grace P. Hagen, and carrying the numbers WYdown 4-0029 and WYdown 4-0136.

3. The application stated that "William Spinelli is known to this affiant and to federal law enforcement agents and local law enforcement agents as a bookmaker, an associate of bookmakers, a gambler, and an associate of gamblers."

4. Finally it was stated that the FBI "has been informed by a confidential reliable informant that William Spinelli is operating a handbook and accepting wagers and disseminating wagering information by means of the telephones which have been assigned the numbers WYdown 4-0029 and WYdown 4-0136."

There can be no question that the last item mentioned, detailing the informant's tip, has a fundamental place in this warrant application. Without it, probable cause could not be established. The first two items reflect only innocent-seeming activity and data. Spinelli's travels to and from the apartment building and his entry into a particular apartment on one occasion could hardly be taken as bespeaking gambling activity; and there is surely nothing unusual about an apartment containing two separate telephones. Many a householder indulges himself in this petty luxury. Finally, the allegation that Spinelli was "known" to the affiant and to other federal and local law enforcement officers as a gambler and an associate of gamblers is but a bald and unilluminating assertion of suspicion that is entitled to no weight in appraising the magistrate's decision. *Nathanson v. United States* (1933).

■ ■ ■

The informer's report must first be measured against *Aguilar*'s standards so that its probative value can be assessed. If the tip is found inadequate under *Aguilar*, the other allegations which corroborate the information contained in the hearsay report should then be considered. At this stage as well, however, the standards enunciated in *Aguilar* must inform the magistrate's decision. He must ask: Can it fairly be said that the tip, even when certain parts of it have been corroborated by independent sources, is as trustworthy as a tip which would pass *Aguilar*'s tests without independent corroboration? *Aguilar* is relevant at this stage of the inquiry as well because the tests it establishes were designed to implement the long-standing principle that probable cause must be determined by a "neutral and detached magistrate," and not by "the officer engaged in the often competitive enterprise of ferreting out crime."

■ ■ ■

Applying these principles to the present case, we first consider the weight to be given the informer's tip when it is considered apart from the rest of the affidavit. It is clear that a Commissioner could not credit it without abdicating his constitutional function. Though the affiant swore that his confidant was "reliable," he offered the magistrate no reason in support of this conclusion. Perhaps even more important is the fact that *Aguilar*'s other test has not been satisfied. The tip does not contain a sufficient statement of the underlying circumstances from which the informer concluded that Spinelli was running a bookmaking operation. We are not told how the FBI's source received his information—it is not alleged that the informant personally observed Spinelli at work or that he had ever placed a bet with him. Moreover, if the informant came by the information indirectly, he did not explain why his sources were reliable. In the absence of a statement detailing the manner in which the information was gathered, it is especially important that the tip describe the accused's criminal activity in sufficient detail that the magistrate may know that he is relying on something more substantial than a casual rumor circulating in the underworld or an accusation based merely on an individual's general reputation.

The detail provided by the informant in *Draper v. United States* (1959) provides a suitable benchmark. While Hereford, the Government's informer in that case, did not state the way in which he had obtained his information, he reported that Draper had gone to Chicago the day before by train and that he would return to Denver by train with three ounces of heroin on one of two specified mornings. Moreover, Hereford went on to describe, with minute particularity, the clothes that Draper would be wearing upon his arrival at the Denver station. A magistrate, when confronted with such detail, could reasonably infer that the informant had gained his information in a reliable way. Such an inference cannot be made in the present case. Here, the only facts supplied were that Spinelli was using two specified telephones and that these phones were being used in gambling operations. This meager report could easily have been obtained from an offhand remark heard at a neighborhood bar.

Nor do we believe that the patent doubts *Aguilar* raises as to the report's reliability are adequately resolved by a consideration of the allegations detailing the FBI's independent investigative efforts. At most, these allegations indicated that Spinelli could have used the telephones specified by the informant for some purpose. This cannot by itself be said to support both the inference that the informer was generally trustworthy and that he had made his charge against Spinelli on the basis of information obtained in a reliable way. Once again, *Draper* provides a relevant comparison. Independent police work in that case corroborated much more than one small detail that had been provided by the informant. There, the police, upon meeting the inbound Denver train on the second morning specified by informer Hereford, saw a man whose dress corresponded precisely to Hereford's detailed description. It was then apparent that the informant had not been fabricating his report out of whole cloth; since the report was of the sort which in common experience may be recognized as having been obtained in a reliable way, it was perfectly clear that probable cause had been established.

We conclude, then, that in the present case the informant's tip—even when corroborated to the extent indicated—was not sufficient to provide the basis for a finding of probable cause. This is not to say that the tip was so insubstantial that it could not properly have counted in the magistrate's determination. Rather, it needed some further support. When we look to the other parts of the application, however, we find nothing alleged which would permit the suspicions engendered by the informant's report to ripen into a judgment that a crime was probably being committed. As we have already seen, the allegations detailing the FBI's surveillance of Spinelli and its investigation of the telephone company records contain no suggestion of criminal conduct when taken by themselves—and they are not endowed with an aura of suspicion by virtue of the informer's tip. Nor do we find that the FBI's reports take on a sinister color when read in light of common knowledge that bookmaking is often carried on over the telephone and from premises ostensibly used by others for perfectly normal purposes. Such an argument would carry weight in a situation in which the premises contain an unusual number of telephones or abnormal activity is observed, but it does not fit this case where neither of these factors is present. All that remains to be considered is the flat statement that Spinelli was "known" to the FBI and others as a gambler. But just as a simple assertion of police suspicion is not itself a sufficient basis for a magistrate's finding of probable cause, we do not believe it may be used to give additional weight to allegations that would otherwise be insufficient.

The affidavit, then, falls short of the standards set forth in *Aguilar, Draper,* and our other decisions that give content to the notion of probable cause. In holding as we have done, we do not retreat from the established propositions that only the probability, and not a prima facie showing, of criminal activity is the standard of probable cause, that affidavits of probable cause are tested by much less rigorous standards than those governing the admissibility of evidence at trial, that in judging probable cause issuing magistrates are not to be confined by niggardly limitations or by restrictions on the use of their common sense, and that their determination of probable cause should be paid great deference by reviewing courts. But we cannot sustain this warrant without diluting important safeguards that assure that the judgment of a disinterested judicial officer will interpose itself between the police and the citizenry.

The judgment of the Court of Appeals is reversed and the case is remanded to that court for further proceedings consistent with this opinion.

It is so ordered.

Reversed and remanded.

Justice BLACK, dissenting.

In my view, this Court's decision in *Aguilar v. Texas* was bad enough. That decision went very far toward elevating the magistrate's hearing for issuance of a search warrant to a full-fledged trial, where witnesses must be brought forward to attest personally to all the facts alleged. But not content with this, the Court today expands *Aguilar* to almost unbelievable proportions. Of course, it would strengthen the probable-cause presentation if eyewitnesses could testify that they saw the defendant commit the crime. It would be stronger still if these witnesses could explain in detail the nature of the sensual perceptions on which they based their "conclusion" that the person they had seen was the defendant and that he was responsible for the events they observed. Nothing in our Constitution, however, requires that the facts be established with that degree of certainty and with such elaborate specificity before a policeman can be authorized by a disinterested magistrate to conduct a carefully limited search.

The Fourth Amendment provides that "no Warrants shall issue, but upon probable cause, supported by Oath or affirmation, and particularly describing the place to be searched, and the persons or things to be seized." In this case a search warrant was issued supported by an oath and particularly describing the place to be searched and the things to be seized. The supporting oath was three printed pages and the full text of it is included in an Appendix to the Court's opinion. The magistrate, I think properly, held the information set forth sufficient facts to show "probable cause" that the defendant was violating the law. Six members of the Court of Appeals also agreed that the affidavit was sufficient to show probable cause. A majority of this Court today holds, however, that the magistrate and all of these judges were wrong. In doing so, they substitute their own opinion for that of the local magistrate and the circuit judges, and reject the en banc factual conclusion of the Eighth Circuit and reverse the judgment based upon that factual conclusion. I cannot join in any such disposition of an issue so vital to the administration of justice, and dissent as vigorously as I can.

I repeat my belief that the affidavit given the magistrate was more than ample to show probable cause of the petitioner's guilt. The affidavit meticulously set out facts sufficient to show the following:

1. The petitioner had been shown going to and coming from a room in an apartment which contained two telephones listed under the name of another person. Nothing in the record indicates that the apartment was of that large and luxurious type which could only be occupied by a person to whom it would be a "petty luxury" to have two separate telephones, with different numbers, both listed under the name of a person who did not live there.

2. The petitioner's car had been observed parked in the apartment's parking lot. This fact was, of course, highly relevant in showing that the petitioner was extremely interested in some enterprise which was located in the apartment.

3. The FBI had been informed by a reliable informant that the petitioner was accepting wagering information by telephones—the particular telephones located in the apartment the defendant had been repeatedly visiting. Unless the Court, going beyond the requirements of the Fourth Amendment, wishes to require magistrates to hold trials before issuing warrants, it is not necessary—as the Court holds—to have the affiant explain "the underlying circumstances from which the informer concluded that Spinelli was running a bookmaking operation."

4. The petitioner was known by federal and local law enforcement agents as a bookmaker and an associate of gamblers. I cannot agree with the Court that this knowledge was only a "bald and unilluminating assertion of suspicion that is entitled to no weight in appraising the magistrate's decision." Although the statement is hearsay that might not be admissible in a regular trial, everyone knows, unless he shuts his eyes to the realities of life, that this is a relevant fact which, together with other circumstances, might indicate a factual probability that gambling is taking place.

The foregoing facts should be enough to constitute probable cause for anyone who does not believe that the only way to obtain a search warrant is to prove beyond a reasonable doubt that a defendant is guilty. Even *Aguilar*, on which the Court relies, cannot support the contrary result, at least as that decision was written before today's massive escalation of it. In *Aguilar* the Court dealt with an affidavit that stated only:

> "Affiants have received reliable information from a credible person and do believe that heroin and other narcotics and narcotic paraphernalia are being kept at the above described premises for the purpose of sale and use contrary to the provisions of the law."

The Court held, over the dissent of Mr. Justice Clark, Mr. Justice Stewart, and myself, that this unsupported conclusion of an unidentified informant provided no basis for the magistrate to make an independent judgment as to the persuasiveness of the facts relied upon to show probable cause. Here, of course, we have much more, and the Court in *Aguilar* was careful to point out that additional information of the kind presented in the affidavit before us now would be highly relevant:

> "If the fact and results of such a surveillance had been appropriately presented to the magistrate, this would, of course, present an entirely different case."

In the present case even the two-judge minority of the court below recognized, as this Court seems to recognize today, that this additional information took the case beyond the rule of *Aguilar*. Six of the other circuit judges disagreed with the two dissenting judges, finding that all the circumstances considered together could support a reasonable judgment that gambling probably was taking place. I fully agree with this carefully considered opinion of the court below. . . .

> "If the teachings of the Court's cases are to be followed and the constitutional policy served, affidavits for search warrants must be tested and interpreted by magistrates and courts in a common-sense and realistic fashion. Technical requirements of elaborate specificity once exacted under common law pleadings have no proper place in this area."

In fact, I believe the Court is moving rapidly, through complex analyses and obfuscatory language, toward the holding that no magistrate can issue a warrant unless according to some unknown standard of proof he can be persuaded that the suspect defendant is actually guilty of a crime. I would affirm this conviction.

Illinois v. Gates

462 U.S. 213 (1983)

Rehnquist, J., delivered the opinion of the Court, in which Burger, C.J., Blackmun, Powell, and O'Connor, JJ., joined. White, J., concurred only in the judgment and filed a dissent. Brennan, J., filed a dissenting opinion, in which Marshall, J., joined.

Stevens, J., filed a dissenting opinion, in which Brennan, J., joined.

Respondents Lance and Susan Gates were indicted for violation of state drug laws after police officers, executing a search warrant, discovered marijuana and other contraband in their automobile and home. Prior to trial the Gateses moved to suppress evidence seized during this search. The Illinois Supreme Court affirmed the decisions of lower state courts, granting the motion. It held that the affidavit submitted in support of the State's application for a warrant to search the Gateses' property was inadequate under this Court's decisions in *Aguilar v. Texas* (1964) and *Spinelli v. United States* (1969).

We granted certiorari to consider the application of the Fourth Amendment to a magistrate's issuance of a search warrant on the basis of a partially corroborated anonymous informant's tip.

■ ■ ■

We . . . turn to the question presented in the State's original petition for certiorari, which requires us to decide whether respondents' rights under the Fourth and Fourteenth Amendments were violated by the search of their car and house. A chronological statement of events usefully introduces the issues at stake. Bloomingdale, Ill., is a suburb of Chicago located in DuPage County. On May 3, 1978, the Bloomingdale Police Department received by mail an anonymous handwritten letter which read as follows:

> "This letter is to inform you that you have a couple in your town who strictly make their living on selling drugs. They are Sue and Lance Gates, they live on Greenway, off Bloomingdale Rd. in the condominiums. Most of their buys are done in Florida. Sue his wife drives their car to Florida, where she leaves it to be loaded up with drugs, then Lance flys down and drives it back. Sue flys back after she drops the car off in Florida. May 3 she is driving down there again and Lance will be flying down in a few days to drive it back. At the time Lance drives the car back he has the trunk loaded with over $100,000.00 in drugs. Presently they have over $100,000.00 worth of drugs in their basement.
>
> They brag about the fact they never have to work, and make their entire living on pushers.
>
> I guarantee if you watch them carefully you will make a big catch. They are friends with some big drugs dealers, who visit their house often.
> Lance & Susan Gates
> Greenway
> in Condominiums"

The letter was referred by the Chief of Police of the Bloomingdale Police Department to Detective Mader, who decided to pursue the tip. Mader learned, from the office of the Illinois Secretary of State, that an Illinois driver's license had been issued to one Lance Gates, residing at a stated address in Bloomingdale. He contacted a confidential informant, whose examination of certain financial records revealed a more recent address for the Gateses, and he also learned from a police officer assigned to O'Hare Airport that "L. Gates" had made a reservation on Eastern Airlines flight 245 to West Palm Beach, Fla., scheduled to depart from Chicago on May 5 at 4:15 p.m.

Mader then made arrangements with an agent of the Drug Enforcement Administration for surveillance of the May 5 Eastern Airlines flight. The agent later reported to Mader that Gates had boarded the flight, and that federal agents in Florida had observed him arrive in West Palm Beach and take a taxi to the nearby Holiday Inn. They also reported that Gates went to a room registered to one Susan Gates and that, at 7:00 a.m. the next morning, Gates and an unidentified woman left the motel in a Mercury bearing Illinois license plates and drove northbound on an interstate frequently used by travelers to the Chicago area. In addition, the DEA agent informed Mader that the license plate number on the Mercury was registered to a Hornet station wagon owned by Gates. The agent also advised Mader that the driving time between West Palm Beach and Bloomingdale was approximately 22 to 24 hours.

Mader signed an affidavit setting forth the foregoing facts, and submitted it to a judge of the Circuit Court of DuPage County, together with a copy of the anonymous letter. The judge of that court thereupon issued a search warrant for the Gateses' residence and for their automobile. The judge, in deciding to issue the warrant, could have determined that the *modus operandi* of the Gateses had been substantially corroborated. As the anonymous letter predicted, Lance Gates had flown from Chicago to West Palm Beach late in the afternoon of May 5th, had checked into a hotel room registered in the name of his wife, and, at 7:00 a.m. the following morning, had headed north, accompanied by an unidentified woman, out of West Palm Beach on an interstate highway used by travelers from South Florida to Chicago in an automobile bearing a license plate issued to him.

At 5:15 a.m. on March 7th, only 36 hours after he had flown out of Chicago, Lance Gates, and his wife, returned to their home in Bloomingdale, driving the car in which they had left West Palm Beach some 22 hours earlier. The Bloomingdale police were awaiting them, searched the trunk of the Mercury, and uncovered approximately 350 pounds of marijuana. A search of the Gateses' home revealed marijuana, weapons, and other contraband. The Illinois Circuit Court ordered suppression of all these items, on the ground that the affidavit submitted to the Circuit Judge failed to support the necessary determination of probable cause to believe that the Gateses' automobile and home contained the contraband in question. This decision was affirmed in turn by the Illinois Appellate Court and by a divided vote of the Supreme Court of Illinois.

The Illinois Supreme Court concluded—and we are inclined to agree—that, standing alone, the anonymous letter sent to the Bloomingdale Police Department would not provide the basis for a magistrate's determination that there was probable cause to believe contraband would be found in the Gateses' car and home. The letter provides virtually nothing from which one might conclude that its author is either honest or his information reliable; likewise, the letter gives absolutely no indication of the basis for the writer's predictions regarding the Gateses' criminal activities. Something more was required, then, before a magistrate could conclude that there was probable cause to believe that contraband would be found in the Gateses' home and car. See *Aguilar v. Texas; Nathanson v. United States* (1933).

The Illinois Supreme Court also properly recognized that Detective Mader's affidavit might be capable of supplementing the anonymous letter with information sufficient to permit a determination of probable cause. In holding that the affidavit in fact did not contain sufficient additional information to sustain a determination of probable cause, the Illinois court applied a "two-pronged test," derived from our decision in *Spinelli v. United States*. The Illinois Supreme Court, like some others, apparently understood *Spinelli* as requiring that the anonymous letter satisfy each of two independent require-ments before it could be relied on. According to this view, the letter, as sup-plemented by Mader's affidavit, first had to adequately reveal the "basis of knowledge" of the letter writer—the particular means by which he came by the information given in his report. Second, it had to provide facts sufficiently establishing either the "veracity" of the affiant's informant, or, alternatively, the "reliability" of the informant's report in this particular case.

■ ■ ■

The Illinois court, alluding to an elaborate set of legal rules that have developed among various lower courts to enforce the "two-pronged test," found that the test had not been satisfied. First, the "veracity" prong was not satisfied because, "there was simply no basis [for] ... conclud[ing] that the anonymous person [who wrote the letter to the Bloomingdale Police Depart-ment] was credible." The court indicated that corroboration by police of details contained in the letter might never satisfy the "veracity" prong, and in any event, could not do so if, as in the present case, only "innocent" details are corroborated. In addition, the letter gave no indication of the basis of its writer's knowledge of the Gateses' activities. The Illinois court under-stood *Spinelli* as permitting the detail contained in a tip to be used to infer that the informant had a reliable basis for his statements, but it thought that the anonymous letter failed to provide sufficient detail to permit such an inference. Thus, it concluded that no showing of probable cause had been made.

■ ■ ■

We agree with the Illinois Supreme Court that an informant's "veracity," "reliability" and "basis of knowledge" are all highly relevant in determining the value of his report. We do not agree, however, that these elements should be understood as entirely separate and independent requirements to be rigidly exacted in every case, which the opinion of the Supreme Court of Illinois would imply. Rather, as detailed below, they should be understood simply as closely intertwined issues that may usefully illuminate the commonsense, practical question whether there is "probable cause" to believe that contraband or evidence is located in a particular place.

■ ■ ■

This totality-of-the-circumstances approach is far more consistent with our prior treatment of probable cause than is any rigid demand that specific "tests" be satisfied by every informant's tip. Perhaps the central teaching of our deci-sions bearing on the probable cause standard is that it is a "practical, nontech-nical conception." "In dealing with probable cause, ... as the very name implies, we deal with probabilities. These are not technical; they are the factual and practical considerations of everyday life on which reasonable and prudent men, not legal technicians, act." *Brinegar v. United States* (1949). Our observa-tion in *United States v. Cortez* (1981), regarding "particularized suspicion," is also applicable to the probable cause standard.

■ ■ ■

The process does not deal with hard certainties, but with probabilities. Long before the law of probabilities was articulated as such, practical people formulated certain common-sense conclusions about human behavior; jurors as factfinders are permitted to do the same—and so are law enforcement officers. Finally, the evidence thus collected must be seen and weighed not in terms of library analysis by scholars, but as understood by those versed in the field of law enforcement.

As these comments illustrate, probable cause is a fluid concept—turning on the assessment of probabilities in particular factual contexts—not readily, or even usefully, reduced to a neat set of legal rules. Informants' tips doubtless come in many shapes and sizes from many different types of persons.

■ ■ ■

Moreover, the "two-pronged test" directs analysis into two largely independent channels—the informant's "veracity" or "reliability" and his "basis of knowledge." There are persuasive arguments against according these two elements such independent status. Instead, they are better understood as relevant considerations in the totality-of-the-circumstances analysis that traditionally has guided probable cause determinations: a deficiency in one may be compensated for, in determining the overall reliability of a tip, by a strong showing as to the other, or by some other indicia of reliability.

If, for example, a particular informant is known for the unusual reliability of his predictions of certain types of criminal activities in a locality, his failure, in a particular case, to thoroughly set forth the basis of his knowledge surely should not serve as an absolute bar to a finding of probable cause based on his tip. Likewise, if an unquestionably honest citizen comes forward with a report of criminal activity—which if fabricated would subject him to criminal liability—we have found rigorous scrutiny of the basis of his knowledge unnecessary. Conversely, even if we entertain some doubt as to an informant's motives, his explicit and detailed description of alleged wrongdoing, along with a statement that the event was observed first-hand, entitles his tip to greater weight than might otherwise be the case. Unlike a totality-of-the-circumstances analysis, which permits a balanced assessment of the relative weights of all the various indicia of reliability (and unreliability) attending an informant's tip, the "two-pronged test" has encouraged an excessively technical dissection of informants' tips, with undue attention being focused on isolated issues that cannot sensibly be divorced from the other facts presented to the magistrate.

■ ■ ■

We . . . have recognized that affidavits "are normally drafted by nonlawyers in the midst and haste of a criminal investigation. Technical requirements of elaborate specificity once exacted under common law pleading have no proper place in this area." *United States v. Ventresca* (1965). Likewise, search and arrest warrants long have been issued by persons who are neither lawyers nor judges, and who certainly do not remain abreast of each judicial refinement of the nature of "probable cause." See *Shadwick v. City of Tampa* (1972).

The rigorous inquiry into the *Spinelli* prongs and the complex superstructure of evidentiary and analytical rules that some have seen implicit in our *Spinelli* decision, cannot be reconciled with the fact that many warrants are—quite properly—issued on the basis of nontechnical, common-sense judgments of laymen applying a standard less demanding than those used in more formal legal proceedings. Likewise, given the informal, often hurried context in which it must be applied, the "built-in subtleties" of the "two-pronged test" are particularly unlikely to assist magistrates in determining probable cause.

Similarly, we have repeatedly said that after-the-fact scrutiny by courts of the sufficiency of an affidavit should not take the form of *de novo* review. A magistrate's "determination of probable cause should be paid great deference by reviewing courts." "A grudging or negative attitude by reviewing courts toward warrants" is inconsistent with the Fourth Amendment's strong preference for searches conducted pursuant to a warrant; "courts should not invalidate . . . warrant[s] by interpreting affidavit[s] in a hypertechnical, rather than a commonsense, manner."

If the affidavits submitted by police officers are subjected to the type of scrutiny some courts have deemed appropriate, police might well resort to warrantless searches, with the hope of relying on consent or some other exception to the warrant clause that might develop at the time of the search. In addition, the possession of a warrant by officers conducting an arrest or search greatly reduces the perception of unlawful or intrusive police conduct, by assuring "the individual whose property is searched or seized of the lawful authority of the executing officer, his need to search, and the limits of his power to search." Reflecting this preference for the warrant process, the traditional standard for review of an issuing magistrate's probable cause determination has been that so long as the magistrate had a "substantial basis for . . . conclud[ing]" that a search would uncover evidence of wrongdoing, the Fourth Amendment requires no more. We think reaffirmation of this standard better serves the purpose of encouraging recourse to the warrant procedure and is more consistent with our traditional deference to the probable cause determinations of magistrates than is the "two-pronged test."

■ ■ ■

For all these reasons, we conclude that it is wiser to abandon the "two-pronged test" established by our decisions in *Aguilar* and *Spinelli*. In its place we reaffirm the totality-of-the-circumstances analysis that traditionally has informed probable cause determinations. The task of the issuing magistrate is simply to make a practical, common-sense decision whether, given all the circumstances set forth in the affidavit before him, including the "veracity" and "basis of knowledge" of persons supplying hearsay information, there is a fair probability that contraband or evidence of a crime will be found in a particular place. And the duty of a reviewing court is simply to ensure that the magistrate had a "substantial basis for . . . conclud[ing]" that probable cause existed. We are convinced that this flexible, easily applied standard will better achieve the accommodation of public and private interests that the

Fourth Amendment requires than does the approach that has developed from *Aguilar* and *Spinelli.*

■ ■ ■

Justice Brennan's dissent suggests in several places that the approach we take today somehow downgrades the role of the neutral magistrate, because *Aguilar* and *Spinelli* "preserve the role of magistrates as independent arbiters of probable cause. . . ." Quite the contrary, we believe, is the case. The essential protection of the warrant requirement of the Fourth Amendment, as stated in *Johnson v. United States* (1948), is in "requiring that [the usual inferences which reasonable men draw from evidence] be drawn by a neutral and detached magistrate instead of being judged by the officer engaged in the often competitive enterprise of ferreting out crime." Nothing in our opinion in any way lessens the authority of the magistrate to draw such reasonable inferences as he will from the material supplied to him by applicants for a warrant; indeed, he is freer than under the regime of *Aguilar* and *Spinelli* to draw such inferences, or to refuse to draw them if he is so minded.

The real gist of Justice Brennan's criticism seems to be a second argument, somewhat at odds with the first, that magistrates should be restricted in their authority to make probable cause determinations by the standards laid down in *Aguilar* and *Spinelli,* and that such findings "should not be authorized unless there is some assurance that the information on which they are based has been obtained in a reliable way by an honest or credible person." However, under our opinion magistrates remain perfectly free to exact such assurances as they deem necessary, as well as those required by this opinion, in making probable cause determinations. Justice Brennan would apparently prefer that magistrates be restricted in their findings of probable cause by the development of an elaborate body of case law dealing with the "veracity" prong of the *Spinelli* test, which in turn is broken down into two "spurs"—the informant's "credibility" and the "reliability" of his information, together with the "basis of knowledge" prong of the *Spinelli* test. That such a labyrinthine body of judicial refinement bears any relationship to familiar definitions of probable cause is hard to imagine. Probable cause deals "with probabilities. These are not technical; they are the factual and practical considerations of everyday life on which reasonable and prudent men, not legal technicians, act."

Justice Brennan's dissent also suggests that "words such as 'practical,' 'nontechnical,' and 'common sense,' as used in the Court's opinion, are but code words for an overly-permissive attitude towards police practices in derogation of the rights secured by the Fourth Amendment." . . . More fundamentally, no one doubts that "under our Constitution only measures consistent with the Fourth Amendment may be employed by government to cure [the horrors of drug trafficking]"; but this agreement does not advance the inquiry as to which measures are, and which measures are not, consistent with the Fourth Amendment. "Fidelity" to the commands of the Constitution suggests balanced judgment rather than exhortation. The highest "fidelity" is achieved neither by the judge who instinctively goes furthest in upholding even the most bizarre claim of individual constitutional rights, any more than it is achieved by a judge who instinctively goes furthest in accepting the most restrictive claims of governmental authorities. The task of this Court, as of other courts, is to "hold the balance true," and we think we have done that in this case.

Our decisions applying the totality-of-the-circumstances analysis outlined above have consistently recognized the value of corroboration of details of an informant's tip by independent police work. We held that an affidavit relying on hearsay "is not to be deemed insufficient on that score, so long as a substantial basis for crediting the hearsay is presented." We went on to say that even in making a warrantless arrest an officer "may rely upon information received through an informant, rather than upon his direct observations, so long as the informant's statement is reasonably corroborated by other matters within the officer's knowledge." Likewise, we recognized the probative value of corroborative efforts of police officials in *Aguilar*—the source of the "two-pronged test"—by observing that if the police had made some effort to corroborate the informant's report at issue, "an entirely different case" would have been presented.

Our decision in *Draper v. United States* (1959), however, is the classic case on the value of corroborative efforts of police officials. There, an informant named Hereford reported that Draper would arrive in Denver on a train from Chicago on one of two days, and that he would be carrying a quantity of heroin. The informant also supplied a fairly detailed physical description of Draper, and predicted that he would be wearing a light colored raincoat, brown slacks and black shoes, and would be walking "real fast." Hereford gave no indication of the basis for his information.

■ ■ ■

In addition, the magistrate could rely on the anonymous letter, which had been corroborated in major part by Mader's efforts—just as had occurred in *Draper*. The Supreme Court of Illinois reasoned that *Draper* involved an informant who had given reliable information on previous occasions, while the honesty and reliability of the anonymous informant in this case were unknown to the Bloomingdale police. While this distinction might be an apt one at the time the police department received the anonymous letter, it became far less significant after Mader's independent investigative work occurred. The corroboration of the letter's predictions that the Gateses' car would be in Florida, that Lance Gates would fly to Florida in the next day or so, and that he would drive the car north toward Bloomingdale all indicated, albeit not with certainty, that the informant's other assertions also were true. "Because an informant is right about some things, he is more probably right about other facts"—including the claim regarding the Gateses' illegal activity. This may well not be the type of "reliability" or "veracity" necessary to satisfy some views of the "veracity prong" of *Spinelli*, but we think it suffices for the practical, common-sense judgment called for in making a probable cause determination. It is enough, for purposes of assessing probable cause, that "corroboration through other sources of information reduced the chances of a reckless or prevaricating tale," thus providing "a substantial basis for crediting the hearsay."

■ ■ ■

Finally, the anonymous letter contained a range of details relating not just to easily obtained facts and conditions existing at the time of the tip, but to future actions of third parties ordinarily not easily predicted. The letter writer's accurate information as to the travel plans of each of the Gateses was of a character likely obtained only from the Gateses themselves, or from someone familiar with their not entirely ordinary travel plans. If the informant had access to accurate information of this type a magistrate could properly conclude that it was not unlikely that he also had access to reliable information of the Gateses' alleged illegal activities. Of course, the Gateses' travel plans might have been learned from a talkative neighbor or travel agent; under the "two-pronged test" developed from *Spinelli,* the character of the details in the anonymous letter might well not permit a sufficiently clear inference regarding the letter writer's "basis of knowledge." But, as discussed previously, probable cause does not demand the certainty we associate with formal trials. It is enough that there was a fair probability that the writer of the anonymous letter had obtained his entire story either from the Gateses or someone they trusted. And corroboration of major portions of the letter's predictions provides just this probability. It is apparent, therefore, that the judge issuing the warrant had a "substantial basis for . . . conclud[ing]" that probable cause to search the Gateses' home and car existed. The judgment of the Supreme Court of Illinois therefore must be

Reversed.

Justice WHITE, concurring in the judgment.

■ ■ ■

Since a majority of the Court deems it inappropriate to address the good faith issue, I briefly address the question that the Court does reach—whether the warrant authorizing the search and seizure of respondents' car and home was constitutionally valid. Abandoning the "two-pronged test" of *Aguilar v. Texas* and *Spinelli v. United States,* the Court upholds the validity of the warrant under a new "totality of the circumstances" approach. Although I agree that the warrant should be upheld, I reach this conclusion in accordance with the *Aguilar-Spinelli* framework.

A

For present purposes, the *Aguilar-Spinelli* rules can be summed up as follows. First, an affidavit based on an informer's tip, standing alone, cannot provide probable cause for issuance of a warrant unless the tip includes information that apprises the magistrate of the informant's basis for concluding that the contraband is where he claims it is (the "basis of knowledge" prong), *and* the affiant informs the magistrate of his basis for believing that the informant is credible (the "veracity" prong). Second, if a tip fails under either or both of the two prongs, probable cause may yet be established by independent police investigatory work that corroborates the tip to such an extent that it supports "both the inference that the informer was generally trustworthy and that he made his charge on the basis of information obtained in a reliable way." In instances where the officers rely on corroboration, the ultimate question is whether the corroborated tip "is as trustworthy as a tip which would pass *Aguilar*'s tests without independent corroboration."

■ ■ ■

In the present case, it is undisputed that the anonymous tip, by itself, did not furnish probable cause. The question is whether those portions of the affidavit describing the results of the police investigation of the respondents, when considered in light of the tip, "would permit the suspicions engendered by the informant's report to ripen into a judgment that a crime was probably being committed." The Illinois Supreme Court concluded that the corroboration was insufficient to permit such a ripening. The court reasoned as follows:

> "[T]he nature of the corroborating evidence in this case would satisfy neither the "basis of knowledge" nor the "veracity" prong of *Aguilar*. Looking to the affidavit submitted as support for Detective Mader's request that a search warrant issue, we note that the corroborative evidence here was only of innocent activity. Mader's independent investigation revealed only that Lance and Sue Gates lived on Greenway Drive; that Lance Gates booked passage on a flight to Florida; that upon arriving he entered a room registered to his wife; and that he and his wife left the hotel together by car. The corroboration of innocent activity is insufficient to support a finding of probable cause."

In my view, the lower court's characterization of the Gateses' activity here as totally "innocent" is dubious. In fact, the behavior was quite suspicious. I agree with the Court that Lance Gates' flight to Palm Beach, an area known to be a source of narcotics, the brief overnight stay in a motel, and apparent immediate return North, suggest a pattern that trained law-enforcement officers have recognized as indicative of illicit drug-dealing activity.

Even, however, had the corroboration related only to completely innocuous activities, this fact alone would not preclude the issuance of a valid warrant. The critical issue is not whether the activities observed by the police are innocent or suspicious. Instead, the proper focus should be on whether the actions of the suspects, whatever their nature, give rise to an inference that the informant is credible and that he obtained his information in a reliable manner.

Thus, in *Draper v. United States*, an informant stated on Sept. 7 that Draper would be carrying narcotics when he arrived by train in Denver on the morning of Sept. 8 or Sept. 9. The informant also provided the police with a detailed physical description of the clothes Draper would be wearing when he alighted from the train. The police observed Draper leaving a train on the morning of Sept. 9, and he was wearing the precise clothing described by the informant. The Court held that the police had probable cause to arrest Draper at this point, even though the police had seen nothing more than the totally innocent act of a man getting off a train carrying a briefcase. As we later explained in *Spinelli*, the important point was that the corroboration showed both that the informant was credible, *i.e.*, that he "had not been fabricating his report out of whole cloth," and that he had an adequate basis of knowledge for his allegations, "since the report was of the sort which in common experience may be recognized as having been obtained in a reliable way." The fact that the informer was able to predict, two days in advance, the exact clothing Draper would be wearing dispelled the possibility that his tip was just based on rumor or "an off-hand remark heard at a neighborhood bar." Probably Draper had planned in advance to wear these specific clothes so that an accomplice could identify him. A clear inference could therefore be drawn that the informant was either involved in the criminal scheme himself or that he otherwise had access to reliable, inside information.

■ ■ ■

As in *Draper*, the police investigation in the present case satisfactorily demonstrated that the informant's tip was as trustworthy as one that would alone satisfy the *Aguilar* tests. The tip predicted that Sue Gates would drive to Florida, that Lance Gates would fly there a few days after May 3, and that Lance would then drive the car back. After the police corroborated these facts, the magistrate could reasonably have inferred, as he apparently did, that the informant, who had specific knowledge of these unusual travel plans, did not make up his story and that he obtained his information in a reliable way. It is theoretically possible, as respondents insist, that the tip could have been supplied by a "vindictive travel agent" and that the Gateses' activities, although unusual, might not have been unlawful. But *Aguilar* and *Spinelli*, like our other cases, do not require that certain guilt be established before a warrant may properly be issued. "[O]nly the probability, and not a prima facie showing, of criminal activity is the standard of probable cause." I therefore conclude that the judgment of the Illinois Supreme Court invalidating the warrant must be reversed.

■ ■ ■

Thus, as I read the majority opinion, it appears that the question whether the probable cause standard is to be diluted is left to the common-sense judgments of issuing magistrates. I am reluctant to approve any standard that does not expressly require, as a prerequisite to issuance of a warrant, some showing of facts from which an inference may be drawn that the informant is credible and that his information was obtained in a reliable way. The Court is correctly concerned with the fact that some lower courts have been applying *Aguilar-Spinelli* in an unduly rigid manner. I believe, however, that with clarification of the rule of corroborating information, the lower courts are fully able to properly interpret *Aguilar-Spinelli* and avoid such unduly-rigid applications. I may be wrong; it ultimately may prove to be the case that the only profitable instruction we can provide to magistrates is to rely on common sense. But the question whether a particular anonymous tip provides the basis for issuance of a warrant will often be a difficult one, and I would at least attempt to provide more precise guidance by clarifying *Aguilar-Spinelli* and the relationship of those cases with *Draper* before totally abdicating our responsibility in this area. Hence, I do not join the Court's opinion rejecting the *Aguilar-Spinelli* rules.

Justice STEVENS, with whom Justice BRENNAN joins, dissenting.

The fact that Lance and Sue Gates made a 22-hour nonstop drive from West Palm Beach, Florida, to Bloomingdale, Illinois, only a few hours after Lance had flown to Florida provided persuasive evidence that they were engaged in illicit activity. That fact, however, was not known to the magistrate when he issued the warrant to search their home.

What the magistrate did know at that time was that the anonymous informant had not been completely accurate in his or her predictions. The informant had indicated that "Sue drives their car to Florida *where she leaves it to be loaded up with drugs. . . . Sue flies back after she drops the car off in Florida*" . . . (emphasis added). Yet Detective Mader's affidavit reported that she "left the West Palm Beach area driving the Mercury northbound."

The discrepancy between the informant's predictions and the facts known to Detective Mader is significant for three reasons. First, it cast doubt on the informant's hypothesis that the Gates already had "over $100,000 worth of drugs in their basement." The informant had predicted an itinerary that always kept one spouse in Bloomingdale, suggesting that the Gates did not want to leave their home unguarded because something valuable was hidden within. That inference obviously could not be drawn when it was known that the pair was actually together over a thousand miles from home.

Second, the discrepancy made the Gates' conduct seem substantially less unusual than the informant had predicted it would be. It would have been odd if, as predicted, Sue had driven down to Florida on Wednesday, left the car, and flown right back to Illinois. But the mere facts that Sue was in West Palm Beach with the car, that she was joined by her husband at the Holiday Inn on Friday, and that the couple drove north together the next morning are neither unusual nor probative of criminal activity.

■ ■ ■

Third, the fact that the anonymous letter contained a material mistake undermines the reasonableness of relying on it as a basis for making a forcible entry into a private home.

Of course, the activities in this case did not stop when the magistrate issued the warrant. The Gates drove all night to Bloomingdale, the officers searched the car and found 400 pounds of marijuana, and then they searched the house. However, none of these subsequent events may be considered in evaluating the warrant, and the search of the house was legal only if the warrant was valid. I cannot accept the Court's casual conclusion that, *before the Gates arrived in Bloomingdale,* there was probable cause to justify a valid entry and search of a private home. No one knows who the informant in this case was, or what motivated him or her to write the note. Given that the note's predictions were faulty in one significant respect, and were corroborated by nothing except ordinary innocent activity, I must surmise that the Court's evaluation of the warrant's validity has been colored by subsequent events.

■ ■ ■

Although the foregoing analysis is determinative as to the house search, the car search raises additional issues because "there is a constitutional difference between houses and cars." *Chambers v. Maroney* (1970). An officer who has probable cause to suspect that a highly movable automobile contains contraband does not need a valid warrant in order to search it. This point was developed in our opinion in *United States v. Ross* (1982), which was not decided until after the Illinois Supreme Court rendered its decision in this case. Under *Ross*, the car search may have been valid if the officers had probable cause *after* the Gates arrived.

In apologizing for its belated realization that we should not have ordered reargument in this case, the Court today shows high regard for the appropriate relationship of this Court to state courts. When the Court discusses the merits, however, it attaches no weight to the conclusions of the Circuit Judge of DuPage County, Illinois, of the three judges of the Second District of the Illinois Appellate Court, or of the five justices of the Illinois Supreme Court, all of whom concluded that the warrant was not based on probable cause. In a fact-bound inquiry of this sort, the judgment of three levels of state courts, all of whom are better able to evaluate the probable reliability of anonymous informants in Bloomingdale, Illinois, than we are, should be entitled to at least a presumption of accuracy. I would simply vacate the judgment of the Illinois Supreme Court and remand the case for reconsideration in the light of our intervening decision in *United States v. Ross*.

United States v. Grubbs

547 U.S. 90 (2006)

SCALIA, J., delivered the opinion of the Court, in which ROBERTS, C.J., and KENNEDY, THOMAS, and BREYER, JJ., joined, and in which STEVENS, SOUTER, and GINSBURG, JJ., joined as to Parts I and II. SOUTER, J., filed an opinion concurring in part and concurring in the judgment, in which STEVENS and GINSBURG, JJ., joined. ALITO, J., took no part in the consideration or decision of the case.

Federal law enforcement officers obtained a search warrant for respondent's house on the basis of an affidavit explaining that the warrant would be executed only after a controlled delivery of contraband to that location. We address two challenges to the constitutionality of this anticipatory warrant.

I

facts

Respondent Jeffrey Grubbs purchased a videotape containing child pornography from a Web site operated by an undercover postal inspector. Officers from the Postal Inspection Service arranged a controlled delivery of a package containing the videotape to Grubbs' residence. A postal inspector submitted a search warrant application to a Magistrate Judge for the Eastern District of California, accompanied by an affidavit describing the proposed operation in detail. The affidavit stated:

> "Execution of this search warrant will not occur unless and until the parcel has been received by a person(s) and has been physically taken into the residence....At that time, and not before, this search warrant will be executed by me and other United States Postal inspectors, with appropriate assistance from other law enforcement officers in accordance with this warrant's command."

In addition to describing this triggering condition, the affidavit referred to two attachments, which described Grubbs' residence and the items officers would seize. These attachments, but not the body of the affidavit, were incorporated into the requested warrant. The affidavit concluded:

> "Based upon the foregoing facts, I respectfully submit there exists probable cause to believe that the items set forth in Attachment B to this affidavit and the search warrant, will be found [at Grubbs' residence], which residence is further described at Attachment A."

Warrant issued

The Magistrate Judge issued the warrant as requested. Two days later, an undercover postal inspector delivered the package. Grubbs' wife signed for it and took the unopened package inside. The inspectors detained Grubbs as he left his home a few minutes later, then entered the house and commenced the search. Roughly 30 minutes into the search, Grubbs was provided with a copy of the warrant, which included both attachments but not the supporting affidavit that explained when the warrant would be executed. Grubbs consented to interrogation by the postal inspectors and admitted ordering the videotape. He was placed under arrest, and various items were seized, including the videotape.

A grand jury for the Eastern District of California indicted Grubbs on one count of receiving a visual depiction of a minor engaged in sexually explicit conduct. He moved to suppress the evidence seized during the search of his residence, arguing as relevant here that the warrant was invalid because it failed to list the triggering condition. After an evidentiary hearing, the District Court denied the motion. Grubbs pleaded guilty, but reserved his right to appeal the denial of his motion to suppress.

reversed

The Court of Appeals for the Ninth Circuit reversed. Relying on Circuit precedent, it held that "the particularity requirement of the Fourth Amendment applies with full force to the conditions precedent to an anticipatory search warrant." An anticipatory warrant defective for that reason may be "cur[ed]" if the conditions precedent are set forth in an affidavit that is incorporated in the warrant and "presented to the person whose property is being searched." Because the postal inspectors "failed to present the affidavit—the only document in which the triggering conditions were listed"—to Grubbs or his wife, the "warrant was . . . inoperative, and the search was illegal." We granted certiorari.

II

Before turning to the Ninth Circuit's conclusion that the warrant at issue here ran afoul of the Fourth Amendment's particularity requirement, we address the antecedent question whether anticipatory search warrants are categorically unconstitutional. An anticipatory warrant is "a warrant based upon an affidavit showing probable cause that at some future time (but not presently) certain evidence of crime will be located at a specified place." 2 W. LaFave, Search and Seizure § 3.7(c), p. 398 (4th ed. 2004). Most anticipatory warrants subject their execution to some condition precedent other than the mere passage of time—a so-called "triggering condition." The affidavit at issue here, for instance, explained that "[e]xecution of th[e] search warrant will not occur unless and until the parcel [containing child pornography] has been received by a person(s) and has been physically taken into the residence." If the government were to execute an anticipatory warrant before the triggering condition occurred, there would be no reason to believe the item described in the warrant could be found at the searched location; by definition, the triggering condition which establishes probable cause has not yet been satisfied when the warrant is issued. Grubbs argues that for this reason anticipatory warrants contravene the Fourth Amendment's provision that "no Warrants shall issue, but upon probable cause."

■ ■ ■

We reject this view, as has every Court of Appeals to confront the issue. Probable cause exists when "there is a fair probability that contraband or evidence of a crime will be found in a particular place." Because the probable-cause requirement looks to whether evidence will be found *when the search is conducted*, all warrants are, in a sense, "anticipatory." In the typical case where the police seek permission to search a house for an item they believe is already located there, the magistrate's determination that there is probable cause for the search amounts to a prediction that the item will still be there when the warrant is executed. The anticipatory nature of warrants is even clearer in the context of electronic surveillance. When police request approval to tap a telephone line, they do so based on the probability that, during the course of the surveillance, the subject *will* use the phone to engage in crime-related conversations. The relevant federal provision requires a judge authorizing "interception of wire, oral, or electronic communications" to determine that "there is probable cause for belief that particular communications concerning [one of various listed offenses] *will be obtained* through such interception."

■ ■ ■

Anticipatory warrants are, therefore, no different in principle from ordinary warrants. They require the magistrate to determine (1) that it is *now probable* that (2) contraband, evidence of a crime, or a fugitive *will be* on the described premises (3) when the warrant is executed. It should be noted, however, that where the anticipatory warrant places a condition (other than the mere passage of time) upon its execution, the first of these determinations goes not merely to what will probably be found *if* the condition is met. (If that were the extent of the probability determination, an anticipatory warrant could be issued for every house in the country, authorizing search and seizure *if* contraband should be delivered—though for any single location there is no likelihood that contraband will be delivered.) Rather, the probability determination for a conditioned anticipatory warrant looks also to the likelihood that the condition will occur, and thus that a proper object of seizure will be on the described premises. In other words, for a conditioned anticipatory warrant to comply with the Fourth Amendment's requirement of probable cause, two prerequisites of probability must be satisfied. It must be true not only that *if* the triggering condition occurs "there is a fair probability that contraband or evidence of a crime will be found in a particular place," but also that there is probable cause to believe the triggering condition *will occur*. The supporting affidavit must provide the magistrate with sufficient information to evaluate both aspects of the probable-cause determination.

In this case, the occurrence of the triggering condition—successful delivery of the videotape to Grubbs' residence—would plainly establish probable cause for the search. In addition, the affidavit established probable cause to believe the triggering condition would be satisfied. Although it is possible that Grubbs could have refused delivery of the videotape he had ordered, that was unlikely. The Magistrate therefore "had a 'substantial basis for . . . conclud[ing]' that probable cause existed."

III

The Ninth Circuit invalidated the anticipatory search warrant at issue here because the warrant failed to specify the triggering condition. The Fourth Amendment's particularity requirement, it held, "applies with full force to the conditions precedent to an anticipatory search warrant."

■ ■ ■

Respondent, drawing upon the Ninth Circuit's analysis below, relies primarily on two related policy rationales. First, he argues, setting forth the triggering condition in the warrant itself is necessary "to delineate the limits of the executing officer's power." This is an application, respondent asserts, of the following principle: "[I]f there is a precondition to the valid exercise of executive power, that precondition must be particularly identified on the face of the warrant." That principle is not to be found in the Constitution. The Fourth Amendment does not require that the warrant set forth the magistrate's basis for finding probable cause, even though probable cause is the quintessential "precondition to the valid exercise of executive power." Much less does it require description of a triggering condition.

Second, respondent argues that listing the triggering condition in the warrant is necessary to " 'assur[e] the individual whose property is searched or seized of the lawful authority of the executing officer, his need to search, and the limits of his power to search.' "

■ ■ ■

Because the Fourth Amendment does not require that the triggering condition for an anticipatory search warrant be set forth in the warrant itself, the Court of Appeals erred in invalidating the warrant at issue here. The judgment of the Court of Appeals is reversed, and the case is remanded for further proceedings consistent with this opinion.

It is so ordered.

Justice Souter, with whom Justice Stevens and Justice Ginsburg join, concurring in part and concurring in the judgment.

I agree with the Court that anticipatory warrants are constitutional for the reasons stated in Part II of the Court's opinion, and I join in the disposition of this case. But I would qualify some points made in Part III.

The Court notes that a warrant's failure to specify the place to be searched and the objects sought violates an express textual requirement of the Fourth Amendment, whereas the text says nothing about a condition placed by the issuing magistrate on the authorization to search (here, delivery of the package of contraband). That textual difference is, however, no authority for neglecting to specify the point or contingency intended by the magistrate to trigger authorization, and the government should beware of banking on the terms of a warrant without such specification. The notation of a starting date was an established feature even of the objectionable 18th-century writs of assistance.

An issuing magistrate's failure to mention that condition can lead to several untoward consequences with constitutional significance. To begin with, a warrant that fails to tell the truth about what a magistrate authorized cannot inform the police officer's responsibility to respect the limits of authorization, a failing assuming real significance when the warrant is not executed by the official who applied for it and happens to know the unstated condition. The peril is that if an officer simply takes such a warrant on its face and makes the ostensibly authorized search before the unstated condition has been met, the search will be held unreasonable. It is true that we have declined to apply the exclusionary rule when a police officer reasonably relies on the product of a magistrate's faulty judgment or sloppy practice, see *Massachusetts v. Sheppard* (1984). But when a government officer obtains what the magistrate says is an anticipatory warrant, he must know or should realize when it omits the condition on which authorization depends, and it is hard to see why the government should not be held to the condition despite the unconditional face of the warrant. *Groh v. Ramirez* (2004) (declaring unconstitutional a search conducted pursuant to a warrant failing to specify the items the government asked the magistrate permission to seize in part because "officers leading a search team must 'make sure that they have a proper warrant that in fact authorizes the search and seizure they are about to conduct'" (brackets omitted)).

Nor does an incomplete anticipatory warrant address an owner's interest in an accurate statement of the government's authority to search property. To be sure, the extent of that interest is yet to be settled; in *Groh v. Ramirez*, the Court was careful to note that the right of an owner to demand to see a copy of the warrant before making way for the police had not been determined, and it remains undetermined today. But regardless of any right on the owner's part, showing an accurate warrant reliably "assures the individual whose property is searched or seized of the lawful authority of the executing officer, his need to search, and the limits of his power to search."

2. Pretext and Scope of Probable Cause

Maryland v. Pringle

540 U.S. 366 (2003)

REHNQUIST, C.J., delivered the opinion for a unanimous Court.

In the early morning hours a passenger car occupied by three men was stopped for speeding by a police officer. The officer, upon searching the car, seized $763 of rolled-up cash from the glove compartment and five glassine baggies of cocaine from between the back-seat armrest and the back seat. After all three men denied ownership of the cocaine and money, the officer arrested each of them. We hold that the officer had probable cause to arrest Pringle— one of the three men.

At 3:16 a.m. on August 7, 1999, a Baltimore County Police officer stopped a Nissan Maxima for speeding. There were three occupants in the car: Donte Partlow, the driver and owner, respondent Pringle, the front-seat passenger, and Otis Smith, the back-seat passenger. The officer asked Partlow for his license and registration. When Partlow opened the glove compartment to retrieve the vehicle registration, the officer observed a large amount of rolled-up money in the glove compartment. The officer returned to his patrol car with Partlow's license and registration to check the computer system for outstanding violations. The computer check did not reveal any violations. The officer returned to the stopped car, had Partlow get out, and issued him an oral warning.

After a second patrol car arrived, the officer asked Partlow if he had any weapons or narcotics in the vehicle. Partlow indicated that he did not. Partlow then consented to a search of the vehicle. The search yielded $763 from the glove compartment and five plastic glassine baggies containing cocaine from behind the back-seat armrest. When the officer began the search the armrest was in the upright position flat against the rear seat. The officer pulled down the armrest and found the drugs, which had been placed between the armrest and the back seat of the car.

The officer questioned all three men about the ownership of the drugs and money, and told them that if no one admitted to ownership of the drugs he was going to arrest them all. The men offered no information regarding the ownership of the drugs or money. All three were placed under arrest and transported to the police station.

Later that morning, Pringle waived his rights under *Miranda v. Arizona* (1966), and gave an oral and written confession in which he acknowledged that the cocaine belonged to him, that he and his friends were going to a party, and that he intended to sell the cocaine or "[u]se it for sex." Pringle maintained that the other occupants of the car did not know about the drugs, and they were released.

The trial court denied Pringle's motion to suppress his confession as the fruit of an illegal arrest, holding that the officer had probable cause to arrest Pringle. A jury convicted Pringle of possession with intent to distribute cocaine and possession of cocaine. He was sentenced to 10 years' incarceration without the possibility of parole. The Court of Special Appeals of Maryland affirmed.

The Court of Appeals of Maryland, by divided vote, reversed, holding that, absent specific facts tending to show Pringle's knowledge and dominion or control over the drugs, "the mere finding of cocaine in the back armrest when [Pringle] was a front seat passenger in a car being driven by its owner is insufficient to establish probable cause for an arrest for possession." We granted certiorari, and now reverse.

■ ■ ■

It is uncontested in the present case that the officer, upon recovering the five plastic glassine baggies containing suspected cocaine, had probable cause to believe a felony had been committed.

■ ■ ■

The long-prevailing standard of probable cause protects "citizens from rash and unreasonable interferences with privacy and from unfounded charges of crime," while giving "fair leeway for enforcing the law in the community's protection." On many occasions, we have reiterated that the probable-cause standard is a " 'practical, nontechnical conception' " that deals with " 'the factual and practical considerations of everyday life on which reasonable and prudent men, not legal technicians, act.' " *Illinois v. Gates* (1983).

■ ■ ■

The probable-cause standard is incapable of precise definition or quantification into percentages because it deals with probabilities and depends on the totality of the circumstances. We have stated, however, that "[t]he substance of all the definitions of probable cause is a reasonable ground for belief of guilt," and that the belief of guilt must be particularized with respect to the person to be searched or seized.

■ ■ ■

To determine whether an officer had probable cause to arrest an individual, we examine the events leading up to the arrest, and then decide "whether these historical facts, viewed from the standpoint of an objectively reasonable police officer, amount to" probable cause.

■ ■ ■

In this case, Pringle was one of three men riding in a Nissan Maxima at 3:16 a.m. There was $763 of rolled-up cash in the glove compartment directly in front of Pringle. Five plastic glassine baggies of cocaine were behind the back-seat armrest and accessible to all three men. Upon questioning, the three men failed to offer any information with respect to the ownership of the cocaine or the money.

We think it an entirely reasonable inference from these facts that any or all three of the occupants had knowledge of, and exercised dominion and control over, the cocaine. Thus, a reasonable officer could conclude that there was probable cause to believe Pringle committed the crime of possession of cocaine, either solely or jointly.

Pringle's attempt to characterize this case as a guilt-by-association case is unavailing. His reliance on *Ybarra v. Illinois* (1979) . . . is misplaced. In *Ybarra*, police officers obtained a warrant to search a tavern and its bartender for evidence of possession of a controlled substance. Upon entering the tavern, the officers conducted patdown searches of the customers present in the tavern, including Ybarra. Inside a cigarette pack retrieved from Ybarra's pocket, an officer found six tinfoil packets containing heroin. We stated:

> "[A] person's mere propinquity to others independently suspected of criminal activity does not, without more, give rise to probable cause to search that person. Where the standard is probable cause, a search or seizure of a person must be supported by probable cause particularized with respect to that person. This requirement cannot be undercut or avoided by simply pointing to the fact that coincidentally there exists probable cause to search or seize another or to search the premises where the person may happen to be."

We held that the search warrant did not permit body searches of all of the tavern's patrons and that the police could not pat down the patrons for weapons, absent individualized suspicion.

This case is quite different from *Ybarra*. Pringle and his two companions were in a relatively small automobile, not a public tavern. In *Wyoming v. Houghton* (1999), we noted that "a car passenger—unlike the unwitting tavern patron in *Ybarra*—will often be engaged in a common enterprise with the driver, and have the same interest in concealing the fruits or the evidence of their wrongdoing." Here we think it was reasonable for the officer to infer a common enterprise among the three men. The quantity of drugs and cash in the car indicated the likelihood of drug dealing, an enterprise to which a dealer would be unlikely to admit an innocent person with the potential to furnish evidence against him. . . .

We hold that the officer had probable cause to believe that Pringle had committed the crime of possession of a controlled substance. Pringle's arrest therefore did not contravene the Fourth and Fourteenth Amendments. Accordingly, the judgment of the Court of Appeals of Maryland is reversed, and the case is remanded for further proceedings not inconsistent with this opinion.

It is so ordered.

Whren v. United States

517 U.S. 806 (1996)

SCALIA, J., delivered the opinion for a unanimous Court.

In this case we decide whether the temporary detention of a motorist who the police have probable cause to believe has committed a civil traffic violation is inconsistent with the Fourth Amendment's prohibition against unreasonable seizures unless a reasonable officer would have been motivated to stop the car by a desire to enforce the traffic laws.

On the evening of June 10, 1993, plainclothes vice-squad officers of the District of Columbia Metropolitan Police Department were patrolling a "high drug area" of the city in an unmarked car. Their suspicions were aroused when they passed a dark Pathfinder truck with temporary license plates and youthful occupants waiting at a stop sign, the driver looking down into the lap of the passenger at his right. The truck remained stopped at the intersection for what seemed an unusually long time—more than 20 seconds. When the police car executed a U-turn in order to head back toward the truck, the Pathfinder turned suddenly to its right, without signaling, and sped off at an "unreasonable" speed. The policemen followed, and in a short while overtook the Pathfinder when it stopped behind other traffic at a red light. They pulled up alongside, and Officer Ephraim Soto stepped out and approached the driver's door, identifying himself as a police officer and directing the driver, petitioner Brown, to put the vehicle in park. When Soto drew up to the driver's window, he immediately observed two large plastic bags of what appeared to be crack cocaine in petitioner Whren's hands. Petitioners were arrested, and quantities of several types of illegal drugs were retrieved from the vehicle.

Petitioners were charged in a four-count indictment with violating various federal drug laws. At a pretrial suppression hearing, they challenged the legality of the stop and the resulting seizure of the drugs. They argued that the stop had not been justified by probable cause to believe, or even reasonable suspicion, that petitioners were engaged in illegal drug-dealing activity; and that Officer Soto's asserted ground for approaching the vehicle—to give the driver a warning concerning traffic violations—was pretextual. The District Court denied the suppression motion, concluding that "the facts of the stop were not controverted," and "[t]here was nothing to really demonstrate that the actions of the officers were contrary to a normal traffic stop."

Petitioners were convicted of the counts at issue here. The Court of Appeals affirmed the convictions, holding with respect to the suppression issue that, "regardless of whether a police officer subjectively believes that the occupants of an automobile may be engaging in some other illegal behavior, a traffic stop is permissible as long as a reasonable officer in the same circumstances *could have* stopped the car for the suspected traffic violation." We granted certiorari....

■ ■ ■

Petitioners accept that Officer Soto had probable cause to believe that various provisions of the District of Columbia traffic code had been violated. They argue, however, that "in the unique context of civil traffic regulations" probable cause is not enough. Since, they contend, the use of automobiles is so heavily and minutely regulated that total compliance with traffic and safety rules is nearly impossible, a police officer will almost invariably be able to catch any given motorist in a technical violation. This creates the temptation to use traffic stops as a means of investigating other law violations, as to which no probable cause or even articulable suspicion exists. Petitioners, who are both black, further contend that police officers might decide which motorists to stop based on decidedly impermissible factors, such as the race of the car's occupants. To avoid this danger, they say, the Fourth Amendment test for traffic stops should be, not the normal one (applied by the Court of Appeals) of whether probable cause existed to justify the stop; but rather, whether a police officer, acting reasonably, would have made the stop for the reason given.

Petitioners contend that the standard they propose is consistent with our past cases' disapproval of police attempts to use valid bases of action against citizens as pretexts for pursuing other investigatory agendas. We are reminded that in *Florida v. Wells* (1990), we stated that "an inventory search" must not be a ruse for a general rummaging in order to discover incriminating evidence"; that in *Colorado v. Bertine* (1987), in approving an inventory search, we apparently thought it significant that there had been "no showing that the police, who were following standardized procedures, acted in bad faith or for the sole purpose of investigation."

■ ■ ■

Recognizing that we have been unwilling to entertain Fourth Amendment challenges based on the actual motivations of individual officers, petitioners disavow any intention to make the individual officer's subjective good faith the touchstone of "reasonableness." They insist that the standard they have put forward—whether the officer's conduct deviated materially from usual police practices, so that a reasonable officer in the same circumstances would not have made the stop for the reasons given—is an "objective" one.

But although framed in empirical terms, this approach is plainly and indisputably driven by subjective considerations. Its whole purpose is to prevent the police from doing under the guise of enforcing the traffic code what they would like to do for different reasons. Petitioners' proposed standard may not use the word "pretext," but it is designed to combat nothing other than the perceived "danger" of the pretextual stop, albeit only indirectly and over the run of cases. Instead of asking whether the individual officer had the proper state of mind, the petitioners would have us ask, in effect, whether (based on general police practices) it is plausible to believe that the officer had the proper state of mind.

Why one would frame a test designed to combat pretext in such fashion that the court cannot take into account *actual and admitted pretext* is a curiosity that can only be explained by the fact that our cases have foreclosed the more sensible option. If those cases were based only upon the evidentiary difficulty of establishing subjective intent, petitioners' attempt to root out subjective vices through objective means might make sense. But they were not based only upon that, or indeed even principally upon that. Their principal basis—which applies equally to attempts to reach subjective intent through ostensibly objective means—is simply that the Fourth Amendment's concern with "reasonableness" allows certain actions to be taken in certain circumstances, *whatever* the subjective intent. But even if our concern had been only an evidentiary one, petitioners' proposal would by no means assuage it. Indeed, it seems to us somewhat easier to figure out the intent of an individual officer than to plumb the collective consciousness of law enforcement in order to determine whether a "reasonable officer" would have been moved to act upon the traffic violation. While police manuals and standard procedures may sometimes provide objective assistance, ordinarily one would be reduced to speculating about the hypothetical reaction of a hypothetical constable—an exercise that might be called virtual subjectivity.

Moreover, police enforcement practices, even if they could be practicably assessed by a judge, vary from place to place and from time to time. We cannot accept that the search and seizure protections of the Fourth Amendment are so variable, and can be made to turn upon such trivialities. The difficulty is illustrated by petitioners' arguments in this case. Their claim that a reasonable officer would not have made this stop is based largely on District of Columbia police regulations which permit plainclothes officers in unmarked vehicles to enforce traffic laws "only in the case of a violation that is so grave as to pose an *immediate threat* to the safety of others."

■ ■ ■

In what would appear to be an elaboration on the "reasonable officer" test, petitioners argue that the balancing inherent in any Fourth Amendment inquiry requires us to weigh the governmental and individual interests implicated in a traffic stop such as we have here. That balancing, petitioners claim, does not support investigation of minor traffic infractions by plainclothes police in unmarked vehicles; such investigation only minimally advances the government's interest in traffic safety, and may indeed retard it by producing motorist confusion and alarm—a view said to be supported by the Metropolitan Police Department's own regulations generally prohibiting this practice. And as for the Fourth Amendment interests of the individuals concerned, petitioners point out that our cases acknowledge that even ordinary traffic stops entail "a possibly unsettling show of authority"; that they at best "interfere with freedom of movement, are inconvenient, and consume time" and at worst "may create substantial anxiety." That anxiety is likely to be even more pronounced when the stop is conducted by plainclothes officers in unmarked cars.

It is of course true that in principle every Fourth Amendment case, since it turns upon a "reasonableness" determination, involves a balancing of all relevant factors. With rare exceptions not applicable here, however, the result of that balancing is not in doubt where the search or seizure is based upon probable cause. That is why petitioners must rely upon cases like *Delaware v. Prouse* (1979) to provide examples of actual "balancing" analysis. There, the police action in question was a random traffic stop for the purpose of checking a motorist's license and vehicle registration, a practice that—like the practices at issue in the inventory search and administrative inspection cases upon which petitioners rely in making their "pretext" claim—involves police intrusion *without the probable cause that is its traditional justification.* Our opinion in *Prouse* expressly distinguished the case from a stop based on precisely what is at issue here: "probable cause to believe that a driver is violating any one of the multitude of applicable traffic and equipment regulations." It noted approvingly that "[t]he foremost method of enforcing traffic and vehicle safety regulations . . . is acting upon observed violations," which afford the " 'quantum of individualized suspicion' " necessary to ensure that police discretion is sufficiently constrained. . . .

Where probable cause has existed, the only cases in which we have found it necessary actually to perform the "balancing" analysis involved searches or seizures conducted in an extraordinary manner, unusually harmful to an individual's privacy or even physical interests—such as, for example, seizure by means of deadly force, see *Tennessee v. Garner* (1985), unannounced entry into a home, see *Wilson v. Arkansas* (1995), entry into a home without a warrant, see *Welsh v. Wisconsin* (1984), or physical penetration of the body, see *Winston v. Lee* (1985). The making of a traffic stop out of uniform does not remotely qualify as such an extreme practice, and so is governed by the usual rule that probable cause to believe the law has been broken "outbalances" private interest in avoiding police contact.

Petitioners urge as an extraordinary factor in this case that the "multitude of applicable traffic and equipment regulations" is so large and so difficult to obey perfectly that virtually everyone is guilty of violation, permitting the police to single out almost whomever they wish for a stop. But we are aware of no principle that would allow us to decide at what point a code of law becomes so expansive and so commonly violated that infraction itself can no longer be the ordinary measure of the lawfulness of enforcement. And even if we could identify such exorbitant codes, we do not know by what standard (or what right) we would decide, as petitioners would have us do, which particular provisions are sufficiently important to merit enforcement.

For the run-of-the-mine case, which this surely is, we think there is no realistic alternative to the traditional common-law rule that probable cause justifies a search and seizure.

■ ■ ■

Here the District Court found that the officers had probable cause to believe that petitioners had violated the traffic code. That rendered the stop reasonable under the Fourth Amendment, the evidence thereby discovered admissible, and the upholding of the convictions by the Court of Appeals for the District of Columbia Circuit correct. The judgment is
Affirmed.

Atwater v. City of Lago Vista

532 U.S. 318 (2001)

SOUTER, J., delivered the opinion of the Court, in which REHNQUIST, C.J., SCALIA, KENNEDY, and THOMAS, JJ., joined. O'CONNOR, J., filed a dissenting opinion, in which STEVENS, GINSBURG, and BREYER, JJ., joined.

■ ■ ■

The question is whether the Fourth Amendment forbids a warrantless arrest for a minor criminal offense, such as a misdemeanor seatbelt violation punishable only by a fine. We hold that it does not.

In Texas, if a car is equipped with safety belts, a front-seat passenger must wear one, and the driver must secure any small child riding in front. Violation of either provision is "a misdemeanor punishable by a fine not less than $25 or more than $50." Texas law expressly authorizes "[a]ny peace officer [to] arrest without warrant a person found committing a violation" of these seatbelt laws, although it permits police to issue citations in lieu of arrest.

In March 1997, petitioner Gail Atwater was driving her pickup truck in Lago Vista, Texas, with her 3-year-old son and 5-year-old daughter in the front seat. None of them was wearing a seatbelt. Respondent Bart Turek, a Lago Vista police officer at the time, observed the seatbelt violations and pulled Atwater over. According to Atwater's complaint (the allegations of which we assume to be true for present purposes), Turek approached the truck and "yell[ed]" something to the effect of "[w]e've met before" and "[y]ou're going to jail." He then called for backup and asked to see Atwater's driver's license and insurance documentation, which state law required her to carry. When Atwater told Turek that she did not have the papers because her purse had been stolen the day before, Turek said that he had "heard that story two-hundred times."

■ ■ ■

Atwater asked to take her "frightened, upset, and crying" children to a friend's house nearby, but Turek told her, "[y]ou're not going anywhere." As it turned out, Atwater's friend learned what was going on and soon arrived to take charge of the children. Turek then handcuffed Atwater, placed her in his squad car, and drove her to the local police station, where booking officers had her remove her shoes, jewelry, and eyeglasses, and empty her pockets. Officers took Atwater's "mug shot" and placed her, alone, in a jail cell for about one hour, after which she was taken before a magistrate and released on $310 bond.

Atwater was charged with driving without her seatbelt fastened, failing to secure her children in seatbelts, driving without a license, and failing to provide proof of insurance. She ultimately pleaded no contest to the misdemeanor seatbelt offenses and paid a $50 fine; the other charges were dismissed.

Atwater and her husband, petitioner Michael Haas, filed suit in a Texas state court under 42 U.S.C. § 1983 against Turek and respondents City of Lago Vista and Chief of Police Frank Miller. So far as concerns us, petitioners (whom we will simply call Atwater) alleged that respondents (for simplicity, the City) had violated Atwater's Fourth Amendment "right to be free from unreasonable seizure," and sought compensatory and punitive damages.

The City removed the suit to the United States District Court for the Western District of Texas. Given Atwater's admission that she had "violated the law" and the absence of any allegation "that she was harmed or detained in any way inconsistent with the law," the District Court ruled the Fourth Amendment claim "meritless" and granted the City's summary judgment motion. A panel of the United States Court of Appeals for the Fifth Circuit reversed. It concluded that "an arrest for a first-time seat belt offense" was an unreasonable seizure within the meaning of the Fourth Amendment, and held that Turek was not entitled to qualified immunity

Sitting en banc, the Court of Appeals vacated the panel's decision and affirmed the District Court's summary judgment for the City. Relying on *Whren v. United States* (1996), the en banc court observed that, although the Fourth Amendment generally requires a balancing of individual and governmental interests, where "an arrest is based on probable cause then 'with rare exceptions . . . the result of that balancing is not in doubt.' " . . .

We granted certiorari to consider whether the Fourth Amendment, either by incorporating common-law restrictions on misdemeanor arrests or otherwise, limits police officers' authority to arrest without warrant for minor criminal offenses. We now affirm.

■ ■ ■

We begin with the state of pre-founding English common law and find that, even after making some allowance for variations in the common-law usage of the term "breach of the peace," the "founding-era common-law rules" were not nearly as clear as Atwater claims; on the contrary, the common-law commentators (as well as the sparsely reported cases) reached divergent conclusions with respect to officers' warrantless misdemeanor arrest power. Moreover, in the years leading up to American independence, Parliament repeatedly extended express warrantless arrest authority to cover misdemeanor-level offenses not amounting to or involving any violent breach of the peace.

■ ■ ■

Atwater's historical argument begins with our quotation from Halsbury in *Carroll v. United States* (1925), that

> " '[i]n cases of misdemeanor, a peace officer like a private person has at common law no power of arresting without a warrant except when a breach of the peace has been committed in his presence or there is reasonable ground for supposing that a breach of peace is about to be committed or renewed in his presence.' " (quoting 9 Halsbury, Laws of England §612, p. 299 (1909)).

But the isolated quotation tends to mislead. In *Carroll* itself we spoke of the common-law rule as only "sometimes expressed" that way, and, indeed, in the very same paragraph, we conspicuously omitted any reference to a breach-of-the-peace limitation in stating that the "usual rule" at common law was that "a police officer [could] arrest without warrant . . . one guilty of a misdemeanor if committed in his presence." Thus, what *Carroll* illustrates, and what others have recognized, is that statements about the common law of warrantless misdemeanor arrest simply are not uniform. Rather, "[a]t common law there is a difference of opinion among the authorities as to whether this right to arrest [without a warrant] extends to all misdemeanors." American Law Institute, Code of Criminal Procedure, Commentary to §21, p. 231 (1930).

On one side of the divide there are certainly eminent authorities supporting Atwater's position. In addition to Lord Halsbury, quoted in *Carroll*, James Fitzjames Stephen and Glanville Williams both seemed to indicate that the common law confined warrantless misdemeanor arrests to actual breaches of the peace. See 1 J. Stephen, A History of the Criminal Law of England 193 (1883).

■ ■ ■

Sir William Blackstone and Sir Edward East might also be counted on Atwater's side, although they spoke only to the sufficiency of breach of the peace as a condition to warrantless misdemeanor arrest, not to its necessity. Blackstone recognized that at common law "[t]he constable . . . hath great original and inherent authority with regard to arrests," but with respect to non-felony offenses said only that "[h]e may, without warrant, arrest any one for a breach of the peace, and carry him before a justice of the peace." 4 Blackstone 289. Not long after the framing of the Fourth Amendment, East characterized peace officers' common-law arrest power in much the same way: "A constable or other known conservator of the peace may lawfully interpose upon his own view to prevent a breach of the peace, or to quiet an affray. . . ." 1 E. East, Pleas of the Crown §71, p. 303 (1803).

The great commentators were not unanimous, however, and there is also considerable evidence of a broader conception of common-law misdemeanor arrest authority unlimited by any breach-of-the-peace condition. Sir Matthew Hale, Chief Justice of King's Bench from 1671 to 1676, wrote in his History of the Pleas of the Crown that, by his "original and inherent power," a constable could arrest without a warrant "for breach of the peace and some misdemeanors, less than felony." 2 M. Hale, Pleas of the Crown 88 (1736).

■ ■ ■

As will be seen later, the view of warrantless arrest authority as extending to at least "some misdemeanors" beyond breaches of the peace was undoubtedly informed by statutory provisions authorizing such arrests, but it reflected common law in the strict, judge-made sense as well, for such was the holding of at least one case reported before Hale had even become a judge but which, like Hale's own commentary, continued to be cited well after the ratification of the Fourth Amendment. In *Holyday v. Oxenbridge* (1631), the Court of King's Bench held that even a private person (and thus *a fortiori* a peace officer) needed no warrant to arrest a "common cheater" whom he discovered "cozen[ing] with false dice." The court expressly rejected the contention that warrantless arrests were improper "unless in felony," and said instead that "there was good cause [for] staying" the gambler and, more broadly, that "it is *pro bono publico* to stay such offenders." In the edition nearest to the date of the Constitution's framing, Sergeant William Hawkins's widely read Treatise of the Pleas of the Crown generalized from *Holyday* that "from the reason of this case it seems to follow, That the [warrantless] arrest of any other offenders . . . for offences in like manner scandalous and prejudicial to the public, may be justified." 2 Hawkins, ch. 12, §20, at 122.

■ ■ ■

We thus find disagreement, not unanimity, among both the common-law jurists and the text writers who sought to pull the cases together and summarize accepted practice. Having reviewed the relevant English decisions, as well as English and colonial American legal treatises, legal dictionaries, and procedure manuals, we simply are not convinced that Atwater's is the correct, or even necessarily the better, reading of the common-law history.

■ ■ ■

The significance of these early English statutes lies not in proving that any common-law rule barring warrantless misdemeanor arrests that might have existed would have been subject to statutory override; the sovereign Parliament could of course have wiped away any judge-made rule. The point is that the statutes riddle Atwater's supposed common-law rule with enough exceptions to unsettle any contention that the law of the mother country would have left the Fourth Amendment's Framers of a view that it would necessarily have been unreasonable to arrest without warrant for a misdemeanor unaccompanied by real or threatened violence.

An examination of specifically American evidence is to the same effect. Neither the history of the framing era nor subsequent legal development indicates that the Fourth Amendment was originally understood, or has traditionally been read, to embrace Atwater's position.

To begin with, Atwater has cited no particular evidence that those who framed and ratified the Fourth Amendment sought to limit peace officers' warrantless misdemeanor arrest authority to instances of actual breach of the peace, and our own review of the recent and respected compilations of framing-era documentary history has likewise failed to reveal any such design.

■ ■ ■

The evidence of actual practice also counsels against Atwater's position. During the period leading up to and surrounding the framing of the Bill of Rights, colonial and state legislatures, like Parliament before them, regularly authorized local peace officers to make warrantless misdemeanor arrests without conditioning statutory authority on breach of the peace.

■ ■ ■

What we have here, then, is just the opposite of what we had in *Wilson v. Arkansas* (1914). There, we emphasized that during the founding era a number of States had "enacted statutes specifically embracing" the common-law knock-and-announce rule; here, by contrast, those very same States passed laws extending warrantless arrest authority to a host of nonviolent misdemeanors, and in so doing acted very much inconsistently with Atwater's claims about the Fourth Amendment's object. Of course, the Fourth Amendment did not originally apply to the States, but that does not make state practice irrelevant in unearthing the Amendment's original meaning. A number of state constitutional search-and-seizure provisions served as models for the Fourth Amendment, see, *e.g.,* N.H. Const. of 1784, pt. I, Art. XIX; Pa. Const. of 1776 (Declaration of Rights), Art. X, and the fact that many of the original States with such constitutional limitations continued to grant their own peace officers broad warrantless misdemeanor arrest authority undermines Atwater's contention that the founding generation meant to bar federal law enforcement officers from exercising the same authority. Given the early state practice, it is likewise troublesome for Atwater's view that just one year after the ratification of the Fourth Amendment, Congress vested federal marshals with "the same powers in executing the laws of the United States, as sheriffs and their deputies in the several states have by law, in executing the laws of their respective states." Act of May 2, 1792, ch. 28, §9, 1 Stat. 265. Thus, as we have said before in only slightly different circumstances, the Second Congress apparently "saw no inconsistency between the Fourth Amendment and legislation giving United States marshals the same power as local peace officers" to make warrantless arrests.

■ ■ ■

The record thus supports Justice Powell's observation that "[t]here is no historical evidence that the Framers or proponents of the Fourth Amendment, outspokenly opposed to the infamous general warrants and writs of assistance, were at all concerned about warrantless arrests by local constables and other peace officers." We simply cannot conclude that the Fourth Amendment, as originally understood, forbade peace officers to arrest without a warrant for misdemeanors not amounting to or involving breach of the peace.

Nor does Atwater's argument from tradition pick up any steam from the historical record as it has unfolded since the framing, there being no indication that her claimed rule has ever become "woven . . . into the fabric" of American law.... *Payton v. New York* (1980) (... "the clear consensus among the States adhering to [a] well-settled common-law rule"). The story, on the contrary, is of two centuries of uninterrupted (and largely unchallenged) state and federal practice permitting warrantless arrests for misdemeanors not amounting to or involving breach of the peace.

First, there is no support for Atwater's position in this Court's cases (apart from the isolated sentence in *Carroll,* already explained). Although the Court has not had much to say about warrantless misdemeanor arrest authority, what little we have said tends to cut against Atwater's argument. In discussing this authority, we have focused on the circumstance that an offense was committed in an officer's presence, to the omission of any reference to a breach-of-the-peace limitation.

■ ■ ■

Finally, both the legislative tradition of granting warrantless misdemeanor arrest authority and the judicial tradition of sustaining such statutes against constitutional attack are buttressed by legal commentary that, for more than a century now, has almost uniformly recognized the constitutionality of extending warrantless arrest power to misdemeanors without limitation to breaches of the peace. See, *e.g.,* E. Fisher, Laws of Arrest §59, p. 130 (1967) ("[I]t is generally recognized today that the common law authority to arrest without a warrant in misdemeanor cases may be enlarged by statute, and this has been done in many of the states.").

Small wonder, then, that today in all 50 States and the District of Columbia permit warrantless misdemeanor arrests by at least some (if not all) peace officers without requiring any breach of the peace, as do a host of congressional enactments.

■ ■ ■

While it is true here that history, if not unequivocal, has expressed a decided, majority view that the police need not obtain an arrest warrant merely because a misdemeanor stopped short of violence or a threat of it, Atwater does not wager all on history. Instead, she asks us to mint a new rule of constitutional law on the understanding that when historical practice fails to speak conclusively to a claim grounded on the Fourth Amendment, courts are left to strike a current balance between individual and societal interests by subjecting particular contemporary circumstances to traditional standards of reasonableness.

■ ■ ■

If we were to derive a rule exclusively to address the uncontested facts of this case, Atwater might well prevail. She was a known and established resident of Lago Vista with no place to hide and no incentive to flee, and common sense says she would almost certainly have buckled up as a condition of driving off with a citation. In her case, the physical incidents of arrest were merely gratuitous humiliations imposed by a police officer who was (at best) exercising extremely poor judgment. Atwater's claim to live free of pointless indignity and confinement clearly outweighs anything the City can raise against it specific to her case.

But we have traditionally recognized that a responsible Fourth Amendment balance is not well served by standards requiring sensitive, case-by-case determinations of government need, lest every discretionary judgment in the field be converted into an occasion for constitutional review. Often enough, the Fourth Amendment has to be applied on the spur (and in the heat) of the moment, and the object in implementing its command of reasonableness is to draw standards sufficiently clear and simple to be applied with a fair prospect of surviving judicial second-guessing months and years after an arrest or search is made. Courts attempting to strike a reasonable Fourth Amendment balance thus credit the government's side with an essential interest in readily administrable rules.

At first glance, Atwater's argument may seem to respect the values of clarity and simplicity, so far as she claims that the Fourth Amendment generally forbids warrantless arrests for minor crimes not accompanied by violence or some demonstrable threat of it (whether "minor crime" be defined as a fine-only traffic offense, a fine-only offense more generally, or a misdemeanor). But the claim is not ultimately so simple, nor could it be, for complications arise the moment we begin to think about the possible applications of the several criteria Atwater proposes for drawing a line between minor crimes with limited arrest authority and others not so restricted.

One line, she suggests, might be between "jailable" and "fine-only" offenses, between those for which conviction could result in commitment and those for which it could not. The trouble with this distinction, of course, is that an officer on the street might not be able to tell. It is not merely that we cannot expect every police officer to know the details of frequently complex penalty schemes, see *Berkemer v. McCarty* (1984) ("[O]fficers in the field frequently 'have neither the time nor the competence to determine' the severity of the offense for which they are considering arresting a person"), but that penalties for ostensibly identical conduct can vary on account of facts difficult (if not impossible) to know at the scene of an arrest. Is this the first offense or is the suspect a repeat offender? Is the weight of the marijuana a gram above or a gram below the fine-only line? Where conduct could implicate more than one criminal prohibition, which one will the district attorney ultimately decide to charge? And so on.

■ ■ ■

But Atwater's refinements would not end there. She represents that if the line were drawn at nonjailable traffic offenses, her proposed limitation should be qualified by a proviso authorizing warrantless arrests where "necessary for enforcement of the traffic laws or when [an] offense would otherwise continue and pose a danger to others on the road." The proviso only compounds the difficulties. Would, for instance, either exception apply to speeding? At oral argument, Atwater's counsel said that "it would not be reasonable to arrest a driver for speeding unless the speeding rose to the level of reckless driving. But is it not fair to expect that the chronic speeder will speed again despite a citation in his pocket, and should that not qualify as showing that the "offense

would . . . continue" under Atwater's rule? And why, as a constitutional matter, should we assume that only reckless driving will "pose a danger to others
on the road" while speeding will not?

There is no need for more examples to show that Atwater's general rule
and limiting proviso promise very little in the way of administrability. It is no
answer that the police routinely make judgments on grounds like risk of
immediate repetition; they surely do and should. But there is a world of difference between making that judgment in choosing between the discretionary
leniency of a summons in place of a clearly lawful arrest, and making the same
judgment when the question is the lawfulness of the warrantless arrest itself. It
is the difference between no basis for legal action challenging the discretionary
judgment, on the one hand, and the prospect of evidentiary exclusion or (as
here) personal § 1983 liability for the misapplication of a constitutional standard, on the other. Atwater's rule therefore would not only place police in an
almost impossible spot but would guarantee increased litigation over many of
the arrests that would occur. For all these reasons, Atwater's various distinctions between permissible and impermissible arrests for minor crimes strike us
as "very unsatisfactory line[s]" to require police officers to draw on a moment's
notice.

■ ■ ■

Just how easily the costs could outweigh the benefits may be shown by
asking, as one Member of this Court did at oral argument, "how bad the problem is out there." The very fact that the law has never jelled the way Atwater
would have it leads one to wonder whether warrantless misdemeanor arrests
need constitutional attention, and there is cause to think the answer is no. So far
as such arrests might be thought to pose a threat to the probable-cause requirement, anyone arrested for a crime without formal process, whether for felony or
misdemeanor, is entitled to a magistrate's review of probable cause within 48
hours, and there is no reason to think the procedure in this case atypical in
giving the suspect a prompt opportunity to request release. . . .

The upshot of all these influences, combined with the good sense (and,
failing that, the political accountability) of most local lawmakers and law-
enforcement officials, is a dearth of horribles demanding redress. Indeed,
when Atwater's counsel was asked at oral argument for any indications of
comparably foolish, warrantless misdemeanor arrests, he could offer only
one. We are sure that there are others, but just as surely the country is not
confronting anything like an epidemic of unnecessary minor-offense arrests.
That fact caps the reasons for rejecting Atwater's request for the development
of a new and distinct body of constitutional law.

Accordingly, we confirm today what our prior cases have intimated: the
standard of probable cause "applie[s] to all arrests, without the need to 'balance' the interests and circumstances involved in particular situations."
Dunaway v. New York (1979). If an officer has probable cause to believe that
an individual has committed even a very minor criminal offense in his presence, he may, without violating the Fourth Amendment, arrest the offender.

Atwater's arrest satisfied constitutional requirements. There is no dispute that Officer Turek had probable cause to believe that Atwater had committed a crime in his presence. She admits that neither she nor her children were wearing seatbelts, as required by Tex. Transp. Code Ann. § 545.413 (1999). Turek was accordingly authorized (not required, but authorized) to make a custodial arrest without balancing costs and benefits or determining whether or not Atwater's arrest was in some sense necessary.

Nor was the arrest made in an "extraordinary manner, unusually harmful to [her] privacy or . . . physical interests." *Whren v. United States.* . . . Atwater's arrest was surely "humiliating," as she says in her brief, but it was no more "harmful to . . . privacy or . . . physical interests" than the normal custodial arrest. She was handcuffed, placed in a squad car, and taken to the local police station, where officers asked her to remove her shoes, jewelry, and glasses, and to empty her pockets. They then took her photograph and placed her in a cell, alone, for about an hour, after which she was taken before a magistrate, and released on $310 bond. The arrest and booking were inconvenient and embarrassing to Atwater, but not so extraordinary as to violate the Fourth Amendment.

The Court of Appeals en banc judgment is affirmed.

It is so ordered.

■ ■ ■

Justice O'CONNOR, with whom Justice STEVENS, Justice GINSBURG, and Justice BREYER join, dissenting.

The Fourth Amendment guarantees the right to be free from "unreasonable searches and seizures." The Court recognizes that the arrest of Gail Atwater was a "pointless indignity" that served no discernible state interest, *ante,* at 347, and yet holds that her arrest was constitutionally permissible. Because the Court's position is inconsistent with the explicit guarantee of the Fourth Amendment, I dissent.

A full custodial arrest, such as the one to which Ms. Atwater was subjected, is the quintessential seizure.

■ ■ ■

The majority gives a brief nod to this bedrock principle of our Fourth Amendment jurisprudence, and even acknowledges that "Atwater's claim to live free of pointless indignity and confinement clearly outweighs anything the City can raise against it specific to her case." But instead of remedying this imbalance, the majority allows itself to be swayed by the worry that "every discretionary judgment in the field [will] be converted into an occasion for constitutional review." It therefore mints a new rule that "[i]f an officer has probable cause to believe that an individual has committed even a very minor criminal offense in his presence, he may, without violating the Fourth Amendment, arrest the offender." This rule is not only unsupported by our precedent, but runs contrary to the principles that lie at the core of the Fourth Amendment.

■ ■ ■

A custodial arrest exacts an obvious toll on an individual's liberty and privacy, even when the period of custody is relatively brief. The arrestee is subject to a full search of her person and confiscation of her possessions. If the arrestee is the occupant of a car, the entire passenger compartment of the car, including packages therein, is subject to search as well.

We have said that "the penalty that may attach to any particular offense seems to provide the clearest and most consistent indication of the State's interest in arresting individuals suspected of committing that offense." *Welsh v. Wisconsin* (1984). If the State has decided that a fine, and not imprisonment, is the appropriate punishment for an offense, the State's interest in taking a person suspected of committing that offense into custody is surely limited, at best. This is not to say that the State will never have such an interest. A full custodial arrest may on occasion vindicate legitimate state interests, even if the crime is punishable only by fine. Arrest is the surest way to abate criminal conduct. It may also allow the police to verify the offender's identity and, if the offender poses a flight risk, to ensure her appearance at trial. But when such considerations are not present, a citation or summons may serve the State's remaining law enforcement interests every bit as effectively as an arrest.

Because a full custodial arrest is such a severe intrusion on an individual's liberty, its reasonableness hinges on "the degree to which it is needed for the promotion of legitimate governmental interests." *Wyoming v. Houghton* (1999). In light of the availability of citations to promote a State's interests when a fine-only offense has been committed, I cannot concur in a rule which deems a full custodial arrest to be reasonable in every circumstance. Giving police officers constitutional carte blanche to effect an arrest whenever there is probable cause to believe a fine-only misdemeanor has been committed is irreconcilable with the Fourth Amendment's command that seizures be reasonable. Instead, I would require that when there is probable cause to believe that a fine-only offense has been committed, the police officer should issue a citation unless the officer is "able to point to specific and articulable facts which, taken together with rational inferences from those facts, reasonably warrant [the additional] intrusion" of a full custodial arrest.

The majority insists that a bright-line rule focused on probable cause is necessary to vindicate the State's interest in easily administrable law enforcement rules. Probable cause itself, however, is not a model of precision. "The quantum of information which constitutes probable cause—evidence which would 'warrant a man of reasonable caution in the belief' that a [crime] has been committed—must be measured by the facts of the particular case." (citation omitted). The rule I propose—which merely requires a legitimate reason for the decision to escalate the seizure into a full custodial arrest—thus does not undermine an otherwise "clear and simple" rule.

While clarity is certainly a value worthy of consideration in our Fourth Amendment jurisprudence, it by no means trumps the values of liberty and privacy at the heart of the Amendment's protections. What the *Terry* rule lacks in precision it makes up for in fidelity to the Fourth Amendment's command of reasonableness and sensitivity to the competing values protected by that Amendment. Over the past 30 years, it appears that the *Terry* rule has been workable and easily applied by officers on the street.

At bottom, the majority offers two related reasons why a bright-line rule is necessary: the fear that officers who arrest for fine-only offenses will be subject to "personal liability for the misapplication of a constitutional standard," and the resulting "systematic disincentive to arrest...where...arresting would serve an important societal interest." These concerns are certainly valid, but they are more than adequately resolved by the doctrine of qualified immunity.

■ ■ ■

In *Anderson v. Creighton* (1987), we made clear that the standard of reasonableness for a search or seizure under the Fourth Amendment is distinct from the standard of reasonableness for qualified immunity purposes. If a law enforcement officer "reasonably but mistakenly conclude[s]" that the constitutional predicate for a search or seizure is present, he "should not be held personally liable."

■ ■ ■

The record in this case makes it abundantly clear that Ms. Atwater's arrest was constitutionally unreasonable. Atwater readily admits—as she did when Officer Turek pulled her over—that she violated Texas' seatbelt law.

There is no question that Officer Turek's actions severely infringed Atwater's liberty and privacy. Turek was loud and accusatory from the moment he approached Atwater's car. Atwater's young children were terrified and hysterical. Yet when Atwater asked Turek to lower his voice because he was scaring the children, he responded by jabbing his finger in Atwater's face and saying, "You're going to jail." Having made the decision to arrest, Turek did not inform Atwater of her right to remain silent. He instead asked for her license and insurance information.

Atwater asked if she could at least take her children to a friend's house down the street before going to the police station. But Turek—who had just castigated Atwater for not caring for her children—refused and said he would take the children into custody as well. Only the intervention of neighborhood children who had witnessed the scene and summoned one of Atwater's friends saved the children from being hauled to jail with their mother.

With the children gone, Officer Turek handcuffed Ms. Atwater with her hands behind her back, placed her in the police car, and drove her to the police station. Ironically, Turek did not secure Atwater in a seatbelt for the drive. At the station, Atwater was forced to remove her shoes, relinquish her possessions, and wait in a holding cell for about an hour. A judge finally informed Atwater of her rights and the charges against her, and released her when she posted bond. Atwater returned to the scene of the arrest, only to find that her car had been towed.

Ms. Atwater ultimately pleaded no contest to violating the seatbelt law and was fined $50. Even though that fine was the maximum penalty for her crime, and even though Officer Turek has never articulated any justification for his actions, the city contends that arresting Atwater was constitutionally reasonable because it advanced two legitimate interests: "the enforcement of child safety laws and encouraging [Atwater] to appear for trial."

It is difficult to see how arresting Atwater served either of these goals any more effectively than the issuance of a citation. With respect to the goal of law enforcement generally, Atwater did not pose a great danger to the community. She had been driving very slowly—approximately 15 miles per hour—in broad daylight on a residential street that had no other traffic. Nor was she a repeat offender; until that day, she had received one traffic citation in her life—a ticket, more than 10 years earlier, for failure to signal a lane change. Although Officer Turek had stopped Atwater approximately three months earlier because he thought that Atwater's son was not wearing a seatbelt, Turek had been mistaken. Moreover, Atwater immediately accepted responsibility and apologized for her conduct. Thus, there was every indication that Atwater would have buckled herself and her children in had she been cited and allowed to leave.

With respect to the related goal of child welfare, the decision to arrest Atwater was nothing short of counterproductive. Atwater's children witnessed Officer Turek yell at their mother and threaten to take them all into custody. Ultimately, they were forced to leave her behind with Turek, knowing that she was being taken to jail. Understandably, the 3-year-old boy was "very, very, very traumatized." After the incident, he had to see a child psychologist regularly, who reported that the boy "felt very guilty that he couldn't stop this horrible thing...he was powerless to help his mother or sister." Both of Atwater's children are now terrified at the sight of any police car. According to Atwater, the arrest "just never leaves us. It's a conversation we have every other day, once a week, and it's—it raises its head constantly in our lives."

Citing Atwater surely would have served the children's interests well. It would have taught Atwater to ensure that her children were buckled up in the future. It also would have taught the children an important lesson in accepting responsibility and obeying the law. Arresting Atwater, though, taught the children an entirely different lesson: that "the bad person could just as easily be the policeman as it could be the most horrible person they could imagine."

■ ■ ■

The city's justifications fall far short of rationalizing the extraordinary intrusion on Gail Atwater and her children. Measuring "the degree to which [Atwater's custodial arrest was] needed for the promotion of legitimate governmental interests" against "the degree to which it intrud[ed] upon [her] privacy," it can hardly be doubted that Turek's actions were disproportionate to Atwater's crime. The majority's assessment that "Atwater's claim to live free of pointless indignity and confinement clearly outweighs anything the City can raise against it specific to her case," is quite correct. In my view, the Fourth Amendment inquiry ends there.

■ ■ ■

Such unbounded discretion carries with it grave potential for abuse. The majority takes comfort in the lack of evidence of "an epidemic of unnecessary minor-offense arrests." But the relatively small number of published cases dealing with such arrests proves little and should provide little solace. Indeed, as the recent debate over racial profiling demonstrates all too clearly, a relatively minor traffic infraction may often serve as an excuse for stopping and harassing an individual. After today, the arsenal available to any officer extends to a full arrest and the searches permissible concomitant to that arrest. An officer's subjective motivations for making a traffic stop are not relevant considerations in determining the reasonableness of the stop. See *Whren v. United States*. But it is precisely because these motivations are beyond our purview that we must vigilantly ensure that officers' poststop actions—which are properly within our reach—comport with the Fourth Amendment's guarantee of reasonableness.

■ ■ ■

The Court neglects the Fourth Amendment's express command in the name of administrative ease. In so doing, it cloaks the pointless indignity that Gail Atwater suffered with the mantle of reasonableness. I respectfully dissent.

Virginia v. Moore

553 U.S. 164 (2008)

SCALIA, J., delivered the opinion of the Court, in which ROBERTS, C.J., STEVENS, KENNEDY, SOUTER, THOMAS, BREYER, and ALITO, JJ., joined. GINSBURG, J., filed an opinion concurring in judgment.

We consider whether a police officer violates the Fourth Amendment by making an arrest based on probable cause but prohibited by state law. . . .

On February 20, 2003, two City of Portsmouth police officers stopped a car driven by David Lee Moore. They had heard over the police radio that a person known as "Chubs" was driving with a suspended license, and one of the officers knew Moore by that nickname. The officers determined that Moore's license was in fact suspended, and arrested him for the misdemeanor of driving on a suspended license, which is punishable under Virginia law by a year in jail and a $2,500 fine. The officers subsequently searched Moore and found that he was carrying 16 grams of crack cocaine and $516 in cash.

Under state law, the officers should have issued Moore a summons instead of arresting him. Driving on a suspended license, like some other misdemeanors, is not an arrestable offense except as to those who "fail or refuse to discontinue" the violation, and those whom the officer reasonably believes to be likely to disregard a summons, or likely to harm themselves or others. The intermediate appellate court found none of these circumstances applicable, and Virginia did not appeal that determination. . . .

Moore was charged with possessing cocaine with the intent to distribute it in violation of Virginia law. He filed a pretrial motion to suppress the evidence from the arrest search. Virginia law does not, as a general matter, require suppression of evidence obtained in violation of state law. Moore argued, however, that suppression was required by the Fourth Amendment. The trial court denied the motion, and after a bench trial found Moore guilty of the drug charge and sentenced him to a 5-year prison term, with one year and six months of the sentence suspended. The conviction was reversed by a panel of Virginia's intermediate court on Fourth Amendment grounds, reinstated by the intermediate court sitting en banc, and finally reversed again by the Virginia Supreme Court. The Court reasoned that since the arresting officers should have issued Moore a citation under state law, and the Fourth Amendment does not permit search incident to citation, the arrest search violated the Fourth Amendment. We granted certiorari. . . .

When history has not provided a conclusive answer, we have analyzed a search or seizure in light of traditional standards of reasonableness "by assessing, on the one hand, the degree to which it intrudes upon an individual's privacy and, on the other, the degree to which it is needed for the promotion of legitimate governmental interests." That methodology provides no support for Moore's Fourth Amendment claim. In a long line of cases, we have said that when an officer has probable cause to believe a person committed even a minor crime in his presence, the balancing of private and public interests is not in doubt. The arrest is constitutionally reasonable. . . .

Our decisions counsel against changing this calculus when a State chooses to protect privacy beyond the level that the Fourth Amendment requires. We have treated additional protections exclusively as matters of state law. In *Cooper v. California* (1967), we reversed a state court that had held the search of a seized vehicle to be in violation of the Fourth Amendment because state law did not explicitly authorize the search. We concluded that whether state law authorized the search was irrelevant. States, we said, remained free "to impose higher standards on searches and seizures than required by the Federal Constitution," but regardless of state rules, police could search a lawfully seized vehicle as a matter of federal constitutional law.

In *California v. Greenwood* (1988), we held that search of an individual's garbage forbidden by California's Constitution was not forbidden by the Fourth Amendment. "[W]hether or not a search is reasonable within the meaning of the Fourth Amendment," we said, has never "depend[ed] on the law of the particular State in which the search occurs." While "[i]ndividual States may surely construe their own constitutions as imposing more stringent constraints on police conduct than does the Federal Constitution," state law did not alter the content of the Fourth Amendment.

We have applied the same principle in the seizure context. *Whren v. United States* (1996) held that police officers had acted reasonably in stopping a car, even though their action violated regulations limiting the authority of plainclothes officers in unmarked vehicles. We thought it obvious that the Fourth

Amendment's meaning did not change with local law enforcement practices—even practices set by rule. While those practices "vary from place to place and from time to time," Fourth Amendment protections are not "so variable" and cannot "be made to turn upon such trivialities."

■ ■ ■

We are convinced that the approach of our prior cases is correct, because an arrest based on probable cause serves interests that have long been seen as sufficient to justify the seizure. *Whren; Atwater v. City of Lago Vista* (2001). Arrest ensures that a suspect appears to answer charges and does not continue a crime, and it safeguards evidence and enables officers to conduct an in-custody investigation.

■ ■ ■

If we concluded otherwise, we would often frustrate rather than further state policy. Virginia chooses to protect individual privacy and dignity more than the Fourth Amendment requires, but it also chooses not to attach to violations of its arrest rules the potent remedies that federal courts have applied to Fourth Amendment violations. Virginia does not, for example, ordinarily exclude from criminal trials evidence obtained in violation of its statutes. Moore would allow Virginia to accord enhanced protection against arrest only on pain of accompanying that protection with federal remedies for Fourth Amendment violations, which often include the exclusionary rule. States unwilling to lose control over the remedy would have to abandon restrictions on arrest altogether. This is an odd consequence of a provision designed to protect against searches and seizures. . . .

Incorporating state-law arrest limitations into the Constitution would produce a constitutional regime no less vague and unpredictable than the one we rejected in *Atwater*. The constitutional standard would be only as easy to apply as the underlying state law, and state law can be complicated indeed. The Virginia statute in this case, for example, calls on law enforcement officers to weigh just the sort of case-specific factors that *Atwater* said would deter legitimate arrests if made part of the constitutional inquiry. It would authorize arrest if a misdemeanor suspect fails or refuses to discontinue the unlawful act, or if the officer believes the suspect to be likely to disregard a summons. *Atwater* specifically noted the "extremely poor judgment" displayed in arresting a local resident who would "almost certainly" have discontinued the offense and who had "no place to hide and no incentive to flee." It nonetheless declined to make those considerations part of the constitutional calculus. *Atwater* differs from this case in only one significant respect: It considered (and rejected) federal constitutional remedies for *all* minor-misdemeanor arrests; Moore seeks them in only that *subset* of minor-misdemeanor arrests in which there is the least to be gained—that is, where the State has already acted to constrain officers' discretion and prevent abuse. Here we confront fewer horribles than in *Atwater*, and less of a need for redress.

Finally, linking Fourth Amendment protections to state law would cause them to "vary from place to place and from time to time." Even at the same place and time, the Fourth Amendment's protections might vary if federal officers were not subject to the same statutory constraints as state officers.

■ ■ ■

We conclude that warrantless arrests for crimes committed in the presence of an arresting officer are reasonable under the Constitution, and that while States are free to regulate such arrests however they desire, state restrictions do not alter the Fourth Amendment's protections.

■ ■ ■

We reaffirm against a novel challenge what we have signaled for more than half a century. When officers have probable cause to believe that a person has committed a crime in their presence, the Fourth Amendment permits them to make an arrest, and to search the suspect in order to safeguard evidence and ensure their own safety. The judgment of the Supreme Court of Virginia is reversed, and the case is remanded for further proceedings not inconsistent with this opinion.

It is so ordered.

Florence v. Burlington

132 S. Ct. 1510 (2012)

Kennedy, J., delivered the opinion of the Court. Roberts, C.J., and Scalia and Alito, JJ., joined that opinion in full, and Thomas, J., Roberts, C.J., and Alito, J., filed concurring opinions. Breyer, J., filed a dissenting opinion, in which Ginsburg, Sotomayor, and Kagan, JJ., joined.

Correctional officials have a legitimate interest, indeed a responsibility, to ensure that jails are not made less secure by reason of what new detainees may carry in on their bodies. Facility personnel, other inmates, and the new detainee himself or herself may be in danger if these threats are introduced into the jail population. This case presents the question of what rules, or limitations, the Constitution imposes on searches of arrested persons who are to be held in jail while their cases are being processed. The term "jail" is used here in a broad sense to include prisons and other detention facilities. The specific measures being challenged will be described in more detail; but, in broad terms, the controversy concerns whether every detainee who will be admitted to the general population may be required to undergo a close visual inspection while undressed.

■ ■ ■

I

In 1998, seven years before the incidents at issue, petitioner Albert Florence was arrested after fleeing from police officers in Essex County, New Jersey. He was charged with obstruction of justice and use of a deadly weapon. Petitioner entered a plea of guilty to two lesser offenses and was sentenced to pay a fine in monthly installments. In 2003, after he fell behind on his payments and failed to appear at an enforcement hearing, a bench warrant was issued for his arrest. He paid the outstanding balance less than a week later; but, for some unexplained reason, the warrant remained in a statewide computer database.

Two years later, in Burlington County, New Jersey, petitioner and his wife were stopped in their automobile by a state trooper. Based on the outstanding warrant in the computer system, the officer arrested petitioner and took him to the Burlington County Detention Center. He was held there for six days and then was transferred to the Essex County Correctional Facility. It is not the arrest or confinement but the search process at each jail that gives rise to the claims before the Court.

Burlington County jail procedures required every arrestee to shower with a delousing agent. Officers would check arrestees for scars, marks, gang tattoos, and contraband as they disrobed. Petitioner claims he was also instructed to open his mouth, lift his tongue, hold out his arms, turn around, and lift his genitals. . . .

The Essex County Correctional Facility, where petitioner was taken after six days, is the largest county jail in New Jersey. . . . When petitioner was transferred there, all arriving detainees passed through a metal detector and waited in a group holding cell for a more thorough search. When they left the holding cell, they were instructed to remove their clothing while an officer looked for body markings, wounds, and contraband. Apparently without touching the detainees, an officer looked at their ears, nose, mouth, hair, scalp, fingers, hands, arms, armpits, and other body openings. This policy applied regardless of the circumstances of the arrest, the suspected offense, or the detainee's behavior, demeanor, or criminal history. Petitioner alleges he was required to lift his genitals, turn around, and cough in a squatting position as part of the process. After a mandatory shower, during which his clothes were inspected, petitioner was admitted to the facility. . . . He was released the next day, when the charges against him were dismissed.

Petitioner sued the governmental entities that operated the jails, one of the wardens, and certain other defendants. The suit was commenced in the United States District Court for the District of New Jersey. Seeking relief under 42 U.S.C. § 1983 for violations of his Fourth and Fourteenth Amendment rights, petitioner maintained that persons arrested for a minor offense could not be required to remove their clothing and expose the most private areas of their bodies to close visual inspection as a routine part of the intake process. Rather, he contended, officials could conduct this kind of search only if they had reason to suspect a particular inmate of concealing a weapon, drugs, or other contraband. The District Court certified a class of individuals who were charged with a nonindictable offense under New Jersey law, processed at either the Burlington County or Essex County jail, and directed to strip naked even though an officer had not articulated any reasonable suspicion they were concealing contraband.

After discovery, the court granted petitioner's motion for summary judgment on the unlawful search claim. It concluded that any policy of "strip searching" nonindictable offenders without reasonable suspicion violated the Fourth Amendment. A divided panel of the United States Court of Appeals for the Third Circuit reversed, holding that the procedures described by the District Court struck a reasonable balance between inmate privacy and the security needs of the two jails. The case proceeds on the understanding that the officers searched detainees prior to their admission to the general population, as the Court of Appeals seems to have assumed.

■ ■ ■

II

■ ■ ■

The Court's opinion in *Bell v. Wolfish* (1979), is the starting point for understanding how this framework applies to Fourth Amendment challenges. That case addressed a rule requiring pretrial detainees in any correctional facility run by the Federal Bureau of Prisons "to expose their body cavities for visual inspection as a part of a strip search conducted after every contact visit with a person from outside the institution." . . . There had been but one instance in which an inmate attempted to sneak contraband back into the facility. . . . The Court nonetheless upheld the search policy. It deferred to the judgment of correctional officials that the inspections served not only to discover but also to deter the smuggling of weapons, drugs, and other prohibited items inside. The Court explained that there is no mechanical way to determine whether intrusions on an inmate's privacy are reasonable. The need for a particular search must be balanced against the resulting invasion of personal rights.

■ ■ ■

Policies designed to keep contraband out of jails and prisons have been upheld in cases decided since *Bell*. In *Block v. Rutherford* (1984), for example, the Court concluded that the Los Angeles County Jail could ban all contact visits because of the threat they posed:

> "They open the institution to the introduction of drugs, weapons, and other contraband. Visitors can easily conceal guns, knives, drugs, or other contraband in countless ways and pass them to an inmate unnoticed by even the most vigilant observers. And these items can readily be slipped from the clothing of an innocent child, or transferred by other visitors permitted close contact with inmates."

The Court has also recognized that deterring the possession of contraband depends in part on the ability to conduct searches without predictable exceptions. In *Hudson v. Palmer* (1984), it addressed the question of whether prison officials could perform random searches of inmate lockers and cells even without reason to suspect a particular individual of concealing a prohibited item. . . . The Court upheld the constitutionality of the practice, recognizing that " '[f]or one to advocate that prison searches must be conducted only pursuant to an enunciated general policy or when suspicion is directed at a particular inmate is to ignore the realities of prison operation.' " . . .

These cases establish that correctional officials must be permitted to devise reasonable search policies to detect and deter the possession of contraband in their facilities.

■ ■ ■

Persons arrested for minor offenses may be among the detainees processed at these facilities. This is, in part, a consequence of the exercise of state authority that was the subject of *Atwater v. Lago Vista* (2001). *Atwater* addressed the perhaps more fundamental question of who may be deprived of liberty and taken to jail in the first place. The case involved a woman who was arrested after a police officer noticed neither she nor her children were wearing their seatbelts. The arrestee argued the Fourth Amendment prohibited her custodial arrest without a warrant when an offense could not result in jail time and there was no compelling need for immediate detention. The Court held that a Fourth Amendment restriction on this power would put officers in an "almost impossible spot." Their ability to arrest a suspect would depend in some cases on the precise weight of drugs in his pocket, whether he was a repeat offender, and the scope of what counted as a compelling need to detain someone. The Court rejected the proposition that the Fourth Amendment barred custodial arrests in a set of these cases as a matter of constitutional law. It ruled, based on established principles, that officers may make an arrest based upon probable cause to believe the person has committed a criminal offense in their presence. The Court stated that "a responsible Fourth Amendment balance is not well served by standards requiring sensitive, case-by-case determinations of government need, lest every discretionary judgment in the field be converted into an occasion for constitutional review."

Atwater did not address whether the Constitution imposes special restrictions on the searches of offenders suspected of committing minor offenses once they are taken to jail. Some Federal Courts of Appeals have held that corrections officials may not conduct a strip search of these detainees, even if no touching is involved, absent reasonable suspicion of concealed contraband. The Courts of Appeals to address this issue in the last decade, however, have come to the opposite conclusion. . . . The current case is set against this precedent and governed by the principles announced in *Turner* and *Bell*.

III

The question here is whether undoubted security imperatives involved in jail supervision override the assertion that some detainees must be exempt from the more invasive search procedures at issue absent reasonable suspicion of a concealed weapon or other contraband. The Court has held that deference must be given to the officials in charge of the jail unless there is "substantial evidence" demonstrating their response to the situation is exaggerated. Petitioner has not met this standard, and the record provides full justifications for the procedures used.

A

Correctional officials have a significant interest in conducting a thorough search as a standard part of the intake process. The admission of inmates creates numerous risks for facility staff, for the existing detainee population, and for a new detainee himself or herself. . . .

■ ■ ■

It is not surprising that correctional officials have sought to perform thorough searches at intake for disease, gang affiliation, and contraband. Jails are often crowded, unsanitary, and dangerous places. There is a substantial interest in preventing any new inmate, either of his own will or as a result of coercion, from putting all who live or work at these institutions at even greater risk when he is admitted to the general population.

B

Petitioner acknowledges that correctional officials must be allowed to conduct an effective search during the intake process and that this will require at least some detainees to lift their genitals or cough in a squatting position. These procedures, similar to the ones upheld in *Bell*, are designed to uncover contraband that can go undetected by a patdown, metal detector, and other less invasive searches. Petitioner maintains there is little benefit to conducting these more invasive steps on a new detainee who has not been arrested for a serious crime or for any offense involving a weapon or drugs. In his view these detainees should be exempt from this process unless they give officers a particular reason to suspect them of hiding contraband. It is reasonable, however, for correctional officials to conclude this standard would be unworkable. The record provides evidence that the seriousness of an offense is a poor predictor of who has contraband and that it would be difficult in practice to determine whether individual detainees fall within the proposed exemption.

1

People detained for minor offenses can turn out to be the most devious and dangerous criminals. . . .

Experience shows that people arrested for minor offenses have tried to smuggle prohibited items into jail, sometimes by using their rectal cavities or genitals for the concealment. They may have some of the same incentives as a serious criminal to hide contraband. A detainee might risk carrying cash, cigarettes, or a penknife to survive in jail. Others may make a quick decision to hide unlawful substances to avoid getting in more trouble at the time of their arrest. . . .

2

It also may be difficult, as a practical matter, to classify inmates by their current and prior offenses before the intake search. Jails can be even more dangerous than prisons because officials there know so little about the people they admit at the outset. . . .

The laborious administration of prisons would become less effective, and likely less fair and evenhanded, were the practical problems inevitable from the rules suggested by petitioner to be imposed as a constitutional mandate. Even if they had accurate information about a detainee's current and prior arrests, officers, under petitioner's proposed regime, would encounter serious implementation difficulties. They would be required, in a few minutes, to determine whether any of the underlying offenses were serious enough to authorize the more invasive search protocol. . . .

The Court addressed an analogous problem in *Atwater*. The petitioner in that case argued the Fourth Amendment prohibited a warrantless arrest when being convicted of the suspected crime "could not ultimately carry any jail time" and there was "no compelling need for immediate detention." That rule "promise[d] very little in the way of administrability." Officers could not be expected to draw the proposed lines on a moment's notice, and the risk of violating the Constitution would have discouraged them from arresting criminals in any questionable circumstances. ("An officer not quite sure the drugs weighed enough to warrant jail time or not quite certain about a suspect's risk of flight would not arrest, even though it could perfectly well turn out that, in fact, the offense called for incarceration and the defendant was long gone on the day of trial"). The Fourth Amendment did not compel this result in *Atwater*. The Court held that officers who have probable cause to believe even a minor criminal offense has been committed in their presence may arrest the offender. Individual jurisdictions can of course choose "to impose more restrictive safeguards through statutes limiting warrantless arrests for minor offenders."

One of the central principles in *Atwater* applies with equal force here. Officers who interact with those suspected of violating the law have an "essential interest in readily administrable rules." The officials in charge of the jails in this case urge the Court to reject any complicated constitutional scheme requiring them to conduct less thorough inspections of some detainees based on their behavior, suspected offense, criminal history, and other factors. They offer significant reasons why the Constitution must not prevent them from conducting the same search on any suspected offender who will be admitted to the general population in their facilities. The restrictions suggested by petitioner would limit the intrusion on the privacy of some detainees but at the risk of increased danger to everyone in the facility, including the less serious offenders themselves.

The judgment of the Court of Appeals for the Third Circuit is affirmed.

It is so ordered.

Justice Breyer, with whom Justice Ginsburg, Justice Sotomayor, and Justice Kagan join, dissenting.

The petition for certiorari asks us to decide "[w]hether the Fourth Amendment permits a . . . suspicionless strip search of every individual arrested for any minor offense." . . . This question is phrased more broadly than what is at issue. The case is limited to strip searches of those arrestees entering a jail's general population, and the kind of strip search in question involves more than undressing and taking a shower (even if guards monitor the shower area for threatened disorder). Rather, the searches here involve close observation of the private areas of a person's body and for that reason constitute a far more serious invasion of that person's privacy.

■ ■ ■

In my view, such a search of an individual arrested for a minor offense that does not involve drugs or violence say a traffic offense, a regulatory offense, an essentially civil matter, or any other such misdemeanor is an "unreasonable searc[h]" forbidden by the Fourth Amendment, unless prison authorities have reasonable suspicion to believe that the individual possesses drugs or other contraband. And I dissent from the Court's contrary determination.

■ ■ ■

II

A strip search that involves a stranger peering without consent at a naked individual, and in particular at the most private portions of that person's body, is a serious invasion of privacy. We have recently said, in respect to a school-child (and a less intrusive search), that the "meaning of such a search, and the degradation its subject may reasonably feel, place a search that intrusive in a category of its own demanding its own specific suspicions." *Safford Unified School Dist. # 1 v. Redding* (2009). . . . Even when carried out in a respectful manner, and even absent any physical touching, see *ante* at 4-5, 19, such searches are inherently harmful, humiliating, and degrading. And the harm to privacy interests would seem particularly acute where the person searched may well have no expectation of being subject to such a search, say, because she had simply received a traffic ticket for failing to buckle a seatbelt, because he had not previously paid a civil fine, or because she had been arrested for a minor trespass.

In *Atwater v. Lago Vista* (2001), for example, police arrested a mother driving with her two children because their seat belts were not buckled. This Court held that the Constitution did not forbid an arrest for a minor seatbelt offense. But, in doing so, it pointed out that the woman was held for only an hour (before being taken to a magistrate and released on bond) and that the search she had to remove her shoes, jewelry, and the contents of her pockets was not " 'unusually harmful to [her] privacy or . . . physical interests.' " . . . Would this Court have upheld the arrest had the magistrate not been immediately available, had the police housed her overnight in the jail, and had they subjected her to a search of the kind at issue here?

The petitioner, Albert W. Florence, states that his present arrest grew out of an (erroneous) report that he had failed to pay a minor civil fine previously assessed because he had hindered a prosecution (by fleeing police officers in his automobile). . . . He alleges that he was held for six days in jail before being taken to a magistrate and that he was subjected to two strip searches of the kind in question.

Amicus briefs present other instances in which individuals arrested for minor offenses have been subjected to the humiliations of a visual strip search. They include a nun, a Sister of Divine Providence for 50 years, who was arrested for trespassing during an antiwar demonstration.... They include women who were strip-searched during periods of lactation or menstruation. *Id.*, at 11-12 (describing humiliating experience of female student who was strip searched while menstruating. I need not go on....

I doubt that we seriously disagree about the nature of the strip search or about the serious affront to human dignity and to individual privacy that it presents. The basic question before us is whether such a search is nonetheless justified when an individual arrested for a minor offense is involuntarily placed in the general jail or prison population.

III

■ ■ ■

The lack of justification is fairly obvious with respect to the first two penological interests advanced. The searches already employed at Essex and Burlington include: (a) pat-frisking all inmates; (b) making inmates go through metal detectors (including the Body Orifice Screening System (BOSS) chair used at Essex County Correctional Facility that identifies metal hidden within the body); (c) making inmates shower and use particular delousing agents or bathing supplies; and (d) searching inmates' clothing. In addition, petitioner concedes that detainees could be lawfully subject to being viewed in their under-garments by jail officers or during showering (for security purposes). ("Showering in the presence of officers is not something that requires reasonable suspicion".) No one here has offered any reason, example, or empirical evidence suggesting the inadequacy of such practices for detecting injuries, diseases, or tattoos. In particular, there is no connection between the genital lift and the "squat and cough" that Florence was allegedly subjected to and health or gang concerns.

■ ■ ■

Nor do I find the majority's lack of examples surprising. After all, those arrested for minor offenses are often stopped and arrested unexpectedly. And they consequently will have had little opportunity to hide things in their body cavities. Thus, the widespread advocacy by prison experts and the widespread application in many States and federal circuits of "reasonable suspicion" requirements indicates an ability to apply such standards in practice without unduly interfering with the legitimate penal interest in preventing the smuggling of contraband.

■ ■ ■

For the reasons set forth, I cannot find justification for the strip search policy at issue here a policy that would subject those arrested for minor offenses to serious invasions of their personal privacy. I consequently dissent.

B. REASONABLE SUSPICION

1. Overview

Camara v. Municipal Court of San Francisco

387 U.S. 523 (1967)

WHITE, J., delivered the opinion of the Court, in which WARREN, C.J., FORTAS, BLACK, BRENNAN, and DOUGLAS, JJ., joined. CLARK, HARLAN, and STEWART, JJ., dissented.

In *Frank v. State of Maryland* (1959), this Court upheld, by a five-to-four vote, a state court conviction of a homeowner who refused to permit a municipal health inspector to enter and inspect his premises without a search warrant. In *Ohio ex rel. Eaton v. Price* (1960), a similar conviction was affirmed by an equally divided Court. Since those closely divided decisions, more intensive efforts at all levels of government to contain and eliminate urban blight have led to increasing use of such inspection techniques, while numerous decisions of this Court have more fully defined the Fourth Amendment's effect on state and municipal action. In view of the growing nationwide importance of the problem, we noted probable jurisdiction in this case and in *See v. City of Seattle* (1967) to re-examine whether administrative inspection programs, as presently authorized and conducted, violate Fourth Amendment rights as those rights are enforced against the States through the Fourteenth Amendment.

Appellant brought this action in a California Superior Court alleging that he was awaiting trial on a criminal charge of violating the San Francisco Housing Code by refusing to permit a warrantless inspection of his residence, and that a writ of prohibition should issue to the criminal court because the ordinance authorizing such inspections is unconstitutional on its face. The Superior Court denied the writ, the District Court of Appeal affirmed, and the Supreme Court of California denied a petition for hearing. Appellant properly raised and had considered by the California courts the federal constitutional questions he now presents to this Court.

■ ■ ■

On November 6, 1963, an inspector of the Division of Housing Inspection of the San Francisco Department of Public Health entered an apartment building to make a routine annual inspection for possible violations of the city's Housing Code. The building's manager informed the inspector that appellant, lessee of the ground floor, was using the rear of his leasehold as a personal residence. Claiming that the building's occupancy permit did not allow residential use of the ground floor, the inspector confronted appellant and demanded that he permit an inspection of the premises. Appellant refused to allow the inspection because the inspector lacked a search warrant.

The inspector returned on November 8, again without a warrant, and appellant again refused to allow an inspection. A citation was then mailed ordering appellant to appear at the district attorney's office. When appellant failed to appear, two inspectors returned to his apartment on November 22. They informed appellant that he was required by law to permit an inspection under § 503 of the Housing Code:

> "Sec. 503 RIGHT TO ENTER BUILDING. Authorized employees of the City departments or City agencies, so far as may be necessary for the performance of their duties, shall, upon presentation of proper credentials, have the right to enter, at reasonable times, any building, structure, or premises in the City to perform any duty imposed upon them by the Municipal Code."

Appellant nevertheless refused the inspectors access to his apartment without a search warrant. Thereafter, a complaint was filed charging him with refusing to permit a lawful inspection in violation of § 507 of the Code. Appellant was arrested on December 2 and released on bail. When his demurrer to the criminal complaint was denied, appellant filed this petition for a writ of prohibition.

Appellant has argued throughout this litigation that § 503 is contrary to the Fourth and Fourteenth Amendments in that it authorizes municipal officials to enter a private dwelling without a search warrant and without probable cause to believe that a violation of the Housing Code exists therein. Consequently, appellant contends, he may not be prosecuted under § 507 for refusing to permit an inspection unconstitutionally authorized by § 503.

■ ■ ■

Though there has been general agreement as to the fundamental purpose of the Fourth Amendment, translation of the abstract prohibition against "unreasonable searches and seizures" into workable guidelines for the decision of particular cases is a difficult task which has for many years divided the members of this Court. Nevertheless, one governing principle, justified by history and by current experience, has consistently been followed: except in certain carefully defined classes of cases, a search of private property without proper consent is "unreasonable" unless it has been authorized by a valid search warrant.

■ ■ ■

> "The right of officers to thrust themselves into a home is also a grave concern, not only to the individual but to a society which chooses to dwell in reasonable security and freedom from surveillance. When the right of privacy must reasonably yield to the right of search is, as a rule, to be decided by a judicial officer, not by a policeman or government enforcement agent."

In *Frank v. State of Maryland*, this Court upheld the conviction of one who refused to permit a warrantless inspection of private premises for the purposes of locating and abating a suspected public nuisance. Although *Frank* can arguably be distinguished from this case on its facts, the *Frank* opinion has generally been interpreted as carving out an additional exception to the rule that warrantless searches are unreasonable under the Fourth Amendment.

■ ■ ■

To the *Frank* majority, municipal fire, health, and housing inspection programs "touch at most upon the periphery of the important interests safeguarded by the Fourteenth Amendment's protection against official intrusion," because the inspections are merely to determine whether physical conditions exist which do not comply with minimum standards prescribed in local regulatory ordinances. Since the inspector does not ask that the property owner open his doors to a search for "evidence of criminal action" which may be used to secure the owner's criminal conviction, historic interests of "self-protection" jointly protected by the Fourth and Fifth Amendments are said not to be involved, but only the less intense "right to be secure from intrusion into personal privacy."

We may agree that a routine inspection of the physical condition of private property is a less hostile intrusion than the typical policeman's search for the fruits and instrumentalities of crime. For this reason alone, *Frank* differed from the great bulk of Fourth Amendment cases which have been considered by this Court. But we cannot agree that the Fourth Amendment interests at stake in these inspection cases are merely "peripheral." It is surely anomalous to say that the individual and his private property are fully protected by the Fourth Amendment only when the individual is suspected of criminal behavior.

■ ■ ■

The *Frank* majority suggested, and appellee reasserts, two other justifications for permitting administrative health and safety inspections without a warrant. First, it is argued that these inspections are "designed to make the least possible demand on the individual occupant." The ordinances authorizing inspections are hedged with safeguards, and at any rate the inspector's particular decision to enter must comply with the constitutional standard of reasonableness even if he may enter without a warrant. In addition, the argument proceeds, the warrant process could not function effectively in this field. The decision to inspect an entire municipal area is based upon legislative or administrative assessment of broad factors such as the area's age and condition. Unless the magistrate is to review such policy matters, he must issue a "rubber stamp" warrant which provides no protection at all to the property owner.

In our opinion, these arguments unduly discount the purposes behind the warrant machinery contemplated by the Fourth Amendment. Under the present system, when the inspector demands entry, the occupant has no way of knowing whether enforcement of the municipal code involved requires inspection of his premises, no way of knowing the lawful limits of the inspector's power to search, and no way of knowing whether the inspector himself is acting under proper authorization. These are questions which may be reviewed by a neutral magistrate without any reassessment of the basic agency decision to canvass an area. Yet, only by refusing entry and risking a criminal conviction can the occupant at present challenge the inspector's decision to search. And even if the occupant possesses sufficient fortitude to take this risk, as appellant did here, he may never learn any more about the reason for the inspection than that the law generally allows housing inspectors to gain entry. The practical effect of this system is to leave the occupant subject to the discretion of the official in the field. This is precisely the discretion to invade private property which we have consistently circumscribed by a requirement that a disinterested party warrant the need to search.

■ ■ ■

The final justification suggested for warrantless administrative searches is that the public interest demands such a rule: it is vigorously argued that the health and safety of entire urban populations is dependent upon enforcement of minimum fire, housing, and sanitation standards, and that the only effective means of enforcing such codes is by routine systematized inspection of all physical structures. Of course, in applying any reasonableness standard, including one of constitutional dimension, an argument that the public interest demands a particular rule must receive careful consideration. But we think this argument misses the mark. The question is not, at this stage at least, whether these inspections may be made, but whether they may be made without a warrant. For example, to say that gambling raids may not be made at the discretion of the police without a warrant is not necessarily to say that gambling raids may never be made. In assessing whether the public interest demands creation of a general exception to the Fourth Amendment's warrant requirement, the question is not whether the public interest justifies the type of search in question, but whether the authority to search should be evidenced by a warrant, which in turn depends in part upon whether the burden of obtaining a warrant is likely to frustrate the governmental purpose behind the search.

■ ■ ■

In summary, we hold that administrative searches of the kind at issue here are significant intrusions upon the interests protected by the Fourth Amendment, that such searches when authorized and conducted without a warrant procedure lack the traditional safeguards which the Fourth Amendment guarantees to the individual, and that the reasons put forth in *Frank v. State of Maryland* and in other cases for upholding these warrantless searches are insufficient to justify so substantial a weakening of the Fourth Amendment's protections. Because of the nature of the municipal programs under consideration, however, these conclusions must be the beginning, not the end, of our inquiry. The *Frank* majority gave recognition to the unique character of these inspection programs by refusing to require search warrants; to reject that disposition does not justify ignoring the question whether some other accommodation between public need and individual rights is essential.

■ ■ ■

In cases in which the Fourth Amendment requires that a warrant to search be obtained, "probable cause" is the standard by which a particular decision to search is tested against the constitutional mandate of reasonableness. To apply this standard, it is obviously necessary first to focus upon the governmental interest which allegedly justifies official intrusion upon the constitutionally protected interests of the private citizen. For example, in a criminal investigation, the police may undertake to recover specific stolen or contraband goods. But that public interest would hardly justify a sweeping search of an entire city conducted in the hope that these goods might be found. Consequently, a search for these goods, even with a warrant, is "reasonable" only when there is "probable cause" to believe that they will be uncovered in a particular dwelling.

Unlike the search pursuant to a criminal investigation, the inspection programs at issue here are aimed at securing city-wide compliance with minimum physical standards for private property. The primary governmental interest at stake is to prevent even the unintentional development of conditions which are hazardous to public health and safety. Because fires and epidemics may ravage large urban areas, because unsightly conditions adversely affect the economic values of neighboring structures, numerous courts have upheld the police power of municipalities to impose and enforce such minimum standards even upon existing structures. In determining whether a particular inspection is reasonable—and thus in determining whether there is probable cause to issue a warrant for that inspection—the need for the inspection must be weighed in terms of these reasonable goals of code enforcement.

There is unanimous agreement among those most familiar with this field that the only effective way to seek universal compliance with the minimum standards required by municipal codes is through routine periodic inspections of all structures. It is here that the probable cause debate is focused, for the agency's decision to conduct an area inspection is unavoidably based on its appraisal of conditions in the area as a whole, not on its knowledge of conditions in each particular building. Appellee contends that, if the probable cause standard urged by appellant is adopted, the area inspection will be eliminated as a means of seeking compliance with code standards and the reasonable goals of code enforcement will be dealt a crushing blow.

[A]ppellant argues . . . that the area inspection is an unreasonable search. Unfortunately, there can be no ready test for determining reasonableness other than by balancing the need to search against the invasion which the search entails. But we think that a number of persuasive factors combine to support the reasonableness of area code-enforcement inspections. First, such programs have a long history of judicial and public acceptance. See Frank v. State of Maryland. Second, the public interest demands that all dangerous conditions be prevented or abated, yet it is doubtful that any other canvassing technique would achieve acceptable results. Many such conditions-faulty wiring is an obvious example-are not observable from outside the building and indeed may not be apparent to the inexpert occupant himself. Finally, because the inspections are neither personal in nature nor aimed at the discovery of evidence of crime, they involve a relatively limited invasion of the urban citizen's privacy. . . .

Having concluded that the area inspection is a "reasonable" search of private property within the meaning of the Fourth Amendment, it is obvious that "probable cause" to issue a warrant to inspect must exist if reasonable legislative or administrative standards for conducting an area inspection are satisfied with respect to a particular dwelling. Such standards, which will vary with the municipal program being enforced, may be based upon the passage of time, the nature of the building (e.g., a multifamily apartment house), or the condition of the entire area, but they will not necessarily depend upon specific knowledge of the condition of the particular dwelling. It has been suggested that so to vary the probable cause test from the standard applied in criminal cases would be to authorize a "synthetic search warrant" and thereby to lessen the overall protections of the Fourth Amendment. But we do not agree. The warrant procedure is designed to guarantee that a decision to search private property is justified by a reasonable governmental interest. But reasonableness is still the ultimate standard. If a valid public interest justifies the intrusion contemplated, then there is probable cause to issue a suitably restricted search warrant. Such an approach neither endangers time-honored doctrines applicable to criminal investigations nor makes a nullity of the probable cause requirement in this area. It merely gives full recognition to the competing public and private interests here at stake and, in so doing, best fulfills the historic purpose behind the constitutional right to be free from unreasonable government invasions of privacy. . . .

The judgment is vacated and the case is remanded for further proceedings not inconsistent with this opinion. It is so ordered.

Judgment vacated and case remanded.

Terry v. Ohio

392 U.S. 1 (1968)

WARREN, C.J., delivered the opinion of the Court, in which BLACK, BRENNAN, STEWART, FORTAS, WHITE, and MARSHALL, JJ., joined. HARLAN, J., filed a concurring opinion. DOUGLAS, J., filed a dissenting opinion.

This case presents serious questions concerning the role of the Fourth Amendment in the confrontation on the street between the citizen and the policeman investigating suspicious circumstances.

Petitioner Terry was convicted of carrying a concealed weapon and sentenced to the statutorily prescribed term of one to three years in the penitentiary. Following the denial of a pretrial motion to suppress, the prosecution introduced in evidence two revolvers and a number of bullets seized from Terry and a codefendant, Richard Chilton, by Cleveland Police Detective Martin McFadden. At the hearing on the motion to suppress this evidence, Officer McFadden testified that while he was patrolling in plain clothes in downtown Cleveland at approximately 2:30 in the afternoon of October 31, 1963, his attention was attracted by two men, Chilton and Terry, standing on the corner of Huron Road and Euclid Avenue. He had never seen the two men before, and he was unable to say precisely what first drew his eye to them. However, he testified that he had been a policeman for 39 years and a detective for 35 and that he had been assigned to patrol this vicinity of downtown Cleveland for shoplifters and pickpockets for 30 years. He explained that he had developed routine habits of observation over the years and that he would "stand and watch people or walk and watch people at many intervals of the day." He added: "Now, in this case when I looked over they didn't look right to me at the time."

His interest aroused, Officer McFadden took up a post of observation in the entrance to a store 300 to 400 feet away from the two men. "I get more purpose to watch them when I seen their movements," he testified. He saw one of the men leave the other one and walk southwest on Huron Road, past some stores. The man paused for a moment and looked in a store window, then walked on a short distance, turned around and walked back toward the corner, pausing once again to look in the same store window. He rejoined his companion at the corner, and the two conferred briefly. Then the second man went through the same series of motions, strolling down Huron Road, looking in the same window, walking on a short distance, turning back, peering in the store window again, and returning to confer with the first man at the corner. The two men repeated this ritual alternately between five and six times apiece—in all, roughly a dozen trips. At one point, while the two were standing together on the corner, a third man approached them and engaged them briefly in conversation. This man then left the two others and walked west on Euclid Avenue. Chilton and Terry resumed their measured pacing, peering and conferring. After this had gone on for 10 to 12 minutes, the two men walked off together, heading west on Euclid Avenue, following the path taken earlier by the third man.

By this time Officer McFadden had become thoroughly suspicious. He testified that after observing their elaborately casual and oft-repeated reconnaissance of the store window on Huron Road, he suspected the two men of "casing a job, a stick-up," and that he considered it his duty as a police officer to investigate further. He added that he feared "they may have a gun." Thus, Officer McFadden followed Chilton and Terry and saw them stop in front of Zucker's store to talk to the same man who had conferred with them earlier on the street corner. Deciding that the situation was ripe for direct action, Officer McFadden approached the three men, identified himself as a police officer and asked for their names. At this point his knowledge was confined to what he had observed. He was not acquainted with any of the three men by name or by sight, and he had received no information concerning them from any other source. When the men "mumbled something" in response to his inquiries, Officer McFadden grabbed petitioner Terry, spun him around so that they were facing the other two, with Terry between McFadden and the others, and patted down the outside of his clothing. In the left breast pocket of Terry's overcoat Officer McFadden felt a pistol. He reached inside the overcoat pocket, but was unable to remove the gun. At this point, keeping Terry between himself and the others, the officer ordered all three men to enter Zucker's store. As they went in, he removed Terry's overcoat completely, removed a .38-caliber revolver from the pocket and ordered all three men to face the wall with their hands raised. Officer McFadden proceeded to pat down the outer clothing of Chilton and the third man, Katz. He discovered another revolver in the outer pocket of Chilton's overcoat, but no weapons were found on Katz. The officer testified that he only patted the men down to see whether they had weapons, and that he did not put his hands beneath the outer garments of either Terry or Chilton until he felt their guns. So far as appears from the record, he never placed his hands beneath Katz' outer garments. Officer McFadden seized Chilton's gun, asked the proprietor of the store to call a police wagon, and took all three men to the station, where Chilton and Terry were formally charged with carrying concealed weapons.

On the motion to suppress the guns the prosecution took the position that they had been seized following a search incident to a lawful arrest. The trial court rejected this theory, stating that it "would be stretching the facts beyond reasonable comprehension" to find that Officer McFadden had had probable cause to arrest the men before he patted them down for weapons. However, the court denied the defendants' motion on the ground that Officer McFadden, on the basis of his experience, "had reasonable cause to believe that the defendants were conducting themselves suspiciously, and some interrogation should be made of their action." Purely for his own protection, the court held, the officer had the right to pat down the outer clothing of these men, who he had reasonable cause to believe might be armed. The court distinguished between an investigatory "stop" and an arrest, and between a "frisk" of the outer clothing for weapons and a full-blown search for evidence of crime. The frisk, it held, was essential to the proper performance of the officer's investigatory duties, for without it "the answer to the police officer may be a bullet, and a loaded pistol discovered during the frisk is admissible."

After the court denied their motion to suppress, Chilton and Terry waived jury trial and pleaded not guilty. The court adjudged them guilty, and the Court of Appeals for the Eighth Judicial District, Cuyahoga County, affirmed. The Supreme Court of Ohio dismissed their appeal on the ground that no "substantial constitutional question" was involved. We granted certiorari to determine whether the admission of the revolvers in evidence violated petitioner's rights under the Fourth Amendment, made applicable to the States by the Fourteenth. We affirm the conviction.

■ ■ ■

We have recently held that "the Fourth Amendment protects people, not places," *Katz v. United States* (1967), and wherever an individual may harbor a reasonable "expectation of privacy," he is entitled to be free from unreasonable governmental intrusion. Of course, the specific content and incidents of this right must be shaped by the context in which it is asserted. For "what the Constitution forbids is not all searches and seizures, but unreasonable searches and seizures." Unquestionably petitioner was entitled to the protection of the Fourth Amendment as he walked down the street in Cleveland. The question is whether in all the circumstances of this on-the-street encounter, his right to personal security was violated by an unreasonable search and seizure.

We would be less than candid if we did not acknowledge that this question thrusts to the fore difficult and troublesome issues regarding a sensitive area of police activity—issues which have never before been squarely presented to this Court. Reflective of the tensions involved are the practical and constitutional arguments pressed with great vigor on both sides of the public debate over the power of the police to "stop and frisk"—as it is sometimes euphemistically termed—suspicious persons.

On the one hand, it is frequently argued that in dealing with the rapidly unfolding and often dangerous situations on city streets the police are in need of an escalating set of flexible responses, graduated in relation to the amount of information they possess. For this purpose it is urged that distinctions should be made between a "stop" and an "arrest" (or a "seizure" of a person), and between a "frisk" and a "search." Thus, it is argued, the police should be allowed to "stop" a person and detain him briefly for questioning upon suspicion that he may be connected with criminal activity. Upon suspicion that the person may be armed, the police should have the power to "frisk" him for weapons. If the "stop" and the "frisk" give rise to probable cause to believe that the suspect has committed a crime, then the police should be empowered to make a formal "arrest," and a full incident "search" of the person. This scheme is justified in part upon the notion that a "stop" and a "frisk" amount to a mere "minor inconvenience and petty indignity," which can properly be imposed upon the citizen in the interest of effective law enforcement on the basis of a police officer's suspicion.

On the other side the argument is made that the authority of the police must be strictly circumscribed by the law of arrest and search as it has developed to date in the traditional jurisprudence of the Fourth Amendment. It is contended with some force that there is not—and cannot be—a variety of police activity which does not depend solely upon the voluntary cooperation of the citizen and yet which stops short of an arrest based upon probable cause to make such an arrest. The heart of the Fourth Amendment, the argument runs, is a severe requirement of specific justification for any intrusion upon protected personal security, coupled with a highly developed system of judicial controls to enforce upon the agents of the State the commands of the Constitution. Acquiescence by the courts in the compulsion inherent in the field interrogation practices at issue here, it is urged, would constitute an abdication of judicial control over, and indeed an encouragement of, substantial interference with liberty and personal security by police officers whose judgment is necessarily colored by their primary involvement in "the often competitive enterprise of ferreting out crime."

■ ■ ■

In this context we approach the issues in this case mindful of the limitations of the judicial function in controlling the myriad daily situations in which policemen and citizens confront each other on the street. The State has characterized the issue here as "the right of a police officer to make an on-the-street stop, interrogate and pat down for weapons (known in street vernacular as 'stop and frisk')." But this is only partly accurate. For the issue is not the abstract propriety of the police conduct, but the admissibility against petitioner of the evidence uncovered by the search and seizure. Ever since its inception, the rule excluding evidence seized in violation of the Fourth Amendment has been recognized as a principal mode of discouraging lawless police conduct. Thus its major thrust is a deterrent one, and experience has taught that it is the only effective deterrent to police misconduct in the criminal context, and that without it the constitutional guarantee against unreasonable searches and seizures would be a mere "form of words." *Mapp v. Ohio* (1961). The rule also serves another vital function—"the imperative of judicial integrity." *Elkins v. United States* (1960). Courts which sit under our Constitution cannot and will not be made party to lawless invasions of the constitutional rights of citizens by permitting unhindered governmental use of the fruits of such invasions. Thus in our system evidentiary rulings provide the context in which the judicial process of inclusion and exclusion approves some conduct as comporting with constitutional guarantees and disapproves other actions by state agents. A ruling admitting evidence in a criminal trial, we recognize, has the necessary effect of legitimizing the conduct which produced the evidence, while an application of the exclusionary rule withholds the constitutional imprimatur.

■ ■ ■

Proper adjudication of cases in which the exclusionary rule is invoked demands a constant awareness of these limitations. The wholesale harassment by certain elements of the police community, of which minority groups, particularly Negroes, frequently complain,[11] will not be stopped by the exclusion of any evidence from any criminal trial. Yet a rigid and unthinking application of the exclusionary rule, in futile protest against practices which it can never be used effectively to control, may exact a high toll in human injury and frustration of efforts to prevent crime. No judicial opinion can comprehend the protean variety of the street encounter, and we can only judge the facts of the case before us. Nothing we say today is to be taken as indicating approval of police conduct outside the legitimate investigative sphere. Under our decision, courts still retain their traditional responsibility to guard against police conduct

---

11. The President's Commission on Law Enforcement and Administration of Justice found that "[i]n many communities, field interrogations are a major source of friction between the police and minority groups." President's Commission on Law Enforcement and Administration of Justice, Task Force Report: The Police 183 (1967). It was reported that the friction caused by "[m]isuse of field interrogations" increases "as more police departments adopt 'aggressive patrol' in which officers are encouraged routinely to stop and question persons on the street who are unknown to them, who are suspicious, or whose purpose for being abroad is not readily evident." While the frequency with which "frisking" forms a part of field interrogation practice varies tremendously with the locale, the objective of the interrogation, and the particular officer, see Tiffany, McIntyre & Rotenberg, supra, n.9, at 47-48, it cannot help but be a severely exacerbating factor in police-community tensions. This is particularly true in situations where the "stop and frisk" of youths or minority group members is "motivated by the officers'" perceived need to maintain the power image of the beat officer, an aim sometimes accomplished by humiliating anyone who attempts to undermine police control of the streets. Ibid.

which is over-bearing or harassing, or which trenches upon personal security without the objective evidentiary justification which the Constitution requires. When such conduct is identified, it must be condemned by the judiciary and its fruits must be excluded from evidence in criminal trials. And, of course, our approval of legitimate and restrained investigative conduct undertaken on the basis of ample factual justification should in no way discourage the employment of other remedies than the exclusionary rule to curtail abuses for which that sanction may prove inappropriate.

Having thus roughly sketched the perimeters of the constitutional debate over the limits on police investigative conduct in general and the background against which this case presents itself, we turn our attention to the quite narrow question posed by the facts before us: whether it is always unreasonable for a policeman to seize a person and subject him to a limited search for weapons unless there is probable cause for an arrest. Given the narrowness of this question, we have no occasion to canvass in detail the constitutional limitations upon the scope of a policeman's power when he confronts a citizen without probable cause to arrest him. . . .

Our first task is to establish at what point in this encounter the Fourth Amendment becomes relevant. That is, we must decide whether and when Officer McFadden "seized" Terry and whether and when he conducted a "search." There is some suggestion in the use of such terms as "stop" and "frisk" that such police conduct is outside the purview of the Fourth Amendment because neither action rises to the level of a "search" or "seizure" within the meaning of the Constitution. We emphatically reject this notion. It is quite plain that the Fourth Amendment governs "seizures" of the person which do not eventuate in a trip to the station house and prosecution for crime—"arrests" in traditional terminology. It must be recognized that whenever a police officer accosts an individual and restrains his freedom to walk away, he has "seized" that person. And it is nothing less than sheer torture of the English language to suggest that a careful exploration of the outer surfaces of a person's clothing all over his or her body in an attempt to find weapons is not a "search." Moreover, it is simply fantastic to urge that such a procedure performed in public by a policeman while the citizen stands helpless, perhaps facing a wall with his hands raised, is a "petty indignity." It is a serious intrusion upon the sanctity of the person, which may inflict great indignity and arouse strong resentment, and it is not to be undertaken lightly.

■ ■ ■

The distinctions of classical "stop-and-frisk" theory thus serve to divert attention from the central inquiry under the Fourth Amendment—the reasonableness in all the circumstances of the particular governmental invasion of a citizen's personal security. "Search" and "seizure" are not talismans. We therefore reject the notions that the Fourth Amendment does not come into play at all as a limitation upon police conduct if the officers stop short of something called a "technical arrest" or a "full-blown search."

In this case there can be no question, then, that Officer McFadden "seized" petitioner and subjected him to a "search" when he took hold of him and patted down the outer surfaces of his clothing. We must decide whether at that point it was reasonable for Officer McFadden to have interfered with petitioner's personal security as he did.[16] And in determining whether the seizure and search were "unreasonable" our inquiry is a dual one—whether the officer's action was justified at its inception, and whether it was reasonably related in scope to the circumstances which justified the interference in the first place.

■   ■   ■

If this case involved police conduct subject to the Warrant Clause of the Fourth Amendment, we would have to ascertain whether "probable cause" existed to justify the search and seizure which took place. However, that is not the case. We do not retreat from our holdings that the police must, whenever practicable, obtain advance judicial approval of searches and seizures through the warrant procedure, or that in most instances failure to comply with the warrant requirement can only be excused by exigent circumstances. But we deal here with an entire rubric of police conduct—necessarily swift action predicated upon the on-the-spot observations of the officer on the beat—which historically has not been, and as a practical matter could not be, subjected to the warrant procedure. Instead, the conduct involved in this case must be tested by the Fourth Amendment's general proscription against unreasonable searches and seizures.

Nonetheless, the notions which underlie both the warrant procedure and the requirement of probable cause remain fully relevant in this context. In order to assess the reasonableness of Officer McFadden's conduct as a general proposition, it is necessary "first to focus upon the governmental interest which allegedly justifies official intrusion upon the constitutionally protected interests of the private citizen," for there is "no ready test for determining reasonableness other than by balancing the need to search (or seize) against the invasion which the search (or seizure) entails." *Camara v. Municipal Court* (1967). And in justifying the particular intrusion the police officer must be able to point to specific and articulable facts which, taken together with rational inferences from those facts, reasonably warrant that intrusion. The scheme of the Fourth Amendment becomes meaningful only when it is assured that at some point the conduct of those charged with enforcing the laws can be subjected to the more detached, neutral scrutiny of a judge who must evaluate the reasonableness of a particular search or seizure in light of the particular

---

16. We thus decide nothing today concerning the constitutional propriety of an investigative "seizure" upon less than probable cause for purposes of "detention" and/or interrogation. Obviously, not all personal intercourse between policemen and citizens involves "seizures" of persons. Only when the officer, by means of physical force or show of authority, has in some way restrained the liberty of a citizen may we conclude that a "seizure" has occurred. We cannot tell with any certainty upon this record whether any such "seizure" took place here prior to Officer McFadden's initiation of physical contact for purposes of searching Terry for weapons, and we thus may assume that up to that point no intrusion upon constitutionally protected rights had occurred.

circumstances. And in making that assessment it is imperative that the facts be judged against an objective standard: would the facts available to the officer at the moment of the seizure or the search "warrant a man of reasonable caution in the belief" that the action taken was appropriate? Anything less would invite intrusions upon constitutionally guaranteed rights based on nothing more substantial than inarticulate hunches, a result this Court has consistently refused to sanction. And simple

> " 'good faith on the part of the arresting officer is not enough.' . . . If subjective good faith alone were the test, the protections of the Fourth Amendment would evaporate, and the people would be 'secure in their persons, houses, papers and effects,' only in the discretion of the police."

Applying these principles to this case, we consider first the nature and extent of the governmental interests involved. One general interest is of course that of effective crime prevention and detection; it is this interest which underlies the recognition that a police officer may in appropriate circumstances and in an appropriate manner approach a person for purposes of investigating possibly criminal behavior even though there is no probable cause to make an arrest. It was this legitimate investigative function Officer McFadden was discharging when he decided to approach petitioner and his companions. He had observed Terry, Chilton, and Katz go through a series of acts, each of them perhaps innocent in itself, but which taken together warranted further investigation. There is nothing unusual in two men standing together on a street corner, perhaps waiting for someone. Nor is there anything suspicious about people in such circumstances strolling up and down the street, singly or in pairs. Store windows, moreover, are made to be looked in. But the story is quite different where, as here, two men hover about a street corner for an extended period of time, at the end of which it becomes apparent that they are not waiting for anyone or anything; where these men pace alternately along an identical route, pausing to stare in the same store window roughly 24 times; where each completion of this route is followed immediately by a conference between the two men on the corner; where they are joined in one of these conferences by a third man who leaves swiftly; and where the two men finally follow the third and rejoin him a couple of blocks away. It would have been poor police work indeed for an officer of 30 years' experience in the detection of thievery from stores in this same neighborhood to have failed to investigate this behavior further.

The crux of this case, however, is not the propriety of Officer McFadden's taking steps to investigate petitioner's suspicious behavior, but rather, whether there was justification for McFadden's invasion of Terry's personal security by searching him for weapons in the course of that investigation. We are now concerned with more than the governmental interest in investigating crime; in addition, there is the more immediate interest of the police officer in taking steps to assure himself that the person with whom he is dealing is not armed with a weapon that could unexpectedly and fatally be used against him.

Certainly it would be unreasonable to require that police officers take unnecessary risks in the performance of their duties. American criminals have a long tradition of armed violence, and every year in this country many law enforcement officers are killed in the line of duty, and thousands more are wounded. Virtually all of these deaths and a substantial portion of the injuries are inflicted with guns and knives.

In view of these facts, we cannot blind ourselves to the need for law enforcement officers to protect themselves and other prospective victims of violence in situations where they may lack probable cause for an arrest. When an officer is justified in believing that the individual whose suspicious behavior he is investigating at close range is armed and presently dangerous to the officer or to others, it would appear to be clearly unreasonable to deny the officer the power to take necessary measures to determine whether the person is in fact carrying a weapon and to neutralize the threat of physical harm.

We must still consider, however, the nature and quality of the intrusion on individual rights which must be accepted if police officers are to be conceded the right to search for weapons in situations where probable cause to arrest for crime is lacking. Even a limited search of the outer clothing for weapons constitutes a severe, though brief, intrusion upon cherished personal security, and it must surely be an annoying, frightening, and perhaps humiliating experience. Petitioner contends that such an intrusion is permissible only incident to a lawful arrest, either for a crime involving the possession of weapons or for a crime the commission of which led the officer to investigate in the first place. However, this argument must be closely examined.

■ ■ ■

Our evaluation of the proper balance that has to be struck in this type of case leads us to conclude that there must be a narrowly drawn authority to permit a reasonable search for weapons for the protection of the police officer, where he has reason to believe that he is dealing with an armed and dangerous individual, regardless of whether he has probable cause to arrest the individual for a crime. The officer need not be absolutely certain that the individual is armed; the issue is whether a reasonably prudent man in the circumstances would be warranted in the belief that his safety or that of others was in danger. And in determining whether the officer acted reasonably in such circumstances, due weight must be given, not to his inchoate and unparticularized suspicion or "hunch," but to the specific reasonable inferences which he is entitled to draw from the facts in light of his experience.

■ ■ ■

We must now examine the conduct of Officer McFadden in this case to determine whether his search and seizure of petitioner were reasonable, both at their inception and as conducted. He had observed Terry, together with Chilton and another man, acting in a manner he took to be preface to a "stick-up." We think on the facts and circumstances Officer McFadden detailed before the trial judge a reasonably prudent man would have been warranted in believing petitioner was armed and thus presented a threat to the officer's safety while he was investigating his suspicious behavior. The actions of Terry and Chilton were consistent with McFadden's hypothesis that these men were contemplating a daylight robbery—which, it is reasonable to assume, would be likely to involve the use of weapons—and nothing in their conduct from the time he first noticed them until the time he confronted them and identified himself as a police officer gave him sufficient reason to negate that hypothesis. Although the trio had departed the original scene, there was nothing to indicate abandonment of an intent to commit a robbery at some point. Thus, when Officer McFadden approached the three men gathered before the display window at Zucker's store he had observed enough to make it quite reasonable to fear that they were armed; and nothing in their response to his hailing them, identifying himself as a police officer, and asking their names served to dispel that reasonable belief. We cannot say his decision at that point to seize Terry and pat his clothing for weapons was the product of a volatile or inventive imagination, or was undertaken simply as an act of harassment; the record evidences the tempered act of a policeman who in the course of an investigation had to make a quick decision as to how to protect himself and others from possible danger, and took limited steps to do so.

The manner in which the seizure and search were conducted is, of course, as vital a part of the inquiry as whether they were warranted at all. The Fourth Amendment proceeds as much by limitations upon the scope of governmental action as by imposing preconditions upon its initiation. The entire deterrent purpose of the rule excluding evidence seized in violation of the Fourth Amendment rests on the assumption that "limitations upon the fruit to be gathered tend to limit the quest itself." Thus, evidence may not be introduced if it was discovered by means of a seizure and search which were not reasonably related in scope to the justification for their initiation.

We need not develop at length in this case, however, the limitations which the Fourth Amendment places upon a protective seizure and search for weapons. These limitations will have to be developed in the concrete factual circumstances of individual cases. . . . Suffice it to note that such a search, unlike a search without a warrant incident to a lawful arrest, is not justified by any need to prevent the disappearance or destruction of evidence of crime. The sole justification of the search in the present situation is the protection of the police officer and others nearby, and it must therefore be confined in scope to an intrusion reasonably designed to discover guns, knives, clubs, or other hidden instruments for the assault of the police officer.

The scope of the search in this case presents no serious problem in light of these standards. Officer McFadden patted down the outer clothing of petitioner and his two companions. He did not place his hands in their pockets or under the outer surface of their garments until he had felt weapons, and then he merely reached for and removed the guns. He never did invade Katz' person beyond the outer surfaces of his clothes, since he discovered nothing in his patdown which might have been a weapon. Officer McFadden confined his search strictly to what was minimally necessary to learn whether the men were armed and to disarm them once he discovered the weapons. He did not conduct a general exploratory search for whatever evidence of criminal activity he might find.

■ ■ ■

We conclude that the revolver seized from Terry was properly admitted in evidence against him. At the time he seized petitioner and searched him for weapons, Officer McFadden had reasonable grounds to believe that petitioner was armed and dangerous, and it was necessary for the protection of himself and others to take swift measures to discover the true facts and neutralize the threat of harm if it materialized. The policeman carefully restricted his search to what was appropriate to the discovery of the particular items which he sought. Each case of this sort will, of course, have to be decided on its own facts. We merely hold today that where a police officer observes unusual conduct which leads him reasonably to conclude in light of his experience that criminal activity may be afoot and that the persons with whom he is dealing may be armed and presently dangerous, where in the course of investigating this behavior he identifies himself as a policeman and makes reasonable inquiries, and where nothing in the initial stages of the encounter serves to dispel his reasonable fear for his own or others' safety, he is entitled for the protection of himself and others in the area to conduct a carefully limited search of the outer clothing of such persons in an attempt to discover weapons which might be used to assault him. Such a search is a reasonable search under the Fourth Amendment, and any weapons seized may properly be introduced in evidence against the person from whom they were taken.

Affirmed.

Justice HARLAN, concurring.

While I unreservedly agree with the Court's ultimate holding in this case, I am constrained to fill in a few gaps, as I see them, in its opinion. I do this because what is said by this Court today will serve as initial guidelines for law enforcement authorities and courts throughout the land as this important new field of law develops.

A police officer's right to make an on-the-street "stop" and an accompanying "frisk" for weapons is of course bounded by the protections afforded by the Fourth and Fourteenth Amendments. The Court holds, and I agree, that while the right does not depend upon possession by the officer of a valid warrant, nor upon the existence of probable cause, such activities must be reasonable under the circumstances as the officer credibly relates them in court. Since the question in this and most cases is whether evidence produced by a frisk is admissible, the problem is to determine what makes a frisk reasonable.

■ ■ ■

In the first place, if the frisk is justified in order to protect the officer during an encounter with a citizen, the officer must first have constitutional grounds to insist on an encounter, to make a forcible stop. Any person, including a policeman, is at liberty to avoid a person he considers dangerous. If and when a policeman has a right instead to disarm such a person for his own protection, he must first have a right not to avoid him but to be in his presence. That right must be more than the liberty (again, possessed by every citizen) to address questions to other persons, for ordinarily the person addressed has an equal right to ignore his interrogator and walk away; he certainly need not submit to a frisk for the questioner's protection. I would make it perfectly clear that the right to frisk in this case depends upon the reasonableness of a forcible stop to investigate a suspected crime.

Where such a stop is reasonable, however, the right to frisk must be immediate and automatic if the reason for the stop is, as here, an articulable suspicion of a crime of violence. Just as a full search incident to a lawful arrest requires no additional justification, a limited frisk incident to a lawful stop must often be rapid and routine. There is no reason why an officer, rightfully but forcibly confronting a person suspected of a serious crime, should have to ask one question and take the risk that the answer might be a bullet.

The facts of this case are illustrative of a proper stop and an incident frisk. Officer McFadden had no probable cause to arrest Terry for anything, but he had observed circumstances that would reasonably lead an experienced, prudent policeman to suspect that Terry was about to engage in burglary or robbery. His justifiable suspicion afforded a proper constitutional basis for accosting Terry, restraining his liberty of movement briefly, and addressing questions to him, and Officer McFadden did so. When he did, he had no reason whatever to suppose that Terry might be armed, apart from the fact that he suspected him of planning a violent crime. McFadden asked Terry his name, to which Terry "mumbled something." Whereupon McFadden, without asking Terry to speak louder and without giving him any chance to explain his presence or his actions, forcibly frisked him.

I would affirm this conviction for what I believe to be the same reasons the Court relies on. I would, however, make explicit what I think is implicit in affirmance on the present facts. Officer McFadden's right to interrupt Terry's freedom of movement and invade his privacy arose only because circumstances warranted forcing an encounter with Terry in an effort to prevent or investigate a crime. Once that forced encounter was justified, however, the officer's right to take suitable measures for his own safety followed automatically.

Upon the foregoing premises, I join the opinion of the Court....

Justice DOUGLAS, dissenting.

I agree that petitioner was "seized" within the meaning of the Fourth Amendment. I also agree that frisking petitioner and his companions for guns was a "search." But it is a mystery how that "search" and that "seizure" can be constitutional by Fourth Amendment standards, unless there was "probable cause" to believe that (1) a crime had been committed or (2) a crime was in the process of being committed or (3) a crime was about to be committed.

The opinion of the Court disclaims the existence of "probable cause." If loitering were in issue and that was the offense charged, there would be "probable cause" shown. But the crime here is carrying concealed weapons; and there is no basis for concluding that the officer had "probable cause" for believing that that crime was being committed. Had a warrant been sought, a magistrate would, therefore, have been unauthorized to issue one, for he can act only if there is a showing of "probable cause." We hold today that the police have greater authority to make a "seizure" and conduct a "search" than a judge has to authorize such action. We have said precisely the opposite over and over again.

In other words, police officers up to today have been permitted to effect arrests or searches without warrants only when the facts within their personal knowledge would satisfy the constitutional standard of probable cause. At the time of their "seizure" without a warrant they must possess facts concerning the person arrested that would have satisfied a magistrate that "probable cause" was indeed present. The term "probable cause" rings a bell of certainty that is not sounded by phrases such as "reasonable suspicion." Moreover, the meaning of "probable cause" is deeply imbedded in our constitutional history.

■ ■ ■

The infringement on personal liberty of any "seizure" of a person can only be "reasonable" under the Fourth Amendment if we require the police to possess "probable cause" before they seize him. Only that line draws a meaningful distinction between an officer's mere inkling and the presence of facts within the officer's personal knowledge which would convince a reasonable man that the person seized has committed, is committing, or is about to commit a particular crime. "In dealing with probable cause, as the very name implies, we deal with probabilities. These are not technical; they are the factual and practical considerations of everyday life on which reasonable and prudent men, not legal technicians, act."

To give the police greater power than a magistrate is to take a long step down the totalitarian path. Perhaps such a step is desirable to cope with modern forms of lawlessness. But if it is taken, it should be the deliberate choice of the people through a constitutional amendment. Until the Fourth Amendment, which is closely allied with the Fifth, is rewritten, the person and the effects of the individual are beyond the reach of all government agencies until there are reasonable grounds to believe (probable cause) that a criminal venture has been launched or is about to be launched.

There have been powerful hydraulic pressures throughout our history that bear heavily on the Court to water down constitutional guarantees and give the police the upper hand. That hydraulic pressure has probably never been greater than it is today.

Yet if the individual is no longer to be sovereign, if the police can pick him up whenever they do not like the cut of his jib, if they can "seize" and "search" him in their discretion, we enter a new regime. The decision to enter it should be made only after a full debate by the people of this country.

2. When Does a Stop Implicate the Fourth Amendment?

United States v. Mendenhall

446 U.S. 544 (1980)

STEWART, J., announced the judgment of the Court, in which REHNQUIST, J., joined. POWELL, J., filed an opinion concurring in part and in the judgment, in which BURGER, C.J., and BLACKMUN, J., joined. WHITE, J., filed a dissenting opinion, in which BRENNAN, MARSHALL, and STEVENS, JJ., joined.

The respondent was brought to trial in the United States District Court for the Eastern District of Michigan on a charge of possessing heroin with intent to distribute it. She moved to suppress the introduction at trial of the heroin as evidence against her on the ground that it had been acquired from her through an unconstitutional search and seizure by agents of the Drug Enforcement Administration (DEA). The District Court denied the respondent's motion, and she was convicted after a trial upon stipulated facts. The Court of Appeals reversed, finding the search of the respondent's person to have been unlawful. We granted certiorari to consider whether any right of the respondent guaranteed by the Fourth Amendment was violated in the circumstances presented by this case....

At the hearing in the trial court on the respondent's motion to suppress, it was established how the heroin she was charged with possessing had been obtained from her. The respondent arrived at the Detroit Metropolitan Airport on a commercial airline flight from Los Angeles early in the morning on February 10, 1976. As she disembarked from the airplane, she was observed by two agents of the DEA, who were present at the airport for the purpose of detecting unlawful traffic in narcotics. After observing the respondent's conduct, which appeared to the agents to be characteristic of persons unlawfully carrying narcotics, the agents approached her as she was walking through the concourse, identified themselves as federal agents, and asked to see her identification and airline ticket. The respondent produced her driver's license, which was in the name of Sylvia Mendenhall, and, in answer to a question of one of the agents, stated that she resided at the address appearing on the license. The airline ticket was issued in the name of "Annette Ford." When asked why the ticket bore a name different from her own, the respondent stated that she "just felt like using that name." In response to a further question, the respondent indicated that she had been in California only two days. Agent Anderson then specifically identified himself as a federal narcotics agent and, according to his testimony, the respondent "became quite shaken, extremely nervous. She had a hard time speaking."

After returning the airline ticket and driver's license to her, Agent Anderson asked the respondent if she would accompany him to the airport DEA office for further questions. She did so, although the record does not indicate a verbal response to the request. The office, which was located up one flight of stairs about 50 feet from where the respondent had first been approached, consisted of a reception area adjoined by three other rooms. At the office the agent asked the respondent if she would allow a search of her person and handbag and told her that she had the right to decline the search if she desired. She responded: "Go ahead." She then handed Agent Anderson her purse, which contained a receipt for an airline ticket that had been issued to "F. Bush" three days earlier for a flight from Pittsburgh through Chicago to Los Angeles. The agent asked whether this was the ticket that she had used for her flight to California, and the respondent stated that it was.

A female police officer then arrived to conduct the search of the respondent's person. She asked the agents if the respondent had consented to be searched. The agents said that she had, and the respondent followed the policewoman into a private room. There the policewoman again asked the respondent if she consented to the search, and the respondent replied that she did. The policewoman explained that the search would require that the respondent remove her clothing. The respondent stated that she had a plane to catch and was assured by the policewoman that if she were carrying no narcotics, there would be no problem. The respondent then began to disrobe without further comment. As the respondent removed her clothing, she took from her undergarments two small packages, one of which appeared to contain heroin, and handed both to the policewoman. The agents then arrested the respondent for possessing heroin.

It was on the basis of this evidence that the District Court denied the respondent's motion to suppress. The court concluded that the agents' conduct in initially approaching the respondent and asking to see her ticket and identification was a permissible investigative stop under the standards of *Terry v. Ohio* (1967) . . . finding that this conduct was based on specific and articulable facts that justified a suspicion of criminal activity. The court also found that the respondent had not been placed under arrest or otherwise detained when she was asked to accompany the agents to the DEA office, but had accompanied the agents " 'voluntarily in a spirit of apparent cooperation.' " It was the court's view that no arrest occurred until after the heroin had been found. Finally, the trial court found that the respondent "gave her consent to the search [in the DEA office] and . . . such consent was freely and voluntarily given."

The Court of Appeals reversed the respondent's subsequent conviction. . . .

. . . Here the Government concedes that its agents had neither a warrant nor probable cause to believe that the respondent was carrying narcotics when the agents conducted a search of the respondent's person. It is the Government's position, however, that the search was conducted pursuant to the respondent's consent, and thus was excepted from the requirements of both a warrant and probable cause. See *Schneckloth v. Bustamonte* (1973). Evidently, the Court of Appeals concluded that the respondent's apparent consent to the search was in fact not voluntarily given and was in any event the product of earlier official conduct violative of the Fourth Amendment. We must first consider, therefore, whether such conduct occurred, either on the concourse or in the DEA office at the airport.

■ ■ ■

The Fourth Amendment's requirement that searches and seizures be founded upon an objective justification, governs all seizures of the person, "including seizures that involve only a brief detention short of traditional arrest. Accordingly, if the respondent was "seized" when the DEA agents approached her on the concourse and asked questions of her, the agents' conduct in doing so was constitutional only if they reasonably suspected the respondent of wrongdoing. But "[o]bviously, not all personal intercourse between policemen and citizens involves 'seizures' of persons. Only when the officer, by means of physical force or show of authority, has in some way restrained the liberty of a citizen may we conclude that a 'seizure' has occurred."

■ ■ ■

We adhere to the view that a person is "seized" only when, by means of physical force or a show of authority, his freedom of movement is restrained. Only when such restraint is imposed is there any foundation whatever for invoking constitutional safeguards. The purpose of the Fourth Amendment is not to eliminate all contact between the police and the citizenry, but "to prevent arbitrary and oppressive interference by enforcement officials with the privacy and personal security of individuals." As long as the person to whom questions are put remains free to disregard the questions and walk away, there has been no intrusion upon that person's liberty or privacy as would under the Constitution require some particularized and objective justification.

Moreover, characterizing every street encounter between a citizen and the police as a "seizure," while not enhancing any interest secured by the Fourth Amendment, would impose wholly unrealistic restrictions upon a wide variety of legitimate law enforcement practices. The Court has on other occasions referred to the acknowledged need for police questioning as a tool in the effective enforcement of the criminal laws.

> "Without such investigation, those who were innocent might be falsely accused, those who were guilty might wholly escape prosecution, and many crimes would go unsolved. In short, the security of all would be diminished. *Haynes v. Washington* (1963)." *Schneckloth.*

We conclude that a person has been "seized" within the meaning of the Fourth Amendment only if, in view of all of the circumstances surrounding the incident, a reasonable person would have believed that he was not free to leave. Examples of circumstances that might indicate a seizure, even where the person did not attempt to leave, would be the threatening presence of several officers, the display of a weapon by an officer, some physical touching of the person of the citizen, or the use of language or tone of voice indicating that compliance with the officer's request might be compelled. In the absence of some such evidence, otherwise inoffensive contact between a member of the public and the police cannot, as a matter of law, amount to a seizure of that person.

On the facts of this case, no "seizure" of the respondent occurred. The events took place in the public concourse. The agents wore no uniforms and displayed no weapons. They did not summon the respondent to their presence, but instead approached her and identified themselves as federal agents. They requested, but did not demand to see the respondent's identification and ticket. Such conduct without more, did not amount to an intrusion upon any constitutionally protected interest. The respondent was not seized simply by reason of the fact that the agents approached her, asked her if she would show them her ticket and identification, and posed to her a few questions. Nor was it enough to establish a seizure that the person asking the questions was a law enforcement official.

■ ■ ■

Our conclusion that no seizure occurred is <u>not affected</u> by the fact that the respondent was not expressly told by the agents that she was free to decline to cooperate with their inquiry, for the voluntariness of her responses does not depend upon her having been so informed. We also reject the argument that the only inference to be drawn from the fact that the respondent acted in a manner so contrary to her self-interest is that she was compelled to answer the agents' questions. It may happen that a person makes statements to law enforcement officials that he later regrets, but the issue in such cases is not whether the statement was self-protective, but rather whether it was made voluntarily.

■ ■ ■

Although we have concluded that the initial encounter between the DEA agents and the respondent on the concourse at the Detroit Airport did not constitute an unlawful seizure, it is still arguable that the respondent's Fourth Amendment protections were violated when she went from the concourse to the DEA office. Such a violation might in turn infect the subsequent search of the respondent's person.

The District Court specifically found that the respondent accompanied the agents to the office " 'voluntarily in a spirit of apparent cooperation.' " . . . Notwithstanding this determination by the trial court, the Court of Appeals evidently concluded that the agents' request that the respondent accompany them converted the situation into an arrest requiring probable cause in order to be found lawful. But because the trial court's finding was sustained by the record, the Court of Appeals was mistaken in substituting for that finding its view of the evidence.

The question whether the respondent's consent to accompany the agents was in fact voluntary or was the product of duress or coercion, express or implied, is to be determined by the totality of all the circumstances, *Schneckloth v. Bustamonte,* and is a matter which the Government has the burden of proving. The respondent herself did not testify at the hearing. The Government's evidence showed that the respondent was not told that she had to go to the office, but was simply asked if she would accompany the officers. There were neither threats nor any show of force. The respondent had been questioned only briefly, and her ticket and identification were returned to her before she was asked to accompany the officers.

On the other hand, it is argued that the incident would reasonably have appeared coercive to the respondent, who was 22 years old and had not been graduated from high school. It is additionally suggested that the respondent, a female and a Negro, may have felt unusually threatened by the officers, who were white males. While these factors were not irrelevant, neither were they decisive, and the totality of the evidence in this case was plainly adequate to support the District Court's finding that the respondent voluntarily consented to accompany the officers to the DEA office.

Because the search of the respondent's person was not preceded by an impermissible seizure of her person, it cannot be contended that her apparent consent to the subsequent search was infected by an unlawful detention.

■ ■ ■

We conclude that the District Court's determination that the respondent consented to the search of her person "freely and voluntarily" was sustained by the evidence and that the Court of Appeals was, therefore, in error in setting it aside. Accordingly, the judgment of the Court of Appeals is reversed, and the case is remanded to that court for further proceedings.

It is so ordered.

Justice POWELL, with whom Chief Justice BURGER and Justice BLACKMUN join, concurring in part and concurring in the judgment.

Because neither of the courts below considered the question, I do not reach the Government's contention that the agents did not "seize" the respondent within the meaning of the Fourth Amendment. In my view, we may assume for present purposes that the stop did constitute a seizure. I would hold—as did the District Court—that the federal agents had reasonable suspicion that the respondent was engaging in criminal activity, and, therefore, that they did not violate the Fourth Amendment by stopping the respondent for routine questioning.

■ ■ ■

Justice WHITE, with whom Justice BRENNAN, Justice MARSHALL, and Justice STEVENS join, dissenting.

The Court today concludes that agents of the Drug Enforcement Administration (DEA) acted lawfully in stopping a traveler changing planes in an airport terminal and escorting her to a DEA office for a strip-search of her person. This result is particularly curious because a majority of the Members of the Court refuse to reject the conclusion that Ms. Mendenhall was "seized," while a separate majority decline to hold that there were reasonable grounds to justify a seizure. Mr. Justice Stewart concludes that the DEA agents acted lawfully, regardless of whether there were any reasonable grounds for suspecting Ms. Mendenhall of criminal activity, because he finds that Ms.

Mendenhall was not "seized" by the DEA agents, even though throughout the proceedings below the Government never questioned the fact that a seizure had occurred necessitating a showing of antecedent reasonable suspicion. Mr. Justice Powell's opinion concludes that even though Ms. Mendenhall may have been "seized," the seizure was lawful because her behavior while changing planes in the airport provided reasonable suspicion that she was engaging in criminal activity. The Court then concludes, based on the absence of evidence that Ms. Mendenhall resisted her detention, that she voluntarily consented to being taken to the DEA office, even though she in fact had no choice in the matter. This conclusion is inconsistent with our recognition that consent cannot be presumed from a showing of acquiescence to authority.

■ ■ ■

Throughout the lower court proceedings in this case, the Government never questioned that the initial stop of Ms. Mendenhall was a "seizure" that required reasonable suspicion. Rather, the Government sought to justify the stop by arguing that Ms. Mendenhall's behavior had given rise to reasonable suspicion because it was consistent with portions of the so-called "drug courier profile," an informal amalgam of characteristics thought to be associated with persons carrying illegal drugs. Having failed to convince the Court of Appeals that the DEA agents had reasonable suspicion for the stop, the Government seeks reversal here by arguing for the first time that no "seizure" occurred, an argument that Mr. Justice Stewart now accepts, thereby pretermitting the question whether there was reasonable suspicion to stop Ms. Mendenhall. Mr. Justice Stewart's opinion not only is inconsistent with our usual refusal to reverse judgments on grounds not raised below, but it also addresses a fact-bound question with a totality-of-circumstances assessment that is best left in the first instance to the trial court, particularly since the question was not litigated below and hence we cannot be sure is adequately addressed by the record before us.

Mr. Justice Stewart believes that a "seizure" within the meaning of the Fourth Amendment occurs when an individual's freedom of movement is restrained by means of physical force or a show of authority. Although it is undisputed that Ms. Mendenhall was not free to leave after the DEA agents stopped her and inspected her identification, Mr. Justice Stewart concludes that she was not "seized" because he finds that, under the totality of the circumstances, a reasonable person would have believed that she was free to leave. While basing this finding on an alleged absence from the record of objective evidence indicating that Ms. Mendenhall was not free to ignore the officer's inquiries and continue on her way, Mr. Justice Stewart's opinion brushes off the fact that this asserted evidentiary deficiency may be largely attributable to the fact that the "seizure" question was never raised below. In assessing what the record does reveal, the opinion discounts certain objective factors that would tend to support a "seizure" finding, while relying on contrary factors inconclusive even under its own illustrations of how a "seizure" may be established. Moreover, although Mr. Justice Stewart's opinion purports to make its "seizure" finding turn on objective factors known to the person accosted, in distinguishing prior decisions holding that investigatory stops constitute "seizures," it does not rely on differences in the extent to which persons accosted could reasonably believe that they were free to leave. Even if one believes the Government should be permitted to raise the "seizure" question in this Court, the proper course would be to direct a remand to the District Court for an evidentiary hearing on the question, rather than to decide it in the first instance in this Court.

Assuming, as we should, that Ms. Mendenhall was "seized" within the meaning of the Fourth Amendment when she was stopped by the DEA agents, the legality of that stop turns on whether there were reasonable grounds for suspecting her of criminal activity at the time of the stop. To establish that there was reasonable suspicion for the stop, it was necessary for the police at least to "be able to point to specific and articulable facts which, taken together with rational inferences from those facts, reasonably warrant that intrusion." *Terry v. Ohio.*

At the time they stopped Ms. Mendenhall, the DEA agents' suspicion that she was engaged in criminal activity was based solely on their brief observations of her conduct at the airport. The officers had no advance information that Ms. Mendenhall, or anyone on her flight, would be carrying drugs. What the agents observed Ms. Mendenhall do in the airport was not "unusual conduct" which would lead an experienced officer reasonably to conclude that criminal activity was afoot, rather the kind of behavior that could reasonably be expected of anyone changing planes in an airport terminal.

None of the aspects of Ms. Mendenhall's conduct, either alone or in combination, were sufficient to provide reasonable suspicion that she was engaged in criminal activity. The fact that Ms. Mendenhall was the last person to alight from a flight originating in Los Angeles was plainly insufficient to provide a basis for stopping her. Nor was the fact that her flight originated from a "major source city," for the mere proximity of a person to areas with a high incidence of drug activity or to persons known to be drug addicts, does not provide the necessary reasonable suspicion for an investigatory stop. Under the circumstances of this case, the DEA agents' observations that Ms. Mendenhall claimed no luggage and changed airlines were also insufficient to provide reasonable suspicion. Unlike the situation in *Terry v. Ohio*, where "nothing in [the suspects'] conduct from the time [the officer] first noticed them until the time he confronted them and identified himself as a police officer gave him sufficient reason to negate [his] hypothesis" of criminal behavior, Ms. Mendenhall's subsequent conduct negated any reasonable inference that she was traveling a long distance without luggage or changing her ticket to a different airline to avoid detection. Agent Anderson testified that he heard the ticket agent tell Ms. Mendenhall that her ticket to Pittsburgh already was in order and that all she needed was a boarding pass for the flight. Thus it should have been plain to an experienced observer that Ms. Mendenhall's failure to claim luggage was attributable to the fact that she was already ticketed through to Pittsburgh on a different airline. Because Agent Anderson's suspicion that Ms. Mendenhall was transporting narcotics could be based only on "his inchoate and unparticularized suspicion or 'hunch,'" rather than "specific reasonable inferences which he is entitled to draw from the facts in light of his experience," he was not justified in "seizing" Ms. Mendenhall.

Because Ms. Mendenhall was being illegally detained at the time of the search of her person, her suppression motion should have been granted in the absence of evidence to dissipate the taint.

California v. Hodari D.

499 U.S. 621 (1991)

SCALIA, J., delivered the opinion of the Court, in which REHNQUIST, C.J., BLACKMUN, KENNEDY, SOUTER, WHITE, and O'CONNOR, JJ., joined. STEVENS, J., filed a dissenting opinion, in which MARSHALL, J., joined.

Late one evening in April 1988, Officers Brian McColgin and Jerry Pertoso were on patrol in a high-crime area of Oakland, California. They were dressed in street clothes but wearing jackets with "Police" embossed on both front and back. Their unmarked car proceeded west on Foothill Boulevard, and turned south onto 63rd Avenue. As they rounded the corner, they saw four or five youths huddled around a small red car parked at the curb. When the youths saw the officers' car approaching they apparently panicked, and took flight. The respondent here, Hodari D., and one companion ran west through an alley; the others fled south. The red car also headed south, at a high rate of speed.

The officers were suspicious and gave chase. McColgin remained in the car and continued south on 63rd Avenue; Pertoso left the car, ran back north along 63rd, then west on Foothill Boulevard, and turned south on 62nd Avenue. Hodari, meanwhile, emerged from the alley onto 62nd and ran north. Looking behind as he ran, he did not turn and see Pertoso until the officer was almost upon him, whereupon he tossed away what appeared to be a small rock. A moment later, Pertoso tackled Hodari, handcuffed him, and radioed for assistance. Hodari was found to be carrying $130 in cash and a pager; and the rock he had discarded was found to be crack cocaine.

In the juvenile proceeding brought against him, Hodari moved to suppress the evidence relating to the cocaine. The court denied the motion without opinion. The California Court of Appeal reversed, holding that Hodari had been "seized" when he saw Officer Pertoso running towards him, that this seizure was unreasonable under the Fourth Amendment, and that the evidence of cocaine had to be suppressed as the fruit of that illegal seizure. The California Supreme Court denied the State's application for review. We granted certiorari.

As this case comes to us, the only issue presented is whether, at the time he dropped the drugs, Hodari had been "seized" within the meaning of the

Fourth Amendment. If so, respondent argues, the drugs were the fruit of that seizure and the evidence concerning them was properly excluded. If not, the drugs were abandoned by Hodari and lawfully recovered by the police, and the evidence should have been admitted. (In addition, of course, Pertoso's seeing the rock of cocaine, at least if he recognized it as such, would provide reasonable suspicion for the unquestioned seizure that occurred when he tackled Hodari.)

■ ■ ■

To say that an arrest is effected by the slightest application of physical force, despite the arrestee's escape, is not to say that for Fourth Amendment purposes there is a *continuing* arrest during the period of fugitivity. If, for example, Pertoso had laid his hands upon Hodari to arrest him, but Hodari had broken away and had *then* cast away the cocaine, it would hardly be realistic to say that that disclosure had been made during the course of an arrest. . . . The present case, however, is even one step further removed. It does not involve the application of any physical force; Hodari was untouched by Officer Pertoso at the time he discarded the cocaine. His defense relies instead upon the proposition that a seizure occurs "when the officer, by means of physical force *or show of authority,* has in some way restrained the liberty of a citizen." Hodari contends (and we accept as true for purposes of this decision) that Pertoso's pursuit qualified as a "show of authority" calling upon Hodari to halt. The narrow question before us is whether, with respect to a show of authority as with respect to application of physical force, a seizure occurs even though the subject does not yield. We hold that it does not.

The language of the Fourth Amendment, of course, cannot sustain respondent's contention. The word "seizure" readily bears the meaning of a laying on of hands or application of physical force to restrain movement, even when it is ultimately unsuccessful. ("She seized the purse-snatcher, but he broke out of her grasp.") It does not remotely apply, however, to the prospect of a policeman yelling "Stop, in the name of the law!" at a fleeing form that continues to flee. That is no seizure. Nor can the result respondent wishes to achieve be produced—indirectly, as it were—by suggesting that Pertoso's uncomplied-with show of authority was a common-law arrest, and then appealing to the principle that all common-law arrests are seizures. An arrest requires *either* physical force (as described above) *or,* where that is absent, *submission* to the assertion of authority.

■ ■ ■

We do not think it desirable, even as a policy matter, to stretch the Fourth Amendment beyond its words and beyond the meaning of arrest, as respondent urges. Street pursuits always place the public at some risk, and compliance with police orders to stop should therefore be encouraged. Only a few of those orders, we must presume, will be without adequate basis, and since the addressee has no ready means of identifying the deficient ones it almost invariably is the responsible course to comply. Unlawful orders will not be deterred, moreover, by sanctioning through the exclusionary rule those of them that are *not* obeyed. Since policemen do not command "Stop!" expecting to be ignored, or give chase hoping to be outrun, it fully suffices to apply the deterrent to their genuine, successful seizures.

Respondent contends that his position is sustained by the so-called *Mendenhall* test, formulated by Justice Stewart's opinion in *United States v. Mendenhall* (1980), and adopted by the Court in later cases, see *Michigan v. Chesternut* (1988)... "[A] person has been 'seized' within the meaning of the Fourth Amendment only if, in view of all the circumstances surrounding the incident, a reasonable person would have believed that he was not free to leave."

■ ■ ■

Quite relevant to the present case, however, was our decision in *Brower v. Inyo County* (1989). In that case, police cars with flashing lights had chased the decedent for 20 miles—surely an adequate "show of authority"—but he did not stop until his fatal crash into a police-erected blockade. The issue was whether his death could be held to be the consequence of an unreasonable seizure in violation of the Fourth Amendment. We did not even consider the possibility that a seizure could have occurred during the course of the chase because, as we explained, that "show of authority" did not produce his stop. And we discussed an opinion of Justice Holmes, involving a situation not much different from the present case, where revenue agents had picked up containers dropped by moonshiners whom they were pursuing without adequate warrant. The containers were not excluded as the product of an unlawful seizure because "[t]he defendant's own acts, and those of his associates, disclosed the jug, the jar and the bottle—and there was no seizure in the sense of the law when the officers examined the contents of each after they had been abandoned." *Hester v. United States* (1924). The same is true here.

In sum, assuming that Pertoso's pursuit in the present case constituted a "show of authority" enjoining Hodari to halt, since Hodari did not comply with that injunction he was not seized until he was tackled. The cocaine abandoned while he was running was in this case not the fruit of a seizure, and his motion to exclude evidence of it was properly denied. We reverse the decision of the California Court of Appeal, and remand for further proceedings not inconsistent with this opinion.

It is so ordered.

Justice STEVENS, with whom Justice MARSHALL joins, dissenting.

The Court's narrow construction of the word "seizure" represents a significant, and in my view, unfortunate, departure from prior case law construing the Fourth Amendment. Almost a quarter of a century ago, in two landmark cases—one broadening the protection of individual privacy, and the other broadening the powers of law enforcement officers—we rejected the method of Fourth Amendment analysis that today's majority endorses. In particular, the Court now adopts a definition of "seizure" that is unfaithful to a long line of Fourth Amendment cases. Even if the Court were defining seizure for the first time, which it is not, the definition that it chooses today is profoundly unwise. In its decision, the Court assumes, without acknowledging, that a police officer may now fire his weapon at an innocent citizen and not implicate the Fourth Amendment—as long as he misses his target.

■ ■ ■

The expansive construction of the word "seizure" in the *Katz* case [(1967)] provided an appropriate predicate for the Court's holding in *Terry v. Ohio* (1968), the following year. Prior to *Terry*, the Fourth Amendment proscribed any seizure of the person that was not supported by the same probable-cause showing that would justify a custodial arrest. Given the fact that street encounters between citizens and police officers "are incredibly rich in diversity," the Court recognized the need for flexibility and held that "reasonable" suspicion—a quantum of proof less demanding than probable cause—was adequate to justify a stop for investigatory purposes. As a corollary to the lesser justification for the stop, the Court necessarily concluded that the word "seizure" in the Fourth Amendment encompasses official restraints on individual freedom that fall short of a common-law arrest. Thus, *Terry* broadened the range of encounters between the police and the citizen encompassed within the term "seizure," while at the same time, lowering the standard of proof necessary to justify a "stop" in the newly expanded category of seizures now covered by the Fourth Amendment.

■ ■ ■

The decisions in *Katz* and *Terry* unequivocally reject the notion that the common law of arrest defines the limits of the term "seizure" in the Fourth Amendment. In *Katz*, the Court abandoned the narrow view that would have limited a seizure to a material object, and, instead, held that the Fourth Amendment extended to the recording of oral statements. And in *Terry*, the Court abandoned its traditional view that a seizure under the Fourth Amendment required probable cause, and, instead, expanded the definition of a seizure to include an investigative stop made on less than probable cause. Thus, the major premise underpinning the majority's entire analysis today—that the common law of arrest should define the term "seizure" for Fourth Amendment purposes—is seriously flawed. The Court mistakenly hearkens back to common law, while ignoring the expansive approach that the Court has taken in Fourth Amendment analysis since *Katz* and *Terry*.

The Court fares no better when it tries to explain why the proper definition of the term "seizure" has been an open question until today. In *Terry*, in addition to stating that a seizure occurs "whenever a police officer accosts an individual and restrains his freedom to walk away," the Court noted that a seizure occurs "when the officer, by means of physical force or show of authority, has in some way restrained the liberty of a citizen." ... The touchstone of a seizure is the restraint of an individual's personal liberty *"in some way."* Today the Court's reaction to respondent's reliance on *Terry* is to demonstrate that in "show of force" cases no common-law arrest occurs unless the arrestee *submits.* That answer, however, is plainly insufficient given the holding in *Terry* that the

Fourth Amendment applies to stops that need not be justified by probable cause in the absence of a full-blown arrest.

In *United States v. Mendenhall*, the Court "adhere[d] to the view that a person is 'seized' only when, by means of physical force or a show of authority, his freedom of movement is restrained." Court looked to whether the citizen who is questioned "remains free to disregard the questions and walk away," and if he or she is able to do so, then "there has been no intrusion upon that person's liberty or privacy" that would require some "particularized and objective justification" under the Constitution. The test for a "seizure," as formulated by the Court in *Mendenhall*, was whether, "in view of all of the circumstances surrounding the incident, a reasonable person would have believed that he was not free to leave." Examples of seizures include "the threatening presence of several officers, the display of a weapon by an officer, some physical touching of the person of the citizen, or the use of language or tone of voice indicating that compliance with the officer's request might be compelled." The Court's unwillingness today to adhere to the "reasonable person" standard, as formulated by Justice Stewart in *Mendenhall*, marks an unnecessary departure from Fourth Amendment case law.

The Court today draws the novel conclusion that even though no seizure can occur *unless* the *Mendenhall* reasonable person standard is met, the fact that the standard has been met does not necessarily mean that a seizure has occurred. . . .

> "As we have noted elsewhere:
>
> Obviously, not all personal intercourse between policemen and citizens involves 'seizures' of persons. Only when the officer, by means of physical force or show of authority, has restrained the liberty of a citizen may we conclude that a 'seizure' has occurred.
>
> While applying such a test is relatively straightforward in a situation resembling a traditional arrest, the protection against unreasonable seizures also extends to 'seizures that involve only a brief detention short of traditional arrest.' What has evolved from our cases is a determination that an initially consensual encounter between a police officer and a citizen can be transformed into a seizure or detention within the meaning of the Fourth Amendment, 'if, in view of all the circumstances surrounding the incident, a reasonable person would have believed that he was not free to leave.' . . ."

Even though momentary, a seizure occurs whenever an objective evaluation of a police officer's show of force conveys the message that the citizen is not entirely free to leave—in other words, that his or her liberty is being restrained in a significant way. . . .

Finally, it is noteworthy that in *Michigan v. Chesternut*, the State asked us to repudiate the reasonable person standard developed in *Terry, Mendenhall, Delgado* (1984), and *Royer* (1983). We decided, however, to "adhere to our traditional contextual approach." In our opinion, we described Justice Stewart's analysis in *Mendenhall* as "a test to be applied in determining whether 'a person has been "seized" within the meaning of the Fourth Amendment'" and noted that "[t]he

Court has since embraced this test." Moreover, in commenting on the virtues of the test, we explained that it focused on the police officer's conduct....

Whatever else one may think of today's decision, it unquestionably represents a departure from earlier Fourth Amendment case law. The notion that our prior cases contemplated a distinction between seizures effected by a touching on the one hand, and those effected by a show of force on the other hand, and that all of our repeated descriptions of the *Mendenhall* test stated only a necessary, but not a sufficient, condition for finding seizures in the latter category, is nothing if not creative lawmaking. Moreover, by narrowing the definition of the term seizure, instead of enlarging the scope of reasonable justifications for seizures, the Court has significantly limited the protection provided to the ordinary citizen by the Fourth Amendment....

In some cases, of course, it is immediately apparent at which moment the suspect submitted to an officer's show of force. For example, if the victim is killed by an officer's gunshot, as in *Tennessee v. Garner* (1985)....

It is too early to know the consequences of the Court's holding. If carried to its logical conclusion, it will encourage unlawful displays of force that will frighten countless innocent citizens into surrendering whatever privacy rights they may still have. It is not too soon, however, to note the irony in the fact that the Court's own justification for its result is its analysis of the rules of the common law of arrest that antedated our decisions in *Katz* and *Terry*. Yet, even in those days the common law provided the citizen with protection against an attempt to make an unlawful arrest. The central message of *Katz* and *Terry* was that the protection the Fourth Amendment provides to the average citizen is not rigidly confined by ancient common-law precept. The message that today's literal-minded majority conveys is that the common law, rather than our understanding of the Fourth Amendment as it has developed over the last quarter of a century, defines, and limits, the scope of a seizure. The Court today defines a seizure as commencing, not with egregious police conduct, but rather with submission by the citizen. Thus, it both delays the point at which "the Fourth Amendment becomes relevant" to an encounter and limits the range of encounters that will come under the heading of "seizure." Today's qualification of the Fourth Amendment means that innocent citizens may remain "secure in their persons... against unreasonable searches and seizures" only at the discretion of the police.

Some sacrifice of freedom always accompanies an expansion in the Executive's unreviewable law enforcement powers. A court more sensitive to the purposes of the Fourth Amendment would insist on greater rewards to society before decreeing the sacrifice it makes today. Alexander Bickel presciently wrote that "many actions of government have two aspects: their immediate, necessarily intended, practical effects, and their perhaps unintended or unappreciated bearing on values we hold to have more general and permanent interest." The Court's immediate concern with containing criminal activity poses a substantial, though unintended, threat to values that are fundamental and enduring.

I respectfully dissent.

United States v. Drayton

536 U.S. 194 (2002)

KENNEDY, J., delivered the opinion of the Court, in which REHNQUIST, C.J., and O'CONNOR, SCALIA, THOMAS, and BREYER, JJ., joined. SOUTER, J., filed a dissenting opinion, in which STEVENS and GINSBURG, JJ., joined.

The Fourth Amendment permits police officers to approach bus passengers at random to ask questions and to request their consent to searches, provided a reasonable person would understand that he or she is free to refuse. This case requires us to determine whether officers must advise bus passengers during these encounters of their right not to cooperate.

■ ■ ■

On February 4, 1999, respondents Christopher Drayton and Clifton Brown, Jr., were traveling on a Greyhound bus en route from Ft. Lauderdale, Florida, to Detroit, Michigan. The bus made a scheduled stop in Tallahassee, Florida. The passengers were required to disembark so the bus could be refueled and cleaned. As the passengers reboarded, the driver checked their tickets and then left to complete paperwork inside the terminal. As he left, the driver allowed three members of the Tallahassee Police Department to board the bus as part of a routine drug and weapons interdiction effort. The officers were dressed in plain clothes and carried concealed weapons and visible badges.

Once onboard Officer Hoover knelt on the driver's seat and faced the rear of the bus. He could observe the passengers and ensure the safety of the two other officers without blocking the aisle or otherwise obstructing the bus exit. Officers Lang and Blackburn went to the rear of the bus. Blackburn remained stationed there, facing forward. Lang worked his way toward the front of the bus, speaking with individual passengers as he went. He asked the passengers about their travel plans and sought to match passengers with luggage in the overhead racks. To avoid blocking the aisle, Lang stood next to or just behind each passenger with whom he spoke.

According to Lang's testimony, passengers who declined to cooperate with him or who chose to exit the bus at any time would have been allowed to do so without argument. In Lang's experience, however, most people are willing to cooperate. Some passengers go so far as to commend the police for their efforts to ensure the safety of their travel. Lang could recall five to six instances in the previous year in which passengers had declined to have their luggage searched. It also was common for passengers to leave the bus for a cigarette or a snack while the officers were on board. Lang sometimes informed passengers of their right to refuse to cooperate. On the day in question, however, he did not.

Respondents were seated next to each other on the bus. Drayton was in the aisle seat, Brown in the seat next to the window. Lang approached respondents from the rear and leaned over Drayton's shoulder. He held up his badge long enough for respondents to identify him as a police officer. With his face 12-to-

18 inches away from Drayton's, Lang spoke in a voice just loud enough for respondents to hear:

> "I'm Investigator Lang with the Tallahassee Police Department. We're conducting bus interdiction [sic], attempting to deter drugs and illegal weapons being transported on the bus. Do you have any bags on the bus?"

Both respondents pointed to a single green bag in the overhead luggage rack. Lang asked, "Do you mind if I check it?" and Brown responded, "Go ahead." Lang handed the bag to Officer Blackburn to check. The bag contained no contraband.

Officer Lang noticed that both respondents were wearing heavy jackets and baggy pants despite the warm weather. In Lang's experience drug traffickers often use baggy clothing to conceal weapons or narcotics. The officer thus asked Brown if he had any weapons or drugs in his possession. And he asked Brown, "Do you mind if I check your person?" Brown answered, "Sure," and cooperated by leaning up in his seat, pulling a cell phone out of his pocket, and opening up his jacket. Lang reached across Drayton and patted down Brown's jacket and pockets, including his waist area, sides, and upper thighs. In both thigh areas, Lang detected hard objects similar to drug packages detected on other occasions. Lang arrested and handcuffed Brown. Officer Hoover escorted Brown from the bus.

Lang then asked Drayton, "Mind if I check you?" Drayton responded by lifting his hands about eight inches from his legs. Lang conducted a patdown of Drayton's thighs and detected hard objects similar to those found on Brown. He arrested Drayton and escorted him from the bus. A further search revealed that respondents had duct-taped plastic bundles of powder cocaine between several pairs of their boxer shorts. Brown possessed three bundles containing 483 grams of cocaine. Drayton possessed two bundles containing 295 grams of cocaine.

Respondents . . . moved to suppress the cocaine, arguing that the consent to the patdown search was invalid. Following a hearing at which only Officer Lang testified, the United States District Court for the Northern District of Florida denied their motions to suppress. The District Court determined that the police conduct was not coercive and respondents' consent to the search was voluntary. The District Court pointed to the fact that the officers were dressed in plain clothes, did not brandish their badges in an authoritative manner, did not make a general announcement to the entire bus, and did not address anyone in a menacing tone of voice. It noted that the officers did not block the aisle or the exit, and stated that it was "obvious that [respondents] can get up and leave, as can the people ahead of them." The District Court concluded: "[E]verything that took place between Officer Lang and Mr. Drayton and Mr. Brown suggests that it was cooperative. There was nothing coercive, there was nothing confrontational about it."

The Court of Appeals for the Eleventh Circuit reversed and remanded with instructions to grant respondents' motions to suppress.

■ ■ ■

We granted certiorari. The respondents, we conclude, were not seized and their consent to the search was voluntary; and we reverse.

II

Law enforcement officers do not violate the Fourth Amendment's prohibition of unreasonable seizures merely by approaching individuals on the street or in other public places and putting questions to them if they are willing to listen. *Florida v. Royer* (1983). Even when law enforcement officers have no basis for suspecting a particular individual, they may pose questions, ask for identification, and request consent to search luggage—provided they do not induce cooperation by coercive means....

The Court has addressed on a previous occasion the specific question of drug interdiction efforts on buses. In [*Florida v.*] *Bostick* (1991), two police officers requested a bus passenger's consent to a search of his luggage. The passenger agreed, and the resulting search revealed cocaine in his suitcase. The Florida Supreme Court suppressed the cocaine. In doing so it adopted a *per se* rule that due to the cramped confines onboard a bus the act of questioning would deprive a person of his or her freedom of movement and so constitute a seizure under the Fourth Amendment.

This Court reversed. *Bostick* first made it clear that for the most part *per se* rules are inappropriate in the Fourth Amendment context. The proper inquiry necessitates a consideration of "all the circumstances surrounding the encounter." The Court noted next that the traditional rule, which states that a seizure does not occur so long as a reasonable person would feel free "to disregard the police and go about his business," *California v. Hodari D.* (1991), is not an accurate measure of the coercive effect of a bus encounter. A passenger may not want to get off a bus if there is a risk it will depart before the opportunity to reboard. *Bostick*. A bus rider's movements are confined in this sense, but this is the natural result of choosing to take the bus; it says nothing about whether the police conduct is coercive. The proper inquiry "is whether a reasonable person would feel free to decline the officers' requests or otherwise terminate the encounter." Finally, the Court rejected Bostick's argument that he must have been seized because no reasonable person would consent to a search of luggage containing drugs. The reasonable person test, the Court explained, is objective and "presupposes an *innocent* person."

In light of the limited record, *Bostick* refrained from deciding whether a seizure occurred. The Court, however, identified two factors "particularly worth noting" on remand. First, although it was obvious that an officer was armed, he did not remove the gun from its pouch or use it in a threatening way. Second, the officer advised the passenger that he could refuse consent to the search. [*Bostick factor* — handwritten marginal note]

Relying upon this latter factor, the Eleventh Circuit has adopted what is in effect a *per se* rule that evidence obtained during suspicionless drug interdiction efforts aboard buses must be suppressed unless the officers have advised passengers of their right not to cooperate and to refuse consent to a search....

Although the Court of Appeals has disavowed a *per se* requirement, the lack of an explicit warning to passengers is the only element common to all its cases. *United States v. Washington* (1998) ("It seems obvious to us that if police officers genuinely want to ensure that their encounters with bus passengers remain absolutely voluntary, they can simply say so. Without such notice in this case, we do not feel a reasonable person would have felt able to decline the agents' requests").... The Court of Appeals erred in adopting this approach.

Applying the *Bostick* framework to the facts of this particular case, we conclude that the police did not seize respondents when they boarded the bus and began questioning passengers. The officers gave the passengers no reason to believe that they were required to answer the officers' questions. When Officer Lang approached respondents, he did not brandish a weapon or make any intimidating movements. He left the aisle free so that respondents could exit. He spoke to passengers one by one and in a polite, quiet voice. Nothing he said would suggest to a reasonable person that he or she was barred from leaving the bus or otherwise terminating the encounter.

There were ample grounds for the District Court to conclude that "everything that took place between Officer Lang and [respondents] suggests that it was cooperative" and that there "was nothing coercive [or] confrontational" about the encounter. There was no application of force, no intimidating movement, no overwhelming show of force, no brandishing of weapons, no blocking of exits, no threat, no command, not even an authoritative tone of voice. It is beyond question that had this encounter occurred on the street, it would be constitutional. The fact that an encounter takes place on a bus does not on its own transform standard police questioning of citizens into an illegal seizure. Indeed, because many fellow passengers are present to witness officers' conduct, a reasonable person may feel even more secure in his or her decision not to cooperate with police on a bus than in other circumstances....

Drayton contends that even if Brown's cooperation with the officers was consensual, Drayton was seized because no reasonable person would feel free to terminate the encounter with the officers after Brown had been arrested. The Court of Appeals did not address this claim; and in any event the argument fails. The arrest of one person does not mean that everyone around him has been seized by police. If anything, Brown's arrest should have put Drayton on notice of the consequences of continuing the encounter by answering the officers' questions. Even after arresting Brown, Lang addressed Drayton in a polite manner and provided him with no indication that he was required to answer Lang's questions....

The judgment of the Court of Appeals is reversed, and the case is remanded for further proceedings consistent with this opinion.

It is so ordered.

Justice SOUTER, with whom Justice STEVENS and Justice GINSBURG join, dissenting.

Anyone who travels by air today submits to searches of the person and luggage as a condition of boarding the aircraft. It is universally accepted that such intrusions are necessary to hedge against risks that, nowadays, even small children understand. The commonplace precautions of air travel have not, thus far, been justified for ground transportation, however, and no such conditions have been placed on passengers getting on trains or buses. There is therefore an air of unreality about the Court's explanation that bus passengers consent to searches of their luggage to "enhanc[e] their own safety and the safety of those around them." Nor are the other factual assessments underlying the Court's conclusion in favor of the Government more convincing.

The issue we took to review is whether the police's examination of the bus passengers, including respondents, amounted to a suspicionless seizure under the Fourth Amendment. If it did, any consent to search was plainly invalid as a product of the illegal seizure.

■ ■ ■

Florida v. Bostick established the framework for determining whether the bus passengers were seized in the constitutional sense. In that case, we rejected the position that police questioning of bus passengers was a *per se* seizure, and held instead that the issue of seizure was to be resolved under an objective test considering all circumstances: whether a reasonable passenger would have felt "free to decline the officers' requests or otherwise terminate the encounter." We thus applied to a bus passenger the more general criterion, whether the person questioned was free "to ignore the police presence and go about his business."

■ ■ ■

When the bus in question made its scheduled stop in Tallahassee, the passengers were required to disembark while the vehicle was cleaned and refueled. When the passengers returned, they gave their tickets to the driver, who kept them and then left himself, after giving three police officers permission to board the bus in his absence. Although they were not in uniform, the officers displayed badges and identified themselves as police. One stationed himself in the driver's seat by the door at the front, facing back to observe the passengers. The two others went to the rear, from which they worked their way forward, with one of them speaking to passengers, the other backing him up. They necessarily addressed the passengers at very close range; the aisle was only 15 inches wide, and each seat only 18. The quarters were cramped further by the overhead rack, 19 inches above the top of the passenger seats. The passenger by the window could not have stood up straight and the face of the nearest officer was only a foot or 18 inches from the face of the nearest passenger being addressed. During the exchanges, the officers looked down, and the passengers had to look up if they were to face the police. The officer asking the questions spoke quietly. He prefaced his requests for permission to search luggage and do a body patdown by identifying himself by name as a police investigator "conducting bus interdiction" and saying, " 'We would like for your cooperation. Do you have any luggage on the bus?' "

Thus, for reasons unexplained, the driver with the tickets entitling the passengers to travel had yielded his custody of the bus and its seated travelers to three police officers, whose authority apparently superseded the driver's own. The officers took control of the entire passenger compartment, one stationed at the door keeping surveillance of all the occupants, the others working forward from the back. With one officer right behind him and the other one forward, a third officer accosted each passenger at quarters extremely close and so cramped that as many as half the passengers could not even have stood to face the speaker. None was asked whether he was willing to converse with the police or to take part in the enquiry. Instead the officer said the police were "conducting bus interdiction," in the course of which they "would like... cooperation." The reasonable inference was that the "interdiction" was not a consensual exercise, but one the police would carry out whatever the circumstances; that they would prefer "cooperation" but would not let the lack of it stand in their way. There was no contrary indication that day, since no passenger had refused the cooperation requested, and there was no reason for any passenger to believe that the driver would return and the trip resume until the police were satisfied. The scene was set and an atmosphere of obligatory participation was established by this introduction. Later requests to search prefaced with "Do you mind..." would naturally have been understood in the terms with which the encounter began.

It is very hard to imagine that either Brown or Drayton would have believed that he stood to lose nothing if he refused to cooperate with the police, or that he had any free choice to ignore the police altogether. No reasonable passenger could have believed that, only an uncomprehending one. It is neither here nor there that the interdiction was conducted by three officers, not one, as a safety precaution. The fact was that there were three, and when Brown and Drayton were called upon to respond, each one was presumably conscious of an officer in front watching, one at his side questioning him, and one behind for cover, in case he became unruly, perhaps, or "cooperation" was not forthcoming. The situation is much like the one in the alley, with civilians in close quarters, unable to move effectively, being told their cooperation is expected. While I am not prepared to say that no bus interrogation and search can pass the *Bostick* test without a warning that passengers are free to say no, the facts here surely required more from the officers than a quiet tone of voice. A police officer who is certain to get his way has no need to shout.

It is true of course that the police testified that a bus passenger sometimes says no, but that evidence does nothing to cast the facts here in a different light. We have no way of knowing the circumstances in which a passenger elsewhere refused a request; maybe that has happened only when the police have told passengers they had a right to refuse (as the officers sometimes advised them).

■ ■ ■

In any event, I am less concerned to parse this case against [*INS v.*] *Delgado* [(1984)] than to apply *Bostick's* totality of circumstances test, and to ask whether a passenger would reasonably have felt free to end his encounter with the three officers by saying no and ignoring them thereafter. In my view the answer is clear. The Court's contrary conclusion tells me that the majority cannot see what Justice Stewart saw, and I respectfully dissent.

3. Reasonable Suspicion Standard

United States v. Arvizu

534 U.S. 266 (2002)

R<small>EHNQUIST</small>, C.J., delivered the opinion for a unanimous Court.

Respondent Ralph Arvizu was stopped by a border patrol agent while driving on an unpaved road in a remote area of southeastern Arizona. A search of his vehicle turned up more than 100 pounds of marijuana. The District Court for the District of Arizona denied respondent's motion to suppress, but the Court of Appeals for the Ninth Circuit reversed. In the course of its opinion, it categorized certain factors relied upon by the District Court as simply out of bounds in deciding whether there was "reasonable suspicion" for the stop. We hold that the Court of Appeals' methodology was contrary to our prior decisions and that it reached the wrong result in this case.

On an afternoon in January 1998, Agent Clinton Stoddard was working at a border patrol checkpoint along U.S. Highway 191 approximately 30 miles north of Douglas, Arizona. Douglas has a population of about 13,000 and is situated on the United States-Mexico border in the southeastern part of the State. Only two highways lead north from Douglas. Highway 191 leads north to Interstate 10, which passes through Tucson and Phoenix. State Highway 80 heads northeast through less populated areas toward New Mexico, skirting south and east of the portion of the Coronado National Forest that lies approximately 20 miles northeast of Douglas.

■ ■ ■

Around 2:15 p.m., Stoddard received a report via Douglas radio that a Leslie Canyon Road sensor had been triggered. This was significant to Stoddard for two reasons. First, it suggested to him that a vehicle might be trying to circumvent the checkpoint. Second, the timing coincided with the point when agents begin heading back to the checkpoint for a shift change, which leaves the area unpatrolled. Stoddard knew that alien smugglers did extensive scouting and seemed to be most active when agents were en route back to the checkpoint. Another border patrol agent told Stoddard that the same sensor had gone off several weeks before and that he had apprehended a minivan using the same route and witnessed the occupants throwing bundles of marijuana out the door.

Stoddard drove eastbound on Rucker Canyon Road to investigate. As he did so, he received another radio report of sensor activity. It indicated that the vehicle that had triggered the first sensor was heading westbound on Rucker Canyon Road. He continued east, passing Kuykendall Cutoff Road. He saw the dust trail of an approaching vehicle about a half mile away. Stoddard had not seen any other vehicles and, based on the timing, believed that this was the one that had tripped the sensors. He pulled off to the side of the road at a slight slant so he could get a good look at the oncoming vehicle as it passed by.

It was a minivan, a type of automobile that Stoddard knew smugglers used. As it approached, it slowed dramatically, from about 50-55 to 25-30 miles per hour. He saw five occupants inside. An adult man was driving, an adult woman sat in the front passenger seat, and three children were in the back. The driver appeared stiff and his posture very rigid. He did not look at Stoddard and seemed to be trying to pretend that Stoddard was not there. Stoddard thought this suspicious because in his experience on patrol most persons look over and see what is going on, and in that area most drivers give border patrol agents a friendly wave. Stoddard noticed that the knees of the two children sitting in the very back seat were unusually high, as if their feet were propped up on some cargo on the floor.

At that point, Stoddard decided to get a closer look, so he began to follow the vehicle as it continued westbound on Rucker Canyon Road toward Kuy-kendall Cutoff Road. Shortly thereafter, all of the children, though still facing forward, put their hands up at the same time and began to wave at Stoddard in an abnormal pattern. It looked to Stoddard as if the children were being instructed. Their odd waving continued on and off for about four to five minutes.

Several hundred feet before the Kuykendall Cutoff Road intersection, the driver signaled that he would turn. At one point, the driver turned the signal off, but just as he approached the intersection he put it back on and abruptly turned north onto Kuykendall. The turn was significant to Stoddard because it was made at the last place that would have allowed the minivan to avoid the checkpoint. Also, Kuykendall, though passable by a sedan or van, is rougher than either Rucker Canyon or Leslie Canyon Roads, and the normal traffic is four-wheel-drive vehicles. Stoddard did not recognize the minivan as part of the local traffic agents encounter on patrol, and he did not think it likely that the minivan was going to or coming from a picnic outing. He was not aware of any picnic grounds on Turkey Creek, which could be reached by following Kuykendall Cutoff all the way up. He knew of picnic grounds and a Boy Scout camp east of the intersection of Rucker Canyon and Leslie Canyon Roads, but the minivan had turned west at that intersection. And he had never seen any-one picnicking or sightseeing near where the first sensor went off.

Stoddard radioed for a registration check and learned that the minivan was registered to an address in Douglas that was four blocks north of the border in an area notorious for alien and narcotics smuggling. After receiving the infor-mation, Stoddard decided to make a vehicle stop. He approached the driver and learned that his name was Ralph Arvizu. Stoddard asked if respondent would mind if he looked inside and searched the vehicle. Respondent agreed, and Stoddard discovered marijuana in a black duffel bag under the feet of the two children in the back seat. Another bag containing marijuana was behind the rear seat. In all, the van contained 128.85 pounds of marijuana, worth an estimated $99,080.

Respondent was charged with possession with intent to distribute marijuana.... He moved to suppress the marijuana, arguing among other things that Stoddard did not have reasonable suspicion to stop the vehicle as required by the Fourth Amendment. After holding a hearing where Stoddard and respondent testified, the District Court for the District of Arizona ruled otherwise. It pointed to a number of the facts described above and noted particularly that any recreational areas north of Rucker Canyon would have been accessible from Douglas via 191 and another paved road, making it unnecessary to take a 40-to-50-mile trip on dirt roads.

The Court of Appeals for the Ninth Circuit reversed. In its view, fact-specific weighing of circumstances or other multifactor tests introduced "a troubling degree of uncertainty and unpredictability" into the Fourth Amendment analysis. It therefore "attempt[ed] . . . to describe and clearly delimit the extent to which certain factors may be considered by law enforcement officers in making stops such as the stop involv[ing]" respondent. After characterizing the District Court's analysis as relying on a list of 10 factors, the Court of Appeals proceeded to examine each in turn. It held that seven of the factors, including respondent's slowing down, his failure to acknowledge Stoddard, the raised position of the children's knees, and their odd waving carried little or no weight in the reasonable-suspicion calculus. The remaining factors—the road's use by smugglers, the temporal proximity between respondent's trip and the agents' shift change, and the use of minivans by smugglers—were not enough to render the stop permissible. We granted certiorari to review the decision of the Court of Appeals because of its importance to the enforcement of federal drug and immigration laws.

The Fourth Amendment prohibits "unreasonable searches and seizures" by the Government, and its protections extend to brief investigatory stops of persons or vehicles that fall short of traditional arrest. *Terry v. Ohio* (1968); *United States v. Cortez* (1981). Because the "balance between the public interest and the individual's right to personal security," *United States v. Brignoni-Ponce* (1975), tilts in favor of a standard less than probable cause in such cases, the Fourth Amendment is satisfied if the officer's action is supported by reasonable suspicion to believe that criminal activity " 'may be afoot.' "

When discussing how reviewing courts should make reasonable-suspicion determinations, we have said repeatedly that they must look at the "totality of the circumstances" of each case to see whether the detaining officer has a "particularized and objective basis" for suspecting legal wrongdoing. This process allows officers to draw on their own experience and specialized training to make inferences from and deductions about the cumulative information available to them that "might well elude an untrained person." Although an officer's reliance on a mere " 'hunch' " is insufficient to justify a stop, the likelihood of criminal activity need not rise to the level required for probable cause, and it falls considerably short of satisfying a preponderance of the evidence standard.

Our cases have recognized that the concept of reasonable suspicion is somewhat abstract. . . . But we have deliberately avoided reducing it to " 'a neat set of legal rules.' "

■ ■ ■

We think that the approach taken by the Court of Appeals here departs sharply from the teachings of these cases. The court's evaluation and rejection of seven of the listed factors in isolation from each other does not take into account the "totality of the circumstances," as our cases have understood that phrase. The court appeared to believe that each observation by Stoddard that was by itself readily susceptible to an innocent explanation was entitled to "no weight." *Terry*, however, precludes this sort of divide-and-conquer analysis. The officer in *Terry* observed the petitioner and his companions repeatedly walk back and forth, look into a store window, and confer with one another. Although each of the series of acts was "perhaps innocent in itself," we held that, taken together, they "warranted further investigation."

The Court of Appeals' view that it was necessary to "clearly delimit" an officer's consideration of certain factors to reduce "troubling . . . uncertainty" also runs counter to our cases and underestimates the usefulness of the reasonable-suspicion standard in guiding officers in the field. . . .

But the Court of Appeals' approach would . . . seriously undercut the "totality of the circumstances" principle which governs the existence *vel non* of "reasonable suspicion." Take, for example, the court's positions that respondent's deceleration could not be considered because "slowing down after spotting a law enforcement vehicle is an entirely normal response that is in no way indicative of criminal activity" and that his failure to acknowledge Stoddard's presence provided no support because there were "no 'special circumstances' rendering 'innocent avoidance . . . improbable.' " We think it quite reasonable that a driver's slowing down, stiffening of posture, and failure to acknowledge a sighted law enforcement officer might well be unremarkable in one instance (such as a busy San Francisco highway) while quite unusual in another (such as a remote portion of rural southeastern Arizona). Stoddard was entitled to make an assessment of the situation in light of his specialized training and familiarity with the customs of the area's inhabitants. To the extent that a totality of the circumstances approach may render appellate review less circumscribed by precedent than otherwise, it is the nature of the totality rule.

In another instance, the Court of Appeals chose to dismiss entirely the children's waving on grounds that odd conduct by children was all too common to be probative in a particular case. . . . ("If every odd act engaged in by one's children . . . could contribute to a finding of reasonable suspicion, the vast majority of American parents might be stopped regularly within a block of their homes"). Yet this case did not involve simply any odd act by children. At the suppression hearing, Stoddard testified about the children's waving several times, and the record suggests that he physically demonstrated it as well. The District Court Judge, who saw and heard Stoddard, then characterized the waving as "methodical," "mechanical," "abnormal," and "certainly . . . a fact that is odd and would lead a reasonable officer to wonder why they are doing this." Though the issue of this case does not turn on the children's idiosyncratic actions, the Court of Appeals should not have casually rejected this factor in light of the District Court's superior access to the evidence and the well-recognized inability of reviewing courts to reconstruct what happened in the courtroom.

Having considered the totality of the circumstances and given due weight to the factual inferences drawn by the law enforcement officer and District Court Judge, we hold that Stoddard had reasonable suspicion to believe that respondent was engaged in illegal activity. It was reasonable for Stoddard to infer from his observations, his registration check, and his experience as a border patrol agent that respondent had set out from Douglas along a little-traveled route used by smugglers to avoid the 191 checkpoint. Stoddard's knowledge further supported a commonsense inference that respondent intended to pass through the area at a time when officers would be leaving their backroads patrols to change shifts. The likelihood that respondent and his family were on a picnic outing was diminished by the fact that the minivan had turned away from the known recreational areas accessible to the east on Rucker Canyon Road. Corroborating this inference was the fact that recreational areas farther to the north would have been easier to reach by taking 191, as opposed to the 40-to-50-mile trip on unpaved and primitive roads. The children's elevated knees suggested the existence of concealed cargo in the passenger compartment. Finally, for the reasons we have given, Stoddard's assessment of respondent's reactions upon seeing him and the children's mechanical-like waving, which continued for a full four to five minutes, were entitled to some weight.

Respondent argues that we must rule in his favor because the facts suggested a family in a minivan on a holiday outing. A determination that reasonable suspicion exists, however, need not rule out the possibility of innocent conduct. Undoubtedly, each of these factors alone is susceptible of innocent explanation, and some factors are more probative than others. Taken together, we believe they sufficed to form a particularized and objective basis for Stoddard's stopping the vehicle, making the stop reasonable within the meaning of the Fourth Amendment.

The judgment of the Court of Appeals is therefore reversed, and the case is remanded for further proceedings consistent with this opinion.

It is so ordered.

Illinois v. Wardlow

528 U.S. 119 (2000)

REHNQUIST, C.J., delivered the opinion of the Court, in which O'CONNOR, SCALIA, KENNEDY, and THOMAS, JJ., joined. STEVENS, J., filed an opinion concurring in part and dissenting in part, in which SOUTER, GINSBURG, and BREYER, JJ., joined.

Respondent Wardlow fled upon seeing police officers patrolling an area known for heavy narcotics trafficking. Two of the officers caught up with him, stopped him and conducted a protective patdown search for weapons.

stop did not violate 4th

Discovering a .38-caliber handgun, the officers arrested Wardlow. We hold that the officers' stop did not violate the Fourth Amendment to the United States Constitution.

On September 9, 1995, Officers Nolan and Harvey were working as uniformed officers in the special operations section of the Chicago Police Department. The officers were driving the last car of a four car caravan converging on an area known for heavy narcotics trafficking in order to investigate drug transactions. The officers were traveling together because they expected to find a crowd of people in the area, including lookouts and customers.

As the caravan passed 4035 West Van Buren, Officer Nolan observed respondent Wardlow standing next to the building holding an opaque bag. Respondent looked in the direction of the officers and fled. Nolan and Harvey turned their car southbound, watched him as he ran through the gangway and an alley, and eventually cornered him on the street. Nolan then exited his car and stopped respondent. He immediately conducted a protective patdown search for weapons because in his experience it was common for there to be weapons in the near vicinity of narcotics transactions. During the frisk, Officer Nolan squeezed the bag respondent was carrying and felt a heavy, hard object similar to the shape of a gun. The officer then opened the bag and discovered a .38-caliber handgun with five live rounds of ammunition. The officers arrested Wardlow.

bag squeeze

The Illinois trial court denied respondent's motion to suppress, finding the gun was recovered during a lawful stop and frisk. Following a stipulated bench trial, Wardlow was convicted of unlawful use of a weapon by a felon. The Illinois Appellate Court reversed Wardlow's conviction, concluding that the gun should have been suppressed because Officer Nolan did not have reasonable suspicion sufficient to justify an investigative stop.

TC: AC:

■ ■ ■

The Illinois Supreme Court agreed. While rejecting the Appellate Court's conclusion that Wardlow was not in a high crime area, the Illinois Supreme Court determined that sudden flight in such an area does not create a reasonable suspicion justifying a *Terry* stop.

■ ■ ■

This case, involving a brief encounter between a citizen and a police officer on a public street, is governed by the analysis we first applied in *Terry* [*v. Ohio* (1968)]. In *Terry*, we held that an officer may, consistent with the Fourth Amendment, conduct a brief, investigatory stop when the officer has a reasonable, articulable suspicion that criminal activity is afoot. While "reasonable suspicion" is a less demanding standard than probable cause and requires a showing considerably less than preponderance of the evidence, the Fourth Amendment requires at least a minimal level of objective justification for making the stop. The officer must be able to articulate more than an "inchoate and unparticularized suspicion or 'hunch'" of criminal activity.

Nolan and Harvey were among eight officers in a four-car caravan that was converging on an area known for heavy narcotics trafficking, and the officers anticipated encountering a large number of people in the area, including drug customers and individuals serving as lookouts. App. 8. It was in this context that Officer Nolan decided to investigate Wardlow after observing him flee. An individual's presence in an area of expected criminal activity, standing alone, is not enough to support a reasonable, particularized suspicion that the person is committing a crime. But officers are not required to ignore the relevant characteristics of a location in determining whether the circumstances are sufficiently suspicious to warrant further investigation. Accordingly, we have previously noted the fact that the stop occurred in a "high crime area" among the relevant contextual considerations in a *Terry* analysis.

In this case, moreover, it was not merely respondent's presence in an area of heavy narcotics trafficking that aroused the officers' suspicion, but his unprovoked flight upon noticing the police. Our cases have also recognized that nervous, evasive behavior is a pertinent factor in determining reasonable suspicion. Headlong flight—wherever it occurs—is the consummate act of evasion: It is not necessarily indicative of wrongdoing, but it is certainly suggestive of such. In reviewing the propriety of an officer's conduct, courts do not have available empirical studies dealing with inferences drawn from suspicious behavior, and we cannot reasonably demand scientific certainty from judges or law enforcement officers where none exists. Thus, the determination of reasonable suspicion must be based on commonsense judgments and inferences about human behavior. We conclude Officer Nolan was justified in suspecting that Wardlow was involved in criminal activity, and, therefore, in investigating further.

■ ■ ■

In allowing such detentions, *Terry* accepts the risk that officers may stop innocent people. Indeed, the Fourth Amendment accepts that risk in connection with more drastic police action; persons arrested and detained on probable cause to believe they have committed a crime may turn out to be innocent. The *Terry* stop is a far more minimal intrusion, simply allowing the officer to briefly investigate further. If the officer does not learn facts rising to the level of probable cause, the individual must be allowed to go on his way. But in this case the officers found respondent in possession of a handgun, and arrested him for violation of an Illinois firearms statute. No question of the propriety of the arrest itself is before us.

The judgment of the Supreme Court of Illinois is reversed, and the cause is remanded for further proceedings not inconsistent with this opinion.

It is so ordered.

Justice STEVENS, with whom Justice SOUTER, Justice GINSBURG, and Justice BREYER join, concurring in part and dissenting in part.

The State of Illinois asks this Court to announce a "bright-line rule" authorizing the temporary detention of anyone who flees at the mere sight of a police officer. Respondent counters by asking us to adopt the opposite *per se* rule— that the fact that a person flees upon seeing the police can never, by itself, be sufficient to justify a temporary investigative stop of the kind authorized by *Terry v. Ohio.*

The Court today wisely endorses neither *per se* rule. Instead, it rejects the proposition that "flight is . . . necessarily indicative of ongoing criminal activity," *ante,* this page, adhering to the view that "[t]he concept of reasonable suspicion . . . is not readily, or even usefully, reduced to a neat set of legal rules," but must be determined by looking to "the totality of the circumstances—the whole picture."

■ ■ ■

Although I agree with the Court's rejection of the *per se* rules proffered by the parties, unlike the Court, I am persuaded that in this case the brief testimony of the officer who seized respondent does not justify the conclusion that he had reasonable suspicion to make the stop. Before discussing the specific facts of this case, I shall comment on the parties' requests for a *per se* rule.

The question in this case concerns "the degree of suspicion that attaches to" a person's flight—or, more precisely, what "commonsense conclusions" can be drawn respecting the motives behind that flight. A pedestrian may break into a run for a variety of reasons—to catch up with a friend a block or two away, to seek shelter from an impending storm, to arrive at a bus stop before the bus leaves, to get home in time for dinner, to resume jogging after a pause for rest, to avoid contact with a bore or a bully, or simply to answer the call of nature— any of which might coincide with the arrival of an officer in the vicinity. A pedestrian might also run because he or she has just sighted one or more police officers. In the latter instance, the State properly points out "that the fleeing person may be, *inter alia,* (1) an escapee from jail; (2) wanted on a warrant; (3) in possession of contraband (i.e. drugs, weapons, stolen goods, etc.); or (4) someone who has just committed another type of crime." In short, there are unquestionably circumstances in which a person's flight is suspicious, and undeniably instances in which a person runs for entirely innocent reasons.

Given the diversity and frequency of possible motivations for flight, it would be profoundly unwise to endorse either *per se* rule. The inference we can reasonably draw about the motivation for a person's flight, rather, will depend on a number of different circumstances. Factors such as the time of day, the number of people in the area, the character of the neighborhood, whether the officer was in uniform, the way the runner was dressed, the direction and speed of the flight, and whether the person's behavior was otherwise unusual might be relevant in specific cases. This number of variables is surely sufficient to preclude either a bright-line rule that always justifies, or that never justifies, an investigative stop based on the sole fact that flight began after a police officer appeared nearby.

■ ■ ■

Among some citizens, particularly minorities and those residing in high crime areas, there is also the possibility that the fleeing person is entirely innocent, but, with or without justification, believes that contact with the police can itself be dangerous, apart from any criminal activity associated with the officer's sudden presence. For such a person, unprovoked flight is neither "aberrant" nor "abnormal." Moreover, these concerns and fears are known to the police officers themselves, and are validated by law enforcement investigations into their own practices. Accordingly, the evidence supporting the reasonableness of these beliefs is too pervasive to be dismissed as random or rare, and too persuasive to be disparaged as inconclusive or insufficient. In any event, just as we do not require "scientific certainty" for our commonsense conclusion that unprovoked flight can sometimes indicate suspicious motives, neither do we require scientific certainty to conclude that unprovoked flight can occur for other, innocent reasons.

■ ■ ■

The probative force of the inferences to be drawn from flight is a function of the varied circumstances in which it occurs. Sometimes those inferences are entirely consistent with the presumption of innocence, sometimes they justify further investigation, and sometimes they justify an immediate stop and search for weapons. These considerations have led us to avoid categorical rules concerning a person's flight and the presumptions to be drawn therefrom.

■ ■ ■

I therefore respectfully dissent from the Court's judgment to reverse the court below.

Florida v. J.L.

529 U.S. 266 (2000)

GINSBURG, J., delivered the opinion for a unanimous Court. KENNEDY, J., filed a concurring opinion, in which REHNQUIST, C.J., joined.

The question presented in this case is whether an anonymous tip that a person is carrying a gun is, without more, sufficient to justify a police officer's stop and frisk of that person. We hold that it is not.

On October 13, 1995, an anonymous caller reported to the Miami-Dade Police that a young black male standing at a particular bus stop and wearing a plaid shirt was carrying a gun. So far as the record reveals, there is no audio recording of the tip, and nothing is known about the informant. Sometime after the police received the tip—the record does not say how long—two officers were instructed to respond. They arrived at the bus stop about six minutes later and saw three black males "just hanging out [there]." One of the three, respondent J.L., was wearing a plaid shirt. Apart from the tip, the officers had no reason to suspect any of the three of illegal conduct. The officers did not see a firearm, and J.L. made no threatening or otherwise unusual movements. One of the officers approached J.L., told him to put his hands up on the bus stop, frisked him, and seized a gun from J.L.'s pocket. The second officer frisked the other two individuals, against whom no allegations had been made, and found nothing.

J.L., who was at the time of the frisk "10 days shy of his 16th birth[day]," was charged under state law with carrying a concealed firearm without a license and possessing a firearm while under the age of 18. He moved to suppress the gun as the fruit of an unlawful search, and the trial court granted his motion. The intermediate appellate court reversed, but the Supreme Court of Florida quashed that decision and held the search invalid under the Fourth Amendment.

Anonymous tips, the Florida Supreme Court stated, are generally less reliable than tips from known informants and can form the basis for reasonable suspicion only if accompanied by specific indicia of reliability, for example, the correct forecast of a subject's " 'not easily predicted' " movements. The tip leading to the frisk of J.L., the court observed, provided no such predictions, nor did it contain any other qualifying indicia of reliability. Two justices dissented. The safety of the police and the public, they maintained, justifies a "firearm exception" to the general rule barring investigatory stops and frisks on the basis of bare-boned anonymous tips.

Seeking review in this Court, the State of Florida noted that the decision of the State's Supreme Court conflicts with decisions of other courts declaring similar searches compatible with the Fourth Amendment.

■ ■ ■

Our "stop and frisk" decisions begin with *Terry v. Ohio* (1968).

■ ■ ■

In the instant case, the officers' suspicion that J.L. was carrying a weapon arose not from any observations of their own but solely from a call made from an unknown location by an unknown caller. Unlike a tip from a known informant whose reputation can be assessed and who can be held responsible if her allegations turn out to be fabricated "an anonymous tip alone seldom demonstrates the informant's basis of knowledge or veracity." *Alabama v. White* (1990). As we have recognized, however, there are situations in which an anonymous tip, suitably corroborated, exhibits "sufficient indicia of reliability to provide reasonable suspicion to make the investigatory stop." . . .

In *White,* the police received an anonymous tip asserting that a woman was carrying cocaine and predicting that she would leave an apartment building at a specified time, get into a car matching a particular description, and drive to a named motel. Standing alone, the tip would not have justified a *Terry* stop. Only after police observation showed that the informant had accurately predicted the woman's movements, we explained, did it become reasonable to think the tipster had inside knowledge about the suspect and therefore to credit his assertion about the cocaine. Although the Court held that the suspicion in *White* became reasonable after police surveillance, we regarded the case as borderline. Knowledge about a person's future movements indicates some familiarity with that person's affairs, but having such knowledge does not necessarily imply that the informant knows, in particular, whether that person is carrying hidden contraband. We accordingly classified *White* as a "close case."

The tip in the instant case lacked the moderate indicia of reliability present in *White* and essential to the Court's decision in that case. The anonymous call concerning J.L. provided no predictive information and therefore left the police without means to test the informant's knowledge or credibility. That the allegation about the gun turned out to be correct does not suggest that the officers, prior to the frisks, had a reasonable basis for suspecting J.L. of engaging in unlawful conduct: The reasonableness of official suspicion must be measured by what the officers knew before they conducted their search. All the police had to go on in this case was the bare report of an unknown, unaccountable informant who neither explained how he knew about the gun nor supplied any basis for believing he had inside information about J.L. If *White* was a close case on the reliability of anonymous tips, this one surely falls on the other side of the line.

■ ■ ■

An accurate description of a subject's readily observable location and appearance is of course reliable in this limited sense: It will help the police correctly identify the person whom the tipster means to accuse. Such a tip, however, does not show that the tipster has knowledge of concealed criminal activity. The reasonable suspicion here at issue requires that a tip be reliable in its assertion of illegality, not just in its tendency to identify a determinate person . . . (distinguishing reliability as to identification, which is often important in other criminal law contexts, from reliability as to the likelihood of criminal activity, which is central in anonymous-tip cases).

■ ■ ■

The judgment of the Florida Supreme Court is affirmed.
It is so ordered.

Virginia v. Harris

130 S. Ct. 10 (2009)

Motion of respondent for leave to proceed *in forma pauperis* granted. Petition for writ of certiorari to the Supreme Court of Virginia denied.

ROBERTS, C.J., with whom SCALIA, J., joins, dissenting from denial of certiorari.

Every year, close to 13,000 people die in alcohol-related car crashes—roughly one death every 40 minutes. See Dept. of Transp., Nat. Hwy. Traffic Safety Admin., Traffic Safety Facts, 2007 Traffic Safety Annual Assessment—Alcohol-Impaired Driving Fatalities 1 (No. 81106, Aug. 2008). Ordinary citizens are well aware of the dangers posed by drunk driving, and they frequently report such conduct to the police. A number of States have adopted programs specifically designed to encourage such tips—programs such as the "Drunkbusters Hotline" in New Mexico and the REDDI program (Report Every Drunk Driver Immediately) in force in several States. See Dept. of

Transp., Nat. Hwy. Traffic Safety Admin., *Programs Across the United States That Aid Motorists in the Reporting of Impaired Drivers to Law Enforcement* (2007).

By a 4-to-3 vote, the Virginia Supreme Court below adopted a rule that will undermine such efforts to get drunk drivers off the road. The decision below commands that police officers following a driver reported to be drunk do nothing until they see the driver actually do something unsafe on the road—by which time it may be too late.

Here, a Richmond police officer pulled Joseph Harris over after receiving an anonymous tip that Harris was driving while intoxicated. The tip described Harris, his car, and the direction he was traveling in considerable detail. The officer did not personally witness Harris violate any traffic laws. When Harris was pulled over, however, he reeked of alcohol, his speech was slurred, he almost fell over in attempting to exit his car, and he failed the sobriety tests the officer administered on the scene. Harris was convicted of driving while intoxicated, but the Virginia Supreme Court overturned the conviction. It concluded that because the officer had failed to independently verify that Harris was driving dangerously, the stop violated the Fourth Amendment's prohibition on unreasonable searches and seizures.

I am not sure that the Fourth Amendment requires such independent corroboration before the police can act, at least in the special context of anonymous tips reporting drunk driving. This is an important question that is not answered by our past decisions, and that has deeply divided federal and state courts. The Court should grant the petition for certiorari to answer the question and resolve the conflict.

On the one hand, our cases allow police to conduct investigative stops based on reasonable suspicion, viewed under the totality of the circumstances. *Terry v. Ohio* (1968); *Alabama v. White* (1990). In *Florida v. J.L.* (2000), however, we explained that anonymous tips, in the absence of additional corroboration, typically lack the "indicia of reliability" needed to justify a stop under the reasonable suspicion standard. In *J.L.*, the Court suppressed evidence seized by police after receiving an anonymous tip alleging that a young man, wearing a plaid shirt and waiting at a particular bus stop, was carrying a gun. The majority below relied extensively on *J.L.* in reversing Harris's conviction.

But it is not clear that *J.L.* applies to anonymous tips reporting drunk or erratic driving. *J.L.* itself suggested that the Fourth Amendment analysis might be different in other situations. The Court declined "to speculate about the circumstances under which the danger alleged in an anonymous tip might be so great as to justify a search even without a showing of reliability." It also hinted that "in quarters where the reasonable expectation of Fourth Amendment privacy is diminished," it might be constitutionally permissible to "conduct protective searches on the basis of information insufficient to justify searches elsewhere."

There is no question that drunk driving is a serious and potentially deadly crime, as our cases have repeatedly emphasized. . . . The imminence of the danger posed by drunk drivers exceeds that at issue in other types of cases.

In a case like *J.L.*, the police can often observe the subject of a tip and step in before actual harm occurs; with drunk driving, such a wait-and-see approach may prove fatal. Drunk driving is always dangerous, as it is occurring. This Court has in fact recognized that the dangers posed by drunk drivers are unique, frequently upholding anti-drunk-driving policies that might be constitutionally problematic in other, less exigent circumstances.

In the absence of controlling precedent on point, a sharp disagreement has emerged among federal and state courts over how to apply the Fourth Amendment in this context. The majority of courts examining the question have upheld investigative stops of allegedly drunk or erratic drivers, even when the police did not personally witness any traffic violations before conducting the stops. These courts have typically distinguished *J.L.*'s general rule based on some combination of (1) the especially grave and imminent dangers posed by drunk driving; (2) the enhanced reliability of tips alleging illegal activity in public, to which the tipster was presumably an eyewitness; (3) the fact that traffic stops are typically less invasive than searches or seizures of individuals on foot; and (4) the diminished expectation of privacy enjoyed by individuals driving their cars on public roads. A minority of jurisdictions, meanwhile, take the same position as the Virginia Supreme Court, requiring that officers first confirm an anonymous tip of drunk or erratic driving through their own independent observation. This conflict has been expressly noted by the lower courts.

The conflict is clear and the stakes are high. The effect of the rule below will be to grant drunk drivers "one free swerve" before they can legally be pulled over by police. It will be difficult for an officer to explain to the family of a motorist killed by that swerve that the police had a tip that the driver of the other car was drunk, but that they were powerless to pull him over, even for a quick check.

Maybe the decision of the Virginia Supreme Court below was correct, and the Fourth Amendment bars police from acting on anonymous tips of drunk driving unless they can verify each tip. If so, then the dangerous consequences of this rule are unavoidable. But the police should have every legitimate tool at their disposal for getting drunk drivers off the road. I would grant certiorari to determine if this is one of them.

4. Scope of *Terry* Stop

Hiibel v. Sixth Judicial District Court of Nevada, Humboldt County

542 U.S. 177 (2004)

KENNEDY, J., delivered the opinion of the Court, in which REHNQUIST, C.J., and O'CONNOR, SCALIA, and THOMAS, JJ., joined. STEVENS, J., filed a dissenting opinion. BREYER, J., filed a dissenting opinion, in which SOUTER and GINSBURG, JJ., joined.

The petitioner was arrested and convicted for refusing to identify himself during a stop allowed by *Terry v. Ohio* (1968). He challenges his conviction under the Fourth and Fifth Amendments to the United States Constitution, applicable to the States through the Fourteenth Amendment. . . .

The sheriff's department in Humboldt County, Nevada, received an afternoon telephone call reporting an assault. The caller reported seeing a man assault a woman in a red and silver GMC truck on Grass Valley Road. Deputy Sheriff Lee Dove was dispatched to investigate. When the officer arrived at the scene, he found the truck parked on the side of the road. A man was standing by the truck, and a young woman was sitting inside it. The officer observed skid marks in the gravel behind the vehicle, leading him to believe it had come to a sudden stop.

The officer approached the man and explained that he was investigating a report of a fight. The man appeared to be intoxicated. The officer asked him if he had "any identification on [him]," which we understand as a request to produce a driver's license or some other form of written identification. The man refused and asked why the officer wanted to see identification. The officer responded that he was conducting an investigation and needed to see some identification. The unidentified man became agitated and insisted he had done nothing wrong. The officer explained that he wanted to find out who the man was and what he was doing there. After continued refusals to comply with the officer's request for identification, the man began to taunt the officer by placing his hands behind his back and telling the officer to arrest him and take him to jail. This routine kept up for several minutes: The officer asked for identification 11 times and was refused each time. After warning the man that he would be arrested if he continued to refuse to comply, the officer placed him under arrest.

We now know that the man arrested on Grass Valley Road is Larry Dudley Hiibel. Hiibel was charged with "willfully resist[ing], delay[ing] or obstruct[ing] a public officer in discharging or attempting to discharge any legal duty of his office" in violation of Nev. Rev. Stat. (NRS) § 199.280 (2003). The government reasoned that Hiibel had obstructed the officer in carrying out his duties under a Nevada statute that defines the legal rights and duties of a police officer in the context of an investigative stop. . . .

Hiibel was tried in the Justice Court of Union Township. The court agreed that Hiibel's refusal to identify himself . . . "obstructed and delayed Dove as a public officer in attempting to discharge his duty" in violation of § 199.280. App. 5. Hiibel was convicted and fined $250. The Sixth Judicial District Court affirmed, rejecting Hiibel's argument that . . . his case violated the Fourth and Fifth Amendments. On review the Supreme Court of Nevada rejected the Fourth Amendment challenge in a divided opinion. . . .

The Court has recognized similar constitutional limitations on the scope and operation of stop and identify statutes. In *Brown v. Texas* (1979), the Court invalidated a conviction for violating a Texas stop and identify statute on Fourth Amendment grounds. The Court ruled that the initial stop was not based on specific, objective facts establishing reasonable suspicion to believe the suspect was involved in criminal activity. Absent that factual basis for detaining the defendant, the Court held, the risk of "arbitrary and abusive police practices" was too great and the stop was impermissible. Four Terms later, the Court invalidated a modified stop and identify statute on vagueness grounds. See *Kolender v. Lawson* (1983). The California law in *Kolender* required a suspect to give an officer " 'credible and reliable' " identification when asked to identify himself. The Court held that the statute was void because it provided no standard for determining what a suspect must do to comply with it, resulting in " 'virtually unrestrained power to arrest and charge persons with a violation.' " (quoting *Lewis v. New Orleans* (1974) (Powell, J., concurring in result)).

The present case begins where our prior cases left off. Here there is no question that the initial stop was based on reasonable suspicion, satisfying the Fourth Amendment requirements noted in *Brown*. Further, the petitioner has not alleged that the statute is unconstitutionally vague, as in *Kolender*. Here the Nevada statute is narrower and more precise. The statute in *Kolender* had been interpreted to require a suspect to give the officer "credible and reliable" identification. In contrast, the Nevada Supreme Court has interpreted the instant statute to require only that a suspect disclose his name.

■ ■ ■

Hiibel argues that his conviction cannot stand because the officer's conduct violated his Fourth Amendment rights. We disagree.

Asking questions is an essential part of police investigations. In the ordinary course a police officer is free to ask a person for identification without implicating the Fourth Amendment. "[I]nterrogation relating to one's identity or a request for identification by the police does not, by itself, constitute a Fourth Amendment seizure." Beginning with *Terry v. Ohio*, the Court has recognized that a law enforcement officer's reasonable suspicion that a person may be involved in criminal activity permits the officer to stop the person for a brief time and take additional steps to investigate further. To ensure that the resulting seizure is constitutionally reasonable, a *Terry* stop must be limited. The officer's action must be " 'justified at its inception, and . . . reasonably related in scope to the circumstances which justified the interference in the first place.' " *United States v. Sharpe* (1985).

■ ■ ■

Our decisions make clear that questions concerning a suspect's identity are a routine and accepted part of many *Terry* stops. . . . *Hayes v. Florida* (1985) ("[I]f there are articulable facts supporting a reasonable suspicion that a person has committed a criminal offense, that person may be stopped in order to identify him, to question him briefly, or to detain him briefly while attempting to obtain additional information"); *Adams v. Williams* (1972) ("A brief stop of a suspicious individual, in order to determine his identity or to maintain the status quo momentarily while obtaining more information, may be most reasonable in light of the facts known to the officer at the time").

Obtaining a suspect's name in the course of a *Terry* stop serves important government interests. Knowledge of identity may inform an officer that a suspect is wanted for another offense, or has a record of violence or mental disorder. On the other hand, knowing identity may help clear a suspect and allow the police to concentrate their efforts elsewhere. Identity may prove particularly important in cases such as this, where the police are investigating what appears to be a domestic assault. Officers called to investigate domestic disputes need to know whom they are dealing with in order to assess the situation, the threat to their own safety, and possible danger to the potential victim.

Although it is well established that an officer may ask a suspect to identify himself in the course of a *Terry* stop, it has been an open question whether the suspect can be arrested and prosecuted for refusal to answer. Petitioner draws our attention to statements in prior opinions that, according to him, answer the question in his favor. In *Terry,* Justice White stated in a concurring opinion that a person detained in an investigative stop can be questioned but is "not obliged to answer, answers may not be compelled, and refusal to answer furnishes no basis for an arrest." . . . In the course of explaining why *Terry* stops have not been subject to *Miranda,* the Court suggested reasons why *Terry* stops have a "nonthreatening character," among them the fact that a suspect detained during a *Terry* stop "is not obliged to respond" to questions. According to petitioner, these statements establish a right to refuse to answer questions during a *Terry* stop.

We do not read these statements as controlling. The passages recognize that the Fourth Amendment does not impose obligations on the citizen but instead provides rights against the government. As a result, the Fourth Amendment itself cannot require a suspect to answer questions. This case concerns a different issue, however. Here, the source of the legal obligation arises from Nevada state law, not the Fourth Amendment. Further, the statutory obligation does not go beyond answering an officer's request to disclose a name.

■ ■ ■

The principles of *Terry* permit a State to require a suspect to disclose his name in the course of a *Terry* stop. The reasonableness of a seizure under the Fourth Amendment is determined "by balancing its intrusion on the individual's Fourth Amendment interests against its promotion of legitimate government interests." The Nevada statute satisfies that standard. The request for identity has an immediate relation to the purpose, rationale, and practical demands of a *Terry* stop. The threat of criminal sanction helps ensure that the request for identity does not become a legal nullity. On the other hand, the Nevada statute does not alter the nature of the stop itself: it does not change its duration, or its location. A state law requiring a suspect to disclose his name in the course of a valid *Terry* stop is consistent with Fourth Amendment prohibitions against unreasonable searches and seizures.

■ ■ ■

The judgment of the Nevada Supreme Court is
Affirmed.

Justice BREYER, with whom Justice SOUTER and Justice GINSBURG join, dissenting.

Notwithstanding the vagrancy statutes to which the majority refers, this Court's Fourth Amendment precedents make clear that police may conduct a *Terry* stop only within circumscribed limits. And one of those limits invalidates laws that compel responses to police questioning.

In *Terry v. Ohio*, the Court considered whether police, in the absence of probable cause, can stop, question, or frisk an individual at all. The Court recognized that the Fourth Amendment protects the " 'right of every individual to the possession and control of his own person.' "

■ ■ ■

About 10 years later, the Court, in *Brown v. Texas*, held that police lacked "any reasonable suspicion" to detain the particular petitioner and require him to identify himself.

■ ■ ■

Then, five years later, the Court wrote that an "officer may ask the [*Terry*] detainee a moderate number of questions to determine his identity and to try to obtain information confirming or dispelling the officer's suspicions. *But the detainee is not obliged to respond.*" *Berkemer v. McCarty* (1984).

■ ■ ■

This lengthy history—of concurring opinions, of references, and of clear explicit statements—means that the Court's statement in *Berkemer*, while technically dicta, is the kind of strong dicta that the legal community typically takes as a statement of the law. And that law has remained undisturbed for more than 20 years.

There is no good reason now to reject this generation-old statement of the law. There are sound reasons rooted in Fifth Amendment considerations for adhering to this Fourth Amendment legal condition circumscribing police authority to stop an individual against his will. Administrative considerations also militate against change. Can a State, in addition to requiring a stopped individual to answer "What's your name?" also require an answer to "What's your license number?" or "Where do you live?" Can a police officer, who must know how to make a *Terry* stop, keep track of the constitutional answers? After all, answers to any of these questions may, or may not, incriminate, depending upon the circumstances.

Indeed, as the Court points out, a name itself—even if it is not "Killer Bill" or "Rough 'em up Harry"—will sometimes provide the police with "a link in the chain of evidence needed to convict the individual of a separate offense." The majority reserves judgment about whether compulsion is permissible in such instances. How then is a police officer in the midst of a *Terry* stop to distinguish between the majority's ordinary case and this special case where the majority reserves judgment?

The majority presents no evidence that the rule enunciated by Justice White and then by the *Berkemer* Court, which for nearly a generation has set forth a settled *Terry* stop condition, has significantly interfered with law enforcement. Nor has the majority presented any other convincing justification for change. I would not begin to erode a clear rule with special exceptions.

I consequently dissent.

Michigan v. Long

463 U.S. 1032 (1983)

O'CONNOR, J., delivered the opinion of the Court, in which BURGER, C.J., WHITE, POWELL, and REHNQUIST, JJ., joined. BLACKMUN, J., concurred in part and dissented in part and filed an opinion. BRENNAN, J., filed a dissenting opinion, in which MARSHALL, J., joined. STEVENS, J., filed a dissenting opinion.

In *Terry v. Ohio* (1968), we upheld the validity of a protective search for weapons in the absence of probable cause to arrest because it is unreasonable to deny a police officer the right "to neutralize the threat of physical harm" when he possesses an articulable suspicion that an individual is armed and dangerous. We did not, however, expressly address whether such a protective search for weapons could extend to an area beyond the person in the absence of probable cause to arrest. In the present case, respondent David Long was convicted for possession of marijuana found by police in the passenger compartment and trunk of the automobile that he was driving. The police searched the passenger compartment because they had reason to believe that the vehicle contained weapons potentially dangerous to the officers. We hold that the protective search of the passenger compartment was reasonable under the principles articulated in *Terry* and other decisions of this Court. We also examine Long's argument that the decision below rests upon an adequate and independent state ground, and we decide in favor of our jurisdiction.

■ ■ ■

The court below held, and respondent Long contends, that Deputy Howell's entry into the vehicle cannot be justified under the principles set forth in *Terry* because "*Terry* authorized only a limited pat-down search of a *person* suspected of criminal activity" rather than a search of an area. Although *Terry* did involve the protective frisk of a person, we believe that the police action in this case is justified by the principles that we have already established in *Terry* and other cases.

In *Terry*, the Court examined the validity of a "stop and frisk" in the absence of probable cause and a warrant. The police officer in *Terry* detained several suspects to ascertain their identities after the officer had observed the suspects for a brief period of time and formed the conclusion that they were about to engage in criminal activity. Because the officer feared that the suspects were armed, he patted down the outside of the suspects' clothing and discovered two revolvers.

Examining the reasonableness of the officer's conduct in *Terry*, we held that there is " 'no ready test for determining reasonableness other than by balancing the need to search [or seize] against the invasion which the search [or seizure] entails.' " Although the conduct of the officer in *Terry* involved a "severe, though brief, intrusion upon cherished personal security," we found that the conduct was reasonable when we weighed the interest of the individual against the legitimate interest in "crime prevention and detection," and the "need for law enforcement officers to protect themselves and other prospective victims of violence in situations where they lack probable cause for an arrest." When the officer has a reasonable belief "that the individual whose suspicious behavior he is investigating at close range is armed and presently dangerous to the officer or to others, it would appear to be clearly unreasonable to deny the officer the power to take necessary measures to determine whether the person is in fact carrying a weapon and to neutralize the threat of physical harm."

Although *Terry* itself involved the stop and subsequent pat-down search of a person, we were careful to note that "[w]e need not develop at length in this case, however, the limitations which the Fourth Amendment places upon a protective search and seizure for weapons. These limitations will have to be developed in the concrete factual circumstances of individual cases." Contrary to Long's view, *Terry* need not be read as restricting the preventative search to the person of the detained suspect.

In two cases in which we applied *Terry* to specific factual situations, we recognized that investigative detentions involving suspects in vehicles are especially fraught with danger to police officers. In *Pennsylvania v. Mimms* (1977), we held that police may order persons out of an automobile during a stop for a traffic violation, and may frisk those persons for weapons if there is a reasonable belief that they are armed and dangerous. Our decision rested in part on the "inordinate risk confronting an officer as he approaches a person seated in an automobile." In *Adams v. Williams* (1972), we held that the police, acting on an informant's tip, may reach into the passenger compartment of an automobile to remove a gun from a driver's waistband even where the gun was not apparent to police from outside the car and the police knew of its existence only because of the tip. Again, our decision rested in part on our view of the danger presented to police officers in "traffic stop" and automobile situations.

■ ■ ■

Our past cases indicate then that protection of police and others can justify protective searches when police have a reasonable belief that the suspect poses a danger, that roadside encounters between police and suspects are especially hazardous, and that danger may arise from the possible presence of weapons in the area surrounding a suspect. These principles compel our conclusion that the search of the passenger compartment of an automobile, limited to those areas in which a weapon may be placed or hidden, is permissible if the police officer possesses a reasonable belief based on "specific and articulable facts which, taken together with the rational inferences from those facts, reasonably warrant" the officers in believing that the suspect is dangerous and the suspect may gain immediate control of weapons. "[T]he issue is whether a reasonably prudent man in the circumstances would be warranted in the belief that his safety or that of others was in danger." If a suspect is "dangerous," he is no less dangerous simply because he is not arrested. If, while conducting a legitimate *Terry* search of the interior of the automobile, the officer should, as here, discover contraband other than weapons, he clearly cannot be required to ignore the contraband, and the Fourth Amendment does not require its suppression in such circumstances.

The circumstances of this case clearly justified Deputies Howell and Lewis in their reasonable belief that Long posed a danger if he were permitted to reenter his vehicle. The hour was late and the area rural. Long was driving his automobile at excessive speed, and his car swerved into a ditch. The officers had to repeat their questions to Long, who appeared to be "under the influence" of some intoxicant. Long was not frisked until the officers observed that there was a large knife in the interior of the car into which Long was about to reenter. The subsequent search of the car was restricted to those areas to which Long would generally have immediate control, and that could contain a weapon. The trial court determined that the leather pouch containing marijuana could have contained a weapon. It is clear that the intrusion was "strictly circumscribed by the exigencies which justifi[ed] its initiation."

■ ■ ■

The decision of the Michigan Supreme Court is reversed, and the case is remanded for further proceedings not inconsistent with this opinion.

It is so ordered.

Justice Brennan, with whom Justice Marshall joins, dissenting.

The Court today holds that "the protective search of the passenger compartment" of the automobile involved in this case "was reasonable under the principles articulated in *Terry* and other decisions of this Court." I disagree. *Terry v. Ohio* does not support the Court's conclusion and the reliance on "other decisions" is patently misplaced. Plainly, the Court is simply continuing the process of distorting *Terry* beyond recognition and forcing it into service as an unlikely weapon against the Fourth Amendment's fundamental requirement that searches and seizures be based on probable cause.

■ ■ ■

In *Terry*, the Court confronted the "quite narrow question" of "whether it is always unreasonable for a policeman to seize a person and subject him to a *limited* search for weapons unless there is probable cause for an arrest." Because the Court was dealing "with an entire rubric of police conduct . . . which historically [had] not been, and as a practical matter could not be, subjected to the warrant procedure," the Court tested the conduct at issue "by the Fourth Amendment's general proscription against unreasonable searches and seizures." In considering the "reasonableness" of the conduct, the Court balanced " 'the need to search [or seize] against the invasion which the search [or seizure] entails.' " It deserves emphasis that in discussing the "invasion" at issue, the Court stated that "[e]ven *a limited search of the outer clothing for weapons* constitutes a severe, though brief, intrusion upon cherished personal security...." Ultimately, the Court concluded that "there must be *a narrowly drawn authority* to permit a reasonable search for weapons for the protection of the police officer, where he has reason to believe that he is dealing with an armed and dangerous individual, regardless of whether he has probable cause to arrest the individual for a crime." The Court expressed its holding as follows:

> "We merely hold today that where a police officer observes unusual conduct which leads him reasonably to conclude in light of his experience that criminal activity may be afoot and that the persons with whom he is dealing may be armed and presently dangerous, where in the course of investigating this behavior he identifies himself as a policeman and makes reasonable inquiries, and where nothing in the initial stages of the encounter serves to dispel his reasonable fear for his own or others' safety, he is entitled for the protection of himself and others in the area to conduct *a carefully limited search of the outer clothing of such persons* in an attempt to discover weapons which might be used to assault him."

It is clear that *Terry* authorized only limited searches of the person for weapons. In light of what *Terry* said, relevant portions of which the Court neglects to quote, the Court's suggestion that "*Terry* need not be read as restricting the preventive search to the person of the detained suspect" can only be described as disingenuous. Nothing in *Terry* authorized police officers to search a suspect's car based on reasonable suspicion. The Court confirmed this this very Term in *United States v. Place* [(1983)], where it described the search authorized by *Terry* as a "limited search for weapons, or 'frisk'...." The search at issue in this case is a far cry from a "frisk" and certainly was not "limited."

■ ■ ■

The Court suggests no limit on the "area search" it now authorizes. The Court states that a "search of the passenger compartment of an automobile, limited to those areas in which a weapon may be placed or hidden, is permissible if the police officer possesses a reasonable belief based on 'specific and articulable facts which, taken together with the rational inferences from those facts, reasonably warrant' the officers to believe that the suspect is dangerous and the suspect may gain immediate control of weapons." Presumably a weapon "may be placed or hidden" anywhere in a car. A weapon also might be hidden in a container in the car. In this case, the Court upholds the officer's search of a leather pouch because it "could have contained a weapon." In addition, the Court's requirement that an officer have a reasonable suspicion that a suspect is armed and dangerous does little to check the initiation of an area search. In this case, the officers saw a hunting knife in the car, but the Court does not base its holding that the subsequent search was permissible on the ground that possession of the knife may have been illegal under state law.

An individual can lawfully possess many things that can be used as weapons. A hammer, or a baseball bat, can be used as a very effective weapon. Finally, the Court relies on the following facts to conclude that the officers had a reasonable suspicion that respondent was presently dangerous: the hour was late; the area was rural; respondent had been driving at an excessive speed; he had been involved in an accident; he was not immediately responsive to the officers' questions; and he appeared to be under the influence of some intoxicant. Based on these facts, one might reasonably conclude that respondent was drunk. A drunk driver is indeed dangerous while driving, but not while stopped on the roadside by the police. Even when an intoxicated person lawfully has in his car an object that could be used as a weapon, it requires imagination to conclude that he is presently dangerous. Even assuming that the facts in this case justified the officers' initial "frisk" of respondent, they hardly provide adequate justification for a search of a suspect's car and the containers within it. This represents an intrusion not just different in degree, but in kind, from the intrusion sanctioned by *Terry*. In short, the implications of the Court's decision are frightening.

■ ■ ■

Today's decision disregards the Court's warning in *Almeida-Sanchez* (1973): "The needs of law enforcement stand in constant tension with the Constitution's protections of the individual against certain exercises of official power. It is precisely the predictability of these pressures that counsels a resolute loyalty to constitutional safeguards." Of course, police should not be exposed to unnecessary danger in the performance of their duties. But a search of a car and the containers within it based on nothing more than reasonable suspicion, even under the circumstances present here, cannot be sustained without doing violence to the requirements of the Fourth Amendment. There is no reason in this case why the officers could not have pursued less intrusive, but equally effective, means of insuring their safety. The Court takes a long step today toward "balancing" into oblivion the protections the Fourth Amendment affords. I dissent, for as Justice Jackson said in *Brinegar v. United States* (1949):

> "[Fourth Amendment rights] are not mere second-class rights but belong in the catalog of indispensable freedoms. Among deprivations of rights, none is so effective in cowing a population, crushing the spirit of the individual and putting terror in every heart. Uncontrolled search and seizure is one of the first and most effective weapons in the arsenal of every arbitrary government."

United States v. Place

462 U.S. 696 (1983)

See also Chapter 2.B.3.a.

Justice O'CONNOR delivered the opinion of the Court, in which BURGER, C.J., REHNQUIST, POWELL, STEVENS, and WHITE, JJ., joined. BRENNAN, J., filed an opinion concurring in the result, in which MARSHALL, J., joined. BLACKMUN, J., filed an opinion concurring in the judgment, in which MARSHALL, J., joined.

Raymond J. Place's behavior aroused the suspicions of law enforcement officers as he waited in line at Miami International Airport to purchase a ticket to New York's LaGuardia Airport. Two Drug Enforcement Administration (DEA) agents waited for Place at LaGuardia Airport. Place refused to consent to a search of his luggage and one of the agents told him that they were going to take the luggage to a federal judge to obtain a search warrant. The agents then took the luggage to Kennedy Airport where they subjected the bags to a "sniff test" by a trained narcotics detection dog. Approximately 90 minutes elapsed between the seizure of Place's luggage and the sniff test.

This case presents the issue whether the Fourth Amendment prohibits law enforcement authorities from temporarily detaining personal luggage for exposure to a trained narcotics detection dog on the basis of reasonable suspicion that the luggage contains narcotics. Given the enforcement problems associated with the detection of narcotics trafficking and the minimal intrusion that a properly limited detention would entail, we conclude that the Fourth Amendment does not prohibit such a detention. On the facts of this case, however, we hold that the police conduct exceeded the bounds of a permissible investigative detention of the luggage.

■ ■ ■

Place was indicted for possession of cocaine with intent to distribute in violation of 21 U.S.C. § 841(a)(1). In the District Court, Place moved to suppress the contents of the luggage seized from him at LaGuardia Airport, claiming that the warrantless seizure of the luggage violated his Fourth Amendment rights. The District Court denied the motion. Applying the standard of *Terry v. Ohio* (1968) to the detention of personal property, it concluded that detention of the bags could be justified if based on reasonable suspicion to believe that the bags contained narcotics. Finding reasonable suspicion, the District Court held that Place's Fourth Amendment rights were not violated by seizure of the bags by the DEA agents. Place pleaded guilty to the possession charge, reserving the right to appeal the denial of his motion to suppress.

On appeal of the conviction, the United States Court of Appeals for the Second Circuit reversed. The majority assumed both that *Terry* principles could be applied to justify a warrantless seizure of baggage on less than probable cause and that reasonable suspicion existed to justify the investigatory stop of Place. The majority concluded, however, that the prolonged seizure of Place's baggage exceeded the permissible limits of a *Terry*-type investigative stop and consequently amounted to a seizure without probable cause in violation of the Fourth Amendment.

We granted certiorari, and now affirm.

■ ■ ■

In this case, the Government asks us to recognize the reasonableness under the Fourth Amendment of warrantless seizures of personal luggage from the custody of the owner on the basis of less than probable cause, for the purpose of pursuing a limited course of investigation, short of opening the luggage, that would quickly confirm or dispel the authorities' suspicion. Specifically, we are asked to apply the principles of *Terry v. Ohio*, to permit such seizures on the basis of reasonable, articulable suspicion, premised on objective facts, that the luggage contains contraband or evidence of a crime. In our view, such application is appropriate.

In *Terry* the Court first recognized "the narrow authority of police officers who suspect criminal activity to make limited intrusions on an individual's personal security based on less than probable cause." In approving the limited search for weapons, or "frisk," of an individual the police reasonably believed to be armed and dangerous, the Court implicitly acknowledged the authority of the police to make a *forcible stop* of a person when the officer has reasonable, articulable suspicion that the person has been, is, or is about to be engaged in criminal activity. . . .

The exception to the probable-cause requirement for limited seizures of the person recognized in *Terry* and its progeny rests on a balancing of the competing interests to determine the reasonableness of the type of seizure involved within the meaning of "the Fourth Amendment's general proscription against unreasonable searches and seizures." We must balance the nature and quality of the intrusion on the individual's Fourth Amendment interests against the importance of the governmental interests alleged to justify the intrusion. When the nature and extent of the detention are minimally intrusive of the individual's Fourth Amendment interests, the opposing law enforcement interests can support a seizure based on less than probable cause.

We examine first the governmental interest offered as a justification for a brief seizure of luggage from the suspect's custody for the purpose of pursuing a limited course of investigation. The Government contends that, where the authorities possess specific and articulable facts warranting a reasonable belief that a traveler's luggage contains narcotics, the governmental interest in seizing the luggage briefly to pursue further investigation is substantial. We agree. . . .

Respondent suggests that, absent some special law enforcement interest such as officer safety, a generalized interest in law enforcement cannot justify an intrusion on an individual's Fourth Amendment interests in the absence of probable cause. Our prior cases, however, do not support this proposition. In *Terry*, we described the governmental interests supporting the initial seizure of the person as "effective crime prevention and detection; it is this interest which underlies the recognition that a police officer may in appropriate circumstances and in an appropriate manner approach a person for purposes of investigating possibly criminal behavior even though there is no probable cause to make an arrest." Similarly, in *Michigan v. Summers* (1981) we identified three law enforcement interests that justified limited detention of the occupants of the premises during execution of a valid search warrant: "preventing flight in the event that incriminating evidence is found," "minimizing the risk of harm" both to the officers and the occupants, and "orderly completion of the search." . . . Cf. *Florida v. Royer* (1983) ("The predicate permitting seizures on suspicion short of probable cause is that law enforcement interests warrant a limited intrusion on the personal security of the suspect"). The test is whether those interests are sufficiently "substantial," not whether they are independent of the interest in investigating crimes effectively and apprehending suspects. The context of a particular law enforcement practice, of course, may affect the determination whether a brief intrusion on Fourth Amendment interests on less than probable cause is essential to effective criminal investigation. Because of the inherently transient nature of drug courier activity at airports, allowing police to make brief investigative stops of persons at airports on reasonable suspicion of drug-trafficking substantially enhances the likelihood that police will be able to prevent the flow of narcotics into distribution channels.

Against this strong governmental interest, we must weigh the nature and extent of the intrusion upon the individual's Fourth Amendment rights when the police briefly detain luggage for limited investigative purposes. On this point, respondent Place urges that the rationale for a *Terry* stop of the person is wholly inapplicable to investigative detentions of personalty. Specifically, the *Terry* exception to the probable-cause requirement is premised on the notion that a *Terry*-type stop of the person is substantially less intrusive of a person's liberty interests than a formal arrest. In the property context, however, Place urges, there are no degrees of intrusion. Once the owner's property is seized, the dispossession is absolute.

We disagree. The intrusion on possessory interests occasioned by a seizure of one's personal effects can vary both in its nature and extent. The seizure may be made after the owner has relinquished control of the property to a third party or, as here, from the immediate custody and control of the owner. Moreover, the police may confine their investigation to an on-the-spot inquiry—for example, immediate exposure of the luggage to a trained narcotics detection dog—or transport the property to another location. Given the fact that seizures of property can vary in intrusiveness, some brief detentions of personal effects may be so minimally intrusive of Fourth Amendment interests that strong countervailing governmental interests will justify a seizure based only on specific articulable facts that the property contains contraband or evidence of a crime.

In sum, we conclude that when an officer's observations lead him reasonably to believe that a traveler is carrying luggage that contains narcotics, the principles of *Terry* and its progeny would permit the officer to detain the luggage briefly to investigate the circumstances that aroused his suspicion, provided that the investigative detention is properly limited in scope.

■ ■ ■

There is no doubt that the agents made a "seizure" of Place's luggage for purposes of the Fourth Amendment when, following his refusal to consent to a search, the agent told Place that he was going to take the luggage to a federal judge to secure issuance of a warrant. As we observed in *Terry*, "[t]he manner in which the seizure . . . [was] conducted is, of course, as vital a part of the inquiry as whether [it was] warranted at all." We therefore examine whether the agents' conduct in this case was such as to place the seizure within the general rule requiring probable cause for a seizure or within *Terry*'s exception to that rule.

■ ■ ■

The length of the detention of respondent's luggage alone precludes the conclusion that the seizure was reasonable in the absence of probable cause. Although we have recognized the reasonableness of seizures longer than the momentary ones . . . the brevity of the invasion of the individual's Fourth Amendment interests is an important factor in determining whether the seizure is so minimally intrusive as to be justifiable on reasonable suspicion. Moreover, in assessing the effect of the length of the detention, we take into account whether the police diligently pursue their investigation. We note that here the New York agents knew the time of Place's scheduled arrival at LaGuardia, had ample time to arrange for their additional investigation at that location, and thereby could have minimized the intrusion on respondent's Fourth Amendment interests. Thus, although we decline to adopt any outside time limitation for a permissible *Terry* stop, we have never approved a seizure of the person for the prolonged 90-minute period involved here and cannot do so on the facts presented by this case.

Although the 90-minute detention of respondent's luggage is sufficient to render the seizure unreasonable, the violation was exacerbated by the failure of the agents to accurately inform respondent of the place to which they were transporting his luggage, of the length of time he might be dispossessed, and of what arrangements would be made for return of the luggage if the investigation dispelled the suspicion. In short, we hold that the detention of respondent's luggage in this case went beyond the narrow authority possessed by police to detain briefly luggage reasonably suspected to contain narcotics.

■ ■ ■

We conclude that, under all of the circumstances of this case, the seizure of respondent's luggage was unreasonable under the Fourth Amendment. Consequently, the evidence obtained from the subsequent search of his luggage was inadmissible, and Place's conviction must be reversed. The judgment of the Court of Appeals, accordingly, is affirmed.

It is so ordered.

Minnesota v. Dickerson

508 U.S. 366 (1993)

Justice WHITE delivered the unanimous opinion of the Court.

In this case, we consider whether the Fourth Amendment permits the seizure of contraband detected through a police officer's sense of touch during a protective patdown search. . . .

On the evening of November 9, 1989, two Minneapolis police officers were patrolling an area on the city's north side in a marked squad car. At about 8:15 p.m., one of the officers observed respondent leaving a 12-unit apartment building on Morgan Avenue North. The officer, having previously responded to complaints of drug sales in the building's hallways and having executed several search warrants on the premises, considered the building to be a notorious "crack house." According to testimony credited by the trial court, respondent began walking toward the police but, upon spotting the squad car and making eye contact with one of the officers, abruptly halted and began walking in the opposite direction. His suspicion aroused, this officer watched as respondent turned and entered an alley on the other side of the apartment building. Based upon respondent's seemingly evasive actions and the fact that he had just left a building known for cocaine traffic, the officers decided to stop respondent and investigate further.

The officers pulled their squad car into the alley and ordered respondent to stop and submit to a patdown search. The search revealed no weapons, but the officer conducting the search did take an interest in a small lump in respondent's nylon jacket. The officer later testified:

> "[A]s I pat-searched the front of his body, I felt a lump, a small lump, in the front pocket. I examined it with my fingers and it slid and it felt to be a lump of crack cocaine in cellophane."

The officer then reached into respondent's pocket and retrieved a small plastic bag containing one-fifth of one gram of crack cocaine. Respondent was arrested and charged in Hennepin County District Court with possession of a controlled substance.

Before trial, respondent moved to suppress the cocaine. The trial court first concluded that the officers were justified under *Terry v. Ohio* (1968) in stopping respondent to investigate whether he might be engaged in criminal activity. The court further found that the officers were justified in frisking respondent to ensure that he was not carrying a weapon. Finally, analogizing to the "plain-view" doctrine, under which officers may make a warrantless seizure of contraband found in plain view during a lawful search for other items, the trial court ruled that the officers' seizure of the cocaine did not violate the Fourth Amendment.

■ ■ ■

His suppression motion having failed, respondent proceeded to trial and was found guilty.

On appeal, the Minnesota Court of Appeals reversed. The court agreed with the trial court that the investigative stop and protective patdown search of respondent were lawful under *Terry* because the officers had a reasonable belief based on specific and articulable facts that respondent was engaged in criminal behavior and that he might be armed and dangerous. The court concluded, however, that the officers had overstepped the bounds allowed by

Terry in seizing the cocaine. In doing so, the Court of Appeals "decline[d] to adopt the plain feel exception" to the warrant requirement.

The Minnesota Supreme Court affirmed. Like the Court of Appeals, the State Supreme Court held that both the stop and the frisk of respondent were valid under *Terry*, but found the seizure of the cocaine to be unconstitutional. The court expressly refused "to extend the plain view doctrine to the sense of touch" on the grounds that "the sense of touch is inherently less immediate and less reliable than the sense of sight" and that "the sense of touch is far more intrusive into the personal privacy that is at the core of the [F]ourth [A]mendment."

■ ■ ■

We granted certiorari to resolve a conflict among the state and federal courts over whether contraband detected through the sense of touch during a patdown search may be admitted into evidence. We now affirm. . . .

We have already held that police officers, at least under certain circumstances, may seize contraband detected during the lawful execution of a *Terry* (1968) search. In *Michigan v. Long,* for example, police approached a man who had driven his car into a ditch and who appeared to be under the influence of some intoxicant. As the man moved to reenter the car from the roadside, police spotted a knife on the floorboard. The officers stopped the man, subjected him to a patdown search, and then inspected the interior of the vehicle for other weapons. During the search of the passenger compartment, the police discovered an open pouch containing marijuana and seized it. This Court upheld the validity of the search and seizure under *Terry.* The Court held first that, in the context of a roadside encounter, where police have reasonable suspicion based on specific and articulable facts to believe that a driver may be armed and dangerous, they may conduct a protective search for weapons not only of the driver's person but also of the passenger compartment of the automobile. Of course, the protective search of the vehicle, being justified solely by the danger that weapons stored there could be used against the officers or bystanders, must be "limited to those areas in which a weapon may be placed or hidden." The Court then held: "If, while conducting a legitimate *Terry* search of the interior of the automobile, the officer should, as here, discover contraband other than weapons, he clearly cannot be required to ignore the contraband, and the Fourth Amendment does not require its suppression in such circumstances."

The Court in *Long* justified this latter holding by reference to our cases under the "plain-view" doctrine. Under that doctrine, if police are lawfully in a position from which they view an object, if its incriminating character is immediately apparent, and if the officers have a lawful right of access to the object, they may seize it without a warrant. If, however, the police lack probable cause to believe that an object in plain view is contraband without conducting some further search of the object—*i.e.,* if "its incriminating character [is not] 'immediately apparent,' " . . . the plain-view doctrine cannot justify its seizure.

We think that this doctrine has an obvious application by analogy to cases in which an officer discovers contraband through the sense of touch during an otherwise lawful search. The rationale of the plain-view doctrine is that if contraband is left in open view and is observed by a police officer from a lawful vantage point, there has been no invasion of a legitimate expectation of privacy and thus no "search" within the meaning of the Fourth Amendment—or at least no search independent of the initial intrusion that gave the officers their vantage point. The warrantless seizure of contraband that presents itself in this manner is deemed justified by the realization that resort to a neutral magistrate under such circumstances would often be impracticable and would do little to promote the objectives of the Fourth Amendment. The same can be said of tactile discoveries of contraband. If a police officer lawfully pats down a suspect's outer clothing and feels an object whose contour or mass makes its identity immediately apparent, there has been no invasion of the suspect's privacy beyond that already authorized by the officer's search for weapons; if the object is contraband, its warrantless seizure would be justified by the same practical considerations that inhere in the plain-view context.

The Minnesota Supreme Court rejected an analogy to the plain-view doctrine on two grounds: first, its belief that "the sense of touch is inherently less immediate and less reliable than the sense of sight," and second, that "the sense of touch is far more intrusive into the personal privacy that is at the core of the [F]ourth [A]mendment." We have a somewhat different view. First, *Terry* itself demonstrates that the sense of touch is capable of revealing the nature of an object with sufficient reliability to support a seizure. The very premise of *Terry*, after all, is that officers will be able to detect the presence of weapons through the sense of touch and *Terry* upheld precisely such a seizure. Even if it were true that the sense of touch is generally less reliable than the sense of sight, that only suggests that officers will less often be able to justify seizures of unseen contraband. Regardless of whether the officer detects the contraband by sight or by touch, however, the Fourth Amendment's requirement that the officer have probable cause to believe that the item is contraband before seizing it ensures against excessively speculative seizures. The court's second concern—that touch is more intrusive into privacy than is sight—is inapposite in light of the fact that the intrusion the court fears has already been authorized by the lawful search for weapons. The seizure of an item whose identity is already known occasions no further invasion of privacy.

■　■　■

It remains to apply these principles to the facts of this case. Respondent has not challenged the finding made by the trial court and affirmed by both the Court of Appeals and the State Supreme Court that the police were justified under *Terry* in stopping him and frisking him for weapons. Thus, the dispositive question before this Court is whether the officer who conducted the search was acting within the lawful bounds marked by *Terry* at the time he gained probable cause to believe that the lump in respondent's jacket was contraband. The State District Court did not make precise findings on this point, instead finding simply that the officer, after feeling "a small, hard object wrapped in plastic" in respondent's pocket, "formed the opinion that the object . . . was crack . . . cocaine." The District Court also noted that the officer made "no claim that he suspected this object to be a weapon," a finding affirmed on appeal (the officer "never thought the lump was a weapon"). The Minnesota Supreme Court, after "a close examination of the record," held that the officer's own testimony "belies any notion that he 'immediately' " recognized the lump as crack cocaine. Rather, the court concluded, the officer determined that the lump was contraband only after "squeezing, sliding and otherwise manipulating the contents of the defendant's pocket"—a pocket which the officer already knew contained no weapon.

Under the State Supreme Court's interpretation of the record before it, it is clear that the court was correct in holding that the police officer in this case overstepped the bounds of the "strictly circumscribed" search for weapons allowed under *Terry*. Where, as here, "an officer who is executing a valid search for one item seizes a different item," this Court rightly "has been sensitive to the danger . . . that officers will enlarge a specific authorization, furnished by a warrant or an exigency, into the equivalent of a general warrant to rummage and seize at will." Here, the officer's continued exploration of respondent's pocket after having concluded that it contained no weapon was unrelated to "[t]he sole justification of the search [under *Terry*:] . . . the protection of the police officer and others nearby." It therefore amounted to the sort of evidentiary search that *Terry* expressly refused to authorize, and that we have condemned in subsequent cases.

Once again, the analogy to the plain-view doctrine is apt. In *Arizona v. Hicks* (1987), this Court held invalid the seizure of stolen stereo equipment found by police while executing a valid search for other evidence. Although the police were lawfully on the premises, they obtained probable cause to believe that the stereo equipment was contraband only after moving the equipment to permit officers to read its serial numbers. The subsequent seizure of the equipment could not be justified by the plain-view doctrine, this Court explained, because the incriminating character of the stereo equipment was not immediately apparent; rather, probable cause to believe that the equipment was stolen arose only as a result of a further search—the moving of the equipment—that was not authorized by a search warrant or by any exception to the warrant requirement. The facts of this case are very similar. Although the officer was lawfully in a position to feel the lump in respondent's pocket, because *Terry* entitled him to place his hands upon respondent's jacket, the court below determined that the incriminating character of the object was not immediately apparent to him. Rather, the officer determined that the item was contraband only after conducting a further search, one not authorized by *Terry* or by any other exception to the warrant requirement. Because this further search of respondent's pocket was constitutionally invalid, the seizure of the cocaine that followed is likewise unconstitutional. . . .

For these reasons, the judgment of the Minnesota Supreme Court is *Affirmed*.

Illinois v. Caballes

543 U.S. 405 (2005)

See also Chapter 2.B.3.a.

STEVENS, J., delivered the opinion of the Court, in which O'CONNOR, SCALIA, KENNEDY, THOMAS, and BREYER, JJ., joined. SOUTER, J., filed a dissenting opinion. GINSBURG, J., filed a dissenting opinion, in which SOUTER, J., joined. REHNQUIST, C.J., took no part in the decision of the case.

Illinois State Trooper Daniel Gillette stopped respondent for speeding on an interstate highway. Craig Graham, of the Illinois State Police Drug Interdiction Team overheard Gillette's radio transmission and headed for the scene with his narcotics-detection dog. When they arrived, respondent was in Gillette's vehicle and Gillette was in the process of writing a warning ticket. Respondent's car was on the shoulder of the road. Graham walked his dog around respondent's car, and the dog alerted at the trunk. A search of the trunk revealed marijuana, and respondent was arrested. The incident lasted less than ten minutes.

The question on which we granted certiorari is narrow: "Whether the Fourth Amendment requires reasonable, articulable suspicion to justify using a drug-detection dog to sniff a vehicle during a legitimate traffic stop." Thus, we proceed on the assumption that the officer conducting the dog sniff had no information about respondent except that he had been stopped for speeding; accordingly, we have omitted any reference to facts about respondent that might have triggered a modicum of suspicion.

Here, the initial seizure of respondent when he was stopped on the highway was based on probable cause and was concededly lawful. It is nevertheless clear that a seizure that is lawful at its inception can violate the Fourth Amendment if its manner of execution unreasonably infringes interests protected by the Constitution. A seizure that is justified solely by the interest in issuing a warning ticket to the driver can become unlawful if it is prolonged beyond the time reasonably required to complete that mission. In an earlier case involving a dog sniff that occurred during an unreasonably prolonged traffic stop, the Illinois Supreme Court held that use of the dog and the subsequent discovery of contraband were the product of an unconstitutional seizure. We may assume that a similar result would be warranted in this case if the dog sniff had been conducted while respondent was being unlawfully detained.

In the state-court proceedings, however, the judges carefully reviewed the details of Officer Gillette's conversations with respondent and the precise timing of his radio transmissions to the dispatcher to determine whether he had improperly extended the duration of the stop to enable the dog sniff to occur. We have not recounted those details because we accept the state court's conclusion that the duration of the stop in this case was entirely justified by the traffic offense and the ordinary inquiries incident to such a stop.

■ ■ ■

The judgment of the Illinois Supreme Court is vacated, and the case is remanded for further proceedings not inconsistent with this opinion.

■ ■ ■

It is so ordered.

Justice GINSBURG, with whom Justice SOUTER joins, dissenting.

The Supreme Court of Illinois held that the drug evidence should have been suppressed. . . . [T]he court employed a two-part test taken from *Terry v. Ohio* (1968) to determine the overall reasonableness of the stop. The court asked first "whether the officer's action was justified at its inception," and second "whether it was reasonably related in scope to the circumstances which justified the interference in the first place." "[I]t is undisputed," the court observed, "that the traffic stop was properly initiated"; thus, the dispositive inquiry trained on the "second part of the *Terry* test," in which "[t]he State bears the burden of establishing that the conduct remained within the scope of the stop."

The court concluded that the State failed to offer sufficient justification for the canine sniff: "The police did not detect the odor of marijuana in the car or note any other evidence suggesting the presence of illegal drugs." Lacking "specific and articulable facts" supporting the canine sniff, the court ruled, "the police impermissibly broadened the scope of the traffic stop in this case into a drug investigation." I would affirm the Illinois Supreme Court's judgment and hold that the drug sniff violated the Fourth Amendment.

In *Terry v. Ohio*, the Court upheld the stop and subsequent frisk of an individual based on an officer's observation of suspicious behavior and his reasonable belief that the suspect was armed. In a *Terry*-type investigatory stop, "the officer's action [must be] justified at its inception, and . . . reasonably related in scope to the circumstances which justified the interference in the first place." In applying *Terry*, the Court has several times indicated that the limitation on "scope" is not confined to the duration of the seizure; it also encompasses the manner in which the seizure is conducted. See, *e.g., Hiibel v. Sixth Judicial Dist. Court of Nev., Humboldt Cty.* (2004) (an officer's request that an individual identify himself "has an immediate relation to the purpose, rationale, and practical demands of a *Terry* stop"); *United States v. Hensley* (1985) (examining . . . both "the length and intrusiveness of the stop and detention"); *Florida v. Royer* (1983) ("[A]n investigative detention must be temporary and last no longer than is necessary to effectuate the purpose of the stop [and] the investigative methods employed should be the least intrusive means reasonably available to verify or dispel the officer's suspicion." . . .).

"A routine traffic stop," the Court has observed, "is a relatively brief encounter and 'is more analogous to a so-called *Terry* stop . . . than to a formal arrest.' " . . . see also *ante* (The government may not "take advantage of a suspect's immobility to search for evidence unrelated to the reason for the detention."). I would apply *Terry's* reasonable-relation test, as the Illinois Supreme Court did, to determine whether the canine sniff impermissibly expanded the scope of the initially valid seizure of Caballes.

It is hardly dispositive that the dog sniff in this case may not have lengthened the duration of the stop. Cf. *ante* ("A seizure ... can become unlawful if it is prolonged beyond the time reasonably required to complete [the initial] mission."). *Terry*, it merits repetition, instructs that any investigation must be "reasonably related in *scope* to the circumstances which justified the interference in the first place." The unwarranted and nonconsensual expansion of the seizure here from a routine traffic stop to a drug investigation broadened the scope of the investigation in a manner that, in my judgment, runs afoul of the Fourth Amendment.

The Court rejects the Illinois Supreme Court's judgment and, implicitly, the application of *Terry* to a traffic stop converted, by calling in a dog, to a drug search. The Court so rules, holding that a dog sniff does not render a seizure that is reasonable in time unreasonable in scope. Dog sniffs that detect only the possession of contraband may be employed without offense to the Fourth Amendment, the Court reasons, because they reveal no lawful activity and hence disturb no legitimate expectation of privacy.

In my view, the Court diminishes the Fourth Amendment's force by abandoning the second *Terry* inquiry (was the police action "reasonably related in scope to the circumstances [justifiying] the [initial] interference"). A drug-detection dog is an intimidating animal. Injecting such an animal into a routine traffic stop changes the character of the encounter between the police and the motorist. The stop becomes broader, more adversarial, and (in at least some cases) longer. Caballes—who, as far as Troopers Gillette and Graham knew, was guilty solely of driving six miles per hour over the speed limit—was exposed to the embarrassment and intimidation of being investigated, on a public thoroughfare, for drugs. Even if the drug sniff is not characterized as a Fourth Amendment "search," the sniff surely broadened the scope of the traffic-violation-related seizure.

The Court has never removed police action from Fourth Amendment control on the ground that the action is well calculated to apprehend the guilty. See, *e.g., United States v. Karo* (1984) (Fourth Amendment warrant requirement applies to police monitoring of a beeper in a house even if "the facts [justify] believing that a crime is being or will be committed and that monitoring the beeper wherever it goes is likely to produce evidence of criminal activity."); see also *Minnesota v. Carter* (1998) ("Fourth Amendment protection, reserved for the innocent only, would have little force in regulating police behavior toward either the innocent or the guilty."). Under today's decision, every traffic stop could become an occasion to call in the dogs, to the distress and embarrassment of the law-abiding population.

The Illinois Supreme Court, it seems to me, correctly apprehended the danger in allowing the police to search for contraband despite the absence of cause to suspect its presence. Today's decision, in contrast, clears the way for suspicionless, dog-accompanied drug sweeps of parked cars along sidewalks and in parking lots. . . . Nor would motorists have constitutional grounds for complaint should police with dogs, stationed at long traffic lights, circle cars waiting for the red signal to turn green.

This Court has distinguished between the general interest in crime control and more immediate threats to public safety. In *Michigan Dept. of State Police v. Sitz* (1990), this Court upheld the use of a sobriety traffic checkpoint. Balancing the State's interest in preventing drunk driving, the extent to which that could be accomplished through the checkpoint program, and the degree of intrusion the stops involved, the Court determined that the State's checkpoint program was consistent with the Fourth Amendment. Ten years after *Sitz*, in *Indianapolis v. Edmond* (2001), this Court held that a drug interdiction checkpoint violated the Fourth Amendment. Despite the illegal narcotics traffic that the Nation is struggling to stem, the Court explained, a "general interest in crime control" did not justify the stops. The Court distinguished the sobriety checkpoints in *Sitz* on the ground that those checkpoints were designed to eliminate an "immediate, vehicle-bound threat to life and limb."

The use of bomb-detection dogs to check vehicles for explosives without doubt has a closer kinship to the sobriety checkpoints in *Sitz* than to the drug checkpoints in *Edmond*. As the Court observed in *Edmond*: "[T]he Fourth Amendment would almost certainly permit an appropriately tailored roadblock set up to thwart an imminent terrorist attack. . . ." Even if the Court were to change course and characterize a dog sniff as an independent Fourth Amendment search, the immediate, present danger of explosives would likely justify a bomb sniff under the special needs doctrine.

■ ■ ■

For the reasons stated, I would hold that the police violated Caballes' Fourth Amendment rights when, without cause to suspect wrongdoing, they conducted a dog sniff of his vehicle. I would therefore affirm the judgment of the Illinois Supreme Court.

Arizona v. United States

132 S. Ct. 2492 (2012)

KENNEDY, J., delivered the opinion of the Court, in which ROBERTS, C.J., and GINSBURG, BREYER, and SOTOMAYOR, JJ., joined. SCALIA, J., THOMAS, J., and ALITO, J., filed opinions concurring in part and dissenting in part. KAGAN, J., took no part in the consideration or decision of the case.

To address pressing issues related to the large number of aliens within its borders who do not have a lawful right to be in this country, the State of Arizona in 2010 enacted a statute called the Support Our Law Enforcement and Safe Neighborhoods Act. The law is often referred to as S.B. 1070, the version introduced in the state senate. Its stated purpose is to "discourage and deter the unlawful entry and presence of aliens and economic activity by persons unlawfully present in the United States." The law's provisions establish an official state policy of "attrition through enforcement."

The question before the Court is whether federal law preempts and renders invalid four separate provisions of the state law.

Note—The excerpt of this decision will only deal with one of the sections.

I

The United States filed this suit against Arizona, seeking to enjoin S.B. 1070 as preempted. . . . Four provisions of the law are at issue here. Two create new state offenses. Section 3 makes failure to comply with federal alien-registration requirements a state misdemeanor. Section 5, in relevant part, makes it a misdemeanor for an unauthorized alien to seek or engage in work in the State; this provision is referred to as §5(C). See §13-2928(C). Two other provisions give specific arrest authority and investigative duties with respect to certain aliens to state and local law enforcement officers. Section 6 authorizes officers to arrest without a warrant a person "the officer has probable cause to believe . . . has committed any public offense that makes the person removable from the United States." §13-3883(A)(5). Section 2(B) provides that officers who conduct a stop, detention, or arrest must in some circumstances make efforts to verify the person's immigration status with the Federal Government.

The United States District Court for the District of Arizona issued a preliminary injunction preventing the four provisions at issue from taking effect. The Court of Appeals for the Ninth Circuit affirmed. It agreed that the United States had established a likelihood of success on its preemption claims. The Court of Appeals was unanimous in its conclusion that §§3 and 5(C) were likely preempted. Judge Bea dissented from the decision to uphold the preliminary injunction against §§2(B) and 6. This Court granted certiorari to resolve important questions concerning the interaction of state and federal power with respect to the law of immigration and alien status.

II

A

The Government of the United States has broad, undoubted power over the subject of immigration and the status of aliens. This authority rests, in part, on the National Government's constitutional power to "establish an uniform Rule of Naturalization," U.S. Const., Art. I, §8, cl. 4, and its inherent power as sovereign to control and conduct relations with foreign nations.

The federal power to determine immigration policy is well settled. Immigration policy can affect trade, investment, tourism, and diplomatic relations for the entire Nation, as well as the perceptions and expectations of aliens in this country who seek the full protection of its laws. Perceived mistreatment of aliens in the United States may lead to harmful reciprocal treatment of American citizens abroad.

It is fundamental that foreign countries concerned about the status, safety, and security of their nationals in the United States must be able to confer and communicate on this subject with one national sovereign, not the 50 separate States. This Court has reaffirmed that "[o]ne of the most important and delicate of all international relationships . . . has to do with the protection of the just rights of a country's own nationals when those nationals are in another country." *Hines v. Davidowitz* (1941).

Federal governance of immigration and alien status is extensive and complex. Congress has specified categories of aliens who may not be admitted to the United States. Unlawful entry and unlawful reentry into the country are federal offenses. Once here, aliens are required to register with the Federal Government and to carry proof of status on their person. Failure to do so is a federal misdemeanor. Federal law also authorizes States to deny noncitizens a range of public benefits, § 1622; and it imposes sanctions on employers who hire unauthorized workers, § 1324a.

Congress has specified which aliens may be removed from the United States and the procedures for doing so. Aliens may be removed if they were inadmissible at the time of entry, have been convicted of certain crimes, or meet other criteria set by federal law. Removal is a civil, not criminal, matter. A principal feature of the removal system is the broad discretion exercised by immigration officials. Federal officials, as an initial matter, must decide whether it makes sense to pursue removal at all. If removal proceedings commence, aliens may seek asylum and other discretionary relief allowing them to remain in the country or at least to leave without formal removal.

Discretion in the enforcement of immigration law embraces immediate human concerns. Unauthorized workers trying to support their families, for example, likely pose less danger than alien smugglers or aliens who commit a serious crime. The equities of an individual case may turn on many factors, including whether the alien has children born in the United States, long ties to the community, or a record of distinguished military service. Some discretionary decisions involve policy choices that bear on this Nation's international relations. Returning an alien to his own country may be deemed inappropriate even where he has committed a removable offense or fails to meet the criteria for admission. The foreign state may be mired in civil war, complicit in political persecution, or enduring conditions that create a real risk that the alien or his family will be harmed upon return. The dynamic nature of relations with other countries requires the Executive Branch to ensure that enforcement policies are consistent with this Nation's foreign policy with respect to these and other realities.

Agencies in the Department of Homeland Security play a major role in enforcing the country's immigration laws. United States Customs and Border Protection (CBP) is responsible for determining the admissibility of aliens and securing the country's borders. In 2010, CBP's Border Patrol apprehended almost half a million people. Immigration and Customs Enforcement (ICE), a second agency, "conducts criminal investigations involving the enforcement of immigration-related statutes." ICE also operates the Law Enforcement Support Center. LESC, as the Center is known, provides immigration status information to federal, state, and local officials around the clock. ICE officers are responsible "for the identification, apprehension, and removal of illegal aliens from the United States." See Dept. of Homeland Security, Office of Immigration Statistics, Immigration Enforcement Actions: 2010, p. 2 (2011)

B

The pervasiveness of federal regulation does not diminish the importance of immigration policy to the States. Arizona bears many of the consequences of unlawful immigration. Hundreds of thousands of deportable aliens are apprehended in Arizona each year.

Statistics alone do not capture the full extent of Arizona's concerns. Accounts in the record suggest there is an "epidemic of crime, safety risks, serious property damage, and environmental problems" associated with the influx of illegal migration across private land near the Mexican border.

These concerns are the background for the formal legal analysis that follows. The issue is whether, under preemption principles, federal law permits Arizona to implement the state-law provisions in dispute.

III

Federalism, central to the constitutional design, adopts the principle that both the National and State Governments have elements of sovereignty the other is bound to respect. From the existence of two sovereigns follows the possibility that laws can be in conflict or at cross-purposes. The Supremacy Clause provides a clear rule that federal law "shall be the supreme Law of the Land; and the Judges in every State shall be bound thereby, any Thing in the Constitution or Laws of any State to the Contrary notwithstanding." Art. VI, cl. 2. Under this principle, Congress has the power to preempt state law. There is no doubt that Congress may withdraw specified powers from the States by enacting a statute containing an express preemption provision.

State law must also give way to federal law in at least two other circumstances. First, the States are precluded from regulating conduct in a field that Congress, acting within its proper authority, has determined must be regulated by its exclusive governance. The intent to displace state law altogether can be inferred from a framework of regulation "so pervasive . . . that Congress left no room for the States to supplement it" or where there is a "federal interest . . . so dominant that the federal system will be assumed to preclude enforcement of state laws on the same subject." *Rice v. Santa Fe Elevator Corp.* (1947).

Second, state laws are preempted when they conflict with federal law. This includes cases where "compliance with both federal and state regulations is a physical impossibility," *Florida Lime & Avocado Growers, Inc. v. Paul* (1963), and those instances where the challenged state law "stands as an obstacle to the accomplishment and execution of the full purposes and objectives of Congress," *Hines*, 312 U.S., at 67.

The four challenged provisions of the state law each must be examined under these preemption principles.

IV

Section 2(B)

Section 2(B) of S.B. 1070 requires state officers to make a "reasonable attempt . . . to determine the immigration status" of any person they stop, detain, or arrest on some other legitimate basis if "reasonable suspicion exists that the person is an alien and is unlawfully present in the United States." Ariz. Rev. Stat. Ann. § 11-1051(B) (West 2012). The law also provides that "[a]ny person who is arrested shall have the person's immigration status determined before the person is released." Ibid. The accepted way to perform these status checks is to contact ICE, which maintains a database of immigration records.

Three limits are built into the state provision. First, a detainee is presumed not to be an alien unlawfully present in the United States if he or she provides a valid Arizona driver's license or similar identification. Second, officers "may not consider race, color or national origin . . . except to the extent permitted by the United States [and] Arizona Constitution[s]." Third, the provisions must be "implemented in a manner consistent with federal law regulating immigration, protecting the civil rights of all persons and respecting the privileges and immunities of United States citizens." § 11-1051(L) (West 2012).

The United States and its *amici* contend that, even with these limits, the State's verification requirements pose an obstacle to the framework Congress put in place. The first concern is the mandatory nature of the status checks. The second is the possibility of prolonged detention while the checks are being performed.

1

Consultation between federal and state officials is an important feature of the immigration system. Congress has made clear that no formal agreement or special training needs to be in place for state officers to "communicate with the [Federal Government] regarding the immigration status of any individual, including reporting knowledge that a particular alien is not lawfully present in the United States." 8 U.S.C. § 1357(g)(10)(A). And Congress has obligated ICE to respond to any request made by state officials for verification of a person's citizenship or immigration status. ICE's Law Enforcement Support Center operates "24 hours a day, seven days a week, 365 days a year" and provides, among other things, "immigration status, identity information and real-time assistance to local, state and federal law enforcement agencies." ICE, Fact Sheet,

The United States argues that making status verification mandatory interferes with the federal immigration scheme. It is true that § 2(B) does not allow state officers to consider federal enforcement priorities in deciding whether to contact ICE about someone they have detained. In other words, the officers must make an inquiry even in cases where it seems unlikely that the Attorney General would have the alien removed. This might be the case, for example, when an alien is an elderly veteran with significant and longstanding ties to the community.

Congress has done nothing to suggest it is inappropriate to communicate with ICE in these situations, however. Indeed, it has encouraged the sharing of information about possible immigration violations. A federal statute regulating the public benefits provided to qualified aliens in fact instructs that "no State or local government entity may be prohibited, or in any way restricted, from sending to or receiving from [ICE] information regarding the immigration status, lawful or unlawful, of an alien in the United States." §1644. The federal scheme thus leaves room for a policy requiring state officials to contact ICE as a routine matter.

2

Some who support the challenge to §2(B) argue that, in practice, state officers will be required to delay the release of some detainees for no reason other than to verify their immigration status. Detaining individuals solely to verify their immigration status would raise constitutional concerns. And it would disrupt the federal framework to put state officers in the position of holding aliens in custody for possible unlawful presence without federal direction and supervision.

But §2(B) could be read to avoid these concerns. To take one example, a person might be stopped for jaywalking in Tucson and be unable to produce identification. The first sentence of §2(B) instructs officers to make a "reasonable" attempt to verify his immigration status with ICE if there is reasonable suspicion that his presence in the United States is unlawful. The state courts may conclude that, unless the person continues to be suspected of some crime for which he may be detained by state officers, it would not be reasonable to prolong the stop for the immigration inquiry.

To take another example, a person might be held pending release on a charge of driving under the influence of alcohol. As this goes beyond a mere stop, the arrestee (unlike the jaywalker) would appear to be subject to the categorical requirement in the second sentence of §2(B) that "[a]ny person who is arrested shall have the person's immigration status determined before [he] is released." State courts may read this as an instruction to initiate a status check every time someone is arrested, or in some subset of those cases, rather than as a command to hold the person until the check is complete no matter the circumstances. Even if the law is read as an instruction to complete a check while the person is in custody, moreover, it is not clear at this stage and on this record that the verification process would result in prolonged detention.

However the law is interpreted, if §2(B) only requires state officers to conduct a status check during the course of an authorized, lawful detention or after a detainee has been released, the provision likely would survive preemption—at least absent some showing that it has other consequences that are adverse to federal law and its objectives. There is no need in this case to address whether reasonable suspicion of illegal entry or another immigration crime would be a legitimate basis for prolonging a detention, . . . or whether this too would be preempted by federal law.

The nature and timing of this case counsel caution in evaluating the validity of §2(B). The Federal Government has brought suit against a sovereign State to challenge the provision even before the law has gone into effect. There is a basic uncertainty about what the law means and how it will be enforced. At this stage, without the benefit of a definitive interpretation from the state courts, it would be inappropriate to assume §2(B) will be construed in a way that creates a conflict with federal law.

■ ■ ■

V

Immigration policy shapes the destiny of the Nation. On May 24, 2012, at one of this Nation's most distinguished museums of history, a dozen immigrants stood before the tattered flag that inspired Francis Scott Key to write the National Anthem. There they took the oath to become American citizens. These naturalization ceremonies bring together men and women of different origins who now share a common destiny. They swear a common oath to renounce fidelity to foreign princes, to defend the Constitution, and to bear arms on behalf of the country when required by law. The history of the United States is in part made of the stories, talents, and lasting contributions of those who crossed oceans and deserts to come here.

The National Government has significant power to regulate immigration. With power comes responsibility, and the sound exercise of national power over immigration depends on the Nation's meeting its responsibility to base its laws on a political will informed by searching, thoughtful, rational civic discourse. Arizona may have understandable frustrations with the problems caused by illegal immigration while that process continues, but the State may not pursue policies that undermine federal law.

■ ■ ■

The United States has established that §§3, 5(C), and 6 of S.B. 1070 are preempted. It was improper, however, to enjoin §2(B) before the state courts had an opportunity to construe it and without some showing that enforcement of the provision in fact conflicts with federal immigration law and its objectives.

The judgment of the Court of Appeals for the Ninth Circuit is affirmed in part and reversed in part. The case is remanded for further proceedings consistent with this opinion.

It is so ordered.

Justice KAGAN took no part in the consideration or decision of this case.

Justice SCALIA, concurring in part and dissenting in part.

The United States is an indivisible "Union of sovereign States." *Hinderlider v. La Plata River & Cherry Creek Ditch Co.* (1938). Today's opinion, approving virtually all of the Ninth Circuit's injunction against enforcement of the four challenged provisions of Arizona's law, deprives States of what most would consider the defining characteristic of sovereignty: the power to exclude from the sovereign's territory people who have no right to be there. Neither the Constitution itself nor even any law passed by Congress supports this result. I dissent.

I

As a sovereign, Arizona has the inherent power to exclude persons from its territory, subject only to those limitations expressed in the Constitution or constitutionally imposed by Congress. That power to exclude has long been recognized as inherent in sovereignty. Emer de Vattel's seminal 1758 treatise on the Law of Nations stated:

> "The sovereign may forbid the entrance of his territory either to foreigners in general, or in particular cases, or to certain persons, or for certain particular purposes, according as he may think it advantageous to the state. There is nothing in all this, that does not flow from the rights of domain and sovereignty: every one is obliged to pay respect to the prohibition; and whoever dares violate it, incurs the penalty decreed to render it effectual." The Law of Nations, bk. II, ch. VII, § 94, p. 309 (B. Kapossy & R. Whatmore eds. 2008).

There is no doubt that "before the adoption of the constitution of the United States" each State had the authority to "prevent [itself] from being burdened by an influx of persons." *Mayor of New York v. Miln* (1837). And the Constitution did not strip the States of that authority. To the contrary, two of the Constitution's provisions were designed to enable the States to prevent "the intrusion of obnoxious aliens through other States." Letter from James Madison to Edmund Randolph (Aug. 27, 1782), in 1 The Writings of James Madison 226 (1900); accord, The Federalist No. 42, pp. 269-271 (C. Rossiter ed. 1961) (J. Madison). The Articles of Confederation had provided that "the free inhabitants of each of these States, paupers, vagabonds and fugitives from justice excepted, shall be entitled to all privileges and immunities of free citizens in the several States." Articles of Confederation, Art. IV. This meant that an unwelcome alien could obtain all the rights of a citizen of one State simply by first becoming an *inhabitant* of another. To remedy this, the Constitution's Privileges and Immunities Clause provided that "[t]he *Citizens* of each State shall be entitled to all Privileges and Immunities of Citizens in the several States." Art. IV, § 2, cl. 1 (emphasis added). But if one State had particularly lax citizenship standards, it might still serve as a gateway for the entry of "obnoxious aliens" into other States. This problem was solved "by authorizing the general government to establish a uniform rule of naturalization throughout the United States." The Federalist No. 42, *supra*, at 271; see Art. I, § 8, cl. 4.

In other words, the naturalization power was given to Congress not to abrogate States' power to exclude those they did not want, but to vindicate it.

Two other provisions of the Constitution are an acknowledgment of the States' sovereign interest in protecting their borders. Article I provides that "[n]o State shall, without the Consent of the Congress, lay any Imposts or Duties on Imports or Exports, *except what may be absolutely necessary for executing its inspection Laws.*" Art. I, §10, cl. 2 (emphasis added). This assumed what everyone assumed: that the States could exclude from their territory dangerous or unwholesome goods. A later portion of the same section provides that "[n]o State shall, without the Consent of Congress, ... engage in War, *unless actually invaded, or in such imminent Danger as will not admit of delay.*" Art. I, §10, cl. 3 (emphasis added). This limits the States' sovereignty (in a way not relevant here) but leaves intact their inherent power to protect their territory.

Notwithstanding "[t]he myth of an era of unrestricted immigration" in the first 100 years of the Republic, the States enacted numerous laws restricting the immigration of certain classes of aliens, including convicted criminals, indigents, persons with contagious diseases, and (in Southern States) freed blacks. Neuman, The Lost Century of American Immigration (1776-1875), 93 Colum. L. Rev. (1993). State laws not only provided for the removal of unwanted immigrants but also imposed penalties on unlawfully present aliens and those who aided their immigration.

In fact, the controversy surrounding the Alien and Sedition Acts involved a debate over whether, under the Constitution, the States had *exclusive* authority to enact such immigration laws. Criticism of the Sedition Act has become a prominent feature of our First Amendment jurisprudence, but one of the Alien Acts[3] also aroused controversy at the time:

> *"Be it enacted by the Senate and House of Representatives of the United States of America in Congress assembled,* That it shall be lawful for the President of the United States at any time during the continuance of this act, to *order* all such *aliens* as he shall judge dangerous to the peace and safety of the United States, or shall have reasonable grounds to suspect are concerned in any treasonable or secret machinations against the government thereof, to depart out of the territory of the United States. ..." An Act concerning Aliens, 1 Stat. 570, 570-571.

The Kentucky and Virginia Resolutions, written in denunciation of these Acts, insisted that the power to exclude unwanted aliens rested solely in the States. Jefferson's Kentucky Resolutions insisted "that alien friends are under the jurisdiction and protection of the laws of the state wherein they are [and] that no power over them has been delegated to the United States, nor prohibited to the individual states, distinct from their power over citizens." Kentucky Resolutions of 1798 (1991). Madison's Virginia Resolutions likewise contended that the Alien Act purported to give the President "a power nowhere delegated

---

3. There were two Alien Acts, one of which dealt only with enemy aliens. An Act respecting Alien Enemies, 1 Stat. 577.

to the federal government." Virginia Resolutions of 1798, reprinted in Powell, *supra*, at 134 (emphasis omitted). Notably, moreover, the Federalist proponents of the Act defended it primarily on the ground that "[t]he removal of aliens is the usual preliminary of hostility" and could therefore be justified in exercise of the Federal Government's war powers.

In *Mayor of New York v. Miln*, this Court considered a New York statute that required the commander of any ship arriving in New York from abroad to disclose "the name, place of birth, and last legal settlement, age and occupation ... of all passengers ... with the intention of proceeding to the said city." 11 Pet., at 130-131. After discussing the sovereign authority to regulate the entrance of foreigners described by De Vattel, the Court said:

> "The power ... of New York to pass this law having undeniably existed at the formation of the constitution, the simply inquiry is, whether by that instrument it was taken from the states, and granted to congress; for if it were not, it yet remains with them." Id., at 132, 11 Pet. 102, 9 L. Ed. 648.

And the Court held that it remains. Id., at 139, 11 Pet. 102, 9 L. Ed. 648.

II

One would conclude from the foregoing that after the adoption of the Constitution there was some doubt about the power of the Federal Government to control immigration, but no doubt about the power of the States to do so. Since the founding era (though not immediately), doubt about the Federal Government's power has disappeared. Indeed, primary responsibility for immigration policy has shifted from the States to the Federal Government. Congress exercised its power "[t]o establish an uniform Rule of Naturalization," Art. I, §8, cl. 4, very early on, see An Act to establish an uniform Rule of Naturalization, 1 Stat. 103. But with the fleeting exception of the Alien Act, Congress did not enact any legislation regulating *immigration* for the better part of a century. In 1862, Congress passed "An Act to prohibit the 'Coolie Trade' by American Citizens in American Vessels," which prohibited "procuring [Chinese nationals] ... to be disposed of, or sold, or transferred, for any term of years or for any time whatever, as servants or apprentices, or to be held to service or labor." 12 Stat. 340. Then, in 1875, Congress amended that act to bar admission to Chinese, Japanese, and other Asian immigrants who had "entered into a contract or agreement for a term of service within the United States, for lewd and immoral purposes." An act supplementary to the acts in relation to immigration, ch. 141, 18 Stat. 477. And in 1882, Congress enacted the first general immigration statute. See An act to regulate Immigration, 22 Stat. 214. Of course, it hardly bears mention that Federal immigration law is now extensive.

I accept that as a valid exercise of federal power—not because of the Naturalization Clause (it has no necessary connection to citizenship) but because it is an inherent attribute of sovereignty no less for the United States than for the States. As this Court has said, it is an " 'accepted maxim of international law, that every sovereign nation has the power, as inherent in sovereignty, and essential to self-preservation, to forbid the entrance of foreigners within its dominions.'" *Fong Yue Ting v. United States*, 1892. That is why there was no need to set forth control of immigration as one of the enumerated powers of Congress, although an acknowledgment of that power (as well as of the States' similar power, subject to federal abridgment) was contained in Art. I, §9, which provided that "[t]he Migration or Importation of such Persons as any of the States now existing shall think proper to admit, shall not be prohibited by the Congress prior to the Year one thousand eight hundred and eight...."

In light of the predominance of federal immigration restrictions in modern times, it is easy to lose sight of the States' traditional role in regulating immigration—and to overlook their sovereign prerogative to do so. I accept as a given that State regulation is excluded by the Constitution when (1) it has been prohibited by a valid federal law, or (2) it conflicts with federal regulation—when, for example, it admits those whom federal regulation would exclude, or excludes those whom federal regulation would admit.

Possibility (1) need not be considered here: there is no federal law prohibiting the States' sovereign power to exclude (assuming federal authority to enact such a law). The mere existence of federal action in the immigration area—and the so-called field preemption arising from that action, upon which the Court's opinion so heavily relies, *ante*, at 9-11—cannot be regarded as such a prohibition. We are not talking here about a federal law prohibiting the States from regulating bubble-gum advertising, or even the construction of nuclear plants. We are talking about a federal law going to the *core* of state sovereignty: the power to exclude. Like elimination of the States' other inherent sovereign power, immunity from suit, elimination of the States' sovereign power to exclude requires that "Congress...unequivocally expres[s] its intent to abrogate," *Seminole Tribe of Fla. v. Florida* (1996) (internal quotation marks and citation omitted). Implicit "field preemption" will not do.

Nor can federal power over illegal immigration be deemed exclusive because of what the Court's opinion solicitously calls "foreign countries['] concern[s] about the status, safety, and security of their nationals in the United States," *ante*, at 3. The Constitution gives all those on our shores the protections of the Bill of Rights—but just as those rights are not expanded for foreign nationals because of their countries' views (some countries, for example, have recently discovered the death penalty to be barbaric), neither are the fundamental sovereign powers of the States abridged to accommodate foreign countries' views. Even in its international relations, the Federal Government must live with the inconvenient fact that it is a Union of independent States, who have their own sovereign powers. This is not the first time it has found that a nuisance and a bother in the conduct of foreign policy. Four years ago, for example, the Government importuned us to interfere with thoroughly constitutional state judicial procedures in the criminal trial of foreign nationals because the international community, and even an opinion of the International Court of Justice, disapproved them. See *Medellin v. Texas* (2008). We rejected that request, as we should reject the Executive's invocation of foreign-affairs considerations here. Though it may upset foreign powers—and even when the Federal Government desperately wants to avoid upsetting foreign powers—the States have the right to protect their borders against foreign nationals, just as they have the right to execute foreign nationals for murder.

What this case comes down to, then, is whether the Arizona law conflicts with federal immigration law—whether it excludes those whom federal law would admit, or admits those whom federal law would exclude. It does not purport to do so. It applies only to aliens who neither possess a privilege to be present under federal law nor have been removed pursuant to the Federal Government's inherent authority. I proceed to consider the challenged provisions in detail.

§2(B)

"For any lawful stop, detention or arrest made by a law enforcement official . . . in the enforcement of any other law or ordinance of a county, city or town or this state where reasonable suspicion exists that the person is an alien and is unlawfully present in the United States, a reasonable attempt shall be made, when practicable, to determine the immigration status of the person, except if the determination may hinder or obstruct an investigation. Any person who is arrested shall have the person's immigration status determined before the person is released . . . ." S.B. 1070, §2(B), as amended, Ariz. Rev. Stat. Ann. §11-1051(B) (West 2012).

The Government has conceded that "even before Section 2 was enacted, state and local officers had state-law authority to inquire of DHS [the Department of Homeland Security] about a suspect's unlawful status and otherwise cooperate with federal immigration officers." Brief for United States 47 (citing App. 62, 82). That concession, in my view, obviates the need for further inquiry. The Government's conflict-pre-emption claim calls on us "to determine whether, under the circumstances of this particular case, [the State's] law stands as an obstacle to the accomplishment and execution of the full purposes and objectives of Congress." *Hines v. Davidowitz* (1941). . . . It is impossible to make such a finding without a factual record concerning the manner in which Arizona is implementing these provisions-something the Government's pre-enforcement challenge has pretermitted. "The fact that [a law] might operate unconstitutionally under some conceivable set of circumstances is insufficient to render it wholly invalid, since we have not recognized an 'overbreadth' doctrine outside the limited context of the First Amendment." *United States v. Salerno* (1987). And on its face, §2(B) merely tells state officials that they are authorized to do something that they were, by the Government's concession, already authorized to do.

The Court therefore properly rejects the Government's challenge, recognizing that, "[a]t this stage, without the benefit of a definitive interpretation from the state courts, it would be inappropriate to assume §2(B) will be construed in a way that creates a conflict with federal law." *Ante*, at 23. Before reaching that conclusion, however, the Court goes to great length to assuage fears that "state officers will be required to delay the release of some detainees for no reason other than to verify their immigration status." *Ante,* at 22. Of course, any investigatory detention, including one under § 2(B), may become an "unreasonable...seizur[e]," U.S. Const., Amdt. IV, if it lasts too long. See *Illinois v. Caballes,* (2005). But that has nothing to do with this case, in which the Government claims that § 2(B) is pre-empted by federal immigration law, not that anyone's Fourth Amendment rights have been violated. And I know of no reason why a protracted detention that does not violate the Fourth Amendment would contradict or conflict with any federal immigration law.

■ ■ ■

The brief for the Government in this case asserted that "the Executive Branch's ability to exercise discretion and set priorities is particularly important because of the need to allocate scarce enforcement resources wisely." Brief for United States 21. Of course there is no reason why the Federal Executive's need to allocate its scarce enforcement resources should disable Arizona from devoting its resources to illegal immigration in Arizona that in its view the Federal Executive has given short shrift. Despite Congress's prescription that "the immigration laws of the United States should be enforced vigorously and uniformly," IRCA § 115, 100 Stat. 3384, Arizona asserts without contradiction and with supporting citations:

> "[I]n the last decade federal enforcement efforts have focused primarily on areas in California and Texas, leaving Arizona's border to suffer from comparative neglect. The result has been the funneling of an increasing tide of illegal border crossings into Arizona. Indeed, over the past decade, over a third of the Nation's illegal border crossings occurred in Arizona." Brief for Petitioners 2-3 (footnote omitted).

Must Arizona's ability to protect its borders yield to the reality that Congress has provided inadequate funding for federal enforcement—or, even worse, to the Executive's unwise targeting of that funding?

But leave that aside. It has become clear that federal enforcement priorities—in the sense of priorities based on the need to allocate "scarce enforcement resources"—is not the problem here. After this case was argued and while it was under consideration, the Secretary of Homeland Security announced a program exempting from immigration enforcement some 1.4 million illegal immigrants under the age of 30.[4] If an individual unlawfully present in the United States

> "...came to the United States under the age of sixteen;
> has continuously resided in the United States for at least five years...,

---

4. Preston & Cushman, Obama to Permit Young Migrants to Remain in U.S., N.Y. Times, June 16, 2012, p. A1.

is currently in school, has graduated from high school, has obtained a general education development certificate, or is an honorably discharged veteran . . . ,

has not been convicted of a [serious crime]; and

is not above the age of thirty,"[5]

then U.S. immigration officials have been directed to "defe[r] action" against such individual "for a period of two years, subject to renewal."[6] The husbanding of scarce enforcement resources can hardly be the justification for this, since the considerable administrative cost of conducting as many as 1.4 million background checks, and ruling on the biennial requests for dispensation that the nonenforcement program envisions, will necessarily be deducted from immigration enforcement. The President said at a news conference that the new program is "the right thing to do" in light of Congress's failure to pass the Administration's proposed revision of the Immigration Act.[7] Perhaps it is, though Arizona may not think so. But to say, as the Court does, that Arizona contradicts federal law by enforcing applications of the Immigration Act that the President declines to enforce boggles the mind.

The Court opinion's looming specter of inutterable horror—"[i]f § 3 of the Arizona statute were valid, every State could give itself independent authority to prosecute federal registration violations," *ante*, at 10—seems to me not so horrible and even less looming. But there has come to pass, and is with us today, the specter that Arizona and the States that support it predicted: A Federal Government that does not want to enforce the immigration laws as written, and leaves the States' borders unprotected against immigrants whom those laws would exclude. So the issue is a stark one. Are the sovereign States at the mercy of the Federal Executive's refusal to enforce the Nation's immigration laws?

A good way of answering that question is to ask: Would the States conceivably have entered into the Union if the Constitution itself contained the Court's holding? Today's judgment surely fails that test. At the Constitutional Convention of 1787, the delegates contended with "the jealousy of the states with regard to their sovereignty." 1 Records of the Federal Convention 19 (M. Farrand ed. 1911) (statement of Edmund Randolph). Through ratification of the fundamental charter that the Convention produced, the States ceded much of their sovereignty to the Federal Government. But much of it remained jealously guarded—as reflected in the innumerable proposals that never left Independence Hall. Now, imagine a provision—perhaps inserted right after Art. I,

---

5. Memorandum from Janet Napolitano, Secretary of Homeland Security, to David V. Aguilar, Acting Commissioner, U.S. Customs and Border Protection; Alejandro Mayorkas, Director, U.S. Citizenship and Immigration Services; and John Morton, Director, U.S. Immigration and Customs Enforcement, p. 1 (June 15, 2012), online at http://www.dhs.gov (all Internet materials as visited June 22, 2012, and available in Clerk of Court's case file).

6. *Id.*, at 2.

7. Remarks by the President on Immigration (June 15, 2012), online at http://www.whitehouse.gov.

§ 8, cl. 4, the Naturalization Clause—which included among the enumerated powers of Congress "To establish Limitations upon Immigration that will be exclusive and that will be enforced only to the extent the President deems appropriate." The delegates to the Grand Convention would have rushed to the exits.

As is often the case, discussion of the dry legalities that are the proper object of our attention suppresses the very human realities that gave rise to the suit. Arizona bears the brunt of the country's illegal immigration problem. Its citizens feel themselves under siege by large numbers of illegal immigrants who invade their property, strain their social services, and even place their lives in jeopardy. Federal officials have been unable to remedy the problem, and indeed have recently shown that they are unwilling to do so. Thousands of Arizona's estimated 400,000 illegal immigrants—including not just children but men and women under 30—are now assured immunity from enforcement, and will be able to compete openly with Arizona citizens for employment.

Arizona has moved to protect its sovereignty—not in contradiction of federal law, but in complete compliance with it. The laws under challenge here do not extend or revise federal immigration restrictions, but merely enforce those restrictions more effectively. If securing its territory in this fashion is not within the power of Arizona, we should cease referring to it as a sovereign State. I dissent.

Justice THOMAS, concurring in part and dissenting in part.

I agree with Justice Scalia that federal immigration law does not pre-empt any of the challenged provisions of S. B. 1070. I reach that conclusion, however, for the simple reason that there is no conflict between the "ordinary meanin[g]" of the relevant federal laws and that of the four provisions of Arizona law at issue here.

■ ■ ■

Section 2(B) of S. B. 1070 provides that, when Arizona law enforcement officers reasonably suspect that a person they have lawfully stopped, detained, or arrested is unlawfully present, "a reasonable attempt shall be made, when practicable, to determine the immigration status of the person" pursuant to the verification procedure established by Congress in 8 U.S.C. § 1373(c). Nothing in the text of that or any other federal statute prohibits Arizona from directing its officers to make immigration-related inquiries in these situations. To the contrary, federal law expressly states that "no State or local government entity may be prohibited, or in any way restricted, from sending to or receiving from" federal officials "information regarding the immigration status" of an alien. 8 U.S.C. § 1644. And, federal law imposes an affirmative obligation on federal officials to respond to a State's immigration-related inquiries. § 1373(c).

■ ■ ■

Despite the lack of any conflict between the ordinary meaning of the Arizona law and that of the federal laws at issue here, the Court holds that various provisions of the Arizona law are pre-empted because they "stan[d] as an obstacle to the accomplishment and execution of the full purposes and objectives of Congress." *Hines, supra,* at 6, 61 S. Ct. 399, 85 L. Ed. 5817. I have explained that the "purposes and objectives" theory of implied pre-emption is inconsistent with the Constitution because it invites courts to engage in freewheeling speculation about congressional purpose that roams well beyond statutory text. See *Wyeth,* 555 U.S., at 604, 129 S. Ct. 1187, 173 L. Ed. 2d 51 (opinion concurring in judgment). Under the Supremacy Clause, pre-emptive effect is to be given to congressionally enacted laws, not to judicially divined legislative purposes. Thus, even assuming the existence of some tension between Arizona's law and the supposed "purposes and objectives" of Congress, I would not hold that any of the provisions of the Arizona law at issue here are pre-empted on that basis.

Justice Aʟɪᴛᴏ, concurring in part and dissenting in part.

This case concerns four provisions of Arizona's Support Our Law Enforcement and Safe Neighborhoods Act, S.B. 1070. Section 2(B) requires Arizona law enforcement officers to make a "reasonable attempt," "when practicable," to ascertain the immigration status of any person whom an officer lawfully stops, detains, or arrests "where reasonable suspicion exists that the person is an alien and is unlawfully present in the United States." Ariz. Rev. Stat. Ann. § 11-1051(B) (West 2012).

I agree with the Court that § 2(B) is not pre-empted. That provision does not authorize or require Arizona law enforcement officers to do anything they are not already allowed to do under existing federal law. The United States' argument that § 2(B) is pre-empted, not by any federal statute or regulation, but simply by the Executive's current enforcement policy is an astounding assertion of federal executive power that the Court rightly rejects.

Section 2(B)
A

Although § 2(B) of the Arizona law has occasioned much controversy, it adds nothing to the authority that Arizona law enforcement officers, like officers in all other States, already possess under federal law. For that reason, I agree with the Court that § 2(B) is not pre-empted.

Section 2(B) quite clearly does not expand the authority of Arizona officers to make stops or arrests. It is triggered only when a "lawful stop, detention or arrest [is] made . . . in the enforcement of *any other [state or local] law or ordinance.*" Ariz. Rev. Stat. Ann. § 11-1051(B) (emphasis added). Section 2(B) thus comes into play only when an officer has reasonable suspicion or probable cause to believe that a person has committed a nonimmigration offense. Arizona officers plainly possessed this authority before § 2(B) took effect.

Section 2(B) also does not expand the authority of Arizona officers to inquire about the immigration status of persons who are lawfully detained. When a person is stopped or arrested and "reasonable suspicion exists that the person is an alien and is unlawfully present in the United States," § 2(B) instructs Arizona officers to make a "reasonable attempt," "when practicable," to ascertain that person's immigration status. Ariz. Rev. Stat. Ann. § 11-1051(B). Even before the Arizona Legislature enacted § 2(B), federal law permitted state and local officers to make such inquiries. In 8 U.S.C. § 1357(g)(10)(A), Congress has made clear that state and local governments need not enter into formal agreements with the Federal Government in order "to communicate with the [Federal Government] regarding the immigration status of any individual." In addition, Congress has mandated that neither the Federal Government nor any state or local government may "prohibit, or in any way restrict, any government entity or official from sending to, or receiving from, [the Federal Government] information regarding the citizenship or immigration status, lawful or unlawful, of any individual." § 1373(a); see also § 1644 (providing that "no State or local government entity may be prohibited, or in any way restricted, from sending to or receiving from [the Federal Government] information regarding the immigration status, lawful or unlawful, of an alien in the United States"). And while these provisions preserve the authority of state and local officers to seek immigration-status information from the Federal Government, another federal statute, § 1373(c), requires that the Federal Government respond to any such inquiries "by providing the requested verification or status information." It comes as no surprise, therefore, that many States and localities permit their law enforcement officers to make the kinds of inquiries that § 2(B) prescribes. See App. 294-298 (reporting that officers in 59 surveyed state and local jurisdictions "generally" ask arrestees about their immigration status while 34 do not and that officers in 78 jurisdictions "generally" inform Immigration and Customs Enforcement (ICE) when they believe an arrestee to be an undocumented alien while only 17 do not). Congress has invited state and local governments to make immigration-related inquiries and has even obligated the Federal Government to respond. Through § 2(B), Arizona has taken Congress up on that invitation.

The United States does not deny that officers may, at their own discretion, inquire about the immigration status of persons whom they lawfully detain. Instead, the United States argues that § 2(B) is pre-empted because it impedes federal-state cooperation by *mandating* that officers verify the immigration status of every detained person if there is reason to believe that the person is unlawfully present in the country. The United States claims that § 2(B)'s mandate runs contrary to federal law in that it "precludes officers from taking [the Federal Government's] priorities and discretion into account." Brief for United States 50. "[B]y interposing a mandatory state law between state and local officers and their federal counterparts," writes the United States, § 2(B) "stands as an obstacle to the accomplishment of the federal requirement of cooperation and the full effectuation of the enforcement judgment and discretion Congress has vested in the Executive Branch." *Ibid.* (internal quotation marks and citation omitted).

The underlying premise of the United States' argument seems to be that state and local officers, when left to their own devices, generally take federal enforcement priorities into account. But there is no reason to think that this premise is true. And even if it were, it would not follow that § 2(B)'s blanket mandate is at odds with federal law. Nothing in the relevant federal statutes *requires* state and local officers to consider the Federal Government's priorities before requesting verification of a person's immigration status. Neither 8 U.S.C. § 1357(g)(10) nor § 1373(a) conditions the right of state and local officers to communicate with the Federal Government on their first taking account of its priorities. Nor does § 1373(c) condition the Federal Government's obligation to answer requests for information on the sensitivity of state and local officers to its enforcement discretion. In fact, § 1373(c) dictates that the Federal Government "shall respond" to any inquiry seeking verification of immigration status, and that command applies whether or not the requesting officer has bothered to consider federal priorities. Because no federal statute requires such consideration, § 2(B) does not conflict with federal law.

In any event, it is hard to see how state and local officers could proceed in conformity with the Federal Government's enforcement priorities without making an inquiry into a suspected alien's immigration status. For example, one of the Federal Government's highest priorities is the apprehension and removal of aliens who have failed to comply with a final order of removal. See App. 108. How can an officer identify those persons without first inquiring about their status? At bottom, the discretion that ultimately matters is not whether to verify a person's immigration status but whether to act once the person's status is known. For that reason, § 2(B)'s verification requirement is not contrary to federal law because the Federal Government retains the discretion that matters most—that is, the discretion to enforce the law in particular cases. If an Arizona officer contacts the Federal Government to verify a person's immigration status and federal records reveal that the person is in the country unlawfully, the Federal Government decides, presumably based on its enforcement priorities, whether to have the person released or transferred to federal custody. Enforcement discretion thus lies with the Federal Government, not with Arizona. Nothing in § 2(B) suggests otherwise.

The United States' attack on § 2(B) is quite remarkable. The United States suggests that a state law may be pre-empted, not because it conflicts with a federal statute or regulation, but because it is inconsistent with a federal agency's current enforcement priorities. Those priorities, however, are not law. They are nothing more than agency policy. I am aware of no decision of this Court recognizing that mere policy can have pre-emptive force. If § 2(B) were pre-empted at the present time because it is out of sync with the Federal Government's current priorities, would it be unpre-empted at some time in the future if the agency's priorities changed?

Like most law enforcement agencies, ICE does not set out inflexible rules for its officers to follow. To the contrary, it provides a list of factors to guide its officers' enforcement discretion on a case-by-case basis. Among those factors is "the agency's civil immigration enforcement priorities," *ibid.*, which change from administration to administration. If accepted, the United States' preemption argument would give the Executive unprecedented power to invalidate state laws that do not meet with its approval, even if the state laws are otherwise consistent with federal statutes and duly promulgated regulations. This argument, to say the least, is fundamentally at odds with our federal system.

■ ■ ■

B

It has been suggested that § 2(B) will cause some persons who are lawfully stopped to be detained in violation of their constitutional rights while a prolonged investigation of their immigration status is undertaken. But nothing on the face of the law suggests that it will be enforced in a way that violates the Fourth Amendment or any other provision of the Constitution. The law instructs officers to make a "reasonable attempt" to investigate immigration status, and this language is best understood as incorporating the Fourth Amendment's standard of reasonableness. Indeed, the Arizona Legislature has directed that § 2(B) "shall be implemented in a manner consistent with federal laws . . . protecting the civil rights of all persons and respecting the privileges and immunities of United States citizens." Ariz. Rev. Stat. Ann. § 11-1051(L).

In the situations that seem most likely to occur, enforcement of § 2(B) will present familiar Fourth Amendment questions. To take a common situation, suppose that a car is stopped for speeding, a nonimmigration offense. (Recall that § 2(B) comes into play only where a stop or arrest is made for a nonimmigration offense.) Suppose also that the officer who makes the stop subsequently acquires reasonable suspicion to believe that the driver entered the country illegally, which is a federal crime. See 8 U.S.C. § 1325(a).

It is well established that state and local officers generally have authority to make stops and arrests for violations of federal criminal laws. I see no reason why this principle should not apply to immigration crimes as well. Lower courts have so held. And the United States, consistent with the position long taken by the Office of Legal Counsel (OLC) in the Department of Justice, does not contend otherwise.

More importantly, no federal statute casts doubt on this authority. To be sure, there are a handful of statutes that purport to authorize state and local officers to make immigration-related arrests in *certain* situations. But a grant of federal arrest authority in some cases does not manifest a clear congressional intent to displace the States' police powers in all other cases. Without more, such an inference is too weak to overcome our presumption against pre-emption where traditional state police powers are at stake. Accordingly, in our hypothetical case, the Arizona officer may arrest the driver for violating § 1325(a) if the officer has probable cause. And if the officer has reasonable suspicion, the officer may detain the driver, to the extent permitted by the Fourth Amendment, while the question of illegal entry is investigated.

■ ■ ■

We have held that a detention based on reasonable suspicion that the detainee committed a particular crime "can become unlawful if it is prolonged beyond the time reasonably required to complete that mission." *Illinois v. Caballes* (2005). But if during the course of a stop an officer acquires suspicion that a detainee committed a different crime, the detention may be extended for a reasonable time to verify or dispel that suspicion. In our hypothetical case, therefore, if the officer, after initially stopping the car for speeding, has a reasonable suspicion that the driver entered the country illegally, the officer may investigate for evidence of illegal entry. But the length and nature of this investigation must remain within the limits set out in our Fourth Amendment cases. An investigative stop, if prolonged, can become an arrest and thus require probable cause. Similarly, if a person is moved from the site of the stop, probable cause will likely be required.

If properly implemented, § 2(B) should not lead to federal constitutional violations, but there is no denying that enforcement of § 2(B) will multiply the occasions on which sensitive Fourth Amendment issues will crop up. These civil-liberty concerns, I take it, are at the heart of most objections to § 2(B). Close and difficult questions will inevitably arise as to whether an officer had reasonable suspicion to believe that a person who is stopped for some other reason entered the country illegally, and there is a risk that citizens, lawful permanent residents, and others who are lawfully present in the country will be detained. To mitigate this risk, Arizona could issue guidance to officers detailing the circumstances that typically give rise to reasonable suspicion of unlawful presence. And in the spirit of the federal-state cooperation that the United States champions, the Federal Government could share its own guidelines. Arizona could also provide officers with a nonexclusive list containing forms of identification sufficient under § 2(B) to dispel any suspicion of unlawful presence. If Arizona accepts licenses from most States as proof of legal status, the problem of roadside detentions will be greatly mitigated.[1]

Arizona v. Johnson

555 U.S. 323 (2009)

GINSBURG, J., delivered the opinion for a unanimous Court.

This case concerns the authority of police officers to "stop and frisk" a passenger in a motor vehicle temporarily seized upon police detection of a traffic infraction. In a pathmarking decision, *Terry v. Ohio* (1968), the Court considered whether an investigatory stop (temporary detention) and frisk

---

1. When the Real ID Act takes effect, the Federal Government will no longer accept state forms of identification that fail to meet certain federal requirements. § 202(a)(1), 119 Stat. 312. One requirement is that any identification be issued only on proof that the applicant is lawfully present in the United States. § 202(c)(2)(B), id., at 313. I anticipate that most, if not all, States will eventually issue forms of identification that suffice to establish lawful presence under § 2(B).

(patdown for weapons) may be conducted without violating the Fourth Amendment's ban on unreasonable searches and seizures. The Court upheld "stop and frisk" as constitutionally permissible if two conditions are met. First, the investigatory stop must be lawful. That requirement is met in an on-the-street encounter, *Terry* determined, when the police officer reasonably suspects that the person apprehended is committing or has committed a criminal offense. Second, to proceed from a stop to a frisk, the police officer must reasonably suspect that the person stopped is armed and dangerous.

For the duration of a traffic stop, we recently confirmed, a police officer effectively seizes "everyone in the vehicle," the driver and all passengers. *Brendlin v. California* (2007). Accordingly, we hold that, in a traffic-stop setting, the first *Terry* condition—a lawful investigatory stop—is met whenever it is lawful for police to detain an automobile and its occupants pending inquiry into a vehicular violation. The police need not have, in addition, cause to believe any occupant of the vehicle is involved in criminal activity. To justify a patdown of the driver or a passenger during a traffic stop, however, just as in the case of a pedestrian reasonably suspected of criminal activity, the police must harbor reasonable suspicion that the person subjected to the frisk is armed and dangerous.

On April 19, 2002, Officer Maria Trevizo and Detectives Machado and Gittings, all members of Arizona's gang task force, were on patrol in Tucson near a neighborhood associated with the Crips gang. At approximately 9 p.m., the officers pulled over an automobile after a license plate check revealed that the vehicle's registration had been suspended for an insurance-related violation. Under Arizona law, the violation for which the vehicle was stopped constituted a civil infraction warranting a citation. At the time of the stop, the vehicle had three occupants—the driver, a front-seat passenger, and a passenger in the back seat, Lemon Montrea Johnson, the respondent here. In making the stop the officers had no reason to suspect anyone in the vehicle of criminal activity.

The three officers left their patrol car and approached the stopped vehicle. Machado instructed all of the occupants to keep their hands visible. He asked whether there were any weapons in the vehicle; all responded no. Machado then directed the driver to get out of the car. Gittings dealt with the front-seat passenger, who stayed in the vehicle throughout the stop. While Machado was getting the driver's license and information about the vehicle's registration and insurance, Trevizo attended to Johnson.

Trevizo noticed that, as the police approached, Johnson looked back and kept his eyes on the officers. When she drew near, she observed that Johnson was wearing clothing, including a blue bandana, that she considered consistent with Crips membership. She also noticed a scanner in Johnson's jacket pocket, which "struck [her] as highly unusual and cause [for] concern," because "most people" would not carry around a scanner that way "unless they're going to be involved in some kind of criminal activity or [are] going to try to evade the police by listening to the scanner." In response to Trevizo's questions, Johnson provided his name and date of birth but said he had no identification with him. He volunteered that he was from Eloy, Arizona, a place Trevizo knew was home to a Crips gang. Johnson further told Trevizo that he had served time in prison for burglary and had been out for about a year.

Trevizo wanted to question Johnson away from the front-seat passenger to gain "intelligence about the gang [Johnson] might be in." For that reason, she asked him to get out of the car. Johnson complied. Based on Trevizo's observations and Johnson's answers to her questions while he was still seated in the car, Trevizo suspected that "he might have a weapon on him." When he exited the vehicle, she therefore "patted him down for officer safety." During the patdown, Trevizo felt the butt of a gun near Johnson's waist. At that point Johnson began to struggle, and Trevizo placed him in handcuffs.

Johnson was charged in state court with, *inter alia,* possession of a weapon by a prohibited possessor. He moved to suppress the evidence as the fruit of an unlawful search. The trial court denied the motion, concluding that the stop was lawful and that Trevizo had cause to suspect Johnson was armed and dangerous. A jury convicted Johnson of the gun-possession charge.

A divided panel of the Arizona Court of Appeals reversed Johnson's conviction. Recognizing that "Johnson was [lawfully] seized when the officers stopped the car," the court nevertheless concluded that prior to the frisk the detention had "evolved into a separate, consensual encounter stemming from an unrelated investigation by Trevizo of Johnson's possible gang affiliation." Absent "reason to believe Johnson was involved in criminal activity," the Arizona appeals court held, Trevizo "had no right to pat him down for weapons, even if she had reason to suspect he was armed and dangerous."

■ ■ ■

The Arizona Supreme Court denied review.

■ ■ ■

We begin our consideration of the constitutionality of Officer Trevizo's patdown of Johnson by looking back to the Court's leading decision in *Terry v. Ohio.* *Terry* involved a stop for interrogation of men whose conduct had attracted the attention of a patrolling police officer. The officer's observation led him reasonably to suspect that the men were casing a jewelry shop in preparation for a robbery. He conducted a patdown, which disclosed weapons concealed in the men's overcoat pockets. This Court upheld the lower courts' determinations that the interrogation was warranted and the patdown, permissible.

Terry established the legitimacy of an investigatory stop "in situations where [the police] may lack probable cause for an arrest." When the stop is justified by suspicion (reasonably grounded, but short of probable cause) that criminal activity is afoot, the Court explained, the police officer must be positioned to act instantly on reasonable suspicion that the persons temporarily detained are armed and dangerous. Recognizing that a limited search of outer clothing for weapons serves to protect both the officer and the public, the Court held the patdown reasonable under the Fourth Amendment.

"[M]ost traffic stops," this Court has observed, "resemble, in duration and atmosphere, the kind of brief detention authorized in *Terry*." *Berkemer v. McCarty* (1984). Furthermore, the Court has recognized that traffic stops are "especially fraught with danger to police officers." " 'The risk of harm to both the police and the occupants [of a stopped vehicle] is minimized,' " we have stressed, " 'if the officers routinely exercise unquestioned command of the situation.' " Three decisions cumulatively portray *Terry*'s application in a traffic-stop setting: *Pennsylvania v. Mimms* (1977) *(per curiam); Maryland v. Wilson* (1997); and *Brendlin v. California.*

In *Mimms,* the Court held that "once a motor vehicle has been lawfully detained for a traffic violation, the police officers may order the driver to get out of the vehicle without violating the Fourth Amendment's proscription of unreasonable searches and seizures." The government's "legitimate and weighty" interest in officer safety, the Court said, outweighs the *"de minimis"* additional intrusion of requiring a driver, already lawfully stopped, to exit the vehicle. Citing *Terry* as controlling, the Court further held that a driver, once outside the stopped vehicle, may be patted down for weapons if the officer reasonably concludes that the driver "might be armed and presently dangerous."

Wilson held that the *Mimms* rule applied to passengers as well as to drivers. Specifically, the Court instructed that "an officer making a traffic stop may order passengers to get out of the car pending completion of the stop." "[T]he same weighty interest in officer safety," the Court observed, "is present regardless of whether the occupant of the stopped car is a driver or passenger."

It is true, the Court acknowledged, that in a lawful traffic stop, "[t]here is probable cause to believe that the driver has committed a minor vehicular offense," but "there is no such reason to stop or detain the passengers." On the other hand, the Court emphasized, the risk of a violent encounter in a traffic-stop setting "stems not from the ordinary reaction of a motorist stopped for a speeding violation, but from the fact that evidence of a more serious crime might be uncovered during the stop." "[T]he motivation of a passenger to employ violence to prevent apprehension of such a crime," the Court stated, "is every bit as great as that of the driver." Moreover, the Court noted, "as a practical matter, the passengers are already stopped by virtue of the stop of the vehicle," so "the additional intrusion on the passenger is minimal."

Completing the picture, *Brendlin* held that a passenger is seized, just as the driver is, "from the moment [a car stopped by the police comes] to a halt on the side of the road." A passenger therefore has standing to challenge a stop's constitutionality.

After *Wilson,* but before *Brendlin,* the Court had stated, in dictum, that officers who conduct "routine traffic stop[s]" may "perform a 'patdown' of a driver and any passengers upon reasonable suspicion that they may be armed and dangerous." That forecast, we now confirm, accurately captures the combined thrust of the Court's decisions in *Mimms, Wilson,* and *Brendlin.*

The Arizona Court of Appeals recognized that, initially, Johnson was lawfully detained incident to the legitimate stop of the vehicle in which he was a passenger. But, that court concluded, once Officer Trevizo undertook to question Johnson on a matter unrelated to the traffic stop, *i.e.*, Johnson's gang affiliation, patdown authority ceased to exist, absent reasonable suspicion that Johnson had engaged, or was about to engage, in criminal activity. In support of the Arizona court's portrayal of Trevizo's interrogation of Johnson as "consensual," Johnson emphasizes Trevizo's testimony at the suppression hearing. Responding to the prosecutor's questions, Trevizo affirmed her belief that Johnson could have "refused to get out of the car" and "to turn around for the pat down."

It is not clear why the prosecutor, in opposing the suppression motion, sought to portray the episode as consensual. In any event, Trevizo also testified that she never advised Johnson he did not have to answer her questions or otherwise cooperate with her. And during cross-examination, Trevizo did not disagree when defense counsel asked "in fact you weren't seeking [Johnson's] permission . . . ?" As the dissenting judge observed, "consensual" is an "unrealistic" characterization of the Trevizo-Johnson interaction. "[T]he encounter . . . took place within minutes of the stop"; the patdown followed "within mere moments" of Johnson's exit from the vehicle; beyond genuine debate, the point at which Johnson could have felt free to leave had not yet occurred.

A lawful roadside stop begins when a vehicle is pulled over for investigation of a traffic violation. The temporary seizure of driver and passengers ordinarily continues, and remains reasonable, for the duration of the stop. Normally, the stop ends when the police have no further need to control the scene, and inform the driver and passengers they are free to leave. An officer's inquiries into matters unrelated to the justification for the traffic stop, this Court has made plain, do not convert the encounter into something other than a lawful seizure, so long as those inquiries do not measurably extend the duration of the stop.

In sum, as stated in *Brendlin*, a traffic stop of a car communicates to a reasonable passenger that he or she is not free to terminate the encounter with the police and move about at will. Nothing occurred in this case that would have conveyed to Johnson that, prior to the frisk, the traffic stop had ended or that he was otherwise free "to depart without police permission." Officer Trevizo surely was not constitutionally required to give Johnson an opportunity to depart the scene after he exited the vehicle without first ensuring that, in so doing, she was not permitting a dangerous person to get behind her.

For the reasons stated, the judgment of the Arizona Court of Appeals is reversed, and the case is remanded for further proceedings not inconsistent with this opinion.

It is so ordered.

C. ADMINISTRATIVE SEARCHES

1. Housing

Camara v. Municipal Court of San Francisco

387 U.S. 523 (1967)

See Chapter 3.B.1.

2. Schools

Safford Unified School District #1 v. Redding

557 U.S. 364 (2009)

Souter, J., delivered the opinion of the Court, in which Roberts, C.J., Scalia, Kennedy, Breyer, and Alito, JJ., joined. Stevens and Ginsburg, JJ., concurred on the Fourth Amendment issue. Thomas, J., filed an opinion concurring in judgment and dissenting on the Fourth Amendment issue.

The issue here is whether a 13-year-old student's Fourth Amendment right was violated when she was subjected to a search of her bra and underpants by school officials acting on reasonable suspicion that she had brought forbidden prescription and over-the-counter drugs to school. Because there were no reasons to suspect the drugs presented a danger or were concealed in her underwear, we hold that the search did violate the Constitution, but because there is reason to question the clarity with which the right was established, the official who ordered the unconstitutional search is entitled to qualified immunity from liability.

■ ■ ■

The events immediately prior to the search in question began in 13-year-old Savana Redding's math class at Safford Middle School one October day in 2003. The assistant principal of the school, Kerry Wilson, came into the room and asked Savana to go to his office. There, he showed her a day planner, unzipped and open flat on his desk, in which there were several knives, lighters, a permanent marker, and a cigarette. Wilson asked Savana whether the planner was hers; she said it was, but that a few days before she had lent it to her friend, Marissa Glines. Savana stated that none of the items in the planner belonged to her.

Wilson then showed Savana four white prescription-strength ibuprofen 400-mg pills, and one over-the-counter blue naproxen 200-mg pill, all used for pain and inflammation but banned under school rules without advance permission. He asked Savana if she knew anything about the pills. Savana answered that she did not. Wilson then told Savana that he had received a report that she was giving these pills to fellow students; Savana denied it and agreed to let Wilson search her belongings. Helen Romero, an administrative assistant, came into the office, and together with Wilson they searched Savana's backpack, finding nothing.

At that point, Wilson instructed Romero to take Savana to the school nurse's office to search her clothes for pills. Romero and the nurse, Peggy Schwallier, asked Savana to remove her jacket, socks, and shoes, leaving her in stretch pants and a T-shirt (both without pockets), which she was then asked to remove. Finally, Savana was told to pull her bra out and to the side and shake it, and to pull out the elastic on her underpants, thus exposing her breasts and pelvic area to some degree. No pills were found.

Savana's mother filed suit against Safford Unified School District . . . for conducting a strip search in violation of Savana's Fourth Amendment rights. The individuals (hereinafter petitioners) moved for summary judgment, raising a defense of qualified immunity. The District Court for the District of Arizona granted the motion on the ground that there was no Fourth Amendment violation, and a panel of the Ninth Circuit affirmed.

A closely divided Circuit sitting en banc, however, reversed.

■ ■ ■

In [*New Jersey v.*] *T.L.O.* [(1985)], we recognized that the school setting "requires some modification of the level of suspicion of illicit activity needed to justify a search," and held that for searches by school officials "a careful balancing of governmental and private interests suggests that the public interest is best served by a Fourth Amendment standard of reasonableness that stops short of probable cause." We have thus applied a standard of reasonable suspicion to determine the legality of a school administrator's search of a student, and have held that a school search "will be permissible in its scope when the measures adopted are reasonably related to the objectives of the search and not excessively intrusive in light of the age and sex of the student and the nature of the infraction."

■ ■ ■

In this case, the school's policies strictly prohibit the nonmedical use, possession, or sale of any drug on school grounds, including " '[a]ny prescription or over-the-counter drug, except those for which permission to use in school has been granted pursuant to Board policy.' " A week before Savana was searched, another student, Jordan Romero (no relation of the school's administrative assistant), told the principal and Assistant Principal Wilson that "certain students were bringing drugs and weapons on campus," and that he had been sick after taking some pills that "he got from a classmate." On the morning of October 8, the same boy handed Wilson a white pill that he said Marissa Glines had given him. He told Wilson that students were planning to take the pills at lunch.

Wilson learned from Peggy Schwallier, the school nurse, that the pill was Ibuprofen 400 mg, available only by prescription. Wilson then called Marissa out of class. Outside the classroom, Marissa's teacher handed Wilson the day planner, found within Marissa's reach, containing various contraband items. Wilson escorted Marissa back to his office.

In the presence of Helen Romero, Wilson requested Marissa to turn out her pockets and open her wallet. Marissa produced a blue pill, several white ones, and a razor blade. Wilson asked where the blue pill came from, and Marissa answered, " 'I guess it slipped in when *she* gave me the IBU 400s.' " When Wilson asked whom she meant, Marissa replied, " 'Savana Redding.' " Wilson then enquired about the day planner and its contents; Marissa denied knowing anything about them. Wilson did not ask Marissa any followup questions to determine whether there was any likelihood that Savana presently had pills: neither asking when Marissa received the pills from Savana nor where Savana might be hiding them.

Schwallier did not immediately recognize the blue pill, but information provided through a poison control hotline indicated that the pill was a 200-mg dose of an anti-inflammatory drug, generically called naproxen, available over the counter. At Wilson's direction, Marissa was then subjected to a search of her bra and underpants by Romero and Schwallier, as Savana was later on. The search revealed no additional pills.

It was at this juncture that Wilson called Savana into his office and showed her the day planner. Their conversation established that Savana and Marissa were on friendly terms: while she denied knowledge of the contraband, Savana admitted that the day planner was hers and that she had lent it to Marissa. Wilson had other reports of their friendship from staff members, who had identified Savana and Marissa as part of an unusually rowdy group at the school's opening dance in August, during which alcohol and cigarettes were found in the girls' bathroom. Wilson had reason to connect the girls with this contraband, for Wilson knew that Jordan Romero had told the principal that before the dance, he had been at a party at Savana's house where alcohol was served. Marissa's statement that the pills came from Savana was thus sufficiently plausible to warrant suspicion that Savana was involved in pill distribution.

This suspicion of Wilson's was enough to justify a search of Savana's backpack and outer clothing. If a student is reasonably suspected of giving out contraband pills, she is reasonably suspected of carrying them on her person and in the carryall that has become an item of student uniform in most places today. If Wilson's reasonable suspicion of pill distribution were not understood to support searches of outer clothes and backpack, it would not justify any search worth making. And the look into Savana's bag, in her presence and in the relative privacy of Wilson's office, was not excessively intrusive, any more than Romero's subsequent search of her outer clothing.

■ ■ ■

Here it is that the parties part company, with Savana's claim that extending the search at Wilson's behest to the point of making her pull out her underwear was constitutionally unreasonable. The exact label for this final step in the intrusion is not important, though strip search is a fair way to speak of it. Romero and Schwallier directed Savana to remove her clothes down to her underwear, and then "pull out" her bra and the elastic band on her underpants. Although Romero and Schwallier stated that they did not see anything when

Savana followed their instructions, we would not define strip search and its Fourth Amendment consequences in a way that would guarantee litigation about who was looking and how much was seen. The very fact of Savana's pulling her underwear away from her body in the presence of the two officials who were able to see her necessarily exposed her breasts and pelvic area to some degree, and both subjective and reasonable societal expectations of personal privacy support the treatment of such a search as categorically distinct, requiring distinct elements of justification on the part of school authorities for going beyond a search of outer clothing and belongings.

■ ■ ■

The indignity of the search does not, of course, outlaw it, but it does implicate the rule of reasonableness as stated in *T.L.O.*, that "the search as actually conducted [be] reasonably related in scope to the circumstances which justified the interference in the first place." The scope will be permissible, that is, when it is "not excessively intrusive in light of the age and sex of the student and the nature of the infraction."

Here, the content of the suspicion failed to match the degree of intrusion. Wilson knew beforehand that the pills were prescription-strength ibuprofen and over-the-counter naproxen, common pain relievers equivalent to two Advil, or one Aleve. He must have been aware of the nature and limited threat of the specific drugs he was searching for, and while just about anything can be taken in quantities that will do real harm, Wilson had no reason to suspect that large amounts of the drugs were being passed around, or that individual students were receiving great numbers of pills.

Nor could Wilson have suspected that Savana was hiding common painkillers in her underwear. . . . [W]hen the categorically extreme intrusiveness of a search down to the body of an adolescent requires some justification in suspected facts, general background possibilities fall short; a reasonable search that extensive calls for suspicion that it will pay off. But nondangerous school contraband does not raise the specter of stashes in intimate places, and there is no evidence in the record of any general practice among Safford Middle School students of hiding that sort of thing in underwear; neither Jordan nor Marissa suggested to Wilson that Savana was doing that, and the preceding search of Marissa that Wilson ordered yielded nothing. Wilson never even determined when Marissa had received the pills from Savana; if it had been a few days before, that would weigh heavily against any reasonable conclusion that Savana presently had the pills on her person, much less in her underwear.

In sum, what was missing from the suspected facts that pointed to Savana was any indication of danger to the students from the power of the drugs or their quantity, and any reason to suppose that Savana was carrying pills in her underwear. We think that the combination of these deficiencies was fatal to finding the search reasonable.

■ ■ ■

We do mean, though, to make it clear that the *T.L.O.* concern to limit a school search to reasonable scope requires the support of reasonable suspicion of danger or of resort to underwear for hiding evidence of wrongdoing before a search can reasonably make the quantum leap from outer clothes and backpacks to exposure of intimate parts. The meaning of such a search, and the degradation its subject may reasonably feel, place a search that intrusive in a category of its own demanding its own specific suspicions.

■ ■ ■

Justice STEVENS, with whom Justice GINSBURG joins, concurring in part and dissenting in part.

In *New Jersey v. T.L.O.*, the Court established a two-step inquiry for determining the reasonableness of a school official's decision to search a student. First, the Court explained, the search must be " 'justified at its inception' " by the presence of "reasonable grounds for suspecting that the search will turn up evidence that the student has violated or is violating either the law or the rules of the school." Second, the search must be "permissible in its scope," which is achieved "when the measures adopted are reasonably related to the objectives of the search and *not excessively intrusive in light of the age and sex of the student and the nature of the infraction.*"

Nothing the Court decides today alters this basic framework. It simply applies *T.L.O.* to declare unconstitutional a strip search of a 13-year-old honors student that was based on a groundless suspicion that she might be hiding medicine in her underwear. This is, in essence, a case in which clearly established law meets clearly outrageous conduct. I have long believed that " '[i]t does not require a constitutional scholar to conclude that a nude search of a 13-year-old child is an invasion of constitutional rights of some magnitude.' " The strip search of Savana Redding in this case was both more intrusive and less justified than the search of the student's purse in *T.L.O.* Therefore, while I join Parts I-III of the Court's opinion, I disagree with its decision to extend qualified immunity to the school official who authorized this unconstitutional search.

■ ■ ■

Justice THOMAS, concurring in the judgment in part and dissenting in part.

I agree with the Court that the judgment against the school officials with respect to qualified immunity should be reversed. Unlike the majority, however, I would hold that the search of Savana Redding did not violate the Fourth Amendment. The majority imposes a vague and amorphous standard on school administrators. It also grants judges sweeping authority to second-guess the measures that these officials take to maintain discipline in their schools and ensure the health and safety of the students in their charge. This deep intrusion into the administration of public schools exemplifies why the Court should return to the common-law doctrine of *in loco parentis* under which "the judiciary was reluctant to interfere in the routine business of school administration, allowing schools and teachers to set and enforce rules and to maintain order." But even under the prevailing Fourth Amendment test established by *New Jersey v. T.L.O.*, all petitioners, including the school district, are entitled to judgment as a matter of law in their favor.

> "Although the underlying command of the Fourth Amendment is always that searches and seizures be reasonable, what is reasonable depends on the context within which a search takes place." Thus, although public school students retain Fourth Amendment rights under this Court's precedent, those rights "are different...than elsewhere; the 'reasonableness' inquiry cannot disregard the schools' custodial and tutelary responsibility for children." For nearly 25 years this Court has understood that "[m]aintaining order in the classroom has never been easy, but in more recent years, school disorder has often taken particularly ugly forms: drug use and violent crime in the schools have become major social problems."

■ ■ ■

For this reason, school officials retain broad authority to protect students and preserve "order and a proper educational environment" under the Fourth Amendment. This authority requires that school officials be able to engage in the "close supervision of schoolchildren, as well as...enforc[e] rules against conduct that would be perfectly permissible if undertaken by an adult." Seeking to reconcile the Fourth Amendment with this unique public school setting, the Court in *T.L.O.* held that a school search is "reasonable" if it is " 'justified at its inception' " and "reasonably related in scope to the circumstances which justified the interference in the first place." The search under review easily meets this standard.

■ ■ ■

A "search of a student by a teacher or other school official will be 'justified at its inception' when there are reasonable grounds for suspecting that the search will turn up evidence that the student has violated or is violating either the law or the rules of the school." As the majority rightly concedes, this search was justified at its inception because there were reasonable grounds to suspect that Redding possessed medication that violated school rules. A finding of reasonable suspicion "does not deal with hard certainties, but with probabilities." To satisfy this standard, more than a mere "hunch" of wrongdoing is required, but "considerably" less suspicion is needed than would be required to "satisf[y] a preponderance of the evidence standard."

Furthermore, in evaluating whether there is a reasonable "particularized and objective" basis for conducting a search based on suspected wrongdoing, government officials must consider the "totality of the circumstances." School officials have a specialized understanding of the school environment, the habits of the students, and the concerns of the community, which enables them to " 'formulat[e] certain common-sense conclusions about human behavior.' " And like police officers, school officials are "entitled to make an assessment of the situation in light of [this] specialized training and familiarity with the customs of the [school]."

Here, petitioners had reasonable grounds to suspect that Redding was in possession of prescription and nonprescription drugs in violation of the school's prohibition of the "non-medical use, possession, or sale of a drug" on school property or at school events.

■ ■ ■

The remaining question is whether the search was reasonable in scope. Under *T.L.O.*, "a search will be permissible in its scope when the measures adopted are reasonably related to the objectives of the search and not excessively intrusive in light of the age and sex of the student and the nature of the infraction." The majority concludes that the school officials' search of Redding's underwear was not "'reasonably related in scope to the circumstances which justified the interference in the first place,'" notwithstanding the officials' reasonable suspicion that Redding "was involved in pill distribution." According to the majority, to be reasonable, this school search required a showing of "danger to the students from the power of the drugs or their quantity" or a "reason to suppose that [Redding] was carrying pills in her underwear." Each of these additional requirements is an unjustifiable departure from bedrock Fourth Amendment law in the school setting, where this Court has heretofore read the Fourth Amendment to grant considerable leeway to school officials. Because the school officials searched in a location where the pills could have been hidden, the search was reasonable in scope under *T.L.O.*

The majority finds that "subjective and reasonable societal expectations of personal privacy support . . . treat[ing]" this type of search, which it labels a "strip search," as "categorically distinct, requiring distinct elements of justification on the part of school authorities for going beyond a search of clothing and belongings." Thus, in the majority's view, although the school officials had reasonable suspicion to believe that Redding had the pills on her person, they needed some greater level of particularized suspicion to conduct this "strip search." There is no support for this contortion of the Fourth Amendment.

The Court has generally held that the reasonableness of a search's scope depends only on whether it is limited to the area that is capable of concealing the object of the search. See, *e.g., Wyoming v. Houghton* (1999) (Police officers "may inspect passengers' belongings found in the car that are capable of concealing the object of the search").

■ ■ ■

In keeping with this longstanding rule, the "nature of the infraction" referenced in *T.L.O.* delineates the proper scope of a search of students in a way that is identical to that permitted for searches outside the school—*i.e.,* the search must be limited to the areas where the object of that infraction could be concealed. See *Horton v. California* (1990) ("Police with a warrant for a rifle may search only places where rifles might be" (internal quotation marks omitted)).

■ ■ ■

The analysis of whether the scope of the search here was permissible under that standard is straightforward. Indeed, the majority does not dispute that "general background possibilities" establish that students conceal "contraband in their underwear." It acknowledges that school officials had reasonable suspicion to look in Redding's backpack and outer clothing because if "Wilson's reasonable suspicion of pill distribution were not understood to support searches of outer clothes and backpack, it would not justify any search worth making." The majority nevertheless concludes that proceeding any further with the search was unreasonable.

■ ■ ■

The majority compounds its error by reading the "nature of the infraction" aspect of the *T.L.O.* test as a license to limit searches based on a judge's assessment of a particular school policy. According to the majority, the scope of the search was impermissible because the school official "must have been aware of the nature and limited threat of the specific drugs he was searching for" and because he "had no reason to suspect that large amounts of the drugs were being passed around, or that individual students were receiving great numbers of pills."

■ ■ ■

Even accepting the majority's assurances that it is not attacking the rule's reasonableness, it certainly is attacking the rule's importance. This approach directly conflicts with *T.L.O.* in which the Court was "unwilling to adopt a standard under which the legality of a search is dependent upon a judge's evaluation of the relative importance of school rules."

■ ■ ■

The majority has placed school officials in this "impossible spot" by questioning whether possession of Ibuprofen and Naproxen causes a severe enough threat to warrant investigation. Had the suspected infraction involved a street drug, the majority implies that it would have approved the scope of the search.

■ ■ ■

A rule promulgated by a school board represents the judgment of school officials that the rule is needed to maintain "school order" and "a proper educational environment." *T.L.O.* Teachers, administrators, and the local school board are called upon both to "protect the...safety of students and school personnel" and "maintain an environment conducive to learning."

■ ■ ■

In determining whether the search's scope was reasonable under the Fourth Amendment, it is therefore irrelevant whether officials suspected Redding of possessing prescription-strength Ibuprofen, nonprescription-strength Naproxen, or some harder street drug. Safford prohibited its possession on school property. Reasonable suspicion that Redding was in possession of drugs in violation of these policies, therefore, justified a search extending to any area where small pills could be concealed. The search did not violate the Fourth Amendment.

■ ■ ■

By declaring the search unreasonable in this case, the majority has " 'surrender[ed] control of the American public school system to public school students' " by invalidating school policies that treat all drugs equally and by second-guessing swift disciplinary decisions made by school officials.

■ ■ ■

"[T]he nationwide drug epidemic makes the war against drugs a pressing concern in every school." *Board of Ed. of Independent School Dist. No. 92 of Pottawatomie Cty. v. Earls* (2002). And yet the Court has limited the authority of school officials to conduct searches for the drugs that the officials believe pose a serious safety risk to their students. By doing so, the majority has confirmed that a return to the doctrine of *in loco parentis* is required to keep the judiciary from essentially seizing control of public schools. Only then will teachers again be able to " 'govern the[ir] pupils, quicken the slothful, spur the indolent, restrain the impetuous, and control the stubborn' " by making " 'rules, giv[ing] commands, and punish[ing] disobedience' " without interference from judges. By deciding that it is better equipped to decide what behavior should be permitted in schools, the Court has undercut student safety and undermined the authority of school administrators and local officials. Even more troubling, it has done so in a case in which the underlying response by school administrators was reasonable and justified. I cannot join this regrettable decision. I, therefore, respectfully dissent from the Court's determination that this search violated the Fourth Amendment.

Board of Education of Independent School District No. 92 of Pottawatomie County v. Earls

536 U.S. 822 (2002)

THOMAS, J., delivered the opinion of the Court, in which REHNQUIST, C.J., and SCALIA, KENNEDY, and BREYER, JJ., joined. BREYER, J., filed a concurring opinion. O'CONNOR, J., filed a dissenting opinion, in which SOUTER, J., joined. GINSBURG, J., filed a dissenting opinion, in which STEVENS, O'CONNOR, and SOUTER, JJ., joined.

The Student Activities Drug Testing Policy implemented by the Board of Education of Independent School District No. 92 of Pottawatomie County (School District) requires all students who participate in competitive extracurricular activities to submit to drug testing. Because this Policy reasonably serves the School District's important interest in detecting and preventing drug use among its students, we hold that it is constitutional.

■ ■ ■

The city of Tecumseh, Oklahoma, is a rural community located approximately 40 miles southeast of Oklahoma City. The School District administers all Tecumseh public schools. In the fall of 1998, the School District adopted the Student Activities Drug Testing Policy (Policy), which requires all middle and high school students to consent to drug testing in order to participate in any extracurricular activity. In practice, the Policy has been applied only to competitive extracurricular activities sanctioned by the Oklahoma Secondary Schools Activities Association, such as the Academic Team, Future Farmers of America, Future Homemakers of America, band, choir, pom-pom, cheerleading, and athletics. Under the Policy, students are required to take a drug test before participating in an extracurricular activity, must submit to random drug testing while participating in that activity, and must agree to be tested at any time upon reasonable suspicion. The urinalysis tests are designed to detect only the use of illegal drugs, including amphetamines, marijuana, cocaine, opiates, and barbituates, not medical conditions or the presence of authorized prescription medications.

At the time of their suit, both respondents attended Tecumseh High School. Respondent Lindsay Earls was a member of the show choir, the marching band, the Academic Team, and the National Honor Society. Respondent Daniel James sought to participate in the Academic Team. Together with their parents, Earls and James brought a 42 U.S.C. § 1983 action against the School District, challenging the Policy both on its face and as applied to their participation in extracurricular activities. They alleged that the Policy violates the Fourth Amendment as incorporated by the Fourteenth Amendment and requested injunctive and declarative relief. They also argued that the School District failed to identify a special need for testing students who participate in extracurricular activities, and that the "Drug Testing Policy neither addresses a proven problem nor promises to bring any benefit to students or the school."

Applying the principles articulated in *Vernonia School Dist. 47J v. Acton* (1995), in which we upheld the suspicionless drug testing of school athletes, the United States District Court for the Western District of Oklahoma rejected respondents' claim that the Policy was unconstitutional and granted summary judgment to the School District. The court noted that "special needs" exist in the public school context and that, although the School District did "not show a drug problem of epidemic proportions," there was a history of drug abuse starting in 1970 that presented "legitimate cause for concern." The District Court also held that the Policy was effective because "[i]t can scarcely be disputed that the drug problem among the student body is effectively addressed by making sure that the large number of students participating in competitive, extracurricular activities do not use drugs."

The United States Court of Appeals for the Tenth Circuit reversed, holding that the Policy violated the Fourth Amendment. The Court of Appeals agreed with the District Court that the Policy must be evaluated in the unique environment of the school setting," but reached a different conclusion as to the Policy's constitutionality. Before imposing a suspicionless drug testing program, the Court of Appeals concluded that a school "must demonstrate that there is some identifiable drug abuse problem among a sufficient number of those subject to the testing, such that testing that group of students will actually redress its drug problem." The Court of Appeals then held that because the School District failed to demonstrate such a problem existed among Tecumseh students participating in competitive extracurricular activities, the Policy was unconstitutional. We granted certiorari, and now reverse.

■ ■ ■

Given that the School District's Policy is not in any way related to the conduct of criminal investigations, respondents do not contend that the School District requires probable cause before testing students for drug use. Respondents instead argue that drug testing must be based at least on some level of individualized suspicion. It is true that we generally determine the reasonableness of a search by balancing the nature of the intrusion on the individual's privacy against the promotion of legitimate governmental interests. But we have long held that "the Fourth Amendment imposes no irreducible requirement of [individualized] suspicion." "[I]n certain limited circumstances, the Government's need to discover such latent or hidden conditions, or to prevent their development, is sufficiently compelling to justify the intrusion on privacy entailed by conducting such searches without any measure of individualized suspicion." [*Treasury Employees v.*] *Von Raab* [(1989)]; see also *Skinner* [*v. Railway Labor Executives' Assn.* (1989)]. Therefore, in the context of safety and administrative regulations, a search unsupported by probable cause may be reasonable "when 'special needs, beyond the normal need for law enforcement, make the warrant and probable-cause requirement impracticable.' "

Significantly, this Court has previously held that "special needs" inhere in the public school context. . . .

In *Vernonia*, this Court held that the suspicionless drug testing of athletes was constitutional. The Court, however, did not simply authorize all school drug testing, but rather conducted a fact-specific balancing of the intrusion on the children's Fourth Amendment rights against the promotion of legitimate governmental interests. Applying the principles of *Vernonia* to the somewhat different facts of this case, we conclude that Tecumseh's Policy is also constitutional.

■ ■ ■

We first consider the nature of the privacy interest allegedly compromised by the drug testing. As in *Vernonia*, the context of the public school environment serves as the backdrop for the analysis of the privacy interest at stake and the reasonableness of the drug testing policy in general. ("Central . . . is the fact that the subjects of the Policy are (1) children, who (2) have been committed to the temporary custody of the State as schoolmaster"); ("The most significant element in this case is the first we discussed: that the Policy was undertaken in furtherance of the government's responsibilities, under a public school system, as guardian and tutor of children entrusted to its care"); ("[W]hen the government acts as guardian and tutor the relevant question is whether the search is one that a reasonable guardian and tutor might undertake").

A student's privacy interest is limited in a public school environment where the State is responsible for maintaining discipline, health, and safety. Schoolchildren are routinely required to submit to physical examinations and vaccinations against disease. Securing order in the school environment sometimes requires that students be subjected to greater controls than those appropriate for adults.

■ ■ ■

Respondents argue that because children participating in nonathletic extracurricular activities are not subject to regular physicals and communal undress, they have a stronger expectation of privacy than the athletes tested in *Vernonia*. This distinction, however, was not essential to our decision in *Vernonia*, which depended primarily upon the school's custodial responsibility and authority.

In any event, students who participate in competitive extracurricular activities voluntarily subject themselves to many of the same intrusions on their privacy as do athletes. Some of these clubs and activities require occasional off-campus travel and communal undress. All of them have their own rules and requirements for participating students that do not apply to the student body as a whole. For example, each of the competitive extracurricular activities governed by the Policy must abide by the rules of the Oklahoma Secondary Schools Activities Association, and a faculty sponsor monitors the students for compliance with the various rules dictated by the clubs and activities. This regulation of extracurricular activities further diminishes the expectation of privacy among schoolchildren. Cf. *Vernonia* ("Somewhat like adults who choose to participate in a closely regulated industry, students who voluntarily participate in school athletics have reason to expect intrusions upon normal rights and privileges, including privacy" (internal quotation marks omitted)). We therefore conclude that the students affected by this Policy have a limited expectation of privacy.

■ ■ ■

Next, we consider the character of the intrusion imposed by the Policy. Urination is "an excretory function traditionally shielded by great privacy." But the "degree of intrusion" on one's privacy caused by collecting a urine sample "depends upon the manner in which production of the urine sample is monitored."

Under the Policy, a faculty monitor waits outside the closed restroom stall for the student to produce a sample and must "listen for the normal sounds of urination in order to guard against tampered specimens and to insure an accurate chain of custody." The monitor then pours the sample into two bottles that are sealed and placed into a mailing pouch along with a consent form signed by the student. This procedure is virtually identical to that reviewed in *Vernonia*, except that it additionally protects privacy by allowing male students to produce their samples behind a closed stall. Given that we considered the method of collection in *Vernonia* a "negligible" intrusion, the method here is even less problematic.

In addition, the Policy clearly requires that the test results be kept in confidential files separate from a student's other educational records and released to school personnel only on a "need to know" basis. Respondents nonetheless contend that the intrusion on students' privacy is significant because the Policy fails to protect effectively against the disclosure of confidential information and, specifically, that the school "has been careless in protecting that information: for example, the Choir teacher looked at students' prescription drug lists and left them where other students could see them." But the choir teacher is someone with a "need to know," because during off-campus trips she needs to know what medications are taken by her students. Even before the Policy was enacted the choir teacher had access to this information. In any event, there is no allegation that any other student did see such information. This one example of alleged carelessness hardly increases the character of the intrusion.

Moreover, the test results are not turned over to any law enforcement authority. Nor do the test results here lead to the imposition of discipline or have any academic consequences. Rather, the only consequence of a failed drug test is to limit the student's privilege of participating in extracurricular activities. Indeed, a student may test positive for drugs twice and still be allowed to participate in extracurricular activities. After the first positive test, the school contacts the student's parent or guardian for a meeting. The student may continue to participate in the activity if within five days of the meeting the student shows proof of receiving drug counseling and submits to a second drug test in two weeks. For the second positive test, the student is suspended from participation in all extracurricular activities for 14 days, must complete four hours of substance abuse counseling, and must submit to monthly drug tests. Only after a third positive test will the student be suspended from participating in any extracurricular activity for the remainder of the school year, or 88 school days, whichever is longer.

Given the minimally intrusive nature of the sample collection and the limited uses to which the test results are put, we conclude that the invasion of students' privacy is not significant.

■ ■ ■

Finally, this Court must consider the nature and immediacy of the government's concerns and the efficacy of the Policy in meeting them. This Court has already articulated in detail the importance of the governmental concern in preventing drug use by schoolchildren. The drug abuse problem among our Nation's youth has hardly abated since *Vernonia* was decided in 1995. In fact, evidence suggests that it has only grown worse. As in *Vernonia*, "the necessity for the State to act is magnified by the fact that this evil is being visited not just upon individuals at large, but upon children for whom it has undertaken a special responsibility of care and direction." The health and safety risks identified in *Vernonia* apply with equal force to Tecumseh's children. Indeed, the nationwide drug epidemic makes the war against drugs a pressing concern in every school.

Additionally, the School District in this case has presented specific evidence of drug use at Tecumseh schools. Teachers testified that they had seen students who appeared to be under the influence of drugs and that they had heard students speaking openly about using drugs. A drug dog found marijuana cigarettes near the school parking lot. Police officers once found drugs or drug paraphernalia in a car driven by a Future Farmers of America member. And the school board president reported that people in the community were calling the board to discuss the "drug situation." We decline to second-guess the finding of the District Court that "[v]iewing the evidence as a whole, it cannot be reasonably disputed that the [School District] was faced with a 'drug problem' when it adopted the Policy."

Respondents consider the proffered evidence insufficient and argue that there is no "real and immediate interest" to justify a policy of drug testing nonathletes. We have recognized, however, that "[a] demonstrated problem of drug abuse . . . [is] not in all cases necessary to the validity of a testing regime," but that some showing does "shore up an assertion of special need for a suspicionless general search program." *Chandler v. Miller* (1997). The School District has provided sufficient evidence to shore up the need for its drug testing program.

■ ■ ■

Given the nationwide epidemic of drug use, and the evidence of increased drug use in Tecumseh schools, it was entirely reasonable for the School District to enact this particular drug testing policy. We reject the Court of Appeals' novel test that "any district seeking to impose a random suspicionless drug testing policy as a condition to participation in a school activity must demonstrate that there is some identifiable drug abuse problem among a sufficient number of those subject to the testing, such that testing that group of students will actually redress its drug problem." Among other problems, it would be difficult to administer such a test. As we cannot articulate a threshold level of drug use that would suffice to justify a drug testing program for schoolchildren, we refuse to fashion what would in effect be a constitutional quantum of drug use necessary to show a "drug problem."

Respondents also argue that the testing of nonathletes does not implicate any safety concerns, and that safety is a "crucial factor" in applying the special needs framework. They contend that there must be "surpassing safety interests," . . . or "extraordinary safety and national security hazards," . . . in order to override the usual protections of the Fourth Amendment. Respondents are correct that safety factors into the special needs analysis, but the safety interest furthered by drug testing is undoubtedly substantial for all children, athletes and nonathletes alike. We know all too well that drug use carries a variety of health risks for children, including death from overdose.

We also reject respondents' argument that drug testing must presumptively be based upon an individualized reasonable suspicion of wrongdoing because such a testing regime would be less intrusive. In this context, the Fourth Amendment does not require a finding of individualized suspicion, and we decline to impose such a requirement on schools attempting to prevent and detect drug use by students. Moreover, we question whether testing based on individualized suspicion in fact would be less intrusive. Such a regime would place an additional burden on public school teachers who are already tasked with the difficult job of maintaining order and discipline. A program of individualized suspicion might unfairly target members of unpopular groups. The fear of lawsuits resulting from such targeted searches may chill enforcement of the program, rendering it ineffective in combating drug use.

■   ■   ■

Finally, we find that testing students who participate in extracurricular activities is a reasonably effective means of addressing the School District's legitimate concerns in preventing, deterring, and detecting drug use. While in *Vernonia* there might have been a closer fit between the testing of athletes and the trial court's finding that the drug problem was "fueled by the 'role model' effect of athletes' drug use," such a finding was not essential to the holding. *Vernonia* did not require the school to test the group of students most likely to use drugs, but rather considered the constitutionality of the program in the context of the public school's custodial responsibilities. Evaluating the Policy in this context, we conclude that the drug testing of Tecumseh students who participate in extracurricular activities effectively serves the School District's interest in protecting the safety and health of its students.

■   ■   ■

Within the limits of the Fourth Amendment, local school boards must assess the desirability of drug testing schoolchildren. In upholding the constitutionality of the Policy, we express no opinion as to its wisdom. Rather, we hold only that Tecumseh's Policy is a reasonable means of furthering the School District's important interest in preventing and deterring drug use among its schoolchildren. Accordingly, we reverse the judgment of the Court of Appeals.

It is so ordered.

Justice Breyer, concurring.

I agree with the Court that *Vernonia School Dist. 47J v. Acton* governs this case and requires reversal of the Tenth Circuit's decision. The school's drug testing program addresses a serious national problem by focusing upon demand, avoiding the use of criminal or disciplinary sanctions, and relying upon professional counseling and treatment. In my view, this program does not violate the Fourth Amendment's prohibition of "unreasonable searches and seizures." I reach this conclusion primarily for the reasons given by the Court, but I would emphasize several underlying considerations, which I understand to be consistent with the Court's opinion.

■   ■   ■

In respect to the school's need for the drug testing program, I would emphasize the following: First, the drug problem in our Nation's schools is serious in terms of size, the kinds of drugs being used, and the consequences of that use both for our children and the rest of us.

■   ■   ■

Third, public school systems must find effective ways to deal with this problem. Today's public expects its schools not simply to teach the fundamentals, but "to shoulder the burden of feeding students breakfast and lunch, offering before and after school child care services, and providing medical and psychological services," all in a school environment that is safe and encourages learning.

■ ■ ■

Fourth, the program at issue here seeks to discourage demand for drugs by changing the school's environment in order to combat the single most important factor leading schoolchildren to take drugs, namely, peer pressure. Malignant Neglect 4 (students "whose friends use illicit drugs are more than 10 times likelier to use illicit drugs than those whose friends do not"). It offers the adolescent a nonthreatening reason to decline his friend's drug-use invitations, namely, that he intends to play baseball, participate in debate, join the band, or engage in any one of half a dozen useful, interesting, and important activities.

■ ■ ■

In respect to the privacy-related burden that the drug testing program imposes upon students, I would emphasize the following: First, not everyone would agree with this Court's characterization of the privacy-related significance of urine sampling as " 'negligible.' " Some find the procedure no more intrusive than a routine medical examination, but others are seriously embarrassed by the need to provide a urine sample with someone listening "outside the closed restroom stall." When trying to resolve this kind of close question involving the interpretation of constitutional values, I believe it important that the school board provided an opportunity for the airing of these differences at public meetings designed to give the entire community "the opportunity to be able to participate" in developing the drug policy. App. 87. The board used this democratic, participatory process to uncover and to resolve differences, giving weight to the fact that the process, in this instance, revealed little, if any, objection to the proposed testing program.

Second, the testing program avoids subjecting the entire school to testing. And it preserves an option for a conscientious objector. He can refuse testing while paying a price (nonparticipation) that is serious, but less severe than expulsion from the school.

Third, a contrary reading of the Constitution, as requiring "individualized suspicion" in this public school context, could well lead schools to push the boundaries of "individualized suspicion" to its outer limits, using subjective criteria that may "unfairly target members of unpopular groups," or leave those whose behavior is slightly abnormal stigmatized in the minds of others.

■ ■ ■

I cannot know whether the school's drug testing program will work. But, in my view, the Constitution does not prohibit the effort. Emphasizing the considerations I have mentioned, along with others to which the Court refers, I conclude that the school's drug testing program, constitutionally speaking, is not "unreasonable." And I join the Court's opinion.

Justice O'CONNOR, with whom Justice SOUTER joins, dissenting.

I dissented in *Vernonia School Dist. 47J v. Acton*, and continue to believe that case was wrongly decided. Because *Vernonia* is now this Court's precedent, and because I agree that petitioners' program fails even under the balancing approach adopted in that case, I join Justice Ginsburg's dissent.

Justice GINSBURG, with whom Justice STEVENS, Justice O'CONNOR, and Justice SOUTER join, dissenting.

Seven years ago, in *Vernonia School Dist. 47J v. Acton*, this Court determined that a school district's policy of randomly testing the urine of its student athletes for illicit drugs did not violate the Fourth Amendment. In so ruling, the Court emphasized that drug use "increase[d] the risk of sports-related injury" and that Vernonia's athletes were the "leaders" of an aggressive local "drug culture" that had reached "'epidemic proportions.'" Today, the Court relies upon *Vernonia* to permit a school district with a drug problem its superintendent repeatedly described as "not . . . major" to test the urine of an academic team member solely by reason of her participation in a nonathletic, competitive extracurricular activity—participation associated with neither special dangers from, nor particular predilections for, drug use.

"[T]he legality of a search of a student," this Court has instructed, "should depend simply on the reasonableness, under all the circumstances, of the search." *New Jersey v. T.L.O.* (1985). Although "'special needs' inhere in the public school context," those needs are not so expansive or malleable as to render reasonable any program of student drug testing a school district elects to install. The particular testing program upheld today is not reasonable; it is capricious, even perverse: Petitioners' policy targets for testing a student population least likely to be at risk from illicit drugs and their damaging effects. I therefore dissent. . . .

The *Vernonia* Court concluded that a public school district facing a disruptive and explosive drug abuse problem sparked by members of its athletic teams had "special needs" that justified suspicionless testing of district athletes as a condition of their athletic participation.

This case presents circumstances dispositively different from those of *Vernonia*. True, as the Court stresses, Tecumseh students participating in competitive extracurricular activities other than athletics share two relevant characteristics with the athletes of *Vernonia*. First, both groups attend public schools. "[O]ur decision in *Vernonia*," the Court states, "depended primarily upon the school's custodial responsibility and authority." Concern for student health and safety is basic to the school's caretaking, and it is undeniable that "drug use carries a variety of health risks for children, including death from overdose."

Those risks, however, are present for *all* schoolchildren. *Vernonia* cannot be read to endorse invasive and suspicionless drug testing of all students upon any evidence of drug use, solely because drugs jeopardize the life and health of those who use them. Many children, like many adults, engage in dangerous activities on their own time; that the children are enrolled in school scarcely allows government to monitor all such activities. If a student has a reasonable subjective expectation of privacy in the personal items she brings to school, surely she has a similar expectation regarding the chemical composition of her urine.

■ ■ ■

The second commonality to which the Court points is the voluntary character of both interscholastic athletics and other competitive extracurricular activities. "By choosing to 'go out for the team,' [school athletes] voluntarily subject themselves to a degree of regulation even higher than that imposed on students generally." Comparably, the Court today observes, "students who participate in competitive extracurricular activities voluntarily subject themselves to" additional rules not applicable to other students.

The comparison is enlightening. While extracurricular activities are "voluntary" in the sense that they are not required for graduation, they are part of the school's educational program; for that reason, the petitioner (hereinafter School District) is justified in expending public resources to make them available. Participation in such activities is a key component of school life, essential in reality for students applying to college, and, for all participants, a significant contributor to the breadth and quality of the educational experience. Students "volunteer" for extracurricular pursuits in the same way they might volunteer for honors classes: They subject themselves to additional requirements, but they do so in order to take full advantage of the education offered them. Cf. *Lee v. Weisman* (1992) ("Attendance may not be required by official decree, yet it is apparent that a student is not free to absent herself from the graduation exercise in any real sense of the term 'voluntary,' for absence would require forfeiture of those intangible benefits which have motivated the student through youth and all her high school years.").

Voluntary participation in athletics has a distinctly different dimension: Schools regulate student athletes discretely because competitive school sports by their nature require communal undress and, more important, expose students to physical risks that schools have a duty to mitigate. For the very reason that schools cannot offer a program of competitive athletics without intimately affecting the privacy of students, *Vernonia* reasonably analogized school athletes to "adults who choose to participate in a closely regulated industry." Industries fall within the closely regulated category when the nature of their activities requires substantial government oversight. Interscholastic athletics similarly require close safety and health regulation; a school's choir, band, and academic team do not.

In short, *Vernonia* applied, it did not repudiate, the principle that "the legality of a search of a student should depend simply on the reasonableness, *under all the circumstances,* of the search." Enrollment in a public school, and election to participate in school activities beyond the bare minimum that the curriculum requires, are indeed factors relevant to reasonableness, but they do not on their own justify intrusive, suspicionless searches. *Vernonia,* accordingly, did not rest upon these factors; instead, the Court performed what today's majority aptly describes as a "fact-specific balancing." Balancing of that order, applied to the facts now before the Court, should yield a result other than the one the Court announces today.

■ ■ ■

Competitive extracurricular activities other than athletics, however, serve students of all manner: the modest and shy along with the bold and uninhibited. Activities of the kind plaintiff-respondent Lindsay Earls pursued—choir, show choir, marching band, and academic team—afford opportunities to gain self-assurance, to "come to know faculty members in a less formal setting than the typical classroom," and to acquire "positive social supports and networks [that] play a critical role in periods of heightened stress."

On "occasional out-of-town trips," students like Lindsay Earls "must sleep together in communal settings and use communal bathrooms." But those situations are hardly equivalent to the routine communal undress associated with athletics; the School District itself admits that when such trips occur, "public-like restroom facilities," which presumably include enclosed stalls, are ordinarily available for changing, and that "more modest students" find other ways to maintain their privacy.

After describing school athletes' reduced expectation of privacy, the *Vernonia* Court turned to "the character of the intrusion . . . complained of." Observing that students produce urine samples in a bathroom stall with a coach or teacher outside, *Vernonia* typed the privacy interests compromised by the process of obtaining samples "negligible." As to the required pretest disclosure of prescription medications taken, the Court assumed that "the School District would have permitted [a student] to provide the requested information in a confidential manner—for example, in a sealed envelope delivered to the testing lab." On that assumption, the Court concluded that Vernonia's athletes faced no significant invasion of privacy.

In this case, however, Lindsay Earls and her parents allege that the School District handled personal information collected under the policy carelessly, with little regard for its confidentiality. Information about students' prescription drug use, they assert, was routinely viewed by Lindsay's choir teacher, who left files containing the information unlocked and unsealed, where others, including students, could see them; and test results were given out to all activity sponsors whether or not they had a clear "need to know."

■ ■ ■

Finally, the "nature and immediacy of the governmental concern" faced by the Vernonia School District dwarfed that confronting Tecumseh administrators. Vernonia initiated its drug testing policy in response to an alarming situation: "[A] large segment of the student body, particularly those involved in interscholastic athletics, was in a state of rebellion . . . fueled by alcohol and drug abuse as well as the student[s'] misperceptions about the drug culture." (internal quotation marks omitted). Tecumseh, by contrast, repeatedly reported to the Federal Government during the period leading up to the adoption of the policy that "types of drugs [other than alcohol and tobacco] including controlled dangerous substances, are present [in the schools] but have not identified themselves as major problems at this time." 1998-1999 Tecumseh School's Application for Funds under the Safe and Drug-Free Schools and Communities Program.

■ ■ ■

Not only did the Vernonia and Tecumseh districts confront drug problems of distinctly different magnitudes, they also chose different solutions: Vernonia limited its policy to athletes; Tecumseh indiscriminately subjected to testing all participants in competitive extracurricular activities. Urging that "the safety interest furthered by drug testing is undoubtedly substantial for all children, athletes and nonathletes alike," the Court cuts out an element essential to the *Vernonia* judgment. Citing medical literature on the effects of combining illicit drug use with physical exertion, the *Vernonia* Court emphasized that "the particular drugs screened by [Vernonia's] Policy have been demonstrated to pose substantial physical risks to athletes." We have since confirmed that these special risks were necessary to our decision in *Vernonia*. See *Chandler* [*v. Miller* (1997)] (*Vernonia* "emphasized the importance of deterring drug use by schoolchildren and the risk of injury a drug-using student athlete cast on himself and those engaged with him on the playing field"); see also *Ferguson v. Charleston* (2001) (Kennedy, J., concurring) (Vernonia's policy had goal of " '[d]eterring drug use by our Nation's schoolchildren,' and particularly by student-athletes, because 'the risk of immediate physical harm to the drug user or those with whom he is playing his sport is particularly high' ").

At the margins, of course, no policy of *random* drug testing is perfectly tailored to the harms it seeks to address. The School District cites the dangers faced by members of the band, who must "perform extremely precise routines with heavy equipment and instruments in close proximity to other students," and by Future Farmers of America, who "are required to individually control and restrain animals as large as 1500 pounds." Brief for Petitioners 43. For its part, the United States acknowledges that "the linebacker faces a greater risk of serious injury if he takes the field under the influence of drugs than the drummer in the halftime band," but parries that "the risk of injury to a student who is under the influence of drugs while playing golf, cross country, or volleyball (sports covered by the policy in *Vernonia*) is scarcely any greater than the risk of injury to a student . . . handling a 1500-pound steer (as [Future Farmers of America] members do) or working with cutlery or other sharp instruments (as [Future Homemakers of America] members do)." . . . One can demur to the Government's view of the risks drug use poses to golfers, . . . for golfers were surely as marginal among the linebackers, sprinters, and basketball players targeted for testing in Vernonia as steer-handlers are among the choristers, musicians, and academic-team members subject to urinalysis in Tecumseh. Notwithstanding nightmarish images of out-of-control flatware, livestock run amok, and colliding tubas disturbing the peace and quiet of Tecumseh, the great majority of students the School District seeks to test in truth are engaged in activities that are not safety sensitive to an unusual degree. There is a difference between imperfect tailoring and no tailoring at all.

The Vernonia district, in sum, had two good reasons for testing athletes: Sports team members faced special health risks and they "were the leaders of the drug culture."

■ ■ ■

Nationwide, students who participate in extracurricular activities are significantly less likely to develop substance abuse problems than are their less-involved peers . . . (tenth graders "who reported spending no time in school-sponsored activities were . . . 49 percent more likely to have used drugs" than those who spent 1-4 hours per week in such activities). Even if students might be deterred from drug use in order to preserve their extracurricular eligibility, it is at least as likely that other students might forgo their extracurricular involvement in order to avoid detection of their drug use. Tecumseh's policy thus falls short doubly if deterrence is its aim: It invades the privacy of students who need deterrence least, and risks steering students at greatest risk for substance abuse away from extracurricular involvement that potentially may palliate drug problems.

To summarize, this case resembles *Vernonia* only in that the School Districts in both cases conditioned engagement in activities outside the obligatory curriculum on random subjection to urinalysis. The defining characteristics of the two programs, however, are entirely dissimilar. The Vernonia district sought to test a subpopulation of students distinguished by their reduced expectation of privacy, their special susceptibility to drug-related injury, and their heavy involvement with drug use. The Tecumseh district seeks to test a much larger population associated with none of these factors. It does so, moreover, without carefully safeguarding student confidentiality and without regard to the program's untoward effects. A program so sweeping is not sheltered by *Vernonia*; its unreasonable reach renders it impermissible under the Fourth Amendment.

■ ■ ■

In *Chandler,* this Court inspected "Georgia's requirement that candidates for state office pass a drug test"; we held that the requirement "d[id] not fit within the closely guarded category of constitutionally permissible suspicion-less searches." Georgia's testing prescription, the record showed, responded to no "concrete danger," was supported by no evidence of a particular problem, and targeted a group not involved in "high-risk, safety-sensitive tasks." We concluded:

> "What is left, after close review of Georgia's scheme, is the image the State seeks to project. By requiring candidates for public office to submit to drug testing, Georgia displays its commitment to the struggle against drug abuse. . . . The need revealed, in short, is symbolic, not 'special,' as that term draws meaning from our case law."

Close review of Tecumseh's policy compels a similar conclusion. That policy was not shown to advance the " 'special needs' [existing] in the public school context [to maintain] ... swift and informal disciplinary procedures ... [and] order in the schools." What is left is the School District's undoubted purpose to heighten awareness of its abhorrence of, and strong stand against, drug abuse. But the desire to augment communication of this message does not trump the right of persons—even of children within the schoolhouse gate—to be "secure in their persons ... against unreasonable searches and seizures." U.S. Const., Amdt. 4.

In *Chandler,* the Court referred to a pathmarking dissenting opinion in which "Justice Brandeis recognized the importance of teaching by example: 'Our Government is the potent, the omnipresent teacher. For good or for ill, it teaches the whole people by its example.' " (quoting *Olmstead v. United States* (1928)). That wisdom should guide decisionmakers in the instant case: The government is nowhere more a teacher than when it runs a public school.

It is a sad irony that the petitioning School District seeks to justify its edict here by trumpeting "the schools' custodial and tutelary responsibility for children." In regulating an athletic program or endeavoring to combat an exploding drug epidemic, a school's custodial obligations may permit searches that would otherwise unacceptably abridge students' rights. When custodial duties are not ascendant, however, schools' tutelary obligations to their students require them to "teach by example" by avoiding symbolic measures that diminish constitutional protections. "That [schools] are educating the young for citizenship is reason for scrupulous protection of Constitutional freedoms of the individual, if we are not to strangle the free mind at its source and teach youth to discount important principles of our government as mere platitudes."

■ ■ ■

For the reasons stated, I would affirm the judgment of the Tenth Circuit declaring the testing policy at issue unconstitutional.

3. Roadways

Michigan Department of State Police v. Sitz

496 U.S. 444 (1990)

REHNQUIST, C.J., delivered the opinion of the Court, in which WHITE, O'CONNOR, SCALIA, and KENNEDY, JJ., joined. BLACKMUN, J., filed an opinion concurring in the judgment. BRENNAN, J., filed a dissenting opinion, in which MARSHALL, J., joined. STEVENS, J., filed a dissenting opinion, in which BRENNAN and MARSHALL, JJ., joined as to Parts I and II.

This case poses the question whether a State's use of highway sobriety checkpoints violates the Fourth and Fourteenth Amendments to the United States Constitution. We hold that it does not and therefore reverse the contrary holding of the Court of Appeals of Michigan.

Petitioners, the Michigan Department of State Police and its director, established a sobriety checkpoint pilot program in early 1986. The director appointed a Sobriety Checkpoint Advisory Committee comprising representatives of the State Police force, local police forces, state prosecutors, and the University of Michigan Transportation Research Institute. Pursuant to its charge, the advisory committee created guidelines setting forth procedures governing checkpoint operations, site selection, and publicity.

Under the guidelines, checkpoints would be set up at selected sites along state roads. All vehicles passing through a checkpoint would be stopped and their drivers briefly examined for signs of intoxication. In cases where a checkpoint officer detected signs of intoxication, the motorist would be directed to a location out of the traffic flow where an officer would check the motorist's driver's license and car registration and, if warranted, conduct further sobriety tests. Should the field tests and the officer's observations suggest that the driver was intoxicated, an arrest would be made. All other drivers would be permitted to resume their journey immediately.

The first—and to date the only—sobriety checkpoint operated under the program was conducted in Saginaw County with the assistance of the Saginaw County Sheriff's Department. During the 75-minute duration of the checkpoint's operation, 126 vehicles passed through the checkpoint. The average delay for each vehicle was approximately 25 seconds. Two drivers were detained for field sobriety testing, and one of the two was arrested for driving under the influence of alcohol. A third driver who drove through without stopping was pulled over by an officer in an observation vehicle and arrested for driving under the influence. . . .

Petitioners concede, correctly in our view, that a Fourth Amendment "seizure" occurs when a vehicle is stopped at a checkpoint . . . ; see [*United States v.*] *Martinez-Fuerte* [(1976)] ("It is agreed that checkpoint stops are 'seizures' within the meaning of the Fourth Amendment"); *Brower v. County of Inyo* (1989) (Fourth Amendment seizure occurs "when there is a governmental termination of freedom of movement *through means intentionally applied*" (emphasis in original)). The question thus becomes whether such seizures are "reasonable" under the Fourth Amendment.

It is important to recognize what our inquiry is *not* about. No allegations are before us of unreasonable treatment of any person after an actual detention at a particular checkpoint. See *Martinez-Fuerte* ("[C]laim that a particular exercise of discretion in locating or operating a checkpoint is unreasonable is subject to post-stop judicial review"). As pursued in the lower courts, the instant action challenges only the use of sobriety checkpoints generally. We address only the initial stop of each motorist passing through a checkpoint and the associated preliminary questioning and observation by checkpoint officers. Detention of particular motorists for more extensive field sobriety testing may require satisfaction of an individualized suspicion standard.

No one can seriously dispute the magnitude of the drunken driving problem or the States' interest in eradicating it. Media reports of alcohol-related death and mutilation on the Nation's roads are legion. The anecdotal is confirmed by the statistical. "Drunk drivers cause an annual death toll of over 25,000 and in the same time span cause nearly one million personal injuries and more than five billion dollars in property damage."

■ ■ ■

Conversely, the weight bearing on the other scale—the measure of the intrusion on motorists stopped briefly at sobriety checkpoints—is slight. We reached a similar conclusion as to the intrusion on motorists subjected to a brief stop at a highway checkpoint for detecting illegal aliens. We see virtually no difference between the levels of intrusion on law-abiding motorists from the brief stops necessary to the effectuation of these two types of checkpoints, which to the average motorist would seem identical save for the nature of the questions the checkpoint officers might ask. The trial court and the Court of Appeals, thus, accurately gauged the "objective" intrusion, measured by the duration of the seizure and the intensity of the investigation, as minimal.

With respect to what it perceived to be the "subjective" intrusion on motorists, however, the Court of Appeals found such intrusion substantial. The court first affirmed the trial court's finding that the guidelines governing checkpoint operation minimize the discretion of the officers on the scene. But the court also agreed with the trial court's conclusion that the checkpoints have the potential to generate fear and surprise in motorists. This was so because the record failed to demonstrate that approaching motorists would be aware of their option to make U-turns or turnoffs to avoid the checkpoints. On that basis, the court deemed the subjective intrusion from the checkpoints unreasonable.

We believe the Michigan courts misread our cases concerning the degree of "subjective intrusion" and the potential for generating fear and surprise. The "fear and surprise" to be considered are not the natural fear of one who has been drinking over the prospect of being stopped at a sobriety checkpoint but, rather, the fear and surprise engendered in law-abiding motorists by the nature of the stop. This was made clear in *Martinez-Fuerte.* Comparing checkpoint stops to roving patrol stops considered in prior cases, we said:

■ ■ ■

" '[T]he circumstances surrounding a checkpoint stop and search are far less intrusive than those attending a roving-patrol stop. Roving patrols often operate at night on seldom-traveled roads, and their approach may frighten motorists. At traffic checkpoints the motorist can see that other vehicles are being stopped, he can see visible signs of the officers' authority, and he is much less likely to be frightened or annoyed by the intrusion.' " *Martinez-Fuerte.*

■ ■ ■

The Court of Appeals went on to consider as part of the balancing analysis the "effectiveness" of the proposed checkpoint program. Based on extensive testimony in the trial record, the court concluded that the checkpoint program failed the "effectiveness" part of the test, and that this failure materially discounted petitioners' strong interest in implementing the program. We think the Court of Appeals was wrong on this point as well.

The actual language from *Brown v. Texas* (1979), upon which the Michigan courts based their evaluation of "effectiveness," describes the balancing factor as "the degree to which the seizure advances the public interest." This passage from *Brown* was not meant to transfer from politically accountable officials to the courts the decision as to which among reasonable alternative law enforcement techniques should be employed to deal with a serious public danger. Experts in police science might disagree over which of several methods of apprehending drunken drivers is preferable as an ideal....

In sum, the balance of the State's interest in preventing drunken driving, the extent to which this system can reasonably be said to advance that interest, and the degree of intrusion upon individual motorists who are briefly stopped, weighs in favor of the state program. We therefore hold that it is consistent with the Fourth Amendment. The judgment of the Michigan Court of Appeals is accordingly reversed, and the cause is remanded for further proceedings not inconsistent with this opinion.

It is so ordered.

Justice BLACKMUN, concurring in the judgment.

I concur only in the judgment.

I fully agree with the Court's lamentations about the slaughter on our highways and about the dangers posed to almost everyone by the driver who is under the influence of alcohol or other drug. I add this comment only to remind the Court that it has been almost 20 years since, in *Perez v. Campbell* (1971), in writing for three others (no longer on the Court) and myself, I noted that the "slaughter on the highways of this Nation exceeds the death toll of all our wars," and that I detected "little genuine public concern about what takes place in our very midst and on our daily travel routes." . . .

Justice BRENNAN, with whom Justice MARSHALL joins, dissenting.

Today, the Court rejects a Fourth Amendment challenge to a sobriety checkpoint policy in which police stop all cars and inspect all drivers for signs of intoxication without *any* individualized suspicion that a specific driver is intoxicated. The Court does so by balancing "the State's interest in preventing drunken driving, the extent to which this system can reasonably be said to advance that interest, and the degree of intrusion upon individual motorists who are briefly stopped." For the reasons stated by Justice Stevens in Parts I and II of his dissenting opinion, I agree that the Court misapplies that test by undervaluing the nature of the intrusion and exaggerating the law enforcement need to use the roadblocks to prevent drunken driving.

■ ■ ■

The majority opinion creates the impression that the Court generally engages in a balancing test in order to determine the constitutionality of all seizures, or at least those "dealing with police stops of motorists on public highways."

■ ■ ■

Indeed, the opinion reads as if the minimal nature of the seizure *ends* rather than begins the inquiry into reasonableness. Once the Court establishes that the seizure is "slight," it asserts without explanation that the balance "weighs in favor of the state program." The Court ignores the fact that in this class of minimally intrusive searches, we have generally required the Government to prove that it had reasonable suspicion for a minimally intrusive seizure to be considered reasonable. . . . By holding that no level of suspicion is necessary before the police may stop a car for the purpose of preventing drunken driving, the Court potentially subjects the general public to arbitrary or harassing conduct by the police. I would have hoped that before taking such a step, the Court would carefully explain how such a plan fits within our constitutional framework.

■ ■ ■

I do not dispute the immense social cost caused by drunken drivers, nor do I slight the government's efforts to prevent such tragic losses. Indeed, I would hazard a guess that today's opinion will be received favorably by a majority of our society, who would willingly suffer the minimal intrusion of a sobriety checkpoint stop in order to prevent drunken driving. But consensus that a particular law enforcement technique serves a laudable purpose has never been the touchstone of constitutional analysis.

■ ■ ■

In the face of the "momentary evil" of drunken driving, the Court today abdicates its role as the protector of that fundamental right. I respectfully dissent.

Justice STEVENS, with whom Justice BRENNAN and Justice MARSHALL join, dissenting.

A sobriety checkpoint is usually operated at night at an unannounced location. Surprise is crucial to its method. The test operation conducted by the Michigan State Police and the Saginaw County Sheriff's Department began shortly after midnight and lasted until about 1 a.m. During that period, the 19 officers participating in the operation made two arrests and stopped and questioned 124 other unsuspecting and innocent drivers. It is, of course, not known how many arrests would have been made during that period if those officers had been engaged in normal patrol activities. However, the findings of the trial court, based on an extensive record and affirmed by the Michigan Court of Appeals, indicate that the net effect of sobriety checkpoints on traffic safety is infinitesimal and possibly negative.

Indeed, the record in this case makes clear that a decision holding these suspicionless seizures unconstitutional would not impede the law enforcement community's remarkable progress in reducing the death toll on our highways. Because the Michigan program was patterned after an older program in Maryland, the trial judge gave special attention to that State's experience. Over a period of several years, Maryland operated 125 checkpoints; of the 41,000 motorists passing through those checkpoints, only 143 persons (0.3%) were arrested. The number of man-hours devoted to these operations is not in the record, but it seems inconceivable that a higher arrest rate could not have been achieved by more conventional means. Yet, even if the 143 checkpoint arrests were assumed to involve a net increase in the number of drunken driving arrests per year, the figure would still be insignificant by comparison to the 71,000 such arrests made by Michigan State Police without checkpoints in 1984 alone.

Any relationship between sobriety checkpoints and an actual reduction in highway fatalities is even less substantial than the minimal impact on arrest rates. As the Michigan Court of Appeals pointed out: "Maryland had conducted a study comparing traffic statistics between a county using checkpoints and a control county. The results of the study showed that alcohol-related accidents in the checkpoint county decreased by ten percent, whereas the control county saw an eleven percent decrease; and while fatal accidents in the control county fell from sixteen to three, fatal accidents in the checkpoint county actually doubled from the prior year."

In light of these considerations, it seems evident that the Court today misapplies the balancing test announced in *Brown v. Texas*. The Court overvalues the law enforcement interest in using sobriety checkpoints, undervalues the citizen's interest in freedom from random, unannounced investigatory seizures, and mistakenly assumes that there is "virtually no difference" between a routine stop at a permanent, fixed checkpoint and a surprise stop at a sobriety checkpoint.

I

There is a critical difference between a seizure that is preceded by fair notice and one that is effected by surprise. That is one reason why a border search, or indeed any search at a permanent and fixed checkpoint, is much less intrusive than a random stop. A motorist with advance notice of the location of a permanent checkpoint has an opportunity to avoid the search entirely, or at least to prepare for, and limit, the intrusion on her privacy.

No such opportunity is available in the case of a random stop or a temporary checkpoint, which both depend for their effectiveness on the element of surprise. A driver who discovers an unexpected checkpoint on a familiar local road will be startled and distressed. She may infer, correctly, that the checkpoint is not simply "business as usual," and may likewise infer, again correctly, that the police have made a discretionary decision to focus their law enforcement efforts upon her and others who pass the chosen point.

This element of surprise is the most obvious distinction between the sobriety checkpoints permitted by today's majority and the interior border checkpoints approved by this Court in *Martinez-Fuerte*. The distinction casts immediate doubt upon the majority's argument, for *Martinez-Fuerte* is the only case in which we have upheld suspicionless seizures of motorists. But the difference between notice and surprise is only one of the important reasons for distinguishing between permanent and mobile checkpoints. With respect to the former, there is no room for discretion in either the timing or the location of the stop—it is a permanent part of the landscape. In the latter case, however, although the checkpoint is most frequently employed during the hours of darkness on weekends (because that is when drivers with alcohol in their blood are most apt to be found on the road), the police have extremely broad discretion in determining the exact timing and placement of the roadblock.

There is also a significant difference between the kind of discretion that the officer exercises after the stop is made. A check for a driver's license, or for identification papers at an immigration checkpoint, is far more easily standardized than is a search for evidence of intoxication. A Michigan officer who questions a motorist at a sobriety checkpoint has virtually unlimited discretion to detain the driver on the basis of the slightest suspicion. A ruddy complexion, an unbuttoned shirt, bloodshot eyes, or a speech impediment may suffice to prolong the detention. Any driver who had just consumed a glass of beer, or even a sip of wine, would almost certainly have the burden of demonstrating to the officer that his or her driving ability was not impaired.

Finally, it is significant that many of the stops at permanent checkpoints occur during daylight hours, whereas the sobriety checkpoints are almost invariably operated at night. A seizure followed by interrogation and even a cursory search at night is surely more offensive than a daytime stop that is almost as routine as going through a tollgate. Thus we thought it important to point out that the random stops at issue in *Ortiz* (1975) frequently occurred at night.

■ ■ ■

II

The Court, unable to draw any persuasive analogy to *Martinez-Fuerte*, rests its decision today on application of a more general balancing test taken from *Brown v. Texas*. In that case the appellant, a pedestrian, had been stopped for questioning in an area of El Paso, Texas, that had "a high incidence of drug traffic" because he "looked suspicious." He was then arrested and convicted for refusing to identify himself to police officers. We set aside his conviction because the officers stopped him when they lacked any reasonable suspicion that he was engaged in criminal activity. In our opinion, we stated:

> "Consideration of the constitutionality of such seizures involves a weighing of the gravity of the public concerns served by the seizure, the degree to which the seizure advances the public interest, and the severity of the interference with individual liberty."

The gravity of the public concern with highway safety that is implicated by this case is, of course, undisputed. Yet, that same grave concern was implicated in *Delaware v. Prouse* [(1979)]. Moreover, I do not understand the Court to have placed any lesser value on the importance of the drug problem implicated in *Brown v. Texas* or on the need to control the illegal border crossings that were at stake in *Almeida-Sanchez* [*v. United States* (1973)] and its progeny. A different result in this case must be justified by the other two factors in the *Brown* formulation.

As I have already explained, I believe the Court is quite wrong in blithely asserting that a sobriety checkpoint is no more intrusive than a permanent checkpoint. In my opinion, unannounced investigatory seizures are, particularly when they take place at night, the hallmark of regimes far different from ours; the surprise intrusion upon individual liberty is not minimal. On that issue, my difference with the Court may amount to nothing less than a difference in our respective evaluations of the importance of individual liberty, a serious, albeit inevitable, source of constitutional disagreement. On the degree to which the sobriety checkpoint seizures advance the public interest, however, the Court's position is wholly indefensible.

The Court's analysis of this issue resembles a business decision that measures profits by counting gross receipts and ignoring expenses. The evidence in this case indicates that sobriety checkpoints result in the arrest of a fraction of one percent of the drivers who are stopped, but there is absolutely no evidence that this figure represents an increase over the number of arrests that would have been made by using the same law enforcement resources in conventional patrols. Thus, although the *gross* number of arrests is more than zero, there is a complete failure of proof on the question whether the wholesale seizures have produced any *net* advance in the public interest in arresting intoxicated drivers.

Indeed, the position adopted today by the Court is not one endorsed by any of the law enforcement authorities to whom the Court purports to defer. The Michigan police do not rely, as the Court does, on the *arrest rate* at sobriety checkpoints to justify the stops made there. Colonel Hough, the commander of the Michigan State Police and a leading proponent of the checkpoints, admitted at trial that the arrest rate at the checkpoints was "very low." Instead, Colonel Hough and the State have maintained that the mere *threat* of such arrests is sufficient to deter drunk-driving and so to reduce the accident rate. The Maryland police officer who testified at trial took the same position with respect to his State's program. There is, obviously, nothing wrong with a law enforcement technique that reduces crime by pure deterrence without punishing anybody; on the contrary, such an approach is highly commendable. One cannot, however, prove its efficacy by counting the arrests that were made. One must instead measure the number of crimes that were avoided. Perhaps because the record is wanting, the Court simply ignores this point. . . .

III

The most disturbing aspect of the Court's decision today is that it appears to give no weight to the citizen's interest in freedom from suspicionless unannounced investigatory seizures. Although the author of the opinion does not reiterate his description of that interest as "diaphanous," see *Delaware v. Prouse* (Rehnquist, J., dissenting), the Court's opinion implicitly adopts that characterization. On the other hand, the Court places a heavy thumb on the law enforcement interest by looking only at gross receipts instead of net benefits. Perhaps this tampering with the scales of justice can be explained by the Court's obvious concern about the slaughter on our highways and a resultant tolerance for policies designed to alleviate the problem by "setting an example" of a few motorists.

■ ■ ■

This is a case that is driven by nothing more than symbolic state action—an insufficient justification for an otherwise unreasonable program of random seizures. Unfortunately, the Court is transfixed by the wrong symbol—the illusory prospect of punishing countless intoxicated motorists—when it should keep its eyes on the road plainly marked by the Constitution.

I respectfully dissent.

City of Indianapolis v. Edmond

531 U.S. 32 (2000)

O'CONNOR, J., delivered the opinion of the Court, in which STEVENS, KENNEDY, SOUTER, GINSBURG, and BREYER, JJ., joined. REHNQUIST, C.J., filed a dissenting opinion, in which THOMAS, J., joined, and in which SCALIA, J., joined as to Part I. THOMAS, J., filed a dissenting opinion.

In *Michigan Dept. of State Police v. Sitz* (1990) and *United States v. Martinez-Fuerte* (1976), we held that brief, suspicionless seizures at highway checkpoints for the purposes of combating drunk driving and intercepting illegal immigrants were constitutional. We now consider the constitutionality of a highway checkpoint program whose primary purpose is the discovery and interdiction of illegal narcotics.

I

In August 1998, the city of Indianapolis began to operate vehicle checkpoints on Indianapolis roads in an effort to interdict unlawful drugs. The city conducted six such roadblocks between August and November that year, stopping 61 vehicles and arresting 104 motorists. Fifty-five arrests were for drug-related crimes, while 49 were for offenses unrelated to drugs. The overall "hit rate" of the program was thus approximately nine percent.

The parties stipulated to the facts concerning the operation of the checkpoints by the Indianapolis Police Department (IPD) for purposes of the preliminary injunction proceedings instituted below. At each checkpoint location, the police stop a predetermined number of vehicles. Approximately 30 officers are stationed at the checkpoint. Pursuant to written directives issued by the chief of police, at least one officer approaches the vehicle, advises the driver that he or she is being stopped briefly at a drug checkpoint, and asks the driver to produce a license and registration. The officer also looks for signs of impairment and conducts an open-view examination of the vehicle from the outside. A narcotics-detection dog walks around the outside of each stopped vehicle.

The directives instruct the officers that they may conduct a search only by consent or based on the appropriate quantum of particularized suspicion. The officers must conduct each stop in the same manner until particularized suspicion develops, and the officers have no discretion to stop any vehicle out of sequence. The city agreed in the stipulation to operate the checkpoints in such a way as to ensure that the total duration of each stop, absent reasonable suspicion or probable cause, would be five minutes or less. . . .

Respondents James Edmond and Joell Palmer were each stopped at a narcotics checkpoint in late September 1998. Respondents then filed a lawsuit on behalf of themselves and the class of all motorists who had been stopped or were subject to being stopped in the future at the Indianapolis drug checkpoints. Respondents claimed that the roadblocks violated the Fourth Amendment of the United States Constitution and the search and seizure provision of the Indiana Constitution. Respondents requested declaratory and injunctive relief for the class, as well as damages and attorney's fees for themselves. . . .

. . . The United States District Court for the Southern District of Indiana agreed to class certification and denied the motion for a preliminary injunction, holding that the checkpoint program did not violate the Fourth Amendment. A divided panel of the United States Court of Appeals for the Seventh Circuit reversed, holding that the checkpoints contravened the Fourth Amendment. The panel denied rehearing. We granted certiorari, and now affirm.

■ ■ ■

In *Sitz*, we evaluated the constitutionality of a Michigan highway sobriety checkpoint program. The *Sitz* checkpoint involved brief, suspicionless stops of motorists so that police officers could detect signs of intoxication and remove impaired drivers from the road. Motorists who exhibited signs of intoxication were diverted for a license and registration check and, if warranted, further sobriety tests. This checkpoint program was clearly aimed at reducing the immediate hazard posed by the presence of drunk drivers on the highways, and there was an obvious connection between the imperative of highway safety and the law enforcement practice at issue. The gravity of the drunk driving problem and the magnitude of the State's interest in getting drunk drivers off the road weighed heavily in our determination that the program was constitutional. . . .

■ ■ ■

It is well established that a vehicle stop at a highway checkpoint effectuates a seizure within the meaning of the Fourth Amendment. The fact that officers walk a narcotics-detection dog around the exterior of each car at the Indianapolis checkpoints does not transform the seizure into a search. . . .

As petitioners concede, the Indianapolis checkpoint program unquestionably has the primary purpose of interdicting illegal narcotics. In their stipulation of facts, the parties repeatedly refer to the checkpoints as "drug checkpoints" and describe them as "being operated by the City of Indianapolis in an effort to interdict unlawful drugs in Indianapolis." In addition, the first document attached to the parties' stipulation is entitled "DRUG CHECK-POINT CONTACT OFFICER DIRECTIVES BY ORDER OF THE CHIEF OF POLICE." These directives instruct officers to "[a]dvise the citizen that they are being stopped briefly at a drug checkpoint." The second document attached to the stipulation is entitled "1998 Drug Road Blocks" and contains a statistical breakdown of information relating to the checkpoints conducted. Further, according to Sergeant DePew, the checkpoints are identified with lighted signs reading, "'NARCOTICS CHECKPOINT MILE AHEAD, NARCOTICS K-9 IN USE, BE PREPARED TO STOP.'" Finally, both the District Court and the Court of Appeals recognized that the primary purpose of the roadblocks is the interdiction of narcotics . . . (noting that both parties "stress the primary purpose of the roadblocks as the interdiction of narcotics" and that "[t]he IPD has made it clear that the purpose for its checkpoints is to interdict narcotics traffic"); . . . (observing that "the City concedes that its proximate goal is to catch drug offenders").

We have never approved a checkpoint program whose primary purpose was to detect evidence of ordinary criminal wrongdoing. Rather, our checkpoint cases have recognized only limited exceptions to the general rule that a seizure must be accompanied by some measure of individualized suspicion. . . .

Nor can the narcotics-interdiction purpose of the checkpoints be rationalized in terms of a highway safety concern similar to that present in *Sitz.* The detection and punishment of almost any criminal offense serves broadly the safety of the community, and our streets would no doubt be safer but for the scourge of illegal drugs. Only with respect to a smaller class of offenses, however, is society confronted with the type of immediate, vehicle-bound threat to life and limb that the sobriety checkpoint in *Sitz* was designed to eliminate.

■ ■ ■

The primary purpose of the Indianapolis narcotics checkpoints is in the end to advance "the general interest in crime control." We decline to suspend the usual requirement of individualized suspicion where the police seek to employ a checkpoint primarily for the ordinary enterprise of investigating crimes. We cannot sanction stops justified only by the generalized and ever-present possibility that interrogation and inspection may reveal that any given motorist has committed some crime.

Of course, there are circumstances that may justify a law enforcement checkpoint where the primary purpose would otherwise, but for some emergency, relate to ordinary crime control. For example, as the Court of Appeals noted, the Fourth Amendment would almost certainly permit an appropriately tailored roadblock set up to thwart an imminent terrorist attack or to catch a dangerous criminal who is likely to flee by way of a particular route. The exigencies created by these scenarios are far removed from the circumstances under which authorities might simply stop cars as a matter of course to see if there just happens to be a felon leaving the jurisdiction. While we do not limit the purposes that may justify a checkpoint program to any rigid set of categories, we decline to approve a program whose primary purpose is ultimately indistinguishable from the general interest in crime control.

■ ■ ■

Petitioners argue that the Indianapolis checkpoint program is justified by its lawful secondary purposes of keeping impaired motorists off the road and verifying licenses and registrations. If this were the case, however, law enforcement authorities would be able to establish checkpoints for virtually any purpose so long as they also included a license or sobriety check. For this reason, we examine the available evidence to determine the primary purpose of the checkpoint program. While we recognize the challenges inherent in a purpose inquiry, courts routinely engage in this enterprise in many areas of constitutional jurisprudence as a means of sifting abusive governmental conduct from that which is lawful. As a result, a program driven by an impermissible purpose may be proscribed while a program impelled by licit purposes is permitted, even though the challenged conduct may be outwardly similar. While reasonableness under the Fourth Amendment is predominantly an objective inquiry, our special needs and administrative search cases demonstrate that purpose is often relevant when suspicionless intrusions pursuant to a general scheme are at issue.

■ ■ ■

Our holding also does not affect the validity of border searches or searches at places like airports and government buildings, where the need for such measures to ensure public safety can be particularly acute. Nor does our opinion speak to other intrusions aimed primarily at purposes beyond the general interest in crime control. Our holding also does not impair the ability of police officers to act appropriately upon information that they properly learn during a checkpoint stop justified by a lawful primary purpose, even where such action may result in the arrest of a motorist for an offense unrelated to that purpose. Finally, we caution that the purpose inquiry in this context is to be conducted only at the programmatic level and is not an invitation to probe the minds of individual officers acting at the scene.

Because the primary purpose of the Indianapolis checkpoint program is ultimately indistinguishable from the general interest in crime control, the checkpoints violate the Fourth Amendment. The judgment of the Court of Appeals is, accordingly, affirmed.

It is so ordered.

Chief Justice REHNQUIST, with whom Justice THOMAS joins, and with whom Justice SCALIA joins as to Part I, dissenting.

The State's use of a drug-sniffing dog, according to the Court's holding, annuls what is otherwise plainly constitutional under our Fourth Amendment

jurisprudence: brief, standardized, discretionless, roadblock seizures of automobiles, seizures which effectively serve a weighty state interest with only
minimal intrusion on the privacy of their occupants. Because these seizures
serve the State's accepted and significant interests of preventing drunken driving and checking for driver's licenses and vehicle registrations, and because
there is nothing in the record to indicate that the addition of the dog sniff
lengthens these otherwise legitimate seizures, I dissent.

I

As it is nowhere to be found in the Court's opinion, I begin with blackletter
roadblock seizure law. "The principal protection of Fourth Amendment rights
at checkpoints lies in appropriate limitations on the scope of the stop." *United
States v. Martinez-Fuerte*. Roadblock seizures are consistent with the Fourth
Amendment if they are "carried out pursuant to a plan embodying explicit,
neutral limitations on the conduct of individual officers." *Brown v. Texas* (1979).
Specifically, the constitutionality of a seizure turns upon "a weighing of the
gravity of the public concerns served by the seizure, the degree to which the
seizure advances the public interest, and the severity of the interference with
individual liberty." . . .

This case follows naturally from *Martinez-Fuerte* and *Sitz*. Petitioners
acknowledge that the "primary purpose" of these roadblocks is to interdict
illegal drugs, but this fact should not be controlling. Even accepting the Court's
conclusion that the checkpoints at issue in *Martinez-Fuerte* and *Sitz* were not
primarily related to criminal law enforcement, the question whether a law
enforcement purpose could support a roadblock seizure is not presented in
this case.

■ ■ ■

Because of the valid reasons for conducting these roadblock seizures, it is
constitutionally irrelevant that petitioners also hoped to interdict drugs.
In *Whren v. United States* (1996), we held that an officer's subjective intent
would not invalidate an otherwise objectively justifiable stop of an automobile.
The reasonableness of an officer's discretionary decision to stop an automobile,
at issue in *Whren*, turns on whether there is probable cause to believe that a
traffic violation has occurred. The reasonableness of highway checkpoints, at
issue here, turns on whether they effectively serve a significant state interest
with minimal intrusion on motorists. The stop in *Whren* was objectively reasonable because the police officers had witnessed traffic violations; so too the
roadblocks here are objectively reasonable because they serve the substantial
interests of preventing drunken driving and checking for driver's licenses and
vehicle registrations with minimal intrusion on motorists.

■ ■ ■

These stops effectively serve the State's legitimate interests; they are executed in a regularized and neutral manner; and they only minimally intrude
upon the privacy of the motorists. They should therefore be constitutional.

II

The Court, unwilling to adopt the straightforward analysis that these precedents dictate, adds a new non-law-enforcement primary purpose test lifted from a distinct area of Fourth Amendment jurisprudence relating to the *searches* of homes and businesses. As discussed above, the question that the Court answers is not even posed in this case given the accepted reasons for the seizures. But more fundamentally, whatever sense a non-law-enforcement primary purpose test may make in the search setting, it is ill suited to brief roadblock seizures, where we have consistently looked at "the scope of the stop" in assessing a program's constitutionality.

■ ■ ■

Petitioners' program complies with our decisions regarding roadblock seizures of automobiles, and the addition of a dog sniff does not add to the length or the intrusion of the stop. Because such stops are consistent with the Fourth Amendment, I would reverse the decision of the Court of Appeals.

Justice THOMAS, dissenting.

Taken together, our decisions in *Michigan Dept. of State Police v. Sitz* and *United States v. Martinez-Fuerte* stand for the proposition that suspicionless roadblock seizures are constitutionally permissible if conducted according to a plan that limits the discretion of the officers conducting the stops. I am not convinced that *Sitz* and *Martinez-Fuerte* were correctly decided. Indeed, I rather doubt that the Framers of the Fourth Amendment would have considered "reasonable" a program of indiscriminate stops of individuals not suspected of wrongdoing.

Respondents did not, however, advocate the overruling of *Sitz* and *Martinez-Fuerte,* and I am reluctant to consider such a step without the benefit of briefing and argument. For the reasons given by The Chief Justice, I believe that those cases compel upholding the program at issue here. I, therefore, join his opinion.

Illinois v. Lidster

540 U.S. 419 (2004)

BREYER, J., delivered the opinion of the Court, in which REHNQUIST, C.J., and O'CONNOR, SCALIA, KENNEDY, and THOMAS, JJ., joined, and in which STEVENS, SOUTER, and GINSBURG, JJ., joined as to Parts I and II. STEVENS, J., filed an opinion concurring in part and dissenting in part, in which SOUTER and GINSBURG, JJ., joined.

This Fourth Amendment case focuses upon a highway checkpoint where police stopped motorists to ask them for information about a recent hit-and-run accident. We hold that the police stops were reasonable, hence, constitutional.

I

The relevant background is as follows: On Saturday, August 23, 1997, just after midnight, an unknown motorist traveling eastbound on a highway in Lombard, Illinois, struck and killed a 70-year-old bicyclist. The motorist drove off without identifying himself. About one week later at about the same time of night and at about the same place, local police set up a highway checkpoint designed to obtain more information about the accident from the motoring public.

Police cars with flashing lights partially blocked the eastbound lanes of the highway. The blockage forced traffic to slow down, leading to lines of up to 15 cars in each lane. As each vehicle drew up to the checkpoint, an officer would stop it for 10 to 15 seconds, ask the occupants whether they had seen anything happen there the previous weekend, and hand each driver a flyer. The flyer said "ALERT...FATAL HIT & RUN ACCIDENT" and requested "ASSISTANCE IN IDENTIFYING THE VEHICLE AND DRIVER INVOLVED IN THIS ACCIDENT WHICH KILLED A 70 YEAR OLD BICYCLIST."

Robert Lidster, the respondent, drove a minivan toward the checkpoint. As he approached the checkpoint, his van swerved, nearly hitting one of the officers. The officer smelled alcohol on Lidster's breath. He directed Lidster to a side street where another officer administered a sobriety test and then arrested Lidster. Lidster was tried and convicted in Illinois state court of driving under the influence of alcohol.

Lidster challenged the lawfulness of his arrest and conviction on the ground that the government had obtained much of the relevant evidence through use of a checkpoint stop that violated the Fourth Amendment. The trial court rejected that challenge. But an Illinois appellate court reached the opposite conclusion. The Illinois Supreme Court agreed with the appellate court. It held (by a vote of 4 to 3) that our decision in *Indianapolis v. Edmond* (2000) required it to find the stop unconstitutional.

Because lower courts have reached different conclusions about this matter, we granted certiorari. We now reverse the Illinois Supreme Court's determination.

II

The Illinois Supreme Court basically held that our decision in *Edmond* governs the outcome of this case. We do not agree. *Edmond* involved a checkpoint at which police stopped vehicles to look for evidence of drug crimes committed by occupants of those vehicles. After stopping a vehicle at the checkpoint, police would examine (from outside the vehicle) the vehicle's interior; they would walk a drug-sniffing dog around the exterior; and, if they found sufficient evidence of drug (or other) crimes, they would arrest the vehicle's occupants. We found that police had set up this checkpoint primarily for general "crime control" purposes, *i.e.*, "to detect evidence of ordinary criminal wrongdoing." We noted that the stop was made without individualized suspicion. And we held that the Fourth Amendment forbids such a stop, in the absence of special circumstances.

The checkpoint stop here differs significantly from that in *Edmond*. The stop's primary law enforcement purpose was *not* to determine whether a vehicle's occupants were committing a crime, but to ask vehicle occupants, as members of the public, for their help in providing information about a crime in all likelihood committed by others. The police expected the information elicited to help them apprehend, not the vehicle's occupants, but other individuals.

Edmond's language, as well as its context, makes clear that the constitutionality of this latter, information-seeking kind of stop was not then before the Court. *Edmond* refers to the subject matter of its holding as "stops justified only by the generalized and ever-present possibility that interrogation and inspection may reveal that *any given motorist has committed some crime.*" We concede that *Edmond* describes the law enforcement objective there in question as a "general interest in crime control," but it specifies that the phrase "general interest in crime control" does not refer to every "law enforcement" objective. We must read this and related general language in *Edmond* as we often read general language in judicial opinions—as referring in context to circumstances similar to the circumstances then before the Court and not referring to quite different circumstances that the Court was not then considering.

Neither do we believe, *Edmond* aside, that the Fourth Amendment would have us apply an *Edmond*-type rule of automatic unconstitutionality to brief, information-seeking highway stops of the kind now before us. For one thing, the fact that such stops normally lack individualized suspicion cannot by itself determine the constitutional outcome. As in *Edmond*, the stop here at issue involves a motorist. The Fourth Amendment does not treat a motorist's car as his castle.

■ ■ ■

For another thing, information-seeking highway stops are less likely to provoke anxiety or to prove intrusive. The stops are likely brief. The police are not likely to ask questions designed to elicit self-incriminating information. And citizens will often react positively when police simply ask for their help as "responsible citizen[s]" to "give whatever information they may have to aid in law enforcement."

Further, the law ordinarily permits police to seek the voluntary cooperation of members of the public in the investigation of a crime. "[L]aw enforcement officers do not violate the Fourth Amendment by merely approaching an individual on the street or in another public place, by asking him if he is willing to answer some questions, [or] by putting questions to him if the person is willing to listen."

■ ■ ■

The importance of soliciting the public's assistance is offset to some degree by the need to stop a motorist to obtain that help—a need less likely present where a pedestrian, not a motorist, is involved. The difference is significant in light of our determinations that such an involuntary stop amounts to a "seizure" in Fourth Amendment terms. That difference, however, is not important enough to justify an *Edmond*-type rule here. After all, as we have said, the motorist stop will likely be brief. Any accompanying traffic delay should prove no more onerous than many that typically accompany normal traffic congestion. And the resulting voluntary questioning of a motorist is as likely to prove important for police investigation as is the questioning of a pedestrian. Given these considerations, it would seem anomalous were the law (1) ordinarily to allow police freely to seek the voluntary cooperation of pedestrians but (2) ordinarily to forbid police to seek similar voluntary cooperation from motorists.

Finally, we do not believe that an *Edmond*-type rule is needed to prevent an unreasonable proliferation of police checkpoints. Practical considerations— namely, limited police resources and community hostility to related traffic tieups—seem likely to inhibit any such proliferation. . . .

These considerations, taken together, convince us that an *Edmond*-type presumptive rule of unconstitutionality does not apply here. That does not mean the stop is automatically, or even presumptively, constitutional. It simply means that we must judge its reasonableness, hence, its constitutionality, on the basis of the individual circumstances. And as this Court said in *Brown v. Texas* (1979), in judging reasonableness, we look to "the gravity of the public concerns served by the seizure, the degree to which the seizure advances the public interest, and the severity of the interference with individual liberty."

III

We now consider the reasonableness of the checkpoint stop before us in light of the factors just mentioned, an issue that, in our view, has been fully argued here. We hold that the stop was constitutional.

The relevant public concern was grave. Police were investigating a crime that had resulted in a human death. No one denies the police's need to obtain more information at that time. And the stop's objective was to help find the perpetrator of a specific and known crime, not of unknown crimes of a general sort.

The stop advanced this grave public concern to a significant degree. The police appropriately tailored their checkpoint stops to fit important criminal investigatory needs. The stops took place about one week after the hit-and-run accident, on the same highway near the location of the accident, and at about the same time of night. And police used the stops to obtain information from drivers, some of whom might well have been in the vicinity of the crime at the time it occurred.

Most importantly, the stops interfered only minimally with liberty of the sort the Fourth Amendment seeks to protect. Viewed objectively, each stop required only a brief wait in line—a very few minutes at most. Contact with the police lasted only a few seconds. . . .

For these reasons we conclude that the checkpoint stop was constitutional.

The judgment of the Illinois Supreme Court is
Reversed.

Justice STEVENS, with whom Justice SOUTER and Justice GINSBURG join, concurring in part and dissenting in part.

There is a valid and important distinction between seizing a person to determine whether she has committed a crime and seizing a person to ask whether she has any information about an unknown person who committed a crime a week earlier. I therefore join Parts I and II of the Court's opinion explaining why our decision in *Indianapolis v. Edmond* is not controlling in this case. However, I find the issue discussed in Part III of the opinion closer than the Court does and believe it would be wise to remand the case to the Illinois state courts to address that issue in the first instance.

In contrast to pedestrians, who are free to keep walking when they encounter police officers handing out flyers or seeking information, motorists who confront a roadblock are required to stop, and to remain stopped for as long as the officers choose to detain them. Such a seizure may seem relatively innocuous to some, but annoying to others who are forced to wait for several minutes when the line of cars is lengthened—for example, by a surge of vehicles leaving a factory at the end of a shift. Still other drivers may find an unpublicized roadblock at midnight on a Saturday somewhat alarming.

On the other side of the equation, the likelihood that questioning a random sample of drivers will yield useful information about a hit-and-run accident that occurred a week earlier is speculative at best. To be sure, the sample in this case was not entirely random: The record reveals that the police knew that the victim had finished work at the Post Office shortly before the fatal accident, and hoped that other employees of the Post Office or the nearby industrial park might work on similar schedules and, thus, have been driving the same route at the same time the previous week. That is a plausible theory, but there is no evidence in the record that the police did anything to confirm that the nearby businesses in fact had shift changes at or near midnight on Saturdays, or that they had reason to believe that a roadblock would be more effective than, say, placing flyers on the employees' cars.

In short, the outcome of the multifactor test prescribed in *Brown v. Texas* is by no means clear on the facts of this case. Because the Illinois Appellate Court and the State Supreme Court held that the Lombard roadblock was *per se* unconstitutional under *Indianapolis v. Edmond,* neither court attempted to apply the *Brown* test. "We ordinarily do not decide in the first instance issues not resolved below." We should be especially reluctant to abandon our role as a court of review in a case in which the constitutional inquiry requires analysis of local conditions and practices more familiar to judges closer to the scene. I would therefore remand the case to the Illinois courts to undertake the initial analysis of the issue that the Court resolves in Part III of its opinion. To that extent, I respectfully dissent.

4. Workplace

Skinner v. Railway Labor

489 U.S. 602 (1989)

KENNEDY, J., delivered the opinion of the Court, in which REHNQUIST, C.J., and WHITE, BLACKMUN, O'CONNOR, and SCALIA, JJ., joined, and in all but portions of Part III of which STEVENS, J., joined. STEVENS, J., filed an opinion concurring in part and concurring in the judgment. MARSHALL, J., filed a dissenting opinion, in which BRENNAN, J., joined.

The Federal Railroad Safety Act of 1970 authorizes the Secretary of Transportation to "prescribe, as necessary, appropriate rules, regulations, orders, and standards for all areas of railroad safety." Finding that alcohol and drug abuse by railroad employees poses a serious threat to safety, the Federal Railroad Administration (FRA) has promulgated regulations that mandate blood and urine tests of employees who are involved in certain train accidents. The FRA also has adopted regulations that do not require, but do authorize, railroads to administer breath and urine tests to employees who violate certain safety rules. The question presented by this case is whether these regulations violate the Fourth Amendment.

The problem of alcohol use on American railroads is as old as the industry itself, and efforts to deter it by carrier rules began at least a century ago. For many years, railroads have prohibited operating employees from possessing alcohol or being intoxicated while on duty and from consuming alcoholic beverages while subject to being called for duty. More recently, these proscriptions have been expanded to forbid possession or use of certain drugs. These restrictions are embodied in "Rule G," an industry-wide operating rule promulgated by the Association of American Railroads, and are enforced, in various formulations, by virtually every railroad in the country. The customary sanction for Rule G violations is dismissal.

In July 1983, the FRA expressed concern that these industry efforts were not adequate to curb alcohol and drug abuse by railroad employees. The FRA pointed to evidence indicating that on-the-job intoxication was a significant problem in the railroad industry. The FRA also found, after a review of accident investigation reports, that from 1972 to 1983 "the nation's railroads experienced at least 21 significant train accidents involving alcohol or drug use as a probable cause or contributing factor," and that these accidents "resulted in 25 fatalities, 61 non-fatal injuries, and property damage estimated at $19 million (approximately $27 million in 1982 dollars)." The FRA further identified "an additional 17 fatalities to operating employees working on or around rail rolling stock that involved alcohol or drugs as a contributing factor." In light of these problems, the FRA solicited comments from interested parties on various regulatory approaches to the problems of alcohol and drug abuse throughout the Nation's railroad system.

■ ■ ■

After reviewing further comments from representatives of the railroad industry, labor groups, and the general public, the FRA, in 1985, promulgated regulations addressing the problem of alcohol and drugs on the railroads.... The regulations prohibit covered employees from using or possessing alcohol or any controlled substance. The regulations further prohibit those employees from reporting for covered service while under the influence of, or impaired by, alcohol, while having a blood alcohol concentration of .04 or more, or while under the influence of, or impaired by, any controlled substance. The regulations do not restrict, however, a railroad's authority to impose an absolute prohibition on the presence of alcohol or any drug in the body fluids of persons in its employ.

■ ■ ■

To the extent pertinent here, two subparts of the regulations relate to testing. Subpart C, which is entitled "Post-Accident Toxicological Testing," is mandatory. It provides that railroads "shall take all practicable steps to assure that all covered employees of the railroad directly involved ... provide blood and urine samples for toxicological testing by FRA," upon the occurrence of certain specified events. Toxicological testing is required following a "major train accident," which is defined as any train accident that involves (i) a fatality, (ii) the release of hazardous material accompanied by an evacuation or a reportable injury, or (iii) damage to railroad property of $500,000 or more. The railroad has the further duty of collecting blood and urine samples for testing after an "impact accident," which is defined as a collision that results in a reportable injury, or in damage to railroad property of $50,000 or more. Finally, the railroad is also obligated to test after "[a]ny train incident that involves a fatality to any on-duty railroad employee."

■ ■ ■

The regulations require that the FRA notify employees of the results of the tests and afford them an opportunity to respond in writing before preparation of any final investigative report. Employees who refuse to provide required blood or urine samples may not perform covered service for nine months, but they are entitled to a hearing concerning their refusal to take the test.

■ ■ ■

Respondents, the Railway Labor Executives' Association and various of its member labor organizations, brought the instant suit in the United States District Court for the Northern District of California, seeking to enjoin the FRA's regulations on various statutory and constitutional grounds. In a ruling from the bench, the District Court granted summary judgment in petitioners' favor. The court concluded that railroad employees "have a valid interest in the integrity of their own bodies" that deserved protection under the Fourth Amendment. The court held, however, that this interest was outweighed by the competing "public and governmental interest in the ... promotion of ... railway safety, safety for employees, and safety for the general public that is involved with the transportation." The District Court found respondents' other constitutional and statutory arguments meritless.

A divided panel of the Court of Appeals for the Ninth Circuit reversed. The court held, first, that tests mandated by a railroad in reliance on the authority conferred by Subpart D involve sufficient Government action to implicate the Fourth Amendment, and that the breath, blood, and urine tests contemplated by the FRA regulations are Fourth Amendment searches. The court also "agre[ed] that the exigencies of testing for the presence of alcohol and drugs in blood, urine or breath require prompt action which precludes obtaining a warrant." The court further held that "accommodation of railroad employees' privacy interest with the significant safety concerns of the government does not require adherence to a probable cause requirement," and, accordingly, that the legality of the searches contemplated by the FRA regulations depends on their reasonableness under all the circumstances.

The court concluded, however, that particularized suspicion is essential to a finding that toxicological testing of railroad employees is reasonable. A requirement of individualized suspicion, the court stated, would impose "no insuperable burden on the government," and would ensure that the tests are confined to the detection of current impairment, rather than to the discovery of "the metabolites of various drugs, which are not evidence of current intoxication and may remain in the body for days or weeks after the ingestion of the drug." Except for the provisions authorizing breath and urine tests on a "reasonable suspicion" of drug or alcohol impairment, the FRA regulations did not require a showing of individualized suspicion, and, accordingly, the court invalidated them. . . .

We granted the federal parties' petition for a writ of certiorari, to consider whether the regulations invalidated by the Court of Appeals violate the Fourth Amendment. We now reverse.

II

We are unwilling to conclude, in the context of this facial challenge, that breath and urine tests required by private railroads in reliance on Subpart D will not implicate the Fourth Amendment. Whether a private party should be deemed an agent or instrument of the Government for Fourth Amendment purposes necessarily turns on the degree of the Government's participation in the private party's activities. . . .

The regulations, including those in Subpart D, pre-empt state laws, rules, or regulations covering the same subject matter, and are intended to supersede "any provision of a collective bargaining agreement, or arbitration award construing such an agreement." They also confer upon the FRA the right to receive certain biological samples and test results procured by railroads pursuant to Subpart D. § 219.11(c). In addition, a railroad may not divest itself of, or otherwise compromise by contract, the authority conferred by Subpart D. As the FRA explained, such "authority . . . is conferred for the purpose of promoting the public safety, and a railroad may not shackle itself in a way inconsistent with its duty to promote the public safety." Nor is a covered employee free to decline his employer's request to submit to breath or urine tests under the conditions set forth in Subpart D. An employee who refuses to submit to the tests must be withdrawn from covered service.

In light of these provisions, we are unwilling to accept petitioners' submission that tests conducted by private railroads in reliance on Subpart D will be primarily the result of private initiative....

We have long recognized that a "compelled intrusio[n] into the body for blood to be analyzed for alcohol content" must be deemed a Fourth Amendment search. See *Schmerber v. California* (1966).

■ ■ ■

Unlike the blood-testing procedure at issue in *Schmerber*, the procedures prescribed by the FRA regulations for collecting and testing urine samples do not entail a surgical intrusion into the body. It is not disputed, however, that chemical analysis of urine, like that of blood, can reveal a host of private medical facts about an employee, including whether he or she is epileptic, pregnant, or diabetic. Nor can it be disputed that the process of collecting the sample to be tested, which may in some cases involve visual or aural monitoring of the act of urination, itself implicates privacy interests....

Because it is clear that the collection and testing of urine intrudes upon expectations of privacy that society has long recognized as reasonable, the Federal Courts of Appeals have concluded unanimously, and we agree, that these intrusions must be deemed searches under the Fourth Amendment.

In view of our conclusion that the collection and subsequent analysis of the requisite biological samples must be deemed Fourth Amendment searches, we need not characterize the employer's antecedent interference with the employee's freedom of movement as an independent Fourth Amendment seizure. As our precedents indicate, not every governmental interference with an individual's freedom of movement raises such constitutional concerns that there is a seizure of the person....

III

In most criminal cases, we strike this balance in favor of the procedures described by the Warrant Clause of the Fourth Amendment. Except in certain well-defined circumstances, a search or seizure in such a case is not reasonable unless it is accomplished pursuant to a judicial warrant issued upon probable cause. We have recognized exceptions to this rule, however, "when 'special needs, beyond the normal need for law enforcement, make the warrant and probable-cause requirement impracticable.'" When faced with such special needs, we have not hesitated to balance the governmental and privacy interests to assess the practicality of the warrant and probable-cause requirements in the particular context.

The Government's interest in regulating the conduct of railroad employees to ensure safety, like its supervision of probationers or regulated industries, or its operation of a government office, school, or prison, "likewise presents 'special needs' beyond normal law enforcement that may justify departures from the usual warrant and probable-cause requirements."

■ ■ ■

The FRA has prescribed toxicological tests, not to assist in the prosecution of employees, but rather "to prevent accidents and casualties in railroad operations that result from impairment of employees by alcohol or drugs." This governmental interest in ensuring the safety of the traveling public and of the employees themselves plainly justifies prohibiting covered employees from using alcohol or drugs on duty, or while subject to being called for duty. This interest also "require[s] and justif[ies] the exercise of supervision to assure that the restrictions are in fact observed." The question that remains, then, is whether the Government's need to monitor compliance with these restrictions justifies the privacy intrusions at issue absent a warrant or individualized suspicion.

■ ■ ■

An essential purpose of a warrant requirement is to protect privacy interests by assuring citizens subject to a search or seizure that such intrusions are not the random or arbitrary acts of government agents. A warrant assures the citizen that the intrusion is authorized by law, and that it is narrowly limited in its objectives and scope.

■ ■ ■

We have recognized, moreover, that the government's interest in dispensing with the warrant requirement is at its strongest when, as here, "the burden of obtaining a warrant is likely to frustrate the governmental purpose behind the search." As the FRA recognized, alcohol and other drugs are eliminated from the bloodstream at a constant rate, and blood and breath samples taken to measure whether these substances were in the bloodstream when a triggering event occurred must be obtained as soon as possible. Although the metabolites of some drugs remain in the urine for longer periods of time and may enable the FRA to estimate whether the employee was impaired by those drugs at the time of a covered accident, incident, or rule violation, the delay necessary to procure a warrant nevertheless may result in the destruction of valuable evidence.

The Government's need to rely on private railroads to set the testing process in motion also indicates that insistence on a warrant requirement would impede the achievement of the Government's objective. Railroad supervisors, like school officials, and hospital administrators, are not in the business of investigating violations of the criminal laws or enforcing administrative codes, and otherwise have little occasion to become familiar with the intricacies of this Court's Fourth Amendment jurisprudence. "Imposing unwieldy warrant procedures . . . upon supervisors, who would otherwise have no reason to be familiar with such procedures, is simply unreasonable."

In sum, imposing a warrant requirement in the present context would add little to the assurances of certainty and regularity already afforded by the regulations, while significantly hindering, and in many cases frustrating, the objectives of the Government's testing program. We do not believe that a warrant is essential to render the intrusions here at issue reasonable under the Fourth Amendment.

Our cases indicate that even a search that may be performed without a warrant must be based, as a general matter, on probable cause to believe that the person to be searched has violated the law. When the balance of interests precludes insistence on a showing of probable cause, we have usually required "some quantum of individualized suspicion" before concluding that a search is reasonable. We made it clear, however, that a showing of individualized suspicion is not a constitutional floor, below which a search must be presumed unreasonable. In limited circumstances, where the privacy interests implicated by the search are minimal, and where an important governmental interest furthered by the intrusion would be placed in jeopardy by a requirement of individualized suspicion, a search may be reasonable despite the absence of such suspicion. We believe this is true of the intrusions in question here.

By and large, intrusions on privacy under the FRA regulations are limited. To the extent transportation and like restrictions are necessary to procure the requisite blood, breath, and urine samples for testing, this interference alone is minimal given the employment context in which it takes place. Ordinarily, an employee consents to significant restrictions in his freedom of movement where necessary for his employment, and few are free to come and go as they please during working hours. Any additional interference with a railroad employee's freedom of movement that occurs in the time it takes to procure a blood, breath, or urine sample for testing cannot, by itself, be said to infringe significant privacy interests.

Our decision in *Schmerber v. California* indicates that the same is true of the blood tests required by the FRA regulations. In that case, we held that a State could direct that a blood sample be withdrawn from a motorist suspected of driving while intoxicated, despite his refusal to consent to the intrusion. We noted that the test was performed in a reasonable manner, as the motorist's "blood was taken by a physician in a hospital environment according to accepted medical practices." We said also that the intrusion occasioned by a blood test is not significant, since such "tests are a commonplace in these days of periodic physical examinations and experience with them teaches that the quantity of blood extracted is minimal, and that for most people the procedure involves virtually no risk, trauma, or pain."

■ ■ ■

The breath tests authorized by Subpart D of the regulations are even less intrusive than the blood tests prescribed by Subpart C. Unlike blood tests, breath tests do not require piercing the skin and may be conducted safely outside a hospital environment and with a minimum of inconvenience or embarrassment. Further, breath tests reveal the level of alcohol in the employee's bloodstream and nothing more. Like the blood-testing procedures mandated by Subpart C, which can be used only to ascertain the presence of alcohol or controlled substances in the bloodstream, breath tests reveal no other facts in which the employee has a substantial privacy interest.

■ ■ ■

A more difficult question is presented by urine tests. Like breath tests, urine tests are not invasive of the body and, under the regulations, may not be used as an occasion for inquiring into private facts unrelated to alcohol or drug use. We recognize, however, that the procedures for collecting the necessary samples, which require employees to perform an excretory function traditionally shielded by great privacy, raise concerns not implicated by blood or breath tests. While we would not characterize these additional privacy concerns as minimal in most contexts, we note that the regulations endeavor to reduce the intrusiveness of the collection process. The regulations do not require that samples be furnished under the direct observation of a monitor, despite the desirability of such a procedure to ensure the integrity of the sample.

■ ■ ■

More importantly, the expectations of privacy of covered employees are diminished by reason of their participation in an industry that is regulated pervasively to ensure safety, a goal dependent, in substantial part, on the health and fitness of covered employees.

■ ■ ■

We do not suggest, of course, that the interest in bodily security enjoyed by those employed in a regulated industry must always be considered minimal. Here, however, the covered employees have long been a principal focus of regulatory concern.

■ ■ ■

By contrast, the Government interest in testing without a showing of individualized suspicion is compelling. Employees subject to the tests discharge duties fraught with such risks of injury to others that even a momentary lapse of attention can have disastrous consequences. Much like persons who have routine access to dangerous nuclear power facilities . . . employees who are subject to testing under the FRA regulations can cause great human loss before any signs of impairment become noticeable to supervisors or others. An impaired employee, the FRA found, will seldom display any outward "signs detectable by the lay person or, in many cases, even the physician."

■ ■ ■

While no procedure can identify all impaired employees with ease and perfect accuracy, the FRA regulations supply an effective means of deterring employees engaged in safety-sensitive tasks from using controlled substances or alcohol in the first place. The railroad industry's experience with Rule G persuasively shows, and common sense confirms, that the customary dismissal sanction that threatens employees who use drugs or alcohol while on duty cannot serve as an effective deterrent unless violators know that they are likely to be discovered. By ensuring that employees in safety-sensitive positions know they will be tested upon the occurrence of a triggering event, the timing of which no employee can predict with certainty, the regulations significantly increase the deterrent effect of the administrative penalties associated with the prohibited conduct, concomitantly increasing the likelihood that employees will forgo using drugs or alcohol while subject to being called for duty.

The testing procedures contemplated by Subpart C also help railroads obtain invaluable information about the causes of major accidents, and to take appropriate measures to safeguard the general public.

■ ■ ■

A requirement of particularized suspicion of drug or alcohol use would seriously impede an employer's ability to obtain this information, despite its obvious importance. Experience confirms the FRA's judgment that the scene of a serious rail accident is chaotic. Investigators who arrive at the scene shortly after a major accident has occurred may find it difficult to determine which members of a train crew contributed to its occurrence. Obtaining evidence that might give rise to the suspicion that a particular employee is impaired, a difficult endeavor in the best of circumstances, is most impracticable in the aftermath of a serious accident. While events following the rule violations that activate the testing authority of Subpart D may be less chaotic, objective indicia of impairment are absent in these instances as well. Indeed, any attempt to gather evidence relating to the possible impairment of particular employees likely would result in the loss or deterioration of the evidence furnished by the tests. It would be unrealistic, and inimical to the Government's goal of ensuring safety in rail transportation, to require a showing of individualized suspicion in these circumstances.

Without quarreling with the importance of these governmental interests, the Court of Appeals concluded that the postaccident testing regulations were unreasonable because "[b]lood and urine tests intended to establish drug use other than alcohol . . . cannot measure current drug intoxication or degree of impairment." The court based its conclusion on its reading of certain academic journals that indicate that the testing of urine can disclose only drug metabolites, which "may remain in the body for days or weeks after the ingestion of the drug." We find this analysis flawed for several reasons.

As we emphasized in *New Jersey v. T.L.O.* (1985), "it is universally recognized that evidence, to be relevant to an inquiry, need not conclusively prove the ultimate fact in issue, but only have 'any tendency to make the existence of any fact that is of consequence to the determination [of the point in issue] more probable or less probable than it would be without the evidence.' " . . .

More importantly, the Court of Appeals overlooked the FRA's policy of placing principal reliance on the results of blood tests, which unquestionably can identify very recent drug use, while relying on urine tests as a secondary source of information designed to guard against the possibility that certain drugs will be eliminated from the bloodstream before a blood sample can be obtained. The court also failed to recognize that the FRA regulations are designed not only to discern impairment but also to deter it. Because the record indicates that blood and urine tests, taken together, are highly effective means of ascertaining on-the-job impairment and of deterring the use of drugs by railroad employees, we believe the Court of Appeals erred in concluding that the postaccident testing regulations are not reasonably related to the Government objectives that support them.

We conclude that the compelling Government interests served by the FRA's regulations would be significantly hindered if railroads were required to point to specific facts giving rise to a reasonable suspicion of impairment before testing a given employee. In view of our conclusion that, on the present record, the toxicological testing contemplated by the regulations is not an undue infringement on the justifiable expectations of privacy of covered employees, the Government's compelling interests outweigh privacy concerns.

IV

The possession of unlawful drugs is a criminal offense that the Government may punish, but it is a separate and far more dangerous wrong to perform certain sensitive tasks while under the influence of those substances. Performing those tasks while impaired by alcohol is, of course, equally dangerous, though consumption of alcohol is legal in most other contexts. The Government may take all necessary and reasonable regulatory steps to prevent or deter that hazardous conduct, and since the gravamen of the evil is performing certain functions while concealing the substance in the body, it may be necessary, as in the case before us, to examine the body or its fluids to accomplish the regulatory purpose. The necessity to perform that regulatory function with respect to railroad employees engaged in safety-sensitive tasks, and the reasonableness of the system for doing so, have been established in this case.

Alcohol and drug tests conducted in reliance on the authority of Subpart D cannot be viewed as private action outside the reach of the Fourth Amendment. Because the testing procedures mandated or authorized by Subparts C and D effect searches of the person, they must meet the Fourth Amendment's reasonableness requirement. In light of the limited discretion exercised by the railroad employers under the regulations, the surpassing safety interests served by toxicological tests in this context, and the diminished expectation of privacy that attaches to information pertaining to the fitness of covered employees, we believe that it is reasonable to conduct such tests in the absence of a warrant or reasonable suspicion that any particular employee may be impaired. We hold that the alcohol and drug tests contemplated by Subparts C and D of the FRA's regulations are reasonable within the meaning of the Fourth Amendment. The judgment of the Court of Appeals is accordingly reversed.

It is so ordered.

Justice STEVENS, concurring in part and concurring in the judgment.

In my opinion the public interest in determining the causes of serious railroad accidents adequately supports the validity of the challenged regulations. I am not persuaded, however, that the interest in deterring the use of alcohol or drugs is either necessary or sufficient to justify the searches authorized by these regulations. . . .

Justice MARSHALL, with whom Justice BRENNAN joins, dissenting.

The issue in this case is not whether declaring a war on illegal drugs is good public policy. The importance of ridding our society of such drugs is, by now, apparent to all. Rather, the issue here is whether the Government's deployment in that war of a particularly Draconian weapon—the compulsory collection and chemical testing of railroad workers' blood and urine—comports with the Fourth Amendment. Precisely because the need for action against the drug scourge is manifest, the need for vigilance against unconstitutional excess is great. History teaches that grave threats to liberty often come in times of urgency, when constitutional rights seem too extravagant to endure. The World War II relocation-camp cases, *Hirabayashi v. United States* (1943); *Korematsu v. United States* (1944), and the Red scare and McCarthy-era internal subversion cases, *Schenck v. United States* (1919); *Dennis v. United States* (1951), are only the most extreme reminders that when we allow fundamental freedoms to be sacrificed in the name of real or perceived exigency, we invariably come to regret it.

In permitting the Government to force entire railroad crews to submit to invasive blood and urine tests, even when it lacks any evidence of drug or alcohol use or other wrongdoing, the majority today joins those shortsighted courts which have allowed basic constitutional rights to fall prey to momentary emergencies. The majority holds that the need of the Federal Railroad Administration (FRA) to deter and diagnose train accidents outweighs any "minimal" intrusions on personal dignity and privacy posed by mass toxicological testing of persons who have given no indication whatsoever of impairment. In reaching this result, the majority ignores the text and doctrinal history of the Fourth Amendment, which require that highly intrusive searches of this type be based on probable cause, not on the evanescent cost-benefit calculations of agencies or judges. But the majority errs even under its own utilitarian standards, trivializing the raw intrusiveness of, and overlooking serious conceptual and operational flaws in, the FRA's testing program. These flaws cast grave doubts on whether that program, though born of good intentions, will do more than ineffectually symbolize the Government's opposition to drug use. . . .

The Court today takes its longest step yet toward reading the probable-cause requirement out of the Fourth Amendment. For the fourth time in as many years, a majority holds that a "'special nee[d], beyond the normal need for law enforcement,'" makes the "'requirement'" of probable cause "'impracticable.'" With the recognition of "[t]he Government's interest in regulating the conduct of railroad employees to ensure safety" as such a need, the Court has now permitted "special needs" to displace constitutional text in each of the four categories of searches enumerated in the Fourth Amendment: searches of "persons," "houses," "papers," and "effects."

The process by which a constitutional "requirement" can be dispensed with as "impracticable" is an elusive one to me. The Fourth Amendment provides that "[t]he right of the people to be secure in their persons, houses, papers, and effects, against unreasonable searches and seizures, shall not be violated; and no Warrants shall issue, but upon probable cause, supported by Oath or affirmation, and particularly describing the place to be searched, and the persons or things to be seized." The majority's recitation of the Amendment, remarkably, leaves off after the word "violated," but the remainder of the Amendment—the Warrant Clause—is not so easily excised. As this Court has long recognized, the Framers intended the provisions of that Clause—a warrant and probable cause—to "provide the yardstick against which official searches and seizures are to be measured." Without the content which those provisions give to the Fourth Amendment's overarching command that searches and seizures be "reasonable," the Amendment lies virtually devoid of meaning, subject to whatever content shifting judicial majorities, concerned about the problems of the day, choose to give to that supple term. . . .

Until recently, an unbroken line of cases had recognized probable cause as an indispensable prerequisite for a full-scale search, regardless of whether such a search was conducted pursuant to a warrant or under one of the recognized exceptions to the warrant requirement. . . .

In the four years since this Court, in *T.L.O.*, first began recognizing "special needs" exceptions to the Fourth Amendment, the clarity of Fourth Amendment doctrine has been badly distorted, as the Court has eclipsed the probable-cause requirement in a patchwork quilt of settings: public school principals' searches of students' belongings, *T.L.O.*; public employers' searches of employees' desks, *O'Connor* (1987); and probation officers' searches of probationers' homes, *Griffin* (1987). Tellingly, each time the Court has found that "special needs" counseled ignoring the literal requirements of the Fourth Amendment for such full-scale searches in favor of a formless and unguided "reasonableness" balancing inquiry, it has concluded that the search in question satisfied that test. I have joined dissenting opinions in each of these cases, protesting the "jettison[ing of] . . . the only standard that finds support in the text of the Fourth Amendment" and predicting that the majority's "Rohrschach-like 'balancing test'" portended "a dangerous weakening of the purpose of the Fourth Amendment to protect the privacy and security of our citizens."

The majority's decision today bears out that prophecy. After determining that the Fourth Amendment applies to the FRA's testing regime, the majority embarks on an extended inquiry into whether that regime is "reasonable," an inquiry in which it balances " 'all the circumstances surrounding the search or seizure and the nature of the search or seizure itself.' " The result is "special needs" balancing analysis' deepest incursion yet into the core protections of the Fourth Amendment. Until today, it was conceivable that, when a government search was aimed at a person and not simply the person's possessions, balancing analysis had no place. No longer: with nary a word of explanation or acknowledgment of the novelty of its approach, the majority extends the "special needs" framework to a regulation involving compulsory blood withdrawal and urinary excretion, and chemical testing of the bodily fluids collected through these procedures. And until today, it was conceivable that a prerequisite for surviving "special needs" analysis was the existence of individualized suspicion. No longer: in contrast to the searches in *T.L.O., O'Connor,* and *Griffin,* which were supported by individualized evidence suggesting the culpability of the persons whose property was searched, the regulatory regime upheld today requires the postaccident collection and testing of the blood and urine of *all* covered employees—even if every member of this group gives every indication of sobriety and attentiveness.

In widening the "special needs" exception to probable cause to authorize searches of the human body unsupported by *any* evidence of wrongdoing, the majority today completes the process begun in *T.L.O.* of eliminating altogether the probable-cause requirement for civil searches—those undertaken for reasons "beyond the normal need for law enforcement." In its place, the majority substitutes a manipulable balancing inquiry under which, upon the mere assertion of a "special need," even the deepest dignitary and privacy interests become vulnerable to governmental incursion. By its terms, however, the Fourth Amendment—unlike the Fifth and Sixth—does not confine its protections to either criminal or civil actions. Instead, it protects generally "[t]he right of the people to be secure."

■ ■ ■

The proper way to evaluate the FRA's testing regime is to use the same analytic framework which we have traditionally used to appraise Fourth Amendment claims involving full-scale searches, at least until the recent "special needs" cases. Under that framework, we inquire, serially, whether a search has taken place, whether the search was based on a valid warrant or undertaken pursuant to a recognized exception to the warrant requirement, whether the search was based on probable cause or validly based on lesser suspicion because it was minimally intrusive, and, finally, whether the search was conducted in a reasonable manner.

The majority's threshold determination that "covered" railroad employees have been searched under the FRA's testing program is certainly correct. Who among us is not prepared to consider reasonable a person's expectation of privacy with respect to the extraction of his blood, the collection of his urine, or the chemical testing of these fluids? The majority's ensuing conclusion that the warrant requirement may be dispensed with, however, conveniently overlooks the fact that there are three distinct searches at issue. Although the importance of collecting blood and urine samples before drug or alcohol metabolites disappear justifies waiving the warrant requirement for those two searches under the narrow "exigent circumstances" exception, see *Schmerber v. California* ("[T]he delay necessary to obtain a warrant...threaten[s] 'the destruction of evidence' "), no such exigency prevents railroad officials from securing a warrant before chemically testing the samples they obtain. Blood and urine do not spoil if properly collected and preserved, and there is no reason to doubt the ability of railroad officials to grasp the relatively simple procedure of obtaining a warrant authorizing, where appropriate, chemical analysis of the extracted fluids. It is therefore wholly unjustified to dispense with the warrant requirement for this final search.

It is the probable-cause requirement, however, that the FRA's testing regime most egregiously violates, a fact which explains the majority's ready acceptance and expansion of the countertextual "special needs" exception. By any measure, the FRA's highly intrusive collection and testing procedures qualify as full-scale personal searches. Under our precedents, a showing of probable cause is therefore clearly required. But even if these searches were viewed as entailing only minimal intrusions on the order, say, of a police stop-and-frisk, the FRA's program would still fail to pass constitutional muster, for we have, without exception, demanded that even minimally intrusive searches of the person be founded on individualized suspicion. The federal parties concede it does not satisfy this standard. Only if one construes the FRA's collection and testing procedures as akin to the routinized and fleeting regulatory interactions which we have permitted in the absence of individualized suspicion. . . .

■ ■ ■

In recognition of the intrusiveness of this procedure, we specifically required in *Schmerber* that police have evidence of a drunken-driving suspect's impairment before forcing him to endure a blood test:

> "The interests in human dignity and privacy which the Fourth Amendment protects forbid any such intrusions on the mere chance that desired evidence might be obtained. In the absence of a clear indication that in fact such evidence will be found, these fundamental human interests require law officers to suffer the risk that such evidence may disappear. . . ."

■ ■ ■

Compelling a person to produce a urine sample on demand also intrudes deeply on privacy and bodily integrity. Urination is among the most private of activities. It is generally forbidden in public, eschewed as a matter of conversation, and performed in places designed to preserve this tradition of personal seclusion. The FRA, however, gives scant regard to personal privacy, for its Field Manual instructs supervisors monitoring urination that railroad workers must provide urine samples *"under direct observation* by the physician/ technician."

■ ■ ■

The majority's characterization of the privacy interests implicated by urine collection as "minimal" is nothing short of startling. This characterization is, furthermore, belied by the majority's own prior explanation of why compulsory urination constitutes a search for the purposes of the Fourth Amendment:

> "'There are few activities in our society more personal or private than the passing of urine. Most people describe it by euphemisms if they talk about

it at all. It is a function traditionally performed without public observation; indeed, its performance in public is generally prohibited by law as well as social custom.' "

The fact that the majority can invoke this powerful passage in the context of deciding that a search has occurred, and then ignore it in deciding that the privacy interests this search implicates are "minimal," underscores the shameless manipulability of its balancing approach.

Finally, the chemical analysis the FRA performs upon the blood and urine samples implicates strong privacy interests apart from those intruded upon by the collection of bodily fluids. Technological advances have made it possible to uncover, through analysis of chemical compounds in these fluids, not only drug or alcohol use, but also medical disorders such as epilepsy, diabetes, and clinical depression....

By any reading of our precedents, the intrusiveness of these three searches demands that they—like other full-scale searches—be justified by probable cause. It is no answer to suggest, as does the majority, that railroad workers have relinquished the protection afforded them by this Fourth Amendment requirement, either by "participat[ing] in an industry that is regulated pervasively to ensure safety" or by undergoing periodic fitness tests pursuant to state law or to collective-bargaining agreements.

Our decisions in the regulatory search area refute the suggestion that the heavy regulation of the railroad industry eclipses workers' rights under the Fourth Amendment to insist upon a showing of probable cause when their bodily fluids are being extracted. This line of cases has exclusively involved searches of employer *property*, with respect to which "[c]ertain industries have such a history of government oversight that no reasonable expectation of privacy could exist for a *proprietor* over the *stock* of such an enterprise."

■ ■ ■

Even accepting the majority's view that the FRA's collection and testing program is appropriately analyzed under a multifactor balancing test, and not under the literal terms of the Fourth Amendment, I would still find the program invalid. The benefits of suspicionless blood and urine testing are far outstripped by the costs imposed on personal liberty by such sweeping searches. Only by erroneously deriding as "minimal" the privacy and dignity interests at stake, and by uncritically inflating the likely efficacy of the FRA's testing program, does the majority strike a different balance.

For the reasons stated above, I find nothing minimal about the intrusion on individual liberty that occurs whenever the Government forcibly draws and analyzes a person's blood and urine. Several aspects of the FRA's testing program exacerbate the intrusiveness of these procedures. Most strikingly, the agency's regulations not only do not forbid, but, in fact, appear to invite criminal prosecutors to obtain the blood and urine samples drawn by the FRA and use them as the basis of criminal investigations and trials.

■ ■ ■

The majority also overlooks needlessly intrusive aspects of the testing process itself. Although the FRA requires the collection and testing of both blood and urine, the agency concedes that mandatory urine tests—unlike blood tests—do not measure current impairment and therefore cannot differentiate on-duty impairment from prior drug or alcohol use which has ceased to affect the user's behavior. . . .

The majority's trivialization of the intrusions on worker privacy posed by the FRA's testing program is matched at the other extreme by its blind acceptance of the Government's assertion that testing will "dete[r] employees engaged in safety-sensitive tasks from using controlled substances or alcohol," and "help railroads obtain invaluable information about the causes of major accidents." . . . As Justice Stevens observes in his concurring opinion:

> "Most people—and I would think most railroad employees as well—do not go to work with the expectation that they may be involved in a major accident, particularly one causing such catastrophic results as loss of life or the release of hazardous material requiring an evacuation. Moreover, even if they are conscious of the possibilities that such an accident might occur and that alcohol or drug use might be a contributing factor, if the risk of serious personal injury does not deter their use of these substances, it seems highly unlikely that the additional threat of loss of employment would have any effect on their behavior."

Under the majority's deterrence rationale, people who skip school or work to spend a sunny day at the zoo will not taunt the lions because their truancy or absenteeism might be discovered in the event they are mauled. It is, of course, the fear of the accident, not the fear of a postaccident revelation, that deters. The majority's credulous acceptance of the FRA's deterrence rationale is made all the more suspect by the agency's failure to introduce, in an otherwise ample administrative record, *any* studies explaining or supporting its theory of accident deterrence.

The poverty of the majority's deterrence rationale leaves the Government's interest in diagnosing the causes of major accidents as the sole remaining justification for the FRA's testing program. I do not denigrate this interest, but it seems a slender thread from which to hang such an intrusive program, particularly given that the knowledge that one or more workers were impaired at the time of an accident falls far short of proving that substance abuse caused or exacerbated that accident. Some corroborative evidence is needed: witness or co-worker accounts of a worker's misfeasance, or at least indications that the cause of the accident was within a worker's area of responsibility. Such particularized facts are, of course, the very essence of the individualized suspicion requirement which the respondent railroad workers urge, and which the Court of Appeals found to "pos[e] no insuperable burden on the government." Furthermore, reliance on the importance of diagnosing the causes of an accident as a critical basis for upholding the FRA's testing plan is especially hard to square with our frequent admonition that the interest in ascertaining the causes of a criminal episode does not justify departure from the Fourth Amendment's requirements.

■ ■ ■

In his first dissenting opinion as a Member of this Court, Oliver Wendell Holmes observed:

> "Great cases, like hard cases, make bad law. For great cases are called great, not by reason of their real importance in shaping the law of the future, but because of some accident of immediate overwhelming interest which appeals to the feelings and distorts the judgment. These immediate interests exercise a kind of hydraulic pressure which makes what previously was clear seem doubtful, and before which even well settled principles of law will bend." *Northern Securities Co. v. United States* (1904).

A majority of this Court, swept away by society's obsession with stopping the scourge of illegal drugs, today succumbs to the popular pressures described by Justice Holmes. In upholding the FRA's plan for blood and urine testing, the majority bends time-honored and textually based principles of the Fourth Amendment—principles the Framers of the Bill of Rights designed to ensure that the Government has a strong and individualized justification when it seeks to invade an individual's privacy. I believe the Framers would be appalled by the vision of mass governmental intrusions upon the integrity of the human body that the majority allows to become reality. The immediate victims of the majority's constitutional timorousness will be those railroad workers whose bodily fluids the Government may now forcibly collect and analyze. But ultimately, today's decision will reduce the privacy all citizens may enjoy, for, as Justice Holmes understood, principles of law, once bent, do not snap back easily. I dissent.

Chandler v. Miller

520 U.S. 305 (1997)

GINSBURG, J., delivered the opinion of the Court, in which STEVENS, O'CONNOR, SCALIA, KENNEDY, SOUTER, THOMAS, and BREYER, JJ., joined. REHNQUIST, C.J., filed a dissenting opinion.

Georgia requires candidates for designated state offices to certify that they have taken a drug test and that the test result was negative. We confront in this case the question whether that requirement ranks among the limited circumstances in which suspicionless searches are warranted....

Petitioners were Libertarian Party nominees in 1994 for state offices subject to the requirement.... The Party nominated Walker L. Chandler for the office of Lieutenant Governor, Sharon T. Harris for the office of Commissioner of Agriculture, and James D. Walker for the office of member of the General Assembly. In May 1994, about one month before the deadline for submission of the certificates required by [statute], petitioners Chandler, Harris, and Walker filed this action in the United States District Court for the Northern District of Georgia. They asserted, *inter alia,* that the drug tests . . . violated their rights under the First, Fourth, and Fourteenth Amendments to the United States Constitution. Naming as defendants Governor Zell D. Miller and two other state officials involved in the administration . . . petitioners requested declaratory and injunctive relief barring enforcement of the statute.

In June 1994, the District Court denied petitioners' motion for a preliminary injunction. Stressing the importance of the state offices sought and the relative unintrusiveness of the testing procedure, the court found it unlikely that petitioners would prevail on the merits of their claims. . . .

A divided Eleventh Circuit panel affirmed. It is settled law, the court accepted, that the drug tests required by the statute rank as searches. But, as was true of the drug-testing programs at issue in *Skinner* [*v. Railway Labor Executives' Assn.* (1989)] and [*National Treasury Employees Union v.*] *Von Raab* [(1989)], the court reasoned, [the statute] serves "special needs," interests other than the ordinary needs of law enforcement. The court therefore endeavored to " 'balance the individual's privacy expectations against the Government's interests to determine whether it [was] impractical to require a warrant or some level of individualized suspicion in the particular context.' "

Examining the state interests involved, the court acknowledged the absence of any record of drug abuse by elected officials in Georgia. Nonetheless, the court observed, "[t]he people of Georgia place in the trust of their elected officials . . . their liberty, their safety, their economic well-being, [and] ultimate responsibility for law enforcement." Consequently, "those vested with the highest executive authority to make public policy in general and frequently to supervise Georgia's drug interdiction efforts in particular must be persons appreciative of the perils of drug use." The court further noted that "[t]he nature of high public office in itself demands the highest levels of honesty, clear-sightedness, and clear-thinking." Reciting responsibilities of the offices petitioners sought, the Court of Appeals perceived those "positions [as] particularly susceptible to the 'risks of bribery and blackmail against which the Government is entitled to guard.' "

Turning to petitioners' privacy interests, the Eleventh Circuit emphasized that the tests could be conducted in the office of the candidate's private physician, making the "intrusion here . . . even less than that approved in *Von Raab.*" The court also noted the statute's reference to federally approved drug-testing guidelines. The drug test itself would reveal only the presence or absence of indicia of the use of particular drugs, and not any other information about the health of the candidate. Furthermore, the candidate would control release of the test results: Should the candidate test positive, he or she could forfeit the opportunity to run for office, and in that event, nothing would be divulged to law enforcement officials. Another consideration, the court said, is the reality that "candidates for high office must expect the voters to demand some disclosures about their physical, emotional, and mental fitness for the position." Concluding that the State's interests outweighed the privacy intrusion caused by the required certification, the court held the statute, as applied to petitioners, not inconsistent with the Fourth and Fourteenth Amendments.

■ ■ ■

We granted the petition for certiorari, and now reverse.

We begin our discussion of this case with an uncontested point: Georgia's drug-testing requirement, imposed by law and enforced by state officials, effects a search within the meaning of the Fourth and Fourteenth Amendments.

■ ■ ■

To be reasonable under the Fourth Amendment, a search ordinarily must be based on individualized suspicion of wrongdoing. But particularized exceptions to the main rule are sometimes warranted based on "special needs, beyond the normal need for law enforcement." When such "special needs"—concerns other than crime detection—are alleged in justification of a Fourth Amendment intrusion, courts must undertake a context-specific inquiry, examining closely the competing private and public interests advanced by the parties. As *Skinner* stated: "In limited circumstances, where the privacy interests implicated by the search are minimal, and where an important governmental interest furthered by the intrusion would be placed in jeopardy by a requirement of individualized suspicion, a search may be reasonable despite the absence of such suspicion."

In evaluating Georgia's ballot-access, drug-testing statute—a measure plainly not tied to individualized suspicion—the Eleventh Circuit sought to " 'balance the individual's privacy expectations against the [State's] interests,' " in line with our precedents most immediately in point: *Skinner, Von Raab,* and *Vernonia* [*School Dist. 47J v. Acton* (1995)]. We review those decisions before inspecting Georgia's law.

■ ■ ■

Skinner concerned Federal Railroad Administration (FRA) regulations that required blood and urine tests of rail employees involved in train accidents; the regulations also authorized railroads to administer breath and urine tests to employees who violated certain safety rules. The FRA adopted the drug-testing program in response to evidence of drug and alcohol abuse by some railroad employees, the obvious safety hazards posed by such abuse, and the documented link between drug- and alcohol-impaired employees and the incidence of train accidents. Recognizing that the urinalysis tests, most conspicuously, raised evident privacy concerns, the Court noted two offsetting considerations: First, the regulations reduced the intrusiveness of the collection process, and, more important, railway employees, "by reason of their participation in an industry that is regulated pervasively to ensure safety," had diminished expectations of privacy....

In *Von Raab,* the Court sustained a United States Customs Service program that made drug tests a condition of promotion or transfer to positions directly involving drug interdiction or requiring the employee to carry a firearm. While the Service's regime was not prompted by a demonstrated drug abuse problem, it was developed for an agency with an "almost unique mission," as the "first line of defense" against the smuggling of illicit drugs into the United States. Work directly involving drug interdiction and posts that require the employee to carry a firearm pose grave safety threats to employees who hold those positions, and also expose them to large amounts of illegal narcotics and to persons engaged in crime; illicit drug users in such high-risk positions might be unsympathetic to the Service's mission, tempted by bribes, or even threatened with blackmail. The Court held that the Government had a "compelling" interest in assuring that employees placed in these positions would not include drug users. Individualized suspicion would not work in this setting, the Court determined, because it was "not feasible to subject [these] employees and their work product to the kind of day-to-day scrutiny that is the norm in more traditional office environments."

Finally, in *Vernonia,* the Court sustained a random drug-testing program for high school students engaged in interscholastic athletic competitions. The program's context was critical, for a local government bears large "responsibilities, under a public school system, as guardian and tutor of children entrusted to its care." An "immediate crisis," caused by "a sharp increase in drug use" in the school district sparked installation of the program. District Court findings established that student athletes were not only "among the drug users," they were "leaders of the drug culture." Our decision noted that " 'students within the school environment have a lesser expectation of privacy than members of the population generally.' " We emphasized the importance of deterring drug use by schoolchildren and the risk of injury a drug-using student athlete cast on himself and those engaged with him on the playing field.

■ ■ ■

Respondents urge that the precedents just examined are not the sole guides for assessing the constitutional validity of the Georgia statute. The "special needs" analysis, they contend, must be viewed through a different lens because §21-2-140 implicates Georgia's sovereign power, reserved to it under the Tenth Amendment, to establish qualifications for those who seek state office.

■ ■ ■

Turning to those guides, we note, first, that the testing method the Georgia statute describes is relatively noninvasive; therefore, if the "special needs" showing had been made, the State could not be faulted for excessive intrusion.

■ ■ ■

Our precedents establish that the proffered special need for drug testing must be substantial—important enough to override the individual's acknowledged privacy interest, sufficiently vital to suppress the Fourth Amendment's normal requirement of individualized suspicion. Georgia has failed to show, in justification of § 21-2-140, a special need of that kind.

Respondents' defense of the statute rests primarily on the incompatibility of unlawful drug use with holding high state office. The statute is justified, respondents contend, because the use of illegal drugs draws into question an official's judgment and integrity; jeopardizes the discharge of public functions, including antidrug law enforcement efforts; and undermines public confidence and trust in elected officials. The statute, according to respondents, serves to deter unlawful drug users from becoming candidates and thus stops them from attaining high state office. Notably lacking in respondents' presentation is any indication of a concrete danger demanding departure from the Fourth Amendment's main rule.

Nothing in the record hints that the hazards respondents broadly describe are real and not simply hypothetical for Georgia's polity.

■ ■ ■

In contrast to the effective testing regimes upheld in *Skinner, Von Raab,* and *Vernonia,* Georgia's certification requirement is not well designed to identify candidates who violate antidrug laws. Nor is the scheme a credible means to deter illicit drug users from seeking election to state office.

■ ■ ■

Respondents and the United States as *amicus curiae* rely most heavily on our decision in *Von Raab,* which sustained a drug-testing program for Customs Service officers prior to promotion or transfer to certain high-risk positions, despite the absence of any documented drug abuse problem among Service employees.

■ ■ ■

Respondents overlook a telling difference between *Von Raab* and Georgia's candidate drug-testing program. In *Von Raab* it was "not feasible to subject employees [required to carry firearms or concerned with interdiction of controlled substances] and their work product to the kind of day-to-day scrutiny that is the norm in more traditional office environments." Candidates for public office, in contrast, are subject to relentless scrutiny—by their peers, the public, and the press. Their day-to-day conduct attracts attention notably beyond the norm in ordinary work environments.

What is left, after close review of Georgia's scheme, is the image the State seeks to project. By requiring candidates for public office to submit to drug testing, Georgia displays its commitment to the struggle against drug abuse. The suspicionless tests, according to respondents, signify that candidates, if elected, will be fit to serve their constituents free from the influence of illegal drugs. But Georgia asserts no evidence of a drug problem among the State's elected officials, those officials typically do not perform high-risk, safety-sensitive tasks, and the required certification immediately aids no interdiction effort. The need revealed, in short, is symbolic, not "special," as that term draws meaning from our case law.

■ ■ ■

In a pathmarking dissenting opinion, Justice Brandeis recognized the importance of teaching by example: "Our Government is the potent, the omnipresent teacher. For good or for ill, it teaches the whole people by its example." *Olmstead v. United States* (1928). Justice Brandeis explained in *Olmstead* why the Government set a bad example when it introduced in a criminal proceeding evidence obtained through an unlawful Government wiretap:

> "[I]t is . . . immaterial that the intrusion was in aid of law enforcement. Experience should teach us to be most on our guard to protect liberty when the Government's purposes are beneficent. Men born to freedom are naturally alert to repel invasion of their liberty by evil-minded rulers. The greatest dangers to liberty lurk in insidious encroachment by men of zeal, well-meaning but without understanding."

However well meant, the candidate drug test Georgia has devised diminishes personal privacy for a symbol's sake. The Fourth Amendment shields society against that state action.

■ ■ ■

We reiterate, too, that where the risk to public safety is substantial and real, blanket suspicionless searches calibrated to the risk may rank as "reasonable"—for example, searches now routine at airports and at entrances to courts and other official buildings. See *Von Raab*. But where, as in this case, public safety is not genuinely in jeopardy, the Fourth Amendment precludes the suspicionless search, no matter how conveniently arranged.

■ ■ ■

For the reasons stated, the judgment of the Court of Appeals for the Eleventh Circuit is

Reversed.

Chief Justice Rehnquist, dissenting.

I fear that the novelty of this Georgia law has led the Court to distort Fourth Amendment doctrine in order to strike it down. The Court notes, impliedly turning up its nose, that "Georgia was the first, and apparently remains the only, State to condition candidacy for state office on a drug test."

■ ■ ■

The test under the Fourth Amendment, as these cases have held, is whether the search required by the Georgia statute is "reasonable." Today's opinion speaks of a "closely guarded" class of permissible suspicionless searches which must be justified by a "special need." But this term, as used in *Skinner* and *Von Raab* and on which the Court now relies, was used in a quite different sense than it is used by the Court today. In *Skinner* and *Von Raab* it was used to describe a basis for a search apart from the regular needs of law enforcement. The "special needs" inquiry as delineated there has not required especially great "importan[ce]," unless one considers "the supervision of probationers" or the "operation of a government office."

■ ■ ■

Under normal Fourth Amendment analysis, the individual's expectation of privacy is an important factor in the equation. But here, the Court perversely relies on the fact that a candidate for office *gives up* so much privacy—"[c]andidates for public office . . . are subject to relentless scrutiny—by their peers, the public, and the press"—as a reason for *sustaining* a Fourth Amendment claim. The Court says, in effect, that the kind of drug test for candidates required by the Georgia law is unnecessary, because the scrutiny to which they are already subjected by reason of their candidacy will enable people to detect any drug use on their part. But this is a strange holding, indeed. One might just as easily say that the railroad employees in *Skinner*, or the Customs officials in *Von Raab*, would be subjected to the same sort of scrutiny from their fellow employees and their supervisors. But the clear teaching of those cases is that the government is not required to settle for that sort of a vague and uncanalized scrutiny; if in fact preventing persons who use illegal drugs from concealing that fact from the public is a legitimate government interest, these cases indicate that the government may require a drug test.

The privacy concerns ordinarily implicated by urinalysis drug testing are "negligible," *Vernonia*, when the procedures used in collecting and analyzing the urine samples are set up "to reduce the intrusiveness" of the process, *Skinner*. Under the Georgia law, the candidate may produce the test specimen at his own doctor's office, which must be one of the least intrusive types of urinalysis drug tests conceivable. But although the Court concedes this, it nonetheless manages to count this factor against the State, because with this kind of test the person tested will have advance notice of its being given, and will therefore be able to abstain from drug use during the necessary period of time. But one may be sure that if the test were random—and therefore apt to ensnare more users—the Court would then fault it for its intrusiveness.

■ ■ ■

Lest readers expect the holding of this case to be extended to any other case, the Court notes that the drug test here is not a part of a medical examination designed to provide certification of a candidate's general health. It is all but inconceivable that a case involving that sort of requirement could be decided differently than the present case; the same sort of urinalysis would be involved. The only possible basis for distinction is to say that the State has a far greater interest in the candidate's "general health" than it does with respect to his propensity to use illegal drugs. But this is the sort of policy judgment that surely must be left to legislatures, rather than being announced from on high by the Federal Judiciary.

Nothing in the Fourth Amendment or in any other part of the Constitution prevents a State from enacting a statute whose principal vice is that it may seem misguided or even silly to the Members of this Court. I would affirm the judgment of the Court of Appeals.

5. Probation

Samson v. California

547 U.S. 843 (2006)

THOMAS, J., delivered the opinion of the Court, in which ROBERTS, C.J., and SCALIA, KENNEDY, GINSBURG, and ALITO, JJ., joined. STEVENS, J., filed a dissenting opinion, in which SOUTER and BREYER, JJ., joined.

California law provides that every prisoner eligible for release on state parole "shall agree in writing to be subject to search or seizure by a parole officer or other peace officer at any time of the day or night, with or without a search warrant and with or without cause." We granted certiorari to decide whether a suspicionless search, conducted under the authority of this statute, violates the Constitution. We hold that it does not. . . .

In September 2002, petitioner Donald Curtis Samson was on state parole in California, following a conviction for being a felon in possession of a firearm. On September 6, 2002, Officer Alex Rohleder of the San Bruno Police Department observed petitioner walking down a street with a woman and a child. Based on a prior contact with petitioner, Officer Rohleder was aware that petitioner was on parole and believed that he was facing an at large warrant. Accordingly, Officer Rohleder stopped petitioner and asked him whether he had an outstanding parole warrant. Petitioner responded that there was no outstanding warrant and that he "was in good standing with his parole agent." Officer Rohleder confirmed, by radio dispatch, that petitioner was on parole and that he did not have an outstanding warrant. Nevertheless . . . based solely on petitioner's status as a parolee, Officer Rohleder searched petitioner. During the search, Officer Rohleder found a cigarette box in petitioner's left breast pocket. Inside the box he found a plastic baggie containing methamphetamine.

The State charged petitioner with possession of methamphetamine. . . . The trial court denied petitioner's motion to suppress the methamphetamine evidence. . . . A jury convicted petitioner of the possession charge and the trial court sentenced him to seven years' imprisonment.

The California Court of Appeal affirmed. . . .

We granted certiorari to answer a variation of the question this Court left open in *United States v. Knights* (2001)—whether a condition of release can so diminish or eliminate a released prisoner's reasonable expectation of privacy that a suspicionless search by a law enforcement officer would not offend the Fourth Amendment. Answering that question in the affirmative today, we affirm the judgment of the California Court of Appeal. . . .

"[U]nder our general Fourth Amendment approach" we "examin[e] the totality of the circumstances" to determine whether a search is reasonable within the meaning of the Fourth Amendment. [*United States v. Knights* (2001).] Whether a search is reasonable "is determined by assessing, on the one hand, the degree to which it intrudes upon an individual's privacy and, on the other, the degree to which it is needed for the promotion of legitimate governmental interests." *Id.* (internal quotation marks omitted).

We recently applied this approach in *United States v. Knights*. In that case, California law required Knights, as a probationer, to " '[s]ubmit his . . . person, property, place of residence, vehicle, personal effects, to search anytime, with or without a search warrant, warrant of arrest or reasonable cause by any probation officer or law enforcement officer.' " Several days after Knights had been placed on probation, police suspected that he had been involved in several incidents of arson and vandalism. Based upon that suspicion and pursuant to the search condition of his probation, a police officer conducted a warrantless search of Knights' apartment and found arson and drug paraphernalia.

We concluded that the search of Knights' apartment was reasonable. In evaluating the degree of intrusion into Knights' privacy, we found Knights' probationary status "salient," observing that "[p]robation is 'one point . . . on a continuum of possible punishments ranging from solitary confinement in a maximum-security facility to a few hours of mandatory community service.' "

■ ■ ■

We also concluded that probation searches, such as the search of Knights' apartment, are necessary to the promotion of legitimate governmental interests. Noting the State's dual interest in integrating probationers back into the community and combating recidivism, we credited the " 'assumption' " that, by virtue of his status, a probationer " 'is more likely than the ordinary citizen to violate the law.' " We further found that "probationers have even more of an incentive to conceal their criminal activities and quickly dispose of incriminating evidence than the ordinary criminal because probationers are aware that they may be subject to supervision and face revocation of probation, and possible incarceration, in proceedings in which the trial rights of a jury and proof beyond a reasonable doubt, among other things, do not apply." We explained that the State did not have to ignore the reality of recidivism or suppress its interests in "protecting potential victims of criminal enterprise" for fear of running afoul of the Fourth Amendment.

Balancing these interests, we held that "[w]hen an officer has reasonable suspicion that a probationer subject to a search condition is engaged in criminal activity, there is enough likelihood that criminal conduct is occurring that an intrusion on the probationer's significantly diminished privacy interests is reasonable." Because the search at issue in *Knights* was predicated on both the probation search condition and reasonable suspicion, we did not reach the question whether the search would have been reasonable under the Fourth Amendment had it been solely predicated upon the condition of probation. Our attention is directed to that question today, albeit in the context of a parolee search.

■ ■ ■

A California inmate may serve his parole period either in physical custody, or elect to complete his sentence out of physical custody and subject to certain conditions. Under the latter option, an inmate-turned-parolee remains in the legal custody of the California Department of Corrections through the remainder of his term and must comply with all of the terms and conditions of parole, including mandatory drug tests, restrictions on association with felons or gang members, and mandatory meetings with parole officers. . . . General conditions of parole also require a parolee to report to his assigned parole officer immediately upon release, inform the parole officer within 72 hours of any change in employment status, request permission to travel a distance of more than 50 miles from the parolee's home, and refrain from criminal conduct and possession of firearms, specified weapons, or knives unrelated to employment. Parolees may also be subject to special conditions, including psychiatric treatment programs, mandatory abstinence from alcohol, residence approval, and "[a]ny other condition deemed necessary by the Board [of Parole Hearings] or the Department [of Corrections and Rehabilitation] due to unusual circumstances." The extent and reach of these conditions clearly demonstrate that parolees like petitioner have severely diminished expectations of privacy by virtue of their status alone.

Additionally, as we found "salient" in *Knights* with respect to the probation search condition, the parole search condition under California law—requiring inmates who opt for parole to submit to suspicionless searches by a parole officer or other peace officer "at any time." . . . He signed an order submitting to the condition and thus was "unambiguously" aware of it. In *Knights,* we found that acceptance of a clear and unambiguous search condition "significantly diminished Knights' reasonable expectation of privacy." Examining the totality of the circumstances pertaining to petitioner's status as a parolee, "an established variation on imprisonment," including the plain terms of the parole search condition, we conclude that petitioner did not have an expectation of privacy that society would recognize as legitimate.

■ ■ ■

The State's interests, by contrast, are substantial. This Court has repeatedly acknowledged that a State has an "overwhelming interest" in supervising parolees because "parolees . . . are more likely to commit future criminal offenses." *Pennsylvania Bd. of Probation and Parole* (1998) (explaining that the interest in combating recidivism "is the very premise behind the system of close parole supervision"). Similarly, this Court has repeatedly acknowledged that a State's interests in reducing recidivism and thereby promoting reintegration and positive citizenship among probationers and parolees warrant privacy intrusions that would not otherwise be tolerated under the Fourth Amendment.

The empirical evidence presented in this case clearly demonstrates the significance of these interests to the State of California. As of November 30, 2005, California had over 130,000 released parolees. California's parolee population has a 68-to-70 percent recidivism rate. See California Attorney General, Crime in California 37 (Apr. 2001) (explaining that 68 percent of adult parolees are returned to prison, 55 percent for a parole violation, 13 percent for the commission of a new felony offense).

■ ■ ■

As we made clear in *Knights,* the Fourth Amendment does not render the States powerless to address these concerns *effectively.* Contrary to petitioner's contention, California's ability to conduct suspicionless searches of parolees serves its interest in reducing recidivism, in a manner that aids, rather than hinders, the reintegration of parolees into productive society. . . .

Petitioner observes that the majority of States and the Federal Government have been able to further similar interests in reducing recidivism and promoting re-integration, despite having systems that permit parolee searches based upon some level of suspicion. Thus, petitioner contends, California's system is constitutionally defective by comparison. Petitioner's reliance on the practices of jurisdictions other than California, however, is misplaced. That some States and the Federal Government require a level of individualized suspicion is of little relevance to our determination whether California's supervisory system is drawn to meet its needs and is reasonable, taking into account a parolee's substantially diminished expectation of privacy.

Nor is there merit to the argument that California's parole search law permits "a blanket grant of discretion untethered by any procedural safeguards," *post* (Stevens, J., dissenting). The concern that California's suspicionless search system gives officers unbridled discretion to conduct searches, thereby inflicting dignitary harms that arouse strong resentment in parolees and undermine their ability to reintegrate into productive society, is belied by California's prohibition on "arbitrary, capricious or harassing" searches. . . .

Thus, we conclude that the Fourth Amendment does not prohibit a police officer from conducting a suspicionless search of a parolee. Accordingly, we affirm the judgment of the California Court of Appeal.

It is so ordered.

Justice STEVENS, with whom Justice SOUTER and Justice BREYER join, dissenting.

Our prior cases have consistently assumed that the Fourth Amendment provides some degree of protection for probationers and parolees. The protection is not as robust as that afforded to ordinary citizens; we have held that probationers' lowered expectation of privacy may justify their warrantless search upon reasonable suspicion of wrongdoing, see *United States v. Knights.* We have also recognized that the supervisory responsibilities of probation officers, who are required to provide "'individualized counseling'" and to monitor their charges' progress, and who are in a unique position to judge "how close a supervision the probationer requires," may give rise to special needs justifying departures from Fourth Amendment strictures. [*Griffin v. Wisconsin* (1987)] ("Although a probation officer is not an impartial magistrate, neither is he the police officer who normally conducts searches against the ordinary citizen"). But neither *Knights* nor *Griffin* supports a regime of suspicionless searches, conducted pursuant to a blanket grant of discretion untethered by any procedural safeguards, by law enforcement personnel who have no special interest in the welfare of the parolee or probationer.

What the Court sanctions today is an unprecedented curtailment of liberty. Combining faulty syllogism with circular reasoning, the Court concludes that parolees have no more legitimate an expectation of privacy in their persons than do prisoners. However superficially appealing that parity in treatment may seem, it runs roughshod over our precedent. It also rests on an intuition that fares poorly under scrutiny. And once one acknowledges that parolees do have legitimate expectations of privacy beyond those of prisoners, our Fourth Amendment jurisprudence does not permit the conclusion, reached by the Court here for the first time, that a search supported by neither individualized suspicion nor "special needs" is nonetheless "reasonable."

■ ■ ■

Not surprisingly, the majority does not seek to justify the search of petitioner on "special needs" grounds. Although the Court has in the past relied on special needs to uphold warrantless searches of probationers, it has never gone so far as to hold that a probationer or parolee may be subjected to full search at the whim of any law enforcement officer he happens to encounter, whether or not the officer has reason to suspect him of wrongdoing. *Griffin,* after all, involved a search *by a probation officer* that was supported by *reasonable suspicion.* The special role of probation officers was critical to the analysis; "we deal with a situation," the Court explained, "in which there is an ongoing supervisory relationship—and one that is not, or at least not entirely, adversarial— between the object of the search and the decisionmaker." The State's interest or "special need," as articulated in *Griffin,* was an interest in supervising the wayward probationer's reintegration into society—not, or at least not principally, the general law enforcement goal of detecting crime.

■ ■ ■

It is no accident, then, that when we later upheld the search of a probationer *by a law enforcement officer* . . . we forwent any reliance on the special needs doctrine. Even if the supervisory relationship between a probation officer and her charge may properly be characterized as one giving rise to needs "divorced from the State's general interest in law enforcement," the relationship between an ordinary law enforcement officer and a probationer unknown to him may not. "None of our special needs precedents has sanctioned the routine inclusion of law enforcement, both in the design of the policy and in using arrests, either threatened or real, to implement the system designed for the special needs objectives."

Ignoring just how "closely guarded" is that "category of constitutionally permissible suspicionless searches," *Chandler v. Miller* (1997), the Court for the first time upholds an entirely suspicionless search unsupported by any special need. And it goes further: In special needs cases we have at least insisted upon programmatic safeguards designed to ensure evenhandedness in application; if individualized suspicion is to be jettisoned, it must be replaced with measures to protect against the state actor's unfettered discretion.

■ ■ ■

The Court is able to make this unprecedented move only by making another. Coupling the dubious holding of *Hudson v. Palmer* (1984), with the bald statement that "parolees have fewer expectations of privacy than probationers," the Court two-steps its way through a faulty syllogism and, thus, avoids the application of Fourth Amendment principles altogether. The logic, apparently, is this: Prisoners have no legitimate expectation of privacy; parolees are like prisoners; therefore, parolees have no legitimate expectation of privacy. The conclusion is remarkable not least because we have long embraced its opposite. It also rests on false premises. First, it is simply not true that a parolee's status, vis-à-vis either the State or the Constitution, is tantamount to that of a prisoner or even materially distinct from that of a probationer.

■ ■ ■

In any event, the notion that a parolee legitimately expects only so much privacy as a prisoner is utterly without foundation. *Hudson v. Palmer* does stand for the proposition that "[a] right of privacy in traditional Fourth Amendment terms" is denied individuals who are incarcerated. But this is because it "is necessary, as a practical matter, to accommodate a myriad of 'institutional needs and objectives' of prison facilities, . . . chief among which is internal security."

■ ■ ■

Nor is it enough, in deciding whether someone's expectation of privacy is "legitimate," to rely on the existence of the offending condition or the individual's notice thereof. The Court's reasoning in this respect is entirely circular. The mere fact that a particular State refuses to acknowledge a parolee's privacy interest cannot mean that a parolee in that State has no expectation of privacy that society is willing to recognize as legitimate—especially when the measure that invades privacy is both the *subject* of the Fourth Amendment challenge and a clear outlier. With only one or two arguable exceptions, neither the Federal Government nor any other State subjects parolees to searches of the kind to which petitioner was subjected. And the fact of notice hardly cures the circularity; the loss of a subjective expectation of privacy would play "no meaningful role" in analyzing the legitimacy of expectations, for example, "if the Government were suddenly to announce on nationwide television that all homes henceforth would be subject to warrantless entry."

Threaded through the Court's reasoning is the suggestion that deprivation of Fourth Amendment rights is part and parcel of any convict's punishment. If a person may be subject to random and suspicionless searches in prison, the Court seems to assume, then he cannot complain when he is subject to the same invasion outside of prison, so long as the State still *can* imprison him. Punishment, though, is not the basis on which *Hudson* was decided. (Indeed, it is settled that a prison inmate " 'retains those [constitutional] rights that are not inconsistent with his status as a prisoner or with the legitimate penological objectives of the corrections system.' " Nor, to my knowledge, have we ever sanctioned the use of any search as a punitive measure. Instead, the question in every case must be whether the balance of legitimate expectations of privacy, on the one hand, and the State's interests in conducting the relevant search, on the other, justifies dispensing with the warrant and probable-cause requirements that are otherwise dictated by the Fourth Amendment. That balance is not the same in prison as it is out. We held in *Knights*—without recourse to *Hudson*—that the balance favored allowing the State to conduct searches based on reasonable suspicion. Never before have we plunged below that floor absent a demonstration of "special needs."

Had the State imposed as a condition of parole a requirement that petitioner submit to random searches by his parole officer, who is "supposed to have in mind the welfare of the [parolee]" and guide the parolee's transition back into society, condition might have been justified either under the special needs doctrine or because at least part of the requisite "reasonable suspicion" is supplied in this context by the individual-specific knowledge gained through the supervisory relationship. . . . Likewise, this might have been a different case had a court or parole board imposed the condition at issue based on specific knowledge of the individual's criminal history and projected likelihood of reoffending, or if the State had had in place programmatic safeguards to ensure evenhandedness. Under either of those scenarios, the State would at least have gone some way toward averting the greatest mischief wrought by officials' unfettered discretion. But the search condition here is imposed on *all* parolees—whatever the nature of their crimes, whatever their likelihood of recidivism, and whatever their supervisory needs—without any programmatic procedural protections.

The Court seems to acknowledge that unreasonable searches "inflic[t] dignitary harms that arouse strong resentment in parolees and undermine their ability to reintegrate into productive society." It is satisfied, however, that the California courts' prohibition against " 'arbitrary, capricious or harassing' " searches suffices to avert those harms—which are of course counterproductive to the State's purported aim of rehabilitating former prisoners and reintegrating them into society. I am unpersuaded. The requirement of individualized suspicion, in all its iterations, is the shield the Framers selected to guard against the evils of arbitrary action, caprice, and harassment. To say that those evils may be averted without that shield is, I fear, to pay lipservice to the end while withdrawing the means.

Respectfully, I dissent.

6. Borders

United States v. Martinez-Fuerte

428 U.S. 543 (1976)

Powell, J., delivered the opinion of the Court, in which Burger, C.J., Stewart, White, Blackmun, Rehnquist, and Stevens, JJ., joined. Brennan, J., filed a dissenting opinion, in which Marshall, J., joined.

These cases involve criminal prosecutions for offenses relating to the transportation of illegal Mexican aliens. Each defendant was arrested at a permanent checkpoint operated by the Border Patrol away from the international border with Mexico, and each sought the exclusion of certain evidence on the ground that the operation of the checkpoint was incompatible with the Fourth Amendment. In each instance whether the Fourth Amendment was violated turns primarily on whether a vehicle may be stopped at a fixed checkpoint for brief questioning of its occupants even though there is no reason to believe the particular vehicle contains illegal aliens. . . . We hold today that such stops are consistent with the Fourth Amendment. We also hold that the operation of a fixed checkpoint need not be authorized in advance by a judicial warrant.

■ ■ ■

> " 'Approximately one mile south of the checkpoint is a large black on yellow sign with flashing yellow lights over the highway stating "ALL VEHICLES, STOP AHEAD, 1 MILE." Three-quarters of a mile further north are two black on yellow signs suspended over the highway with flashing lights stating "WATCH FOR BRAKE LIGHTS." At the checkpoint, which is also the location of a State of California weighing station, are two large signs with flashing red lights suspended over the highway. These signs each state "STOP HERE U.S. OFFICERS." Placed on the highway are a number of orange traffic cones funneling traffic into two lanes where a Border Patrol agent in full dress uniform, standing behind a white on red "STOP" sign checks traffic. Blocking traffic in the unused lanes are official U.S. Border Patrol vehicles with flashing red lights. In addition, there is a permanent building which houses the Border Patrol office and temporary detention facilities. There are also floodlights for nighttime operation.' " *United States v. Ortiz* (1975), quoting *United States v. Baca* (1973).

The "point" agent standing between the two lanes of traffic visually screens all northbound vehicles, which the checkpoint brings to a virtual, if not a complete, halt. Most motorists are allowed to resume their progress without any oral inquiry or close visual examination. In a relatively small number of cases the "point" agent will conclude that further inquiry is in order. He directs these cars to a secondary inspection area, where their occupants are asked about their citizenship and immigration status. The Government informs us that at San Clemente the average length of an investigation in the secondary inspection area is three to five minutes. A direction to stop in the secondary inspection area could be based on something suspicious about a particular car passing through the checkpoint, but the Government concedes that none of the three stops at issue . . . was based on any articulable suspicion. During the period when these stops were made, the checkpoint was operating under a magistrate's "warrant of inspection," which authorized the Border Patrol to conduct a routine-stop operation at the San Clemente location.

■ ■ ■

The Border Patrol conducts three kinds of inland traffic-checking operations in an effort to minimize illegal immigration. Permanent checkpoints, such as those at San Clemente and Sarita, are maintained at or near intersections of important roads leading away from the border. They operate on a coordinated basis designed to avoid circumvention by smugglers and others who transport the illegal aliens. Temporary checkpoints, which operate like permanent ones, occasionally are established in other strategic locations. Finally, roving patrols are maintained to supplement the checkpoint system. . . .

We are concerned here with permanent checkpoints, the locations of which are chosen on the basis of a number of factors. The Border Patrol believes that to assure effectiveness, a checkpoint must be (i) distant enough from the border to avoid interference with traffic in populated areas near the border, (ii) close to the confluence of two or more significant roads leading away from the border, (iii) situated in terrain that restricts vehicle passage around the checkpoint, (iv) on a stretch of highway compatible with safe operation, and (v) beyond the 25-mile zone in which "border passes" are valid. . . .

The Fourth Amendment imposes limits on search-and-seizure powers in order to prevent arbitrary and oppressive interference by enforcement officials with the privacy and personal security of individuals. . . .

In *Almeida-Sanchez v. United States* (1973), the question was whether a roving-patrol unit constitutionally could search a vehicle for illegal aliens simply because it was in the general vicinity of the border. We recognized that important law enforcement interests were at stake but held that searches by roving patrols impinged so significantly on Fourth Amendment privacy interests that a search could be conducted without consent only if there was probable cause to believe that a car contained illegal aliens, at least in the absence of a judicial warrant authorizing random searches by roving patrols in a given area.

■ ■ ■

In *United States v. Brignoni-Ponce* (1975), however, we recognized that other traffic-checking practices involve a different balance of public and private interests and appropriately are subject to less stringent constitutional safeguards. The question was under what circumstances a roving patrol could stop motorists in the general area of the border for brief inquiry into their residence status. We found that the interference with Fourth Amendment interests involved in such a stop was "modest," while the inquiry served significant law enforcement needs. We therefore held that a roving-patrol stop need not be justified by probable cause and may be undertaken if the stopping officer is "aware of specific articulable facts, together with rational inferences from those facts, that reasonably warrant suspicion" that a vehicle contains illegal aliens.

■ ■ ■

Our previous cases have recognized that maintenance of a traffic-checking program in the interior is necessary because the flow of illegal aliens cannot be controlled effectively at the border. We note here only the substantiality of the public interest in the practice of routine stops for inquiry at permanent checkpoints, a practice which the Government identifies as the most important of the traffic-checking operations.

■ ■ ■

A requirement that stops on major routes inland always be based on reasonable suspicion would be impractical because the flow of traffic tends to be too heavy to allow the particularized study of a given car that would enable it to be identified as a possible carrier of illegal aliens. In particular, such a requirement would largely eliminate any deterrent to the conduct of well-disguised smuggling operations, even though smugglers are known to use these highways regularly.

■ ■ ■

While the need to make routine checkpoint stops is great, the consequent intrusion on Fourth Amendment interests is quite limited. The stop does intrude to a limited extent on motorists' right to "free passage without interruption."

■ ■ ■

Neither the vehicle nor its occupants are searched, and visual inspection of the vehicle is limited to what can be seen without a search. This objective intrusion—the stop itself, the questioning, and the visual inspection—also existed in roving-patrol stops. But we view checkpoint stops in a different light because the subjective intrusion—the generating of concern or even fright on the part of lawful travelers—is appreciably less in the case of a checkpoint stop. In *Ortiz*, we noted:

> "[T]he circumstances surrounding a checkpoint stop and search are far less intrusive than those attending a roving-patrol stop. Roving patrols often operate at night on seldom-traveled roads, and their approach may frighten motorists. At traffic checkpoints the motorist can see that other vehicles are being stopped, he can see visible signs of the officers' authority, and he is much less likely to be frightened or annoyed by the intrusion."

■ ■ ■

Routine checkpoint stops do not intrude similarly on the motoring public. First, the potential interference with legitimate traffic is minimal. Motorists using these highways are not taken by surprise as they know, or may obtain knowledge of, the location of the checkpoints and will not be stopped elsewhere. Second, checkpoint operations both appear to and actually involve less discretionary enforcement activity. The regularized manner in which established checkpoints are operated is visible evidence, reassuring to law-abiding motorists, that the stops are duly authorized and believed to serve the public interest. The location of a fixed checkpoint is not chosen by officers in the field, but by officials responsible for making overall decisions as to the most effective allocation of limited enforcement resources. We may assume that such officials will be unlikely to locate a checkpoint where it bears arbitrarily or oppressively on motorists as a class. And since field officers may stop only those cars passing the checkpoint, there is less room for abusive or harassing stops of individuals than there was in the case of roving-patrol stops. Moreover, a claim that a particular exercise of discretion in locating or operating a checkpoint is unreasonable is subject to post-stop judicial review.

The defendants arrested at the San Clemente checkpoint suggest that its operation involves a significant extra element of intrusiveness in that only a small percentage of cars are referred to the secondary inspection area, thereby "stigmatizing" those diverted and reducing the assurances provided by equal treatment of all motorists. We think defendants overstate the consequences. Referrals are made for the sole purpose of conducting a routine and limited inquiry into residence status that cannot feasibly be made of every motorist where the traffic is heavy. The objective intrusion of the stop and inquiry thus remains minimal. Selective referral may involve some annoyance, but it remains true that the stops should not be frightening or offensive because of their public and relatively routine nature. Moreover, selective referrals rather than questioning the occupants of every car tend to advance some Fourth Amendment interests by minimizing the intrusion on the general motoring public.

■ ■ ■

The defendants note correctly that to accommodate public and private interests some quantum of individualized suspicion is usually a prerequisite to a constitutional search or seizure.

■ ■ ■

We think the same conclusion is appropriate here, where we deal neither with searches nor with the sanctity of private dwellings, ordinarily afforded the most stringent Fourth Amendment protection. As we have noted earlier, one's expectation of privacy in an automobile and of freedom in its operation are significantly different from the traditional expectation of privacy and freedom in one's residence. . . . And the reasonableness of the procedures followed in making these checkpoint stops makes the resulting intrusion on the interests of motorists minimal. On the other hand, the purpose of the stops is legitimate and in the public interest, and the need for this enforcement technique is demonstrated by the records in the cases before us. Accordingly, we hold that the stops and questioning at issue may be made in the absence of any individualized suspicion at reasonably located checkpoints.

We further believe that it is constitutional to refer motorists selectively to the secondary inspection area at the San Clemente checkpoint on the basis of criteria that would not sustain a roving-patrol stop. Thus, even if it be assumed that such referrals are made largely on the basis of apparent Mexican ancestry, we perceive no constitutional violation.

■ ■ ■

In summary, we hold that stops for brief questioning routinely conducted at permanent checkpoints are consistent with the Fourth Amendment and need not be authorized by warrant. The principal protection of Fourth Amendment rights at checkpoints lies in appropriate limitations on the scope of the stop. We have held that checkpoint searches are constitutional only if justified by consent or probable cause to search. And our holding today is limited to the type of stops described in this opinion. "[A]ny further detention...must be based on consent or probable cause." None of the defendants in these cases argues that the stopping officers exceeded these limitations. Consequently, we affirm the judgment of the Court of Appeals for the Fifth Circuit, which had affirmed the conviction of Sifuentes. We reverse the judgment of the Court of Appeals for the Ninth Circuit and remand the case with directions to affirm the conviction of Martinez-Fuerte and to remand the other cases to the District Court for further proceedings.

It is so ordered.

Justice BRENNAN, with whom Justice MARSHALL joins, dissenting.

Today's decision is the ninth this Term marking the continuing evisceration of Fourth Amendment protections against unreasonable searches and seizures. Early in the Term, *Texas v. White* (1975) permitted the warrantless search of an automobile in police custody despite the unreasonableness of the custody and opportunity to obtain a warrant. *United States v. Watson* (1976) held that regardless of whether opportunity exists to obtain a warrant, an arrest in a public place for a previously committed felony never requires a warrant, a result certainly not fairly supported by either history or precedent. *United States v. Santana* (1976) went further and approved the warrantless arrest for a felony of a person standing on the front porch of her residence. *United States v. Miller* (1976) narrowed the Fourth Amendment's protection of privacy by denying the existence of a protectible interest in the compilation of checks, deposit slips, and other records pertaining to an individual's bank account. *Stone v. Powell* (1976) precluded the assertion of Fourth Amendment claims in federal collateral relief proceedings. *United States v. Janis* (1976) held that evidence unconstitutionally seized by a state officer is admissible in a civil proceeding by or against the United States. *South Dakota v. Opperman* (1976) approved sweeping inventory searches of automobiles in police custody irrespective of the particular circumstances of the case. Finally, in *Andresen v. Maryland* (1976), the Court, in practical effect, weakened the Fourth Amendment prohibition against general warrants.

Consistent with this purpose to debilitate Fourth Amendment protections, the Court's decision today virtually empties the Amendment of its reasonableness requirement by holding that law enforcement officials manning fixed checkpoint stations who make standardless seizures of persons do not violate the Amendment.

■ ■ ■

Terry [*v. Ohio* (1968)] thus made clear what common sense teaches: Conduct, to be reasonable, must pass muster under objective standards applied to specific facts.

We are told today, however, that motorists without number may be individually stopped, questioned, visually inspected, and then further detained without even a showing of articulable suspicion, let alone the heretofore constitutional minimum of reasonable suspicion, a result that permits search and seizure to rest upon "nothing more substantial than inarticulate hunches." This defacement of Fourth Amendment protections is arrived at by a balancing process that overwhelms the individual's protection against unwarranted official intrusion by a governmental interest said to justify the search and seizure. But that method is only a convenient cover for condoning arbitrary official conduct, for the governmental interests relied on as warranting intrusion here are the same as those in *Almeida-Sanchez* and *Ortiz*, which required a showing of probable cause for roving-patrol and fixed checkpoint searches, and *Brignoni-Ponce*, which required at least a showing of reasonable suspicion based on specific articulable facts to justify roving-patrol stops. Absent some difference in the nature of the intrusion, the same minimal requirement should be imposed for checkpoint stops.

The Court assumes, and I certainly agree, that persons stopped at fixed checkpoints, whether or not referred to a secondary detention area, are "seized" within the meaning of the Fourth Amendment. Moreover, since the vehicle and its occupants are subjected to a "visual inspection," the intrusion clearly exceeds mere physical restraint, for officers are able to see more in a stopped vehicle than in vehicles traveling at normal speeds down the highway. As the Court concedes, the checkpoint stop involves essentially the same intrusions as a roving-patrol stop, yet the Court provides no principled basis for distinguishing checkpoint stops.

Certainly that basis is not provided in the Court's reasoning that the subjective intrusion here is appreciably less than in the case of a stop by a roving patrol. *Brignoni-Ponce* nowhere bases the requirement of reasonable suspicion upon the subjective nature of the intrusion. In any event, the subjective aspects of checkpoint stops, even if different from the subjective aspects of roving-patrol stops, just as much require some principled restraint on law enforcement conduct. The motorist whose conduct has been nothing but innocent and this is overwhelmingly the case surely resents his own detention and inspection. And checkpoints, unlike roving stops, detain thousands of motorists, a dragnet-like procedure offensive to the sensibilities of free citizens. Also, the delay occasioned by stopping hundreds of vehicles on a busy highway is particularly irritating.

■ ■ ■

Every American citizen of Mexican ancestry and every Mexican alien lawfully in this country must know after today's decision that he travels the fixed checkpoint highways at the risk of being subjected not only to a stop, but also to detention and interrogation, both prolonged and to an extent far more than for non-Mexican appearing motorists. To be singled out for referral and to be detained and interrogated must be upsetting to any motorist. One wonders what actual experience supports my Brethren's conclusion that referrals "should not be frightening or offensive because of their public and relatively routine nature." In point of fact, referrals, viewed in context, are not relatively routine; thousands are otherwise permitted to pass. But for the arbitrarily selected motorists who must suffer the delay and humiliation of detention and interrogation, the experience can obviously be upsetting. And that experience is particularly vexing for the motorist of Mexican ancestry who is selectively referred, knowing that the officers' target is the Mexican alien. That deep resentment will be stirred by a sense of unfair discrimination is not difficult to foresee.

■ ■ ■

The Court also attempts to justify its approval of standardless conduct on the ground that checkpoint stops "involve less discretionary enforcement activity" than roving stops. This view is at odds with its later more revealing statement that "officers must have wide discretion in selecting the motorists to be diverted for the brief questioning involved." Similarly unpersuasive is the statement that "since field officers may stop only those cars passing the checkpoint, there is less room for abusive or harassing stops of individuals than there was in the case of roving-patrol stops." The Fourth Amendment standard of reasonableness admits of neither intrusion at the discretion of law enforcement personnel nor abusive or harassing stops, however infrequent. Action based merely on whatever may pique the curiosity of a particular officer is the antithesis of the objective standards requisite to reasonable conduct and to avoiding abuse and harassment. Such action, which the Court now permits, has expressly been condemned as contrary to basic Fourth Amendment principles.

■ ■ ■

The cornerstone of this society, indeed of any free society, is orderly procedure. The Constitution, as originally adopted, was therefore, in great measure, a procedural document. For the same reasons the drafters of the Bill of Rights largely placed their faith in procedural limitations on government action. The Fourth Amendment's requirement that searches and seizures be reasonable enforces this fundamental understanding in erecting its buffer against the arbitrary treatment of citizens by government. But to permit, as the Court does today, police discretion to supplant the objectivity of reason and, thereby, expediency to reign in the place of order, is to undermine Fourth Amendment safeguards and threaten erosion of the cornerstone of our system of a government, for, as Mr. Justice Frankfurter reminded us, "[t]he history of American freedom is, in no small measure, the history of procedure."

United States v. Flores-Montano

541 U.S. 149 (2004)

REHNQUIST, C.J., delivered the opinion for a unanimous Court....

Customs officials seized 37 kilograms—a little more than 81 pounds—of marijuana from respondent Manuel Flores-Montano's gas tank at the international border. The Court of Appeals for the Ninth Circuit, relying on an earlier decision by a divided panel of that court, *United States v. Molina-Tarazon* (2002), held that the Fourth Amendment forbade the fuel tank search absent reasonable suspicion. We hold that the search in question did not require reasonable suspicion. . . .

In *Molina-Tarazon*, the Court of Appeals decided a case presenting similar facts to the one at bar. It asked "whether [the removal and dismantling of the defendant's fuel tank] is a 'routine' border search for which no suspicion whatsoever is required." The Court of Appeals stated that "[i]n order to conduct a search that goes beyond the routine, an inspector must have reasonable suspicion," and the "critical factor" in determining whether a search is "routine" is the "degree of intrusiveness."

The Court of Appeals seized on language from our opinion in *United States v. Montoya de Hernandez* (1985), in which we used the word "routine" as a descriptive term in discussing border searches. ("Routine searches of the persons and effects of entrants are not subject to any requirement of reasonable suspicion, probable cause, or warrant"); ("Because the issues are not presented today we suggest no view on what level of suspicion, if any, is required for nonroutine border searches such as strip, body-cavity, or involuntary x-ray searches"). The Court of Appeals took the term "routine," fashioned a new balancing test, and extended it to searches of vehicles. But the reasons that might support a requirement of some level of suspicion in the case of highly intrusive searches of the person—dignity and privacy interests of the person being searched—simply do not carry over to vehicles. Complex balancing tests to determine what is a "routine" search of a vehicle, as opposed to a more "intrusive" search of a person, have no place in border searches of vehicles.

The Government's interest in preventing the entry of unwanted persons and effects is at its zenith at the international border. Time and again, we have stated that "searches made at the border, pursuant to the longstanding right of the sovereign to protect itself by stopping and examining persons and property crossing into this country, are reasonable simply by virtue of the fact that they occur at the border." *United States v. Ramsey* (1977). Congress, since the beginning of our Government, "has granted the Executive plenary authority to conduct routine searches and seizures at the border, without probable cause or a warrant, in order to regulate the collection of duties and to prevent the introduction of contraband into this country." . . .

Respondent asserts two main arguments with respect to his Fourth Amendment interests. First, he urges that he has a privacy interest in his fuel tank, and that the suspicionless disassembly of his tank is an invasion of his privacy. But on many occasions, we have noted that the expectation of privacy is less at the border than it is in the interior. *Montoya de Hernandez*. We have long recognized that automobiles seeking entry into this country may be searched. See *Carroll v. United States* (1925) ("Travellers may be so stopped in crossing an international boundary because of national self protection reasonably requiring one entering the country to identify himself as entitled to come in, and his belongings as effects which may be lawfully brought in"). It is difficult to imagine how the search of a gas tank, which should be solely a repository for fuel, could be more of an invasion of privacy than the search of the automobile's passenger compartment.

Second, respondent argues that the Fourth Amendment "protects property as well as privacy," *Soldal v. Cook County* (1992), and that the disassembly and reassembly of his gas tank is a significant deprivation of his property interest because it may damage the vehicle. He does not, and on the record cannot, truly contend that the procedure of removal, disassembly, and reassembly of the fuel tank in this case or any other has resulted in serious damage to, or destruction of, the property. According to the Government, for example, in fiscal year 2003, 348 gas tank searches conducted along the southern border were negative (*i.e.*, no contraband was found), the gas tanks were reassembled, and the vehicles continued their entry into the United States without incident. Brief for United States 31.

Respondent cites not a single accident involving the vehicle or motorist in the many thousands of gas tank disassemblies that have occurred at the border. A gas tank search involves a brief procedure that can be reversed without damaging the safety or operation of the vehicle. If damage to a vehicle were to occur, the motorist might be entitled to recovery. While the interference with a motorist's possessory interest is not insignificant when the Government removes, disassembles, and reassembles his gas tank, it nevertheless is justified by the Government's paramount interest in protecting the border.

For the reasons stated, we conclude that the Government's authority to conduct suspicionless inspections at the border includes the authority to remove, disassemble, and reassemble a vehicle's fuel tank. While it may be true that some searches of property are so destructive as to require a different result, this was not one of them. The judgment of the United States Court of Appeals for the Ninth Circuit is therefore reversed, and the case is remanded for further proceedings consistent with this opinion.

It is so ordered. . . .

CHAPTER 4

Warrants

Introduction

This chapter deals with the warrant requirements of the Fourth Amendment and ways in which those requirements can be avoided, often referred to as exceptions to the warrant requirement. The decisions in this chapter depict the significant differences between the Warren Court and the Burger, Rehnquist, and Roberts Courts. Originally, exceptions to warrant requirements were limited to practicality concerns, and the scope of the warrant exceptions were specifically tailored to those concerns. Brennan's dissent in *T.L.O* exemplifies this conservatism: "Warrantless searches are *per se* unreasonable, subject only to a few specifically delineated and well-recognized exceptions." However, more recently, warrantless searches are often the norm and no longer so limited in scope.

Section A of this chapter explores arrest warrants. *Chimel* and *Buie* discuss the scope of a search when executing an arrest warrant at a home. *Payton* holds that arrest warrants are generally required for home arrests. *Steagald* limits arrest warrants when the arrestee is at the home of a third party. *Watson*, covered by the *Payton* excerpt in this chapter, establishes that arrest warrants are not required for a public arrest.

Section B of this chapter analyzes the various requirements for a search warrant. *Lo-Ji Sales* looks into the neutrality of the issuing magistrate. *Andresen* and *Messerschmidt* involve the interpretation of "particularity" in the Fourth Amendment. Execution of the warrant is dealt with in *Banks* (knock requirement) and *McArthur* (detention of occupant while securing the warrant). *Hudson* examines the exclusionary rule ramifications of a failure-to-knock violation.

Section C examines the many exceptions to the warrant requirement or ways in which it can be avoided. The major way to avoid warrants and the justification requirement discussed in Chapter 3 is through consent. Consent is an important law enforcement tool. *Schneckloth* deals with the requirements for waiver of Fourth Amendment rights through consenting to a search. *Rodriguez* and *Randolph* consider third-party consent, and *Jimeno* explores the scope of consent to search. The use of "plain view" will often extend the scope of a lawful search. This is explored in *Hicks* and *Dickerson*.

The scope of a search incident to arrest, originally discussed in *Chimel*, is extended in *Robinson*. The Massachusetts Statute represents a state's reaction to the *Robinson* decision. In *Buie*, the search incident to an arrest is extended to include the area of arrest to protect police from people lurking. The scope of a search incident to an arrest in the automobile context was greatly expanded in *Belton* and *Thornton* and then reduced in the most recent case of *Gant*. These automobile cases provide an interesting insight into the expansion of the scope of a search incident to an arrest and then a sudden retrenchment to that expansion. When there is probable cause to search an automobile, *Carroll* develops the initial automobile exception, which was based on the mobility concern. *Chambers* and *Acevedo* represent a movement beyond the original justification for the automobile exception to the warrant requirement.

Finally, *Welsh*, *Stuart*, *Fisher*, and *King* examine the most obvious exception to a warrant: the "exigent circumstances" or "emergency" exception, when it is just not practical to get a warrant.

A. ARREST WARRANTS

Chimel v. California

395 U.S. 752 (1969)

STEWART, J., delivered the opinion of the Court, in which WARREN, C.J., DOUGLAS, HARLAN, BRENNAN, FORTAS, and MARSHALL, JJ., joined. WHITE, J., filed a dissenting opinion, in which BLACK, J., joined.

This case raises basic questions concerning the permissible scope under the Fourth Amendment of a search incident to a lawful arrest. The relevant facts are essentially undisputed. Late in the afternoon of September 13, 1965, three police officers arrived at the Santa Ana, California, home of the petitioner with a warrant authorizing his arrest for the burglary of a coin shop. The officers knocked on the door, identified themselves to the petitioner's wife, and asked if they might come inside. She ushered them into the house, where they waited 10 or 15 minutes until the petitioner returned home from work. When the petitioner entered the house, one of the officers handed him the arrest warrant and asked for permission to "look around." The petitioner objected, but was advised that "on the basis of the lawful arrest," the officers would nonetheless conduct a search. No search warrant had been issued.

Accompanied by the petitioner's wife, the officers then looked through the entire three-bedroom house, including the attic, the garage, and a small workshop. In some rooms the search was relatively cursory. In the master bedroom and sewing room, however, the officers directed the petitioner's wife to open drawers and "to physically move contents of the drawers from side to side so that [they] might view any items that would have come from [the] burglary." After completing the search, they seized numerous items—primarily coins, but also several medals, tokens, and a few other objects. The entire search took between 45 minutes and an hour.

At the petitioner's subsequent state trial on two charges of burglary, the items taken from his house were admitted into evidence against him, over his objection that they had been unconstitutionally seized. He was convicted, and the judgments of conviction were affirmed by both the California Court of Appeal, and the California Supreme Court. Both courts accepted the petitioner's contention that the arrest warrant was invalid because the supporting affidavit was set out in conclusory terms.

■ ■ ■

Without deciding the question, we proceeded on the hypothesis that the California courts were correct in holding that the arrest of the petitioner was valid under the Constitution. This brings us directly to the question whether the warrantless search of the petitioner's entire house can be constitutionally justified as incident to that arrest. The decisions of this Court bearing upon that question have been far from consistent, as even the most cursory review makes evident.

Approval of a warrantless search incident to a lawful arrest seems first to have been articulated by the Court in 1914 as dictum in *Weeks v. United States* (1914), in which the Court stated:

> "What then is the present case? Before answering that inquiry specifically, it may be well by a process of exclusion to state what it is not. It is not an assertion of the right on the part of the Government, always recognized under English and American law, to search the person of the accused when legally arrested to discover and seize the fruits or evidences of crime....
>
> Plainly the case before us is essentially different from *Marron v. United States* (1927). There, officers executing a valid search warrant for intoxicating liquors found and arrested one Birdsall who in pursuance of a conspiracy was actually engaged in running a saloon. As an incident to the arrest they seized a ledger in a closet where the liquor or some of it was kept and some bills beside the cash register. These things were visible and accessible and in the offender's immediate custody. There was no threat of force or general search or rummaging of the place."

■ ■ ■

The limiting views expressed in *Go-Bart* [*Importing Co. v. United States*] (1931) and [*United States v.*] *Lefkowitz* (1932) were thrown to the winds, however, in *Harris v. United States*, decided in 1947. In that case, officers had obtained a warrant for Harris' arrest on the basis of his alleged involvement with the cashing and interstate transportation of a forged check. He was arrested in the living room of his four-room apartment, and in an attempt to recover two canceled checks thought to have been used in effecting the forgery, the officers undertook a thorough search of the entire apartment. Inside a desk drawer they found a sealed envelope marked "George Harris, personal papers." The envelope, which was then torn open, was found to contain altered Selective Service documents, and those documents were used to secure Harris' conviction for violating the Selective Training and Service Act of 1940. The Court rejected Harris' Fourth Amendment claim, sustaining the search as "incident to arrest."

Only a year after *Harris*, however, the pendulum swung again. In *Trupiano v. United States* (1948), agents raided the site of an illicit distillery, saw one of several conspirators operating the still, and arrested him, contemporaneously "seiz[ing] the illicit distillery." The Court held that the arrest and others made subsequently had been valid, but that the unexplained failure of the agents to procure a search warrant—in spite of the fact that they had had more than enough time before the raid to do so—rendered the search unlawful. The opinion stated:

> "It is a cardinal rule that, in seizing goods and articles, law enforcement agents must secure and use search warrants wherever reasonably practicable. This rule rests upon the desirability of having magistrates rather than police officers determine when searches and seizures are permissible and what limitations should be placed upon such activities. To provide the necessary security against unreasonable intrusions upon the private lives of individuals, the framers of the Fourth Amendment required adherence to judicial processes wherever possible. And subsequent history has confirmed the wisdom of that requirement.
>
> A search or seizure without a warrant as an incident to a lawful arrest has always been considered to be a strictly limited right. It grows out of the inherent necessities of the situation at the time of the arrest. But there must be something more in the way of necessity than merely a lawful arrest."

In 1950, two years after *Trupiano*, came *United States v. Rabinowitz* (1950), the decision upon which California primarily relies in the case now before us. In *Rabinowitz*, federal authorities had been informed that the defendant was dealing in stamps bearing forged overprints. On the basis of that information they secured a warrant for his arrest, which they executed at his one-room business office. At the time of the arrest, the officers "searched the desk, safe, and file cabinets in the office for about an hour and a half," and seized 573 stamps with forged overprints. The stamps were admitted into evidence at the defendant's trial, and this Court affirmed his conviction, rejecting the contention that the warrantless search had been unlawful. The Court held that the search in its entirety fell within the principle giving law enforcement authorities "[t]he right 'to search the place where the arrest is made in order to find and seize things connected with the crime. . . .' " *Harris* was regarded as "ample authority" for that conclusion. The opinion rejected the rule of *Trupiano* that " 'in seizing goods and articles, law enforcement agents must secure and use search warrants wherever reasonably practicable.' The test, said the Court, 'is not whether it is reasonable to procure a search warrant, but whether the search was reasonable.' "

Rabinowitz has come to stand for the proposition, inter alia, that a warrantless search "incident to a lawful arrest" may generally extend to the area that is considered to be in the "possession" or under the "control" of the person arrested. And it was on the basis of that proposition that the California courts upheld the search of the petitioner's entire house in this case. That doctrine, however, at least in the broad sense in which it was applied by the California courts in this case, can withstand neither historical nor rational analysis.

Even limited to its own facts, the *Rabinowitz* decision was, as we have seen, hardly founded on an unimpeachable line of authority. As Mr. Justice Frankfurter commented in dissent in that case, the "hint" contained in *Weeks* was, without persuasive justification, "loosely turned into dictum and finally elevated to a decision." And the approach taken in cases such as *Go-Bart, Lefkowitz,* and *Trupiano* was essentially disregarded by the *Rabinowitz* Court.

Nor is the rationale by which the State seeks here to sustain the search of the petitioner's house supported by a reasoned view of the background and purpose of the Fourth Amendment. Mr. Justice Frankfurter wisely pointed out in his *Rabinowitz* dissent that the Amendment's proscription of "unreasonable searches and seizures" must be read in light of "the history that gave rise to the words"—a history of "abuses so deeply felt by the Colonies as to be one of the potent causes of the Revolution." The Amendment was in large part a reaction to the general warrants and warrantless searches that had so alienated the colonists and had helped speed the movement for independence. In the scheme of the Amendment, therefore, the requirement that "no Warrants shall issue, but upon probable cause," plays a crucial part.

Only last Term in *Terry v. Ohio* (1967), we emphasized that "the police must, whenever practicable, obtain advance judicial approval of searches and seizures through the warrant procedure," and that "[t]he scope of [a] search must be 'strictly tied to and justified by' the circumstances which rendered its initiation permissible."

■ ■ ■

A similar analysis underlies the "search incident to arrest" principle, and marks its proper extent. When an arrest is made, it is reasonable for the arresting officer to search the person arrested in order to remove any weapons that the latter might seek to use in order to resist arrest or effect his escape. Otherwise, the officer's safety might well be endangered, and the arrest itself frustrated. In addition, it is entirely reasonable for the arresting officer to search for and seize any evidence on the arrestee's person in order to prevent its concealment or destruction. And the area into which an arrestee might reach in order to grab a weapon or evidentiary items must, of course, be governed by a like rule. A gun on a table or in a drawer in front of one who is arrested can be as dangerous to the arresting officer as one concealed in the clothing of the person arrested. There is ample justification, therefore, for a search of the arrestee's person and the area "within his immediate control"—construing that phrase to mean the area from within which he might gain possession of a weapon or destructible evidence.

There is no comparable justification, however, for routinely searching any room other than that in which an arrest occurs—or, for that matter, for searching through all the desk drawers or other closed or concealed areas in that room itself. Such searches, in the absence of well-recognized exceptions, may be made only under the authority of a search warrant. The "adherence to judicial processes" mandated by the Fourth Amendment requires no less.

■ ■ ■

It is argued in the present case that it is "reasonable" to search a man's house when he is arrested in it. But that argument is founded on little more than a subjective view regarding the acceptability of certain sorts of police conduct, and not on consideration relevant to Fourth Amendment interests. Under such an unconfined analysis, Fourth Amendment protection in this area would approach the evaporation point. It is not easy to explain why, for instance, it is less subjectively "reasonable" to search a man's house when he is arrested on his front lawn—or just down the street—than it is when he happens to be in the house at the time of arrest. As Mr. Justice Frankfurter put it:

> "To say that the search must be reasonable is to require some criterion of reason. It is no guide at all either for a jury or for district judges or the police to say that an 'unreasonable search' is forbidden—that the search must be reasonable. What is the test of reason which makes a search reasonable? The test is the reason underlying and expressed by the Fourth Amendment: the history and experience which it embodies and the safeguards afforded by it against the evils to which it was a response."

Thus, although "[t]he recurring questions of the reasonableness of searches" depend upon "the facts and circumstances—the total atmosphere of the case," those facts and circumstances must be viewed in the light of established Fourth Amendment principles.

It would be possible, of course, to draw a line between *Rabinowitz* and *Harris* on the one hand, and this case on the other. For *Rabinowitz* involved a single room, and *Harris* a four-room apartment, while in the case before us an entire house was searched. But such a distinction would be highly artificial. The rationale that allowed the searches and seizures in *Rabinowitz* and *Harris* would allow the searches and seizures in this case. No consideration relevant to the Fourth Amendment suggests any point of rational limitation, once the search is allowed to go beyond the area from which the person arrested might obtain weapons or evidentiary items. The only reasoned distinction is one between a search of the person arrested and the area within his reach on the one hand, and more extensive searches on the other.

The petitioner correctly points out that one result of decisions such as *Rabinowitz* and *Harris* is to give law enforcement officials the opportunity to engage in searches not justified by probable cause, by the simple expedient of arranging to arrest suspects at home rather than elsewhere. We do not suggest that the petitioner is necessarily correct in his assertion that such a strategy was utilized here, but the fact remains that had he been arrested earlier in the day, at his place of employment rather than at home, no search of his house could have been made without a search warrant.

■ ■ ■

"After arresting a man in his house, to rummage at will among his papers in search of whatever will convict him, appears to us to be indistinguishable from what might be done under a general warrant; indeed, the warrant would give more protection, for presumably it must be issued by a magistrate. True, by hypothesis the power would not exist, if the supposed offender were not found on the premises; but it is small consolation to know that one's papers are safe only so long as one is not at home."

■ ■ ■

Application of sound Fourth Amendment principles to the facts of this case produces a clear result. The search here went far beyond the petitioner's person and the area from within which he might have obtained either a weapon or something that could have been used as evidence against him. There was no constitutional justification, in the absence of a search warrant, for extending the search beyond that area. The scope of the search was, therefore, "unreasonable" under the Fourth and Fourteenth Amendments and the petitioner's conviction cannot stand.

Reversed.

Justice WHITE, with whom Justice BLACK joins, dissenting.

Few areas of the law have been as subject to shifting constitutional standards over the last 50 years as that of the search "incident to an arrest." There has been a remarkable instability in this whole area, which has seen at least four major shifts in emphasis. Today's opinion makes an untimely fifth. In my view, the Court should not now abandon the old rule....

The modern odyssey of doctrine in this field is detailed in the majority opinion. It began with *Weeks v. United States*, where the Court paused to note what the case before it was not. "It is not an assertion of the right on the part of the Government, always recognized under English and American law, to search the person of the accused when legally arrested to discover and seize the fruits or evidences of crime. This right has been uniformly maintained in many cases. Nor is it the case of burglar's tools or other proofs of guilt found upon his arrest within the control of the accused." This scope of search incident to arrest, extending to all items under the suspect's "control," was reaffirmed in a dictum in *Carroll v. United States* (1925). Accord, *Agnello v. United States* (1925) (holding that "the place where the arrest is made" may be searched "is not to be doubted"). The rule was reaffirmed in *Marron v. United States*, where the Court asserted that authority to search incident to an arrest "extended to all parts of the premises used for the unlawful purpose."

■ ■ ■

Within five years, this rule was qualified by two Prohibition Act cases, *Go-Bart Importing Co. v. United States*, and *United States v. Lefkowitz*.

The rule which has prevailed, but for very brief or doubtful periods of aberration, is that a search incident to an arrest may extend to those areas under the control of the defendant and where items subject to constitutional seizure may be found. The justification for this rule must, under the language of the Fourth Amendment, lie in the reasonableness of the rule. *Terry v. Ohio.*

■ ■ ■

In terms, then, the Court must decide whether a given search is reasonable. The Amendment does not proscribe "warrantless searches" but instead it proscribes "unreasonable searches" and this Court has never held nor does the majority today assert that warrantless searches are necessarily unreasonable.

Applying this reasonableness test to the area of searches incident to arrests, one thing is clear at the outset. Search of an arrested man and of the items within his immediate reach must in almost every case be reasonable. There is always a danger that the suspect will try to escape, seizing concealed weapons with which to overpower and injure the arresting officers, and there is a danger that he may destroy evidence vital to the prosecution. Circumstances in which these justifications would not apply are sufficiently rare that inquiry is not made into searches of this scope, which have been considered reasonable throughout.

The justifications which make such a search reasonable obviously do not apply to the search of areas to which the accused does not have ready physical access. This is not enough, however, to prove such searches unconstitutional. The Court has always held, and does not today deny, that when there is probable cause to search and it is "impracticable" for one reason or another to get a search warrant, then a warrantless search may be reasonable. E.g., even *Trupiano v. United States.* This is the case whether an arrest was made at the time of the search or not.

This is not to say that a search can be reasonable without regard to the probable cause to believe that seizable items are on the premises. But when there are exigent circumstances, and probable cause, then the search may be made without a warrant, reasonably. An arrest itself may often create an emergency situation making it impracticable to obtain a warrant before embarking on a related search. Again assuming that there is probable cause to search premises at the spot where a suspect is arrested, it seems to me unreasonable to require the police to leave the scene in order to obtain a search warrant when they are already legally there to make a valid arrest, and when there must almost always be a strong possibility that confederates of the arrested man will in the meanwhile remove the items for which the police have probable cause to search. This must so often be the case that it seems to me as unreasonable to require a warrant for a search of the premises as to require a warrant for search of the person and his very immediate surroundings.

This case provides a good illustration of my point that it is unreasonable to require police to leave the scene of an arrest in order to obtain a search warrant when they already have probable cause to search and there is a clear danger that the items for which they may reasonably search will be removed before they return with a warrant. Petitioner was arrested in his home after an arrest whose validity will be explored below, but which I will now assume was valid. There was doubtless probable cause not only to arrest petitioner, but also to search his house. He had obliquely admitted, both to a neighbor and to the owner of the burglarized store, that he had committed the burglary. In light of this, and the fact that the neighbor had seen other admittedly stolen property in petitioner's house, there was surely probable cause on which a warrant could have issued to search the house for the stolen coins. Moreover, had the police simply arrested petitioner, taken him off to the station house, and later returned with a warrant, it seems very likely that petitioner's wife, who in view of petitioner's generally garrulous nature must have known of the robbery, would have removed the coins. For the police to search the house while the evidence they had probable cause to search out and seize was still there cannot be considered unreasonable.

■ ■ ■

If circumstances so often require the warrantless arrest that the law generally permits it, the typical situation will find the arresting officers lawfully on the premises without arrest or search warrant. Like the majority, I would permit the police to search the person of a suspect and the area under his immediate control either to assure the safety of the officers or to prevent the destruction of evidence. And like the majority, I see nothing in the arrest alone furnishing probable cause for a search of any broader scope. However, where as here the existence of probable cause is independently established and would justify a warrant for a broader search for evidence, I would follow past cases and permit such a search to be carried out without a warrant, since the fact of arrest supplies an exigent circumstance justifying police action before the evidence can be removed, and also alerts the suspect to the fact of the search so that he can immediately seek judicial determination of probable cause in an adversary proceeding, and appropriate redress.

This view, consistent with past cases, would not authorize the general search against which the Fourth Amendment was meant to guard, nor would it broaden or render uncertain in any way whatsoever the scope of searches permitted under the Fourth Amendment. The issue in this case is not the breadth of the search, since there was clearly probable cause for the search which was carried out. No broader search than if the officers had a warrant would be permitted. The only issue is whether a search warrant was required as a precondition to that search. It is agreed that such a warrant would be required absent exigent circumstances. I would hold that the fact of arrest supplies such an exigent circumstance, since the police had lawfully gained entry to the premises to effect the arrest and since delaying the search to secure a warrant would have involved the risk of not recovering the fruits of the crime.

The majority today proscribes searches for which there is probable cause and which may prove fruitless unless carried out immediately. This rule will have no added effect whatsoever in protecting the rights of the criminal accused at trial against introduction of evidence seized without probable cause. Such evidence could not be introduced under the old rule. Nor does the majority today give any added protection to the right of privacy of those whose houses there is probable cause to search. A warrant would still be sworn out for those houses, and the privacy of their owners invaded. The only possible justification for the majority's rule is that in some instances arresting officers may search when they have no probable cause to do so and that such unlawful searches might be prevented if the officers first sought a warrant from a magistrate. Against the possible protection of privacy in that class of cases, in which the privacy of the house has already been invaded by entry to make the arrest—an entry for which the majority does not assert that any warrant is necessary—must be weighed the risk of destruction of evidence for which there is probable cause to search, as a result of delays in obtaining a search warrant. Without more basis for radical change than the Court's opinion reveals, I would not upset the balance of these interests which has been struck by the former decisions of this Court.

■ ■ ■

An arrested man, by definition conscious of the police interest in him, and provided almost immediately with a lawyer and a judge, is in an excellent position to dispute the reasonableness of his arrest and contemporaneous search in a full adversary proceeding. I would uphold the constitutionality of this search contemporaneous with an arrest since there were probable cause both for the search and for the arrest, exigent circumstances involving the removal or destruction of evidence, and satisfactory opportunity to dispute the issues of probable cause shortly thereafter. In this case, the search was reasonable.

Maryland v. Buie

494 U.S. 325 (1990)

WHITE, J., delivered the opinion of the Court, in which REHNQUIST, BLACKMUN, STEVENS, O'CONNOR, SCALIA, and KENNEDY, JJ., joined. STEVENS and KENNEDY, JJ., filed concurring opinions. BRENNAN, J., filed a dissenting opinion, in which MARSHALL, J., joined.

A "protective sweep" is a quick and limited search of premises, incident to an arrest and conducted to protect the safety of police officers or others. It is narrowly confined to a cursory visual inspection of those places in which a person might be hiding. In this case we must decide what level of justification is required by the Fourth and Fourteenth Amendments before police officers, while effecting the arrest of a suspect in his home pursuant to an arrest warrant, may conduct a warrantless protective sweep of all or part of the premises. The Court of Appeals of Maryland held that a running suit seized in plain view during such a protective sweep should have been suppressed at respondent's armed robbery trial because the officer who conducted the sweep did not have probable cause to believe that a serious and demonstrable potentiality for danger existed. We conclude that the Fourth Amendment would permit the protective sweep undertaken here if the searching officer "possesse[d] a reasonable belief based on 'specific and articulable facts which, taken together with the rational inferences from those facts, reasonably warrant[ed]' the officer in believing," that the area swept harbored an individual posing a danger to the officer or others. We accordingly vacate the judgment below and remand for application of this standard.

■ ■ ■

On February 3, 1986, two men committed an armed robbery of a Godfather's Pizza restaurant in Prince George's County, Maryland. One of the robbers was wearing a red running suit. That same day, Prince George's County police obtained arrest warrants for respondent Jerome Edward Buie and his suspected accomplice in the robbery, Lloyd Allen. Buie's house was placed under police surveillance.

On February 5, the police executed the arrest warrant for Buie. They first had a police department secretary telephone Buie's house to verify that he was home. The secretary spoke to a female first, then to Buie himself. Six or seven officers proceeded to Buie's house. Once inside, the officers fanned out through the first and second floors. Corporal James Rozar announced that he would "freeze" the basement so that no one could come up and surprise the officers. With his service revolver drawn, Rozar twice shouted into the basement, ordering anyone down there to come out. When a voice asked who was calling, Rozar announced three times: "this is the police, show me your hands." App. 5. Eventually, a pair of hands appeared around the bottom of the stairwell and Buie emerged from the basement. He was arrested, searched, and handcuffed by Rozar. Thereafter, Detective Joseph Frolich entered the basement "in case there was someone else" down there. He noticed a red running suit lying in plain view on a stack of clothing and seized it.

The trial court denied Buie's motion to suppress the running suit, stating in part: "The man comes out from a basement, the police don't know how many other people are down there. He is charged with a serious offense." The State introduced the running suit into evidence at Buie's trial. A jury convicted Buie of robbery with a deadly weapon and using a handgun in the commission of a felony.

The Court of Special Appeals of Maryland affirmed the trial court's denial of the suppression motion. The court stated that Detective Frolich did not go into the basement to search for evidence, but to look for the suspected accomplice or anyone else who might pose a threat to the officers on the scene.

■ ■ ■

The Court of Appeals of Maryland reversed by a 4-to-3 vote. The court acknowledged that "when the intrusion is slight, as in the case of a brief stop and frisk on a public street, and the public interest in prevention of crime is substantial, reasonable articulable suspicion may be enough to pass constitutional muster." The court, however, stated that when the sanctity of the home is involved, the exceptions to the warrant requirement are few, and held: "[T]o justify a protective sweep of a home, the government must show that there is probable cause to believe that 'a serious and demonstrable potentiality for danger' exists." The court went on to find that the State had not satisfied that probable-cause requirement.

■ ■ ■

It is not disputed that until the point of Buie's arrest the police had the right, based on the authority of the arrest warrant, to search anywhere in the house that Buie might have been found, including the basement. "If there is sufficient evidence of a citizen's participation in a felony to persuade a judicial officer that his arrest is justified, it is constitutionally reasonable to require him to open his doors to the officers of the law." There is also no dispute that if Detective Frolich's entry into the basement was lawful, the seizure of the red running suit, which was in plain view and which the officer had probable cause to believe was evidence of a crime, was also lawful under the Fourth Amendment. The issue in this case is what level of justification the Fourth Amendment required before Detective Frolich could legally enter the basement to see if someone else was there.

■ ■ ■

The *Terry* (1968) case is most instructive for present purposes. There we held that an on-the-street "frisk" for weapons must be tested by the Fourth Amendment's general proscription against unreasonable searches because such a frisk involves "an entire rubric of police conduct—necessarily swift action predicated upon the on-the-spot observations of the officer on the beat—which historically has not been, and as a practical matter could not be, subjected to the warrant procedure." We stated that there is " 'no ready test for determining reasonableness other than by balancing the need to search . . . against the invasion which the search . . . entails.' " Applying that balancing test, it was held that although a frisk for weapons "constitutes a severe, though brief, intrusion upon cherished personal security," such a frisk is reasonable when weighed against the "need for law enforcement officers to protect themselves and other prospective victims of violence in situations where they may lack probable cause for an arrest." We therefore authorized a limited patdown for weapons where a reasonably prudent officer would be warranted in the belief, based on "specific and articulable facts," and not on a mere "inchoate and unparticularized suspicion or 'hunch,' " "that he is dealing with an armed and dangerous individual."

In *Michigan v. Long* (1983), the principles of *Terry* were applied in the context of a roadside encounter: "[T]he search of the passenger compartment of an automobile, limited to those areas in which a weapon may be placed or hidden, is permissible if the police officer possesses a reasonable belief based on 'specific and articulable facts which, taken together with the rational inferences from those facts, reasonably warrant' the officer in believing that the suspect is dangerous and the suspect may gain immediate control of weapons."

■ ■ ■

We agree with the State, as did the court below, that a warrant was not required. We also hold that as an incident to the arrest the officers could, as a precautionary matter and without probable cause or reasonable suspicion, look in closets and other spaces immediately adjoining the place of arrest from which an attack could be immediately launched. Beyond that, however, we hold that there must be articulable facts which, taken together with the ~~hold~~ rational inferences from those facts, would warrant a reasonably prudent officer in believing that the area to be swept harbors an individual posing a danger to those on the arrest scene. This is no more and no less than was required in *Terry* and *Long*, and as in those cases, we think this balance is the proper one.

We should emphasize that such a protective sweep, aimed at protecting the arresting officers, if justified by the circumstances, is nevertheless not a full search of the premises, but may extend only to a cursory inspection of those spaces where a person may be found. The sweep lasts no longer than is necessary to dispel the reasonable suspicion of danger and in any event no longer than it takes to complete the arrest and depart the premises.

■ ■ ■

Affirmance is not required by *Chimel v. California* (1969), where it was held that in the absence of a search warrant, the justifiable search incident to an in-home arrest could not extend beyond the arrestee's person and the area from within which the arrestee might have obtained a weapon. First, *Chimel* was concerned with a full-blown search of the entire house for evidence of the crime for which the arrest was made, not the more limited intrusion contemplated by a protective sweep. Second, the justification for the search incident to arrest considered in *Chimel* was the threat posed by the arrestee, not the safety threat posed by the house, or more properly by unseen third parties in the house. To reach our conclusion today, therefore, we need not disagree with the Court's statement in *Chimel*, that "the invasion of privacy that results from a top-to-bottom search of a man's house [cannot be characterized] as 'minor,'" nor hold that "simply because some interference with an individual's privacy and freedom of movement has lawfully taken place, further intrusions should automatically be allowed despite the absence of a warrant that the Fourth Amendment would otherwise require." The type of search we authorize today is far removed from the "top-to-bottom" search involved in *Chimel*; moreover, it is decidedly not "automati[c]," but may be conducted only when justified by a reasonable, articulable suspicion that the house is harboring a person posing a danger to those on the arrest scene.

■ ■ ■

We conclude that by requiring a protective sweep to be justified by probable cause to believe that a serious and demonstrable potentiality for danger existed, the Court of Appeals of Maryland applied an unnecessarily strict Fourth Amendment standard. The Fourth Amendment permits a properly limited protective sweep in conjunction with an in-home arrest when the searching officer possesses a reasonable belief based on specific and articulable facts that the area to be swept harbors an individual posing a danger to those on the arrest scene. We therefore vacate the judgment below and remand this case to the Court of Appeals of Maryland for further proceedings not inconsistent with this opinion.

It is so ordered.

Justice STEVENS, concurring.

Today the Court holds that reasonable suspicion, rather than probable cause, is necessary to support a protective sweep while an arrest is in progress. I agree with that holding and with the Court's opinion, but I believe it is important to emphasize that the standard applies only to *protective* sweeps. Officers conducting such a sweep must have a reasonable basis for believing that their search will reduce the danger of harm to themselves or of violent interference with their mission; in short, the search must be protective. . . .

Justice BRENNAN, with whom Justice MARSHALL joins, dissenting.

Today the Court for the first time extends *Terry v. Ohio* into the home, dispensing with the Fourth Amendment's general requirements of a warrant and probable cause and carving a "reasonable suspicion" exception for protective sweeps in private dwellings. In *Terry*, the Court held that a police officer may briefly detain a suspect based on a reasonable suspicion of criminal activity and may conduct a limited "frisk" of the suspect for concealed weapons in order to protect herself from personal danger. The Court deemed such a frisk "reasonable" under the Fourth Amendment in light of the special "need for law enforcement officers to protect themselves and other prospective victims of violence" during investigative detentions, and the "brief, though far from inconsiderable, intrusion upon the sanctity of the person."

Terry and its early progeny "permit[ted] only brief investigative stops and extremely limited searches based on reasonable suspicion."

■ ■ ■

The Court today holds that *Terry's* "reasonable suspicion" standard "strikes the proper balance between officer safety and citizen privacy" for protective sweeps in private dwellings. I agree with the majority that officers executing an arrest warrant within a private dwelling have an interest in protecting themselves against potential ambush by third parties, but the majority offers no support for its assumption that the danger of ambush during planned home arrests approaches the danger of unavoidable "on-the-beat" confrontations in "the myriad daily situations in which policemen and citizens confront each other on the street." In any event, the Court's implicit judgment that a protective sweep constitutes a "minimally intrusive" search akin to that involved in *Terry* markedly undervalues the nature and scope of the privacy interests involved.

While the Fourth Amendment protects a person's privacy interests in a variety of settings, "physical entry of the home is the chief evil against which the wording of the Fourth Amendment is directed." The Court discounts the nature of the intrusion because it believes that the scope of the intrusion is limited. The Court explains that a protective sweep's scope is "narrowly confined to a cursory visual inspection of those places in which a person might be hiding," and confined in duration to a period "no longer than is necessary to dispel the reasonable suspicion of danger and in any event no longer than it takes to complete the arrest and depart the premises." But these spatial and temporal restrictions are not particularly limiting. A protective sweep would bring within police purview virtually all personal possessions within the house not hidden from view in a small enclosed space. Police officers searching for potential ambushers might enter every room including basements and attics; open up closets, lockers, chests, wardrobes, and cars; and peer under beds and behind furniture. The officers will view letters, documents, and personal effects that are on tables or desks or are visible inside open drawers; books, records, tapes, and pictures on shelves; and clothing, medicines, toiletries and other paraphernalia not carefully stored in dresser drawers or bathroom cupboards. While perhaps not a "full-blown" or "top-to-bottom" search, a protective sweep is much closer to it than to a "limited patdown for weapons" or a "'frisk' of an automobile." Because the nature and scope of the intrusion sanctioned here are far greater than those upheld in *Terry* and *Long*, the Court's conclusion that "[t]he ingredients to apply the balance struck in *Terry* and *Long* are present in this case" is unwarranted. The "ingredient" of a minimally intrusive search is absent, and the Court's holding today therefore unpalatably deviates from *Terry* and its progeny.

In light of the special sanctity of a private residence and the highly intrusive nature of a protective sweep, I firmly believe that police officers must have probable cause to fear that their personal safety is threatened by a hidden confederate of an arrestee before they may sweep through the entire home. Given the state-court determination that the officers searching Buie's home lacked probable cause to perceive such a danger and therefore were not lawfully present in the basement, I would affirm the state court's decision to suppress the incriminating evidence. I respectfully dissent.

Payton v. New York

445 U.S. 573 (1980)

STEVENS, J., delivered the opinion of the Court, in which POWELL, BRENNAN, MARSHALL, and STEWART, JJ., joined. BLACKMUN, J., filed a concurring opinion. WHITE, J., filed a dissenting opinion, in which BURGER, C.J., and REHNQUIST, J., joined. REHNQUIST, J., filed a dissenting opinion.

These appeals challenge the constitutionality of New York statutes that authorize police officers to enter a private residence without a warrant and with force, if necessary, to make a routine felony arrest.

The important constitutional question presented by this challenge has been expressly left open in a number of our prior opinions. In *United States v. Watson* (1976), we upheld a warrantless "midday public arrest," expressly noting that the case did not pose "the still unsettled question . . . 'whether and under what circumstances an officer may enter a suspect's home to make a warrantless arrest.'" The question has been answered in different ways by other appellate courts. The Supreme Court of Florida rejected the constitutional attack, as did the New York Court of Appeals, in this case. The courts of last resort in 10 other States, however, have held that unless special circumstances are present, warrantless arrests in the home are unconstitutional. Of the seven United States Courts of Appeals that have considered the question, five have expressed the opinion that such arrests are unconstitutional.

■ ■ ■

On January 14, 1970, after two days of intensive investigation, New York detectives had assembled evidence sufficient to establish probable cause to believe that Theodore Payton had murdered the manager of a gas station two days earlier. At about 7:30 a.m. on January 15, six officers went to Payton's apartment in the Bronx, intending to arrest him. They had not obtained a warrant. Although light and music emanated from the apartment, there was no response to their knock on the metal door. They summoned emergency assistance and, about 30 minutes later, used crowbars to break open the door and enter the apartment. No one was there. In plain view, however, was a .30-caliber shell casing that was seized and later admitted into evidence at Payton's murder trial.

In due course Payton surrendered to the police, was indicted for murder, and moved to suppress the evidence taken from his apartment. The trial judge held that the warrantless and forcible entry was authorized by the New York Code of Criminal Procedure, and that the evidence in plain view was properly seized. He found that exigent circumstances justified the officers' failure to announce their purpose before entering the apartment as required by the statute. He had no occasion, however, to decide whether those circumstances also would have justified the failure to obtain a warrant, because he concluded that the warrantless entry was adequately supported by the statute without regard to the circumstances. The Appellate Division, First Department, summarily affirmed.

■ ■ ■

Before addressing the narrow question presented by these appeals, we put to one side other related problems that are *not* presented today. Although it is arguable that the warrantless entry to effect Payton's arrest might have been justified by exigent circumstances, none of the New York courts relied on any such justification. The Court of Appeals majority treated Payton's . . . case as involving [a] routine arrest in which there was ample time to obtain a warrant, and we will do the same. Accordingly, we have no occasion to consider the sort of emergency or dangerous situation, described in our case as "exigent circumstances," that would justify a warrantless entry into a home for the purpose of either arrest or search.

Nor do[es] th[is] case raise any question concerning the authority of the police, without either a search or arrest warrant, to enter a third party's home to arrest a suspect. The police broke into Payton's apartment intending to arrest Payton. . . . We also note that . . . it [is not] argued that the police lacked probable cause to believe that the suspect was at home when they entered. Finally . . . we are dealing with entries into homes made without the consent of any occupant. In *Payton*, the police used crowbars to break down the door. . . .

■　■　■

It is thus perfectly clear that the evil the Amendment was designed to prevent was broader than the abuse of a general warrant. Unreasonable searches or seizures conducted without any warrant at all are condemned by the plain language of the first clause of the Amendment. Almost a century ago the Court stated in resounding terms that the principles reflected in the Amendment "reached farther than the concrete form" of the specific cases that gave it birth, and "apply to all invasions on the part of the government and its employés of the sanctity of a man's home and the privacies of life." *Boyd v. United States* [(1886)].

■　■　■

The simple language of the Amendment applies equally to seizures of persons and to seizures of property. Our analysis in this case may therefore properly commence with rules that have been well established in Fourth Amendment litigation involving tangible items. As the Court reiterated just a few years ago, the "physical entry of the home is the chief evil against which the wording of the Fourth Amendment is directed." And we have long adhered to the view that the warrant procedure minimizes the danger of needless intrusions of that sort.

It is a "basic principle of Fourth Amendment law" that searches and seizures inside a home without a warrant are presumptively unreasonable. Yet it is also well settled that objects such as weapons or contraband found in a public place may be seized by the police without a warrant. The seizure of property in plain view involves no invasion of privacy and is presumptively reasonable, assuming that there is probable cause to associate the property with criminal activity.

■　■　■

As the late Judge Leventhal recognized, this distinction has equal force when the seizure of a person is involved. Writing on the constitutional issue now before us for the United States Court of Appeals for the District of Columbia Circuit sitting en banc, *Dorman v. United States* (1970), Judge Leventhal first noted the settled rule that warrantless arrests in public places are valid. He immediately recognized, however, that "[a] greater burden is placed . . . on officials who enter a home or dwelling without consent. Freedom from intrusion into the home or dwelling is the archetype of the privacy protection secured by the Fourth Amendment."

His analysis of this question then focused on the long-settled premise that, absent exigent circumstances, a warrantless entry to search for weapons or contraband is unconstitutional even when a felony has been committed and there is probable cause to believe that incriminating evidence will be found within. He reasoned that the constitutional protection afforded to the individual's interest in the privacy of his own home is equally applicable to a warrantless entry for the purpose of arresting a resident of the house; for it is inherent in such an entry that a search for the suspect may be required before he can be apprehended. Judge Leventhal concluded that an entry to arrest and an entry to search for and to seize property implicate the same interest in preserving the privacy and the sanctity of the home, and justify the same level of constitutional protection.

■ ■ ■

The majority of the New York Court of Appeals, however, suggested that there is a substantial difference in the relative intrusiveness of an entry to search for property and an entry to search for a person. It is true that the area that may legally be searched is broader when executing a search warrant than when executing an arrest warrant in the home. This difference may be more theoretical than real, however, because the police may need to check the entire premises for safety reasons, and sometimes they ignore the restrictions on searches incident to arrest.

But the critical point is that any differences in the intrusiveness of entries to search and entries to arrest are merely ones of degree rather than kind. The two intrusions share this fundamental characteristic: the breach of the entrance to an individual's home. The Fourth Amendment protects the individual's privacy in a variety of settings. In none is the zone of privacy more clearly defined than when bounded by the unambiguous physical dimensions of an individual's home—a zone that finds its roots in clear and specific constitutional terms: "The right of the people to be secure in their . . . houses . . . shall not be violated."

■ ■ ■

A study of the common law on the question whether a constable had the authority to make warrantless arrests in the home on mere suspicion of a felony—as distinguished from an officer's right to arrest for a crime committed in his presence—reveals a surprising lack of judicial decisions and a deep divergence among scholars.

■ ■ ■

Thus, our study of the relevant common law does not provide the same guidance that was present in *Watson*. Whereas the rule concerning the validity of an arrest in a public place was supported by cases directly in point and by the unanimous views of the commentators, we have found no direct authority supporting forcible entries into a home to make a routine arrest and the weight of the scholarly opinion is somewhat to the contrary. Indeed, the absence of any 17th- or 18th-century English cases directly in point, together with the unequivocal endorsement of the tenet that "a man's house is his castle," strongly suggests that the prevailing practice was not to make such arrests except in hot pursuit or when authorized by a warrant.

■ ■ ■

A majority of the States that have taken a position on the question permit warrantless entry into the home to arrest even in the absence of exigent circumstances. At this time, 24 States permit such warrantless entries; 15 States clearly prohibit them, though 3 States do so on federal constitutional grounds alone; and 11 States have apparently taken no position on the question.

■ ■ ■

But these current figures reflect a significant decline during the last decade in the number of States permitting warrantless entries for arrest. Recent dicta in this Court raising questions about the practice, and Federal Courts of Appeals' decisions on point, have led state courts to focus on the issue. Virtually all of the state courts that have had to confront the constitutional issue directly have held warrantless entries into the home to arrest to be invalid in the absence of exigent circumstances.

■ ■ ■

A longstanding, widespread practice is not immune from constitutional scrutiny. But neither is it to be lightly brushed aside. This is particularly so when the constitutional standard is as amorphous as the word "reasonable," and when custom and contemporary norms necessarily play such a large role in the constitutional analysis. In this case, although the weight of state-law authority is clear, there is by no means the kind of virtual unanimity on this question that was present in *United States v. Watson*, with regard to warrantless arrests in public places. Only 24 of the 50 States currently sanction warrantless entries into the home to arrest, and there is an obvious declining trend. Further, the strength of the trend is greater than the numbers alone indicate. Seven state courts have recently held that warrantless home arrests violate their respective *State* Constitutions. That is significant because by invoking a state constitutional provision, a state court immunizes its decision from review by this Court. This heightened degree of immutability underscores the depth of the principle underlying the result.

■ ■ ■

Justice POWELL, concurring in *United States v. Watson*, stated:

> "But logic sometimes must defer to history and experience. The Court's opinion emphasizes the historical sanction accorded warrantless felony arrests [in public places]."

In this case, however, neither history nor this Nation's experience requires us to disregard the overriding respect for the sanctity of the home that has been embedded in our traditions since the origins of the Republic....

Because no arrest warrant was obtained in either of these cases, the judgments must be reversed and the cases remanded to the New York Court of Appeals for further proceedings not inconsistent with this opinion.

It is so ordered.

■ ■ ■

Justice WHITE, with whom Chief Justice BURGER and Justice REHNQUIST join, dissenting.

The Court today holds that absent exigent circumstances officers may never enter a home during the daytime to arrest for a dangerous felony unless they have first obtained a warrant. This hard-and-fast rule, founded on erroneous assumptions concerning the intrusiveness of home arrest entries, finds little or no support in the common law or in the text and history of the Fourth Amendment. I respectfully dissent.

■ ■ ■

The history of the Fourth Amendment does not support the rule announced today. At the time that Amendment was adopted the constable possessed broad inherent powers to arrest. The limitations on those powers derived, not from a warrant "requirement," but from the generally ministerial nature of the constable's office at common law. Far from restricting the constable's arrest power, the institution of the warrant was used to expand that authority by giving the constable delegated powers of a superior officer such as a justice of the peace. Hence at the time of the Bill of Rights, the warrant functioned as a powerful tool of law enforcement rather than as a protection for the rights of criminal suspects.

In fact, it was the abusive use of the warrant power, rather than any excessive zeal in the discharge of peace officers' inherent authority, that precipitated the Fourth Amendment. That Amendment grew out of colonial opposition to the infamous general warrants known as writs of assistance, which empowered customs officers to search at will, and to break open receptacles or packages, wherever they suspected uncustomed goods to be. *United States v. Chadwick* (1977). . . . The writs did not specify where searches could occur and they remained effective throughout the sovereign's lifetime. In effect, the writs placed complete discretion in the hands of executing officials. Customs searches of this type were beyond the inherent power of common-law officials and were the subject of court suits when performed by colonial customs agents not acting pursuant to a writ.

The common law was the colonists' ally in their struggle against writs of assistance. Hale and Blackstone had condemned general warrants, and fresh in the colonists' minds were decisions granting recovery to parties arrested or searched under general warrants on suspicion of seditious libel. When James Otis, Jr., delivered his courtroom oration against writs of assistance in 1761, he looked to the common law in asserting that the writs, if not construed specially, were void as a form of general warrant.

■ ■ ■

"It has been sometimes contended, that an arrest of this character, without a warrant, was a violation of the great fundamental principles of our national and state constitutions, forbidding unreasonable searches and arrests, except by warrant founded upon a complaint made under oath. Those provisions doubtless had another and different purpose, being in restraint of general warrants to make searches, and requiring warrants to issue only upon a complaint made under oath. They do not conflict with the authority of constables or other peace-officers . . . to arrest without warrant those who have committed felonies. The public safety, and the due apprehension of criminals, charged with heinous offences, imperiously require that such arrests should be made without warrant by officers of the law." *Rohan v. Sawin* (1851).

That the Framers were concerned about warrants, and not about the constable's inherent power to arrest, is also evident from the text and legislative history of the Fourth Amendment. That provision first reaffirms the basic principle of common law, that "[t]he right of the people to be secure in their persons, houses, papers, and effects, against unreasonable searches and seizures, shall not be violated. . . ." The Amendment does not here purport to limit or restrict the peace officer's inherent power to arrest or search, but rather assumes an existing right against actions in excess of that inherent power and ensures that it remain inviolable. As I have noted, it was not generally considered "unreasonable" at common law for officers to break doors in making warrantless felony arrests. The Amendment's second clause is directed at the actions of officers taken in their ministerial capacity pursuant to writs of assistance and other warrants. In contrast to the first Clause, the second Clause does purport to alter colonial practice: "and no Warrants shall issue, but upon probable cause, supported by Oath or affirmation, and particularly describing the place to be searched, and the persons or things to be seized."

That the Fourth Amendment was directed towards safeguarding the rights at common law, and restricting the warrant practice which gave officers vast new powers beyond their inherent authority, is evident from the legislative history of that provision. As originally drafted by James Madison, it was directed *only* at warrants; so deeply ingrained was the basic common-law premise that it was not even expressed:

"The rights of the people to be secure in their persons[,] their houses, their papers, and their other property, from all unreasonable searches and seizures, shall not be violated by warrants issued without probable cause, supported by oath or affirmation, or not particularly describing the places to be searched, or the persons or things to be seized."

The Committee of Eleven reported the provision as follows:

"The right of the people to be secure in their persons, houses, papers, and effects, shall not be violated by warrants issuing without probable cause, supported by oath or affirmation, and not particularly describing the place to be searched, and the persons or things to be seized."

The present language was adopted virtually at the last moment by the Committee of Three, which had been appointed only to arrange the Amendments rather than to make substantive changes in them. The Amendment passed the House; but "the House seems never to have consciously agreed to the Amendment in its present form." In any event, because the sanctity of the common-law protections was assumed from the start, it is evident that the change made by the Committee of Three was a cautionary measure without substantive content.

In sum, the background, text, and legislative history of the Fourth Amendment demonstrate that the purpose was to restrict the abuses that had developed with respect to warrants; the Amendment preserved common-law rules of arrest. Because it was not considered generally unreasonable at common law for officers to break doors to effect a warrantless felony arrest, I do not believe that the Fourth Amendment was intended to outlaw the types of police conduct at issue in the present cases. . . .

Today's decision rests, in large measure, on the premise that warrantless arrest entries constitute a particularly severe invasion of personal privacy. I do not dispute that the home is generally a very private area or that the common law displayed a special "reverence . . . for the individual's right of privacy in his house." However, the Fourth Amendment is concerned with protecting people, not places, and no talismanic significance is given to the fact that an arrest occurs in the home rather than elsewhere. It is necessary in each case to assess realistically the actual extent of invasion of constitutionally protected privacy. Further, as Mr. Justice POWELL observed in *United States v. Watson* (concurring opinion), all arrests involve serious intrusions into an individual's privacy and dignity. Yet we settled in *Watson* that the intrusiveness of a public arrest is not enough to mandate the obtaining of a warrant. The inquiry in the present case, therefore, is whether the incremental intrusiveness that results from an arrest's being made *in the dwelling* is enough to support an inflexible constitutional rule requiring warrants for such arrests whenever exigent circumstances are not present.

Today's decision ignores the carefully crafted restrictions on the common-law power of arrest entry and thereby overestimates the dangers inherent in that practice. At common law, absent exigent circumstances, entries to arrest could be made only for felony. Even in cases of felony, the officers were required to announce their presence, demand admission, and be refused entry before they were entitled to break doors. Further, it seems generally accepted that entries could be made only during daylight hours. And, in my view, the officer entering to arrest must have reasonable grounds to believe, not only that the arrestee has committed a crime, but also that the person suspected is present in the house at the time of the entry.

■ ■ ■

While exaggerating the invasion of personal privacy involved in home arrests, the Court fails to account for the danger that its rule will "severely hamper effective law enforcement." The policeman on his beat must now make subtle discriminations that perplex even judges in their chambers. As Mr. Justice Powell noted, concurring in *United States v. Watson*, police will sometimes delay making an arrest, even after probable cause is established, in order to be sure that they have enough evidence to convict. Then, if they suddenly have to arrest, they run the risk that the subsequent exigency will not excuse their prior failure to obtain a warrant. This problem cannot effectively be cured by obtaining a warrant as soon as probable cause is established because of the chance that the warrant will go stale before the arrest is made.

Further, police officers will often face the difficult task of deciding whether the circumstances are sufficiently exigent to justify their entry to arrest without a warrant. This is a decision that must be made quickly in the most trying of circumstances. If the officers mistakenly decide that the circumstances are exigent, the arrest will be invalid and any evidence seized incident to the arrest or in plain view will be excluded at trial. On the other hand, if the officers mistakenly determine that exigent circumstances are lacking, they may refrain from making the arrest, thus creating the possibility that a dangerous criminal will escape into the community. The police could reduce the likelihood of escape by staking out all possible exits until the circumstances become clearly exigent or a warrant is obtained. But the costs of such a stakeout seem excessive in an era of rising crime and scarce police resources.

The uncertainty inherent in the exigent-circumstances determination burdens the judicial system as well. In the case of searches, exigent circumstances are sufficiently unusual that this Court has determined that the benefits of a warrant outweigh the burdens imposed, including the burdens on the judicial system. In contrast, arrests recurringly involve exigent circumstances, and this Court has heretofore held that a warrant can be dispensed with without undue sacrifice in Fourth Amendment values. The situation should be no different with respect to arrests in the home. Under today's decision, whenever the police have made a warrantless home arrest there will be the possibility of "endless litigation with respect to the existence of exigent circumstances, whether it was practicable to get a warrant, whether the suspect was about to flee, and the like."

Our cases establish that the ultimate test under the Fourth Amendment is one of "reasonableness." I cannot join the Court in declaring unreasonable a practice which has been thought entirely reasonable by so many for so long. It would be far preferable to adopt a clear and simple rule: after knocking and announcing their presence, police may enter the home to make a daytime arrest without a warrant when there is probable cause to believe that the person to be arrested committed a felony and is present in the house. This rule would best comport with the common-law background, with the traditional practice in the States, and with the history and policies of the Fourth Amendment. Accordingly, I respectfully dissent.

Steagald v. United States

451 U.S. 204 (1981)

MARSHALL, J., delivered the opinion of the Court, in which BLACKMUN, POWELL, BRENNAN, STEVENS, and STEWART, JJ., joined. BURGER, C.J., filed an opinion concurring in the judgment. REHNQUIST, J., filed a dissenting opinion, in which WHITE, J., joined.

The issue in this case is whether, under the Fourth Amendment, a law enforcement officer may legally search for the subject of an arrest warrant in the home of a third party without first obtaining a search warrant. Concluding that a search warrant must be obtained absent exigent circumstances or consent, we reverse the judgment of the United States Court of Appeals for the Fifth Circuit affirming petitioner's conviction.

■ ■ ■

In early January 1978, an agent of the Drug Enforcement Administration (DEA) was contacted in Detroit, Mich., by a confidential informant who suggested that he might be able to locate Ricky Lyons, a federal fugitive wanted on drug charges. On January 14, 1978, the informant called the agent again, and gave him a telephone number in the Atlanta, Ga., area where, according to the informant, Ricky Lyons could be reached during the next 24 hours. On January 16, 1978, the agent called fellow DEA Agent Kelly Goodowens in Atlanta and relayed the information he had obtained from the informant. Goodowens contacted Southern Bell Telephone Co., and secured the address corresponding to the telephone number obtained by the informant. Goodowens also discovered that Lyons was the subject of a 6-month-old arrest warrant.

Two days later, Goodowens and 11 other officers drove to the address supplied by the telephone company to search for Lyons. The officers observed two men standing outside the house to be searched. These men were Hoyt Gaultney and petitioner Gary Steagald. The officers approached with guns drawn, frisked both men, and, after demanding identification, determined that neither man was Lyons. Several agents proceeded to the house. Gaultney's wife answered the door, and informed the agents that she was alone in the house. She was told to place her hands against the wall and was guarded in that position while one agent searched the house. Ricky Lyons was not found, but during the search of the house the agent observed what he believed to be cocaine. Upon being informed of this discovery, Agent Goodowens sent an officer to obtain a search warrant and in the meantime conducted a second search of the house, which uncovered additional incriminating evidence. During a third search conducted pursuant to a search warrant, the agents uncovered 43 pounds of cocaine. Petitioner was arrested and indicted on federal drug charges.

■ ■ ■

The question before us is a narrow one. The search at issue here took place in the absence of consent or exigent circumstances. Except in such special situations, we have consistently held that the entry into a home to conduct a search or make an arrest is unreasonable under the Fourth Amendment unless done pursuant to a warrant. *Payton v. New York* (1980). . . . Thus, as we recently observed: "In terms that apply equally to seizures of property and to seizures of persons, the Fourth Amendment has drawn a firm line at the entrance to the house. Absent exigent circumstances, that threshold may not reasonably be crossed without a warrant." Here, of course, the agents had a warrant—one authorizing the arrest of Ricky Lyons. However, the Fourth Amendment claim here is not being raised by Ricky Lyons. Instead, the challenge to the search is asserted by a person not named in the warrant who was convicted on the basis of evidence uncovered during a search of his residence for Ricky Lyons. Thus, the narrow issue before us is whether an arrest warrant—as opposed to a search warrant—is adequate to protect the Fourth Amendment interests of persons not named in the warrant, when their homes are searched without their consent and in the absence of exigent circumstances.

The purpose of a warrant is to allow a neutral judicial officer to assess whether the police have probable cause to make an arrest or conduct a search. As we have often explained, the placement of this checkpoint between the Government and the citizen implicitly acknowledges that an "officer engaged in the often competitive enterprise of ferreting out crime," *Johnson v. United States* (1948), may lack sufficient objectivity to weigh correctly the strength of the evidence supporting the contemplated action against the individual's interests in protecting his own liberty and the privacy of his home. However, while an arrest warrant and a search warrant both serve to subject the probable-cause determination of the police to judicial review, the interests protected by the two warrants differ. An arrest warrant is issued by a magistrate upon a showing that probable cause exists to believe that the subject of the warrant has committed an offense and thus the warrant primarily serves to protect an individual from an unreasonable seizure. A search warrant, in contrast, is issued upon a showing of probable cause to believe that the legitimate object of a search is located in a particular place, and therefore safeguards an individual's interest in the privacy of his home and possessions against the unjustified intrusion of the police.

Thus, whether the arrest warrant issued in this case adequately safeguarded the interests protected by the Fourth Amendment depends upon what the warrant authorized the agents to do. To be sure, the warrant embodied a judicial finding that there was probable cause to believe that Ricky Lyons had committed a felony, and the warrant therefore authorized the officers to seize Lyons. However, the agents sought to do more than use the warrant to arrest Lyons in a public place or in his home; instead, they relied on the warrant as legal authority to enter the home of a third person based on their belief that Ricky Lyons might be a guest there. Regardless of how reasonable this belief might have been, it was never subjected to the detached scrutiny of a judicial officer. Thus, while the warrant in this case may have protected Lyons from an unreasonable seizure, it did absolutely nothing to protect petitioner's privacy interest in being free from an unreasonable invasion and search of his home. Instead, petitioner's only protection from an illegal entry and search was the agent's personal determination of probable cause. In the absence of exigent circumstances, we have consistently held that such judicially untested determinations are not reliable enough to justify an entry into a person's home to arrest him without a warrant, or a search of a home for objects in the absence of a search warrant. We see no reason to depart from this settled course when the search of a home is for a person rather than an object.

A contrary conclusion—that the police, acting alone and in the absence of exigent circumstances, may decide when there is sufficient justification for searching the home of a third party for the subject of an arrest warrant— would create a significant potential for abuse. Armed solely with an arrest warrant for a single person, the police could search all the homes of that individual's friends and acquaintances. Moreover, an arrest warrant may serve as the pretext for entering a home in which the police have a suspicion, but not probable cause to believe, that illegal activity is taking place. The Government recognizes the potential for such abuses, but contends that existing remedies—such as motions to suppress illegally procured evidence and damages actions for Fourth Amendment violations—provide adequate means of redress. We do not agree.

■ ■ ■

In sum, two distinct interests were implicated by the search at issue here— Ricky Lyons' interest in being free from an unreasonable seizure and petitioner's interest in being free from an unreasonable search of his home. Because the arrest warrant for Lyons addressed only the former interest, the search of petitioner's home was no more reasonable from petitioner's perspective than it would have been if conducted in the absence of any warrant. Since warrantless searches of a home are impermissible absent consent or exigent circumstances, we conclude that the instant search violated the Fourth Amendment.

■ ■ ■

The Government also suggests that practical problems might arise if law enforcement officers are required to obtain a search warrant before entering the home of a third party to make an arrest. The basis of this concern is that persons, as opposed to objects, are inherently mobile, and thus officers seeking to effect an arrest may be forced to return to the magistrate several times as the subject of the arrest warrant moves from place to place. We are convinced, however, that a search warrant requirement will not significantly impede effective law enforcement efforts.

First, the situations in which a search warrant will be necessary are few. As noted in *Payton v. New York*, an arrest warrant alone will suffice to enter a suspect's own residence to effect his arrest. Furthermore, if probable cause exists, no warrant is required to apprehend a suspected felon in a public place. *United States v. Watson* (1976). Thus, the subject of an arrest warrant can be readily seized before entering or after leaving the home of a third party. Finally, the exigent-circumstances doctrine significantly limits the situations in which a search warrant would be needed. For example, a warrantless entry of a home would be justified if the police were in "hot pursuit" of a fugitive. Thus, to the extent that searches for persons pose special problems, we believe that the exigent-circumstances doctrine is adequate to accommodate legitimate law enforcement needs.

Moreover, in those situations in which a search warrant is necessary, the inconvenience incurred by the police is simply not that significant. First, if the police know of the location of the felon when they obtain an arrest warrant, the additional burden of obtaining a search warrant at the same time is miniscule. The inconvenience of obtaining such a warrant does not increase significantly when an outstanding arrest warrant already exists. In this case, for example, Agent Goodowens knew the address of the house to be searched two days in advance, and planned the raid from the federal courthouse in Atlanta where, we are informed, three full-time magistrates were on duty. In routine search cases such as this, the short time required to obtain a search warrant from a magistrate will seldom hinder efforts to apprehend a felon. Finally, if a magistrate is not nearby, a telephonic search warrant can usually be obtained. See Fed. Rule Crim. Proc. 41(c)(1), (2).

Whatever practical problems remain, however, cannot outweigh the constitutional interests at stake. Any warrant requirement impedes to some extent the vigor with which the Government can seek to enforce its laws, yet the Fourth Amendment recognizes that this restraint is necessary in some cases to protect against unreasonable searches and seizures. We conclude that this is such a case. The additional burden imposed on the police by a warrant requirement is minimal. In contrast, the right protected—that of presumptively innocent people to be secure in their homes from unjustified, forcible intrusions by the Government—is weighty. Thus, in order to render the instant search reasonable under the Fourth Amendment, a search warrant was required.

Accordingly, the judgment of the Court of Appeals is reversed, and the case is remanded to that court for further proceedings consistent with this opinion.

So ordered.

■ ■ ■

Justice REHNQUIST, with whom Justice WHITE joins, dissenting.

■ ■ ■

The government's interests in the warrantless entry of a third-party dwelling to execute an arrest warrant are compelling. The basic problem confronting police in such situations is the inherent mobility of the fugitive. By definition, the police have probable cause to believe that the fugitive is in a dwelling which is not his home. He may stay there for a week, a day, or 10 minutes. Fugitives from justice tend to be mobile, and police officers will generally have no way of knowing whether the subject of an arrest warrant will be at the dwelling when they return from seeking a search warrant. Imposition of a search warrant requirement in such circumstances will frustrate the compelling interests of the government and indeed the public in the apprehension of those subject to outstanding arrest warrants.

The Court's responses to these very real concerns are singularly unpersuasive. It first downplays them by stating that "the situations in which a search warrant will be necessary are few," because no search warrant is necessary to arrest a suspect at his home and, if the suspect is at another's home, the police need only wait until he leaves, since no search warrant is needed to arrest him in a public place. These beguilingly simple answers to a serious law enforcement problem simply will not wash. Criminals who know or suspect they are subject to arrest warrants would not be likely to return to their homes, and while "[t]he police could reduce the likelihood of escape by staking out all possible exits . . . the costs of such a stakeout seems excessive in an era of rising crime and scarce police resources." *Payton v. New York* (White, J., dissenting). The Court's ivory tower misconception of the realities of the apprehension of fugitives from justice reaches its apogee when it states: "In routine search cases such as this, the short time required to obtain a search warrant from a magistrate will seldom hinder efforts to apprehend a felon." The cases we are considering are *not* "routine search cases." They are cases of attempted arrest, pursuant to a warrant, when the object of the arrest may flee at any time—including the "short time" during which the police are endeavoring to obtain a search warrant.

At the same time the interference with the Fourth Amendment privacy interests of those whose homes are entered to apprehend the felon is not nearly as significant as suggested by the Court. The arrest warrant serves some of the functions a separate search warrant would. It assures the occupants that the police officer is present on official business. The arrest warrant also limits the scope of the search, specifying what the police may search for—*i.e.*, the subject of the arrest warrant. No general search is permitted, but only a search of those areas in which the object of the search might hide. Indeed there may be no intrusion on the occupant's privacy at all, since if present the suspect will have the opportunity to voluntarily surrender at the door. Even if the suspect does not surrender but secretes himself within the house, the occupant can limit the search by pointing him out to the police. It is important to remember that the contraband discovered during the entry and search for Lyons was in plain view, and was discovered during a "sweep search" for Lyons, not a probing of drawers or cabinets for contraband.

Because the burden on law enforcement officers to obtain a separate search warrant before entering the dwelling of a third party to execute a concededly valid arrest warrant is great, and carries with it a high possibility that the fugitive named in the arrest warrant will escape apprehension, I would conclude that the application of the traditional "reasonableness" standard of the Fourth Amendment does not require a separate search warrant in a case such as this.

■ ■ ■

On the one side *Payton* makes clear that an arrest warrant is all that is needed to enter the suspect's "home" to effect the arrest. If a suspect has been living in a particular dwelling for any significant period, say a few days, it can certainly be considered his "home" for Fourth Amendment purposes, even if the premises are owned by a third party and others are living there, and even if the suspect concurrently maintains a residence elsewhere as well. In such a case the police could enter the premises with only an arrest warrant. On the other side, the more fleeting a suspect's connection with the premises, such as when he is a mere visitor, the more likely that exigent circumstances will exist justifying immediate police action without departing to obtain a search warrant. The practical damage done to effective law enforcement by today's decision, without any basis in the Constitution, may well be minimal if courts carefully consider the various congeries of facts in the actual case before them.

The genuinely unfortunate aspect of today's ruling is not that fewer fugitives will be brought to book, or fewer criminals apprehended, though both of these consequences will undoubtedly occur; the greater misfortune is the increased uncertainty imposed on police officers in the field, committing magistrates, and trial judges, who must confront variations and permutations of this factual situation on a day-to-day basis. They will, in their various capacities, have to weigh the time during which a suspect for whom there is an outstanding arrest warrant has been in the building, whether the dwelling is the suspect's home, how long he has lived there, whether he is likely to leave immediately, and a number of related and equally imponderable questions. Certainty and repose, as Justice Holmes said, may not be the destiny of man, but one might have hoped for a higher degree of certainty in this one narrow but important area of the law than is offered by today's decision.

B. SEARCH WARRANTS

Lo-Ji Sales, Inc. v. New York

442 U.S. 319 (1979)

Burger, C.J., delivered the opinion of the unanimous Court.

We granted certiorari on claims that the seizure of magazines, films, and other objects from petitioner's bookstore violated guarantees of the First, Fourth, and Fourteenth Amendments. . . .

On June 20, 1976, an investigator for the New York State Police purchased two reels of film from petitioner's so-called "adult" bookstore. Upon viewing them, he concluded the films violated New York's obscenity laws. On June 25, he took them to a Town Justice for a determination whether there was reasonable cause to believe the films violated the state obscenity laws so as to justify a warrant to search the seller's store. The Town Justice viewed both films in their entirety, and he apparently concluded they were obscene. Based upon an affidavit of the investigator subscribed before the Town Justice after this viewing, a warrant issued authorizing the search of petitioner's store and the seizure of other copies of the two films exhibited to the Town Justice.

The investigator's affidavit also contained an assertion that "similar" films and printed matter portraying similar activities could be found on the premises, and a statement of the affiant's belief that the items were possessed in violation of the obscenity laws. The warrant application requested that the Town Justice accompany the investigator to petitioner's store for the execution of the search warrant. The stated purpose was to allow the Town Justice to determine independently if any other items at the store were possessed in violation of law and subject to seizure. The Town Justice agreed. Accordingly, the warrant also contained a recital that authorized the seizure of "[t]he following items that the Court independently [on examination] has determined to be possessed in violation of Article 235 of the Penal Law...." However, at the time the Town Justice signed the warrant there were no items listed or described following this statement. As noted earlier, the only "things to be seized" that were described in the warrant were copies of the two films the state investigator had purchased. Before going to the store, the Town Justice also signed a warrant for the arrest of the clerk who operated the store for having sold the two films to the investigator.

The Town Justice and the investigator enlisted three other State Police investigators, three uniformed State Police officers, and three members of the local prosecutor's office—a total of 11—and the search party converged on the bookstore. The store clerk was immediately placed under arrest and advised of the search warrant. He was the only employee present; he was free to continue working in the store to the extent the search permitted, and the store remained open to the public while the party conducted its search mission which was to last nearly six hours.

The search began in an area of the store which contained booths in which silent films were shown by coin-operated projectors. The clerk adjusted the machines so that the films could be viewed by the Town Justice without coins; it is disputed whether he volunteered or did so under compulsion of the arrest or the warrant. The Town Justice viewed 23 films for two to three minutes each and, satisfied there was probable cause to believe they were obscene, then ordered the films and the projectors seized.

The Town Justice next focused on another area containing four coin-operated projectors showing both soundless and sound films. After viewing each film for two to five minutes, again without paying, he ordered them seized along with their projectors.

The search party then moved to an area in which books and magazines were on display. The magazines were encased in clear plastic or cellophane wrappers which the Town Justice had two police officers remove prior to his examination of the books. Choosing only magazines that did not contain significant amounts of written material, he spent not less than 10 seconds nor more than a minute looking through each one. When he was satisfied that probable cause existed, he immediately ordered the copy which he had reviewed, along with other copies of the same or "similar" magazines, seized. An investigator wrote down the titles of the items seized. All told, 397 magazines were taken.

The final area searched was one in which petitioner displayed films and other items for sale behind a glass enclosed case. When it was announced that each box of film would be opened, the clerk advised that a picture on the outside of the box was representative of what the film showed. Therefore, if satisfied from the picture that there was probable cause to believe the film in the box was obscene, the Town Justice ordered the seizure of all copies of that film. As with the magazines, an investigator wrote down the titles of the films seized, a total of 431 reels. Miscellaneous other items, including business records, were also seized, but no issue concerning them is raised here.

Throughout the day, two or three marked police cars were parked in front of the store and persons who entered the store were asked to show identification and their names were taken by the police. Not surprisingly, no sales were made during the period the search party was at the store, and no customers or potential customers remained in the store for any appreciable time after becoming aware of the police presence.

After the search and seizure was completed, the seized items were taken to a State Police barracks where they were inventoried. Each item was then listed on the search warrant, and late the same night the completed warrant was given to the Town Justice. The warrant, which had consisted of 2 pages when he signed it before the search, by late in the day contained 16 pages. It is clear, therefore, that the particular description of "things to be seized" was entered in the document after the seizure and impoundment of the books and other articles.

The items seized formed the basis for a three-count information charging petitioner with obscenity in the second degree under New York law.

■ ■ ■

This search warrant and what followed the entry on petitioner's premises are reminiscent of the general warrant or writ of assistance of the 18th century against which the Fourth Amendment was intended to protect. Except for the specification of copies of the two films previously purchased, the warrant did not purport to "PARTICULARLY DESCRIB[E] . . . THE . . . THINGS to be seized." U.S. Const., Amdt. 4. Based on the conclusory statement of the police investigator that other similarly obscene materials would be found at the store, the warrant left it entirely to the discretion of the officials conducting the search to decide what items were likely obscene and to accomplish their seizure. The Fourth Amendment does not permit such action. Nor does the Fourth Amendment countenance open-ended warrants, to be completed while a search is being conducted and items seized or after the seizure has been carried out. . . .

We have repeatedly said that a warrant authorized by a neutral and detached judicial officer is "a more reliable safeguard against improper searches than the hurried judgment of a law enforcement officer 'engaged in the often competitive enterprise of ferreting out crime.' *Johnson v. United States* (1948)." The State contends that the presence and participation of the Town Justice in the search ensured that no items would be seized absent probable cause to believe they were obscene, and that his presence enabled petitioner to enjoy an immediate adversary hearing on the issue.

The Town Justice did not manifest that neutrality and detachment demanded of a judicial officer when presented with a warrant application for a search and seizure. *Coolidge v. New Hampshire* (1971). We need not question the subjective belief of the Town Justice in the propriety of his actions, but the objective facts of record manifest an erosion of whatever neutral and detached posture existed at the outset. He allowed himself to become a member, if not the leader, of the search party which was essentially a police operation. Once in the store, he conducted a generalized search under authority of an invalid warrant; he was not acting as a judicial officer but as an adjunct law enforcement officer. When he ordered an item seized because he believed it was obscene, he instructed the police officers to seize all "similar" items as well, leaving determination of what was "similar" to the officer's discretion. Indeed, he yielded to the State Police even the completion of the general provision of the warrant. Though it would not have validated the warrant in any event, the Town Justice admitted at the hearing to suppress evidence that he could not verify that the inventory prepared by the police and presented to him late that evening accurately reflected what he had ordered seized.

■ ■ ■

In contrast, the local justice here undertook to telescope the processes of the application for a warrant, the issuance of the warrant, and its execution. It is difficult to discern when he was acting as a "neutral and detached" judicial officer and when he was one with the police and prosecutors in the executive seizure, and indeed even whether he thought he was conducting, *ex parte*, the "prompt" postseizure hearings on obscenity called for by *Heller v. New York* (1973). *Heller* does not permit the kind of activities revealed by this record.[6]

The judgment of the Appellate Term of the Supreme Court of the State of New York for the Ninth and Tenth Judicial Districts is reversed, and the case is remanded for further proceedings not inconsistent with this opinion.

Reversed and remanded.

---

6. We do not suggest, of course, that a "neutral and detached magistrate," *Shadwick v. Tampa* (1972), loses his character as such merely because he leaves his regular office in order to make himself readily available to law enforcement officers who may wish to seek the issuance of warrants by him. For example, in *Heller*, the judge signed the search warrant for the seizure of the film in the theater itself. But as we have just pointed out, *Heller* cannot control this case where the local Town Justice undertook not merely to issue a warrant, but to participate with the police and prosecutors in its execution. . . .

Andresen v. Maryland

427 U.S. 463 (1976)

BLACKMUN, J., delivered the opinion of the Court, in which BURGER, C.J., STEWART, WHITE, POWELL, REHNQUIST, and STEVENS, JJ., joined. BRENNAN and MARSHALL, JJ., filed dissenting opinions.

This case presents the issue whether the introduction into evidence of a person's business records, seized during a search of his offices, violates the Fifth Amendment's command that "[n]o person...shall be compelled in any criminal case to be a witness against himself." We also must determine whether the particular searches and seizures here were "unreasonable" and thus violated the prohibition of the Fourth Amendment.

■ ■ ■

In early 1972, a Bi-County Fraud Unit, acting under the joint auspices of the State's Attorneys' Offices of Montgomery and Prince George's Counties, Md., began an investigation of real estate settlement activities in the Washington, D. C., area. At the time, petitioner Andresen was an attorney who, as a sole practitioner, specialized in real estate settlements in Montgomery County. During the Fraud Unit's investigation, his activities came under scrutiny, particularly in connection with a transaction involving Lot 13T in the Potomac Woods subdivision of Montgomery County. The investigation, which included interviews with the purchaser, the mortgage holder, and other lienholders of Lot 13T, as well as an examination of county land records, disclosed that petitioner, acting as settlement attorney, had defrauded Standard-Young Associates, the purchaser of Lot 13T. Petitioner had represented that the property was free of liens and that, accordingly, no title insurance was necessary, when in fact, he knew that there were two outstanding liens on the property. In addition, investigators learned that the lienholders, by threatening to foreclose their liens, had forced a halt to the purchaser's construction on the property. When Standard-Young had confronted petitioner with this information, he responded by issuing, as an agent of a title insurance company, a title policy guaranteeing clear title to the property. By this action, petitioner also defrauded that insurance company by requiring it to pay the outstanding liens.

The investigators, concluding that there was probable cause to believe that petitioner had committed the state crime of false pretenses against Standard-Young, applied for warrants to search petitioner's law office and the separate office of Mount Vernon Development Corporation, of which petitioner was incorporator, sole shareholder, resident agent, and director. The application sought permission to search for specified documents pertaining to the sale and conveyance of Lot 13T. A judge of the Sixth Judicial Circuit of Montgomery County concluded that there was probable cause and issued the warrants.

The searches of the two offices were conducted simultaneously during daylight hours on October 31, 1972. Petitioner was present during the search of his law office and was free to move about. Counsel for him was present during the latter half of the search. Between 2% and 3% of the files in the office were seized. A single investigator, in the presence of a police officer, conducted the search of Mount Vernon Development Corporation. This search, taking about four hours, resulted in the seizure of less than 5% of the corporation's files.

Petitioner eventually was charged, partly by information and partly by indictment, with the crime of false pretenses, based on his misrepresentation to Standard-Young concerning Lot 13T, and with fraudulent misappropriation by a fiduciary, based on similar false claims made to three home purchasers. Before trial began, petitioner moved to suppress the seized documents.

■ ■ ■

With respect to all the items not suppressed or returned, the trial court ruled that admitting them into evidence would not violate the Fifth and Fourth Amendments. It reasoned that the searches and seizures did not force petitioner to be a witness against himself because he had not been required to produce the seized documents, nor would he be compelled to authenticate them. Moreover, the search warrants were based on probable cause, and the documents not returned or suppressed were either directly related to Lot 13T, and therefore within the express language of the warrants, or properly seized and otherwise admissible to show a pattern of criminal conduct relevant to the charge concerning Lot 13T.

■ ■ ■

After a trial by jury, petitioner was found guilty upon five counts of false pretenses and three counts of fraudulent misappropriation by a fiduciary. He was sentenced to eight concurrent two-year prison terms.

On appeal to the Court of Special Appeals of Maryland, four of the five false-pretenses counts were reversed because the indictment had failed to allege intent to defraud, a necessary element of the state offense. Only the count pertaining to Standard-Young's purchase of Lot 13T remained. With respect to this count of false pretenses and the three counts of misappropriation by a fiduciary, the Court of Special Appeals rejected petitioner's Fourth and Fifth Amendment Claims. Specifically, it held that the warrants were supported by probable cause, that they did not authorize a general search in violation of the Fourth Amendment, and that the items admitted into evidence against petitioner at trial were within the scope of the warrants or were otherwise properly seized....

We turn next to petitioner's contention that rights guaranteed him by the Fourth Amendment were violated because the descriptive terms of the search warrants were so broad as to make them impermissible "general" warrants, and because certain items were seized in violation of the principles of *Warden v. Hayden* (1967).

The specificity of the search warrants. Although petitioner concedes that the warrants for the most part were models of particularity, he contends that they were rendered fatally "general" by the addition, in each warrant, to the exhaustive list of particularly described documents, of the phrase "together with other fruits, instrumentalities and evidence of crime at this [time] unknown." The quoted language, it is argued, must be read in isolation and without reference to the rest of the long sentence at the end of which it appears. When read "properly," petitioner contends, it permits the search for and seizure of any evidence of any crime.

General warrants, of course, are prohibited by the Fourth Amendment. "[T]he problem [posed by the general warrant] is not that of intrusion per se, but of a general, exploratory rummaging in a person's belongings. . . . [The Fourth Amendment addresses the problem] by requiring a 'particular description' of the things to be seized." *Coolidge v. New Hampshire* (1971). This requirement " 'makes general searches . . . impossible and prevents the seizure of one thing under a warrant describing another. As to what is to be taken, nothing is left to the discretion of the officer executing the warrant.' " *Stanford v. Texas* (1965).

■ ■ ■

In this case we agree with the determination of the Court of Special Appeals of Maryland that the challenged phrase must be read as authorizing only the search for and seizure of evidence relating to "the crime of false pretenses with respect to Lot 13T." The challenged phrase is not a separate sentence. Instead, it appears in each warrant at the end of a sentence containing a lengthy list of specified and particular items to be seized, all pertaining to Lot 13T. We think it clear from the context that the term "crime" in the warrants refers only to the crime of false pretenses with respect to the sale of Lot 13T. The "other fruits" clause is one of a series that follows the colon after the word "Maryland." All clauses in the series are limited by what precedes that colon, namely, "items pertaining to . . . lot 13, block T." The warrants, accordingly, did not authorize the executing officers to conduct a search for evidence of other crimes but only to search for and seize evidence relevant to the crime of false pretenses and Lot 13T.

The admissibility of certain items of evidence in light of Warden v. Hayden. Petitioner charges that the seizure of documents pertaining to a lot other than Lot 13T violated the principles of *Warden v. Hayden* and therefore should have been suppressed. His objection appears to be that these papers were not relevant to the Lot 13T charge and were admissible only to prove another crime with which he was charged after the search. The fact that these documents were used to help form the evidentiary basis for another charge, it is argued, shows that the documents were seized solely for that purpose.

The State replies that *Warden v. Hayden* was not violated and that this is so because the challenged evidence is relevant to the question whether petitioner committed the crime of false pretenses with respect to Lot 13T. In Maryland, the crime is committed when a person makes a false representation of a past or existing fact, with intent to defraud and knowledge of its falsity, and obtains any chattel, money, or valuable security from another, who relies on the false representation to his detriment. Thus, the State is required to prove intent to defraud beyond a reasonable doubt. The State consequently argues that the documents pertaining to another lot in the Potomac Woods subdivision demonstrate that the misrepresentation with respect to Lot 13T was not the result of mistake on the part of petitioner.

In *Warden v. Hayden*, the Court stated that when the police seize " 'mere evidence,' probable cause must be examined in terms of cause to believe that the evidence sought will aid in a particular apprehension or conviction. In so doing, consideration of police purposes will be required." In this case, we conclude that the trained special investigators reasonably could have believed that the evidence specifically dealing with another lot in the Potomac Woods subdivision could be used to show petitioner's intent with respect to the Lot 13T transaction.

■ ■ ■

In the present case, when the special investigators secured the search warrants, they had been informed of a number of similar charges against petitioner arising out of Potomac Woods transactions. And, by reading numerous documents and records supplied by the Lot 13T and other complainants, and by interviewing witnesses, they had become familiar with petitioner's method of operation. Accordingly, the relevance of documents pertaining specifically to a lot other than Lot 13T, and their admissibility to show the Lot 13T offense, would have been apparent. Lot 13T and the other lot had numerous features in common. Both were in the same section of the Potomac Woods subdivision; both had been owned by the same person; and transactions concerning both had been handled extensively by petitioner. Most important was the fact that there were two deeds of trust in which both lots were listed as collateral. Unreleased liens respecting both lots were evidenced by these deeds of trusts. Petitioner's transactions relating to the other lot, subject to the same liens as Lot 13T, therefore, were highly relevant to the question whether his failure to deliver title to Lot 13T free of all encumbrances was mere inadvertence. Although these records subsequently were used to secure additional charges against petitioner, suppression of this evidence in this case was not required. The fact that the records could be used to show intent to defraud with respect to Lot 13T permitted the seizure and satisfied the requirements of *Warden v. Hayden*.

The judgment of the Court of Special Appeals of Maryland is affirmed.

It is so ordered.

Justice BRENNAN, dissenting.

■ ■ ■

Even if a Fifth Amendment violation is not to be recognized in the seizure of petitioner's papers, a violation of Fourth Amendment protections clearly should be, for the warrants under which those papers were seized were impermissibly general. General warrants are specially prohibited by the Fourth Amendment. The problem to be avoided is "not that of intrusion *per se*, but of a general, exploratory rummaging in a person's belongings." *Coolidge v. New Hampshire*. Thus the requirement plainly appearing on the face of the Fourth

Amendment that a warrant specify with particularity the place to be searched and the things to be seized is imposed to the end that "unauthorized invasions of 'the sanctity of a man's home and the privacies of life'" be prevented.

■ ■ ■

The Court recites these requirements, but their application in this case renders their limitation on unlawful governmental conduct an empty promise. After a lengthy and admittedly detailed listing of items to be seized, the warrants in this case further authorized the seizure of "other fruits, instrumentalities and evidence of crime at this [time] unknown." The Court construes this sweeping authorization to be limited to evidence pertaining to the crime of false pretenses with respect to the sale of Lot 13T. However, neither this Court's construction of the warrants nor the similar construction by the Court of Special Appeals of Maryland was available to the investigators at the time they executed the warrants. The question is not how those warrants are to be viewed in hindsight, but how they were in fact viewed by those executing them. The overwhelming quantity of seized material that was either suppressed or returned to petitioner is irrefutable testimony to the unlawful generality of the warrants. The Court's attempt to cure this defect by *post hoc* judicial construction evades principles settled in this Court's Fourth Amendment decisions. "The scheme of the Fourth Amendment becomes meaningful only when it is assured that at some point the conduct of those charged with enforcing the laws can be subjected to the more detached, neutral scrutiny of a judge. . . ." *Terry v. Ohio* (1968). See . . . *Johnson v. United States* (1948). It is not the function of a detached and neutral review to give effect to warrants whose terms unassailably authorize the far-reaching search and seizure of a person's papers especially where that has in fact been the result of executing those warrants. . . .

Messerschmidt v. Millender

132 S. Ct. 1235 (2012)

Roberts, C.J., delivered the opinion of the Court, in which Scalia, Kennedy, Thomas, Breyer, and Alito, JJ., joined. Breyer, J., filed a concurring opinion. Kagan, J., filed an opinion concurring in part and dissenting in part. Sotomayor, J., filed a dissenting opinion, in which Ginsburg, J., joined.

Petitioner police officers conducted a search of respondents' home pursuant to a warrant issued by a neutral magistrate. The warrant authorized a search for all guns and gang-related material, in connection with the investigation of a known gang member for shooting at his ex-girlfriend with a pistol-gripped sawed-off shotgun, because she had "call[ed] the cops" on him. Respondents brought an action seeking to hold the officers personally liable under 42 U.S.C. § 1983, alleging that the search violated their Fourth Amendment rights because there was not sufficient probable cause to believe the items sought were evidence of a crime. In particular, respondents argued that there was no basis to search for all guns simply because the suspect owned and had used a sawed-off shotgun, and no reason to search for gang material because the shooting at the ex-girlfriend for "call[ing] the cops" was solely a domestic dispute. The Court of Appeals for the Ninth Circuit held that the warrant was invalid, and that the officers were not entitled to immunity from personal liability because this invalidity was so obvious that any reasonable officer would have recognized it, despite the magistrate's approval. We disagree and reverse.

I

A

Shelly Kelly decided to break off her romantic relationship with Jerry Ray Bowen and move out of her apartment, to which Bowen had a key. Kelly feared an attack from Bowen, who had previously assaulted her and had been convicted of multiple violent felonies. She therefore asked officers from the Los Angeles County Sheriff's Department to accompany her while she gathered her things. Deputies from the Sheriff's Department came to assist Kelly but were called away to respond to an emergency before the move was complete.

As soon as the officers left, an enraged Bowen appeared at the bottom of the stairs to the apartment, yelling "I told you never to call the cops on me bitch!" Bowen then ran up the stairs to Kelly, grabbed her by her shirt, and tried to throw her over the railing of the second-story landing. When Kelly successfully resisted, Bowen bit her on the shoulder and attempted to drag her inside the apartment by her hair. Kelly again managed to escape Bowen's grasp, and ran to her car. By that time, Bowen had retrieved a black sawed-off shotgun with a pistol grip. He ran in front of Kelly's car, pointed the shotgun at her, and told Kelly that if she tried to leave he would kill her. Kelly leaned over, fully depressed the gas pedal, and sped away. Bowen fired at the car a total of five times, blowing out the car's left front tire in the process, but Kelly managed to escape.

Kelly quickly located police officers and reported the assault. She told the police what had happened—that Bowen had attacked her after becoming "angry because she had called the Sheriff's Department"—and she mentioned that Bowen was "an active member of the 'Mona Park Crips,'" a local street gang . . . Kelly also provided the officers with photographs of Bowen.

Detective Curt Messerschmidt was assigned to investigate the incident. Messerschmidt met with Kelly to obtain details of the assault and information about Bowen. Kelly described the attack and informed Messerschmidt that she thought Bowen was staying at his foster mother's home at 2234 East 120th Street. Kelly also informed Messerschmidt of Bowen's previous assaults on her and of his gang ties.

Messerschmidt then conducted a background check on Bowen by consulting police records, California Department of Motor Vehicles records, and the "cal-gang" database. Based on this research, Messerschmidt confirmed

Bowen's connection to the 2234 East 120th Street address. He also confirmed that Bowen was an "active" member of the Mona Park Crips and a "secondary" member of the Dodge City Crips. Finally, Messerschmidt learned that Bowen had been arrested and convicted for numerous violent and firearm-related offenses. Indeed, at the time of the investigation, Bowen's "rapsheet" spanned over 17 printed pages, and indicated that he had been arrested at least 31 times. Nine of these arrests were for firearms offenses and six were for violent crimes, including three arrests for assault with a deadly weapon (firearm).

Messerschmidt prepared two warrants: one to authorize Bowen's arrest and one to authorize the search of 2234 East 120th Street. An attachment to the search warrant described the property that would be the object of the search:

> "All handguns, rifles, or shotguns of any caliber, or any firearms capable of firing ammunition, or firearms or devices modified or designed to allow it [sic] to fire ammunition. All caliber of ammunition, miscellaneous gun parts, gun cleaning kits, holsters which could hold or have held any caliber handgun being sought. Any receipts or paperwork, showing the purchase, ownership, or possession of the handguns being sought. Any firearm for which there is no proof of ownership. Any firearm capable of firing or chambered to fire any caliber ammunition.
>
> Articles of evidence showing street gang membership or affiliation with any Street Gang to include but not limited to any reference to 'Mona Park Crips', including writings or graffiti depicting gang membership, activity or identity. Articles of personal property tending to establish the identity of person [sic] in control of the premise or premises. Any photographs or photograph albums depicting persons, vehicles, weapons or locations, which may appear relevant to gang membership, or which may depict the item being sought and or believed to be evidence in the case being investigated on this warrant, or which may depict evidence of criminal activity. Additionally to include any gang indicia that would establish the persons being sought in this warrant, affiliation or membership with the 'Mona Park Crips' street gang."

Two affidavits accompanied Messerschmidt's warrant applications. The first affidavit described Messerschmidt's extensive law enforcement experience, including that he had served as a peace officer for 14 years, that he was then assigned to a "specialized unit" "investigating gang related crimes and arresting gang members for various violations of the law," that he had been involved in "hundreds of gang related incidents, contacts, and or arrests" during his time on the force, and that he had "received specialized training in the field of gang related crimes" and training in "gang related shootings."

The second affidavit—expressly incorporated into the search warrant—explained why Messerschmidt believed there was sufficient probable cause to support the warrant. That affidavit described the facts of the incident involving Kelly and Bowen in great detail, including the weapon used in the assault. The affidavit recounted that Kelly had identified Bowen as the assailant and that she thought Bowen might be found at 2234 East 120th Street. It also reported that Messerschmidt had "conducted an extensive background search on the suspect by utilizing departmental records, state computer records, and other police agency records," and that from that information he had concluded that Bowen resided at 2234 East 120th Street.

The affidavit requested that the search warrant be endorsed for night service because "information provided by the victim and the cal-gang data base" indicated that Bowen had "gang ties to the Mona Park Crip gang" and that "night service would provide an added element of safety to the community as well as for the deputy personnel serving the warrant." The affidavit concluded by noting that Messerschmidt "believe[d] that the items sought" would be in Bowen's possession and that "recovery of the weapon could be invaluable in the successful prosecution of the suspect involved in this case, and the curtailment of further crimes being committed."

Messerschmidt submitted the warrants to his supervisors—Sergeant Lawrence and Lieutenant Ornales—for review. Deputy District Attorney Janet Wilson also reviewed the materials and initialed the search warrant, indicating that she agreed with Messerschmidt's assessment of probable cause. Finally, Messerschmidt submitted the warrants to a magistrate. The magistrate approved the warrants and authorized night service.

The search warrant was served two days later by a team of officers that included Messerschmidt and Lawrence. Sheriff's deputies forced open the front door of 2234 East 120th Street and encountered Augusta Millender— awoman in her seventies—and Millender's daughter and grandson. As instructed by the police, the Millenders went outside while the residence was secured but remained in the living room while the search was conducted. Bowen was not found in the residence. The search did, however, result in the seizure of Augusta Millender's shotgun, a California Social Services letter addressed to Bowen, and a box of .45-caliber ammunition.

Bowen was arrested two weeks later after Messerschmidt found him hiding under a bed in a motel room.

B

The Millenders filed suit in Federal District Court against the County of Los Angeles, the sheriff's department, the sheriff, and a number of individual officers, including Messerschmidt and Lawrence. The complaint alleged, as relevant here, that the search warrant was invalid under the Fourth Amendment. It sought damages from Messerschmidt and Lawrence, among others.

The parties filed cross motions for summary judgment on the validity of the search warrant. The District Court found the warrant defective in two respects. The District Court concluded that the warrant's authorization to search for firearms was unconstitutionally overbroad because the "crime specified here was a physical assault with a very specific weapon"—a black sawed-off shotgun with a pistol grip—negating any need to "search for all firearms". The court also found the warrant overbroad with respect to the search for gang-related materials, because there "was no evidence that the crime at issue was gang-related." As a result, the District Court granted summary judgment to the Millenders on their constitutional challenges to the firearm and gang material aspects of the search warrant. The District Court also rejected the officers' claim that they were entitled to qualified immunity from damages.

Messerschmidt and Lawrence appealed, and a divided panel of the Court of Appeals for the Ninth Circuit reversed the District Court's denial of qualified immunity. The court held that the officers were entitled to qualified immunity because "they reasonably relied on the approval of the warrant by a deputy district attorney and a judge."

The Court of Appeals granted rehearing en banc and affirmed the District Court's denial of qualified immunity. The en banc court concluded that the warrant's authorization was unconstitutionally overbroad because the affidavit and the warrant failed to "establish [ ] probable cause that the broad categories of firearms, firearm-related material, and gang-related material described in the warrant were contraband or evidence of a crime." In the en banc court's view, "the deputies had probable cause to search for a single, identified weapon. . . . They had no probable cause to search for the broad class of firearms and firearm-related materials described in the warrant." In addition, "[b]ecause the deputies failed to establish any link between gang-related materials and a crime, the warrant authorizing the search and seizure of all gang-related evidence [was] likewise invalid." Concluding that "a reasonable officer in the deputies' position would have been well aware of this deficiency," the en banc court held that the officers were not entitled to qualified immunity.

■ ■ ■

II

The Millenders allege that they were subjected to an unreasonable search in violation of the Fourth Amendment because the warrant authorizing the search of their home was not supported by probable cause. They seek damages from Messerschmidt and Lawrence for their roles in obtaining and executing this warrant. The validity of the warrant is not before us. The question instead is whether Messerschmidt and Lawrence are entitled to immunity from damages, even assuming that the warrant should not have been issued.

■ ■ ■

Where the alleged Fourth Amendment violation involves a search or seizure pursuant to a warrant, the fact that a neutral magistrate has issued a warrant is the clearest indication that the officers acted in an objectively reasonable manner or, as we have sometimes put it, in "objective good faith." *United States v. Leon* (1984). Nonetheless, under our precedents, the fact that a neutral magistrate has issued a warrant authorizing the allegedly unconstitutional search or seizure does not end the inquiry into objective reasonableness. Rather, we have recognized an exception allowing suit when "it is obvious that no reasonably competent officer would have concluded that a warrant should issue." The "shield of immunity" otherwise conferred by the warrant, will be lost, for example, where the warrant was "based on an affidavit so lacking in indicia of probable cause as to render official belief in its existence entirely unreasonable." *Leon.*

Our precedents make clear, however, that the threshold for establishing this exception is a high one, and it should be. As we explained in *Leon,* "[i]n the ordinary case, an officer cannot be expected to question the magistrate's probable-cause determination" because "[i]t is the magistrate's responsibility to determine whether the officer's allegations establish probable cause and, if so, to issue a warrant comporting in form with the requirements of the Fourth Amendment."

III

The Millenders contend, and the Court of Appeals held, that their case falls into this narrow exception. According to the Millenders, the officers "failed to provide *any* facts or circumstances from which a magistrate could properly conclude that there was probable cause to seize the broad classes of items being sought," and "[n]o reasonable officer would have presumed that such a warrant was valid." We disagree.

A

With respect to the warrant's authorization to search for and seize all firearms, the Millenders argue that "a reasonably well-trained officer would have readily perceived that there was no probable cause to search the house for *all* firearms and firearm-related items." Noting that "the affidavit indicated exactly what item was evidence of a crime—the 'black sawed off shotgun with a pistol grip,'" they argue that "[n]o facts established that Bowen possessed any other firearms, let alone that such firearms (if they existed) were 'contraband or evidence of a crime.'"

Even if the scope of the warrant were overbroad, in authorizing a search for all guns when there was information only about a specific one, that specific one was a sawed-off shotgun with a pistol grip, owned by a known gang member, who had just fired the weapon five times in public in an attempt to murder another person, on the asserted ground that she had "call[ed] the cops" on him. Under these circumstances—set forth in the warrant—it would not have been unreasonable for an officer to conclude that there was a "fair probability" that the sawed-off shotgun was not the only firearm Bowen owned. *Illinois v. Gates* (1983). And it certainly would have been reasonable for an officer to assume that Bowen's sawed-off shotgun was illegal. Evidence of one crime is not always evidence of several, but given Bowen's possession of one illegal gun, his gang membership, his willingness to use the gun to kill someone, and his concern about the police, a reasonable officer could conclude that there would be additional illegal guns among others that Bowen owned.

A reasonable officer also could believe that seizure of the firearms was necessary to prevent further assaults on Kelly. California law allows a magistrate to issue a search warrant for items "in the possession of any person with the intent to use them as a means of committing a public offense," and the warrant application submitted by the officers specifically referenced this provision as a basis for the search. Bowen had already attempted to murder Kelly once with a firearm, and had yelled "I'll kill you" as she tried to escape from him. A reasonable officer could conclude that Bowen would make another attempt on Kelly's life and that he possessed other firearms "with the intent to use them" to that end.

Given the foregoing, it would not have been "entirely unreasonable" for an officer to believe, in the particular circumstances of this case, that there was probable cause to search for all firearms and firearm-related materials.

■ ■ ■

It would therefore not have been unreasonable—based on the facts set out in the affidavit—for an officer to believe that evidence regarding Bowen's gang affiliation would prove helpful in prosecuting him for the attack on Kelly. Not only would such evidence help to establish motive, either apart from or in addition to any domestic dispute, it would also support the bringing of additional, related charges against Bowen for the assault.

In addition, a reasonable officer could believe that evidence demonstrating Bowen's membership in a gang might prove helpful in impeaching Bowen or rebutting various defenses he could raise at trial. For example, evidence that Bowen had ties to a gang that uses guns such as the one he used to assault Kelly would certainly be relevant to establish that he had familiarity with or access to this type of weapon.

■ ■ ■

Whatever the use to which evidence of Bowen's gang involvement might ultimately have been put, it would not have been "entirely unreasonable" for an officer to believe that the facts set out in the affidavit established a fair probability that such evidence would aid the prosecution of Bowen for the criminal acts at issue.

B

Whether any of these facts, standing alone or taken together, actually establish probable cause is a question we need not decide. Qualified immunity "gives government officials breathing room to make reasonable but mistaken judgments." The officers' judgment that the scope of the warrant was supported by probable cause may have been mistaken, but it was not "plainly incompetent."

On top of all this, the fact that the officers sought and obtained approval of the warrant application from a superior and a deputy district attorney before submitting it to the magistrate provides further support for the conclusion that an officer could reasonably have believed that the scope of the warrant was supported by probable cause. Before seeking to have the warrant issued by a magistrate, Messerschmidt conducted an extensive investigation into Bowen's background and the facts of the crime. Based on this investigation, Messerschmidt prepared a detailed warrant application that truthfully laid out the pertinent facts. The only facts omitted—the officers' knowledge of Bowen's arrest and conviction records, would only have strengthened the warrant. Messerschmidt then submitted the warrant application for review by Lawrence, another superior officer, and a deputy district attorney, all of whom approved the application without any apparent misgivings. Only after this did Messerschmidt seek the approval of a neutral magistrate, who issued the requested warrant. The officers thus "took every step that could reasonably be expected of them." *Massachusetts v. Sheppard* (1984). In light of the foregoing, it cannot be said that "no officer of reasonable competence would have requested the warrant." Indeed, a contrary conclusion would mean not only that Messerschmidt and Lawrence were "plainly incompetent," but that their supervisor, the deputy district attorney, and the magistrate were as well.

■ ■ ■

C

In holding that the warrant in this case was so obviously defective that no reasonable officer could have believed it was valid, the court below relied heavily on our decision in *Groh v. Ramirez* (2004), but that precedent is far afield. There, we held that officers who carried out a warrant-approved search were not entitled to qualified immunity because the warrant in question failed to describe the items to be seized *at all*. We explained that "[i]n the portion of the form that called for a description of the 'person or property' to be seized, [the applicant] typed a description of [the target's] two-story blue house rather than the alleged stockpile of firearms." . . .

This case is not remotely similar. In contrast to *Groh*, any defect here would not have been obvious from the face of the warrant. Rather, any arguable defect would have become apparent only upon a close parsing of the warrant application, and a comparison of the affidavit to the terms of the warrant to determine whether the affidavit established probable cause to search for all the items listed in the warrant. This is not an error that "just a simple glance" would have revealed. Indeed, unlike in *Groh*, the officers here did not merely submit their application to a magistrate. They also presented it for review by a superior officer, and a deputy district attorney, before submitting it to the magistrate. The fact that none of the officials who reviewed the application expressed concern about its validity demonstrates that any error was not obvious. *Groh* plainly does not control the result here.

The question in this case is not whether the magistrate erred in believing there was sufficient probable cause to support the scope of the warrant he issued. It is instead whether the magistrate so obviously erred that any reasonable officer would have recognized the error. The occasions on which this standard will be met may be rare, but so too are the circumstances in which it will be appropriate to impose personal liability on a lay officer in the face of judicial approval of his actions. Even if the warrant in this case were invalid, it was not so obviously lacking in probable cause that the officers can be considered "plainly incompetent" for concluding otherwise. The judgment of the Court of Appeals denying the officers qualified immunity must therefore be reversed.

It is so ordered.

Justice BREYER, concurring.

The Court concludes that the officers acted reasonably in searching the house for " 'all firearms and firearm-related items.' " In support of this conclusion, it cites two sets of circumstances. First, the majority points to "Bowen's possession of one illegal gun, his gang membership, his willingness to use the gun to kill someone, and his concern about the police. . . ." Second, the majority notes that "[a] reasonable officer also could believe that seizure of the firearms was necessary to prevent further assaults on Kelly," because "Bowen had already attempted to murder Kelly once with a firearm, and had yelled 'I'll kill you' as she tried to escape from him." In my view, given all these circumstances together, the officers could reasonably have believed that the scope of their search was supported by probable cause. On that basis, I concur.

Justice KAGAN, concurring in part and dissenting in part.

Both the Court and the dissent view this case as an all-or-nothing affair: The Court awards immunity across the board to Messerschmidt and his colleagues, while the dissent would grant them none at all. I think the right answer lies in between, although the Court makes the more far-reaching error.

I agree with the Court that a reasonably competent police officer could have thought this warrant valid in authorizing a search for all firearms and related items. The warrant application recounted that a known gang member had used a sawed-off shotgun—an illegal weapon under California law—to try to kill another person. Perhaps gang ties plus possession of an unlawful gun plus use of that gun to commit a violent assault do not add up to what was needed for this search: probable cause to believe that Bowen had additional illegal firearms (or legal firearms that he intended to use to violate the law) at the place he was staying. But because our and the Ninth Circuit's decisions leave that conclusion debatable, a reasonable police officer could have found the warrant adequately supported by "indicia of probable cause." So Messerschmidt and his fellow officers should receive qualified immunity for their search for firearms.

The Court, however, goes astray when it holds that a reasonable officer could have thought the warrant valid in approving a search for evidence of "street gang membership." Membership in even the worst gang does not violate California law, so the officers could not search for gang paraphernalia just to establish Bowen's ties to the Crips. Instead, the police needed probable cause to believe that such items would provide evidence of an actual crime—and as the Court acknowledges, the only crime mentioned in the warrant application was the assault on Kelly. The problem for the Court is that nothing in the application supports a link between Bowen's gang membership and that shooting. . . .

To fill this vacuum, the Court proposes an alternative, but similarly inadequate justification—that gang paraphernalia could have demonstrated Bowen's connection to the Millender residence and to any evidence of the assault found there. The dissent rightly notes one difficulty with this argument: The discovery of gang items would not have established that Bowen was staying at the house, given that several other gang members regularly did so. And even setting that issue aside, the Court's reasoning proves far too much: It would sanction equally well a search for *any* of Bowen's possessions on the premises—a result impossible to square with the Fourth Amendment. See, *e.g.*, *Andresen v. Maryland*, (1976) (disapproving " 'a general, exploratory rummaging in a person's belongings.' " In authorizing a search for all gang-related items, the warrant far outstripped the officers' probable cause. Because a reasonable officer would have recognized that defect, I would not award qualified immunity to Messerschmidt and his colleagues for this aspect of their search.

■ ■ ■

For these reasons, I would reverse in part and affirm in part the judgment of the Court of Appeals, and I would remand this case for further proceedings.

■ ■ ■

Justice SOTOMAYOR, with whom Justice GINSBURG joins, dissenting.

The fundamental purpose of the Fourth Amendment's warrant clause is "to protect against all general searches." The Fourth Amendment was adopted specifically in response to the Crown's practice of using general warrants and writs of assistance to search "suspected places" for evidence of smuggling, libel, or other crimes. Early patriots railed against these practices as "the worst instrument of arbitrary power" and John Adams later claimed that "the child Independence was born" from colonists' opposition to their use.

To prevent the issue of general warrants on "loose, vague or doubtful bases of fact," the Framers established the inviolable principle that should resolve this case: "no Warrants shall issue, but upon probable cause . . . and particularly describing the . . . things to be seized." U.S. Const., Amdt. 4. That is, the police must articulate an adequate reason to search for specific items related to specific crimes.

In this case, police officers investigating a specific, non-gang-related assault committed with a specific firearm (a sawed-off shotgun) obtained a warrant to search for all evidence related to "any Street Gang," "[a]ny photographs . . . which may depict evidence of criminal activity," and "any firearms." They did so for the asserted reason that the search might lead to evidence related to other gang members and other criminal activity, and that other "[v]alid warrants commonly allow police to search for 'firearms and ammunition.' " That kind of general warrant is antithetical to the Fourth Amendment.

The Court nonetheless concludes that the officers are entitled to qualified immunity because their conduct was "objectively reasonable." I could not disagree more. All 13 federal judges who previously considered this case had little difficulty concluding that the police officers' search for any gang-related material violated the Fourth Amendment. And a substantial majority agreed that the police's search for both gang-related material and all firearms not only violated the Fourth Amendment, but was objectively unreasonable. Like them, I believe that any "reasonably well-trained officer in petitioner's position would have known that his affidavit failed to establish probable cause." *Malley v. Briggs* (1986).

The Court also hints that a police officer's otherwise unreasonable conduct may be excused by the approval of a magistrate, or more disturbingly, another police officer. That is inconsistent with our focus on the objective reasonableness of an officer's decision to submit a warrant application to a magistrate, and we long ago rejected it.

The Court's analysis bears little relationship to the record in this case, our precedents, or the purposes underlying qualified immunity analysis. For all these reasons, I respectfully dissent.

I

The Court holds that a well-trained officer could have reasonably concluded that there was probable cause to search the Millenders' residence for any evidence of affiliation with "any Street Gang," and "all handguns, rifles, or shotguns of any caliber, or any firearms capable of firing ammunition. I cannot agree.

A

Most troubling is the Court's determination that petitioners reasonably could have concluded that they had probable cause to search for all evidence of any gang affiliation in the Millenders' home. The Court reaches this result only by way of an unprecedented, *post hoc* reconstruction of the crime that wholly ignores the police's own conclusions, as well as the undisputed facts presented to the District Court.

The Court primarily theorizes that "[a] reasonable officer could certainly view Bowen's attack as motivated not by the souring of his romantic relationship with Kelly but instead by a desire to prevent her from disclosing details of his gang activity to the police." The majority therefore dismisses as "misleading" the Millenders' characterization of the case as a "domestic dispute," insisting that Detective Messerschmidt could have reasonably thought that the crime was gang related.

The police flatly rejected that hypothesis, however, concluding that the crime was a domestic dispute that was not in any way gang related. Detective Messerschmidt's deposition is illustrative.

> "*Q*: So as far as you knew, it was just sort of a spousal-abuse-type case where the perpetrator happened to be in a gang, right?
> *A*: Correct.
> *Q*: So you didn't have any reason to believe that the assault on Kelly was any sort of gang crime, did you?
> *A*: No."

The "Crime Analysis" forms prepared by the police likewise identified Bowen as a "Mona Park Crip" gang member, but did not check off "gang-related" as a motive for the attack. And the District Court noted it was undisputed that Detective Messerschmidt "had no reason to believe Bowen's crime was a 'gang' crime."

The police's conclusions matched the victim's own account of the attack. Kelly asked police officers to help her move out because Bowen "ha[d] a domestic violence on his record," had "hit [her] once or twice" already, had repeatedly threatened her "You'll never leave me. I'll kill you if you leave me," and she was "planning on breaking up" with him. As Kelly described the confrontation, it was only after she fled to her car in order to leave that Bowen reemerged from their shared apartment with the shotgun and told her "I'm gonna kill your ass right here if you take off," consistent with his prior threats. Every piece of information, therefore, accorded with Detective Messerschmidt's conclusion: The crime was domestic violence that was not gang related.

Unlike the Members of this Court, Detective Messerschmidt alone had 14 years of experience as a peace officer, "hundreds of hours of instruction on the dynamics of gangs and gang trends," received "specialized training in the field of gang related crimes," and had been "involved in hundreds of gang related incidents, contacts, and or arrests." The Court provides no justification for sweeping aside the conclusions he reached on the basis of his far greater expertise, let alone the facts found by the District Court. We have repeatedly and recently warned appellate courts, "far removed from the scene," against second-guessing the judgments made by the police or reweighing the facts as they stood before the district court. The majority's decision today is totally inconsistent with those principles.

■ ■ ■

The Court offers two secondary explanations for why a search for gang-related items might have been justified, but they are equally unpersuasive. First, the majority suggests that such evidence hypothetically "might prove helpful in impeaching Bowen or rebutting various defenses he could raise at trial." That is a non-starter. The Fourth Amendment does not permit the police to search for evidence solely because it could be admissible for impeachment or rebuttal purposes. If it did, the police would be equally entitled to obtain warrants to rifle through the papers of anyone reasonably suspected of a crime for all evidence of his bad character, Fed. Rule Evid. 404(a)(2)(B)(i), or any evidence of any "crime, wrong, or other act" that might prove the defendant's "motive, opportunity, intent, preparation, plan, knowledge, identity, absence of mistake, or lack of accident," Fed. Rule Evid. 404(b)(2). Indeed, the majority's rationale presumably would authorize the police to search the residence of every member of Bowen's street gang for similar weapons—which likewise "might [have] prove[d] helpful in impeaching Bowen or rebutting various defenses he could raise at trial." It has long been the case, however, that such general searches, detached from probable cause, are impermissible.

■   ■   ■

Finally, the Court concludes that "even if this were merely a domestic dispute, a reasonable officer could still conclude that gang paraphernalia found at the Millenders' residence would aid in the prosecution of Bowen by, for example, demonstrating Bowen's connection to other [unspecified] evidence found there." That is difficult to understand. The police were well aware before obtaining a warrant that "other persons associated with the home, the Millender family members, were active Mona Park Crip gang members." Simply finding gang-related paraphernalia, therefore, would have done little to establish probable cause that particular evidence found in the home was connected to Bowen, rather than any of the several other active gang members who resided full time at the Millender home. Moreover, it would have done nothing to establish that Bowen had committed the non-gang-related crime specified in the warrant.

B

The Court also errs by concluding that petitioners could have reasonably concluded that they had probable cause to search for all firearms. Notably absent from the Court's discussion is any acknowledgment of the actual basis for petitioners' search. The police officers searched for all firearms not for the reasons hypothesized by the majority, but because they determined that "[v]alid warrants commonly allow police to search for 'firearms and ammunition,'" and that "[h]ere, any caliber of shotgun or receipts would show possession of and/or purchase of guns." . . . It bears repeating that the Founders adopted the Fourth Amendment to protect against searches for evidence of unspecified crimes. And merely possessing other firearms is not a crime at all.

By justifying the officers' actions on reasons of its own invention, the Court ignores the reasons the officers actually gave, as well as the facts upon which this case was decided below. The majority's analysis—akin to a rational-basis test—is thus far removed from what qualified immunity analysis demands. Even if the police had searched for the reasons the Court proposes, however, I still would find it inappropriate to afford them qualified immunity.

■   ■   ■

The majority has little difficulty concluding that because Bowen fired one firearm, it was reasonable for the police to conclude not only that Bowen must have possessed others, but that he must be storing these other weapons at his 73-year-old former foster mother's home. Again, however, this is not what the police actually concluded, as Detective Messerschmidt's deposition makes clear.

"Q: Did you have any reason to believe there would be any automatic weapons in the house?
A: No.

Q: Did you have any reason to believe there would be any hand guns in the house?

A: I wasn't given information that there were."

Undaunted, the majority finds that a well-trained officer could have concluded on this information that he had probable cause to search for "[a]ll hand guns, . . . [a]11 caliber of ammunition, miscellaneous gun parts, gun cleaning kits, holsters which could hold or have held any caliber handgun being sought," and "[a]ny receipts or paperwork, showing the purchase, ownership, or possession of the handguns being sought." That is puzzling. If any aspect of the Fourth Amendment is clearly established, it is that the police cannot reasonably search—even pursuant to a warrant—for items that they do not have "any reason to believe" will be present. The Court's conclusion to the contrary simply reads the "probable cause" requirement out of the Fourth Amendment.

■ ■ ■

II

The Court also finds error in the Court of Appeals' failure to find "pertinent" the fact that the officer sought approval of his warrant from a magistrate. Whether Detective Messerschmidt presented his warrant application to a magistrate surely would be "pertinent" to demonstrating his subjective good faith. But qualified immunity does not turn on whether an officer is motivated by good intentions or malice, but rather on the "objective reasonableness of an official's conduct."

The majority asserts, without citation, that the magistrate's approval is relevant to objective reasonableness. That view, however, is expressly contradicted by our holding in *Malley v. Briggs* [(1986)]. There, we found that a police officer is not "entitled to rely on the judgment of a judicial officer in finding that probable cause exists and hence issuing the warrant," and explained that "[that] view of objective reasonableness is at odds with our development of that. . . . The appropriate qualified immunity analysis, we held, was not whether an officer reasonably relied on a magistrate's probable cause determination, but rather "whether a reasonably well-trained officer in petitioner's position would have known that his affidavit failed to establish probable cause and that he should not have *applied* for the warrant." (emphasis added). In such a case, "the officer's application for a warrant [would] not [be] objectively reasonable, because it create[s] the unnecessary danger of an unlawful arrest." When "no officer of reasonable competence would have requested the warrant," a "magistrate [who] issues the warrant [makes] not just a reasonable mistake, but an unacceptable error indicating gross incompetence or neglect of duty." In such cases, "[t]he officer . . . cannot excuse his own default by pointing to the greater incompetence of the magistrate."

In cases in which it would be not only wrong but unreasonable for any well-trained officer to seek a warrant, allowing a magistrate's approval to immunize the police officer's unreasonable action retrospectively makes little sense. By motivating an officer "to reflect, before submitting a request for a warrant, upon whether he has a reasonable basis for believing that his affidavit establishes probable cause," we recognized that our qualified immunity precedents had the "desirable" effect of "reduc[ing] the likelihood that the officer's request for a warrant will be premature," leading to "a waste of judicial resources" or "premature arrests" To the extent it proposes to cut back upon *Malley*, the majority will promote the opposite result-encouraging sloppy police work and exacerbating the risk that searches will not comport with the requirements of the Fourth Amendment.

The Court also makes much of the fact that Detective Messerschmidt sent his proposed warrant application to two superior police officers and a district attorney for review. Giving weight to that fact would turn the Fourth Amendment on its head. This Court made clear in *Malley* that a police officer acting unreasonably cannot obtain qualified immunity on the basis of a neutral magistrate's approval. It would be passing strange, therefore, to immunize an officer's conduct instead based upon the approval of other police officers and prosecutors. . . .

III

Police officers perform a difficult and essential service to society, frequently at substantial risk to their personal safety. And criminals like Bowen are not sympathetic figures. But the Fourth Amendment "protects all, those suspected or known to be offenders as well as the innocent." *Go-Bart Importing Co. [v. United States* (1931)]. And this Court long ago recognized that efforts "to bring the guilty to punishment, praiseworthy as they are, are not to be aided by the sacrifice of those great principles established by years of endeavor and suffering which have resulted in their embodiment in the fundamental law of the land." *Weeks v. United States* (1914).

Qualified immunity properly affords police officers protection so long as their conduct is objectively reasonable. But it is not objectively reasonable for police investigating a specific, non-gang-related assault committed with a particular firearm to search for all evidence related to "any Street Gang," "photographs . . . which may depict evidence of criminal activity," and all firearms. The Court reaches a contrary result not because it thinks that these police officers' stated reasons for searching were objectively reasonable, but because it thinks different conclusions might be drawn from the crime scene that reasonably might have led different officers to search for different reasons. That analysis, however, is far removed from qualified immunity's proper focus on whether *petitioners* acted in an objectively reasonable manner.

Because petitioners did not, I would affirm the judgment of the Court of Appeals.

United States v. Banks

540 U.S. 31 (2003)

Justice SOUTER delivered the opinion of the unanimous Court.

Officers executing a warrant to search for cocaine in respondent Banks's apartment knocked and announced their authority. The question is whether their 15-to-20-second wait before a forcible entry satisfied the Fourth Amendment.... We hold that it did.

With information that Banks was selling cocaine at home, North Las Vegas Police Department officers and Federal Bureau of Investigation agents got a warrant to search his two-bedroom apartment. As soon as they arrived there, about 2 o'clock on a Wednesday afternoon, officers posted in front called out "police search warrant" and rapped hard enough on the door to be heard by officers at the back door. Brief for United States 3 (internal quotation marks omitted). There was no indication whether anyone was home, and after waiting for 15 to 20 seconds with no answer, the officers broke open the front door with a battering ram. Banks was in the shower and testified that he heard nothing until the crash of the door, which brought him out dripping to confront the police. The search produced weapons, crack cocaine, and other evidence of drug dealing.

In response to drug and firearms charges, Banks moved to suppress evidence, arguing that the officers executing the search warrant waited an unreasonably short time before forcing entry, and so violated ... the Fourth Amendment.... The District Court denied the motion, and Banks pleaded guilty, reserving his right to challenge the search on appeal.

A divided panel of the Ninth Circuit reversed and ordered suppression of the evidence found. In assessing the reasonableness of the execution of the warrant, the panel majority set out a nonexhaustive list of "factors that an officer reasonably should consider" in deciding when to enter premises identified in a warrant, after knocking and announcing their presence but receiving no express acknowledgment:

> "(a) size of the residence; (b) location of the residence; (c) location of the officers in relation to the main living or sleeping areas of the residence; (d) time of day; (e) nature of the suspected offense; (f) evidence demonstrating the suspect's guilt; (g) suspect's prior convictions and, if any, the type of offense for which he was convicted; and (h) any other observations triggering the senses of the officers that reasonably would lead one to believe that immediate entry was necessary."

The majority also defined four categories of intrusion after knock and announcement, saying that the classification "aids in the resolution of the essential question whether the entry made herein was reasonable under the circumstances":

> "(1) entries in which exigent circumstances exist and non-forcible entry is possible, permitting entry to be made simultaneously with or shortly after

announcement; (2) entries in which exigent circumstances exist and forced entry by destruction of property is required, necessitating more specific inferences of exigency; (3) entries in which no exigent circumstances exist and non-forcible entry is possible, requiring an explicit refusal of admittance or a lapse of a significant amount of time; and (4) entries in which no exigent circumstances exist and forced entry by destruction of property is required, mandating an explicit refusal of admittance or a lapse of an even more substantial amount of time." . . .

We granted certiorari to consider how to go about applying the standard of reasonableness to the length of time police with a warrant must wait before entering without permission after knocking and announcing their intent in a felony case. We now reverse.

■ ■ ■

There has never been a dispute that these officers were obliged to knock and announce their intentions when executing the search warrant, an obligation they concededly honored. Despite this agreement, we start with a word about standards for requiring or dispensing with a knock and announcement, since the same criteria bear on when the officers could legitimately enter after knocking.

The Fourth Amendment says nothing specific about formalities in exercising a warrant's authorization, speaking to the manner of searching as well as to the legitimacy of searching at all simply in terms of the right to be "secure . . . against unreasonable searches and seizures." Although the notion of reasonable execution must therefore be fleshed out, we have done that case by case, largely avoiding categories and protocols for searches. Instead, we have treated reasonableness as a function of the facts of cases so various that no template is likely to produce sounder results than examining the totality of circumstances in a given case; it is too hard to invent categories without giving short shrift to details that turn out to be important in a given instance, and without inflating marginal ones.

■ ■ ■

In *Wilson v. Arkansas* (1995), we held that the common law knock-and-announce principle is one focus of the reasonableness enquiry; and we subsequently decided that although the standard generally requires the police to announce their intent to search before entering closed premises, the obligation gives way when officers "have a reasonable suspicion that knocking and announcing their presence, under the particular circumstances, would be dangerous or futile, or . . . would inhibit the effective investigation of the crime by, for example, allowing the destruction of evidence," *Richards v. Wisconsin* (1997). When a warrant applicant gives reasonable grounds to expect futility or to suspect that one or another such exigency already exists or will arise instantly upon knocking, a magistrate judge is acting within the Constitution to authorize a "no-knock" entry. And even when executing a warrant silent about that, if circumstances support a reasonable suspicion of exigency when the officers arrive at the door, they may go straight in.

Since most people keep their doors locked, entering without knocking will normally do some damage, a circumstance too common to require a heightened justification when a reasonable suspicion of exigency already justifies an unwarned entry. We have accordingly held that police in exigent circumstances may damage premises so far as necessary for a no-knock entrance without demonstrating the suspected risk in any more detail than the law demands for an unannounced intrusion simply by lifting the latch. Either way, it is enough that the officers had a reasonable suspicion of exigent circumstances.

■ ■ ■

Banks does not, of course, deny that exigency may develop in the period beginning when officers with a warrant knock to be admitted, and the issue comes down to whether it was reasonable to suspect imminent loss of evidence after the 15 to 20 seconds the officers waited prior to forcing their way. Though we agree with Judge Fisher's dissenting opinion that this call is a close one, we think that after 15 or 20 seconds without a response, police could fairly suspect that cocaine would be gone if they were reticent any longer. Courts of Appeals have, indeed, routinely held similar wait times to be reasonable in drug cases with similar facts including easily disposable evidence (and some courts have found even shorter ones to be reasonable enough).

A look at Banks's counterarguments shows why these courts reached sensible results, for each of his reasons for saying that 15 to 20 seconds was too brief rests on a mistake about the relevant enquiry: the fact that he was actually in the shower and did not hear the officers is not to the point, and the same is true of the claim that it might have taken him longer than 20 seconds if he had heard the knock and headed straight for the door. As for the shower, it is enough to say that the facts known to the police are what count in judging reasonable waiting time, cf., *e.g.*, *Graham v. Connor* (1989) ("The 'reasonableness' of a particular use of force must be judged from the perspective of a reasonable officer on the scene, rather than with the 20/20 vision of hindsight"), and there is no indication that the police knew that Banks was in the shower and thus unaware of an impending search that he would otherwise have tried to frustrate.

And the argument that 15 to 20 seconds was too short for Banks to have come to the door ignores the very risk that justified prompt entry. True, if the officers were to justify their timing here by claiming that Banks's failure to admit them fairly suggested a refusal to let them in, Banks could at least argue that no such suspicion can arise until an occupant has had time to get to the door, a time that will vary with the size of the establishment, perhaps five seconds to open a motel room door, or several minutes to move through a townhouse. In this case, however, the police claim exigent need to enter, and the crucial fact in examining their actions is not time to reach the door but the particular exigency claimed. On the record here, what matters is the opportunity to get rid of cocaine, which a prudent dealer will keep near a commode or kitchen sink. The significant circumstances include the arrival of the police during the day, when anyone inside would probably have been up and around, and the sufficiency of 15 to 20 seconds for getting to the bathroom or the kitchen to start flushing cocaine down the drain. That is, when circumstances are exigent because a pusher may be near the point of putting his drugs beyond reach, it is imminent disposal, not travel time to the entrance, that governs when the police may reasonably enter; since the bathroom and kitchen are usually in the interior of a dwelling, not the front hall, there is no reason generally to peg the travel time to the location of the door, and no reliable basis for giving the proprietor of a mansion a longer wait than the resident of a bungalow, or an apartment like Banks's. And 15 to 20 seconds does not seem an unrealistic guess about the time someone would need to get in a position to rid his quarters of cocaine.

■ ■ ■

Our emphasis on totality analysis necessarily rejects positions taken on each side of this case. . . . One point in making an officer knock and announce, then, is to give a person inside the chance to save his door. That is why, in the case with no reason to suspect an immediate risk of frustration or futility in waiting at all, the reasonable wait time may well be longer when police make a forced entry, since they ought to be more certain the occupant has had time to answer the door. It is hard to be more definite than that, without turning the notion of a reasonable time under all the circumstances into a set of sub-rules as the Ninth Circuit has been inclined to do. Suffice it to say that the need to damage property in the course of getting in is a good reason to require more patience than it would be reasonable to expect if the door were open. Police seeking a stolen piano may be able to spend more time to make sure they really need the battering ram.

On the other side, we disapprove of the Court of Appeals's four-part scheme for vetting knock-and-announce entries. To begin with, the demand for enhanced evidence of exigency before a door can reasonably be damaged by a warranted no-knock intrusion was already bad law before the Court of Appeals decided this case.

■ ■ ■

The judgment of the Court of Appeals is reversed.
So ordered.

Illinois v. McArthur

531 U.S. 326 (2001)

BREYER, J., delivered the opinion of the Court, in which REHNQUIST, C.J., KENNEDY, THOMAS, GINSBURG, SCALIA, and O'CONNOR, JJ., joined. SOUTER, J., filed a concurring opinion. STEVENS, J., filed a dissenting opinion.

Police officers, with probable cause to believe that a man had hidden marijuana in his home, prevented that man from entering the home for about two hours while they obtained a search warrant. We must decide whether those officers violated the Fourth Amendment. We conclude that the officers acted reasonably. They did not violate the Amendment's requirements. And we reverse an Illinois court's holding to the contrary.

■ ■ ■

On April 2, 1997, Tera McArthur asked two police officers to accompany her to the trailer where she lived with her husband, Charles, so that they could keep the peace while she removed her belongings. The two officers, Assistant Chief John Love and Officer Richard Skidis, arrived with Tera at the trailer at about 3:15 p.m. Tera went inside, where Charles was present. The officers remained outside.

When Tera emerged after collecting her possessions, she spoke to Chief Love, who was then on the porch. She suggested he check the trailer because "Chuck had dope in there." She added (in Love's words) that she had seen Chuck "slid[e] some dope underneath the couch."

Love knocked on the trailer door, told Charles what Tera had said, and asked for permission to search the trailer, which Charles denied. Love then sent Officer Skidis with Tera to get a search warrant.

Love told Charles, who by this time was also on the porch, that he could not reenter the trailer unless a police officer accompanied him. Charles subsequently reentered the trailer two or three times (to get cigarettes and to make phone calls), and each time Love stood just inside the door to observe what Charles did.

Officer Skidis obtained the warrant by about 5 p.m. He returned to the trailer and, along with other officers, searched it. The officers found under the sofa a marijuana pipe, a box for marijuana (called a "one-hitter" box), and a small amount of marijuana. They then arrested Charles.

■ ■ ■

The Fourth Amendment says that the "right of the people to be secure in their persons, houses, papers, and effects, against unreasonable searches and seizures, shall not be violated." Its "central requirement" is one of reasonableness. In order to enforce that requirement, this Court has interpreted the Amendment as establishing rules and presumptions designed to control conduct of law enforcement officers that may significantly intrude upon privacy interests. Sometimes those rules require warrants. We have said, for example, that in "the ordinary case," seizures of personal property are "unreasonable within the meaning of the Fourth Amendment," without more, "unless... accomplished pursuant to a judicial warrant," issued by a neutral magistrate after finding probable cause.

We nonetheless have made it clear that there are exceptions to the warrant requirement. When faced with special law enforcement needs, diminished expectations of privacy, minimal intrusions, or the like, the Court has found that certain general, or individual, circumstances may render a warrantless search or seizure reasonable.

■ ■ ■

In the circumstances of the case before us, we cannot say that the warrantless seizure was *per se* unreasonable. It involves a plausible claim of specially pressing or urgent law enforcement need, *i.e.*, "exigent circumstances." . . . Moreover, the restraint at issue was tailored to that need, being limited in time and scope, cf. *Terry v. Ohio* (1968), and avoiding significant intrusion into the home itself, cf. *Payton v. New York* (1980) ('[T]he chief evil against which the . . . Fourth Amendment is directed' is warrantless entry and search of home).

■ ■ ■

We conclude that the restriction at issue was reasonable, and hence lawful, in light of the following circumstances, which we consider in combination. First, the police had probable cause to believe that McArthur's trailer home contained evidence of a crime and contraband, namely, unlawful drugs. The police had had an opportunity to speak with Tera McArthur and make at least a very rough assessment of her reliability. They knew she had had a firsthand opportunity to observe her husband's behavior, in particular with respect to the drugs at issue. And they thought, with good reason, that her report to them reflected that opportunity.

Second, the police had good reason to fear that, unless restrained, McArthur would destroy the drugs before they could return with a warrant. They reasonably might have thought that McArthur realized that his wife knew about his marijuana stash; observed that she was angry or frightened enough to ask the police to accompany her; saw that after leaving the trailer she had spoken with the police; and noticed that she had walked off with one policeman while leaving the other outside to observe the trailer. They reasonably could have concluded that McArthur, consequently suspecting an imminent search, would, if given the chance, get rid of the drugs fast.

Third, the police made reasonable efforts to reconcile their law enforcement needs with the demands of personal privacy. They neither searched the trailer nor arrested McArthur before obtaining a warrant. Rather, they imposed a significantly less restrictive restraint, preventing McArthur only from entering the trailer unaccompanied. They left his home and his belongings intact—until a neutral Magistrate, finding probable cause, issued a warrant.

Fourth, the police imposed the restraint for a limited period of time, namely, two hours. As far as the record reveals, this time period was no longer than reasonably necessary for the police, acting with diligence, to obtain the warrant.

■ ■ ■

In sum, the police officers in this case had probable cause to believe that a home contained contraband, which was evidence of a crime. They reasonably believed that the home's resident, if left free of any restraint, would destroy that evidence. And they imposed a restraint that was both limited and tailored reasonably to secure law enforcement needs while protecting privacy interests. In our view, the restraint met the Fourth Amendment's demands.

The judgment of the Illinois Appellate Court is reversed, and the case is remanded for further proceedings not inconsistent with this opinion.

It is so ordered.

Hudson v. Michigan

547 U.S. 586 (2006)

See also Chapter 1.F.

SCALIA, J., delivered the opinion of the Court with respect to Parts I, II, and III, in which ROBERTS, C.J., and KENNEDY, THOMAS, and ALITO, JJ., joined, and an opinion with respect to Part IV, in which ROBERTS, C.J., and THOMAS and ALITO, JJ., joined. KENNEDY, J., filed an opinion concurring in part and concurring in the judgment. BREYER, J., filed a dissenting opinion, in which STEVENS, SOUTER, and GINSBURG, JJ., joined.

We decide whether violation of the "knock-and-announce" rule requires the suppression of all evidence found in the search.

I

Police obtained a warrant authorizing a search for drugs and firearms at the home of petitioner Booker Hudson. They discovered both. Large quantities of drugs were found, including cocaine rocks in Hudson's pocket. A loaded gun was lodged between the cushion and armrest of the chair in which he was sitting. Hudson was charged under Michigan law with unlawful drug and firearm possession.

This case is before us only because of the method of entry into the house. When the police arrived to execute the warrant, they announced their presence, but waited only a short time—perhaps "three to five seconds," App. 15—before turning the knob of the unlocked front door and entering Hudson's home. Hudson moved to suppress all the inculpatory evidence, arguing that the premature entry violated his Fourth Amendment rights.

The Michigan trial court granted his motion. On interlocutory review, the Michigan Court of Appeals reversed, relying on Michigan Supreme Court cases holding that suppression is inappropriate when entry is made pursuant to warrant but without proper " 'knock and announce.' " . . . He renewed his Fourth Amendment claim on appeal, but the Court of Appeals rejected it and affirmed the conviction. The Michigan Supreme Court again declined review. We granted certiorari.

II

The common-law principle that law enforcement officers must announce their presence and provide residents an opportunity to open the door is an ancient one. See *Wilson v. Arkansas* (1995). . . .

We recognized that the new constitutional rule we had announced is not easily applied. *Wilson* and cases following it have noted the many situations in which it is not necessary to knock and announce. It is not necessary when "circumstances presen[t] a threat of physical violence," or if there is "reason to believe that evidence would likely be destroyed if advance notice were given."

When the knock-and-announce rule does apply, it is not easy to determine precisely what officers must do. How many seconds' wait are too few? Our "reasonable wait time" standard, see *United States v. Banks* (2003), is necessarily vague. *Banks* (a drug case, like this one) held that the proper measure was not how long it would take the resident to reach the door, but how long it would take to dispose of the suspected drugs—but that such a time (15 to 20 seconds in that case) would necessarily be extended when, for instance, the suspected contraband was not easily concealed. If our *ex post* evaluation is subject to such calculations, it is unsurprising that, *ex ante*, police officers about to encounter someone who may try to harm them will be uncertain how long to wait.

Happily, these issues do not confront us here. From the trial level onward, Michigan has conceded that the entry was a knock-and-announce violation. The issue here is remedy. *Wilson* specifically declined to decide whether the exclusionary rule is appropriate for violation of the knock-and-announce requirement. That question is squarely before us now.

III

A

In *Weeks v. United States* (1914), we adopted the federal exclusionary rule for evidence that was unlawfully seized from a home without a warrant in violation of the Fourth Amendment. We began applying the same rule to the States, through the Fourteenth Amendment, in *Mapp v. Ohio* (1961).

Suppression of evidence, however, has always been our last resort, not our first impulse. The exclusionary rule generates "substantial social costs," *United States v. Leon* (1984), which sometimes include setting the guilty free and the dangerous at large. We have therefore been "cautio[us] against expanding" it, *Colorado v. Connelly* (1986), and "have repeatedly emphasized that the rule's 'costly toll' upon truth-seeking and law enforcement objectives presents a high obstacle for those urging [its] application," *Pennsylvania Bd. of Probation and Parole v. Scott* (1998). We have rejected "[i]ndiscriminate application" of the rule, *Leon*, and have held it to be applicable only "where its remedial objectives are thought most efficaciously served," *United States v. Calandra* (1974)—that is, "where its deterrence benefits outweigh its 'substantial social costs.'"...

We did not always speak so guardedly. Expansive dicta in *Mapp*, for example, suggested wide scope for the exclusionary rule...("[A]ll evidence obtained by searches and seizures in violation of the Constitution is, by that same authority, inadmissible in a state court"). *Whiteley v. Warden, Wyo. State Penitentiary* (1971) was to the same effect. But we have long since rejected that approach. As explained in *Arizona v. Evans* (1995): "In *Whiteley*, the Court treated identification of a Fourth Amendment violation as synonymous with application of the exclusionary rule to evidence secured incident to that violation. Subsequent case law has rejected this reflexive application of the exclusionary rule." (Citation omitted.) We had said as much in *Leon*, a decade earlier, when we explained that "[w]hether the exclusionary sanction is appropriately imposed in a particular case . . . is 'an issue separate from the question whether the Fourth Amendment rights of the party seeking to invoke the rule were violated by police conduct.' "

In other words, exclusion may not be premised on the mere fact that a constitutional violation was a "but-for" cause of obtaining evidence. Our cases show that but-for causality is only a necessary, not a sufficient, condition for suppression. In this case, of course, the constitutional violation of an illegal *manner* of entry was *not* a but-for cause of obtaining the evidence. Whether that preliminary misstep had occurred *or not*, the police would have executed the warrant they had obtained, and would have discovered the gun and drugs inside the house. But even if the illegal entry here could be characterized as a but-for cause of discovering what was inside, we have "never held that evidence is 'fruit of the poisonous tree' simply because 'it would not have come to light but for the illegal actions of the police.' " *Segura v. United States* (1984).

■ ■ ■

Attenuation can occur, of course, when the causal connection is remote. See . . . *Nardone v. United States* (1939). Attenuation also occurs when, even given a direct causal connection, the interest protected by the constitutional guarantee that has been violated would not be served by suppression of the evidence obtained. "The penalties visited upon the Government, and in turn upon the public, because its officers have violated the law must bear some relation to the purposes which the law is to serve." Thus, in *New York v. Harris* (1990), where an illegal warrantless arrest was made in Harris' house, we held that

> "suppressing [Harris'] statement taken outside the house would not serve the purpose of the rule that made Harris' in-house arrest illegal. The warrant requirement for an arrest in the home is imposed to protect the home, and anything incriminating the police gathered from arresting Harris in his home, rather than elsewhere, has been excluded, as it should have been; the purpose of the rule has thereby been vindicated."

For this reason, cases excluding the fruits of unlawful warrantless searches . . . say nothing about the appropriateness of exclusion to vindicate the interests protected by the knock-and-announce requirement. . . . Exclusion of the evidence obtained by a warrantless search vindicates that entitlement. The interests protected by the knock-and-announce requirement are quite different—and do not include the shielding of potential evidence from the government's eyes.

One of those interests is the protection of human life and limb, because an unannounced entry may provoke violence in supposed self-defense by the surprised resident. Another interest is the protection of property. Breaking a house (as the old cases typically put it) absent an announcement would penalize someone who " 'did not know of the process, of which, if he had notice, it is to be presumed that he would obey it. . . .' *Wilson*." . . . And thirdly, the knock-and-announce rule protects those elements of privacy and dignity that can be destroyed by a sudden entrance. It gives residents the "opportunity to prepare themselves for" the entry of the police. *Richards v. Wisconsin* [(1997)].

■ ■ ■

What the knock-and-announce rule has never protected, however, is one's interest in preventing the government from seeing or taking evidence described in a warrant. Since the interests that *were* violated in this case have nothing to do with the seizure of the evidence, the exclusionary rule is inapplicable.

■ ■ ■

Quite apart from the requirement of unattenuated causation, the exclusionary rule has never been applied except "where its deterrence benefits outweigh its 'substantial social costs.'" The costs here are considerable. In addition to the grave adverse consequence that exclusion of relevant incriminating evidence always entails (viz., the risk of releasing dangerous criminals into society), imposing that massive remedy for a knock-and-announce violation would generate a constant flood of alleged failures to observe the rule, and claims that any asserted *Richards* justification for a no-knock entry . . . had inadequate support. The cost of entering this lottery would be small, but the jackpot enormous: suppression of all evidence, amounting in many cases to a get-out-of-jail-free card. Courts would experience as never before the reality that "[t]he exclusionary rule frequently requires extensive litigation to determine whether particular evidence must be excluded." Unlike the warrant or *Miranda* requirements, compliance with which is readily determined (either there was or was not a warrant; either the *Miranda* warning was given, or it was not), what constituted a "reasonable wait time" in a particular case . . . (or, for that matter, how many seconds the police in fact waited), or whether there was "reasonable suspicion" of the sort that would invoke the *Richards* exceptions, is difficult for the trial court to determine and even more difficult for an appellate court to review.

Another consequence of the incongruent remedy Hudson proposes would be police officers' refraining from timely entry after knocking and announcing. As we have observed, the amount of time they must wait is necessarily uncertain. If the consequences of running afoul of the rule were so massive, officers would be inclined to wait longer than the law requires—producing preventable violence against officers in some cases, and the destruction of evidence in many others. We deemed these consequences severe enough to produce our unanimous agreement that a mere "reasonable suspicion" that knocking and announcing "under the particular circumstances, would be dangerous or futile, or that it would inhibit the effective investigation of the crime," will cause the requirement to yield.

Next to these "substantial social costs" we must consider the deterrence benefits, existence of which is a necessary condition for exclusion. (It is not, of course, a sufficient condition: "[I]t does not follow that the Fourth Amendment requires adoption of every proposal that might deter police misconduct." *Calandra*.) To begin with, the value of deterrence depends upon the strength of the incentive to commit the forbidden act. Viewed from this perspective, deterrence of knock-and-announce violations is not worth a lot. Violation of the warrant requirement sometimes produces incriminating evidence that could not otherwise be obtained. But ignoring knock-and-announce can realistically be expected to achieve absolutely nothing except the prevention of destruction of evidence and the avoidance of life-threatening resistance by occupants of the premises—dangers which, if there is even "reasonable suspicion" of their existence, *suspend the knock-and-announce requirement anyway.* Massive deterrence is hardly required.

It seems to us not even true, as Hudson contends, that without suppression there will be no deterrence of knock-and-announce violations at all. Of course even if this assertion were accurate, it would not necessarily justify suppression. Assuming (as the assertion must) that civil suit is not an effective deterrent, one can think of many forms of police misconduct that are similarly "undeterred." When, for example, a confessed suspect in the killing of a police officer, arrested (along with incriminating evidence) in a lawful warranted search, is subjected to physical abuse at the station house, would it seriously be suggested that the evidence must be excluded, since that is the only "effective deterrent"? And what, other than civil suit, is the "effective deterrent" of police violation of an already-confessed suspect's Sixth Amendment rights by denying him prompt access to counsel? Many would regard these violated rights as more significant than the right not to be intruded upon in one's nightclothes—and yet nothing but "ineffective" civil suit is available as a deterrent. And the police incentive for those violations is arguably greater than the incentive for disregarding the knock-and-announce rule.

We cannot assume that exclusion in this context is necessary deterrence simply because we found that it was necessary deterrence in different contexts and long ago. That would be forcing the public today to pay for the sins and inadequacies of a legal regime that existed almost half a century ago. Dollree Mapp could not turn to 42 U.S.C. § 1983 for meaningful relief; *Monroe v. Pape* (1961), which began the slow but steady expansion of that remedy, was decided the same Term as *Mapp*. It would be another 17 years before the § 1983 remedy was extended to reach the deep pocket of municipalities, *Monell v. New York City Dept. of Social Servs* (1978). Citizens whose Fourth Amendment rights were violated by federal officers could not bring suit until 10 years after *Mapp*, with this Court's decision in *Bivens v. Six Unknown Fed. Narcotics Agents* (1971).

Hudson complains that "it would be very hard to find a lawyer to take a case such as this." . . . Since some civil-rights violations would yield damages too small to justify the expense of litigation, Congress has authorized attorney's fees for civil-rights plaintiffs. This remedy was unavailable in the heydays of our exclusionary-rule jurisprudence, because it is tied to the availability of a cause of action. For years after *Mapp*, "very few lawyers would even consider representation of persons who had civil rights claims against the police," but now "much has changed. Citizens and lawyers are much more willing to seek relief in the courts for police misconduct." The number of public-interest law firms and lawyers who specialize in civil-rights grievances has greatly expanded.

Hudson points out that few published decisions to date announce huge awards for knock-and-announce violations. But this is an unhelpful statistic. Even if we thought that only large damages would deter police misconduct (and that police somehow are deterred by "damages" but indifferent to the prospect of large § 1988 attorney's fees), we do not know how many claims have been settled, or indeed how many violations have occurred that produced anything more than nominal injury. It is clear, at least, that the lower courts are allowing colorable knock-and-announce suits to go forward, unimpeded by assertions of qualified immunity.

■ ■ ■

Another development over the past half-century that deters civil-rights violations is the increasing professionalism of police forces, including a new emphasis on internal police discipline. Even as long ago as 1980 we felt it proper to "assume" that unlawful police behavior would "be dealt with appropriately" by the authorities, *United States v. Payner* (1980), but we now have increasing evidence that police forces across the United States take the constitutional rights of citizens seriously. . . .

In sum, the social costs of applying the exclusionary rule to knock-and-announce violations are considerable; the incentive to such violations is minimal to begin with, and the extant deterrences against them are substantial—incomparably greater than the factors deterring warrantless entries when *Mapp* was decided. Resort to the massive remedy of suppressing evidence of guilt is unjustified.

IV

A trio of cases—*Segura v. United States* (1984); *New York v. Harris*; and *United States v. Ramirez* (1998)—confirms our conclusion that suppression is unwarranted in this case.

Like today's case, *Segura* involved a concededly illegal entry. Police conducting a drug crime investigation waited for Segura outside an apartment building; when he arrived, he denied living there. The police arrested him and brought him to the apartment where they suspected illegal activity. An officer knocked. When someone inside opened the door, the police entered, taking Segura with them. They had neither a warrant nor consent to enter, and they did not announce themselves as police—an entry as illegal as can be. Officers then stayed in the apartment for *19 hours* awaiting a search warrant. Once alerted that the search warrant had been obtained, the police—still inside, having secured the premises so that no evidence could be removed—conducted a search. We refused to exclude the resulting evidence. We recognized that only the evidence gained from the particular violation could be excluded, and therefore distinguished the effects of the illegal entry from the effects of the legal search: "None of the information on which the warrant was secured was derived from or related in any way to the initial entry into petitioners' apartment. . . ." It was therefore "beyond dispute that the information possessed by the agents before they entered the apartment constituted an independent source for the discovery and seizure of the evidence now challenged."

If the search in *Segura* could be "wholly unrelated to the prior entry," when the only entry was warrantless, it would be bizarre to treat more harshly the actions in this case, where the only entry was *with* a warrant. If the probable cause backing a warrant that was issued *later in time* could be an "independent source" for a search that proceeded after the officers illegally entered and waited, a search warrant obtained *before* going in must have at least this much effect.

In the second case, *Harris*, the police violated the defendant's Fourth Amendment rights by arresting him at home without a warrant, contrary to *Payton v. New York* (1980). Once taken to the station house, he gave an incriminating statement. We refused to exclude it. Like the illegal entry which led to discovery of the evidence in today's case, the illegal arrest in *Harris* began a process that culminated in acquisition of the evidence sought to be excluded. While Harris's statement was "the product of an arrest and being in custody," it "was not the fruit of the fact that the arrest was made in the house rather than someplace else." Likewise here: While acquisition of the gun and drugs was the product of a search pursuant to warrant, it was not the fruit of the fact that the entry was not preceded by knock and announce.

■ ■ ■

It is so ordered.

Justice KENNEDY, concurring in part and concurring in the judgment.

Two points should be underscored with respect to today's decision. First, the knock-and-announce requirement protects rights and expectations linked to ancient principles in our constitutional order. See *Wilson v. Arkansas*. The Court's decision should not be interpreted as suggesting that violations of the requirement are trivial or beyond the law's concern. Second, the continued operation of the exclusionary rule, as settled and defined by our precedents, is not in doubt. Today's decision determines only that in the specific context of the knock-and-announce requirement, a violation is not sufficiently related to the later discovery of evidence to justify suppression.

As to the basic right in question, privacy and security in the home are central to the Fourth Amendment's guarantees as explained in our decisions and as understood since the beginnings of the Republic. This common understanding ensures respect for the law and allegiance to our institutions, and it is an instrument for transmitting our Constitution to later generations undiminished in meaning and force. It bears repeating that it is a serious matter if law enforcement officers violate the sanctity of the home by ignoring the requisites of lawful entry. Security must not be subject to erosion by indifference or contempt.

Our system, as the Court explains, has developed procedures for training police officers and imposing discipline for failures to act competently and lawfully. If those measures prove ineffective, they can be fortified with more detailed regulations or legislation. Supplementing these safeguards are civil remedies, such as those available under 42 U.S.C. § 1983, that provide restitution for discrete harms. These remedies apply to all violations, including, of course, exceptional cases in which unannounced entries cause severe fright and humiliation.

Suppression is another matter. Under our precedents the causal link between a violation of the knock-and-announce requirement and a later search is too attenuated to allow suppression. Cf. *United States v. Ramirez* (1998) (application of the exclusionary rule depends on the existence of a "sufficient causal relationship" between the unlawful conduct and the discovery of evidence). When, for example, a violation results from want of a 20-second pause but an ensuing, lawful search lasting five hours discloses evidence of criminality, the failure to wait at the door cannot properly be described as having caused the discovery of evidence.

Today's decision does not address any demonstrated pattern of knock-and-announce violations. If a widespread pattern of violations were shown, and particularly if those violations were committed against persons who lacked the means or voice to mount an effective protest, there would be reason for grave concern. Even then, however, the Court would have to acknowledge that extending the remedy of exclusion to all the evidence seized following a knock-and-announce violation would mean revising the requirement of causation that limits our discretion in applying the exclusionary rule. That type of extension also would have significant practical implications, adding to the list of issues requiring resolution at the criminal trial questions such as whether police officers entered a home after waiting 10 seconds or 20.

In this case the relevant evidence was discovered not because of a failure to knock-and-announce, but because of a subsequent search pursuant to a lawful warrant.

■   ■   ■

Justice BREYER, with whom Justice STEVENS, Justice SOUTER, and Justice GINSBURG join, dissenting.

In *Wilson v. Arkansas*, a unanimous Court held that the Fourth Amendment normally requires law enforcement officers to knock and announce their presence before entering a dwelling. Today's opinion holds that evidence seized from a home following a violation of this requirement need not be suppressed.

As a result, the Court destroys the strongest legal incentive to comply with the Constitution's knock-and-announce requirement. And the Court does so without significant support in precedent. At least I can find no such support in the many Fourth Amendment cases the Court has decided in the near century since it first set forth the exclusionary principle in *Weeks v. United States.*

Today's opinion is thus doubly troubling. It represents a significant departure from the Court's precedents. And it weakens, perhaps destroys, much of the practical value of the Constitution's knock-and-announce protection.

■ ■ ■

This Court has set forth the legal principles that ought to have determined the outcome of this case in two sets of basic Fourth Amendment cases. I shall begin by describing that underlying case law.

■ ■ ■

The first set of cases describes the constitutional knock-and-announce requirement, a requirement that this Court initially set forth only 11 years ago in *Wilson v. Arkansas.*

■ ■ ■

And we held that the "common-law 'knock and announce' principle forms a part of the reasonableness inquiry under the Fourth Amendment." Thus, "a search or seizure of a dwelling might be constitutionally defective if police officers enter without prior announcement."

■ ■ ■

The second set of cases sets forth certain well-established principles that are relevant here. They include:

Boyd v. United States (1886). In this seminal Fourth Amendment case, decided 120 years ago, the Court wrote, in frequently quoted language, that the Fourth Amendment's prohibitions apply

> "to all invasions on the part of the government and its employés of the sanctity of a man's home and the privacies of life. It is not the breaking of his doors, and the rummaging of his drawers, that constitutes the essence of the offence; but it is the invasion of his indefeasible right of personal security, personal liberty and private property."

Weeks. This case, decided 28 years after *Boyd,* originated the exclusionary rule. The Court held that the Federal Government could not retain evidence seized unconstitutionally and use that evidence in a federal criminal trial. The Court pointed out that "[i]f letters and private documents" could be unlawfully seized from a home "and used in evidence against a citizen accused of an offense, the protection of the Fourth Amendment declaring his right to be secure against such searches and seizures is of no value, and . . . might as well be stricken from the Constitution."

Silverthorne Lumber Co. v. United States (1920). This case created an exception to (or a qualification of) *Weeks'* exclusionary rule. The Court held that the Government could not use information obtained during an illegal search to subpoena documents that they illegally viewed during that search. Writing for the Court, Justice Holmes noted that the exclusionary rule "does not mean that the facts [unlawfully] obtained become sacred and inaccessible. If knowledge of them is gained from an independent source they may be proved like any others...." *Silverthorne* thus stands for the proposition that the exclusionary rule does not apply if the evidence in question (or the "fruits" of that evidence) was obtained through a process unconnected with, and untainted by, the illegal search.

Wolf v. Colorado (1949) and *Mapp v. Ohio*. Both of these cases considered whether *Weeks'* exclusionary rule applies to the States. In *Wolf*, the Court held that it did not. It said that "[t]he security of one's privacy against arbitrary intrusion by the police...is...implicit in 'the concept of ordered liberty' and as such enforceable against the States through the Due Process Clause." But the Court held that the exclusionary rule is not enforceable against the States as "an essential ingredient of the right." In *Mapp*, the Court overruled *Wolf*. Experience, it said, showed that alternative methods of enforcing the Fourth Amendment's requirements had failed.

■ ■ ■

Reading our knock-and-announce cases, Part I-A, in light of this foundational Fourth Amendment case law, Part I-B, *supra*, it is clear that the exclusionary rule should apply. For one thing, elementary logic leads to that conclusion. We have held that a court must "conside[r]" whether officers complied with the knock-and-announce requirement "in assessing the reasonableness of a search or seizure." The Fourth Amendment insists that an unreasonable search or seizure is, constitutionally speaking, an illegal search or seizure. And ever since *Weeks* (in respect to federal prosecutions) and *Mapp* (in respect to state prosecutions), "the use of evidence secured through an illegal search and seizure" is "barred" in criminal trials.

For another thing, the driving legal purpose underlying the exclusionary rule, namely, the deterrence of unlawful government behavior, argues strongly for suppression. See *Elkins v. United States* (1960) (purpose of the exclusionary rule is "to deter—to compel respect for the constitutional guaranty...by removing the incentive to disregard it"). In *Weeks, Silverthorne*, and *Mapp*, the Court based its holdings requiring suppression of unlawfully obtained evidence upon the recognition that admission of that evidence would seriously undermine the Fourth Amendment's promise. All three cases recognized that failure to apply the exclusionary rule would make that promise a hollow one, reducing it to "a form of words" ... "of no value" to those whom it seeks to protect. Indeed, this Court in *Mapp* held that the exclusionary rule applies to the States in large part due to its belief that alternative state mechanisms for enforcing the Fourth Amendment's guarantees had proved "worthless and futile."

Why is application of the exclusionary rule any the less necessary here? Without such a rule, as in *Mapp*, police know that they can ignore the Constitution's requirements without risking suppression of evidence discovered after an unreasonable entry. As in *Mapp*, some government officers will find it easier, or believe it less risky, to proceed with what they consider a necessary search immediately and without the requisite constitutional (say, warrant or knock-and-announce) compliance.

■ ■ ■

To argue, as the majority does, that new remedies, such as 42 U.S.C. § 1983 actions or better trained police, make suppression unnecessary is to argue that *Wolf*, not *Mapp*, is now the law. (The Court recently rejected a similar argument in *Dickerson v. United States* (2000).) To argue that there may be few civil suits because violations may produce nothing "more than nominal injury" is to confirm, not to deny, the inability of civil suits to deter violations. And to argue without evidence (and despite myriad reported cases of violations, no reported case of civil damages, and Michigan's concession of their nonexistence) that civil suits may provide deterrence because claims *may* "have been settled" is, perhaps, to search in desperation for an argument. Rather, the majority, as it candidly admits, has simply "assumed" that, "[a]s far as [it] know[s], civil liability is an effective deterrent," a support-free assumption that *Mapp* and subsequent cases make clear does not embody the Court's normal approach to difficult questions of Fourth Amendment law.

It is not surprising, then, that after looking at virtually every pertinent Supreme Court case decided since *Weeks*, I can find no precedent that might offer the majority support for its contrary conclusion. The Court has, of course, recognized that not every Fourth Amendment violation necessarily triggers the exclusionary rule ... (application of the exclusionary rule is a separate question from whether the Fourth Amendment has been violated). But the class of Fourth Amendment violations that do not result in suppression of the evidence seized, however, is limited.

The Court has declined to apply the exclusionary rule only:

(1) where there is a specific reason to believe that application of the rule would "not result in appreciable deterrence," *United States v. Janis* (1976); see, *e.g., United States v. Leon* (exception where searching officer executes defective search warrant in "good faith"); *Arizona v. Evans* (exception for clerical errors by court employees); *Walder v. United States* (1954) (exception for impeachment purposes), or

(2) where admissibility in proceedings other than criminal trials was at issue, see, *e.g., Pennsylvania Bd. of Probation and Parole v. Scott* (exception for parole revocation proceedings); *INS v. Lopez-Mendoza* (1984) (plurality opinion) (exception for deportation proceedings); *Janis* (exception for civil tax proceedings); *United States v. Calandra* (exception for grand jury proceedings); *Stone v. Powell* (1976) (exception for federal habeas proceedings).

Neither of these two exceptions applies here. The second does not apply because this case is an ordinary criminal trial. The first does not apply because (1) officers who violate the rule are not acting "as a reasonable officer would and should act in similar circumstances," *Leon*, (2) this case does not involve government employees other than police, *Evans*, and (3), most importantly, the key rationale for any exception, "lack of deterrence," is missing, see

Pennsylvania Bd. of Probation (noting that the rationale for not applying the rule in noncriminal cases has been that the deterrence achieved by having the rule apply in those contexts is "minimal" *because* "application of the rule in the criminal trial context already provides significant deterrence of unconstitutional searches").

■ ■ ■

I am aware of no other basis for an exception. The Court has decided more than 300 Fourth Amendment cases since *Weeks*. The Court has found constitutional violations in nearly a third of them. The nature of the constitutional violation varies. In most instances officers lacked a warrant; in others, officers possessed a warrant based on false affidavits; in still others, the officers executed the search in an unconstitutional manner. But in every case involving evidence seized during an illegal search of a home (federally since *Weeks*, nationally since *Mapp*), the Court, with the exceptions mentioned, has either explicitly or implicitly upheld (or required) the suppression of the evidence at trial.

■ ■ ■

I can find nothing persuasive in the majority's opinion that could justify its refusal to apply the rule. It certainly is not a justification for an exception here (as the majority finds) to find odd instances in *other* areas of law that do not automatically demand suppression.

■ ■ ■

Neither can the majority justify its failure to respect the need for deterrence, as set forth consistently in the Court's prior case law, through its claim of "substantial social costs"—at least if it means that those "social costs" are somehow special here. The only costs it mentions are those that typically accompany *any* use of the Fourth Amendment's exclusionary principle: (1) that where the constable blunders, a guilty defendant may be set free (consider *Mapp* itself); (2) that defendants may assert claims where Fourth Amendment rights are uncertain (consider the Court's qualified immunity jurisprudence); and (3) that sometimes it is difficult to decide the merits of those uncertain claims. In fact, the "no-knock" warrants that are provided by many States, by diminishing uncertainty, may make application of the knock-and-announce principle less "cost[ly]" on the whole than application of comparable Fourth Amendment principles, such as determining whether a particular warrantless search was justified by exigency. The majority's "substantial social costs" argument is an argument against the Fourth Amendment's exclusionary principle itself. And it is an argument that this Court, until now, has consistently rejected.

■ ■ ■

The majority, Michigan, and the United States point out that the officers here possessed a warrant authorizing a search. That fact, they argue, means that the evidence would have been discovered independently or somehow diminishes the need to suppress the evidence. But I do not see why that is so. The warrant in question was not a "no-knock" warrant, which many States (but not Michigan) issue to assure police that a prior knock is not necessary. It did not authorize a search that fails to comply with knock-and-announce requirements. Rather, it was an ordinary search warrant. It authorized a search that *complied with*, not a search that *disregarded*, the Constitution's knock-and-announce rule.

Would a warrant that authorizes entry into a home on Tuesday permit the police to enter on Monday? Would a warrant that authorizes entry during the day authorize the police to enter during the middle of the night? It is difficult for me to see how the presence of a warrant that does not authorize the entry in question has anything to do with the "inevitable discovery" exception or otherwise diminishes the need to enforce the knock-and-announce requirement through suppression.

■ ■ ■

The majority and the United States set forth a policy-related variant of the causal connection theme: The United States argues that the law should suppress evidence only insofar as a Fourth Amendment violation causes the kind of harm that the particular Fourth Amendment rule seeks to protect against. It adds that the constitutional purpose of the knock-and-announce rule is to prevent needless destruction of property (such as breaking down a door) and to avoid unpleasant surprise. And it concludes that the exclusionary rule should suppress evidence of, say, damage to property, the discovery of a defendant in an "intimate or compromising moment," or an excited utterance from the occupant caught by surprise, but nothing more.

The majority makes a similar argument. It says that evidence should not be suppressed once the causal connection between unlawful behavior and discovery of the evidence becomes too "attenuated." But the majority then makes clear that it is not using the word "attenuated" to mean what this Court's precedents have typically used that word to mean, namely, that the discovery of the evidence has come about long after the unlawful behavior took place or in an independent way, *i.e.*, through " 'means sufficiently distinguishable to be purged of the primary taint.' "

Rather, the majority gives the word "attenuation" a new meaning (thereby, in effect, making the same argument as the United States). "Attenuation," it says, "also occurs when, even given a direct causal connection, the interest protected by the constitutional guarantee that has been violated would not be served by suppression of the evidence obtained." The interests the knock-and-announce rule seeks to protect, the Court adds, are "human life" (at stake when a householder is "surprised"), "property" (such as the front door), and "those elements of privacy and dignity that can be destroyed by a sudden entrance," namely, "the opportunity to collect oneself before answering the door." Since none of those interests led to the discovery of the evidence seized here, there is no reason to suppress it.

There are three serious problems with this argument. First, it does not fully describe the constitutional values, purposes, and objectives underlying the knock-and-announce requirement. That rule does help to protect homeowners from damaged doors; it does help to protect occupants from surprise. But it does more than that. It protects the occupants' privacy by assuring them that government agents will not enter their home without complying with those requirements (among others) that diminish the offensive nature of any such intrusion. Many years ago, Justice Frankfurter wrote for the Court that the "knock at the door, . . . as a prelude to a search, with-out authority of law . . . [is] inconsistent with the conception of human rights enshrined in [our] history" and Constitution. *Wolf.*

■ ■ ■

Over a century ago this Court wrote that "it is not the breaking of his doors" that is the "essence of the offence," but the "invasions on the part of the government . . . of the sanctity of a man's home and the privacies of life." *Boyd.*

■ ■ ■

Second, whether the interests underlying the knock-and-announce rule are implicated in any given case is, in a sense, beside the point. As we have explained, failure to comply with the knock-and-announce rule renders the related search unlawful.

■ ■ ■

Third, the majority's interest-based approach departs from prior law. Ordinarily a court will simply look to see if the unconstitutional search produced the evidence. The majority does not refer to any relevant case in which, beyond that, suppression turned on the far more detailed relation between, say, (1) a particular materially false statement made to the magistrate who issued a (consequently) invalid warrant and (2) evidence found after a search with that warrant.

■ ■ ■

The United States, in its brief and at oral argument, has argued that suppression is "an especially harsh remedy given the nature of the violation in this case." This argument focuses upon the fact that entering a house after knocking and announcing can, in some cases, prove dangerous to a police officer. Perhaps someone inside has a gun, as turned out to be the case here. The majority adds that police officers about to encounter someone who may try to harm them will be "uncertain" as to how long to wait. It says that, "[i]f the consequences of running afoul" of the knock-and-announce "rule were so massive," *i.e.*, would lead to the exclusion of evidence, then "officers would be inclined to wait longer than the law requires—producing preventable violence against officers in some cases."

To argue that police efforts to assure compliance with the rule may prove dangerous, however, is not to argue against evidence suppression. It is to argue against the validity of the rule itself. Similarly, to argue that enforcement means uncertainty, which in turn means the potential for dangerous and longer-than-necessary delay, is (if true) to argue against meaningful compliance with the rule.

The answer to the first argument is that the rule itself does not require police to knock or to announce their presence where police have a "reasonable suspicion" that doing so "would be dangerous or futile" or "would inhibit the effective investigation of the crime by, for example, allowing the destruction of evidence."

The answer to the second argument is that States can, and many do, reduce police uncertainty while assuring a neutral evaluation of concerns about risks to officers or the destruction of evidence by permitting police to obtain a "no-knock" search warrant from a magistrate judge, thereby assuring police that a prior announcement is not necessary.

Of course, even without such a warrant, police maintain the backup "authority to exercise independent judgment concerning the wisdom of a no-knock entry at the time the warrant is being executed." *Richards.* "[I]f circumstances support a reasonable suspicion of exigency when the officers arrive at the door, they may go straight in." *Banks.*

■ ■ ■

Consider this very case. The police obtained a search warrant that authorized a search, not only for drugs, but also for *guns*. If probable cause justified a search for guns, why would it not also have justified a no-knock warrant, thereby diminishing any danger to the officers? Why (in a State such as Michigan that lacks no-knock warrants) would it not have justified the very no-knock entry at issue here? Indeed, why did the prosecutor not argue in this very case that, given the likelihood of guns, the no-knock entry was lawful? From what I have seen in the record, he would have won. And had he won, there would have been no suppression here.

That is the right way to win. The very process of arguing the merits of the violation would help to clarify the contours of the knock-and-announce rule, contours that the majority believes are too fuzzy.

■ ■ ■

There is perhaps one additional argument implicit in the majority's approach. The majority says, for example, that the "cost" to a defendant of "entering this lottery," *i.e.*, of claiming a "knock-and-announce" violation, "would be small, but the jackpot enormous"—namely, a potential "get-out-of-jail-free card." It adds that the "social costs" of applying the exclusionary rule here are not worth the deterrence benefits. Leaving aside what I believe are invalid arguments based on precedent or the majority's own estimate that suppression is not necessary to deter constitutional violations, one is left with a simple unvarnished conclusion, namely, that in this kind of case, a knock-and-announce case, "[r]esort to the massive remedy of suppressing evidence of guilt is unjustified." Why is that judicial judgment, taken on its own, inappropriate? Could it not be argued that the knock-and-announce rule, a subsidiary Fourth Amendment rule, is simply not important enough to warrant a suppression remedy? Could the majority not simply claim that the suppression game is not worth the candle?

The answer, I believe, is "no." That "no" reflects history, a history that shows the knock-and-announce rule is important. That "no" reflects precedent, precedent that shows there is no pre-existing legal category of exceptions to the exclusionary rule into which the knock-and-announce cases might fit. That "no" reflects empirical fact, experience that provides confirmation of what common sense suggests: without suppression there is little to deter knock-and-announce violations.

There may be instances in the law where text or history or tradition leaves room for a judicial decision that rests upon little more than an unvarnished judicial instinct. But this is not one of them. Rather, our Fourth Amendment traditions place high value upon protecting privacy in the home. They emphasize the need to assure that its constitutional protections are effective, lest the Amendment "sound the word of promise to the ear but break it to the hope." They include an exclusionary principle, which since *Weeks* has formed the centerpiece of the criminal law's effort to ensure the _____ _____ _____ of those promises. That is why the Court should assure itsel_____ from that principle is firmly grounded in logic, in history, _____ empirical fact. It has not done so. That is why, with resp_____

■ ■ ■

C. EXCEPTIONS TO WARRANT REQUIREMEN

1. Consent

Schneckloth v. Bustamonte

412 U.S. 218 (1973)

STEWART, J., delivered the opinion of the Court, in which B____ REHNQUIST, BLACKMUN and POWELL, JJ., joined. DOUGLAS, BRENNAN, and MARSHALL, JJ., filed dissenting opinions.

The constitutional question in the present case concerns the definition of "consent" in this Fourth and Fourteenth Amendment context.

While on routine patrol in Sunnyvale, California, at approximately 2:40 in the morning, Police Officer James Rand stopped an automobile when he observed that one headlight and its license plate light were burned out. Six men were in the vehicle. Joe Alcala and the respondent, Robert Bustamonte, were in the front seat with Joe Gonzales, the driver. Three older men were seated in the rear. When, in response to the policeman's question, Gonzales could not produce a driver's license, Officer Rand asked if any of the other five had any evidence of identification. Only Alcala produced a license, and he explained that the car was his brother's. After the six occupants had stepped out of the car at the officer's request and after two additional policemen had arrived, Officer Rand asked Alcala if he could search the car. Alcala replied, "Sure, go ahead." Prior to the search no one was threatened with arrest and, according to Officer Rand's uncontradicted testimony, it "was all very congenial at this time." Gonzales testified that Alcala actually helped in the search of the car, by opening the trunk and glove compartment. In Gonzales' words: "[T]he police officer asked Joe [Alcala], he goes, 'Does the trunk open?' And Joe said, 'Yes.' He went to the car and got the keys and opened up the trunk." Wadded up under the left rear seat, the police officers found three checks that had previously been stolen from a car wash.

The trial judge denied the motion to suppress, and the checks in question were admitted in evidence at Bustamonte's trial. On the basis of this and other evidence he was convicted, and the California Court of Appeal for the First Appellate District affirmed the conviction. In agreeing that the search and seizure were constitutionally valid, the appellate court applied the standard earlier formulated by the Supreme Court of California in an opinion by then Justice Traynor: "Whether in a particular case an apparent consent was in fact voluntarily given or was in submission to an express or implied assertion of authority, is a question of fact to be determined in the light of all the circumstances." The appellate court found that "[i]n the instant case the prosecution met the necessary burden of showing consent . . . since there were clearly circumstances from which the trial court could ascertain that consent had been freely given without coercion or submission to authority. Not only officer Rand, but Gonzales, the driver of the automobile, testified that Alcala's assent to the search of his brother's automobile was freely, even casually given. At the time of the request to search the automobile the atmosphere, according to Rand, was 'congenial' and there has been no discussion of any crime. As noted, Gonzales said Alcala even attempted to aid in the search." The California Supreme Court denied review.

Thereafter, the respondent sought a writ of habeas corpus in a federal district court. It was denied. On appeal, the Court of Appeals for the Ninth Circuit set aside the District Court's order. The appellate court reasoned that a consent was a waiver of a person's Fourth and Fourteenth Amendment rights, and that the State was under an obligation to demonstrate, not only that the consent had been uncoerced, but that it had been given with an understanding that it could be freely and effectively withheld. Consent could not be found, the court held, solely from the absence of coercion and a verbal expression of assent. Since the District Court had not determined that Alcala had known that his consent could have been withheld and that he could have refused to have his vehicle searched, the Court of Appeals vacated the order denying the writ and remanded the case for further proceedings. We granted certiorari to determine whether the Fourth and Fourteenth Amendments require the showing thought necessary by the Court of Appeals. . . .

It is important to make it clear at the outset what is not involved in this case. The respondent concedes that a search conducted pursuant to a valid consent is constitutionally permissible. . . .

The precise question in this case, then, is what must the prosecution prove to demonstrate that a consent was "voluntarily" given. And upon that question there is a square conflict of views between the state and federal courts that have reviewed the search involved in the case before us. The Court of Appeals for the Ninth Circuit concluded that it is an essential part of the State's initial burden to prove that a person knows he has a right to refuse consent. The California courts have followed the rule that voluntariness is a question of fact to be determined from the totality of all the circumstances, and that the state of a defendant's knowledge is only one factor to be taken into account in assessing the voluntariness of a consent.

■ ■ ■

The most extensive judicial exposition of the meaning of "voluntariness" has been developed in those cases in which the Court has had to determine the "voluntariness" of a defendant's confession for purposes of the Fourteenth Amendment. Almost 40 years ago, in *Brown v. Mississippi* (1936), the Court held that a criminal conviction based upon a confession obtained by brutality and violence was constitutionally invalid under the Due Process Clause of the Fourteenth Amendment.

■ ■ ■

Those cases yield no talismanic definition of "voluntariness," mechanically applicable to the host of situations where the question has arisen. "The notion of 'voluntariness,'" Mr. Justice Frankfurter once wrote, "is itself an amphibian." *Culombe v. Connecticut* (1961). It cannot be taken literally to mean a "knowing" choice.

> "Except where a person is unconscious or drugged or otherwise lacks capacity for conscious choice, all incriminating statements—even those made under brutal treatment—are 'voluntary' in the sense of representing a choice of alternatives. On the other hand, if 'voluntariness' incorporates notions of 'but for' cause, the question should be whether the statement would have been made even absent inquiry or other official action. Under such a test, virtually no statement would be voluntary because very few people give incriminating statements in the absence of official action of some kind."

Bator & Vorenberg, Arrest, Detention, Interrogation and the Right to Counsel: Basic Problems and Possible Legislative Solutions, 66 Col. L. Rv. 62, 72-73. It is thus evident that neither linguistics nor epistemology will provide a ready definition of the meaning of "voluntariness."

Rather, "voluntariness" has reflected an accommodation of the complex of values implicated in police questioning of a suspect. At one end of the spectrum is the acknowledged need for police questioning as a tool for the effective enforcement of criminal laws.

■ ■ ■

This Court's decisions reflect a frank recognition that the Constitution requires the sacrifice of neither security nor liberty. The Due Process Clause does not mandate that the police forgo all questioning, or that they be given carte blanche to extract what they can from a suspect. "The ultimate test remains that which has been the only clearly established test in Anglo-American courts for two hundred years: the test of voluntariness. Is the confession the product of an essentially free and unconstrained choice by its maker? If it is, if he has willed to confess, it may be used against him. If it is not, if his will has been overborne and his capacity for self-determination critically impaired, the use of his confession offends due process."

In determining whether a defendant's will was overborne in a particular case, the Court has assessed the totality of all the surrounding circumstances—both the characteristics of the accused and the details of the interrogation.

■ ■ ■

Similar considerations lead us to agree with the courts of California that the question whether a consent to a search was in fact "voluntary" or was the product of duress or coercion, express or implied, is a question of fact to be determined from the totality of all the circumstances. While knowledge of the right to refuse consent is one factor to be taken into account, the government need not establish such knowledge as the sine qua non of an effective consent. As with police questioning, two competing concerns must be accommodated in determining the meaning of a "voluntary" consent—the legitimate need for such searches and the equally important requirement of assuring the absence of coercion.

In situations where the police have some evidence of illicit activity, but lack probable cause to arrest or search, a search authorized by a valid consent may be the only means of obtaining important and reliable evidence. In the present case for example, while the police had reason to stop the car for traffic violations, the State does not contend that there was probable cause to search the vehicle or that the search was incident to a valid arrest of any of the occupants. Yet, the search yielded tangible evidence that served as a basis for a prosecution, and provided some assurance that others, wholly innocent of the crime, were not mistakenly brought to trial. And in those cases where there is probable cause to arrest or search, but where the police lack a warrant, a consent search may still be valuable. If the search is conducted and proves fruitless, that in itself may convince the police that an arrest with its possible stigma and embarrassment is unnecessary, or that a far more extensive search pursuant to a warrant is not justified. In short, a search pursuant to consent may result in considerably less inconvenience for the subject of the search, and, properly conducted, is a constitutionally permissible and wholly legitimate aspect of effective police activity.

But the Fourth and Fourteenth Amendments require that a consent not be coerced, by explicit or implicit means, by implied threat or covert force. For, no matter how subtly the coercion was applied, the resulting "consent" would be no more than a pretext for the unjustified police intrusion against which the Fourth Amendment is directed.

■ ■ ■

The problem of reconciling the recognized legitimacy of consent searches with the requirement that they be free from any aspect of official coercion cannot be resolved by any infallible touchstone. To approve such searches without the most careful scrutiny would sanction the possibility of official coercion; to place artificial restrictions upon such searches would jeopardize their basic validity. Just as was true with confessions, the requirement of a "voluntary" consent reflects a fair accommodation of the constitutional requirements involved. In examining all the surrounding circumstances to determine if in fact the consent to search was coerced, account must be taken of subtly coercive police questions, as well as the possibly vulnerable subjective state of the person who consents. Those searches that are the product of police coercion can thus be filtered out without undermining the continuing validity of consent searches. In sum, there is no reason for us to depart in the area of consent searches, from the traditional definition of "voluntariness."

The approach of the Court of Appeals for the Ninth Circuit finds no support in any of our decisions that have attempted to define the meaning of "voluntariness." Its ruling, that the State must affirmatively prove that the subject of the search knew that he had a right to refuse consent, would, in practice, create serious doubt whether consent searches could continue to be conducted. There might be rare cases where it could be proved from the record that a person in fact affirmatively knew of his right to refuse—such as a case where he announced to the police that if he didn't sign the consent form, "you [police] are going to get a search warrant;" or a case where by prior experience and training a person had clearly and convincingly demonstrated such knowledge. But more commonly where there was no evidence of any coercion, explicit or implicit, the prosecution would nevertheless be unable to demonstrate that the subject of the search in fact had known of his right to refuse consent.

■ ■ ■

One alternative that would go far toward proving that the subject of a search did know he had a right to refuse consent would be to advise him of that right before eliciting his consent. That, however, is a suggestion that has been almost universally repudiated by both federal and state courts, and, we think, rightly so. For it would be thoroughly impractical to impose on the normal consent search the detailed requirements of an effective warning. Consent searches are part of the standard investigatory techniques of law enforcement agencies. They normally occur on the highway, or in a person's home or office, and under informal and unstructured conditions. The circumstances that prompt the initial request to search may develop quickly or be a logical extension of investigative police questioning. The police may seek to investigate further suspicious circumstances or to follow up leads developed in questioning persons at the scene of a crime.

■ ■ ■

"Our decision is not intended to hamper the traditional function of police officers in investigating crime. . . . When an individual is in custody on probable cause, the police may, of course, seek out evidence in the field to be used at trial against him. Such investigation may include inquiry of persons not under restraint. General on-the-scene questioning as to facts surrounding a crime or other general questioning of citizens in the fact-finding process is not affected by our holding. It is an act of responsible citizenship for individuals to give whatever information they may have to aid in law enforcement." *Miranda v. Arizona* (1966).

Consequently, we cannot accept the position of the Court of Appeals in this case that proof of knowledge of the right to refuse consent is a necessary prerequisite to demonstrating a "voluntary" consent. Rather it is only by analyzing all the circumstances of an individual consent that it can be ascertained whether in fact it was voluntary or coerced. It is this careful sifting of the unique facts and circumstances of each case that is evidenced in our prior decisions involving consent searches.

■ ■ ■

In short, neither this Court's prior cases nor the traditional definition of "voluntariness" requires proof of knowledge of a right to refuse as the sine qua non of an effective consent to a search.

■ ■ ■

It is said, however, that a "consent" is a "waiver" of a person's rights under the Fourth and Fourteenth Amendments. The argument is that by allowing the police to conduct a search, a person "waives" whatever right he had to prevent the police from searching.

■ ■ ■

But these standards were enunciated in the context of the safeguards of a fair criminal trial. Our cases do not reflect an uncritical demand for a knowing and intelligent waiver in every situation where a person has failed to invoke a constitutional protection.

■ ■ ■

The requirement of a "knowing" and "intelligent" waiver was articulated in a case involving the validity of a defendant's decision to forego a right constitutionally guaranteed to protect a fair trial and the reliability of the truth-determining process. *Johnson v. Zerbst* (1938) dealt with the denial of counsel in a federal criminal trial. There the Court held that under the Sixth Amendment a criminal defendant is entitled to the assistance of counsel, and that if he lacks sufficient funds to retain counsel, it is the Government's obligation to furnish him with a lawyer. As Mr. Justice Black wrote for the Court: "The Sixth Amendment stands as a constant admonition that if the constitutional safeguards it provides be lost, justice will not 'still be done.' It embodies a realistic recognition of the obvious truth that the average defendant does not have the professional legal skill to protect himself when brought before a tribunal with power to take his life or liberty, wherein the prosecution is presented by experienced and learned counsel. That which is simple, orderly, and necessary to the lawyer—to the untrained layman may appear intricate, complex and mysterious." To preserve the fairness of the trial process the Court established an appropriately heavy burden on the Government before waiver could be found—"an intentional relinquishment or abandonment of a known right or privilege."

■ ■ ■

There is a vast difference between those rights that protect a fair criminal trial and the rights guaranteed under the Fourth Amendment. Nothing, either in the purposes behind requiring a "knowing" and "intelligent" waiver of trial rights, or in the practical application of such a requirement suggests that it ought to be extended to the constitutional guarantee against unreasonable searches and seizures.

A strict standard of waiver has been applied to those rights guaranteed to a criminal defendant to insure that he will be accorded the greatest possible opportunity to utilize every facet of the constitutional model of a fair criminal trial. Any trial conducted in derogation of that model leaves open the possibility that the trial reached an unfair result precisely because all the protections specified in the Constitution were not provided. A prime example is the right to counsel. For without that right, a wholly innocent accused faces the real and substantial danger that simply because of his lack of legal expertise he may be convicted. As Mr. Justice Harlan once wrote: "The sound reason why [the right to counsel] is so freely extended for a criminal trial is the severe injustice risked by confronting an untrained defendant with a range of technical points of law, evidence, and tactics familiar to the prosecutor but not to himself." *Miranda* (dissenting opinion). The Constitution requires that every effort be made to see to it that a defendant in a criminal case has not unknowingly relinquished the basic protections that the Framers thought indispensable to a fair trial.

The protections of the Fourth Amendment are of a wholly different order, and have nothing whatever to do with promoting the fair ascertainment of truth at a criminal trial. Rather, as Mr. Justice Frankfurter's opinion for the Court put it in *Wolf v. Colorado* (1949), the Fourth Amendment protects the "security of one's privacy against arbitrary intrusion by the police. . . ." In declining to apply the exclusionary rule of *Mapp v. Ohio* (1961) to convictions that had become final before rendition of that decision, the Court emphasized that "there is no likelihood of unreliability or coercion present in a search-and-seizure case," *Linkletter v. Walker* (1965). In *Linkletter*, the Court indicated that those cases that had been given retroactive effect went to "the fairness of the trial—the very integrity of the fact-finding process. Here . . . the fairness of the trial is not under attack." The Fourth Amendment "is not an adjunct to the ascertainment of truth." The guarantees of the Fourth Amendment stand "as a protection of quite different constitutional values—values reflecting the concern of our society for the right of each individual to be let alone. To recognize this is no more than to accord those values undiluted respect."

Nor can it even be said that a search, as opposed to an eventual trial, is somehow "unfair" if a person consents to a search. While the Fourth and Fourteenth Amendments limit the circumstances under which the police can conduct a search, there is nothing constitutionally suspect in a person's voluntarily allowing a search. The actual conduct of the search may be precisely the same as if the police had obtained a warrant. And, unlike those constitutional guarantees that protect a defendant at trial, it cannot be said every reasonable presumption ought to be indulged against voluntary relinquishment. We have only recently stated: "[I]t is no part of the policy underlying the Fourth and Fourteenth Amendments to discourage citizens from aiding to the utmost of their ability in the apprehension of criminals." *Coolidge v. New Hampshire* (1971). Rather, the community has a real interest in encouraging consent, for the resulting search may yield necessary evidence for the solution and prosecution of crime, evidence that may insure that a wholly innocent person is not wrongly charged with a criminal offense.

■ ■ ■

Much of what has already been said disposes of the argument that the Court's decision in the *Miranda* case requires the conclusion that knowledge of a right to refuse is an indispensable element of a valid consent. The considerations that informed the Court's holding in *Miranda* are simply inapplicable in the present case. In *Miranda* the Court found that the techniques of police questioning and the nature of custodial surroundings produce an inherently coercive situation. The Court concluded that "[u]nless adequate protective devices are employed to dispel the compulsion inherent in custodial surroundings, no statement obtained from the defendant can truly be the product of his free choice." And at another point the Court noted that "without proper safeguards the process of in-custody interrogation of persons suspected or accused of crime contains inherently compelling pressures which work to undermine the individual's will to resist and to compel him to speak where he would not otherwise do so freely."

In this case, there is no evidence of any inherently coercive tactics—either from the nature of the police questioning or the environment in which it took place. Indeed, since consent searches will normally occur on a person's own familiar territory, the specter of incommunicado police interrogation in some remote station house is simply inapposite. There is no reason to believe, under circumstances such as are present here, that the response to a policeman's question is presumptively coerced; and there is, therefore, no reason to reject the traditional test for determining the voluntariness of a person's response. *Miranda*, of course, did not reach investigative questioning of a person not in custody, which is most directly analogous to the situation of a consent search, and it assuredly did not indicate that such questioning ought to be deemed inherently coercive.

■ ■ ■

Our decision today is a narrow one. We hold only that when the subject of a search is not in custody and the State attempts to justify a search on the basis of his consent, the Fourth and Fourteenth Amendments require that it demonstrate that the consent was in fact voluntarily given, and not the result of duress or coercion, express or implied. Voluntariness is a question of fact to be determined from all the circumstances, and while the subject's knowledge of a right to refuse is a factor to be taken into account, the prosecution is not required to demonstrate such knowledge as a prerequisite to establishing a voluntary consent. Because the California court followed these principles in affirming the respondent's conviction, and because the Court of Appeals for the Ninth Circuit in remanding for an evidentiary hearing required more, its judgment must be reversed.

It is so ordered.

■ ■ ■

Justice BRENNAN, dissenting.

The Fourth Amendment specifically guarantees "[t]he right of the people to be secure in their persons, houses, papers and effects, against unreasonable searches and seizures. . . ." We have consistently held that governmental searches conducted pursuant to a validly obtained warrant or reasonably incident to a valid arrest do not violate this guarantee. Here, however, as the Court itself recognizes, no search warrant was obtained and the State does not even suggest "that there was probable cause to search the vehicle or that the search was incident to a valid arrest of any of the occupants." As a result, the search of the vehicle can be justified solely on the ground that the owner's brother gave his consent—that is, that he waived his Fourth Amendment right "to be secure" against an otherwise "unreasonable" search. The Court holds today that an individual can effectively waive this right even though he is totally ignorant of the fact that, in the absence of his consent, such invasions of his privacy would be constitutionally prohibited. It wholly escapes me how our citizens can meaningfully be said to have waived something as precious as a constitutional guarantee without ever being aware of its existence. In my view, the Court's conclusion is supported neither by "linguistics," nor by "epistemology," nor, indeed, by "common sense." I respectfully dissent.

Justice MARSHALL, dissenting.

■ ■ ■

I believe that the Court misstates the true issue in this case. That issue is not, as the Court suggests, whether the police overbore Alcala's will in eliciting his consent, but rather whether a simple statement of assent to search, without more, should be sufficient to permit the police to search and thus act as a relinquishment of Alcala's constitutional right to exclude the police. This Court has always scrutinized with great care claims that a person has forgone the opportunity to assert constitutional rights.

■ ■ ■

To begin, it is important to understand that the opinion of the Court is misleading in its treatment of the issue here in three ways. First, it derives its criterion for determining when a verbal statement of assent to search operates as a relinquishment of a person's right to preclude entry from a justification of consent searches that is inconsistent with our treatment in earlier cases of exceptions to the requirements of the Fourth Amendment, and that is not responsive to the unique nature of the consent-search exception. Second, it applies a standard of voluntariness that was developed in a very different context, where the standard was based on policies different from those involved in this case. Third, it mischaracterizes our prior cases involving consent searches.

■ ■ ■

The Court assumes that the issue in this case is: what are the standards by which courts are to determine that consent is voluntarily given? It then imports into the law of search and seizure standards developed to decide entirely different questions about coerced confessions.

The Fifth Amendment, in terms, provides that no person "shall be compelled in any criminal case to be a witness against himself." Nor is the interest protected by the Due Process Clause of the Fourteenth Amendment any different. The inquiry in a case where a confession is challenged as having been elicited in an unconstitutional manner is, therefore, whether the behavior of the police amounted to compulsion of the defendant. Because of the nature of the right to be free of compulsion, it would be pointless to ask whether a defendant knew of it before he made a statement; no sane person would knowingly relinquish a right to be free of compulsion. Thus, the questions of compulsion and of violation of the right itself are inextricably intertwined. The cases involving coerced confessions, therefore, pass over the question of knowledge of that right as irrelevant, and turn directly to the question of compulsion. . . .

In contrast, this case deals not with "coercion," but with "consent," a subtly different concept to which different standards have been applied in the past. Freedom from coercion is a substantive right, guaranteed by the Fifth and Fourteenth Amendments. Consent, however, is a mechanism by which substantive requirements, otherwise applicable, are avoided. In the context of the Fourth Amendment, the relevant substantive requirements are that searches be conducted only after evidence justifying them has been submitted to an impartial magistrate for a determination of probable cause. There are, of course, exceptions to these requirements based on a variety of exigent circumstances that make it impractical to invalidate a search simply because the police failed to get a warrant. But none of the exceptions relating to the overriding needs of law enforcement are applicable when a search is justified solely by consent. On the contrary, the needs of law enforcement are significantly more attenuated, for probable cause to search may be lacking but a search permitted if the subject's consent has been obtained. Thus, consent searches are permitted, not because such an exception to the requirements of probable cause and warrant is essential to proper law enforcement, but because we permit our citizens to choose whether or not they wish to exercise their constitutional rights. Our prior decisions simply do not support the view that a meaningful choice has been made solely because no coercion was brought to bear on the subject.

■ ■ ■

My approach to the case is straight-forward and, to me, obviously required by the notion of consent as a relinquishment of Fourth Amendment rights. I am at a loss to understand why consent "cannot be taken literally to mean a 'knowing' choice." In fact, I have difficulty in comprehending how a decision made without knowledge of available alternatives can be treated as a choice at all.

If consent to search means that a person has chosen to forgo his right to exclude the police from the place they seek to search, it follows that his consent cannot be considered a meaningful choice unless he knew that he could in fact exclude the police. The Court appears, however, to reject even the modest proposition that, if the subject of a search convinces the trier of fact that he did not know of his right to refuse assent to a police request for permission to search, the search must be held unconstitutional. For it says only that "knowledge of the right to refuse consent is one factor to be taken into account." I find this incomprehensible. I can think of no other situation in which we would say that a person agreed to some course of action if he convinced us that he did not know that there was some other course he might have pursued. I would therefore hold, at a minimum, that the prosecution may not rely on a purported consent to search if the subject of the search did not know that he could refuse to give consent. That, I think, is the import of *Bumper v. North Carolina* [(1968)]. Where the police claim authority to search yet in fact lack such authority, the subject does not know that he may permissibly refuse them entry, and it is this lack of knowledge that invalidates the consent.

■ ■ ■

I must conclude with some reluctance that when the Court speaks of practicality, what it really is talking of is the continued ability of the police to capitalize on the ignorance of citizens so as to accomplish by subterfuge what they could not achieve by relying only on the knowing relinquishment of constitutional rights. Of course it would be "practical" for the police to ignore the commands of the Fourth Amendment, if by practicality we mean that more criminals will be apprehended, even though the constitutional rights of innocent people also go by the board. But such a practical advantage is achieved only at the cost of permitting the police to disregard the limitations that the Constitution places on their behavior, a cost that a constitutional democracy cannot long absorb.

■ ■ ■

It is regrettable that the obsession with validating searches like that conducted in this case, so evident in the Court's hyperbole, has obscured the Court's vision of how the Fourth Amendment was designed to govern the relationship between police and citizen in our society. I believe that experience and careful reflection show how narrow and inaccurate that vision is, and I respectfully dissent.

Illinois v. Rodriguez

497 U.S. 177 (1990)

SCALIA, J., delivered the opinion of the Court, in which REHNQUIST, C.J., and WHITE, BLACKMUN, O'CONNOR, and KENNEDY, JJ., joined. MARSHALL, J., filed a dissenting opinion, in which BRENNAN and STEVENS, JJ., joined.

In *United States v. Matlock* (1974), this Court reaffirmed that a warrantless entry and search by law enforcement officers does not violate the Fourth Amendment's proscription of "unreasonable searches and seizures" if the officers have obtained the consent of a third party who possesses common authority over the premises. The present case presents an issue we expressly reserved in *Matlock* . . . : Whether a warrantless entry is valid when based upon the consent of a third party whom the police, at the time of the entry, reasonably believe to possess common authority over the premises, but who in fact does not do so.

■ ■ ■

Respondent Edward Rodriguez was arrested in his apartment by law enforcement officers and charged with possession of illegal drugs. The police gained entry to the apartment with the consent and assistance of Gail Fischer, who had lived there with respondent for several months. The relevant facts leading to the arrest are as follows.

On July 26, 1985, police were summoned to the residence of Dorothy Jackson on South Wolcott in Chicago. They were met by Ms. Jackson's daughter, Gail Fischer, who showed signs of a severe beating. She told the officers that she had been assaulted by respondent Edward Rodriguez earlier that day in an apartment on South California. Fischer stated that Rodriguez was then asleep in the apartment, and she consented to travel there with the police in order to unlock the door with her key so that the officers could enter and arrest him. During this conversation, Fischer several times referred to the apartment on South California as "our" apartment, and said that she had clothes and furniture there. It is unclear whether she indicated that she currently lived at the apartment, or only that she used to live there.

The police officers drove to the apartment on South California, accompanied by Fischer. They did not obtain an arrest warrant for Rodriguez, nor did they seek a search warrant for the apartment. At the apartment, Fischer unlocked the door with her key and gave the officers permission to enter. They moved through the door into the living room, where they observed in plain view drug paraphernalia and containers filled with white powder that they believed (correctly, as later analysis showed) to be cocaine. They proceeded to the bedroom, where they found Rodriguez asleep and discovered additional containers of white powder in two open attaché cases. The officers arrested Rodriguez and seized the drugs and related paraphernalia. . . .

On the merits of the issue, respondent asserts that permitting a reasonable belief of common authority to validate an entry would cause a defendant's Fourth Amendment rights to be "vicariously waived." We disagree.

We have been unyielding in our insistence that a defendant's waiver of his trial rights cannot be given effect unless it is "knowing" and "intelligent." *Colorado v. Spring* (1987); *Johnson v. Zerbst* (1938). We would assuredly not permit, therefore, evidence seized in violation of the Fourth Amendment to be introduced on the basis of a trial court's mere "reasonable belief"—derived from statements by unauthorized persons—that the defendant has waived his objection. But one must make a distinction between, on the one hand, trial rights that *derive* from the violation of constitutional guarantees and, on the other hand, the nature of those constitutional guarantees themselves. As we said in *Schneckloth [v. Bustamonte* (1973)]:

> "There is a vast difference between those rights that protect a fair criminal trial and the rights guaranteed under the Fourth Amendment. Nothing, either in the purposes behind requiring 'knowing' and 'intelligent' waiver of trial rights, or in the practical application of such a requirement suggests that it ought to be extended to the constitutional guarantee against unreasonable searches and seizures."

What Rodriguez is assured by the trial right of the exclusionary rule, where it applies, is that no evidence seized in violation of the Fourth Amendment will be introduced at his trial unless he consents. What he is assured by the Fourth Amendment itself, however, is not that no government search of his house will occur unless he consents; but that no such search will occur that is "unreasonable." There are various elements, of course, that can make a search of a person's house "reasonable"—one of which is the consent of the person or his cotenant. The essence of respondent's argument is that we should impose upon this element a requirement that we have not imposed upon other elements that regularly compel government officers to exercise judgment regarding the facts: namely, the requirement that their judgment be not only responsible but correct.

■ ■ ■

It is apparent that in order to satisfy the "reasonableness" requirement of the Fourth Amendment, what is generally demanded of the many factual determinations that must regularly be made by agents of the government— whether the magistrate issuing a warrant, the police officer executing a warrant, or the police officer conducting a search or seizure under one of the exceptions to the warrant requirement—is not that they always be correct, but that they always be reasonable.

■ ■ ■

> "Because many situations which confront officers in the course of executing their duties are more or less ambiguous, room must be allowed for some mistakes on their part. But the mistakes must be those of reasonable men, acting on facts leading sensibly to their conclusions of probability." *Brinegar v. United States* (1949).

We see no reason to depart from this general rule with respect to facts bearing upon the authority to consent to a search. Whether the basis for such authority exists is the sort of recurring factual question to which law enforcement officials must be expected to apply their judgment; and all the Fourth Amendment requires is that they answer it reasonably. The Constitution is no more violated when officers enter without a warrant because they reasonably (though erroneously) believe that the person who has consented to their entry is a resident of the premises, than it is violated when they enter without a warrant because they reasonably (though erroneously) believe they are in pursuit of a violent felon who is about to escape.

Stoner v. California (1964) is in our view not to the contrary. There, in holding that police had improperly entered the defendant's hotel room based on the consent of a hotel clerk, we stated that "the rights protected by the Fourth Amendment are not to be eroded ... by unrealistic doctrines of 'apparent authority.'" It is ambiguous, of course, whether the word "unrealistic" is descriptive or limiting—that is, whether we were condemning as unrealistic all reliance upon apparent authority, or whether we were condemning only such reliance upon apparent authority as is unrealistic. Similarly ambiguous is the opinion's earlier statement that "there [is no] substance to the claim that the search was reasonable because the police, relying upon the night clerk's expressions of consent, had a reasonable basis for the belief that the clerk had authority to consent to the search." Was there no substance to it because it failed as a matter of law, or because the facts could not possibly support it? At one point the opinion does seem to speak clearly:

> "It is important to bear in mind that it was the petitioner's constitutional right which was at stake here, and not the night clerk's nor the hotel's. It was a right, therefore, which only the petitioner could waive by word or deed, either directly or through an agent."

But as we have discussed, what is at issue when a claim of apparent consent is raised is not whether the right to be free of searches has been *waived*, but whether the right to be free of *unreasonable* searches has been *violated*. Even if one does not think the *Stoner* opinion had this subtlety in mind, the supposed clarity of its foregoing statement is immediately compromised, as follows:

> "It is true that the night clerk clearly and unambiguously consented to the search. But there is nothing in the record to indicate that *the police had any basis whatsoever to believe that* the night clerk had been authorized by the petitioner to permit the police to search the petitioner's room."

■ ■ ■

As *Stoner* demonstrates, what we hold today does not suggest that law enforcement officers may always accept a person's invitation to enter premises. Even when the invitation is accompanied by an explicit assertion that the person lives there, the surrounding circumstances could conceivably be such that a reasonable person would doubt its truth and not act upon it without further inquiry. As with other factual determinations bearing upon search and seizure, determination of consent to enter must "be judged against an objective standard: would the facts available to the officer at the moment . . . 'warrant a man of reasonable caution in the belief' " that the consenting party had authority over the premises?

In the present case, the Appellate Court found it unnecessary to determine whether the officers reasonably believed that Fischer had the authority to consent, because it ruled as a matter of law that a reasonable belief could not validate the entry. Since we find that ruling to be in error, we remand for consideration of that question. The judgment of the Illinois Appellate Court is reversed, and the case is remanded for further proceedings not inconsistent with this opinion.

So ordered.

Justice MARSHALL, with whom Justice BRENNAN and Justice STEVENS join, dissenting.

Dorothy Jackson summoned police officers to her house to report that her daughter Gail Fischer had been beaten. Fischer told police that Ed Rodriguez, her boyfriend, was her assaulter. During an interview with Fischer, one of the officers asked if Rodriguez dealt in narcotics. Fischer did not respond. Fischer did agree, however, to the officers' request to let them into Rodriguez's apartment so that they could arrest him for battery. The police, without a warrant and despite the absence of an exigency, entered Rodriguez's home to arrest him. As a result of their entry, the police discovered narcotics that the State subsequently sought to introduce in a drug prosecution against Rodriguez.

The majority agrees with the Illinois Appellate Court's determination that Fischer did not have authority to consent to the officers' entry of Rodriguez's apartment. The Court holds that the warrantless entry into Rodriguez's home was nonetheless valid if the officers reasonably believed that Fischer had authority to consent. The majority's defense of this position rests on a misconception of the basis for third-party consent searches. That such searches do not give rise to claims of constitutional violations rests not on the premise that they are "reasonable" under the Fourth Amendment, but on the premise that a person may voluntarily limit his expectation of privacy by allowing others to exercise authority over his possessions.

■ ■ ■

The baseline for the reasonableness of a search or seizure in the home is the presence of a warrant.

■ ■ ■

The Court has tolerated departures from the warrant requirement only when an exigency makes a warrantless search imperative to the safety of the police and of the community. . . . The Court has often heard, and steadfastly rejected, the invitation to carve out further exceptions to the warrant requirement for searches of the home because of the burdens on police investigation and prosecution of crime. Our rejection of such claims is not due to a lack of appreciation of the difficulty and importance of effective law enforcement, but rather to our firm commitment to "the view of those who wrote the Bill of Rights that the privacy of a person's home and property may not be totally sacrificed in the name of maximum simplicity in enforcement of the criminal law."

In the absence of an exigency, then, warrantless home searches and seizures are unreasonable under the Fourth Amendment. The weighty constitutional interest in preventing unauthorized intrusions into the home overrides any law enforcement interest in relying on the reasonable but potentially mistaken belief that a third party has authority to consent to such a search or seizure. Indeed, as the present case illustrates, only the minimal interest in avoiding the inconvenience of obtaining a warrant weighs in on the law enforcement side.

■ ■ ■

Unlike searches conducted pursuant to the recognized exceptions to the warrant requirement, third-party consent searches are not based on an exigency and therefore serve no compelling social goal. Police officers, when faced with the choice of relying on consent by a third party or securing a warrant, should secure a warrant and must therefore accept the risk of error should they instead choose to rely on consent.

■ ■ ■

Our prior cases discussing searches based on third-party consent have never suggested that such searches are "reasonable." In *United States v. Matlock* [(1974)], this Court upheld a warrantless search conducted pursuant to the consent of a third party who was living with the defendant. The Court rejected the defendant's challenge to the search, stating that a person who permits others to have "joint access or control for most purposes . . . assume[s] the risk that [such persons] might permit the common area to be searched."

■ ■ ■

A search conducted pursuant to an officer's reasonable but mistaken belief that a third party had authority to consent is thus on an entirely different constitutional footing from one based on the consent of a third party who in fact has such authority. Even if the officers reasonably believed that Fischer had authority to consent, she did not, and Rodriguez's expectation of privacy was therefore undiminished. Rodriguez accordingly can challenge the warrantless intrusion into his home as a violation of the Fourth Amendment.

■ ■ ■

Acknowledging that the third party in this case lacked authority to consent, the majority seeks to rely on cases suggesting that reasonable but mistaken factual judgments by police will not invalidate otherwise reasonable searches. The majority reads these cases as establishing a "general rule" that "what is generally demanded of the many factual determinations that must regularly be made by agents of the government—whether the magistrate issuing a warrant, the police officer executing a warrant, or the police officer conducting a search or seizure under one of the exceptions to the warrant requirement—is not that they always be correct, but that they always be reasonable."

■ ■ ■

Our cases demonstrate that third-party consent searches are free from constitutional challenge only to the extent that they rest on consent by a party empowered to do so. The majority's conclusion to the contrary ignores the legitimate expectations of privacy on which individuals are entitled to rely. That a person who allows another joint access to his property thereby limits his expectation of privacy does not justify trampling the rights of a person who has not similarly relinquished any of his privacy expectation.

Instead of judging the validity of consent searches, as we have in the past, based on whether a defendant has in fact limited his expectation of privacy, the Court today carves out an additional exception to the warrant requirement for third-party consent searches without pausing to consider whether " 'the exigencies of the situation' make the needs of law enforcement so compelling that the warrantless search is objectively reasonable under the Fourth Amendment." Where this free-floating creation of "reasonable" exceptions to the warrant requirement will end, now that the Court has departed from the balancing approach that has long been part of our Fourth Amendment jurisprudence, is unclear. But by allowing a person to be subjected to a warrantless search in his home without his consent and without exigency, the majority has taken away some of the liberty that the Fourth Amendment was designed to protect.

Georgia v. Randolph

547 U.S. 103 (2006)

SOUTER, J., delivered the opinion of the Court, in which STEVENS, KENNEDY, GINSBURG, and BREYER, JJ., joined. STEVENS and BREYER, JJ., filed concurring opinions. ROBERTS, C.J., filed a dissenting opinion, in which SCALIA, J., joined. SCALIA and THOMAS, JJ., filed dissenting opinions. ALITO, J., did not participate.

The Fourth Amendment recognizes a valid warrantless entry and search of premises when police obtain the voluntary consent of an occupant who shares, or is reasonably believed to share, authority over the area in common with a co-occupant who later objects to the use of evidence so obtained. *Illinois v. Rodriguez* (1990). The question here is whether such an evidentiary seizure is likewise lawful with the permission of one occupant when the other, who later seeks to suppress the evidence, is present at the scene and expressly refuses to consent. We hold that, in the circumstances here at issue, a physically present co-occupant's stated refusal to permit entry prevails, rendering the warrantless search unreasonable and invalid as to him.

Respondent Scott Randolph and his wife, Janet, separated in late May 2001, when she left the marital residence in Americus, Georgia, and went to stay with her parents in Canada, taking their son and some belongings. In July, she returned to the Americus house with the child, though the record does not reveal whether her object was reconciliation or retrieval of remaining possessions.

On the morning of July 6, she complained to the police that after a domestic dispute her husband took their son away, and when officers reached the house she told them that her husband was a cocaine user whose habit had caused financial troubles. She mentioned the marital problems and said that she and their son had only recently returned after a stay of several weeks with her parents. Shortly after the police arrived, Scott Randolph returned and explained that he had removed the child to a neighbor's house out of concern that his wife might take the boy out of the country again; he denied cocaine use, and countered that it was in fact his wife who abused drugs and alcohol.

One of the officers, Sergeant Murray, went with Janet Randolph to reclaim the child, and when they returned she not only renewed her complaints about her husband's drug use, but also volunteered that there were " 'items of drug evidence' " in the house. Sergeant Murray asked Scott Randolph for permission to search the house, which he unequivocally refused.

The sergeant turned to Janet Randolph for consent to search, which she readily gave. She led the officer upstairs to a bedroom that she identified as Scott's, where the sergeant noticed a section of a drinking straw with a powdery residue he suspected was cocaine. He then left the house to get an evidence bag from his car and to call the district attorney's office, which instructed him to stop the search and apply for a warrant. When Sergeant Murray returned to the house, Janet Randolph withdrew her consent. The police took the straw to the police station, along with the Randolphs. After getting a search warrant, they returned to the house and seized further evidence of drug use, on the basis of which Scott Randolph was indicted for possession of cocaine.

He moved to suppress the evidence, as products of a warrantless search of his house unauthorized by his wife's consent over his express refusal. The trial court denied the motion, ruling that Janet Randolph had common authority to consent to the search.

The Court of Appeals of Georgia reversed, and was itself sustained by the State Supreme Court, principally on the ground that "the consent to conduct a warrantless search of a residence given by one occupant is not valid in the face of the refusal of another occupant who is physically present at the scene to permit a warrantless search."

■ ■ ■

We granted certiorari to resolve a split of authority on whether one occupant may give law enforcement effective consent to search shared premises, as against a co-tenant who is present and states a refusal to permit the search. We now affirm.

■ ■ ■

Although we have not dealt directly with the reasonableness of police entry in reliance on consent by one occupant subject to immediate challenge by another, we took a step toward the issue in an earlier case dealing with the Fourth Amendment rights of a social guest arrested at premises the police entered without a warrant or the benefit of any exception to the warrant requirement. *Minnesota v. Olson* (1990) held that overnight houseguests have a legitimate expectation of privacy in their temporary quarters because "it is unlikely that [the host] will admit someone who wants to see or meet with the guest over the objection of the guest. If that customary expectation of courtesy or deference is a foundation of Fourth Amendment rights of a houseguest, it presumably should follow that an inhabitant of shared premises may claim at least as much, and it turns out that the co-inhabitant naturally has an even stronger claim.

To begin with, it is fair to say that a caller standing at the door of shared premises would have no confidence that one occupant's invitation was a sufficiently good reason to enter when a fellow tenant stood there saying, "stay out." Without some very good reason, no sensible person would go inside under those conditions. Fear for the safety of the occupant issuing the invitation, or of someone else inside, would be thought to justify entry, but the justification then would be the personal risk, the threats to life or limb, not the disputed invitation.

The visitor's reticence without some such good reason would show not timidity but a realization that when people living together disagree over the use of their common quarters, a resolution must come through voluntary accommodation, not by appeals to authority. Unless the people living together fall within some recognized hierarchy, like a household of parent and child or barracks housing military personnel of different grades, there is no societal understanding of superior and inferior, a fact reflected in a standard formulation of domestic property law, that "[e]ach cotenant . . . has the right to use and enjoy the entire property as if he or she were the sole owner, limited only by the same right in the other cotenants."

■ ■ ■

Since the co-tenant wishing to open the door to a third party has no recognized authority in law or social practice to prevail over a present and objecting co-tenant, his disputed invitation, without more, gives a police officer no better claim to reasonableness in entering than the officer would have in the absence of any consent at all. Accordingly, in the balancing of competing individual and governmental interests entailed by the bar to unreasonable searches, the cooperative occupant's invitation adds nothing to the government's side to counter the force of an objecting individual's claim to security against the government's intrusion into his dwelling place. Since we hold to the "centuries-old principle of respect for the privacy of the home, . . . it is beyond dispute that the home is entitled to special protection as the center of the private lives of our people." . . .

■ ■ ■

Nor should this established policy of Fourth Amendment law be undermined by the principal dissent's claim that it shields spousal abusers and other violent co-tenants who will refuse to allow the police to enter a dwelling when their victims ask the police for help. It is not that the dissent exaggerates violence in the home; we recognize that domestic abuse is a serious problem in the United States. See U.S. Dept. of Justice, National Institute of Justice, P. Tjaden & N. Thoennes, Full Report of the Prevalence, Incidence, and Consequences of Violence Against Women 25-26 (2000) (noting that over 20 million women and 6 million men will, in the course of their lifetimes, be the victims of intimate-partner abuse); U.S. Dept. of Health and Human Services, Centers for Disease Control and Prevention, National Center for Injury Prevention and Control, Costs of Intimate Partner Violence Against Women in the United States 19 (2003) (finding that nearly 5.3 million intimate-partner victimizations, which result in close to 2 million injuries and 1,300 deaths, occur among women in the United States each year); U.S. Dept. of Justice, Bureau of Justice Statistics, Crime Data Brief, C. Rennison, Intimate Partner Violence, 1993-2001 (Feb. 2003) (noting that in 2001 intimate-partner violence made up 20% of violent crime against women).

■ ■ ■

But this case has no bearing on the capacity of the police to protect domestic victims. The dissent's argument rests on the failure to distinguish two different issues: when the police may enter without committing a trespass, and when the police may enter to search for evidence. No question has been raised, or reasonably could be, about the authority of the police to enter a dwelling to protect a resident from domestic violence; so long as they have good reason to believe such a threat exists, it would be silly to suggest that the police would commit a tort by entering, say, to give a complaining tenant the opportunity to collect belongings and get out safely, or to determine whether violence (or threat of violence) has just occurred or is about to (or soon will) occur, however much a spouse or other co-tenant objected.

■ ■ ■

None of the cases cited by the dissent supports its improbable view that recognizing limits on merely evidentiary searches would compromise the capacity to protect a fearful occupant. In the circumstances of those cases, there is no danger that the fearful occupant will be kept behind the closed door of the house simply because the abusive tenant refuses to consent to a search.

■ ■ ■

The dissent's red herring aside, we know, of course, that alternatives to disputed consent will not always open the door to search for evidence that the police suspect is inside. The consenting tenant may simply not disclose enough information, or information factual enough, to add up to a showing of probable cause, and there may be no exigency to justify fast action. But nothing in social custom or its reflection in private law argues for placing a higher value on delving into private premises to search for evidence in the face of disputed consent, than on requiring clear justification before the government searches private living quarters over a resident's objection. We therefore hold that a warrantless search of a shared dwelling for evidence over the express refusal of consent by a physically present resident cannot be justified as reasonable as to him on the basis of consent given to the police by another resident.

■ ■ ■

This is the line we draw, and we think the formalism is justified. So long as there is no evidence that the police have removed the potentially objecting tenant from the entrance for the sake of avoiding a possible objection, there is practical value in the simple clarity of complementary rules, one recognizing the co-tenant's permission when there is no fellow occupant on hand, the other according dispositive weight to the fellow occupant's contrary indication when he expresses it. For the very reason that *Rodriguez* held it would be unjustifiably impractical to require the police to take affirmative steps to confirm the actual authority of a consenting individual whose authority was apparent, we think it would needlessly limit the capacity of the police to respond to ostensibly legitimate opportunities in the field if we were to hold that reasonableness required the police to take affirmative steps to find a potentially objecting co-tenant before acting on the permission they had already received.... The pragmatic decision to accept the simplicity of this line is, moreover, supported by the substantial number of instances in which suspects who are asked for permission to search actually consent, albeit imprudently, a fact that undercuts any argument that the police should try to locate a suspected inhabitant because his denial of consent would be a foregone conclusion.

This case invites a straightforward application of the rule that a physically present inhabitant's express refusal of consent to a police search is dispositive as to him, regardless of the consent of a fellow occupant. Scott Randolph's refusal is clear, and nothing in the record justifies the search on grounds independent of Janet Randolph's consent. The State does not argue that she gave any indication to the police of a need for protection inside the house that might have justified entry into the portion of the premises where the police found the powdery straw (which, if lawfully seized, could have been used when attempting to establish probable cause for the warrant issued later). Nor does the State claim that the entry and search should be upheld under the rubric of exigent circumstances, owing to some apprehension by the police officers that Scott Randolph would destroy evidence of drug use before any warrant could be obtained.

The judgment of the Supreme Court of Georgia is therefore affirmed.

It is so ordered.

Justice BREYER, concurring.

If Fourth Amendment law forced us to choose between two bright-line rules, (1) a rule that always found one tenant's consent sufficient to justify a search without a warrant and (2) a rule that never did, I believe we should choose the first. That is because, as The Chief Justice's dissent points out, a rule permitting such searches can serve important law enforcement needs (for example, in domestic abuse cases), and the consenting party's joint tenancy diminishes the objecting party's reasonable expectation of privacy.

But the Fourth Amendment does not insist upon bright-line rules. Rather, it recognizes that no single set of legal rules can capture the ever changing complexity of human life. It consequently uses the general terms "unreasonable searches and seizures." And this Court has continuously emphasized that "[r]easonableness... is measured... by examining the totality of the circumstances."

■ ■ ■

If a possible abuse victim invites a responding officer to enter a home or consents to the officer's entry request, that invitation (or consent) itself could reflect the victim's fear about being left alone with an abuser. It could also indicate the availability of evidence, in the form of an immediate willingness to speak, that might not otherwise exist. In that context, an invitation (or consent) would provide a special reason for immediate, rather than later, police entry. And, entry following invitation or consent by one party ordinarily would be reasonable even in the face of direct objection by the other. That being so, contrary to The Chief Justice's suggestion, today's decision will not adversely affect ordinary law enforcement practices.

Chief Justice ROBERTS, with whom Justice SCALIA joins, dissenting.

The Court creates constitutional law by surmising what is typical when a social guest encounters an entirely atypical situation. The rule the majority fashions does not implement the high office of the Fourth Amendment to protect privacy, but instead provides protection on a random and happenstance basis, protecting, for example, a co-occupant who happens to be at the front door when the other occupant consents to a search, but not one napping or watching television in the next room. And the cost of affording such random protection is great, as demonstrated by the recurring cases in which abused spouses seek to authorize police entry into a home they share with a nonconsenting abuser.

The correct approach to the question presented is clearly mapped out in our precedents: The Fourth Amendment protects privacy. If an individual shares information, papers, *or places* with another, he assumes the risk that the other person will in turn share access to that information or those papers *or places* with the government. And just as an individual who has shared illegal plans or incriminating documents with another cannot interpose an objection when that other person turns the information over to the government, just because the individual happens to be present at the time, so too someone who shares a place with another cannot interpose an objection when that person decides to grant access to the police, simply because the objecting individual happens to be present.

A warrantless search is reasonable if police obtain the voluntary consent of a person authorized to give it. Co-occupants have "assumed the risk that one of their number might permit [a] common area to be searched." *United States v. Matlock* (1974). Just as Mrs. Randolph could walk upstairs, come down, and turn her husband's cocaine straw over to the police, she can consent to police entry and search of what is, after all, her home, too.

In *Illinois v. Rodriguez*, this Court stated that "[w]hat [a person] is assured by the Fourth Amendment . . . is not that no government search of his house will occur unless he consents; but that no such search will occur that is 'unreasonable.'" One element that can make a warrantless government search of a home "'reasonable'" is voluntary consent.

■ ■ ■

This exception is based on what the majority describes as "widely shared social expectations" that "when people living together disagree over the use of their common quarters, a resolution must come through voluntary accommodation." But this fundamental predicate to the majority's analysis gets us nowhere: Does the objecting co-tenant accede to the consenting co-tenant's wishes, or the other way around? The majority's assumption about voluntary accommodation simply leads to the common stalemate of two gentlemen insisting that the other enter a room first.

Nevertheless, the majority is confident in assuming—confident enough to incorporate its assumption into the Constitution—that an invited social guest who arrives at the door of a shared residence, and is greeted by a disagreeable co-occupant shouting "'stay out,'" would simply go away. The Court observes that "no sensible person would go inside under those conditions," and concludes from this that the inviting co-occupant has no "authority" to insist on getting her way over the wishes of her co-occupant. But it seems equally accurate to say—based on the majority's conclusion that one does not have a right to prevail over the express wishes of his co-occupant—that the objector has no "authority" to insist on getting *his* way over his co-occupant's wish that her guest be admitted.

The fact is that a wide variety of differing social situations can readily be imagined, giving rise to quite different social expectations. A relative or good friend of one of two feuding roommates might well enter the apartment over the objection of the other roommate. The reason the invitee appeared at the door also affects expectations: A guest who came to celebrate an occupant's birthday, or one who had traveled some distance for a particular reason, might not readily turn away simply because of a roommate's objection. The nature of the place itself is also pertinent: Invitees may react one way if the feuding roommates share one room, differently if there are common areas from which the objecting roommate could readily be expected to absent himself. Altering the numbers might well change the social expectations: Invitees might enter if two of three co-occupants encourage them to do so, over one dissenter.

The possible scenarios are limitless, and slight variations in the fact pattern yield vastly different expectations about whether the invitee might be expected to enter or to go away. Such shifting expectations are not a promising foundation on which to ground a constitutional rule, particularly because the majority has no support for its basic assumption—that an invited guest encountering two disagreeing co-occupants would flee—beyond a hunch about how people would typically act in an atypical situation.

And in fact the Court has not looked to such expectations to decide questions of consent under the Fourth Amendment, but only to determine when a search has occurred and whether a particular person has standing to object to a search. For these latter inquiries, we ask whether a person has a subjective expectation of privacy in a particular place, and whether "the expectation [is] one that society is prepared to recognize as 'reasonable.'"

■ ■ ■

The majority suggests that "widely shared social expectations" are a "constant element in assessing Fourth Amendment reasonableness" (citing *Rakas v. Illinois* (1978)), but that is not the case; the Fourth Amendment precedents the majority cites refer instead to a "legitimate expectation of *privacy*" ... (emphasis added; internal quotation marks omitted). Whatever social expectation the majority seeks to protect, it is not one of privacy. The very predicate giving rise to the question in cases of shared information, papers, containers, or places is that privacy has been shared with another. Our common social expectations may well be that the other person will not, in turn, share what we have shared with them with another—including the police—but that is the risk we take in sharing. If two friends share a locker and one keeps contraband inside, he might trust that his friend will not let others look inside. But by sharing private space, privacy has "already been frustrated" with respect to the lockermate.

■ ■ ■

A wide variety of often subtle social conventions may shape expectations about how we act when another shares with us what is otherwise private, and those conventions go by a variety of labels—courtesy, good manners, custom, protocol, even honor among thieves. The Constitution, however, protects not these but privacy, and once privacy has been shared, the shared information, documents, or places remain private only at the discretion of the confidant.

■ ■ ■

The majority states its rule as follows: "[A] warrantless search of a shared dwelling for evidence over the express refusal of consent by a physically present resident cannot be justified as reasonable as to him on the basis of consent given to the police by another resident."

Just as the source of the majority's rule is not privacy, so too the interest it protects cannot reasonably be described as such. That interest is not protected if a co-owner happens to be absent when the police arrive, in the backyard gardening, asleep in the next room, or listening to music through earphones so that only his co-occupant hears the knock on the door. That the rule is so random in its application confirms that it bears no real relation to the privacy protected by the Fourth Amendment. What the majority's rule protects is not so much privacy as the good luck of a co-owner who just happens to be present at the door when the police arrive. Usually when the development of Fourth Amendment jurisprudence leads to such arbitrary lines, we take it as a signal that the rules need to be rethought.

■　■　■

Rather than draw such random and happenstance lines—and pretend that the Constitution decreed them—the more reasonable approach is to adopt a rule acknowledging that shared living space entails a limited yielding of privacy to others, and that the law historically permits those to whom we have yielded our privacy to in turn cooperate with the government. Such a rule flows more naturally from our cases concerning Fourth Amendment reasonableness and is logically grounded in the concept of privacy underlying that Amendment.

■　■　■

Perhaps the most serious consequence of the majority's rule is its operation in domestic abuse situations, a context in which the present question often arises. While people living together might typically be accommodating to the wishes of their co-tenants, requests for police assistance may well come from co-inhabitants who are having a disagreement. The Court concludes that because "no sensible person would go inside" in the face of disputed consent, and the consenting co-tenant thus has "no recognized authority" to insist on the guest's admission, a "police officer [has] no better claim to reasonableness in entering than the officer would have in the absence of any consent at all." But the police officer's superior claim to enter is obvious: Mrs. Randolph did not invite the police to join her for dessert and coffee; the officer's precise purpose in knocking on the door was to assist with a dispute between the Randolphs— one in which Mrs. Randolph felt the need for the protective presence of the police. The majority's rule apparently forbids police from entering to assist with a domestic dispute if the abuser whose behavior prompted the request for police assistance objects.

The majority acknowledges these concerns, but dismisses them on the ground that its rule can be expected to give rise to exigent situations, and police can then rely on an exigent circumstances exception to justify entry. This is a strange way to justify a rule, and the fact that alternative justifications for entry might arise does not show that entry pursuant to consent is unreasonable. In addition, it is far from clear that an exception for emergency entries suffices to protect the safety of occupants in domestic disputes. . . .

Rather than give effect to a consenting spouse's authority to permit entry into her house to avoid such situations, the majority again alters established Fourth Amendment rules to defend giving veto power to the objecting spouse. In response to the concern that police might be turned away under its rule before entry can be justified based on exigency, the majority creates a new rule: A "good reason" to enter, coupled with one occupant's consent, will ensure that a police officer is "lawfully in the premises."

The majority's analysis alters a great deal of established Fourth Amendment law. The majority imports the concept of "social expectations," previously used only to determine when a search has occurred and whether a particular person has standing to object to a search, into questions of consent. To determine whether entry and search are reasonable, the majority considers a police officer's subjective motive in asking for consent, which we have otherwise refrained from doing in assessing Fourth Amendment questions. And the majority creates a new exception to the warrant requirement to justify warrantless entry short of exigency in potential domestic abuse situations.

Considering the majority's rule is solely concerned with protecting a person who happens to be present at the door when a police officer asks his co-occupant for consent to search, but not one who is asleep in the next room or in the backyard gardening, the majority has taken a great deal of pain in altering Fourth Amendment doctrine, for precious little (if any) gain in privacy. Perhaps one day, as the consequences of the majority's analytic approach become clearer, today's opinion will be treated the same way the majority treats our opinions in *Matlock* and *Rodriguez*—as a "loose end" to be tied up.

■ ■ ■

Our third-party consent cases have recognized that a person who shares common areas with others "assume[s] the risk that one of their number might permit the common area to be searched." The majority reminds us, in high tones, that a man's home is his castle, but even under the majority's rule, it is not his castle if he happens to be absent, asleep in the keep, or otherwise engaged when the constable arrives at the gate. Then it is his co-owner's castle. And, of course, it is not his castle if he wants to consent to entry, but his co-owner objects. Rather than constitutionalize such an arbitrary rule, we should acknowledge that a decision to share a private place, like a decision to share a secret or a confidential document, necessarily entails the risk that those with whom we share may in turn choose to share—for their own protection or for other reasons—with the police.

I respectfully dissent.

Justice Thomas, dissenting.

The Court has long recognized that "[i]t is an act of responsible citizenship for individuals to give whatever information they may have to aid in law enforcement." *Miranda v. Arizona* (1966).

■ ■ ■

In the instant case, Mrs. Randolph told police responding to a domestic dispute that respondent was using a substantial quantity of cocaine. Upon police request, she consented to a general search of her residence to investigate her statements. However, as the Court's recitation of the facts demonstrates, the record is clear that no such general search occurred. Instead, Sergeant Brett Murray asked Mrs. Randolph where the cocaine was located, and she showed him to an upstairs bedroom, where he saw the "piece of cut straw" on a dresser.

Sergeant Murray's entry into the Randolphs' home at the invitation of Mrs. Randolph to be shown evidence of respondent's cocaine use does not constitute a Fourth Amendment search. Under this Court's precedents, only the action of an agent of the government can constitute a search within the meaning of the Fourth Amendment, because that Amendment "was intended as a restraint upon the activities of *sovereign authority*, and was not intended to be a limitation upon other than governmental agencies."

Florida v. Jimeno

500 U.S. 248 (1991)

REHNQUIST, C.J., delivered the opinion of the Court, in which WHITE, BLACKMUN, O'CONNOR, SCALIA, KENNEDY, and SOUTER, JJ., joined. MARSHALL, J., filed a dissenting opinion, in which STEVENS, J., joined.

In this case we decide whether a criminal suspect's Fourth Amendment right to be free from unreasonable searches is violated when, after he gives a police officer permission to search his automobile, the officer opens a closed container found within the car that might reasonably hold the object of the search. We find that it is not. The Fourth Amendment is satisfied when, under the circumstances, it is objectively reasonable for the officer to believe that the scope of the suspect's consent permitted him to open a particular container within the automobile.

This case began when a Dade County police officer, Frank Trujillo, overheard respondent, Enio Jimeno, arranging what appeared to be a drug transaction over a public telephone. Believing that respondent might be involved in illegal drug trafficking, Officer Trujillo followed his car. The officer observed respondent make a right turn at a red light without stopping. He then pulled respondent over to the side of the road in order to issue him a traffic citation. Officer Trujillo told respondent that he had been stopped for committing a traffic infraction. The officer went on to say that he had reason to believe that respondent was carrying narcotics in his car, and asked permission to search the car. He explained that respondent did not have to consent to a search of the car. Respondent stated that he had nothing to hide and gave Trujillo permission to search the automobile. After two passengers stepped out of respondent's car, Officer Trujillo went to the passenger side, opened the door, and saw a folded, brown paper bag on the floorboard. The officer picked up the bag, opened it, and found a kilogram of cocaine inside.

■ ■ ■

The Florida District Court of Appeal affirmed the trial court's decision to suppress the evidence of the cocaine. In doing so, the court established a *per se* rule that "consent to a general search for narcotics does not extend to 'sealed containers within the general area agreed to by the defendant.'" The Florida Supreme Court affirmed.

■ ■ ■

The touchstone of the Fourth Amendment is reasonableness. The Fourth Amendment does not proscribe all state-initiated searches and seizures; it merely proscribes those which are unreasonable. *Illinois v. Rodriguez* (1990). Thus, we have long approved consensual searches because it is no doubt reasonable for the police to conduct a search once they have been permitted to do so. *Schneckloth v. Bustamonte* (1973). The standard for measuring the scope of a suspect's consent under the Fourth Amendment is that of "objective" reasonableness—what would the typical reasonable person have understood by the exchange between the officer and the suspect?

The scope of a search is generally defined by its expressed object. In this case, the terms of the search's authorization were simple. Respondent granted Officer Trujillo permission to search his car, and did not place any explicit limitation on the scope of the search. Trujillo had informed respondent that he believed respondent was carrying narcotics, and that he would be looking for narcotics in the car. We think that it was objectively reasonable for the police to conclude that the general consent to search respondent's car included consent to search containers within that car which might bear drugs. A reasonable person may be expected to know that narcotics are generally carried in some form of a container. "Contraband goods rarely are strewn across the trunk or floor of a car." [*United States v. Ross* (1982)]. The authorization to search in this case, therefore, extended beyond the surfaces of the car's interior to the paper bag lying on the car's floor.

■ ■ ■

Respondent argues, and the Florida trial court agreed with him, that if the police wish to search closed containers within a car they must separately request permission to search each container. But we see no basis for adding this sort of superstructure to the Fourth Amendment's basic test of objective reasonableness. A suspect may of course delimit as he chooses the scope of the search to which he consents. But if his consent would reasonably be understood to extend to a particular container, the Fourth Amendment provides no grounds for requiring a more explicit authorization. "[T]he community has a real interest in encouraging consent, for the resulting search may yield necessary evidence for the solution and prosecution of crime, evidence that may insure that a wholly innocent person is not wrongly charged with a criminal offense."

The judgment of the Supreme Court of Florida is accordingly reversed, and the case is remanded for further proceedings not inconsistent with this opinion.

It is so ordered.

Justice MARSHALL, with whom Justice STEVENS joins, dissenting.

The question in this case is whether an individual's general consent to a search of the interior of his car for narcotics should reasonably be understood as consent to a search of closed containers inside the car. Nothing in today's opinion dispels my belief that the two are not one and the same from the consenting individual's standpoint. Consequently, an individual's consent to a search of the interior of his car should not be understood to authorize a search of closed containers inside the car. I dissent.

In my view, analysis of this question must start by identifying the differing expectations of privacy that attach to cars and closed containers. It is well established that an individual has but a limited expectation of privacy in the interior of his car. A car ordinarily is not used as a residence or repository for one's personal effects, and its passengers and contents are generally exposed to public view.

■ ■ ■

In contrast, it is equally well established that an individual has a heightened expectation of privacy in the contents of a closed container. *United States v. Chadwick* (1977). Luggage, handbags, paper bags, and other containers are common repositories for one's papers and effects, and the protection of these items from state intrusion lies at the heart of the Fourth Amendment. U.S. Const., Amdt. 4 ("The right of the people to be secure in their . . . papers, and effects, against unreasonable searches and seizures, shall not be violated"). By placing his possessions inside a container, an individual manifests an intent that his possessions be "preserve[d] as private," *Katz v. United States* (1967), and thus kept "free from public examination."

The distinct privacy expectations that a person has in a car as opposed to a closed container do not merge when the individual uses his car to transport the container. In this situation, the individual still retains a heightened expectation of privacy in the container.

■ ■ ■

Because an individual's expectation of privacy in a container is distinct from, and far greater than, his expectation of privacy in the interior of his car, it follows that an individual's consent to a search of the interior of his car cannot necessarily be understood as extending to containers in the car. At the very least, general consent to search the car is ambiguous with respect to containers found inside the car. In my view, the independent and divisible nature of the privacy interests in cars and containers mandates that a police officer who wishes to search a suspicious container found during a consensual automobile search obtain additional consent to search the container. If the driver intended to authorize search of the container, he will say so; if not, then he will say no. The only objection that the police could have to such a rule is that it would prevent them from exploiting the ignorance of a citizen who simply did not anticipate that his consent to search the car would be understood to authorize the police to rummage through his packages.

■ ■ ■

Almost 20 years ago, this Court held that an individual could validly "consent" to a search—or, in other words, waive his right to be free from an otherwise unlawful search—without being told that he had the right to withhold his consent. See *Schneckloth v. Bustamonte*. In *Schneckloth*, as in this case, the Court cited the practical interests in efficacious law enforcement as the basis for not requiring the police to take meaningful steps to establish the basis of an individual's consent. I dissented in *Schneckloth*, and what I wrote in that case applies with equal force here.

> "I must conclude, with some reluctance, that when the Court speaks of practicality, what it really is talking of is the continued ability of the police to capitalize on the ignorance of citizens so as to accomplish by subterfuge what they could not achieve by relying only on the knowing relinquishment of constitutional rights. Of course it would be "practical" for the police to ignore the commands of the Fourth Amendment, if by practicality we mean that more criminals will be apprehended, even though the constitutional rights of innocent people also go by the board. But such a practical advantage is achieved only at the cost of permitting the police to disregard the limitations that the Constitution places on their behavior, a cost that a constitutional democracy cannot long absorb."

I dissent.

2. Plain View

Arizona v. Hicks

480 U.S. 321 (1987)

Scalia, J., delivered the opinion of the Court, in which Brennan, White, Marshall, Blackmun, and Stevens, JJ., joined.... Powell, J., filed a dissenting opinion, in which Rehnquist, C.J., and O'Connor, J., joined. O'Connor, J., filed a dissenting opinion, in which Rehnquist, C.J., and Powell, J., joined.

In *Coolidge v. New Hampshire* (1971), we said that in certain circumstances a warrantless seizure by police of an item that comes within plain view during their lawful search of a private area may be reasonable under the Fourth Amendment. We granted certiorari in the present case to decide whether this "plain view" doctrine may be invoked when the police have less than probable cause to believe that the item in question is evidence of a crime or is contraband.

On April 18, 1984, a bullet was fired through the floor of respondent's apartment, striking and injuring a man in the apartment below. Police officers arrived and entered respondent's apartment to search for the shooter, for other victims, and for weapons. They found and seized three weapons, including a sawed-off rifle, and in the course of their search also discovered a stocking-cap mask.

One of the policemen, Officer Nelson, noticed two sets of expensive stereo components, which seemed out of place in the squalid and otherwise ill-appointed four-room apartment. Suspecting that they were stolen, he read and recorded their serial numbers—moving some of the components, including a Bang and Olufsen turntable, in order to do so—which he then reported by phone to his headquarters. On being advised that the turntable had been taken in an armed robbery, he seized it immediately. It was later determined that some of the other serial numbers matched those on other stereo equipment taken in the same armed robbery, and a warrant was obtained and executed to seize that equipment as well. Respondent was subsequently indicted for the robbery.

The state trial court granted respondent's motion to suppress the evidence that had been seized. The Court of Appeals of Arizona affirmed. It was conceded that the initial entry and search, although warrantless, were justified by the exigent circumstance of the shooting. The Court of Appeals viewed the obtaining of the serial numbers, however, as an additional search, unrelated to that exigency.... Both courts—the trial court explicitly and the Court of Appeals by necessary implication—rejected the State's contention that Officer Nelson's actions were justified under the "plain view" doctrine of *Coolidge v. New Hampshire.* The Arizona Supreme Court denied review, and the State filed this petition.

■ ■ ■

Officer Nelson's moving of the equipment . . . did constitute a "search" separate and apart from the search for the shooter, victims, and weapons that was the lawful objective of his entry into the apartment. Merely inspecting those parts of the turntable that came into view during the latter search would not have constituted an independent search, because it would have produced no additional invasion of respondent's privacy interest. But taking action, unrelated to the objectives of the authorized intrusion, which exposed to view concealed portions of the apartment or its contents, did produce a new invasion of respondent's privacy unjustified by the exigent circumstance that validated the entry. This is why, contrary to Justice Powell's suggestion, the "distinction between 'looking' at a suspicious object in plain view and 'moving' it even a few inches" is much more than trivial for purposes of the Fourth Amendment. It matters not that the search uncovered nothing of any great personal value to respondent—serial numbers rather than . . . letters or photographs. A search is a search, even if it happens to disclose nothing but the bottom of a turntable.

■ ■ ■

The remaining question is whether the search was "reasonable" under the Fourth Amendment.

On this aspect of the case we reject, at the outset, the apparent position of the Arizona Court of Appeals that because the officers' action directed to the stereo equipment was unrelated to the justification for their entry into respondent's apartment, it was *ipso facto* unreasonable. That lack of relationship *always* exists with regard to action validated under the "plain view" doctrine; where action is taken for the purpose justifying the entry, invocation of the doctrine is superfluous.

■ ■ ■

We turn, then, to application of the doctrine to the facts of this case. "It is well established that under certain circumstances the police may *seize* evidence in plain view without a warrant." Those circumstances include situations "[w]here the initial intrusion that brings the police within plain view of such [evidence] is supported . . . by one of the recognized exceptions to the warrant requirement," such as the exigent-circumstances intrusion here. It would be absurd to say that an object could lawfully be seized and taken from the premises, but could not be moved for closer examination. It is clear, therefore, that the search here was valid if the "plain view" doctrine would have sustained a seizure of the equipment.

There is no doubt it would have done so if Officer Nelson had probable cause to believe that the equipment was stolen. The State has conceded, however, that he had only a "reasonable suspicion," by which it means something less than probable cause. We have not ruled on the question whether probable cause is required in order to invoke the "plain view" doctrine.

■ ■ ■

We now hold that probable cause is required. To say otherwise would be to cut the "plain view" doctrine loose from its theoretical and practical moorings. The theory of that doctrine consists of extending to nonpublic places such as the home, where searches and seizures without a warrant are presumptively unreasonable, the police's longstanding authority to make warrantless seizures in public places of such objects as weapons and contraband.

■ ■ ■

We do not say, of course, that a seizure can never be justified on less than probable cause. We have held that it can—where, for example, the seizure is minimally intrusive and operational necessities render it the only practicable means of detecting certain types of crime. No special operational necessities are relied on here, however—but rather the mere fact that the items in question came lawfully within the officer's plain view. That alone cannot supplant the requirement of probable cause.

■ ■ ■

Justice O'Connor's dissent suggests that we uphold the action here on the ground that it was a "cursory inspection" rather than a "full-blown search," and could therefore be justified by reasonable suspicion instead of probable cause. As already noted, a truly cursory inspection—one that involves merely looking at what is already exposed to view, without disturbing it—is not a "search" for Fourth Amendment purposes, and therefore does not even require reasonable suspicion. We are unwilling to send police and judges into a new thicket of Fourth Amendment law, to seek a creature of uncertain description that is neither a "plain view" inspection nor yet a "full-blown search."

■ ■ ■

Justice Powell's dissent reasonably asks what it is we would have had Officer Nelson do in these circumstances. The answer depends, of course, upon whether he had probable cause to conduct a search, a question that was not preserved in this case. If he had, then he should have done precisely what he did. If not, then he should have followed up his suspicions, if possible, by means other than a search—just as he would have . . . to do if, while walking along the street, he had noticed the same suspicious stereo equipment sitting inside a house a few feet away from him, beneath an open window. It may well be that, in such circumstances, no effective means short of a search exist. But there is nothing new in the realization that the Constitution sometimes insulates the criminality of a few in order to protect the privacy of us all. Our disagreement with the dissenters pertains to where the proper balance should be struck; we choose to adhere to the textual and traditional standard of probable cause.

The State contends that, even if Officer Nelson's search violated the Fourth Amendment, the court below should have admitted the evidence thus obtained under the "good faith" exception to the exclusionary rule. That was not the question on which certiorari was granted, and we decline to consider it.

For the reasons stated, the judgment of the Court of Appeals of Arizona is *Affirmed.*

■ ■ ■

Justice POWELL, with whom THE CHIEF JUSTICE and Justice O'CONNOR join, dissenting.

I join Justice O'Connor's dissenting opinion, and write briefly to highlight what seem to me the unfortunate consequences of the Court's decision.

Today the Court holds for the first time that the requirement of probable cause operates as a separate limitation on the application of the plain-view doctrine. The plurality opinion in *Coolidge v. New Hampshire* required only that it be "immediately apparent to the police that they have evidence before them; the 'plain view' doctrine may not be used to extend a general exploratory search from one object to another until something incriminating at last emerges." There was no general exploratory search in this case, and I would not approve such a search. All the pertinent objects were in plain view and could be identified as objects frequently stolen. There was no looking into closets, opening of drawers or trunks, or other "rummaging around." Justice O'Connor properly emphasizes that the moving of a suspicious object in plain view results in a minimal invasion of privacy. The Court nevertheless holds that "merely looking at" an object in plain view is lawful, but "moving" or "disturbing" the object to investigate a reasonable suspicion is not. The facts of this case well illustrate the unreasonableness of this distinction.

The officers' suspicion that the stereo components at issue were stolen was both reasonable and based on specific, articulable facts. Indeed, the State was unwise to concede the absence of probable cause. The police lawfully entered respondent's apartment under exigent circumstances that arose when a bullet fired through the floor of the apartment struck a man in the apartment below.

What they saw in the apartment hardly suggested that it was occupied by law-abiding citizens. A .25-caliber automatic pistol lay in plain view on the living room floor. During a concededly lawful search, the officers found a .45-caliber automatic, a .22-caliber, sawed-off rifle, and a stocking-cap mask. The apartment was littered with drug paraphernalia. The officers also observed two sets of expensive stereo components of a type that frequently was stolen.

■ ■ ■

Justice O'CONNOR, with whom THE CHIEF JUSTICE and Justice POWELL join, dissenting.

The Court today gives the right answer to the wrong question. The Court asks whether the police must have probable cause before either seizing an object in plain view or conducting a full-blown search of that object, and concludes that they must. I agree. In my view, however, this case presents a different question: whether police must have probable cause before conducting a cursory inspection of an item in plain view. Because I conclude that such an inspection is reasonable if the police are aware of facts or circumstances that justify a reasonable suspicion that the item is evidence of a crime, I would reverse the judgment of the Arizona Court of Appeals, and therefore dissent.

■ ■ ■

The purpose of the "immediately apparent" requirement is to prevent "general, exploratory rummaging in a person's belongings." If an officer could indiscriminately search every item in plain view, a search justified by a limited purpose—such as exigent circumstances—could be used to eviscerate the protections of the Fourth Amendment. In order to prevent such a general search, therefore, we require that the relevance of the item be "immediately apparent." As Justice Stewart explained:

> "Of course, the extension of the original justification [for being present] is legitimate only where it is immediately apparent to the police that they have evidence before them; the 'plain view' doctrine may not be used to extend a general exploratory search from one object to another until something incriminating at last emerges. Cf. *Stanley v. Georgia* (1969) (Stewart, J., concurring in result)." *Coolidge.*

Thus, I agree with the Court that even under the plain-view doctrine, probable cause is required before the police seize an item, or conduct a full-blown search of evidence in plain view. Such a requirement of probable cause will prevent the plain-view doctrine from authorizing general searches. This is not to say, however, that even a mere inspection of a suspicious item must be supported by probable cause. When a police officer makes a cursory inspection of a suspicious item in plain view in order to determine whether it is indeed evidence of a crime, there is no "exploratory rummaging." Only those items that the police officer "reasonably suspects" as evidence of a crime may be inspected, and perhaps more importantly, the scope of such an inspection is quite limited. In short, if police officers have a reasonable, articulable suspicion that an object they come across during the course of a lawful search is evidence of crime, in my view they may make a cursory examination of the object to verify their suspicion. If the officers wish to go beyond such a cursory examination of the object, however, they must have probable cause.

■ ■ ■

In my view, the balance of the governmental and privacy interests strongly supports a reasonable-suspicion standard for the cursory examination of items in plain view. The additional intrusion caused by an inspection of an item in plain view for its serial number is miniscule. Indeed, the intrusion in this case was even more transitory and less intrusive than the seizure of luggage from a suspected drug dealer in *United States v. Place* [(1983)], and the "severe, though brief, intrusion upon cherished personal security" in *Terry v. Ohio* [(1968)].

Weighed against this minimal additional invasion of privacy are rather major gains in law enforcement. The use of identification numbers in tracing stolen property is a powerful law enforcement tool. Serial numbers are far more helpful and accurate in detecting stolen property than simple police recollection of the evidence.

Minnesota v. Dickerson

508 U.S. 366 (1993)

See also Chapter 3.B.

WHITE, J., delivered the opinion of the Court, in which KENNEDY, SOUTER, and O'CONNOR, JJ., joined. REHNQUIST, C.J., filed an opinion concurring in part and dissenting in part, in which BLACKMUN and THOMAS, JJ., joined.

> *On the evening of November 9, 1989, two Minneapolis police officers stopped the respondent based on his seemingly evasive actions and the fact that he had just left a building known for cocaine traffic. A patdown search revealed a small lump in the respondent's nylon jacket. The officer later testified: "I examined it with my fingers and it slid and it felt to be a lump of crack cocaine in cellophane." The officer then reached into the respondent's pocket and retrieved a small plastic bag containing one-fifth of one gram of crack cocaine.*

■ ■ ■

We granted certiorari to resolve a conflict among the state and federal courts over whether contraband detected through the sense of touch during a patdown search may be admitted into evidence.

■ ■ ■

These principles were settled 25 years ago when, on the same day, the Court announced its decisions in *Terry* [*v. Ohio* (1968)] and *Sibron* [*v. New York* (1968)]. The question presented today is whether police officers may seize nonthreatening contraband detected during a protective patdown search of the sort permitted by *Terry*. We think the answer is clearly that they may, so long as the officers' search stays within the bounds marked by *Terry*.

■ ■ ■

We think that this doctrine has an obvious application by analogy to cases in which an officer discovers contraband through the sense of touch during an otherwise lawful search. The rationale of the plain-view doctrine is that if contraband is left in open view and is observed by a police officer from a lawful vantage point, there has been no invasion of a legitimate expectation of privacy and thus no "search" within the meaning of the Fourth Amendment—or at least no search independent of the initial intrusion that gave the officers their vantage point. The warrantless seizure of contraband that presents itself in this manner is deemed justified by the realization that resort to a neutral magistrate under such circumstances would often be impracticable and would do little to promote the objectives of the Fourth Amendment. The same can be said of tactile discoveries of contraband. If a police officer lawfully pats down a suspect's outer clothing and feels an object whose contour or mass makes its identity immediately apparent, there has been no invasion of the suspect's privacy beyond that already authorized by the officer's search for weapons; if the object is contraband, its warrantless seizure would be justified by the same practical considerations that inhere in the plain-view context.

It remains to apply these principles to the facts of this case. Respondent has not challenged the finding made by the trial court and affirmed by both the Court of Appeals and the State Supreme Court that the police were justified under *Terry* in stopping him and frisking him for weapons. Thus, the dispositive question before this Court is whether the officer who conducted the search was acting within the lawful bounds marked by *Terry* at the time he gained probable cause to believe that the lump in respondent's jacket was contraband. The State District Court did not make precise findings on this point, instead finding simply that the officer, after feeling "a small, hard object wrapped in plastic" in respondent's pocket, "formed the opinion that the object . . . was crack . . . cocaine." The District Court also noted that the officer made "no claim that he suspected this object to be a weapon," a finding affirmed on appeal (the officer "never thought the lump was a weapon"). The Minnesota Supreme Court, after "a close examination of the record," held that the officer's own testimony "belies any notion that he 'immediately' " recognized the lump as crack cocaine. Rather, the court concluded, the officer determined that the lump was contraband only after "squeezing, sliding and otherwise manipulating the contents of the defendant's pocket"—a pocket which the officer already knew contained no weapon.

Under the State Supreme Court's interpretation of the record before it, it is clear that the court was correct in holding that the police officer in this case overstepped the bounds of the "strictly circumscribed" search for weapons allowed under *Terry*. Where, as here, "an officer who is executing a valid search for one item seizes a different item," this Court rightly "has been sensitive to the danger . . . that officers will enlarge a specific authorization, furnished by a warrant or an exigency, into the equivalent of a general warrant to rummage and seize at will." Here, the officer's continued exploration of respondent's pocket after having concluded that it contained no weapon was unrelated to "[t]he sole justification of the search [under *Terry*:] . . . the protection of the police officer and others nearby."

■ ■ ■

Once again, the analogy to the plain-view doctrine is apt. In *Arizona v. Hicks* (1987), this Court held invalid the seizure of stolen stereo equipment found by police while executing a valid search for other evidence. Although the police were lawfully on the premises, they obtained probable cause to believe that the stereo equipment was contraband only after moving the equipment to permit officers to read its serial numbers. The subsequent seizure of the equipment could not be justified by the plain-view doctrine, this Court explained, because the incriminating character of the stereo equipment was not immediately apparent; rather, probable cause to believe that the equipment was stolen arose only as a result of a further search—the moving of the equipment— that was not authorized by a search warrant or by any exception to the warrant requirement. The facts of this case are very similar. Although the officer was lawfully in a position to feel the lump in respondent's pocket, because *Terry* entitled him to place his hands upon respondent's jacket, the court below determined that the incriminating character of the object was not immediately apparent to him. Rather, the officer determined that the item was contraband only after conducting a further search, one not authorized by *Terry* or by any other exception to the warrant requirement.

■ ■ ■

For these reasons, the judgment of the Minnesota Supreme Court is *Affirmed.*

3. Search Incident to Arrest

Chimel v. California

395 U.S. 752 (1969)
See Chapter 4.A.

United States v. Robinson

414 U.S. 218 (1973)

REHNQUIST, J., delivered the opinion of the Court, in which BURGER, C.J., BLACKMUN, WHITE, and STEWART, JJ., joined. POWELL, J., filed a concurring opinion (414 U.S. 260). MARSHALL, J., filed a dissenting opinion, in which DOUGLAS and BRENNAN, JJ., joined.

On April 23, 1968, at approximately 11 p.m., Officer Richard Jenks, a 15-year veteran of the District of Columbia Metropolitan Police Department, observed the respondent driving a 1965 Cadillac near the intersection of 8th and C Streets, N.E., in the District of Columbia. Jenks, as a result of previous investigation following a check of respondent's operator's permit four days earlier, determined there was reason to believe that respondent was operating a motor vehicle after the revocation of his operator's permit. This is an offense defined by statute in the District of Columbia which carries a mandatory minimum jail term, a mandatory minimum fine, or both.

Jenks signaled respondent to stop the automobile, which respondent did, and all three of the occupants emerged from the car. At that point Jenks informed respondent that he was under arrest for "operating after revocation and obtaining a permit by misrepresentation." It was assumed by the Court of Appeals, and is conceded by the respondent here, that Jenks had probable cause to arrest respondent, and that he effected a full custody arrest.

In accordance with procedures prescribed in police department instructions, Jenks then began to search respondent. He explained at a subsequent hearing that he was "face-to-face" with the respondent, and "placed [his] hands on [the respondent], my right hand to his left breast like this (demonstrating) and proceeded to pat him down thus [with the right hand]." During this patdown, Jenks felt an object in the left breast pocket of the heavy coat respondent was wearing, but testified that he "couldn't tell what it was" and also that he "couldn't actually tell the size of it." Jenks then reached into the pocket and pulled out the object, which turned out to be a "crumpled up cigarette package." Jenks testified that at this point he still did not know what was in the package:

> "As I felt the package I could feel objects in the package but I couldn't tell what they were. . . . I knew they weren't cigarettes."

The officer then opened the cigarette pack and found 14 gelatin capsules of white powder which he thought to be, and which later analysis proved to be, heroin. Jenks then continued his search of respondent to completion, feeling around his waist and trouser legs, and examining the remaining pockets. The heroin seized from the respondent was admitted into evidence at the trial which resulted in his conviction in the District Court. . . .

It is well settled that a search incident to a lawful arrest is a traditional exception to the warrant requirement of the Fourth Amendment. This general exception has historically been formulated into two distinct propositions. The first is that a search may be made of the person of the arrestee by virtue of the lawful arrest. The second is that a search may be made of the area within the control of the arrestee.

Examination of this Court's decisions shows that these two propositions have been treated quite differently. The validity of the search of a person incident to a lawful arrest has been regarded as settled from its first enunciation, and has remained virtually unchallenged until the present case. The validity of the second proposition, while likewise conceded in principle, has been subject to differing interpretations as to the extent of the area which may be searched.

Because the rule requiring exclusion of evidence obtained in violation of the Fourth Amendment was first enunciated in *Weeks v. United States* (1914), it is understandable that virtually all of this Court's search-and-seizure law has been developed since that time. In *Weeks*, the Court made clear its recognition of the validity of a search incident to a lawful arrest:

> "What then is the present case? Before answering that inquiry specifically, it may be well by a process of exclusion to state what it is not. It is not an assertion of the right on the part of the Government, always recognized under English and American law, to search the person of the accused when legally arrested to discover and seize the fruits or evidences of crime...."

■ ■ ■

> "When an arrest is made, it is reasonable for the arresting officer to search the person arrested in order to remove any weapons that the latter might seek to use in order to resist arrest or effect his escape. Otherwise, the officer's safety might well be endangered, and the arrest itself frustrated. In addition, it is entirely reasonable for the arresting officer to search for and seize any evidence on the arrestee's person in order to prevent its concealment or destruction." *Chimel v. California* (1969).

■ ■ ■

In its decision of this case, the Court of Appeals decided that even after a police officer lawfully places a suspect under arrest for the purpose of taking him into custody, he may not ordinarily proceed to fully search the prisoner. He must, instead, conduct a limited frisk of the outer clothing and remove such weapons that he may, as a result of that limited frisk, reasonably believe and ascertain that the suspect has in his possession. While recognizing that *Terry v. Ohio* (1968) dealt with a permissible "frisk" incident to an investigative stop based on less than probable cause to arrest, the Court of Appeals felt that the principles of that case should be carried over to this probable-cause arrest for driving while one's license is revoked. Since there would be no further evidence of such a crime to be obtained in a search of the arrestee, the court held that only a search for weapons could be justified.

■ ■ ■

> "... An arrest is a wholly different kind of intrusion upon individual freedom from a limited search for weapons, and the interests each is designed to serve are likewise quite different. An arrest is the initial stage of a criminal prosecution. It is intended to vindicate society's interest in having its laws obeyed, and it is inevitably accompanied by future interference with the individual's freedom of movement, whether or not trial or conviction ultimately follows. The protective search for weapons, on the other hand, constitutes brief, though far from inconsiderable, intrusion upon the sanctity of the person." *Terry*.

Terry, therefore, affords no basis to carry over to a probable-cause arrest the limitations this Court placed on a stop-and-frisk search permissible without probable cause.

■ ■ ■

The justification or reason for the authority to search incident to a lawful arrest rests quite as much on the need to disarm the suspect in order to take him into custody as it does on the need to preserve evidence on his person for later use at trial. *Agnello v. United States* (1925)....The standards traditionally governing a search incident to lawful arrest are not, therefore, commuted to the stricter *Terry* standards by the absence of probable fruits or further evidence of the particular crime for which the arrest is made.

Nor are we inclined, on the basis of what seems to us to be a rather speculative judgment, to qualify the breadth of the general authority to search incident to a lawful custodial arrest on an assumption that persons arrested for the offense of driving while their licenses have been revoked are less likely to possess dangerous weapons than are those arrested for other crimes. It is scarcely open to doubt that the danger to an officer is far greater in the case of the extended exposure which follows the taking of a suspect into custody and transporting him to the police station than in the case of the relatively fleeting contact resulting from the typical *Terry*-type stop. This is an adequate basis for treating all custodial arrests alike for purposes of search justification.

But quite apart from these distinctions, our more fundamental disagreement with the Court of Appeals arises from its suggestion that there must be litigated in each case the issue of whether or not there was present one of the reasons supporting the authority for a search of the person incident to a lawful arrest. We do not think the long line of authorities of this Court dating back to *Weeks*, or what we can glean from the history of practice in this country and in England, requires such a case-by-case adjudication. A police officer's determination as to how and where to search the person of a suspect whom he has arrested is necessarily a quick ad hoc judgment which the Fourth Amendment does not require to be broken down in each instance into an analysis of each step in the search. The authority to search the person incident to a lawful custodial arrest, while based upon the need to disarm and to discover evidence, does not depend on what a court may later decide was the probability in a particular arrest situation that weapons or evidence would in fact be found upon the person of the suspect. A custodial arrest of a suspect based on probable cause is a reasonable intrusion under the Fourth Amendment; that intrusion being lawful, a search incident to the arrest requires no additional justification. It is the fact of the lawful arrest which establishes the authority to search, and we hold that in the case of a lawful custodial arrest a full search of the person is not only an exception to the warrant requirement of the Fourth Amendment, but is also a "reasonable" search under that Amendment....

The search of respondent's person conducted by Officer Jenks in this case and the seizure from him of the heroin, were permissible under established Fourth Amendment law. While thorough, the search partook of none of the extreme or patently abusive characteristics which were held to violate the Due Process Clause of the Fourteenth Amendment in *Rochin v. California* (1952). Since it is the fact of custodial arrest which gives rise to the authority to search, it is of no moment that Jenks did not indicate any subjective fear of the respondent or that he did not himself suspect that respondent was armed. Having in the course of a lawful search come upon the crumpled package of cigarettes, he was entitled to inspect it; and when his inspection revealed the heroin capsules, he was entitled to seize them as "fruits, instrumentalities, or contraband" probative of criminal conduct. . . .

Reversed.

Justice MARSHALL, with whom Justice DOUGLAS and Justice BRENNAN join, dissenting.

Certain fundamental principles have characterized this Court's Fourth Amendment jurisprudence over the years. Perhaps the most basic of these was expressed by Mr. Justice Butler, speaking for a unanimous Court in *Go-Bart Co. v. United States* (1931): "There is no formula for the determination of reasonableness. Each case is to be decided on its own facts and circumstances." As we recently held: "The constitutional validity of a warrantless search is preeminently the sort of question which can only be decided in the concrete factual context of the individual case." *Sibron v. New York* (1968). And the intensive, at times painstaking, case-by-case analysis characteristic of our Fourth Amendment decisions bespeaks our "jealous regard for maintaining the integrity of individual rights."

■ ■ ■

In the present case, however, the majority turns its back on these principles, holding that "the fact of the lawful arrest" always establishes the authority to conduct a full search of the arrestee's person, regardless of whether in a particular case "there was present one of the reasons supporting the authority for a search of the person incident to a lawful arrest." The majority's approach represents a clear and marked departure from our long tradition of case-by-case adjudication of the reasonableness of searches and seizures under the Fourth Amendment. I continue to believe that "[t]he scheme of the Fourth Amendment becomes meaningful only when it is assured that at some point the conduct of those charged with enforcing the laws can be subjected to the more detached, neutral scrutiny of a judge who must evaluate the reasonableness of a particular search or seizure in light of the particular circumstances." *Terry v. Ohio.* Because I find the majority's reasoning to be at odds with these fundamental principles, I must respectfully dissent.

■ ■ ■

Mr. Justice Jackson, writing for the Court in *Johnson v. United States* (1948), explained:

"The point of the Fourth Amendment, which often is not grasped by zealous officers, is not that it denies law enforcement the support of the usual inferences which reasonable men draw from evidence. Its protection consists in requiring that those inferences be drawn by a neutral and detached magistrate instead of being judged by the officer engaged in the often competitive enterprise of ferreting out crime.... When the right of privacy must reasonably yield to the right of search is, as a rule, to be decided by a judicial officer, not by a policeman or government enforcement agent."

■ ■ ■

Carrying out our mandate of delineating the proper scope of the search-incident-to-arrest exception requires consideration of the purposes of that exception as they apply to the particular search that occurred in this case. See *Chimel v. California*; *Preston v. United States* (1964). Yet the majority, rather than focusing on the facts of this case, places great emphasis on the police department order which instructed Officer Jenks to conduct a full search and to examine carefully everything he found whenever making an in-custody arrest.

■ ■ ■

The majority's attempt to avoid case-by-case adjudication of Fourth Amendment issues is not only misguided as a matter of principle, but is also doomed to fail as a matter of practical application. As the majority itself is well aware, the powers granted the police in this case are strong ones, subject to potential abuse. Although, in this particular case, Officer Jenks was required by police department regulations to make an in-custody arrest rather than to issue a citation, in most jurisdictions and for most traffic offenses the determination of whether to issue a citation or effect a full arrest is discretionary with the officer. There is always the possibility that a police officer, lacking probable cause to obtain a search warrant, will use a traffic arrest as a pretext to conduct a search. See, e.g., *Amador-Gonzalez v. United States* [(1968)]. I suggest this possibility not to impugn the integrity of our police, but merely to point out that case-by-case adjudication will always be necessary to determine whether a full arrest was effected for purely legitimate reasons or, rather, as a pretext for searching the arrestee....

The majority states that "[a] police officer's determination as to how and where to search the person of a suspect whom he has arrested is necessarily a quick ad hoc judgment which the Fourth Amendment does not require to be broken down in each instance into an analysis of each step in the search." No precedent is cited for this broad assertion—not surprisingly, since there is none. Indeed, we only recently rejected such "a rigid all-or-nothing model of justification and regulation under the Amendment, [for] it obscures the utility of limitations upon the scope, as well as the initiation, of police action as a means of constitutional regulation. This Court has held in the past that a search which is reasonable at its inception may violate the Fourth Amendment by virtue of its intolerable intensity and scope." *Terry v. Ohio*. As we there concluded, "in determining whether the seizure and search were 'unreasonable' our inquiry is a dual one—whether the officer's action was justified at its inception, and whether it was reasonably related in scope to the circumstances which justified the interference in the first place."

As I view the matter, the search in this case divides into three distinct phases: the patdown of respondent's coat pocket; the removal of the unknown object from the pocket; and the opening of the crumpled-up cigarette package.

■ ■ ■

No question is raised here concerning the lawfulness of the patdown of respondent's coat pocket. The Court of Appeals unanimously affirmed the right of a police officer to conduct a limited frisk for weapons when making an in-custody arrest, regardless of the nature of the crime for which the arrest was made. As it said:

> "[I]t would seem clearly unreasonable to expect a police officer to place a suspect in his squad car for transportation to the stationhouse without first taking reasonable measures to insure that the suspect is unarmed. We therefore conclude that whenever a police officer, acting within the bounds of his authority, makes an in-custody arrest, he may also conduct a limited frisk of the suspect's outer clothing in order to remove any weapons the suspect may have in his possession."

■ ■ ■

With respect to the removal of the unknown object from the coat pocket, the first issue presented is whether that aspect of the search can be sustained as part of the limited frisk for weapons. The weapons search approved by the Court of Appeals was modeled upon the narrowly drawn protective search for weapons authorized in *Terry*, which consists "of a limited patting of the outer clothing of the suspect for concealed objects which might be used as instruments of assault."

It appears to have been conceded by the Government below that the removal of the object from respondent's coat pocket exceeded the scope of a *Terry* frisk for weapons, since, under *Terry*, an officer may not remove an object from the suspect's pockets unless he has reason to believe it to be a dangerous weapon.

■ ■ ■

In the present case, however, Officer Jenks had no reason to believe and did not in fact believe that the object in respondent's coat pocket was a weapon. He admitted later that the object did not feel like a gun. In fact, he did not really have any thoughts one way or another about what was in the pocket. As Jenks himself testified, "I just searched him. I didn't think about what I was looking for. I just searched him." Since the removal of the object from the pocket cannot be justified as part of a limited *Terry* weapons frisk, the question arises whether it is reasonable for a police officer, when effecting an in-custody arrest of a traffic offender, to make a fuller search of the person than is permitted pursuant to *Terry*.

The underlying rationale of a search incident to arrest of a traffic offender initially suggests as reasonable a search whose scope is similar to the protective weapons frisk permitted in *Terry*. A search incident to arrest, as the majority indicates, has two basic functions: the removal of weapons the arrestee might use to resist arrest or effect an escape, and the seizure of evidence or fruits of the crime for which the arrest is made, so as to prevent their concealment or destruction.

The Government does not now contend that the search of respondent's pocket can be justified by any need to find and seize evidence in order to prevent its concealment or destruction, for, as the Court of Appeals found, there is no evidence or fruits of the offense with which respondent was charged. The only rationale for a search in this case, then, is the removal of weapons which the arrestee might use to harm the officer and attempt an escape. This rationale, of course, is identical to the rationale of the search permitted in *Terry*. As we said there, "The sole justification of the search in the present situation is the protection of the police officer and others nearby, and it must therefore be confined in scope to an intrusion reasonably designed to discover guns, knives, clubs, or other hidden instruments for the assault of the police officer." Since the underlying rationale of a *Terry* search and the search of a traffic violator are identical, the Court of Appeals held that the scope of the searches must be the same. And in view of its conclusion that the removal of the object from respondent's coat pocket exceeded the scope of a lawful *Terry* frisk, a conclusion not disputed by the Government or challenged by the majority here, the plurality of the Court of Appeals held that the removal of the package exceeded the scope of a lawful search incident to arrest of a traffic violator.

The problem with this approach, however, is that it ignores several significant differences between the context in which a search incident to arrest for a traffic violation is made, and the situation presented in *Terry*. Some of these differences would appear to suggest permitting a more thorough search in this case than was permitted in *Terry*; other differences suggest a narrower, more limited right to search than was there recognized.

The most obvious difference between the two contexts relates to whether the officer has cause to believe that the individual he is dealing with possesses weapons which might be used against him. *Terry* did not permit an officer to conduct a weapons frisk of anyone he lawfully stopped on the street, but rather, only where "he has reason to believe that he is dealing with an armed and dangerous individual. . . ." While the policeman who arrests a suspected rapist or robber may well have reason to believe he is dealing with an armed and dangerous person, certainly this does not hold true with equal force with respect to a person arrested for a motor vehicle violation of the sort involved in this case.

Nor was there any particular reason in this case to believe that respondent was dangerous. He had not attempted to evade arrest, but had quickly complied with the police both in bringing his car to a stop after being signaled to do so and in producing the documents Officer Jenks requested. In fact, Jenks admitted that he searched respondent face to face rather than in spread-eagle fashion because he had no reason to believe respondent would be violent.

While this difference between the situation presented in *Terry* and the context presented in this case would tend to suggest a lesser authority to search here than was permitted in *Terry*, other distinctions between the two cases suggest just the opposite. As the Court of Appeals noted, a crucial feature distinguishing the in-custody arrest from the *Terry* context "is not the greater likelihood that a person taken into custody is armed, but rather the increased likelihood of danger to the officer if in fact the person is armed." A *Terry* stop involves a momentary encounter between officer and suspect, while an in-custody arrest places the two in close proximity for a much longer period of time. If the individual happens to have a weapon on his person, he will certainly have much more opportunity to use it against the officer in the in-custody situation. The prolonged proximity also makes it more likely that the individual will be able to extricate any small hidden weapon which might go undetected in a weapons frisk, such as a safety pin or razor blade. In addition, a suspect taken into custody may feel more threatened by the serious restraint on his liberty than a person who is simply stopped by an officer for questioning, and may therefore be more likely to resort to force.

Thus, in some senses there is less need for a weapons search in the in-custody traffic arrest situation than in a *Terry* context; while in other ways, there is a greater need. Balancing these competing considerations in order to determine what is a reasonable warrantless search in the traffic arrest context is a difficult process, one for which there may be no easy analytical guideposts. We are dealing with factors not easily quantified and, therefore, not easily weighed one against the other. And the competing interests we are protecting—the individual's interest in remaining free from unnecessarily intrusive invasions of privacy and society's interest that police officers not take unnecessary risks in the performance of their duties—are each deserving of our most serious attention and do not themselves tip the balance in any particular direction. . . .

The majority opinion fails to recognize that the search conducted by Officer Jenks did not merely involve a search of respondent's person. It also included a separate search of effects found on his person. And even were we to assume, arguendo, that it was reasonable for Jenks to remove the object he felt in respondent's pocket, clearly there was no justification consistent with the Fourth Amendment which would authorize his opening the package and looking inside.

To begin with, after Jenks had the cigarette package in his hands, there is no indication that he had reason to believe or did in fact believe that the package contained a weapon. More importantly, even if the crumpled-up cigarette package had in fact contained some sort of small weapon, it would have been impossible for respondent to have used it once the package was in the officer's hands. Opening the package, therefore, did not further the protective purpose of the search. Even the dissenting opinion in the Court of Appeals conceded that "since the package was now in the officer's possession, any risk of the prisoner's use of a weapon in this package had been eliminated."

It is suggested, however, that since the custodial arrest itself represents a significant intrusion into the privacy of the person, any additional intrusion by way of opening or examining effects found on the person is not worthy of constitutional protection. But such an approach was expressly rejected by the Court in *Chimel*. There it was suggested that since the police had lawfully entered petitioner's house to effect an arrest, the additional invasion of privacy stemming from an accompanying search of the entire house was inconsequential. The Court answered: "[W]e can see no reason why, simply because some interference with an individual's privacy and freedom of movement has lawfully taken place, further intrusions should automatically be allowed despite the absence of a warrant that the Fourth Amendment would otherwise require."

The Fourth Amendment preserves the right of "the people to be secure in their persons, houses, papers, and effects, against unreasonable searches and seizures. . . ." *Chimel* established the principle that the lawful right of the police to interfere with the security of the person did not, standing alone, automatically confer the right to interfere with the security and privacy of his house. Hence, the mere fact of an arrest should be no justification, in and of itself, for invading the privacy of the individual's personal effects.

The Government argues that it is difficult to see what constitutionally protected "expectation of privacy" a prisoner has in the interior of a cigarette pack. One wonders if the result in this case would have been the same were respondent a businessman who was lawfully taken into custody for driving without a license and whose wallet was taken from him by the police. Would it be reasonable for the police officer, because of the possibility that a razor blade was hidden somewhere in the wallet, to open it, remove all the contents, and examine each item carefully? Or suppose a lawyer lawfully arrested for a traffic offense is found to have a sealed envelope on his person. Would it be permissible for the arresting officer to tear open the envelope in order to make sure that it did not contain a clandestine weapon—perhaps a pin or a razor blade? Would it not be more consonant with the purpose of the Fourth Amendment and the legitimate needs of the police to require the officer, if he has any question whatsoever about what the wallet or letter contains, to hold on to it until the arrestee is brought to the precinct station?

I, for one, cannot characterize any of these intrusions into the privacy of an individual's papers and effects as being negligible incidents to the more serious intrusion into the individual's privacy stemming from the arrest itself. Nor can any principled distinction be drawn between the hypothetical searches I have posed and the search of the cigarette package in this case. The only reasoned distinction is between warrantless searches which serve legitimate protective and evidentiary functions and those that do not.

The search conducted by Officer Jenks in this case went far beyond what was reasonably necessary to protect him from harm or to ensure that respondent would not effect an escape from custody. In my view, it therefore fell outside the scope of a properly drawn "search incident to arrest" exception to the Fourth Amendment's warrant requirement. I would affirm the judgment of the Court of Appeals holding that the fruits of the search should have been suppressed at respondent's trial.

Note how the Massachusetts legislature in response to Robinson *passed the following law:*

Mass. Gen. Laws ch. 276, § 1
A search conducted incident to an arrest may be made only for the purposes of seizing fruits, instrumentalities, contraband and other evidence of the crime for which the arrest has been made, in order to prevent its destruction or concealment; and removing any weapons that the arrestee might use to resist arrest or effect his escape. Property seized as a result of a search in violation of the provisions of this paragraph shall not be admissible in evidence in criminal proceedings.

Florence v. Burlington

132 S. Ct. 1510 (2012)

See Chapter 3.A.2

Maryland v. Buie

494 U.S. 325 (1990)

See Chapter 4.A.

4. Automobile—Search Incident to Arrest

New York v. Belton

453 U.S. 454 (1981)

STEWART, J., delivered the opinion of the Court, in which BURGER, C.J., REHNQUIST, BLACKMUN, POWELL, and O'CONNOR, JJ., joined. STEVENS, J., filed a statement concurring in the judgment. BRENNAN, J., filed a dissenting opinion, in which MARSHALL, J., joined. WHITE, J., filed a dissenting opinion, in which MARSHALL, J., joined.

When the occupant of an automobile is subjected to a lawful custodial arrest, does the constitutionally permissible scope of a search incident to his arrest include the passenger compartment of the automobile in which he was riding? That is the question at issue in the present case. . . .

On April 9, 1978, Trooper Douglas Nicot, a New York State policeman driving an unmarked car on the New York Thruway, was passed by another automobile traveling at an excessive rate of speed. Nicot gave chase, overtook the speeding vehicle, and ordered its driver to pull it over to the side of the road and stop. There were four men in the car, one of whom was Roger Belton, the respondent in this case. The policeman asked to see the driver's license and automobile registration, and discovered that none of the men owned the vehicle or was related to its owner. Meanwhile, the policeman had smelled burnt marihuana and had seen on the floor of the car an envelope marked "Supergold" that he associated with marihuana. He therefore directed the men to get out of the car, and placed them under arrest for the unlawful possession of marihuana. He patted down each of the men and "split them up into four separate areas of the Thruway at this time so they would not be in physical touching area of each other." He then picked up the envelope marked "Supergold" and found that it contained marihuana. After giving the arrestees the warnings required by *Miranda v. Arizona* (1966), the state policeman searched each one of them. He then searched the passenger compartment of the car. On the back seat he found a black leather jacket belonging to Belton. He unzipped one of the pockets of the jacket and discovered cocaine. Placing the jacket in his automobile, he drove the four arrestees to a nearby police station.

Belton was subsequently indicted for criminal possession of a controlled substance. In the trial court he moved that the cocaine the trooper had seized from the jacket pocket be suppressed. The court denied the motion. Belton then pleaded guilty to a lesser included offense, but preserved his claim that the cocaine had been seized in violation of the Fourth and Fourteenth Amendments. The Appellant Division of the New York Supreme Court upheld the constitutionality of the search and seizure, reasoning that "[o]nce defendant was validly arrested for possession of marihuana, the officer was justified in searching the immediate area for other contraband."

The New York Court of Appeals reversed, holding that "[a] warrantless search of the zippered pockets of an unaccessible jacket may not be upheld as a search incident to a lawful arrest where there is no longer any danger that the arrestee or a confederate might gain access to the article."

■ ■ ■

It is a first principle of Fourth Amendment jurisprudence that the police may not conduct a search unless they first convince a neutral magistrate that there is probable cause to do so. This Court has recognized, however, that "the exigencies of the situation" may sometimes make exemption from the warrant requirement "imperative." Specifically, the Court held in *Chimel v. California* [(1969)] that a lawful custodial arrest creates a situation which justifies the contemporaneous search without a warrant of the person arrested and of the immediately surrounding area. Such searches have long been considered valid because of the need "to remove any weapons that [the arrestee] might seek to use in order to resist arrest or effect his escape" and the need to prevent the concealment or destruction of evidence.

The Court's opinion in *Chimel* emphasized the principle that, as the Court had said in *Terry v. Ohio* (1968), "the scope of [a] search must be 'strictly tied to and justified by' the circumstances which rendered its initiation permissible." Thus while the Court in *Chimel* found "ample justification" for a search of "the area from within which [an arrestee] might gain possession of a weapon or destructible evidence," the Court found "no comparable justification . . . for routinely searching any room other than that in which an arrest occurs—or, for that matter, for searching through all the desk drawers or other closed or concealed areas in that room itself."

Although the principle that limits a search incident to a lawful custodial arrest may be stated clearly enough, courts have discovered the principle difficult to apply in specific cases. Yet, as one commentator has pointed out, the protection of the Fourth and Fourteenth Amendments "can only be realized if the police are acting under a set of rules which, in most instances, makes it possible to reach a correct determination beforehand as to whether an invasion of privacy is justified in the interest of law enforcement." This is because "Fourth Amendment doctrine, given force and effect by the exclusionary rule, is primarily intended to regulate the police in their day-to-day activities and thus ought to be expressed in terms that are readily applicable by the police in the context of the law enforcement activities in which they are necessarily engaged. A highly sophisticated set of rules, qualified by all sorts of ifs, ands, and buts and requiring the drawing of subtle nuances and hairline distinctions, may be the sort of heady stuff upon which the facile minds of lawyers and judges eagerly feed, but they may be 'literally impossible of application by the officer in the field.' " LaFave, "Case-By-Case Adjudication" Versus "Standardized Procedures": The *Robinson* Dilemma, 1974 S. Ct. Rev. 127, 142.

In short, "[a] single, familiar standard is essential to guide police officers, who have only limited time and expertise to reflect on and balance the social and individual interests involved in the specific circumstances they confront." *Dunaway v. New York* [(1979)].

So it was that, in *United States v. Robinson* (1973), the Court hewed to a straightforward rule, easily applied, and predictably enforced: "[I]n the case of a lawful custodial arrest a full search of the person is not only an exception to the warrant requirement of the Fourth Amendment, but is also a 'reasonable' search under that Amendment." In so holding, the Court rejected the suggestion that "there must be litigated in each case the issue of whether or not there was present one of the reasons supporting the authority for a search of the person incident to a lawful arrest."

■ ■ ■

When a person cannot know how a court will apply a settled principle to a recurring factual situation, that person cannot know the scope of his constitutional protection, nor can a policeman know the scope of his authority. While the *Chimel* case established that a search incident to an arrest may not stray beyond the area within the immediate control of the arrestee, courts have found no workable definition of "the area within the immediate control of the arrestee" when that area arguably includes the interior of an automobile and the arrestee is its recent occupant. Our reading of the cases suggests the generalization that articles inside the relatively narrow compass of the passenger compartment of an automobile are in fact generally, even if not inevitably, within "the area into which an arrestee might reach in order to grab a weapon or evidentiary ite[m]." In order to establish the workable rule this category of cases requires, we read *Chimel*'s definition of the limits of the area that may be searched in light of that generalization. Accordingly, we hold that when a policeman has made a lawful custodial arrest of the occupant of an automobile, he may, as a contemporaneous incident of that arrest, search the passenger compartment of that automobile.

It follows from this conclusion that the police may also examine the contents of any containers found within the passenger compartment, for if the passenger compartment is within reach of the arrestee, so also will containers in it be within his reach. Such a container may, of course, be searched whether it is open or closed, since the justification for the search is not that the arrestee has no privacy interest in the container, but that the lawful custodial arrest justifies the infringement of any privacy interest the arrestee may have. Thus, while the Court in *Chimel* held that the police could not search all the drawers in an arrestee's house simply because the police had arrested him at home, the Court noted that drawers within an arrestee's reach could be searched because of the danger their contents might pose to the police.

It is true, of course, that these containers will sometimes be such that they could hold neither a weapon nor evidence of the criminal conduct for which the suspect was arrested. However, in *United States v. Robinson*, the Court rejected the argument that such a container—there a "crumpled up cigarette package"—located during a search of Robinson incident to his arrest could not be searched: "The authority to search the person incident to a lawful custodial arrest, while based upon the need to disarm and to discover evidence, does not depend on what a court may later decide was the probability in a particular arrest situation that weapons or evidence would in fact be found upon the person of the suspect. A custodial arrest of a suspect based on probable cause is a reasonable intrusion under the Fourth Amendment; that intrusion being lawful, a search incident to the arrest requires no additional justification."

■ ■ ■

It is not questioned that the respondent was the subject of a lawful custodial arrest on a charge of possessing marihuana. The search of the respondent's jacket followed immediately upon that arrest. The jacket was located inside the passenger compartment of the car in which the respondent had been a passenger just before he was arrested. The jacket was thus within the area which we have concluded was "within the arrestee's immediate control" within the meaning of the *Chimel* case. The search of the jacket, therefore, was a search incident to a lawful custodial arrest, and it did not violate the Fourth and Fourteenth Amendments. Accordingly, the judgment is reversed.

It is so ordered.

Justice BRENNAN, with whom Justice MARSHALL joins, dissenting.

In *Chimel v. California*, this Court carefully analyzed more than 50 years of conflicting precedent governing the permissible scope of warrantless searches incident to custodial arrest. The Court today turns its back on the product of that analysis, formulating an arbitrary "bright-line" rule applicable to "recent" occupants of automobiles that fails to reflect *Chimel*'s underlying policy justifications. While the Court claims to leave *Chimel* intact, I fear that its unwarranted abandonment of the principles underlying that decision may signal a wholesale retreat from our carefully developed search-incident-to-arrest analysis. I dissent.

■ ■ ■

It has long been a fundamental principle of Fourth Amendment analysis that exceptions to the warrant requirement are to be narrowly construed. . . . Second, in determining whether to grant an exception to the warrant requirement, courts should carefully consider the facts and circumstances of each search and seizure, focusing on the reasons supporting the exception rather than on any bright-line rule of general application.

The *Chimel* exception to the warrant requirement was designed with two principal concerns in mind: the safety of the arresting officer and the preservation of easily concealed or destructible evidence. Recognizing that a suspect might have access to weapons or contraband at the time of arrest, the Court declared:

> "When an arrest is made, it is reasonable for the arresting officer to search the person arrested in order to remove any weapons that the latter might seek to use in order to resist arrest or effect his escape. Otherwise, the officer's safety might well be endangered, and the arrest itself frustrated. In addition, it is entirely reasonable for the arresting officer to search for and seize any evidence on the arrestee's person in order to prevent its concealment or destruction. And the area into which an arrestee might reach in order to grab a weapon or evidentiary items must, of course, be governed by a like rule."

The *Chimel* standard was narrowly tailored to address these concerns: it permits police officers who have effected a custodial arrest to conduct a warrantless search "of the arrestee's person and the area 'within his immediate control'—construing that phrase to mean the area from within which he might gain possession of a weapon or destructible evidence." It thus places a temporal and a spatial limitation on searches incident to arrest, excusing compliance with the warrant requirement only when the search " 'is substantially contemporaneous with the arrest and is confined to the *immediate* vicinity of the arrest.' "

■ ■ ■

As the facts of this case make clear, the Court today substantially expands the permissible scope of searches incident to arrest by permitting police officers to search areas and containers the arrestee could not possibly reach at the time of arrest. These facts demonstrate that at the time Belton and his three companions were placed under custodial arrest—which was *after* they had been removed from the car, patted down, and separated—none of them could have reached the jackets that had been left on the back seat of the car.

■ ■ ■

By approving the constitutionality of the warrantless search in this case, the Court carves out a dangerous precedent that is not justified by the concerns underlying *Chimel*. Disregarding the principle "that the scope of a warrantless search must be commensurate with the rationale that excepts the search from the warrant requirement," the Court for the first time grants police officers authority to conduct a warrantless "area" search under circumstances where there is no chance that the arrestee "might gain possession of a weapon or destructible evidence." *Chimel v. California*. Under the approach taken today, the result would presumably be the same even if Officer Nicot had handcuffed Belton and his companions in the patrol car before placing them under arrest, and even if his search had extended to locked luggage or other inaccessible containers located in the back seat of the car.

This expansion of the *Chimel* exception is both analytically unsound and inconsistent with every significant search-incident-to-arrest case we have decided in which the issue was whether the police could lawfully conduct a warrantless search of the area surrounding the arrestee.

■ ■ ■

The Court seeks to justify its departure from the principles underlying *Chimel* by proclaiming the need for a new "bright-line" rule to guide the officer in the field. As we pointed out in *Mincey v. Arizona* (1977), however, "the mere fact that law enforcement may be made more efficient can never by itself justify disregard of the Fourth Amendment." Moreover, the Court's attempt to forge a "bright-line" rule fails on its own terms. While the "interior/trunk" distinction may provide a workable guide in certain routine cases—for example, where the officer arrests the driver of a car and then immediately searches the seats and floor—in the long run, I suspect it will create far more problems than it solves. The Court's new approach leaves open too many questions and, more important, it provides the police and the courts with too few tools with which to find the answers.

■ ■ ■

The standard announced in *Chimel* is not nearly as difficult to apply as the Court suggests. To the contrary, I continue to believe that *Chimel* provides a sound, workable rule for determining the constitutionality of a warrantless search incident to arrest. Under *Chimel*, searches incident to arrest may be conducted without a warrant only if limited to the person of the arrestee, see *United States v. Robinson* (1973), or to the area within the arrestee's "immediate control." While it may be difficult in some cases to measure the exact scope of the arrestee's immediate control, relevant factors would surely include the relative number of police officers and arrestees, the manner of restraint placed on the arrestee, and the ability of the arrestee to gain access to a particular area or container. Certainly there will be some close cases, but when in doubt the police can always turn to the rationale underlying *Chimel*—the need to prevent the arrestee from reaching weapons or contraband—before exercising their judgment. A rule based on that rationale should provide more guidance than the rule announced by the Court today. Moreover, unlike the Court's rule, it would be faithful to the Fourth Amendment.

Thornton v. United States

541 U.S. 615 (2004)

Rehnquist, C.J., delivered the opinion of the Court except as to footnote 4. Kennedy, Thomas, and Breyer, JJ., joined that opinion in full. O'Connor, J., filed an opinion concurring in part. Scalia, J., filed an opinion concurring in the judgment, in which Ginsburg, J., joined. Stevens, J., filed a dissenting opinion, in which Souter, J., joined.

In *New York v. Belton* (1981), we held that when a police officer has made a lawful custodial arrest of an occupant of an automobile, the Fourth Amendment allows the officer to search the passenger compartment of that vehicle as a contemporaneous incident of arrest. We have granted certiorari twice before to determine whether *Belton*'s rule is limited to situations where the officer makes contact with the occupant while the occupant is inside the vehicle, or whether it applies as well when the officer first makes contact with the arrestee after the latter has stepped out of his vehicle.

Officer Deion Nichols of the Norfolk, Virginia, Police Department, who was in uniform but driving an unmarked police car, first noticed petitioner Marcus Thornton when petitioner slowed down so as to avoid driving next to him. Nichols suspected that petitioner knew he was a police officer and for some reason did not want to pull next to him. His suspicions aroused, Nichols pulled off onto a side street and petitioner passed him. After petitioner passed him, Nichols ran a check on petitioner's license tags, which revealed that the tags had been issued to a 1982 Chevy two-door and not to a Lincoln Town Car, the model of car petitioner was driving. Before Nichols had an opportunity to pull him over, petitioner drove into a parking lot, parked, and got out of the vehicle. Nichols saw petitioner leave his vehicle as he pulled in behind him. He parked the patrol car, accosted petitioner, and asked him for his driver's license. He also told him that his license tags did not match the vehicle that he was driving.

Petitioner appeared nervous. He began rambling and licking his lips; he was sweating. Concerned for his safety, Nichols asked petitioner if he had any narcotics or weapons on him or in his vehicle. Petitioner said no. Nichols then asked petitioner if he could pat him down, to which petitioner agreed. Nichols felt a bulge in petitioner's left front pocket and again asked him if he had any illegal narcotics on him. This time petitioner stated that he did, and he reached into his pocket and pulled out two individual bags, one containing three bags of marijuana and the other containing a large amount of crack cocaine. Nichols handcuffed petitioner, informed him that he was under arrest, and placed him in the back seat of the patrol car. He then searched petitioner's vehicle and found a BryCo 9-millimeter handgun under the driver's seat.

■ ■ ■

Petitioner sought to suppress, *inter alia*, the firearm as the fruit of an unconstitutional search. After a hearing, the District Court denied petitioner's motion to suppress, holding that the automobile search was valid under *New York v. Belton*, and alternatively that Nichols could have conducted an inventory search of the automobile.

■ ■ ■

Petitioner appealed, challenging only the District Court's denial of the suppression motion. He argued that *Belton* was limited to situations where the officer initiated contact with an arrestee while he was still an occupant of the car. The United States Court of Appeals for the Fourth Circuit affirmed. . . . We granted certiorari, and now affirm.

In *Belton*, an officer overtook a speeding vehicle on the New York Thruway and ordered its driver to pull over. Suspecting that the occupants possessed marijuana, the officer directed them to get out of the car and arrested them for unlawful possession. He searched them and then searched the passenger compartment of the car. We considered the constitutionally permissible scope of a search in these circumstances and sought to lay down a workable rule governing that situation.

We first referred to *Chimel v. California* (1969), a case where the arrestee was arrested in his home, and we had described the scope of a search incident to a lawful arrest as the person of the arrestee and the area immediately surrounding him. This rule was justified by the need to remove any weapon the arrestee might seek to use to resist arrest or to escape, and the need to prevent the concealment or destruction of evidence. Although easily stated, the *Chimel* principle had proved difficult to apply in specific cases. We pointed out that in *United States v. Robinson* (1973), a case dealing with the scope of the search of the arrestee's person, we had rejected a suggestion that " 'there must be litigated in each case the issue of whether or not there was present one of the reasons supporting the authority' " to conduct such a search. Similarly, because "courts ha[d] found no workable definition of 'the area within the immediate control of the arrestee' when that area arguably include[d] the interior of an automobile and the arrestee [wa]s its recent occupant," we sought to set forth a clear rule for police officers and citizens alike. We therefore held that "when a policeman has made a lawful custodial arrest of the occupant of an automobile, he may, as a contemporaneous incident of that arrest, search the passenger compartment of that automobile."

In so holding, we placed no reliance on the fact that the officer in *Belton* ordered the occupants out of the vehicle, or initiated contact with them while they remained within it. Nor do we find such a factor persuasive in distinguishing the current situation, as it bears no logical relationship to *Belton*'s rationale. There is simply no basis to conclude that the span of the area generally within the arrestee's immediate control is determined by whether the arrestee exited the vehicle at the officer's direction, or whether the officer initiated contact with him while he remained in the car.

■ ■ ■

In all relevant aspects, the arrest of a suspect who is next to a vehicle presents identical concerns regarding officer safety and the destruction of evidence as the arrest of one who is inside the vehicle. An officer may search a suspect's vehicle under *Belton* only if the suspect is arrested. A custodial arrest is fluid and "[t]he danger to the police officer flows from *the fact of the arrest,* and its attendant proximity, stress, and uncertainty." . . .

Petitioner argues, however, that *Belton* will fail to provide a "bright-line" rule if it applies to more than vehicle "occupants." But *Belton* allows police to search the passenger compartment of a vehicle incident to a lawful custodial arrest of both "occupant[s]" and "recent occupant[s]." Indeed, the respondent in *Belton* was not inside the car at the time of the arrest and search; he was standing on the highway. In any event, while an arrestee's status as a "recent occupant" may turn on his temporal or spatial relationship to the car at the time of the arrest and search, it certainly does not turn on whether he was inside or outside the car at the moment that the officer first initiated contact with him.

To be sure, not all contraband in the passenger compartment is likely to be readily accessible to a "recent occupant." It is unlikely in this case that petitioner could have reached under the driver's seat for his gun once he was outside of his automobile. But the firearm and the passenger compartment in general were no more inaccessible than were the contraband and the passenger compartment in *Belton.* The need for a clear rule, readily understood by police officers and not depending on differing estimates of what items were or were not within reach of an arrestee at any particular moment, justifies the sort of generalization which *Belton* enunciated. Once an officer determines that there is probable cause to make an arrest, it is reasonable to allow officers to ensure their safety and to preserve evidence by searching the entire passenger compartment.

Rather than clarifying the constitutional limits of a *Belton* search, petitioner's "contact initiation" rule would obfuscate them. Under petitioner's proposed rule, an officer approaching a suspect who has just alighted from his vehicle would have to determine whether he actually confronted or signaled confrontation with the suspect while he remained in the car, or whether the suspect exited his vehicle unaware of, and for reasons unrelated to, the officer's presence. This determination would be inherently subjective and highly fact specific, and would require precisely the sort of ad hoc determinations on the part of officers in the field and reviewing courts that *Belton* sought to avoid. Experience has shown that such a rule is impracticable, and we refuse to adopt it. So long as an arrestee is the sort of "recent occupant" of a vehicle such as petitioner was here, officers may search that vehicle incident to the arrest.[4]

The judgment of the Court of Appeals is affirmed.

It is so ordered.

■ ■ ■

Justice SCALIA, with whom Justice GINSBURG joins, concurring in the judgment.

In *Chimel v. California*, we held that a search incident to arrest was justified only as a means to find weapons the arrestee might use or evidence he might conceal or destroy. We accordingly limited such searches to the area within the suspect's " 'immediate control' "—*i.e.*, "the area into which an arrestee might reach in order to grab a weapon or evidentiary ite[m]." In *New York v. Belton*, we set forth a bright-line rule for arrests of automobile occupants, holding that, because the vehicle's entire passenger compartment is "in fact generally, even if not inevitably," within the arrestee's immediate control, a search of the whole compartment is justified in every case.

When petitioner's car was searched in this case, he was neither in, nor anywhere near, the passenger compartment of his vehicle. Rather, he was handcuffed and secured in the back of the officer's squad car. The risk that he would nevertheless "grab a weapon or evidentiary ite[m]" from his car was remote in the extreme. The Court's effort to apply our current doctrine to this search stretches it beyond its breaking point, and for that reason I cannot join the Court's opinion.

■ ■ ■

I see three reasons why the search in this case might have been justified to protect officer safety or prevent concealment or destruction of evidence. None ultimately persuades me.

The first is that, despite being handcuffed and secured in the back of a squad car, petitioner might have escaped and retrieved a weapon or evidence from his vehicle—a theory that calls to mind Judge Goldberg's reference to the mythical arrestee "possessed of the skill of Houdini and the strength of Hercules."

■ ■ ■

Of course, the Government need not document specific instances in order to justify measures that avoid obvious risks. But the risk here is far from obvious, and in a context as frequently recurring as roadside arrests, the

---

4. Whatever the merits of Justice Scalia's opinion concurring in the judgment, this is the wrong case in which to address them. Petitioner has never argued that *Belton* should be limited "to cases where it is reasonable to believe evidence relevant to the crime of arrest might be found in the vehicle," nor did any court below consider Justice Scalia's reasoning. . . . Under these circumstances, it would be imprudent to overrule, for all intents and purposes, our established constitutional precedent, which governs police authority in a common occurrence such as automobile searches pursuant to arrest, and we decline to do so at this time.

Government's inability to come up with even a single example of a handcuffed arrestee's retrieval of arms or evidence from his vehicle undermines its claims. The risk that a suspect handcuffed in the back of a squad car might escape and recover a weapon from his vehicle is surely no greater than the risk that a suspect handcuffed in his residence might escape and recover a weapon from the next room—a danger we held insufficient to justify a search in *Chimel*.

The second defense of the search in this case is that, since the officer could have conducted the search at the time of arrest (when the suspect was still near the car), he should not be penalized for having taken the sensible precaution of securing the suspect in the squad car first. As one Court of Appeals put it: " '[I]t does not make sense to prescribe a constitutional test that is entirely at odds with safe and sensible police procedures.' " The weakness of this argument is that it assumes that, one way or another, the search must take place. But conducting a *Chimel* search is not the Government's right; it is an exception— justified by necessity—to a rule that would otherwise render the search unlawful. If "sensible police procedures" require that suspects be handcuffed and put in squad cars, then police should handcuff suspects, put them in squad cars, and not conduct the search. Indeed, if an officer leaves a suspect unrestrained nearby just to manufacture authority to search, one could argue that the search is unreasonable *precisely because* the dangerous conditions justifying it existed only by virtue of the officer's failure to follow sensible procedures.

The third defense of the search is that, even though the arrestee posed no risk here, *Belton* searches in general are reasonable, and the benefits of a bright-line rule justify upholding that small minority of searches that, on their particular facts, are not reasonable. The validity of this argument rests on the accuracy of *Belton*'s claim that the passenger compartment is "in fact generally, even if not inevitably," within the suspect's immediate control. By the United States' own admission, however, "[t]he practice of restraining an arrestee on the scene before searching a car that he just occupied is so prevalent that holding that *Belton* does not apply in that setting would . . . 'largely render *Belton* a dead letter.' "

■　■　■

The popularity of the practice is not hard to fathom. If *Belton entitles* an officer to search a vehicle upon arresting the driver despite having taken measures that eliminate any danger, what rational officer would not take those measures?

■　■　■

There is nothing irrational about broader police authority to search for evidence when and where the perpetrator of a crime is lawfully arrested. The fact of prior lawful arrest distinguishes the arrestee from society at large, and distinguishes a search for evidence of *his* crime from general rummaging. Moreover, it is not illogical to assume that evidence of a crime is most likely to be found where the suspect was apprehended.

■　■　■

In short, both [*United States v.*] *Rabinowitz* [(1969)] and *Chimel* are plausible accounts of what the Constitution requires, and neither is so persuasive as to justify departing from settled law. But if we are going to continue to allow *Belton* searches on *stare decisis* grounds, we should at least be honest about why we are doing so. *Belton* cannot reasonably be explained as a mere application of *Chimel*. Rather, it is a return to the broader sort of search incident to arrest that we allowed before *Chimel*—limited, of course, to searches of motor vehicles, a category of "effects" which give rise to a reduced expectation of privacy, see *Wyoming v. Houghton* (1999), and heightened law enforcement needs, *Rabinowitz* (Frankfurter, J., dissenting).

Recasting *Belton* in these terms would have at least one important practical consequence. In *United States v. Robinson*, we held that authority to search an arrestee's person does not depend on the actual presence of one of *Chimel*'s two rationales in the particular case; rather, the fact of arrest alone justifies the search. That holding stands in contrast to *Rabinowitz*, where we did not treat the fact of arrest alone as sufficient, but upheld the search only after noting that it was "not general or exploratory for whatever might be turned up" but reflected a reasonable belief that evidence would be found.

■ ■ ■

In this case, as in *Belton*, petitioner was lawfully arrested for a drug offense. It was reasonable for Officer Nichols to believe that further contraband or similar evidence relevant to the crime for which he had been arrested might be found in the vehicle from which he had just alighted and which was still within his vicinity at the time of arrest. I would affirm the decision below on that ground.

Justice STEVENS, with whom Justice SOUTER joins, dissenting.

Prior to our decision in *New York v. Belton*, there was a widespread conflict among both federal and state courts over the question "whether, in the course of a search incident to the lawful custodial arrest of the occupants of an automobile, police may search inside the automobile after the arrestees are no longer in it." In answering that question, the Court expanded the authority of the police in two important respects. It allowed the police to conduct a broader search than our decision in *Chimel v. California* would have permitted, and it authorized them to open closed containers that might be found in the vehicle's passenger compartment.

Belton's basic rationale for both expansions rested not on a concern for officer safety, but rather on an overriding desire to hew "to a straightforward rule, easily applied, and predictably enforced." When the case was decided, I was persuaded that the important interest in clarity and certainty adequately justified the modest extension of the *Chimel* rule to permit an officer to examine the interior of a car pursuant to an arrest for a traffic violation. But I took a different view with respect to the search of containers within the car absent probable cause, because I thought "it palpably unreasonable to require the driver of a car to open his briefcase or his luggage for inspection by the officer." I remain convinced that this aspect of the *Belton* opinion was both unnecessary and erroneous. Whether one agrees or disagrees with that view, however, the interest in certainty that supports *Belton*'s bright-line rule surely does not justify an expansion of the rule that only blurs those clear lines. Neither the rule in *Chimel* nor *Belton*'s modification of that rule would have allowed the search of petitioner's car.

A fair reading of the *Belton* opinion itself, and of the conflicting cases that gave rise to our grant of certiorari, makes clear that we were not concerned with the situation presented in this case. The Court in *Belton* noted that the lower courts had discovered *Chimel*'s reaching-distance principle difficult to apply in the context of automobile searches incident to arrest, and that "no straightforward rule ha[d] emerged from the litigated cases." None of the cases cited by the Court to demonstrate the disarray in the lower courts involved a pedestrian who was in the vicinity, but outside the reaching distance, of his or her car. Nor did any of the decisions cited in the petition for a writ of certiorari present such a case. Thus, *Belton* was demonstrably concerned only with the narrow but common circumstance of a search occasioned by the arrest of a suspect who was seated in or driving an automobile at the time the law enforcement official approached. Normally, after such an arrest has occurred, the officer's safety is no longer in jeopardy, but he must decide what, if any, search for incriminating evidence he should conduct. *Belton* provided previously unavailable and therefore necessary guidance for that category of cases.

The bright-line rule crafted in *Belton* is not needed for cases in which the arrestee is first accosted when he is a pedestrian, because *Chimel* itself provides all the guidance that is necessary. The only genuine justification for extending *Belton* to cover such circumstances is the interest in uncovering potentially valuable evidence. In my opinion, that goal must give way to the citizen's constitutionally protected interest in privacy when there is already in place a well-defined rule limiting the permissible scope of a search of an arrested pedestrian. The *Chimel* rule should provide the same protection to a "recent occupant" of a vehicle as to a recent occupant of a house.

Unwilling to confine the *Belton* rule to the narrow class of cases it was designed to address, the Court extends *Belton*'s reach without supplying any guidance for the future application of its swollen rule. We are told that officers may search a vehicle incident to arrest "[s]o long as [the] arrestee is the sort of 'recent occupant' of a vehicle such as petitioner was here."

■ ■ ■

Accordingly, I respectfully dissent.

Arizona v. Gant

556 U.S. 332 (2009)

STEVENS, J., delivered the opinion of the Court, in which SCALIA, SOUTER, THOMAS, and GINSBURG, JJ., joined. SCALIA, J., filed a concurring opinion. BREYER, J., filed a dissenting opinion. ALITO, J., filed a dissenting opinion, in which ROBERTS, C.J., and KENNEDY, J., joined, and in which BREYER, J., joined except as to Part II-E.

After Rodney Gant was arrested for driving with a suspended license, handcuffed, and locked in the back of a patrol car, police officers searched his car and discovered cocaine in the pocket of a jacket on the backseat. Because Gant could not have accessed his car to retrieve weapons or evidence at the time of the search, the Arizona Supreme Court held that the search-incident-to-arrest exception to the Fourth Amendment's warrant requirement, as defined in *Chimel v. California* (1969), and applied to vehicle searches in *New York v. Belton* (1981), did not justify the search in this case. We agree with that conclusion.

Under *Chimel*, police may search incident to arrest only the space within an arrestee's "'immediate control,'" meaning "the area from within which he might gain possession of a weapon or destructible evidence." The safety and evidentiary justifications underlying *Chimel*'s reaching-distance rule determine *Belton*'s scope. Accordingly, we hold that *Belton* does not authorize a vehicle search incident to a recent occupant's arrest after the arrestee has been secured and cannot access the interior of the vehicle. Consistent with the holding in *Thornton v. United States* (2004), and following the suggestion in Justice Scalia's opinion concurring in the judgment in that case, we also conclude that circumstances unique to the automobile context justify a search incident to arrest when it is reasonable to believe that evidence of the offense of arrest might be found in the vehicle.

On August 25, 1999, acting on an anonymous tip that the residence at 2524 North Walnut Avenue was being used to sell drugs, Tucson police officers Griffith and Reed knocked on the front door and asked to speak to the owner. Gant answered the door and, after identifying himself, stated that he expected the owner to return later. The officers left the residence and conducted a records check, which revealed that Gant's driver's license had been suspended and there was an outstanding warrant for his arrest for driving with a suspended license.

When the officers returned to the house that evening, they found a man near the back of the house and a woman in a car parked in front of it. After a third officer arrived, they arrested the man for providing a false name and the woman for possessing drug paraphernalia. Both arrestees were handcuffed and secured in separate patrol cars when Gant arrived. The officers recognized his car as it entered the driveway, and Officer Griffith confirmed that Gant was the driver by shining a flashlight into the car as it drove by him. Gant parked at the end of the driveway, got out of his car, and shut the door. Griffith, who was about 30 feet away, called to Gant, and they approached each other, meeting 10-to-12 feet from Gant's car. Griffith immediately arrested Gant and hand-cuffed him.

Because the other arrestees were secured in the only patrol cars at the scene, Griffith called for backup. When two more officers arrived, they locked Gant in the backseat of their vehicle. After Gant had been handcuffed and placed in the back of a patrol car, two officers searched his car: One of them found a gun, and the other discovered a bag of cocaine in the pocket of a jacket on the backseat.

Gant was charged with two offenses—possession of a narcotic drug for sale and possession of drug paraphernalia (*i.e.*, the plastic bag in which the cocaine was found). He moved to suppress the evidence seized from his car on the ground that the warrantless search violated the Fourth Amendment. Among other things, Gant argued that *Belton* did not authorize the search of his vehicle because he posed no threat to the officers after he was handcuffed in the patrol car and because he was arrested for a traffic offense for which no evidence could be found in his vehicle. When asked at the suppression hearing why the search was conducted, Officer Griffith responded: "Because the law says we can do it."

The trial court rejected the State's contention that the officers had probable cause to search Gant's car for contraband when the search began, but it denied the motion to suppress. Relying on the fact that the police saw Gant commit the crime of driving without a license and apprehended him only shortly after he exited his car, the court held that the search was permissible as a search inci-dent to arrest. A jury found Gant guilty on both drug counts, and he was sentenced to a 3-year term of imprisonment.

After protracted state-court proceedings, the Arizona Supreme Court con-cluded that the search of Gant's car was unreasonable within the meaning of the Fourth Amendment....

The chorus that has called for us to revisit *Belton* includes courts, scholars, and Members of this Court who have questioned that decision's clarity and its fidelity to Fourth Amendment principles. We therefore granted the State's petition for certiorari.

Consistent with our precedent, our analysis begins, as it should in every case addressing the reasonableness of a warrantless search, with the basic rule that "searches conducted outside the judicial process, without prior approval by judge or magistrate, are *per se* unreasonable under the Fourth Amendment—subject only to a few specifically established and well-delineated exceptions." *Katz v. United States* (1967). Among the exceptions to the warrant requirement is a search incident to a lawful arrest. The exception derives from interests in officer safety and evidence preservation that are typi-cally implicated in arrest situations. See *United States v. Robinson* (1973).

In *Chimel*, we held that a search incident to arrest may only include "the arrestee's person and the area 'within his immediate control'—construing that phrase to mean the area from within which he might gain possession of a weapon or destructible evidence." That limitation, which continues to define the boundaries of the exception, ensures that the scope of a search incident to arrest is commensurate with its purposes of protecting arresting officers and safeguarding any evidence of the offense of arrest that an arrestee might conceal or destroy. If there is no possibility that an arrestee could reach into the area that law enforcement officers seek to search, both justifications for the search-incident-to-arrest exception are absent and the rule does not apply.

In *Belton*, we considered *Chimel*'s application to the automobile context. A lone police officer in that case stopped a speeding car in which Belton was one of four occupants. While asking for the driver's license and registration, the officer smelled burnt marijuana and observed an envelope on the car floor marked "Supergold"—a name he associated with marijuana. Thus having probable cause to believe the occupants had committed a drug offense, the officer ordered them out of the vehicle, placed them under arrest, and patted them down. Without handcuffing the arrestees, the officer " 'split them up into four separate areas of the Thruway . . . so they would not be in physical touching area of each other' " and searched the vehicle, including the pocket of a jacket on the backseat, in which he found cocaine.

The New York Court of Appeals found the search unconstitutional, concluding that after the occupants were arrested the vehicle and its contents were "safely within the exclusive custody and control of the police." The State asked this Court to consider whether the exception recognized in *Chimel* permits an officer to search "a jacket found inside an automobile while the automobile's four occupants, all under arrest, are standing unsecured around the vehicle." We granted certiorari because "courts ha[d] found no workable definition of 'the area within the immediate control of the arrestee' when that area arguably includes the interior of an automobile."

In its brief, the State argued that the Court of Appeals erred in concluding that the jacket was under the officer's exclusive control. Focusing on the number of arrestees and their proximity to the vehicle, the State asserted that it was reasonable for the officer to believe the arrestees could have accessed the vehicle and its contents, making the search permissible under *Chimel*. The United States, as *amicus curiae* in support of the State, argued for a more permissive standard, but it maintained that any search incident to arrest must be " 'substantially contemporaneous' " with the arrest—a requirement it deemed "satisfied if the search occurs during the period in which the arrest is being consummated and before the situation has so stabilized that it could be said that the arrest was completed." There was no suggestion by the parties or *amici* that *Chimel* authorizes a vehicle search incident to arrest when there is no realistic possibility that an arrestee could access his vehicle.

After considering these arguments, we held that when an officer lawfully arrests "the occupant of an automobile, he may, as a contemporaneous incident of that arrest, search the passenger compartment of the automobile" and any containers therein. That holding was based in large part on our assumption "that articles inside the relatively narrow compass of the passenger compartment of an automobile are in fact generally, even if not inevitably, within 'the area into which an arrestee might reach.'"

The Arizona Supreme Court read our decision in *Belton* as merely delineating "the proper scope of a search of the interior of an automobile" incident to an arrest. That is, *when* the passenger compartment is within an arrestee's reaching distance, *Belton* supplies the generalization that the entire compartment and any containers therein may be reached. On that view of *Belton*, the state court concluded that the search of Gant's car was unreasonable because Gant clearly could not have accessed his car at the time of the search. It also found that no other exception to the warrant requirement applied in this case.

Gant now urges us to adopt the reading of *Belton* followed by the Arizona Supreme Court.

■ ■ ■

Despite the textual and evidentiary support for the Arizona Supreme Court's reading of *Belton*, our opinion has been widely understood to allow a vehicle search incident to the arrest of a recent occupant even if there is no possibility the arrestee could gain access to the vehicle at the time of the search. This reading may be attributable to Justice Brennan's dissent in *Belton*, in which he characterized the Court's holding as resting on the "fiction . . . that the interior of a car is *always* within the immediate control of an arrestee who has recently been in the car." Under the majority's approach, he argued, "the result would presumably be the same even if [the officer] had handcuffed Belton and his companions in the patrol car" before conducting the search.

Since we decided *Belton*, Courts of Appeals have given different answers to the question whether a vehicle must be within an arrestee's reach to justify a vehicle search incident to arrest, but Justice Brennan's reading of the Court's opinion has predominated. As Justice O'Connor observed, "lower court decisions seem now to treat the ability to search a vehicle incident to the arrest of a recent occupant as a police entitlement rather than as an exception justified by the twin rationales of *Chimel*." Justice Scalia has similarly noted that, although it is improbable that an arrestee could gain access to weapons stored in his vehicle after he has been handcuffed and secured in the backseat of a patrol car, cases allowing a search in "this precise factual scenario . . . are legion." Indeed, some courts have upheld searches under *Belton* "even when . . . the handcuffed arrestee has already left the scene."

Under this broad reading of *Belton*, a vehicle search would be authorized incident to every arrest of a recent occupant notwithstanding that in most cases the vehicle's passenger compartment will not be within the arrestee's reach at the time of the search. To read *Belton* as authorizing a vehicle search incident to every recent occupant's arrest would thus untether the rule from the justifications underlying the *Chimel* exception—a result clearly incompatible with our statement in *Belton* that it "in no way alters the fundamental principles established in the *Chimel* case regarding the basic scope of searches incident to lawful custodial arrests." Accordingly, we reject this reading of *Belton* and hold that the *Chimel* rationale authorizes police to search a vehicle incident to a recent occupant's arrest only when the arrestee is unsecured and within reaching distance of the passenger compartment at the time of the search.

Although it does not follow from *Chimel*, we also conclude that circumstances unique to the vehicle context justify a search incident to a lawful arrest when it is "reasonable to believe evidence relevant to the crime of arrest might be found in the vehicle." *Thornton* (Scalia, J., concurring in judgment). In many cases, as when a recent occupant is arrested for a traffic violation, there will be no reasonable basis to believe the vehicle contains relevant evidence. But in others, including *Belton* and *Thornton*, the offense of arrest will supply a basis for searching the passenger compartment of an arrestee's vehicle and any containers therein.

Neither the possibility of access nor the likelihood of discovering offense-related evidence authorized the search in this case. Unlike in *Belton*, which involved a single officer confronted with four unsecured arrestees, the five officers in this case outnumbered the three arrestees, all of whom had been handcuffed and secured in separate patrol cars before the officers searched Gant's car. Under those circumstances, Gant clearly was not within reaching distance of his car at the time of the search. An evidentiary basis for the search was also lacking in this case. Whereas Belton and Thornton were arrested for drug offenses, Gant was arrested for driving with a suspended license—an offense for which police could not expect to find evidence in the passenger compartment of Gant's car. Because police could not reasonably have believed either that Gant could have accessed his car at the time of the search or that evidence of the offense for which he was arrested might have been found therein, the search in this case was unreasonable.

■ ■ ■

The State does not seriously disagree with the Arizona Supreme Court's conclusion that Gant could not have accessed his vehicle at the time of the search, but it nevertheless asks us to uphold the search of his vehicle under the broad reading of *Belton* discussed above. The State argues that *Belton* searches are reasonable regardless of the possibility of access in a given case because that expansive rule correctly balances law enforcement interests, including the interest in a bright-line rule, with an arrestee's limited privacy interest in his vehicle.

For several reasons, we reject the State's argument. First, the State seriously undervalues the privacy interests at stake. Although we have recognized that a motorist's privacy interest in his vehicle is less substantial than in his home, the former interest is nevertheless important and deserving of constitutional protection. It is particularly significant that *Belton* searches authorize police officers to search not just the passenger compartment but every purse, briefcase, or other container within that space. A rule that gives police the power to conduct such a search whenever an individual is caught committing a traffic offense, when there is no basis for believing evidence of the offense might be found in the vehicle, creates a serious and recurring threat to the privacy of countless individuals. Indeed, the character of that threat implicates the central concern underlying the Fourth Amendment—the concern about giving police officers unbridled discretion to rummage at will among a person's private effects.

At the same time as it undervalues these privacy concerns, the State exaggerates the clarity that its reading of *Belton* provides. Courts that have read *Belton* expansively are at odds regarding how close in time to the arrest and how proximate to the arrestee's vehicle an officer's first contact with the arrestee must be to bring the encounter within *Belton*'s purview and whether a search is reasonable when it commences or continues after the arrestee has been removed from the scene. The rule has thus generated a great deal of uncertainty, particularly for a rule touted as providing a "bright line."

Contrary to the State's suggestion, a broad reading of *Belton* is also unnecessary to protect law enforcement safety and evidentiary interests. Under our view, *Belton* and *Thornton* permit an officer to conduct a vehicle search when an arrestee is within reaching distance of the vehicle or it is reasonable to believe the vehicle contains evidence of the offense of arrest. Other established exceptions to the warrant requirement authorize a vehicle search under additional circumstances when safety or evidentiary concerns demand.

■ ■ ■

Our dissenting colleagues argue that the doctrine of *stare decisis* requires adherence to a broad reading of *Belton* even though the justifications for searching a vehicle incident to arrest are in most cases absent. The doctrine of *stare decisis* is of course "essential to the respect accorded to the judgments of the Court and to the stability of the law," but it does not compel us to follow a past decision when its rationale no longer withstands "careful analysis." *Lawrence v. Texas* (2003).

We have never relied on *stare decisis* to justify the continuance of an unconstitutional police practice. And we would be particularly loath to uphold an unconstitutional result in a case that is so easily distinguished from the decisions that arguably compel it. The safety and evidentiary interests that supported the search in *Belton* simply are not present in this case. Indeed, it is hard to imagine two cases that are factually more distinct, as *Belton* involved one officer confronted by four unsecured arrestees suspected of committing a drug offense and this case involves several officers confronted with a securely detained arrestee apprehended for driving with a suspended license. This case is also distinguishable from *Thornton*, in which the petitioner was arrested for a drug offense. It is thus unsurprising that Members of this Court who concurred in the judgments in *Belton* and *Thornton* also concur in the decision in this case.

We do not agree with the contention in Justice Alito's dissent (hereinafter dissent) that consideration of police reliance interests requires a different result. Although it appears that the State's reading of *Belton* has been widely taught in police academies and that law enforcement officers have relied on the rule in conducting vehicle searches during the past 28 years, many of these searches were not justified by the reasons underlying the *Chimel* exception. Countless individuals guilty of nothing more serious than a traffic violation have had their constitutional right to the security of their private effects violated as a result. The fact that the law enforcement community may view the State's version of the *Belton* rule as an entitlement does not establish the sort of reliance interest that could outweigh the countervailing interest that all individuals share in having their constitutional rights fully protected. If it is clear that a practice is unlawful, individuals' interest in its discontinuance clearly outweighs any law enforcement "entitlement" to its persistence.

■ ■ ■

The experience of the 28 years since we decided *Belton* has shown that the generalization underpinning the broad reading of that decision is unfounded. We now know that articles inside the passenger compartment are rarely "within 'the area into which an arrestee might reach,' " and blind adherence to *Belton*'s faulty assumption would authorize myriad unconstitutional searches. The doctrine of *stare decisis* does not require us to approve routine constitutional violations.

■ ■ ■

Police may search a vehicle incident to a recent occupant's arrest only if the arrestee is within reaching distance of the passenger compartment at the time of the search or it is reasonable to believe the vehicle contains evidence of the offense of arrest. When these justifications are absent, a search of an arrestee's vehicle will be unreasonable unless police obtain a warrant or show that another exception to the warrant requirement applies. The Arizona Supreme Court correctly held that this case involved an unreasonable search. Accordingly, the judgment of the State Supreme Court is affirmed.

It is so ordered.

Justice SCALIA, concurring.

To determine what is an "unreasonable" search within the meaning of the Fourth Amendment, we look first to the historical practices the Framers sought to preserve; if those provide inadequate guidance, we apply traditional standards of reasonableness. See *Virginia v. Moore* (2008). Since the historical scope of officers' authority to search vehicles incident to arrest is uncertain, see *Thornton v. United States* (Scalia, J., concurring in judgment), traditional standards of reasonableness govern. It is abundantly clear that those standards do not justify what I take to be the rule set forth in *New York v. Belton*, and *Thornton*: that arresting officers may always search an arrestee's vehicle in order to protect themselves from hidden weapons. When an arrest is made in connection with a roadside stop, police virtually always have a less intrusive and more effective means of ensuring their safety—and a means that is virtually always employed: ordering the arrestee away from the vehicle, patting him down in the open, handcuffing him, and placing him in the squad car.

Law enforcement officers face a risk of being shot whenever they pull a car over. But that risk is at its height at the time of the initial confrontation; and it is *not at all* reduced by allowing a search of the stopped vehicle after the driver has been arrested and placed in the squad car. I observed in *Thornton* that the government had failed to provide a single instance in which a formerly restrained arrestee escaped to retrieve a weapon from his own vehicle; Arizona and its *amici* have not remedied that significant deficiency in the present case.

It must be borne in mind that we are speaking here only of a rule automatically permitting a search when the driver or an occupant is arrested. Where no arrest is made, we have held that officers may search the car if they reasonably believe "the suspect is dangerous and . . . may gain immediate control of weapons." *Michigan v. Long* (1983). In the no-arrest case, the possibility of access to weapons in the vehicle always exists, since the driver or passenger will be allowed to return to the vehicle when the interrogation is completed. The rule of *Michigan v. Long* is not at issue here.

Justice Stevens acknowledges that an officer-safety rationale cannot justify all vehicle searches incident to arrest, but asserts that that is not the rule *Belton* and *Thornton* adopted. Justice Stevens would therefore retain the application of *Chimel v. California* in the car-search context but would apply in the future what he believes our cases held in the past: that officers making a roadside stop may search the vehicle so long as the "arrestee is within reaching distance of the passenger compartment at the time of the search." I believe that this standard fails to provide the needed guidance to arresting officers and also leaves much room for manipulation, inviting officers to leave the scene unsecured (at least where dangerous suspects are not involved) in order to conduct a vehicle search. In my view we should simply abandon the *Belton-Thornton* charade of officer safety and overrule those cases. I would hold that a vehicle search incident to arrest is *ipso facto* "reasonable" only when the object of the search is evidence of the crime for which the arrest was made, or of another crime that the officer has probable cause to believe occurred. Because respondent was arrested for driving without a license (a crime for which no evidence could be expected to be found in the vehicle), I would hold in the present case that the search was unlawful.

Justice Alito insists that the Court must demand a good reason for abandoning prior precedent. That is true enough, but it seems to me ample reason that the precedent was badly reasoned and produces erroneous (in this case unconstitutional) results. We should recognize *Belton*'s fanciful reliance upon officer safety for what it was: "a return to the broader sort of [evidence-gathering] search incident to arrest that we allowed before *Chimel*."

Justice Alito argues that there is no reason to adopt a rule limiting automobile-arrest searches to those cases where the search's object is evidence of the crime of arrest. I disagree. This formulation of officers' authority both preserves the outcomes of our prior cases and tethers the scope and rationale of the doctrine to the triggering event. *Belton*, by contrast, allowed searches precisely when its exigency-based rationale was least applicable: The fact of the arrest in the automobile context makes searches on exigency grounds *less* reasonable, not more. I also disagree with Justice Alito's conclusory assertion that this standard will be difficult to administer in practice; the ease of its application in this case would suggest otherwise.

No other Justice, however, shares my view that application of *Chimel* in this context should be entirely abandoned. It seems to me unacceptable for the Court to come forth with a 4-to-1-to-4 opinion that leaves the governing rule uncertain. I am therefore confronted with the choice of either leaving the current understanding of *Belton* and *Thornton* in effect, or acceding to what seems to me the artificial narrowing of those cases adopted by Justice Stevens. The latter, as I have said, does not provide the degree of certainty I think desirable in this field; but the former opens the field to what I think are plainly unconstitutional searches—which is the greater evil. I therefore join the opinion of the Court.

Justice BREYER, dissenting.

I agree with Justice Alito that *New York v. Belton* is best read as setting forth a bright-line rule that permits a warrantless search of the passenger compartment of an automobile incident to the lawful arrest of an occupant—regardless of the danger the arrested individual in fact poses. I also agree with Justice Stevens, however, that the rule can produce results divorced from its underlying Fourth Amendment rationale.

■ ■ ■

The matter, however, is not one of first impression, and that fact makes a substantial difference. The *Belton* rule has been followed not only by this Court in *Thornton v. United States*, but also by numerous other courts. Principles of *stare decisis* must apply, and those who wish this Court to change a well-established legal precedent—where, as here, there has been considerable reliance on the legal rule in question—bear a heavy burden.

■ ■ ■

Justice ALITO, with whom Chief Justice ROBERTS and Justice KENNEDY join, and with whom Justice BREYER joins except as to Part II-E, dissenting.

Twenty-eight years ago, in *New York v. Belton*, this Court held that "when a policeman has made a lawful custodial arrest of the occupant of an automobile, he may, as a contemporaneous incident of that arrest, search the passenger compartment of that automobile." Five years ago, in *Thornton v. United States*—a case involving a situation not materially distinguishable from the situation here—the Court not only reaffirmed but extended the holding of *Belton*, making it applicable to recent occupants. Today's decision effectively overrules those important decisions, even though respondent Gant has not asked us to do so.

To take the place of the overruled precedents, the Court adopts a new two-part rule under which a police officer who arrests a vehicle occupant or recent occupant may search the passenger compartment if (1) the arrestee is within reaching distance of the vehicle at the time of the search or (2) the officer has reason to believe that the vehicle contains evidence of the offense of arrest. The first part of this new rule may endanger arresting officers and is truly endorsed by only four Justices; Justice Scalia joins solely for the purpose of avoiding a "4-to-1-to-4 opinion." The second part of the new rule is taken from

Justice Scalia's separate opinion in *Thornton* without any independent explanation of its origin or justification and is virtually certain to confuse law enforcement officers and judges for some time to come. The Court's decision will cause the suppression of evidence gathered in many searches carried out in good-faith reliance on well-settled case law, and although the Court purports to base its analysis on the landmark decision in *Chimel v. California*, the Court's reasoning undermines *Chimel*. I would follow *Belton*, and I therefore respectfully dissent.

I

Although the Court refuses to acknowledge that it is overruling *Belton* and *Thornton*, there can be no doubt that it does so.

■ ■ ■

The precise holding in *Belton* could not be clearer. The Court stated unequivocally: "[W]e hold that when a policeman has made a lawful custodial arrest of the occupant of an automobile, he may, as a contemporaneous incident of that arrest, search the passenger compartment of that automobile."

Despite this explicit statement, the opinion of the Court in the present case curiously suggests that *Belton* may reasonably be read as adopting a holding that is narrower than the one explicitly set out in the *Belton* opinion, namely, that an officer arresting a vehicle occupant may search the passenger compartment "*when* the passenger compartment is within an arrestee's reaching distance." According to the Court, the broader reading of *Belton* that has gained wide acceptance "may be attributable to Justice Brennan's dissent."

Contrary to the Court's suggestion, however, Justice Brennan's *Belton* dissent did not mischaracterize the Court's holding in that case or cause that holding to be misinterpreted. As noted, the *Belton* Court explicitly stated precisely what it held. In *Thornton*, the Court recognized the scope of *Belton*'s holding.... ("In [*Belton*] we set forth a bright-line rule for arrests of automobile occupants, holding that... a search of the whole [passenger] compartment is justified in every case".)

II

Because the Court has substantially overruled *Belton* and *Thornton*, the Court must explain why its departure from the usual rule of *stare decisis* is justified. I recognize that *stare decisis* is not an "inexorable command," *Payne v. Tennessee* (1991), and applies less rigidly in constitutional cases.... But the Court has said that a constitutional precedent should be followed unless there is a "'special justification'" for its abandonment. *Dickerson v. United States* (2000). Relevant factors identified in prior cases include whether the precedent has engendered reliance, whether there has been an important change in circumstances in the outside world... whether the precedent has proved to be unworkable... whether the precedent has been undermined by later decisions... and whether the decision was badly reasoned. These factors weigh in favor of retaining the rule established in *Belton*.

A

Reliance. While reliance is most important in "cases involving property and contract rights," the Court has recognized that reliance by law enforcement officers is also entitled to weight. In *Dickerson*, the Court held that principles of *stare decisis* "weigh[ed]" heavily against overruling *Miranda v. Arizona* (1966), because the *Miranda* rule had become "embedded in routine police practice."

If there was reliance in *Dickerson*, there certainly is substantial reliance here. The *Belton* rule has been taught to police officers for more than a quarter century. Many searches—almost certainly including more than a few that figure in cases now on appeal—were conducted in scrupulous reliance on that precedent. It is likely that, on the very day when this opinion is announced, numerous vehicle searches will be conducted in good faith by police officers who were taught the *Belton* rule.

The opinion of the Court recognizes that "*Belton* has been widely taught in police academies and that law enforcement officers have relied on the rule in conducting vehicle searches during the past 28 years." But for the Court, this seemingly counts for nothing. The Court states that "[w]e have never relied on *stare decisis* to justify the continuance of an unconstitutional police practice," but of course the Court routinely relies on decisions sustaining the constitutionality of police practices without doing what the Court has done here—*sua sponte* considering whether those decisions should be overruled. And the Court cites no authority for the proposition that *stare decisis* may be disregarded or provides only lesser protection when the precedent that is challenged is one that sustained the constitutionality of a law enforcement practice.

The Court also errs in arguing that the reliance interest that was given heavy weight in *Dickerson* was not "police reliance on a rule requiring them to provide warnings but to the broader societal reliance on that individual right." The *Dickerson* opinion makes no reference to "societal reliance," and petitioner in that case contended that there had been reliance on *Miranda* because, among other things, "[f]or nearly thirty-five years, *Miranda's* requirements ha[d] shaped law enforcement training [and] police conduct."

B

Changed circumstances. Abandonment of the *Belton* rule cannot be justified on the ground that the dangers surrounding the arrest of a vehicle occupant are different today than they were 28 years ago. The Court claims that "[w]e now know that articles inside the passenger compartment are rarely 'within "the area into which an arrestee might reach," ' " but surely it was well known in 1981 that a person who is taken from a vehicle, handcuffed, and placed in the back of a patrol car is unlikely to make it back into his own car to retrieve a weapon or destroy evidence.

C

Workability. The *Belton* rule has not proved to be unworkable. On the contrary, the rule was adopted for the express purpose of providing a test that would be relatively easy for police officers and judges to apply. The Court correctly notes that even the *Belton* rule is not perfectly clear in all situations. Specifically, it is sometimes debatable whether a search is or is not contemporaneous with an arrest, but that problem is small in comparison with the problems that the Court's new two-part rule will produce.

The first part of the Court's new rule—which permits the search of a vehicle's passenger compartment if it is within an arrestee's reach at the time of the search—reintroduces the same sort of case-by-case, fact-specific decision making that the *Belton* rule was adopted to avoid. As the situation in *Belton* illustrated, there are cases in which it is unclear whether an arrestee could retrieve a weapon or evidence in the passenger compartment of a car.

Even more serious problems will also result from the second part of the Court's new rule, which requires officers making roadside arrests to determine whether there is reason to believe that the vehicle contains evidence of the crime of arrest. What this rule permits in a variety of situations is entirely unclear.

D

Consistency with later cases. The *Belton* bright-line rule has not been undermined by subsequent cases. On the contrary, that rule was reaffirmed and extended just five years ago in *Thornton.*

E

Bad reasoning. The Court is harshly critical of *Belton*'s reasoning, but the problem that the Court perceives cannot be remedied simply by overruling *Belton*. *Belton* represented only a modest—and quite defensible—extension of *Chimel*, as I understand that decision.

Prior to *Chimel*, the Court's precedents permitted an arresting officer to search the area within an arrestee's "possession" and "control" for the purpose of gathering evidence. Based on this "abstract doctrine," the Court had sustained searches that extended far beyond an arrestee's grabbing area. See *United States v. Rabinowitz* (1950).

■ ■ ■

The *Chimel* Court, in an opinion written by Justice Stewart, overruled these cases. Concluding that there are only two justifications for a warrantless search incident to arrest—officer safety and the preservation of evidence—the Court stated that such a search must be confined to "the arrestee's person" and "the area from within which he might gain possession of a weapon or destructible evidence."

Unfortunately, *Chimel* did not say whether "the area from within which [an arrestee] might gain possession of a weapon or destructible evidence" is to be measured at the time of the arrest or at the time of the search, but unless the *Chimel* rule was meant to be a specialty rule, applicable to only a few unusual cases, the Court must have intended for this area to be measured at the time of arrest.

This is so because the Court can hardly have failed to appreciate the following two facts. First, in the great majority of cases, an officer making an arrest is able to handcuff the arrestee and remove him to a secure place before conducting a search incident to the arrest. Second, because it is safer for an arresting officer to secure an arrestee before searching, it is likely that this is what arresting officers do in the great majority of cases. . . . Thus, if the area within an arrestee's reach were assessed, not at the time of arrest, but at the time of the search, the *Chimel* rule would rarely come into play.

■ ■ ■

The *Belton* Court, in my view, proceeded on the basis of this interpretation of *Chimel*. Again speaking through Justice Stewart, the *Belton* Court reasoned that articles in the passenger compartment of a car are "generally, even if not inevitably" within an arrestee's reach. This is undoubtedly true at the time of the arrest of a person who is seated in a car but plainly not true when the person has been removed from the car and placed in handcuffs. Accordingly, the *Belton* Court must have proceeded on the assumption that the *Chimel* rule was to be applied at the time of arrest. And that is why the *Belton* Court was able to say that its decision "in no way alter[ed] the fundamental principles established in the *Chimel* case regarding the basic scope of searches incident to lawful custodial arrests." Viewing *Chimel* as having focused on the time of arrest, *Belton*'s only new step was to eliminate the need to decide on a case-by-case basis whether a particular person seated in a car actually could have reached the part of the passenger compartment where a weapon or evidence was hidden. For this reason, if we are going to reexamine *Belton*, we should also reexamine the reasoning in *Chimel* on which *Belton* rests.

F

The second part of the Court's new rule, which the Court takes uncritically from Justice Scalia's separate opinion in *Thornton*, raises doctrinal and practical problems that the Court makes no effort to address. Why, for example, is the standard for this type of evidence-gathering search "reason to believe" rather than probable cause? And why is this type of search restricted to evidence of the offense of arrest? It is true that an arrestee's vehicle is probably more likely to contain evidence of the crime of arrest than of some other crime, but if reason-to-believe is the governing standard for an evidence-gathering search incident to arrest, it is not easy to see why an officer should not be able to search when the officer has reason to believe that the vehicle in question possesses evidence of a crime other than the crime of arrest.

Nor is it easy to see why an evidence-gathering search incident to arrest should be restricted to the passenger compartment. The *Belton* rule was limited in this way because the passenger compartment was considered to be the area that vehicle occupants can generally reach, but since the second part of the new rule is not based on officer safety or the preservation of evidence, the ground for this limitation is obscure.

III

Respondent in this case has not asked us to overrule *Belton*, much less *Chimel*. Respondent's argument rests entirely on an interpretation of *Belton* that is plainly incorrect, an interpretation that disregards *Belton*'s explicit delineation of its holding. I would therefore leave any reexamination of our prior precedents for another day, if such a reexamination is to be undertaken at all. In this case, I would simply apply *Belton* and reverse the judgment below.

5. Probable Cause to Search an Automobile   4/15/14

Carroll v. United States

267 U.S. 132 (1925)

Chief Justice TAFT delivered the opinion of the Court.

On reason and authority the true rule is that if the search and seizure without a warrant are made upon probable cause, that is, upon a belief, reasonably arising out of circumstances known to the seizing officer, that an automobile or other vehicle contains that which by law is subject to seizure and destruction, the search and seizure are valid. The Fourth Amendment is to be construed in the light of what was deemed an unreasonable search and seizure when it was adopted, and in a manner which will conserve public interests as well as the interests and rights of individual citizens.

■ ■ ■

We have made a somewhat extended reference to these statutes to show that the guaranty of freedom from unreasonable searches and seizures by the Fourth Amendment has been construed, practically since the beginning of the Government, as recognizing a necessary difference between a search of a store, dwelling house or other structure in respect of which a proper official warrant readily may be obtained, and a search of a ship, motor boat, wagon or automobile, for contraband goods, where it is not practicable to secure a warrant because the vehicle can be quickly moved out of the locality or jurisdiction in which the warrant must be sought.

Having thus established that contraband goods concealed and illegally transported in an automobile or other vehicle may be searched for without a warrant, we come now to consider under what circumstances such search may be made. . . .

Chambers v. Maroney

399 U.S. 42 (1970)

WHITE, J., delivered the opinion of the Court, in which BURGER, C.J., BLACK, DOUGLAS, BRENNAN, STEWART, MARSHALL, and BLACKMUN, JJ., joined. STEWART, J., filed a concurring opinion. HARLAN, J., filed an opinion concurring in part and dissenting in part.

The principal question in this case concerns the admissibility of evidence seized from an automobile, in which petitioner was riding at the time of his arrest, after the automobile was taken to a police station and was there thoroughly searched without a warrant. The Court of Appeals for the Third Circuit found no violation of petitioner's Fourth Amendment rights. We affirm.

■ ■ ■

Even so, the search that produced the incriminating evidence was made at the police station some time after the arrest and cannot be justified as a search incident to arrest: "Once an accused is under arrest and in custody, then a search made at another place, without a warrant, is simply not incident to the arrest." *Preston v. United States* (1964).

■ ■ ■

In terms of the circumstances justifying a warrantless search, the Court has long distinguished between an automobile and a home or office. In *Carroll v. United States* (1925), the issue was the admissibility in evidence of contraband liquor seized in a warrantless search of a car on the highway. After surveying the law from the time of the adoption of the Fourth Amendment onward, the Court held that automobiles and other conveyances may be searched without a warrant in circumstances that would not justify the search without a warrant of a house or an office, provided that there is probable cause to believe that the car contains articles that the officers are entitled to seize. The Court expressed its holding as follows:

> "We have made a somewhat extended reference to these statutes to show that the guaranty of freedom from unreasonable searches and seizures by the Fourth Amendment has been construed, practically since the beginning of the government, as recognizing a necessary difference between a search of a store, dwelling house, or other structure in respect of which a proper official warrant readily may be obtained and a search of a ship, motor boat, wagon, or automobile for contraband goods, where it is not practicable to secure a warrant, because the vehicle can be quickly moved out of the locality or jurisdiction in which the warrant must be sought.
>
> Having thus established that contraband goods concealed and illegally transported in an automobile or other vehicle may be searched for without a warrant, we come now to consider under what circumstances such search may be made. [T]hose lawfully within the country, entitled to use the public highways, have a right to free passage without interruption or search unless there is known to a competent official, authorized to search, probable cause

for believing that their vehicles are carrying contraband or illegal merchandise."

■ ■ ■

"The measure of legality of such a seizure is, therefore, that the seizing officer shall have reasonable or probable cause for believing that the automobile which he stops and seizes has contraband liquor therein which is being illegally transported."

The Court also noted that the search of an auto on probable cause proceeds on a theory wholly different from that justifying the search incident to an arrest:

> "The right to search and the validity of the seizure are not dependent on the right to arrest. They are dependent on the reasonable cause the seizing officer has for belief that the contents of the automobile offend against the law."

Finding that there was probable cause for the search and seizure at issue before it, the Court affirmed the convictions.

■ ■ ■

Neither *Carroll* nor other cases in this Court require or suggest that in every conceivable circumstance the search of an auto even with probable cause may be made without the extra protection for privacy that a warrant affords. But the circumstances that furnish probable cause to search a particular auto for particular articles are most often unforeseeable; moreover, the opportunity to search is fleeting since a car is readily movable. Where this is true, as in *Carroll* and the case before us now, if an effective search is to be made at any time, either the search must be made immediately without a warrant or the car itself must be seized and held without a warrant for whatever period is necessary to obtain a warrant for the search.

In enforcing the Fourth Amendment's prohibition against unreasonable searches and seizures, the Court has insisted upon probable cause as a minimum requirement for a reasonable search permitted by the Constitution. As a general rule, it has also required the judgment of a magistrate on the probable-cause issue and the issuance of a warrant before a search is made. Only in exigent circumstances will the judgment of the police as to probable cause serve as a sufficient authorization for a search. *Carroll* holds a search warrant unnecessary where there is probable cause to search an automobile stopped on the highway; the car is movable, the occupants are alerted, and the car's contents may never be found again if a warrant must be obtained. Hence an immediate search is constitutionally permissible.

Arguably, because of the preference for a magistrate's judgment, only the immobilization of the car should be permitted until a search warrant is obtained; arguably, only the "lesser" intrusion is permissible until the magistrate authorizes the "greater." But which is the "greater" and which the "lesser" intrusion is itself a debatable question and the answer may depend on a variety of circumstances. For constitutional purposes, we see no difference between on the one hand seizing and holding a car before presenting the probable cause issue to a magistrate and on the other hand carrying out an immediate search without a warrant. Given probable cause to search, either course is reasonable under the Fourth Amendment.

On the facts before us, the blue station wagon could have been searched on the spot when it was stopped since there was probable cause to search and it was a fleeting target for a search. The probable-cause factor still obtained at the station house and so did the mobility of the car unless the Fourth Amendment permits a warrantless seizure of the car and the denial of its use to anyone until a warrant is secured. In that event there is little to choose in terms of practical consequences between an immediate search without a warrant and the car's immobilization until a warrant is obtained. The same consequences may not follow where there is unforeseeable cause to search a house. But as *Carroll* held, for the purposes of the Fourth Amendment there is a constitutional difference between houses and cars.

■ ■ ■

Justice HARLAN, concurring in part and dissenting in part.

I find myself in disagreement with the Court's disposition of this case in two respects.

■ ■ ■

In sustaining the search of the automobile I believe the Court ignores the framework of our past decisions circumscribing the scope of permissible search without a warrant. The Court has long read the Fourth Amendment's proscription of "unreasonable" searches as imposing a general principle that a search without a warrant is not justified by the mere knowledge by the searching officers of facts showing probable cause. The "general requirement that a search warrant be obtained" is basic to the Amendment's protection of privacy, and "the burden is on those seeking [an] exemption to show the need for it."

Fidelity to this established principle requires that, where exceptions are made to accommodate the exigencies of particular situations, those exceptions be no broader than necessitated by the circumstances presented. For example, the Court has recognized that an arrest creates an emergency situation justifying a warrantless search of the arrestee's person and of "the area from within which he might gain possession of a weapon or destructible evidence"; however, because the exigency giving rise to this exception extends only that far, the search may go no further. *Chimel v. California* (1969); *Trupiano v. United States* (1948). Similarly we held in *Terry v. Ohio* (1968) that a warrantless search in a "stop and frisk" situation must "be strictly circumscribed by the exigencies which justify its initiation." . . .

Where officers have probable cause to search a vehicle on a public way, a further limited exception to the warrant requirement is reasonable because "the vehicle can be quickly moved out of the locality or jurisdiction in which the warrant must be sought." *Carroll v. United States.* Because the officers might be deprived of valuable evidence if required to obtain a warrant before effecting any search or seizure, I agree with the Court that they should be permitted to take the steps necessary to preserve evidence and to make a search possible. The Court holds that those steps include making a warrantless search of the entire vehicle on the highway—a conclusion reached by the Court in *Carroll* without discussion—and indeed appears to go further and to condone the removal of the car to the police station for a warrantless search there at the convenience of the police. I cannot agree that this result is consistent with our insistence in other areas that departures from the warrant requirement strictly conform to the exigency presented.

The Court concedes that the police could prevent removal of the evidence by temporarily seizing the car for the time necessary to obtain a warrant. It does not dispute that such a course would fully protect the interests of effective law enforcement; rather, it states that whether temporary seizure is a "lesser" intrusion than warrantless search "is itself a debatable question and the answer may depend on a variety of circumstances." I believe it clear that a warrantless search involves the greater sacrifice of Fourth Amendment values.

The Fourth Amendment proscribes, to be sure, unreasonable "seizures" as well as "searches." However, in the circumstances in which this problem is likely to occur, the lesser intrusion will almost always be the simple seizure of the car for the period—perhaps a day—necessary to enable the officers to obtain a search warrant. In the first place, as this case shows, the very facts establishing probable cause to search will often also justify arrest of the occupants of the vehicle. Since the occupants themselves are to be taken into custody, they will suffer minimal further inconvenience from the temporary immobilization of their vehicle. Even where no arrests are made, persons who wish to avoid a search—either to protect their privacy or to conceal incriminating evidence—will almost certainly prefer a brief loss of the use of the vehicle in exchange for the opportunity to have a magistrate pass upon the justification for the search. To be sure, one can conceive of instances in which the occupant, having nothing to hide and lacking concern for the privacy of the automobile, would be more deeply offended by a temporary immobilization of his vehicle than by a prompt search of it. However, such a person always remains free to consent to an immediate search, thus avoiding any delay. Where consent is not forthcoming, the occupants of the car have an interest in privacy that is protected by the Fourth Amendment even where the circumstances justify a temporary seizure. The Court's endorsement of a warrantless invasion of that privacy where another course would suffice is simply inconsistent with our repeated stress on the Fourth Amendment's mandate of "adherence to judicial processes."

California v. Acevedo

500 U.S. 565 (1991)

BLACKMUN, J., delivered the opinion of the Court, in which REHNQUIST, C.J., and O'CONNOR, KENNEDY, and SOUTER, JJ., joined. SCALIA, J., filed an opinion concurring in the judgment. WHITE, J., filed a dissenting opinion. STEVENS, J., filed a dissenting opinion, in which MARSHALL, J., joined.

This case requires us once again to consider the so-called "automobile exception" to the warrant requirement of the Fourth Amendment and its application to the search of a closed container in the trunk of a car.

On October 28, 1987, Officer Coleman of the Santa Ana, Cal., Police Department received a telephone call from a federal drug enforcement agent in Hawaii. The agent informed Coleman that he had seized a package containing marijuana which was to have been delivered to the Federal Express Office in Santa Ana and which was addressed to J.R. Daza at 805 West Stevens Avenue in that city. The agent arranged to send the package to Coleman instead. Coleman then was to take the package to the Federal Express office and arrest the person who arrived to claim it.

Coleman received the package on October 29, verified its contents, and took it to the Senior Operations Manager at the Federal Express office. At about 10:30 a.m. on October 30, a man, who identified himself as Jamie Daza, arrived to claim the package. He accepted it and drove to his apartment on West Stevens. He carried the package into the apartment.

At 11:45 a.m., officers observed Daza leave the apartment and drop the box and paper that had contained the marijuana into a trash bin. Coleman at that point left the scene to get a search warrant. About 12:05 p.m., the officers saw Richard St. George leave the apartment carrying a blue knapsack which appeared to be half full. The officers stopped him as he was driving off, searched the knapsack, and found 1½ pounds of marijuana.

At 12:30 p.m., respondent Charles Steven Acevedo arrived. He entered Daza's apartment, stayed for about 10 minutes, and reappeared carrying a brown paper bag that looked full. The officers noticed that the bag was the size of one of the wrapped marijuana packages sent from Hawaii. Acevedo walked to a silver Honda in the parking lot. He placed the bag in the trunk of the car and started to drive away. Fearing the loss of evidence, officers in a marked police car stopped him. They opened the trunk and the bag, and found marijuana.

The California Court of Appeal, Fourth District, concluded that the marijuana found in the paper bag in the car's trunk should have been suppressed.

The Supreme Court of California denied the State's petition for review.

We granted certiorari to reexamine the law applicable to a closed container in an automobile, a subject that has troubled courts and law enforcement officers since it was first considered in [*United States v.*] *Chadwick* (1977).

The Fourth Amendment protects the "right of the people to be secure in their persons, houses, papers, and effects, against unreasonable searches and seizures." Contemporaneously with the adoption of the Fourth Amendment, the First Congress, and, later, the Second and Fourth Congresses, distinguished between the need for a warrant to search for contraband concealed in "a dwelling house or similar place" and the need for a warrant to search for contraband concealed in a movable vessel. In *Carroll* [*v. United States* (1925)], this Court established an exception to the warrant requirement for moving vehicles, for it recognized

> "a necessary difference between a search of a store, dwelling house or other structure in respect of which a proper official warrant readily may be obtained, and a search of a ship, motor boat, wagon or automobile, for contraband goods, where it is not practicable to secure a warrant because the vehicle can be quickly moved out of the locality or jurisdiction in which the warrant must be sought."

It therefore held that a warrantless search of an automobile, based upon probable cause to believe that the vehicle contained evidence of crime in the light of an exigency arising out of the likely disappearance of the vehicle, did not contravene the Warrant Clause of the Fourth Amendment.

The Court refined the exigency requirement in *Chambers v. Maroney* (1970), when it held that the existence of exigent circumstances was to be determined at the time the automobile is seized. The car search at issue in *Chambers* took place at the police station, where the vehicle was immobilized, some time after the driver had been arrested. Given probable cause and exigent circumstances at the time the vehicle was first stopped, the Court held that the later warrantless search at the station passed constitutional muster. The validity of the later search derived from the ruling in *Carroll* that an immediate search without a warrant at the moment of seizure would have been permissible.

In *United States v. Ross*, decided in 1982, we held that a warrantless search of an automobile under the *Carroll* doctrine could include a search of a container or package found inside the car when such a search was supported by probable cause. The warrantless search of Ross' car occurred after an informant told the police that he had seen Ross complete a drug transaction using drugs stored in the trunk of his car. The police stopped the car, searched it, and discovered in the trunk a brown paper bag containing drugs. We decided that the search of Ross' car was not unreasonable under the Fourth Amendment: "The scope of a warrantless search based on probable cause is no narrower—and no broader—than the scope of a search authorized by a warrant supported by probable cause." Thus, "[i]f probable cause justifies the search of a lawfully stopped vehicle, it justifies the search of every part of the vehicle and its contents that may conceal the object of the search." In *Ross*, therefore, we clarified the scope of the *Carroll* doctrine as properly including a "probing search" of compartments and containers within the automobile so long as the search is supported by probable cause.

In addition to this clarification, *Ross* distinguished the *Carroll* doctrine from the separate rule that governed the search of closed containers. The Court had announced this separate rule, unique to luggage and other closed packages, bags, and containers, in *United States v. Chadwick*. In *Chadwick*, federal narcotics agents had probable cause to believe that a 200-pound double-locked footlocker contained marijuana. The agents tracked the locker as the defendants removed it from a train and carried it through the station to a waiting car. As soon as the defendants lifted the locker into the trunk of the car, the agents arrested them, seized the locker, and searched it. In this Court, the United States did not contend that the locker's brief contact with the automobile's trunk sufficed to make the *Carroll* doctrine applicable. Rather, the United States urged that the search of movable luggage could be considered analogous to the search of an automobile.

The Court rejected this argument because, it reasoned, a person expects more privacy in his luggage and personal effects than he does in his automobile. Moreover, it concluded that as "may often not be the case when automobiles are seized," secure storage facilities are usually available when the police seize luggage.

In *Arkansas v. Sanders* (1979), the Court extended *Chadwick*'s rule to apply to a suitcase actually being transported in the trunk of a car. In *Sanders*, the police had probable cause to believe a suitcase contained marijuana. They watched as the defendant placed the suitcase in the trunk of a taxi and was driven away. The police pursued the taxi for several blocks, stopped it, found the suitcase in the trunk, and searched it. Although the Court had applied the *Carroll* doctrine to searches of integral parts of the automobile itself (indeed, in *Carroll*, contraband whiskey was in the upholstery of the seats), . . . it did not extend the doctrine to the warrantless search of personal luggage "merely because it was located in an automobile lawfully stopped by the police." Again, the *Sanders* majority stressed the heightened privacy expectation in personal luggage and concluded that the presence of luggage in an automobile did not diminish the owner's expectation of privacy in his personal items.

In *Ross*, the Court endeavored to distinguish between *Carroll*, which governed the *Ross* automobile search, and *Chadwick*, which governed the *Sanders* automobile search. It held that the *Carroll* doctrine covered searches of automobiles when the police had probable cause to search an entire vehicle, but that the *Chadwick* doctrine governed searches of luggage when the officers had probable cause to search only a container within the vehicle. Thus, in a *Ross* situation, the police could conduct a reasonable search under the Fourth Amendment without obtaining a warrant, whereas in a *Sanders* situation, the police had to obtain a warrant before they searched.

Justice Stevens is correct, of course, that *Ross* involved the scope of an automobile search. *Ross* held that closed containers encountered by the police during a warrantless search of a car pursuant to the automobile exception could also be searched. Thus, this Court in *Ross* took the critical step of saying that closed containers in cars could be searched without a warrant because of their presence within the automobile. Despite the protection that *Sanders* purported to extend to closed containers, the privacy interest in those closed containers yielded to the broad scope of an automobile search.

The facts in this case closely resemble the facts in *Ross*. In *Ross*, the police had probable cause to believe that drugs were stored in the trunk of a particular car. Here, the California Court of Appeal concluded that the police had probable cause to believe that respondent was carrying marijuana in a bag in his car's trunk. Furthermore, for what it is worth, in *Ross*, as here, the drugs in the trunk were contained in a brown paper bag.

This Court in *Ross* rejected *Chadwick*'s distinction between containers and cars. It concluded that the expectation of privacy in one's vehicle is equal to one's expectation of privacy in the container, and noted that "the privacy interests in a car's trunk or glove compartment may be no less than those in a movable container." It also recognized that it was arguable that the same exigent circumstances that permit a warrantless search of an automobile would justify the warrantless search of a movable container. In deference to the rule of *Chadwick* and *Sanders*, however, the Court put that question to one side. It concluded that the time and expense of the warrant process would be misdirected if the police could search every cubic inch of an automobile until they discovered a paper sack, at which point the Fourth Amendment required them to take the sack to a magistrate for permission to look inside. We now must decide the question deferred in *Ross*: whether the Fourth Amendment requires the police to obtain a warrant to open the sack in a movable vehicle simply because they lack probable cause to search the entire car. We conclude that it does not.

Dissenters in *Ross* asked why the suitcase in *Sanders* was "more private, less difficult for police to seize and store, or in any other relevant respect more properly subject to the warrant requirement, than a container that police discover in a probable-cause search of an entire automobile?" We now agree that a container found after a general search of the automobile and a container found in a car after a limited search for the container are equally easy for the police to store and for the suspect to hide or destroy. In fact, we see no principled distinction in terms of either the privacy expectation or the exigent circumstances between the paper bag found by the police in *Ross* and the paper bag found by the police here. Furthermore, by attempting to distinguish between a container for which the police are specifically searching and a container which they come across in a car, we have provided only minimal protection for privacy and have impeded effective law enforcement.

The line between probable cause to search a vehicle and probable cause to search a package in that vehicle is not always clear, and separate rules that govern the two objects to be searched may enable the police to broaden their power to make warrantless searches and disserve privacy interests. We noted this in *Ross* in the context of a search of an entire vehicle. Recognizing that under *Carroll*, the "entire vehicle itself . . . could be searched without a warrant," we concluded that "prohibiting police from opening immediately a container in which the object of the search is most likely to be found and instead forcing them first to comb the entire vehicle would actually exacerbate the intrusion on privacy interests." At the moment when officers stop an automobile, it may be less than clear whether they suspect with a high degree of certainty that the vehicle contains drugs in a bag or simply contains drugs. If the police know that they may open a bag only if they are actually searching the entire car, they may search more extensively than they otherwise would in order to establish the general probable cause required by *Ross.*

Such a situation is not farfetched. In *United States v. Johns* (1985), Customs agents saw two trucks drive to a private airstrip and approach two small planes. The agents drew near the trucks, smelled marijuana, and then saw in the backs of the trucks packages wrapped in a manner that marijuana smugglers customarily employed. The agents took the trucks to headquarters and searched the packages without a warrant. Relying on *Chadwick,* the defendants argued that the search was unlawful. The defendants contended that *Ross* was inapplicable because the agents lacked probable cause to search anything but the packages themselves and supported this contention by noting that a search of the entire vehicle never occurred. We rejected that argument and found *Chadwick* and *Sanders* inapposite because the agents had probable cause to search the entire body of each truck, although they had chosen not to do so. We cannot see the benefit of a rule that requires law enforcement officers to conduct a more intrusive search in order to justify a less intrusive one.

To the extent that the *Chadwick-Sanders* rule protects privacy, its protection is minimal. Law enforcement officers may seize a container and hold it until they obtain a search warrant. "Since the police, by hypothesis, have probable cause to seize the property, we can assume that a warrant will be routinely forthcoming in the overwhelming majority of cases (dissenting opinion). And the police often will be able to search containers without a warrant, despite the *Chadwick-Sanders* rule, as a search incident to a lawful arrest. In *New York v. Belton* (1981), the Court said:

> "[W]e hold that when a policeman has made a lawful custodial arrest of the occupant of an automobile, he may, as a contemporaneous incident of that arrest, search the passenger compartment of that automobile.
>
> It follows from this conclusion that the police may also examine the contents of any containers found within the passenger compartment."

Under *Belton,* the same probable cause to believe that a container holds drugs will allow the police to arrest the person transporting the container and search it.

Finally, the search of a paper bag intrudes far less on individual privacy than does the incursion sanctioned long ago in *Carroll.* In that case, prohibition agents slashed the upholstery of the automobile. This Court nonetheless found their search to be reasonable under the Fourth Amendment. If destroying the interior of an automobile is not unreasonable, we cannot conclude that looking inside a closed container is. In light of the minimal protection to privacy afforded by the *Chadwick-Sanders* rule, and our serious doubt whether that rule substantially serves privacy interests, we now hold that the Fourth Amendment does not compel separate treatment for an automobile search that extends only to a container within the vehicle.

■ ■ ■

The discrepancy between the two rules has led to confusion for law enforcement officers. For example, when an officer, who has developed probable cause to believe that a vehicle contains drugs, begins to search the vehicle and immediately discovers a closed container, which rule applies? The defendant will argue that the fact that the officer first chose to search the container indicates that his probable cause extended only to the container and that *Chadwick* and *Sanders* therefore require a warrant. On the other hand, the fact that the officer first chose to search in the most obvious location should not restrict the propriety of the search. The *Chadwick* rule, as applied in *Sanders*, has devolved into an anomaly such that the more likely the police are to discover drugs in a container, the less authority they have to search it. We have noted the virtue of providing " '"clear and unequivocal" guidelines to the law enforcement profession.' "

■ ■ ■

The interpretation of the *Carroll* doctrine set forth in *Ross* now applies to all searches of containers found in an automobile. In other words, the police may search without a warrant if their search is supported by probable cause. The Court in *Ross* put it this way:

> "The scope of a warrantless search of an automobile . . . is not defined by the nature of the container in which the contraband is secreted. Rather, it is defined by the object of the search and the places in which there is probable cause to believe that it may be found."

It went on to note: "Probable cause to believe that a container placed in the trunk of a taxi contains contraband or evidence does not justify a search of the entire cab." We reaffirm that principle. In the case before us, the police had probable cause to believe that the paper bag in the automobile's trunk contained marijuana. That probable cause now allows a warrantless search of the paper bag. The facts in the record reveal that the police did not have probable cause to believe that contraband was hidden in any other part of the automobile and a search of the entire vehicle would have been without probable cause and unreasonable under the Fourth Amendment.

Our holding today neither extends the *Carroll* doctrine nor broadens the scope of the permissible automobile search delineated in *Carroll, Chambers*, and *Ross.* It remains a "cardinal principle that 'searches conducted outside the judicial process, without prior approval by judge or magistrate, are *per se* unreasonable under the Fourth Amendment—subject only to a few specifically established and well-delineated exceptions.' "

Until today, this Court has drawn a curious line between the search of an automobile that coincidentally turns up a container and the search of a container that coincidentally turns up in an automobile. The protections of the Fourth Amendment must not turn on such coincidences. We therefore interpret *Carroll* as providing one rule to govern all automobile searches. The police may search an automobile and the containers within it where they have probable cause to believe contraband or evidence is contained.

The judgment of the California Court of Appeal is reversed, and the case is remanded to that court for further proceedings not inconsistent with this opinion.

It is so ordered.

Justice SCALIA, concurring in the judgment.

I agree with the dissent that it is anomalous for a briefcase to be protected by the "general requirement" of a prior warrant when it is being carried along the street, but for that same briefcase to become unprotected as soon as it is carried into an automobile. On the other hand, I agree with the Court that it would be anomalous for a locked compartment in an automobile to be unprotected by the "general requirement" of a prior warrant, but for an unlocked briefcase within the automobile to be protected. I join in the judgment of the Court because I think its holding is more faithful to the text and tradition of the Fourth Amendment, and if these anomalies in our jurisprudence are ever to be eliminated that is the direction in which we should travel.

■ ■ ■

Although the Fourth Amendment does not explicitly impose the requirement of a warrant, it is of course textually possible to consider that implicit within the requirement of reasonableness. For some years after the (still continuing) explosion in Fourth Amendment litigation that followed our announcement of the exclusionary rule in *Weeks v. United States* (1914), our jurisprudence lurched back and forth between imposing a categorical warrant requirement and looking to reasonableness alone. (The opinions preferring a warrant involved searches of structures.)

The victory was illusory. Even before today's decision, the "warrant requirement" had become so riddled with exceptions that it was basically unrecognizable. In 1985, one commentator cataloged nearly 20 such exceptions, including "searches incident to arrest . . . automobile searches . . . border searches . . . administrative searches of regulated businesses . . . exigent circumstances . . . search[es] incident to nonarrest when there is probable cause to arrest . . . boat boarding for document checks . . . welfare searches . . . inventory searches . . . airport searches . . . school search[es] . . ." Our intricate body of law regarding "reasonable expectation of privacy" has been developed largely as a means of creating these exceptions, enabling a search to be denominated not a Fourth Amendment "search" and therefore not subject to the general warrant requirement.

Unlike the dissent, therefore, I do not regard today's holding as some momentous departure, but rather as merely the continuation of an inconsistent jurisprudence that has been with us for years.

■ ■ ■

I would reverse the judgment in the present case, not because a closed container carried inside a car becomes subject to the "automobile" exception to the general warrant requirement, but because the search of a closed container, outside a privately owned building, with probable cause to believe that the container contains contraband, and when it in fact does contain contraband, is not one of those searches whose Fourth Amendment reasonableness depends upon a warrant. For that reason I concur in the judgment of the Court.

Justice WHITE, dissenting.

Agreeing as I do with most of Justice Stevens' opinion and with the result he reaches, I dissent and would affirm the judgment below.

Justice Stevens, with whom Justice Marshall joins, dissenting.

At the end of its opinion, the Court pays lipservice to the proposition that should provide the basis for a correct analysis of the legal question presented by this case: It is "a cardinal principle that 'searches conducted outside the judicial process, without prior approval by judge or magistrate, are *per se* unreasonable under the Fourth Amendment—subject only to a few specifically established and well-delineated exceptions.'"

Relying on arguments that conservative judges have repeatedly rejected in past cases, the Court today—despite its disclaimer to the contrary—enlarges the scope of the automobile exception to this "cardinal principle," which undergirded our Fourth Amendment jurisprudence prior to the retirement of the author of the landmark opinion in *United States v. Chadwick*. As a preface to my response to the Court's arguments, it is appropriate to restate the basis for the warrant requirement, the significance of the *Chadwick* case, and the reasons why the limitations on the automobile exception that were articulated in *United States v. Ross* represent a fair accommodation between the basic rule requiring prior judicial approval of searches and the automobile exception.

Our decisions have always acknowledged that the warrant requirement imposes a burden on law enforcement. And our cases have not questioned that trained professionals normally make reliable assessments of the existence of probable cause to conduct a search. We have repeatedly held, however, that these factors are outweighed by the individual interest in privacy that is protected by advance judicial approval. The Fourth Amendment dictates that the privacy interest is paramount, no matter how marginal the risk of error might be if the legality of warrantless searches were judged only after the fact.

In the concluding paragraph of his opinion in *Chadwick*, Chief Justice Burger made the point this way:

"Even though on this record the issuance of a warrant by a judicial officer was reasonably predictable, a line must be drawn. In our view, when no exigency is shown to support the need for an immediate search, the Warrant Clause places the line at the point where the property to be searched comes under the exclusive dominion of police authority. Respondents were therefore entitled to the protection of the Warrant Clause with the evaluation of a neutral magistrate, before their privacy interests in the contents of [their luggage] were invaded."

In *Chadwick*, the Department of Justice had mounted a frontal attack on the warrant requirement. The Government's principal contention was that "the Fourth Amendment Warrant Clause protects only interests traditionally identified with the home." We categorically rejected that contention, relying on the history and text of the Amendment, the policy underlying the warrant requirement, and a line of cases spanning over a century of our jurisprudence. We also rejected the Government's alternative argument that the rationale of our automobile search cases demonstrated the reasonableness of permitting warrantless searches of luggage.

■ ■ ■

We concluded that neither of the justifications for the automobile exception could support a similar exception for luggage. We first held that the privacy interest in luggage is "substantially greater than in an automobile." Unlike automobiles and their contents, we reasoned, "[l]uggage contents are not open to public view, except as a condition to a border entry or common carrier travel; nor is luggage subject to regular inspections and official scrutiny on a continuing basis." Indeed, luggage is specifically intended to safeguard the privacy of personal effects, unlike an automobile, "whose primary function is transportation."

We then held that the mobility of luggage did not justify creating an additional exception to the Warrant Clause. Unlike an automobile, luggage can easily be seized and detained pending judicial approval of a search. Once the police have luggage "under their exclusive control, there [i]s not the slightest danger that the [luggage] or its contents could [be] removed before a valid search warrant could be obtained.... With the [luggage] safely immobilized, it [i]s unreasonable to undertake the additional and greater intrusion of a search without a warrant" (footnote omitted).

Two Terms after *Chadwick*, we decided a case in which the relevant facts were identical to those before the Court today. In *Arkansas v. Sanders*, the police had probable cause to search a green suitcase that had been placed in the trunk of a taxicab at the Little Rock Airport. Several blocks from the airport, they stopped the cab, arrested the passengers, seized the suitcase and, without obtaining a warrant, opened and searched it.

The Arkansas Supreme Court held that the search was unconstitutional. Relying on *Chadwick*, the state court had no difficulty in concluding that there was "nothing in this set of circumstances that would lend credence to an assertion of impracticability in obtaining a search warrant." *Sanders v. State* (1977). Over the dissent of Justice Blackmun and then-Justice Rehnquist, both of whom had also dissented in *Chadwick*, this Court affirmed. In his opinion for the Court, Justice Powell noted that the seizure of the green suitcase was entirely proper, but that the State nevertheless had the burden of justifying the warrantless search, and that it had "failed to carry its burden of demonstrating the need for warrantless searches of luggage properly taken from automobiles." *Arkansas v. Sanders.*

Chief Justice Burger wrote separately to identify the distinction between cases in which police have probable cause to believe contraband is located somewhere in a vehicle—the typical automobile exception case—and cases like *Chadwick* and *Sanders* in which they had probable cause to search a particular container before it was placed in the car. He wrote:

> "Because the police officers had probable cause to believe that respondent's green suitcase contained marihuana before it was placed in the trunk of the taxicab, their duty to obtain a search warrant before opening it is clear under *United States v. Chadwick* (1977). The essence of our holding in *Chadwick* is that there is a legitimate expectation of privacy in the contents of a trunk or suitcase accompanying or being carried by a person; that expectation of privacy is not diminished simply because the owner's arrest occurs in a public place. Whether arrested in a hotel lobby, an airport, a railroad terminal, or on a public street, as here, the owner has the right to expect that the contents of his luggage will not, without his consent, be exposed on demand of the police."

■ ■ ■

We held in *Ross* that "the scope of the warrantless search authorized by [the automobile] exception is no broader and no narrower than a magistrate could legitimately authorize by warrant." The inherent mobility of the vehicle justified the immediate search without a warrant, but did not affect the scope of the search. Thus, the search could encompass containers, which might or might not conceal the object of the search, as well as the remainder of the vehicle.

Our conclusion was supported not only by prior cases defining the proper scope of searches authorized by warrant, as well as cases involving the automobile exception, but also by practical considerations that apply to searches in which the police have only generalized probable cause to believe that contraband is somewhere in a vehicle. We explained that, in such instances, "prohibiting police from opening immediately a container in which the object of the search is most likely to be found and instead forcing them first to comb the entire vehicle would actually exacerbate the intrusion on privacy interests." Indeed, because "the police could never be certain that the contraband was not secreted in a yet undiscovered portion of the vehicle," the most likely result would be that "the vehicle would need to be secured while a warrant was obtained."

These concerns that justified our holding in *Ross* are not implicated in cases like *Chadwick* and *Sanders* in which the police have probable cause to search a *particular* container rather than the *entire* vehicle. Because the police can seize the container which is the object of their search, they have no need either to search or to seize the entire vehicle. Indeed, as even the Court today recognizes, they have no authority to do so.

In reaching our conclusion in *Ross*, we therefore did not retreat at all from the holding in either *Chadwick* or *Sanders*. Instead, we expressly endorsed the reasoning in Chief Justice Burger's separate opinion in *Sanders*. We explained repeatedly that *Ross* involved the *scope* of the warrantless search authorized by the automobile exception, and, unlike *Chadwick* and *Sanders*, did not involve the *applicability* of the exception to closed containers.

■ ■ ■

Thus, we recognized in *Ross* that *Chadwick* and *Sanders* had not created a special rule for container searches, but rather had merely applied the cardinal principle that warrantless searches are per se unreasonable unless justified by an exception to the general rule. *Ross* dealt with the scope of the automobile exception; *Chadwick* and *Sanders* were cases in which the exception simply did not apply.

The Privacy Argument

The Court's statement that *Chadwick* and *Sanders* provide only "minimal protection to privacy" is also unpersuasive. Every citizen clearly has an interest in the privacy of the contents of his or her luggage, briefcase, handbag or any other container that conceals private papers and effects from public scrutiny. That privacy interest has been recognized repeatedly in cases spanning more than a century.

Under the Court's holding today, the privacy interest that protects the contents of a suitcase or a briefcase from a warrantless search when it is in public view simply vanishes when its owner climbs into a taxicab. Unquestionably the rejection of the *Sanders* line of cases by today's decision will result in a significant loss of individual privacy.

■ ■ ■

Even if the warrant requirement does inconvenience the police to some extent, that fact does not distinguish this constitutional requirement from any other procedural protection secured by the Bill of Rights. It is merely a part of the price that our society must pay in order to preserve its freedom. Thus, in a unanimous opinion that relied on both *Johnson* [*v. United States* (1948)] and *Chadwick*, Justice Stewart wrote:

> "Moreover, the mere fact that law enforcement may be made more efficient can never by itself justify disregard of the Fourth Amendment. Cf. *Coolidge v. New Hampshire* (1971). The investigation of crime would always be simplified if warrants were unnecessary. But the Fourth Amendment reflects the view of those who wrote the Bill of Rights that the privacy of a person's home and property may not be totally sacrificed in the name of maximum simplicity in enforcement of the criminal law."

It is too early to know how much freedom America has lost today. The magnitude of the loss is, however, not nearly as significant as the Court's willingness to inflict it without even a colorable basis for its rejection of prior law.

I respectfully dissent.

6. Exigent Circumstances

Welsh v. Wisconsin

466 U.S. 740 (1984)

BRENNAN, J., delivered the opinion of the Court, in which MARSHALL, BLACKMUN, POWELL, STEVENS, and O'CONNOR, JJ., joined. BLACKMUN, J., filed a concurring opinion. WHITE, J., filed a dissenting opinion, in which REHNQUIST, J., joined. BURGER, C.J., would have dismissed the writ and wrote a separate statement.

Payton v. New York (1980) held that, absent probable cause and exigent circumstances, warrantless arrests in the home are prohibited by the Fourth Amendment. But the Court in that case explicitly refused "to consider the sort of emergency or dangerous situation, described in our cases as 'exigent circumstances,' that would justify a warrantless entry into a home for the purpose of either arrest or search." Certiorari was granted in this case to decide at least one aspect of the unresolved question: whether, and if so under what circumstances, the Fourth Amendment prohibits the police from making a warrantless night entry of a person's home in order to arrest him for a nonjailable traffic offense. . . .

Shortly before 9 o'clock on the rainy night of April 24, 1978, a lone witness, Randy Jablonic, observed a car being driven erratically. After changing speeds and veering from side to side, the car eventually swerved off the road and came to a stop in an open field. No damage to any person or property occurred. Concerned about the driver and fearing that the car would get back on the highway, Jablonic drove his truck up behind the car so as to block it from returning to the road. Another passerby also stopped at the scene, and Jablonic asked her to call the police. Before the police arrived, however, the driver of the car emerged from his vehicle, approached Jablonic's truck, and asked Jablonic for a ride home. Jablonic instead suggested that they wait for assistance in removing or repairing the car. Ignoring Jablonic's suggestion, the driver walked away from the scene.

A few minutes later, the police arrived and questioned Jablonic. He told one officer what he had seen, specifically noting that the driver was either very inebriated or very sick. The officer checked the motor vehicle registration of the abandoned car and learned that it was registered to the petitioner, Edward G. Welsh. In addition, the officer noted that the petitioner's residence was a short distance from the scene, and therefore easily within walking distance.

Without securing any type of warrant, the police proceeded to the petitioner's home, arriving about 9 p.m. When the petitioner's stepdaughter answered the door, the police gained entry into the house. Proceeding upstairs to the petitioner's bedroom, they found him lying naked in bed. At this point, the petitioner was placed under arrest for driving or operating a motor vehicle while under the influence of an intoxicant. . . . The petitioner was taken to the police station, where he refused to submit to a breath-analysis test.

■ ■ ■

It is axiomatic that the "physical entry of the home is the chief evil against which the wording of the Fourth Amendment is directed." *United States v. United States District Court* (1972). And a principal protection against unnecessary intrusions into private dwellings is the warrant requirement imposed by the Fourth Amendment on agents of the government who seek to enter the home for purposes of search or arrest. See *Johnson v. United States* (1948). It is not surprising, therefore, that the Court has recognized, as "a 'basic principle of Fourth Amendment law[,]' that searches and seizures inside a home without a warrant are presumptively unreasonable." *Payton v. New York.*

■ ■ ■

Consistently with these long-recognized principles, the Court decided in *Payton v. New York* that warrantless felony arrests in the home are prohibited by the Fourth Amendment, absent probable cause and exigent circumstances. At the same time, the Court declined to consider the scope of any exception for exigent circumstances that might justify warrantless home arrests, thereby leaving to the lower courts the initial application of the exigent-circumstances exception.

■ ■ ■

Our hesitation in finding exigent circumstances, especially when warrantless arrests in the home are at issue, is particularly appropriate when the underlying offense for which there is probable cause to arrest is relatively minor. Before agents of the government may invade the sanctity of the home, the burden is on the government to demonstrate exigent circumstances that overcome the presumption of unreasonableness that attaches to all warrantless home entries. When the government's interest is only to arrest for a minor offense, that presumption of unreasonableness is difficult to rebut, and the government usually should be allowed to make such arrests only with a warrant issued upon probable cause by a neutral and detached magistrate.

■ ■ ■

We therefore conclude that the common-sense approach utilized by most lower courts is required by the Fourth Amendment prohibition on "unreasonable searches and seizures," and hold that an important factor to be considered when determining whether any exigency exists is the gravity of the underlying offense for which the arrest is being made. Moreover, although no exigency is created simply because there is probable cause to believe that a serious crime has been committed, see *Payton*, application of the exigent-circumstances exception in the context of a home entry should rarely be sanctioned when there is probable cause to believe that only a minor offense, such as the kind at issue in this case, has been committed.

Application of this principle to the facts of the present case is relatively straightforward. The petitioner was arrested in the privacy of his own bedroom for a noncriminal, traffic offense. The State attempts to justify the arrest by relying on the hot-pursuit doctrine, on the threat to public safety, and on the need to preserve evidence of the petitioner's blood-alcohol level. On the facts of this case, however, the claim of hot pursuit is unconvincing because there was no immediate or continuous pursuit of the petitioner from the scene of a crime. Moreover, because the petitioner had already arrived home, and had abandoned his car at the scene of the accident, there was little remaining threat to the public safety. Hence, the only potential emergency claimed by the State was the need to ascertain the petitioner's blood-alcohol level.

■ ■ ■

The Supreme Court of Wisconsin let stand a warrantless, nighttime entry into the petitioner's home to arrest him for a civil traffic offense. Such an arrest, however, is clearly prohibited by the special protection afforded the individual in his home by the Fourth Amendment. The petitioner's arrest was therefore invalid, the judgment of the Supreme Court of Wisconsin is vacated, and the case is remanded for further proceedings not inconsistent with this opinion.

It is so ordered.

Brigham City, Utah v. Stuart

547 U.S. 398 (2006)

ROBERTS, C.J., delivered the opinion for a unanimous Court.

In this case we consider whether police may enter a home without a warrant when they have an objectively reasonable basis for believing that an occupant is seriously injured or imminently threatened with such injury. We conclude that they may.

This case arises out of a melee that occurred in a Brigham City, Utah, home in the early morning hours of July 23, 2000. At about 3 a.m., four police officers responded to a call regarding a loud party at a residence. Upon arriving at the house, they heard shouting from inside, and proceeded down the driveway to investigate. There, they observed two juveniles drinking beer in the backyard. They entered the backyard, and saw—through a screen door and windows—an altercation taking place in the kitchen of the home. According to the testimony of one of the officers, four adults were attempting, with some difficulty, to restrain a juvenile. The juvenile eventually "broke free, swung a fist and struck one of the adults in the face." The officer testified that he observed the victim of the blow spitting blood into a nearby sink. The other adults continued to try to restrain the juvenile, pressing him up against a refrigerator with such force that the refrigerator began moving across the floor. At this point, an officer opened the screen door and announced the officers' presence. Amid the tumult, nobody noticed. The officer entered the kitchen and again cried out, and as the occupants slowly became aware that the police were on the scene, the altercation ceased.

The officers subsequently arrested respondents and charged them with contributing to the delinquency of a minor, disorderly conduct, and intoxication. In the trial court, respondents filed a motion to suppress all evidence obtained after the officers entered the home, arguing that the warrantless entry violated the Fourth Amendment. The court granted the motion, and the Utah Court of Appeals affirmed.

■ ■ ■

. . . Although [the Supreme Court of Utah] found the case "a close and difficult call," the court nevertheless concluded that the officers' entry was not justified by exigent circumstances.

We granted certiorari, in light of differences among state courts and the Courts of Appeals concerning the appropriate Fourth Amendment standard governing warrantless entry by law enforcement in an emergency situation.

■ ■ ■

One exigency obviating the requirement of a warrant is the need to assist persons who are seriously injured or threatened with such injury. "The need to protect or preserve life or avoid serious injury is justification for what would be otherwise illegal absent an exigency or emergency." Accordingly, law enforcement officers may enter a home without a warrant to render emergency assistance to an injured occupant or to protect an occupant from imminent injury.

■ ■ ■

Respondents do not take issue with these principles, but instead advance two reasons why the officers' entry here was unreasonable. First, they argue that the officers were more interested in making arrests than quelling violence. They urge us to consider, in assessing the reasonableness of the entry, whether the officers were "indeed motivated primarily by a desire to save lives and property."

■ ■ ■

Our cases have repeatedly rejected this approach. An action is "reasonable" under the Fourth Amendment, regardless of the individual officer's state of mind, "as long as the circumstances, viewed *objectively*, justify [the] action."

■ ■ ■

Respondents . . . contend that their conduct was not serious enough to justify the officers' intrusion into the home. They rely on *Welsh v. Wisconsin* (1984), in which we held that "an important factor to be considered when determining whether any exigency exists is the gravity of the underlying offense for which the arrest is being made." This contention, too, is misplaced. *Welsh* involved a warrantless entry by officers to arrest a suspect for driving while intoxicated. There, the "only potential emergency" confronting the officers was the need to preserve evidence (*i.e.*, the suspect's blood-alcohol level)—an exigency that we held insufficient under the circumstances to justify entry into the suspect's home. Here, the officers were confronted with *ongoing* violence occurring *within* the home. *Welsh* did not address such a situation.

We think the officers' entry here was plainly reasonable under the circumstances. The officers were responding, at 3 o'clock in the morning, to complaints about a loud party. As they approached the house, they could hear from within "an altercation occurring, some kind of a fight." "It was loud and it was tumultuous." The officers heard "thumping and crashing" and people yelling "stop, stop" and "get off me." As the trial court found, "it was obvious that . . . knocking on the front door" would have been futile. The noise seemed to be coming from the back of the house; after looking in the front window and seeing nothing, the officers proceeded around back to investigate further. They found two juveniles drinking beer in the backyard. From there, they could see that a fracas was taking place inside the kitchen. A juvenile, fists clenched, was being held back by several adults. As the officers watch, he breaks free and strikes one of the adults in the face, sending the adult to the sink spitting blood.

In these circumstances, the officers had an objectively reasonable basis for believing both that the injured adult might need help and that the violence in the kitchen was just beginning. Nothing in the Fourth Amendment required them to wait until another blow rendered someone "unconscious" or "semi-conscious" or worse before entering. The role of a peace officer includes preventing violence and restoring order, not simply rendering first aid to casualties; an officer is not like a boxing (or hockey) referee, poised to stop a bout only if it becomes too one-sided.

The manner of the officers' entry was also reasonable. After witnessing the punch, one of the officers opened the screen door and "yelled in police." When nobody heard him, he stepped into the kitchen and announced himself again. Only then did the tumult subside. The officer's announcement of his presence was at least equivalent to a knock on the screen door. Indeed, it was probably the only option that had even a chance of rising above the din. Under these circumstances, there was no violation of the Fourth Amendment's knock-and-announce rule. Furthermore, once the announcement was made, the officers were free to enter; it would serve no purpose to require them to stand dumbly at the door awaiting a response while those within brawled on, oblivious to their presence.

Accordingly, we reverse the judgment of the Supreme Court of Utah, and remand the case for further proceedings not inconsistent with this opinion.

It is so ordered.

Michigan v. Fisher

130 S. Ct. 546 (2009)

PER CURIAM.

Police officers responded to a complaint of a disturbance near Allen Road in Brownstown, Michigan.[*] Officer Christopher Goolsby later testified that, as he and his partner approached the area, a couple directed them to a residence where a man was "going crazy." Upon their arrival, the officers found a household in considerable chaos: a pickup truck in the driveway with its front

---

[*] We have taken the facts from the opinion of the Michigan Court of Appeals. Except where indicated, the parties do not dispute the facts.

smashed, damaged fenceposts along the side of the property, and three broken house windows, the glass still on the ground outside. The officers also noticed blood on the hood of the pickup and on clothes inside of it, as well as on one of the doors to the house. (It is disputed whether they noticed this immediately upon reaching the house, but undisputed that they noticed it before the allegedly unconstitutional entry.) Through a window, the officers could see respondent, Jeremy Fisher, inside the house, screaming and throwing things. The back door was locked, and a couch had been placed to block the front door.

The officers knocked, but Fisher refused to answer. They saw that Fisher had a cut on his hand, and they asked him whether he needed medical attention. Fisher ignored these questions and demanded, with accompanying profanity, that the officers go to get a search warrant. Officer Goolsby then pushed the front door partway open and ventured into the house. Through the window of the open door he saw Fisher pointing a long gun at him. Officer Goolsby withdrew.

Fisher was charged under Michigan law with assault with a dangerous weapon and possession of a firearm during the commission of a felony. The trial court concluded that Officer Goolsby violated the Fourth Amendment when he entered Fisher's house, and granted Fisher's motion to suppress the evidence obtained as a result—that is, Officer Goolsby's statement that Fisher pointed a rifle at him. The Michigan Court of Appeals initially remanded for an evidentiary hearing, after which the trial court reinstated its order. The Court of Appeals then affirmed over a dissent by Judge Talbot. See 2008 Mich. App. LEXIS 633, [WL], at *2; 2005 Mich. App. LEXIS 3172, [WL], at *2-*5. The Michigan Supreme Court granted leave to appeal, but, after hearing oral argument, it vacated its prior order and denied leave instead; three justices, however, would have taken the case and reversed on the ground that the Court of Appeals misapplied the Fourth Amendment. See 483 Mich. 1007, 765 N.W.2d 19 (2009). Because the decision of the Michigan Court of Appeals is indeed contrary to our Fourth Amendment case law, particularly *Brigham City v. Stuart* (2006), we grant the State's petition for certiorari and reverse.

> "[T]he ultimate touchstone of the Fourth Amendment," we have often said, "is 'reasonableness.'" Therefore, although "searches and seizures inside a home without a warrant are presumptively unreasonable," that presumption can be overcome. For example, "the exigencies of the situation [may] make the needs of law enforcement so compelling that the warrantless search is objectively reasonable."

Brigham City identified one such exigency: "the need to assist persons who are seriously injured or threatened with such injury." Thus, law enforcement officers "may enter a home without a warrant to render emergency assistance to an injured occupant or to protect an occupant from imminent injury." This "emergency aid exception" does not depend on the officers' subjective intent or the seriousness of any crime they are investigating when the emergency arises.

It requires only "an objectively reasonable basis for believing" that "a person within [the house] is in need of immediate aid."

■ ■ ■

A straightforward application of the emergency aid exception, as in *Brigham City*, dictates that the officer's entry was reasonable. Just as in *Brigham City*, the police officers here were responding to a report of a disturbance. Just as in *Brigham City*, when they arrived on the scene they encountered a tumultuous situation in the house—and here they also found signs of a recent injury, perhaps from a car accident, outside. And just as in *Brigham City*, the officers could see violent behavior inside. Although Officer Goolsby and his partner did not see punches thrown, as did the officers in *Brigham City*, they did see Fisher screaming and throwing things. It would be objectively reasonable to believe that Fisher's projectiles might have a human target (perhaps a spouse or a child), or that Fisher would hurt himself in the course of his rage. In short, we find it as plain here as we did in *Brigham City* that the officer's entry was reasonable under the Fourth Amendment.

The Michigan Court of Appeals, however, thought the situation "did not rise to a level of emergency justifying the warrantless intrusion into a residence." Although the Court of Appeals conceded that "there was evidence an injured person was on the premises," it found it significant that "the mere drops of blood did not signal a likely serious, life-threatening injury." The court added that the cut Officer Goolsby observed on Fisher's hand "likely explained the trail of blood" and that Fisher "was very much on his feet and apparently able to see to his own needs."

Even a casual review of *Brigham City* reveals the flaw in this reasoning. Officers do not need ironclad proof of "a likely serious, life-threatening" injury to invoke the emergency aid exception. The only injury police could confirm in *Brigham City* was the bloody lip they saw the juvenile inflict upon the adult. Fisher argues that the officers here could not have been motivated by a perceived need to provide medical assistance, since they never summoned emergency medical personnel. This would have no bearing, of course, upon their need to assure that Fisher was not endangering someone else in the house. Moreover, even if the failure to summon medical personnel conclusively established that Goolsby did not subjectively believe, when he entered the house, that Fisher or someone else was seriously injured (which is doubtful), the test, as we have said, is not what Goolsby believed, but whether there was "an objectively reasonable basis for believing" that medical assistance was needed, or persons were in danger.

It was error for the Michigan Court of Appeals to replace that objective inquiry into appearances with its hindsight determination that there was in fact no emergency. It does not meet the needs of law enforcement or the demands of public safety to require officers to walk away from a situation like the one they encountered here. Only when an apparent threat has become an actual harm can officers rule out innocuous explanations for ominous circumstances. But "[t]he role of a peace officer includes preventing violence and restoring order, not simply rendering first aid to casualties." It sufficed to invoke the emergency aid exception that it was reasonable to believe that Fisher had hurt himself (albeit nonfatally) and needed treatment that in his rage he was unable to provide, or that Fisher was about to hurt, or had already hurt, someone else. The Michigan Court of Appeals required more than what the Fourth Amendment demands.

The petition for certiorari is granted. The judgment of the Michigan Court of Appeals is reversed, and the case is remanded for further proceedings not inconsistent with this opinion.

It is so ordered.

Justice STEVENS, with whom Justice SOTOMAYOR joins, dissenting.

As a matter of Michigan law it is well settled that police officers may enter a home without a warrant "when they reasonably believe that a person within is in need of immediate aid." We have stated the rule in the same way under federal law, *Mincey v. Arizona* [(1978)], and have explained that a warrantless entry is justified by the "'need to protect or preserve life or avoid serious injury.'" The State bears the burden of proof on that factual issue and relied entirely on the testimony of Officer Goolsby in its attempt to carry that burden. Since three years had passed, Goolsby was not sure about certain facts—such as whether Fisher had a cut on his hand—but he did remember that Fisher repeatedly swore at the officers and told them to get a warrant, and that Fisher was screaming and throwing things. Goolsby also testified that he saw "mere drops" of blood outside Fisher's home, and that he did not ask whether anyone else was inside. Goolsby did not testify that he had any reason to believe that anyone else was in the house. Thus, the factual question was whether Goolsby had "an objectively reasonable basis for believing that [Fisher was] seriously injured or imminently threatened with such injury."

After hearing the testimony, the trial judge was "even more convinced" that the entry was unlawful. He noted the issue was "whether or not there was a reasonable basis to [enter the house] or whether [Goolsby] was just acting on some possibilities," and evidently found the record supported the latter rather than the former. He found the police decision to leave the scene and not return for several hours—without resolving any potentially dangerous situation and without calling for medical assistance—inconsistent with a reasonable belief that Fisher was in need of immediate aid. In sum, the one judge who heard Officer Goolsby's testimony was not persuaded that Goolsby had an objectively reasonable basis for believing that entering Fisher's home was necessary to avoid *serious* injury.

The Michigan Court of Appeals affirmed, concluding that the State had not met its burden. Perhaps because one judge dissented, the Michigan Supreme Court initially granted an application for leave to appeal. After considering briefs and oral argument, however, the majority of that Court vacated its earlier order because it was "no longer persuaded that the questions presented should be reviewed by this Court."

Today, without having heard Officer Goolsby's testimony, this Court decides that the trial judge got it wrong. I am not persuaded that he did, but even if we make that assumption, it is hard to see how the Court is justified in micromanaging the day-to-day business of state tribunals making fact-intensive decisions of this kind. We ought not usurp the role of the factfinder when faced with a close question of the reasonableness of an officer's actions, particularly in a case tried in a state court. I therefore respectfully dissent.

Kentucky v. King

131 S. Ct. 1849 (2011)

Justice ALITO delivered the opinion of the Court, in which ROBERTS, C.J., and SCALIA, KENNEDY, THOMAS, BREYER, SOTOMAYOR, and KAGAN, JJ., joined. GINSBURG, J., filed a dissenting opinion.

It is well established that "exigent circumstances," including the need to prevent the destruction of evidence, permit police officers to conduct an otherwise permissible search without first obtaining a warrant. In this case, we consider whether this rule applies when police, by knocking on the door of a residence and announcing their presence, cause the occupants to attempt to destroy evidence. The Kentucky Supreme Court held that the exigent circumstances rule does not apply in the case at hand because the police should have foreseen that their conduct would prompt the occupants to attempt to destroy evidence. We reject this interpretation of the exigent circumstances rule. The conduct of the police prior to their entry into the apartment was entirely lawful. They did not violate the Fourth Amendment or threaten to do so. In such a situation, the exigent circumstances rule applies.

I

A

This case concerns the search of an apartment in Lexington, Kentucky. Police officers set up a controlled buy of crack cocaine outside an apartment complex. Undercover Officer Gibbons watched the deal take place from an unmarked car in a nearby parking lot. After the deal occurred, Gibbons radioed uniformed officers to move in on the suspect. He told the officers that the suspect was moving quickly toward the breezeway of an apartment building, and he urged them to "hurry up and get there" before the suspect entered an apartment.

In response to the radio alert, the uniformed officers drove into the nearby parking lot, left their vehicles, and ran to the breezeway. Just as they entered the breezeway, they heard a door shut and detected a very strong odor of burnt marijuana. At the end of the breezeway, the officers saw two apartments, one on the left and one on the right, and they did not know which apartment the suspect had entered. Gibbons had radioed that the suspect was running into the apartment on the right, but the officers did not hear this statement because they had already left their vehicles. Because they smelled marijuana smoke emanating from the apartment on the left, they approached the door of that apartment.

Officer Steven Cobb, one of the uniformed officers who approached the door, testified that the officers banged on the left apartment door "as loud as [they] could" and announced, "This is the police" or "Police, police, police." Cobb said that "[a]s soon as [the officers] started banging on the door," they "could hear people inside moving," and "it sounded as though things were being moved inside the apartment." These noises, Cobb testified, led the officers to believe that drug-related evidence was about to be destroyed.

At that point, the officers announced that they "were going to make entry inside the apartment." Cobb then kicked in the door, the officers entered the apartment, and they found three people in the front room: respondent Hollis King, respondent's girlfriend, and a guest who was smoking marijuana. The officers performed a protective sweep of the apartment during which they saw marijuana and powder cocaine in plain view. In a subsequent search, they also discovered crack cocaine, cash, and drug paraphernalia.

Police eventually entered the apartment on the right. Inside, they found the suspected drug dealer who was the initial target of their investigation.

B

In the Fayette County Circuit Court, a grand jury charged respondent with trafficking in marijuana, first-degree trafficking in a controlled substance, and second-degree persistent felony offender status. Respondent filed a motion to suppress the evidence from the warrantless search, but the Circuit Court denied the motion. The Circuit Court concluded that the officers had probable cause to investigate the marijuana odor and that the officers "properly conducted the investigation by initially knocking on the door of the apartment unit and awaiting the response or consensual entry." Exigent circumstances justified the warrantless entry, the court held, because "there was no response at all to the knocking," and because "Officer Cobb heard movement in the apartment which he reasonably concluded were persons in the act of destroying evidence, particularly narcotics because of the smell." Respondent then entered a conditional guilty plea, reserving his right to appeal the denial of his suppression motion. The court sentenced respondent to 11 years' imprisonment.

The Kentucky Court of Appeals affirmed. It held that exigent circumstances justified the warrantless entry because the police reasonably believed that evidence would be destroyed. The police did not impermissibly create the exigency, the court explained, because they did not deliberately evade the warrant requirement.

The Supreme Court of Kentucky reversed. As a preliminary matter, the court observed that there was "certainly some question as to whether the sound of persons moving inside the apartment was sufficient to establish that evidence was being destroyed." But the court did not answer that question. Instead, it "assume[d] for the purpose of argument that exigent circumstances existed."

To determine whether police impermissibly created the exigency, the Supreme Court of Kentucky announced a two-part test. First, the court held, police cannot "deliberately creat[e] the exigent circumstances with the bad faith intent to avoid the warrant requirement." Second, even absent bad faith, the court concluded, police may not rely on exigent circumstances if "it was reasonably foreseeable that the investigative tactics employed by the police would create the exigent circumstances." Although the court found no evidence of bad faith, it held that exigent circumstances could not justify the search because it was reasonably foreseeable that the occupants would destroy evidence when the police knocked on the door and announced their presence.

We granted certiorari.

II

A

. . . [t]he text of the Amendment . . . expressly imposes two requirements. First, all searches and seizures must be reasonable. Second, a warrant may not be issued unless probable cause is properly established and the scope of the authorized search is set out with particularity.

Although the text of the Fourth Amendment does not specify when a search warrant must be obtained, this Court has inferred that a warrant must generally be secured. "It is a basic principle of Fourth Amendment law, we have often said, that searches and seizures inside a home without a warrant are presumptively unreasonable." *Brigham City v. Stuart* (2006). But we have also recognized that this presumption may be overcome in some circumstances because the ultimate touchstone of the Fourth Amendment is reasonableness. Accordingly, the warrant requirement is subject to certain reasonable exceptions.

One well-recognized exception applies when the exigencies of the situation make the needs of law enforcement so compelling that a warrantless search is objectively reasonable under the Fourth Amendment.

This Court has identified several exigencies that may justify a warrantless search of a home. Under the "emergency aid" exception, for example, "officers may enter a home without a warrant to render emergency assistance to an injured occupant or to protect an occupant from imminent injury." Police officers may enter premises without a warrant when they are in hot pursuit of a fleeing suspect. See *United States v. Santana* (1976). And—what is relevant here—the need "to prevent the imminent destruction of evidence" has long been recognized as a sufficient justification for a warrantless search. *Brigham City.*

B

Over the years, lower courts have developed an exception to the exigent circumstances rule, the so-called "police-created exigency" doctrine. Under this doctrine, police may not rely on the need to prevent destruction of evidence when that exigency was "created" or "manufactured" by the conduct of the police.

In applying this exception for the "creation" or "manufacturing" of an exigency by the police, courts require something more than mere proof that fear of detection by the police caused the destruction of evidence. An additional showing is obviously needed because, as the Eighth Circuit has recognized, "in some sense the police always create the exigent circumstances." *United States v. Duchi* (1990). That is to say, in the vast majority of cases in which evidence is destroyed by persons who are engaged in illegal conduct, the reason for the destruction is fear that the evidence will fall into the hands of law enforcement. Destruction of evidence issues probably occur most frequently in drug cases because drugs may be easily destroyed by flushing them down a toilet or rinsing them down a drain. Persons in possession of valuable drugs are unlikely to destroy them unless they fear discovery by the police. Consequently, a rule that precludes the police from making a warrantless entry to prevent the destruction of evidence whenever their conduct causes the exigency would unreasonably shrink the reach of this well-established exception to the warrant requirement.

Presumably for the purpose of avoiding such a result, the lower courts have held that the police-created exigency doctrine requires more than simple causation, but the lower courts have not agreed on the test to be applied. Indeed, the petition in this case maintains that "[t]here are currently five different tests being used by the United States Courts of Appeals," and that some state courts have crafted additional tests.

III

A

Despite the welter of tests devised by the lower courts, the answer to the question presented in this case follows directly and clearly from the principle that permits warrantless searches in the first place. As previously noted, warrantless searches are allowed when the circumstances make it reasonable, within the meaning of the Fourth Amendment, to dispense with the warrant requirement. Therefore, the answer to the question before us is that the exigent circumstances rule justifies a warrantless search when the conduct of the police preceding the exigency is reasonable in the same sense. Where, as here, the police did not create the exigency by engaging or threatening to engage in conduct that violates the Fourth Amendment, warrantless entry to prevent the destruction of evidence is reasonable and thus allowed.[4]

■ ■ ■

---

4. There is a strong argument to be made that, at least in most circumstances, the exigent circumstances rule should not apply where the police, without a warrant or any legally sound basis for a warrantless entry, threaten that they will enter without permission unless admitted. In this case, however, no such actual threat was made, and therefore we have no need to reach that question.

B

Some lower courts have adopted a rule that is similar to the one that we recognize today. But others, including the Kentucky Supreme Court, have imposed additional requirements that are unsound and that we now reject.

Bad faith. Some courts, including the Kentucky Supreme Court, ask whether law enforcement officers "deliberately created the exigent circumstances with the bad faith intent to avoid the warrant requirement."

This approach is fundamentally inconsistent with our Fourth Amendment jurisprudence. "Our cases have repeatedly rejected" a subjective approach, asking only whether "the circumstances, viewed *objectively,* justify the action." *Brigham City.* Indeed, we have never held, outside limited contexts such as an "inventory search or administrative inspection . . . that an officer's motive invalidates objectively justifiable behavior under the Fourth Amendment." *Whren v. United States* (1996).

The reasons for looking to objective factors, rather than subjective intent, are clear. Legal tests based on reasonableness are generally objective, and this Court has long taken the view that "evenhanded law enforcement is best achieved by the application of objective standards of conduct, rather than standards that depend upon the subjective state of mind of the officer."

Reasonable foreseeability. Some courts, again including the Kentucky Supreme Court, hold that police may not rely on an exigency if "it was reasonably foreseeable that the investigative tactics employed by the police would create the exigent circumstances." Courts applying this test have invalidated warrantless home searches on the ground that it was reasonably foreseeable that police officers, by knocking on the door and announcing their presence, would lead a drug suspect to destroy evidence.

Contrary to this reasoning, however, we have rejected the notion that police may seize evidence without a warrant only when they come across the evidence by happenstance. In *Horton* (1990) . . . we held that the police may seize evidence in plain view even though the officers may be "interested in an item of evidence and fully expec[t] to find it in the course of a search."

Adoption of a reasonable foreseeability test would also introduce an unacceptable degree of unpredictability. For example, whenever law enforcement officers knock on the door of premises occupied by a person who may be involved in the drug trade, there is *some* possibility that the occupants may possess drugs and may seek to destroy them. Under a reasonable foreseeability test, it would be necessary to quantify the degree of predictability that must be reached before the police-created exigency doctrine comes into play.

A simple example illustrates the difficulties that such an approach would produce. Suppose that the officers in the present case did not smell marijuana smoke and thus knew only that there was a 50% chance that the fleeing suspect had entered the apartment on the left rather than the apartment on the right. Under those circumstances, would it have been reasonably foreseeable that the occupants of the apartment on the left would seek to destroy evidence upon learning that the police were at the door? Or suppose that the officers knew only that the suspect had disappeared into one of the apartments on a floor with 3, 5, 10, or even 20 units? If the police chose a door at random and knocked for the purpose of asking the occupants if they knew a person who fit the description of the suspect, would it have been reasonably foreseeable that the occupants would seek to destroy evidence?

We have noted that "[t]he calculus of reasonableness must embody allowance for the fact that police officers are often forced to make split-second judgments—in circumstances that are tense, uncertain, and rapidly evolving." The reasonable foreseeability test would create unacceptable and unwarranted difficulties for law enforcement officers who must make quick decisions in the field, as well as for judges who would be required to determine after the fact whether the destruction of evidence in response to a knock on the door was reasonably foreseeable based on what the officers knew at the time.

Probable cause and time to secure a warrant. Some courts, in applying the police-created exigency doctrine, fault law enforcement officers if, after acquiring evidence that is sufficient to establish probable cause to search particular premises, the officers do not seek a warrant but instead knock on the door and seek either to speak with an occupant or to obtain consent to search.

This approach unjustifiably interferes with legitimate law enforcement strategies. There are many entirely proper reasons why police may not want to seek a search warrant as soon as the bare minimum of evidence needed to establish probable cause is acquired. Without attempting to provide a comprehensive list of these reasons, we note a few.

First, the police may wish to speak with the occupants of a dwelling before deciding whether it is worthwhile to seek authorization for a search. They may think that a short and simple conversation may obviate the need to apply for and execute a warrant. Second, the police may want to ask an occupant of the premises for consent to search because doing so is simpler, faster, and less burdensome than applying for a warrant. A consensual search also "may result in considerably less inconvenience" and embarrassment to the occupants than a search conducted pursuant to a warrant. Third, law enforcement officers may wish to obtain more evidence before submitting what might otherwise be considered a marginal warrant application. Fourth, prosecutors may wish to wait until they acquire evidence that can justify a search that is broader in scope than the search that a judicial officer is likely to authorize based on the evidence then available. And finally, in many cases, law enforcement may not want to execute a search that will disclose the existence of an investigation because doing so may interfere with the acquisition of additional evidence against those already under suspicion or evidence about additional but as yet unknown participants in a criminal scheme.

We have said that "[l]aw enforcement officers are under no constitutional duty to call a halt to criminal investigation the moment they have the minimum evidence to establish probable cause." *Hoffa v. United States* (1966). Faulting the police for failing to apply for a search warrant at the earliest possible time after obtaining probable cause imposes a duty that is nowhere to be found in the Constitution.

Standard or good investigative tactics. Finally, some lower court cases suggest that law enforcement officers may be found to have created or manufactured an exigency if the court concludes that the course of their investigation was "contrary to standard or good law enforcement practices (or to the policies or practices of their jurisdictions)." This approach fails to provide clear guidance for law enforcement officers and authorizes courts to make judgments on matters that are the province of those who are responsible for federal and state law enforcement agencies.

C

Respondent argues for a rule that differs from those discussed above, but his rule is also flawed. Respondent contends that law enforcement officers impermissibly create an exigency when they "engage in conduct that would cause a reasonable person to believe that entry is imminent and inevitable." In respondent's view, relevant factors include the officers' tone of voice in announcing their presence and the forcefulness of their knocks. But the ability of law enforcement officers to respond to an exigency cannot turn on such subtleties.

Police officers may have a very good reason to announce their presence loudly and to knock on the door with some force. A forceful knock may be necessary to alert the occupants that someone is at the door. Furthermore, unless police officers identify themselves loudly enough, occupants may not know who is at their doorstep. Officers are permitted—indeed, encouraged—to identify themselves to citizens, and "in many circumstances this is cause for assurance, not discomfort. Citizens who are startled by an unexpected knock on the door or by the sight of unknown persons in plain clothes on their door-step may be relieved to learn that these persons are police officers. Others may appreciate the opportunity to make an informed decision about whether to answer the door to the police.

If respondent's test were adopted, it would be extremely difficult for police officers to know how loudly they may announce their presence or how force-fully they may knock on a door without running afoul of the police-created exigency rule. And in most cases, it would be nearly impossible for a court to determine whether that threshold had been passed. The Fourth Amendment does not require the nebulous and impractical test that respondent proposes.

D

For these reasons, we conclude that the exigent circumstances rule applies when the police do not gain entry to premises by means of an actual or threa-tened violation of the Fourth Amendment. This holding provides ample pro-tection for the privacy rights that the Amendment protects.

When law enforcement officers who are not armed with a warrant knock on a door, they do no more than any private citizen might do. And whether the person who knocks on the door and requests the opportunity to speak is a police officer or a private citizen, the occupant has no obligation to open the door or to speak. When the police knock on a door but the occupants choose not to respond or to speak, "the investigation will have reached a conspicuously low point," and the occupants "will have the kind of warning that even the most elaborate security system cannot provide." And even if an occupant chooses to open the door and speak with the officers, the occupant need not allow the officers to enter the premises and may refuse to answer any questions at any time.

Occupants who choose not to stand on their constitutional rights but instead elect to attempt to destroy evidence have only themselves to blame for the warrantless exigent-circumstances search that may ensue.

IV

■ ■ ■

We need not decide whether exigent circumstances existed in this case. Any warrantless entry based on exigent circumstances must, of course, be supported by a genuine exigency. The trial court and the Kentucky Court of Appeals found that there was a real exigency in this case, but the Kentucky Supreme Court expressed doubt on this issue, observing that there was "certainly some question as to whether the sound of persons moving [inside the apartment] was sufficient to establish that evidence was being destroyed." The Kentucky Supreme Court "assume[d] for the purpose of argument that exigent circumstances existed," and it held that the police had impermissibly manufactured the exigency.

We, too, assume for purposes of argument that an exigency existed. We decide only the question on which the Kentucky Supreme Court ruled and on which we granted certiorari: Under what circumstances do police impermissibly create an exigency? Any question about whether an exigency actually existed is better addressed by the Kentucky Supreme Court on remand.

■ ■ ■

Like the court below, we assume for purposes of argument that an exigency existed. Because the officers in this case did not violate or threaten to violate the Fourth Amendment prior to the exigency, we hold that the exigency justified the warrantless search of the apartment.

The judgment of the Kentucky Supreme Court is reversed, and the case is remanded for further proceedings not inconsistent with this opinion.

It is so ordered.

Justice GINSBURG, dissenting.

The Court today arms the police with a way routinely to dishonor the Fourth Amendment's warrant requirement in drug cases. In lieu of presenting their evidence to a neutral magistrate, police officers may now knock, listen, then break the door down, nevermind that they had ample time to obtain a warrant. I dissent from the Court's reduction of the Fourth Amendment's force.

■ ■ ■

This case involves a principal exception to the warrant requirement, the exception applicable in "exigent circumstances." "[C]arefully delineated," the exception should govern only in genuine emergency situations. Circumstances qualify as "exigent" when there is an imminent risk of death or serious injury, or danger that evidence will be immediately destroyed, or that a suspect will escape. *Brigham City v. Stuart*. The question presented: May police, who could pause to gain the approval of a neutral magistrate, dispense with the need to get a warrant by themselves creating exigent circumstances? I would answer no, as did the Kentucky Supreme Court. The urgency must exist, I would rule, when the police come on the scene, not subsequent to their arrival, prompted by their own conduct.

I

Two pillars of our Fourth Amendment jurisprudence should have controlled the Court's ruling: First, "whenever practical, the police must obtain advance judicial approval of searches and seizures through the warrant procedure," *Terry v. Ohio* (1968); second, unwarranted "searches and seizures inside a home" bear heightened scrutiny, *Payton v. New York* (1980). The warrant requirement, Justice Jackson observed, ranks among the "fundamental distinctions between our form of government, where officers are under the law, and the police-state where they are the law." *Johnson v. United States* (1948). The Court has accordingly declared warrantless searches, in the main, "*per se* unreasonable." *Mincey v. Arizona* (1978). "[T]he police bear a heavy burden," the Court has cautioned, "when attempting to demonstrate an urgent need that might justify warrantless searches." *Welsh v. Wisconsin* (1984).

That heavy burden has not been carried here. There was little risk that drug-related evidence would have been destroyed had the police delayed the search pending a magistrate's authorization. As the Court recognizes, "[p]ersons in possession of valuable drugs are unlikely to destroy them unless they fear discovery by the police." Nothing in the record shows that, prior to the knock at the apartment door, the occupants were apprehensive about police proximity.

In no quarter does the Fourth Amendment apply with greater force than in our homes, our most private space which, for centuries, has been regarded as "entitled to special protection." *Georgia v. Randolph* (2006). Home intrusions, the Court has said, are indeed "the chief evil against which...the Fourth Amendment is directed." *Payton*. How "secure" do our homes remain if police, armed with no warrant, can pound on doors at will and, on hearing sounds indicative of things moving, forcibly enter and search for evidence of unlawful activity?

II

As above noted, to justify the police activity in this case, Kentucky invoked the once-guarded exception for emergencies "in which the delay necessary to obtain a warrant...threatens 'the destruction of evidence.'" To fit within this exception, "police action literally must be [taken] 'now or never' to preserve the evidence of the crime." *Roaden v. Kentucky* (1973).

The existence of a genuine emergency depends not only on the state of necessity at the time of the warrantless search; it depends, first and foremost, on "actions taken by the police *preceding* the warrantless search." "[W]asting a clear opportunity to obtain a warrant," therefore, "disentitles the officer from relying on subsequent exigent circumstances." S. Saltzburg & D. Capra, American Criminal Procedure 376 (8th ed. 2007).

Under an appropriately reined-in "emergency" or "exigent circumstances" exception, the result in this case should not be in doubt. The target of the investigation's entry into the building, and the smell of marijuana seeping under the apartment door into the hallway, the Kentucky Supreme Court rightly determined, gave the police "probable cause . . . sufficient . . . to obtain a warrant to search the . . . apartment." As that court observed, nothing made it impracticable for the police to post officers on the premises while proceeding to obtain a warrant authorizing their entry. Before this Court, Kentucky does not urge otherwise.

■ ■ ■

. . . When possible, "a warrant must generally be secured," the Court acknowledges. There is every reason to conclude that securing a warrant was entirely feasible in this case, and no reason to contract the Fourth Amendment's dominion.

CHAPTER 5

Interrogation

Introduction

The U.S. Supreme Court has analyzed questionable police interrogation in three ways: (1) by focusing on the voluntariness of both the interrogation and any confession obtained, using the due process clause of the Fifth and Fourteenth Amendments; (2) by applying the *Miranda* warning requirement, arising from the Court's interpretation of the Fifth Amendment self-incrimination clause; and (3) by determining whether the Sixth Amendment right to counsel has been preserved.

Section A deals with the "voluntariness" standard, the original way of analyzing police interrogation and resulting confessions by determining whether a suspect's will has been overborne. The federal system uses the Fifth Amendment self-incrimination clause in making this determination, while the state system uses Fourteenth Amendment due process. In this analysis, the Court originally focused on the reliability of the confession. For example, in *Brown*, the police conduct was so egregious that it was likely the confession was unreliable. In *Rogers*, the Court focuses on abuse by the police rather than reliability of the confession. *Connelly* suggests that there needs to be some sort of police coercion to establish a lack of voluntariness. *Fulminante*, the most recent case involving voluntariness, finds a confession to be involuntary due to a threat of violence. As a result of the threat posed by 9/11, torture similar to that witnessed in *Brown* has reemerged. Included in this section is a portion of a decision by Justice Barak of the Israeli Supreme Court to illustrate how Israel deals with issues of terrorism.

Section B illustrates the Court's departure from the voluntariness test due to its subjectivity. *Massiah* and *Escobedo* represent approaches taken by the Warren Court to deal with this subjectivity. This effort culminated in the *Miranda* decision. *Malloy* incorporates the Fifth Amendment requirement to the states.

Section C explores *Miranda* and how the decision has been interpreted or, some might say, cut back by later Supreme Court decisions. In looking at the different approaches taken by the Court, it is useful to take the specific language of the *Miranda* decision and see how later Courts have interpreted that language.

Miranda requires warnings when there is a custodial interrogation. The recent *Powell* case illustrates how the Court applies the *Miranda* warnings requirement. *Berkemer, Bruder,* and *Yarborough,* and *J.D.B. v. North Carolina* address the custody component. *Innis, Mauro, Perkins,* and *Muniz* elaborate on the interrogation component. *Howes* deals with custody within a prison setting. *Miranda* discusses the state's heavy burden to demonstrate an explicit waiver of the *Miranda* protections. The heavy burden was defined as preponderance of the evidence in *Connelly,* and the explicit waiver is explored in *Butler, Spring,* and *Barrett. Mosley* and *Edwards* further explore the waiver issue with regard to the right to silence and to an attorney, respectively. *Bradshaw* and *Davis* expand the *Edwards* decision. *Davis* requires an unambiguous invocation of counsel. *Shatzer* refused to extend the *Edwards* presumption of coercion where there had been a sufficient break in custody. *Berghuis* further extends a suspect's invocation of the right to remain silent. The *Berghuis* case, a 5-4 decision, provides a good indication of how the Court aligns on *Miranda* issues.

The thrust of the exclusionary rule for a *Miranda* violation is the topic of discussion in *Elstad,* which analyzes confessions derived from an initial violation, under the so-called fruits doctrine. *Quarles* creates the public safety exception to *Miranda* warnings. Finally, the modern approach to *Miranda* is explored by the cases in subsection 7. *Dickerson* discusses the constitutionality of *Miranda. Chavez* attempts to reconcile *Dickerson* with many of the cases after *Miranda. Seibert* observes the ramifications of some of the cutbacks to *Miranda. Patane* further limits the fruits analysis beyond *Elstad* when the evidence derived from a violation is real evidence.

Section D begins with *Massiah,* which held the government may not deliberately elicit a statement once the right to a lawyer has attached. This Sixth Amendment mechanism to analyze interrogation originated in *Massiah. Brewer,* sometimes referred to as the "Christian Burial Case" (previously discussed in Chapter 1.F), demonstrates how this approach is used for direct police action as opposed to use of an informant (*Massiah*). *Moulton* discusses the offense-specific requirement of this right, and *Cobb* defines what an offense entails. *Henry* and *Kuhlmann* deal with what constitutes deliberate elicitation of the right to counsel in a jail or prison setting. Waiver of the Sixth Amendment right to counsel is explored in *Jackson, Patterson,* and the recent *Montejo* case. Finally, the applicability of the Sixth Amendment exclusionary rule is explored in *Fellers* and *Ventris.*

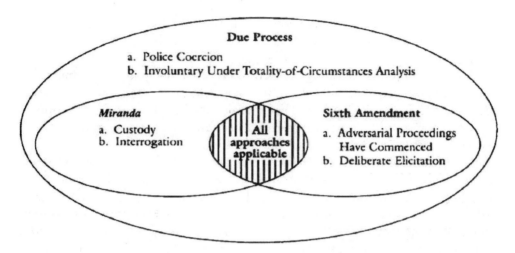

This image is taken from Robert M. Bloom and Mark S. Brodin, *The Constitution and the Police* (6th ed., Aspen Publishers).

A. VOLUNTARINESS

1. Historical

Brown v. State of Mississippi

297 U.S. 278 (1936)

HUGHES, C.J., delivered the opinion of the unanimous Court.

The question in this case is whether convictions, which rest solely upon confessions shown to have been extorted by officers of the state by brutality and violence, are consistent with the due process of law required by the Fourteenth Amendment of the Constitution of the United States.

Petitioners were indicted for the murder of one Raymond Stewart, whose death occurred on March 30, 1934. They were indicted on April 4, 1934, and were then arraigned and pleaded not guilty. Counsel were appointed by the court to defend them. Trial was begun the next morning and was concluded on the following day, when they were found guilty and sentenced to death.

Aside from the confessions, there was no evidence sufficient to warrant the submission of the case to the jury. After a preliminary inquiry, testimony as to the confessions was received over the objection of defendants' counsel. Defendants then testified that the confessions were false and had been procured by physical torture. The case went to the jury with instructions, upon the request of defendants' counsel, that, if the jury had reasonable doubt as to the confessions' having resulted from coercion, and that they were not true, they were not to be considered as evidence. On their appeal to the Supreme Court of the

State, defendants assigned as error the inadmissibility of the confessions. The judgment was affirmed.

Defendants then moved in the Supreme Court of the State to arrest the judgment and for a new trial on the ground that all the evidence against them was obtained by coercion and brutality known to the court and to the district attorney, and that defendants had been denied the benefit of counsel or opportunity to confer with counsel in a reasonable manner. The motion was supported by affidavits. At about the same time, defendants filed in the Supreme Court a "suggestion of error" explicitly challenging the proceedings of the trial, in the use of the confessions and with respect to the alleged denial of representation by counsel, as violating the due process clause of the Fourteenth Amendment of the Constitution of the United States. The state court entertained the suggestion of error, considered the federal question, and decided it against defendants' contentions. . . . We granted a writ of certiorari.

The grounds of the decision were (1) that immunity from self-incrimination is not essential to due process of law; and (2) that the failure of the trial court to exclude the confessions after the introduction of evidence showing their incompetency, in the absence of a request for such exclusion, did not deprive the defendants of life or liberty without due process of law; and that even if the trial court had erroneously overruled a motion to exclude the confessions, the ruling would have been mere error reversible on appeal, but not a violation of constitutional right.

The opinion of the state court did not set forth the evidence as to the circumstances in which the confessions were procured. That the evidence established that they were procured by coercion was not questioned. The state court said: "After the state closed its case on the merits, the appellants, for the first time, introduced evidence from which it appears that the confessions were not made voluntarily but were coerced." There is no dispute as to the facts upon this point, and as they are clearly and adequately stated in the dissenting opinion of Judge Griffith (with whom Judge Anderson concurred), showing both the extreme brutality of the measures to extort the confessions and the participation of the state authorities, we quote this part of his opinion in full, as follows:

> "The crime with which these defendants, all ignorant negroes, are charged, was discovered about 1 o'clock p.m. on Friday, March 30, 1934. On that night one Dial, a deputy sheriff, accompanied by others, came to the home of Ellington, one of the defendants, and requested him to accompany them to the house of the deceased, and there a number of white men were gathered, who began to accuse the defendant of the crime. Upon his denial they seized him, and with the participation of the deputy they hanged him by a rope to the limb of a tree, and, having let him down, they hung him again, and when he was let down the second time, and he still protested his innocence, he was tied to a tree and whipped, and, still declining to accede to the demands that he confess, he was finally released, and he returned with some difficulty to his home, suffering intense pain and agony. The record of the testimony shows

that the signs of the rope on his neck were plainly visible during the so-called trial. A day or two thereafter the said deputy, accompanied by another, returned to the home of the said defendant and arrested him, and departed with the prisoner towards the jail in an adjoining county, but went by a route which led into the state of Alabama; and while on the way, in that state, the deputy stopped and again severely whipped the defendant, declaring that he would continue the whipping until he confessed, and the defendant then agreed to confess to such a statement as the deputy would dictate, and he did so, after which he was delivered to jail.

The other two defendants, Ed Brown and Henry Shields, were also arrested and taken to the same jail. On Sunday night, April 1, 1934, the same deputy, accompanied by a number of white men, one of whom was also an officer, and by the jailer, came to the jail, and the two last named defendants were made to strip and they were laid over chairs and their backs were cut to pieces with a leather strap with buckles on it, and they were likewise made by the said deputy definitely to understand that the whipping would be continued unless and until they confessed, and not only confessed, but confessed in every matter of detail as demanded by those present; and in this manner the defendants confessed the crime, and, as the whippings progressed and were repeated, they changed or adjusted their confession in all particulars of detail so as to conform to the demands of their torturers. When the confessions had been obtained in the exact form and contents as desired by the mob, they left with the parting admonition and warning that, if the defendants changed their story at any time in any respect from that last stated, the perpetrators of the outrage would administer the same or equally effective treatment.

Further details of the brutal treatment to which these helpless prisoners were subjected need not be pursued. It is sufficient to say that in pertinent respects the transcript reads more like pages torn from some medieval account than a record made within the confines of a modern civilization which aspires to an enlightened constitutional government.

All this having been accomplished, on the next day, that is, on Monday, April 2, when the defendants had been given time to recuperate somewhat from the tortures to which they had been subjected, the two sheriffs, one of the county where the crime was committed, and the other of the county of the jail in which the prisoners were confined, came to the jail, accompanied by eight other persons, some of them deputies, there to hear the free and voluntary confession of these miserable and abject defendants. The sheriff of the county of the crime admitted that he had heard of the whipping, but averred that he had no personal knowledge of it. He admitted that one of the defendants, when brought before him to confess, was limping and did not sit down, and that this particular defendant then and there stated that he had been strapped so severely that he could not sit down, and, as already stated, the signs of the rope on the neck of another of the defendants were plainly visible to all. Nevertheless the solemn farce of hearing the free and voluntary confessions was gone through with, and these two sheriffs and one other person then present were the three witnesses used in court to establish the so-called confessions, which were received by the court and admitted in evidence over the objections of the defendants duly entered of record as each of the said three witnesses delivered their alleged testimony. There was thus enough before the court when these confessions were first offered to make known to the court that they were not, beyond all reasonable doubt, free and voluntary; and the failure of the court then to exclude the confessions is sufficient to reverse the judgment, under every rule of procedure that has heretofore been prescribed, and hence it was not necessary subsequently to renew the objections by motion or otherwise.

The spurious confessions having been obtained—and the farce last mentioned having been gone through with on Monday, April 2d—the court, then in session, on the following day, Tuesday, April 3, 1934, ordered the grand jury to reassemble on the succeeding day, April 4, 1934, at 9 o'clock, and on the morning of the day last mentioned the grand jury returned an indictment against the defendants for murder. Late that afternoon the defendants were brought from the jail in the adjoining county and arraigned, when one or more of them offered to plead guilty, which the court declined to accept, and, upon inquiry whether they had or desired counsel, they stated that they had none, and did not suppose that counsel could be of any assistance to them. The court thereupon appointed counsel, and set the case for trial for the following morning at 9 o'clock, and the defendants were returned to the jail in the adjoining county about thirty miles away.

The defendants were brought to the courthouse of the county on the following morning, April 5th, and the so-called trial was opened, and was concluded on the next day, April 6, 1934, and resulted in a pretended conviction with death sentences. The evidence upon which the conviction was obtained was the so-called confessions. Without this evidence, a peremptory instruction to find for the defendants would have been inescapable. The defendants were put on the stand, and by their testimony the facts and the details thereof as to the manner by which the confessions were extorted from them were fully developed, and it is further disclosed by the record that the same deputy Dial under whose guiding hand and active participation the tortures to coerce the confessions were administered, was actively in the performance of the supposed duties of a court deputy in the courthouse and in the presence of the prisoners during what is denominated, in complimentary terms, the trial of these defendants. This deputy was put on the stand by the state in rebuttal, and admitted the whippings. It is interesting to note that in his testimony with reference to the whipping of the defendant Ellington, and in response to the inquiry as to how severely he was whipped, the deputy stated, 'Not too much for a negro; not as much as I would have done if it were left to me.' Two others who had participated in these whippings were introduced and admitted it—not a single witness was introduced who denied it. The facts are not only undisputed, they are admitted, and admitted to have been done by officers of the state, in conjunction with other participants, and all this was definitely well known to everybody connected with the trial, and during the trial, including the state's prosecuting attorney and the trial judge presiding."

■ ■ ■

The state is free to regulate the procedure of its courts in accordance with its own conceptions of policy, unless in so doing it "offends some principle of justice so rooted in the traditions and conscience of our people as to be ranked as fundamental." *Snyder v. Massachusetts* (1934). But the freedom of the state in establishing its policy is the freedom of constitutional government and is limited by the requirement of due process of law. Because a state may dispense with a jury trial, it does not follow that it may substitute trial by ordeal. The rack and torture chamber may not be substituted for the witness stand. The state may not permit an accused to be hurried to conviction under mob domination—where the whole proceeding is but a mask—without supplying corrective process. The state may not deny to the accused the aid of counsel. *Powell v. Alabama* (1932). Nor may a state, through the action of its officers, contrive a conviction through the pretense of a trial which in truth is "but used as a means of depriving a defendant of liberty through a deliberate deception of court and jury by the presentation of testimony known to be perjured." *Mooney v. Holohan* [(1935)]. And the trial equally is a mere pretense where the state authorities have contrived a conviction resting solely upon confessions obtained by violence. The due process clause requires "that state action, whether through one agency or another, shall be consistent with the fundamental principles of liberty and justice which lie at the base of all our civil and political institutions." It would be difficult to conceive of methods more revolting to the sense of justice than those taken to procure the confessions of these petitioners, and the use of the confessions thus obtained as the basis for conviction and sentence was a clear denial of due process.

■ ■ ■

It is in this view that the further contention of the State must be considered.

■ ■ ■

The court thus denied a federal right fully established and specially set up and claimed, and the judgment must be reversed.

It is so ordered.

Rogers v. Richmond

365 U.S. 534 (1961)

FRANKFURTER, J., delivered the opinion of the Court, in which WARREN, C.J, BLACK, BRENNAN, DOUGLAS, WHITAKER, and HARLAN, JJ., joined. STEWART, J., wrote a dissenting opinion, in which CLARK, J., joined.

This case has a long history. It must be told with some particularity in order to unravel issues ensnarled in protracted litigation in both state and federal courts, turning essentially on the admissibility of confessions.

The Trial.—Petitioner was found guilty of murder by a jury in the Superior Court, New Haven County, Connecticut. The undisputed evidence leading to the conviction may be briefly told. On January 9, 1954, New Haven,

Connecticut, police arrested petitioner on charges of committing attempted robbery and other crimes on that day at a local hotel. At the time of his arrest petitioner had in his possession a revolver. Subsequent ballistic tests tended to show that this weapon, which had been reported stolen from the home of petitioner's nephew, was used in a fatal shooting during a liquor store robbery in West Haven, Connecticut, on November 21, 1953, the same day its disappearance was discovered.

Petitioner was lodged in the New Haven County Jail pending trial on the charges that prompted his arrest. On January 30, 1954, he was transported without court order from the jail to the office of the State's Attorney for questioning in connection with the West Haven killing. The interrogation commenced at approximately 2 p.m. of that day and continued throughout the afternoon and evening. During the interrogation petitioner was allowed to smoke, was brought a sandwich and coffee, and was at no time subjected to violence or threat of violence.

After petitioner had been intermittently questioned without success by a team of at least three police officers from 2 p.m. to 8 p.m., New Haven Assistant Chief of Police Eagan was called in to conduct the investigation. When petitioner persisted in his denial that he had done the shooting, Chief Eagan pretended, in petitioner's hearing, to place a telephone call to police officers, directing them to stand in readiness to bring in petitioner's wife for questioning. After the passage of approximately one hour, during which petitioner remained silent, Chief Eagan indicated that he was about to have petitioner's wife taken into custody. At this point petitioner announced his willingness to confess and did confess in a statement which was taken down in shorthand by an official court reporter.

The following morning the Coroner of New Haven County issued an order that petitioner be held incommunicado at the jail. When a lawyer associated with counsel whom petitioner had previously retained to defend him on the attempted robbery charge called at the jail to see petitioner, he was turned away on the authority of the Coroner's order. Petitioner was then transported to the County Court House for interrogation by the Coroner, who had been informed of his confession of the previous night. There he was put on oath to tell the truth but warned that he might refuse to say anything further and advised that he might obtain the assistance of counsel. Petitioner again confessed to the shooting in a statement recorded by the same official court reporter.

Petitioner's defense at the trial was directed toward discrediting the confessions as the product of coercion. In accordance with Connecticut practice, the trial judge heard the evidence bearing on admissibility of the confessions without the jury present. At this hearing petitioner testified that shortly after the commencement of the interrogation he asked to see a lawyer but was never permitted to do so. He also testified, with reference to Chief Eagen's pretense of bringing petitioner's wife in for questioning, that this move took the form of a threat to do so unless he confessed and that in making this threat Chief Eagan told him that he would be "less than a man" if he failed to confess and thereby caused her to be taken into custody. According to petitioner his wife suffered from arthritis, and he confessed to spare her being transported to the scene of the interrogation.

The State met petitioner's account with the testimony of Chief Eagan. He testified that petitioner made no request to see a lawyer during his presence in the room. However, it will be recalled that Chief Eagan did not arrive until the questioning had run a course of six hours and that petitioner claimed to have requested counsel during that period. Chief Eagan also denied that he had framed his remarks about bringing petitioner's wife in for questioning as a threat or that he had suggested that petitioner would be "less than a man," etc.

On the basis of the evidence summarized, the trial judge concluded that the confessions were voluntary and allowed them to go to the jury for consideration of the weight to be given them under all the circumstances that led to them. Conviction of petitioner for murder followed. . . .

Our decisions under [the Fourteenth] Amendment have made clear that convictions following the admission into evidence of confessions which are involuntary, *i.e.*, the product of coercion, either physical or psychological, cannot stand. This is so not because such confessions are unlikely to be true but because the methods used to extract them offend an underlying principle in the enforcement of our criminal law: that ours is an accusatorial and not an inquisitorial system—a system in which the State must establish guilt by evidence independently and freely secured and may not by coercion prove its charge against an accused out of his own mouth. To be sure, confessions cruelly extorted may be and have been, to an unascertained extent, found to be untrustworthy. But the constitutional principle of excluding confessions that are not voluntary does not rest on this consideration. Indeed, in many of the cases in which the command of the Due Process Clause has compelled us to reverse state convictions involving the use of confessions obtained by impermissible methods, independent corroborating evidence left little doubt of the truth of what the defendant had confessed. Despite such verification, confessions were found to be the product of constitutionally impermissible methods in their inducement. Since a defendant had been subjected to pressures to which, under our accusatorial system, an accused should not be subjected, we were constrained to find that the procedures leading to his conviction had failed to afford him that due process of law which the Fourteenth Amendment guarantees.

In the present case, while the trial judge ruled that each of petitioner's confessions was "freely and voluntarily made and accordingly was admissible in evidence," he reached that conclusion on the basis of considerations that undermine its validity. He found that the pretense of bringing petitioner's wife in for questioning "had no tendency to produce a confession that was not in accord with the truth." Again, in his charge to the jury, he thus enunciated the reasoning which had guided him in admitting the confessions for its consideration:

"No confession or admission of an accused is admissible in evidence unless made freely and voluntarily and not under the influence of promises or threats. The fact that a confession was procured by the employment of some artifice or deception does not exclude the confession if it was not calculated, that is to say, if the artifice or deception was not calculated to procure an untrue statement. The motive of a person in confessing is of no importance provided the particular confession does not result from threats, fear or promises made by persons in actual or seeming authority. The object of evidence is to get at the truth, and a trick or device which has no tendency to produce a confession except one in accordance with the truth does not render the confession inadmissible. The rules which surround the use of a confession are designed and put into operation because of the desire expressed in the law that the confession, if used, be probably a true confession."

The same view—that the probable reliability of a confession is a circumstance of weight in determining its voluntariness—entered the opinion of the Supreme Court of Errors of Connecticut in sustaining the trial judge's admission of the confession:

"If we concede that this [petitioner's claims of illegal removal from jail and incommunicado detention] was all true and that such conduct was unlawful, it does not, standing alone, render the defendant's confessions inadmissible. The question is whether, under these and other circumstances of the case, that conduct induced the defendant to confess falsely that he had committed the crime being investigated. Unless it did, it cannot be said that its illegality vitiated his confessions."

And again:

"Proper court authorization should have been secured before the defendant was removed from the jail. There is nothing about his illegal removal, however, to demonstrate that he was thereby forced to make an untrue statement. The same can be said concerning the refusal to admit counsel to see the defendant on the morning of January 31 before he was brought before the coroner."

Concerning the feigned phone call that petitioner's wife be brought in to headquarters, the Supreme Court concluded:

"Here again, the question for the court to decide was whether this conduct induced the defendant to make an involuntary and hence untrue statement."

From a fair reading of these expressions, we cannot but conclude that the question whether Rogers' confessions were admissible into evidence was answered by reference to a legal standard which took into account the circumstance of probable truth or falsity. And this is not a permissible standard under the Due Process Clause of the Fourteenth Amendment. The attention of the trial judge should have been focused, for purposes of the Federal Constitution, on the question whether the behavior of the State's law enforcement officials was such as to overbear petitioner's will to resist and bring about confessions not freely self-determined—a question to be answered with complete disregard of whether or not petitioner in fact spoke the truth. The employment instead, by the trial judge and the Supreme Court of Errors, of a standard infected by the inclusion of references to probable reliability resulted in a constitutionally invalid conviction, pursuant to which Rogers is now detained "in violation of the Constitution." A defendant has the right to be tried according to the substantive and procedural due process requirements of the Fourteenth Amendment. This means that a vital confession, such as is involved in this case, may go to the jury only if it is subjected to screening in accordance with correct constitutional standards. To the extent that in the trial of Rogers evidence was allowed to go to the jury on the basis of standards that departed from constitutional requirements, to that extent he was unconstitutionally tried and the conviction was vitiated by error of constitutional dimension.

It is not for this Court, any more than for a Federal District Court, in habeas corpus proceedings, to make an independent appraisal of the legal significance of facts gleaned from the record after such a conviction. We are barred from speculating—it would be an irrational process—about the weight attributed to the impermissible consideration of truth and falsity which, entering into the Connecticut trial court's deliberations concerning the admissibility of the confessions, may well have distorted, by putting in improper perspective, even its findings of historical fact. Any consideration of this "reliability" element was constitutionally precluded, precisely because the force which it carried with the trial judge cannot be known.

As a matter of abstract logic it is arguable that Rogers may not have been deprived of a constitutional right, nor held in custody in violation of the Constitution . . . solely because the Connecticut trial court applied an impermissible constitutional standard in admitting his confession—that Rogers was not so deprived, or so held, unless "in fact" his confession was coerced, a "fact" to be ascertained from the state record on direct review here, or de novo by a federal district judge in habeas corpus proceedings. Such a view ignores both the volatile and amorphous character of "fact" as fact is found by courts, and the distributive functions of the dual judicial system in our federalism for the finding of fact and the application of law to fact. In coerced confession cases coming directly to this Court from the highest court of a State in which review may be had, we look for "fact" to the undisputed, the uncontested evidence of record.

■ ■ ■

Reversed.

Justice STEWART, whom Justice CLARK joins, dissenting.

Although the matter is not free from doubt, I accept the Court's conclusion that both state courts gave some weight to the probable truth of the confessions in determining that they were voluntary. But I cannot accept the proposition that the petitioner is entitled to his release by way of federal habeas corpus merely because of the state courts' failure properly to verbalize the correct Fourteenth Amendment test of admissibility.

■ ■ ■

I would, therefore, remand the case to the District Court for a plenary hearing to determine this question. Where, as here, the state trial court's determination of admissibility was at least partly affected by the impermissible factor of probable reliability, I think there can be no question of the federal court's duty to hold such a hearing. While the state court's failure to enunciate the correct standard was not itself an error of constitutional dimensions, it did make impossible the federal court's unquestioning reliance on the trial court's findings of fact.

■ ■ ■

2. Modern

Colorado v. Connelly

479 U.S. 157 (1986)

REHNQUIST, C.J., delivered the opinion of the Court, in which WHITE, POWELL, O'CONNOR, and SCALIA, JJ., joined, and in all but Part III-A of which BLACKMUN, J., joined. BLACKMUN, J., filed an opinion concurring in part and concurring in the judgment. STEVENS, J., filed an opinion concurring in part and dissenting in part. BRENNAN, J., filed a dissenting opinion, in which MARSHALL, J., joined.

In this case, the Supreme Court of Colorado held that the United States Constitution requires a court to suppress a confession when the mental state of the defendant, at the time he made the confession, interfered with his "rational intellect" and his "free will." Because this decision seemed to conflict with prior holdings of this Court, we granted certiorari. We conclude that the admissibility of this kind of statement is governed by state rules of evidence, rather than by our previous decisions regarding coerced confessions and *Miranda* waivers. We therefore reverse.

On August 18, 1983, Officer Patrick Anderson of the Denver Police Department was in uniform, working in an off-duty capacity in downtown Denver. Respondent Francis Connelly approached Officer Anderson and, without any prompting, stated that he had murdered someone and wanted to talk about it. Anderson immediately advised respondent that he had the right to remain silent, that anything he said could be used against him in court, and that he had the right to an attorney prior to any police questioning. See *Miranda v. Arizona* (1966). Respondent stated that he understood these rights but he still wanted to talk about the murder. Understandably bewildered by this confession, Officer Anderson asked respondent several questions. Connelly denied that he had been drinking, denied that he had been taking any drugs, and stated that, in the past, he had been a patient in several mental hospitals. Officer Anderson again told Connelly that he was under no obligation to say anything. Connelly replied that it was "all right," and that he would talk to Officer Anderson because his conscience had been bothering him. To Officer Anderson, respondent appeared to understand fully the nature of his acts.

Shortly thereafter, Homicide Detective Stephen Antuna arrived. Respondent was again advised of his rights, and Detective Antuna asked him "what he had on his mind." Respondent answered that he had come all the way from Boston to confess to the murder of Mary Ann Junta, a young girl whom he had killed in Denver sometime during November 1982. Respondent was taken to police headquarters, and a search of police records revealed that the body of an unidentified female had been found in April 1983. Respondent openly detailed his story to Detective Antuna and Sergeant Thomas Haney, and readily agreed to take the officers to the scene of the killing. Under Connelly's sole direction, the two officers and respondent proceeded in a police vehicle to the location of the crime. Respondent pointed out the exact location of the murder. Throughout this episode, Detective Antuna perceived no indication whatsoever that respondent was suffering from any kind of mental illness.

Respondent was held overnight. During an interview with the public defender's office the following morning, he became visibly disoriented. He began giving confused answers to questions, and for the first time, stated that "voices" had told him to come to Denver and that he had followed the directions of these voices in confessing. Respondent was sent to a state hospital for evaluation. He was initially found incompetent to assist in his own defense. By March 1984, however, the doctors evaluating respondent determined that he was competent to proceed to trial.

At a preliminary hearing, respondent moved to suppress all of his statements. Dr. Jeffrey Metzner, a psychiatrist employed by the state hospital, testified that respondent was suffering from chronic schizophrenia and was in a psychotic state at least as of August 17, 1983, the day before he confessed. Metzner's interviews with respondent revealed that respondent was following the "voice of God." This voice instructed respondent to withdraw money from the bank, to buy an airplane ticket, and to fly from Boston to Denver. When respondent arrived from Boston, God's voice became stronger and told respondent either to confess to the killing or to commit suicide. Reluctantly following the command of the voices, respondent approached Officer Anderson and confessed.

Dr. Metzner testified that, in his expert opinion, respondent was experiencing "command hallucinations." This condition interfered with respondent's "volitional abilities; that is, his ability to make free and rational choices." Dr. Metzner further testified that Connelly's illness did not significantly impair his cognitive abilities. Thus, respondent understood the rights he had when Officer Anderson and Detective Antuna advised him that he need not speak. Dr. Metzner admitted that the "voices" could in reality be Connelly's interpretation of his own guilt, but explained that in his opinion, Connelly's psychosis motivated his confession.

On the basis of this evidence the Colorado trial court decided that respondent's statements must be suppressed because they were "involuntary."

■ ■ ■

The Colorado Supreme Court affirmed. In that court's view, the proper test for admissibility is whether the statements are "the product of a rational intellect and a free will." Indeed, "the absence of police coercion or duress does not foreclose a finding of involuntariness. One's capacity for rational judgment and free choice may be overborne as much by certain forms of severe mental illness as by external pressure." The court found that the very admission of the evidence in a court of law was sufficient state action to implicate the Due Process Clause of the Fourteenth Amendment to the United States Constitution. The evidence fully supported the conclusion that respondent's initial statement was not the product of a rational intellect and a free will. The court then considered respondent's attempted waiver of his constitutional rights and found that respondent's mental condition precluded his ability to make a valid waiver. The Colorado Supreme Court thus affirmed the trial court's decision to suppress all of Connelly's statements.

The Due Process Clause of the Fourteenth Amendment provides that no State shall "deprive any person of life, liberty, or property, without due process of law." Just last term, in *Miller v. Fenton* (1985), we held that by virtue of the Due Process Clause "certain interrogation techniques, either in isolation or as applied to the unique characteristics of a particular suspect, are so offensive to a civilized system of justice that they must be condemned."

Indeed, coercive government misconduct was the catalyst for this Court's seminal confession case, *Brown v. Mississippi* (1936). In that case, police officers extracted confessions from the accused through brutal torture. The Court had little difficulty concluding that even though the Fifth Amendment did not at that time apply to the States, the actions of the police were "revolting to the sense of justice."

■ ■ ■

Thus the cases considered by this Court over the 50 years since *Brown v. Mississippi* have focused upon the crucial element of police overreaching. While each confession case has turned on its own set of factors justifying the conclusion that police conduct was oppressive, all have contained a substantial element of coercive police conduct. Absent police conduct causally related to the confession, there is simply no basis for concluding that any state actor has deprived a criminal defendant of due process of law. Respondent correctly notes that as interrogators have turned to more subtle forms of psychological persuasion, courts have found the mental condition of the defendant a more significant factor in the "voluntariness" calculus. See *Spano v. New York* (1959). But this fact does not justify a conclusion that a defendant's mental condition, by itself and apart from its relation to official coercion, should ever dispose of the inquiry into constitutional "voluntariness."

Respondent relies on *Blackburn v. Alabama* (1960) and *Townsend v. Sain* (1963) for the proposition that the "deficient mental condition of the defendants in those cases was sufficient to render their confessions involuntary." But respondent's reading of *Blackburn* and *Townsend* ignores the integral element of police overreaching present in both cases. In *Blackburn*, the Court found that the petitioner was probably insane at the time of his confession and the police learned during the interrogation that he had a history of mental problems. The police exploited this weakness with coercive tactics: "the eight- to nine-hour sustained interrogation in a tiny room which was upon occasion literally filled with police officers; the absence of Blackburn's friends, relatives, or legal counsel; [and] the composition of the confession by the Deputy Sheriff rather than by Blackburn." These tactics supported a finding that the confession was involuntary. Indeed, the Court specifically condemned police activity that "wrings a confession out of an accused against his will." *Townsend* presented a similar instance of police wrongdoing. In that case, a police physician had given Townsend a drug with truth-serum properties. The subsequent confession, obtained by officers who knew that Townsend had been given drugs, was held involuntary. These two cases demonstrate that while mental condition is surely relevant to an individual's susceptibility to police coercion, mere examination of the confessant's state of mind can never conclude the due process inquiry.

Our "involuntary confession" jurisprudence is entirely consistent with the settled law requiring some sort of "state action" to support a claim of violation of the Due Process Clause of the Fourteenth Amendment. The Colorado trial court, of course, found that the police committed no wrongful acts, and that finding has been neither challenged by respondent nor disturbed by the Supreme Court of Colorado. The latter court, however, concluded that sufficient state action was present by virtue of the admission of the confession into evidence in a court of the State.

The difficulty with the approach of the Supreme Court of Colorado is that it fails to recognize the essential link between coercive activity of the State, on the one hand, and a resulting confession by a defendant, on the other. The flaw in respondent's constitutional argument is that it would expand our previous line of "voluntariness" cases into a far-ranging requirement that courts must divine a defendant's motivation for speaking or acting as he did even though there be no claim that governmental conduct coerced his decision.

The most outrageous behavior by a private party seeking to secure evidence against a defendant does not make that evidence inadmissible under the Due Process Clause. . . .

We have previously cautioned against expanding "currently applicable exclusionary rules by erecting additional barriers to placing truthful and probative evidence before state juries. . . ." We abide by that counsel now. "[T]he central purpose of a criminal trial is to decide the factual question of the defendant's guilt or innocence," and while we have previously held that exclusion of evidence may be necessary to protect constitutional guarantees, both the necessity for the collateral inquiry and the exclusion of evidence deflect a criminal trial from its basic purpose. Respondent would now have us require sweeping inquiries into the state of mind of a criminal defendant who has confessed, inquiries quite divorced from any coercion brought to bear on the defendant by the State. We think the Constitution rightly leaves this sort of inquiry to be resolved by state laws governing the admission of evidence and erects no standard of its own in this area. A statement rendered by one in the condition of respondent might be proved to be quite unreliable, but this is a matter to be governed by the evidentiary laws of the forum, and not by the Due Process Clause of the Fourteenth Amendment. "The aim of the requirement of due process is not to exclude presumptively false evidence, but to prevent fundamental unfairness in the use of evidence, whether true or false."

We hold that coercive police activity is a necessary predicate to the finding that a confession is not "voluntary" within the meaning of the Due Process Clause of the Fourteenth Amendment. We also conclude that the taking of respondent's statements, and their admission into evidence, constitute no violation of that Clause.

III

A

The Supreme Court of Colorado went on to affirm the trial court's ruling that respondent's later statements made while in custody should be suppressed because respondent had not waived his right to consult an attorney and his right to remain silent. That court held that the State must bear its burden of proving waiver of these *Miranda* rights by "clear and convincing evidence." Although we have stated in passing that the State bears a "heavy" burden in proving waiver, *Tague v. Louisiana* (1980) (*per curiam*); *North Carolina v. Butler* (1979); *Miranda v. Arizona*, we have never held that the "clear and convincing evidence" standard is the appropriate one.

■ ■ ■

We now reaffirm our holding: Whenever the State bears the burden of proof in a motion to suppress a statement that the defendant claims was obtained in violation of our *Miranda* doctrine, the State need prove waiver only by a preponderance of the evidence.

■ ■ ■

We also think that the Supreme Court of Colorado was mistaken in its analysis of the question whether respondent had waived his *Miranda* rights in this case. Of course, a waiver must at a minimum be "voluntary" to be effective against an accused. The Supreme Court of Colorado in addressing this question relied on the testimony of the court-appointed psychiatrist to the effect that respondent was not capable of making a "free decision with respect to his constitutional right of silence . . . and his constitutional right to confer with a lawyer before talking to the police."

We think that the Supreme Court of Colorado erred in importing into this area of constitutional law notions of "free will" that have no place there. There is obviously no reason to require more in the way of a "voluntariness" inquiry in the *Miranda* waiver context than in the Fourteenth Amendment confession context. The sole concern of the Fifth Amendment, on which *Miranda* was based, is governmental coercion.

■ ■ ■

The judgment of the Supreme Court of Colorado is accordingly reversed, and the cause is remanded for further proceedings not inconsistent with this opinion.

It is so ordered.

Justice BLACKMUN, concurring in part and concurring in the judgment.

I join Parts I, II, III-B, and IV of the Court's opinion and its judgment.

I refrain, however, from joining Part III-A of the opinion. Whatever may be the merits of the issue discussed there, which concerns the level of the State's burden of proof in showing that respondent had waived his rights under *Miranda v. Arizona*, that issue was neither raised nor briefed by the parties, and, in my view, it is not necessary to the decision.

Justice STEVENS, concurring in the judgment in part and dissenting in part.

Respondent made incriminatory statements both before and after he was handcuffed and taken into custody. The only question presented by the Colorado District Attorney in his certiorari petition concerned the admissibility of respondent's precustodial statements. I agree with the State of Colorado that the United States Constitution does not require suppression of those statements, but in reaching that conclusion, unlike the Court, I am perfectly willing to accept the state trial court's finding that the statements were involuntary.

The state trial court found that, in view of the "overwhelming evidence presented by the Defense," the prosecution did not meet its burden of demonstrating that respondent's initial statements to Officer Anderson were voluntary. Nevertheless, in my opinion, the use of these involuntary precustodial statements does not violate the Fifth Amendment because they were not the product of state compulsion. Although they may well be so unreliable that they could not support a conviction, at this stage of the proceeding I could not say that they have no probative force whatever. The fact that the statements were involuntary—just as the product of Lady Macbeth's nightmare was involuntary—does not mean that their use for whatever evidentiary value they may have is fundamentally unfair or a denial of due process.

The postcustodial statements raise an entirely distinct question. When the officer whom respondent approached elected to handcuff him and to take him into custody, the police assumed a fundamentally different relationship with him. Prior to that moment, the police had no duty to give respondent *Miranda* warnings and had every right to continue their exploratory conversation with him. Once the custodial relationship was established, however, the questioning assumed a presumptively coercive character.

The Court seems to believe that a waiver can be voluntary even if it is not the product of an exercise of the defendant's " 'free will.' " The Court's position is not only incomprehensible to me; it is also foreclosed by the Court's recent pronouncement in *Moran v. Burbine* (1986) that "the relinquishment of the right must have been voluntary in the sense that it was the product of a free and deliberate choice...." Because respondent's waiver was not voluntary in that sense, his custodial interrogation was presumptively coercive. The Colorado Supreme Court was unquestionably correct in concluding that his post-custodial incriminatory statements were inadmissible.

Accordingly, I concur in the judgment insofar as it applies to respondent's precustodial statements but respectfully dissent from the Court's disposition of the question that was not presented by the certiorari petition.

Justice BRENNAN, with whom Justice MARSHALL joins, dissenting.

Today the Court denies Mr. Connelly his fundamental right to make a vital choice with a sane mind, involving a determination that could allow the State to deprive him of liberty or even life. This holding is unprecedented: "Surely in the present stage of our civilization a most basic sense of justice is affronted by the spectacle of incarcerating a human being upon the basis of a statement he made while insane...." Because I believe that the use of a mentally ill person's involuntary confession is antithetical to the notion of fundamental fairness embodied in the Due Process Clause, I dissent.

■ ■ ■

The absence of police wrongdoing should not, by itself, determine the voluntariness of a confession by a mentally ill person. The requirement that a confession be voluntary reflects a recognition of the importance of free will and of reliability in determining the admissibility of a confession, and thus demands an inquiry into the totality of the circumstances surrounding the confession.

Today's decision restricts the application of the term "involuntary" to those confessions obtained by police coercion. Confessions by mentally ill individuals or by persons coerced by parties other than police officers are now considered "voluntary." The Court's failure to recognize all forms of involuntariness or coercion as antithetical to due process reflects a refusal to acknowledge free will as a value of constitutional consequence. But due process derives much of its meaning from a conception of fundamental fairness that emphasizes the right to make vital choices voluntarily: "The Fourteenth Amendment secures against state invasion... the right of a person to remain silent unless he chooses to speak in the unfettered exercise of his own will...." This right requires vigilant protection if we are to safeguard the values of private conscience and human dignity.

■ ■ ■

"The ultimate test remains that which has been the only clearly established test in Anglo-American courts for two hundred years: the test of voluntariness. Is the confession the product of an essentially free and unconstrained choice by its maker?... The line of distinction is that at which governing self-direction is lost *and compulsion, of whatever nature or however infused*, propels or helps to propel the confession."

what B thinks to should h

A true commitment to fundamental fairness requires that the inquiry be "not whether the conduct of state officers in obtaining the confession is shocking, but whether the confession was 'free and voluntary'...."

We have never confined our focus to police coercion, because the value of freedom of will has demanded a broader inquiry. See *Blackburn v. Alabama*. The confession cases decided by this Court over the 50 years since *Brown v. Mississippi* have focused upon both police overreaching and free will. While it is true that police overreaching has been an element of every confession case to date, it is also true that in every case the Court has made clear that ensuring that a confession is a product of free will is an independent concern. The fact that involuntary confessions have always been excluded in part because of police overreaching signifies only that this is a case of first impression. Until today, we have never upheld the admission of a confession that does not reflect the exercise of free will.

The Court cites *Townsend v. Sain* and *Blackburn* in support of its view that police wrongdoing should be the central focus of inquiry. In *Townsend*, we overturned a murder conviction because the defendant's conviction was determined to be involuntary. The defendant suffered from stomach pains induced by heroin withdrawal. The police properly contacted a physician who administered medications alleviating the withdrawal symptoms. The defendant then confessed. Although the physician denied that he purposely administered "truth serum," there was an indication that the medications could have had such a side effect upon a narcotic addict.

The *Townsend* Court examined "many relevant circumstances": "Among these are [the defendant's] lack of counsel at the time, his drug addiction, the fact that he was a 'near mental defective,' and his youth and inexperience." According to today's Court, the police wrongdoing in *Townsend* was that the police physician had allegedly given the defendant a drug with truth-serum properties, and that the confession was obtained by officers who knew that the defendant had been given drugs.

■ ■ ■

Furthermore, in prescient refutation of this Court's "police wrongdoing" theory, the *Townsend* Court analyzed *Blackburn*, the other case relied upon by this Court to "demonstrate" that police wrongdoing was a more important factor than the defendant's state of mind. The Court in *Townsend* stated:

> "[I]n *Blackburn v. Alabama*, we held *irrelevant* the absence of evidence of improper purpose on the part of the questioning officers. There the evidence indicated that the interrogating officers thought the defendant sane when he confessed, but we judged the confession inadmissible because the probability was that the defendant was *in fact* insane at the time."

Thus the *Townsend* Court interpreted *Blackburn* as a case involving a confession by a mentally ill defendant in which the police harbored no improper purpose.

This Court abandons this precedent in favor of the view that only confessions rendered involuntary by some state action are inadmissible, and that the only relevant form of state action is police conduct.

■ ■ ■

Since the Court redefines voluntary confessions to include confessions by mentally ill individuals, the reliability of these confessions becomes a central concern. A concern for reliability is inherent in our criminal justice system, which relies upon accusatorial rather than inquisitorial practices. While an inquisitorial system prefers obtaining confessions from criminal defendants, an accusatorial system must place its faith in determinations of "guilt by evidence independently and freely secured."

■ ■ ■

Our distrust for reliance on confessions is due, in part, to their decisive impact upon the adversarial process. Triers of fact accord confessions such heavy weight in their determinations that "the introduction of a confession makes the other aspects of a trial in court superfluous, and the real trial, for all practical purposes, occurs when the confession is obtained." E. Cleary, McCormick on Evidence 316 (2d ed. 1972)....

■ ■ ■

The instant case starkly highlights the danger of admitting a confession by a person with a severe mental illness. The trial court made no findings concerning the reliability of Mr. Connelly's involuntary confession, since it believed that the confession was excludable on the basis of involuntariness. However, the overwhelming evidence in the record points to the unreliability of Mr. Connelly's delusional mind. Mr. Connelly was found incompetent to stand trial because he was unable to relate accurate information, and the court-appointed psychiatrist indicated that Mr. Connelly was actively hallucinating and exhibited delusional thinking at the time of his confession. The Court, in fact, concedes that "[a] statement rendered by one in the condition of respondent might be proved to be quite unreliable. . . ."

Moreover, the record is barren of any corroboration of the mentally ill defendant's confession. No physical evidence links the defendant to the alleged crime. Police did not identify the alleged victim's body as the woman named by the defendant. Mr. Connelly identified the alleged scene of the crime, but it has not been verified that the unidentified body was found there or that a crime actually occurred there. There is not a shred of competent evidence in this record linking the defendant to the charged homicide. There is only Mr. Connelly's confession.

Minimum standards of due process should require that the trial court find substantial indicia of reliability, on the basis of evidence extrinsic to the confession itself, before admitting the confession of a mentally ill person into evidence. I would require the trial court to make such a finding on remand. To hold otherwise allows the State to imprison and possibly to execute a mentally ill defendant based solely upon an inherently unreliable confession.

■ ■ ■

In holding that the government need only prove the voluntariness of the waiver of *Miranda* rights by a preponderance of the evidence, the Court ignores the explicit command of *Miranda*:

> "If the interrogation continues without the presence of an attorney and a statement is taken, a *heavy* burden rests on the government to demonstrate that the defendant knowingly and intelligently waived his privilege against self-incrimination and his right to retained or appointed counsel. This Court has always set *high* standards of proof for the waiver of constitutional rights, and we re-assert these standards as applied to in-custody interrogation."

In recognition of the importance of the Due Process Clause and the Fifth Amendment, we always have characterized the State's burden of proof on a *Miranda* waiver as "great" and "heavy."

■ ■ ■

The ultimate irony is that, even accepting the preponderance of the evidence as the correct standard, the prosecution still failed to meet this burden of proof. The Colorado Supreme Court found that Dr. Metzner, the court-appointed psychiatrist and the only expert to testify, "clearly established" that Mr. Connelly "was incapable" of making a "free decision" respecting his *Miranda* rights. Thus the prosecution failed—even by the modest standard imposed today—to prove that Mr. Connelly voluntarily waived his *Miranda* rights.

The Court imports its voluntariness analysis, which makes police coercion a requirement for a finding of involuntariness, into its evaluation of the waiver of *Miranda* rights.

■ ■ ■

I turn then to the second requirement, apart from the voluntariness requirement, that the State must satisfy to establish a waiver of *Miranda* rights. Besides being voluntary, the waiver must be knowing and intelligent. See *Moran v. Burbine*. We recently noted that "the waiver must have been made with a full awareness both of the nature of the right being abandoned and the consequences of the decision to abandon it." The two requirements are independent: "Only if the 'totality of the circumstances surrounding the interrogation' reveals *both* an uncoerced choice *and* the requisite level of comprehension may a court properly conclude that the *Miranda* rights have been waived." *Moran*.

Since the Colorado Supreme Court found that Mr. Connelly was "clearly" unable to make an "intelligent" decision, clearly its judgment should be affirmed. The Court reverses the entire judgment, however, without explaining how a "mistaken view of voluntariness" could "taint" this independent justification for suppressing the custodial confession, but leaving the Colorado Supreme Court free on remand to reconsider other issues, not inconsistent with the Court's opinion. Such would include, in my view, whether the requirement of a knowing and intelligent waiver was satisfied. Moreover, on the remand, today's holding does not, of course, preclude a contrary resolution of this case based upon the State's separate interpretation of its own Constitution.

I dissent.

Arizona v. Fulminante

499 U.S. 279 (1991)

WHITE, J., delivered an opinion, Parts I, II, and IV of which are for the Court, and filed a dissenting opinion in Part III. MARSHALL, BLACKMUN, and STEVENS, JJ., joined Parts I, II, III, and IV of that opinion; SCALIA, J., joined Parts I and II; and KENNEDY, J., joined Parts I and IV. REHNQUIST, C.J., delivered an opinion, Part II of which is for the Court, and filed a dissenting opinion in Parts I and III. O'CONNOR, J., joined Parts I, II, and III of that opinion; KENNEDY and SOUTER, JJ., joined Parts I and II; and SCALIA, J., joined Parts II and III. KENNEDY, J., filed an opinion concurring in the judgment.

Note—Pay special attention to the breakdown of Justices; especially Justices Kennedy and Scalia.

■ ■ ■

The Arizona Supreme Court ruled in this case that respondent Oreste Fulminante's confession, received in evidence at his trial for murder, had been coerced and that its use against him was barred by the Fifth and Fourteenth Amendments to the United States Constitution. The court also held that the harmless-error rule could not be used to save the conviction. We affirm the judgment of the Arizona court, although for different reasons than those upon which that court relied.

I

Early in the morning of September 14, 1982, Fulminante called the Mesa, Arizona, Police Department to report that his 11-year-old stepdaughter, Jeneane Michelle Hunt, was missing. He had been caring for Jeneane while his wife, Jeneane's mother, was in the hospital. Two days later, Jeneane's body was found in the desert east of Mesa. She had been shot twice in the head at close range with a large caliber weapon, and a ligature was around her neck. Because of the decomposed condition of the body, it was impossible to tell whether she had been sexually assaulted.

Fulminante's statements to police concerning Jeneane's disappearance and his relationship with her contained a number of inconsistencies, and he became a suspect in her killing. When no charges were filed against him, Fulminante left Arizona for New Jersey. Fulminante was later convicted in New Jersey on federal charges of possession of a firearm by a felon.

Fulminante was incarcerated in the Ray Brook Federal Correctional Institution in New York. There he became friends with another inmate, Anthony Sarivola, then serving a 60-day sentence for extortion. The two men came to spend several hours a day together. Sarivola, a former police officer, had been involved in loansharking for organized crime but then became a paid informant for the Federal Bureau of Investigation. While at Ray Brook, he masqueraded as an organized crime figure. After becoming friends with Fulminante, Sarivola heard a rumor that Fulminante was suspected of killing a child in Arizona. Sarivola then raised the subject with Fulminante in several conversations, but Fulminante repeatedly denied any involvement in Jeneane's death. During one conversation, he told Sarivola that Jeneane had been killed by bikers looking for drugs; on another occasion, he said he did not know what had happened. Sarivola passed this information on to an agent of the Federal Bureau of Investigation, who instructed Sarivola to find out more.

Sarivola learned more one evening in October 1983, as he and Fulminante walked together around the prison track. Sarivola said that he knew Fulminante was "starting to get some tough treatment and whatnot" from other inmates because of the rumor. Sarivola offered to protect Fulminante from his fellow inmates, but told him, " 'You have to tell me about it,' you know. I mean, in other words, 'For me to give you any help.' " Fulminante then admitted to Sarivola that he had driven Jeneane to the desert on his motorcycle, where he choked her, sexually assaulted her, and made her beg for her life, before shooting her twice in the head.

Sarivola was released from prison in November 1983. Fulminante was released the following May, only to be arrested the next month for another weapons violation. On September 4, 1984, Fulminante was indicted in Arizona for the first-degree murder of Jeneane.

Prior to trial, Fulminante moved to suppress the statement he had given Sarivola in prison, as well as a second confession he had given to Donna Sarivola, then Anthony Sarivola's fiancée and later his wife, following his May 1984 release from prison. He asserted that the confession to Sarivola was coerced, and that the second confession was the "fruit" of the first. Following the hearing, the trial court denied the motion to suppress, specifically finding that, based on the stipulated facts, the confessions were voluntary. The State introduced both confessions as evidence at trial, and on December 19, 1985, Fulminante was convicted of Jeneane's murder. He was subsequently sentenced to death.

Fulminante appealed, arguing, among other things, that his confession to Sarivola was the product of coercion and that its admission at trial violated his rights to due process under the Fifth and Fourteenth Amendments to the United States Constitution. After considering the evidence at trial as well as the stipulated facts before the trial court on the motion to suppress, the Arizona Supreme Court held that the confession was coerced, but initially determined that the admission of the confession at trial was harmless error, because of the overwhelming nature of the evidence against Fulminante. Upon Fulminante's motion for reconsideration, however, the court ruled that this Court's precedent precluded the use of the harmless-error analysis in the case of a coerced confession. The court therefore reversed the conviction and ordered that Fulminante be retried without the use of the confession to Sarivola. Because of differing views in the state and federal courts over whether the admission at trial of a coerced confession is subject to a harmless-error analysis, we granted the State's petition for certiorari. Although a majority of this Court finds that such a confession is subject to a harmless-error analysis, for the reasons set forth below, we affirm the judgment of the Arizona court.

■ ■ ■

II

We deal first with the State's contention that the court below erred in holding Fulminante's confession to have been coerced. The State argues that it is the totality of the circumstances that determines whether Fulminante's confession was coerced, but contends that rather than apply this standard, the Arizona court applied a "but for" test, under which the court found that but for the promise given by Sarivola, Fulminante would not have confessed. In support of this argument, the State points to the Arizona court's reference to *Bram v. United States* (1897). Although the Court noted in *Bram* that a confession cannot be obtained by " 'any direct or implied promises, however slight, nor by the exertion of any improper influence,' " it is clear that this passage from *Bram*, which under current precedent does not state the standard for determining the voluntariness of a confession, was not relied on by the Arizona court in reaching its conclusion. Rather, the court cited this language as part of a longer quotation from an Arizona case which accurately described the State's burden of proof for establishing voluntariness. Indeed, the Arizona Supreme Court stated that a "determination regarding the voluntariness of a confession . . . must be viewed in a totality of the circumstances," and under that standard plainly found that Fulminante's statement to Sarivola had been coerced.

In applying the totality of the circumstances test to determine that the confession to Sarivola was coerced, the Arizona Supreme Court focused on a number of relevant facts. First, the court noted that "because [Fulminante] was an alleged child murderer, he was in danger of physical harm at the hands of other inmates." In addition, Sarivola was aware that Fulminante had been receiving " 'rough treatment from the guys.' " Using his knowledge of these threats, Sarivola offered to protect Fulminante in exchange for a confession to Jeneane's murder, and "[i]n response to Sarivola's offer of protection, [Fulminante] confessed." Agreeing with Fulminante that "Sarivola's promise was 'extremely coercive,' " the Arizona court declared: "[T]he confession was obtained as a direct result of extreme coercion and was tendered in the belief that the defendant's life was in jeopardy if he did not confess. This is a true coerced confession in every sense of the word...."

We normally give great deference to the factual findings of the state court. Nevertheless, "the ultimate issue of 'voluntariness' is a legal question requiring independent federal determination."

Although the question is a close one, we agree with the Arizona Supreme Court's conclusion that Fulminante's confession was coerced. The Arizona Supreme Court found a credible threat of physical violence unless Fulminante confessed. Our cases have made clear that a finding of coercion need not depend upon actual violence by a government agent; a credible threat is sufficient. As we have said, "coercion can be mental as well as physical, and . . . the blood of the accused is not the only hallmark of an unconstitutional inquisition." *Blackburn v. Alabama* (1960).... Accepting the Arizona court's finding, permissible on this record, that there was a credible threat of physical violence, we agree with its conclusion that Fulminante's will was overborne in such a way as to render his confession the product of coercion.

■ ■ ■

III

Four of us, Justices MARSHALL, BLACKMUN, STEVENS, and myself, would affirm the judgment of the Arizona Supreme Court on the ground that the harmless-error rule is inapplicable to erroneously admitted coerced confessions. We thus disagree with the Justices who have a contrary view.

The majority today abandons what until now the Court has regarded as the "axiomatic [proposition] that a defendant in a criminal case is deprived of due process of law if his conviction is founded, in whole or in part, upon an involuntary confession, without regard for the truth or falsity of the confession.

■ ■ ■

In extending to coerced confessions the harmless-error rule of *Chapman v. California* (1967), the majority declares that because the Court has applied that analysis to numerous other "trial errors," there is no reason that it should not apply to an error of this nature as well. The four of us remain convinced, however, that we should abide by our cases that have refused to apply the harmless-error rule to coerced confessions, for a coerced confession is fundamentally different from other types of erroneously admitted evidence to which the rule has been applied. Indeed, as the majority concedes, *Chapman* itself recognized that prior cases "have indicated that there are some constitutional rights so basic to a fair trial that their infraction can *never* be treated as harmless error," and it placed in that category the constitutional rule against using a defendant's coerced confession against him at his criminal trial. Moreover, cases since *Chapman* have reiterated the rule that using a defendant's coerced confession against him is a denial of due process of law regardless of the other evidence in the record aside from the confession.

Chapman specifically noted three constitutional errors that could not be categorized as harmless error: using a coerced confession against a defendant in a criminal trial, depriving a defendant of counsel, and trying a defendant before a biased judge. The majority attempts to distinguish the use of a coerced confession from the other two errors listed in *Chapman* first by distorting the decision in *Payne* [*v. Arkansas* (1958)], and then by drawing a meaningless dichotomy between "trial errors" and "structural defects" in the trial process. Viewing *Payne* as merely rejecting a test whereby the admission of a coerced confession could stand if there were "sufficient evidence," other than the confession, to support the conviction, the majority suggests that the Court in *Payne* might have reached a different result had it been considering a harmless-error test. It is clear, though, that in *Payne* the Court recognized that *regardless* of the amount of other evidence, "the admission in evidence, over objection, of the coerced confession vitiates the judgment," because "where, as here, a coerced confession constitutes a part of the evidence before the jury and a general verdict is returned, no one can say what credit and weight the jury gave to the confession." The inability to assess its effect on a conviction causes the admission at trial of a coerced confession to "defy analysis by 'harmless-error' standards," just as certainly as do deprivation of counsel and trial before a biased judge.

The majority also attempts to distinguish "trial errors" which occur "during the presentation of the case to the jury," and which it deems susceptible to harmless-error analysis, from "structural defects in the constitution of the trial mechanism," which the majority concedes cannot be so analyzed. This effort fails, for our jurisprudence on harmless error has not classified so neatly the errors at issue. For example, we have held susceptible to harmless-error analysis the failure to instruct the jury on the presumption of innocence. . . . These cases cannot be reconciled by labeling the former "trial error" and the latter not, for both concern the exact same stage in the trial proceedings. Rather, these cases can be reconciled only by considering the nature of the right at issue and the effect of an error upon the trial. A jury instruction on the presumption of innocence is not constitutionally required in every case to satisfy due process, because such an instruction merely offers an additional safeguard beyond that provided by the constitutionally required instruction on reasonable doubt. While it may be possible to analyze as harmless the omission of a presumption of innocence instruction when the required reasonable-doubt instruction has been given, it is impossible to assess the effect on the jury of the omission of the more fundamental instruction on reasonable doubt. In addition, omission of a reasonable-doubt instruction, though a "trial error," distorts the very structure of the trial because it creates the risk that the jury will convict the defendant even if the State has not met its required burden of proof.

These same concerns counsel against applying harmless-error analysis to the admission of a coerced confession. A defendant's confession is "probably the most probative and damaging evidence that can be admitted against him," so damaging that a jury should not be expected to ignore it even if told to do so, and because in any event it is impossible to know what credit and weight the jury gave to the confession. Concededly, this reason is insufficient to justify a *per se* bar to the use of *any* confession. . . .

As the majority concedes, there are other constitutional errors that invalidate a conviction even though there may be no reasonable doubt that the defendant is guilty and would be convicted absent the trial error. For example, a judge in a criminal trial "is prohibited from entering a judgment of conviction or directing the jury to come forward with such a verdict, regardless of how overwhelmingly the evidence may point in that direction." A defendant is entitled to counsel at trial, and as *Chapman* recognized, violating this right can never be harmless error . . . where a conviction was set aside because the defendant had not had counsel at a preliminary hearing without regard to the showing of prejudice. In *Vasquez v. Hillery* (1986), a defendant was found guilty beyond reasonable doubt, but the conviction had been set aside because of the unlawful exclusion of members of the defendant's race from the grand jury that indicted him, despite overwhelming evidence of his guilt. The error at the grand jury stage struck at fundamental values of our society and "undermine[d] the structural integrity of the criminal tribunal itself, and [was] not amenable to harmless-error review." *Vasquez*, like *Chapman*, also noted that rule of automatic reversal when a defendant is tried before a judge with a financial interest in the outcome. . . .

The search for truth is indeed central to our system of justice, but "certain constitutional rights are not, and should not be, subject to harmless-error analysis because those rights protect important values that are unrelated to the truth-seeking function of the trial." . . .

For the foregoing reasons, the four of us would adhere to the consistent line of authority that has recognized as a basic tenet of our criminal justice system, before and after both *Miranda* and *Chapman*, the prohibition against using a defendant's coerced confession against him at his criminal trial. *Stare decisis* is "of fundamental importance to the rule of law"; the majority offers no convincing reason for overturning our long line of decisions requiring the exclusion of coerced confessions.

IV

Since five Justices have determined that harmless-error analysis applies to coerced confessions, it becomes necessary to evaluate under that ruling the admissibility of Fulminante's confession to Sarivola. . . . *Chapman* made clear that, "before a federal constitutional error can be held harmless, the court must be able to declare a belief that it was harmless beyond a reasonable doubt." The Court has the power to review the record *de novo* in order to determine an error's harmlessness. In so doing, it must be determined whether the State has met its burden of demonstrating that the admission of the confession to Sarivola did not contribute to Fulminante's conviction. Five of us are of the view that the State has not carried its burden and accordingly affirm the judgment of the court below reversing respondent's conviction. . . .

In the Arizona Supreme Court's initial opinion, in which it determined that harmless-error analysis could be applied to the confession, the court found that the admissible second confession to Donna Sarivola rendered the first confession to Anthony Sarivola cumulative. The court also noted that circumstantial physical evidence concerning the wounds, the ligature around Jeneane's neck, the location of the body, and the presence of motorcycle tracks at the scene corroborated the second confession. The court concluded that "due to the overwhelming evidence adduced from the second confession, if there had not been a first confession, the jury would still have had the same basic evidence to convict" Fulminante.

We have a quite different evaluation of the evidence. Our review of the record leads us to conclude that the State has failed to meet its burden of establishing, beyond a reasonable doubt, that the admission of Fulminante's confession to Anthony Sarivola was harmless error. Three considerations compel this result.

First, the transcript discloses that both the trial court and the State recognized that a successful prosecution depended on the jury believing the two confessions. Absent the confessions, it is unlikely that Fulminante would have been prosecuted at all, because the physical evidence from the scene and other circumstantial evidence would have been insufficient to convict. Indeed, no indictment was filed until nearly two years after the murder. Although the police had suspected Fulminante from the beginning, as the prosecutor acknowledged in his opening statement to the jury, "[W]hat brings us to Court, what makes this case fileable, and prosecutable and triable is that later, Mr. Fulminante confesses this crime to Anthony Sarivola and later, to Donna Sarivola, his wife." After trial began, during a renewed hearing on Fulminante's motion to suppress, the trial court opined, "You know, I think from what little I know about this trial, the character of this man [Sarivola] for truthfulness or untruthfulness and his credibility is the centerpiece of this case, is it not?" The prosecutor responded, "It's very important, there's no doubt." Finally, in his closing argument, the prosecutor prefaced his discussion of the two confessions by conceding: "[W]e have a lot of [circumstantial] evidence that indicates that this is our suspect, this is the fellow that did it, but it's a little short as far as saying that it's proof that he actually put the gun to the girl's head and killed her. So it's a little short of that. We recognize that."

Second, the jury's assessment of the confession to Donna Sarivola could easily have depended in large part on the presence of the confession to Anthony Sarivola. Absent the admission at trial of the first confession, the jurors might have found Donna Sarivola's story unbelievable. Fulminante's confession to Donna Sarivola allegedly occurred in May 1984, on the day he was released from Ray Brook, as she and Anthony Sarivola drove Fulminante from New York to Pennsylvania. Donna Sarivola testified that Fulminante, whom she had never before met, confessed in detail about Jeneane's brutal murder in response to her casual question concerning why he was going to visit friends in Pennsylvania instead of returning to his family in Arizona.

Although she testified that she was "disgusted" by Fulminante's disclosures, she stated that she took no steps to notify authorities of what she had learned. In fact, she claimed that she barely discussed the matter with Anthony Sarivola, who was in the car and overheard Fulminante's entire conversation with Donna. Despite her disgust for Fulminante, Donna Sarivola later went on a second trip with him. Although Sarivola informed authorities that he had driven Fulminante to Pennsylvania, he did not mention Donna's presence in the car or her conversation with Fulminante. Only when questioned by authorities in June 1985 did Anthony Sarivola belatedly recall the confession to Donna more than a year before, and only then did he ask if she would be willing to discuss the matter with authorities.

Although some of the details in the confession to Donna Sarivola were corroborated by circumstantial evidence, many, including details that Jeneane was choked and sexually assaulted, were not. As to other aspects of the second confession, including Fulminante's motive and state of mind, the *only* corroborating evidence was the first confession to Anthony Sarivola. Thus, contrary to what the Arizona Supreme Court found, it is clear that the jury might have believed that the two confessions reinforced and corroborated each other. For this reason, one confession was *not* merely cumulative of the other.

■ ■ ■

The jurors could also have believed that Donna Sarivola had a motive to lie about the confession in order to assist her husband. Anthony Sarivola received significant benefits from federal authorities, including payment for information, immunity from prosecution, and eventual placement in the federal Witness Protection Program.

■ ■ ■

Third, the admission of the first confession led to the admission of other evidence prejudicial to Fulminante. For example, the State introduced evidence that Fulminante knew of Sarivola's connections with organized crime in an attempt to explain why Fulminante would have been motivated to confess to Sarivola in seeking protection. Absent the confession, this evidence would have had no relevance and would have been inadmissible at trial. The Arizona Supreme Court found that the evidence of Sarivola's connections with organized crime reflected on Sarivola's character, not Fulminante's, and noted that the evidence could have been used to impeach Sarivola. This analysis overlooks the fact that had the confession not been admitted, there would have been no reason for Sarivola to testify and thus no need to impeach his testimony. Moreover, we cannot agree that the evidence did not reflect on Fulminante's character as well, for it depicted him as someone who willingly sought out the company of criminals. It is quite possible that this evidence led the jury to view Fulminante as capable of murder.

■ ■ ■

Because a majority of the Court has determined that Fulminante's confession to Anthony Sarivola was coerced and because a majority has determined that admitting this confession was not harmless beyond a reasonable doubt, we agree with the Arizona Supreme Court's conclusion that Fulminante is entitled to a new trial at which the confession is not admitted. Accordingly the judgment of the Arizona Supreme Court is

Affirmed.

Chief Justice REHNQUIST, with whom Justice O'CONNOR joins, Justice KENNEDY and Justice SOUTER join as to Parts I and II, and Justice SCALIA joins as to Parts II and III, delivered the opinion of the Court with respect to Part II, and a dissenting opinion with respect to Parts I and III.

The Court today properly concludes that the admission of an "involuntary" confession at trial is subject to harmless-error analysis. Nonetheless, the independent review of the record which we are required to make shows that respondent Fulminante's confession was not in fact involuntary. And even if the confession were deemed to be involuntary, the evidence offered at trial, including a second, untainted confession by Fulminante, supports the conclusion that any error here was certainly harmless.

I

The question whether respondent Fulminante's confession was voluntary is one of federal law. "Without exception, the Court's confession cases hold that the ultimate issue of 'voluntariness' is a legal question requiring independent federal determination."

■   ■   ■

The admissibility of a confession such as that made by respondent Fulminante depends upon whether it was voluntarily made. "The ultimate test remains that which has been the only clearly established test in Anglo-American courts for two hundred years: the test of voluntariness. Is the confession the product of an essentially free and unconstrained choice by its maker? If it is, if he has willed to confess, it may be used against him. If it is not, if his will has been overborne and his capacity for self-determination critically impaired, the use of his confession offends due process." *Culombe v. Connecticut* (1961).

In this case the parties stipulated to the basic facts at the hearing in the Arizona trial court on respondent's motion to suppress the confession. Anthony Sarivola, an inmate at the Ray Brook Prison, was a paid confidential informant for the FBI. While at Ray Brook, various rumors reached Sarivola that Oreste Fulminante, a fellow inmate who had befriended Sarivola, had killed his stepdaughter in Arizona. Sarivola passed these rumors on to his FBI contact, who told him "to find out more about it." Sarivola, having already discussed the rumors with respondent on several occasions, asked him whether the rumors were true, adding that he might be in a position to protect Fulminante from physical recriminations in prison, but that "[he] must tell him the truth." Fulminante then confessed to Sarivola that he had in fact killed his stepdaughter in Arizona, and provided Sarivola with substantial details about the manner in which he killed the child. At the suppression hearing,

Fulminante stipulated to the fact that "[a]t no time did the defendant indicate he was in fear of other inmates nor did he ever seek Mr. Sarivola's 'protection.'" The trial court was also aware, through an excerpt from Sarivola's interview testimony which respondent appended to his reply memorandum, that Sarivola believed Fulminante's time was "running short" and that he would "have went out of the prison horizontally." The trial court found that respondent's confession was voluntary.

The Supreme Court of Arizona stated that the trial court committed no error in finding the confession voluntary based on the record before it. But it overturned the trial court's finding of voluntariness based on the more comprehensive trial record before it, which included, in addition to the facts stipulated at the suppression hearing, a statement made by Sarivola at the trial that "the defendant had been receiving 'rough treatment from the guys, and if the defendant would tell the truth, he could be protected.'" It also had before it the presentence report, which showed that Fulminante was no stranger to the criminal justice system: He had six prior felony convictions and had been imprisoned on three prior occasions.

On the basis of the record before it, the Supreme Court stated:

> "Defendant contends that because he was an alleged child murderer, he was in danger of physical harm at the hands of other inmates. Sarivola was aware that defendant faced the possibility of retribution from other inmates, and that in return for the confession with respect to the victim's murder, Sarivola would protect him. Moreover, the defendant maintains that Sarivola's promise was 'extremely coercive' because the 'obvious' inference from the promise was that his life would be in jeopardy if he did not confess. We agree."

Exercising our responsibility to make the independent examination of the record necessary to decide this federal question, I am at a loss to see how the Supreme Court of Arizona reached the conclusion that it did. Fulminante offered no evidence that he believed that his life was in danger or that he in fact confessed to Sarivola in order to obtain the proffered protection. Indeed, he had stipulated that "[a]t no time did the defendant indicate he was in fear of other inmates nor did he ever seek Mr. Sarivola's 'protection.'" Sarivola's testimony that he told Fulminante that "if [he] would tell the truth, he could be protected," adds little if anything to the substance of the parties' stipulation. The decision of the Supreme Court of Arizona rests on an assumption that is squarely contrary to this stipulation, and one that is not supported by any testimony of Fulminante.

The facts of record in the present case are quite different from those present in cases where we have found confessions to be coerced and involuntary. Since Fulminante was unaware that Sarivola was an FBI informant, there existed none of "the danger of coercion result[ing] from the interaction of custody and official interrogation." The fact that Sarivola was a Government informant does not by itself render Fulminante's confession involuntary, since we have consistently accepted the use of informants in the discovery of evidence of a crime as a legitimate investigatory procedure consistent with the Constitution. The conversations between Sarivola and Fulminante were not lengthy, and the defendant was free at all times to leave Sarivola's company. Sarivola at no time threatened him or demanded that he confess; he simply requested that he speak the truth about the matter. Fulminante was an experienced habitue of prisons, and presumably able to fend for himself. In concluding on these facts that Fulminante's confession was involuntary, the Court today embraces a more expansive definition of that term than is warranted by any of our decided cases.

II

Since this Court's landmark decision in *Chapman v. California*, in which we adopted the general rule that a constitutional error does not automatically require reversal of a conviction, the Court has applied harmless-error analysis to a wide range of errors and has recognized that most constitutional errors can be harmless.

■ ■ ■

The common thread connecting these cases is that each involved "trial error"—error which occurred during the presentation of the case to the jury, and which may therefore be quantitatively assessed in the context of other evidence presented in order to determine whether its admission was harmless beyond a reasonable doubt. In applying harmless-error analysis to these many different constitutional violations, the Court has been faithful to the belief that the harmless-error doctrine is essential to preserve the "principle that the central purpose of a criminal trial is to decide the factual question of the defendant's guilt or innocence, and promotes public respect for the criminal process by focusing on the underlying fairness of the trial rather than on the virtually inevitable presence of immaterial error."

■ ■ ■

It is on the basis of this language in *Chapman* that Justice White in dissent concludes that the principle of *stare decisis* requires us to hold that an involuntary confession is not subject to harmless-error analysis. We believe that there are several reasons which lead to a contrary conclusion. In the first place, the quoted language from *Chapman* does not by its terms adopt any such rule in that case. The language that "[a]lthough our prior cases have indicated," coupled with the relegation of the cases themselves to a footnote, is more appropriately regarded as a historical reference to the holdings of these cases. This view is buttressed by an examination of the opinion in *Payne v. Arkansas*, which is the case referred to for the proposition that an involuntary confession may not be subject to harmless-error analysis.

■ ■ ■

It is apparent that the State's argument which the Court rejected in *Payne* is not the harmless-error analysis later adopted in *Chapman*, but a much more lenient rule which would allow affirmance of a conviction if the evidence other than the involuntary confession was sufficient to sustain the verdict.

This is confirmed by the dissent of Justice Clark in that case, which adopted the more lenient test. Such a test would, of course—unlike the harmless-error test—make the admission of an involuntary confession virtually risk-free for the State.

The admission of an involuntary confession—a classic "trial error"—is markedly different from the other two constitutional violations referred to in the *Chapman* footnote as not being subject to harmless-error analysis. One of those violations, involved in *Gideon v. Wainwright* (1963), was the total deprivation of the right to counsel at trial. The other violation, involved in *Tumey v. Ohio* (1927), was a judge who was not impartial. These are structural defects in the constitution of the trial mechanism, which defy analysis by "harmless-error" standards. The entire conduct of the trial from beginning to end is obviously affected by the absence of counsel for a criminal defendant, just as it is by the presence on the bench of a judge who is not impartial. Since our decision in *Chapman*, other cases have added to the category of constitutional errors which are not subject to harmless error the following: unlawful exclusion of members of the defendant's race from a grand jury, the right to self-representation at trial, and the right to public trial. Each of these constitutional deprivations is a similar structural defect affecting the framework within which the trial proceeds, rather than simply an error in the trial process itself. "Without these basic protections, a criminal trial cannot reliably serve its function as a vehicle for determination of guilt or innocence, and no criminal punishment may be regarded as fundamentally fair."

It is evident from a comparison of the constitutional violations which we have held subject to harmless error, and those which we have held not, that involuntary statements or confessions belong in the former category. The admission of an involuntary confession is a "trial error," similar in both degree and kind to the erroneous admission of other types of evidence. The evidentiary impact of an involuntary confession, and its effect upon the composition of the record, is indistinguishable from that of a confession obtained in violation of the Sixth Amendment—of evidence seized in violation of the Fourth Amendment—or of a prosecutor's improper comment on a defendant's silence at trial in violation of the Fifth Amendment. When reviewing the erroneous admission of an involuntary confession, the appellate court, as it does with the admission of other forms of improperly admitted evidence, simply reviews the remainder of the evidence against the defendant to determine whether the admission of the confession was harmless beyond a reasonable doubt.

Nor can it be said that the admission of an involuntary confession is the type of error which "transcends the criminal process." This Court has applied harmless-error analysis to the violation of other constitutional rights similar in magnitude and importance and involving the same level of police misconduct. For instance, we have previously held that the admission of a defendant's statements obtained in violation of the Sixth Amendment is subject to harmless-error analysis.

■　■　■

Of course an involuntary confession may have a more dramatic effect on the course of a trial than do other trial errors—in particular cases it may be devastating to a defendant—but this simply means that a reviewing court will conclude in such a case that its admission was not harmless error; it is not a reason for eschewing the harmless-error test entirely. The Supreme Court of Arizona, in its first opinion in the present case, concluded that the admission of Fulminante's confession *was* harmless error. That court concluded that a second and more explicit confession of the crime made by Fulminante after he was released from prison was not tainted by the first confession, and that the second confession, together with physical evidence from the wounds (the victim had been shot twice in the head with a large caliber weapon at close range and a ligature was found around her neck) and other evidence introduced at trial rendered the admission of the first confession harmless beyond a reasonable doubt.

III

I would agree with the finding of the Supreme Court of Arizona in its initial opinion—in which it believed harmless-error analysis was applicable to the admission of involuntary confessions—that the admission of Fulminante's confession was harmless. Indeed, this seems to me to be a classic case of harmless error: a second confession giving more details of the crime than the first was admitted in evidence and found to be free of any constitutional objection. Accordingly, I would affirm the holding of the Supreme Court of Arizona in its initial opinion and reverse the judgment which it ultimately rendered in this case.

Justice KENNEDY, concurring in the judgment.

For the reasons stated by The Chief Justice, I agree that Fulminante's confession to Anthony Sarivola was not coerced. In my view, the trial court did not err in admitting this testimony. A majority of the Court, however, finds the confession coerced and proceeds to consider whether harmless-error analysis may be used when a coerced confession has been admitted at trial. With the case in this posture, it is appropriate for me to address the harmless-error issue.

Again for the reasons stated by The Chief Justice, I agree that harmless-error analysis should apply in the case of a coerced confession. That said, the court conducting a harmless-error inquiry must appreciate the indelible impact a full confession may have on the trier of fact, as distinguished, for instance, from the impact of an isolated statement that incriminates the defendant only when connected with other evidence. If the jury believes that a defendant has admitted the crime, it doubtless will be tempted to rest its decision on that evidence alone, without careful consideration of the other evidence in the case. Apart, perhaps, from a videotape of the crime, one would have difficulty finding evidence more damaging to a criminal defendant's plea of innocence. For the reasons given by Justice White in Part IV of his opinion, I cannot with confidence find admission of Fulminante's confession to Anthony Sarivola to be harmless error.

The same majority of the Court does not agree on the three issues presented by the trial court's determination to admit Fulminante's first confession: whether the confession was inadmissible because coerced; whether harmless-error analysis is appropriate; and if so whether any error was harmless here. My own view that the confession was not coerced does not command a majority.

In the interests of providing a clear mandate to the Arizona Supreme Court in this capital case, I deem it proper to accept in the case now before us the holding of five Justices that the confession was coerced and inadmissible. I agree with a majority of the Court that admission of the confession could not be harmless error when viewed in light of all the other evidence; and so I concur in the judgment to affirm the ruling of the Arizona Supreme Court.

Torture: Extract from Israeli Supreme Court Ruling

Chief Justice Aharon Barak
September 6, 1999

This decision opened with a description of the difficult reality in which Israel finds herself. We conclude this judgment by revisiting that harsh reality. We are aware that this decision does make it easier to deal with that reality. This is the destiny of a democracy—it does not see all means as acceptable, and the ways of its enemies are not always open before it. A democracy must sometimes fight with one hand tied behind its back. Even so, a democracy has the upper hand. The rule of law and the liberty of an individual constitute important components in its understanding of security. At the end of the day, they strengthen its spirit and this strength allows it to overcome its difficulties.

This having been said, there are those who argue that Israel's security problems are too numerous, and require the authorization of physical means. Whether it is appropriate for Israel, in light of its security difficulties, to sanction physical means is an issue that must be decided by the legislative branch, which represents the people. We do not take any stand on this matter at this time. It is there that various considerations must be weighed. The debate must occur there. It is there that the required legislation may be passed, provided, of course, that the law befit[s] the values of the State of Israel, is enacted for a proper purpose, and [infringes the suspect's liberty] to an extent no greater than required. *See* article 8 of the Basic Law: Human Dignity and Liberty.

B. MOVEMENT AWAY FROM VOLUNTARINESS STANDARD

Malloy v. Hogan

378 U.S. 1 (1964)

BRENNAN, J., delivered the opinion of the Court, in which WARREN, C.J., GOLDBERG, BLACK, and DOUGLAS, JJ., joined. HARLAN, WHITE, STEWART, and CLARK, JJ., dissented.

In this case we are asked to reconsider prior decisions holding that the privilege against self-incrimination is not safeguarded against state action by the Fourteenth Amendment. *Twining v. New Jersey* [(1908)]; *Adamson v. California* [(1947)].

■ ■ ■

The Court has not hesitated to re-examine past decisions according the Fourteenth Amendment a less central role in the preservation of basic liberties than that which was contemplated by its Framers when they added the Amendment to our constitutional scheme. Thus, although the Court as late as 1922 said that "neither the Fourteenth Amendment nor any other provision of the Constitution of the United States imposes upon the States any restrictions about 'freedom of speech,' . . ." three years later, *Gitlow v. New York* (1925) initiated a series of decisions which today hold immune from state invasion every First Amendment protection for the cherished rights of mind and spirit—the freedoms of speech, press, religion, assembly, association, and petition for redress of grievances.

Similarly, *Palko v. Connecticut*, decided in 1937, suggested that the rights secured by the Fourth Amendment were not protected against state action, citing . . . the statement of the Court in 1914 in *Weeks v. United States* (1914), that "the 4th Amendment is not directed to individual misconduct of [state] officials." In 1961, however, the Court held that in the light of later decisions, it was taken as settled that "the Fourth Amendment's right of privacy has been declared enforceable against the States through the Due Process Clause of the Fourteenth Amendment." *Mapp v. Ohio* (1961). Again, although the Court held in 1942 that in a state prosecution for a non-capital offense, "appointment of counsel is not a fundamental right," *Betts v. Brady* 1942); cf. *Powell v. Alabama* (1932), only last Term this decision was re-examined and it was held that provision of counsel in all criminal cases was "a fundamental right, essential to a fair trial," and thus was made obligatory on the States by the Fourteenth Amendment. *Gideon v. Wainwright* (1963).

We hold today that the Fifth Amendment's exception from compulsory self-incrimination is also protected by the Fourteenth Amendment against abridgment by the States. Decisions of the Court since *Twining* and *Adamson* have departed from the contrary view expressed in those cases. We discuss first the decisions which forbid the use of coerced confessions in state criminal prosecutions.

Brown v. Mississippi (1936) was the first case in which the Court held that the Due Process Clause prohibited the States from using the accused's coerced confessions against him. The Court in *Brown* felt impelled, in light of *Twining*, to say that its conclusion did not involve the privilege against self-incrimination. "Compulsion by torture to extort a confession is a different matter." But this distinction was soon abandoned, and today the admissibility of a confession in a state criminal prosecution is tested by the same standard applied in federal prosecutions since 1897, when, in *Bram v. United States* (1897), the Court held that "[i]n criminal trials, in the courts of the United States, wherever a question arises whether a confession is incompetent because not voluntary, the issue is controlled by that portion of the Fifth Amendment to the Constitution of the United States commanding that no person 'shall be compelled in any criminal case to be a witness against himself.'" Under this test, the constitutional inquiry is not whether the conduct of state officers in obtaining the confession was shocking, but whether the confession was "free and voluntary; that is, [it] must not be extracted by any sort of threats or violence, nor obtained by any direct or implied promises, however slight, nor by the exertion of any improper influence." In other words the person must not have been compelled to incriminate himself. We have held inadmissible even a confession secured by so mild a whip as the refusal, under certain circumstances, to allow a suspect to call his wife until he confessed.

The marked shift to the federal standard in state cases began with *Lisenba v. California* (1941), where the Court spoke of the accused's "free choice to admit, to deny, or to refuse to answer." The shift reflects recognition that the American system of criminal prosecution is accusatorial, not inquisitorial, and that the Fifth Amendment privilege is its essential mainstay. *Rogers v. Richmond* (1961). Governments, state and federal, are thus constitutionally compelled to establish guilt by evidence independently and freely secured, and may not by coercion prove a charge against an accused out of his own mouth. Since the Fourteenth Amendment prohibits the States from inducing a person to confess through "sympathy falsely aroused," or other like inducement far short of "compulsion by torture," it follows a fortiori that it also forbids the States to resort to imprisonment, as here, to compel him to answer questions that might incriminate him. The Fourteenth Amendment secures against state invasion the same privilege that the Fifth Amendment guarantees against federal infringement—the right of a person to remain silent unless he chooses to speak in the unfettered exercise of his own will, and to suffer no penalty, as held in *Twining*, for such silence.

This conclusion is fortified by our recent decision in *Mapp v. Ohio*, overruling *Wolf v. Colorado* (1949), which had held "that in a prosecution in a State court for a State crime the Fourteenth Amendment does not forbid the admission of evidence obtained by an unreasonable search and seizure." *Mapp* held that the Fifth Amendment privilege against self-incrimination implemented the Fourth Amendment in such cases, and that the two guarantees of personal security conjoined in the Fourteenth Amendment to make the exclusionary rule obligatory upon the States. . . . We said in *Mapp*:

> "We find that, as to the Federal Government the Fourth and Fifth Amendments and, as to the States, the freedom from unconscionable invasions of privacy and the freedom from convictions based upon coerced confessions do enjoy an 'intimate relation' in their perpetuation of 'principles of humanity and civil liberty [secured] only after years of struggle.' The philosophy of each Amendment and of each freedom is complementary to, although not dependent upon, that of the other in its sphere of influence—the very least that together they assure in either sphere is that no man is to be convicted on unconstitutional evidence."

In thus returning to the *Boyd* [*v. United States* (1886)] view that the privilege is one of the "principles of a free government," *Mapp* necessarily repudiated the *Twining* concept of the privilege as a mere rule of evidence "best defended not as an unchangeable principle of universal justice, but as a law proved by experience to be expedient."

■ ■ ■

Reversed.

Massiah v. United States

377 U.S. 201 (1964)

STEWART, J., delivered the opinion of the Court, in which WARREN, C.J., GOLDBERG, BRENNAN, DOUGLAS, and BLACK, JJ., joined. WHITE, J., wrote a dissenting opinion, in which CLARK and HARLAN, JJ., joined.

The petitioner was indicted for violating the federal narcotics laws. He retained a lawyer, pleaded not guilty, and was released on bail. While he was free on bail a federal agent succeeded by surreptitious means in listening to incriminating statements made by him. Evidence of these statements was introduced against the petitioner at his trial over his objection. He was convicted, and the Court of Appeals affirmed. We granted certiorari to consider whether, under the circumstances here presented, the prosecution's use at the trial of evidence of the petitioner's own incriminating statements deprived him of any right secured to him under the Federal Constitution.

The petitioner, a merchant seaman, was in 1958 a member of the crew of the S.S. Santa Maria. In April of that year federal customs officials in New York received information that he was going to transport a quantity of narcotics aboard that ship from South America to the United States. As a result of this and other information, the agents searched the Santa Maria upon its arrival in New York and found in the afterpeak of the vessel five packages containing about three and a half pounds of cocaine. They also learned of circumstances, not here relevant, tending to connect the petitioner with the cocaine. He was arrested, promptly arraigned, and subsequently indicted for possession of narcotics aboard a United States vessel. In July a superseding indictment was returned, charging the petitioner and a man named Colson with the same substantive offense, and in separate counts charging the petitioner, Colson, and others with having conspired to possess narcotics aboard a United States vessel, and to import, conceal, and facilitate the sale of narcotics. The petitioner, who had retained a lawyer, pleaded not guilty and was released on bail, along with Colson.

A few days later, and quite without the petitioner's knowledge, Colson decided to cooperate with the government agents in their continuing investigation of the narcotics activities in which the petitioner, Colson, and others had allegedly been engaged. Colson permitted an agent named Murphy to install a Schmidt radio transmitter under the front seat of Colson's automobile, by means of which Murphy, equipped with an appropriate receiving device, could overhear from some distance away conversations carried on in Colson's car.

On the evening of November 19, 1959, Colson and the petitioner held a lengthy conversation while sitting in Colson's automobile, parked on a New York street. By prearrangement with Colson, and totally unbeknown to the petitioner, the agent Murphy sat in a car parked out of sight down the street and listened over the radio to the entire conversation. The petitioner made several incriminating statements during the course of this conversation. At the petitioner's trial these incriminating statements were brought before the jury through Murphy's testimony, despite the insistent objection of defense counsel. The jury convicted the petitioner of several related narcotics offenses, and the convictions were affirmed by the Court of Appeals.

■ ■ ■

Ever since this Court's decision in the *Spano* [*v. New York* (1959)] case, the New York courts have unequivocally followed this constitutional rule. "Any secret interrogation of the defendant, from and after the finding of the indictment, without the protection afforded by the presence of counsel, contravenes the basic dictates of fairness in the conduct of criminal causes and the fundamental rights of persons charged with crime." *People v. Waterman* [(1961)].

This view no more than reflects a constitutional principle established as long ago as *Powell v. Alabama* [(1932)], where the Court noted that "... during perhaps the most critical period of the proceedings ... that is to say, from the time of their arraignment until the beginning of their trial, when consultation, thorough-going investigation and preparation [are] vitally important, the defendants ... [are] as much entitled to such aid [of counsel] during that period as at the trial itself."

■ ■ ■

Here we deal not with a state court conviction, but with a federal case, where the specific guarantee of the Sixth Amendment directly applies. We hold that the petitioner was denied the basic protections of that guarantee when there was used against him at his trial evidence of his own incriminating words, which federal agents had deliberately elicited from him after he had been indicted and in the absence of his counsel. It is true that in the *Spano* case the defendant was interrogated in a police station, while here the damaging testimony was elicited from the defendant without his knowledge while he was free on bail. But, as Judge Hays pointed out in his dissent in the Court of Appeals, "if such a rule is to have any efficacy it must apply to indirect and surreptitious interrogations as well as those conducted in the jailhouse. In this case, Massiah was more seriously imposed upon . . . because he did not even know that he was under interrogation by a government agent."

[T]he Solicitor General, in his brief and oral argument, has strenuously contended that the federal law enforcement agents had the right, if not indeed the duty, to continue their investigation of the petitioner and his alleged criminal associates even though the petitioner had been indicted. He points out that the Government was continuing its investigation in order to uncover not only the source of narcotics found on the S. S. Santa Maria, but also their intended buyer. He says that the quantity of narcotics involved was such as to suggest that the petitioner was part of a large and well-organized ring, and indeed that the continuing investigation confirmed this suspicion, since it resulted in criminal charges against many defendants. Under these circumstances the Solicitor General concludes that the Government agents were completely "justified in making use of Colson's cooperation by having Colson continue his normal associations and by surveilling them."

We may accept and, at least for present purposes, completely approve all that this argument implies, Fourth Amendment problems to one side. We do not question that in this case, as in many cases, it was entirely proper to continue an investigation of the suspected criminal activities of the defendant and his alleged confederates, even though the defendant had already been indicted. All that we hold is that the defendant's own incriminating statements, obtained by federal agents under the circumstances here disclosed, could not constitutionally be used by the prosecution as evidence against him at his trial.

Reversed.

Justice WHITE, with whom Justice CLARK and Justice HARLAN join, dissenting.

The current incidence of serious violations of the law represents not only an appalling waste of the potentially happy and useful lives of those who engage in such conduct but also an overhanging, dangerous threat to those unidentified and innocent people who will be the victims of crime today and tomorrow. This is a festering problem for which no adequate cures have yet been devised. At the very least there is much room for discontent with remedial measures so far undertaken. And admittedly there remains much to be settled concerning the disposition to be made of those who violate the law.

But dissatisfaction with preventive programs aimed at eliminating crime and profound dispute about whether we should punish, deter, rehabilitate or cure cannot excuse concealing one of our most menacing problems until the millennium has arrived. In my view, a civilized society must maintain its ~~IMO~~ capacity to discover transgressions of the law and to identify those who flout it. This much is necessary even to know the scope of the problem, much less to formulate intelligent counter-measures. It will just not do to sweep these disagreeable matters under the rug or to pretend they are not there at all.

It is therefore a rather portentous occasion when a constitutional rule is established barring the use of evidence which is relevant, reliable and highly probative of the issue which the trial court has before it—whether the accused committed the act with which he is charged. Without the evidence, the quest for truth may be seriously impeded and in many cases the trial court, although aware of proof showing defendant's guilt, must nevertheless release him because the crucial evidence is deemed inadmissible. This result is entirely justified in some circumstances because exclusion serves other policies of over-riding importance, as where evidence seized in an illegal search is excluded, not because of the quality of the proof, but to secure meaningful enforcement of the Fourth Amendment. But this only emphasizes that the soundest of reasons is necessary to warrant the exclusion of evidence otherwise admissible and the creation of another area of privileged testimony. With all due deference, I am not at all convinced that the additional barriers to the pursuit of truth which the Court today erects rest on anything like the solid foundations which decisions of this gravity should require.

The importance of the matter should not be underestimated, for today's rule promises to have wide application well beyond the facts of this case. The reason given for the result here—the admissions were obtained in the absence of counsel—would seem equally pertinent to statements obtained at any time after the right to counsel attaches, whether there has been an indict-ment or not; to admissions made prior to arraignment, at least where the defendant has counsel or asks for it; to the fruits of admissions improperly obtained under the new rule; to criminal proceedings in state courts; and to defendants long since convicted upon evidence including such admissions. The new rule will immediately do service in a great many cases.

Whatever the content or scope of the rule may prove to be, I am unable to see how this case presents an unconstitutional interference with Massiah's right to counsel. Massiah was not prevented from consulting with counsel as often as he wished. No meetings with counsel were disturbed or spied upon. Preparation for trial was in no way obstructed. It is only a sterile syllogism—an unsound one, besides—to say that because Massiah had a right to counsel's aid before and during the trial, his out-of-court conversations and admissions must be excluded if obtained without counsel's consent or presence.

■ ■ ■

Since the new rule would exclude all admissions made to the police, no matter how voluntary and reliable, the requirement of counsel's presence or approval would seem to rest upon the probability that counsel would foreclose any admissions at all. This is nothing more than a thinly disguised constitutional policy of minimizing or entirely prohibiting the use in evidence of voluntary out-of-court admissions and confessions made by the accused. Carried as far as blind logic may compel some to go, the notion that statements from the mouth of the defendant should not be used in evidence would have a severe and unfortunate impact upon the great bulk of criminal cases.

Viewed in this light, the Court's newly fashioned exclusionary principle goes far beyond the constitutional privilege against self-incrimination, which neither requires nor suggests the barring of voluntary pretrial admissions. The Fifth Amendment states that no person "shall be compelled in any criminal case to be a witness against himself. . . ." The defendant may thus not be compelled to testify at his trial, but he may if he wishes. Likewise he may not be compelled or coerced into saying anything before trial; but until today he could if he wished to, and if he did, it could be used against him. Whether as a matter of self-incrimination or of due process, the proscription is against compulsion-coerced incrimination. Under the prior law, announced in countless cases in this Court, the defendant's pretrial statements were admissible evidence if voluntarily made, inadmissible if not the product of his free will.

■ ■ ■

The Court presents no facts, no objective evidence, no reasons to warrant scrapping the voluntary-involuntary test for admissibility in this area. Without such evidence I would retain it in its present form.

■ ■ ■

This is a wiser rule than the automatic rule announced by the Court, which requires courts and juries to disregard voluntary admissions which they might well find to be the best possible evidence in discharging their responsibility for ascertaining truth.

Escobedo v. Illinois

378 U.S. 478 (1964)

GOLDBERG, J., delivered the opinion of the Court, in which WARREN, C.J., BLACK, DOUGLAS, and BRENNAN, JJ., joined. HARLAN, STEWART, and WHITE, JJ., dissented.

The critical question in this case is whether, under the circumstances, the refusal by the police to honor petitioner's request to consult with his lawyer during the course of an interrogation constitutes a denial of "the Assistance of Counsel" in violation of the Sixth Amendment to the Constitution as "made obligatory upon the States by the Fourteenth Amendment," *Gideon v. Wainwright* (1963), and thereby renders inadmissible in a state criminal trial any incriminating statement elicited by the police during the interrogation.

On the night of January 19, 1960, petitioner's brother-in-law was fatally shot. In the early hours of the next morning, at 2:30 a.m., petitioner was arrested without a warrant and interrogated. Petitioner made no statement to the police and was released at 5 that afternoon pursuant to a state court writ of habeas corpus obtained by Mr. Warren Wolfson, a lawyer who had been retained by petitioner.

On January 30, Benedict DiGerlando, who was then in police custody and who was later indicted for the murder along with petitioner, told the police that petitioner had fired the fatal shots. Between 8 and 9 that evening, petitioner and his sister, the widow of the deceased, were arrested and taken to police headquarters. En route to the police station, the police "had handcuffed the defendant behind his back," and "one of the arresting officers told defendant that DiGerlando had named him as the one who shot" the deceased. Petitioner testified, without contradiction, that the "detective said they had us pretty well, up pretty tight, and we might as well admit to this crime," and that he replied, "I am sorry but I would like to have advice from my lawyer." A police officer testified that although petitioner was not formally charged "he was in custody" and "couldn't walk out the door."

Shortly after petitioner reached police headquarters, his retained lawyer arrived. The lawyer described the ensuing events in the following terms:

> "On that day I received a phone call [from 'the mother of another defendant'] and pursuant to that phone call I went to the Detective Bureau at 11th and State. The first person I talked to was the Sergeant on duty at the Bureau Desk, Sergeant Pidgeon. I asked Sergeant Pidgeon for permission to speak to my client, Danny Escobedo.... Sergeant Pidgeon made a call to the Bureau lockup and informed me that the boy had been taken from the lockup to the Homicide Bureau. This was between 9:30 and 10:00 in the evening. Before I went anywhere, he called the Homicide Bureau and told them there was an attorney waiting to see Escobedo. He told me I could not see him. Then I went upstairs to the Homicide Bureau. There were several Homicide Detectives around and I talked to them. I identified myself as Escobedo's attorney and asked permission to see him. They said I could not.... The police officer told me to see Chief Flynn who was on duty. I identified myself to Chief Flynn and asked permission to see my client. He said I could not.... I think it was approximately 11:00 o'clock. He said I couldn't see him because they hadn't completed questioning.... [F]or a second or two I spotted him in an office in the Homicide Bureau. The door was open and I could see through the office.... I waved to him and he waved back and then the door was closed, by one of the officers at Homicide. There were four or five officers milling around the Homicide Detail that night. As to whether I talked to Captain Flynn any later that day, I waited around for another hour or two and went back again and renewed by [sic] request to see my client. He again told me I could not.... I filed an official complaint with Commissioner Phelan of the Chicago Police Department. I had a conversation with every police officer I could find. I was told at Homicide that I couldn't see him and I would have to get a writ of habeas corpus. I left the Homicide Bureau and from the Detective Bureau at 11th and State at

approximately 1:00 a.m. (Sunday morning) I had no opportunity to talk to my client that night. I quoted to Captain Flynn the Section of the Criminal Code which allows an attorney the right to see his client."

Petitioner testified that during the course of the interrogation he repeatedly asked to speak to his lawyer and that the police said that his lawyer "didn't want to see" him. The testimony of the police officers confirmed these accounts in substantial detail.

Notwithstanding repeated requests by each, petitioner and his retained lawyer were afforded no opportunity to consult during the course of the entire interrogation. At one point, as previously noted, petitioner and his attorney came into each other's view for a few moments but the attorney was quickly ushered away. Petitioner testified "that he heard a detective telling the attorney the latter would not be allowed to talk to [him] 'until they were done'" and that he heard the attorney being refused permission to remain in the adjoining room. A police officer testified that he had told the lawyer that he could not see petitioner until "we were through interrogating" him.

There is testimony by the police that during the interrogation, petitioner, a 22-year-old of Mexican extraction with no record of previous experience with the police, "was handcuffed" in a standing position and that he "was nervous, he had circles under his eyes and he was upset" and was "agitated" because "he had not slept well in over a week."

It is undisputed that during the course of the interrogation Officer Montejano, who "grew up" in petitioner's neighborhood, who knew his family, and who uses "Spanish language in [his] police work," conferred alone with petitioner "for about a quarter of an hour...." Petitioner testified that the officer said to him "in Spanish that my sister and I could go home if I pinned it on Benedict DiGerlando," that "he would see to it that we would go home and be held only as witnesses, if anything, if we had made a statement against DiGerlando,...that we would be able to go home that night." Petitioner testified that he made the statement in issue because of this assurance. Officer Montejano denied offering any such assurance.

A police officer testified that during the interrogation the following occurred:

> "I informed him of what DiGerlando told me and when I did, he told me that DiGerlando was [lying] and I said, 'Would you care to tell DiGerlando that?' and he said, 'Yes, I will.' So, I brought...Escobedo in and he confronted DiGerlando and he told him that he was lying and said, 'I didn't shoot Manuel, you did it.'"

In this way, petitioner, for the first time admitted to some knowledge of the crime. After that he made additional statements further implicating himself in the murder plot. At this point an Assistant State's Attorney, Theodore J. Cooper, was summoned "to take" a statement. Mr. Cooper, an experienced lawyer who was assigned to the Homicide Division to take "statements from some defendants and some prisoners that they had in custody," "took" petitioner's statement by asking carefully framed questions apparently designed to assure the admissibility into evidence of the resulting answers. Mr. Cooper testified that he did not advise petitioner of his constitutional rights, and it is undisputed that no one during the course of the interrogation so advised him.

Petitioner moved both before and during trial to suppress the incriminating statement, but the motions were denied. Petitioner was convicted of murder and he appealed the conviction.

■ ■ ■

In *Massiah v. United States* (1964), this Court observed that "a Constitution which guarantees a defendant the aid of counsel at . . . trial could surely vouchsafe no less to an indicted defendant under interrogation by the police in a completely extrajudicial proceeding. Anything less . . . might deny a defendant 'effective representation by counsel at the only stage when legal aid and advice would help him.'"

The interrogation here was conducted before petitioner was formally indicted. But in the context of this case, that fact should make no difference. When petitioner requested, and was denied, an opportunity to consult with his lawyer, the investigation had ceased to be a general investigation of "an unsolved crime." *Spano v. New York* (1959). Petitioner had become the accused, and the purpose of the interrogation was to "get him" to confess his guilt despite his constitutional right not to do so. At the time of his arrest and throughout the course of the interrogation, the police told petitioner that they had convincing evidence that he had fired the fatal shots. Without informing him of his absolute right to remain silent in the face of this accusation, the police urged him to make a statement. As this Court observed many years ago:

> "It cannot be doubted that, placed in the position in which the accused was when the statement was made to him that the other suspected person had charged him with crime, the result was to produce upon his mind the fear that, if he remained silent, it would be considered an admission of guilt, and therefore render certain his being committed for trial as the guilty person, and it cannot be conceived that the converse impression would not also have naturally arisen that, by denying, there was hope of removing the suspicion from himself." *Bram v. United States* (1887).

■ ■ ■

In *Gideon v. Wainwright* (1963), we held that every person accused of a crime, whether state or federal, is entitled to a lawyer at trial. The rule sought by the State here, however, would make the trial no more than an appeal from the interrogation; and the "right to use counsel at the formal trial [would be] a very hollow thing [if], for all practical purposes, the conviction is already assured by pretrial examination." In re *Groban* [(1957)] (Black, J., dissenting). 'One can imagine a cynical prosecutor saying: "Let them have the most illustrious counsel, now. They can't escape the noose. There is nothing that counsel can do for them at the trial."' Ex Parte *Sullivan* ([1952]).

It is argued that if the right to counsel is afforded prior to indictment, the number of confessions obtained by the police will diminish significantly, because most confessions are obtained during the period between arrest and indictment, and "any lawyer worth his salt will tell the suspect in no uncertain terms to make no statement to police under any circumstances." This argument, of course, cuts two ways. The fact that many confessions are obtained during this period points up its critical nature as a "stage when legal aid and advice" are surely needed. The right to counsel would indeed be hollow if it began at a period when few confessions were obtained. There is necessarily a direct relationship between the importance of a stage to the police in their quest for a confession and the criticalness of that stage to the accused in his need for legal advice. Our Constitution, unlike some others, strikes the balance in favor of the right of the accused to be advised by his lawyer of his privilege against self-incrimination.

We have learned the lesson of history, ancient and modern, that a system of criminal law enforcement, which comes to depend on the "confession" will, in the long run, be less reliable and more subject to abuses than a system which depends on extrinsic evidence independently secured through skillful investigation. As Dean Wigmore so wisely said:

> "[A]ny system of administration which permits the prosecution to trust habitually to compulsory self-disclosure as a source of proof must itself suffer morally thereby. The inclination develops to rely mainly upon such evidence, and to be satisfied with an incomplete investigation of the other sources. The exercise of the power to extract answers begets a forgetfulness of the just limitations of that power. The simple and peaceful process of questioning breeds a readiness to resort to bullying and to physical force and torture. If there is a right to an answer, there soon seems to be a right to the expected answer—that is, to a confession of guilt. Thus the legitimate use grows into the unjust abuse; ultimately, the innocent are jeopardized by the encroachments of a bad system. Such seems to have been the course of experience in those legal systems where the privilege was not recognized." 8 Wigmore, Evidence (3d ed. 1940), 309. (Emphasis in original.)

■ ■ ■

We have also learned the companion lesson of history that no system of criminal justice can, or should, survive if it comes to depend for its continued effectiveness on the citizens' abdication through unawareness of their constitutional rights. No system worth preserving should have to fear that if an accused is permitted to consult with a lawyer, he will become aware of, and exercise, these rights. If the exercise of constitutional rights will thwart the effectiveness of a system of law enforcement, then there is something very wrong with that system.

We hold, therefore, that where, as here, the investigation is no longer a general inquiry into an unsolved crime but has begun to focus on a particular suspect, the suspect has been taken into police custody, the police carry out a process of interrogations that lends itself to eliciting incriminating statements, the suspect has requested and been denied an opportunity to consult with his lawyer, and the police have not effectively warned him of his absolute constitutional right to remain silent, the accused has been denied "The Assistance of Counsel" in violation of the Sixth Amendment to the Constitution as "made obligatory upon the States by the Fourteenth Amendment," *Gideon v. Wainwright*, and that no statement elicited by the police during the interrogation may be used against him at a criminal trial.

■ ■ ■

Nothing we have said today affects the powers of the police to investigate "an unsolved crime," by gathering information from witnesses and by other "proper investigative efforts." We hold only that when the process shifts from investigatory to accusatory—when its focus is on the accused and its purpose is to elicit a confession—our adversary system begins to operate, and, under the circumstances here, the accused must be permitted to consult with his lawyer.

The judgment of the Illinois Supreme Court is reversed and the case remanded for proceedings not inconsistent with this opinion.

Reversed and remanded.

C. MIRANDA

1. Miranda v. Arizona

Miranda v. Arizona

384 U.S. 436 (1966)

Warren, C.J., delivered the opinion of the Court, in which Black, Douglas, Brennan, and Fortas, JJ., joined. Clark, J., dissented in part. Harlan, J., wrote a dissenting opinion, in which Stewart and White, JJ., joined. White, J., wrote a dissenting opinion, in which Harlan and Stewart, JJ., joined.

The cases before us raise questions which go to the roots of our concepts of American criminal jurisprudence: the restraints society must observe consistent with the Federal Constitution in prosecuting individuals for crime. More specifically, we deal with the admissibility of statements obtained from an individual who is subjected to custodial police interrogation and the necessity for procedures which assure that the individual is accorded his privilege under the Fifth Amendment to the Constitution not to be compelled to incriminate himself.

We dealt with certain phases of this problem recently in *Escobedo v. State of Illinois* (1964). There, as in the four cases before us, law enforcement officials took the defendant into custody and interrogated him in a police station for the purpose of obtaining a confession. The police did not effectively advise him of his right to remain silent or of his right to consult with his attorney. Rather, they confronted him with an alleged accomplice who accused him of having perpetrated a murder. When the defendant denied the accusation and said "I didn't shoot Manuel, you did it," they handcuffed him and took him to an interrogation room. There, while handcuffed and standing, he was questioned for four hours until he confessed. During this interrogation, the police denied his request to speak to his attorney, and they prevented his retained attorney, who had come to the police station, from consulting with him. At his trial, the State, over his objection, introduced the confession against him. We held that the statements thus made were constitutionally inadmissible.

This case has been the subject of judicial interpretation and spirited legal debate since it was decided two years ago. Both state and federal courts, in assessing its implications, have arrived at varying conclusions. A wealth of scholarly material has been written tracing its ramifications and underpinnings. Police and prosecutor have speculated on its range and desirability. We granted certiorari in these cases in order further to explore some facets of the problems, thus exposed, of applying the privilege against self-incrimination to in-custody interrogation, and to give concrete constitutional guidelines for law enforcement agencies and courts to follow.

■ ■ ■

We start here, as we did in *Escobedo*, with the premise that our holding is not an innovation in our jurisprudence, but is an application of principles long recognized and applied in other settings. We have undertaken a thorough re-examination of the *Escobedo* decision and the principles it announced, and we reaffirm it. That case was but an explication of basic rights that are enshrined in our Constitution—that "No person shall be compelled in any criminal case to be a witness against himself," and that "the accused shall have the Assistance of Counsel"—rights which were put in jeopardy in that case through official overbearing. These precious rights were fixed in our Constitution only after centuries of persecution and struggle.

■ ■ ■

Over 70 years ago, our predecessors on this Court eloquently stated:

"The maxim 'Nemo tenetur seipsum accusare,' had its origin in a protest against the inquisitorial and manifestly unjust methods of interrogating accused persons, which [have] long obtained in the continental system, and, until the expulsion of the Stuarts from the British throne in 1688, and the erection of additional barriers for the protection of the people against the exercise of arbitrary power, [were] not uncommon even in England. While the admissions or confessions of the prisoner, when voluntarily and freely made, have always ranked high in the scale of incriminating evidence, if an accused person be asked to explain his apparent connection with a crime under investigation, the ease with which the questions put to him may assume an inquisitorial character, the temptation to press the witness unduly, to browbeat him if he be timid or reluctant, to push him into a corner, and to entrap him into fatal contradictions, which is so painfully evident in many of the earlier state trials, notably in those of Sir Nicholas Throckmorton, and Udal, the Puritan minister, made the system so odious as to give rise to a demand for its total abolition. The change in the English criminal procedure in that particular seems to be founded upon no statute and no judicial opinion, but upon a general and silent acquiescence of the courts in a popular demand. But, however adopted, it has become firmly embedded in English, as well as in American jurisprudence. . . ." *Brown v. Walker* (1896).

Our holding will be spelled out with some specificity in the pages which follow but briefly stated it is this: the prosecution may not use statements, whether exculpatory or inculpatory, stemming from custodial interrogation of the defendant unless it demonstrates the use of procedural safeguards effective to secure the privilege against self-incrimination. By custodial interrogation, we mean questioning initiated by law enforcement officers after a person has been taken into custody or otherwise deprived of his freedom of action in any significant way. As for the procedural safeguards to be employed, unless other fully effective means are devised to inform accused persons of their right of silence and to assure a continuous opportunity to exercise it, the following measures are required. Prior to any questioning, the person must be warned that he has a right to remain silent, that any statement he does make may be used as evidence against him, and that he has a right to the presence of an attorney, either retained or appointed. The defendant may waive effectuation of these rights, provided the waiver is made voluntarily, knowingly and intelligently. If, however, he indicates in any manner and at any stage of the process that he wishes to consult with an attorney before speaking there can be no questioning. Likewise, if the individual is alone and indicates in any manner that he does not wish to be interrogated, the police may not question him. The mere fact that he may have answered some questions or volunteered some statements on his own does not deprive him of the right to refrain from answering any further inquiries until he has consulted with an attorney and thereafter consents to be questioned.

■ ■ ■

The constitutional issue we decide in each of these cases is the admissibility of statements obtained from a defendant questioned while in custody or otherwise deprived of his freedom of action in any significant way. In each, the defendant was questioned by police officers, detectives, or a prosecuting attorney in a room in which he was cut off from the outside world. In none of these cases was the defendant given a full and effective warning of his rights at the outset of the interrogation process. In all the cases, the questioning elicited oral admissions, and in three of them, signed statements as well which were admitted at their trials. They all thus share salient features—incommunicado interrogation of individuals in a police-dominated atmosphere, resulting in self-incriminating statements without full warnings of constitutional rights.

An understanding of the nature and setting of this in-custody interrogation is essential to our decisions today. The difficulty in depicting what transpires at such interrogations stems from the fact that in this country they have largely taken place incommunicado. From extensive factual studies undertaken in the early 1930's, including the famous Wickersham Report to Congress by a Presidential Commission, it is clear that police violence and the "third degree" flourished at that time. In a series of cases decided by this Court long after these studies, the police resorted to physical brutality—beatings, hanging, whipping—and to sustained and protracted questioning incommunicado in order to extort confessions. The Commission on Civil Rights in 1961 found much evidence to indicate that "some policemen still resort to physical force to obtain confessions." The use of physical brutality and violence is not, unfortunately, relegated to the past or to any part of the country. Only recently in Kings County, New York, the police brutally beat, kicked and placed lighted cigarette butts on the back of a potential witness under interrogation for the purpose of securing a statement incriminating a third party.

The examples given above are undoubtedly the exception now, but they are sufficiently widespread to be the object of concern. Unless a proper limitation upon custodial interrogation is achieved—such as these decisions will advance—there can be no assurance that practices of this nature will be eradicated in the foreseeable future.

■ ■ ■

Again we stress that the modern practice of in-custody interrogation is psychologically rather than physically oriented. As we have stated before, ". . . [T]his Court has recognized that coercion can be mental as well as physical, and that the blood of the accused is not the only hallmark of an unconstitutional inquisition." *Blackburn v. Alabama* (1960). Interrogation still takes place in privacy. Privacy results in secrecy and this in turn results in a gap in our knowledge as to what in fact goes on in the interrogation rooms. A valuable source of information about present police practices, however, may be found in various police manuals and texts which document procedures employed with success in the past, and which recommend various other effective tactics. These texts are used by law enforcement agencies themselves as guides. It should be noted that these texts professedly present the most enlightened and effective means presently used to obtain statements through custodial interrogation. By considering these texts and other data, it is possible to describe procedures observed and noted around the country.

The officers are told by the manuals that the "principal psychological factor contributing to a successful interrogation is privacy—being alone with the person under interrogation." The efficacy of this tactic has been explained as follows:

> "If at all practicable, the interrogation should take place in the investigator's office or at least in a room of his own choice. The subject should be deprived of every psychological advantage. In his own home he may be confident, indignant, or recalcitrant. He is more keenly aware of his rights and more reluctant to tell of his indiscretions of criminal behavior within the walls of

his home. Moreover his family and other friends are nearby, their presence lending moral support. In his office, the investigator possesses all the advantages. The atmosphere suggests the invincibility of the forces of the law." [O'Hara, Fundamentals of Criminal Investigation (1956).]

To highlight the isolation and unfamiliar surroundings, the manuals instruct the police to display an air of confidence in the suspect's guilt and from outward appearance to maintain only an interest in confirming certain details. The guilt of the subject is to be posited as a fact. The interrogator should direct his comments toward the reasons why the subject committed the act, rather than court failure by asking the subject whether he did it. Like other men, perhaps the subject has had a bad family life, had an unhappy childhood, had too much to drink, had an unrequited desire for women. The officers are instructed to minimize the moral seriousness of the offense, to cast blame on the victim or on society. These tactics are designed to put the subject in a psychological state where his story is but an elaboration of what the police purport to know already—that he is guilty. Explanations to the contrary are dismissed and discouraged.

The texts thus stress that the major qualities an interrogator should possess are patience and perseverance. One writer describes the efficacy of these characteristics in this manner:

> "In the preceding paragraphs emphasis has been placed on kindness and stratagems. The investigator will, however, encounter many situations where the sheer weight of his personality will be the deciding factor. Where emotional appeals and tricks are employed to no avail, he must rely on an oppressive atmosphere of dogged persistence. He must interrogate steadily and without relent, leaving the subject no prospect of surcease. He must dominate his subject and overwhelm him with his inexorable will to obtain the truth. He should interrogate for a spell of several hours pausing only for the subject's necessities in acknowledgment of the need to avoid a charge of duress that can be technically substantiated. In a serious case, the interrogation may continue for days, with the required intervals for food and sleep, but with no respite from the atmosphere of domination. It is possible in this way to induce the subject to talk without resorting to duress or coercion. The method should be used only when the guilt of the subject appears highly probable." O'Hara.

The manuals suggest that the suspect be offered legal excuses for his actions in order to obtain an initial admission of guilt. Where there is a suspected revenge-killing, for example, the interrogator may say:

> "Joe, you probably didn't go out looking for this fellow with the purpose of shooting him. My guess is, however, that you expected something from him and that's why you carried a gun—for your own protection. You knew him for what he was, no good. Then when you met him he probably started using foul, abusive language and he gave some indication that he was about to pull a gun on you, and that's when you had to act to save your own life. That's about it, isn't it, Joe?"

Having then obtained the admission of shooting, the interrogator is advised to refer to circumstantial evidence which negates the self-defense explanation. This should enable him to secure the entire story. One text notes that "Even if he fails to do so, the inconsistency between the subject's original denial of the shooting and his present admission of at least doing the shooting will serve to deprive him of a self-defense 'out' at the time of trial."

When the techniques described above prove unavailing, the texts recommend they be alternated with a show of some hostility. One ploy often used has been termed the "friendly-unfriendly" or the "Mutt and Jeff" act:

> "In this technique, two agents are employed. Mutt, the relentless investigator, who knows the subject is guilty and is not going to waste any time. He's sent a dozen men away for this crime and he's going to send the subject away for the full term. Jeff, on the other hand, is obviously a kindhearted man. He has a family himself. He has a brother who was involved in a little scrape like this. He disapproves of Mutt and his tactics and will arrange to get him off the case if the subject will cooperate. He can't hold Mutt off for very long. The subject would be wise to make a quick decision. The technique is applied by having both investigators present while Mutt acts out his role. Jeff may stand by quietly and demur at some of Mutt's tactics. When Jeff makes his plea for cooperation, Mutt is not present in the room."

The interrogators sometimes are instructed to induce a confession out of trickery. The technique here is quite effective in crimes which require identification or which run in series. In the identification situation, the interrogator may take a break in his questioning to place the subject among a group of men in a line-up. "The witness or complainant (previously coached, if necessary) studies the line-up and confidently points out the subject as the guilty party." Then the questioning resumes "as though there were now no doubt about the guilt of the subject." A variation on this technique is called the "reverse line-up":

> "The accused is placed in a line-up, but this time he is identified by several fictitious witnesses or victims who associated him with different offenses. It is expected that the subject will become desperate and confess to the offense under investigation in order to escape from the false accusations."

The manuals also contain instructions for police on how to handle the individual who refuses to discuss the matter entirely, or who asks for an attorney or relatives. The examiner is to concede him the right to remain silent. "This usually has a very undermining effect. First of all, he is disappointed in his expectation of an unfavorable reaction on the part of the interrogator. Secondly, a concession of this right to remain silent impresses the subject with the apparent fairness of his interrogator." After this psychological conditioning, however, the officer is told to point out the incriminating significance of the suspect's refusal to talk:

> "Joe, you have a right to remain silent. That's your privilege and I'm the last person in the world who'll try to take it away from you. If that's the way you

want to leave this, O.K. But let me ask you this. Suppose you were in my shoes and I were in yours and you called me in to ask me about this and I told you, 'I don't want to answer any of your questions.' You'd think I had something to hide, and you'd probably be right in thinking that. That's exactly what I'll have to think about you, and so will everybody else. So let's sit here and talk this whole thing over."

Few will persist in their initial refusal to talk, it is said, if this monologue is employed correctly.

In the event that the subject wishes to speak to a relative or an attorney, the following advice is tendered:

"[T]he interrogator should respond by suggesting that the subject first tell the truth to the interrogator himself rather than get anyone else involved in the matter. If the request is for an attorney, the interrogator may suggest that the subject save himself or his family the expense of any such professional service, particularly if he is innocent of the offense under investigation. The interrogator may also add, 'Joe, I'm only looking for the truth, and if you're telling the truth, that's it. You can handle this by yourself.' "

From these representative samples of interrogation techniques, the setting prescribed by the manuals and observed in practice becomes clear. In essence, it is this: To be alone with the subject is essential to prevent distraction and to deprive him of any outside support. The aura of confidence in his guilt undermines his will to resist. He merely confirms the preconceived story the police seek to have him describe. Patience and persistence, at times relentless questioning, are employed. To obtain a confession, the interrogator must "patiently maneuver himself or his quarry into a position from which the desired objective may be attained." When normal procedures fail to produce the needed result, the police may resort to deceptive stratagems such as giving false legal advice. It is important to keep the subject off balance, for example, by trading on his insecurity about himself or his surroundings. The police then persuade, trick, or cajole him out of exercising his constitutional rights.

Even without employing brutality, the "third degree" or the specific stratagems described above, the very fact of custodial interrogation exacts a heavy toll on individual liberty and trades on the weakness of individuals.

■ ■ ■

In the cases before us today, given this background, we concern ourselves primarily with this interrogation atmosphere and the evils it can bring. In No. 759, *Miranda v. Arizona*, the police arrested the defendant and took him to a special interrogation room where they secured a confession. In No. 760, *Vignera v. New York*, the defendant made oral admissions to the police after interrogation in the afternoon, and then signed an inculpatory statement upon being questioned by an assistant district attorney later the same evening. In No. 761, *Westover v. United States*, the defendant was handed over to the Federal Bureau of Investigation by local authorities after they had detained and interrogated him for a lengthy period, both at night and the following morning. After some two hours of questioning, the federal officers had obtained signed statements from the defendant. Lastly, in No. 584, *California v. Stewart*, the local police held the defendant five days in the station and interrogated him on nine separate occasions before they secured his inculpatory statement.

In these cases, we might not find the defendants' statements to have been involuntary in traditional terms. Our concern for adequate safeguards to protect precious Fifth Amendment rights is, of course, not lessened in the slightest. In each of the cases, the defendant was thrust into an unfamiliar atmosphere and run through menacing police interrogation procedures. The potentiality for compulsion is forcefully apparent, for example, in *Miranda*, where the indigent Mexican defendant was a seriously disturbed individual with pronounced sexual fantasies, and in *Stewart*, in which the defendant was an indigent Los Angeles Negro who had dropped out of school in the sixth grade. To be sure, the records do not evince overt physical coercion or patent psychological ploys. The fact remains that in none of these cases did the officers undertake to afford appropriate safeguards at the outset of the interrogation to insure that the statements were truly the product of free choice.

It is obvious that such an interrogation environment is created for no purpose other than to subjugate the individual to the will of his examiner. This atmosphere carries its own badge of intimidation. To be sure, this is not physical intimidation, but it is equally destructive of human dignity. The current practice of incommunicado interrogation is at odds with one of our Nation's most cherished principles—that the individual may not be compelled to incriminate himself. Unless adequate protective devices are employed to dispel the compulsion inherent in custodial surroundings, no statement obtained from the defendant can truly be the product of his free choice.

From the foregoing, we can readily perceive an intimate connection between the privilege against self-incrimination and police custodial questioning. It is fitting to turn to history and precedent underlying the Self-Incrimination Clause to determine its applicability in this situation.

■ ■ ■

The question in these cases is whether the privilege is fully applicable during a period of custodial interrogation. In this Court, the privilege has consistently been accorded a liberal construction. We are satisfied that all the principles embodied in the privilege apply to informal compulsion exerted by law-enforcement officers during in-custody questioning. An individual swept from familiar surroundings into police custody, surrounded by antagonistic forces, and subjected to the techniques of persuasion described above cannot be otherwise than under compulsion to speak. As a practical matter, the compulsion to speak in the isolated setting of the police station may well be greater than in courts or other official investigations, where there are often impartial observers to guard against intimidation or trickery.

■ ■ ■

Today, then, there can be no doubt that the Fifth Amendment privilege is available outside of criminal court proceedings and serves to protect persons in all settings in which their freedom of action is curtailed in any significant way from being compelled to incriminate themselves. We have concluded that without proper safeguards the process of in-custody interrogation of persons suspected or accused of crime contains inherently compelling pressures which work to undermine the individual's will to resist and to compel him to speak where he would not otherwise do so freely. In order to combat these pressures and to permit a full opportunity to exercise the privilege against self-incrimination, the accused must be adequately and effectively apprised of his rights and the exercise of those rights must be fully honored.

It is impossible for us to foresee the potential alternatives for protecting the privilege which might be devised by Congress or the States in the exercise of their creative rule-making capacities. Therefore we cannot say that the Constitution necessarily requires adherence to any particular solution for the inherent compulsions of the interrogation process as it is presently conducted. Our decision in no way creates a constitutional straitjacket which will handicap sound efforts at reform, nor is it intended to have this effect. We encourage Congress and the States to continue their laudable search for increasingly effective ways of protecting the rights of the individual while promoting efficient enforcement of our criminal laws. However, unless we are shown other procedures which are at least as effective in apprising accused persons of their right of silence and in assuring a continuous opportunity to exercise it, the following safeguards must be observed.

At the outset, if a person in custody is to be subjected to interrogation, he must first be informed in clear and unequivocal terms that he has the right to remain silent. For those unaware of the privilege, the warning is needed simply to make them aware of it—the threshold requirement for an intelligent decision as to its exercise. More important, such a warning is an absolute prerequisite in overcoming the inherent pressures of the interrogation atmosphere. It is not just the subnormal or woefully ignorant who succumb to an interrogator's imprecations, whether implied or expressly stated, that the interrogation will continue until a confession is obtained or that silence in the face of accusation is itself damning and will bode ill when presented to a jury. Further, the warning will show the individual that his interrogators are prepared to recognize his privilege should he choose to exercise it.

The Fifth Amendment privilege is so fundamental to our system of constitutional rule and the expedient of giving an adequate warning as to the availability of the privilege so simple, we will not pause to inquire in individual cases whether the defendant was aware of his rights without a warning being given. Assessments of the knowledge the defendant possessed, based on information as to his age, education, intelligence, or prior contact with authorities, can never be more than speculation; a warning is a clear-cut fact. More important, whatever the background of the person interrogated, a warning at the time of the interrogation is indispensable to overcome its pressures and to insure that the individual knows he is free to exercise the privilege at that point in time.

The warning of the right to remain silent must be accompanied by the explanation that anything said can and will be used against the individual in court. This warning is needed in order to make him aware not only of the privilege, but also of the consequences of forgoing it. It is only through an awareness of these consequences that there can be any assurance of real understanding and intelligent exercise of the privilege. Moreover, this warning may serve to make the individual more acutely aware that he is faced with a phase of the adversary system—that he is not in the presence of persons acting solely in his interest.

The circumstances surrounding in-custody interrogation can operate very quickly to overbear the will of one merely made aware of his privilege by his interrogators. Therefore, the right to have counsel present at the interrogation is indispensable to the protection of the Fifth Amendment privilege under the system we delineate today. Our aim is to assure that the individual's right to choose between silence and speech remains unfettered throughout the interrogation process. A once-stated warning, delivered by those who will conduct the interrogation, cannot itself suffice to that end among those who most require knowledge of their rights. A mere warning given by the interrogators is not alone sufficient to accomplish that end. Prosecutors themselves claim that the admonishment of the right to remain silent without more "will benefit only the recidivist and the professional." Even preliminary advice given to the accused by his own attorney can be swiftly overcome by the secret interrogation process. Thus, the need for counsel to protect the Fifth Amendment privilege comprehends not merely a right to consult with counsel prior to questioning, but also to have counsel present during any questioning if the defendant so desires.

The presence of counsel at the interrogation may serve several significant subsidiary functions as well. If the accused decides to talk to his interrogators, the assistance of counsel can mitigate the dangers of untrustworthiness. With a lawyer present the likelihood that the police will practice coercion is reduced, and if coercion is nevertheless exercised the lawyer can testify to it in court. The presence of a lawyer can also help to guarantee that the accused gives a fully accurate statement to the police and that the statement is rightly reported by the prosecution at trial.

An individual need not make a pre-interrogation request for a lawyer. While such request affirmatively secures his right to have one, his failure to ask for a lawyer does not constitute a waiver. No effective waiver of the right to counsel during interrogation can be recognized unless specifically made after the warnings we here delineate have been given. The accused who does not know his rights and therefore does not make a request may be the person who most needs counsel.

■ ■ ■

right to counsel

Accordingly we hold that an individual held for interrogation must be clearly informed that he has the right to consult with a lawyer and to have the lawyer with him during interrogation under the system for protecting the privilege we delineate today. As with the warnings of the right to remain silent and that anything stated can be used in evidence against him, this warning is an absolute prerequisite to interrogation. No amount of circumstantial evidence that the person may have been aware of this right will suffice to stand in its stead. Only through such a warning is there ascertainable assurance that the accused was aware of this right.

If an individual indicates that he wishes the assistance of counsel before any interrogation occurs, the authorities cannot rationally ignore or deny his request on the basis that the individual does not have or cannot afford a retained attorney. The financial ability of the individual has no relationship to the scope of the rights involved here. The privilege against self-incrimination secured by the Constitution applies to all individuals. The need for counsel in order to protect the privilege exists for the indigent as well as the affluent. In fact, were we to limit these constitutional rights to those who can retain an attorney, our decisions today would be of little significance. The cases before us as well as the vast majority of confession cases with which we have dealt in the past involve those unable to retain counsel. While authorities are not required to relieve the accused of his poverty, they have the obligation not to take advantage of indigence in the administration of justice. Denial of counsel to the indigent at the time of interrogation while allowing an attorney to those who can afford one would be no more supportable by reason or logic than the similar situation at trial and on appeal struck down in *Gideon v. Wainwright* (1963), and *Douglas v. People of State of California* (1963).

In order fully to apprise a person interrogated of the extent of his rights under this system then, it is necessary to warn him not only that he has the right to consult with an attorney, but also that if he is indigent a lawyer will be appointed to represent him. Without this additional warning, the admonition of the right to consult with counsel would often be understood as meaning only that he can consult with a lawyer if he has one or has the funds to obtain one. The warning of a right to counsel would be hollow if not couched in terms that would convey to the indigent—the person most often subjected to interrogation—the knowledge that he too has a right to have counsel present. As with the warnings of the right to remain silent and of the general right to counsel, only by effective and express explanation to the indigent of this right can there be assurance that he was truly in a position to exercise it.

Once warnings have been given, the subsequent procedure is clear. If the individual indicates in any manner, at any time prior to or during questioning, that he wishes to remain silent, the interrogation must cease. At this point he has shown that he intends to exercise his Fifth Amendment privilege; any statement taken after the person invokes his privilege cannot be other than the product of compulsion, subtle or otherwise. Without the right to cut off questioning, the setting of in-custody interrogation operates on the individual to overcome free choice in producing a statement after the privilege has been once invoked. If the individual states that he wants an attorney, the interrogation must cease until an attorney is present. At that time, the individual must have an opportunity to confer with the attorney and to have him present during any subsequent questioning. If the individual cannot obtain an attorney and he indicates that he wants one before speaking to police, they must respect his decision to remain silent.

This does not mean, as some have suggested, that each police station must have a "station house lawyer" present at all times to advise prisoners. It does mean, however, that if police propose to interrogate a person they must make known to him that he is entitled to a lawyer and that if he cannot afford one, a lawyer will be provided for him prior to any interrogation. If authorities conclude that they will not provide counsel during a reasonable period of time in which investigation in the field is carried out, they may refrain from doing so without violating the person's Fifth Amendment privilege so long as they do not question him during that time.

If the interrogation continues without the presence of an attorney and a statement is taken, a heavy burden rests on the government to demonstrate that the defendant knowingly and intelligently waived his privilege against self-incrimination and his right to retained or appointed counsel. *Escobedo v. State of Illinois.* This Court has always set high standards of proof for the waiver of constitutional rights, *Johnson v. Zerbst* (1938), and we reassert these standards as applied to in-custody interrogation. Since the State is responsible for establishing the isolated circumstances under which the interrogation takes place and has the only means of making available corroborated evidence of warnings given during incommunicado interrogation, the burden is rightly on its shoulders.

An express statement that the individual is willing to make a statement and does not want an attorney followed closely by a statement could constitute a waiver. But a valid waiver will not be presumed simply from the silence of the accused after warnings are given or simply from the fact that a confession was in fact eventually obtained.

■ ■ ■

Whatever the testimony of the authorities as to waiver of rights by an accused, the fact of lengthy interrogation or incommunicado incarceration before a statement is made is strong evidence that the accused did not validly waive his rights. In these circumstances the fact that the individual eventually made a statement is consistent with the conclusion that the compelling influence of the interrogation finally forced him to do so. It is inconsistent with any notion of a voluntary relinquishment of the privilege. Moreover, any evidence that the accused was threatened, tricked, or cajoled into a waiver will, of course, show that the defendant did not voluntarily waive his privilege. The requirement of warnings and waiver of rights is a fundamental with respect to the Fifth Amendment privilege and not simply a preliminary ritual to existing methods of interrogation.

The warnings required and the waiver necessary in accordance with our opinion today are, in the absence of a fully effective equivalent, prerequisites to the admissibility of any statement made by a defendant. No distinction can be drawn between statements which are direct confessions and statements which amount to "admissions" of part or all of an offense. The privilege against self-incrimination protects the individual from being compelled to incriminate himself in any manner; it does not distinguish degrees of incrimination. Similarly, for precisely the same reason, no distinction may be drawn between inculpatory statements and statements alleged to be merely "exculpatory." If a statement made were in fact truly exculpatory it would, of course, never be used by the prosecution. In fact, statements merely intended to be exculpatory by the defendant are often used to impeach his testimony at trial or to demonstrate untruths in the statement given under interrogation and thus to prove guilt by implication. These statements are incriminating in any meaningful sense of the word and may not be used without the full warnings and effective waiver required for any other statement. In *Escobedo* itself, the defendant fully intended his accusation of another as the slayer to be exculpatory as to himself.

The principles announced today deal with the protection which must be given to the privilege against self-incrimination when the individual is first subjected to police interrogation while in custody at the station or otherwise deprived of his freedom of action in any significant way. It is at this point that our adversary system of criminal proceedings commences, distinguishing itself at the outset from the inquisitorial system recognized in some countries. Under the system of warnings we delineate today or under any other system which may be devised and found effective, the safeguards to be erected about the privilege must come into play at this point.

Our decision is not intended to hamper the traditional function of police officers in investigating crime. When an individual is in custody on probable cause, the police may, of course, seek out evidence in the field to be used at trial against him. Such investigation may include inquiry of persons not under restraint. General on-the-scene questioning as to facts surrounding a crime or other general questioning of citizens in the fact-finding process is not affected by our holding. It is an act of responsible citizenship for individuals to give whatever information they may have to aid in law enforcement. In such situations the compelling atmosphere inherent in the process of in-custody interrogation is not necessarily present.

In dealing with statements obtained through interrogation, we do not purport to find all confessions inadmissible. Confessions remain a proper element in law enforcement. Any statement given freely and voluntarily without any compelling influences is, of course, admissible in evidence. The fundamental import of the privilege while an individual is in custody is not whether he is allowed to talk to the police without the benefit of warnings and counsel, but whether he can be interrogated. There is no requirement that police stop a person who enters a police station and states that he wishes to confess to a crime, or a person who calls the police to offer a confession or any other statement he desires to make. Volunteered statements of any kind are not barred by the Fifth Amendment and their admissibility is not affected by our holding today.

To summarize, we hold that when an individual is taken into custody or otherwise deprived of his freedom by the authorities in any significant way and is subjected to questioning, the privilege against self-incrimination is jeopardized. Procedural safeguards must be employed to protect the privilege and unless other fully effective means are adopted to notify the person of his right of silence and to assure that the exercise of the right will be scrupulously honored, the following measures are required. He must be warned prior to any questioning that he has the right to remain silent, that anything he says can be used against him in a court of law, that he has the right to the presence of an attorney, and that if he cannot afford an attorney one will be appointed for him prior to any questioning if he so desires. Opportunity to exercise these rights must be afforded to him throughout the interrogation. After such warnings have been given, and such opportunity afforded him, the individual may knowingly and intelligently waive these rights and agree to answer questions or make a statement. But unless and until such warnings and waiver are demonstrated by the prosecution at trial, no evidence obtained as a result of interrogation can be used against him.

■ ■ ■

A recurrent argument made in these cases is that society's need for interrogation outweighs the privilege. This argument is not unfamiliar to this Court. The whole thrust of our foregoing discussion demonstrates that the Constitution has prescribed the rights of the individual when confronted with the power of government when it provided in the Fifth Amendment that an individual cannot be compelled to be a witness against himself. That right cannot be abridged. As Mr. Justice Brandeis once observed:

> "Decency, security, and liberty alike demand that government officials shall be subjected to the same rules of conduct that are commands to the citizen. In a government of laws, existence of the government will be imperilled if it fails to observe the law scrupulously. Our government is the potent, the omnipresent teacher. For good or for ill, it teaches the whole people by its example. Crime is contagious. If the government becomes a lawbreaker, it breeds contempt for law; it invites every man to become a law unto himself; it invites anarchy. To declare that in the administration of the criminal law the end justifies the means would bring terrible retribution. Against that pernicious doctrine this court should resolutely set its face." *Olmstead v. United States* (1928) (dissenting opinion).

■ ■ ■

In announcing these principles, we are not unmindful of the burdens which law enforcement officials must bear, often under trying circumstances. We also fully recognize the obligation of all citizens to aid in enforcing the criminal laws. This Court, while protecting individual rights, has always given ample latitude to law enforcement agencies in the legitimate exercise of their duties. The limits we have placed on the interrogation process should not constitute an undue interference with a proper system of law enforcement. As we have noted, our decision does not in any way preclude police from carrying out their traditional investigatory functions. Although confessions may play an important role in some convictions, the cases before us present graphic examples of the overstatement of the "need" for confessions. In each case authorities conducted interrogations ranging up to five days in duration despite the presence, through standard investigating practices, of considerable evidence against each defendant.

■ ■ ■

Over the years the Federal Bureau of Investigation has compiled an exemplary record of effective law enforcement while advising any suspect or arrested person, at the outset of an interview, that he is not required to make a statement, that any statement may be used against him in court, that the individual may obtain the services of an attorney of his own choice and, more recently, that he has a right to free counsel if he is unable to pay. A letter received from the Solicitor General in response to a question from the Bench makes it clear that the present pattern of warnings and respect for the rights of the individual followed as a practice by the FBI is consistent with the procedure which we delineate today.

■ ■ ■

The practice of the FBI can readily be emulated by state and local enforcement agencies. The argument that the FBI deals with different crimes than are dealt with by state authorities does not mitigate the significance of the FBI experience.

The experience in some other countries also suggests that the danger to law enforcement in curbs on interrogation is overplayed. The English procedure since 1912 under the Judges' Rules is significant. As recently strengthened, the Rules require that a cautionary warning be given an accused by a police officer as soon as he has evidence that affords reasonable grounds for suspicion; they also require that any statement made be given by the accused without questioning by police. The right of the individual to consult with an attorney during this period is expressly recognized.

The safeguards present under Scottish law may be even greater than in England. Scottish judicial decisions bar use in evidence of most confessions obtained through police interrogation. In India, confessions made to police not in the presence of a magistrate have been excluded by rule of evidence since 1872, at a time when it operated under British law. Identical provisions appear in the Evidence Ordinance of Ceylon, enacted in 1895. Similarly, in our country the Uniform Code of Military Justice has long provided that no suspect may be interrogated without first being warned of his right not to make a statement and that any statement he makes may be used against him. Denial of the right to consult counsel during interrogation has also been proscribed by military tribunals. There appears to have been no marked detrimental effect on criminal law enforcement in these jurisdictions as a result of these rules. Conditions of law enforcement in our country are sufficiently similar to permit reference to this experience as assurance that lawlessness will not result from warning an individual of his rights or allowing him to exercise them. Moreover, it is consistent with our legal system that we give at least as much protection to these rights as is given in the jurisdictions described. We deal in our country with rights grounded in a specific requirement of the Fifth Amendment of the Constitution, whereas other jurisdictions arrived at their conclusions on the basis of principles of justice not so specifically defined. . . .

Justice CLARK, dissenting.

It is with regret that I find it necessary to write in these cases. However, I am unable to join the majority because its opinion goes too far on too little, while my dissenting brethren do not go quite far enough. Nor can I join in the Court's criticism of the present practices of police and investigatory agencies as to custodial interrogation. The materials it refers to as "police manuals" are, as I read them, merely writings in this field by professors and some police officers. Not one is shown by the record here to be the official manual of any police department, much less in universal use in crime detection. Moreover the examples of police brutality mentioned by the Court are rare exceptions to the thousands of cases that appear every year in the law reports. The police agencies—all the way from municipal and state forces to the federal bureaus—are responsible for law enforcement and public safety in this country. I am proud of their efforts, which in my view are not fairly characterized by the Court's opinion.

■ ■ ■

I would continue to follow that rule. Under the "totality of circumstances" rule . . . I would consider in each case whether the police officer prior to custodial interrogation added the warning that the suspect might have counsel present at the interrogation and, further, that a court would appoint one at his request if he was too poor to employ counsel. In the absence of warnings, the burden would be on the State to prove that counsel was knowingly and intelligently waived or that in the totality of the circumstances, including the failure to give the necessary warnings, the confession was clearly voluntary.

Rather than employing the arbitrary Fifth Amendment rule which the Court lays down I would follow the more pliable dictates of the Due Process Clauses of the Fifth and Fourteenth Amendments which we are accustomed to administering and which we know from our cases are effective instruments in protecting persons in police custody. In this way we would not be acting in the dark nor in one full sweep changing the traditional rules of custodial interrogation which this Court has for so long recognized as a justifiable and proper tool in balancing individual rights against the rights of society. It will be soon enough to go further when we are able to appraise with somewhat better accuracy the effect of such a holding. . . .

Justice HARLAN, whom Justice STEWART and Justice WHITE join, dissenting.

I believe the decision of the Court represents poor constitutional law and entails harmful consequences for the country at large. How serious these consequences may prove to be only time can tell. But the basic flaws in the Court's justification seem to me readily apparent now once all sides of the problem are considered.

I. INTRODUCTION

At the outset, it is well to note exactly what is required by the Court's new constitutional code of rules for confessions. The foremost requirement, upon which later admissibility of a confession depends, is that a fourfold warning be given to a person in custody before he is questioned, namely, that he has a right to remain silent, that anything he says may be used against him, that he has a right to have present an attorney during the questioning, and that if indigent he has a right to a lawyer without charge. To forgo these rights, some affirmative statement of rejection is seemingly required, and threats, tricks, or cajolings to obtain this waiver are forbidden. If before or during questioning the suspect seeks to invoke his right to remain silent, interrogation must be forgone or cease; a request for counsel brings about the same result until a lawyer is procured. Finally, there are a miscellany of minor directives, for example, the burden of proof of waiver is on the State, admissions and exculpatory statements are treated just like confessions, withdrawal of a waiver is always permitted, and so forth.

While the fine points of this scheme are far less clear than the Court admits, the tenor is quite apparent. The new rules are not designed to guard against police brutality or other unmistakably banned forms of coercion. Those who use third-degree tactics and deny them in court are equally able and destined to lie as skillfully about warnings and waivers. Rather, the thrust of the new rules is to negate all pressures, to reinforce the nervous or ignorant suspect, and ultimately to discourage any confession at all. The aim in short is toward "voluntariness" in a utopian sense, or to view it from a different angle, voluntariness with a vengeance.

To incorporate this notion into the Constitution requires a strained reading of history and precedent and a disregard of the very pragmatic concerns that alone may on occasion justify such strains. I believe that reasoned examination will show that the Due Process Clauses provide an adequate tool for coping with confessions and that, even if the Fifth Amendment privilege against self-incrimination be invoked, its precedents taken as a whole do not sustain the present rules. Viewed as a choice based on pure policy, these new rules prove to be a highly debatable, if not one-sided, appraisal of the competing interests, imposed over widespread objection, at the very time when judicial restraint is most called for by the circumstances.

II. CONSTITUTIONAL PREMISES

■ ■ ■

I turn now to the Court's asserted reliance on the Fifth Amendment, an approach which I frankly regard as a trompe l'oeil. The Court's opinion in my view reveals no adequate basis for extending the Fifth Amendment's privilege against self-incrimination to the police station. Far more important, it fails to show that the Court's new rules are well supported, let alone compelled, by Fifth Amendment precedents. Instead, the new rules actually derive from quotation and analogy drawn from precedents under the Sixth Amendment, which should properly have no bearing on police interrogation.

The Court's opening contention, that the Fifth Amendment governs police station confessions, is perhaps not an impermissible extension of the law but it has little to commend itself in the present circumstances. Historically, the privilege against self-incrimination did not bear at all on the use of extra-legal confessions, for which distinct standards evolved; indeed, "the history of the two principles is wide apart, differing by one hundred years in origin, and derived through separate lines of precedents...."

■ ■ ■

III. POLICY CONSIDERATIONS

Examined as an expression of public policy, the Court's new regime proves so dubious that there can be no due compensation for its weakness in constitutional law. The foregoing discussion has shown, I think, how mistaken is the Court in implying that the Constitution has struck the balance in favor of the approach the Court takes. Rather, precedent reveals that the Fourteenth Amendment in practice has been construed to strike a different balance, that the Fifth Amendment gives the Court little solid support in this context, and that the Sixth Amendment should have no bearing at all. Legal history has been stretched before to satisfy deep needs of society. In this instance, however, the Court has not and cannot make the powerful showing that its new rules are plainly desirable in the context of our society, something which is surely demanded before those rules are engrafted onto the Constitution and imposed on every State and county in the land.

Without at all subscribing to the generally black picture of police conduct painted by the Court, I think it must be frankly recognized at the outset that police questioning allowable under due process precedents may inherently entail some pressure on the suspect and may seek advantage in his ignorance or weaknesses. The atmosphere and questioning techniques, proper and fair though they be, can in themselves exert a tug on the suspect to confess, and in this light "[t]o speak of any confessions of crime made after arrest as being 'voluntary' or 'uncoerced' is somewhat inaccurate, although traditional. A confession is wholly and incontestably voluntary only if a guilty person gives himself up to the law and becomes his own accuser." *Ashcraft v. Tennessee*

[(1944)] (Jackson, J., dissenting). Until today, the role of the Constitution has been only to sift out undue pressure, not to assure spontaneous confessions.

The Court's new rules aim to offset these minor pressures and disadvantages intrinsic to any kind of police interrogation. The rules do not serve due process interests in preventing blatant coercion since, as I noted earlier, they do nothing to contain the policeman who is prepared to lie from the start. The rules work for reliability in confessions almost only in the Pickwickian sense that they can prevent some from being given at all. In short, the benefit of this new regime is simply to lessen or wipe out the inherent compulsion and inequalities to which the Court devotes some nine pages of description.

What the Court largely ignores is that its rules impair, if they will not eventually serve wholly to frustrate, an instrument of law enforcement that has long and quite reasonably been thought worth the price paid for it. There can be little doubt that the Court's new code would markedly decrease the number of confessions. To warn the suspect that he may remain silent and remind him that his confession may be used in court are minor obstructions. To require also an express waiver by the suspect and an end to questioning whenever he demurs must heavily handicap questioning. And to suggest or provide counsel for the suspect simply invites the end of the interrogation.

How much harm this decision will inflict on law enforcement cannot fairly be predicted with accuracy. Evidence on the role of confessions is notoriously incomplete . . . and little is added by the Court's reference to the FBI experience and the resources believed wasted in interrogation. We do know that some crimes cannot be solved without confessions, that ample expert testimony attests to their importance in crime control, and that the Court is taking a real risk with society's welfare in imposing its new regime on the country. The social costs of crime are too great to call the new rules anything but a hazardous experimentation. . . .

This brief statement of the competing considerations seems to me ample proof that the Court's preference is highly debatable at best and therefore not to be read into the Constitution. However, it may make the analysis more graphic to consider the actual facts of one of the four cases reversed by the Court. *Miranda v. Arizona* serves best, being neither the hardest nor easiest of the four under the Court's standards.

On March 3, 1963, an 18-year-old girl was kidnapped and forcibly raped near Phoenix, Arizona. Ten days later, on the morning of March 13, petitioner Miranda was arrested and taken to the police station. At this time Miranda was 23 years old, indigent, and educated to the extent of completing half the ninth grade. He had "an emotional illness" of the schizophrenic type, according to the doctor who eventually examined him; the doctor's report also stated that Miranda was "alert and oriented as to time, place, and person," intelligent within normal limits, competent to stand trial, and sane within the legal definition. At the police station, the victim picked Miranda out of a lineup, and two officers then took him into a separate room to interrogate him, starting about 11:30 a.m. Though at first denying his guilt, within a short time Miranda gave a detailed oral confession and then wrote out in his own hand and signed a brief statement admitting and describing the crime. All this was accomplished in two hours or less without any force, threats or promises and—I will assume this though the record is uncertain . . . —without any effective warnings at all.

Miranda's oral and written confessions are now held inadmissible under the Court's new rules. One is entitled to feel astonished that the Constitution can be read to produce this result. These confessions were obtained during brief, daytime questioning conducted by two officers and unmarked by any of the traditional indicia of coercion. They assured a conviction for a brutal and unsettling crime, for which the police had and quite possibly could obtain little evidence other than the victim's identifications, evidence which is frequently unreliable. There was, in sum, a legitimate purpose, no perceptible unfairness, and certainly little risk of injustice in the interrogation. Yet the resulting confessions, and the responsible course of police practice they represent, are to be sacrificed to the Court's own finespun conception of fairness which I seriously doubt is shared by many thinking citizens in this country.

■ ■ ■

IV.   CONCLUSIONS

. . . In conclusion: Nothing in the letter or the spirit of the Constitution or in the precedents squares with the heavy-handed and one-sided action that is so precipitously taken by the Court in the name of fulfilling its constitutional responsibilities. The foray which the Court makes today brings to mind the wise and farsighted words of Mr. Justice Jackson in *Douglas v. City of Jeannette* [(1943)] (separate opinion): "This Court is forever adding new stories to the temples of constitutional law, and the temples have a way of collapsing when one story too many is added."

WHITE, J., with whom HARLAN, J., and STEWART, J., join, dissenting.

■ ■ ■

That the Court's holding today is neither compelled nor even strongly suggested by the language of the Fifth Amendment, is at odds with American and English legal history, and involves a departure from a long line of precedent does not prove either that the Court has exceeded its powers or that the Court is wrong or unwise in its present reinterpretation of the Fifth Amendment. It does, however, underscore the obvious—that the Court has not discovered or found the law in making today's decision, nor has it derived it from some irrefutable sources; what it has done is to make new law and new public policy in much the same way that it has in the course of interpreting other great clauses of the Constitution. This is what the Court historically has done. Indeed, it is what it must do and will continue to do until and unless there is some fundamental change in the constitutional distribution of governmental powers.

■ ■ ■

Although in the Court's view in-custody interrogation is inherently coercive, the Court says that the spontaneous product of the coercion of arrest and detention is still to be deemed voluntary. An accused, arrested on probable cause, may blurt out a confession which will be admissible despite the fact that he is alone and in custody, without any showing that he had any notion of his right to remain silent or of the consequences of his admission. Yet, under the Court's rule, if the police ask him a single question such as "Do you have anything to say?" or "Did you kill your wife?" his response, if there is one, has somehow been compelled, even if the accused has been clearly warned of his right to remain silent. Common sense informs us to the contrary. While one may say that the response was "involuntary" in the sense the question provoked or was the occasion for the response and thus the defendant was induced to speak out when he might have remained silent if not arrested and not questioned, it is patently unsound to say the response is compelled.

Today's result would not follow even if it were agreed that to some extent custodial interrogation is inherently coercive. The test has been whether the totality of circumstances deprived the defendant of a "free choice to admit, to deny, or to refuse to answer," and whether physical or psychological coercion was of such a degree that "the defendant's will was overborne at the time he confessed."

■ ■ ■

If the rule announced today were truly based on a conclusion that all confessions resulting from custodial interrogation are coerced, then it would simply have no rational foundation. . . . A fortiori that would be true of the extension of the rule to exculpatory statements, which the Court effects after a brief discussion of why, in the Court's view, they must be deemed incriminatory but without any discussion of why they must be deemed coerced. Even if one were to postulate that the Court's concern is not that all confessions induced by police interrogation are coerced but rather that some such confessions are coerced and present judicial procedures are believed to be inadequate to identify the confessions that are coerced and those that are not, it would still not be essential to impose the rule that the Court has now fashioned. Transcripts or observers could be required, specific time limits, tailored to fit the cause, could be imposed, or other devices could be utilized to reduce the chances that otherwise indiscernible coercion will produce an inadmissible confession.

On the other hand, even if one assumed that there was an adequate factual basis for the conclusion that all confessions obtained during in-custody interrogation are the product of compulsion, the rule propounded by the Court will still be irrational, for, apparently, it is only if the accused is also warned of his right to counsel and waives both that right and the right against self-incrimination that the inherent compulsiveness of interrogation disappears. But if the defendant may not answer without a warning a question such as "Where were you last night?" without having his answer be a compelled one, how can the Court ever accept his negative answer to the question of whether he wants to consult his retained counsel or counsel whom the court will appoint? And why if counsel is present and the accused nevertheless confesses, or counsel tells the accused to tell the truth, and that is what the accused does, is the situation any less coercive insofar as the accused is concerned? The Court apparently realizes its dilemma of foreclosing questioning without the necessary warnings but at the same time permitting the accused, sitting in the same chair in front of the same policemen, to waive his right to consult an attorney. It expects, however, that the accused will not often waive the right; and if it is claimed that he has, the State faces a severe, if not impossible burden of proof.

All of this makes very little sense in terms of the compulsion which the Fifth Amendment proscribes. That amendment deals with compelling the accused himself. It is his free will that is involved. Confessions and incriminating admissions, as such, are not forbidden evidence; only those which are compelled are banned. I doubt that the Court observes these distinctions today. By considering any answers to any interrogation to be compelled regardless of the content and course of examination and by escalating the requirements to prove waiver, the Court not only prevents the use of compelled confessions but for all practical purposes forbids interrogation except in the presence of counsel. That is, instead of confining itself to protection of the right against compelled self-incrimination the Court has created a limited Fifth Amendment right to counsel—or, as the Court expresses it, a "need for counsel to protect the Fifth Amendment privilege." The focus then is not on the will of the accused but on the will of counsel and how much influence he can have on the accused. Obviously there is no warrant in the Fifth Amendment for thus installing counsel as the arbiter of the privilege.

In sum, for all the Court's expounding on the menacing atmosphere of police interrogation procedures, it has failed to supply any foundation for the conclusions it draws or the measures it adopts.

■ ■ ■

2. Warnings

Florida v. Powell

130 S. Ct. 1195 (2009)

GINSBURG, J., delivered the opinion of the Court, in which ROBERTS, C.J., and SCALIA, KENNEDY, THOMAS, ALITO, and SOTOMAYOR, JJ., joined, and in which BREYER, J., joined in part. STEVENS, J., filed a dissenting opinion, in which BREYER, J., joined in part.

In a pathmarking decision, *Miranda v. Arizona* [(1966)], the Court held that an individual must be "clearly informed," prior to custodial questioning, that he has, among other rights, "the right to consult with a lawyer and to have the

Q + A

lawyer with him during interrogation." The question presented in this case is whether advice that a suspect has "the right to talk to a lawyer before answering any of [the law enforcement officers'] questions," and that he can invoke this right "at any time . . . during th[e] interview," satisfies *Miranda*. We hold that it does.

(fact)

On August 10, 2004, law enforcement officers in Tampa, Florida, seeking to apprehend respondent Kevin Dewayne Powell in connection with a robbery investigation, entered an apartment rented by Powell's girlfriend. After spotting Powell coming from a bedroom, the officers searched the room and discovered a loaded nine-millimeter handgun under the bed.

The officers arrested Powell and transported him to the Tampa Police headquarters. Once there, and before asking Powell any questions, the officers read Powell the standard Tampa Police Department Consent and Release Form 310. The form states:

> "You have the right to remain silent. If you give up the right to remain silent, anything you say can be used against you in court. You have the right to talk to a lawyer before answering any of our questions. If you cannot afford to hire a lawyer, one will be appointed for you without cost and before any questioning. You have the right to use any of these rights at any time you want during this interview."

Standard Tampa form

Acknowledging that he had been informed of his rights, that he "underst[oo]d them," and that he was "willing to talk" to the officers, Powell signed the form. He then admitted that he owned the handgun found in the apartment. Powell knew he was prohibited from possessing a gun because he had previously been convicted of a felony, but said he had nevertheless purchased and carried the firearm for his protection.

■ ■ ■

To give force to the Constitution's protection against compelled self-incrimination, the Court established in *Miranda* "certain procedural safeguards that require police to advise criminal suspects of their rights under the Fifth and Fourteenth Amendments before commencing custodial interrogation." *Duckworth v. Eagan* [(1989)]. Intent on "giv[ing] concrete constitutional guidelines for law enforcement agencies and courts to follow," *Miranda* prescribed the following four now-familiar warnings:

> "[A suspect] must be warned prior to any questioning [1] that he has the right to remain silent, [2] that anything he says can be used against him in a court of law, [3] that he has the right to the presence of an attorney, and [4] that if he cannot afford an attorney one will be appointed for him prior to any questioning if he so desires."

Miranda's third warning—the only one at issue here—addresses our particular concern that "[t]he circumstances surrounding in-custody interrogation can operate very quickly to overbear the will of one merely made aware of his privilege [to remain silent] by his interrogators." Responsive to that concern, we stated, as "an absolute prerequisite to interrogation," that an individual held for questioning "must be clearly informed that he has the right to consult with a lawyer and to have the lawyer with him during interrogation." The question before us is whether the warnings Powell received satisfied this requirement.

The four warnings *Miranda* requires are invariable, but this Court has not dictated the words in which the essential information must be conveyed. See *California v. Prysock* (19810) (*per curiam*) ("This Court has never indicated that the rigidity of *Miranda* extends to the precise formulation of the warnings given a criminal defendant." (internal quotation marks omitted)); *Rhode Island v. Innis* (1980) (safeguards against self-incrimination include "*Miranda* warnings . . . or their equivalent"). In determining whether police officers adequately conveyed the four warnings, we have said, reviewing courts are not required to examine the words employed "as if construing a will or defining the terms of an easement. The inquiry is simply whether the warnings reasonably 'conve[y] to [a suspect] his rights as required by *Miranda*.'"

Our decisions in *Prysock* and *Duckworth* inform our judgment here. Both concerned a suspect's entitlement to adequate notification of the right to appointed counsel. In *Prysock*, an officer informed the suspect of, *inter alia*, his right to a lawyer's presence during questioning and his right to counsel appointed at no cost. The Court of Appeals held the advice inadequate to comply with *Miranda* because it lacked an express statement that the appointment of an attorney would occur prior to the impending interrogation. We reversed. "[N]othing in the warnings," we observed, "suggested any limitation on the right to the presence of appointed counsel different from the clearly conveyed rights to a lawyer in general, including the right to a lawyer before [the suspect is] questioned, . . . while [he is] being questioned, and all during the questioning."

Similarly, in *Duckworth*, we upheld advice that, in relevant part, communicated the right to have an attorney present during the interrogation and the right to an appointed attorney, but also informed the suspect that the lawyer would be appointed "if and when [the suspect goes] to court." "The Court of Appeals thought th[e] 'if and when you go to court' language suggested that only those accused who can afford an attorney have the right to have one present before answering any questions." We thought otherwise. Under the relevant state law, we noted, "counsel is appointed at [a] defendant's initial appearance in court." The "if and when you go to court" advice, we said, "simply anticipate[d]" a question the suspect might be expected to ask after receiving *Miranda* warnings, i.e., "*when* [will he] obtain counsel." Reading the "if and when" language together with the other information conveyed, we held that the warnings, "in their totality, satisfied *Miranda*."

We reach the same conclusion in this case. The Tampa officers did not "entirely omi[t]" any information *Miranda* required them to impart. They informed Powell that he had "the right to talk to a lawyer before answering any of [their] questions" and "the right to use any of [his] rights at any time [he] want[ed] during th[e] interview." The first statement communicated that Powell could consult with a lawyer before answering any particular question, and the second statement confirmed that he could exercise that right while the interrogation was underway. In combination, the two warnings reasonably conveyed Powell's right to have an attorney present, not only at the outset of interrogation, but at all times. . .

The Florida Supreme Court found the warning misleading because it believed the temporal language—that Powell could "talk to a lawyer before answering any of [the officers'] questions"—suggested Powell could consult with an attorney only before the interrogation started. In context, however, the term "before" merely conveyed when Powell's right to an attorney became effective—namely, before he answered any questions at all. Nothing in the words used indicated that counsel's presence would be restricted after the questioning commenced. Instead, the warning communicated that the right to counsel carried forward to and through the interrogation: Powell could seek his attorney's advice before responding to "*any* of [the officers'] questions" and "*at any time . . . during* th[e] interview." . . .

Pursuing a different line of argument, Powell points out that most jurisdictions in Florida and across the Nation expressly advise suspects of the right to have counsel present both before and during interrogation. If we find the advice he received adequate, Powell suggests, law enforcement agencies, hoping to obtain uninformed waivers, will be tempted to end-run *Miranda* by amending their warnings to introduce ambiguity. But as the United States explained as *amicus curiae* in support of the State of Florida, "law enforcement agencies have little reason to assume the litigation risk of experimenting with novel *Miranda* formulations"; instead, it is "desirable police practice" and "in law enforcement's own interest" to state warnings with maximum clarity.

For these reasons, "all . . . federal law enforcement agencies explicitly advise . . . suspect[s] of the full contours of each [*Miranda*] right, including the right to the presence of counsel during questioning." The standard warnings used by the Federal Bureau of Investigation are exemplary. They provide, in relevant part: "You have the right to talk to a lawyer for advice before we ask you any questions. You have the right to have a lawyer with you during questioning." This advice is admirably informative, but we decline to declare its precise formulation necessary to meet *Miranda*'s requirements. Different words were used in the advice Powell received, but they communicated the same essential message.

For the reasons stated, the judgment of the Supreme Court of Florida is reversed, and the case is remanded for further proceedings not inconsistent with this opinion.

It is so ordered.

Justice STEVENS, with whom Justice BREYER joins in part, dissenting.

■ ■ ■

The Court's decision on the merits is also unpersuasive. As we recognized in *Miranda*, "the right to have counsel present at [an] interrogation is indispensable to the protection of the Fifth Amendment privilege." *Miranda v. Arizona*. Furthermore, "the need for counsel to protect the Fifth Amendment privilege comprehends not merely a right to consult with counsel prior to questioning, but also to have counsel present during any questioning." Because the "accused who does not know his rights and therefore does not make a request may be the person who most needs counsel," a defendant "must be clearly informed" regarding two aspects of his right to consult an attorney: "the right to consult with a lawyer and to have the lawyer with him during interrogation."

In this case, the form regularly used by the Tampa police warned Powell that he had "the right to talk to a lawyer before answering any of our questions." This informed him only of the right to consult with a lawyer before questioning, the very right the *Miranda* Court identified as insufficient to protect the Fifth Amendment privilege. The warning did not say anything about the right to have counsel present during interrogation. Although we have never required "rigidity in the *form* of the required warnings," *California v. Prysock*, this is, I believe, the first time the Court has approved a warning which, if given its natural reading, entirely omitted an essential element of a suspect's rights.

Despite the failure of the warning to mention it, in the Court's view the warning "reasonably conveyed" to Powell that he had the right to a lawyer's presence during the interrogation. The Court cobbles together this conclusion from two elements of the warning. First, the Court assumes the warning regarding Powell's right "to talk to a lawyer before answering any of [the officers'] questions," conveyed that "Powell could consult with a lawyer before answering any *particular* question." Second, in the Court's view, the addition of a catchall clause at the end of the recitation of rights "confirmed" that Powell could use his right to consult an attorney "while the interrogation was underway."

The more natural reading of the warning Powell was given, which (1) contained a temporal limit and (2) failed to mention his right to the presence of counsel in the interrogation room, is that Powell only had the right to consult with an attorney before the interrogation began, not that he had the right to have an attorney with him during questioning. Even those few Courts of Appeals that have approved warnings that did not expressly mention the right to an attorney's presence during interrogation have found language of the sort used in Powell's warning to be misleading. For instance, petitioner cites the Second Circuit's decision in *United States v. Lamia* (1970) as an example of a court applying the properly flexible approach to *Miranda*. But in that case, the Second Circuit expressly distinguished a warning that a suspect " 'could consult an attorney prior to any question,' " which was "affirmatively misleading since it was thought to imply that the attorney could not be present during questioning." That even the Courts of Appeals taking the most flexible approach to *Miranda* have found warnings like Powell's misleading should caution the Court against concluding that such a warning reasonably conveyed Powell's right to have an attorney with him during the interrogation.

When the relevant clause of the warning in this case is given its most natural reading, the catchall clause does not meaningfully clarify Powell's rights. It communicated that Powell could exercise the previously listed rights at any time. Yet the only previously listed right was the "right to talk to a lawyer *before* answering any of [the officers'] questions." Informing Powell that he could exercise, at any time during the interview, the right to talk to a lawyer *before* answering any questions did not reasonably convey the right to talk to a lawyer *after* answering some questions, much less implicitly inform Powell of his right to have a lawyer with him at all times during interrogation. An intelligent suspect could reasonably conclude that all he was provided was a one-time right to consult with an attorney, not a right to have an attorney present with him in the interrogation room at all times.

The Court relies on *Duckworth v. Eagan* (1989) and *Prysock*, but in neither case did the warning at issue completely omit one of a suspect's rights. In *Prysock*, the warning regarding the right to an appointed attorney contained no temporal limitation, which clearly distinguishes that case from Powell's. In *Duckworth*, the suspect was explicitly informed that he had the right "to talk to a lawyer for advice before we ask you any questions, and to have him with you during questioning," and that he had "this right to the advice and presence of a lawyer even if you cannot afford to hire one." The warning thus conveyed in full the right to appointed counsel before and during the interrogation. Although the warning was arguably undercut by the addition of a statement that an attorney would be appointed "if and when you go to court," the Court found the suspect was informed of his full rights and the warning simply added additional, truthful information regarding when counsel would be appointed. Unlike the *Duckworth* warning, Powell's warning did not convey his *Miranda* rights in full with the addition of some arguably misleading statement. Rather, the warning entirely failed to inform him of the separate and distinct right "to have counsel present during any questioning."

In sum, the warning at issue in this case did not reasonably convey to Powell his right to have a lawyer with him during the interrogation. "The requirement of warnings . . . [is] fundamental with respect to the Fifth Amendment privilege and not simply a preliminary ritual to existing methods of interrogation." In determining that the warning implied what it did not say, it is the Court "that is guilty of attaching greater importance to the form of the *Miranda* ritual than to the substance of the message it is intended to convey."

Whether we focus on Powell's particular case, or the use of the warning form as the standard used in one jurisdiction, it is clear that the form is imperfect. As the majority's decision today demonstrates, reasonable judges may well differ over the question whether the deficiency is serious enough to violate the Federal Constitution. That difference of opinion, in my judgment, falls short of providing a justification for reviewing this case when the judges of the highest court of the State have decided the warning is insufficiently protective of the rights of the State's citizens. In my view, respect for the independence of state courts, and their authority to set the rules by which their citizens are protected, should result in a dismissal of this petition.

I respectfully dissent.

3. Custody

Berkemer v. McCarty

468 U.S. 420 (1984)

Marshall, J., delivered the opinion of the unanimous Court.

This case presents two related questions: First, does our decision in *Miranda v. Arizona* (1966) govern the admissibility of statements made during custodial interrogation by a suspect accused of a misdemeanor traffic offense? Second, does the roadside questioning of a motorist detained pursuant to a traffic stop constitute custodial interrogation for the purposes of the doctrine enunciated in *Miranda*?

■ ■ ■

. . . On the evening of March 31, 1980, Trooper Williams of the Ohio State Highway Patrol observed respondent's car weaving in and out of a lane on Interstate Highway 270. After following the car for two miles, Williams forced respondent to stop and asked him to get out of the vehicle. When respondent complied, Williams noticed that he was having difficulty standing. At that point, "Williams concluded that [respondent] would be charged with a traffic offense and, therefore, his freedom to leave the scene was terminated." However, respondent was not told that he would be taken into custody. Williams then asked respondent to perform a field sobriety test, commonly known as a "balancing test." Respondent could not do so without falling.

While still at the scene of the traffic stop, Williams asked respondent whether he had been using intoxicants. Respondent replied that "he had consumed two beers and had smoked several joints of marijuana a short time before." Respondent's speech was slurred, and Williams had difficulty understanding him. Williams thereupon formally placed respondent under arrest and transported him in the patrol car to the Franklin County Jail.

At the jail, respondent was given an intoxilyzer test to determine the concentration of alcohol in his blood. The test did not detect any alcohol whatsoever in respondent's system. Williams then resumed questioning respondent in order to obtain information for inclusion in the State Highway Patrol Alcohol Influence Report. Respondent answered affirmatively a question whether he had been drinking. When then asked if he was under the influence of alcohol, he said, "I guess, barely." Williams next asked respondent to indicate on the form whether the marihuana he had smoked had been treated with any chemicals. In the section of the report headed "Remarks," respondent wrote, "No ang[el] dust or PCP in the pot. Rick McCarty."

At no point in this sequence of events did Williams or anyone else tell respondent that he had a right to remain silent, to consult with an attorney, and to have an attorney appointed for him if he could not afford one.

■ ■ ■

We granted certiorari to resolve confusion in the federal and state courts regarding the applicability of our ruling in *Miranda* to interrogations involving minor offenses and to questioning of motorists detained pursuant to traffic stops.

■ ■ ■

In the years since the decision in *Miranda*, we have frequently reaffirmed the central principle established by that case: if the police take a suspect into custody and then ask him questions without informing him of the rights enumerated above, his responses cannot be introduced into evidence to establish his guilt.

■ ■ ■

Petitioner asks us to carve an exception out of the foregoing principle. When the police arrest a person for allegedly committing a misdemeanor traffic offense and then ask him questions without telling him his constitutional rights, petitioner argues, his responses should be admissible against him. We cannot agree.

One of the principal advantages of the doctrine that suspects must be given warnings before being interrogated while in custody is the clarity of that rule.

> "*Miranda*'s holding has the virtue of informing police and prosecutors with specificity as to what they may do in conducting custodial interrogation, and of informing courts under what circumstances statements obtained during such interrogation are not admissible. This gain in specificity, which benefits the accused and the State alike, has been thought to outweigh the burdens that the decision in *Miranda* imposes on law enforcement agencies and the courts by requiring the suppression of trustworthy and highly probative evidence even though the confession might be voluntary under traditional Fifth Amendment analysis." *Fare v. Michael C.* (1979).

The exception to *Miranda* proposed by petitioner would substantially undermine this crucial advantage of the doctrine. The police often are unaware when they arrest a person whether he may have committed a misdemeanor or a felony.

■ ■ ■

Equally importantly, the doctrinal complexities that would confront the courts if we accepted petitioner's proposal would be Byzantine. Difficult questions quickly spring to mind: For instance, investigations into seemingly minor offenses sometimes escalate gradually into investigations into more serious matters; at what point in the evolution of an affair of this sort would the police be obliged to give *Miranda* warnings to a suspect in custody? What evidence would be necessary to establish that an arrest for a misdemeanor offense was merely a pretext to enable the police to interrogate the suspect (in hopes of obtaining information about a felony) without providing him the safeguards prescribed by *Miranda*? The litigation necessary to resolve such matters would be time-consuming and disruptive of law enforcement. And the end result would be an elaborate set of rules, interlaced with exceptions and subtle distinctions, discriminating between different kinds of custodial interrogations. Neither the police nor criminal defendants would benefit from such a development.

■ ■ ■

We hold therefore that a person subjected to custodial interrogation is entitled to the benefit of the procedural safeguards enunciated in *Miranda*, regardless of the nature or severity of the offense of which he is suspected or for which he was arrested.

The implication of this holding is that the Court of Appeals was correct in ruling that the statements made by respondent at the County Jail were inadmissible. There can be no question that respondent was "in custody" at least as of the moment he was formally placed under arrest and instructed to get into the police car. Because he was not informed of his constitutional rights at that juncture, respondent's subsequent admissions should not have been used against him.

■ ■ ■

To assess the admissibility of the self-incriminating statements made by respondent prior to his formal arrest, we are obliged to address a second issue concerning the scope of our decision in *Miranda*: whether the roadside questioning of a motorist detained pursuant to a routine traffic stop should be considered "custodial interrogation." Respondent urges that it should, on the ground that *Miranda* by its terms applies whenever "a person has been taken into custody or otherwise deprived of his freedom of action in any significant way." Petitioner contends that a holding that every detained motorist must be advised of his rights before being questioned would constitute an unwarranted extension of the *Miranda* doctrine.

It must be acknowledged at the outset that a traffic stop significantly curtails the "freedom of action" of the driver and the passengers, if any, of the detained vehicle. Under the law of most States, it is a crime either to ignore a policeman's signal to stop one's car or, once having stopped, to drive away without permission. Certainly few motorists would feel free either to disobey a directive to pull over or to leave the scene of a traffic stop without being told they might do so. Partly for these reasons, we have long acknowledged that "stopping an automobile and detaining its occupants constitute a 'seizure' within the meaning of [the Fourth] Amendmen[t], even though the purpose of the stop is limited and the resulting detention quite brief."

However, we decline to accord talismanic power to the phrase in the *Miranda* opinion emphasized by respondent. Fidelity to the doctrine announced in *Miranda* requires that it be enforced strictly, but only in those types of situations in which the concerns that powered the decision are implicated. Thus, we must decide whether a traffic stop exerts upon a detained person pressures that sufficiently impair his free exercise of his privilege against self-incrimination to require that he be warned of his constitutional rights.

Two features of an ordinary traffic stop mitigate the danger that a person questioned will be induced "to speak where he would not otherwise do so freely," *Miranda v. Arizona.* First, detention of a motorist pursuant to a traffic stop is presumptively temporary and brief. The vast majority of roadside detentions last only a few minutes. A motorist's expectations, when he sees a policeman's light flashing behind him, are that he will be obliged to spend a short period of time answering questions and waiting while the officer checks his license and registration, that he may then be given a citation, but that in the end he most likely will be allowed to continue on his way. In this respect, questioning incident to an ordinary traffic stop is quite different from station-house interrogation, which frequently is prolonged, and in which the detainee often is aware that questioning will continue until he provides his interrogators the answers they seek.

Second, circumstances associated with the typical traffic stop are not such that the motorist feels completely at the mercy of the police. To be sure, the aura of authority surrounding an armed, uniformed officer and the knowledge that the officer has some discretion in deciding whether to issue a citation, in combination, exert some pressure on the detainee to respond to questions. But other aspects of the situation substantially offset these forces. Perhaps most importantly, the typical traffic stop is public, at least to some degree. Passersby, on foot or in other cars, witness the interaction of officer and motorist. This exposure to public view both reduces the ability of an unscrupulous policeman to use illegitimate means to elicit self-incriminating statements and diminishes the motorist's fear that, if he does not cooperate, he will be subjected to abuse. The fact that the detained motorist typically is confronted by only one or at most two policemen further mutes his sense of vulnerability. In short, the atmosphere surrounding an ordinary traffic stop is substantially less "police dominated" than that surrounding the kinds of interrogation at issue in *Miranda* itself, and in the subsequent cases in which we have applied *Miranda.*

In both of these respects, the usual traffic stop is more analogous to a so-called "*Terry* stop," see *Terry v. Ohio* (1968), than to a formal arrest. Under the Fourth Amendment, we have held, a policeman who lacks probable cause but whose "observations lead him reasonably to suspect" that a particular person has committed, is committing, or is about to commit a crime, may detain that person briefly in order to "investigate the circumstances that provoke suspicion." *United States v. Brignoni-Ponce* (1975). "[T]he stop and inquiry must be 'reasonably related in scope to the justification for their initiation.' " *Ibid.* (quoting *Terry v. Ohio*). Typically, this means that the officer may ask the detainee a moderate number of questions to determine his identity and to try to obtain information confirming or dispelling the officer's suspicions. But the detainee is not obliged to respond. And, unless the detainee's answers provide the officer with probable cause to arrest him, he must then be released. The comparatively nonthreatening character of detentions of this sort explains the absence of any suggestion in our opinions that *Terry* stops are subject to the dictates of *Miranda*. The similarly noncoercive aspect of ordinary traffic stops prompts us to hold that persons temporarily detained pursuant to such stops are not "in custody" for the purposes of *Miranda*.

■ ■ ■

Turning to the case before us, we find nothing in the record that indicates that respondent should have been given *Miranda* warnings at any point prior to the time Trooper Williams placed him under arrest. For the reasons indicated above, we reject the contention that the initial stop of respondent's car, by itself, rendered him "in custody." And respondent has failed to demonstrate that, at any time between the initial stop and the arrest, he was subjected to restraints comparable to those associated with a formal arrest. Only a short period of time elapsed between the stop and the arrest. At no point during that interval was respondent informed that his detention would not be temporary. Although Trooper Williams apparently decided as soon as respondent stepped out of his car that respondent would be taken into custody and charged with a traffic offense, Williams never communicated his intention to respondent. A policeman's unarticulated plan has no bearing on the question whether a suspect was "in custody" at a particular time; the only relevant inquiry is how a reasonable man in the suspect's position would have understood his situation. Nor do other aspects of the interaction of Williams and respondent support the contention that respondent was exposed to "custodial interrogation" at the scene of the stop. From aught that appears in the stipulation of facts, a single police officer asked respondent a modest number of questions and requested him to perform a simple balancing test at a location visible to passing motorists. Treatment of this sort cannot fairly be characterized as the functional equivalent of formal arrest.

We conclude, in short, that respondent was not taken into custody for the purposes of *Miranda* until Williams arrested him. Consequently, the statements respondent made prior to that point were admissible against him. . . .

Yarborough v. Alvarado

541 U.S. 652 (2004)

KENNEDY, J., delivered the opinion of the Court, in which REHNQUIST, C.J., and O'CONNOR, SCALIA, and THOMAS, JJ., joined. O'CONNOR, J., filed a concurring opinion. BREYER, J., filed a dissenting opinion, in which STEVENS, SOUTER, and GINSBURG, JJ., joined.

Under the Antiterrorism and Effective Death Penalty Act of 1996 (AEDPA), a federal court can grant an application for a writ of habeas corpus on behalf of a person held pursuant to a state-court judgment if the state-court adjudication "resulted in a decision that was contrary to, or involved an unreasonable application of, clearly established Federal law, as determined by the Supreme Court of the United States." 28 U.S.C. §2254(d)(1). The United States Court of Appeals for the Ninth Circuit ruled that a state court unreasonably applied clearly established law when it held that the respondent was not in custody for *Miranda* purposes. We disagree and reverse.

■ ■ ■

Paul Soto and respondent Michael Alvarado attempted to steal a truck in the parking lot of a shopping mall in Santa Fe Springs, California. Soto and Alvarado were part of a larger group of teenagers at the mall that night. Soto decided to steal the truck, and Alvarado agreed to help. Soto pulled out a .357 Magnum and approached the driver, Francisco Castaneda, who was standing near the truck emptying trash into a dumpster. Soto demanded money and the ignition keys from Castaneda. Alvarado, then five months short of his 18th birthday, approached the passenger side door of the truck and crouched down. When Castaneda refused to comply with Soto's demands, Soto shot Castaneda, killing him. Alvarado then helped hide Soto's gun.

Los Angeles County Sheriff's detective Cheryl Comstock led the investigation into the circumstances of Castaneda's death. About a month after the shooting, Comstock left word at Alvarado's house and also contacted Alvarado's mother at work with the message that she wished to speak with Alvarado. Alvarado's parents brought him to the Pico Rivera Sheriff's Station to be interviewed around lunchtime. They waited in the lobby while Alvarado went with Comstock to be interviewed. Alvarado contends that his parents asked to be present during the interview but were rebuffed.

Comstock brought Alvarado to a small interview room and began interviewing him at about 12:30 p.m. The interview lasted about two hours, and was recorded by Comstock with Alvarado's knowledge. Only Comstock and Alvarado were present. Alvarado was not given a warning under *Miranda v. Arizona* (1966). Comstock began the interview by asking Alvarado to recount the events on the night of the shooting. On that night, Alvarado explained, he had been drinking alcohol at a friend's house with some other friends and acquaintances. After a few hours, part of the group went home and the rest walked to a nearby mall to use its public telephones. In Alvarado's initial telling, that was the end of it. The group went back to the friend's home and "just went to bed."

Unpersuaded, Comstock pressed on:

"*Q.* Okay. We did real good up until this point and everything you've said it's pretty accurate till this point, except for you left out the shooting.
A. The shooting?
Q. Uh huh, the shooting.
A. Well I had never seen no shooting.
Q. Well I'm afraid you did.
A. I had never seen no shooting.

Q. Well I beg to differ with you. I've been told quite the opposite and we have witnesses that are saying quite the opposite.

A. That I had seen the shooting?

Q. So why don't you take a deep breath, like I told you before, the very best thing is to be honest. . . . You can't have that many people get involved in a murder and expect that some of them aren't going to tell the truth, okay? Now granted if it was maybe one person, you might be able to keep your fingers crossed and say, god I hope he doesn't tell the truth, but the problem is is that they have to tell the truth, okay? Now all I'm simply doing is giving you the opportunity to tell the truth and when we got that many people telling a story and all of a sudden you tell something way far fetched different."

At this point, Alvarado slowly began to change his story. First he acknowledged being present when the carjacking occurred but claimed that he did not know what happened or who had a gun. When he hesitated to say more, Comstock tried to encourage Alvarado to discuss what happened by appealing to his sense of honesty and the need to bring the man who shot Castaneda to justice. Alvarado then admitted he had helped the other man try to steal the truck by standing near the passenger side door. Next he admitted that the other man was Paul Soto, that he knew Soto was armed, and that he had helped hide the gun after the murder. Alvarado explained that he had expected Soto to scare the driver with the gun, but that he did not expect Soto to kill anyone. Toward the end of the interview, Comstock twice asked Alvarado if he needed to take a break. Alvarado declined. When the interview was over, Comstock returned with Alvarado to the lobby of the sheriff's station where his parents were waiting. Alvarado's father drove him home.

A few months later, the State of California charged Soto and Alvarado with first-degree murder and attempted robbery. Citing *Miranda*, Alvarado moved to suppress his statements from the Comstock interview. The trial court denied the motion on the ground that the interview was noncustodial. Alvarado and Soto were tried together, and Alvarado testified in his own defense. He offered an innocent explanation for his conduct, testifying that he happened to be standing in the parking lot of the mall when a gun went off nearby. The government's cross-examination relied on Alvarado's statement to Comstock. Alvarado admitted having made some of the statements but denied others. When Alvarado denied particular statements, the prosecution countered by playing excerpts from the audio recording of the interview.

During cross-examination, Alvarado agreed that the interview with Comstock "was a pretty friendly conversation," that there was "sort of a free flow between [Alvarado] and Detective Comstock," and that Alvarado did not "feel coerced or threatened in any way" during the interview. The jury convicted Soto and Alvarado of first-degree murder and attempted robbery. The trial judge later reduced Alvarado's conviction to second-degree murder for his comparatively minor role in the offense. The judge sentenced Soto to life in prison and Alvarado to 15-years-to-life.

On direct appeal, the Second Appellate District Court of Appeal (hereinafter state court) affirmed.

■ ■ ■

Alvarado filed a petition for a writ of habeas corpus in the United States District Court for the Central District of California. The District Court agreed with the state court that Alvarado was not in custody for *Miranda* purposes during the interview.

■ ■ ■

The Court of Appeals for the Ninth Circuit reversed. First, the Court of Appeals held that the state court erred in failing to account for Alvarado's youth and inexperience when evaluating whether a reasonable person in his position would have felt free to leave. It noted that this Court has considered a suspect's juvenile status when evaluating the voluntariness of confessions and the waiver of the privilege against self-incrimination. The Court of Appeals held that in light of these authorities, Alvarado's age and experience must be a factor in the *Miranda* custody inquiry. A minor with no criminal record would be more likely to feel coerced by police tactics and conclude he is under arrest than would an experienced adult, the Court of Appeals reasoned. This required extra "safeguards . . . commensurate with the age and circumstances of a juvenile defendant." According to the Court of Appeals, the effect of Alvarado's age and inexperience was so substantial that it turned the interview into a custodial interrogation.

The Court of Appeals next considered whether Alvarado could obtain relief in light of the deference a federal court must give to a state-court determination on habeas review. The deference required by AEDPA did not bar relief, the Court of Appeals held, because the relevance of juvenile status in Supreme Court case law as a whole compelled the "extension of the principle that juvenile status is relevant" to the context of *Miranda* custody determinations. In light of the clearly established law considering juvenile status, it was "simply unreasonable to conclude that a reasonable 17-year-old, with no prior history of arrest or police interviews, would have felt that he was at liberty to terminate the interrogation and leave."

We granted certiorari.

We begin by determining the relevant clearly established law. For purposes of 28 U.S.C. §2254(d)(1), clearly established law as determined by this Court "refers to the holdings, as opposed to the dicta, of this Court's decisions as of the time of the relevant state-court decision."

■ ■ ■

Miranda itself held that preinterrogation warnings are required in the context of custodial interrogations given "the compulsion inherent in custodial surroundings." The Court explained that "custodial interrogation" meant "questioning initiated by law enforcement officers after a person has been taken into custody or otherwise deprived of his freedom of action in any significant way." The *Miranda* decision did not provide the Court with an opportunity to apply that test to a set of facts.

After *Miranda*, the Court first applied the custody test in *Oregon v. Mathiason* (1977) (*per curiam*). In *Mathiason*, a police officer contacted the suspect after a burglary victim identified him. The officer arranged to meet the suspect at a nearby police station. At the outset of the questioning, the officer stated his belief that the suspect was involved in the burglary but that he was not under arrest. During the 30-minute interview, the suspect admitted his guilt. He was then allowed to leave. The Court held that the questioning was not custodial because there was "no indication that the questioning took place in a context where [the suspect's] freedom to depart was restricted in any way." The Court noted that the suspect had come voluntarily to the police station, that he was informed that he was not under arrest, and that he was allowed to leave at the end of the interview.

In *California v. Beheler* (1983) (*per curiam*), the Court reached the same result in a case with facts similar to those in *Mathiason*. In *Beheler*, the state court had distinguished *Mathiason* based on what it described as differences in the totality of the circumstances. The police interviewed Beheler shortly after the crime occurred; Beheler had been drinking earlier in the day; he was emotionally distraught; he was well known to the police; and he was a parolee who knew it was necessary for him to cooperate with the police. The Court agreed that "the circumstances of each case must certainly influence" the custody determination, but reemphasized that "the ultimate inquiry is simply whether there is a formal arrest or restraint on freedom of movement of the degree associated with a formal arrest." The Court found the case indistinguishable from *Mathiason*. It noted that how much the police knew about the suspect and how much time had elapsed after the crime occurred were irrelevant to the custody inquiry.

Our more recent cases instruct that custody must be determined based on how a reasonable person in the suspect's situation would perceive his circumstances. In *Berkemer v. McCarty* (1984), a police officer stopped a suspected drunk driver and asked him some questions. Although the officer reached the decision to arrest the driver at the beginning of the traffic stop, he did not do so until the driver failed a sobriety test and acknowledged that he had been drinking beer and smoking marijuana. The Court held the traffic stop noncustodial despite the officer's intent to arrest because he had not communicated that intent to the driver. "A policeman's unarticulated plan has no bearing on the question whether a suspect was 'in custody' at a particular time," the Court explained. "[T]he only relevant inquiry is how a reasonable man in the suspect's position would have understood his situation."

■ ■ ■

Stansbury v. California (1994) (*per curiam*) confirmed this analytical framework. *Stansbury* explained that "the initial determination of custody depends on the objective circumstances of the interrogation, not on the subjective views harbored by either the interrogating officers or the person being questioned."

Courts must examine "all of the circumstances surrounding the interrogation" and determine "how a reasonable person in the position of the individual being questioned would gauge the breadth of his or her freedom of action."

Finally, in *Thompson v. Keohane* (1995), the Court offered the following description of the *Miranda* custody test:

> "Two discrete inquiries are essential to the determination: first, what were the circumstances surrounding the interrogation; and second, given those circumstances, would a reasonable person have felt he or she was not at liberty to terminate the interrogation and leave. Once the scene is set and the players' lines and actions are reconstructed, the court must apply an objective test to resolve the ultimate inquiry: was there a formal arrest or restraint on freedom of movement of the degree associated with a formal arrest."

We turn now to the case before us and ask if the state-court adjudication of the claim "involved an unreasonable application" of clearly established law when it concluded that Alvarado was not in custody. 28 U.S.C. § 2254(d)(1). See *Williams* [*v. Taylor* (2000)] ("Under the 'unreasonable application' clause, a federal habeas court may grant the writ if the state court identifies the correct governing principle from this Court's decisions but unreasonably applies that principle to the facts of the prisoner's case"). The term " 'unreasonable' " is "a common term in the legal world and, accordingly, federal judges are familiar with its meaning." At the same time, the range of reasonable judgment can depend in part on the nature of the relevant rule. If a legal rule is specific, the range may be narrow. Applications of the rule may be plainly correct or incorrect. Other rules are more general, and their meaning must emerge in application over the course of time. Applying a general standard to a specific case can demand a substantial element of judgment. As a result, evaluating whether a rule application was unreasonable requires considering the rule's specificity. The more general the rule, the more leeway courts have in reaching outcomes in case-by-case determinations.

Based on these principles, we conclude that the state court's application of our clearly established law was reasonable. Ignoring the deferential standard of § 2254(d)(1) for the moment, it can be said that fair-minded jurists could disagree over whether Alvarado was in custody. On one hand, certain facts weigh against a finding that Alvarado was in custody. The police did not transport Alvarado to the station or require him to appear at a particular time. They did not threaten him or suggest he would be placed under arrest. Alvarado's parents remained in the lobby during the interview, suggesting that the interview would be brief. In fact, according to trial counsel for Alvarado, he and his parents were told that the interview was " 'not going to be long.' " During the interview, Comstock focused on Soto's crimes rather than Alvarado's. Instead of pressuring Alvarado with the threat of arrest and prosecution, she appealed to his interest in telling the truth and being helpful to a police officer. In addition, Comstock twice asked Alvarado if he wanted to take a break. At the end of the interview, Alvarado went home. All of these objective facts are consistent with an interrogation environment in which a reasonable person would have felt free to terminate the interview and leave. Indeed, a number of the facts echo those of *Mathiason*, a *per curiam* summary reversal in which we found it "clear from these facts" that the suspect was not in custody.

Other facts point in the opposite direction. Comstock interviewed Alvarado at the police station. The interview lasted two hours, four times longer than the 30-minute interview in *Mathiason*. Unlike the officer in *Mathiason*, Comstock did not tell Alvarado that he was free to leave. Alvarado was brought to the police station by his legal guardians rather than arriving on his own accord, making the extent of his control over his presence unclear. Counsel for Alvarado alleges that Alvarado's parents asked to be present at the interview but were rebuffed, a fact that—if known to Alvarado—might reasonably have led someone in Alvarado's position to feel more restricted than otherwise. These facts weigh in favor of the view that Alvarado was in custody.

These differing indications lead us to hold that the state court's application of our custody standard was reasonable. The Court of Appeals was nowhere close to the mark when it concluded otherwise. Although the question of what an "unreasonable application" of law might be is difficult in some cases, it is not difficult here. The custody test is general, and the state court's application of our law fits within the matrix of our prior decisions. We cannot grant relief under AEDPA by conducting our own independent inquiry into whether the state court was correct as a *de novo* matter.

■ ■ ■

The Court of Appeals reached the opposite result by placing considerable reliance on Alvarado's age and inexperience with law enforcement. Our Court has not stated that a suspect's age or experience is relevant to the *Miranda* custody analysis, and counsel for Alvarado did not press the importance of either factor on direct appeal or in habeas proceedings. According to the Court of Appeals, however, our Court's emphasis on juvenile status in other contexts demanded consideration of Alvarado's age and inexperience here. The Court of Appeals viewed the state court's failure to " 'extend a clearly established legal principle [of the relevance of juvenile status] to a new context' " as objectively unreasonable in this case, requiring issuance of the writ.

■ ■ ■

There is an important conceptual difference between the *Miranda* custody test and the line of cases from other contexts considering age and experience. The *Miranda* custody inquiry is an objective test. As we stated in *Keohane*, "[o]nce the scene is set and the players' lines and actions are reconstructed, the court must apply an objective test to resolve the ultimate inquiry." The objective test furthers "the clarity of [*Miranda*'s] rule," ... ensuring that the police do not need "to make guesses as to [the circumstances] at issue before deciding how they may interrogate the suspect." To be sure, the line between permissible objective facts and impermissible subjective experiences can be indistinct in some cases. It is possible to subsume a subjective factor into an objective test by making the latter more specific in its formulation. Thus the Court of Appeals styled its inquiry as an objective test by considering what a "reasonable 17-year-old, with no prior history of arrest or police interviews," would perceive.

■ ■ ■

At the same time, the objective *Miranda* custody inquiry could reasonably be viewed as different from doctrinal tests that depend on the actual mindset of a particular suspect, where we do consider a suspect's age and experience. For example, the voluntariness of a statement is often said to depend on whether "the defendant's will was overborne."

■ ■ ■

Indeed, reliance on Alvarado's prior history with law enforcement was improper not only under the deferential standard of 28 U.S.C. §2254(d)(1), but also as a *de novo* matter. In most cases, police officers will not know a suspect's interrogation history. Even if they do, the relationship between a suspect's past experiences and the likelihood a reasonable person with that experience would feel free to leave often will be speculative. True, suspects with prior law enforcement experience may understand police procedures and reasonably feel free to leave unless told otherwise. On the other hand, they may view past as prologue and expect another in a string of arrests. We do not ask police officers to consider these contingent psychological factors when deciding when suspects should be advised of their *Miranda* rights. The inquiry turns too much on the suspect's subjective state of mind and not enough on the "objective circumstances of the interrogation."

The state court considered the proper factors and reached a reasonable conclusion. The judgment of the Court of Appeals is

Reversed.

Justice O'CONNOR, concurring.

I join the opinion of the Court, but write separately to express an additional reason for reversal. There may be cases in which a suspect's age will be relevant to the "custody" inquiry under *Miranda v. Arizona*. In this case, however, Alvarado was almost 18 years old at the time of his interview. It is difficult to expect police to recognize that a suspect is a juvenile when he is so close to the age of majority. Even when police do know a suspect's age, it may be difficult for them to ascertain what bearing it has on the likelihood that the suspect would feel free to leave. That is especially true here; 17½-year-olds vary widely in their reactions to police questioning, and many can be expected to behave as adults. Given these difficulties, I agree that the state court's decision in this case cannot be called an unreasonable application of federal law simply because it failed explicitly to mention Alvarado's age.

Justice BREYER, with whom Justice STEVENS, Justice SOUTER, and Justice GINSBURG join, dissenting.

In my view, Michael Alvarado clearly was "in custody" when the police questioned him (without *Miranda* warnings) about the murder of Francisco Castaneda. To put the question in terms of federal law's well-established legal standards: Would a "reasonable person" in Alvarado's "position" have felt he was "at liberty to terminate the interrogation and leave"?

■ ■ ■

I

A

The law in this case asks judges to apply, not arcane or complex legal directives, but ordinary common sense. Would a reasonable person in Alvarado's position have felt free simply to get up and walk out of the small room in the station house at will during his 2-hour police interrogation? I ask the reader to put himself, or herself, in Alvarado's circumstances and then answer that question: Alvarado hears from his parents that he is needed for police questioning. His parents take him to the station. On arrival, a police officer separates him from his parents. His parents ask to come along, but the officer says they may not. Another officer says, " 'What do we have here; we are going to question a suspect.' "

The police take Alvarado to a small interrogation room, away from the station's public area. A single officer begins to question him, making clear in the process that the police have evidence that he participated in an attempted carjacking connected with a murder. When he says that he never saw any shooting, the officer suggests that he is lying, while adding that she is "giving [him] the opportunity to tell the truth" and "tak[e] care of [him]self." Toward the end of the questioning, the officer gives him permission to take a bathroom or water break. After two hours, by which time he has admitted he was involved in the attempted theft, knew about the gun, and helped to hide it, the questioning ends.

What reasonable person in the circumstances—brought to a police station by his parents at police request, put in a small interrogation room, questioned for a solid two hours, and confronted with claims that there is strong evidence that he participated in a serious crime—could have thought to himself, "Well, anytime I want to leave I can just get up and walk out"? If the person harbored any doubts, would he still think he might be free to leave once he recalls that the police officer has just refused to let his parents remain with him during questioning? Would he still think that he, rather than the officer, controls the situation?

There is only one possible answer to these questions. A reasonable person would *not* have thought he was free simply to pick up and leave in the middle of the interrogation. I believe the California courts were clearly wrong to hold the contrary, and the Ninth Circuit was right in concluding that those state courts unreasonably applied clearly established federal law. See 28 U.S.C. § 2254(d)(1).

B

. . . Consider each of the facts [the majority] says "weigh against a finding" of custody:

(1) *"The police did not transport Alvarado to the station or require him to appear at a particular time."* (emphasis added). True. His parents brought him to the station at police request. But why does that matter? The relevant question is whether Alvarado came to the station of his own free will or submitted to questioning voluntarily."

(2) "Alvarado's parents remained in the lobby during the interview, suggesting that the interview would be brief. In fact, [Alvarado] and his parents were told that the interview was 'not going to be long.'" Whatever was communicated to Alvarado before the questioning began, the fact is that the interview was not brief, nor, after the first half hour or so, would Alvarado have expected it to be brief. And those are the relevant considerations.

(3) *"At the end of the interview, Alvarado went home."* As the majority acknowledges, our recent case law makes clear that the relevant question is how a reasonable person would have gauged his freedom to leave *during*, not *after*, the interview.

(4) *"During the interview, [Officer] Comstock focused on Soto's crimes rather than Alvarado's."* In fact, the police officer characterized Soto as the ringleader, while making clear that she knew Alvarado had participated in the attempted carjacking during which Castaneda was killed. Her questioning would have reinforced, not diminished, Alvarado's fear that he was not simply a witness, but also suspected of having been involved in a serious crime.

(5) "[The officer did not] pressur[e] Alvarado with the threat of arrest and prosecution . . . [but instead] appealed to his interest in telling the truth and being helpful to a police officer." This factor might be highly significant were the question one of "coercion." But it is not. The question is whether Alvarado would have felt free to terminate the interrogation and leave. In respect to that question, police politeness, while commendable, does not significantly help the majority.

(6) *"Comstock twice asked Alvarado if he wanted to take a break."* This circumstance, emphasizing the officer's control of Alvarado's movements, makes it *less* likely, not *more* likely, that Alvarado would have thought he was free to leave at will.

The facts to which the majority points make clear what the police did *not* do, for example, come to Alvarado's house, tell him he was under arrest, handcuff him, place him in a locked cell, threaten him, or tell him explicitly that he was not free to leave. But what is important here is what the police *did* do—namely, have Alvarado's parents bring him to the station, put him with a single officer in a small room, keep his parents out, let him know that he was a suspect, and question him for two hours. These latter facts compel a single conclusion: A reasonable person in Alvarado's circumstances would *not* have felt free to terminate the interrogation and leave.

■ ■ ■

What about Alvarado's youth? The fact that Alvarado was 17 helps to show that he was unlikely to have felt free to ignore his parents' request to come to the station. And a 17-year-old is more likely than, say, a 35-year-old, to take a police officer's assertion of authority to keep parents outside the room as an assertion of authority to keep their child inside as well.

The majority suggests that the law might *prevent* a judge from taking account of the fact that Alvarado was 17. I can find nothing in the law that supports that conclusion. Our cases do instruct lower courts to apply a "reasonable person" standard. But the "reasonable person" standard does not require a court to pretend that Alvarado was a 35-year-old with aging parents whose middle-aged children do what their parents ask only out of respect. Nor does it say that a court should pretend that Alvarado was the statistically determined "average person"—a working, married, 35-year-old white female with a high school degree.

Rather, the precise legal definition of "reasonable person" may, depending on legal context, appropriately account for certain personal characteristics. In negligence suits, for example, the question is what would a "reasonable person" do " 'under the same or similar circumstances.' " In answering that question, courts enjoy "latitude" and may make "allowance not only for external facts, but sometimes for certain characteristics of the actor himself," including physical disability, youth, or advanced age.

■ ■ ■

In the present context, that of *Miranda*'s "in custody" inquiry, the law has introduced the concept of a "reasonable person" to avoid judicial inquiry into subjective states of mind, and to focus the inquiry instead upon objective circumstances that are known to both the officer and the suspect and that are likely relevant to the way a person would understand his situation. . . .

In this case, Alvarado's youth is an objective circumstance that was known to the police. It is not a special quality, but rather a widely shared characteristic that generates commonsense conclusions about behavior and perception. To focus on the circumstance of age in a case like this does not complicate the "in custody" inquiry. And to say that courts should ignore widely shared, objective characteristics, like age, on the ground that only a (large) *minority* of the population possesses them would produce absurd results, the present instance being a case in point. I am not surprised that the majority points to no case suggesting any such limitation.

■ ■ ■

Nor am I surprised that the majority makes no real argument at all explaining *why* any court would believe that the objective fact of a suspect's age could *never* be relevant.

■ ■ ■

As I have said, the law in this case is clear. This Court's cases establish that, even if the police do not tell a suspect he is under arrest, do not handcuff him, do not lock him in a cell, and do not threaten him, he may nonetheless reasonably believe he is not free to leave the place of questioning—and thus be in custody for *Miranda* purposes.

Our cases also make clear that to determine how a suspect would have "gaug[ed]" his "freedom of movement," a court must carefully examine "all of the circumstances surrounding the interrogation." . . . In the present case, every one of these factors argues—and argues strongly—that Alvarado was in custody for *Miranda* purposes when the police questioned him.

Common sense, and an understanding of the law's basic purpose in this area, are enough to make clear that Alvarado's age—an objective, widely shared characteristic about which the police plainly knew—is also relevant to the inquiry. Unless one is prepared to pretend that Alvarado is someone he is not, a middle-aged gentleman, well versed in police practices, it seems to me clear that the California courts made a serious mistake. I agree with the Ninth Circuit's similar conclusions. Consequently, I dissent.

J.D.B. v. North Carolina

131 S. Ct. 2394 (2011)

SOTOMAYOR, J., delivered the opinion of the Court, in which KENNEDY, GINSBURG, BREYER, and KAGAN, JJ., joined. ALITO, J., filed a dissenting opinion, in which ROBERTS, C.J., and SCALIA and THOMAS, JJ. joined.

This case presents the question whether the age of a child subjected to police questioning is relevant to the custody analysis of *Miranda v. Arizona* (1966). It is beyond dispute that children will often feel bound to submit to police questioning when an adult in the same circumstances would feel free to leave. Seeing no reason for police officers or courts to blind themselves to that commonsense reality, we hold that a child's age properly informs the *Miranda* custody analysis.

I

A

Petitioner J.D.B. was a 13-year-old, seventh-grade student attending class at Smith Middle School in Chapel Hill, North Carolina when he was removed from his classroom by a uniformed police officer, escorted to a closed-door conference room, and questioned by police for at least half an hour.

This was the second time that police questioned J.D.B. in the span of a week. Five days earlier, two home break-ins occurred, and various items were stolen. Police stopped and questioned J.D.B. after he was seen behind a residence in the neighborhood where the crimes occurred. That same day, police also spoke to J.D.B.'s grandmother—his legal guardian—as well as his aunt.

Police later learned that a digital camera matching the description of one of the stolen items had been found at J.D.B.'s middle school and seen in J.D.B.'s possession. Investigator DiCostanzo, the juvenile investigator with the local police force who had been assigned to the case, went to the school to question J.D.B. Upon arrival, DiCostanzo informed the uniformed police officer on detail to the school (a so-called school resource officer), the assistant principal, and an administrative intern that he was there to question J.D.B. about the break-ins. Although DiCostanzo asked the school administrators to verify J.D.B.'s date of birth, address, and parent contact information from school records, neither the police officers nor the school administrators contacted J.D.B.'s grandmother.

The uniformed officer interrupted J.D.B.'s afternoon social studies class, removed J.D.B. from the classroom, and escorted him to a school conference room. There, J.D.B. was met by DiCostanzo, the assistant principal, and the administrative intern. The door to the conference room was closed. With the two police officers and the two administrators present, J.D.B. was questioned for the next 30 to 45 minutes. Prior to the commencement of questioning, J.D.B. was given neither *Miranda* warnings nor the opportunity to speak to his grandmother. Nor was he informed that he was free to leave the room.

Questioning began with small talk—discussion of sports and J.D.B.'s family life. DiCostanzo asked, and J.D.B. agreed, to discuss the events of the prior weekend. Denying any wrongdoing, J.D.B. explained that he had been in the neighborhood where the crimes occurred because he was seeking work mowing lawns. DiCostanzo pressed J.D.B. for additional detail about his efforts to obtain work; asked J.D.B. to explain a prior incident, when one of the victims returned home to find J.D.B. behind her house; and confronted J.D.B. with the stolen camera. The assistant principal urged J.D.B. to "do the right thing," warning J.D.B. that "the truth always comes out in the end." Eventually, J.D.B. asked whether he would "still be in trouble" if he returned the "stuff." In response, DiCostanzo explained that return of the stolen items would be helpful, but "this thing is going to court" regardless. DiCostanzo then warned that he may need to seek a secure custody order if he believed that J.D.B. would continue to break into other homes. When J.D.B. asked what a secure custody order was, DiCostanzo explained that "it's where you get sent to juvenile detention before court."

After learning of the prospect of juvenile detention, J.D.B. confessed that he and a friend were responsible for the break-ins. DiCostanzo only then informed J.D.B. that he could refuse to answer the investigator's questions and that he was free to leave. Asked whether he understood, J.D.B. nodded and provided further detail, including information about the location of the stolen items. Eventually J.D.B. wrote a statement, at DiCostanzo's request. When the bell rang indicating the end of the school day, J.D.B. was allowed to leave to catch the bus home.

Nonetheless, both parties' submissions to this Court suggest that the warnings came after DiCostanzo raised the possibility of a secure custody order but before J.D.B. confessed for the first time. Because we remand for a determination whether J.D.B. was in custody under the proper analysis, the state courts remain free to revisit whether the trial court made a conclusive finding of fact in this respect.

B

Two juvenile petitions were filed against J.D.B., each alleging one count of breaking and entering and one count of larceny. J.D.B.'s public defender moved to suppress his statements and the evidence derived therefrom, arguing that suppression was necessary because J.D.B. had been "interrogated by police in a custodial setting without being afforded *Miranda* warnings," and because his statements were involuntary under the totality of the circumstances test. After a suppression hearing at which DiCostanzo and J.D.B. testified, the trial court denied the motion, deciding that J.D.B. was not in custody at the time of the schoolhouse interrogation and that his statements were voluntary. As a result, J.D.B. entered a transcript of admission to all four counts, renewing his objection to the denial of his motion to suppress, and the court adjudicated J.D.B. delinquent.

A divided panel of the North Carolina Court of Appeals affirmed. The North Carolina Supreme Court held, over two dissents, that J.D.B. was not in custody when he confessed, "declining to extend the test for custody to include consideration of the age . . . of an individual subjected to questioning by police."

We granted certiorari to determine whether the *Miranda* custody analysis includes consideration of a juvenile suspect's age.

II

A

Any police interview of an individual suspected of a crime has "coercive aspects to it." Only those interrogations that occur while a suspect is in police custody, however, "heighten the risk" that statements obtained are not the product of the suspect's free choice. *Dickerson v. United States* (2000).

By its very nature, custodial police interrogation entails "inherently compelling pressures." *Miranda.* Even for an adult, the physical and psychological isolation of custodial interrogation can "undermine the individual's will to resist and . . . compel him to speak where he would not otherwise do so freely." Indeed, the pressure of custodial interrogation is so immense that it "can induce a frighteningly high percentage of people to confess to crimes they never committed." That risk is all the more troubling—and recent studies suggest, all the more acute—when the subject of custodial interrogation is a juvenile. See Brief for Center on Wrongful Convictions of Youth et al. as *Amici Curiae* 21-22 (collecting empirical studies that "illustrate the heightened risk of false confessions from youth").

Recognizing that the inherently coercive nature of custodial interrogation "blurs the line between voluntary and involuntary statements," this Court in *Miranda* adopted a set of prophylactic measures designed to safeguard the constitutional guarantee against self-incrimination. Prior to questioning, a suspect "must be warned that he has a right to remain silent, that any statement he does make may be used as evidence against him, and that he has a right to the presence of an attorney, either retained or appointed." And, if a suspect makes a statement during custodial interrogation, the burden is on the Government to show, as a "prerequisite" to the statement's admissibility as evidence in the Government's case in chief, that the defendant "voluntarily, knowingly and intelligently" waived his rights.

Because these measures protect the individual against the coercive nature of custodial interrogation, they are required " 'only where there has been such a restriction on a person's freedom as to render him "in custody."' " As we have repeatedly emphasized, whether a suspect is "in custody" is an objective inquiry.

> "Two discrete inquiries are essential to the determination: first, what were the circumstances surrounding the interrogation; and second, given those circumstances, would a reasonable person have felt he or she was at liberty to terminate the interrogation and leave. Once the scene is set and the players' lines and actions are reconstructed, the court must apply an objective test to resolve the ultimate inquiry: was there a formal arrest or restraint on freedom of movement of the degree associated with formal arrest." *Thomson v. Keohane* (1995).

Rather than demarcate a limited set of relevant circumstances, we have required police officers and courts to "examine all of the circumstances surrounding the interrogation," including any circumstance that "would have affected how a reasonable person" in the suspect's position "would perceive his or her freedom to leave." On the other hand, the "subjective views harbored by either the interrogating officers or the person being questioned" are irrelevant. The test, in other words, involves no consideration of the "actual mindset" of the particular suspect subjected to police questioning.

The benefit of the objective custody analysis is that it is "designed to give clear guidance to the police." Police must make in-the-moment judgments as to when to administer *Miranda* warnings. By limiting analysis to the objective circumstances of the interrogation, and asking how a reasonable person in the suspect's position would understand his freedom to terminate questioning and leave, the objective test avoids burdening police with the task of anticipating the idiosyncrasies of every individual suspect and divining how those particular traits affect each person's subjective state of mind.

B

The State and its *amici* contend that a child's age has no place in the custody analysis, no matter how young the child subjected to police questioning. We cannot agree. In some circumstances, a child's age "would have affected how a reasonable person" in the suspect's position "would perceive his or her freedom to leave." That is, a reasonable child subjected to police questioning will sometimes feel pressured to submit when a reasonable adult would feel free to go. We think it clear that courts can account for that reality without doing any damage to the objective nature of the custody analysis.

A child's age is far "more than a chronological fact." It is a fact that "generates commonsense conclusions about behavior and perception." Such conclusions apply broadly to children as a class. And, they are self-evident to anyone who was a child once himself, including any police officer or judge.

Time and again, this Court has drawn these commonsense conclusions for itself. We have observed that children "generally are less mature and responsible than adults," that they "often lack the experience, perspective, and judgment to recognize and avoid choices that could be detrimental to them," that they "are more vulnerable or susceptible to outside pressures" than adults, and so on. See Addressing the specific context of police interrogation, we have observed that events that "would leave a man cold and unimpressed can overawe and overwhelm a lad in his early teens." Describing no one child in particular, these observations restate what "any parent knows"—indeed, what any person knows—about children generally.

Our various statements to this effect are far from unique. The law has historically reflected the same assumption that children characteristically lack the capacity to exercise mature judgment and possess only an incomplete ability to understand the world around them. See, *e.g.*, 1 W. Blackstone, Commentaries on the Laws of England *464-*465 (explaining that limits on children's legal capacity under the common law "secure them from hurting themselves by their own improvident acts"). Like this Court's own generalizations, the legal disqualifications placed on children as a class—*e.g.*, limitations on their ability to alienate property, enter a binding contract enforceable against them, and marry without parental consent—exhibit the settled understanding that the differentiating characteristics of youth are universal.

Indeed, even where a "reasonable person" standard otherwise applies, the common law has reflected the reality that children are not adults. In negligence suits, for instance, where liability turns on what an objectively reasonable person would do in the circumstances, "all American jurisdictions accept the idea that a person's childhood is a relevant circumstance" to be considered. Restatement (Third) of Torts § 10, Comment *b*, p. 117 (2005).

As this discussion establishes, "our history is replete with laws and judicial recognition" that children cannot be viewed simply as miniature adults. We see no justification for taking a different course here. So long as the child's age was known to the officer at the time of the interview, or would have been objectively apparent to any reasonable officer, including age as part of the custody analysis requires officers neither to consider circumstances "unknowable" to them, nor to "anticipate the frailties or idiosyncrasies" of the particular suspect whom they question. The same "wide basis of community experience" that makes it possible, as an objective matter, "to determine what is to be expected" of children in other contexts, likewise makes it possible to know what to expect of children subjected to police questioning.

In other words, a child's age differs from other personal characteristics that, even when known to police, have no objectively discernible relationship to a reasonable person's understanding of his freedom of action. *Alvarado* (2004), holds, for instance, that a suspect's prior interrogation history with law enforcement has no role to play in the custody analysis because such experience could just as easily lead a reasonable person to feel free to walk away as to feel compelled to stay in place. Because the effect in any given case would be "contingent on the psychology" of the individual suspect, the Court explained, such experience cannot be considered without compromising the objective nature of the custody analysis. A child's age, however, is different. Precisely because childhood yields objective conclusions like those we have drawn ourselves—among others, that children are "most susceptible to influence," and "outside pressures"—considering age in the custody analysis in no way involves a determination of how youth "subjectively affects the mindset" of any particular child, Brief for Respondent 14.[7]

In fact, in many cases involving juvenile suspects, the custody analysis would be nonsensical absent some consideration of the suspect's age. This case is a prime example. Were the court precluded from taking J.D.B.'s youth into account, it would be forced to evaluate the circumstances present here through the eyes of a reasonable person of average years. In other words, how would a reasonable adult understand his situation, after being removed from a seventh-grade social studies class by a uniformed school resource officer; being encouraged by his assistant principal to "do the right thing"; and being warned by a police investigator of the prospect of juvenile detention and separation from his guardian and primary caretaker? To describe such an inquiry is to demonstrate its absurdity. Neither officers nor courts can reasonably evaluate the effect of objective circumstances that, by their nature, are specific to children without accounting for the age of the child subjected to those circumstances.

Indeed, although the dissent suggests that concerns "regarding the application of the *Miranda* custody rule to minors can be accommodated by considering the unique circumstances present when minors are questioned in school," the effect of the schoolhouse setting cannot be disentangled from the identity of the person questioned. A student—whose presence at school is compulsory and whose disobedience at school is cause for disciplinary action—is in a far different position than, say, a parent volunteer on school grounds to chaperone an event, or an adult from the community on school grounds to attend a basketball game. Without asking whether the person "questioned in school" is a "minor," the coercive effect of the schoolhouse setting is unknowable.

■ ■ ■

---

7. Thus, contrary to the dissent's protestations, today's holding neither invites consideration of whether a particular suspect is "unusually meek or compliant," nor "expands" the *Miranda* custody analysis into a test that requires officers to anticipate and account for a suspect's every personal characteristic.

holding

Reviewing the question *de novo* today, we hold that so long as the child's age was known to the officer at the time of police questioning, or would have been objectively apparent to a reasonable officer, its inclusion in the custody analysis is consistent with the objective nature of that test.[8] This is not to say that a child's age will be a determinative, or even a significant, factor in every case. It is, however, a reality that courts cannot simply ignore.

III

The State and its *amici* offer numerous reasons that courts must blind themselves to a juvenile defendant's age. None is persuasive.

To start, the State contends that a child's age must be excluded from the custody inquiry because age is a personal characteristic specific to the suspect himself rather than an "external" circumstance of the interrogation. Despite the supposed significance of this distinction, however, at oral argument counsel for the State suggested without hesitation that at least some undeniably personal characteristics—for instance, whether the individual being questioned is blind—are circumstances relevant to the custody analysis. Thus, the State's quarrel cannot be that age is a personal characteristic, without more.[9]

The State further argues that age is irrelevant to the custody analysis because it "go[es] to how a suspect may internalize and perceive the circumstances of an interrogation." But the same can be said of every objective circumstance that the State agrees is relevant to the custody analysis: Each circumstance goes to how a reasonable person would "internalize and perceive" every other. Indeed, this is the very reason that we ask whether the objective circumstances "add up to custody," instead of evaluating the circumstances one by one.

In the same vein, the State and its *amici* protest that the "effect of . . . age on [the] perception of custody is internal." But the whole point of the custody analysis is to determine whether, given the circumstances, "a reasonable person would have felt he or she was at liberty to terminate the interrogation and leave." Because the *Miranda* custody inquiry turns on the mindset of a reasonable person in the suspect's position, it cannot be the case that a circumstance is subjective simply because it has an "internal" or "psychological" impact on

---

8. This approach does not undermine the basic principle that an interrogating officer's unarticulated, internal thoughts are never—in and of themselves—objective circumstances of an interrogation. Unlike a child's youth, an officer's purely internal thoughts have no conceivable effect on how a reasonable person in the suspect's position would understand his freedom of action. Rather than "overturn" that settled principle, the limitation that a child's age may inform the custody analysis only when known or knowable simply reflects our unwillingness to require officers to "make guesses" as to circumstances "unknowable" to them in deciding when to give *Miranda* warnings.

9. The State's purported distinction between blindness and age—that taking account of a suspect's youth requires a court "to get into the mind" of the child, whereas taking account of a suspect's blindness does not—is mistaken. In either case, the question becomes how a reasonable person would understand the circumstances, either from the perspective of a blind person or, as here, a 13-year-old child.

perception. Were that so, there would be no objective circumstances to consider at all.

Relying on our statements that the objective custody test is "designed to give clear guidance to the police," the State next argues that a child's age must be excluded from the analysis in order to preserve clarity. Similarly, the dissent insists that the clarity of the custody analysis will be destroyed unless a "one-size-fits-all reasonable-person test" applies. In reality, however, ignoring a juvenile defendant's age will often make the inquiry more artificial, and thus only add confusion. And in any event, a child's age, when known or apparent, is hardly an obscure factor to assess. Though the State and the dissent worry about gradations among children of different ages, that concern cannot justify ignoring a child's age altogether. Just as police officers are competent to account for other objective circumstances that are a matter of degree such as the length of questioning or the number of officers present, so too are they competent to evaluate the effect of relative age. Indeed, they are competent to do so even though an interrogation room lacks the "reflective atmosphere of a jury deliberation room." The same is true of judges, including those whose childhoods have long since passed. In short, officers and judges need no imaginative powers, knowledge of developmental psychology, training in cognitive science, or expertise in social and cultural anthropology to account for a child's age. They simply need the common sense to know that a 7-year-old is not a 13-year-old and neither is an adult.

There is, however, an even more fundamental flaw with the State's plea for clarity and the dissent's singular focus on simplifying the analysis: Not once have we excluded from the custody analysis a circumstance that we determined was relevant and objective, simply to make the fault line between custodial and noncustodial "brighter." Indeed, were the guiding concern clarity and nothing else, the custody test would presumably ask only whether the suspect had been placed under formal arrest. But we have rejected that "more easily administered line," recognizing that it would simply "enable the police to circumvent the constraints on custodial interrogations established by *Miranda.*"

Finally, the State and the dissent suggest that excluding age from the custody analysis comes at no cost to juveniles' constitutional rights because the due process voluntariness test independently accounts for a child's youth. To be sure, that test permits consideration of a child's age, and it erects its own barrier to admission of a defendant's inculpatory statements at trial. But *Miranda*'s procedural safeguards exist precisely because the voluntariness test is an inadequate barrier when custodial interrogation is at stake. To hold, as the State requests, that a child's age is never relevant to whether a suspect has been taken into custody—and thus to ignore the very real differences between children and adults—would be to deny children the full scope of the procedural safeguards that *Miranda* guarantees to adults.

■ ■ ■

[handwritten: remanded for custody determination]

The question remains whether J.D.B. was in custody when police interrogated him. We remand for the state courts to address that question, this time taking account of all of the relevant circumstances of the interrogation, including J.D.B.'s age at the time.

The judgment of the North Carolina Supreme Court is reversed, and the case is remanded for proceedings not inconsistent with this opinion.

It is so ordered.

Justice ALITO, with whom THE CHIEF JUSTICE, Justice SCALIA, and Justice THOMAS join, dissenting.

The Court's decision in this case may seem on first consideration to be modest and sensible, but in truth it is neither. It is fundamentally inconsistent with one of the main justifications for the *Miranda* rule: the perceived need for a clear rule that can be easily applied in all cases. And today's holding is not needed to protect the constitutional rights of minors who are questioned by the police. *[handwritten: destroys the "clear" Miranda rule]*

Miranda's prophylactic regime places a high value on clarity and certainty. Dissatisfied with the highly fact-specific constitutional rule against the admission of involuntary confessions, the *Miranda* Court set down rigid standards that often require courts to ignore personal characteristics that may be highly relevant to a particular suspect's actual susceptibility to police pressure. This rigidity, however, has brought with it one of *Miranda*'s principal strengths—"the ease and clarity of its application" by law enforcement officials and courts. A key contributor to this clarity, at least up until now, has been *Miranda*'s objective reasonable-person test for determining custody.

Miranda's custody requirement is based on the proposition that the risk of unconstitutional coercion is heightened when a suspect is placed under formal arrest or is subjected to some functionally equivalent limitation on freedom of movement. When this custodial threshold is reached, *Miranda* warnings must precede police questioning. But in the interest of simplicity, the custody analysis considers only whether, under the circumstances, a hypothetical reasonable person would consider himself to be confined.

Many suspects, of course, will differ from this hypothetical reasonable person. Some, including those who have been hardened by past interrogations, may have no need for *Miranda* warnings at all. And for other suspects—those who are unusually sensitive to the pressures of police questioning—*Miranda* warnings may come too late to be of any use. That is a necessary consequence of *Miranda*'s rigid standards, but it does not mean that the constitutional rights of these especially sensitive suspects are left unprotected. A vulnerable defendant can still turn to the constitutional rule against *actual* coercion and contend that that his confession was extracted against his will.

Today's decision shifts the *Miranda* custody determination from a one-size-fits-all reasonable-person test into an inquiry that must account for at least one individualized characteristic—age—that is thought to correlate with susceptibility to coercive pressures. Age, however, is in no way the only personal characteristic that may correlate with pliability, and in future cases the Court will be forced to choose between two unpalatable alternatives. It may choose to limit today's decision by arbitrarily distinguishing a suspect's age from other personal characteristics—such as intelligence, education, occupation, or prior experience with law enforcement—that may also correlate with susceptibility to coercive pressures. Or, if the Court is unwilling to draw these arbitrary lines, it will be forced to effect a fundamental transformation of the *Miranda* custody test—from a clear, easily applied prophylactic rule into a highly fact-intensive standard resembling the voluntariness test that the *Miranda* Court found to be unsatisfactory.

For at least three reasons, there is no need to go down this road. First, many minors subjected to police interrogation are near the age of majority, and for these suspects the one-size-fits-all *Miranda* custody rule may not be a bad fit. Second, many of the difficulties in applying the *Miranda* custody rule to minors arise because of the unique circumstances present when the police conduct interrogations at school. The *Miranda* custody rule has always taken into account the setting in which questioning occurs, and accounting for the school setting in such cases will address many of these problems. Third, in cases like the one now before us, where the suspect is especially young, courts applying the constitutional voluntariness standard can take special care to ensure that incriminating statements were not obtained through coercion.

Safeguarding the constitutional rights of minors does not require the extreme makeover of *Miranda* that today's decision may portend.

I

In the days before *Miranda*, this Court's sole metric for evaluating the admissibility of confessions was a voluntariness standard rooted in both the Fifth Amendment's Self–Incrimination Clause and the Due Process Clause of the Fourteenth Amendment. The question in these voluntariness cases was whether the particular "defendant's will" had been "overborne." Courts took into account both "the details of the interrogation" *and* "the characteristics of the accused," and then "weighed the circumstances of pressure against the power of resistance of the person confessing."

All manner of individualized, personal characteristics were relevant in this voluntariness inquiry. Among the most frequently mentioned factors were the defendant's education, physical condition, intelligence, and mental health. The suspect's age also received prominent attention in several cases, especially when the suspect was a "mere child." The weight assigned to any one consideration varied from case to case. But all of these factors, along with anything else that might have affected the "individual's capacity for effective choice," were relevant in determining whether the confession was coerced or compelled.

The all-encompassing nature of the voluntariness inquiry had its benefits. It allowed courts to accommodate a "complex of values," and to make a careful, highly individualized determination as to whether the police had wrung "a confession out of [the] accused against his will." But with this flexibility came a decrease in both certainty and predictability, and the voluntariness standard proved difficult "for law enforcement officers to conform to, and for courts to apply in a consistent manner."

In *Miranda*, the Court supplemented the voluntariness inquiry with a "set of prophylactic measures" designed to ward off the "inherently compelling pressures of custodial interrogation." *Miranda* greatly simplified matters by requiring police to give suspects standard warnings before commencing any custodial interrogation. Its requirements are no doubt "rigid," and they often require courts to suppress "trustworthy and highly probative" statements that may be perfectly "voluntary under a traditional Fifth Amendment analysis." But with this rigidity comes increased clarity. *Miranda* provides "a workable rule to guide police officers," and an administrable standard for the courts. As has often been recognized, this gain in clarity and administrability is one of *Miranda*'s "principal advantages."

No less than other facets of *Miranda*, the threshold requirement that the suspect be in "custody" is "designed to give clear guidance to the police." Custody under *Miranda* attaches where there is a "formal arrest" or a "restraint on freedom of movement" akin to formal arrest. This standard is "objective" and turns on how a hypothetical "reasonable person in the position of the individual being questioned would gauge the breadth of his or her freedom of action."

Until today, the Court's cases applying this test have focused solely on the "objective circumstances of the interrogation," not the personal characteristics of the interrogated. Relevant factors have included such things as where the questioning occurred, how long it lasted, what was said, any physical restraints placed on the suspect's movement, and whether the suspect was allowed to leave when the questioning was through. The totality of *these* circumstances—the external circumstances, that is, of the interrogation itself—is what has mattered in this Court's cases. Personal characteristics of suspects have consistently been rejected or ignored as irrelevant under a one-size-fits-all reasonable-person standard.

■   ■   ■

The glaring absence of reliance on personal characteristics in these and other custody cases should come as no surprise. To account for such indivi-dualized considerations would be to contradict *Miranda*'s central premise. The *Miranda* Court's decision to adopt its inflexible prophylactic requirements was expressly based on the notion that "assessments of the knowledge the defendant possessed, based on information as to his age, education, intelli-gence, or prior contact with authorities, can never be more than speculation

II

In light of this established practice, there is no denying that, by incc ating age into its analysis, the Court is embarking on a new expansion established custody standard. And since *Miranda* is this Court's rule, constitutional command," it is up to the Court "to justify its expansion." This the Court fails to do.

In its present form, *Miranda*'s prophylactic regime already imposes "high cost[s]" by requiring suppression of confessions that are often "highly probative" and "voluntary" by any traditional standard. Nonetheless, a "core virtue" of *Miranda* has been the clarity and precision of its guidance to "police and courts." The Court has, however, repeatedly cautioned against upsetting the careful "balance" that *Miranda* struck, and it has "refused to sanction attempts to expand the *Miranda* holding" in ways that would reduce its "clarity." Given this practice, there should be a "strong presumption" against the Court's new departure from the established custody test. In my judgment, that presumption cannot be overcome here.

A

The Court's rationale for importing age into the custody standard is that minors tend to lack adults' "capacity to exercise mature judgment" and that failing to account for that "reality" will leave some minors unprotected under *Miranda* in situations where they perceive themselves to be confined. I do not dispute that many suspects who are under 18 will be more susceptible to police pressure than the average adult. As the Court notes, our pre-*Miranda* cases were particularly attuned to this "reality" in applying the constitutional requirement of voluntariness in fact. It is no less a "reality," however, that many persons *over* the age of 18 are also more susceptible to police pressure than the hypothetical reasonable person. Yet the *Miranda* custody standard has never accounted for the personal characteristics of these or any other individual defendants.

Indeed, it has always been the case under *Miranda* that the unusually meek or compliant are subject to the same fixed rules, including the same custody requirement, as those who are unusually resistant to police pressure. *Miranda*'s rigid standards are both overinclusive and underinclusive. They are overinclusive to the extent that they provide a windfall to the most hardened and savvy of suspects, who often have no need for *Miranda*'s protections. And *Miranda*'s requirements are underinclusive to the extent that they fail to account for "frailties," "idiosyncrasies," and other individualized considerations that might cause a person to bend more easily during a confrontation with the police. Members of this Court have seen this rigidity as a major weakness in *Miranda*'s "code of rules for confessions." But if it is, then the weakness is an inescapable consequence of the *Miranda* Court's decision to supplement the more holistic voluntariness requirement with a one-size-fits-all prophylactic rule.

That is undoubtedly why this Court's *Miranda* cases have never before mentioned "the suspect's age" or any other individualized consideration in applying the custody standard. And unless the *Miranda* custody rule is now to be radically transformed into one that takes into account the wide range of individual characteristics that are relevant in determining whether a confession is voluntary, the Court must shoulder the burden of explaining why age is different from these other personal characteristics.

Why, for example, is age different from intelligence? Suppose that an officer, upon going to a school to question a student, is told by the principal that the student has an I.Q. of 75 and is in a special-education class. Are those facts more or less important than the student's age in determining whether he or she "felt at liberty to terminate the interrogation and leave"? An I.Q. score, like age, is more than just a number. And an individual's intelligence can also yield "conclusions" similar to those "we have drawn ourselves" in cases far afield of *Miranda*.

How about the suspect's cultural background? Suppose the police learn (or should have learned) that a suspect they wish to question is a recent immigrant from a country in which dire consequences often befall any person who dares to attempt to cut short any meeting with the police. Is this really less relevant than the fact that a suspect is a month or so away from his 18th birthday?

The defendant's education is another personal characteristic that may generate "conclusions about behavior and perception." Under today's decision, why should police officers and courts "blind themselves," to the fact that a suspect has "only a fifth-grade education"? Alternatively, what if the police know or should know that the suspect is "a college-educated man with law school training"? How are these individual considerations meaningfully different from age in their "relationship to a reasonable person's understanding of his freedom of action"? The Court proclaims that "[a] child's age . . . is different," but the basis for this *ipse dixit* is dubious.

I have little doubt that today's decision will soon be cited by defendants—and perhaps by prosecutors as well—for the proposition that all manner of other individual characteristics should be treated like age and taken into account in the *Miranda* custody calculus. Indeed, there are already lower court decisions that take this approach.

In time, the Court will have to confront these issues, and it will be faced with a difficult choice. It may choose to distinguish today's decision and adhere to the arbitrary proclamation that "age is different." Or it may choose to extend today's holding and, in doing so, further undermine the very rationale for the *Miranda* regime.

B

If the Court chooses the latter course, then a core virtue of *Miranda*—the "ease and clarity of its application"—will be lost. However, even today's more limited departure from *Miranda*'s one-size-fits-all reasonable-person test will produce the very consequences that prompted the *Miranda* Court to abandon exclusive reliance on the voluntariness test in the first place: The Court's test will be hard for the police to follow, and it will be hard for judges to apply.

The Court holds that age must be taken into account when it "was known to the officer at the time of the interview," or when it "would have been objectively apparent" to a reasonable officer. The first half of this test overturns the rule that the "initial determination of custody" does not depend on the "subjective views harbored by interrogating officers." The second half will generate time-consuming satellite litigation over a reasonable officer's perceptions. When, as here, the interrogation takes place in school, the inquiry may be relatively simple. But not all police questioning of minors takes place in schools. In many cases, courts will presumably have to make findings as to whether a particular suspect had a sufficiently youthful look to alert a reasonable officer to the possibility that the suspect was under 18, or whether a reasonable officer would have recognized that a suspect's I.D. was a fake. The inquiry will be both "time-consuming and disruptive" for the police and the courts. It will also be made all the more complicated by the fact that a suspect's dress and manner will often be different when the issue is litigated in court than it was at the time of the interrogation.

Even after courts clear this initial hurdle, further problems will likely emerge as judges attempt to put themselves in the shoes of the average 16-year-old, or 15-year-old, or 13-year-old, as the case may be. Consider, for example, a 60-year-old judge attempting to make a custody determination through the eyes of a hypothetical, average 15-year-old. Forty-five years of personal experience and societal change separate this judge from the days when he or she was 15 years old. And this judge may or may not have been an average 15-year-old. The Court's answer to these difficulties is to state that "no imaginative powers, knowledge of developmental psychology, [or] training in cognitive science" will be necessary. Judges "simply need the common sense," the Court assures, "to know that a 7-year-old is not a 13-year-old and neither is an adult." It is obvious, however, that application of the Court's new rule demands much more than this.

Take a fairly typical case in which today's holding may make a difference. A 16½-year-old moves to suppress incriminating statements made prior to the administration of *Miranda* warnings. The circumstances are such that, if the defendant were at least 18, the court would not find that he or she was in custody, but the defendant argues that a reasonable 16½-year-old would view the situation differently. The judge will not have the luxury of merely saying: "It is common sense that a 16½-year-old is not an 18-year-old. Motion granted." Rather, the judge will be required to determine whether the differences between a typical 16½-year-old and a typical 18-year-old with respect to susceptibility to the pressures of interrogation are sufficient to change the outcome of the custody determination. Today's opinion contains not a word of actual guidance as to how judges are supposed to go about making that determination.

C

Petitioner and the Court attempt to show that this task is not unmanageable by pointing out that age is taken into account in other legal contexts. In particular, the Court relies on the fact that the age of a defendant is a relevant factor under the reasonable-person standard applicable in negligence suits.

But negligence is generally a question for the jury, the members of which can draw on their varied experiences with persons of different ages. It also involves a *post hoc* determination, in the reflective atmosphere of a deliberation room, about whether the defendant conformed to a standard of care. The *Miranda* custody determination, by contrast, must be made in the first instance by police officers in the course of an investigation that may require quick decisionmaking.

■ ■ ■

III

The Court's decision greatly diminishes the clarity and administrability that have long been recognized as "principal advantages" of *Miranda*'s pro-phylactic requirements. But what is worse, the Court takes this step unneces-sarily, as there are other, less disruptive tools available to ensure that minors are not coerced into confessing.

As an initial matter, the difficulties that the Court's standard introduces will likely yield little added protection for most juvenile defendants. Most juveniles who are subjected to police interrogation are teenagers nearing the age of majority. These defendants' reactions to police pressure are unlikely to be much different from the reaction of a typical 18-year-old in similar circum-stances. A one-size-fits-all *Miranda* custody rule thus provides a roughly rea-sonable fit for these defendants.

In addition, many of the concerns that petitioner raises regarding the appli-cation of the *Miranda* custody rule to minors can be accommodated by con-sidering the unique circumstances present when minors are questioned in school. The *Miranda* custody rule has always taken into account the setting in which questioning occurs, restrictions on a suspect's freedom of movement, and the presence of police officers or other authority figures. It can do so here as well.

Finally, in cases like the one now before us, where the suspect is much younger than the typical juvenile defendant, courts should be instructed to take particular care to ensure that incriminating statements were not obtained involuntarily. The voluntariness inquiry is flexible and accommodating by nature, and the Court's precedents already make clear that "special care" must be exercised in applying the voluntariness test where the confession of a "mere child" is at issue. If *Miranda*'s rigid, one-size-fits-all standards fail to account for the unique needs of juveniles, the response should be to rigorously apply the constitutional rule against coercion to ensure that the rights of min-ors are protected. There is no need to run *Miranda* off the rails.

■ ■ ■

The Court rests its decision to inject personal characteristics into the *Miranda* custody inquiry on the principle that judges applying *Miranda* cannot "blind themselves to commonsense reality." But the Court's shift is fundamen-tally at odds with the clear prophylactic rules that *Miranda* has long enforced. *Miranda* frequently requires judges to blind themselves to the reality that many un-Mirandized custodial confessions are "by no means involuntary" or coerced. It also requires police to provide a rote recitation of *Miranda* warnings that many suspects already know and could likely recite from memory.[13] Under today's new, "reality"-based approach to the doctrine, perhaps these and other principles of our *Miranda* jurisprudence will, like the custody standard, now be ripe for modification. Then, bit by bit, *Miranda* will lose the clarity and ease of application that has long been viewed as one of its chief justifications.

I respectfully dissent.

Howes v. Fields

131 S. Ct. 1047 (2011)

ALITO, J. delivered the opinion of the Court, in which ROBERTS, C.J., and SCALIA, KENNEDY, THOMAS, and KAGAN, JJ., joined. GINSBURG, J., filed an opinion concurring in part and dissenting in part, in which BREYER and SOTOMAYOR, JJ., joined.

The United States Court of Appeals for the Sixth Circuit held that our precedents clearly establish that a prisoner is in custody within the meaning of *Miranda v. Arizona* (1966), if the prisoner is taken aside and questioned about events that occurred outside the prison walls. Our decisions, however, do not clearly establish such a rule, and therefore the Court of Appeals erred in holding that this rule provides a permissible basis for federal habeas relief under the relevant provision of the Antiterrorism and Effective Death Penalty Act of 1996 (AEDPA). Indeed, the rule applied by the court below does not represent a correct interpretation of our *Miranda* case law. We therefore reverse.

I

While serving a sentence in a Michigan jail, Randall Fields was escorted by a corrections officer to a conference room where two sheriff's deputies questioned him about allegations that, before he came to prison, he had engaged in sexual conduct with a 12-year-old boy. In order to get to the conference room, Fields had to go down one floor and pass through a locked door that separated two sections of the facility. Fields arrived at the conference room between 7 p.m. and 9 p.m. and was questioned for between five and seven hours. At the beginning of the interview, Fields was told that he was free to leave and return to his cell. Later, he was again told that he could leave whenever he wanted. The two interviewing deputies were armed during the interview, but

---

13. Surveys have shown that "large majorities" of the public are aware that "individuals arrested for a crime" have a right to "remain silent (81%)," a right to "a lawyer (95%)," and a right to have a lawyer "appointed" if the arrestee "cannot afford one (88%)." See Belden, Russonello & Stewart, Developing a National Message for Indigent Defense: Analysis of National Survey 4 (Oct. 2001), online at http://www.nlada.org/DMS/Documents/1211996548.53/Polling results report.pdf.

Fields remained free of handcuffs and other restraints. The door to the conference room was sometimes open and sometimes shut.

About halfway through the interview, after Fields had been confronted with the allegations of abuse, he became agitated and began to yell. Fields testified that one of the deputies, using an expletive, told him to sit down and said that "if [he] didn't want to cooperate, [he] could leave." Fields eventually confessed to engaging in sex acts with the boy. According to Fields' testimony at a suppression hearing, he said several times during the interview that he no longer wanted to talk to the deputies, but he did not ask to go back to his cell prior to the end of the interview.

When he was eventually ready to leave, he had to wait an additional 20 minutes or so because a corrections officer had to be summoned to escort him back to his cell, and he did not return to his cell until well after the hour when he generally retired. At no time was Fields given *Miranda* warnings or advised that he did not have to speak with the deputies.

... The jury convicted Fields of two counts of third-degree criminal sexual conduct, and the judge sentenced him to a term of 10 to 15 years of imprisonment. On direct appeal, the Michigan Court of Appeals affirmed, rejecting Fields' contention that his statements should have been suppressed because he was subjected to custodial interrogation without a *Miranda* warning. The court ruled that Fields had not been in custody for purposes of *Miranda* during the interview, so no *Miranda* warnings were required. The court emphasized that Fields was told that he was free to leave and return to his cell but that he never asked to do so. The Michigan Supreme Court denied discretionary review.

Fields then filed a petition for a writ of habeas corpus in Federal District Court, and the court granted relief. The Sixth Circuit affirmed, holding that the interview in the conference room was a "custodial interrogation" within the meaning of *Miranda* because isolation from the general prison population combined with questioning about conduct occurring outside the prison makes any such interrogation custodial per se. The Court of Appeals reasoned that this Court clearly established in *Mathis v. United States* (1968), that "*Miranda* warnings must be administered when law enforcement officers remove an inmate from the general prison population and interrogate him regarding criminal conduct that took place outside the jail or prison." Because Fields was isolated from the general prison population and interrogated about conduct occurring in the outside world, the Court of Appeals found that the state court's decision was contrary to clearly established federal law as determined by this Court in *Mathis*. . . .

II

Under AEDPA, a federal court may grant a state prisoner's application for a writ of habeas corpus if the state-court adjudication pursuant to which the prisoner is held "resulted in a decision that was contrary to, or involved an unreasonable application of, clearly established Federal law, as determined by the Supreme Court of the United States." 28 U.S.C. § 2254(d)(1). In this context, "clearly established law" signifies "the holdings, as opposed to the dicta, of this Court's decisions."

In this case, it is abundantly clear that our precedents do not clearly establish the categorical rule on which the Court of Appeals relied, *i.e.*, that the questioning of a prisoner is always custodial when the prisoner is removed from the general prison population and questioned about events that occurred outside the prison. On the contrary, we have repeatedly declined to adopt any categorical rule with respect to whether the questioning of a prison inmate is custodial.

In *Illinois v. Perkins* (1990), where we upheld the admission of un-Mirandized statements elicited from an inmate by an undercover officer masquerading as another inmate, we noted that "[t]he bare fact of custody may not in every instance require a warning *even when the suspect is aware that he is speaking to an official, but we do not have occasion to explore that issue here.*" (emphasis added). Instead, we simply "reject[ed] the argument that *Miranda* warnings are required whenever a suspect is in custody in a technical sense and converses with someone who happens to be a government agent."

Most recently, in *Maryland v. Shatzer* (2010), we expressly declined to adopt a bright-line rule for determining the applicability of *Miranda* in prisons. *Shatzer* considered whether a break in custody ends the presumption of involuntariness established in *Edwards v. Arizona* (1981); and, if so, whether a prisoner's return to the general prison population after a custodial interrogation constitutes a break in *Miranda* custody. . . . The answer to this question, we noted, would "depen[d] upon whether [incarceration] exerts the coercive pressure that *Miranda* was designed to guard against—the 'danger of coercion [that] results from the *interaction* of custody and official interrogation.' "

■ ■ ■

The Court of Appeals purported to find support for its *per se* rule in *Shatzer*, relying on our statement that "[n]o one questions that Shatzer was in custody for *Miranda* purposes" when he was interviewed. But this statement means only that the issue of custody was not contested before us. It strains credulity to read the statement as constituting an "unambiguous conclusion" or "finding" by this Court that Shatzer was in custody.

Finally, contrary to respondent's suggestion, *Miranda* itself did not clearly establish the rule applied by the Court of Appeals. *Miranda* adopted a "set of prophylactic measures" designed to ward off the " 'inherently compelling pressures' of custodial interrogation," *Shatzer*, but *Miranda* did not hold that such pressures are always present when a prisoner is taken aside and questioned about events outside the prison walls. Indeed, *Miranda* did not even establish that police questioning of a suspect at the station house is always custodial. See [*Oregon v.*] *Mathiason* [(1977)] (declining to find that *Miranda* warnings are required "simply because the questioning takes place in the station house, or because the questioned person is one whom the police suspect").

In sum, our decisions do not clearly establish that a prisoner is always in custody for purposes of *Miranda* whenever a prisoner is isolated from the general prison population and questioned about conduct outside the prison.

III

Not only does the categorical rule applied below go well beyond anything that is clearly established in our prior decisions, it is simply wrong. The three elements of that rule—(1) imprisonment, (2) questioning in private, and (3) questioning about events in the outside world—are not necessarily enough to create a custodial situation for *Miranda* purposes.

A

As used in our *Miranda* case law, "custody" is a term of art that specifies circumstances that are thought generally to present a serious danger of coercion. In determining whether a person is in custody in this sense, the initial step is to ascertain whether, in light of "the objective circumstances of the interrogation," *Stansbury v. California* (1994) (*per curiam*), a "reasonable person [would] have felt he or she was not at liberty to terminate the interrogation and leave." And in order to determine how a suspect would have "gauge[d]" his "freedom of movement," courts must examine "all of the circumstances surrounding the interrogation." . . .

Determining whether an individual's freedom of movement was curtailed, however, is simply the first step in the analysis, not the last. Not all restraints on freedom of movement amount to custody for purposes of *Miranda*. We have "decline[d] to accord talismanic power" to the freedom-of-movement inquiry, *Berkemer* [*v. McCarty* (1984)], and have instead asked the additional question whether the relevant environment presents the same inherently coercive pressures as the type of station house questioning at issue in *Miranda*. "Our cases make clear . . . that the freedom-of-movement test identifies only a necessary and not a sufficient condition for *Miranda* custody." *Shatzer*.

This important point is illustrated by our decision in *Berkemer v. McCarty*. In that case, we held that the roadside questioning of a motorist who was pulled over in a routine traffic stop did not constitute custodial interrogation. We acknowledged that "a traffic stop significantly curtails the 'freedom of action' of the driver and the passengers," and that it is generally "a crime either to ignore a policeman's signal to stop one's car or, once having stopped, to drive away without permission." "[F]ew motorists," we noted, "would feel free either to disobey a directive to pull over or to leave the scene of a traffic stop without being told they might do so." Nevertheless, we held that a person detained as a result of a traffic stop is not in *Miranda* custody because such detention does not "sufficiently impair [the detained person's] free exercise of his privilege against self-incrimination to require that he be warned of his constitutional rights." As we later put it, the "temporary and relatively non-threatening detention involved in a traffic stop or *Terry* stop does not constitute *Miranda* custody."

It may be thought that the situation in *Berkemer*—the questioning of a motorist subjected to a brief traffic stop—is worlds away from those present when an inmate is questioned in a prison, but the same cannot be said of *Shatzer*, where we again distinguished between restraints on freedom of movement and *Miranda* custody. *Shatzer*, as noted, concerned the *Edwards* prophylactic rule, which limits the ability of the police to initiate further questioning of a suspect in *Miranda* custody once the suspect invokes the right to counsel. We held in *Shatzer* that this rule does not apply when there is a sufficient break in custody between the suspect's invocation of the right to counsel and the initiation of subsequent questioning. And, what is significant for present purposes, we further held that a break in custody may occur while a suspect is serving a term in prison. If a break in custody can occur while a prisoner is serving an uninterrupted term of imprisonment, it must follow that imprisonment alone is not enough to create a custodial situation within the meaning of *Miranda*.

There are at least three strong grounds for this conclusion. First, questioning a person who is already serving a prison term does not generally involve the shock that very often accompanies arrest. In the paradigmatic *Miranda* situation—a person is arrested in his home or on the street and whisked to a police station for questioning—detention represents a sharp and ominous change, and the shock may give rise to coercive pressures. A person who is "cut off from his normal life and companions," *Shatzer*, and abruptly transported from the street into a "police-dominated atmosphere," *Miranda*, may feel coerced into answering questions.

By contrast when a person who is already serving a term of imprisonment is questioned, there is usually no such change. "Interrogated suspects who have previously been convicted of crime live in prison." *Shatzer*. For a person serving a term of incarceration, we reasoned in *Shatzer*, the ordinary restrictions of prison life, while no doubt unpleasant, are expected and familiar and thus do not involve the same "inherently compelling pressures" that are often present when a suspect is yanked from familiar surroundings in the outside world and subjected to interrogation in a police station.

Second, a prisoner, unlike a person who has not been sentenced to a term of incarceration, is unlikely to be lured into speaking by a longing for prompt release. When a person is arrested and taken to a station house for interrogation, the person who is questioned may be pressured to speak by the hope that, after doing so, he will be allowed to leave and go home. On the other hand, when a prisoner is questioned, he knows that when the questioning ceases, he will remain under confinement.

Third, a prisoner, unlike a person who has not been convicted and sentenced, knows that the law enforcement officers who question him probably lack the authority to affect the duration of his sentence. And "where the possibility of parole exists," the interrogating officers probably also lack the power to bring about an early release. "When the suspect has no reason to think that the listeners have official power over him, it should not be assumed that his words are motivated by the reaction he expects from his listeners." [*Illinois v.*]

Perkins [(1990)]. Under such circumstances, there is little "basis for the assumption that a suspect . . . will feel compelled to speak by the fear of reprisal for remaining silent or in the hope of [a] more lenient treatment should he confess."

In short, standard conditions of confinement and associated restrictions on freedom will not necessarily implicate the same interests that the Court sought to protect when it afforded special safeguards to persons subjected to custodial interrogation. Thus, service of a term of imprisonment, without more, is not enough to constitute *Miranda* custody.

B

The two other elements included in the Court of Appeals' rule—questioning in private and questioning about events that took place outside the prison—are likewise insufficient.

Taking a prisoner aside for questioning—as opposed to questioning the prisoner in the presence of fellow inmates—does not necessarily convert a "noncustodial situation . . . to one in which *Miranda* applies." When a person who is not serving a prison term is questioned, isolation may contribute to a coercive atmosphere by preventing family members, friends, and others who may be sympathetic from providing either advice or emotional support. And without any such assistance, the person who is questioned may feel overwhelming pressure to speak and to refrain from asking that the interview be terminated.

By contrast, questioning a prisoner in private does not generally remove the prisoner from a supportive atmosphere. Fellow inmates are by no means necessarily friends. On the contrary, they may be hostile and, for a variety of reasons, may react negatively to what the questioning reveals. In the present case, for example, would respondent have felt more at ease if he had been questioned in the presence of other inmates about the sexual abuse of an adolescent boy? Isolation from the general prison population is often in the best interest of the interviewee and, in any event, does not suggest on its own the atmosphere of coercion that concerned the Court in *Miranda*.

It is true that taking a prisoner aside for questioning may necessitate some additional limitations on his freedom of movement. A prisoner may, for example, be removed from an exercise yard and taken, under close guard, to the room where the interview is to be held. But such procedures are an ordinary and familiar attribute of life behind bars. Escorts and special security precautions may be standard procedures regardless of the purpose for which an inmate is removed from his regular routine and taken to a special location. For example, ordinary prison procedure may require such measures when a prisoner is led to a meeting with an attorney.

Finally, we fail to see why questioning about criminal activity outside the prison should be regarded as having a significantly greater potential for coercion than questioning under otherwise identical circumstances about criminal activity within the prison walls. In both instances, there is the potential for additional criminal liability and punishment. If anything, the distinction would seem to cut the other way, as an inmate who confesses to misconduct that occurred within the prison may also incur administrative penalties, but even this is not enough to tip the scale in the direction of custody. "The threat to a citizen's Fifth Amendment rights that *Miranda* was designed to neutralize" is neither mitigated nor magnified by the location of the conduct about which questions are asked

For these reasons, the Court of Appeals' categorical rule is unsound.

IV

A

When a prisoner is questioned, the determination of custody should focus on all of the features of the interrogation. These include the language that is used in summoning the prisoner to the interview and the manner in which the interrogation is conducted. . . .

"Fidelity to the doctrine announced in *Miranda* requires that it be enforced strictly, but only in those types of situations in which the concerns that powered the decision are implicated." Confessions voluntarily made by prisoners in other situations should not be suppressed. "Voluntary confessions are not merely a proper element in law enforcement, they are an unmitigated good, essential to society's compelling interest in finding, convicting, and punishing those who violate the law."

B

The record in this case reveals that respondent was not taken into custody for purposes of *Miranda*. To be sure, respondent did not invite the interview or consent to it in advance, and he was not advised that he was free to decline to speak with the deputies. The following facts also lend some support to respondent's argument that *Miranda*'s custody requirement was met: The interview lasted for between five and seven hours in the evening and continued well past the hour when respondent generally went to bed; the deputies who questioned respondent were armed; and one of the deputies, according to respondent, "[u]sed a very sharp tone."

These circumstances, however, were offset by others. Most important, respondent was told at the outset of the interrogation, and was reminded again thereafter, that he could leave and go back to his cell whenever he wanted. Moreover, respondent was not physically restrained or threatened and was interviewed in a well-lit, average-sized conference room, where he was "not uncomfortable. He was offered food and water, and the door to the conference room was sometimes left open." "All of these objective facts are consistent with an interrogation environment in which a reasonable person would have felt free to terminate the interview and leave."

Because he was in prison, respondent was not free to leave the conference room by himself and to make his own way through the facility to his cell. Instead, he was escorted to the conference room and, when he ultimately decided to end the interview, he had to wait about 20 minutes for a corrections officer to arrive and escort him to his cell. But he would have been subject to this same restraint even if he had been taken to the conference room for some reason other than police questioning; under no circumstances could he have reasonably expected to be able to roam free. And while respondent testified that he "was told . . . if I did not want to cooperate, I needed to go back to my cell," these words did not coerce cooperation by threatening harsher conditions. Returning to his cell would merely have returned him to his usual environment. See *Shatzer* ("Interrogated suspects who have previously been convicted of crime live in prison. When they are released back into the general prison population, they return to their accustomed surroundings and daily routine—they regain the degree of control they had over their lives prior to the interrogation").

Taking into account all of the circumstances of the questioning—including especially the undisputed fact that respondent was told that he was free to end the questioning and to return to his cell—we hold that respondent was not in custody within the meaning of *Miranda*.

The judgment of the Court of Appeals is
Reversed.

Justice GINSBURG, with whom Justice BREYER and Justice SOTOMAYOR join, concurring in part and dissenting in part.

Given this Court's controlling decisions on what counts as "custody" for *Miranda* purposes, I agree that the law is not "clearly established" in respondent Fields's favor. But I disagree with the Court's further determination that Fields was not in custody under *Miranda*. Were the case here on direct review, I would vote to hold that *Miranda* precludes the State's introduction of Fields's confession as evidence against him.

Miranda v. Arizona reacted to police interrogation tactics that eroded the Fifth Amendment's ban on compulsory self-incrimination. The opinion did so by requiring interrogators to convey to suspects the now-familiar warnings: The suspect is to be informed, prior to interrogation, that he "has a right to remain silent, that any statement he does make may be used as evidence against him, and that he has a right to the presence of an attorney, either retained or appointed."

Under what circumstances are *Miranda* warnings required? *Miranda* tells us "in all settings in which [a person's] freedom of action is curtailed in any significant way." Given the reality that police interrogators "trad[e] on the weakness of individuals," *i.e.*, their "insecurity about [themselves] or [their] surroundings," the Court found the preinterrogation warnings set out in the opinion "indispensable." Those warnings, the Court elaborated, are "an absolute prerequisite in overcoming the inherent pressures of the interrogation atmosphere."

Fields, serving time for disorderly conduct, was, of course, "i[n] custody," but not "for purposes of *Miranda*," the Court concludes. I would not train, as the Court does, on the question whether there can be custody within custody.

Instead, I would ask, as *Miranda* put it, whether Fields was subjected to "incommunicado interrogation . . . in a police-dominated atmosphere," whether he was placed, against his will, in an inherently stressful situation, and whether his "freedom of action [was] curtailed in any significant way." Those should be the key questions, and to each I would answer "Yes."

As the Court acknowledges, Fields did not invite or consent to the interview. He was removed from his cell in the evening, taken to a conference room in the sheriff's quarters, and questioned by two armed deputies long into the night and early morning. He was not told at the outset that he had the right to decline to speak with the deputies. Shut in with the armed officers, Fields felt "trapped." Although told he could return to his cell if he did not want to cooperate, Fields believed the deputies "would not have allowed [him] to leave the room." And with good reason. More than once, "he told the officers . . . he did not want to speak with them anymore." He was given water, but not his evening medications. Yet the Court concludes that Fields was in "an interrogation environment in which a reasonable person would have felt free to terminate the interview and leave."

Critical to the Court's judgment is "the undisputed fact that [Fields] was told that he was free to end the questioning and to return to his cell." Never mind the facts suggesting that Fields's submission to the overnight interview was anything but voluntary. Was Fields "held for interrogation"? Brought to, and left alone with, the gun-bearing deputies, he surely was in my judgment.

Miranda instructed that such a person "must be clearly informed that he has the right to consult with a lawyer and to have the lawyer with him during interrogation." Those warnings, along with "warnings of the right to remain silent and that anything stated can be used in evidence against [the speaker]," *Miranda* explained, are necessary "prerequisite[s] to [an] interrogation" compatible with the Fifth Amendment. Today, for people already in prison, the Court finds it adequate for the police to say: "You are free to terminate this interrogation and return to your cell." Such a statement is no substitute for one ensuring that an individual is aware of his rights.

For the reasons stated, I would hold that the "incommunicado interrogation [of Fields] in a police-dominated atmosphere," without informing him of his rights, dishonored the Fifth Amendment privilege *Miranda* was designed to safeguard.

4. Interrogation

Rhode Island v. Innis

446 U.S. 291 (1980)

STEWART, J., delivered the opinion of the Court, in which BLACKMUN, WHITE, POWELL, and REHNQUIST, JJ., joined. WHITE, J., filed a concurring opinion.

Burger, C.J., filed an opinion concurring in the judgment. Marshall, J., filed a dissenting opinion, in which Brennan, J., joined. Stevens, J., filed a dissenting opinion.

In *Miranda v. Arizona* [(1966)], the Court held that, once a defendant in custody asks to speak with a lawyer, all interrogation must cease until a lawyer is present. The issue in this case is whether the respondent was "interrogated" in violation of the standards promulgated in the *Miranda* opinion.

■   ■   ■

On the night of January 12, 1975, John Mulvaney, a Providence, R.I., taxicab driver, disappeared after being dispatched to pick up a customer. His body was discovered four days later buried in a shallow grave in Coventry, R.I. He had died from a shotgun blast aimed at the back of his head.

On January 17, 1975, shortly after midnight, the Providence police received a telephone call from Gerald Aubin, also a taxicab driver, who reported that he had just been robbed by a man wielding a sawed-off shotgun. Aubin further reported that he had dropped off his assailant near Rhode Island College in a section of Providence known as Mount Pleasant. While at the Providence police station waiting to give a statement, Aubin noticed a picture of his assailant on a bulletin board. Aubin so informed one of the police officers present. The officer prepared a photo array, and again Aubin identified a picture of the same person. That person was the respondent. Shortly thereafter, the Providence police began a search of the Mount Pleasant area.

At approximately 4:30 a.m. on the same date, Patrolman Lovell, while cruising the streets of Mount Pleasant in a patrol car, spotted the respondent standing in the street facing him. When Patrolman Lovell stopped his car, the respondent walked towards it. Patrolman Lovell then arrested the respondent, who was unarmed, and advised him of his so-called *Miranda* rights. While the two men waited in the patrol car for other police officers to arrive, Patrolman Lovell did not converse with the respondent other than to respond to the latter's request for a cigarette.

Within minutes, Sergeant Sears arrived at the scene of the arrest, and he also gave the respondent the *Miranda* warnings. Immediately thereafter, Captain Leyden and other police officers arrived. Captain Leyden advised the respondent of his *Miranda* rights. The respondent stated that he understood those rights and wanted to speak with a lawyer. Captain Leyden then directed that the respondent be placed in a "caged wagon," a four-door police car with a wire screen mesh between the front and rear seats, and be driven to the central police station. Three officers, Patrolmen Gleckman, Williams, and McKenna, were assigned to accompany the respondent to the central station. They placed the respondent in the vehicle and shut the doors. Captain Leyden then instructed the officers not to question the respondent or intimidate or coerce him in any way. The three officers then entered the vehicle, and it departed.

While en route to the central station, Patrolman Gleckman initiated a conversation with Patrolman McKenna concerning the missing shotgun. As Patrolman Gleckman later testified:

"*A.* At this point, I was talking back and forth with Patrolman McKenna stating that I frequent this area while on patrol and [that because a school for handicapped children is located nearby,] there's a lot of handicapped children running around in this area, and God forbid one of them might find a weapon with shells and they might hurt themselves."

Patrolman McKenna apparently shared his fellow officer's concern:

"*A.* I more or less concurred with him [Gleckman] that it was a safety factor and that we should, you know, continue to search for the weapon and try to find it."

While Patrolman Williams said nothing, he overheard the conversation between the two officers:

"*A.* He [Gleckman] said it would be too bad if the little—I believe he said a girl—would pick up the gun, maybe kill herself."

The respondent then interrupted the conversation, stating that the officers should turn the car around so he could show them where the gun was located. At this point, Patrolman McKenna radioed back to Captain Leyden that they were returning to the scene of the arrest and that the respondent would inform them of the location of the gun. At the time the respondent indicated that the officers should turn back, they had traveled no more than a mile, a trip encompassing only a few minutes.

The police vehicle then returned to the scene of the arrest where a search for the shotgun was in progress. There, Captain Leyden again advised the respondent of his *Miranda* rights. The respondent replied that he understood those rights but that he "wanted to get the gun out of the way because of the kids in the area in the school." The respondent then led the police to a nearby field, where he pointed out the shotgun under some rocks by the side of the road.

■ ■ ■

We granted certiorari to address for the first time the meaning of "interrogation" under *Miranda v. Arizona.*

■ ■ ■

In its *Miranda* opinion, the Court concluded that in the context of "custodial interrogation" certain procedural safeguards are necessary to protect a defendant's Fifth and Fourteenth Amendment privilege against compulsory self-incrimination. More specifically, the Court held that "the prosecution may not use statements, whether exculpatory or inculpatory, stemming from custodial interrogation of the defendant unless it demonstrates the use of procedural safeguards effective to secure the privilege against self-incrimination." Those safeguards included the now familiar *Miranda* warnings—namely, that the defendant be informed "that he has the right to remain silent, that anything he says can be used against him in a court of law, that he has the right to the presence of an attorney, and that if he cannot afford an attorney one will be appointed for him prior to any questioning if he so desires"—or their equivalent.

The Court in the *Miranda* opinion also outlined in some detail the consequences that would result if a defendant sought to invoke those procedural safeguards. With regard to the right to the presence of counsel, the Court noted:

> "Once warnings have been given, the subsequent procedure is clear. . . . If the individual states that he wants an attorney, the interrogation must cease until an attorney is present. At that time, the individual must have an opportunity to confer with the attorney and to have him present during any subsequent questioning. If the individual cannot obtain an attorney and he indicates that he wants one before speaking to police, they must respect his decision to remain silent."

he invoked Miranda

In the present case, the parties are in agreement that the respondent was fully informed of his *Miranda* rights and that he invoked his *Miranda* right to counsel when he told Captain Leyden that he wished to consult with a lawyer. It is also uncontested that the respondent was "in custody" while being transported to the police station.

Issue

The issue, therefore, is whether the respondent was "interrogated" by the police officers in violation of the respondent's undisputed right under *Miranda* to remain silent until he had consulted with a lawyer. In resolving this issue, we first define the term "interrogation" under *Miranda* before turning to a consideration of the facts of this case.

■ ■ ■

The starting point for defining "interrogation" in this context is, of course, the Court's *Miranda* opinion. There the Court observed that "[b]y custodial interrogation, we mean *questioning* initiated by law enforcement officers after a person has been taken into custody or otherwise deprived of his freedom of action in any significant way." This passage and other references throughout the opinion to "questioning" might suggest that the *Miranda* rules were to apply only to those police interrogation practices that involve express questioning of a defendant while in custody.

broader reading of Miranda

We do not, however, construe the *Miranda* opinion so narrowly. The concern of the Court in *Miranda* was that the "interrogation environment" created by the interplay of interrogation and custody would "subjugate the individual to the will of his examiner" and thereby undermine the privilege against compulsory self-incrimination. The police practices that evoked this concern included several that did not involve express questioning. For example, one of the practices discussed in *Miranda* was the use of lineups in which a coached witness would pick the defendant as the perpetrator. This was designed to establish that the defendant was in fact guilty as a predicate for further interrogation. A variation on this theme discussed in *Miranda* was the so-called "reverse line-up" in which a defendant would be identified by coached witnesses as the perpetrator of a fictitious crime, with the object of inducing him to confess to the actual crime of which he was suspected in order to escape the false prosecution. The Court in *Miranda* also included in its survey of interrogation practices the use of psychological ploys, such as to "posi[t]" "the guilt of the subject," to "minimize the moral seriousness of the offense," and "to cast blame on the victim or on society." It is clear that these techniques of persuasion, no less than express questioning, were thought, in a custodial setting, to amount to interrogation.

This is not to say, however, that all statements obtained by the police after a person has been taken into custody are to be considered the product of interrogation.

■ ■ ■

It is clear therefore that the special procedural safeguards outlined in *Miranda* are required not where a suspect is simply taken into custody, but rather where a suspect in custody is subjected to interrogation. "Interrogation," as conceptualized in the *Miranda* opinion, must reflect a measure of compulsion above and beyond that inherent in custody itself.

We conclude that the *Miranda* safeguards come into play whenever a person in custody is subjected to either express questioning or its functional equivalent. That is to say, the term "interrogation" under *Miranda* refers not only to express questioning, but also to any words or actions on the part of the police (other than those normally attendant to arrest and custody) that the police should know are reasonably likely to elicit an incriminating response from the suspect. The latter portion of this definition focuses primarily upon the perceptions of the suspect, rather than the intent of the police. This focus reflects the fact that the *Miranda* safeguards were designed to vest a suspect in custody with an added measure of protection against coercive police practices, without regard to objective proof of the underlying intent of the police. A practice that the police should know is reasonably likely to evoke an incriminating response from a suspect thus amounts to interrogation.[7] But, since the police surely cannot be held accountable for the unforeseeable results of their words or actions, the definition of interrogation can extend only to words or actions on the part of police officers that they *should have known* were reasonably likely to elicit an incriminating response. . . .

Turning to the facts of the present case, we conclude that the respondent was not "interrogated" within the meaning of *Miranda*. It is undisputed that the first prong of the definition of "interrogation" was not satisfied, for the conversation between Patrolmen Gleckman and McKenna included no express

---

7. This is not to say that the intent of the police is irrelevant, for it may well have a bearing on whether the police should have known that their words or actions were reasonably likely to evoke an incriminating response. In particular, where a police practice is designed to elicit an incriminating response from the accused, it is unlikely that the practice will not also be one which the police should have known was reasonably likely to have that effect.

questioning of the respondent. Rather, that conversation was, at least in form, nothing more than a dialogue between the two officers to which no response from the respondent was invited.

Moreover, it cannot be fairly concluded that the respondent was subjected to the "functional equivalent" of questioning. It cannot be said, in short, that Patrolmen Gleckman and McKenna should have known that their conversation was reasonably likely to elicit an incriminating response from the respondent. There is nothing in the record to suggest that the officers were aware that the respondent was peculiarly susceptible to an appeal to his conscience concerning the safety of handicapped children. Nor is there anything in the record to suggest that the police knew that the respondent was unusually disoriented or upset at the time of his arrest.[9]

The case thus boils down to whether, in the context of a brief conversation, the officers should have known that the respondent would suddenly be moved to make a self-incriminating response. Given the fact that the entire conversation appears to have consisted of no more than a few off hand remarks, we cannot say that the officers should have known that it was reasonably likely that Innis would so respond. This is not a case where the police carried on a lengthy harangue in the presence of the suspect. Nor does the record support the respondent's contention that, under the circumstances, the officers' comments were particularly "evocative." It is our view, therefore, that the respondent was not subjected by the police to words or actions that the police should have known were reasonably likely to elicit an incriminating response from him.

The Rhode Island Supreme Court erred, in short, in equating "subtle compulsion" with interrogation. That the officers' comments struck a responsive chord is readily apparent. Thus, it may be said, as the Rhode Island Supreme Court did say, that the respondent was subjected to "subtle compulsion." But that is not the end of the inquiry. It must also be established that a suspect's incriminating response was the product of words or actions on the part of the police that they should have known were reasonably likely to elicit an incriminating response. This was not established in the present case.

For the reasons stated, the judgment of the Supreme Court of Rhode Island is vacated, and the case is remanded to that court for further proceedings not inconsistent with this opinion.

It is so ordered.

■ ■ ■

Justice STEVENS, dissenting.

An original definition of an old term coupled with an original finding of fact on a cold record makes it possible for this Court to vacate the judgment of

---

9. The record in no way suggests that the officers' remarks were *designed* to elicit a response. It is significant that the trial judge, after hearing the officers' testimony, concluded that it was "entirely understandable that [the officers] would voice their concern [for the safety of the handicapped children] to each other."

the Supreme Court of Rhode Island. That court, on the basis of the facts in the record before it, concluded that members of the Providence, R.I., police force had interrogated respondent, who was clearly in custody at the time, in the absence of counsel after he had requested counsel. In my opinion the state court's conclusion that there was interrogation rests on a proper interpretation of both the facts and the law; thus, its determination that the products of the interrogation were inadmissible at trial should be affirmed.

■ ■ ■

After a suppression hearing, the trial court assumed, without deciding, that Officer Gleckman's statement constituted interrogation. The court nevertheless allowed the shotgun and testimony concerning respondent's connection to it into evidence on the ground that respondent had waived his *Miranda* rights when he consented to help police locate the gun. On appeal from respondent's conviction for kidnaping, robbery and murder, the Rhode Island Supreme Court held that Officer Gleckman's statement constituted impermissible interrogation and rejected the trial court's waiver analysis. It therefore reversed respondent's conviction and remanded for a new trial. Today, the Court reverses the Rhode Island court's resolution of the interrogation issue, creating a new definition of that term and holding, as a matter of law, that the statement at issue in this case did not constitute interrogation.

■ ■ ■

As the Court recognizes, *Miranda v. Arizona* makes it clear that, once respondent requested an attorney, he had an absolute right to have any type of interrogation cease until an attorney was present. As it also recognizes, *Miranda* requires that the term "interrogation" be broadly construed to include "either express questioning or its functional equivalent." In my view any statement that would normally be understood by the average listener as calling for a response is the functional equivalent of a direct question, whether or not it is punctuated by a question mark. The Court, however, takes a much narrower view. It holds that police conduct is not the "functional equivalent" of direct questioning unless the police should have known that what they were saying or doing was likely to elicit an incriminating response from the suspect. This holding represents a plain departure from the principles set forth in *Miranda*.

■ ■ ■

In short, in order to give full protection to a suspect's right to be free from any interrogation at all, the definition of "interrogation" must include any police statement or conduct that has the same purpose or effect as a direct question. Statements that appear to call for a response from the suspect, as well as those that are designed to do so, should be considered interrogation. By prohibiting only those relatively few statements or actions that a police officer should know are likely to elicit an incriminating response, the Court today accords a suspect considerably less protection. Indeed, since I suppose most suspects are unlikely to incriminate themselves even when questioned directly, this new definition will almost certainly exclude every statement that is not punctuated with a question mark from the concept of "interrogation."

The difference between the approach required by a faithful adherence to *Miranda* and the stinted test applied by the Court today can be illustrated by comparing three different ways in which Officer Gleckman could have communicated his fears about the possible dangers posed by the shotgun to handicapped children. He could have:

(1) directly asked Innis:

Will you please tell me where the shotgun is so we can protect handicapped school children from danger?

(2) announced to the other officers in the wagon:

If the man sitting in the back seat with me should decide to tell us where the gun is, we can protect handicapped children from danger.

or **(3)** stated to the other officers:

It would be too bad if a little handicapped girl would pick up the gun that this man left in the area and maybe kill herself.

In my opinion, all three of these statements should be considered interrogation because all three appear to be designed to elicit a response from anyone who in fact knew where the gun was located. Under the Court's test, on the other hand, the form of the statements would be critical. The third statement would not be interrogation because in the Court's view there was no reason for Officer Gleckman to believe that Innis was susceptible to this type of an implied appeal, therefore, the statement would not be reasonably likely to elicit an incriminating response. Assuming that this is true, then it seems to me that the first two statements, which would be just as unlikely to elicit such a response, should also not be considered interrogation. But, because the first statement is clearly an express question, it *would* be considered interrogation under the Court's test. The second statement, although just as clearly a deliberate appeal to Innis to reveal the location of the gun, would presumably not be interrogation because (a) it was not in form a direct question and (b) it does not fit within the "reasonably likely to elicit an incriminating response" category that applies to indirect interrogation.

As this example illustrates, the Court's test creates an incentive for police to ignore a suspect's invocation of his rights in order to make continued attempts to extract information from him. If a suspect does not appear to be susceptible to a particular type of psychological pressure, the police are apparently free to exert that pressure on him despite his request for counsel, so long as they are careful not to punctuate their statements with question marks. And if, contrary to all reasonable expectations, the suspect makes an incriminating statement, that statement can be used against him at trial. The Court thus turns *Miranda's* unequivocal rule against any interrogation at all into a trap in which unwary suspects may be caught by police deception. . . .

Arizona v. Mauro

481 U.S. 520 (1987)

Powell, J., delivered the opinion of the Court, in which Rehnquist, C.J., and White, O'Connor, and Scalia, JJ., joined. Stevens, J., filed a dissenting opinion, in which Brennan, Marshall, and Blackmun, JJ., joined.

While respondent in this case was in police custody, he indicated that he did not wish to answer any questions until a lawyer was present. The issue presented is whether, in the circumstances of this case, officers interrogated respondent in violation of the Fifth and Fourteenth Amendments when they allowed him to speak with his wife in the presence of a police officer.

On November 23, 1982, the Flagstaff Police Department received a telephone call from a local K Mart store. The caller stated that a man had entered the store claiming to have killed his son. When officers reached the store, respondent Mauro freely admitted that he had killed his son. He directed the officers to the child's body, and then was arrested and advised of his constitutional rights pursuant to *Miranda v. Arizona* (1966). The officers then took Mauro to the police station, where he was advised of his *Miranda* rights again. At that point, Mauro told the officers that he did not wish to make any more statements without having a lawyer present. All questioning then ceased. As no secure detention area was available, Mauro was held in the office of the police captain.

At the same time, one of the officers, Detective Manson, was questioning Mauro's wife in another room. After she finished speaking with Manson, Mrs. Mauro asked if she could speak to her husband. Manson was reluctant to allow the meeting, but after Mrs. Mauro insisted, he discussed the request with his supervisor, Sergeant Allen. Allen testified that he "saw no harm in it and suggested to [Manson] that if she really sincerely wanted to talk to him to go ahead and allow it." Allen instructed Manson not to leave Mr. and Mrs. Mauro alone and suggested that Manson tape-record the conversation.

Manson then "told both Mr. and Mrs. Mauro that they could speak together only if an officer were present in the room to observe and hear what was going on." He brought Mrs. Mauro into the room and seated himself at a desk, placing a tape recorder in plain sight on the desk. He recorded their brief conversation, in which she expressed despair about their situation.

During the conversation, Mauro told his wife not to answer questions until a lawyer was present.[1]

Mauro's defense at trial was that he had been insane at the time of the crime. In rebuttal, the prosecution played the tape of the meeting between Mauro and his wife, arguing that it demonstrated that Mauro was sane on the day of the murder. Mauro sought suppression of the recording on the ground that it was a product of police interrogation in violation of his *Miranda* rights. The trial court refused to suppress the recording. First, it explained the basis of the officers' decision to allow Mrs. Mauro to meet with her husband in the presence of a policeman.

■ ■ ■

We begin by summarizing the relevant legal principles. The Fifth Amendment provides that no "person . . . shall be compelled in any criminal case to be a witness against himself." In *Miranda v. Arizona*, the Court concluded that "without proper safeguards the process of in-custody interrogation of persons suspected or accused of crime contains inherently compelling pressures which work to undermine the individual's will to resist and to compel him to speak where he would not otherwise do so freely." "Accordingly, the Court formulated the now-familiar 'procedural safeguards effective to secure the privilege against self-incrimination.' " Among these is the rule that when an accused has "expressed his desire to deal with the police only through counsel, [he] is not subject to further interrogation by the authorities until counsel has been made available to him, unless the accused himself initiates further communication, exchanges, or conversations with the police." *Edwards v. Arizona* (1981).

One of the questions frequently presented in cases in this area is whether particular police conduct constitutes "interrogation." In *Miranda*, the Court

---

1. The entire conversation proceeded as follows:

"*Mrs. Mauro:* Please—please, I don't know what to do. We should have put David [the victim] in the hospital. Please—I don't know what we're going to do. We should have went for help—we should have went for help."

[Mr. Mauro]: You tried as best you could to stop it.

Mrs. Mauro: I—

[Mr. Mauro]: Shut up.

Mrs. Mauro: —taken him to a mental hospital or something. What'll we do?

[Mr. Mauro]: Shut up.

Det. Manson: Do you know a reverend or a priest or someone you can talk to—take care of David?

Mrs. Mauro: No.

[Mr. Mauro]: Don't answer questions until you get rights of attorney before you find out whats [*sic*] going on. You tried to stop me as best you can. What are you going to do, kill me? You tried the best you can to stop me.

Mrs. Mauro: I don't—we don't—I don't have money.

[Mr. Mauro]: There's a public attorney.

Mrs. Mauro: I don't know.

[Mr. Mauro]: There's a public attorney. Why don't you just be quiet.

Mrs. Mauro: I don't have any money to bury him. I don't have any money. All I got is enough money for the rent for the children and that's it.

Det. Manson: Did you want to talk to your husband any more?

Mrs. Mauro: No, I can't talk to him.

[Mr. Mauro]: Then don't talk to me—get out.

Mrs. Mauro: I don't know what to do. O.K."

suggested in one passage that "interrogation" referred only to actual "questioning initiated by law enforcement officers." But this statement was clarified in *Rhode Island v. Innis* (1980). In that case, the Court reviewed the police practices that had evoked the *Miranda* Court's concern about the coerciveness of the " 'interrogation environment.' " The questioned practices included "the use of lineups in which a coached witness would pick the defendant as the perpetrator . . . [,] the so-called 'reverse line-up' in which a defendant would be identified by coached witnesses as the perpetrator of a fictitious crime," and a variety of "psychological ploys, such as to 'posi[t]' 'the guilt of the subject,' to 'minimize the moral seriousness of the offense,' and 'to cast blame on the victim or on society.' " None of these techniques involves express questioning, and yet the Court found that any of them, coupled with the "interrogation environment," was likely to " 'subjugate the individual to the will of his examiner' and thereby undermine the privilege against compulsory self-incrimination." Thus, the *Innis* Court concluded that the goals of the *Miranda* safeguards could be effectuated if those safeguards extended not only to express questioning, but also to "its functional equivalent." The Court explained the phrase "functional equivalent" of interrogation as including "any words or actions on the part of the police (other than those normally attendant to arrest and custody) that the police should know are reasonably likely to elicit an incriminating response from the suspect." Finally, it noted that "[t]he latter portion of this definition focuses primarily upon the perceptions of the suspect, rather than the intent of the police."

■ ■ ■

We now turn to the case before us. The officers gave Mauro the warnings required by *Miranda*. Mauro indicated that he did not wish to be questioned further without a lawyer present. Mauro never waived his right to have a lawyer present. The sole issue, then, is whether the officers' subsequent actions rose to the level of interrogation—that is, in the language of *Innis*, whether they were the "functional equivalent" of police interrogation. We think it is clear under both *Miranda* and *Innis* that Mauro was not interrogated. The tape recording of the conversation between Mauro and his wife shows that Detective Manson asked Mauro no questions about the crime or his conduct. Nor is it suggested—or supported by any evidence—that Sergeant Allen's decision to allow Mauro's wife to see him was the kind of psychological ploy that properly could be treated as the functional equivalent of interrogation.

There is no evidence that the officers sent Mrs. Mauro in to see her husband for the purpose of eliciting incriminating statements. As the trial court found, the officers tried to discourage her from talking to her husband, but finally "yielded to her insistent demands." Nor was Detective Manson's presence improper. His testimony, that the trial court found credible, indicated a number of legitimate reasons—not related to securing incriminating statements—for having a police officer present. Finally, the weakness of Mauro's claim that he was interrogated is underscored by examining the situation from his perspective. *Rhode Island v. Innis* (suggesting that the suspect's perspective may be relevant in some cases in determining whether police actions constitute interrogation). We doubt that a suspect, told by officers that his wife will be allowed to speak to him, would feel that he was being coerced to incriminate himself in any way.

■ ■ ■

In deciding whether particular police conduct is interrogation, we must remember the purpose behind our decisions in *Miranda* and *Edwards*: preventing government officials from using the coercive nature of confinement to extract confessions that would not be given in an unrestrained environment. The government actions in this case do not implicate this purpose in any way. Police departments need not adopt inflexible rules barring suspects from speaking with their spouses, nor must they ignore legitimate security concerns by allowing spouses to meet in private. In short, the officers in this case acted reasonably and lawfully by allowing Mrs. Mauro to speak with her husband. In this situation, the Federal Constitution does not forbid use of Mauro's subsequent statements at his criminal trial.

■ ■ ■

The judgment of the Arizona Supreme Court is reversed. The case is remanded for further proceedings not inconsistent with this opinion.

It is so ordered.

Justice Stevens, with whom Justice Brennan, Justice Marshall, and Justice Blackmun join, dissenting.

The Supreme Court of Arizona unanimously and unequivocally concluded that the police intended to interrogate respondent. This Court reverses, finding that no interrogation occurred because Mauro "was not subjected to compelling influences, psychological ploys, or direct questioning." The record indicates, however, that the police employed a powerful psychological ploy: they failed to give respondent any advance warning that Mrs. Mauro was coming to talk to him, that a police officer would accompany her, or that their conversation would be recorded. As the transcript of the conversation reveals, respondent would not have freely chosen to speak with her. These facts compel the conclusion that the police took advantage of Mrs. Mauro's request to visit her husband, setting up a confrontation between them at a time when he manifestly desired to remain silent. Because they allowed respondent's conversation with his wife to commence at a time when they knew it was reasonably likely to produce an incriminating statement, the police interrogated him. The Court's opposite conclusion removes an important brick from the wall of protection against police overreaching that surrounds the Fifth Amendment rights of suspects in custody.

■ ■ ■

At the time of the meeting in question between William Mauro and his wife, he was in police custody and had requested an attorney. It is therefore undisputed that he could not be subjected to interrogation until he either received the assistance of counsel or initiated a conversation with the police.

Since neither event occurred, the tape-recorded evidence must be excluded if it was the product of "interrogation" within the meaning of *Rhode Island v. Innis.*

Police conduct may constitute "interrogation" even if the officers do not pose direct questions to the suspect. The Court explained the term in *Rhode Island v. Innis:*

> "[T]he term 'interrogation' under *Miranda* refers not only to express questioning, but also to any words or actions on the part of the police (other than those normally attendant to arrest and custody) that the police should know are reasonably likely to elicit an incriminating response from the suspect. . . . A practice that the police should know is reasonably likely to evoke an incriminating response from a suspect thus amounts to interrogation."

In a footnote, the Court added:

> "By 'incriminating response' we refer to any response—whether inculpatory or exculpatory—that the *prosecution* may seek to introduce at trial."

The Arizona Supreme Court correctly applied the *Innis* standard when it held that "the admission of a tape-recorded conversation between [Mauro] and his wife violated his state and federal rights not to incriminate himself."

■ ■ ■

> "Interrogation includes a 'practice that the police should know is reasonably likely to evoke an incriminating response from a suspect.' *Rhode Island v. Innis* (1980). 'The focus in ascertaining whether particular police conduct amounts to interrogation, then, is not on the form of the words used, but the intent of the police officers and the perceptions of the suspect.' An incriminating response is any response—whether inculpatory or exculpatory—that the prosecution may seek to introduce at trial.
>
> The intent of the detectives is clear from their own testimony. They both knew that if the conversation took place, incriminating statements were likely to be made. With that in mind, they decided to take in a tape recorder, sit near appellant and his wife and allow the conversation to commence.
>
> Since the intent of the detectives is so clear, we need not address appellant's perceptions. Whether the police knew that appellant was unusually disoriented or upset might have been an important factor in this case had the State's intent not been so unambiguous. *Rhode Island v. Innis* (suspect's peculiar susceptibility to the police appeal and whether the police knew that appellant was unusually disoriented or upset are factors to be examined in determining the perceptions of a suspect). We find, therefore, that in allowing the conversation to commence, the police did indirectly what they could not do directly—interrogate appellant."

■ ■ ■

The Court's proffered reasons for disturbing these cogent findings are unpersuasive.

■ ■ ■

It is undisputed that a police decision to place two suspects in the same room and then to listen to or record their conversation may constitute a form of interrogation even if no questions are asked by any police officers. That is exactly what happened here. The police placed respondent and his wife, who was also in police custody, in the same small area. Mr. and Mrs. Mauro were both suspects in the murder of their son. Each of them had been interrogated separately before the officers decided to allow them to converse, an act that surely did not require a tape recorder or the presence of a police officer within hearing range. Under the circumstances, the police knew or should have known that Mrs. Mauro's encounter with respondent was reasonably likely to produce an incriminating response. Indeed, Officer Allen's supervisor testified that the police had a reasonable expectation that the spousal conversation would provide information on the murder investigation.

■ ■ ■

In my opinion, it was not only likely, but highly probable, that one of the suspects would make a statement that the prosecutor might seek to introduce at trial. It follows that the police conduct in this case was the "functional equivalent" of deliberate, direct interrogation.

The State should not be permitted to set aside this conclusion with testimony that merely indicates that the evidence-gathering purpose of the police was mixed with other motives. For example, it is irrelevant to the inquiry whether the police had legitimate security reasons for having an officer present that were "not related to securing incriminating statements." Nor does it matter that the officers lacked a precise expectation of how the statements Mauro would make might be incriminating; much interrogation is exploratory rather than directed at the admission of a fact whose incriminatory import is already known to the officers.

The Court's final proffered reason for disregarding the findings of the Supreme Court of Arizona is that the suspect may not have felt coerced to incriminate himself. The police did not compel or even encourage Mauro to speak with his wife. When they brought her into the room without warning Mauro in advance, however, they expected that the resulting conversation "could shed light on our case." Under the circumstances, the mere fact that respondent's wife made the initial request leading to the conversation does not alter the correctness of the Supreme Court of Arizona's analysis. The officers exercised exclusive control over whether and when the suspects spoke with each other; the police knew that whatever Mauro might wish to convey to his wife at that moment, he would have to say under the conditions unilaterally imposed by the officers. In brief, the police exploited the custodial situation and the understandable desire of Mrs. Mauro to speak with respondent to conduct an interrogation.

I respectfully dissent.

Illinois v. Perkins

496 U.S. 292 (1990)

KENNEDY, J., delivered the opinion of the Court, in which REHNQUIST, C.J., and WHITE, BLACKMUN, STEVENS, O'CONNOR, and SCALIA, JJ., joined. BRENNAN, J., filed an opinion concurring in the judgment. MARSHALL, J., filed a dissenting opinion.

An undercover government agent was placed in the cell of respondent Perkins, who was incarcerated on charges unrelated to the subject of the agent's investigation. Respondent made statements that implicated him in the crime that the agent sought to solve. Respondent claims that the statements should be inadmissible because he had not been given *Miranda* warnings by the agent. We hold that the statements are admissible. *Miranda* warnings are not required when the suspect is unaware that he is speaking to a law enforcement officer and gives a voluntary statement.

■ ■ ■

In November 1984, Richard Stephenson was murdered in a suburb of East St. Louis, Illinois. The murder remained unsolved until March 1986, when one Donald Charlton told police that he had learned about a homicide from a fellow inmate at the Graham Correctional Facility, where Charlton had been serving a sentence for burglary. The fellow inmate was Lloyd Perkins, who is the respondent here. Charlton told police that, while at Graham, he had befriended respondent, who told him in detail about a murder that respondent had committed in East St. Louis. On hearing Charlton's account, the police recognized details of the Stephenson murder that were not well known, and so they treated Charlton's story as a credible one.

By the time the police heard Charlton's account, respondent had been released from Graham, but police traced him to a jail in Montgomery County, Illinois, where he was being held pending trial on a charge of aggravated battery, unrelated to the Stephenson murder. The police wanted to investigate further respondent's connection to the Stephenson murder, but feared that the use of an eavesdropping device would prove impracticable and unsafe. They decided instead to place an undercover agent in the cellblock with respondent and Charlton. The plan was for Charlton and undercover agent John Parisi to pose as escapees from a work release program who had been arrested in the course of a burglary. Parisi and Charlton were instructed to engage respondent in casual conversation and report anything he said about the Stephenson murder.

Parisi, using the alias "Vito Bianco," and Charlton, both clothed in jail garb, were placed in the cellblock with respondent at the Montgomery County jail. The cellblock consisted of 12 separate cells that opened onto a common room. Respondent greeted Charlton who, after a brief conversation with respondent, introduced Parisi by his alias. Parisi told respondent that he "wasn't going to do any more time" and suggested that the three of them escape. Respondent replied that the Montgomery County jail was "rinky-dink" and that they could "break out." The trio met in respondent's cell later that evening, after the other inmates were asleep, to refine their plan. Respondent said that his girlfriend could smuggle in a pistol. Charlton said: "Hey, I'm not a murderer, I'm a burglar. That's your guys' profession." After telling Charlton that he would be responsible for any murder that occurred, Parisi asked respondent if he had ever "done" anybody. Respondent said that he had and proceeded to describe at length the events of the Stephenson murder. Parisi and respondent then engaged in some casual conversation before respondent went to sleep. Parisi did not give respondent *Miranda* warnings before the conversations.

Respondent was charged with the Stephenson murder. Before trial, he moved to suppress the statements made to Parisi in the jail. The trial court granted the motion to suppress, and the State appealed. The Appellate Court of Illinois affirmed.

■ ■ ■

We granted certiorari to decide whether an undercover law enforcement officer must give *Miranda* warnings to an incarcerated suspect before asking him questions that may elicit an incriminating response. We now reverse.

■ ■ ■

Conversations between suspects and undercover agents do not implicate the concerns underlying *Miranda*. The essential ingredients of a "police-dominated atmosphere" and compulsion are not present when an incarcerated person speaks freely to someone whom he believes to be a fellow inmate. Coercion is determined from the perspective of the suspect. When a suspect considers himself in the company of cellmates and not officers, the coercive atmosphere is lacking. *Miranda v. Arizona* [(1966)] ("[T]he 'principal psychological factor contributing to a successful interrogation is *privacy*—being alone with the person under interrogation'"). There is no empirical basis for the assumption that a suspect speaking to those whom he assumes are not officers will feel compelled to speak by the fear of reprisal for remaining silent or in the hope of more lenient treatment should he confess.

■ ■ ■

Miranda forbids coercion, not mere strategic deception by taking advantage of a suspect's misplaced trust in one he supposes to be a fellow prisoner. As we recognized in *Miranda*: "[C]onfessions remain a proper element in law enforcement. Any statement given freely and voluntarily without any compelling influences is, of course, admissible in evidence."

■ ■ ■

Miranda was not meant to protect suspects from boasting about their criminal activities in front of persons whom they believe to be their cellmates. This case is illustrative. Respondent had no reason to feel that undercover agent Parisi had any legal authority to force him to answer questions or that Parisi could affect respondent's future treatment. Respondent viewed the cellmate-agent as an equal and showed no hint of being intimidated by the atmosphere of the jail. In recounting the details of the Stephenson murder, respondent was motivated solely by the desire to impress his fellow inmates. He spoke at his own peril.

The tactic employed here to elicit a voluntary confession from a suspect does not violate the Self-Incrimination Clause. We held in *Hoffa v. United States* (1966) that placing an undercover agent near a suspect in order to gather incriminating information was permissible under the Fifth Amendment. In *Hoffa*, while petitioner Hoffa was on trial, he met often with one Partin, who, unbeknownst to Hoffa, was cooperating with law enforcement officials. Partin reported to officials that Hoffa had divulged his attempts to bribe jury members. We approved using Hoffa's statements at his subsequent trial for jury tampering, on the rationale that "no claim ha[d] been or could [have been] made that [Hoffa's] incriminating statements were the product of any sort of coercion, legal or factual." In addition, we found that the fact that Partin had fooled Hoffa into thinking that Partin was a sympathetic colleague did not affect the voluntariness of the statements. . . . The only difference between this case and *Hoffa* is that the suspect here was incarcerated, but detention, whether or not for the crime in question, does not warrant a presumption that the use of an undercover agent to speak with an incarcerated suspect makes any confession thus obtained involuntary.

Our decision in *Mathis v. United States* (1968) is distinguishable. In *Mathis*, an inmate in a state prison was interviewed by an Internal Revenue Service agent about possible tax violations. No *Miranda* warning was given before questioning. The Court held that the suspect's incriminating statements were not admissible at his subsequent trial on tax fraud charges. The suspect in *Mathis* was aware that the agent was a Government official, investigating the possibility of noncompliance with the tax laws. The case before us now is different. Where the suspect does not know that he is speaking to a government agent there is no reason to assume the possibility that the suspect might feel coerced. (The bare fact of custody may not in every instance require a warning even when the suspect is aware that he is speaking to an official, but we do not have occasion to explore that issue here.)

This Court's Sixth Amendment decisions in *Massiah v. United States* (1964), *United States v. Henry* (1980), and *Maine v. Moulton* (1985) also do not avail respondent. We held in those cases that the government may not use an undercover agent to circumvent the Sixth Amendment right to counsel once a suspect has been charged with the crime. After charges have been filed, the Sixth Amendment prevents the government from interfering with the accused's right to counsel. In the instant case no charges had been filed on the subject of the interrogation, and our Sixth Amendment precedents are not applicable.

■ ■ ■

We hold that an undercover law enforcement officer posing as a fellow inmate need not give *Miranda* warnings to an incarcerated suspect before asking questions that may elicit an incriminating response. The statements at issue in this case were voluntary, and there is no federal obstacle to their admissibility at trial. We now reverse and remand for proceedings not inconsistent with our opinion.

It is so ordered.

Justice BRENNAN, concurring in the judgment.

The Court holds that *Miranda v. Arizona* does not require suppression of a statement made by an incarcerated suspect to an undercover agent. Although I do not subscribe to the majority's characterization of *Miranda* in its entirety, I do agree that when a suspect does not know that his questioner is a police agent, such questioning does not amount to "interrogation" in an "inherently coercive" environment so as to require application of *Miranda*. Since the only issue raised at this stage of the litigation is the applicability of *Miranda*, I concur in the judgment of the Court.

This is not to say that I believe the Constitution condones the method by which the police extracted the confession in this case. To the contrary, the deception and manipulation practiced on respondent raise a substantial claim that the confession was obtained in violation of the Due Process Clause.

■ ■ ■

The deliberate use of deception and manipulation by the police appears to be incompatible "with a system that presumes innocence and assures that a conviction will not be secured by inquisitorial means," and raises serious concerns that respondent's will was overborne. It is open to the lower court on remand to determine whether, under the totality of the circumstances, respondent's confession was elicited in a manner that violated the Due Process Clause. That the confession was not elicited through means of physical torture, see *Brown v. Mississippi* (1936), or overt psychological pressure, see *Payne v. Arkansas* (1958), does not end the inquiry. "[A]s law enforcement officers become more responsible, and the methods used to extract confessions more sophisticated, [a court's] duty to enforce federal constitutional protections does not cease. It only becomes more difficult because of the more delicate judgments to be made."

Justice MARSHALL, dissenting.

This Court clearly and simply stated its holding in *Miranda v. Arizona* (1966): "[T]he prosecution may not use statements, whether exculpatory or inculpatory, stemming from custodial interrogation of the defendant unless it demonstrates the use of procedural safeguards effective to secure the privilege against self-incrimination." The conditions that require the police to apprise a defendant of his constitutional rights—custodial interrogation conducted by an agent of the police—were present in this case. Because Lloyd Perkins received no *Miranda* warnings before he was subjected to custodial interrogation, his confession was not admissible.

The Court reaches the contrary conclusion by fashioning an exception to the *Miranda* rule that applies whenever "an undercover law enforcement officer posing as a fellow inmate . . . ask[s] questions that may elicit an incriminating response" from an incarcerated suspect. This exception is inconsistent with the rationale supporting *Miranda* and allows police officers intentionally to take advantage of suspects unaware of their constitutional rights. I therefore dissent.

The Court does not dispute that the police officer here conducted a custodial interrogation of a criminal suspect. Perkins was incarcerated in county jail during the questioning at issue here; under these circumstances, he was in custody as that term is defined in *Miranda*.

■ ■ ■

The police officer continued the inquiry, asking a series of questions designed to elicit specific information about the victim, the crime scene, the weapon, Perkins' motive, and his actions during and after the shooting. This interaction was not a "conversation"; Perkins, the officer, and the informant were not equal participants in a free-ranging discussion, with each man offering his views on different topics. Rather, it was an interrogation: Perkins was subjected to express questioning likely to evoke an incriminating response.

Because Perkins was interrogated by police while he was in custody, *Miranda* required that the officer inform him of his rights. In rejecting that conclusion, the Court finds that "conversations" between undercover agents and suspects are devoid of the coercion inherent in station house interrogations conducted by law enforcement officials who openly represent the State. *Miranda* was not, however, concerned solely with police *coercion.* It dealt with *any* police tactics that may operate to compel a suspect in custody to make incriminating statements without full awareness of his constitutional rights.

■ ■ ■

Thus, the pressures unique to custody allow the police to use deceptive interrogation tactics to compel a suspect to make an incriminating statement. The compulsion is not eliminated by the suspect's ignorance of his interrogator's true identity. The Court therefore need not inquire past the bare facts of custody and interrogation to determine whether *Miranda* warnings are required.

■ ■ ■

The Court's holding today complicates a previously clear and straightforward doctrine. The Court opines that "[l]aw enforcement officers will have little difficulty putting into practice our holding that undercover agents need not give *Miranda* warnings to incarcerated suspects." Perhaps this prediction is true with respect to fact patterns virtually identical to the one before the Court today. But the outer boundaries of the exception created by the Court are by no means clear. Would *Miranda* be violated, for instance, if an undercover police officer beat a confession out of a suspect, but the suspect thought the officer was another prisoner who wanted the information for his own purposes?

Even if *Miranda*, as interpreted by the Court, would not permit such obviously compelled confessions, the ramifications of today's opinion are still disturbing. The exception carved out of the *Miranda* doctrine today may well result in a proliferation of departmental policies to encourage police officers to conduct interrogations of confined suspects through undercover agents, thereby circumventing the need to administer *Miranda* warnings. Indeed, if *Miranda* now requires a police officer to issue warnings only in those situations in which the suspect might feel compelled "to speak by the fear of reprisal for remaining silent or in the hope of more lenient treatment should he confess," presumably it allows custodial interrogation by an undercover officer posing as a member of the clergy or a suspect's defense attorney. Although such abhorrent tricks would play on a suspect's need to confide in a trusted adviser, neither would cause the suspect to "think that the listeners have official power over him." The Court's adoption of the "undercover agent" exception to the *Miranda* rule thus is necessarily also the adoption of a substantial loophole in our jurisprudence protecting suspects' Fifth Amendment rights.

I dissent.

Pennsylvania v. Muniz

496 U.S. 582 (1990)

BRENNAN, J., announced the judgment of the Court and delivered the opinion of the Court with respect to Parts I, II, III-A, and IV, in which REHNQUIST, C.J., and WHITE, BLACKMUN, STEVENS, O'CONNOR, SCALIA, and KENNEDY, JJ., joined, the opinion of the Court with respect to Part III-B, in which MARSHALL, O'CONNOR, SCALIA, and KENNEDY, JJ., joined, and an opinion with respect to Part III-C, in which O'CONNOR, SCALIA, and KENNEDY, JJ., joined. REHNQUIST, C.J., filed an opinion concurring in part, concurring in the result in part, and dissenting in part, in which WHITE, BLACKMUN, and STEVENS, JJ., joined. MARSHALL, J., filed an opinion concurring in part and dissenting in part.

We must decide in this case whether various incriminating utterances of a drunken-driving suspect, made while performing a series of sobriety tests, constitute testimonial responses to custodial interrogation for purposes of the Self-Incrimination Clause of the Fifth Amendment.

I

During the early morning hours of November 30, 1986, a patrol officer spotted respondent Inocencio Muniz and a passenger parked in a car on the shoulder of a highway. When the officer inquired whether Muniz needed assistance, Muniz replied that he had stopped the car so he could urinate. The officer smelled alcohol on Muniz's breath and observed that Muniz's eyes were glazed and bloodshot and his face was flushed. The officer then directed Muniz to remain parked until his condition improved, and Muniz gave assurances that he would do so. But as the officer returned to his vehicle, Muniz drove off. After the officer pursued Muniz down the highway and pulled him over, the officer asked Muniz to perform three standard field sobriety tests: a "horizontal gaze nystagmus" test, a "walk and turn" test,

Said he had been drinking

and a "one leg stand" test. Muniz performed these tests poorly, and he informed the officer that he had failed the tests because he had been drinking.

The patrol officer arrested Muniz and transported him to the West Shore facility of the Cumberland County Central Booking Center. Following its routine practice for receiving persons suspected of driving while intoxicated, the booking center videotaped the ensuing proceedings. Muniz was informed that his actions and voice were being recorded, but he was not at this time (nor had he been previously) advised of his rights under *Miranda v. Arizona* (1966). Officer Hosterman first asked Muniz his name, address, height, weight, eye color, date of birth, and current age. He responded to each of these questions, stumbling over his address and age. The officer then asked Muniz, "Do you know what the date was of your sixth birthday?" After Muniz offered an inaudible reply, the officer repeated, "When you turned six years old, do you remember what the date was?" Muniz responded, "No, I don't."

not Mirandized yet

Officer Hosterman next requested Muniz to perform each of the three sobriety tests that Muniz had been asked to perform earlier during the initial roadside stop. The videotape reveals that his eyes jerked noticeably during the gaze test, that he did not walk a very straight line, and that he could not balance himself on one leg for more than several seconds. During the latter two tests, he did not complete the requested verbal counts from 1 to 9 and from 1 to 30. Moreover, while performing these tests, Muniz "attempted to explain his difficulties in performing the various tasks, and often requested further clarification of the tasks he was to perform."

■ ■ ■

Both the video and audio portions of the videotape were admitted into evidence at Muniz' bench trial, along with the arresting officer's testimony that Muniz failed the roadside sobriety tests and made incriminating remarks at that time. Muniz was convicted of driving under the influence of alcohol. . . . Muniz filed a motion for a new trial, contending that the court should have excluded the testimony relating to the field sobriety tests and the videotape taken at the booking center "because they were incriminating and completed prior to [Muniz's] receiving his *Miranda* warnings." The trial court denied the motion, holding that " 'requesting a driver, suspected of driving under the influence of alcohol, to perform physical tests or take a breath analysis does not violate [his] privilege against self-incrimination because [the] evidence procured is of a physical nature rather than testimonial, and therefore no *Miranda* warnings are required.' "

On appeal, the Superior Court of Pennsylvania reversed. . . .

II

The Self-Incrimination Clause of the Fifth Amendment provides that no "person . . . shall be compelled in any criminal case to be a witness against himself." Although the text does not delineate the ways in which a person might be made a "witness against himself," cf. *Schmerber v. California* (1966), we have long held that the privilege does not protect a suspect from being compelled by the State to produce "real or physical evidence." Rather, the privilege "protects an accused only from being compelled to testify against himself, or otherwise provide the State with evidence of a testimonial or communicative nature." "[I]n order to be testimonial, an accused's communication must itself, explicitly or implicitly, relate a factual assertion or disclose information. Only then is a person compelled to be a 'witness' against himself."

In *Miranda v. Arizona*, we reaffirmed our previous understanding that the privilege against self-incrimination protects individuals not only from legal compulsion to testify in a criminal courtroom but also from "informal compulsion exerted by law-enforcement officers during in-custody questioning." Of course, voluntary statements offered to police officers "remain a proper element in law enforcement." But "without proper safeguards the process of in-custody interrogation of persons suspected or accused of crime contains inherently compelling pressures which work to undermine the individual's will to resist and to compel him to speak where he would not otherwise do so freely." Accordingly, we held that protection of the privilege against self-incrimination during pretrial questioning requires application of special "procedural safeguards." "Prior to any questioning, the person must be warned that he has a right to remain silent, that any statement he does make may be used as evidence against him, and that he has a right to the presence of an attorney, either retained or appointed." Unless a suspect "voluntarily, knowingly and intelligently" waives these rights, any incriminating responses to questioning may not be introduced into evidence in the prosecution's case in chief in a subsequent criminal proceeding.

This case implicates both the "testimonial" and "compulsion" components of the privilege against self-incrimination in the context of pretrial questioning. Because Muniz was not advised of his *Miranda* rights until after the videotaped proceedings at the booking center were completed, any verbal statements that were both testimonial in nature and elicited during custodial interrogation should have been suppressed. We focus first on Muniz's responses to the initial informational questions, then on his questions and utterances while performing the physical dexterity and balancing tests, and finally on his questions and utterances surrounding the breathalyzer test.

III

In the initial phase of the recorded proceedings, Officer Hosterman asked Muniz his name, address, height, weight, eye color, date of birth, current age, and the date of his sixth birthday. Both the delivery and content of Muniz's answers were incriminating. As the state court found, "Muniz's videotaped responses ... certainly led the finder of fact to infer that his confusion and failure to speak clearly indicated a state of drunkenness that prohibited him from safely operating his vehicle." The Commonwealth argues, however, that admission of Muniz's answers to these questions does not contravene Fifth Amendment principles because Muniz's statement regarding his sixth birthday was not "testimonial" and his answers to the prior questions were not elicited by custodial interrogation. We consider these arguments in turn.

A

We agree with the Commonwealth's contention that Muniz's answers are not rendered inadmissible by *Miranda* merely because the slurred nature of his speech was incriminating. The physical inability to articulate words in a clear manner due to "the lack of muscular coordination of his tongue and mouth" is not itself a testimonial component of Muniz's responses to Officer Hosterman's introductory questions. In *Schmerber v. California*, we drew a distinction between "testimonial" and "real or physical evidence" for purposes of the privilege against self-incrimination.

■ ■ ■

We have since applied the distinction between "real or physical" and "testimonial" evidence in other contexts where the evidence could be produced only through some volitional act on the part of the suspect. . . . [W]e held that a suspect could be compelled to participate in a lineup and to repeat a phrase provided by the police so that witnesses could view him and listen to his voice. We explained that requiring his presence and speech at a lineup reflected "compulsion of the accused to exhibit his physical characteristics, not compulsion to disclose any knowledge he might have."

■ ■ ■

Under *Schmerber* and its progeny, we agree with the Commonwealth that any slurring of speech and other evidence of lack of muscular coordination revealed by Muniz's responses to Officer Hosterman's direct questions constitute nontestimonial components of those responses. Requiring a suspect to reveal the physical manner in which he articulates words, like requiring him to reveal the physical properties of the sound produced by his voice, see *Dionisio, supra*, does not, without more, compel him to provide a "testimonial" response for purposes of the privilege.

B

This does not end our inquiry, for Muniz's answer to the sixth birthday question was incriminating, not just because of his delivery, but also because of his answer's *content*; the trier of fact could infer from Muniz's answer (that he did not *know* the proper date) that his mental state was confused. The Commonwealth and the United States as *amicus curiae* argue that this incriminating inference does not trigger the protections of the Fifth Amendment privilege because the inference concerns "the physiological functioning of [Muniz's] brain," Brief for Petitioner 21, which is asserted to be every bit as "real or physical" as the physiological makeup of his blood and the timbre of his voice.

But this characterization addresses the wrong question; that the "fact" to be inferred might be said to concern the physical status of Muniz's brain merely describes the way in which the inference is incriminating. The correct question for present purposes is whether the incriminating inference of mental confusion is drawn from a testimonial act or from physical evidence. In *Schmerber*, for example, we held that the police could compel a suspect to provide a blood sample in order to determine the physical makeup of his blood and thereby draw an inference about whether he was intoxicated. This compulsion was outside of the Fifth Amendment's protection, not simply because the evidence concerned the suspect's physical body, but rather because the evidence was *obtained* in a manner that did not entail any testimonial act on the part of the suspect: "Not even a shadow of testimonial compulsion upon or enforced communication by the accused was involved either in the extraction or in the chemical analysis." In contrast, had the police instead asked the suspect directly whether his blood contained a high concentration of alcohol, his affirmative response would have been testimonial even though it would have been used to draw the same inference concerning his physiology. . . . In this case, the question is not whether a suspect's "impaired mental faculties" can fairly be characterized as an aspect of his physiology, but rather whether Muniz's response to the sixth birthday question that gave rise to the inference of such an impairment was testimonial in nature.

We recently explained in *Doe v. United States* (1988) that "in order to be testimonial, an accused's communication must itself, explicitly or implicitly, relate a factual assertion or disclose information." We reached this conclusion after addressing our reasoning in *Schmerber* and its progeny.

■ ■ ■

After canvassing the purposes of the privilege recognized in prior cases, we concluded that "[t]hese policies are served when the privilege is asserted to spare the accused from having to reveal, directly or indirectly, his knowledge of facts relating him to the offense or from having to share his thoughts and beliefs with the Government."

■ ■ ■

In contrast, the sixth birthday question in this case required a testimonial response. When Officer Hosterman asked Muniz if he knew the date of his sixth birthday and Muniz, for whatever reason, could not remember or calculate that date, he was confronted with the trilemma. By hypothesis, the inherently coercive environment created by the custodial interrogation precluded the option of remaining silent. Muniz was left with the choice of incriminating himself by admitting that he did not then know the date of his sixth birthday, or answering untruthfully by reporting a date that he did not then believe to be accurate (an incorrect guess would be incriminating as well as untruthful). The content of his truthful answer supported an inference that his mental faculties were impaired, because his assertion (he did not know the date of his sixth birthday) was different from the assertion (he knew the date was (correct date)) that the trier of fact might reasonably have expected a lucid person to provide. Hence, the incriminating inference of impaired mental faculties stemmed, not just from the fact that Muniz slurred his response, but also from a testimonial aspect of that response.

The state court held that the sixth birthday question constituted an unwarned interrogation for purposes of the privilege against self-incrimination, and that Muniz's answer was incriminating. The Commonwealth does not question either conclusion. Therefore, because we conclude that Muniz's response to the sixth birthday question was testimonial, the response should have been suppressed.

C

The Commonwealth argues that the seven questions asked by Officer Hosterman just *prior* to the sixth birthday question—regarding Muniz's name, address, height, weight, eye color, date of birth, and current age—did not constitute custodial interrogation as we have defined the term in *Miranda* and subsequent cases. In *Miranda*, the Court referred to "interrogation" as actual "questioning initiated by law enforcement officers." We have since clarified that definition, finding that the "goals of the *Miranda* safeguards could be effectuated if those safeguards extended not only to express questioning, but also to 'its functional equivalent.' " In *Rhode Island v. Innis* (1980), the Court defined the phrase "functional equivalent" of express questioning to include "any words or actions on the part of the police (other than those normally attendant to arrest and custody) that the police should know are reasonably likely to elicit an incriminating response from the suspect. The latter portion of this definition focuses primarily upon the perceptions of the suspect, rather than the intent of the police." However, "[a]ny knowledge the police may have had concerning the unusual susceptibility of a defendant to a particular form of persuasion might be an important factor in determining" what the police reasonably should have known. Thus, custodial interrogation for purposes of *Miranda* includes both express questioning and words or actions that, given the officer's knowledge of any special susceptibilities of the suspect, the officer knows or reasonably should know are likely to "have . . . the force of a question on the accused," and therefore be reasonably likely to elicit an incriminating response.

We disagree with the Commonwealth's contention that Officer Hosterman's first seven questions regarding Muniz's name, address, height, weight, eye color, date of birth, and current age do not qualify as custodial interrogation as we defined the term in *Innis*, merely because the questions were not intended to elicit information for investigatory purposes. As explained above, the *Innis* test focuses primarily upon "the perspective of the suspect." We agree with *amicus* United States, however, that Muniz's answers to these first seven questions are nonetheless admissible because the questions fall within a "routine booking question" exception which exempts from *Miranda*'s coverage questions to secure the " 'biographical data necessary to complete booking or pretrial services.' " . . .

IV

During the second phase of the videotaped proceedings, Officer Hosterman asked Muniz to perform the same three sobriety tests that he had earlier performed at roadside prior to his arrest: the "horizontal gaze nystagmus" test, the "walk and turn" test, and the "one leg stand" test. While Muniz was attempting to comprehend Officer Hosterman's instructions and then perform the requested sobriety tests, Muniz made several audible and incriminating statements. Muniz argued to the state court that both the videotaped performance of the physical tests themselves and the audiorecorded verbal statements were introduced in violation of *Miranda*.

The court refused to suppress the videotaped evidence of Muniz's paltry performance on the physical sobriety tests, reasoning that "[r]equiring a driver to perform physical [sobriety] tests . . . does not violate the privilege against self-incrimination because the evidence procured is of a physical nature rather than testimonial." With respect to Muniz's verbal statements, however, the court concluded that "none of Muniz's utterances were spontaneous, voluntary verbalizations," and because they were "elicited before Muniz received his *Miranda* warnings, they should have been excluded as evidence."

We disagree. Officer Hosterman's dialogue with Muniz concerning the physical sobriety tests consisted primarily of carefully scripted instructions as to how the tests were to be performed. These instructions were not likely to be perceived as calling for any verbal response and therefore were not "words or actions" constituting custodial interrogation, with two narrow exceptions not relevant here. The dialogue also contained limited and carefully worded inquiries as to whether Muniz understood those instructions, but these focused inquiries were necessarily "attendant to" the police procedure held by the court to be legitimate. Hence, Muniz's incriminating utterances during this phase of the videotaped proceedings were "voluntary" in the sense that they were not elicited in response to custodial interrogation. See *South Dakota v. Neville* (1983) (drawing analogy to "police request to submit to fingerprinting or photography" and holding that police inquiry whether suspect would submit to blood-alcohol test was not "interrogation within the meaning of *Miranda*").

Similarly, we conclude that *Miranda* does not require suppression of the statements Muniz made when asked to submit to a breathalyzer examination. Officer Deyo read Muniz a prepared script explaining how the test worked, the nature of Pennsylvania's Implied Consent Law, and the legal consequences that would ensue should he refuse. Officer Deyo then asked Muniz whether he understood the nature of the test and the law and whether he would like to submit to the test. Muniz asked Officer Deyo several questions concerning the legal consequences of refusal, which Deyo answered directly, and Muniz then commented upon his state of inebriation. After offering to take the test only after waiting a couple of hours or drinking some water, Muniz ultimately refused.

■ ■ ■

V

We agree with the state court's conclusion that *Miranda* requires suppression of Muniz's response to the question regarding the date of his sixth birthday, but we do not agree that the entire audio portion of the videotape must be suppressed. Accordingly, the court's judgment reversing Muniz's conviction is vacated, and the case is remanded for further proceedings not inconsistent with this opinion.

It is so ordered.

Chief Justice REHNQUIST, with whom Justice WHITE, Justice BLACKMUN, and Justice STEVENS join, concurring in part, concurring in the result in part, and dissenting in part.

■ ■ ■

The Court holds that the sixth birthday question Muniz was asked required a testimonial response, and that its admission at trial therefore violated Muniz's privilege against compulsory self-incrimination. The Court says:

> "When Officer Hosterman asked Muniz if he knew the date of his sixth birthday and Muniz, for whatever reason, could not remember or calculate that date, he was confronted with the trilemma [*i.e.*, the ' "trilemma" of truth, falsity, or silence,'] . . . Muniz was left with the choice of incriminating himself by admitting that he did not then know the date of his sixth birthday, or answering untruthfully by reporting a date that he did not then believe to be accurate (an incorrect guess would be incriminating as well as untruthful)."

As an assumption about human behavior, this statement is wrong. Muniz would no more have felt compelled to fabricate a false date than one who cannot read the letters on an eye chart feels compelled to fabricate false letters; nor does a wrong guess call into question a speaker's veracity. The Court's statement is also a flawed predicate on which to base its conclusion that Muniz's answer to this question was "testimonial" for purposes of the Fifth Amendment.

■ ■ ■

The sixth birthday question here was an effort on the part of the police to check how well Muniz was able to do a simple mathematical exercise. Indeed, had the question related only to the date of his birth, it presumably would have come under the "booking exception" to *Miranda v. Arizona*, to which the Court refers elsewhere in its opinion. The Court holds in this very case that Muniz may be required to perform a "horizontal gaze nystagmus" test, the "walk and turn" test, and the "one leg stand" test, all of which are designed to test a suspect's physical coordination. If the police may require Muniz to use his body in order to demonstrate the level of his physical coordination, there is no reason why they should not be able to require him to speak or write in order to determine his mental coordination. That was all that was sought here. Since it was permissible for the police to extract and examine a sample of Schmerber's blood to determine how much that part of his system had been affected by alcohol, I see no reason why they may not examine the functioning of Muniz's mental processes for the same purpose.

Surely if it were relevant, a suspect might be asked to take an eye examination in the course of which he might have to admit that he could not read the letters on the third line of the chart. At worst, he might utter a mistaken guess. Muniz likewise might have attempted to guess the correct response to the sixth birthday question instead of attempting to calculate the date or answer "I don't know." But the potential for giving a bad guess does not subject the suspect to the truth-falsity-silence predicament that renders a response testimonial and, therefore, within the scope of the Fifth Amendment privilege.

For substantially the same reasons, Muniz's responses to the videotaped "booking" questions were not testimonial and do not warrant application of the privilege. Thus, it is unnecessary to determine whether the questions fall within the "routine booking question" exception to *Miranda* Justice Brennan recognizes.

I would reverse in its entirety the judgment of the Superior Court of Pennsylvania. But given the fact that five members of the Court agree that Muniz's response to the sixth birthday question should have been suppressed, I agree that the judgment of the Superior Court should be vacated so that, on remand, the court may consider whether admission of the response at trial was harmless error.

■ ■ ■

5. *Miranda* Waiver

a. Overview

North Carolina v. Butler

441 U.S. 369 (1979)

STEWART, J., delivered the opinion of the Court, in which BURGER, C.J., POWELL, WHITE, and REHNQUIST, JJ., joined. BLACKMUN, J., wrote a concurring opinion. BRENNAN, J., wrote a dissenting opinion, in which MARSHALL and STEVENS, JJ., joined.

In evident conflict with the present view of every other court that has considered the issue, the North Carolina Supreme Court has held that *Miranda v. Arizona* [(1966)] requires that no statement of a person under custodial interrogation may be admitted in evidence against him unless, at the time the statement was made, he explicitly waived the right to the presence of a lawyer. We granted certiorari to consider whether this *per se* rule reflects a proper understanding of the *Miranda* decision.

The prosecution . . . produced evidence of incriminating statements made by the respondent shortly after his arrest by Federal Bureau of Investigation agents in the Bronx, N.Y., on the basis of a North Carolina fugitive warrant. Outside the presence of the jury, FBI Agent Martinez testified that at the time of the arrest he fully advised the respondent of the rights delineated in the

Miranda case. According to the uncontroverted testimony of Martinez, the agents then took the respondent to the FBI office in nearby New Rochelle, N.Y. There, after the agents determined that the respondent had an 11th grade education and was literate, he was given the Bureau's "Advice of Rights" form which he read. When asked if he understood his rights, he replied that he did. The respondent refused to sign the waiver at the bottom of the form. He was told that he need neither speak nor sign the form, but that the agents would like him to talk to them. The respondent replied: "I will talk to you but I am not signing any form." He then made inculpatory statements. Agent Martinez testified that the respondent said nothing when advised of his right to the assistance of a lawyer. At no time did the respondent request counsel or attempt to terminate the agents' questioning.

At the conclusion of this testimony the respondent moved to suppress the evidence of his incriminating statements on the ground that he had not waived his right to the assistance of counsel at the time the statements were made. The court denied the motion, finding that

> "the statement made by the defendant, William Thomas Butler, to Agent David C. Martinez, was made freely and voluntarily to said agent after having been advised of his rights as required by the *Miranda* ruling, including his right to an attorney being present at the time of the inquiry and that the defendant, Butler, understood his rights; [and] that he effectively waived his rights, including the right to have an attorney present during the questioning by his indication that he was willing to answer questions, having read the rights form together with the Waiver of Rights. . . ."

The respondent's statements were then admitted into evidence, and the jury ultimately found the respondent guilty of each offense charged.

On appeal, the North Carolina Supreme Court reversed the convictions and ordered a new trial. It found that the statements had been admitted in violation of the requirements of the *Miranda* decision, noting that the respondent had refused to waive in writing his right to have counsel present and that there had not been a *specific* oral waiver. As it had in at least two earlier cases, the court read the *Miranda* opinion as

> "provid[ing] in plain language that waiver of the right to counsel during interrogation will not be recognized unless such waiver is 'specifically made' after the *Miranda* warnings have been given."

We conclude that the North Carolina Supreme Court erred in its reading of the *Miranda* opinion. There, this Court said:

> "If the interrogation continues without the presence of an attorney and a statement is taken, a heavy burden rests on the government to demonstrate that the defendant knowingly and intelligently waived his privilege against self-incrimination and his right to retained or appointed counsel."

The Court's opinion went on to say:

> "An express statement that the individual is willing to make a statement and does not want an attorney followed closely by a statement could constitute a waiver. But a valid waiver will not be presumed simply from the silence of the accused after warnings are given or simply from the fact that a confession was in fact eventually obtained."

Thus, the Court held that an express statement can constitute a waiver, and that silence alone after such warnings cannot do so. But the Court did not hold that such an express statement is indispensable to a finding of waiver.

An express written or oral statement of waiver of the right to remain silent or of the right to counsel is usually strong proof of the validity of that waiver, but is not inevitably either necessary or sufficient to establish waiver. The question is not one of form, but rather whether the defendant in fact knowingly and voluntarily waived the rights delineated in the *Miranda* case. As was unequivocally said in *Miranda*, mere silence is not enough. That does not mean that the defendant's silence, coupled with an understanding of his rights and a course of conduct indicating waiver, may never support a conclusion that a defendant has waived his rights. The courts must presume that a defendant did not waive his rights; the prosecution's burden is great; but in at least some cases waiver can be clearly inferred from the actions and words of the person interrogated.

The Court's opinion in *Miranda* explained the reasons for the prophylactic rules it created:

> "We have concluded that without proper safeguards the process of in-custody interrogation of persons suspected or accused of crime contains inherently compelling pressures which work to undermine the individual's will to resist and to compel him to speak where he would not otherwise do so freely. In order to combat these pressures and to permit a full opportunity to exercise the privilege against self-incrimination, the accused must be adequately and effectively apprised of his rights and the exercise of those rights must be fully honored."

The *per se* rule that the North Carolina Supreme Court has found in *Miranda* does not speak to these concerns. There is no doubt that this respondent was adequately and effectively apprised of his rights. The only question is whether he waived the exercise of one of those rights, the right to the presence of a lawyer. Neither the state court nor the respondent has offered any reason why there must be a negative answer to that question in the absence of an *express* waiver. This is not the first criminal case to question whether a defendant waived his constitutional rights. It is an issue with which courts must repeatedly deal. Even when a right so fundamental as that to counsel at trial is involved, the question of waiver must be determined on "the particular facts and circumstances surrounding that case, including the background, experience, and conduct of the accused."

We see no reason to discard that standard and replace it with an inflexible *per se* rule in a case such as this. As stated at the outset of this opinion, it appears that every court that has considered this question has now reached the same conclusion. Ten of the eleven United States Courts of Appeals and the courts of at least 17 States have held that an explicit statement of waiver is not invariably necessary to support a finding that the defendant waived the right to remain silent or the right to counsel guaranteed by the *Miranda* case. By creating an inflexible rule that no implicit waiver can ever suffice, the North Carolina Supreme Court has gone beyond the requirements of federal organic law. It follows that its judgment cannot stand, since a state court can neither add to nor subtract from the mandates of the United States Constitution.

Accordingly, the judgment is vacated, and the case is remanded to the North Carolina Supreme Court for further proceedings not inconsistent with this opinion.

It is so ordered.

■ ■ ■

Justice BRENNAN, with whom Justice MARSHALL and Justice STEVENS join, dissenting.

Miranda v. Arizona held that "[n]o effective waiver of the right to counsel during interrogation can be recognized unless *specifically* made after the warnings we here delineate have been given."

■ ■ ■

There is no allegation of an affirmative waiver in this case. As the Court concedes, the respondent here refused to sign the waiver form, and "said nothing when advised of his right to the assistance of a lawyer." Thus, there was no "disputed fact question requiring a hearing," and the trial court erred in holding one. In the absence of an "affirmative waiver" in the form of an express written or oral statement, the Supreme Court of North Carolina correctly granted a new trial. I would, therefore, affirm its decision.

The rule announced by the Court today allows a finding of waiver based upon "infer[ence] from the actions and words of the person interrogated." The Court thus shrouds in half-light the question of waiver, allowing courts to construct inferences from ambiguous words and gestures. But the very premise of *Miranda* requires that ambiguity be interpreted against the interrogator. That premise is the recognition of the "compulsion inherent in custodial" interrogation, and of its purpose "to subjugate the individual to the will of [his] examiner." Under such conditions, only the most explicit waivers of rights can be considered knowingly and freely given.

The instant case presents a clear example of the need for an express waiver requirement. As the Court acknowledges, there is a disagreement over whether respondent was orally advised of his rights at the time he made his statement. The fact that Butler received a written copy of his rights is deemed by the Court to be sufficient basis to resolve the disagreement. But, unfortunately, there is also a dispute over whether Butler could read. And, obviously, if Butler did not have his rights read to him, and could not read them himself, there could be no basis upon which to conclude that he knowingly waived them. Indeed, even if Butler could read there is no reason to believe that his oral statements, which followed a refusal to sign a written waiver form, were intended to signify relinquishment of his rights.

Faced with "actions and words" of uncertain meaning, some judges may find waivers where none occurred. Others may fail to find them where they did. In the former case, the defendant's rights will have been violated; in the latter, society's interest in effective law enforcement will have been frustrated. A simple prophylactic rule requiring the police to obtain an express waiver of the right to counsel before proceeding with interrogation eliminates these difficulties. And since the Court agrees that *Miranda* requires the police to obtain some kind of waiver—whether express or implied—the requirement of an express waiver would impose no burden on the police not imposed by the Court's interpretation. It would merely make that burden explicit. Had Agent Martinez simply elicited a clear answer from Willie Butler to the question, "Do you waive your right to a lawyer?" this journey through three courts would not have been necessary.

Colorado v. Spring

479 U.S. 564 (1987)

Powell, J., delivered the opinion of the Court, in which Rehnquist, C.J., and White, Blackmun, Stevens, O'Connor, and Scalia, JJ., joined. Marshall, J., filed a dissenting opinion, in which Brennan, J., joined.

In *Miranda v. Arizona* (1966), the Court held that a suspect's waiver of the Fifth Amendment privilege against self-incrimination is valid only if it is made voluntarily, knowingly, and intelligently. This case presents the question whether the suspect's awareness of all the crimes about which he may be questioned is relevant to determining the validity of his decision to waive the Fifth Amendment privilege.

■ ■ ■

In February 1979, respondent John Leroy Spring and a companion shot and killed Donald Walker during a hunting trip in Colorado. Shortly thereafter, an informant told agents of the Bureau of Alcohol, Tobacco, and Firearms (ATF) that Spring was engaged in the interstate transportation of stolen firearms. The informant also told the agents that Spring had discussed his participation in the Colorado killing. At the time the ATF agents received this information, Walker's body had not been found and the police had received no report of his disappearance. Based on the information received from the informant relating to the firearms violations, the ATF agents set up an undercover operation to purchase firearms from Spring. On March 30, 1979, ATF agents arrested Spring in Kansas City, Missouri, during the undercover purchase.

An ATF agent on the scene of the arrest advised Spring of his *Miranda* rights. Spring was advised of his *Miranda* rights a second time after he was transported to the ATF office in Kansas City. At the ATF office, the agents also advised Spring that he had the right to stop the questioning at any time or to stop the questioning until the presence of an attorney could be secured. Spring then signed a written form stating that he understood and waived his rights, and that he was willing to make a statement and answer questions.

ATF agents first questioned Spring about the firearms transactions that led to his arrest. They then asked Spring if he had a criminal record. He admitted that he had a juvenile record for shooting his aunt when he was 10 years old. The agents asked if Spring had ever shot anyone else. Spring ducked his head and mumbled, "I shot another guy once." The agents asked Spring if he had ever been to Colorado. Spring said no. The agents asked Spring whether he had shot a man named Walker in Colorado and thrown his body into a snowbank. Spring paused and then ducked his head again and said no. The interview ended at this point.

On May 26, 1979, Colorado law enforcement officials visited Spring while he was in jail in Kansas City pursuant to his arrest on the firearms offenses. The officers gave Spring the *Miranda* warnings, and Spring again signed a written form indicating that he understood his rights and was willing to waive them. The officers informed Spring that they wanted to question him about the Colorado homicide. Spring indicated that he "wanted to get it off his chest." In an interview that lasted approximately 1½ hours, Spring confessed to the Colorado murder. During that time, Spring talked freely to the officers, did not indicate a desire to terminate the questioning, and never requested counsel. The officers prepared a written statement summarizing the interview. Spring read, edited, and signed the statement.

Spring was charged in Colorado state court with first-degree murder. Spring moved to suppress both statements on the ground that his waiver of *Miranda* rights was invalid. The trial court found that the ATF agents' failure to inform Spring before the March 30 interview that they would question him about the Colorado murder did not affect his waiver of his *Miranda* rights. . . .

We granted certiorari to resolve an arguable Circuit conflict and to review the Colorado Supreme Court's determination that a suspect's awareness of the possible subjects of questioning is a relevant and sometimes determinative consideration in assessing whether a waiver of the Fifth Amendment privilege is valid. We now reverse.

■ ■ ■

There is no dispute that the police obtained the May 26 confession after complete *Miranda* warnings and after informing Spring that he would be questioned about the Colorado homicide. The Colorado Supreme Court nevertheless held that the confession should have been suppressed because it was the illegal "fruit" of the March 30 statement. A confession cannot be "fruit of the poisonous tree" if the tree itself is not poisonous. Our inquiry, therefore, centers on the validity of the March 30 statement.

■ ■ ■

A statement is not "compelled" within the meaning of the Fifth Amendment if an individual "voluntarily, knowingly and intelligently" waives his constitutional privilege.

■ ■ ■

There also is no doubt that Spring's waiver of his Fifth Amendment privilege was knowingly and intelligently made: that is, that Spring understood that he had the right to remain silent and that anything he said could be used as evidence against him. The Constitution does not require that a criminal suspect know and understand every possible consequence of a waiver of the Fifth Amendment privilege. *Moran v. Burbine* (1986). The Fifth Amendment's guarantee is both simpler and more fundamental: A defendant may not be compelled to be a witness against himself in any respect. The *Miranda* warnings protect this privilege by ensuring that a suspect knows that he may choose not to talk to law enforcement officers, to talk only with counsel present, or to discontinue talking at any time. The *Miranda* warnings ensure that a waiver of these rights is knowing and intelligent by requiring that the suspect be fully advised of this constitutional privilege, including the critical advice that whatever he chooses to say may be used as evidence against him.

In this case there is no allegation that Spring failed to understand the basic privilege guaranteed by the Fifth Amendment. Nor is there any allegation that he misunderstood the consequences of speaking freely to the law enforcement officials. In sum, we think that the trial court was indisputably correct in finding that Spring's waiver was made knowingly and intelligently within the meaning of *Miranda*.

■ ■ ■

Spring relies on this Court's statement in *Miranda* that "any evidence that the accused was threatened, tricked, or cajoled into a waiver will . . . show that the defendant did not voluntarily waive his privilege." He contends that the failure to inform him of the potential subjects of interrogation constitutes the police trickery and deception condemned in *Miranda*, thus rendering his waiver of *Miranda* rights invalid. Spring, however, reads this statement in *Miranda* out of context and without due regard to the constitutional privilege the *Miranda* warnings were designed to protect.

We note first that the Colorado courts made no finding of official trickery. In fact, as noted above, the trial court expressly found that "there was no element of duress or coercion used to induce Spring's statements." Spring nevertheless insists that the failure of the ATF agents to inform him that he would be questioned about the murder constituted official "trickery" sufficient to invalidate his waiver of his Fifth Amendment privilege, even if the official conduct did not amount to "coercion." Even assuming that Spring's proposed distinction has merit, we reject his conclusion. This Court has never held that mere silence by law enforcement officials as to the subject matter of an interrogation is "trickery" sufficient to invalidate a suspect's waiver of *Miranda* rights, and we expressly decline so to hold today.

Once *Miranda* warnings are given, it is difficult to see how official silence could cause a suspect to misunderstand the nature of his constitutional right— "his right to refuse to answer any question which might incriminate him."

■ ■ ■

This Court's holding in *Miranda* specifically required that the police inform a criminal suspect that he has the right to remain silent and that *anything* he says may be used against him. There is no qualification of this broad and explicit warning. The warning, as formulated in *Miranda*, conveys to a suspect the nature of his constitutional privilege and the consequences of abandoning it. Accordingly, we hold that a suspect's awareness of all the possible subjects of questioning in advance of interrogation is not relevant to determining whether the suspect voluntarily, knowingly, and intelligently waived his Fifth Amendment privilege.

■ ■ ■

The judgment of the Colorado Supreme Court is reversed, and the case is remanded for further proceedings not inconsistent with this opinion.

It is so ordered.

Justice MARSHALL, with whom Justice BRENNAN joins, dissenting.

The Court asserts there is "no doubt" that respondent Spring's decision to waive his Fifth Amendment privilege was voluntarily, knowingly, and intelligently made. I agree, however, with the Colorado Supreme Court that a significant doubt exists in the circumstances of this case and thus the State has failed to carry the "heavy burden" recognized in *Miranda v. Arizona*, for establishing the constitutional validity of Spring's alleged waiver.

Consistent with our prior decisions, the Court acknowledges that a suspect's waiver of fundamental constitutional rights, such as *Miranda*'s protections against self-incrimination during a custodial interrogation, must be examined in light of the "totality of the circumstances." . . . Nonetheless, the Court proceeds to hold that the specific crimes and topics of investigation known to the interrogating officers before questioning begins are "not relevant" to, and in this case "could not affect," the validity of the suspect's decision to waive his Fifth Amendment privilege. It seems to me self-evident that a suspect's decision to waive this privilege will necessarily be influenced by his awareness of the scope and seriousness of the matters under investigation.

To attempt to minimize the relevance of such information by saying that it "could affect only the wisdom of" the suspect's waiver, as opposed to the validity of that waiver, ventures an inapposite distinction. Wisdom and validity in this context are overlapping concepts, as circumstances relevant to assessing the validity of a waiver may also be highly relevant to its wisdom in any given context. Indeed, the admittedly "critical" piece of advice the Court recognizes today—that the suspect be informed that whatever he says may be used as evidence against him—is certainly relevant to the wisdom of any suspect's decision to submit to custodial interrogation without first consulting his lawyer. The Court offers no principled basis for concluding that this is a relevant factor for determining the validity of a waiver but that, under what it calls a *totality* of the circumstances analysis, a suspect's knowledge of the specific crimes and other topics previously identified for questioning can never be.

■ ■ ■

I would include among the relevant factors for consideration whether before waiving his Fifth Amendment rights the suspect was aware, either through the circumstances surrounding his arrest or through a specific advisement from the arresting or interrogating officers, of the crime or crimes he was suspected of committing and about which they intended to ask questions. To hold that such knowledge is relevant would not undermine the " 'virtue of informing police and prosecutors with specificity' as to how a pretrial questioning of a suspect must be conducted," . . . nor would it interfere with the use of legitimate interrogation techniques.

The interrogation tactics utilized in this case demonstrate the relevance of the information Spring did not receive. The agents evidently hoped to obtain from Spring a valid confession to the federal firearms charge for which he was arrested and then parlay this admission into an additional confession of first-degree murder. Spring could not have expected questions about the latter, separate offense when he agreed to waive his rights, as it occurred in a different State and was a violation of state law outside the normal investigative focus of federal Alcohol, Tobacco, and Firearms agents.

■ ■ ■

Not only is the suspect's awareness of the suspected criminal conduct relevant, its absence may be determinative in a given case. The State's burden of proving that a suspect's waiver was voluntary, knowing, and intelligent is a "heavy" one. We are to " 'indulge every reasonable presumption against waiver' of fundamental constitutional rights" and we shall " 'not presume acquiescence in the loss of fundamental rights.' " It is reasonable to conclude that, had Spring known of the federal agents' intent to ask questions about a murder unrelated to the offense for which he was arrested, he would not have consented to interrogation without first consulting his attorney. In this case, I would therefore accept the determination of the Colorado Supreme Court that Spring did not voluntarily, knowingly, and intelligently waive his Fifth Amendment rights.

I dissent.

Connecticut v. Barrett

479 U.S. 523 (1987)

Rehnquist, C.J., delivered the opinion of the Court, in which White, Blackmun, Powell, O'Connor, and Scalia, JJ., joined. Brennan, J., filed an opinion concurring in the judgment. Stevens, J., filed a dissenting opinion, in which Marshall, J., joined.

Respondent William Barrett was convicted after a jury trial of sexual assault, unlawful restraint, and possession of a controlled substance. The Connecticut Supreme Court reversed the convictions. It held that incriminating statements made by Barrett should have been suppressed under our decision in *Edwards v. Arizona* (1981), because Barrett, though stating his willingness to speak to police, had indicated that he would not make a written statement outside the presence of counsel. . . . We reverse.

In the early morning of October 24, 1980, Barrett was transported from New Haven, Connecticut, to Wallingford, where he was a suspect in a sexual assault that had occurred the previous evening. Upon arrival at the Wallingford police station, Officer Peter Cameron advised Barrett of his rights, and Barrett signed and dated an acknowledgment that he had received the warnings required by *Miranda v. Arizona* (1966). Barrett stated that "he would not give the police any written statements but he had no problem in talking about the incident."

Approximately 30 minutes later, Barrett was questioned by Officer Cameron and Officer John Genovese. Before this questioning, he was again advised of his *Miranda* rights and signed a card acknowledging that he had been read the rights. Respondent stated that he understood his rights, and told the officers that he would not give a written statement unless his attorney was present but had "no problem" talking about the incident. Barrett then gave an oral statement admitting his involvement in the sexual assault.

After discovering that a tape recorder used to preserve the statement had malfunctioned, the police conducted a second interview. For the third time, Barrett was advised of his *Miranda* rights by the Wallingford police, and once again stated that "he was willing to talk about [the incident] verbally but he did not want to put anything in writing until his attorney came." He then repeated to the police his confession regarding the previous evening's events. When the officers discovered that their tape recorder had again failed to record the statement, Officer Cameron reduced to writing his recollection of respondent's statement.

The trial court, after a suppression hearing, held that the confession was admissible. It found that respondent not only indicated that he understood the warnings, but also "offered the statements that he did not need anything explained to him because he understood. So it was not merely a passive acquiescence. . . ." Barrett's decision to make no written statement without his attorney "indicate[d] to the Court that he certainly understood from having his rights read to him that . . . he was under no obligation to give any statement." The court held that Barrett had voluntarily waived his right to counsel and thus allowed testimony at trial as to the content of Barrett's statement. Barrett took the stand in his own defense and testified that he had understood his rights as they were read to him.

■ ■ ■

The Connecticut Supreme Court reversed the conviction, holding that respondent had invoked his right to counsel by refusing to make written statements without the presence of his attorney. In the court's view, Barrett's expressed desire for counsel before making a written statement served as an invocation of the right for all purposes.

■ ■ ■

We think that the Connecticut Supreme Court erred in holding that the United States Constitution required suppression of Barrett's statement. Barrett made clear to police his willingness to talk about the crime for which he was a suspect. The trial court found that this decision was a voluntary waiver of his rights, and there is no evidence that Barrett was "threatened, tricked, or cajoled" into this waiver. The Connecticut Supreme Court nevertheless held as a matter of law that respondent's limited invocation of his right to counsel prohibited all interrogation absent initiation of further discussion by Barrett. Nothing in our decisions, however, or in the rationale of *Miranda*, requires authorities to ignore the tenor or sense of a defendant's response to these warnings.

The fundamental purpose of the Court's decision in *Miranda* was "to assure that *the individual's right to choose* between speech and silence remains unfettered throughout the interrogation process."

■ ■ ■

But we know of no constitutional objective that would be served by suppression in this case. It is undisputed that Barrett desired the presence of counsel before making a written statement. Had the police obtained such a statement without meeting the waiver standards of *Edwards*, it would clearly be inadmissible. Barrett's limited requests for counsel, however, were accompanied by affirmative announcements of his willingness to speak with the authorities. The fact that officials took the opportunity provided by Barrett to obtain an oral confession is quite consistent with the Fifth Amendment. *Miranda* gives the defendant a right to choose between speech and silence, and Barrett chose to speak.

The Connecticut Supreme Court's decision to the contrary rested on the view that requests for counsel are not to be narrowly construed. In support of this premise, respondent observes that our prior decisions have given broad effect to requests for counsel that were less than all-inclusive.

■ ■ ■

We also reject the contention that the distinction drawn by Barrett between oral and written statements indicates an understanding of the consequences so incomplete that we should deem his limited invocation of the right to counsel effective for all purposes. This suggestion ignores Barrett's testimony—and the finding of the trial court not questioned by the Connecticut Supreme Court— that respondent fully understood the *Miranda* warnings. These warnings, of course, made clear to Barrett that "[i]f you talk to any police officers, anything you say can and will be used against you in court." The fact that some might find Barrett's decision illogical is irrelevant, for we have never "embraced the theory that a defendant's ignorance of the full consequences of his decisions vitiates their voluntariness."

For the reasons stated, the judgment of the Connecticut Supreme Court is reversed, and the case is remanded for further proceedings not inconsistent with this opinion.

It is so ordered.

Justice BRENNAN, concurring in the judgment.

I concur in the judgment that the Constitution does not require the suppression of Barrett's statements to the police, but for reasons different from those set forth in the opinion of the Court. Barrett's contemporaneous waiver of his right to silence and limited invocation of his right to counsel . . . suggested that he did not understand that anything he *said* could be used against him. However, the State eliminated this apparent ambiguity when it demonstrated that Barrett's waiver of his right to silence was voluntary, knowing, and intelligent. Barrett testified at trial that he understood his *Miranda* rights . . . he knew that he need not talk to the police without a lawyer present and that anything he said could be used against him. Under these circumstances, the waiver of the right to silence and the limited invocation of the right to counsel were valid.

■ ■ ■

In this case, Barrett affirmatively waived his *Miranda* rights. Unlike the defendant in [*North Carolina v.*] *Butler* [(1979)], Barrett orally expressed his willingness to talk with the police *and* willingly signed a form indicating that he understood his rights. The police obtained an explicit oral waiver of the right to silence. Furthermore, the officer who administered the *Miranda* warnings to Barrett testified that the latter understood his rights "[c]ompletely": "I asked [Barrett] several times during my administration of those rights, if, in fact, he understood them; if there were points he wanted me to clarify, and he indicated to me, no, he understood everything fairly well." At trial, one issue was whether Barrett voluntarily, knowingly, and intelligently waived his *Miranda* rights, and Barrett himself testified that he understood his rights as they were read to him.

Had the State been without Barrett's testimony at trial, where he was represented by counsel, I could not reach this conclusion. Barrett's statement to police—that he would talk to them, but allow nothing in writing without counsel—created doubt about whether he actually understood that anything he *said* could be used against him. In other words, the statement is not, on its face, a knowing and intelligent waiver of the right to silence. As a general matter, I believe that this odd juxtaposition (a willingness to talk and an unwillingness to have anything preserved) militates against finding a knowing or intelligent waiver of the right to silence. But Barrett's testimony revealed that he understood that he had rights to remain silent and to have an attorney present, and that anything he said could be used against him; nevertheless he chose to speak.

In sum, the State has carried its "heavy burden" of demonstrating waiver. It has shown that Barrett received the *Miranda* warnings, that he had the capacity to understand them and *in fact* understood them, and that he expressly waived his right to silence, saying that he "had no problem in talking about the incident." In my view, each of these findings was essential to the conclusion that a voluntary, knowing, and intelligent waiver of the *Miranda* rights occurred.

■ ■ ■

For these reasons, I concur in the judgment of the Court.

Justice STEVENS, with whom Justice MARSHALL joins, dissenting.

The Court's disposition of this case raises two troublesome questions.

First, why did the Court decide to exercise its discretion to grant review in this case? The facts of the case are surely unique. They do not give rise to any issue of general or recurring significance. There is no conflict among the state or federal courts on how the narrow question presented should be resolved. It is merely a case in which one State Supreme Court arguably granted more protection to a citizen accused of crime than the Federal Constitution requires. The State "asks us to rule that the state court interpreted federal rights too broadly and 'overprotected' the citizen." *Michigan v. Long* (1983). If this is a sufficient reason for adding a case to our already overcrowded docket, we will need, not one, but several newly fashioned "intercircuit tribunals" to keep abreast of our work.

Second, why was respondent's request for the assistance of counsel any less ambiguous than the request in *Edwards v. Arizona*? In that case, the defendant said that he wanted an attorney " 'before making a deal.' " He also said he would talk to the police " 'but I don't want it on tape.' " The police interrogation complied with the everyday meaning of both of those conditions; it occurred before Edwards made any "deal"—indeed, he never made a deal—and no tape recording of the session was made. The Court nevertheless found the interrogation objectionable. In this case, respondent requested an attorney before signing a written statement. Why the police's compliance with the literal terms of that request makes the request—as opposed to the subsequent waiver—any less of a request for the assistance of counsel than Edwards' is not adequately explained in the Court's opinion. In all events, the Court does not purport to change the governing rule of law that judges must "give a broad, rather than a narrow, interpretation to a defendant's request for counsel." *Michigan v. Jackson* (1986).

I would dismiss the writ of certiorari as improvidently granted.

Davis v. United States

512 U.S. 452 (1994)

O'CONNOR, J., delivered the opinion of the Court, in which REHNQUIST, C.J., and SCALIA, KENNEDY, and THOMAS, JJ., joined. SCALIA, J., filed a concurring opinion, SOUTER, J., filed an opinion concurring in the judgment, in which BLACKMUN, STEVENS, and GINSBURG, JJ., joined.

■ ■ ■

In *Edwards v. Arizona* (1981), we held that law enforcement officers must immediately cease questioning a suspect who has clearly asserted his right to have counsel present during custodial interrogation. In this case we decide how law enforcement officers should respond when a suspect makes a reference to counsel that is insufficiently clear to invoke the *Edwards* prohibition on further questioning.

■ ■ ■

Pool brought trouble—not to River City, but to the Charleston Naval Base. Petitioner, a member of the United States Navy, spent the evening of October 2, 1988, shooting pool at a club on the base. Another sailor, Keith Shackleton, lost a game and a $30 wager to petitioner, but Shackleton refused to pay. After the club closed, Shackleton was beaten to death with a pool cue on a loading dock behind the commissary. The body was found early the next morning.

The investigation by the Naval Investigative Service (NIS) gradually focused on petitioner. Investigative agents determined that petitioner was at the club that evening, and that he was absent without authorization from his duty station the next morning. The agents also learned that only privately owned pool cues could be removed from the club premises, and that petitioner owned two cues—one of which had a bloodstain on it. The agents were told by various people that petitioner either had admitted committing the crime or had recounted details that clearly indicated his involvement in the killing.

On November 4, 1988, petitioner was interviewed at the NIS office. As required by military law, the agents advised petitioner that he was a suspect in the killing, that he was not required to make a statement, that any statement could be used against him at a trial by court-martial, and that he was entitled to speak with an attorney and have an attorney present during questioning. See Art. 31, Uniform Code of Military Justice (UCMJ), Manual for Courts-Martial A22-13 (1984). Petitioner waived his rights to remain silent and to counsel, both orally and in writing.

About an hour and a half into the interview, petitioner said, "Maybe I should talk to a lawyer." According to the uncontradicted testimony of one of the interviewing agents, the interview then proceeded as follows:

> "[We m]ade it very clear that we're not here to violate his rights, that if he wants a lawyer, then we will stop any kind of questioning with him, that we weren't going to pursue the matter unless we have it clarified is he asking for a lawyer or is he just making a comment about a lawyer, and he said, [']No, I'm not asking for a lawyer,' and then he continued on, and said, 'No, I don't want a lawyer.'"

After a short break, the agents reminded petitioner of his rights to remain silent and to counsel. The interview then continued for another hour, until petitioner said, "I think I want a lawyer before I say anything else." At that point, questioning ceased.

■ ■ ■

The Sixth Amendment right to counsel attaches only at the initiation of adversary criminal proceedings, see *United States v. Gouveia* (1984), and before proceedings are initiated a suspect in a criminal investigation has no constitutional right to the assistance of counsel. Nevertheless, we held in *Miranda v. Arizona* (1966) that a suspect subject to custodial interrogation has the right to consult with an attorney and to have counsel present during questioning, and that the police must explain this right to him before questioning begins. The right to counsel established in *Miranda* was one of a "series of recommended 'procedural safeguards'... [that] were not themselves rights protected by the Constitution but were instead measures to insure that the right against compulsory self-incrimination was protected."

The right to counsel recognized in *Miranda* is sufficiently important to suspects in criminal investigations, we have held, that it "requir[es] the special protection of the knowing and intelligent waiver standard."

■ ■ ■

The applicability of the "'rigid' prophylactic rule" of *Edwards* requires courts to "determine whether the accused *actually invoked* his right to counsel." To avoid difficulties of proof and to provide guidance to officers conducting interrogations, this is an objective inquiry. Invocation of the *Miranda* right to counsel "requires, at a minimum, some statement that can reasonably be construed to be an expression of a desire for the assistance of an attorney." But if a suspect makes a reference to an attorney that is ambiguous or equivocal in that a reasonable officer in light of the circumstances would have understood only that the suspect *might* be invoking the right to counsel, our precedents do not require the cessation of questioning.

Rather, the suspect must unambiguously request counsel. As we have observed, "a statement either is such an assertion of the right to counsel or it is not." *Smith v. Illinois* [(1984)]. Although a suspect need not "speak with the discrimination of an Oxford don" (Souter, J., concurring in judgment), he must articulate his desire to have counsel present sufficiently clearly that a reasonable police officer in the circumstances would understand the statement to be a request for an attorney. If the statement fails to meet the requisite level of clarity, *Edwards* does not require that the officers stop questioning the suspect. ("[T]he interrogation must cease until an attorney is present *only* [i]f the individual states that he wants an attorney").

We decline petitioner's invitation to extend *Edwards* and require law enforcement officers to cease questioning immediately upon the making of an ambiguous or equivocal reference to an attorney....

We recognize that requiring a clear assertion of the right to counsel might disadvantage some suspects who—because of fear, intimidation, lack of linguistic skills, or a variety of other reasons—will not clearly articulate their right to counsel although they actually want to have a lawyer present. But the primary protection afforded suspects subject to custodial interrogation is the *Miranda* warnings themselves. "[F]ull comprehension of the rights to remain silent and request an attorney [is] sufficient to dispel whatever coercion is inherent in the interrogation process." A suspect who knowingly and voluntarily waives his right to counsel after having that right explained to him has indicated his willingness to deal with the police unassisted. Although *Edwards* provides an additional protection—if a suspect subsequently requests an attorney, questioning must cease—it is one that must be affirmatively invoked by the suspect.

In considering how a suspect must invoke the right to counsel, we must consider the other side of the *Miranda* equation: the need for effective law enforcement. Although the courts ensure compliance with the *Miranda* requirements through the exclusionary rule, it is police officers who must actually decide whether or not they can question a suspect. The *Edwards* rule—questioning must cease if the suspect asks for a lawyer—provides a bright line that can be applied by officers in the real world of investigation and interrogation without unduly hampering the gathering of information. But if we were to require questioning to cease if a suspect makes a statement that *might* be a request for an attorney, this clarity and ease of application would be lost. Police officers would be forced to make difficult judgment calls about whether the suspect in fact wants a lawyer even though he has not said so, with the threat of suppression if they guess wrong. We therefore hold that, after a knowing and voluntary waiver of the *Miranda* rights, law enforcement officers may continue questioning until and unless the suspect clearly requests an attorney.

Of course, when a suspect makes an ambiguous or equivocal statement it will often be good police practice for the interviewing officers to clarify whether or not he actually wants an attorney. That was the procedure followed by the NIS agents in this case. Clarifying questions help protect the rights of the suspect by ensuring that he gets an attorney if he wants one, and will minimize the chance of a confession being suppressed due to subsequent judicial second-guessing as to the meaning of the suspect's statement regarding counsel. But we decline to adopt a rule requiring officers to ask clarifying questions. If the suspect's statement is not an unambiguous or unequivocal request for counsel, the officers have no obligation to stop questioning him.

To recapitulate: We held in *Miranda* that a suspect is entitled to the assistance of counsel during custodial interrogation even though the Constitution does not provide for such assistance. We held in *Edwards* that if the suspect invokes the right to counsel at any time, the police must immediately cease questioning him until an attorney is present. But we are unwilling to create a third layer of prophylaxis to prevent police questioning when the suspect *might* want a lawyer. Unless the suspect actually requests an attorney, questioning may continue.

The courts below found that petitioner's remark to the NIS agents—"Maybe I should talk to a lawyer"—was not a request for counsel, and we see no reason to disturb that conclusion. The NIS agents therefore were not required to stop questioning petitioner, though it was entirely proper for them to clarify whether petitioner in fact wanted a lawyer. Because there is no ground for suppression of petitioner's statements, the judgment of the Court of Military Appeals is

Affirmed.

■ ■ ■

Justice SOUTER, with whom Justice BLACKMUN, Justice STEVENS, and Justice GINSBURG join, concurring in the judgment.

In the midst of his questioning by naval investigators, petitioner said "Maybe I should talk to a lawyer." The investigators promptly stopped questioning Davis about the killing of Keith Shackleton and instead undertook to determine whether he meant to invoke his right to counsel, see *Miranda v. Arizona.* According to testimony accepted by the courts below, Davis answered the investigators' questions on that point by saying, "I'm not asking for a lawyer," and "No, I don't want to talk to a lawyer." Only then did the interrogation resume (stopping for good when petitioner said, "I think I want a lawyer before I say anything else").

I agree with the majority that the Constitution does not forbid law enforcement officers to pose questions (like those directed at Davis) aimed solely at clarifying whether a suspect's ambiguous reference to counsel was meant to assert his Fifth Amendment right. Accordingly I concur in the judgment affirming Davis's conviction, resting partly on evidence of statements given after agents ascertained that he did not wish to deal with them through counsel. I cannot, however, join in my colleagues' further conclusion that if the investigators here had been so inclined, they were at liberty to disregard Davis's reference to a lawyer entirely, in accordance with a general rule that interrogators have no legal obligation to discover what a custodial subject meant by an ambiguous statement that could reasonably be understood to express a desire to consult a lawyer.

Our own precedent, the reasonable judgments of the majority of the many courts already to have addressed the issue before us, and the advocacy of a considerable body of law enforcement officials are to the contrary. All argue against the Court's approach today, which draws a sharp line between interrogated suspects who "clearly" assert their right to counsel, and those who say something that may, but may not, express a desire for counsel's presence, the former suspects being assured that questioning will not resume without counsel present, the latter being left to fend for themselves. The concerns of fairness and practicality that have long anchored our *Miranda* case law point to a different response: when law enforcement officials "reasonably do not know whether or not the suspect wants a lawyer," they should stop their interrogation and ask him to make his choice clear.

While the question we address today is an open one, its answer requires coherence with nearly three decades of case law addressing the relationship between police and criminal suspects in custodial interrogation. Throughout that period, two precepts have commanded broad assent: that the *Miranda* safeguards exist " 'to assure that *the individual's right to choose* between speech and silence remains unfettered throughout the interrogation process.' "

■ ■ ■

Tested against the same two principles, the approach the Court adopts does not fare so well. First, as the majority expressly acknowledges, criminal suspects who may (in *Miranda*'s words) be "thrust into an unfamiliar atmosphere and run through menacing police interrogation procedures" would seem an odd group to single out for the Court's demand of heightened linguistic care. A substantial percentage of them lack anything like a confident command of the English language, many are "woefully ignorant and many more will be sufficiently intimidated by the interrogation process or overwhelmed by the uncertainty of their predicament that the ability to speak assertively will abandon them. Indeed, the awareness of just these realities has, in the past, dissuaded the Court from placing any burden of clarity upon individuals in custody, but has led it instead to require that requests for counsel be "give[n] a broad, rather than a narrow, interpretation," and that courts "indulge every reasonable presumption," that a suspect has not waived his right to counsel under *Miranda*.

Nor may the standard governing waivers as expressed in these statements be deflected away by drawing a distinction between initial waivers of *Miranda* rights and subsequent decisions to reinvoke them, on the theory that so long as the burden to demonstrate waiver rests on the government, it is only fair to make the suspect shoulder a burden of showing a clear subsequent assertion.

■ ■ ■

The Court defends as tolerable the certainty that some poorly expressed requests for counsel will be disregarded on the ground that *Miranda* warnings suffice to alleviate the inherent coercion of the custodial interrogation. But, "[a] once-stated warning, delivered by those who will conduct the interrogation, cannot itself suffice" to "assure that the . . . right to choose between silence and speech remains unfettered throughout the interrogation process."

■ ■ ■

Indeed, it is easy, amidst the discussion of layers of protection, to lose sight of a real risk in the majority's approach, going close to the core of what the Court has held that the Fifth Amendment provides. The experience of the timid or verbally inept suspect (whose existence the Court acknowledges) may not always closely follow that of the defendant in *Edwards v. Arizona* (whose purported waiver of his right to counsel, made after having invoked the right, was held ineffective, lest police be tempted to "badge[r]" others like him).

■ ■ ■

Nor is it enough to say that a " 'statement either is . . . an assertion of the right to counsel or it is not.' " While it might be fair to say that every statement is meant either to express a desire to deal with police through counsel or not, this fact does not dictate the rule that interrogators who hear a statement consistent with either possibility may presume the latter and forge ahead; on the contrary, clarification is the intuitively sensible course.

The other justifications offered for the "requisite level of clarity" rule, are that, whatever its costs, it will further society's strong interest in "effective law enforcement," and maintain the "ease of application," that has long been a concern of our jurisprudence. With respect to the first point, the margin of difference between the clarification approach advocated here and the one the Court adopts is defined by the class of cases in which a suspect, if asked, would make it plain that he meant to request counsel (at which point questioning would cease). While these lost confessions do extract a real price from society, it is one that *Miranda* itself determined should be borne.

As for practical application, while every approach, including the majority's, will involve some "difficult judgment calls," the rule argued for here would relieve the officer of any responsibility for guessing "whether the suspect in fact wants a lawyer even though he hasn't said so." To the contrary, it would assure that the "judgment call" will be made by the party most competent to resolve the ambiguity, who our case law has always assumed should make it: the individual suspect.

■ ■ ■

Our cases are best respected by a rule that when a suspect under custodial interrogation makes an ambiguous statement that might reasonably be understood as expressing a wish that a lawyer be summoned (and questioning cease), interrogators' questions should be confined to verifying whether the individual meant to ask for a lawyer. While there is reason to expect that trial courts will apply today's ruling sensibly (without requiring criminal suspects to speak with the discrimination of an Oxford don) and that interrogators will continue to follow what the Court rightly calls "good police practice" (compelled up to now by a substantial body of state and Circuit law), I believe that the case law under *Miranda* does not allow them to do otherwise.

b. Silence

Michigan v. Mosley

423 U.S. 96 (1975)

Stewart, J., delivered the opinion of the Court, in which Burger, C.J., Blackmun, Powell, and Douglas, JJ., joined. White, J., filed an opinion concurring in the result. Brennan, J., filed a dissenting opinion, in which Marshall, J., joined.

The respondent, Richard Bert Mosley, was arrested in Detroit, Mich., in the early afternoon of April 8, 1971, in connection with robberies that had recently occurred at the Blue Goose Bar and the White Tower Restaurant on that city's lower east side. The arresting officer, Detective James Cowie of the Armed Robbery Section of the Detroit Police Department, was acting on a tip implicating Mosley and three other men in the robberies.[1] After effecting the arrest,

---

1. The officer testified that information supplied by an anonymous caller was the sole basis for his arrest of Mosley.

Detective Cowie brought Mosley to the Robbery, Breaking and Entering Bureau of the Police Department, located on the fourth floor of the departmental headquarters building. The officer advised Mosley of his rights under this Court's decision in *Miranda v. Arizona* [(1966)], and had him read and sign the department's constitutional rights notification certificate. After filling out the necessary arrest papers, Cowie began questioning Mosley about the robbery of the White Tower Restaurant. When Mosley said he did not want to answer any questions about the robberies, Cowie promptly ceased the interrogation. The completion of the arrest papers and the questioning of Mosley together took approximately 20 minutes. At no time during the questioning did Mosley indicate a desire to consult with a lawyer, and there is no claim that the procedures followed to this point did not fully comply with the strictures of the *Miranda* opinion. Mosley was then taken to a ninth-floor cell block.

Shortly after 6 p.m., Detective Hill of the Detroit Police Department Homicide Bureau brought Mosley from the cell block to the fifth-floor office of the Homicide Bureau for questioning about the fatal shooting of a man named Leroy Williams. Williams had been killed on January 9, 1971, during a holdup attempt outside the 101 Ranch Bar in Detroit. Mosley had not been arrested on this charge or interrogated about it by Detective Cowie.[2] Before questioning Mosley about this homicide, Detective Hill carefully advised him of his "*Miranda* rights." Mosley read the notification form both silently and aloud, and Detective Hill then read and explained the warnings to him and had him sign the form. Mosley at first denied any involvement in the Williams murder, but after the officer told him that Anthony Smith had confessed to participating in the slaying and had named him as the "shooter," Mosley made a statement implicating himself in the homicide.[3] The interrogation by Detective Hill lasted approximately 15 minutes, and at no time during its course did Mosley ask to consult with a lawyer or indicate that he did not want to discuss the homicide. In short, there is no claim that the procedures followed during Detective Hill's interrogation of Mosley, standing alone, did not fully comply with the strictures of the *Miranda* opinion.[4]

Mosley was subsequently charged in a one-count information with first-degree murder. Before the trial he moved to suppress his incriminating statement on a number of grounds, among them the claim that under the doctrine of the *Miranda* case it was constitutionally impermissible for Detective Hill to question him about the Williams murder after he had told Detective Cowie that he did not want to answer any questions about the robberies.[5] The trial

---

2. The original tip to Detective Cowie had, however, implicated Mosley in the Williams murder.

3. During cross-examination by Mosley's counsel at the evidentiary hearing, Detective Hill conceded that Smith in fact had not confessed but had "denied a physical participation in the robbery."

4. But see n. 5, *infra*.

5. In addition to the claim that Detective Hill's questioning violated *Miranda*, Mosley contended that the statement was the product of an illegal arrest, that the statement was inadmissible because he had not been taken before a judicial officer without unnecessary delay, and that it had been obtained through trickery and promises of leniency. He argued that these circumstances, either independently or in combination, required the suppression of his incriminating statement.

court denied the motion to suppress after an evidentiary hearing, and the incriminating statement was subsequently introduced in evidence against Mosley at his trial. The jury convicted Mosley of first-degree murder, and the court imposed a mandatory sentence of life imprisonment.

On appeal to the Michigan Court of Appeals, Mosley renewed his previous objections to the use of his incriminating statement in evidence. The appellate court reversed the judgment of conviction, holding that Detective Hill's interrogation of Mosley had been a per se violation of the *Miranda* doctrine. Accordingly, without reaching Mosley's other contentions, the Court remanded the case for a new trial with instructions that Mosley's statement be suppressed as evidence. After further appeal was denied by the Michigan Supreme Court, the State filed a petition for certiorari here. We granted the writ because of the important constitutional question presented.

In the *Miranda* case this Court promulgated a set of safeguards to protect the there-delineated constitutional rights of persons subjected to custodial police interrogation. In sum, the Court held in that case that unless law enforcement officers give certain specified warnings before questioning a person in custody, and follow certain specified procedures during the course of any subsequent interrogation, any statement made by the person in custody cannot over his objection be admitted in evidence against him as a defendant at trial, even though the statement may in fact be wholly voluntary.

Neither party in the present case challenges the continuing validity of the *Miranda* decision, or of any of the so-called guidelines it established to protect what the Court there said was a person's constitutional privilege against compulsory self-incrimination. The issue in this case, rather, is whether the conduct of the Detroit police that led to Mosley's incriminating statement did in fact violate the *Miranda* "guidelines," so as to render the statement inadmissible in evidence against Mosley at his trial. Resolution of the question turns almost entirely on the interpretation of a single passage in the *Miranda* opinion, upon which the Michigan appellate court relied in finding a per se violation of *Miranda*:

> "Once warnings have been given, the subsequent procedure is clear. If the individual indicates in any manner, at any time prior to or during questioning, that he wishes to remain silent, the interrogation must cease. At this point he has shown that he intends to exercise his Fifth Amendment privilege; any statement taken after the person invokes his privilege cannot be other than the product of compulsion, subtle or otherwise. Without the right to cut off questioning, the setting of in-custody interrogation operates on the individual to overcome free choice in producing a statement after the privilege has been once invoked."

This passage states that "the interrogation must cease" when the person in custody indicates that "he wishes to remain silent." It does not state under what circumstances, if any, a resumption of questioning is permissible. The passage could be literally read to mean that a person who has invoked his "right to silence" can never again be subjected to custodial interrogation by any police officer at any time or place on any subject. Another possible construction of the passage would characterize "any statement taken after the person invokes his privilege" as "the product of compulsion" and would therefore mandate its exclusion from evidence, even if it were volunteered by the person in custody without any further interrogation whatever. Or the passage could be interpreted to require only the immediate cessation of questioning, and to permit a resumption of interrogation after a momentary respite.

It is evident that any of these possible literal interpretations would lead to absurd and unintended results. To permit the continuation of custodial interrogation after a momentary cessation would clearly frustrate the purposes of *Miranda* by allowing repeated rounds of questioning to undermine the will of the person being questioned. At the other extreme, a blanket prohibition against the taking of voluntary statements or a permanent immunity from further interrogation, regardless of the circumstances, would transform the *Miranda* safeguards into wholly irrational obstacles to legitimate police investigative activity, and deprive suspects of an opportunity to make informed and intelligent assessments of their interests. Clearly, therefore, neither this passage nor any other passage in the *Miranda* opinion can sensibly be read to create a per se proscription of indefinite duration upon any further questioning by any police officer on any subject, once the person in custody has indicated a desire to remain silent.

A reasonable and faithful interpretation of the *Miranda* opinion must rest on the intention of the Court in that case to adopt "fully effective means . . . to notify the person of his right of silence and to assure that the exercise of the right will be scrupulously honored. . . ." The critical safeguard identified in the passage at issue is a person's "right to cut off questioning." Through the exercise of his option to terminate questioning he can control the time at which questioning occurs, the subjects discussed, and the duration of the interrogation. The requirement that law enforcement authorities must respect a person's exercise of that option counteracts the coercive pressures of the custodial setting. We therefore conclude that the admissibility of statements obtained after the person in custody has decided to remain silent depends under *Miranda* on whether his "right to cut off questioning" was "scrupulously honored."

A review of the circumstances leading to Mosley's confession reveals that his "right to cut off questioning" was fully respected in this case. Before his initial interrogation, Mosley was carefully advised that he was under no obligation to answer any questions and could remain silent if he wished. He orally acknowledged that he understood the *Miranda* warnings and then signed a printed notification-of-rights form. When Mosley stated that he did not want to discuss the robberies, Detective Cowie immediately ceased the interrogation and did not try either to resume the questioning or in any way to persuade Mosley to reconsider his position. After an interval of more than two hours, Mosley was questioned by another police officer at another location about an unrelated holdup murder. He was given full and complete *Miranda* warnings at the outset of the second interrogation. He was thus reminded again that he could remain silent and could consult with a lawyer, and was carefully given a full and fair opportunity to exercise these options. The subsequent questioning did not undercut Mosley's previous decision not to answer Detective Cowie's inquiries. Detective Hill did not resume the interrogation about the White Tower Restaurant robbery or inquire about the Blue Goose Bar robbery, but instead focused exclusively on the Leroy Williams homicide, a crime different in nature and in time and place of occurrence from the robberies for which Mosley had been arrested and interrogated by Detective Cowie. Although it is not clear from the record how much Detective Hill knew about the earlier interrogation, his questioning of Mosley about an unrelated homicide was quite consistent with a reasonable interpretation of Mosley's earlier refusal to answer any questions about the robberies.

This is not a case, therefore, where the police failed to honor a decision of a person in custody to cut off questioning, either by refusing to discontinue the interrogation upon request or by persisting in repeated efforts to wear down his resistance and make him change his mind. In contrast to such practices, the police here immediately ceased the interrogation, resumed questioning only after the passage of a significant period of time and the provision of a fresh set of warnings, and restricted the second interrogation to a crime that had not been a subject of the earlier interrogation.

■ ■ ■

For these reasons, we conclude that the admission in evidence of Mosley's incriminating statement did not violate the principles of *Miranda v. Arizona*. Accordingly, the judgment of the Michigan Court of Appeals is vacated, and the case is remanded to that court for further proceedings not inconsistent with this opinion.

It is so ordered.

■ ■ ■

Justice Brennan, with whom Justice Marshall joins, dissenting.

The Court focuses on the correct passage from *Miranda v. Arizona*:

> "Once warnings have been given, the subsequent procedure is clear. If the individual indicates in any manner, at any time prior to or during questioning, that he wishes to remain silent, the interrogation must cease. At this point he has shown that he intends to exercise his Fifth Amendment privilege; any statement taken after the person invokes his privilege cannot be other than the product of compulsion, subtle or otherwise. Without the right to cut off questioning, the setting of in-custody interrogation operates on the individual to overcome free choice in producing a statement after the privilege has been once invoked."

But the process of eroding *Miranda* rights, begun with *Harris v. New York* (1971), continues with today's holding that police may renew the questioning of a suspect who has once exercised his right to remain silent, provided the suspect's right to cut off questioning has been "scrupulously honored." Today's distortion of *Miranda*'s constitutional principles can be viewed only as yet another stop in the erosion and, I suppose, ultimate overruling of *Miranda*'s enforcement of the privilege against self-incrimination.

■ ■ ■

The language which the Court finds controlling in this case teaches that renewed questioning itself is part of the process which invariably operates to overcome the will of a suspect. . . . Today's decision uncritically abandons that teaching: The Court assumes, contrary to controlling language, that "scrupulously honoring" an initial exercise of the right to remain silent preserves the efficaciousness of initial and future warnings despite the fact that the suspect has once been subject to interrogation and then has been detained for a lengthy period of time.

■ ■ ■

I agree that *Miranda* is not to be read, on the one hand, to impose an absolute ban on resumption of questioning "at any time or place on any subject," or on the other hand, "to permit a resumption of interrogation after a momentary respite." But this surely cannot justify adoption of a vague and ineffective procedural standard that falls somewhere between those absurd extremes, for *Miranda* in flat and unambiguous terms requires that questioning "cease" when a suspect exercises the right to remain silent. *Miranda*'s terms, however, are not so uncompromising as to preclude the fashioning of guidelines to govern this case. Those guidelines must, of course, necessarily be sensitive to the reality that "[a]s a practical matter, the compulsion to speak in the isolated setting of the police station may well be greater than in courts or other official investigations, where there are often impartial observers to guard against intimidation or trickery."

The fashioning of guidelines for this case is an easy task. Adequate procedures are readily available. Michigan law requires that the suspect be arraigned before a judicial officer "without unnecessary delay," certainly not a burdensome requirement. Alternatively, a requirement that resumption of questioning should await appointment and arrival of counsel for the suspect would be an acceptable and readily satisfied precondition to resumption. *Miranda* expressly held that "[t]he presence of counsel . . . would be the adequate protective device necessary to make the process of police interrogation conform to the dictates of the privilege (against self-incrimination)." The Court expediently bypasses this alternative in its search for circumstances where renewed questioning would be permissible.

Indeed, language in *Miranda* suggests that the presence of counsel is the only appropriate alternative. In categorical language we held in *Miranda*: "If the individual indicates in any manner, at any time prior to or during questioning, that he wishes to remain silent, the interrogation must cease." We then immediately observed:

> "If an individual indicates his desire to remain silent, but has an attorney present, there may be some circumstances in which further questioning

would be permissible. In the absence of evidence of overbearing, statements then made in the presence of counsel might be free of the compelling influence of the interrogation process and might fairly be construed as a waiver of the privilege for purposes of these statements."

This was the only circumstance in which we at all suggested that questioning could be resumed, and even then, further questioning was not permissible in all such circumstances, for compulsion was still the presumption not easily dissipated.

■ ■ ■

In light of today's erosion of *Miranda* standards as a matter of federal constitutional law, it is appropriate to observe that no State is precluded by the decision from adhering to higher standards under state law. Each State has power to impose higher standards governing police practices under state law than is required by the Federal Constitution.

■ ■ ■

Berghuis v. Thompkins

130 S. Ct. 2250 (2010)

KENNEDY, J., delivered the opinion of the Court, in which ROBERTS, C.J., and SCALIA, THOMAS, and ALITO, JJ., joined. SOTOMAYOR, J., filed a dissenting opinion, in which STEVENS, GINSBURG, and BREYER, JJ., joined.

■ ■ ■

On January 10, 2000, a shooting occurred outside a mall in Southfield, Michigan. Among the victims was Samuel Morris, who died from multiple gunshot wounds. The other victim, Frederick France, recovered from his injuries and later testified. Thompkins, who was a suspect, fled. About one year later he was found in Ohio and arrested there.

Two Southfield police officers traveled to Ohio to interrogate Thompkins, then awaiting transfer to Michigan. The interrogation began around 1:30 p.m. and lasted about three hours. The interrogation was conducted in a room that was 8 by 10 feet, and Thompkins sat in a chair that resembled a school desk (it had an arm on it that swings around to provide a surface to write on). At the beginning of the interrogation, one of the officers, Detective Helgert, presented Thompkins with a form derived from the *Miranda* rule. It stated:

"NOTIFICATION OF CONSTITUTIONAL RIGHTS AND STATEMENT

1. You have the right to remain silent.

2. Anything you say can and will be used against you in a court of law.

3. You have a right to talk to a lawyer before answering any questions and you have the right to have a lawyer present with you while you are answering any questions.

4. If you cannot afford to hire a lawyer, one will be appointed to represent you before any questioning, if you wish one.

5. You have the right to decide at any time before or during questioning to use your right to remain silent and your right to talk with a lawyer while you are being questioned."

Helgert asked Thompkins to read the fifth warning out loud. Thompkins complied. Helgert later said this was to ensure that Thompkins could read, and Helgert concluded that Thompkins understood English. Helgert then read the other four *Miranda* warnings out loud and asked Thompkins to sign the form to demonstrate that he understood his rights. Thompkins declined to sign the form. The record contains conflicting evidence about whether Thompkins then verbally confirmed that he understood the rights listed on the form.

Officers began an interrogation. At no point during the interrogation did Thompkins say that he wanted to remain silent, that he did not want to talk with the police, or that he wanted an attorney. Thompkins was "[l]argely" silent during the interrogation, which lasted about three hours. He did give a few limited verbal responses, however, such as "yeah," "no," or "I don't know." And on occasion he communicated by nodding his head. Thompkins also said that he "didn't want a peppermint" that was offered to him by the police and that the chair he was "sitting in was hard."

About 2 hours and 45 minutes into the interrogation, Helgert asked Thompkins, "Do you believe in God?" Thompkins made eye contact with Helgert and said "Yes," as his eyes "well[ed] up with tears." Helgert asked, "Do you pray to God?" Thompkins said "Yes." Helgert asked, "Do you pray to God to forgive you for shooting that boy down?" Thompkins answered "Yes" and looked away. Thompkins refused to make a written confession, and the interrogation ended about 15 minutes later.

Thompkins was charged with first-degree murder, assault with intent to commit murder, and certain firearms-related offenses. He moved to suppress the statements made during the interrogation. He argued that he had invoked his Fifth Amendment right to remain silent, requiring police to end the interrogation at once, see *Michigan v. Mosley* (1975), that he had not waived his right to remain silent, and that his inculpatory statements were involuntary. The trial court denied the motion.

■ ■ ■

Under AEDPA, a federal court may not grant a habeas corpus application "with respect to any claim that was adjudicated on the merits in State court proceedings," 28 U.S.C. §2254(d), unless the state court's decision "was contrary to, or involved an unreasonable application of, clearly established Federal law, as determined by the Supreme Court of the United States," §2254(d)(1), or "was based on an unreasonable determination of the facts in light of the evidence presented in the State court proceeding," §2254(d)(2). See *Knowles v. Mirzayance* (2009). The relevant state-court decision here is the Michigan

Court of Appeals' decision affirming Thompkins's conviction and rejecting his *Miranda* and ineffective-assistance-of-counsel claims on the merits.

The *Miranda* Court formulated a warning that must be given to suspects before they can be subjected to custodial interrogation. The substance of the warning still must be given to suspects today. A suspect in custody must be advised as follows:

> "He must be warned prior to any questioning that he has the right to remain silent, that anything he says can be used against him in a court of law, that he has the right to the presence of an attorney, and that if he cannot afford an attorney one will be appointed for him prior to any questioning if he so desires." [*Miranda v. Arizona* (1966).]

All concede that the warning given in this case was in full compliance with these requirements. The dispute centers on the response—or nonresponse—from the suspect.

Thompkins makes various arguments that his answers to questions from the detectives were inadmissible. He first contends that he "invoke[d] his privilege" to remain silent by not saying anything for a sufficient period of time, so the interrogation should have "cease[d]" before he made his inculpatory statements. . . . see *Mosley* (police must " 'scrupulously hono[r]' " this "critical safeguard" when the accused invokes his or her " 'right to cut off questioning' " (quoting *Miranda*).

This argument is unpersuasive. In the context of invoking the *Miranda* right to counsel, the Court in *Davis v. United States* (1994) held that a suspect must do so "unambiguously." If an accused makes a statement concerning the right to counsel "that is ambiguous or equivocal" or makes no statement, the police are not required to end the interrogation, or ask questions to clarify whether the accused wants to invoke his or her *Miranda* rights.

The Court has not yet stated whether an invocation of the right to remain silent can be ambiguous or equivocal, but there is no principled reason to adopt different standards for determining when an accused has invoked the *Miranda* right to remain silent and the *Miranda* right to counsel at issue in *Davis*. See, *e.g.*, *Solem v. Stumes* (1984) ("[M]uch of the logic and language of [*Mosley*]," which discussed the *Miranda* right to remain silent, "could be applied to the invocation of the [*Miranda* right to counsel]"). Both protect the privilege against compulsory self-incrimination, *Miranda*, by requiring an interrogation to cease when either right is invoked.

There is good reason to require an accused who wants to invoke his or her right to remain silent to do so unambiguously. A requirement of an unambiguous invocation of *Miranda* rights results in an objective inquiry that "avoid[s] difficulties of proof and . . . provide[s] guidance to officers" on how to proceed in the face of ambiguity. If an ambiguous act, omission, or statement could require police to end the interrogation, police would be required to make difficult decisions about an accused's unclear intent and face the consequence of suppression "if they guess wrong." Suppression of a voluntary confession in these circumstances would place a significant burden on society's interest in prosecuting criminal activity. Treating an ambiguous or equivocal act, omission, or statement as an invocation of *Miranda* rights "might add marginally to *Miranda*'s goal of dispelling the compulsion inherent in custodial interrogation." But "as *Miranda* holds, full comprehension of the rights to remain silent and request an attorney are sufficient to dispel whatever coercion is inherent in the interrogation process."

Thompkins did not say that he wanted to remain silent or that he did not want to talk with the police. Had he made either of these simple, unambiguous statements, he would have invoked his " 'right to cut off questioning.' " Here he did neither, so he did not invoke his right to remain silent.

We next consider whether Thompkins waived his right to remain silent. Even absent the accused's invocation of the right to remain silent, the accused's statement during a custodial interrogation is inadmissible at trial unless the prosecution can establish that the accused "in fact knowingly and voluntarily waived [*Miranda*] rights" when making the statement. The waiver inquiry "has two distinct dimensions": waiver must be "voluntary in the sense that it was the product of a free and deliberate choice rather than intimidation, coercion, or deception," and "made with a full awareness of both the nature of the right being abandoned and the consequences of the decision to abandon it."

Some language in *Miranda* could be read to indicate that waivers are difficult to establish absent an explicit written waiver or a formal, express oral statement. *Miranda* said "a valid waiver will not be presumed simply from the silence of the accused after warnings are given or simply from the fact that a confession was in fact eventually obtained." In addition, the *Miranda* Court stated that "a heavy burden rests on the government to demonstrate that the defendant knowingly and intelligently waived his privilege against self-incrimination and his right to retained or appointed counsel."

The course of decisions since *Miranda*, informed by the application of *Miranda* warnings in the whole course of law enforcement, demonstrates that waivers can be established even absent formal or express statements of waiver that would be expected in, say, a judicial hearing to determine if a guilty plea has been properly entered. The main purpose of *Miranda* is to ensure that an accused is advised of and understands the right to remain silent and the right to counsel. Thus, "[i]f anything, our subsequent cases have reduced the impact of the *Miranda* rule on legitimate law enforcement while reaffirming the decision's core ruling that unwarned statements may not be used as evidence in the prosecution's case in chief."

One of the first cases to decide the meaning and import of *Miranda* with respect to the question of waiver was *North Carolina v. Butler* [(1979)]. The *Butler* Court, after discussing some of the problems created by the language in *Miranda*, established certain important propositions. *Butler* interpreted the *Miranda* language concerning the "heavy burden" to show waiver, in accord with usual principles of determining waiver, which can include waiver implied from all the circumstances. And in a later case, the

Court stated that this "heavy burden" is not more than the burden to establish waiver by a preponderance of the evidence. *Colorado v. Connelly* (1986).

The prosecution therefore does not need to show that a waiver of *Miranda* rights was express. An "implicit waiver" of the "right to remain silent" is sufficient to admit a suspect's statement into evidence. *Butler* made clear that a waiver of *Miranda* rights may be implied through "the defendant's silence, coupled with an understanding of his rights and a course of conduct indicating waiver." The Court in *Butler* therefore "retreated" from the "language and tenor of the *Miranda* opinion," which "suggested that the Court would require that a waiver . . . be 'specifically made.' "

If the State establishes that a *Miranda* warning was given and the accused made an uncoerced statement, this showing, standing alone, is insufficient to demonstrate "a valid waiver" of *Miranda* rights. The prosecution must make the additional showing that the accused understood these rights. Where the prosecution shows that a *Miranda* warning was given and that it was understood by the accused, an accused's uncoerced statement establishes an implied waiver of the right to remain silent.

Although *Miranda* imposes on the police a rule that is both formalistic and practical when it prevents them from interrogating suspects without first providing them with a *Miranda* warning, it does not impose a formalistic waiver procedure that a suspect must follow to relinquish those rights. As a general proposition, the law can presume that an individual who, with a full understanding of his or her rights, acts in a manner inconsistent with their exercise has made a deliberate choice to relinquish the protection those rights afford. . . .

The record in this case shows that Thompkins waived his right to remain silent. There is no basis in this case to conclude that he did not understand his rights; and on these facts it follows that he chose not to invoke or rely on those rights when he did speak. First, there is no contention that Thompkins did not understand his rights; and from this it follows that he knew what he gave up when he spoke. There was more than enough evidence in the record to conclude that Thompkins understood his *Miranda* rights. Thompkins received a written copy of the *Miranda* warnings; Detective Helgert determined that Thompkins could read and understand English; and Thompkins was given time to read the warnings. Thompkins, furthermore, read aloud the fifth warning, which stated that "you have the right to decide at any time before or during questioning to use your right to remain silent and your right to talk with a lawyer while you are being questioned." He was thus aware that his right to remain silent would not dissipate after a certain amount of time and that police would have to honor his right to be silent and his right to counsel during the whole course of interrogation. Those rights, the warning made clear, could be asserted at any time. Helgert, moreover, read the warnings aloud.

Second, Thompkins's answer to Detective Helgert's question about whether Thompkins prayed to God for forgiveness for shooting the victim is a "course of conduct indicating waiver" of the right to remain silent. If Thompkins wanted to remain silent, he could have said nothing in response to Helgert's questions, or he could have unambiguously invoked his *Miranda* rights and ended the interrogation. The fact that Thompkins made a statement about three hours after receiving a *Miranda* warning does not overcome the fact that he engaged in a course of conduct indicating waiver. Police are not required to rewarn suspects from time to time. Thompkins's answer to Helgert's question about praying to God for forgiveness for shooting the victim was sufficient to show a course of conduct indicating waiver. This is confirmed by the fact that before then Thompkins had given sporadic answers to questions throughout the interrogation.

Third, there is no evidence that Thompkins's statement was coerced. Thompkins does not claim that police threatened or injured him during the interrogation or that he was in any way fearful. The interrogation was conducted in a standard-sized room in the middle of the afternoon. It is true that apparently he was in a straight-backed chair for three hours, but there is no authority for the proposition that an interrogation of this length is inherently coercive. Indeed, even where interrogations of greater duration were held to be improper, they were accompanied, as this one was not, by other facts indicating coercion, such as an incapacitated and sedated suspect, sleep and food deprivation, and threats. The fact that Helgert's question referred to Thompkins's religious beliefs also did not render Thompkins's statement involuntary. "[T]he Fifth Amendment privilege is not concerned 'with moral and psychological pressures to confess emanating from sources other than official coercion.'" In these circumstances, Thompkins knowingly and voluntarily made a statement to police, so he waived his right to remain silent.

Thompkins next argues that, even if his answer to Detective Helgert could constitute a waiver of his right to remain silent, the police were not allowed to question him until they obtained a waiver first. *Butler* forecloses this argument. The *Butler* Court held that courts can infer a waiver of *Miranda* rights "from the actions and words of the person interrogated." This principle would be inconsistent with a rule that requires a waiver at the outset. The *Butler* Court thus rejected the rule proposed by the *Butler* dissent, which would have "requir[ed] the police to obtain an express waiver of [*Miranda* rights] before proceeding with interrogation." This holding also makes sense given that "the primary protection afforded suspects subject[ed] to custodial interrogation is the *Miranda* warnings themselves." The *Miranda* rule and its requirements are met if a suspect receives adequate *Miranda* warnings, understands them, and has an opportunity to invoke the rights before giving any answers or admissions. Any waiver, express or implied, may be contradicted by an invocation at any time. If the right to counsel or the right to remain silent is invoked at any point during questioning, further interrogation must cease.

Interrogation provides the suspect with additional information that can put his or her decision to waive, or not to invoke, into perspective. As questioning commences and then continues, the suspect has the opportunity to consider the choices he or she faces and to make a more informed decision, either to insist on silence or to cooperate. When the suspect knows that *Miranda* rights can be invoked at any time, he or she has the opportunity to reassess his or her immediate and long-term interests. Cooperation with the police may result in more favorable treatment for the suspect; the apprehension of accomplices; the prevention of continuing injury and fear; beginning steps towards relief or solace for the victims; and the beginning of the suspect's own return to the law and the social order it seeks to protect.

In order for an accused's statement to be admissible at trial, police must have given the accused a *Miranda* warning. If that condition is established, the court can proceed to consider whether there has been an express or implied waiver of *Miranda* rights. In making its ruling on the admissibility of a statement made during custodial questioning, the trial court, of course, considers whether there is evidence to support the conclusion that, from the whole course of questioning, an express or implied waiver has been established. Thus, after giving a *Miranda* warning, police may interrogate a suspect who has neither invoked nor waived his or her *Miranda* rights. On these premises, it follows the police were not required to obtain a waiver of Thompkins's *Miranda* rights before commencing the interrogation.

In sum, a suspect who has received and understood the *Miranda* warnings, and has not invoked his *Miranda* rights, waives the right to remain silent by making an uncoerced statement to the police. Thompkins did not invoke his right to remain silent and stop the questioning. Understanding his rights in full, he waived his right to remain silent by making a voluntary statement to the police. The police, moreover, were not required to obtain a waiver of Thompkins's right to remain silent before interrogating him. The state court's decision rejecting Thompkins's *Miranda* claim was thus correct under *de novo* review and therefore necessarily reasonable under the more deferential AEDPA standard of review (state court's decision was correct under *de novo* review and not unreasonable under AEDPA).

■ ■ ■

The judgment of the Court of Appeals is reversed, and the case is remanded with instructions to deny the petition.

It is so ordered.

Justice SOTOMAYOR, with whom Justice STEVENS, Justice GINSBURG, and Justice BREYER join, dissenting.

The Court concludes today that a criminal suspect waives his right to remain silent if, after sitting tacit and uncommunicative through nearly three hours of police interrogation, he utters a few one-word responses. The Court also concludes that a suspect who wishes to guard his right to remain silent against such a finding of "waiver" must, counterintuitively, speak—and must do so with sufficient precision to satisfy a clear-statement rule that construes ambiguity in favor of the police. Both propositions mark a substantial retreat from the protection against compelled self-incrimination that *Miranda v. Arizona* (1966) has long provided during custodial interrogation....

We granted certiorari to review the judgment of the Court of Appeals for the Sixth Circuit, which held that Thompkins was entitled to habeas relief.... As to the *Miranda* claims, Thompkins argues first that through his conduct during the 3-hour custodial interrogation he effectively invoked his right to remain silent, requiring police to cut off questioning in accordance with *Miranda* and *Michigan v. Mosley* (1975). Thompkins also contends his statements were in any case inadmissible because the prosecution failed to meet its heavy burden under *Miranda* of proving that he knowingly and intelligently waived his right to remain silent. The Sixth Circuit agreed with Thompkins as to waiver and declined to reach the question of invocation. In my view, even if Thompkins cannot prevail on his invocation claim under AEDPA, he is entitled to relief as to waiver. Because I would affirm the judgment of the Sixth Circuit on that ground, I would not reach Thompkins' claim that he received constitutionally ineffective assistance of counsel.

The strength of Thompkins' *Miranda* claims depends in large part on the circumstances of the 3-hour interrogation, at the end of which he made inculpatory statements later introduced at trial. The Court's opinion downplays record evidence that Thompkins remained almost completely silent and unresponsive throughout that session. One of the interrogating officers, Detective Helgert, testified that although Thompkins was administered *Miranda* warnings, the last of which he read aloud, Thompkins expressly declined to sign a written acknowledgment that he had been advised of and understood his rights. There is conflicting evidence in the record about whether Thompkins ever verbally confirmed understanding his rights.[1] The record contains no indication that the officers sought or obtained an express waiver.

As to the interrogation itself, Helgert candidly characterized it as "very, very one-sided" and "nearly a monologue." Thompkins was "[p]eculiar," "[s]ullen," and "[g]enerally quiet." Helgert and his partner "did most of the talking," as Thompkins was "not verbally communicative" and "[l]argely" remained silent. To the extent Thompkins gave any response, his answers consisted of "a word or two. A 'yeah,' or a 'no,' or 'I don't know.' . . . And sometimes . . . he simply sat down . . . with [his] head in [his] hands looking down. Sometimes . . . he would look up and make eye-contact would be the only response." After proceeding in this fashion for approximately 2 hours and 45 minutes, Helgert asked Thompkins three questions relating to his faith in God. The prosecution relied at trial on Thompkins' one-word answers of "yes."

---

1. At the suppression hearing, Detective Helgert testified that after reading Thompkins the warnings, "I believe I asked him if he understood the Rights, and I think I got a verbal answer to that as a 'yes.'" In denying the motion to suppress, the trial court relied on that factual premise. In his later testimony at trial, Helgert remembered the encounter differently. Asked whether Thompkins "indicate[d] that he understood [the warnings]" after they had been read, Helgert stated "I don't know that I orally asked him that question." Nevertheless, the Michigan Court of Appeals stated that Thompkins verbally acknowledged understanding his rights.

Thompkins' nonresponsiveness is particularly striking in the context of the officers' interview strategy, later explained as conveying to Thompkins that "this was his opportunity to explain his side [of the story]" because "[e]verybody else, including [his] co-[d]efendants, had given their version," and asking him "[w]ho is going to speak up for you if you don't speak up for yourself?" Yet, Helgert confirmed that the *only* thing [Thompkins said] relative to his involvement [in the shooting]" occurred near the end of the interview—*i.e.*, in response to the questions about God. The only other responses Helgert could remember Thompkins giving were that " '[h]e didn't want a peppermint' " and " 'the chair that he was sitting in was hard.' " Nevertheless, the Michigan court concluded on this record that Thompkins had not invoked his right to remain silent because "he continued to talk with the officer, albeit sporadically," and that he voluntarily waived that right.

Thompkins' federal habeas petition is governed by AEDPA, under which a federal court may not grant the writ unless the state court's adjudication of the merits of the claim at issue "was contrary to, or involved an unreasonable application of, clearly established Federal law, as determined by the Supreme Court of the United States," or "was based on an unreasonable determination of the facts in light of the evidence presented in the State court proceeding."

The relevant clearly established federal law for purposes of § 2254(d)(1) begins with our landmark *Miranda* decision, which "g[a]ve force to the Constitution's protection against compelled self-incrimination" by establishing " 'certain procedural safeguards that require police to advise criminal suspects of their rights under the Fifth and Fourteenth Amendments before commencing custodial interrogation.' " . . . "If [an] individual indicates in any manner, at any time prior to or during questioning, that he wishes to remain silent" or if he "states that he wants an attorney," the interrogation "must cease."

Even when warnings have been administered and a suspect has not affirmatively invoked his rights, statements made in custodial interrogation may not be admitted as part of the prosecution's case in chief "unless and until" the prosecution demonstrates that an individual "knowingly and intelligently waive[d] [his] rights." "[A] heavy burden rests on the government to demonstrate that the defendant knowingly and intelligently waived his privilege against self-incrimination and his right to retained or appointed counsel." The government must satisfy the "high standar[d] of proof for the waiver of constitutional rights."

The question whether a suspect has validly waived his right is "entirely distinct" as a matter of law from whether he invoked that right. *Smith v. Illinois* (1984) (*per curiam*). The questions are related, however, in terms of the practical effect on the exercise of a suspect's rights. A suspect may at any time revoke his prior waiver of rights—or, closer to the facts of this case, guard against the possibility of a future finding that he implicitly waived his rights—by invoking the rights and thereby requiring the police to cease questioning. . . .

Like the Sixth Circuit, I begin with the question whether Thompkins waived his right to remain silent. Even if Thompkins did not invoke that right, he is entitled to relief because Michigan did not satisfy its burden of establishing waiver.

Miranda's discussion of the prosecution's burden in proving waiver speaks with particular clarity to the facts of this case and therefore merits reproducing at length:

> "If [an] interrogation continues without the presence of an attorney and a statement is taken, a heavy burden rests on the government to demonstrate that the defendant knowingly and intelligently waived his privilege against self-incrimination and his right to retained or appointed counsel. . . . Since the State is responsible for establishing the isolated circumstances under which [an] interrogation takes place and has the only means of making available corroborated evidence of warnings given during incommunicado interrogation, the burden is rightly on its shoulders.
>
> An express statement that the individual is willing to make a statement and does not want an attorney followed closely by a statement could constitute a waiver. But a valid waiver will not be presumed simply from the silence of the accused after warnings are given or simply from the fact that a confession was in fact eventually obtained."

Miranda went further in describing the facts likely to satisfy the prosecution's burden of establishing the admissibility of statements obtained after a lengthy interrogation:

> "Whatever the testimony of the authorities as to waiver of rights by an accused, the fact of lengthy interrogation or incommunicado incarceration before a statement is made is strong evidence that the accused did not validly waive his rights. In these circumstances the fact that the individual eventually made a statement is consistent with the conclusion that the compelling influence of the interrogation finally forced him to do so. It is inconsistent with any notion of a voluntary relinquishment of the privilege."

This Court's decisions subsequent to *Miranda* have emphasized the prosecution's "heavy burden" in proving waiver. We have also reaffirmed that a court may not presume waiver from a suspect's silence or from the mere fact that a confession was eventually obtained. See *North Carolina v. Butler*.

Even in concluding that *Miranda* does not invariably require an express waiver of the right to silence or the right to counsel, this Court in *Butler* made clear that the prosecution bears a substantial burden in establishing an implied waiver. The Federal Bureau of Investigation had obtained statements after advising Butler of his rights and confirming that he understood them. When presented with a written waiver-of-rights form, Butler told the agents, " 'I will talk to you but I am not signing any form.' " He then made inculpatory statements, which he later sought to suppress on the ground that he had not expressly waived his right to counsel.

Although this Court reversed the state-court judgment concluding that the statements were inadmissible, we quoted at length portions of the *Miranda* opinion reproduced above. We cautioned that even an "express written or oral statement of waiver of the right to remain silent or of the right to counsel" is not "inevitably . . . sufficient to establish waiver," emphasizing that "[t]he question is . . . whether the defendant in fact knowingly and voluntarily waived the rights delineated in the *Miranda* case." *Miranda*, we observed, "unequivocally said . . . mere silence is not enough." While we stopped short in *Butler* of announcing a *per se* rule that "the defendant's silence, coupled with an understanding of his rights and a course of conduct indicating waiver, may never support a conclusion that a defendant has waived his rights," we reiterated that "courts must presume that a defendant did not waive his rights; the prosecution's burden is great."

Rarely do this Court's precedents provide clearly established law so closely on point with the facts of a particular case. Together, *Miranda* and *Butler* establish that a court "must presume that a defendant did not waive his right[s]"; the prosecution bears a "heavy burden" in attempting to demonstrate waiver; the fact of a "lengthy interrogation" prior to obtaining statements is "strong evidence" against a finding of valid waiver; "mere silence" in response to questioning is "not enough"; and waiver may not be presumed "simply from the fact that a confession was in fact eventually obtained."

It is undisputed here that Thompkins never expressly waived his right to remain silent. His refusal to sign even an acknowledgment that he understood his *Miranda* rights evinces, if anything, an intent not to waive those rights. That Thompkins did not make the inculpatory statements at issue until after approximately 2 hours and 45 minutes of interrogation serves as "strong evidence" against waiver. *Miranda* and *Butler* expressly preclude the possibility that the inculpatory statements themselves are sufficient to establish waiver.

In these circumstances, Thompkins' "actions and words" preceding the inculpatory statements simply do not evidence a "course of conduct indicating waiver" sufficient to carry the prosecution's burden. See *Butler*. Although the Michigan court stated that Thompkins "sporadically" participated in the interview that court's opinion and the record before us are silent as to the subject matter or context of even a single question to which Thompkins purportedly responded, other than the exchange about God and the statements respecting the peppermint and the chair. Unlike in *Butler*, Thompkins made no initial declaration akin to "I will talk to you." See also [case below] (noting that the case might be different if the record showed Thompkins had responded affirmatively to an invitation to tell his side of the story or described any particular question that Thompkins answered). Indeed, Michigan and the United States concede that no waiver occurred in this case until Thompkins responded "yes" to the questions about God. I believe it is objectively unreasonable under our clearly established precedents to conclude the prosecution met its "heavy burden" of proof on a record consisting of three one-word answers, following 2 hours and 45 minutes of silence punctuated by a few largely nonverbal responses to unidentified questions.

Perhaps because our prior *Miranda* precedents so clearly favor Thompkins, the Court today goes beyond AEDPA's deferential standard of review and announces a new general principle of law. Any new rule, it must be emphasized, is unnecessary to the disposition of this case. If, in the Court's view, the Michigan court did not unreasonably apply our *Miranda* precedents in denying Thompkins relief, it should simply say so and reverse the Sixth Circuit's judgment on that ground. "It is a fundamental rule of judicial restraint . . . that this Court will not reach constitutional questions in advance of the necessity of deciding them." Consistent with that rule, we have frequently declined to address questions beyond what is necessary to resolve a case under AEDPA. No necessity exists to justify the Court's broad announcement today.

The Court concludes that when *Miranda* warnings have been given and understood, "an accused's uncoerced statement establishes an implied waiver of the right to remain silent." More broadly still, the Court states that, "[a]s a general proposition, the law can presume that an individual who, with a full understanding of his or her rights, acts in a manner inconsistent with their exercise has made a deliberate choice to relinquish the protection those rights afford."

These principles flatly contradict our longstanding views that "a valid waiver will not be presumed . . . simply from the fact that a confession was in fact eventually obtained," and that "[t]he courts must presume that a defendant did not waive his rights." Indeed, we have in the past summarily reversed a state-court decision that inverted *Miranda*'s antiwaiver presumption, characterizing the error as "readily apparent." At best, the Court today creates an unworkable and conflicting set of presumptions that will undermine *Miranda*'s goal of providing "concrete constitutional guidelines for law enforcement agencies and courts to follow." At worst, it overrules *sub silentio* an essential aspect of the protections *Miranda* has long provided for the constitutional guarantee against self-incrimination.

The Court's conclusion that Thompkins' inculpatory statements were sufficient to establish an implied waiver finds no support in *Butler*. *Butler* itself distinguished between a sufficient "course of conduct" and inculpatory statements, reiterating *Miranda*'s admonition that " 'a valid waiver will not be presumed simply from . . . the fact that a confession was in fact eventually obtained.' " Michigan suggests Butler's silence " 'when advised of his right to the assistance of a lawyer,' " combined with our remand for the state court to apply the implied-waiver standard, shows that silence followed by statements can be a " 'course of conduct.' " But the evidence of implied waiver in *Butler* was worlds apart from the evidence in this case, because Butler unequivocally said "I will talk to you" after having been read *Miranda* warnings. Thompkins, of course, made no such statement.

The Court also relies heavily on [*Moran v.*] *Burbine* [(1986)] in characterizing the scope of the prosecution's burden in proving waiver. Consistent with *Burbine*, the Court observes, the prosecution must prove that waiver was " 'voluntary in the sense that it was the product of a free and deliberate choice rather than intimidation' " and " 'made with a full awareness of both the nature of the right being abandoned and the consequences of the decision to abandon it.'" I agree with the Court's statement, so far as it goes. What it omits, however, is that the prosecution also bears an antecedent burden of showing there was, in fact, either an express waiver or a "course of conduct" sufficiently clear to support a finding of implied waiver. Nothing in *Burbine* even hints at removing that obligation. The question in that case, rather, was whether a suspect's multiple express waivers of his rights were invalid because police "misinformed an inquiring attorney about their plans concerning the suspect or because they failed to inform the suspect of the attorney's efforts to reach him." The Court's analysis in *Burbine* was predicated on the existence of waiver-in-fact.

Today's dilution of the prosecution's burden of proof to the bare fact that a suspect made inculpatory statements after *Miranda* warnings were given and understood takes an unprecedented step away from the "high standards of proof for the waiver of constitutional rights" this Court has long demanded... cf. *Brewer v. Williams* (1977) ("[C]ourts indulge in every reasonable presumption against waiver"). When waiver is to be inferred during a custodial interrogation, there are sound reasons to require evidence beyond inculpatory statements themselves. *Miranda* and our subsequent cases are premised on the idea that custodial interrogation is inherently coercive. See [*Miranda*] ("Even without employing brutality, the 'third degree' or [other] specific strategems... the very fact of custodial interrogation exacts a heavy toll on individual liberty and trades on the weakness of individuals"). Requiring proof of a course of conduct beyond the inculpatory statements themselves is critical to ensuring that those statements are voluntary admissions and not the dubious product of an overborne will.

Today's decision thus ignores the important interests *Miranda* safeguards. The underlying constitutional guarantee against self-incrimination reflects "many of our fundamental values and most noble aspirations," our society's "preference for an accusatorial rather than an inquisitorial system of criminal justice"; a "fear that self-incriminating statements will be elicited by inhumane treatment and abuses" and a resulting "distrust of self-deprecatory statements"; and a realization that while the privilege is "sometimes a shelter to the guilty, [it] is often a protection to the innocent." For these reasons, we have observed, a criminal law system "which comes to depend on the 'confession' will, in the long run, be less reliable and more subject to abuses than a system relying on independent investigation." "By bracing against 'the possibility of unreliable statements in every instance of in-custody interrogation,'" *Miranda*'s prophylactic rules serve to "'protect the fairness of the trial itself.'" Today's decision bodes poorly for the fundamental principles that *Miranda* protects.

Thompkins separately argues that his conduct during the interrogation invoked his right to remain silent, requiring police to terminate questioning. Like the Sixth Circuit, I would not reach this question because Thompkins is in any case entitled to relief as to waiver. But even if Thompkins would not prevail on his invocation claim under AEDPA's deferential standard of review,

I cannot agree with the Court's much broader ruling that a suspect must clearly invoke his right to silence by speaking. Taken together with the Court's reformulation of the prosecution's burden of proof as to waiver, today's novel clear-statement rule for invocation invites police to question a suspect at length—notwithstanding his persistent refusal to answer questions—in the hope of eventually obtaining a single inculpatory response which will suffice to prove waiver of rights. Such a result bears little semblance to the "fully effective" prophylaxis that *Miranda* requires.

Thompkins' claim for relief under AEDPA rests on the clearly established federal law of *Miranda* and *Mosley*. In *Miranda*, the Court concluded that "[i]f [an] individual indicates in any manner, at any time prior to or during questioning, that he wishes to remain silent, the interrogation must cease . . . [A]ny statement taken after the person invokes his privilege cannot be other than the product of compulsion, subtle or otherwise." In *Mosley*, the Court said that a "critical safeguard" of the right to remain silent is a suspect's " 'right to cut off questioning.' " Thus, "the admissibility of statements obtained after the person in custody has decided to remain silent depends under *Miranda* on whether his 'right to cut off questioning' was 'scrupulously honored.' "

Thompkins contends that in refusing to respond to questions he effectively invoked his right to remain silent, such that police were required to terminate the interrogation prior to his inculpatory statements. In Michigan's view, Thompkins cannot prevail under AEDPA because this Court's precedents have not previously established whether a suspect's ambiguous statements or actions require the police to stop questioning. We have held that a suspect who has " 'invoked his right to have counsel present . . . is not subject to further interrogation by the authorities until counsel has been made available to him, unless [he] initiates further communication, exchanges, or conversations with the police.' " Notwithstanding *Miranda*'s statement that "there can be no questioning" if a suspect "indicates in any manner . . . that he wishes to consult with an attorney," the Court in *Davis v. United States* established a clear-statement rule for invoking the right to counsel. After a suspect has knowingly and voluntarily waived his *Miranda* rights, *Davis* held, police may continue questioning "until and unless the suspect *clearly* requests an attorney."

Because this Court has never decided whether *Davis*' clear-statement rule applies to an invocation of the right to silence, Michigan contends, there was no clearly established federal law prohibiting the state court from requiring an unambiguous invocation. That the state court's decision was not objectively unreasonable is confirmed, in Michigan's view, by the number of federal Courts of Appeals to have applied *Davis* to invocation of the right to silence.

Under AEDPA's deferential standard of review, it is indeed difficult to conclude that the state court's application of our precedents was objectively unreasonable. Although the duration and consistency of Thompkins' refusal to answer questions throughout the 3-hour interrogation provide substantial evidence in support of his claim, Thompkins did not remain absolutely silent, and this Court has not previously addressed whether a suspect can invoke the right to silence by remaining uncooperative and nearly silent for 2 hours and 45 minutes.

The Court, however, eschews this narrow ground of decision, instead extending *Davis* to hold that police may continue questioning a suspect until he unambiguously invokes his right to remain silent. Because Thompkins neither said "he wanted to remain silent" nor said "he did not want to talk with the police," the Court concludes, he did not clearly invoke his right to silence.

I disagree with this novel application of *Davis*. Neither the rationale nor holding of that case compels today's result. *Davis* involved the right to counsel, not the right to silence. The Court in *Davis* reasoned that extending *Edwards'* [*v. Arizona* (1981)] "rigid" prophylactic rule to ambiguous requests for a lawyer would transform *Miranda* into a " 'wholly irrational obstacl[e] to legitimate police investigative activity' " by "needlessly prevent[ing] the police from questioning a suspect in the absence of counsel even if [he] did not wish to have a lawyer present." But *Miranda* itself "distinguished between the procedural safeguards triggered by a request to remain silent and a request for an attorney." *Mosley* upheld the admission of statements when police immediately stopped interrogating a suspect who invoked his right to silence, but reapproached him after a 2-hour delay and obtained inculpatory responses relating to a different crime after administering fresh *Miranda* warnings. The different effects of invoking the rights are consistent with distinct standards for invocation. To the extent *Mosley* contemplates a more flexible form of prophylaxis than *Edwards*—and, in particular, does not categorically bar police from reapproaching a suspect who has invoked his right to remain silent—*Davis'* concern about " 'wholly irrational obstacles' " to police investigation applies with less force.

In addition, the suspect's equivocal reference to a lawyer in *Davis* occurred only *after* he had given express oral and written waivers of his rights. *Davis'* holding is explicitly predicated on that fact. ("We therefore hold that, after a knowing and voluntary waiver of the *Miranda* rights, law enforcement officers may continue questioning until and unless the suspect clearly requests an attorney"). The Court ignores this aspect of *Davis*, as well as the decisions of numerous federal and state courts declining to apply a clear-statement rule when a suspect has not previously given an express waiver of rights.

In my mind, a more appropriate standard for addressing a suspect's ambiguous invocation of the right to remain silent is the constraint *Mosley* places on questioning a suspect who has invoked that right: The suspect's " 'right to cut off questioning' " must be " 'scrupulously honored.' " Such a standard is necessarily precautionary and fact specific. The rule would acknowledge that some statements or conduct are so equivocal that police may scrupulously honor a suspect's rights without terminating questioning—for instance, if a suspect's actions are reasonably understood to indicate a willingness to listen before deciding whether to respond. But other statements or actions—in particular, when a suspect sits silent throughout prolonged interrogation, long past the point when he could be deciding whether to respond—cannot reasonably be understood other than as an invocation of the right to remain silent. Under such circumstances, "scrupulous" respect for the suspect's rights will require police to terminate questioning under *Mosley*.

To be sure, such a standard does not provide police with a bright-line rule. But, as we have previously recognized, *Mosley* itself does not offer clear guidance to police about when and how interrogation may continue after a suspect invokes his rights. Given that police have for nearly 35 years applied *Mosley*'s fact-specific standard in questioning suspects who have invoked their right to remain silent; that our cases did not during that time resolve what statements or actions suffice to invoke that right; and that neither Michigan nor the Solicitor General have provided evidence in this case that the status quo has proved unworkable, I see little reason to believe today's clear-statement rule is necessary to ensure effective law enforcement.

Davis' clear-statement rule is also a poor fit for the right to silence. Advising a suspect that he has a "right to remain silent" is unlikely to convey that he must speak (and must do so in some particular fashion) to ensure the right will be protected. ("What in the world must an individual do to exercise his constitutional right to remain silent beyond actually, in fact, remaining silent?"). By contrast, telling a suspect "he has the right to the presence of an attorney, and that if he cannot afford an attorney one will be appointed for him prior to any questioning if he so desires," implies the need for speech to exercise that right. *Davis'* requirement that a suspect must "clearly reques[t] an attorney" to terminate questioning thus aligns with a suspect's likely understanding of the *Miranda* warnings in a way today's rule does not. The Court suggests Thompkins could have employed the "simple, unambiguous" means of saying "he wanted to remain silent" or "did not want to talk with the police." But the *Miranda* warnings give no hint that a suspect should use those magic words, and there is little reason to believe police—who have ample incentives to avoid invocation—will provide such guidance.

Conversely, the Court's concern that police will face "difficult decisions about an accused's unclear intent" and suffer the consequences of " 'guess[ing] wrong' " is misplaced. If a suspect makes an ambiguous statement or engages in conduct that creates uncertainty about his intent to invoke his right, police can simply ask for clarification. It is hardly an unreasonable burden for police to ask a suspect, for instance, "Do you want to talk to us?" The majority in *Davis* itself approved of this approach as protecting suspects' rights while "minimiz[ing] the chance of a confession [later] being suppressed." Given this straightforward mechanism by which police can "scrupulously hono[r]" a suspect's right to silence, today's clear-statement rule can only be seen as accepting "as tolerable the certainty that some poorly expressed requests [to remain silent] will be disregarded," without any countervailing benefit. Police may well prefer not to seek clarification of an ambiguous statement out of fear that a suspect will invoke his rights. But "our system of justice is not founded on a fear that a suspect will exercise his rights. 'If the exercise of constitutional rights will thwart the effectiveness of a system of law enforcement, then there is something very wrong with that system.' "

The Court asserts in passing that treating ambiguous statements or acts as an invocation of the right to silence will only " 'marginally' " serve *Miranda*'s goals. Experience suggests the contrary. In the 16 years since *Davis* was decided, ample evidence has accrued that criminal suspects often use equivocal or colloquial language in attempting to invoke their right to silence. A number of lower courts that have (erroneously, in my view) imposed a clear-statement requirement for invocation of the right to silence have rejected as ambiguous an array of statements whose meaning might otherwise be thought plain. At a minimum, these decisions suggest that differentiating "clear" from "ambiguous" statements is often a subjective inquiry. Even if some of the cited decisions are themselves in tension with *Davis*' admonition that a suspect need not " 'speak with the discrimination of an Oxford don' " to invoke his rights, they demonstrate that today's decision will significantly burden the exercise of the right to silence. Notably, when a suspect "understands his (expressed) wishes to have been ignored . . . in contravention of the 'rights' just read to him by his interrogator, he may well see further objection as futile and confession (true or not) as the only way to end his interrogation."

For these reasons, I believe a precautionary requirement that police "scrupulously hono[r]" a suspect's right to cut off questioning is a more faithful application of our precedents than the Court's awkward and needless extension of *Davis*.

■ ■ ■

Today's decision turns *Miranda* upside down. Criminal suspects must now unambiguously invoke their right to remain silent—which, counterintuitively, requires them to speak. At the same time, suspects will be legally presumed to have waived their rights even if they have given no clear expression of their intent to do so. Those results, in my view, find no basis in *Miranda* or our subsequent cases and are inconsistent with the fair-trial principles on which those precedents are grounded. Today's broad new rules are all the more unfortunate because they are unnecessary to the disposition of the case before us. I respectfully dissent.

c. *Request for Counsel*

Edwards v. Arizona

451 U.S. 477 (1981)

WHITE, J., delivered the opinion of the Court, in which BRENNAN, STEWART, MARSHALL, BLACKMUN, and STEVENS, JJ., joined. BURGER, C.J., wrote an opinion concurring in the judgment. POWELL, J., wrote an opinion concurring in the result, in which REHNQUIST, J., joined.

On January 19, 1976, a sworn complaint was filed against Edwards in Arizona state court charging him with robbery, burglary, and first-degree murder. An arrest warrant was issued pursuant to the complaint, and Edwards was arrested at his home later that same day. At the police station, he was informed of his rights as required by *Miranda v. Arizona* (1966). Petitioner stated that he understood his rights, and was willing to submit to questioning. After being told that another suspect already in custody had implicated him in the crime, Edwards denied involvement and gave a taped statement presenting an alibi defense. He then sought to "make a deal." The interrogating officer told him that he wanted a statement, but that he did not have the authority to negotiate a deal. The officer provided Edwards with the telephone number of a county attorney. Petitioner made the call, but hung up after a few moments. Edwards then said: "I want an attorney before making a deal." At that point, questioning ceased and Edwards was taken to county jail.

At 9:15 the next morning, two detectives, colleagues of the officer who had interrogated Edwards the previous night, came to the jail and asked to see Edwards. When the detention officer informed Edwards that the detectives wished to speak with him, he replied that he did not want to talk to anyone. The guard told him that "he had" to talk and then took him to meet with the detectives. The officers identified themselves, stated they wanted to talk to him, and informed him of his *Miranda* rights. Edwards was willing to talk, but he first wanted to hear the taped statement of the alleged accomplice who had implicated him. After listening to the tape for several minutes, petitioner said that he would make a statement so long as it was not tape-recorded. The detectives informed him that the recording was irrelevant since they could testify in court concerning whatever he said. Edwards replied: "I'll tell you anything you want to know, but I don't want it on tape." He thereupon implicated himself in the crime.

Prior to trial, Edwards moved to suppress his confession on the ground that his *Miranda* rights had been violated when the officers returned to question him after he had invoked his right to counsel. The trial court initially granted the motion to suppress, but reversed its ruling when presented with a supposedly controlling decision of a higher Arizona court. The court stated without explanation that it found Edwards' statement to be voluntary. Edwards was tried twice and convicted. Evidence concerning his confession was admitted at both trials.

On appeal, the Arizona Supreme Court held that Edwards had invoked both his right to remain silent and his right to counsel during the interrogation conducted on the night of January 19. The court then went on to determine, however, that Edwards had waived both rights.

Because the use of Edwards' confession against him at his trial violated his rights under the Fifth and Fourteenth Amendments as construed in *Miranda v. Arizona*, we reverse the judgment of the Arizona Supreme Court.

In *Miranda v. Arizona*, the Court determined that the Fifth and Fourteenth Amendments' prohibition against compelled self-incrimination required that custodial interrogation be preceded by advice to the putative defendant that he has the right to remain silent and also the right to the presence of an attorney. The Court also indicated the procedures to be followed subsequent to the warnings. If the accused indicates that he wishes to remain silent, "the interrogation must cease." If he requests counsel, "the interrogation must cease until an attorney is present."

Miranda thus declared that an accused has a Fifth and Fourteenth Amendment right to have counsel present during custodial interrogation. Here, the critical facts as found by the Arizona Supreme Court are that Edwards asserted his right to counsel and his right to remain silent on January 19, but that the police, without furnishing him counsel, returned the next morning to confront him and as a result of the meeting secured incriminating oral admissions. Contrary to the holdings of the state courts, Edwards insists that having exercised his right on the 19th to have counsel present during interrogation, he did not validly waive that right on the 20th. For the following reasons, we agree.

We note that in denying petitioner's motion to suppress, the trial court found the admission to have been "voluntary," without separately focusing on whether Edwards had knowingly and intelligently relinquished his right to counsel. The Arizona Supreme Court, in a section of its opinion entitled "Voluntariness of Waiver," stated that in Arizona, confessions are prima facie involuntary and that the State had the burden of showing by a preponderance of the evidence that the confession was freely and voluntarily made. The court stated that the issue of voluntariness should be determined based on the totality of the circumstances as it related to whether an accused's action was "knowing and intelligent and whether his will [was] overborne." Once the trial court determines that "the confession is voluntary, the finding will not be upset on appeal absent clear and manifest error." The court then upheld the trial court's finding that the "waiver and confession were voluntarily and knowingly made."

In referring to the necessity to find Edwards' confession knowing and intelligent, the State Supreme Court cited *Schneckloth v. Bustamonte* (1973). Yet, it is clear that *Schneckloth* does not control the issue presented in this case. The issue in *Schneckloth* was under what conditions an individual could be found to have consented to a search and thereby waived his Fourth Amendment rights. The Court declined to impose the "intentional relinquishment or abandonment of a known right or privilege" standard and required only that the consent be voluntary under the totality of the circumstances. The Court specifically noted that the right to counsel was a prime example of those rights requiring the special protection of the knowing and intelligent waiver standard, but held that "[t]he considerations that informed the Court's holding in *Miranda* are simply inapplicable in the present case." *Schneckloth* itself thus emphasized that the voluntariness of a consent or an admission on the one hand, and a knowing and intelligent waiver on the other, are discrete inquiries. Here, however sound the conclusion of the state courts as to the voluntariness of Edwards' admission may be, neither the trial court nor the Arizona Supreme Court undertook to focus on whether Edwards understood his right to counsel and intelligently and knowingly relinquished it. It is thus apparent that the decision below misunderstood the requirement for finding a valid waiver of the right to counsel, once invoked.

Second, although we have held that after initially being advised of his *Miranda* rights, the accused may himself validly waive his rights and respond to interrogation, see *North Carolina v. Butler* (1979), the Court has strongly indicated that additional safeguards are necessary when the accused asks for counsel; and we now hold that when an accused has invoked his right to have counsel present during custodial interrogation, a valid waiver of that right cannot be established by showing only that he responded to further police-initiated custodial interrogation even if he has been advised of his rights. We further hold that an accused, such as Edwards, having expressed his desire to deal with the police only through counsel, is not subject to further interrogation by the authorities until counsel has been made available to him, unless the accused himself initiates further communication, exchanges, or conversations with the police.

Miranda itself indicated that the assertion of the right to counsel was a significant event and that once exercised by the accused, "the interrogation must cease until an attorney is present." Our later cases have not abandoned that view. In *Michigan v. Mosley* (1975), the Court noted that *Miranda* had distinguished between the procedural safeguards triggered by a request to remain silent and a request for an attorney and had required that interrogation cease until an attorney was present only if the individual stated that he wanted counsel. In *Fare v. Michael C.* (1979), the Court referred to *Miranda*'s "rigid rule that an accused's request for an attorney is *per se* an invocation of his Fifth Amendment rights, requiring that all interrogation cease." And just last Term, in a case where a suspect in custody had invoked his *Miranda* right to counsel, the Court again referred to the "undisputed right" under *Miranda* to remain silent and to be free of interrogation "until he had consulted with a lawyer." *Rhode Island v. Innis* (1980). We reconfirm these views and, to lend them substance, emphasize that it is inconsistent with *Miranda* and its progeny for the authorities, at their instance, to reinterrogate an accused in custody if he has clearly asserted his right to counsel.

In concluding that the fruits of the interrogation initiated by the police on January 20 could not be used against Edwards, we do not hold or imply that Edwards was powerless to countermand his election or that the authorities could in no event use any incriminating statements made by Edwards prior to his having access to counsel. Had Edwards initiated the meeting on January 20, nothing in the Fifth and Fourteenth Amendments would prohibit the police from merely listening to his voluntary, volunteered statements and using them against him at the trial. The Fifth Amendment right identified in *Miranda* is the right to have counsel present at any custodial interrogation. Absent such interrogation, there would have been no infringement of the right that Edwards invoked and there would be no occasion to determine whether there had been a valid waiver. *Rhode Island v. Innis* makes this sufficiently clear.

But this is not what the facts of this case show. Here, the officers conducting the interrogation on the evening of January 19 ceased interrogation when Edwards requested counsel as he had been advised he had the right to do. The Arizona Supreme Court was of the opinion that this was a sufficient invocation of his *Miranda* rights, and we are in accord. It is also clear that without making counsel available to Edwards, the police returned to him the next day. This was not at his suggestion or request. Indeed, Edwards informed the detention officer that he did not want to talk to anyone. At the meeting, the detectives told Edwards that they wanted to talk to him and again advised him of his *Miranda* rights. Edwards stated that he would talk, but what prompted this action does not appear. He listened at his own request to part of the taped statement made by one of his alleged accomplices and then made an incriminating statement, which was used against him at his trial. We think it is clear that Edwards was subjected to custodial interrogation on January 20 within the meaning of *Rhode Island v. Innis* and that this occurred at the instance of the authorities. His statement, made without having had access to counsel, did not amount to a valid waiver, and hence was inadmissible.

Accordingly, the holding of the Arizona Supreme Court that Edwards had waived his right to counsel was infirm, and the judgment of that court is reversed.

So ordered.

Chief Justice BURGER, concurring in the judgment.

I concur only in the judgment because I do not agree that either any constitutional standard or the holding of *Miranda v. Arizona*—as distinguished from its dicta—calls for a special rule as to how an accused in custody may waive the right to be free from interrogation. The extraordinary protections afforded a person in custody suspected of criminal conduct are not without a valid basis, but as with all "good" things they can be carried too far.

On this record the Supreme Court of Arizona erred in holding that the resumption of interrogation was the product of a voluntary waiver, such as I found to be the situation in both *Innis* (concurring opinion) and *Brewer v. Williams* (1977) (dissenting opinion).

Justice POWELL, with whom Justice REHNQUIST joins, concurring in the result.

Although I agree that the judgment of the Arizona Supreme Court must be reversed, I do not join the Court's opinion because I am not sure what it means.

Oregon v. Bradshaw

462 U.S. 1039 (1983)

REHNQUIST, J., announced the judgment of the Court and delivered an opinion in which BURGER, C.J., WHITE, and O'CONNOR, JJ., joined. POWELL, J., filed an opinion concurring in the judgment. MARSHALL, J., filed a dissenting opinion, in which BRENNAN, BLACKMUN, and STEVENS, JJ., joined.

After a bench trial in an Oregon trial court, respondent James Edward Bradshaw was convicted of the offenses of first degree manslaughter, driving while under the influence of intoxicants, and driving while his license was revoked. The Oregon Court of Appeals reversed his conviction, holding that an inquiry he made of a police officer at the time he was in custody did not "initiate" a conversation with the officer, and that therefore statements by the respondent growing out of that conversation should have been excluded from evidence under *Edwards v. Arizona* (1981). We granted certiorari to review this determination.

In September, 1980, Oregon police were investigating the death of one Lowell Reynolds in Tillamook County. Reynolds' body had been found in his wrecked pickup truck, in which he appeared to have been a passenger at the time the vehicle left the roadway, struck a tree and an embankment, and finally came to rest on its side in a shallow creek. Reynolds had died from traumatic injury, coupled with asphyxia by drowning. During the investigation of Reynolds' death, respondent was asked to accompany a police officer to the Rockaway Police Station for questioning.

Once at the station, respondent was advised of his rights as required by *Miranda v. Arizona* (1966). Respondent then repeated to the police his earlier account of the events of the evening of Reynolds' death, admitting that he had provided Reynolds and others with liquor for a party at Reynolds' house, but denying involvement in the traffic accident that apparently killed Reynolds. Respondent suggested that Reynolds might have met with foul play at the hands of the assailant whom respondent alleged had struck him at the party.

At this point, respondent was placed under arrest for furnishing liquor to Reynolds, a minor, and again advised of his *Miranda* rights. A police officer then told respondent the officer's theory of how the traffic accident that killed Reynolds occurred; a theory which placed respondent behind the wheel of the vehicle. Respondent again denied his involvement, and said "I do want an attorney before it goes very much further." The officer immediately terminated the conversation.

Sometime later respondent was transferred from the Rockaway Police Station to the Tillamook County Jail, a distance of some ten or fifteen miles. Either just before, or during, his trip from Rockaway to Tillamook, respondent inquired of a police officer, "Well, what is going to happen to me now?" The officer answered by saying "You do not have to talk to me. You have requested an attorney and I don't want you talking to me unless you so desire because anything you say—because—since you have requested an attorney, you know, it has to be at your own free will." Respondent said he understood. There followed a discussion between respondent and the officer concerning where respondent was being taken and the offense with which he would be charged. The officer suggested that respondent might help himself by taking a polygraph examination. Respondent agreed to take such an examination, saying that he was willing to do whatever he could to clear up the matter.

The next day, following another reading to respondent of his *Miranda* rights, and respondent's signing a written waiver of those rights, the polygraph was administered. At its conclusion, the examiner told respondent that he did not believe respondent was telling the truth. Respondent then recanted his earlier story, admitting that he had been at the wheel of the vehicle in which Reynolds was killed, that he had consumed a considerable amount of alcohol, and that he had passed out at the wheel before the vehicle left the roadway and came to rest in the creek.

Respondent was charged with first degree manslaughter, driving while under the influence of intoxicants, and driving while his license was revoked. His motion to suppress the statements described above was denied, and he was found guilty after a bench trial. The Oregon Court of Appeals, relying on our decision in *Edwards v. Arizona*, reversed, concluding that the statements had been obtained in violation of respondent's Fifth Amendment rights. We now conclude that the Oregon Court of Appeals misapplied our decision in *Edwards*.

In *Edwards* the defendant had voluntarily submitted to questioning but later stated that he wished an attorney before the discussions continued. The following day detectives accosted the defendant in the county jail, and when he refused to speak with them he was told that "he had" to talk. We held that subsequent incriminating statements made without his attorney present violated the rights secured to the defendant by the Fifth and Fourteenth Amendments to the United States Constitution.

■ ■ ■

Respondent's question in the present case, "Well, what is going to happen to me now?", admittedly was asked prior to respondent being "subject[ed] to further interrogation by the authorities." The Oregon Court of Appeals stated that it did not "construe defendant's question about what was going to happen to him to have been a waiver of his right to counsel, invoked only minutes before. . . ."

We think the Oregon Court of Appeals misapprehended the test laid down in *Edwards*. We did not there hold that the "initiation" of a conversation by a defendant such as respondent would amount to a waiver of a previously invoked right to counsel; we held that after the right to counsel had been asserted by an accused, further interrogation of the accused should not take place "unless the accused himself initiates further communication, exchanges, or conversations with the police." This was in effect a prophylactic rule, designed to protect an accused in police custody from being badgered by police officers in the manner in which the defendant in *Edwards* was.

■ ■ ■

But even if a conversation taking place after the accused has "expressed his desire to deal with the police only through counsel" is initiated by the accused, where reinterrogation follows, the burden remains upon the prosecution to show that subsequent events indicated a waiver of the Fifth Amendment right to have counsel present during the interrogation. This is made clear in the following footnote to our *Edwards* opinion:

> "If, as frequently would occur in the course of a meeting initiated by the accused, the conversation is not wholly one-sided, it is likely that the officers will say or do something that clearly would be 'interrogation.' In that event, the question would be whether a valid waiver of the right to counsel and the right to silence had occurred, that is, *whether the purported waiver was knowing and intelligent and found to be so under the totality of the circumstances,* including the necessary fact that the accused, not the police, reopened the dialogue with the authorities."

■ ■ ■

Thus, the Oregon Court of Appeals was wrong in thinking that an "initiation" of a conversation or discussion by an accused not only satisfied the *Edwards* rule, but *ex proprio vigore* sufficed to show a waiver of the previously asserted right to counsel. The inquiries are separate, and clarity of application is not gained by melding them together.

There can be no doubt in this case that in asking, "Well, what is going to happen to me now?", respondent "initiated" further conversation in the ordinary dictionary sense of that word. While we doubt that it would be desirable to build a superstructure of legal refinements around the word "initiate" in this context, there are undoubtedly situations where a bare inquiry by either a defendant or by a police officer should not be held to "initiate" any conversation or dialogue. There are some inquiries, such as a request for a drink of water or a request to use a telephone that are so routine that they cannot be fairly said to represent a desire on the part of an accused to open up a more generalized discussion relating directly or indirectly to the investigation. Such inquiries or statements, by either an accused or a police officer, relating to routine incidents of the custodial relationship, will not generally "initiate" a conversation in the sense in which that word was used in *Edwards*.

Although ambiguous, the respondent's question in this case as to what was going to happen to him evinced a willingness and a desire for a generalized discussion about the investigation; it was not merely a necessary inquiry arising out of the incidents of the custodial relationship. It could reasonably have been interpreted by the officer as relating generally to the investigation. That the police officer so understood it is apparent from the fact that he immediately reminded the accused that "you do not have to talk to me," and only after the accused told him that he "understood" did they have a generalized conversation. On these facts we believe that there was not a violation of the *Edwards* rule.

Since there was no violation of the *Edwards* rule in this case, the next inquiry was "whether a valid waiver of the right to counsel and the right to silence had occurred, that is, whether the purported waiver was knowing and intelligent and found to be so under the totality of the circumstances, including the necessary fact that the accused, not the police, reopened the dialogue with the authorities." *Edwards*. As we have said many times before, this determination depends "upon the particular facts and circumstances surrounding the case, including the background, experience, and conduct of the accused." *North Carolina v. Butler* (1979), quoting *Johnson v. Zerbst* (1938).

The state trial court made this inquiry and, in the words of the Oregon Court of Appeals, "found that the police made no threats, promises or inducements to talk, that defendant was properly advised of his rights and understood them and that within a short time after requesting an attorney he changed his mind without any impropriety on the part of the police. The court held that the statements made to the polygraph examiner were voluntary and the result of a knowing waiver of his right to remain silent."

We have no reason to dispute these conclusions, based as they are upon the trial court's first-hand observation of the witnesses to the events involved. The judgment of the Oregon Court of Appeals is therefore reversed, and the cause remanded for further proceedings.

It is so ordered.

Justice POWELL, concurring in the judgment.

The Court's recent decision in *Edwards v. Arizona* has resulted in disagreement as to whether it announced a new *per se* rule. My hope had been that this case would afford an opportunity to clarify the confusion. As evidenced by the differing readings of *Edwards* by Justices Marshall and Rehnquist in their respective opinions, my hope has not been fully realized. Justice Marshall, and the three Justices who join his opinion, would affirm the Oregon Court of Appeals because it "properly applied *Edwards*." Justice Rehnquist, and the three Justices who join him, would "conclude that the Oregon Court of Appeals misapplied our decision in *Edwards*." In view of the disagreement here, it is not surprising that courts have differed as to whether *Edwards* announced a *per se* rule, and if so what rule. I joined the judgment in *Edwards* because on the facts "it [was] clear that Edwards [had been] taken from his cell against his will and [improperly] subjected to renewed interrogation."

The opinions today reflect the ambiguity of some of the *Edwards* language, particularly on the meaning of "initiation." Justice Marshall reads *Edwards* as requiring not only that the accused initiate further communication, but also that the communication be *"about the subject matter of the criminal investigation."* Justice Rehnquist, however, would require only that the suspect "evinc[e] a willingness and a desire for a generalized discussion about the investigation." This formulation would include an "initiation" of conversation "in the ordinary dictionary sense" of the word, excluding "inquiries...that are so routine that they cannot be fairly said to represent a desire...to open up a more generalized discussion relating directly or indirectly to the investigation."

Both Justices agree in one respect. They view the "initiation" question as the first step of a two-step analysis, the second step being the application of the *Zerbst* standard that requires examination of the "totality of the circumstances."

■ ■ ■

Justice Rehnquist's opinion observes that the initiation and the voluntariness of the waiver under *Zerbst* "are separate, and clarity of application is not gained by melding them together."

This bifurcating of the *Zerbst* standard is not compelled by *Edwards* or any of our other cases. The inquiry in *Edwards* did focus on the reopening of communication with the accused by the police—a reopening that properly was held to be coercive. As there were no other significant facts or circumstances bearing upon the waiver question, there was no occasion for the Court to consider whether a two-step analysis is required in the more customary case. An incarcerated person, accused of crime, does not remain silent and speak only when conversation is initiated by others, whether by fellow prisoners, guards, or law enforcement officers. Jail or prison confinements prior to indictment or trial may extend over days and weeks, and numerous conversations customarily occur, often accompanied by collateral facts and circumstances. Rarely can a Court properly focus on a particular conversation, and intelligently base a judgment on the simplistic inquiry as to who spoke first.

■ ■ ■

My concern is that a two-step analysis could confound the confusion evident from the differing views expressed by other courts and indeed evidenced by the conflicting reading of *Edwards* by Justices Marshall and Rehnquist. The *Zerbst* standard is one that is widely understood and followed. It also comports with common sense. Fragmenting the standard into a novel two-step analysis—if followed literally—often would frustrate justice as well as common sense. Courts should engage in more substantive inquiries than "who said what first." The holding of the Court in *Edwards* cannot in my view fairly be reduced to this.

We are unanimous in agreeing in this case, as in *Edwards*, that "the right to counsel [is] a prime example of those rights requiring the special protection of the knowing and intelligent waiver standard." We also agree that once the accused has requested counsel this right requires additional safeguards, particularly against any coercive form of custodial interrogation. But the question of whether a suspect has waived this important right to counsel is uniquely one of fact, and usually must and should be left to the judgment of the trial court that has had the benefit of hearing the evidence and assessing the weight and credibility of testimony. In the circumstances of this case, I agree that

Bradshaw knowingly and intelligently waived his right to counsel, and that the judgment below therefore should be reversed.

Justice MARSHALL, with whom Justice BRENNAN, Justice BLACKMUN, and Justice STEVENS join, dissenting.

Because in my view the plurality has misapplied *Edwards v. Arizona,* I respectfully dissent.

In *Miranda v. Arizona,* this Court recognized that "[u]nless adequate protective devices are employed to dispel the compulsion inherent in custodial surroundings, no statement obtained from the defendant can truly be the product of his free choice." Access to counsel was held essential to secure the Fifth Amendment privilege against self-incrimination. "If the individual states that he wants an attorney, *the interrogation must cease until an attorney is present.*" *Miranda* thus created a "rigid rule that an accused's request for an attorney is *per se* an invocation of his Fifth Amendment rights, requiring that all interrogation cease."

■ ■ ■

Although an accused may waive his various *Miranda* rights and submit to interrogation, the Court has recognized that "additional safeguards are necessary when the accused asks for counsel." *Edwards* held that a valid waiver of the right to counsel cannot be established by showing only that the accused responded to further police-initiated custodial interrogation, even if he had again been advised of his rights. An accused who invokes his right to counsel is not subject to further interrogation until counsel has been made available, "unless the accused himself initiates further communication, exchanges, or conversations with the police." To establish a waiver, it would thus be a "*necessary fact* that the accused, not the police, reopened the dialogue with the authorities."

In this case, respondent invoked his right to have counsel during custodial interrogation. Shortly thereafter, he asked a police officer, "Well, what is going to happen to me now?" The Oregon Court of Appeals concluded that respondent's question was not "a waiver of his right to counsel, invoked only minutes before, or anything other than a normal reaction to being taken from the police station and placed in a police car, obviously for transport to some destination." Relying on *Edwards,* the Oregon Court held that respondent had not initiated the subsequent interrogation.

The Oregon Court of Appeals properly applied *Edwards.* When this Court in *Edwards* spoke of "initiat[ing] further communication" with the police and "reopen[ing] the dialogue with the authorities," it obviously had in mind communication or dialogue *about the subject matter of the criminal investigation.* The rule announced in *Edwards* was designed to ensure that any interrogation subsequent to an invocation of the right to counsel be at the instance of the accused, not the authorities. Thus, a question or statement which does not invite further interrogation before an attorney is present cannot qualify as "initiation" under *Edwards.* To hold otherwise would drastically undermine the safeguards that *Miranda* and *Edwards* carefully erected around the right to counsel in the custodial setting.

The safeguards identified in *Edwards* hardly pose an insurmountable obstacle to an accused who truly wishes to waive his rights after invoking his right to counsel. A waiver can be established, however, only when the accused himself reopens the dialogue about the subject matter of the criminal investigation. Since our decision in *Edwards*, the lower courts have had no difficulty in identifying such situations.

■ ■ ■

I agree with the plurality that, in order to constitute "initiation" under *Edwards*, an accused's inquiry must demonstrate a desire to discuss the subject matter of the criminal investigation. I am baffled, however, at the plurality's application of that standard to the facts of this case. The plurality asserts that respondent's question, "What is going to happen to me now?", evinced both "a willingness and a desire for a generalized discussion about the investigation." If respondent's question had been posed by Jean-Paul Sartre before a class of philosophy students, it might well have evinced a desire for a "generalized" discussion. But under the circumstances of this case, it is plain that respondent's only "desire" was to find out where the police were going to take him. As the Oregon Court of Appeals stated, respondent's query came only minutes after his invocation of the right to counsel and was simply "a normal reaction to being taken from the police station and placed in a police car, obviously for transport to some destination." On these facts, I fail to see how respondent's question can be considered "initiation" of a conversation about the subject matter of the criminal investigation.

To hold that respondent's question in this case opened a dialogue with the authorities flies in the face of the basic purpose of the *Miranda* safeguards. When someone in custody asks, "What is going to happen to me now?", he is surely responding to his custodial surroundings. The very essence of custody is the loss of control over one's freedom of movement. The authorities exercise virtually unfettered control over the accused. To allow the authorities to recommence an interrogation based on such a question is to permit them to capitalize on the custodial setting. Yet *Miranda*'s procedural protections were adopted precisely in order "to dispel the compulsion inherent in custodial surroundings."

Accordingly, I dissent.

Maryland v. Shatzer

130 S. Ct. 1213 (2010)

SCALIA, J., delivered the opinion of a unanimous Court.

We consider whether a break in custody ends the presumption of involuntariness established in *Edwards v. Arizona* (1981).

In August 2003, a social worker assigned to the Child Advocacy Center in the Criminal Investigation Division of the Hagerstown Police Department referred to the department allegations that respondent Michael Shatzer, Sr., had sexually abused his 3-year-old son. At that time, Shatzer was incarcerated at the Maryland Correctional Institution-Hagerstown, serving a sentence for an unrelated child-sexual-abuse offense. Detective Shane Blankenship was assigned to the investigation and interviewed Shatzer at the correctional institution on August 7, 2003. Before asking any questions, Blankenship reviewed Shatzer's *Miranda* rights with him, and obtained a written waiver of those rights. When Blankenship explained that he was there to question Shatzer about sexually abusing his son, Shatzer expressed confusion—he had thought Blankenship was an attorney there to discuss the prior crime for which he was incarcerated. Blankenship clarified the purpose of his visit, and Shatzer declined to speak without an attorney. Accordingly, Blankenship ended the interview, and Shatzer was released back into the general prison population. Shortly thereafter, Blankenship closed the investigation.

Two years and six months later, the same social worker referred more specific allegations to the department about the same incident involving Shatzer. Detective Paul Hoover, from the same division, was assigned to the investigation. He and the social worker interviewed the victim, then eight years old, who described the incident in more detail. With this new information in hand, on March 2, 2006, they went to the Roxbury Correctional Institute, to which Shatzer had since been transferred, and interviewed Shatzer in a maintenance room outfitted with a desk and three chairs. Hoover explained that he wanted to ask Shatzer about the alleged incident involving Shatzer's son. Shatzer was surprised because he thought that the investigation had been closed, but Hoover explained they had opened a new file. Hoover then read Shatzer his *Miranda* rights and obtained a written waiver on a standard department form.

Hoover interrogated Shatzer about the incident for approximately 30 minutes. Shatzer denied ordering his son to perform fellatio on him, but admitted to masturbating in front of his son from a distance of less than three feet. Before the interview ended, Shatzer agreed to Hoover's request that he submit to a polygraph examination. At no point during the interrogation did Shatzer request to speak with an attorney or refer to his prior refusal to answer questions without one.

Five days later, on March 7, 2006, Hoover and another detective met with Shatzer at the correctional facility to administer the polygraph examination. After reading Shatzer his *Miranda* rights and obtaining a written waiver, the other detective administered the test and concluded that Shatzer had failed. When the detectives then questioned Shatzer, he became upset, started to cry, and incriminated himself by saying, " 'I didn't force him. I didn't force him.' " After making this inculpatory statement, Shatzer requested an attorney, and Hoover promptly ended the interrogation.

■ ■ ■

The Fifth Amendment, which applies to the States by virtue of the Fourteenth Amendment, *Malloy v. Hogan* (1964), provides that "[n]o person . . . shall be compelled in any criminal case to be a witness against himself." U.S. Const., Amdt. 5. In *Miranda v. Arizona* (1966), the Court adopted a set of prophylactic measures to protect a suspect's Fifth Amendment right from the "inherently compelling pressures" of custodial interrogation. The Court observed that "incommunicado interrogation" in an "unfamiliar," "police-dominated atmosphere," involves psychological pressures "which work to undermine the individual's will to resist and to compel him to speak where he would not otherwise do so freely." Consequently, it reasoned, "[u]nless adequate protective devices are employed to dispel the compulsion inherent in custodial surroundings, no statement obtained from the defendant can truly be the product of his free choice."

To counteract the coercive pressure, *Miranda* announced that police officers must warn a suspect prior to questioning that he has a right to remain silent, and a right to the presence of an attorney. After the warnings are given, if the suspect indicates that he wishes to remain silent, the interrogation must cease. Similarly, if the suspect states that he wants an attorney, the interrogation must cease until an attorney is present. Critically, however, a suspect can waive these rights. To establish a valid waiver, the State must show that the waiver was knowing, intelligent, and voluntary under the "high standar[d] of proof for the waiver of constitutional rights [set forth in] *Johnson v. Zerbst* (1938)."

In *Edwards*, the Court determined that *Zerbst*'s traditional standard for waiver was not sufficient to protect a suspect's right to have counsel present at a subsequent interrogation if he had previously requested counsel; "additional safeguards" were necessary. *Edwards* held:

> "[W]hen an accused has invoked his right to have counsel present during custodial interrogation, a valid waiver of that right cannot be established by showing only that he responded to further police-initiated custodial interrogation even if he has been advised of his rights. . . . [He] is not subject to further interrogation by the authorities until counsel has been made available to him, unless the accused himself initiates further communication, exchanges, or conversations with the police."

The rationale of *Edwards* is that once a suspect indicates that "he is not capable of undergoing [custodial] questioning without advice of counsel," "any subsequent waiver that has come at the authorities' behest, and not at the suspect's own instigation, is itself the product of the 'inherently compelling pressures' and not the purely voluntary choice of the suspect." *Arizona v. Roberson* (1988). Under this rule, a voluntary *Miranda* waiver is sufficient at the time of an initial attempted interrogation to protect a suspect's right to have counsel present, but it is not sufficient at the time of subsequent attempts if the suspect initially requested the presence of counsel. The implicit assumption, of course, is that the subsequent requests for interrogation pose a significantly greater risk of coercion. That increased risk results not only from the police's persistence in trying to get the suspect to talk, but also from the continued pressure that begins when the individual is taken into custody as a suspect and sought to be interrogated—pressure likely to "increase as custody is prolonged," *Minnick v. Mississippi* (1990). The *Edwards* presumption of involuntariness ensures that police will not take advantage of the mounting coercive pressures of "prolonged police custody," *Roberson,* by repeatedly attempting to question a suspect who previously requested counsel until the suspect is "badgered into submission" *id.* (Kennedy, J., dissenting).

We have frequently emphasized that the *Edwards* rule is not a constitutional mandate, but judicially prescribed prophylaxis. See, *e.g., Montejo v. Louisiana* (2009); *Michigan v. Harvey* (1990); *Solem v. Stumes* (1984). Because *Edwards* is "our rule, not a constitutional command," "it is our obligation to justify its expansion." *Roberson* (Kennedy, J., dissenting). Lower courts have uniformly held that a break in custody ends the *Edwards* presumption, see, *e.g., People v. Storm* (2002) (collecting state and federal cases).

A judicially crafted rule is "justified only by reference to its prophylactic purpose," *Davis v. United States* (1994) (internal quotation marks omitted), and applies only where its benefits outweigh its costs. We begin with the benefits. *Edwards'* presumption of involuntariness has the incidental effect of "conserv-[ing] judicial resources which would otherwise be expended in making difficult determinations of voluntariness." Its fundamental purpose, however, is to "[p]reserv[e] the integrity of an accused's choice to communicate with police only through counsel," *Patterson v. Illinois* (1988), by "prevent[ing] police from badgering a defendant into waiving his previously asserted *Miranda* rights," *Harvey.* Thus, the benefits of the rule are measured by the number of coerced confessions it suppresses that otherwise would have been admitted.

It is easy to believe that a suspect may be coerced or badgered into abandoning his earlier refusal to be questioned without counsel in the paradigm *Edwards* case. That is a case in which the suspect has been arrested for a particular crime and is held in uninterrupted pretrial custody while that crime is being actively investigated. After the initial interrogation, and up to and including the second one, he remains cut off from his normal life and companions, "thrust into" and isolated in an "unfamiliar," "police-dominated atmosphere," *Miranda,* where his captors "appear to control [his] fate," *Illinois v. Perkins* (1990). That was the situation confronted by the suspects in *Edwards, Roberson,* and *Minnick,* the three cases in which we have held the *Edwards* rule applicable. Edwards was arrested pursuant to a warrant and taken to a police station, where he was interrogated until he requested counsel. *Edwards.* The officer ended the interrogation and took him to the county jail, but at 9:15 the next morning, two of the officer's colleagues reinterrogated Edwards at the jail. Roberson was arrested "at the scene of a just-completed burglary" and interrogated there until he requested a lawyer. A different officer interrogated him three days later while he "was still in custody pursuant to the arrest." Minnick was arrested by local police and taken to the San Diego jail, where two FBI agents interrogated him the next morning until he requested counsel. Two days later a Mississippi Deputy Sheriff reinterrogated him at the jail. None of these suspects regained a sense of control or normalcy after they were initially taken into custody for the crime under investigation.

When, unlike what happened in these three cases, a suspect has been released from his pretrial custody and has returned to his normal life for some time before the later attempted interrogation, there is little reason to think that his change of heart regarding interrogation without counsel has been coerced. He has no longer been isolated. He has likely been able to seek advice from an attorney, family members, and friends. And he knows from his earlier experience that he need only demand counsel to bring the interrogation to a halt; and that investigative custody does not last indefinitely. In these circumstances, it is far-fetched to think that a police officer's asking the suspect whether he would like to waive his *Miranda* rights will any more "wear down the accused," *Smith v. Illinois* (1984) (*per curiam*), than did the first such request at the original attempted interrogation—which is of course not deemed coercive. His change of heart is less likely attributable to "badgering" than it is to the fact that further deliberation in familiar surroundings has caused him to believe (rightly or wrongly) that cooperating with the investigation is in his interest. Uncritical extension of *Edwards* to this situation would not significantly increase the number of genuinely coerced confessions excluded. . . .

At the same time that extending the *Edwards* rule yields diminished benefits, extending the rule also increases its costs: the in-fact voluntary confessions it excludes from trial, and the voluntary confessions it deters law enforcement officers from even trying to obtain. Voluntary confessions are not merely "a proper element in law enforcement," they are an "unmitigated good," " 'essential to society's compelling interest in finding, convicting, and punishing those who violate the law,' " *ibid.* (quoting *Moran v. Burbine* (1986)).

The only logical endpoint of *Edwards* disability is termination of *Miranda* custody and any of its lingering effects. Without that limitation—and barring some purely arbitrary time-limit—every *Edwards* prohibition of custodial interrogation of a particular suspect would be eternal. The prohibition applies, of course, when the subsequent interrogation pertains to a different crime, *Roberson*, when it is conducted by a different law enforcement authority, *Minnick*, and even when the suspect has met with an attorney after the first interrogation. And it not only prevents questioning *ex ante*; it would render invalid *ex post*, confessions invited and obtained from suspects who (unbeknownst to the interrogators) have acquired *Edwards* immunity previously in connection with any offense in any jurisdiction. In a country that harbors a large number of repeat offenders, this consequence is disastrous.

We conclude that such an extension of *Edwards* is not justified; we have opened its "protective umbrella" far enough. The protections offered by *Miranda*, which we have deemed sufficient to ensure that the police respect the suspect's desire to have an attorney present the first time police interrogate him, adequately ensure that result when a suspect who initially requested counsel is reinterrogated after a break in custody that is of sufficient duration to dissipate its coercive effects.

■ ■ ■

The 14-day limitation meets Shatzer's concern that a break-in-custody rule lends itself to police abuse. He envisions that once a suspect invokes his *Miranda* right to counsel, the police will release the suspect briefly (to end the *Edwards* presumption) and then promptly bring him back into custody for reinterrogation. But once the suspect has been out of custody long enough (14 days) to eliminate its coercive effect, there will be nothing to gain by such gamesmanship—nothing, that is, except the entirely appropriate gain of being able to interrogate a suspect who has made a valid waiver of his *Miranda* rights.

Shatzer argues that ending the *Edwards* protections at a break in custody will undermine *Edwards*' purpose to conserve judicial resources. To be sure, we have said that "[t]he merit of the *Edwards* decision lies in the clarity of its command and the certainty of its application." But clarity and certainty are not goals in themselves. They are valuable only when they reasonably further the achievement of some substantive end—here, the exclusion of compelled confessions. Confessions obtained after a 2-week break in custody and a waiver of *Miranda* rights are most unlikely to be compelled, and hence are unreasonably excluded. In any case, a break-in-custody exception will dim only marginally, if at all, the bright-line nature of *Edwards*. In every case involving *Edwards*, the courts must determine whether the suspect was in custody when he requested counsel and when he later made the statements he seeks to suppress. Now, in cases where there is an alleged break in custody, they simply have to repeat the inquiry for the time between the initial invocation and reinterrogation. In most cases that determination will be easy. And when it is determined that the defendant pleading *Edwards* has been out of custody for two weeks before the contested interrogation, the court is spared the fact-intensive inquiry into whether he ever, anywhere, asserted his *Miranda* right to counsel.

The facts of this case present an additional issue. No one questions that Shatzer was in custody for *Miranda* purposes during the interviews with Detective Blankenship in 2003 and Detective Hoover in 2006. Likewise, no one questions that Shatzer triggered the *Edwards* protections when, according to Detective Blankenship's notes of the 2003 interview, he stated that " 'he would not talk about this case without having an attorney present.' " After the 2003 interview, Shatzer was released back into the general prison population where he was serving an unrelated sentence. The issue is whether that constitutes a break in *Miranda* custody.

We have never decided whether incarceration constitutes custody for *Miranda* purposes, and have indeed explicitly declined to address the issue. Whether it does depends upon whether it exerts the coercive pressure that *Miranda* was designed to guard against—the "danger of coercion [that] results from the *interaction* of custody and official interrogation." To determine whether a suspect was in *Miranda* custody we have asked whether "there is a 'formal arrest or restraint on freedom of movement' of the degree associated with a formal arrest." *New York v. Quarles* (1984). This test, no doubt, is satisfied by all forms of incarceration. Our cases make clear, however, that the freedom-of-movement test identifies only a necessary and not a sufficient condition for *Miranda* custody. We have declined to accord it "talismanic power," because *Miranda* is to be enforced "only in those types of situations in which the concerns that powered the decision are implicated." *Berkemer v. McCarty* (1984). Thus, the temporary and relatively nonthreatening detention involved in a traffic stop or *Terry* stop, see *Terry v. Ohio* (1968), does not constitute *Miranda* custody.

Here, we are addressing the interim period during which a suspect was not interrogated, but was subject to a baseline set of restraints imposed pursuant to a prior conviction. Without minimizing the harsh realities of incarceration, we think lawful imprisonment imposed upon conviction of a crime does not create the coercive pressures identified in *Miranda*.

Interrogated suspects who have previously been convicted of crime live in prison. When they are released back into the general prison population, they return to their accustomed surroundings and daily routine—they regain the degree of control they had over their lives prior to the interrogation. Sentenced prisoners, in contrast to the *Miranda* paradigm, are not isolated with their accusers. They live among other inmates, guards, and workers, and often can receive visitors and communicate with people on the outside by mail or telephone.

Their detention, moreover, is relatively disconnected from their prior unwillingness to cooperate in an investigation. The former interrogator has no power to increase the duration of incarceration, which was determined at sentencing. And even where the possibility of parole exists, the former interrogator has no apparent power to decrease the time served. This is in stark contrast to the circumstances faced by the defendants in *Edwards, Roberson*, and *Minnick*, whose continued detention as suspects rested with those controlling their interrogation, and who confronted the uncertainties of what final charges they would face, whether they would be convicted, and what sentence they would receive.

Shatzer's experience illustrates the vast differences between *Miranda* custody and incarceration pursuant to conviction. At the time of the 2003 attempted interrogation, Shatzer was already serving a sentence for a prior conviction. After that, he returned to the general prison population in the Maryland Correctional Institution-Hagerstown and was later transferred, for unrelated reasons, down the street to the Roxbury Correctional Institute. Both are medium-security state correctional facilities. Inmates in these facilities generally can visit the library each week; have regular exercise and recreation periods; can participate in basic adult education and occupational training; are able to send and receive mail; and are allowed to receive visitors twice a week. His continued detention after the 2003 interrogation did not depend on what he said (or did not say) to Detective Blankenship, and he has not alleged that he was placed in a higher level of security or faced any continuing restraints as a result of the 2003 interrogation. The "inherently compelling pressures" of custodial interrogation ended when he returned to his normal life.

■ ■ ■

Because Shatzer experienced a break in *Miranda* custody lasting more than two weeks between the first and second attempts at interrogation, *Edwards* does not mandate suppression of his March 2006 statements. Accordingly, we reverse the judgment of the Court of Appeals of Maryland, and remand the case for further proceedings not inconsistent with this opinion.

It is so ordered.

6. *Miranda* and the Exclusionary Rule

Oregon v. Elstad

470 U.S. 298 (1985)

O'CONNOR, J., delivered the opinion of the Court, in which BURGER, C.J., BLACKMUN, POWELL, WHITE, REHNQUIST, and O'CONNOR, JJ., joined. BRENNAN, J., filed a dissenting opinion, in which MARSHALL, J., joined. STEVENS, J., filed a dissenting opinion.

This case requires us to decide whether an initial failure of law enforcement officers to administer the warnings required by *Miranda v. Arizona* (1966), without more, "taints" subsequent admissions made after a suspect has been fully advised of and has waived his *Miranda* rights. Respondent, Michael James Elstad, was convicted of burglary by an Oregon trial court. The Oregon Court of Appeals reversed, holding that respondent's signed confession, although voluntary, was rendered inadmissible by a prior remark made in response to questioning without benefit of *Miranda* warnings. We granted certiorari, and we now reverse.

In December 1981, the home of Mr. and Mrs. Gilbert Gross, in the town of Salem, Polk County, Ore., was burglarized. Missing were art objects and furnishings valued at $150,000. A witness to the burglary contacted the Polk County Sheriff's office, implicating respondent Michael Elstad, an 18-year-old neighbor and friend of the Grosses' teenage son. Thereupon, Officers Burke and McAllister went to the home of respondent Elstad, with a warrant for his arrest. Elstad's mother answered the door. She led the officers to her son's room where he lay on his bed, clad in shorts and listening to his stereo. The officers asked him to get dressed and to accompany them into the living room. Officer McAllister asked respondent's mother to step into the kitchen, where he explained that they had a warrant for her son's arrest for the burglary of a neighbor's residence. Officer Burke remained with Elstad in the living room. He later testified:

> "I sat down with Mr. Elstad and I asked him if he was aware of why Detective McAllister and myself were there to talk with him. He stated no, he had no idea why we were there. I then asked him if he knew a person by the name of Gross, and he said yes, he did, and also added that he heard that there was a robbery at the Gross house. And at that point I told Mr. Elstad that I felt he was involved in that, and he looked at me and stated, 'Yes, I was there.'"

The officers then escorted Elstad to the back of the patrol car. As they were about to leave for the Polk County Sheriff's office, Elstad's father arrived home and came to the rear of the patrol car. The officers advised him that his son was a suspect in the burglary. Officer Burke testified that Mr. Elstad became quite agitated, opened the rear door of the car and admonished his son: "I told you that you were going to get into trouble. You wouldn't listen to me. You never learn."

Elstad was transported to the Sheriff's headquarters and approximately one hour later, Officers Burke and McAllister joined him in McAllister's office. McAllister then advised respondent for the first time of his *Miranda* rights, reading from a standard card. Respondent indicated he understood his rights, and, having these rights in mind, wished to speak with the officers. Elstad gave a full statement, explaining that he had known that the Gross family was out of town and had been paid to lead several acquaintances to the Gross residence and show them how to gain entry through a defective sliding glass door. The statement was typed, reviewed by respondent, read back to him for correction, initialed and signed by Elstad and both officers. As an afterthought, Elstad added and initialed the sentence, "After leaving the house Robby & I went back to [the] van & Robby handed me a small bag of grass."

■ ■ ■

Respondent was charged with first-degree burglary. He was represented at trial by retained counsel. Elstad waived his right to a jury, and his case was tried by a Circuit Court Judge. Respondent moved at once to suppress his oral statement and signed confession. He contended that the statement he made in response to questioning at his house "let the cat out of the bag," and tainted the subsequent confession as "fruit of the poisonous tree," citing *Wong Sun v. United States* (1963). The judge ruled that the statement, "I was there," had to be excluded because the defendant had not been advised of his *Miranda* rights. The written confession taken after Elstad's arrival at the Sheriff's office, however, was admitted in evidence.

■ ■ ■

The arguments advanced in favor of suppression of respondent's written confession rely heavily on metaphor. One metaphor, familiar from the Fourth Amendment context, would require that respondent's confession, regardless of its integrity, voluntariness, and probative value, be suppressed as the "tainted fruit of the poisonous tree" of the *Miranda* violation. A second metaphor questions whether a confession can be truly voluntary once the "cat is out of the bag." Taken out of context, each of these metaphors can be misleading. They should not be used to obscure fundamental differences between the role of the Fourth Amendment exclusionary rule and the function of *Miranda* in guarding against the prosecutorial use of compelled statements as prohibited by the Fifth Amendment. The Oregon court assumed and respondent here contends that a failure to administer *Miranda* warnings necessarily breeds the same consequences as police infringement of a constitutional right, so that evidence uncovered following an unwarned statement must be suppressed as "fruit of the poisonous tree." We believe this view misconstrues the nature of the protections afforded by *Miranda* warnings and therefore misreads the consequences of police failure to supply them.

■ ■ ■

Respondent's contention that his confession was tainted by the earlier failure of the police to provide *Miranda* warnings and must be excluded as "fruit of the poisonous tree" assumes the existence of a constitutional violation. This figure of speech is drawn from *Wong Sun v. United States,* in which the Court held that evidence and witnesses discovered as a result of a search in violation of the Fourth Amendment must be excluded from evidence. The *Wong Sun* doctrine applies as well when the fruit of the Fourth Amendment violation is a confession. It is settled law that "a confession obtained through custodial interrogation after an illegal arrest should be excluded unless intervening events break the causal connection between the illegal arrest and the confession so that the confession is 'sufficiently an act of free will to purge the primary taint.'"

But as we explained in [*New York v.*] *Quarles* [(1984)] and [*Michigan v.*] *Tucker* [(1974)], a procedural *Miranda* violation differs in significant respects from violations of the Fourth Amendment, which have traditionally mandated a broad application of the "fruits" doctrine. The purpose of the Fourth Amendment exclusionary rule is to deter unreasonable searches, no matter how probative their fruits. "The exclusionary rule,... when utilized to effectuate the Fourth Amendment, serves interests and policies that are distinct from those it serves under the Fifth." Where a Fourth Amendment violation "taints" the confession, a finding of voluntariness for the purposes of the Fifth Amendment is merely a threshold requirement in determining whether the confession may be admitted in evidence. Beyond this, the prosecution must show a sufficient break in events to undermine the inference that the confession was caused by the Fourth Amendment violation.

The *Miranda* exclusionary rule, however, serves the Fifth Amendment and sweeps more broadly than the Fifth Amendment itself. It may be triggered even in the absence of a Fifth Amendment violation. The Fifth Amendment prohibits use by the prosecution in its case in chief only of *compelled* testimony. Failure to administer *Miranda* warnings creates a presumption of compulsion. Consequently, unwarned statements that are otherwise voluntary within the meaning of the Fifth Amendment must nevertheless be excluded from evidence under *Miranda*. Thus, in the individual case, *Miranda*'s preventive medicine provides a remedy even to the defendant who has suffered no identifiable constitutional harm. *New York v. Quarles; Michigan v. Tucker.*

But the *Miranda* presumption, though irrebuttable for purposes of the prosecution's case in chief, does not require that the statements and their fruits be discarded as inherently tainted. Despite the fact that patently *voluntary* statements taken in violation of *Miranda* must be excluded from the prosecution's case, the presumption of coercion does not bar their use for impeachment purposes on cross-examination. *Harris v. New York* (1971). The Court in *Harris* rejected as an "extravagant extension of the Constitution," the theory that a defendant who had confessed under circumstances that made the confession inadmissible, could thereby enjoy the freedom to "deny every fact disclosed or discovered as a 'fruit' of his confession, free from confrontation with his prior statements" and that the voluntariness of his confession would be totally irrelevant.

■ ■ ■

In *Michigan v. Tucker*, the Court was asked to extend the *Wong Sun* fruits doctrine to suppress the testimony of a witness for the prosecution whose identity was discovered as the result of a statement taken from the accused without benefit of full *Miranda* warnings. As in respondent's case, the breach of the *Miranda* procedures in *Tucker* involved no actual compulsion. The Court concluded that the unwarned questioning "did not abridge respondent's constitutional privilege...but departed only from the prophylactic standards later laid down by this Court in *Miranda* to safeguard that privilege."

■ ■ ■

We believe that this reasoning applies with equal force when the alleged "fruit" of a noncoercive *Miranda* violation is neither a witness nor an article of evidence but the accused's own voluntary testimony. As in *Tucker*, the absence of any coercion or improper tactics undercuts the twin rationales—trustworthiness and deterrence—for a broader rule. Once warned, the suspect is free to exercise his own volition in deciding whether or not to make a statement to the authorities. The Court has often noted: " '[A] living witness is not to be mechanically equated with the proffer of inanimate evidentiary objects illegally seized.... [T]he living witness is an individual human personality whose attributes of will, perception, memory and *volition* interact to determine what testimony he will give.' " *United States v. Ceccolini* (1978).

■ ■ ■

The Oregon court nevertheless identified a subtle form of lingering compulsion, the psychological impact of the suspect's conviction that he has let the cat out of the bag and, in so doing, has sealed his own fate. But endowing the psychological effects of *voluntary* unwarned admissions with constitutional implications would, practically speaking, disable the police from obtaining the suspect's informed cooperation even when the official coercion proscribed by the Fifth Amendment played no part in either his warned or unwarned confessions. As the Court remarked in [*United States v.*] *Bayer* [(1947)]:

> "[A]fter an accused has once let the cat out of the bag by confessing, no matter what the inducement, he is never thereafter free of the psychological and practical disadvantages of having confessed. He can never get the cat back in the bag. The secret is out for good. In such a sense, a later confession may always be looked upon as fruit of the first. But this Court has never gone so far as to hold that making a confession under circumstances which preclude its use, perpetually disables the confessor from making a usable one after those conditions have been removed."

■ ■ ■

This Court has never held that the psychological impact of voluntary disclosure of a guilty secret qualifies as state compulsion or compromises the voluntariness of a subsequent informed waiver. The Oregon court, by adopting this expansive view of Fifth Amendment compulsion, effectively immunizes a suspect who responds to pre-*Miranda* warning questions from the consequences of his subsequent informed waiver of the privilege of remaining silent. This immunity comes at a high cost to legitimate law enforcement activity, while adding little desirable protection to the individual's interest in not being *compelled* to testify against himself....

There is a vast difference between the direct consequences flowing from coercion of a confession by physical violence or other deliberate means calculated to break the suspect's will and the uncertain consequences of disclosure of a "guilty secret" freely given in response to an unwarned but noncoercive question, as in this case. Justice Brennan's contention that it is impossible to perceive any causal distinction between this case and one involving a confession that is coerced by torture is wholly unpersuasive. Certainly, in respondent's case, the causal connection between any psychological disadvantage created by his admission and his ultimate decision to cooperate is speculative and attenuated at best. It is difficult to tell with certainty what motivates a suspect to speak. A suspect's confession may be traced to factors as disparate as "a prearrest event such as a visit with a minister," or an intervening event such as the exchange of words respondent had with his father. We must conclude that, absent deliberately coercive or improper tactics in obtaining the initial statement, the mere fact that a suspect has made an unwarned admission does not warrant a presumption of compulsion. A subsequent administration of *Miranda* warnings to a suspect who has given a voluntary but unwarned statement ordinarily should suffice to remove the conditions that precluded admission of the earlier statement. In such circumstances, the finder of fact may reasonably conclude that the suspect made a rational and intelligent choice whether to waive or invoke his rights.

■ ■ ■

The State has conceded the issue of custody and thus we must assume that Burke breached *Miranda* procedures in failing to administer *Miranda* warnings before initiating the discussion in the living room. This breach may have been the result of confusion as to whether the brief exchange qualified as "custodial interrogation" or it may simply have reflected Burke's reluctance to initiate an alarming police procedure before McAllister had spoken with respondent's mother. Whatever the reason for Burke's oversight, the incident had none of the earmarks of coercion. Nor did the officers exploit the unwarned admission to pressure respondent into waiving his right to remain silent.

■ ■ ■

When police ask questions of a suspect in custody without administering the required warnings, *Miranda* dictates that the answers received be presumed compelled and that they be excluded from evidence at trial in the State's case in chief. The Court has carefully adhered to this principle, permitting a narrow exception only where pressing public safety concerns demanded. The Court today in no way retreats from the bright-line rule of *Miranda*. We do not imply that good faith excuses a failure to administer *Miranda* warnings; nor do we condone inherently coercive police tactics or methods offensive to due process that render the initial admission involuntary and undermine the suspect's will to invoke his rights once they are read to him. A handful of courts have, however, applied our precedents relating to confessions obtained under coercive circumstances to situations involving wholly voluntary admissions, requiring a passage of time or break in events before a second, fully warned statement can be deemed voluntary. Far from establishing a rigid rule, we direct courts to avoid one; there is no warrant for presuming coercive effect where the suspect's initial inculpatory statement, though technically in violation of *Miranda*, was voluntary. The relevant inquiry is whether, in fact, the second statement was also voluntarily made. As in any such inquiry, the finder of fact must examine the surrounding circumstances and the entire course of police conduct with respect to the suspect in evaluating the voluntariness of his statements. The fact that a suspect chooses to speak after being informed of his rights is, of course, highly probative. We find that the dictates of *Miranda* and the goals of the Fifth Amendment proscription against use of compelled testimony are fully satisfied in the circumstances of this case by barring use of the unwarned statement in the case in chief. No further purpose is served by imputing "taint" to subsequent statements obtained pursuant to a voluntary and knowing waiver. We hold today that a suspect who has once responded to unwarned yet uncoercive questioning is not thereby disabled from waiving his rights and confessing after he has been given the requisite *Miranda* warnings.

The judgment of the Court of Appeals of Oregon is reversed, and the case is remanded for further proceedings not inconsistent with this opinion.

It is so ordered.

Justice BRENNAN, with whom Justice MARSHALL joins, dissenting.

The Self-Incrimination Clause of the Fifth Amendment guarantees every individual that, if taken into official custody, he shall be informed of important constitutional rights and be given the opportunity knowingly and voluntarily to waive those rights before being interrogated about suspected wrongdoing. This guarantee embodies our society's conviction that "no system of criminal justice can, or should, survive if it comes to depend for its continued effectiveness on the citizens' abdication through unawareness of their constitutional rights."

Even while purporting to reaffirm these constitutional guarantees, the Court has engaged of late in a studied campaign to strip the *Miranda* decision piecemeal and to undermine the rights *Miranda* sought to secure. Today's decision not only extends this effort a further step, but delivers a potentially crippling blow to *Miranda* and the ability of courts to safeguard the rights of persons accused of crime. For at least with respect to successive confessions, the Court today appears to strip remedies for *Miranda* violations of the "fruit of the poisonous tree" doctrine prohibiting the use of evidence presumptively derived from official illegality.

Two major premises undergird the Court's decision. The Court rejects as nothing more than "speculative" the long-recognized presumption that an illegally extracted confession causes the accused to confess again out of the mistaken belief that he already has sealed his fate, and it condemns as " 'extravagant' " the requirement that the prosecution affirmatively rebut the presumption before the subsequent confession may be admitted. The Court instead adopts a new rule that, so long as the accused is given the usual *Miranda* warnings before further interrogation, the taint of a previous confession obtained in violation of *Miranda* "ordinarily" must be viewed as *automatically* dissipated.

In the alternative, the Court asserts that neither the Fifth Amendment itself nor the judicial policy of deterring illegal police conduct requires the suppression of the "fruits" of a confession obtained in violation of *Miranda*, reasoning that to do otherwise would interfere with "legitimate law enforcement activity." As the Court surely understands, however, "[t]o forbid the direct use of methods . . . but to put no curb on their full indirect use would only invite the very methods deemed 'inconsistent with ethical standards and destructive of personal liberty.' " *Nardone v. United States* (1939). If violations of constitutional rights may not be remedied through the well-established rules respecting derivative evidence, as the Court has held today, there is a critical danger that the rights will be rendered nothing more than a mere "form of words." *Silverthorne Lumber Co. v. United States* (1920).

The Court's decision says much about the way the Court currently goes about implementing its agenda. In imposing its new rule, for example, the Court mischaracterizes our precedents, obfuscates the central issues, and altogether ignores the practical realities of custodial interrogation that have led nearly every lower court to reject its simplistic reasoning. Moreover, the Court adopts startling and unprecedented methods of construing constitutional guarantees. Finally the Court reaches out once again to address issues not before us. For example, although the State of Oregon has conceded that the arresting officers broke the law in this case, the Court goes out of its way to suggest that they may have been objectively justified in doing so.

Today's decision, in short, threatens disastrous consequences far beyond the outcome in this case. As the Court has not seen fit to provide a full explanation for this result, I believe it essential to consider in detail the premises, reasoning, and implications of the Court's opinion.

I

The threshold question is this: What effect should an admission or confession of guilt obtained in violation of an accused's *Miranda* rights be presumed to have upon the voluntariness of subsequent confessions that are preceded by *Miranda* warnings? Relying on the "cat out of the bag" analysis, the Oregon Court of Appeals held that the first confession presumptively taints subsequent confessions in such circumstances.

■ ■ ■

If this Court's reversal of the judgment below reflected mere disagreement with the Oregon court's application of the "cat out of the bag" presumption to the particular facts of this case, the outcome, while clearly erroneous, would be of little lasting consequence. But the Court rejects the "cat out of the bag" presumption *entirely* and instead adopts a new rule presuming that "ordinarily" there is *no* causal connection between a confession extracted in violation of *Miranda* and a subsequent confession preceded by the usual *Miranda* warnings. The Court suggests that it is merely following settled lower-court practice in adopting this rule and that the analysis followed by the Oregon Court of Appeals was aberrant. This is simply not so. Most federal courts have rejected the Court's approach and instead held that (1) there is a rebuttable presumption that a confession obtained in violation of *Miranda* taints subsequent confessions, and (2) the taint cannot be dissipated solely by giving *Miranda* warnings. Moreover, those few federal courts that have suggested approaches similar to the Court's have subsequently qualified their positions. Even more significant is the case among state courts. Although a handful have adopted the Court's approach, the overwhelming majority of state courts that have considered the issue have concluded that subsequent confessions are presumptively tainted by a first confession taken in violation of *Miranda* and that *Miranda* warnings alone cannot dissipate the taint.

The Court today sweeps aside this common-sense approach as "speculative" reasoning, adopting instead a rule that "the psychological impact of *voluntary* disclosure of a guilty secret" neither "qualifies as state compulsion" nor "compromises the voluntariness" of subsequent confessions. So long as a suspect receives the usual *Miranda* warnings before further interrogation, the Court reasons, the fact that he "is free to exercise his own volition in deciding whether or not to make" further confessions "ordinarily" is a sufficient "cure" and serves to break any causal connection between the illegal confession and subsequent statements.

The Court's marble-palace psychoanalysis is tidy, but it flies in the face of our own precedents, demonstrates a startling unawareness of the realities of police interrogation, and is completely out of tune with the experience of state and federal courts over the last 20 years. Perhaps the Court has grasped some psychological truth that has eluded persons far more experienced in these matters; if so, the Court owes an explanation of how so many could have been so wrong for so many years.

■ ■ ■

Our precedents did not develop in a vacuum. They reflect an understanding of the realities of police interrogation and the everyday experience of lower courts. Expert interrogators, far from dismissing a first admission or confession as creating merely a "speculative and attenuated" disadvantage for a suspect, understand that such revelations frequently lead directly to a full confession. Standard interrogation manuals advise that "[t]he securing of the first admission is the biggest stumbling block. . . ."

■ ■ ■

Interrogators describe the point of the first admission as the "breakthrough" and the "beachhead," R. Royal & S. Schutt, The Gentle Art of Interviewing and Interrogation: A Professional Manual and Guide 143 (1976), which once obtained will give them enormous "tactical advantages." Thus "[t]he securing of incriminating admissions might well be considered as the beginning of the final stages in crumbling the defenses of the suspect," and the process of obtaining such admissions is described as "the spadework required to motivate the subject into making the full confession."

"Once the initial admission has been made, further inducement in the form of skillfully applied interrogation techniques will motivate the suspect into making the confession." Some of these "skillfully applied" techniques involve direct confrontation of the suspect with the earlier admission, but many of the techniques are more discreet and create leverage without the need of expressly discussing the earlier admission. These techniques are all aimed at reinforcing in the suspect's mind that, as one manual describes it, " 'you're wasting your own time, and you're wasting my time, you're guilty and you know it, I know it, what's more, you know that I know it.' "

The practical experience of state and federal courts confirms the experts' understanding. From this experience, lower courts have concluded that a first confession obtained without proper *Miranda* warnings, far from creating merely some "speculative and attenuated" disadvantage for the accused, frequently enables the authorities to obtain subsequent confessions on a "silver platter."

■ ■ ■

The Court's new view about the "psychological impact" of prior illegalities also is at odds with our Fourth Amendment precedents. For example, it is well established that a confession secured as a proximate result of an illegal arrest must be suppressed. See, *e.g., Taylor v. Alabama* (1982); *Brown v. Illinois* (1975); *Wong Sun v. United States*. We have emphasized in this context that "verbal evidence which derives so immediately from an unlawful entry and an unauthorized arrest... is no less the 'fruit' of official illegality than the more common tangible fruits of the unwarranted intrusion." *Wong Sun v. United States.*

The Court seeks to distinguish these precedents on the ground that Fourth Amendment violations require a broader exclusionary rule than do Fifth Amendment violations. But the question immediately at issue—whether there should be a presumptive rule against finding a causal connection between successive confessions—would surely seem to be controlled by the logic of these Fourth Amendment cases. In part because of the inherent psychological pressures attendant upon an arrest, we have refused to presume that a confession following an illegal arrest is "sufficiently an act of free will to purge the primary taint of the unlawful invasion." If the Court so quickly dismisses the notion of a multiple-confession taint as nothing more than a "speculative and attenuated" disadvantage, what is to prevent it in the future from deciding that, contrary to the settled understanding, the fact of a proximate illegal arrest is presumptively nothing but a "speculative and attenuated" disadvantage to a defendant who is asked to confess?

Similarly, a confession obtained as a proximate result of confronting the accused with illegally seized evidence is inadmissible as the fruit of the illegal seizure.

■ ■ ■

Not content merely to ignore the practical realities of police interrogation and the likely effects of its abolition of the derivative-evidence presumption, the Court goes on to assert that nothing in the Fifth Amendment or the general judicial policy of deterring illegal police conduct "ordinarily" requires the suppression of evidence derived proximately from a confession obtained in violation of *Miranda.* The Court does not limit its analysis to successive confessions, but recurrently refers generally to the "fruits" of the illegal confession. Thus the potential impact of the Court's reasoning might extend far beyond the "cat out of the bag" context to include the discovery of physical evidence and other derivative fruits of *Miranda* violations as well.

The Fifth Amendment requires that an accused in custody be informed of important constitutional rights before the authorities interrogate him. *Miranda v. Arizona.* This requirement serves to combat the "inherently compelling pressures" of custodial questioning "which work to undermine the individual's will to resist and to compel him to speak where he would not otherwise do so freely," and is a prerequisite to securing the accused's informed and voluntary waiver of his rights. Far from serving merely as a prophylactic safeguard, "[t]he requirement of warnings and waiver of rights is a fundamental with respect to the Fifth Amendment privilege...." It is precisely because this requirement embraces rights that are deemed to serve a "central role in the preservation of basic liberties" that it is binding on the States through the Fourteenth Amendment, *Miranda v. Arizona.*

Twice in the last 10 years, however, the Court has suggested that the *Miranda* safeguards are not themselves rights guaranteed by the Fifth Amendment. In *Michigan v. Tucker*, the Court stated that *Miranda* had only prescribed "recommended" procedural safeguards "to provide practical reinforcement for the right against compulsory self-incrimination," the violation of which may not necessarily violate the Fifth Amendment itself. And in *New York v. Quarles*, the Court last Term disturbingly rejected the argument that a confession "must be *presumed* compelled because of ... failure to read [the accused] his *Miranda* warnings."

These assertions are erroneous. *Miranda*'s requirement of warnings and an effective waiver was not merely an exercise of supervisory authority over interrogation practices. As Justice Douglas noted in his *Tucker* dissent:

> "*Miranda*'s purpose was not promulgation of judicially preferred standards for police interrogation, a function we are quite powerless to perform; the decision enunciated '*constitutional* standards for protection of the privilege' against self-incrimination."

Miranda clearly emphasized that warnings and an informed waiver are essential to the Fifth Amendment privilege itself. As noted in *Tucker*, *Miranda* did state that the Constitution does not require "adherence to any particular solution" for providing the required knowledge and obtaining an informed waiver. But to rely solely on this language in concluding that the *Miranda* warnings are not constitutional rights, as did the Court in *Tucker*, ignores the central issue. The Court in *Tucker* omitted to mention that in *Miranda*, after concluding that no "particular solution" is required, we went on to emphasize that "unless we are shown other procedures which are at least as effective in apprising accused persons of their right of silence and in assuring a continuous opportunity to exercise it, the [prescribed] safeguards must be observed."

■ ■ ■

The Court today finally recognizes these flaws in the logic of *Tucker* and *Quarles*. Although disastrous in so many other respects, today's opinion at least has the virtue of rejecting the inaccurate assertion in *Quarles* that confessions extracted in violation of *Miranda* are not presumptively coerced for Fifth Amendment purposes.

■ ■ ■

Unfortunately, the Court takes away with one hand far more than what it has given with the other. Although the Court concedes, as it must, that a confession obtained in violation of *Miranda* is irrebuttably presumed to be coerced and that the Self-Incrimination Clause therefore prevents its use in the prosecution's case in chief, the Court goes on to hold that nothing in the Fifth Amendment prevents the introduction at trial of evidence proximately derived from the illegal confession. It contends, for example, that the Fifth Amendment prohibits introduction "only" of the "compelled testimony," and that this constitutional guarantee "is not concerned with nontestimonial evidence."

■ ■ ■

In short, the Fifth Amendment's rule excluding "the use of compelled testimony and evidence derived therefrom is coextensive with the scope of the privilege" against self-incrimination itself. "The essence of a provision forbidding the acquisition of evidence in a certain way is that not merely evidence so acquired shall not be used before the Court but that it shall not be used *at all*." *Silverthorne Lumber Co. v. United States*. If the authorities were permitted to use an accused's illegal confession to extract additional confessions or to uncover physical evidence against him, the use of these fruits at trial would violate the Self-Incrimination Clause just as surely as if the original confession itself were introduced. Yet that is precisely what today's decision threatens to encourage.

■ ■ ■

For these reasons, the Fifth Amendment itself requires the exclusion of evidence proximately derived from a confession obtained in violation of *Miranda*. The Court today has altogether evaded this constitutional command, the application of which should not turn simply on whether one is "sympathetic" to suspects undergoing custodial interrogation.

Even if I accepted the Court's conclusion that the Fifth Amendment does not command the suppression of evidence proximately derived from a *Miranda* violation, I would nevertheless dissent from the Court's refusal to recognize the importance of deterring *Miranda* violations in appropriate circumstances. Just last Term, in *United States v. Leon* (1984), the Court held that while the Fourth Amendment does not *per se* require the suppression of evidence derived from an unconstitutional search, the exclusionary rule must nevertheless be invoked where the search was objectively unreasonable. Although I do not share the Court's view of the Fourth Amendment, *Leon* at least had the virtue of recognizing that exclusion of derivative evidence is essential to the effective deterrence of objectively unreasonable failures by the authorities to obey the law.

The Court today refuses to apply the derivative-evidence rule even to the extent necessary to deter objectively unreasonable failures by the authorities to honor a suspect's *Miranda* rights. Incredibly, faced with an obvious violation of *Miranda*, the Court asserts that it will not countenance suppression of a subsequent confession in such circumstances where the authorities have acted "legitimate[ly]" and have not used "improper tactics." One can only respond: whither went *Miranda*?

■ ■ ■

The Court's decision today vividly reflects its impatience with the constitutional rights that the authorities attack as standing in the way of combating crime. But the States that adopted the Bill of Rights struck that balance and it is not for this Court to balance the Bill of Rights away on a cost/benefit scale "where the 'costs' of excluding illegally obtained evidence loom to exaggerated heights and where the 'benefits' of such exclusion are made to disappear with a mere wave of the hand." It is precisely in that vein, however, that the Court emphasizes that the subsequent confession in this case was "voluntary" and "highly probative evidence," that application of the derivative-evidence presumption would cause the confession to be "irretrievably lost," and that such a result would come at an impermissibly "high cost to legitimate law enforcement activity."

Failure of government to obey the law cannot ever constitute "legitimate law enforcement activity." In any event, application of the derivative-evidence presumption does not "irretrievably" lead to suppression. If a subsequent confession is truly independent of earlier, illegally obtained confessions, nothing prevents its full use to secure the accused's conviction. If the subsequent confession *did* result from the earlier illegalities, however, there is nothing "voluntary" about it. And even if a tainted subsequent confession is "highly probative," we have never until today permitted probity to override the fact that the confession was "the product of constitutionally impermissible methods in [its] inducement." In such circumstances, the Fifth Amendment makes clear that the prosecutor has *no* entitlement to use the confession in attempting to obtain the accused's conviction.

The lesson of today's decision is that, at least for now, what the Court decrees are "legitimate" violations by authorities of the rights embodied in *Miranda* shall "ordinarily" go undeterred. It is but the latest of the escalating number of decisions that are making this tribunal increasingly irrelevant in the protection of individual rights, and that are requiring other tribunals to shoulder the burden.

■ ■ ■

I dissent.

Justice STEVENS, dissenting.

The Court concludes its opinion with a carefully phrased statement of its holding:

> "We hold today that a suspect who has once responded to unwarned yet uncoercive questioning is not thereby disabled from waiving his rights and confessing after he has been given the requisite *Miranda* warnings."

I find nothing objectionable in such a holding. Moreover, because the Court expressly endorses the "bright-line rule of *Miranda*," which conclusively presumes that incriminating statements obtained from a suspect in custody without administering the required warnings are the product of compulsion, and because the Court places so much emphasis on the special facts of this case, I am persuaded that the Court intends its holding to apply only to a narrow category of cases in which the initial questioning of the suspect was made in a totally uncoercive setting and in which the first confession obviously had no influence on the second. I nevertheless dissent because even such a narrowly confined exception is inconsistent with the Court's prior cases, because the attempt to identify its boundaries in future cases will breed confusion and uncertainty in the administration of criminal justice, and because it denigrates the importance of one of the core constitutional rights that protects every

American citizen from the kind of tyranny that has flourished in other societies.

The desire to achieve a just result in this particular case has produced an opinion that is somewhat opaque and internally inconsistent. If I read it correctly, its conclusion rests on two untenable premises: (1) that the respondent's first confession was not the product of coercion; and (2) that no constitutional right was violated when respondent was questioned in a tranquil, domestic setting.

Even before the decision in *Miranda v. Arizona*, it had been recognized that police interrogation of a suspect who has been taken into custody is presumptively coercive. That presumption had its greatest force when the questioning occurred in a police station, when it was prolonged, and when there was evidence that the prisoner had suffered physical injury. To rebut the presumption, the prosecutor had the burden of proving the absence of any actual coercion. Because police officers are generally more credible witnesses than prisoners and because it is always difficult for triers of fact to disregard evidence of guilt when addressing a procedural question, more often than not the presumption of coercion afforded only slight protection to the accused.

The decision in *Miranda v. Arizona* clarified the law in three important respects. First, it provided the prosecutor with a simple method of overcoming the presumption of coercion. If the police interrogation is preceded by the warning specified in that opinion, the usual presumption does not attach. Second, it provided an important protection to the accused by making the presumption of coercion irrebuttable if the prescribed warnings are not given. Third, the decision made it clear that a self-incriminatory statement made in response to custodial interrogation was always to be considered "compelled" within the meaning of the Fifth Amendment to the Federal Constitution if the interrogation had not been preceded by appropriate warnings. Thus the irrebuttable presumption of coercion that applies to such a self-incriminatory statement, like a finding of actual coercion, renders the resulting confession inadmissible as a matter of federal constitutional law.

■ ■ ■

For me, the most disturbing aspect of the Court's opinion is its somewhat opaque characterization of the police misconduct in this case. The Court appears ambivalent on the question whether there was any constitutional violation. This ambivalence is either disingenuous or completely lawless. This Court's power to require state courts to exclude probative self-incriminatory statements rests entirely on the premise that the use of such evidence violates the Federal Constitution. The same constitutional analysis applies whether the custodial interrogation is actually coercive or irrebuttably presumed to be coercive. If the Court does not accept that premise, it must regard the holding in the *Miranda* case itself, as well as all of the federal jurisprudence that has evolved from that decision, as nothing more than an illegitimate exercise of raw judicial power. If the Court accepts the proposition that respondent's self-incriminatory statement was inadmissible, it must also acknowledge that the

Federal Constitution protected him from custodial police interrogation without first being advised of his right to remain silent.

The source of respondent's constitutional protection is the Fifth Amendment's privilege against compelled self-incrimination that is secured against state invasion by the Due Process Clause of the Fourteenth Amendment. Like many other provisions of the Bill of Rights, that provision is merely a procedural safeguard. It is, however, the specific provision that protects all citizens from the kind of custodial interrogation that was once employed by the Star Chamber, by "the Germans of the 1930's and early 1940's," and by some of our own police departments only a few decades ago. Custodial interrogation that violates that provision of the Bill of Rights is a classic example of a violation of a constitutional right.

I respectfully dissent.

New York v. Quarles

467 U.S. 649 (1984)

REHNQUIST, J., delivered the opinion of the Court, in which BURGER, C.J., BLACKMUN, POWELL, WHITE and REHNQUIST, JJ., joined. O'CONNOR, J., wrote an opinion concurring in part and dissenting in part. MARSHALL, J., wrote a dissenting opinion, in which BRENNAN and STEVENS, JJ., joined.

Respondent Benjamin Quarles was charged in the New York trial court with criminal possession of a weapon. The trial court suppressed the gun in question, and a statement made by respondent, because the statement was obtained by police before they read respondent his "*Miranda* rights." That ruling was affirmed on appeal through the New York Court of Appeals. We granted certiorari, and we now reverse. We conclude that under the circumstances involved in this case, overriding considerations of public safety justify the officer's failure to provide *Miranda* warnings before he asked questions devoted to locating the abandoned weapon.

On September 11, 1980, at approximately 12:30 a.m., Officer Frank Kraft and Officer Sal Scarring were on road patrol in Queens, N.Y., when a young woman approached their car. She told them that she had just been raped by a black male, approximately six feet tall, who was wearing a black jacket with the name "Big Ben" printed in yellow letters on the back. She told the officers that the man had just entered an A & P supermarket located nearby and that the man was carrying a gun.

The officers drove the woman to the supermarket, and Officer Kraft entered the store while Officer Scarring radioed for assistance. Officer Kraft quickly spotted respondent, who matched the description given by the woman, approaching a checkout counter. Apparently upon seeing the officer, respondent turned and ran toward the rear of the store, and Officer Kraft pursued him with a drawn gun. When respondent turned the corner at the end of an aisle, Officer Kraft lost sight of him for several seconds, and upon regaining sight of respondent, ordered him to stop and put his hands over his head.

Although more than three other officers had arrived on the scene by that time, Officer Kraft was the first to reach respondent. He frisked him and discovered that he was wearing a shoulder holster which was then empty. After handcuffing him, Officer Kraft asked him where the gun was. Respondent nodded in the direction of some empty cartons and responded, "the gun is over there." Officer Kraft thereafter retrieved a loaded .38-caliber revolver from one of the cartons, formally placed respondent under arrest, and read him his *Miranda* rights from a printed card. Respondent indicated that he would be willing to answer questions without an attorney present. Officer Kraft then asked respondent if he owned the gun and where he had purchased it. Respondent answered that he did own it and that he had purchased it in Miami, Fla.

In the subsequent prosecution of respondent for criminal possession of a weapon, the judge excluded the statement, "the gun is over there," and the gun because the officer had not given respondent the warnings required by our decision in *Miranda v. Arizona* (1966) before asking him where the gun was located. The judge excluded the other statements about respondent's ownership of the gun and the place of purchase, as evidence tainted by the prior *Miranda* violation.

■ ■ ■

The Fifth Amendment guarantees that "[n]o person . . . shall be compelled in any criminal case to be a witness against himself." In *Miranda* this Court for the first time extended the Fifth Amendment privilege against compulsory self-incrimination to individuals subjected to custodial interrogation by the police. The Fifth Amendment itself does not prohibit all incriminating admissions; "[a]bsent some officially coerced self-accusation, the Fifth Amendment privilege is not violated by even the most damning admissions." The *Miranda* Court, however, presumed that interrogation in certain custodial circumstances is inherently coercive and held that statements made under those circumstances are inadmissible unless the suspect is specifically informed of his *Miranda* rights and freely decides to forgo those rights. The prophylactic *Miranda* warnings therefore are "not themselves rights protected by the Constitution but [are] instead measures to insure that the right against compulsory self-incrimination [is] protected."

■ ■ ■

In this case we have before us no claim that respondent's statements were actually compelled by police conduct which overcame his will to resist.

■ ■ ■

The New York Court of Appeals was undoubtedly correct in deciding that the facts of this case come within the ambit of the *Miranda* decision as we have subsequently interpreted it. We agree that respondent was in police custody because we have noted that "the ultimate inquiry is simply whether there is a 'formal arrest or restraint on freedom of movement' of the degree associated with a formal arrest."

■ ■ ■

We hold that on these facts there is a "public safety" exception to the requirement that *Miranda* warnings be given before a suspect's answers may be admitted into evidence, and that the availability of that exception does not depend upon the motivation of the individual officers involved. In a kaleidoscopic situation such as the one confronting these officers, where spontaneity rather than adherence to a police manual is necessarily the order of the day, the application of the exception which we recognize today should not be made to depend on post hoc findings at a suppression hearing concerning the subjective motivation of the arresting officer. Undoubtedly most police officers, if placed in Officer Kraft's position, would act out of a host of different, instinctive, and largely unverifiable motives—their own safety, the safety of others, and perhaps as well the desire to obtain incriminating evidence from the suspect.

Whatever the motivation of individual officers in such a situation, we do not believe that the doctrinal underpinnings of *Miranda* require that it be applied in all its rigor to a situation in which police officers ask questions reasonably prompted by a concern for the public safety. The *Miranda* decision was based in large part on this Court's view that the warnings which it required police to give to suspects in custody would reduce the likelihood that the suspects would fall victim to constitutionally impermissible practices of police interrogation in the presumptively coercive environment of the station house. The dissenters warned that the requirement of *Miranda* warnings would have the effect of decreasing the number of suspects who respond to police questioning. The *Miranda* majority, however, apparently felt that whatever the cost to society in terms of fewer convictions of guilty suspects, that cost would simply have to be borne in the interest of enlarged protection for the Fifth Amendment privilege.

The police in this case, in the very act of apprehending a suspect, were confronted with the immediate necessity of ascertaining the whereabouts of a gun which they had every reason to believe the suspect had just removed from his empty holster and discarded in the supermarket. So long as the gun was concealed somewhere in the supermarket, with its actual whereabouts unknown, it obviously posed more than one danger to the public safety: an accomplice might make use of it, a customer or employee might later come upon it.

In such a situation, if the police are required to recite the familiar *Miranda* warnings before asking the whereabouts of the gun, suspects in Quarles' position might well be deterred from responding. Procedural safeguards which deter a suspect from responding were deemed acceptable in *Miranda* in order to protect the Fifth Amendment privilege; when the primary social cost of those added protections is the possibility of fewer convictions, the *Miranda* majority was willing to bear that cost. Here, had *Miranda* warnings deterred

Quarles from responding to Officer Kraft's question about the whereabouts of the gun, the cost would have been something more than merely the failure to obtain evidence useful in convicting Quarles. Officer Kraft needed an answer to his question not simply to make his case against Quarles but to insure that further danger to the public did not result from the concealment of the gun in a public area.

We conclude that the need for answers to questions in a situation posing a threat to the public safety outweighs the need for the prophylactic rule protecting the Fifth Amendment's privilege against self-incrimination. We decline to place officers such as Officer Kraft in the untenable position of having to consider, often in a matter of seconds, whether it best serves society for them to ask the necessary questions without the *Miranda* warnings and render whatever probative evidence they uncover inadmissible, or for them to give the warnings in order to preserve the admissibility of evidence they might uncover but possibly damage or destroy their ability to obtain that evidence and neutralize the volatile situation confronting them.

In recognizing a narrow exception to the *Miranda* rule in this case, we acknowledge that to some degree we lessen the desirable clarity of that rule. At least in part in order to preserve its clarity, we have over the years refused to sanction attempts to expand our *Miranda* holding.

■ ■ ■

The facts of this case clearly demonstrate that distinction and an officer's ability to recognize it. Officer Kraft asked only the question necessary to locate the missing gun before advising respondent of his rights. It was only after securing the loaded revolver and giving the warnings that he continued with investigatory questions about the ownership and place of purchase of the gun. The exception which we recognize today, far from complicating the thought processes and the on-the-scene judgments of police officers, will simply free them to follow their legitimate instincts when confronting situations presenting a danger to the public safety.

We hold that the Court of Appeals in this case erred in excluding the statement, "the gun is over there," and the gun because of the officer's failure to read respondent his *Miranda* rights before attempting to locate the weapon. Accordingly we hold that it also erred in excluding the subsequent statements as illegal fruits of a *Miranda* violation. We therefore reverse and remand for further proceedings not inconsistent with this opinion.

It is so ordered.

Justice O'CONNOR, concurring in the judgment in part and dissenting in part.

In *Miranda v. Arizona*, the Court held unconstitutional, because inherently compelled, the admission of statements derived from in-custody questioning not preceded by an explanation of the privilege against self-incrimination and the consequences of forgoing it. Today, the Court concludes that overriding considerations of public safety justify the admission of evidence—oral statements and a gun—secured without the benefit of such warnings. In so holding, the Court acknowledges that it is departing from prior precedent, and that it is "lessen[ing] the desirable clarity of [the *Miranda*] rule." Were the Court writing from a clean slate, I could agree with its holding. But *Miranda* is now the law and, in my view, the Court has not provided sufficient justification for departing from it or for blurring its now clear strictures. Accordingly, I would require suppression of the initial statement taken from respondent in this case. On the other hand, nothing in *Miranda* or the privilege itself requires exclusion of nontestimonial evidence derived from informal custodial interrogation, and I therefore agree with the Court that admission of the gun in evidence is proper.

■ ■ ■

Prior to *Miranda*, the privilege against self-incrimination had not been applied to an accused's statements secured during custodial police interrogation. In these circumstances, the issue of admissibility turned, not on whether the accused had waived his privilege against self-incrimination, but on whether his statements were "voluntary" within the meaning of the Due Process Clause.

■ ■ ■

In my view, a "public safety" exception unnecessarily blurs the edges of the clear line heretofore established and makes *Miranda*'s requirements more difficult to understand. In some cases, police will benefit because a reviewing court will find that an exigency excused their failure to administer the required warnings. But in other cases, police will suffer because, though they thought an exigency excused their noncompliance, a reviewing court will view the "objective" circumstances differently and require exclusion of admissions thereby obtained. The end result will be a finespun new doctrine on public safety exigencies incident to custodial interrogation, complete with the hair-splitting distinctions that currently plague our Fourth Amendment jurisprudence. "While the rigidity of the prophylactic rules was a principal weakness in the view of dissenters and critics outside the Court, . . . that rigidity [has also been called a] strength of the decision. It [has] afforded police and courts clear guidance on the manner in which to conduct a custodial investigation: if it was rigid, it was also precise. . . . [T]his core virtue of *Miranda* would be eviscerated if the prophylactic rules were freely [ignored] by . . . courts under the guise of [reinterpreting] *Miranda*. . . ." *Fare v. Michael* (1978).

The justification the Court provides for upsetting the equilibrium that has finally been achieved—that police cannot and should not balance considerations of public safety against the individual's interest in avoiding compulsory testimonial self-incrimination—really misses the critical question to be decided. *Miranda* has never been read to prohibit the police from asking questions to secure the public safety. Rather, the critical question *Miranda* addresses is who shall bear the cost of securing the public safety when such questions are asked and answered: the defendant or the State. *Miranda*, for better or worse, found the resolution of that question implicit in the prohibition against compulsory self-incrimination and placed the burden on the State.

When police ask custodial questions without administering the required warnings, *Miranda* quite clearly requires that the answers received be presumed compelled and that they be excluded from evidence at trial.

■ ■ ■

The gun respondent was compelled to supply is clearly evidence of the "real or physical" sort. What makes the question of its admissibility difficult is the fact that, in asking respondent to produce the gun, the police also "compelled" him, in the *Miranda* sense, to create an incriminating testimonial response. In other words, the case is problematic because police compelled respondent not only to provide the gun but also to admit that he knew where it was and that it was his.

It is settled that *Miranda* did not itself determine whether physical evidence obtained in this manner would be admissible. But the Court in *Schmerber* [*v. California* (1966)], with *Miranda* fresh on its mind, did address the issue. In concluding that the privilege did not require suppression of compelled blood tests, the Court noted:

> "This conclusion would not necessarily govern had the State tried to show that the accused had incriminated himself when told that he would have to be tested. Such incriminating evidence may be an unavoidable by-product of the compulsion to take the test, especially for an individual who fears the extraction or opposes it on religious grounds. If it wishes to compel persons to submit to such attempts to discover evidence, the State may have to forgo the advantage of any testimonial products of administering the test—products which would fall within the privilege."

Thus, *Schmerber* resolved the dilemma by allowing admission of the non-testimonial, but not the testimonial, products of the State's compulsion. . . .

Justice MARSHALL, with whom Justice BRENNAN and Justice STEVENS join, dissenting.

The police in this case arrested a man suspected of possessing a firearm in violation of New York law. Once the suspect was in custody and found to be unarmed, the arresting officer initiated an interrogation. Without being advised of his right not to respond, the suspect incriminated himself by locating the gun. The majority concludes that the State may rely on this incriminating statement to convict the suspect of possessing a weapon. I disagree. The arresting officers had no legitimate reason to interrogate the suspect without advising him of his rights to remain silent and to obtain assistance of counsel. By finding on these facts justification for unconsented interrogation, the majority abandons the clear guidelines enunciated in *Miranda v. Arizona*, and condemns the American judiciary to a new era of post hoc inquiry into the propriety of custodial interrogations. More significantly and in direct conflict with this Court's longstanding interpretation of the Fifth Amendment, the majority has endorsed the introduction of coerced self-incriminating statements in criminal prosecutions. I dissent.

■ ■ ■

The majority's entire analysis rests on the factual assumption that the public was at risk during Quarles' interrogation. This assumption is completely in conflict with the facts as found by New York's highest court. Before the interrogation began, Quarles had been "reduced to a condition of physical powerlessness." Contrary to the majority's speculations, Quarles was not believed to have, nor did he in fact have, an accomplice to come to his rescue. When the questioning began, the arresting officers were sufficiently confident of their safety to put away their guns. As Officer Kraft acknowledged at the suppression hearing, "the situation was under control." Based on Officer Kraft's own testimony, the New York Court of Appeals found: "Nothing suggests that any of the officers was by that time concerned for his own physical safety." The Court of Appeals also determined that there was no evidence that the interrogation was prompted by the arresting officers' concern for the public's safety.

The majority attempts to slip away from these unambiguous findings of New York's highest court by proposing that danger be measured by objective facts rather than the subjective intentions of arresting officers. Though clever, this ploy was anticipated by the New York Court of Appeals: "[T]here is no evidence in the record before us that there were exigent circumstances posing a risk to the public safety. . . ."

■ ■ ■

The majority's treatment of the legal issues presented in this case is no less troubling than its abuse of the facts. Before today's opinion, the Court had twice concluded that, under *Miranda v. Arizona*, police officers conducting custodial interrogations must advise suspects of their rights before any questions concerning the whereabouts of incriminating weapons can be asked. *Rhode Island v. Innis* (1980) (dicta); *Orozco v. Texas* (1969) (holding). Now the majority departs from these cases and rules that police may withhold *Miranda* warnings whenever custodial interrogations concern matters of public safety.

The majority contends that the law, as it currently stands, places police officers in a dilemma whenever they interrogate a suspect who appears to know of some threat to the public's safety. If the police interrogate the suspect without advising him of his rights, the suspect may reveal information that the authorities can use to defuse the threat, but the suspect's statements will be inadmissible at trial. If, on the other hand, the police advise the suspect of his rights, the suspect may be deterred from responding to the police's questions, and the risk to the public may continue unabated. According to the majority, the police must now choose between establishing the suspect's guilt and safeguarding the public from danger.

The majority proposes to eliminate this dilemma by creating an exception to *Miranda v. Arizona* for custodial interrogations concerning matters of public safety. Under the majority's exception, police would be permitted to interrogate suspects about such matters before the suspects have been advised of their constitutional rights. Without being "deterred" by the knowledge that they have a constitutional right not to respond, these suspects will be likely to answer the questions. Should the answers also be incriminating, the State would be free to introduce them as evidence in a criminal prosecution. Through this "narrow exception to the *Miranda* rule," the majority proposes to protect the public's safety without jeopardizing the prosecution of criminal defendants. I find in this reasoning an unwise and unprincipled departure from our Fifth Amendment precedents.

Before today's opinion, the procedures established in *Miranda v. Arizona* had "the virtue of informing police and prosecutors with specificity as to what they may do in conducting custodial interrogation, and of informing courts under what circumstances statements obtained during such interrogation are not admissible." In a chimerical quest for public safety, the majority has abandoned the rule that brought 18 years of doctrinal tranquility to the field of custodial interrogations. As the majority candidly concedes, a public-safety exception destroys forever the clarity of *Miranda* for both law enforcement officers and members of the judiciary. The Court's candor cannot mask what a serious loss the administration of justice has incurred. . . .

The end result, as Justice O'Connor predicts, will be "a finespun new doctrine on public safety exigencies incident to custodial interrogation, complete with the hairsplitting distinctions that currently plague our Fourth Amendment jurisprudence." In the meantime, the courts will have to dedicate themselves to spinning this new web of doctrines, and the country's law enforcement agencies will have to suffer patiently through the frustrations of another period of constitutional uncertainty.

Though unfortunate, the difficulty of administering the "public-safety" exception is not the most profound flaw in the majority's decision. The majority has lost sight of the fact that *Miranda v. Arizona* and our earlier custodial-interrogation cases all implemented a constitutional privilege against self-incrimination. The rules established in these cases were designed to protect criminal defendants against prosecutions based on coerced self-incriminating statements. The majority today turns its back on these constitutional considerations, and invites the government to prosecute through the use of what necessarily are coerced statements.

The majority's error stems from a serious misunderstanding of *Miranda v. Arizona* and of the Fifth Amendment upon which that decision was based. The majority implies that *Miranda* consisted of no more than a judicial balancing act in which the benefits of "enlarged protection for the Fifth Amendment privilege" were weighed against "the cost to society in terms of fewer convictions of guilty suspects." Supposedly because the scales tipped in favor of the privilege against self-incrimination, the *Miranda* Court erected a prophylactic barrier around statements made during custodial interrogations. The majority now proposes to return to the scales of social utility to calculate whether *Miranda*'s prophylactic rule remains cost-effective when threats to the public's safety are added to the balance. The results of the majority's "test" are announced with pseudoscientific precision:

> "We conclude that the need for answers to questions in a situation posing a threat to the public safety outweighs the need for the prophylactic rule protecting the Fifth Amendment's privilege against self-incrimination."

The majority misreads *Miranda*. Though the *Miranda* dissent prophesized dire consequences, the *Miranda* Court refused to allow such concerns to weaken the protections of the Constitution:

> "A recurrent argument made in these cases is that society's need for interrogation outweighs the privilege. This argument is not unfamiliar to this Court. The whole thrust of our foregoing discussion demonstrates that the Constitution has prescribed the rights of the individual when confronted with the power of government when it provided in the Fifth Amendment that an individual cannot be compelled to be a witness against himself. That right cannot be abridged."

Whether society would be better off if the police warned suspects of their rights before beginning an interrogation or whether the advantages of giving such warnings would outweigh their costs did not inform the *Miranda* decision. On the contrary, the *Miranda* Court was concerned with the proscriptions of the Fifth Amendment, and, in particular, whether the Self-Incrimination Clause permits the government to prosecute individuals based on statements made in the course of custodial interrogations.

Miranda v. Arizona was the culmination of a century-long inquiry into how this Court should deal with confessions made during custodial interrogations. Long before *Miranda*, the Court had recognized that the Federal Government was prohibited from introducing at criminal trials compelled confessions, including confessions compelled in the course of custodial interrogations. In 1924, Justice Brandeis was reciting settled law when he wrote: "[A] confession obtained by compulsion must be excluded whatever may have been the character of the compulsion, and whether the compulsion was applied in a judicial proceeding or otherwise." *Wan v. United States* [(1924)].

Prosecutors in state courts were subject to similar constitutional restrictions.

■ ■ ■

When *Miranda* reached this Court, it was undisputed that both the States and the Federal Government were constitutionally prohibited from prosecuting defendants with confessions coerced during custodial interrogations. As a theoretical matter, the law was clear. In practice, however, the courts found it exceedingly difficult to determine whether a given confession had been coerced. Difficulties of proof and subtleties of interrogation technique made it impossible in most cases for the judiciary to decide with confidence whether the defendant had voluntarily confessed his guilt or whether his testimony had been unconstitutionally compelled. Courts around the country were spending countless hours reviewing the facts of individual custodial interrogations.

   Miranda dealt with these practical problems. After a detailed examination of police practices and a review of its previous decisions in the area, the Court in *Miranda* determined that custodial interrogations are inherently coercive. The Court therefore created a constitutional presumption that statements made during custodial interrogations are compelled in violation of the Fifth Amendment and are thus inadmissible in criminal prosecutions. As a result of the Court's decision in *Miranda*, a statement made during a custodial interrogation may be introduced as proof of a defendant's guilt only if the prosecution demonstrates that the defendant knowingly and intelligently waived his constitutional rights before making the statement. The now-familiar *Miranda* warnings offer law enforcement authorities a clear, easily administered device for ensuring that criminal suspects understand their constitutional rights well enough to waive them and to engage in consensual custodial interrogation.

   In fashioning its "public-safety" exception to *Miranda*, the majority makes no attempt to deal with the constitutional presumption established by that case. The majority does not argue that police questioning about issues of public safety is any less coercive than custodial interrogations into other matters. The majority's only contention is that police officers could more easily protect the public if *Miranda* did not apply to custodial interrogations concerning the public's safety. But *Miranda* was not a decision about public safety; it was a decision about coerced confessions. Without establishing that interrogations concerning the public's safety are less likely to be coercive than other interrogations, the majority cannot endorse the "public-safety" exception and remain faithful to the logic of *Miranda v. Arizona*.

■ ■ ■

   Having determined that the Fifth Amendment renders inadmissible Quarles' response to Officer Kraft's questioning, I have no doubt that our precedents require that the gun discovered as a direct result of Quarles' statement must be presumed inadmissible as well. The gun was the direct product of a coercive custodial interrogation. In *Silverthorne Lumber Co. v. United States* (1920) and *Wong Sun v. United States* (1963), this Court held that the Government may not introduce incriminating evidence derived from an illegally obtained source.

■ ■ ■

   Accordingly, I would affirm the order of the Court of Appeals to the extent that it found Quarles' incriminating statement inadmissible under the Fifth Amendment, would vacate the order to the extent that it suppressed Quarles' gun, and would remand the matter for reconsideration in light of *Nix v. Williams*.

7. *Miranda* Reconsidered

Dickerson v. United States

530 U.S. 428 (2000)

REHNQUIST, C.J., delivered the opinion of the Court, in which STEVENS, O'CONNOR, KENNEDY, SOUTER, GINSBURG, and BREYER, JJ., joined. SCALIA, J., filed a dissenting opinion, in which THOMAS, J., joined.

In *Miranda v. Arizona* (1966), we held that certain warnings must be given before a suspect's statement made during custodial interrogation could be admitted in evidence. In the wake of that decision, Congress enacted 18 U.S.C. §3501, which in essence laid down a rule that the admissibility of such statements should turn only on whether or not they were voluntarily made. We hold that *Miranda*, being a constitutional decision of this Court, may not be in effect overruled by an Act of Congress, and we decline to overrule *Miranda* ourselves. We therefore hold that *Miranda* and its progeny in this Court govern the admissibility of statements made during custodial interrogation in both state and federal courts.

Petitioner Dickerson was indicted for bank robbery, conspiracy to commit bank robbery, and using a firearm in the course of committing a crime of violence, all in violation of the applicable provisions of Title 18 of the United States Code. Before trial, Dickerson moved to suppress a statement he had made at a Federal Bureau of Investigation field office, on the grounds that he had not received "*Miranda* warnings" before being interrogated. The District Court granted his motion to suppress, and the Government took an interlocutory appeal to the United States Court of Appeals for the Fourth Circuit. That court, by a divided vote, reversed the District Court's suppression order. It agreed with the District Court's conclusion that petitioner had not received *Miranda* warnings before making his statement. But it went on to hold that §3501, which in effect makes the admissibility of statements such as Dickerson's turn solely on whether they were made voluntarily, was satisfied in this case. It then concluded that our decision in *Miranda* was not a constitutional holding, and that, therefore, Congress could by statute have the final say on the question of admissibility.

Because of the importance of the questions raised by the Court of Appeals' decision, we granted certiorari, and now reverse.

We begin with a brief historical account of the law governing the admission of confessions. Prior to *Miranda*, we evaluated the admissibility of a suspect's confession under a voluntariness test. The roots of this test developed in the common law, as the courts of England and then the United States recognized that coerced confessions are inherently untrustworthy. Over time, our cases recognized two constitutional bases for the requirement that a confession be voluntary to be admitted into evidence: the Fifth Amendment right against self-incrimination and the Due Process Clause of the Fourteenth Amendment.

See, *e.g., Bram v. United States* (1897) (stating that the voluntariness test "is controlled by that portion of the Fifth Amendment... commanding that no person 'shall be compelled in any criminal case to be a witness against himself'"); *Brown v. Mississippi* (1936) (reversing a criminal conviction under the Due Process Clause because it was based on a confession obtained by physical coercion).

While *Bram* was decided before *Brown* and its progeny, for the middle third of the 20th century our cases based the rule against admitting coerced confessions primarily, if not exclusively, on notions of due process....

We have never abandoned this due process jurisprudence, and thus continue to exclude confessions that were obtained involuntarily. But our decisions in *Malloy v. Hogan* (1964) and *Miranda* changed the focus of much of the inquiry in determining the admissibility of suspects' incriminating statements. In *Malloy*, we held that the Fifth Amendment's Self-Incrimination Clause is incorporated in the Due Process Clause of the Fourteenth Amendment and thus applies to the States. We decided *Miranda* on the heels of *Malloy*.

In *Miranda*, we noted that the advent of modern custodial police interrogation brought with it an increased concern about confessions obtained by coercion. Because custodial police interrogation, by its very nature, isolates and pressures the individual, we stated that "[e]ven without employing brutality, the 'third degree' or [other] specific stratagems,... custodial interrogation exacts a heavy toll on individual liberty and trades on the weakness of individuals." We concluded that the coercion inherent in custodial interrogation blurs the line between voluntary and involuntary statements, and thus heightens the risk that an individual will not be "accorded his privilege under the Fifth Amendment... not to be compelled to incriminate himself." Accordingly, we laid down "concrete constitutional guidelines for law enforcement agencies and courts to follow." Those guidelines established that the admissibility in evidence of any statement given during custodial interrogation of a suspect would depend on whether the police provided the suspect with four warnings. These warnings (which have come to be known colloquially as "*Miranda* rights") are: a suspect "has the right to remain silent, that anything he says can be used against him in a court of law, that he has the right to the presence of an attorney, and that if he cannot afford an attorney one will be appointed for him prior to any questioning if he so desires."

Two years after *Miranda* was decided, Congress enacted § 3501. That section provides, in relevant part:

> "(a) In any criminal prosecution brought by the United States or by the District of Columbia, a confession... shall be admissible in evidence if it is voluntarily given. Before such confession is received in evidence, the trial judge shall, out of the presence of the jury, determine any issue as to voluntariness. If the trial judge determines that the confession was voluntarily made it shall be admitted in evidence and the trial judge shall permit the jury to hear relevant evidence on the issue of voluntariness and shall instruct the jury to

give such weight to the confession as the jury feels it deserves under all the circumstances.

(b) The trial judge in determining the issue of voluntariness shall take into consideration all the circumstances surrounding the giving of the confession, including (1) the time elapsing between arrest and arraignment of the defendant making the confession, if it was made after arrest and before arraignment, (2) whether such defendant knew the nature of the offense with which he was charged or of which he was suspected at the time of making the confession, (3) whether or not such defendant was advised or knew that he was not required to make any statement and that any such statement could be used against him, (4) whether or not such defendant had been advised prior to questioning of his right to the assistance of counsel, and (5) whether or not such defendant was without the assistance of counsel when questioned and when giving such confession.

The presence or absence of any of the above-mentioned factors to be taken into consideration by the judge need not be conclusive on the issue of voluntariness of the confession."

Given express designation of voluntariness as the touchstone of admissibility, its omission of any warning requirement, and the instruction for trial courts to consider a nonexclusive list of factors relevant to the circumstances of a confession, we agree with the Court of Appeals that Congress intended by its enactment to overrule *Miranda*. See also *Davis v. United States* (1994) (Scalia, J., concurring) (stating that, prior to *Miranda*, "voluntariness *vel non* was the touchstone of admissibility of confessions"). Because of the obvious conflict between our decision in *Miranda* and §3501, we must address whether Congress has constitutional authority to thus supersede *Miranda*. If Congress has such authority, §3501's totality-of-the-circumstances approach must prevail over *Miranda*'s requirement of warnings; if not, that section must yield to *Miranda*'s more specific requirements.

The law in this area is clear. This Court has supervisory authority over the federal courts, and we may use that authority to prescribe rules of evidence and procedure that are binding in those tribunals. However, the power to judicially create and enforce nonconstitutional "rules of procedure and evidence for the federal courts exists only in the absence of a relevant Act of Congress." Congress retains the ultimate authority to modify or set aside any judicially created rules of evidence and procedure that are not required by the Constitution.

But Congress may not legislatively supersede our decisions interpreting and applying the Constitution. This case therefore turns on whether the *Miranda* Court announced a constitutional rule or merely exercised its supervisory authority to regulate evidence in the absence of congressional direction. Recognizing this point, the Court of Appeals surveyed *Miranda* and its progeny to determine the constitutional status of the *Miranda* decision. Relying on the fact that we have created several exceptions to *Miranda*'s warnings requirement and that we have repeatedly referred to the *Miranda* warnings as "prophylactic," *New York v. Quarles* (1984), and "not themselves rights protected by the Constitution," *Michigan v. Tucker* (1974), the Court of Appeals concluded that the protections announced in *Miranda* are not constitutionally required.

We disagree with the Court of Appeals' conclusion, although we concede that there is language in some of our opinions that supports the view taken by that court. But first and foremost of the factors on the other side—that *Miranda* is a constitutional decision—is that both *Miranda* and two of its companion cases applied the rule to proceedings in state courts—to wit, Arizona, California, and New York. Since that time, we have consistently applied *Miranda*'s rule to prosecutions arising in state courts. It is beyond dispute that we do not hold a supervisory power over the courts of the several States. With respect to proceedings in state courts, our "authority is limited to enforcing the commands of the United States Constitution."

The *Miranda* opinion itself begins by stating that the Court granted certiorari "to explore some facets of the problems . . . of applying the privilege against self-incrimination to in-custody interrogation, *and to give concrete constitutional guidelines for law enforcement agencies and courts to follow.*" In fact, the majority opinion is replete with statements indicating that the majority thought it was announcing a constitutional rule. Indeed, the Court's ultimate conclusion was that the unwarned confessions obtained in the four cases before the Court in *Miranda* "were obtained from the defendant under circumstances that did not meet constitutional standards for protection of the privilege."

Additional support for our conclusion that *Miranda* is constitutionally based is found in the *Miranda* Court's invitation for legislative action to protect the constitutional right against coerced self-incrimination. After discussing the "compelling pressures" inherent in custodial police interrogation, the *Miranda* Court concluded that, "[i]n order to combat these pressures and to permit a full opportunity to exercise the privilege against self-incrimination, the accused must be adequately and effectively apprised of his rights and the exercise of those rights must be fully honored." However, the Court emphasized that it could not foresee "the potential alternatives for protecting the privilege which might be devised by Congress or the States," and it accordingly opined that the Constitution would not preclude legislative solutions that differed from the prescribed *Miranda* warnings but which were "at least as effective in apprising accused persons of their right of silence and in assuring a continuous opportunity to exercise it."

The Court of Appeals also relied on the fact that we have, after our *Miranda* decision, made exceptions from its rule in cases such as *New York v. Quarles* and *Harris v. New York* (1971). These decisions illustrate the principle—not that *Miranda* is not a constitutional rule—but that no constitutional rule is immutable. No court laying down a general rule can possibly foresee the various circumstances in which counsel will seek to apply it, and the sort of modifications represented by these cases are as much a normal part of constitutional law as the original decision.

The Court of Appeals also noted that in *Oregon v. Elstad* (1985), we stated that " '[t]he *Miranda* exclusionary rule . . . serves the Fifth Amendment and sweeps more broadly than the Fifth Amendment itself.' " Our decision in that case—refusing to apply the traditional "fruits" doctrine developed in Fourth Amendment cases—does not prove that *Miranda* is a nonconstitutional decision, but simply recognizes the fact that unreasonable searches under the Fourth Amendment are different from unwarned interrogation under the Fifth Amendment.

As an alternative argument for sustaining the Court of Appeals' decision, the court-invited *amicus curiae* contends that the section complies with the requirement that a legislative alternative to *Miranda* be equally as effective in preventing coerced confessions. We agree with the *amicus'* contention that there are more remedies available for abusive police conduct than there were at the time *Miranda* was decided. But we do not agree that these additional measures supplement §3501's protections sufficiently to meet the constitutional minimum. *Miranda* requires procedures that will warn a suspect in custody of his right to remain silent and which will assure the suspect that the exercise of that right will be honored. As discussed above, §3501 explicitly eschews a requirement of preinterrogation warnings in favor of an approach that looks to the administration of such warnings as only one factor in determining the voluntariness of a suspect's confession. The additional remedies cited by *amicus* do not, in our view, render them, together with §3501, an adequate substitute for the warnings required by *Miranda*.

The dissent argues that it is judicial overreaching for this Court to hold §3501 unconstitutional unless we hold that the *Miranda* warnings are required by the Constitution, in the sense that nothing else will suffice to satisfy constitutional requirements. But we need not go further than *Miranda* to decide this case.

■ ■ ■

Whether or not we would agree with *Miranda*'s reasoning and its resulting rule, were we addressing the issue in the first instance, the principles of *stare decisis* weigh heavily against overruling it now. *Arizona v. Rumsey* (1984).

■ ■ ■

We do not think there is such justification for overruling *Miranda*. *Miranda* has become embedded in routine police practice to the point where the warnings have become part of our national culture.

■ ■ ■

The disadvantage of the *Miranda* rule is that statements which may be by no means involuntary, made by a defendant who is aware of his "rights," may nonetheless be excluded and a guilty defendant go free as a result. But experience suggests that the totality-of-the-circumstances test which §3501 seeks to revive is more difficult than *Miranda* for law enforcement officers to conform to, and for courts to apply in a consistent manner.

■ ■ ■

In sum, we conclude that *Miranda* announced a constitutional rule that Congress may not supersede legislatively. Following the rule of *stare decisis*, we decline to overrule *Miranda* ourselves. The judgment of the Court of Appeals is therefore

Reversed.

Justice SCALIA, with whom Justice THOMAS joins, dissenting.

Those to whom judicial decisions are an unconnected series of judgments that produce either favored or disfavored results will doubtless greet today's decision as a paragon of moderation, since it declines to overrule *Miranda v. Arizona.* Those who understand the judicial process will appreciate that today's decision is not a reaffirmation of *Miranda*, but a radical revision of the most significant element of *Miranda* (as of all cases): the rationale that gives it a permanent place in our jurisprudence.

Marbury v. Madison (1803) held that an Act of Congress will not be enforced by the courts if what it prescribes violates the Constitution of the United States. That was the basis on which *Miranda* was decided. One will search today's opinion in vain, however, for a statement (surely simple enough to make) that what 18 U.S.C. § 3501 prescribes—the use at trial of a voluntary confession, even when a *Miranda* warning or its equivalent has failed to be given—violates the Constitution. The reason the statement does not appear is not only (and perhaps not so much) that it would be absurd, inasmuch as § 3501 excludes from trial precisely what the Constitution excludes from trial, viz., compelled confessions; but also that Justices whose votes are needed to compose today's majority are on record as believing that a violation of *Miranda* is *not* a violation of the Constitution. And so, to justify today's agreed-upon result, the Court must adopt a significant *new*, if not entirely comprehensible, principle of constitutional law. As the Court chooses to describe that principle, statutes of Congress can be disregarded, not only when what they prescribe violates the Constitution, but when what they prescribe contradicts a decision of this Court that "announced a constitutional rule." As I shall discuss in some detail, the only thing that can possibly mean in the context of this case is that this Court has the power, not merely to apply the Constitution but to expand it, imposing what it regards as useful "prophylactic" restrictions upon Congress and the States. That is an immense and frightening antidemocratic power, and it does not exist.

It takes only a small step to bring today's opinion out of the realm of power-judging and into the mainstream of legal reasoning: The Court need only go beyond its carefully couched iterations that "*Miranda* is a constitutional decision," that "*Miranda* is constitutionally based," that *Miranda* has "constitutional underpinnings," and come out and say quite clearly: "We reaffirm today that custodial interrogation that is not preceded by *Miranda* warnings or their equivalent violates the Constitution of the United States." It cannot say that, because a majority of the Court does not believe it. The Court therefore acts in plain violation of the Constitution when it denies effect to this Act of Congress.

Early in this Nation's history, this Court established the sound proposition that constitutional government in a system of separated powers requires judges to regard as inoperative any legislative Act, even of Congress itself, that is "repugnant to the Constitution."

> "So if a law be in opposition to the constitution; if both the law and the constitution apply to a particular case, so that the court must either decide that case conformably to the law, disregarding the constitution; or conformably to the constitution, disregarding the law; the court must determine which of these conflicting rules governs the case."

The power we recognized in *Marbury* will thus permit us, indeed require us, to "disregar[d]" §3501, a duly enacted statute governing the admissibility of evidence in the federal courts, only if it "be in opposition to the constitution"—here, assertedly, the dictates of the Fifth Amendment.

It was once possible to characterize the so-called *Miranda* rule as resting (however implausibly) upon the proposition that what the statute here before us permits—the admission at trial of un-*Mirandized* confessions—violates the Constitution. That is the fairest reading of the *Miranda* case itself. The Court began by announcing that the Fifth Amendment privilege against self-incrimination applied in the context of extrajudicial custodial interrogation—itself a doubtful proposition as a matter both of history and precedent. Having extended the privilege into the confines of the station house, the Court liberally sprinkled throughout its sprawling 60-page opinion suggestions that, because of the compulsion inherent in custodial interrogation, the privilege was violated by any statement thus obtained that did not conform to the rules set forth in *Miranda*, or some functional equivalent.

■ ■ ■

The dissenters, for their part, also understood *Miranda*'s holding to be based on the "premise . . . that pressure on the suspect must be eliminated though it be only the subtle influence of the atmosphere and surroundings." . . . *id.* ("[I]t has never been suggested, until today, that such questioning was so coercive and accused persons so lacking in hardihood that the very first response to the very first question following the commencement of custody must be conclusively presumed to be the product of an overborne will"). And at least one case decided shortly after *Miranda* explicitly confirmed the view.

So understood, *Miranda* was objectionable for innumerable reasons, not least the fact that cases spanning more than 70 years had rejected its core premise that, absent the warnings and an effective waiver of the right to remain silent and of the (thitherto unknown) right to have an attorney present, a statement obtained pursuant to custodial interrogation was necessarily the product of compulsion. Moreover, history and precedent aside, the decision in *Miranda*, if read as an explication of what the Constitution *requires*, is preposterous. There is, for example, simply no basis in reason for concluding that a response to the very first question asked, by a suspect who already *knows* all of the rights described in the *Miranda* warning, is anything other than a volitional act. And even if one assumes that the elimination of compulsion absolutely requires informing even the most knowledgeable suspect of his right to remain silent, it cannot conceivably require the right to have *counsel* present. There is a world of difference, which the Court recognized under the traditional voluntariness test but ignored in *Miranda*, between compelling a suspect to incriminate himself and preventing him from foolishly doing so of his own accord. Only the latter (which is *not* required by the Constitution) could explain the Court's inclusion of a right to counsel and the requirement that it, too, be knowingly and intelligently waived. Counsel's presence is not required to tell the suspect that he *need* not speak; the interrogators can do that. The only good reason for having counsel there is that he can be counted on to advise the suspect that he *should* not speak.

Preventing foolish (rather than compelled) confessions is likewise the only conceivable basis for the rules (suggested in *Miranda*), that courts must exclude any confession elicited by questioning conducted, without interruption, after the suspect has indicated a desire to stand on his right to remain silent, see *Michigan v. Mosley* (1975), or initiated by police after the suspect has expressed a desire to have counsel present, see *Edwards v. Arizona* (1981). Nonthreatening attempts to persuade the suspect to reconsider that initial decision are not, without more, enough to render a change of heart the product of anything other than the suspect's free will. Thus, what is most remarkable about the *Miranda* decision—and what made it unacceptable as a matter of straightforward constitutional interpretation in the *Marbury* tradition—is its palpable hostility toward the act of confession *per se*, rather than toward what the Constitution abhors, *compelled* confession.

■ ■ ■

For these reasons, and others more than adequately developed in the *Miranda* dissents and in the subsequent works of the decision's many critics, any conclusion that a violation of the *Miranda* rules *necessarily* amounts to a violation of the privilege against compelled self-incrimination can claim no support in history, precedent, or common sense, and as a result would at least presumptively be worth reconsidering even at this late date. But that is unnecessary, since the Court has (thankfully) long since abandoned the notion that failure to comply with *Miranda*'s rules is itself a violation of the Constitution.

As the Court today acknowledges, since *Miranda* we have explicitly, and repeatedly, interpreted that decision as having announced, not the circumstances in which custodial interrogation runs afoul of the Fifth or Fourteenth Amendment, but rather only "prophylactic" rules that go beyond the right against compelled self-incrimination. Of course the seeds of this "prophylactic" interpretation of *Miranda* were present in the decision itself.

■ ■ ■

Michigan v. Tucker, an opinion for the Court written by then-Justice Rehnquist, rejected the true-to-*Marbury*, failure-to-warn-as-constitutional-violation interpretation of *Miranda*. It held that exclusion of the "fruits" of a *Miranda* violation—the statement of a witness whose identity the defendant had revealed while in custody—was not required. The opinion explained that the question whether the "police conduct complained of directly infringed upon respondent's right against compulsory self-incrimination" was a "separate question" from "whether it instead violated only the prophylactic rules developed to protect that right." The "procedural safeguards" adopted in *Miranda*, the Court said, "were not themselves rights protected by the Constitution but were instead measures to insure that the right against compulsory self-incrimination was protected," and to "provide practical reinforcement for the right." Comparing the particular facts of the custodial interrogation with the "historical circumstances underlying the privilege," the Court concluded, unequivocally, that the defendant's statement could not be termed "involuntary as that term has been defined in the decisions of this Court," and thus that there had been no constitutional violation, notwithstanding the clear violation of the "procedural rules later established in *Miranda*." Lest there be any confusion on the point, the Court reiterated that the "police conduct at issue here did not abridge respondent's constitutional privilege against compulsory self-incrimination, but departed only from the prophylactic standards later laid down by this Court in *Miranda* to safeguard that privilege." It is clear from our cases, of course, that if the statement in *Tucker had* been obtained in violation of the Fifth Amendment, the statement and its fruits would have been excluded.

■ ■ ■

Nearly a decade later, in *New York v. Quarles*, the Court relied upon the fact that "[t]he prophylactic *Miranda* warnings . . . are 'not themselves rights protected by the Constitution,'" (quoting *Tucker*) to create a "public safety" exception. In that case, police apprehended, after a chase in a grocery store, a rape suspect known to be carrying a gun. After handcuffing and searching him (and finding no gun)—but before reading him his *Miranda* warnings—the police demanded to know where the gun was. The defendant nodded in the direction of some empty cartons and responded that "the gun is over there." The Court held that both the unwarned statement—"the gun is over there"—and the recovered weapon were admissible in the prosecution's case in chief under a "public safety exception" to the "prophylactic rules enunciated in *Miranda*." It explicitly acknowledged that if the *Miranda* warnings were an imperative of the Fifth Amendment itself, such an exigency exception would be impossible, since the Fifth Amendment's bar on compelled self-incrimination is absolute, and its "'strictures, unlike the Fourth's are not removed by showing reasonableness.'" (For the latter reason, the Court found it necessary to note that respondent did not "claim that [his] statements were actually compelled by police conduct which overcame his will to resist.")

The next year, the Court again declined to apply the "fruit of the poisonous tree" doctrine to a *Miranda* violation, this time allowing the admission of a suspect's properly warned statement even though it had been preceded (and, arguably, induced) by an earlier inculpatory statement taken in violation of *Miranda. Oregon v. Elstad.* As in *Tucker*, the Court distinguished the case from those holding that a confession obtained as a result of an unconstitutional search is inadmissible, on the ground that the violation of *Miranda* does not involve an "actual infringement of the suspect's constitutional rights," the Court explained, "sweeps more broadly than the Fifth Amendment itself," and "*Miranda*'s preventive medicine provides a remedy even to the defendant who has suffered no identifiable constitutional harm."

■ ■ ■

In light of these cases, and our statements to the same effect in others, it is simply no longer possible for the Court to conclude, even if it wanted to, that a violation of *Miranda*'s rules is a violation of the Constitution. But as I explained at the outset, that is what is required before the Court may disregard a law of Congress governing the admissibility of evidence in federal court. The Court today insists that the *decision* in *Miranda* is a "constitutional" one, that it has "constitutional underpinnings," a "constitutional basis" and a "constitutional origin," that it was "constitutionally based," and that it announced a "constitutional rule." It is fine to play these word games; but what makes a decision "constitutional" in the only sense relevant here—in the sense that renders it impervious to supersession by congressional legislation such as § 3501—is the determination that the Constitution *requires* the result that the decision announces and the statute ignores. By disregarding congressional action that concededly does not violate the Constitution, the Court flagrantly offends fundamental principles of separation of powers, and arrogates to itself prerogatives reserved to the representatives of the people.

The Court seeks to avoid this conclusion in two ways: First, by misdescribing these post-*Miranda* cases as mere dicta. The Court concedes only "that there is language in some of our opinions that supports the view" that *Miranda*'s protections are not "constitutionally required." It is not a matter of *language*; it is a matter of *holdings*. The proposition that failure to comply with *Miranda*'s rules does not establish a constitutional violation was central to the *holdings* of *Tucker, Quarles*, and *Elstad*.

The second way the Court seeks to avoid the impact of these cases is simply to disclaim responsibility for reasoned decisionmaking. It says:

> "These decisions illustrate the principle—not that *Miranda* is not a constitutional rule—but that no constitutional rule is immutable. No court laying down a general rule can possibly foresee the various circumstances in which counsel will seek to apply it, and the sort of modifications represented by these cases are as much a normal part of constitutional law as the original decision."

The issue, however, is not whether court rules are "mutable"; they assuredly are. It is not whether, in the light of "various circumstances," they can be "modifi[ed]"; they assuredly can. The issue is whether, *as mutated and modified*, they must *make sense*. The requirement that they do so is the only thing that prevents this Court from being some sort of nine-headed Caesar, giving thumbs-up or thumbs-down to whatever outcome, case by case, suits or offends its collective fancy. And if confessions procured in violation of *Miranda* are confessions "compelled" in violation of the Constitution, the post-*Miranda* decisions I have discussed do not make sense. The only reasoned basis for their outcome was that a violation of *Miranda* is *not* a violation of the Constitution. If, for example, as the Court acknowledges was the holding of *Elstad*, "the traditional 'fruits' doctrine developed in Fourth Amendment cases" (that the fruits of evidence obtained unconstitutionally must be excluded from trial) does *not* apply to the fruits of *Miranda* violations; and if the reason for the difference is *not* that *Miranda* violations are not constitutional violations (which is plainly and flatly what *Elstad* said); then the Court must come up with some *other* explanation for the difference. (That will take quite a bit of doing, by the way, since it is *not* clear on the face of the Fourth Amendment that evidence obtained in violation of that guarantee must be excluded from trial, whereas it *is* clear on the face of the Fifth Amendment that unconstitutionally compelled confessions cannot be used.) To say simply that "unreasonable searches under the Fourth Amendment are different from unwarned interrogation under the Fifth Amendment" is true but supremely unhelpful.

Finally, the Court asserts that *Miranda* must be a "constitutional decision" announcing a "constitutional rule," and thus immune to congressional modification, because we have since its inception applied it to the States. If this argument is meant as an invocation of *stare decisis*, it fails because, though it is true that our cases applying *Miranda* against the States must be reconsidered if *Miranda* is not required by the Constitution, it is likewise true that our cases (discussed above) based on the principle that *Miranda* is *not* required by the Constitution will have to be reconsidered if it *is*. So the *stare decisis* argument is a wash. If, on the other hand, the argument is meant as an appeal to logic rather than *stare decisis*, it is a classic example of begging the question: Congress's attempt to set aside *Miranda*, since it represents an assertion that violation of *Miranda* is not a violation of the Constitution, *also* represents an assertion that the Court has no power to impose *Miranda* on the States. To answer this assertion—not by showing why violation of *Miranda* *is* a violation of the Constitution—but by asserting that *Miranda* *does* apply against the States, is to assume precisely the point at issue. In my view, our continued application of the *Miranda* code to the States despite our consistent statements that running afoul of its dictates does not necessarily—or even usually—result in an actual constitutional violation, represents not the source of *Miranda*'s salvation but rather evidence of its ultimate illegitimacy.

■ ■ ■

But even were I to agree that the old totality-of-the-circumstances test was more cumbersome, it is simply not true that *Miranda* has banished it from the law and replaced it with a new test. Under the current regime, which the Court today retains in its entirety, courts are frequently called upon to undertake *both* inquiries. That is because, as explained earlier, voluntariness remains the *constitutional* standard, and as such continues to govern the admissibility for impeachment purposes of statements taken in violation of *Miranda*, the admissibility of the "fruits" of such statements, and the admissibility of statements challenged as unconstitutionally obtained *despite* the interrogator's compliance with *Miranda*, see, *e.g., Colorado v. Connelly* (1986).

Finally, I am not convinced by petitioner's argument that *Miranda* should be preserved because the decision occupies a special place in the "public's consciousness." As far as I am aware, the public is not under the illusion that we are infallible. I see little harm in admitting that we made a mistake in taking away from the people the ability to decide for themselves what protections (beyond those required by the Constitution) are reasonably afford-able in the criminal investigatory process. And I see much to be gained by reaffirming for the people the wonderful reality that they govern themselves— which means that "[t]he powers not delegated to the United States by the Constitution" that the people adopted, "nor prohibited . . . to the States" by that Constitution, "are reserved to the States respectively, or to the people," U.S. Const., Amdt. 10.

Today's judgment converts *Miranda* from a milestone of judicial overreach-ing into the very Cheops' Pyramid (or perhaps the Sphinx would be a better analogue) of judicial arrogance. In imposing its Court-made code upon the States, the original opinion at least *asserted* that it was demanded by the Con-stitution. Today's decision does not pretend that it is—and yet *still* asserts the right to impose it against the will of the people's representatives in Congress. Far from believing that *stare decisis* compels this result, I believe we cannot allow to remain on the books even a celebrated decision—*especially* a cele-brated decision—that has come to stand for the proposition that the Supreme Court has power to impose extraconstitutional constraints upon Congress and the States. This is not the system that was established by the Framers, or that would be established by any sane supporter of government by the people.

I dissent from today's decision, and, until § 3501 is repealed, will continue to apply it in all cases where there has been a sustainable finding that the defendant's confession was voluntary.

Reversed and remanded.

Chavez v. Martinez

538 U.S. 760 (2003)

THOMAS, J., announced the judgment of the Court and delivered an opinion, which was joined by REHNQUIST, C.J., in full, by O'CONNOR, J., as to Parts I and II-A, and by SCALIA, J., as to Parts I and II. SOUTER, J., delivered an opinion, Part II of which was for the Court and was joined by STEVENS, KENNEDY, GINSBURG, and BREYER, JJ., and Part I of which concurred in the judgment and was joined by BREYER, J. SCALIA, J., filed an opinion concurring in part in the judgment. STEVENS, J., filed an opinion concurring in part and dissenting in part. KENNEDY, J., filed an opinion concurring in part and dissenting in part, which was joined by STEVENS,

J., in full and by GINSBURG, J., as to Parts II and III. GINSBURG, J., filed an opinion concurring in part and dissenting in part.

charges

This case involves a 42 U.S.C. § 1983 suit arising out of petitioner Ben Chavez's allegedly coercive interrogation of respondent Oliverio Martinez. The United States Court of Appeals for the Ninth Circuit held that Chavez was not entitled to a defense of qualified immunity because he violated Martinez's clearly established constitutional rights. We conclude that Chavez did not deprive Martinez of a constitutional right.

I

Facts

On November 28, 1997, police officers Maria Peã and Andrew Salinas were near a vacant lot in a residential area of Oxnard, California, investigating suspected narcotics activity. While Peã and Salinas were questioning an individual, they heard a bicycle approaching on a darkened path that crossed the lot. They ordered the rider, respondent Martinez, to dismount, spread his legs, and place his hands behind his head. Martinez complied. Salinas then conducted a patdown frisk and discovered a knife in Martinez's waistband. An altercation ensued.

There is some dispute about what occurred during the altercation. The officers claim that Martinez drew Salinas' gun from its holster and pointed it at them; Martinez denies this. Both sides agree, however, that Salinas yelled, " 'He's got my gun!' " Peã then drew her gun and shot Martinez several times, causing severe injuries that left Martinez permanently blinded and paralyzed from the waist down. The officers then placed Martinez under arrest.

Petitioner showed up much later

Petitioner Chavez, a patrol supervisor, arrived on the scene minutes later with paramedics. Chavez accompanied Martinez to the hospital and then questioned Martinez there while he was receiving treatment from medical personnel. The interview lasted a total of about 10 minutes, over a 45-minute period, with Chavez leaving the emergency room for periods of time to permit medical personnel to attend to Martinez.

interview

At first, most of Martinez's answers consisted of "I don't know," "I am dying," and "I am choking." Later in the interview, Martinez admitted that he took the gun from the officer's holster and pointed it at the police. He also admitted that he used heroin regularly. At one point, Martinez said "I am not telling you anything until they treat me," yet Chavez continued the interview. At no point during the interview was Martinez given warnings under *Miranda v. Arizona* (1966).

Martinez was never charged with a crime, and his answers were never used against him in any criminal prosecution. Nevertheless, Martinez filed suit under 42 U.S.C. § 1983, maintaining that Chavez's actions violated his Fifth Amendment right not to be "compelled in any criminal case to be a witness against himself," as well as his Fourteenth Amendment substantive due process right to be free from coercive questioning. The District Court granted summary judgment to Martinez as to Chavez's qualified immunity defense on both the Fifth and Fourteenth Amendment claims. Chavez took an interlocutory appeal to the Ninth Circuit, which affirmed the District Court's denial of qualified immunity.

■ ■ ■

The Ninth Circuit then concluded that the Fifth and Fourteenth Amendment rights asserted by Martinez were clearly established by federal law, explaining that a reasonable officer "would have known that persistent interrogation of the suspect despite repeated requests to stop violated the suspect's Fifth and Fourteenth Amendment right to be free from coercive interrogation."

We granted certiorari.

II

In deciding whether an officer is entitled to qualified immunity, we must first determine whether the officer's alleged conduct violated a constitutional right. If not, the officer is entitled to qualified immunity, and we need not consider whether the asserted right was "clearly established." We conclude that Martinez's allegations fail to state a violation of his constitutional rights.

A

■ ■ ■

The Fifth Amendment, made applicable to the States by the Fourteenth Amendment, requires that "[n]o person . . . shall be compelled *in any criminal case* to be a *witness* against himself." U.S. Const., Amdt. 5 (emphases added). We fail to see how, based on the text of the Fifth Amendment, Martinez can allege a violation of this right, since Martinez was never prosecuted for a crime, let alone compelled to be a witness against himself in a criminal case.

Although Martinez contends that the meaning of "criminal case" should encompass the entire criminal investigatory process, including police interrogations, we disagree. In our view, a "criminal case" at the very least requires the initiation of legal proceedings. We need not decide today the precise moment when a "criminal case" commences; it is enough to say that police questioning does not constitute a "case" any more than a private investigator's precomplaint activities constitute a "civil case." Statements compelled by police interrogations of course may not be used against a defendant at trial, see *Brown v. Mississippi* (1936), but it is not until their use in a criminal case that a violation of the Self-Incrimination Clause occurs.

■ ■ ■

Here, Martinez was never made to be a "witness" against himself in violation of the Fifth Amendment's Self-Incrimination Clause because his statements were never admitted as testimony against him in a criminal case. Nor was he ever placed under oath and exposed to " 'the cruel trilemma of self-accusation, perjury or contempt.' " The text of the Self-Incrimination Clause simply cannot support the Ninth Circuit's view that the mere use of compulsive questioning, without more, violates the Constitution.

■ ■ ■

Our views on the proper scope of the Fifth Amendment's Self-Incrimination Clause do not mean that police torture or other abuse that results in a confession is constitutionally permissible so long as the statements are not used at trial; it simply means that the Fourteenth Amendment's Due Process Clause, rather than the Fifth Amendment's Self-Incrimination Clause, would govern the inquiry in those cases and provide relief in appropriate circumstances.

B

The Fourteenth Amendment provides that no person shall be deprived "of life, liberty, or property, without due process of law." Convictions based on evidence obtained by methods that are "so brutal and so offensive to human dignity" that they "shoc[k] the conscience" violate the Due Process Clause.

■ ■ ■

We are satisfied that Chavez's questioning did not violate Martinez's due process rights. Even assuming, *arguendo*, that the persistent questioning of Martinez somehow deprived him of a liberty interest, we cannot agree with Martinez's characterization of Chavez's behavior as "egregious" or "conscience shocking." [T]he official conduct "most likely to rise to the conscience-shocking level" is the "conduct intended to injure in some way unjustifiable by any government interest." Here, there is no evidence that Chavez acted with a purpose to harm Martinez by intentionally interfering with his medical treatment. Medical personnel were able to treat Martinez throughout the interview, and Chavez ceased his questioning to allow tests and other procedures to be performed. Nor is there evidence that Chavez's conduct exacerbated Martinez's injuries or prolonged his stay in the hospital. Moreover, the need to investigate whether there had been police misconduct constituted a justifiable government interest given the risk that key evidence would have been lost if Martinez had died without the authorities ever hearing his side of the story.

We conclude that Martinez has failed to allege a violation of the Fourteenth Amendment, and it is therefore unnecessary to inquire whether the right asserted by Martinez was clearly established.

III

Because Chavez did not violate Martinez's Fifth and Fourteenth Amendment rights, he was entitled to qualified immunity. The judgment of the Court of Appeals for the Ninth Circuit is therefore reversed, and the case is remanded for further proceedings.

It is so ordered.

Justice SOUTER delivered an opinion, Part II of which is the opinion of the Court and Part I of which is an opinion concurring in the judgment. Justice BREYER joins this opinion in its entirety. Justice STEVENS, Justice KENNEDY, and Justice GINSBURG join Part II of this opinion.

I

■ ■ ■

To recognize such a constitutional cause of action for compensation would, of course, be well outside the core of Fifth Amendment protection, but that alone is not a sufficient reason to reject Martinez's claim.

■ ■ ■

I do not, however, believe that Martinez can make the "powerful show-ing," subject to a realistic assessment of costs and risks, necessary to expand protection of the privilege against compelled self-incrimination to the point of the civil liability he asks us to recognize here. The most obvious drawback inherent in Martinez's purely Fifth Amendment claim to damages is its risk of global application in every instance of interrogation producing a statement inadmissible under Fifth and Fourteenth Amendment principles, or violating one of the complementary rules we have accepted in aid of the privilege against evidentiary use. If obtaining Martinez's statement is to be treated as a stand-alone violation of the privilege subject to compensation, why should the same not be true whenever the police obtain any involuntary self-incriminating statement, or whenever the government so much as threatens a penalty in derogation of the right to immunity, or whenever the police fail to honor *Miranda*? Martinez offers no limiting principle or reason to foresee a stopping place short of liability in all such cases.

Recognizing an action for damages in every such instance not only would revolutionize Fifth and Fourteenth Amendment law, but would beg the ques-tion that must inform every extension or recognition of a complementary rule in service of the core privilege: why is this new rule necessary in aid of the basic guarantee? Martinez has offered no reason to believe that the guarantee has been ineffective in all or many of those circumstances in which its vindication has depended on excluding testimonial admissions or barring penalties. And I have no reason to believe the law has been systemically defective in this respect.

But if there is no failure of efficacy infecting the existing body of Fifth Amendment law, any argument for a damages remedy in this case must depend not on its Fifth Amendment feature but upon the particular charge of outrageous conduct by the police, extending from their initial encounter with Martinez through the questioning by Chavez. That claim, however, if it is to be recognized as a constitutional one that may be raised in an action under §1983, must sound in substantive due process.

■ ■ ■

II

Whether Martinez may pursue a claim of liability for a substantive due process violation is thus an issue that should be addressed on remand, along with the scope and merits of any such action that may be found open to him.

■ ■ ■

Justice STEVENS, concurring in part and dissenting in part.

As a matter of fact, the interrogation of respondent was the functional equivalent of an attempt to obtain an involuntary confession from a prisoner by torturous methods. As a matter of law, that type of brutal police conduct constitutes an immediate deprivation of the prisoner's constitutionally protected interest in liberty. Because these propositions are so clear, the District Court and the Court of Appeals correctly held that petitioner is not entitled to qualified immunity.

What follows is an English translation of portions of the tape-recorded questioning in Spanish that occurred in the emergency room of the hospital when, as is evident from the text, both parties believed that respondent was about to die:

"*Chavez:* What happened? Olivero, tell me what happened.
O[liverio] M[artinez]: I don't know.
Chavez: I don't know what happened (sic)?
O. M.: Ay! I am dying. Ay! What are you doing to me? No,...! (unintelligible scream).
Chavez: What happened, sir?
O. M.: My foot hurts...
Chavez: Olivera. Sir, what happened?
O. M.: I am choking.
Chavez: Tell me what happened.
O. M.: I don't know.
Chavez: 'I don't know.'
O. M.: My leg hurts.
Chavez: I don't know what happened (sic)?
O. M.: It hurts...
Chavez: Hey, hey look.
O. M.: I am choking.
Chavez: Can you hear? Look listen, I am Benjamin Chavez with the police here in Oxnard, look.
O. M.: I am dying, please.
Chavez: OK, yes, tell me what happened. If you are going to die, tell me what happened. Look I need to tell (sic) what happened.
O. M.: I don't know.
Chavez: You don't know, I don't know what happened (sic)? Did you talk to the police?
O. M.: Yes.
Chavez: What happened with the police?
O. M.: We fought.
Chavez: Huh? What happened with the police?
O. M.: The police shot me.
Chavez: Why?
O. M.: Because I was fighting with him.
Chavez: Oh, why were you fighting with the police?

O. M.: I am dying . . .

Chavez: OK, yes you are dying, but tell me why you are fighting, were you fighting with the police?

O. M.: Doctor, please I want air, I am dying.

Chavez: OK, OK. I want to know if you pointed the gun [to yourself] at the police.

O. M.: Yes.

Chavez: Yes, and you pointed it [to yourself]? (sic) at the police pointed the gun? (sic) Huh?

O. M.: I am dying, please . . .

. . .

Chavez: OK, listen, listen I want to know what happened, ok?

O. M.: I want them to treat me.

Chavez: OK, they are do it (sic), look when you took out the gun from the tape (sic) of the police . . .

O. M.: I am dying . . .

Chavez: Ok, look, what I want to know if you took out (sic) the gun of the police?

O. M.: I am not telling you anything until they treat me.

Chavez: Look, tell me what happened, I want to know, look well don't you want the police know (sic) what happened with you?

O. M.: Uuuggghhh! my belly hurts . . .

. . .

Chavez: Nothing, why did you run (sic) from the police?

O. M.: I don't want to say anything anymore.

Chavez: No?

O. M.: I want them to treat me, it hurts a lot, please.

Chavez: You don't want to tell (sic) what happened with you over there?

O. M.: I don't want to die, I don't want to die.

Chavez: Well if you are going to die tell me what happened, and right now you think you are going to die?

O. M.: No.

Chavez: No, do you think you are going to die?

O. M.: Aren't you going to treat me or what?

Chavez: Look, think you are going to die, (sic) that's all I want to know, if you think you are going to die? Right now, do you think you are going to die?

O. M.: My belly hurts, please treat me.

Chavez: Sir?

O. M.: If you treat me I tell you everything, if not, no.

Chavez: Sir, I want to know if you think you are going to die right now?

O. M.: I think so.

Chavez: You think (sic) so? Ok. Look, the doctors are going to help you with all they can do, Ok? That they can do.

O. M.: Get moving, I am dying, can't you see me? Come on.

Chavez: Ah, huh, right now they are giving you medication."

The sound recording of this interrogation, which has been lodged with the Court, vividly demonstrates that respondent was suffering severe pain and mental anguish throughout petitioner's persistent questioning.

The Due Process Clause of the Fourteenth Amendment protects individuals against state action that either " 'shocks the conscience,' *Rochin v. California* (1952), or interferes with rights 'implicit in the concept of ordered liberty.' "

■ ■ ■

By its terms, the Fifth Amendment itself has no application to the States. It is, however, one source of the protections against state actions that deprive individuals of rights "implicit in the concept of ordered liberty" that the Fourteenth Amendment guarantees. Indeed, as I pointed out in my dissent in *Oregon v. Elstad* (1985), it is the most specific provision in the Bill of Rights "that protects all citizens from the kind of custodial interrogation that was once employed by the Star Chamber, by 'the Germans of the 1930's and early 1940's,' and by some of our own police departments only a few decades ago." Whenever it occurs, as it did here, official interrogation of that character is a classic example of a violation of a constitutional right "implicit in the concept of ordered liberty."

I respectfully dissent....

Justice KENNEDY, with whom Justice STEVENS joins, and with whom Justice GINSBURG joins as to Parts II and III, concurring in part and dissenting in part.

■ ■ ■

II

Justice Souter and Justice Thomas are wrong, in my view, to maintain that in all instances a violation of the Self-Incrimination Clause simply does not occur unless and until a statement is introduced at trial, no matter how severe the pain or how direct and commanding the official compulsion used to extract it.

■ ■ ■

Our cases and our legal tradition establish that the Self-Incrimination Clause is a substantive constraint on the conduct of the government, not merely an evidentiary rule governing the work of the courts. The Clause must provide more than mere assurance that a compelled statement will not be introduced against its declarant in a criminal trial. Otherwise there will be too little protection against the compulsion the Clause prohibits. The Clause protects an individual from being forced to give answers demanded by an official in any context when the answers might give rise to criminal liability in the future. "It can be asserted in any proceeding, civil or criminal, administrative or judicial, investigatory or adjudicatory; and it protects against any disclosures that the witness reasonably believes could be used in a criminal prosecution or could lead to other evidence that might be so used." The decision in *Kastigar* [*v. United States* (1972)] described the Self-Incrimination Clause as an exemption from the testimonial duty. As the duty is immediate, so must be the privilege. Furthermore, the exercise of the privilege depends on what the witness reasonably believes will be the future use of a statement. Again, this indicates the existence of a present right.

The Clause provides both assurance that a person will not be compelled to testify against himself in a criminal proceeding and a continuing right against government conduct intended to bring about self-incrimination.

■ ■ ■

III

There is no rule against interrogating suspects who are in anguish and pain. The police may have legitimate reasons, borne of exigency, to question a person who is suffering or in distress. Locating the victim of a kidnaping, ascertaining the whereabouts of a dangerous assailant or accomplice, or determining whether there is a rogue police officer at large are some examples. That a suspect is in fear of dying, furthermore, may not show compulsion but just the opposite. The fear may be a motivating factor to volunteer information. The words of a declarant who believes his death is imminent have a special status in the law of evidence. A declarant in Martinez's circumstances may want to tell his story even if it increases his pain and agony to do so. The Constitution does not forbid the police from offering a person an opportunity to volunteer evidence he wishes to reveal.

There are, however, actions police may not take if the prohibition against the use of coercion to elicit a statement is to be respected. The police may not prolong or increase a suspect's suffering against the suspect's will. That conduct would render government officials accountable for the increased pain. The officers must not give the impression that severe pain will be alleviated only if the declarant cooperates, for that, too, uses pain to extract a statement. In a case like this one, recovery should be available under § 1983 if a complainant can demonstrate that an officer exploited his pain and suffering with the purpose and intent of securing an incriminating statement. That showing has been made here.

The transcript of the interrogation set out by Justice Stevens (opinion concurring in part and dissenting in part), and other evidence considered by the District Court demonstrate that the suspect thought his treatment would be delayed, and thus his pain and condition worsened, by refusal to answer questions.

■ ■ ■

The standards governing the interrogation of suspects and witnesses who suffer severe pain must accommodate the exigencies that law enforcement personnel encounter in circumstances like this case. It is clear enough, however, that the police should take the necessary steps to ensure that there is neither the fact nor the perception that the declarant's pain is being used to induce the statement against his will. In this case no reasonable police officer would believe that the law permitted him to prolong or increase pain to obtain a statement. The record supports the ultimate finding that the officer acted with the intent of exploiting Martinez's condition for purposes of extracting a statement.

Accordingly, I would affirm the decision of the Court of Appeals that a cause of action under § 1983 has been stated. . . . I join Part II of Justice SOUTER's opinion and would remand the case for further consideration.

■ ■ ■

Missouri v. Seibert

542 U.S. 600 (2004)

SOUTER, J., announced the judgment of the Court and delivered an opinion, in which STEVENS, GINSBURG, and BREYER, JJ., joined. BREYER, J., filed a concurring opinion. KENNEDY, J., filed an opinion concurring in the judgment. O'CONNOR, J., filed a dissenting opinion, in which REHNQUIST, C.J., and SCALIA and THOMAS, JJ., joined.

This case tests a police protocol for custodial interrogation that calls for giving no warnings of the rights to silence and counsel until interrogation has produced a confession. Although such a statement is generally inadmissible, since taken in violation of *Miranda v. Arizona* (1966), the interrogating officer follows it with *Miranda* warnings and then leads the suspect to cover the same ground a second time. The question here is the admissibility of the repeated statement. Because this midstream recitation of warnings after interrogation and unwarned confession could not effectively comply with *Miranda's* constitutional requirement, we hold that a statement repeated after a warning in such circumstances is inadmissible.

I

Respondent Patrice Seibert's 12-year-old son Jonathan had cerebral palsy, and when he died in his sleep she feared charges of neglect because of bedsores on his body. In her presence, two of her teenage sons and two of their friends devised a plan to conceal the facts surrounding Jonathan's death by incinerating his body in the course of burning the family's mobile home, in which they planned to leave Donald Rector, a mentally ill teenager living with the family, to avoid any appearance that Jonathan had been unattended. Seibert's son Darian and a friend set the fire, and Donald died.

Five days later, the police awakened Seibert at 3 a.m. at a hospital where Darian was being treated for burns. In arresting her, Officer Kevin Clinton followed instructions from Rolla, Missouri, Officer Richard Hanrahan that he refrain from giving *Miranda* warnings. After Seibert had been taken to the police station and left alone in an interview room for 15 to 20 minutes, Officer Hanrahan questioned her without *Miranda* warnings for 30 to 40 minutes, squeezing her arm and repeating "Donald was also to die in his sleep." After Seibert finally admitted she knew Donald was meant to die in the fire, she was given a 20-minute coffee and cigarette break. Officer Hanrahan then turned on a tape recorder, gave Seibert the *Miranda* warnings, and obtained a signed waiver of rights from her. He resumed the questioning with "Ok, 'trice, we've been talking for a little while about what happened on Wednesday the twelfth, haven't we?" and confronted her with her prewarning statements:

Hanrahan: "Now, in discussion you told us, you told us that there was a[n] understanding about Donald."
Seibert: "Yes."
Hanrahan: "Did that take place earlier that morning?"
Seibert: "Yes."
Hanrahan: "And what was the understanding about Donald?"
Seibert: "If they could get him out of the trailer, to take him out of the trailer."
Hanrahan: "And if they couldn't?"
Seibert: "I, I never even thought about it. I just figured they would."
Hanrahan: 'Trice, didn't you tell me that he was supposed to die in his sleep?"
Seibert: "If that would happen, 'cause he was on that new medicine, you know...."
Hanrahan: "The Prozac? And it makes him sleepy. So he was supposed to die in his sleep?"
Seibert: "Yes."

■ ■ ■

The trial court suppressed the prewarning statement but admitted the responses given after the *Miranda* recitation. A jury convicted Seibert of second-degree murder. On appeal, the Missouri Court of Appeals affirmed, treating this case as indistinguishable from *Oregon v. Elstad* (1985).

The Supreme Court of Missouri reversed, holding that "[i]n the circumstances here, where the interrogation was nearly continuous, ... the second statement, clearly the product of the invalid first statement, should have been suppressed." The court distinguished *Elstad* on the ground that warnings had not intentionally been withheld there, and reasoned that "Officer Hanrahan's intentional omission of a *Miranda* warning was intended to deprive Seibert of the opportunity knowingly and intelligently to waive her *Miranda* rights." Since there were "no circumstances that would seem to dispel the effect of the *Miranda* violation," the court held that the postwarning confession was involuntary and therefore inadmissible. To allow the police to achieve an "end run" around *Miranda*, the court explained, would encourage *Miranda* violations and diminish *Miranda*'s role in protecting the privilege against self-incrimination.

■ ■ ■

We granted certiorari to resolve a split in the Courts of Appeals.... We now affirm.

■ ■ ■

"[T]o reduce the risk of a coerced confession and to implement the Self-Incrimination Clause," this Court in *Miranda* concluded that "the accused must be adequately and effectively apprised of his rights and the exercise of those rights must be fully honored." *Miranda* conditioned the admissibility at trial of any custodial confession on warning a suspect of his rights: failure to give the prescribed warnings and obtain a waiver of rights before custodial questioning generally requires exclusion of any statements obtained. Conversely, giving the warnings and getting a waiver has generally produced a virtual ticket of admissibility; maintaining that a statement is involuntary even though given after warnings and voluntary waiver of rights requires unusual stamina, and litigation over voluntariness tends to end with the finding of a valid waiver.

■ ■ ■

The technique of interrogating in successive, unwarned and warned phases raises a new challenge to *Miranda*. Although we have no statistics on the frequency of this practice, it is not confined to Rolla, Missouri. An officer of that police department testified that the strategy of withholding *Miranda* warnings until after interrogating and drawing out a confession was promoted not only by his own department, but by a national police training organization and other departments in which he had worked. Consistently with the officer's testimony, the Police Law Institute, for example, instructs that "officers may conduct a two-stage interrogation. . . . At any point during the pre-*Miranda* interrogation, usually after arrestees have confessed, officers may then read the *Miranda* warnings and ask for a waiver. If the arrestees waive their *Miranda* rights, officers will be able to repeat any *subsequent* incriminating statements later in court." The upshot of all this advice is a question-first practice of some popularity, as one can see from the reported cases describing its use, sometimes in obedience to departmental policy.

When a confession so obtained is offered and challenged, attention must be paid to the conflicting objects of *Miranda* and question-first. *Miranda* addressed "interrogation practices . . . likely . . . to disable [an individual] from making a free and rational choice" about speaking, and held that a suspect must be "adequately and effectively" advised of the choice the Constitution guarantees. The object of question-first is to render *Miranda* warnings ineffective by waiting for a particularly opportune time to give them, after the suspect has already confessed.

Just as "no talismanic incantation [is] required to satisfy [*Miranda*'s] strictures," it would be absurd to think that mere recitation of the litany suffices to satisfy *Miranda* in every conceivable circumstance. "The inquiry is simply whether the warnings reasonably 'conve[y] to [a suspect] his rights as required by *Miranda*.'" The threshold issue when interrogators question first and warn later is thus whether it would be reasonable to find that in these circumstances the warnings could function "effectively" as *Miranda* requires. Could the warnings effectively advise the suspect that he had a real choice about giving an admissible statement at that juncture? Could they reasonably convey that he could choose to stop talking even if he had talked earlier? For unless the warnings could place a suspect who has just been interrogated in a position to make such an informed choice, there is no practical justification for accepting the formal warnings as compliance with *Miranda*, or for treating the second stage of interrogation as distinct from the first, unwarned and inadmissible segment.

There is no doubt about the answer that proponents of question-first give to this question about the effectiveness of warnings given only after successful interrogation, and we think their answer is correct. By any objective measure, applied to circumstances exemplified here, it is likely that if the interrogators employ the technique of withholding warnings until after interrogation succeeds in eliciting a confession, the warnings will be ineffective in preparing the suspect for successive interrogation, close in time and similar in content. After all, the reason that question-first is catching on is as obvious as its manifest purpose, which is to get a confession the suspect would not make if he understood his rights at the outset; the sensible underlying assumption is that with one confession in hand before the warnings, the interrogator can count on getting its duplicate, with trifling additional trouble. Upon hearing warnings only in the aftermath of interrogation and just after making a confession, a suspect would hardly think he had a genuine right to remain silent, let alone persist in so believing once the police began to lead him over the same ground again. A more likely reaction on a suspect's part would be perplexity about the reason for discussing rights at that point, bewilderment being an unpromising frame of mind for knowledgeable decision. What is worse, telling a suspect that "anything you say can and will be used against you," without expressly excepting the statement just given, could lead to an entirely reasonable inference that what he has just said will be used, with subsequent silence being of no avail. Thus, when *Miranda* warnings are inserted in the midst of coordinated and continuing interrogation, they are likely to mislead and "depriv[e] a defendant of knowledge essential to his ability to understand the nature of his rights and the consequences of abandoning them."

■ ■ ■

Missouri argues that a confession repeated at the end of an interrogation sequence envisioned in a question-first strategy is admissible on the authority of *Oregon v. Elstad*, but the argument disfigures that case. In *Elstad*, the police went to the young suspect's house to take him into custody on a charge of burglary. Before the arrest, one officer spoke with the suspect's mother, while the other one joined the suspect in a "brief stop in the living room," where the officer said he "felt" the young man was involved in a burglary. . . . This Court noted that the pause in the living room "was not to interrogate the suspect but to notify his mother of the reason for his arrest," and described the incident as having "none of the earmarks of coercion." The Court, indeed, took care to mention that the officer's initial failure to warn was an "oversight" that "may have been the result of confusion as to whether the brief exchange qualified as 'custodial interrogation' or . . . may simply have reflected . . . reluctance to initiate an alarming police procedure before [an officer] had spoken with respondent's mother." At the outset of a later and systematic stationhouse interrogation going well beyond the scope of the laconic prior admission, the suspect was given *Miranda* warnings and made a full confession. In holding the second statement admissible and voluntary, *Elstad* rejected the "cat out of the bag" theory that any short, earlier admission, obtained in arguably innocent neglect of *Miranda*, determined the character of the later, warned confession; on the facts of that case, the Court thought any causal connection between the first and second responses to the police was "speculative and attenuated." Although the *Elstad* Court expressed no explicit conclusion about either officer's state of mind, it is fair to read *Elstad* as treating the living room conversation as a good-faith *Miranda* mistake, not only open to correction by careful warnings before systematic questioning in that particular case, but posing no threat to warn-first practice generally.

The contrast between *Elstad* and this case reveals a series of relevant facts that bear on whether *Miranda* warnings delivered midstream could be effective enough to accomplish their object: the completeness and detail of the questions and answers in the first round of interrogation, the overlapping content of the two statements, the timing and setting of the first and the second, the continuity of police personnel, and the degree to which the interrogator's questions treated the second round as continuous with the first. In *Elstad*, it was not unreasonable to see the occasion for questioning at the station house as presenting a markedly different experience from the short conversation at home; since a reasonable person in the suspect's shoes could have seen the station house questioning as a new and distinct experience, the *Miranda* warnings could have made sense as presenting a genuine choice whether to follow up on the earlier admission.

At the opposite extreme are the facts here, which by any objective measure reveal a police strategy adapted to undermine the *Miranda* warnings. The unwarned interrogation was conducted in the station house, and the questioning was systematic, exhaustive, and managed with psychological skill. When the police were finished there was little, if anything, of incriminating potential left unsaid. The warned phase of questioning proceeded after a pause of only 15 to 20 minutes, in the same place as the unwarned segment. When the same officer who had conducted the first phase recited the *Miranda* warnings, he said nothing to counter the probable misimpression that the advice that anything Seibert said could be used against her also applied to the details of the inculpatory statement previously elicited. In particular, the police did not advise that her prior statement could not be used. Nothing was said or done to dispel the oddity of warning about legal rights to silence and counsel right after the police had led her through a systematic interrogation, and any uncertainty on her part about a right to stop talking about matters previously discussed would only have been aggravated by the way Officer Hanrahan set the scene by saying "we've been talking for a little while about what happened on Wednesday the twelfth, haven't we?" The impression that the further questioning was a mere continuation of the earlier questions and responses was fostered by references back to the confession already given. It would have been reasonable to regard the two sessions as parts of a continuum, in which it would have been unnatural to refuse to repeat at the second stage what had been said before. These circumstances must be seen as challenging the comprehensibility and efficacy of the *Miranda* warnings to the point that a reasonable person in the suspect's shoes would not have understood them to convey a message that she retained a choice about continuing to talk.

Strategists dedicated to draining the substance out of *Miranda* cannot accomplish by training instructions what *Dickerson* [*v. United States* (2000)] held Congress could not do by statute. Because the question-first tactic effectively threatens to thwart *Miranda*'s purpose of reducing the risk that a coerced confession would be admitted, and because the facts here do not reasonably support a conclusion that the warnings given could have served their purpose, Seibert's postwarning statements are inadmissible. The judgment of the Supreme Court of Missouri is affirmed.

It is so ordered.

Justice BREYER, concurring.

In my view, the following simple rule should apply to the two-stage interrogation technique: Courts should exclude the "fruits" of the initial unwarned questioning unless the failure to warn was in good faith. I believe this is a sound and workable approach to the problem this case presents. Prosecutors and judges have long understood how to apply the "fruits" approach, which they use in other areas of law. See *Wong Sun v. United States* (1963). And in the workaday world of criminal law enforcement the administrative simplicity of the familiar has significant advantages over a more complex exclusionary rule.

■ ■ ■

I consequently join the plurality's opinion in full. I also agree with Justice Kennedy's opinion insofar as it is consistent with this approach and makes clear that a good-faith exception applies.

Justice KENNEDY, concurring in the judgment.

The interrogation technique used in this case is designed to circumvent *Miranda v. Arizona*. It undermines the *Miranda* warning and obscures its meaning. The plurality opinion is correct to conclude that statements obtained through the use of this technique are inadmissible. Although I agree with much in the careful and convincing opinion for the plurality, my approach does differ in some respects, requiring this separate statement.

The *Miranda* rule has become an important and accepted element of the criminal justice system. See *Dickerson v. United States*. At the same time, not every violation of the rule requires suppression of the evidence obtained. Evidence is admissible when the central concerns of *Miranda* are not likely to be implicated and when other objectives of the criminal justice system are best served by its introduction. Thus, we have held that statements obtained in violation of the rule can be used for impeachment, so that the truth-finding function of the trial is not distorted by the defense, that there is an exception to protect countervailing concerns of public safety, and that physical evidence obtained in reliance on statements taken in violation of the rule is admissible, see *United States v. Patane* (2004). These cases, in my view, are correct. They recognize that admission of evidence is proper when it would further important objectives without compromising *Miranda*'s central concerns. Under these precedents, the scope of the *Miranda* suppression remedy depends on a consideration of those legitimate interests and on whether admission of the evidence under the circumstances would frustrate *Miranda*'s central concerns and objectives.

Oregon v. Elstad reflects this approach. In *Elstad*, a suspect made an initial incriminating statement at his home. The suspect had not received a *Miranda* warning before making the statement, apparently because it was not clear whether the suspect was in custody at the time. The suspect was taken to the station house, where he received a proper warning, waived his *Miranda* rights, and made a second statement. He later argued that the postwarning statement should be suppressed because it was related to the unwarned first statement, and likely induced or caused by it. The Court held that, although a *Miranda* violation made the first statement inadmissible, the postwarning statements could be introduced against the accused because "neither the general goal of deterring improper police conduct nor the Fifth Amendment goal of assuring trustworthy evidence would be served by suppression" given the facts of that case.

In my view, *Elstad* was correct in its reasoning and its result. *Elstad* reflects a balanced and pragmatic approach to enforcement of the *Miranda* warning. An officer may not realize that a suspect is in custody and warnings are required. The officer may not plan to question the suspect or may be waiting for a more appropriate time. Skilled investigators often interview suspects multiple times, and good police work may involve referring to prior statements to test their veracity or to refresh recollection. In light of these realities it would be extravagant to treat the presence of one statement that cannot be admitted under *Miranda* as sufficient reason to prohibit subsequent statements preceded by a proper warning.

This case presents different considerations. The police used a two-step questioning technique based on a deliberate violation of *Miranda*. The *Miranda* warning was withheld to obscure both the practical and legal significance of the admonition when finally given. As Justice Souter points out, the two-step technique permits the accused to conclude that the right not to respond did not exist when the earlier incriminating statements were made. The strategy is based on the assumption that *Miranda* warnings will tend to mean less when recited midinterrogation, after inculpatory statements have already been obtained. This tactic relies on an intentional misrepresentation of the protection that *Miranda* offers and does not serve any legitimate objectives that might otherwise justify its use.

Further, the interrogating officer here relied on the defendant's prewarning statement to obtain the postwarning statement used against her at trial. The postwarning interview resembled a cross-examination. The officer confronted the defendant with her inadmissible prewarning statements and pushed her to acknowledge them. This shows the temptations for abuse inherent in the two-step technique. Reference to the prewarning statement was an implicit suggestion that the mere repetition of the earlier statement was not independently incriminating. The implicit suggestion was false.

The technique used in this case distorts the meaning of *Miranda* and furthers no legitimate countervailing interest. The *Miranda* rule would be frustrated were we to allow police to undermine its meaning and effect. The technique simply creates too high a risk that postwarning statements will be obtained when a suspect was deprived of "knowledge essential to his ability to understand the nature of his rights and the consequences of abandoning them." When an interrogator uses this deliberate, two-step strategy, predicated upon violating *Miranda* during an extended interview, postwarning statements that are related to the substance of prewarning statements must be excluded absent specific, curative steps.

The plurality concludes that whenever a two-stage interview occurs, admissibility of the postwarning statement should depend on "whether [the] *Miranda* warnings delivered midstream could have been effective enough to accomplish their object" given the specific facts of the case. This test envisions an objective inquiry from the perspective of the suspect, and applies in the case of both intentional and unintentional two-stage interrogations. In my view, this test cuts too broadly. *Miranda*'s clarity is one of its strengths, and a multifactor test that applies to every two-stage interrogation may serve to undermine that clarity. I would apply a narrower test applicable only in the infrequent case, such as we have here, in which the two-step interrogation technique was used in a calculated way to undermine the *Miranda* warning.

The admissibility of postwarning statements should continue to be governed by the principles of *Elstad* unless the deliberate two-step strategy was employed. If the deliberate two-step strategy has been used, postwarning statements that are related to the substance of prewarning statements must be excluded unless curative measures are taken before the postwarning statement is made. Curative measures should be designed to ensure that a reasonable person in the suspect's situation would understand the import and effect of the *Miranda* warning and of the *Miranda* waiver. For example, a substantial break in time and circumstances between the prewarning statement and the *Miranda* warning may suffice in most circumstances, as it allows the accused to distinguish the two contexts and appreciate that the interrogation has taken a new turn. Alternatively, an additional warning that explains the likely inadmissibility of the prewarning custodial statement may be sufficient. No curative steps were taken in this case, however, so the postwarning statements are inadmissible and the conviction cannot stand.

For these reasons, I concur in the judgment of the Court.

Justice O'CONNOR, with whom Chief Justice REHNQUIST, Justice SCALIA, and Justice THOMAS join, dissenting.

bound by Elstad

The plurality devours *Oregon v. Elstad*, even as it accuses petitioner's argument of "disfigur[ing]" that decision. I believe that we are bound by *Elstad* to reach a different result, and I would vacate the judgment of the Supreme Court of Missouri.

On two preliminary questions I am in full agreement with the plurality. First, the plurality appropriately follows *Elstad* in concluding that Seibert's statement cannot be held inadmissible under a "fruit of the poisonous tree" theory. Second, the plurality correctly declines to focus its analysis on the subjective intent of the interrogating officer.

This Court has made clear that there simply is no place for a robust deterrence doctrine with regard to violations of *Miranda v. Arizona*. See *Dickerson v. United States*.

■ ■ ■

The plurality's rejection of an intent-based test is also, in my view, correct. Freedom from compulsion lies at the heart of the Fifth Amendment, and requires us to assess whether a suspect's decision to speak truly was voluntary. Because voluntariness is a matter of the suspect's state of mind, we focus our analysis on the way in which suspects experience interrogation.

■ ■ ■

Because the isolated fact of Officer Hanrahan's intent could not have had any bearing on Seibert's "capacity to comprehend and knowingly relinquish" her right to remain silent, it could not by itself affect the voluntariness of her confession. Moreover, recognizing an exception to *Elstad* for intentional violations would require focusing constitutional analysis on a police officer's subjective intent, an unattractive proposition that we all but uniformly avoid. In general, "we believe that 'sending state and federal courts on an expedition into the minds of police officers would produce a grave and fruitless misallocation of judicial resources.'" *United States v. Leon* (1984). . . . This case presents the uncommonly straightforward circumstance of an officer openly admitting that the violation was intentional. But the inquiry will be complicated in other situations probably more likely to occur. For example, different officers involved in an interrogation might claim different states of mind regarding the failure to give *Miranda* warnings. Even in the simple case of a single officer who claims that a failure to give *Miranda* warnings was inadvertent, the likelihood of error will be high.

These evidentiary difficulties have led us to reject an intent-based test in several criminal procedure contexts. For example, in *New York v. Quarles*, one of the factors that led us to reject an inquiry into the subjective intent of the police officer in crafting a test for the "public safety" exception to *Miranda* was that officers' motives will be "largely unverifiable." Similarly, our opinion in *Whren v. United States* (1996) made clear that "the evidentiary difficulty of establishing subjective intent" was one of the reasons (albeit not the principal one) for refusing to consider intent in Fourth Amendment challenges generally.

For these reasons, I believe that the approach espoused by Justice Kennedy is ill advised. Justice Kennedy would extend *Miranda*'s exclusionary rule to any case in which the use of the "two-step interrogation technique" was "deliberate" or "calculated." This approach untethers the analysis from facts knowable to, and therefore having any potential directly to affect, the suspect. Far from promoting "clarity," the approach will add a third step to the suppression inquiry. In virtually every two-stage interrogation case, in addition to addressing the standard *Miranda* and voluntariness questions, courts will be forced to conduct the kind of difficult, state-of-mind inquiry that we normally take pains to avoid.

The plurality's adherence to *Elstad*, and mine to the plurality, end there. Our decision in *Elstad* rejected two lines of argument advanced in favor of suppression. The first was based on the "fruit of the poisonous tree" doctrine, discussed above. The second was the argument that the "lingering compulsion" inherent in a defendant's having let the "cat out of the bag" required suppression.

■ ■ ■

I would analyze the two-step interrogation procedure under the voluntariness standards central to the Fifth Amendment and reiterated in *Elstad*. *Elstad* commands that if Seibert's first statement is shown to have been involuntary, the court must examine whether the taint dissipated through the passing of time or a change in circumstances: "When a prior statement is actually coerced, the time that passes between confessions, the change in place of interrogations, and the change in identity of the interrogators all bear on whether that coercion has carried over into the second confession." In addition, Seibert's second statement should be suppressed if she showed that it was involuntary despite the *Miranda* warnings. *Elstad* ("The relevant inquiry is whether, in fact, the second statement was also voluntarily made. As in any such inquiry, the finder of fact must examine the surrounding circumstances and the entire course of police conduct with respect to the suspect in evaluating the voluntariness of his statements"). Although I would leave this analysis for the Missouri courts to conduct on remand, I note that, unlike the officers in *Elstad*, Officer Hanrahan referred to Seibert's unwarned statement during the second part of the interrogation when she made a statement at odds with her unwarned confession.

■ ■ ■

Because I believe that the plurality gives insufficient deference to *Elstad* and that Justice Kennedy places improper weight on subjective intent, I respectfully dissent.

United States v. Patane

542 U.S. 630 (2004)

THOMAS, J., announced the judgment of the Court and delivered an opinion, in which REHNQUIST, C.J., and SCALIA, J., joined. KENNEDY, J., filed an opinion concurring in the judgment, in which O'CONNOR, J., joined. SOUTER, J., filed a dissenting opinion, in which Stevens and Ginsburg, JJ., joined. Breyer, J., filed a dissenting opinion.

In this case we must decide whether a failure to give a suspect the warnings prescribed by *Miranda v. Arizona* (1966) requires suppression of the physical fruits of the suspect's unwarned but voluntary statements. The Court has previously addressed this question but has not reached a definitive conclusion.

■ ■ ■

In June 2001, respondent, Samuel Francis Patane, was arrested for harassing his ex-girlfriend, Linda O'Donnell. He was released on bond, subject to a temporary restraining order that prohibited him from contacting O'Donnell. Respondent apparently violated the restraining order by attempting to telephone O'Donnell. On June 6, 2001, Officer Tracy Fox of the Colorado Springs Police Department began to investigate the matter. On the same day, a county probation officer informed an agent of the Bureau of Alcohol, Tobacco and Firearms (ATF), that respondent, a convicted felon, illegally possessed a .40 Glock pistol. The ATF relayed this information to Detective Josh Benner, who worked closely with the ATF. Together, Detective Benner and Officer Fox proceeded to respondent's residence.

After reaching the residence and inquiring into respondent's attempts to contact O'Donnell, Officer Fox arrested respondent for violating the restraining order. Detective Benner attempted to advise respondent of his *Miranda* rights but got no further than the right to remain silent. At that point, respondent interrupted, asserting that he knew his rights, and neither officer attempted to complete the warning.

Detective Benner then asked respondent about the Glock. Respondent was initially reluctant to discuss the matter, stating: "I am not sure I should tell you anything about the Glock because I don't want you to take it away from me." Detective Benner persisted, and respondent told him that the pistol was in his bedroom. Respondent then gave Detective Benner permission to retrieve the pistol. Detective Benner found the pistol and seized it.

. . . The District Court granted respondent's motion to suppress the firearm, reasoning that the officers lacked probable cause to arrest respondent for violating the restraining order. It therefore declined to rule on respondent's alternative argument that the gun should be suppressed as the fruit of an unwarned statement.

The Court of Appeals reversed the District Court's ruling with respect to probable cause but affirmed the suppression order on respondent's alternative theory. The court rejected the Government's argument that this Court's decisions in [*Oregon v.*] *Elstad* [(1985)] and [*Michigan v.*] *Tucker* [(1974)] foreclosed application of the fruit of the poisonous tree doctrine of *Wong Sun v. United States* (1963) to the present context.

■ ■ ■

As we explain below, the *Miranda* rule is a prophylactic employed to protect against violations of the Self-Incrimination Clause. The Self-Incrimination Clause, however, is not implicated by the admission into evidence of the physical fruit of a voluntary statement. Accordingly, there is no justification for extending the *Miranda* rule to this context. And just as the Self-Incrimination Clause primarily focuses on the criminal trial, so too does the *Miranda* rule. The *Miranda* rule is not a code of police conduct, and police do not violate the Constitution (or even the *Miranda* rule, for that matter) by mere failures to warn. For this reason, the exclusionary rule articulated in cases such as *Wong Sun* does not apply. Accordingly, we reverse the judgment of the Court of Appeals and remand the case for further proceedings.

The Self-Incrimination Clause provides: "No person . . . shall be compelled in any criminal case to be a witness against himself." U.S. Const., Amdt. 5. We need not decide here the precise boundaries of the Clause's protection. For present purposes, it suffices to note that the core protection afforded by the Self-Incrimination Clause is a prohibition on compelling a criminal defendant to testify against himself at trial. See, *e.g.*, *Chavez v. Martinez* (2003) (plurality opinion).

■ ■ ■

Similarly, in *Miranda*, the Court concluded that the possibility of coercion inherent in custodial interrogations unacceptably raises the risk that a suspect's privilege against self-incrimination might be violated. To protect against this danger, the *Miranda* rule creates a presumption of coercion, in the absence of specific warnings, that is generally irrebuttable for purposes of the prosecution's case in chief.

But because these prophylactic rules (including the *Miranda* rule) necessarily sweep beyond the actual protections of the Self-Incrimination Clause, any further extension of these rules must be justified by its necessity for the protection of the actual right against compelled self-incrimination. . . . Indeed, at times the Court has declined to extend *Miranda* even where it has perceived a need to protect the privilege against self-incrimination.

■ ■ ■

Furthermore, the Self-Incrimination Clause contains its own exclusionary rule. It provides that "[n]o person . . . shall be compelled in any criminal case to be a witness against himself." Amdt. 5. Unlike the Fourth Amendment's bar on unreasonable searches, the Self-Incrimination Clause is self-executing. We have repeatedly explained "that those subjected to coercive police interrogations have an *automatic* protection from the use of their involuntary statements (or evidence derived from their statements) in any subsequent criminal trial." . . .

Finally, nothing in *Dickerson* [*v. United States* (2000)], including its characterization of *Miranda* as announcing a constitutional rule, changes any of these observations. Indeed, in *Dickerson*, the Court specifically noted that the Court's "subsequent cases have reduced the impact of the *Miranda* rule on legitimate law enforcement while reaffirming [*Miranda*]'s core ruling that unwarned statements may not be used as evidence in the prosecution's case in chief." This description of *Miranda*, especially the emphasis on the use of "unwarned statements . . . in the prosecution's case in chief," makes clear our continued focus on the protections of the Self-Incrimination Clause. The Court's reliance on our *Miranda* precedents, including both *Tucker* and *Elstad*, further demonstrates the continuing validity of those decisions. In short, nothing in *Dickerson* calls into question our continued insistence that the closest possible fit be maintained between the Self-Incrimination Clause and any rule designed to protect it.)

■ ■ ■

But *Dickerson*'s characterization of *Miranda* as a constitutional rule does not lessen the need to maintain the closest possible fit between the Self-Incrimination Clause and any judge-made rule designed to protect it. And there is no such fit here. Introduction of the nontestimonial fruit of a voluntary statement, such as respondent's Glock, does not implicate the Self-Incrimination Clause. The admission of such fruit presents no risk that a defendant's coerced statements (however defined) will be used against him at a criminal trial. In any case, "[t]he exclusion of unwarned statements . . . is a complete and sufficient remedy" for any perceived *Miranda* violation.

■ ■ ■

Similarly, because police cannot violate the Self-Incrimination Clause by taking unwarned though voluntary statements, an exclusionary rule cannot be justified by reference to a deterrence effect on law enforcement, as the Court of Appeals believed. Our decision not to apply *Wong Sun* to mere failures to give *Miranda* warnings was sound at the time *Tucker* and *Elstad* were decided, and we decline to apply *Wong Sun* to such failures now.

■ ■ ■

Accordingly, we reverse the judgment of the Court of Appeals and remand the case for further proceedings.

It is so ordered.

Justice KENNEDY, with whom Justice O'CONNOR joins, concurring in the judgment.

In *Oregon v. Elstad* . . . evidence obtained following an unwarned interrogation was held admissible. This result was based in large part on our recognition that the concerns underlying the *Miranda v. Arizona* rule must be accommodated to other objectives of the criminal justice system. I agree with the plurality that *Dickerson v. United States* did not undermine these precedents and, in fact, cited them in support. Here, it is sufficient to note that the Government presents an even stronger case for admitting the evidence obtained as the result of Patane's unwarned statement. Admission of nontestimonial physical fruits (the Glock in this case), even more so than the postwarning statements to the police in *Elstad* and *Michigan v. Tucker*, does not run the risk of admitting into trial an accused's coerced incriminating statements against himself. In light of the important probative value of reliable physical evidence, it is doubtful that exclusion can be justified by a deterrence rationale sensitive to both law enforcement interests and a suspect's rights during an in-custody interrogation. Unlike the plurality, however, I find it unnecessary to decide whether the detective's failure to give Patane the full *Miranda* warnings should be characterized as a violation of the *Miranda* rule itself, or whether there is "[any]thing to deter" so long as the unwarned statements are not later introduced at trial.

With these observations, I concur in the judgment of the Court.

Justice SOUTER, with whom Justice STEVENS and Justice GINSBURG join, dissenting.

The plurality repeatedly says that the Fifth Amendment does not address the admissibility of nontestimonial evidence, an overstatement that is beside the point. The issue actually presented today is whether courts should apply the fruit of the poisonous tree doctrine lest we create an incentive for the police to omit *Miranda* warnings before custodial interrogation. In closing their eyes to the consequences of giving an evidentiary advantage to those who ignore *Miranda*, the plurality adds an important inducement for interrogators to ignore the rule in that case.

Miranda rested on insight into the inherently coercive character of custodial interrogation and the inherently difficult exercise of assessing the voluntariness of any confession resulting from it. Unless the police give the prescribed warnings meant to counter the coercive atmosphere, a custodial confession is inadmissible, there being no need for the previous time-consuming and difficult enquiry into voluntariness. That inducement to forestall involuntary statements and troublesome issues of fact can only atrophy if we turn around and recognize an evidentiary benefit when an unwarned statement leads investigators to tangible evidence. There is, of course, a price for excluding evidence, but the Fifth Amendment is worth a price, and in the absence of a very good reason, the logic of *Miranda* should be followed: a *Miranda* violation raises a presumption of coercion, and the Fifth Amendment privilege against compelled self-incrimination extends to the exclusion of derivative evidence.

■ ■ ■

The fact that the books contain some exceptions to the *Miranda* exclusionary rule carries no weight here. In *Harris v. New York* (1971), it was respect for the integrity of the judicial process that justified the admission of unwarned statements as impeachment evidence. But Patane's suppression motion can hardly be described as seeking to "perver[t]" *Miranda* "into a license to use perjury" or otherwise handicap the "traditional truth-testing devices of the adversary process." Nor is there any suggestion that the officers' failure to warn Patane was justified or mitigated by a public emergency or other exigent circumstance, as in *New York v. Quarles* (1984). And of course the premise of *Oregon v. Elstad* is not on point; although a failure to give *Miranda* warnings before one individual statement does not necessarily bar the admission of a subsequent statement given after adequate warnings, that rule obviously does not apply to physical evidence seized once and for all.

■ ■ ■

There is no way to read this case except as an unjustifiable invitation to law enforcement officers to flout *Miranda* when there may be physical evidence to be gained. The incentive is an odd one, coming from the Court on the same day it decides *Missouri v. Seibert* (2004). I respectfully dissent.

Justice BREYER, dissenting.

For reasons similar to those set forth in Justice SOUTER's dissent and in my concurring opinion in *Missouri v. Seibert*, I would extend to this context the "fruit of the poisonous tree" approach, which I believe the Court has come close to adopting in *Seibert*. Under that approach, courts would exclude physical evidence derived from unwarned questioning unless the failure to provide *Miranda v. Arizona* warnings was in good faith. Because the courts below made no explicit finding as to good or bad faith, I would remand for such a determination.

D. SIXTH AMENDMENT

1. Mechanism to Analyze Interrogation

Massiah v. United States

377 U.S. 201 (1964)

See section B of this chapter.

Brewer v. Williams

430 U.S. 387 (1977)

See also Nix v. Williams *(1984), Chapter 1.F, in which the Supreme Court upheld Williams' conviction on his second appeal.*

STEWART, J., delivered the opinion of the Court, in which BRENNAN, J., joined. MARSHALL, POWELL, and STEVENS, JJ., filed concurring opinions. BURGER, C.J., filed a dissenting opinion. WHITE, J., filed a dissenting opinion, in which BLACKMUN and REHNQUIST, JJ., joined. BLACKMUN, J., filed a dissenting opinion, in which WHITE and REHNQUIST, JJ., joined.

On the afternoon of December 24, 1968, a 10-year-old girl named Pamela Powers went with her family to the YMCA in Des Moines, Iowa, to watch a wrestling tournament in which her brother was participating. When she failed to return from a trip to the washroom, a search for her began. The search was unsuccessful.

Robert Williams, who had recently escaped from a mental hospital, was a resident of the YMCA. Soon after the girl's disappearance Williams was seen in the YMCA lobby carrying some clothing and a large bundle wrapped in a blanket. He obtained help from a 14-year-old boy in opening the street door of the YMCA and the door to his automobile parked outside. When Williams placed the bundle in the front seat of his car the boy "saw two legs in it and they were skinny and white." Before anyone could see what was in the bundle Williams drove away. His abandoned car was found the following day in Davenport, Iowa, roughly 160 miles east of Des Moines. A warrant was then issued in Des Moines for his arrest on a charge of abduction.

On the morning of December 26, a Des Moines lawyer named Henry McKnight went to the Des Moines police station and informed the officers present that he had just received a long-distance call from Williams, and that he had advised Williams to turn himself in to the Davenport police. Williams did surrender that morning to the police in Davenport, and they booked him on the charge specified in the arrest warrant and gave him the warnings required by *Miranda v. Arizona*. The Davenport police then telephoned their counterparts in Des Moines to inform them that Williams had surrendered. McKnight, the lawyer, was still at the Des Moines police headquarters, and Williams conversed with McKnight on the telephone. In the presence of the Des Moines chief of police and a police detective named Leaming, McKnight advised Williams that Des Moines police officers would be driving to Davenport to pick him up, that the officers would not interrogate him or mistreat him, and that Williams was not to talk to the officers about Pamela Powers until after consulting with McKnight upon his return to Des Moines. As a result of these conversations, it was agreed between McKnight and the Des Moines police officials that Detective Leaming and a fellow officer would drive to Davenport to pick up Williams, that they would bring him directly back to Des Moines, and that they would not question him during the trip.

In the meantime Williams was arraigned before a judge in Davenport on the outstanding arrest warrant. The judge advised him of his *Miranda* rights and committed him to jail. Before leaving the courtroom, Williams conferred with a lawyer named Kelly, who advised him not to make any statements until consulting with McKnight back in Des Moines.

Detective Leaming and his fellow officer arrived in Davenport about noon to pick up Williams and return him to Des Moines. Soon after their arrival they met with Williams and Kelly, who, they understood, was acting as Williams' lawyer. Detective Leaming repeated the *Miranda* warnings, and told Williams:

> "[W]e both know that you're being represented here by Mr. Kelly and you're being represented by Mr. McKnight in Des Moines, and . . . I want you to remember this because we'll be visiting between here and Des Moines."

Williams then conferred again with Kelly alone, and after this conference Kelly reiterated to Detective Leaming that Williams was not to be questioned about the disappearance of Pamela Powers until after he had consulted with

McKnight back in Des Moines. When Leaming expressed some reservations, Kelly firmly stated that the agreement with McKnight was to be carried out that there was to be no interrogation of Williams during the automobile journey to Des Moines. Kelly was denied permission to ride in the police car back to Des Moines with Williams and the two officers.

The two detectives, with Williams in their charge, then set out on the 160-mile drive. At no time during the trip did Williams express a willingness to be interrogated in the absence of an attorney. Instead, he stated several times that "[w]hen I get to Des Moines and see Mr. McKnight, I am going to tell you the whole story." Detective Leaming knew that Williams was a former mental patient, and knew also that he was deeply religious.

The detective and his prisoner soon embarked on a wide-ranging conversation covering a variety of topics, including the subject of religion. Then, not long after leaving Davenport and reaching the interstate highway, Detective Leaming delivered what has been referred to in the briefs and oral arguments as the "Christian burial speech." Addressing Williams as "Reverend," the detective said:

> "I want to give you something to think about while we're traveling down the road.... Number one, I want you to observe the weather conditions, it's raining, it's sleeting, it's freezing, driving is very treacherous, visibility is poor, it's going to be dark early this evening. They are predicting several inches of snow for tonight, and I feel that you yourself are the only person that knows where this little girl's body is, that you yourself have only been there once, and if you get a snow on top of it you yourself may be unable to find it. And, since we will be going right past the area on the way into Des Moines, I feel that we could stop and locate the body, that the parents of this little girl should be entitled to a Christian burial for the little girl who was snatched away from them on Christmas [E]ve and murdered. And I feel we should stop and locate it on the way in rather than waiting until morning and trying to come back out after a snow storm and possibly not being able to find it at all."

Williams asked Detective Leaming why he thought their route to Des Moines would be taking them past the girl's body, and Leaming responded that he knew the body was in the area of Mitchellville, a town they would be passing on the way to Des Moines. Leaming then stated: "I do not want you to answer me. I don't want to discuss it any further. Just think about it as we're riding down the road."

As the car approached Grinnell, a town approximately 100 miles west of Davenport, Williams asked whether the police had found the victim's shoes. When Detective Leaming replied that he was unsure, Williams directed the officers to a service station where he said he had left the shoes; a search for them proved unsuccessful. As they continued towards Des Moines, Williams asked whether the police had found the blanket, and directed the officers to a rest area where he said he had disposed of the blanket. Nothing was found. The car continued towards Des Moines, and as it approached Mitchellville,

Williams said that he would show the officers where the body was. He then directed the police to the body of Pamela Powers.

Williams was indicted for first-degree murder. Before trial, his counsel moved to suppress all evidence relating to or resulting from any statements Williams had made during the automobile ride from Davenport to Des Moines. After an evidentiary hearing the trial judge denied the motion. He found that "an agreement was made between defense counsel and the police officials to the effect that the Defendant was not to be questioned on the return trip to Des Moines," and that the evidence in question had been elicited from Williams during "a critical stage in the proceedings requiring the presence of counsel on his request." The judge ruled, however, that Williams had "waived his right to have an attorney present during the giving of such information."

■ ■ ■

Specifically, there is no need to review in this case the doctrine of *Miranda v. Arizona* [(1966)], a doctrine designed to secure the constitutional privilege against compulsory self-incrimination. It is equally unnecessary to evaluate the ruling of the District Court that Williams' self-incriminating statements were, indeed, involuntarily made. For it is clear that the judgment before us must in any event be affirmed upon the ground that Williams was deprived of a different constitutional right—the right to the assistance of counsel.

This right, guaranteed by the Sixth and Fourteenth Amendments, is indispensable to the fair administration of our adversary system of criminal justice. Its vital need at the pretrial stage has perhaps nowhere been more succinctly explained than in Mr. Justice Sutherland's memorable words for the Court 44 years ago in *Powell v. Alabama* [(1932)]:

> "[D]uring perhaps the most critical period of the proceedings against these defendants, that is to say, from the time of their arraignment until the beginning of their trial, when consultation, thorough-going investigation and preparation were vitally important, the defendants did not have the aid of counsel in any real sense, although they were as much entitled to such aid during that period as at the trial itself."

There has occasionally been a difference of opinion within the Court as to the peripheral scope of this constitutional right.... But its basic contours, which are identical in state and federal contexts, are too well established to require extensive elaboration here. Whatever else it may mean, the right to counsel granted by the Sixth and Fourteenth Amendments means at least that a person is entitled to the help of a lawyer at or after the time that judicial proceedings have been initiated against him "whether by way of formal charge, preliminary hearing, indictment, information, or arraignment."

■ ■ ■

There can be no doubt in the present case that judicial proceedings had been initiated against Williams before the start of the automobile ride from Davenport to Des Moines. A warrant had been issued for his arrest, he had been arraigned on that warrant before a judge in a Davenport courtroom, and he had been committed by the court to confinement in jail. The State does not contend otherwise.

There can be no serious doubt, either, that Detective Leaming deliberately and designedly set out to elicit information from Williams just as surely as and perhaps more effectively than if he had formally interrogated him. Detective Leaming was fully aware before departing for Des Moines that Williams was being represented in Davenport by Kelly and in Des Moines by McKnight. Yet he purposely sought during Williams' isolation from his lawyers to obtain as much incriminating information as possible. Indeed, Detective Leaming conceded as much when he testified at Williams' trial:

> "Q. In fact, Captain, whether he was a mental patient or not, you were trying to get all the information you could before he got to his lawyer, weren't you?
> A. I was sure hoping to find out where that little girl was, yes, sir.
> Q. Well, I'll put it this way: You was [sic] hoping to get all the information you could before Williams got back to McKnight, weren't you?
> A. Yes, sir."

■ ■ ■

The circumstances of this case are thus constitutionally indistinguishable from those presented in *Massiah v. United States* [(1964)]. The petitioner in that case was indicted for violating the federal narcotics law. He retained a lawyer, pleaded not guilty, and was released on bail. While he was free on bail a federal agent succeeded by surreptitious means in listening to incriminating statements made by him. Evidence of these statements was introduced against the petitioner at his trial, and he was convicted. This Court reversed the conviction, holding "that the petitioner was denied the basic protections of that guarantee [the right to counsel] when there was used against him at his trial evidence of his own incriminating words, which federal agents had deliberately elicited from him after he had been indicted and in the absence of his counsel."

That the incriminating statements were elicited surreptitiously in the *Massiah* case, and otherwise here, is constitutionally irrelevant. Rather, the clear rule of *Massiah* is that once adversary proceedings have commenced against an individual, he has a right to legal representation when the government interrogates him. It thus requires no wooden or technical application of the *Massiah* doctrine to conclude that Williams was entitled to the assistance of counsel guaranteed to him by the Sixth and Fourteenth Amendments.

The Iowa courts recognized that Williams had been denied the constitutional right to the assistance of counsel. They held, however, that he had waived that right during the course of the automobile trip from Davenport to Des Moines. The state trial court explained its determination of waiver as follows:

waiver (7)

> "The time element involved on the trip, the general circumstances of it, and more importantly the absence on the Defendant's part of any assertion of his

right or desire not to give information absent the presence of his attorney, are the main foundations for the Court's conclusion that he voluntarily waived such right."

In its lengthy opinion affirming this determination, the Iowa Supreme Court applied "the totality-of-circumstances test for a showing of waiver of constitutionally-protected rights in the absence of an express waiver," and concluded that "evidence of the time element involved on the trip, the general circumstances of it, and the absence of any request or expressed desire for the aid of counsel before or at the time of giving information, were sufficient to sustain a conclusion that defendant did waive his constitutional rights as alleged."

■ ■ ■

The District Court and the Court of Appeals were correct in the view that the question of waiver was not a question of historical fact, but one which, in the words of Mr. Justice Frankfurter, requires "application of constitutional principles to the facts as found...."

The District Court and the Court of Appeals were also correct in their understanding of the proper standard to be applied in determining the question of waiver as a matter of federal constitutional law—that it was incumbent upon the State to prove "an intentional relinquishment or abandonment of a known right or privilege." That standard has been reiterated in many cases. We have said that the right to counsel does not depend upon a request by the defendant.... This strict standard applies equally to an alleged waiver of the right to counsel whether at trial or at a critical stage of pretrial proceedings.

We conclude, finally, that the Court of Appeals was correct in holding that, judged by these standards, the record in this case falls far short of sustaining petitioner's burden. It is true that Williams had been informed of and appeared to understand his right to counsel. But waiver requires not merely comprehension but relinquishment, and Williams' consistent reliance upon the advice of counsel in dealing with the authorities refutes any suggestion that he waived that right. He consulted McKnight by long-distance telephone before turning himself in. He spoke with McKnight by telephone again shortly after being booked. After he was arraigned, Williams sought out and obtained legal advice from Kelly. Williams again consulted with Kelly after Detective Leaming and his fellow officer arrived in Davenport. Throughout, Williams was advised not to make any statements before seeing McKnight in Des Moines, and was assured that the police had agreed not to question him. His statements while in the car that he would tell the whole story after seeing McKnight in Des Moines were the clearest expressions by Williams himself that he desired the presence of an attorney before any interrogation took place. But even before making these statements, Williams had effectively asserted his right to counsel by having secured attorneys at both ends of the automobile trip, both of whom, acting as his agents, had made clear to the police that no interrogation was to occur during the journey. Williams knew of that agreement and, particularly in view of his consistent reliance on counsel, there is no basis for concluding that he disavowed it.

Despite Williams' express and implicit assertions of his right to counsel, Detective Leaming proceeded to elicit incriminating statements from Williams. Leaming did not preface this effort by telling Williams that he had a right to the presence of a lawyer, and made no effort at all to ascertain whether Williams wished to relinquish that right. The circumstances of record in this case thus provide no reasonable basis for finding that Williams waived his right to the assistance of counsel.

The Court of Appeals did not hold, nor do we, that under the circumstances of this case Williams could not, without notice to counsel, have waived his rights under the Sixth and Fourteenth Amendments. It only held, as do we, that he did not.

■ ■ ■

The crime of which Williams was convicted was senseless and brutal, calling for swift and energetic action by the police to apprehend the perpetrator and gather evidence with which he could be convicted. No mission of law enforcement officials is more important. Yet "[d]isinterested zeal for the public good does not assure either wisdom or right in the methods it pursues." Although we do not lightly affirm the issuance of a writ of habeas corpus in this case, so clear a violation of the Sixth and Fourteenth Amendments as here occurred cannot be condoned. The pressures on state executive and judicial officers charged with the administration of the criminal law are great, especially when the crime is murder and the victim a small child. But it is precisely the predictability of those pressures that makes imperative a resolute loyalty to the guarantees that the Constitution extends to us all.

The judgment of the Court of Appeals is affirmed.

It is so ordered.

■ ■ ■

Chief Justice BURGER, dissenting.

The result in this case ought to be intolerable in any society which purports to call itself an organized society. It continues the Court by the narrowest margin on the much-criticized course of punishing the public for the mistakes and misdeeds of law enforcement officers, instead of punishing the officer directly, if in fact he is guilty of wrongdoing. It mechanically and blindly keeps reliable evidence from juries whether the claimed constitutional violation involves gross police misconduct or honest human error.

Williams is guilty of the savage murder of a small child; no member of the Court contends he is not. While in custody, and after no fewer than five warnings of his rights to silence and to counsel, he led police to the concealed body of his victim. The Court concedes Williams was not threatened or coerced and that he spoke and acted voluntarily and with full awareness of his constitutional rights. In the face of all this, the Court now holds that because Williams was prompted by the detective's statement—not interrogation but a statement—the jury must not be told how the police found the body.

Today's holding fulfills Judge (later Mr. Justice) Cardozo's grim prophecy that someday some court might carry the exclusionary rule to the absurd extent that its operative effect would exclude evidence relating to the body of a murder victim because of the means by which it was found. In so ruling the Court regresses to playing a grisly game of "hide and seek," once more exalting the sporting theory of criminal justice which has been experiencing a decline in our jurisprudence.

■ ■ ■

THE COURT CONCEDES WILLIAMS' DISCLOSURES WERE VOLUNTARY

Under well-settled precedents which the Court freely acknowledges, it is very clear that Williams had made a valid waiver of his Fifth Amendment right to silence and his Sixth Amendment right to counsel when he led police to the child's body. Indeed, even under the Court's analysis I do not understand how a contrary conclusion is possible.

The Court purports to apply as the appropriate constitutional waiver standard the familiar "intentional relinquishment or abandonment of a known right or privilege" test of *Johnson v. Zerbst* (1938). The Court assumes, without deciding, that Williams' conduct and statements were voluntary. It concedes, as it must, *ibid.*, that Williams had been informed of and fully understood his constitutional rights and the consequences of their waiver. Then, having either assumed or found every element necessary to make out a valid waiver under its own test, the Court reaches the astonishing conclusion that no valid waiver has been demonstrated. . . .

The evidence is uncontradicted that Williams had abundant knowledge of his right to have counsel present and of his right to silence. Since the Court does not question his mental competence, it boggles the mind to suggest that Williams could not understand that leading police to the child's body would have other than the most serious consequences. All of the elements necessary to make out a valid waiver are shown by the record and acknowledged by the Court; we thus are left to guess how the Court reached its holding.

One plausible but unarticulated basis for the result reached is that once a suspect has asserted his right not to talk without the presence of an attorney, it becomes legally impossible for him to waive that right until he has seen an attorney. But constitutional rights are personal, and an otherwise valid waiver should not be brushed aside by judges simply because an attorney was not present. The Court's holding operates to "imprison a man in his privileges"; it conclusively presumes a suspect is legally incompetent to change his mind and tell the truth until an attorney is present. It denigrates an individual to a nonperson whose free will has become hostage to a lawyer so that until the lawyer consents, the suspect is deprived of any legal right or power to decide for himself that he wishes to make a disclosure. It denies that the rights to counsel and silence are personal, nondelegable, and subject to a waiver only by that individual. The opinions in support of the Court's judgment do not enlighten us as to why police conduct whether good or bad should operate to suspend Williams' right to change his mind and "tell all" at once rather than waiting until he reached Des Moines.

■ ■ ■

THE EXCLUSIONARY RULE SHOULD NOT BE APPLIED TO NON-EGREGIOUS POLICE CONDUCT

Even if there was no waiver, and assuming a technical violation occurred, the Court errs gravely in mechanically applying the exclusionary rule without considering whether that Draconian judicial doctrine should be invoked in these circumstances, or indeed whether any of its conceivable goals will be furthered by its application here.

The obvious flaws of the exclusionary rule as a judicial remedy are familiar. See *Bivens v. Six Unknown Fed. Narcotics Agents* (1971).

■ ■ ■

Accordingly, unlawfully obtained evidence is not automatically excluded from the factfinding process in all circumstances. In a variety of contexts we inquire whether application of the rule will promote its objectives sufficiently to justify the enormous cost it imposes on society. "As with any remedial device, the application of the rule has been restricted to those areas where its remedial objectives are thought most efficaciously served."

This is, of course, the familiar balancing process applicable to cases in which important competing interests are at stake. It is a recognition, albeit belated, that "the policies behind the exclusionary rule are not absolute." It acknowledges that so serious an infringement of the crucial truth-seeking function of a criminal prosecution should be allowed only when imperative to safeguard constitutional rights. An important factor in this amalgam is whether the violation at issue may properly be classed as "egregious." The Court understandably does not try to characterize the police actions here as "egregious."

Against this background, it is striking that the Court fails even to consider whether the benefits secured by application of the exclusionary rule in this case outweigh its obvious social costs. Perhaps the failure is due to the fact that this case arises not under the Fourth Amendment, but under *Miranda v. Arizona* (1966), and the Sixth Amendment right to counsel. The Court apparently perceives the function of the exclusionary rule to be so different in these varying contexts that it must be mechanically and uncritically applied in all cases arising outside the Fourth Amendment.

But this is demonstrably not the case where police conduct collides with *Miranda*'s procedural safeguards rather than with the Fifth Amendment privilege against compulsory self-incrimination. Involuntary and coerced admissions are suppressed because of the inherent unreliability of a confession wrung from an unwilling suspect by threats, brutality, or other coercion.

■ ■ ■

But use of Williams' disclosures and their fruits carries no risk whatever of unreliability, for the body was found where he said it would be found. Moreover, since the Court makes no issue of voluntariness, no dangers are posed to individual dignity or free will. *Miranda*'s safeguards are premised on presumed unreliability long associated with confessions extorted by brutality or threats; they are not personal constitutional rights, but are simply judicially created prophylactic measures.

Thus, in cases where incriminating disclosures are voluntarily made without coercion, and hence not violative of the Fifth Amendment, but are obtained in violation of one of the *Miranda* prophylaxes, suppression is no longer automatic. Rather, we weigh the deterrent effect on unlawful police conduct, together with the normative Fifth Amendment justifications for suppression, against "the strong interest under any system of justice of making available to the trier of fact all concededly relevant and trustworthy evidence which either party seeks to adduce.... We also 'must consider society's interest in the effective prosecution of criminals....'" This individualized consideration or balancing process with respect to the exclusionary sanction is possible in this case, as in others, because Williams' incriminating disclosures are not infected with any element of compulsion the Fifth Amendment forbids; nor, as noted earlier, does this evidence pose any danger of unreliability to the factfinding process. In short, there is no reason to exclude this evidence.

Similarly, the exclusionary rule is not uniformly implicated in the Sixth Amendment, particularly its pretrial aspects. We have held that

> "the core purpose of the counsel guarantee was to assure 'Assistance' at trial, when the accused was confronted with both the intricacies of the law and the advocacy of the public prosecutor." *United States v. Ash* (1973).

Thus, the right to counsel is fundamentally a "trial" right necessitated by the legal complexities of a criminal prosecution and the need to offset, to the trier of fact, the power of the State as prosecutor.

As we have seen in the Fifth Amendment setting, violations of prophylactic rules designed to safeguard other constitutional guarantees and deter impermissible police conduct need not call for the automatic suppression of evidence without regard to the purposes served by exclusion; nor do Fourth Amendment violations merit uncritical suppression of evidence. In other situations we decline to suppress eyewitness identifications which are the products of unnecessarily suggestive lineups or photo displays unless there is a "very substantial likelihood of irreparable misidentification."

So, too, in the Sixth Amendment sphere failure to have counsel in a pretrial setting should not lead to the "knee-jerk" suppression of relevant and reliable evidence. Just as even uncounseled "critical" pretrial confrontations may often be conducted fairly and not in derogation of Sixth Amendment values, *Stovall v. Denno* (1967), evidence obtained in such proceedings should be suppressed only when its use would imperil the core values the Amendment was written to protect. Having extended Sixth Amendment concepts originally thought to relate to the trial itself to earlier periods when a criminal investigation is focused on a suspect, application of the drastic bar of exclusion should be approached with caution.

In any event, the fundamental purpose of the Sixth Amendment is to safeguard the fairness of the trial and the integrity of the factfinding process. In this case, where the evidence of how the child's body was found is of unquestioned reliability, and since the Court accepts Williams' disclosures as voluntary and uncoerced, there is no issue either of fairness or evidentiary reliability to justify suppression of truth. It appears suppression is mandated here for no other reason than the Court's general impression that it may have a beneficial effect on future police conduct; indeed, the Court fails to say even that much in defense of its holding.

Thus, whether considered under *Miranda* or the Sixth Amendment, there is no more than there was in *Stone v. Powell* [(1976)]; that holding was premised on the utter reliability of evidence sought to be suppressed, the irrelevancy of the constitutional claim to the criminal defendant's factual guilt or innocence, and the minimal deterrent effect of habeas corpus on police misconduct. This case, like *Stone v. Powell*, comes to us by way of habeas corpus after a fair trial and appeal in the state courts. Relevant factors in this case are thus indistinguishable from those in *Stone*, and from those in other Fourth Amendment cases suggesting a balancing approach toward utilization of the exclusionary sanction. Rather than adopting a formalistic analysis varying with the constitutional provision invoked, we should apply the exclusionary rule on the basis of its benefits and costs, at least in those cases where the police conduct at issue is far from being outrageous or egregious.

The bizarre result reached by the Court today recalls Mr. Justice Black's strong dissent in *Kaufman v. United States* (1969). There, too, a defendant sought release after his conviction had been affirmed on appeal. There, as here, the defendant's guilt was manifest, and was not called into question by the constitutional claims presented. This Court granted relief because it thought reliable evidence had been unconstitutionally obtained. Mr. Justice Black's reaction, foreshadowing our long overdue holding in *Stone v. Powell*, serves as a fitting conclusion to the views I have expressed:

> "It is seemingly becoming more and more difficult to gain acceptance for the proposition that punishment of the guilty is desirable, other things being equal. One commentator, who attempted in vain to dissuade this Court from today's holding, thought it necessary to point out that there is 'a strong public interest in convicting the guilty.' . . .
>
> . . . I would not let any criminal conviction become invulnerable to collateral attack where there is left remaining the probability or possibility that constitutional commands related to the integrity of the fact-finding process have been violated. In such situations society has failed to perform its obligation to prove beyond a reasonable doubt that the defendant committed the crime. But it is [quite] a different thing to permit collateral attack on a conviction after a trial according to due process when the defendant clearly is, by the

proof and by his own admission, guilty of the crime charged. . . . In collateral attacks whether by habeas corpus or by § 2255 proceedings, I would always require that the convicted defendant raise the kind of constitutional claim that casts some shadow of a doubt on his guilt. This defendant is permitted to attack his conviction collaterally although he conceded at the trial and does not now deny that he had robbed the savings and loan association and although the evidence makes absolutely clear that he knew what he was doing. Thus, his guilt being certain, surely he does not have a constitutional right to get a new trial. I cannot possibly agree with the Court."

Like Mr. Justice Black in *Kaufman,* I cannot possibly agree with the Court.

Justice WHITE, with whom Justice BLACKMUN and Justice REHNQUIST join, dissenting.

The respondent in this case killed a 10-year-old child. The majority sets aside his conviction, holding that certain statements of unquestioned reliability were unconstitutionally obtained from him, and, under the circumstances, probably makes it impossible to retry him. Because there is nothing in the Constitution or in our previous cases which requires the Court's action, I dissent.

■ ■ ■

The victim in this case disappeared from a YMCA building in Des Moines, Iowa, on Christmas Eve in 1968. Respondent was seen shortly thereafter carrying a bundle wrapped in a blanket from the YMCA to his car. His car was found in Davenport, Iowa, 160 miles away on Christmas Day. A warrant was then issued for his arrest. On the day after Christmas respondent surrendered himself voluntarily to local police in Davenport where he was arraigned. The Des Moines police, in turn, drove to Davenport, picked respondent up and drive him back to Des Moines. During the trip back to Des Moines respondent made statements evidencing his knowledge of the whereabouts of the victim's clothing and body and leading the police to the body. The statements were, of course, made without the presence of counsel since no counsel was in the police car. The issue in this case is whether respondent who was entitled not to make any statements to the police without consultation with and/or presence of counsel validly waived those rights.

■ ■ ■

The strictest test of waiver which might be applied to this case is that set forth in *Johnson v. Zerbst* (1938) and quoted by the majority. In order to show that a right has been waived under this test, the State must prove "an intentional relinquishment or abandonment of a known right or privilege." The majority creates no new rule preventing an accused who has retained a lawyer from waiving his right to the lawyer's presence during questioning. The majority simply finds that no waiver was proved in this case. I disagree. That respondent knew of his right not to say anything to the officers without advice and presence of counsel is established on this record to a moral certainty. He was advised of the right by three officials of the State telling at least one that he understood the right and by two lawyers. Finally, he further demonstrated his knowledge of the right by informing the police that he would tell them the story in the presence of McKnight when they arrived in Des Moines. The issue in this case, then, is whether respondent relinquished that right intentionally.

Respondent relinquished his right not to talk to the police about his crime when the car approached the place where he had hidden the victim's clothes. Men usually intend to do what they do, and there is nothing in the record to support the proposition that respondent's decision to talk was anything but an exercise of his own free will. Apparently, without any prodding from the officers, respondent—who had earlier said that he would tell the whole story when he arrived in Des Moines—spontaneously changed his mind about the timing of his disclosures when the car approached the places where he had hidden the evidence. However, even if his statements were influenced by Detective Leaming's above-quoted statement, respondent's decision to talk in the absence of counsel can hardly be viewed as the product of an overborne will. The statement by Leaming was not coercive; it was accompanied by a request that respondent not respond to it; and it was delivered hours before respondent decided to make any statement. Respondent's waiver was thus knowing and intentional.

The majority's contrary conclusion seems to rest on the fact that respondent "asserted" his right to counsel by retaining and consulting with one lawyer and by consulting with another. How this supports the conclusion that respondent's later relinquishment of his right not to talk in the absence of counsel was unintentional is a mystery. The fact that respondent consulted with counsel on the question whether he should talk to the police in counsel's absence makes his later decision to talk in counsel's absence better informed and, if anything, more intelligent.

The majority recognizes that even after this "assertion" of his right to counsel, it would have found that respondent waived his right not to talk in counsel's absence if his waiver had been express, *i.e.*, if the officers had asked him in the car whether he would be willing to answer questions in counsel's absence and if he had answered "yes." But waiver is not a formalistic concept. Waiver is shown whenever the facts establish that an accused knew of a right and intended to relinquish it. Such waiver, even if not express, was plainly shown here. The only other conceivable basis for the majority's holding is the implicit suggestion, that the right involved in *Massiah v. United States* (1964), as distinguished from the right involved in *Miranda v. Arizona* (1966), is a right not to be asked any questions in counsel's absence rather than a right not to answer any questions in counsel's absence, and that the right not to be asked questions must be waived before the questions are asked. Such wafer-thin distinctions cannot determine whether a guilty murderer should go free. The only conceivable purpose for the presence of counsel during questioning is to protect an accused from making incriminating answers. Questions, unanswered, have no significance at all. Absent coercion no matter how the right involved is defined an accused is amply protected by a rule requiring waiver before or simultaneously with the giving by him of an answer or the making by him of a statement. . . .

There is absolutely no reason to require an additional question to the already cumbersome *Miranda* litany just because the majority finds another case—*Massiah v. United States*—providing exactly the same right to counsel as that involved in *Miranda*. In either event, the issue is, as the majority recognizes, one of the proof necessary to establish waiver. If an intentional relinquishment of the right to counsel under *Miranda* is established by proof that the accused was informed of his right and then voluntarily answered questions in counsel's absence, then similar proof establishes an intentional relinquishment of the *Massiah* right to counsel. . . .

The consequence of the majority's decision is, as the majority recognizes, extremely serious. A mentally disturbed killer whose guilt is not in question may be released. Why? Apparently the answer is that the majority believes that the law enforcement officers acted in a way which involves some risk of injury to society and that such conduct should be deterred. However, the officers' conduct did not, and was not likely to, jeopardize the fairness of respondent's trial or in any way risk the conviction of an innocent man—the risk against which the Sixth Amendment guarantee of assistance of counsel is designed to protect.

■ ■ ■

Justice BLACKMUN, with whom Justice WHITE and Justice REHNQUIST join, dissenting.

■ ■ ■

What the Court chooses to do here, and with which I disagree, is to hold that respondent Williams' situation was in the mold of *Massiah v. United States*, that is, that it was dominated by a denial to Williams of his Sixth Amendment right to counsel after criminal proceedings had been instituted against him. The Court rules that the Sixth Amendment was violated because Detective Leaming "purposely sought during Williams' isolation from his lawyers to obtain as much incriminating information as possible."

First, the police did not deliberately seek to isolate Williams from his lawyers so as to deprive him of the assistance of counsel. The isolation in this case was a necessary incident of transporting Williams to the county where the crime was committed.

Second, Leaming's purpose was not solely to obtain incriminating evidence. The victim had been missing for only two days, and the police could not be certain that she was dead. Leaming, of course, and in accord with his duty, was "hoping to find out where that little girl was," but such motivation does not equate with an intention to evade the Sixth Amendment. Moreover, the Court seems to me to place an undue emphasis and aspersion on what it and the lower courts have chosen to call the "Christian burial speech," and on Williams' "deeply religious" convictions.

Third, not every attempt to elicit information should be regarded as "tantamount to interrogation." I am not persuaded that Leaming's observations and comments, made as the police car traversed the snowy and slippery miles between Davenport and Des Moines that winter afternoon, were an interrogation, direct or subtle, of Williams. Contrary to this Court's statement, the Iowa Supreme Court appears to me to have thought and held otherwise, and I agree. Williams, after all, was counseled by lawyers, and warned by the arraigning judge in Davenport and by the police, and yet it was he who started the travel conversations and brought up the subject of the criminal investigation. Without further reviewing the circumstances of the trip, I would say it is clear there was no interrogation. In this respect, I am in full accord with Judge Webster in his vigorous dissent, and with the views implicitly indicated by Chief Judge Gibson and Judge Stephenson, who joined him in voting for rehearing en banc.

In summary, it seems to me that the Court is holding that *Massiah* is violated whenever police engage in any conduct, in the absence of counsel, with the subjective desire to obtain information from a suspect after arraignment. Such a rule is far too broad. Persons in custody frequently volunteer statements in response to stimuli other than interrogation.

The *Massiah* point thus being of no consequence, I would vacate the judgment of the Court of Appeals and remand the case for consideration of the issue of voluntariness, in the constitutional sense, of Williams' statements, an issue the Court of Appeals did not reach when the case was before it.

United States v. Henry

447 U.S. 264 (1980)

BURGER, C.J., delivered the opinion of the Court, in which BRENNAN, STEVENS, MARSHALL, POWELL, and STEWART, JJ., joined. POWELL, J., filed a concurring opinion. BLACKMUN, J., filed a dissenting opinion, in which WHITE, J., joined. REHNQUIST, J., filed a dissenting opinion.

We granted certiorari to consider whether respondent's Sixth Amendment right to the assistance of counsel was violated by the admission at trial of incriminating statements made by respondent to his cellmate, an undisclosed Government informant, after indictment and while in custody.

The Janaf Branch of the United Virginia Bank/Seaboard National in Norfolk, Va., was robbed in August 1972. Witnesses saw two men wearing masks and carrying guns enter the bank while a third man waited in the car. No witnesses were able to identify respondent Henry as one of the participants. About an hour after the robbery, the getaway car was discovered. Inside was found a rent receipt signed by one "Allen R. Norris" and a lease, also signed by Norris, for a house in Norfolk. Two men, who were subsequently convicted of participating in the robbery, were arrested at the rented house. Discovered with them were the proceeds of the robbery and the guns and masks used by the gunman.

Government agents traced the rent receipt to Henry; on the basis of this information, Henry was arrested in Atlanta, Ga., in November 1972. Two weeks later he was indicted for armed robbery....

On November 21, 1972, shortly after Henry was incarcerated, Government agents working on the Janaf robbery contacted one Nichols, an inmate at the Norfolk city jail, who for some time prior to this meeting had been engaged to provide confidential information to the Federal Bureau of Investigation as a paid informant. Nichols was then serving a sentence on local forgery charges. The record does not disclose whether the agent contacted Nichols specifically to acquire information about Henry or the Janaf robbery.

Nichols informed the agent that he was housed in the same cellblock with several federal prisoners awaiting trial, including Henry. The agent told him to be alert to any statements made by the federal prisoners, but not to initiate any conversation with or question Henry regarding the bank robbery. In early December, after Nichols had been released from jail, the agent again contacted Nichols, who reported that he and Henry had engaged in conversation and that Henry had told him about the robbery of the Janaf bank. Nichols was paid for furnishing the information.

When Henry was tried in March 1973, an agent of the Federal Bureau of Investigation testified concerning the events surrounding the discovery of the rental slip and the evidence uncovered at the rented house. Other witnesses also connected Henry to the rented house, including the rental agent who positively identified Henry as the "Allen R. Norris" who had rented the house and had taken the rental receipt described earlier. A neighbor testified that prior to the robbery she saw Henry at the rented house with John Luck, one of the two men who had by the time of Henry's trial been convicted for the robbery. In addition, palm prints found on the lease agreement matched those of Henry.

Nichols testified at trial that he had "an opportunity to have some conversations with Mr. Henry while he was in the jail," and that Henry told him that on several occasions he had gone to the Janaf Branch to see which employees opened the vault. Nichols also testified that Henry described to him the details of the robbery and stated that the only evidence connecting him to the robbery was the rental receipt. The jury was not informed that Nichols was a paid Government informant.

On the basis of this testimony, Henry was convicted of bank robbery and sentenced to a term of imprisonment of 25 years.

■ ■ ■

This Court has scrutinized postindictment confrontations between Government agents and the accused to determine whether they are "critical stages" of the prosecution at which the Sixth Amendment right to the assistance of counsel attaches. The present case involves incriminating statements made by the accused to an undisclosed and undercover Government informant while in custody and after indictment. The Government characterizes Henry's incriminating statements as voluntary and not the result of any affirmative conduct on the part of Government agents to elicit evidence. From this, the Government argues that Henry's rights were not violated, even assuming the Sixth Amendment applies to such surreptitious confrontations; in short, it is contended that the Government has not interfered with Henry's right to counsel.

This Court first applied the Sixth Amendment to postindictment communications between the accused and agents of the Government in *Massiah v. United States* [(1964)]. There, after the accused had been charged, he made incriminating statements to his codefendant, who was acting as an agent of the Government. In reversing the conviction, the Court held that the accused was denied "the basic protections of [the Sixth Amendment] when there was used against him at his trial evidence of his own incriminating words, which federal agents had deliberately elicited from him." The *Massiah* holding rests squarely on interference with his right to counsel.

The question here is whether under the facts of this case a Government agent "deliberately elicited" incriminating statements from Henry within the meaning of *Massiah*. Three factors are important. First, Nichols was acting under instructions as a paid informant for the Government; second, Nichols was ostensibly no more than a fellow inmate of Henry; and third, Henry was in custody and under indictment at the time he was engaged in conversation by Nichols.

The Court of Appeals viewed the record as showing that Nichols deliberately used his position to secure incriminating information from Henry when counsel was not present and held that conduct attributable to the Government. Nichols had been a paid Government informant for more than a year; moreover, the FBI agent was aware that Nichols had access to Henry and would be able to engage him in conversations without arousing Henry's suspicion. The arrangement between Nichols and the agent was on a contingent-fee basis; Nichols was to be paid only if he produced useful information. This combination of circumstances is sufficient to support the Court of Appeals' determination. Even if the agent's statement that he did not intend that Nichols would take affirmative steps to secure incriminating information is accepted, he must have known that such propinquity likely would lead to that result.

The Government argues that the federal agents instructed Nichols not to question Henry about the robbery. Yet according to his own testimony, Nichols was not a passive listener; rather, he had "some conversations with Mr. Henry" while he was in jail and Henry's incriminatory statements were "the product of this conversation."

■ ■ ■

It is quite a different matter when the Government uses undercover agents to obtain incriminating statements from persons not in custody but suspected of criminal activity prior to the time charges are filed. In *Hoffa v. United States* (1966), for example, this Court held that "no interest legitimately protected by the Fourth Amendment is involved" because "the Fourth Amendment [does not protect] a wrongdoer's misplaced belief that a person to whom he voluntarily confides his wrongdoing will not reveal it." See also *United States v. White* (1971). Similarly, the Fifth Amendment has been held not to be implicated by the use of undercover Government agents before charges are filed because of the absence of the potential for compulsion.

■ ■ ■

It is undisputed that Henry was unaware of Nichols' role as a Government informant. The government argues that this Court should apply a less rigorous standard under the Sixth Amendment where the accused is prompted by an undisclosed undercover informant than where the accused is speaking in the hearing of persons he knows to be Government officers. That line of argument, however, seeks to infuse Fifth Amendment concerns against compelled self-incrimination into the Sixth Amendment protection of the right to the assistance of counsel. An accused speaking to a known Government agent is typically aware that his statements may be used against him. The adversary positions at that stage are well established; the parties are then "arms' length" adversaries.

When the accused is in the company of a fellow inmate who is acting by prearrangement as a Government agent, the same cannot be said. Conversation stimulated in such circumstances may elicit information that an accused would not intentionally reveal to persons known to be Government agents. Indeed, the *Massiah* Court noted that if the Sixth Amendment "is to have any efficacy it must apply to indirect and surreptitious interrogations as well as those conducted in the jailhouse."

■ ■ ■

Finally Henry's incarceration at the time he was engaged in conversation by Nichols is also a relevant factor. As a ground for imposing the prophylactic requirements in *Miranda v. Arizona* (1966), this Court noted the powerful psychological inducements to reach for aid when a person is in confinement. While the concern in *Miranda* was limited to custodial police interrogation, the mere fact of custody imposes pressures on the accused; confinement may bring into play subtle influences that will make him particularly susceptible to the ploys of undercover Government agents. The Court of Appeals determined that on this record the incriminating conversations between Henry and Nichols were facilitated by Nichols' conduct and apparent status as a person sharing a common plight. That Nichols had managed to gain the confidence of Henry, as the Court of Appeals determined, is confirmed by Henry's request that Nichols assist him in his escape plans when Nichols was released from confinement.

Under the strictures of the Court's holdings on the exclusion of evidence, we conclude that the Court of Appeals did not err in holding that Henry's statements to Nichols should not have been admitted at trial. By intentionally creating a situation likely to induce Henry to make incriminating statements without the assistance of counsel, the Government violated Henry's Sixth Amendment right to counsel. This is not a case where, in Justice Cardozo's words, "the constable . . . blundered," rather, it is one where the "constable" planned an impermissible interference with the right to the assistance of counsel.

The judgment of the Court of Appeals for the Fourth Circuit is
Affirmed.

Kuhlmann v. Wilson

477 U.S. 436 (1986)

POWELL, J., announced the judgment of the Court, in which BURGER, C.J., BLACKMUN, POWELL, WHITE, REHNQUIST, and O'CONNOR, JJ., joined. BRENNAN, J., filed a dissenting opinion, in which MARSHALL, J., joined. STEVENS, J., filed a dissenting opinion.

■ ■ ■

In the early morning of July 4, 1970, respondent and two confederates robbed the Star Taxicab Garage in the Bronx, New York, and fatally shot the night dispatcher. Shortly before, employees of the garage had observed respondent, a former employee there, on the premises conversing with two other men. They also witnessed respondent fleeing after the robbery, carrying loose money in his arms. After eluding the police for four days, respondent turned himself in. Respondent admitted that he had been present when the crimes took place, claimed that he had witnessed the robbery, gave the police a description of the robbers, but denied knowing them. Respondent also denied any involvement in the robbery or murder, claiming that he had fled because he was afraid of being blamed for the crimes.

After his arraignment, respondent was confined in the Bronx House of Detention, where he was placed in a cell with a prisoner named Benny Lee. Unknown to respondent, Lee had agreed to act as a police informant. Respondent made incriminating statements that Lee reported to the police. Prior to trial, respondent moved to suppress the statements on the ground that they were obtained in violation of his right to counsel. The trial court held an evidentiary hearing on the suppression motion, which revealed that the statements were made under the following circumstances.

Before respondent arrived in the jail, Lee had entered into an arrangement with Detective Cullen, according to which Lee agreed to listen to respondent's conversations and report his remarks to Cullen. Since the police had positive evidence of respondent's participation, the purpose of placing Lee in the cell was to determine the identities of respondent's confederates. Cullen instructed Lee not to ask respondent any questions, but simply to "keep his ears open" for the names of the other perpetrators. Respondent first spoke to Lee about the crimes after he looked out the cellblock window at the Star Taxicab Garage, where the crimes had occurred. Respondent said, "someone's messing with me," and began talking to Lee about the robbery, narrating the same story that he had given the police at the time of his arrest. Lee advised respondent that this explanation "didn't sound too good," but respondent did not alter his story. Over the next few days, however, respondent changed details of his original account. Respondent then received a visit from his brother, who mentioned that members of his family were upset because they believed that respondent had murdered the dispatcher. After the visit, respondent again described the crimes to Lee. Respondent now admitted that he and two other men, whom he never identified, had planned and carried out the robbery, and had murdered the dispatcher. Lee informed Cullen of respondent's statements and furnished Cullen with notes that he had written surreptitiously while sharing the cell with respondent.

After hearing the testimony of Cullen and Lee, the trial court found that Cullen had instructed Lee "to ask no questions of [respondent] about the crime but merely to listen as to what [respondent] might say in his presence." The court determined that Lee obeyed these instructions, that he "at no time asked any questions with respect to the crime," and that he "only listened to [respondent] and made notes regarding what [respondent] had to say." The trial court also found that respondent's statements to Lee were "spontaneous" and "unsolicited." Under state precedent, a defendant's volunteered statements to a police agent were admissible in evidence because the police were not required to prevent talkative defendants from making incriminating statements.

■ ■ ■

[W]e conclude that it erred in holding that respondent was entitled to relief under *United States v. Henry* (1980). As the District Court observed, *Henry* left open the question whether the Sixth Amendment forbids admission in evidence of an accused's statements to a jailhouse informant who was "placed in close proximity but [made] no effort to stimulate conversations about the crime charged." Our review of the line of cases beginning with *Massiah v. United States* (1964) shows that this question must, as the District Court properly decided, be answered negatively.

■ ■ ■

In *United States v. Henry*, the Court applied the *Massiah* test to incriminating statements made to a jailhouse informant. The Court of Appeals in that case found a violation of *Massiah* because the informant had engaged the defendant in conversations and "had developed a relationship of trust and confidence with [the defendant] such that [the defendant] revealed incriminating information." This Court affirmed, holding that the Court of Appeals reasonably concluded that the Government informant "deliberately used his position to secure incriminating information from [the defendant] when counsel was not present." Although the informant had not questioned the defendant, the informant had "stimulated" conversations with the defendant in order to "elicit" incriminating information. The Court emphasized that those facts, like the facts of *Massiah*, amounted to " 'indirect and surreptitious interrogatio[n]' " of the defendant.

Earlier this Term, we applied the *Massiah* standard in a case involving incriminating statements made under circumstances substantially similar to the facts of *Massiah* itself. In *Maine v. Moulton* (1985), the defendant made incriminating statements in a meeting with his accomplice, who had agreed to cooperate with the police. During that meeting, the accomplice, who wore a wire transmitter to record the conversation, discussed with the defendant the charges pending against him, repeatedly asked the defendant to remind him of the details of the crime, and encouraged the defendant to describe his plan for killing witnesses. The Court concluded that these investigatory techniques denied the defendant his right to counsel on the pending charges. Significantly, the Court emphasized that, because of the relationship between the defendant and the informant, the informant's engaging the defendant "in active conversation about their upcoming trial was certain to elicit" incriminating statements from the defendant. Thus, the informant's participation "in this conversation was 'the functional equivalent of interrogation.'"

■ ■ ■

As our recent examination of this Sixth Amendment issue in *Moulton* makes clear, the primary concern of the *Massiah* line of decisions is secret interrogation by investigatory techniques that are the equivalent of direct police interrogation. Since "the Sixth Amendment is not violated whenever—by luck or happenstance—the State obtains incriminating statements from the accused after the right to counsel has attached," . . . a defendant does not make out a violation of that right simply by showing that an informant, either through prior arrangement or voluntarily, reported his incriminating statements to the police. Rather, the defendant must demonstrate that the police and their informant took some action, beyond merely listening, that was designed deliberately to elicit incriminating remarks.

■ ■ ■

The state court found that Officer Cullen had instructed Lee only to listen to respondent for the purpose of determining the identities of the other participants in the robbery and murder. The police already had solid evidence of respondent's participation. The court further found that Lee followed those instructions, that he "at no time asked any questions" of respondent concerning the pending charges, and that he "only listened" to respondent's "spontaneous" and "unsolicited" statements. The only remark made by Lee that has any support in this record was his comment that respondent's initial version of his participation in the crimes "didn't sound too good." . . . [T]he Court of Appeals focused on that one remark and gave a description of Lee's interaction with respondent that is completely at odds with the facts found by the trial court. In the Court of Appeals' view, "[s]ubtly and slowly, but surely, Lee's ongoing verbal intercourse with [respondent] served to exacerbate [respondent's] already troubled state of mind." After thus revising some of the trial court's findings, and ignoring other more relevant findings, the Court of

Appeals concluded that the police "deliberately elicited" respondent's incriminating statements. This conclusion conflicts with the decision of every other state and federal judge who reviewed this record.

■ ■ ■

The judgment of the Court of Appeals is reversed, and the case is remanded for further proceedings consistent with this opinion.

It is so ordered.

■ ■ ■

Justice BRENNAN, with whom Justice MARSHALL joins, dissenting.

■ ■ ■

The Sixth Amendment guarantees an accused, at least after the initiation of formal charges, the right to rely on counsel as the "medium" between himself and the State. *Maine v. Moulton.* Accordingly, the Sixth Amendment "imposes on the State an affirmative obligation to respect and preserve the accused's choice to seek [the assistance of counsel]," and therefore "[t]he determination whether particular action by state agents violates the accused's right to... counsel must be made in light of this obligation." To be sure, the Sixth Amendment is not violated whenever, "by luck or happenstance," the State obtains incriminating statements from the accused after the right to counsel has attached. It is violated, however, when "the State obtains incriminating statements by knowingly circumventing the accused's right to have counsel present in a confrontation between the accused and a state agent." As we explained in *Henry,* where the accused has not waived his right to counsel, the government knowingly circumvents the defendant's right to counsel where it "deliberately elicit[s]" inculpatory admissions, that is, "intentionally creat[es] a situation likely to induce [the accused] to make incriminating statements without the assistance of counsel."

In *Henry,* we found that the Federal Government had "deliberately elicited" incriminating statements from Henry based on the following circumstances. The jailhouse informant, Nichols, had apparently followed instructions to obtain information without directly questioning Henry and without initiating conversations concerning the charges pending against Henry. We rejected the Government's argument that because Henry initiated the discussion of his crime, no Sixth Amendment violation had occurred. We pointed out that under *Massiah v. United States,* it is irrelevant whether the informant asks pointed questions about the crime or "merely engage[s] in general conversation about it." Nichols, we noted, "was not a passive listener; ... he had 'some conversations with Mr. Henry' while he was in jail and Henry's incriminatory statements were 'the product of this conversation.'"

In deciding that Nichols' role in these conversations amounted to deliberate elicitation, we also found three other factors important. First, Nichols was to be paid for any information he produced and thus had an incentive to extract inculpatory admissions from Henry. Second, Henry was not aware that Nichols was acting as an informant. "Conversation stimulated in such circumstances," we observed, "may elicit information that an accused would not intentionally reveal to persons known to be Government agents." Third, Henry was in custody at the time he spoke with Nichols. This last fact is significant, we stated, because "custody imposes pressures on the accused [and] confinement may bring into play subtle influences that will make him particularly susceptible to the ploys of undercover Government agents." We concluded that by "intentionally creating a situation likely to induce Henry to make incriminating statements without the assistance of counsel, the Government violated Henry's Sixth Amendment right to counsel."

In the instant case, as in *Henry*, the accused was incarcerated and therefore was "susceptible to the ploys of undercover Government agents." Like Nichols, Lee was a secret informant, usually received consideration for the services he rendered the police, and therefore had an incentive to produce the information which he knew the police hoped to obtain. Just as Nichols had done, Lee obeyed instructions not to question respondent and to report to the police any statements made by the respondent in Lee's presence about the crime in question. And, like Nichols, Lee encouraged respondent to talk about his crime by conversing with him on the subject over the course of several days and by telling respondent that his exculpatory story would not convince anyone without more work. However, unlike the situation in *Henry*, a disturbing visit from respondent's brother, rather than a conversation with the informant, seems to have been the immediate catalyst for respondent's confession to Lee. While it might appear from this sequence of events that Lee's comment regarding respondent's story and his general willingness to converse with respondent about the crime were not the *immediate* causes of respondent's admission, I think that the deliberate-elicitation standard requires consideration of the entire course of government behavior.

The State intentionally created a situation in which it was foreseeable that respondent would make incriminating statements without the assistance of counsel, *Henry*—it assigned respondent to a cell overlooking the scene of the crime and designated a secret informant to be respondent's cellmate. The informant, while avoiding direct questions, nonetheless developed a relationship of cellmate camaraderie with respondent and encouraged him to talk about his crime. While the *coup de grace* was delivered by respondent's brother, the groundwork for respondent's confession was laid by the State. Clearly the State's actions had a sufficient nexus with respondent's admission of guilt to constitute deliberate elicitation within the meaning of *Henry*. I would affirm the judgment of the Court of Appeals.

■ ■ ■

Texas v. Cobb

532 U.S. 162 (2001)

REHNQUIST, C.J., delivered the opinion of the Court, in which O'CONNOR, SCALIA, KENNEDY, and THOMAS, JJ., joined. KENNEDY, J., filed a concurring opinion, in which SCALIA and THOMAS, JJ., joined. BREYER, J., filed a dissenting opinion, in which STEVENS, SOUTER, and GINSBURG, JJ., joined.

The Texas Court of Criminal Appeals held that a criminal defendant's Sixth Amendment right to counsel attaches not only to the offense with which he is charged, but to other offenses "closely related factually" to the charged offense. We hold that our decision in *McNeil v. Wisconsin* (1991) meant what it said, and that the Sixth Amendment right is "offense specific."

In December 1993, Lindsey Owings reported to the Walker County, Texas, Sheriff's Office that the home he shared with his wife, Margaret, and their 16-month-old daughter, Kori Rae, had been burglarized. He also informed police that his wife and daughter were missing. Respondent Raymond Levi Cobb lived across the street from the Owings. Acting on an anonymous tip that respondent was involved in the burglary, Walker County investigators questioned him about the events. He denied involvement. In July 1994, while under arrest for an unrelated offense, respondent was again questioned about the incident. Respondent then gave a written statement confessing to the burglary, but he denied knowledge relating to the disappearances. Respondent was subsequently indicted for the burglary, and Hal Ridley was appointed in August 1994 to represent respondent on that charge.

Shortly after Ridley's appointment, investigators asked and received his permission to question respondent about the disappearances. Respondent continued to deny involvement. Investigators repeated this process in September 1995, again with Ridley's permission and again with the same result.

In November 1995, respondent, free on bond in the burglary case, was living with his father in Odessa, Texas. At that time, respondent's father contacted the Walker County Sheriff's Office to report that respondent had confessed to him that he killed Margaret Owings in the course of the burglary. Walker County investigators directed respondent's father to the Odessa police station, where he gave a statement. Odessa police then faxed the statement to Walker County, where investigators secured a warrant for respondent's arrest and faxed it back to Odessa. Shortly thereafter, Odessa police took respondent into custody and administered warnings pursuant to *Miranda v. Arizona* (1966). Respondent waived these rights.

After a short time, respondent confessed to murdering both Margaret and Kori Rae. Respondent explained that when Margaret confronted him as he was attempting to remove the Owings' stereo, he stabbed her in the stomach with a knife he was carrying. Respondent told police that he dragged her body to a wooded area a few hundred yards from the house.

■ ■ ■

Respondent later led police to the location where he had buried the victims' bodies.

■ ■ ■

The Sixth Amendment provides that "[i]n all criminal prosecutions, the accused shall enjoy the right...to have the Assistance of Counsel for his defence." In *McNeil v. Wisconsin*, we explained when this right arises:

"The Sixth Amendment right [to counsel]...is offense specific. It cannot be invoked once for all future prosecutions, for it does not attach until a prosecution is commenced, that is, at or after the initiation of adversary judicial criminal proceedings—whether by way of formal charge, preliminary hearing, indictment, information, or arraignment."

Accordingly, we held that a defendant's statements regarding offenses for which he had not been charged were admissible notwithstanding the attachment of his Sixth Amendment right to counsel on other charged offenses.

Some state courts and Federal Courts of Appeals, however, have read into *McNeil*'s offense-specific definition an exception for crimes that are "factually related" to a charged offense. Several of these courts have interpreted *Brewer v. Williams* (1977) and *Maine v. Moulton* (1985)—both of which were decided well before *McNeil*—to support this view, which respondent now invites us to approve. We decline to do so.

In *Brewer*, a suspect in the abduction and murder of a 10-year-old girl had fled from the scene of the crime in Des Moines, Iowa, some 160 miles east to Davenport, Iowa, where he surrendered to police. An arrest warrant was issued in Des Moines on a charge of abduction, and the suspect was arraigned on that warrant before a Davenport judge. Des Moines police traveled to Davenport, took the man into custody, and began the drive back to Des Moines. Along the way, one of the officers persuaded the suspect to lead police to the victim's body. The suspect ultimately was convicted of the girl's murder. This Court upheld the federal habeas court's conclusion that police had violated the suspect's Sixth Amendment right to counsel. We held that the officer's comments to the suspect constituted interrogation and that the suspect had not validly waived his right to counsel by responding to the officer.

■ ■ ■

Respondent predicts that the offense-specific rule will prove "disastrous" to suspects' constitutional rights and will "permit law enforcement officers almost complete and total license to conduct unwanted and uncounseled interrogations." Besides offering no evidence that such a parade of horribles has occurred in those jurisdictions that have not enlarged upon *McNeil*, he fails to appreciate the significance of two critical considerations. First, there can be no doubt that a suspect must be apprised of his rights against compulsory self-incrimination and to consult with an attorney before authorities may conduct custodial interrogation. In the present case, police scrupulously followed *Miranda*'s dictates when questioning respondent. Second, it is critical to recognize that the Constitution does not negate society's interest in the ability of police to talk to witnesses and suspects, even those who have been charged with other offenses.

Although it is clear that the Sixth Amendment right to counsel attaches only to charged offenses, we have recognized in other contexts that the definition of an "offense" is not necessarily limited to the four corners of a charging instrument. In *Blockburger v. United States* (1932), we explained that "where the same act or transaction constitutes a violation of two distinct statutory provisions, the test to be applied to determine whether there are two offenses or only one, is whether each provision requires proof of a fact which the other does not." We have since applied the *Blockburger* test to delineate the scope of the Fifth Amendment's Double Jeopardy Clause, which prevents multiple or successive prosecutions for the "same offence." We see no constitutional difference between the meaning of the term "offense" in the contexts of double jeopardy and of the right to counsel. Accordingly, we hold that when the Sixth Amendment right to counsel attaches, it does encompass offenses that, even if not formally charged, would be considered the same offense under the *Blockburger* test.

■ ■ ■

It remains only to apply these principles to the facts at hand. At the time he confessed to Odessa police, respondent had been indicted for burglary of the Owings residence, but he had not been charged in the murders of Margaret and Kori Rae. As defined by Texas law, burglary and capital murder are not the same offense under *Blockburger*. . . . Accordingly, the Sixth Amendment right to counsel did not bar police from interrogating respondent regarding the murders, and respondent's confession was therefore admissible.

The judgment of the Court of Criminal Appeals of Texas is reversed.

It is so ordered.

■ ■ ■

Justice BREYER, with whom Justice STEVENS, Justice SOUTER, and Justice GINSBURG join, dissenting.

This case focuses upon the meaning of a single word, "offense," when it arises in the context of the Sixth Amendment. Several basic background principles define that context.

First, the Sixth Amendment right to counsel plays a central role in ensuring the fairness of criminal proceedings in our system of justice. See *Gideon v. Wainwright* (1963); *Powell v. Alabama* (1932).

Second, the right attaches when adversary proceedings, triggered by the government's formal accusation of a crime, begin. See *Brewer v. Williams* (1977); *Kirby v. Illinois* (1972); *Massiah v. United States* (1964).

Third, once this right attaches, law enforcement officials are required, in most circumstances, to deal with the defendant through counsel rather than directly, even if the defendant has waived his Fifth Amendment rights. See *Michigan v. Jackson* (1986).

■ ■ ■

Fourth, the particular aspect of the right here at issue—the rule that the police ordinarily must communicate with the defendant through counsel—has important limits. In particular, recognizing the need for law enforcement officials to investigate "new or additional crimes" not the subject of current proceedings, this Court has made clear that the right to counsel does not attach to any and every crime that an accused may commit or have committed, see *McNeil v. Wisconsin*. The right "cannot be invoked once for all future prosecutions," and it does not forbid "interrogation unrelated to the charge." In a word, as this Court previously noted, the right is "offense specific."

This case focuses upon the last-mentioned principle, in particular upon the meaning of the words "offense specific." These words appear in this Court's Sixth Amendment case law, not in the Sixth Amendment's text. See U.S. Const., Amdt. 6 (guaranteeing right to counsel "[i]n all criminal prosecutions"). The definition of these words is not self-evident. Sometimes the term "offense" may refer to words that are written in a criminal statute; sometimes it may refer generally to a course of conduct in the world, aspects of which constitute the elements of one or more crimes; and sometimes it may refer, narrowly and technically, just to the conceptually severable aspects of the latter. This case requires us to determine whether an "offense"—for Sixth Amendment purposes—includes factually related aspects of a single course of conduct other than those few acts that make up the essential elements of the crime charged.

We should answer this question in light of the Sixth Amendment's basic objectives as set forth in this Court's case law. At the very least, we should answer it in a way that does not undermine those objectives. But the Court today decides that "offense" means the crime set forth within "the four corners of a charging instrument," along with other crimes that "would be considered the same offense" under the test established by *Blockburger v. United States*. In my view, this unnecessarily technical definition undermines Sixth Amendment protections while doing nothing to further effective law enforcement.

■ ■ ■

Jackson focuses upon a suspect—perhaps a frightened or uneducated suspect—who, hesitant to rely upon his own unaided judgment in his dealings with the police, has invoked his constitutional right to legal assistance in such matters. See *Michigan v. Jackson* (" 'The simple fact that [a] defendant has requested an attorney indicates that he does not believe that he is sufficiently capable of dealing with his adversaries singlehandedly' ").... *Jackson* says that, once such a request has been made, the police may not simply throw that suspect—who does not trust his own unaided judgment—back upon his own devices by requiring him to rely for protection upon that same unaided judgment that he previously rejected as inadequate. In a word, the police may not force a suspect who has asked for legal counsel to make a critical legal choice without the legal assistance that he has requested and that the Constitution guarantees.

■ ■ ■

The majority's rule permits law enforcement officials to question those charged with a crime without first approaching counsel, through the simple device of asking questions about any other related crime not actually charged in the indictment. Thus, the police could ask the individual charged with robbery about, say, the assault of the cashier not yet charged, or about any other uncharged offense (unless under *Blockburger*'s definition it counts as the "same crime"), all *without notifying counsel.* Indeed, the majority's rule would permit law enforcement officials to question anyone charged with any crime in any one of the examples just given about his or her conduct on the single relevant occasion without notifying counsel unless the prosecutor has charged every possible crime arising out of that same brief course of conduct. What Sixth Amendment sense—what common sense—does such a rule make? What is left of the "communicate through counsel" rule? The majority's approach is inconsistent with any common understanding of the scope of counsel's representation. It will undermine the lawyer's role as "'medium'" between the defendant and the government. And it will, on a random basis, remove a significant portion of the protection that this Court has found inherent in the Sixth Amendment.

In fact, under the rule today announced by the majority, two of the seminal cases in our Sixth Amendment jurisprudence would have come out differently. In *Maine v. Moulton*, which the majority points out "expressly referred to the offense-specific nature of the Sixth Amendment right to counsel," we treated burglary and theft as the same offense for Sixth Amendment purposes. Despite the opinion's clear statement that "[i]ncriminating statements pertaining to other crimes, as to which the Sixth Amendment right has not yet attached, are, of course, admissible at a trial of those offenses," the Court affirmed the lower court's reversal of both burglary and theft charges even though, at the time that the incriminating statements at issue were made, Moulton had been charged only with theft by receiving. Under the majority's rule, in contrast, because theft by receiving and burglary each required proof of a fact that the other did not, only Moulton's theft convictions should have been overturned.

■ ■ ■

In *Brewer v. Williams*, the effect of the majority's rule would have been even more dramatic. Because first-degree murder and child abduction each required proof of a fact not required by the other, and because at the time of the impermissible interrogation Williams had been charged only with abduction of a child, Williams' murder conviction should have remained undisturbed. This is not to suggest that this Court has previously addressed and decided the question presented by this case. Rather, it is to point out that the Court's conception of the Sixth Amendment right at the time that *Moulton* and *Brewer* were decided naturally presumed that it extended to factually related but uncharged offenses.

■ ■ ■

In theory, the test says that two offenses are the "same offense" unless each requires proof of a fact that the other does not. That means that most of the different crimes mentioned above are not the "same offense." Under many States' laws, for example, the statute defining assault and the statute defining robbery each requires proof of a fact that the other does not.

■ ■ ■

But, more to the point, the simple-sounding *Blockburger* test has proved extraordinarily difficult to administer in practice. Judges, lawyers, and law professors often disagree about how to apply it.

■ ■ ■

There is, of course, an alternative. We can, and should, define "offense" in terms of the conduct that constitutes the crime that the offender committed on a particular occasion, including criminal acts that are "closely related to" or "inextricably intertwined with" the particular crime set forth in the charging instrument. This alternative is not perfect. The language used lacks the precision for which police officers may hope; and it requires lower courts to specify its meaning further as they apply it in individual cases. Yet virtually every lower court in the United States to consider the issue has defined "offense" in the Sixth Amendment context to encompass such closely related acts.

■ ■ ■

One cannot say in favor of this commonly followed approach that it is perfectly clear—only that, because it comports with common sense, it is far easier to apply than that of the majority. One might add that, unlike the majority's test, it is consistent with this Court's assumptions in previous cases. See *Maine v. Moulton.* . . . And, most importantly, the "closely related" test furthers, rather than undermines, the Sixth Amendment's "right to counsel," a right so necessary to the realization in practice of that most "noble ideal," a fair trial.

The Texas Court of Criminal Appeals, following this commonly accepted approach, found that the charged burglary and the uncharged murders were "closely related." All occurred during a short period of time on the same day in the same basic location. The victims of the murders were also victims of the burglary. Cobb committed one of the murders in furtherance of the robbery, the other to cover up the crimes. The police, when questioning Cobb, knew that he already had a lawyer representing him on the burglary charges and had demonstrated their belief that this lawyer also represented Cobb in respect to the murders by asking his permission to question Cobb about the murders on previous occasions. The relatedness of the crimes is well illustrated by the impossibility of questioning Cobb about the murders without eliciting admissions about the burglary.

■ ■ ■

Consequently, I dissent.

2. Waiver

Michigan v. Jackson

475 U.S. 625 (1986)

STEVENS, J., delivered the opinion of the Court, in which BRENNAN, WHITE, MARSHALL, and BLACKMUN, JJ., joined. BURGER, C.J., filed an opinion concurring in the judgment. REHNQUIST, J., filed a dissenting opinion, in which POWELL and O'CONNOR, JJ., joined.

In *Edwards v. Arizona* (1981), we held that an accused person in custody who has "expressed his desire to deal with the police only through counsel, is not subject to further interrogation by the authorities until counsel has been made available to him, unless the accused himself initiates further communication, exchanges, or conversations with the police."

■ ■ ■

The question presented . . . is whether the same rule applies to a defendant who has been formally charged with a crime and who has requested appointment of counsel at his arraignment. In both cases, the Michigan Supreme Court held that postarraignment confessions were improperly obtained—and the Sixth Amendment violated—because the defendants had "requested counsel during their arraignments, but were not afforded an opportunity to consult with counsel before the police initiated further interrogations." We agree with that holding.

■ ■ ■

The relevant facts may be briefly stated. Respondent Bladel was convicted of the murder of three railroad employees at the Amtrak Station in Jackson, Michigan, on December 31, 1978. Bladel, a disgruntled former employee, was arrested on January 1, 1979, and, after being questioned on two occasions, was released on January 3. He was arrested again on March 22, 1979, and agreed to talk to the police that evening without counsel. On the following morning, Friday, March 23, 1979, Bladel was arraigned. He requested that counsel be appointed for him because he was indigent. The detective in charge of the Bladel investigation was present at the arraignment. A notice of appointment was promptly mailed to a law firm, but the law firm did not receive it until Tuesday, March 27. In the interim, on March 26, 1979, two police officers interviewed Bladel in the county jail and obtained a confession from him. Prior to that questioning, the officers properly advised Bladel of his *Miranda* rights. Although he had inquired about his representation several times since the arraignment, Bladel was not told that a law firm had been appointed to represent him.

■ ■ ■

The question is not whether respondents had a right to counsel at their postarraignment, custodial interrogations. The existence of that right is clear. It has two sources. The Fifth Amendment protection against compelled self-incrimination provides the right to counsel at custodial interrogations. *Edwards*; *Miranda v. Arizona* (1966). The Sixth Amendment guarantee of the assistance of counsel also provides the right to counsel at postarraignment interrogations. The arraignment signals "the initiation of adversary judicial proceedings" and thus the attachment of the Sixth Amendment.

■ ■ ■

In *Edwards*, the request for counsel was made to the police during custodial interrogation, and the basis for the Court's holding was the Fifth Amendment privilege against compelled self-incrimination. The Court noted the relevance of various Sixth Amendment precedents, but found it unnecessary to rely on the possible applicability of the Sixth Amendment. In these cases, the request for counsel was made to a judge during arraignment, and the basis for the Michigan Supreme Court opinion was the Sixth Amendment's guarantee of the assistance of counsel. The State argues that the *Edwards* rule should not apply to these circumstances because there are legal differences in the basis for the claims; because there are factual differences in the contexts of the claims; and because respondents signed valid waivers of their right to counsel at the postarraignment custodial interrogations. We consider these contentions in turn.

The State contends that differences in the legal principles underlying the Fifth and Sixth Amendments compel the conclusion that the *Edwards* rule should not apply to a Sixth Amendment claim. *Edwards* flows from the Fifth Amendment's right to counsel at custodial interrogations, the State argues; its relevance to the Sixth Amendment's provision of the assistance of counsel is far less clear, and thus the *Edwards* principle for assessing waivers is unnecessary and inappropriate.

In our opinion, however, the reasons for prohibiting the interrogation of an uncounseled prisoner who has asked for the help of a lawyer are even stronger after he has been formally charged with an offense than before. The State's argument misapprehends the nature of the pretrial protections afforded by the Sixth Amendment. In *United States v. Gouveia*, we explained the significance of the formal accusation, and the corresponding attachment of the Sixth Amendment right to counsel:

> "[G]iven the plain language of the Amendment and its purpose of protecting the unaided layman at critical confrontations with his adversary, our conclusion that the right to counsel attaches at the initiation of adversary judicial criminal proceedings 'is far from a mere formalism.' *Kirby v. Illinois* (1972). It is only at that time 'that the government has committed itself to prosecute, and only then that the adverse positions of government and defendant have solidified. It is then that a defendant finds himself faced with the prosecutorial forces of organized society, and immersed in the intricacies of substantive and procedural criminal law.' "

As a result, the "Sixth Amendment guarantees the accused, at least after the initiation of formal charges, the right to rely on counsel as a 'medium' between him and the State." Thus, the Sixth Amendment right to counsel at a postarraignment interrogation requires at least as much protection as the Fifth Amendment right to counsel at any custodial interrogation.

■ ■ ■

The State also relies on the factual differences between a request for counsel during custodial interrogation and a request for counsel at an arraignment. The State maintains that respondents may not have actually intended their request for counsel to encompass representation during any further questioning by the police. This argument, however, must be considered against the backdrop of our standard for assessing waivers of constitutional rights. Almost a half century ago, in *Johnson v. Zerbst* (1938), a case involving an alleged waiver of a defendant's Sixth Amendment right to counsel, the Court explained that we should "indulge every reasonable presumption against waiver of fundamental constitutional rights." For that reason, it is the State that has the burden of establishing a valid waiver. Doubts must be resolved in favor of protecting the constitutional claim. This settled approach to questions of waiver requires us to give a broad, rather than a narrow, interpretation to a defendant's request for counsel—we presume that the defendant requests the lawyer's services at every critical stage of the prosecution. We thus reject the State's suggestion that respondents' requests for the appointment of counsel should be construed to apply only to representation in formal legal proceedings.

The State points to another factual difference: the police may not know of the defendant's request for attorney at the arraignment. That claimed distinction is similarly unavailing. In the cases at bar, in which the officers in charge of the investigations of respondents were present at the arraignments, the argument is particularly unconvincing. More generally, however, Sixth Amendment principles require that we impute the State's knowledge from one state actor to another. For the Sixth Amendment concerns the confrontation between the State and the individual. One set of state actors (the police) may not claim ignorance of defendants' unequivocal request for counsel to another state actor (the court).

The State also argues that, because of these factual differences, the application of *Edwards* in a Sixth Amendment context will generate confusion. However, we have frequently emphasized that one of the characteristics of *Edwards* is its clear, "bright-line" quality. . . .

Finally, the State maintains that each of the respondents made a valid waiver of his Sixth Amendment rights by signing a postarraignment confession after again being advised of his constitutional rights. In *Edwards*, however, we rejected the notion that, after a suspect's request for counsel, advice of rights and acquiescence in police-initiated questioning could establish a valid waiver. We find no warrant for a different view under a Sixth Amendment analysis. Indeed, our rejection of the comparable argument in *Edwards* was based, in part, on our review of earlier Sixth Amendment cases. Just as written waivers are insufficient to justify police-initiated interrogations after the request for counsel in a Fifth Amendment analysis, so too they are insufficient to justify police-initiated interrogations after the request for counsel in a Sixth Amendment analysis.

Edwards is grounded in the understanding that "the assertion of the right to counsel [is] a significant event," and that "additional safeguards are necessary when the accused asks for counsel." We conclude that the assertion is no less significant, and the need for additional safeguards no less clear, when the request for counsel is made at an arraignment and when the basis for the claim is the Sixth Amendment. We thus hold that, if police initiate interrogation after a defendant's assertion, at an arraignment or similar proceeding, of his right to counsel, any waiver of the defendant's right to counsel for that police-initiated interrogation is invalid.

Although the *Edwards* decision itself rested on the Fifth Amendment and concerned a request for counsel made during custodial interrogation, the Michigan Supreme Court correctly perceived that the reasoning of that case applies with even greater force to these cases. The judgments are accordingly affirmed.

It is so ordered.

■ ■ ■

Justice REHNQUIST, with whom Justice POWELL and Justice O'CONNOR join, dissenting.

The Court's decision today rests on the following deceptively simple line of reasoning: *Edwards v. Arizona* created a bright-line rule to protect a defendant's Fifth Amendment rights; Sixth Amendment rights are even more important than Fifth Amendment rights; therefore, we must also apply the *Edwards* rule to the Sixth Amendment. The Court prefers this neat syllogism to an effort to discuss or answer the only relevant question: Does the *Edwards* rule make sense in the context of the Sixth Amendment? I think it does not, and I therefore dissent from the Court's unjustified extension of the *Edwards* rule to the Sixth Amendment.

My disagreement with the Court stems from our differing understandings of *Edwards*. In *Edwards*, this Court held that once a defendant has invoked his right under *Miranda v. Arizona* to have counsel present during custodial interrogation, "a valid waiver of that right cannot be established by showing only that he responded to further police-initiated custodial interrogation even if he has been advised of his rights." This "prophylactic rule" was deemed necessary to prevent the police from effectively "overriding" a defendant's assertion of his *Miranda* rights by "badgering" him into waiving those rights.

■ ■ ■

What the Court today either forgets or chooses to ignore is that the "constitutional guarantee" ... is the Fifth Amendment's prohibition on compelled self-incrimination. This prohibition, of course, is also the constitutional underpinning for the set of prophylactic rules announced in *Miranda* itself.

■ ■ ■

The dispositive question in the instant cases, and the question the Court should address in its opinion, is whether the same kind of prophylactic rule is needed to protect a defendant's right to counsel under the Sixth Amendment. The answer to this question, it seems to me, is clearly "no." The Court does not even suggest that the police commonly deny defendants their Sixth Amendment right to counsel. Nor, I suspect, would such a claim likely be borne out by empirical evidence. Thus, the justification for the prophylactic rules this Court created in *Miranda* and *Edwards*, namely, the perceived widespread problem that the police were violating, and would probably continue to violate, the Fifth Amendment rights of defendants during the course of custodial interrogations, is conspicuously absent in the Sixth Amendment context. To put it simply, the prophylactic rule set forth in *Edwards* makes no sense at all except when linked to the Fifth Amendment's prohibition against compelled self-incrimination.

Not only does the Court today cut the *Edwards* rule loose from its analytical moorings, it does so in a manner that graphically reveals the illogic of the Court's position. The Court phrases the question presented in these cases as whether the *Edwards* rule applies "to a defendant who has been formally charged with a crime *and who has requested appointment of counsel at his arraignment.*" And the Court ultimately limits its holding to those situations where the police "initiate interrogation *after a defendant's assertion, at an arraignment or similar proceeding, of his right to counsel.*"

In other words, the Court most assuredly does *not* hold that the *Edwards per se* rule prohibiting all police-initiated interrogations applies from the moment the defendant's Sixth Amendment right to counsel attaches, with or without a request for counsel by the defendant. Such a holding would represent, after all, a shockingly dramatic restructuring of the balance this Court has traditionally struck between the rights of the defendant and those of the larger society.

■ ■ ■

This leaves the Court, however, in an analytical straitjacket. The problem with the limitation the Court places on the Sixth Amendment version of the *Edwards* rule is that, unlike a defendant's "right to counsel" under *Miranda*, which does not arise until affirmatively invoked by the defendant during custodial interrogation, a defendant's Sixth Amendment right to counsel does not depend at all on whether the defendant has requested counsel.

■ ■ ■

The Court provides no satisfactory explanation for its decision to extend the *Edwards* rule to the Sixth Amendment, yet limit that rule to those defendants foresighted enough, or just plain lucky enough, to have made an explicit request for counsel which we have always understood to be completely unnecessary for Sixth Amendment purposes. The Court attempts to justify its emphasis on the otherwise legally insignificant request for counsel by stating that "we construe the defendant's request for counsel as an extremely important fact in considering the validity of a subsequent waiver in response to police-initiated interrogation." This statement sounds reasonable, but it is flatly inconsistent with the remainder of the Court's opinion, in which the Court holds that there can be no waiver of the Sixth Amendment right to counsel after a request for counsel has been made. It is obvious that, for the Court, the defendant's request for counsel is not merely an "extremely important fact"; rather, it is the *only* fact that counts.

The truth is that there is no satisfactory explanation for the position the Court adopts in these cases. The glaring inconsistencies in the Court's opinion arise precisely because the Court lacks a coherent, analytically sound basis for its decision. The prophylactic rule of *Edwards*, designed from its inception to protect a defendant's right under the Fifth Amendment not to be compelled to incriminate himself, simply does not meaningfully apply to the Sixth Amendment. I would hold that *Edwards* has no application outside the context of the Fifth Amendment, and would therefore reverse the judgment of the court below.

Patterson v. Illinois

487 U.S. 285 (1988)

WHITE, J., delivered the opinion of the Court, in which REHNQUIST, C.J., and O'CONNOR, SCALIA, and KENNEDY, JJ., joined. BLACKMUN, J., filed a dissenting opinion. STEVENS, J., filed a dissenting opinion, in which BRENNAN and MARSHALL, JJ., joined.

In this case, we are called on to determine whether the interrogation of petitioner after his indictment violated his Sixth Amendment right to counsel.

■ ■ ■

Before dawn on August 21, 1983, petitioner and other members of the "Vice Lords" street gang became involved in a fight with members of a rival gang, the "Black Mobsters." Some time after the fight, a former member of the Black Mobsters, James Jackson, went to the home where the Vice Lords had fled. A second fight broke out there, with petitioner and three other Vice Lords beating Jackson severely. The Vice Lords then put Jackson into a car, drove to the end of a nearby street, and left him face down in a puddle of water. Later that morning, police discovered Jackson, dead, where he had been left.

That afternoon, local police officers obtained warrants for the arrest of the Vice Lords, on charges of battery and mob action, in connection with the first fight. One of the gang members who was arrested gave the police a statement concerning the first fight; the statement also implicated several of the Vice Lords (including petitioner) in Jackson's murder. A few hours later, petitioner was apprehended. Petitioner was informed of his rights under *Miranda v. Arizona* (1966), and volunteered to answer questions put to him by the police. Petitioner gave a statement concerning the initial fight between the rival gangs, but denied knowing anything about Jackson's death. Petitioner was held in custody the following day, August 22, as law enforcement authorities completed their investigation of the Jackson murder.

On August 23, a Cook County grand jury indicted petitioner and two other gang members for the murder of James Jackson. Police Officer Michael Gresham, who had questioned petitioner earlier, removed him from the lockup where he was being held, and told petitioner that because he had been indicted he was being transferred to the Cook County jail. Petitioner asked Gresham which of the gang members had been charged with Jackson's murder, and upon learning that one particular Vice Lord had been omitted from the indictments, asked: "[W]hy wasn't he indicted, he did everything." Petitioner also began to explain that there was a witness who would support his account of the crime.

At this point, Gresham interrupted petitioner, and handed him a *Miranda* waiver form. The form contained five specific warnings, as suggested by this Court's *Miranda* decision, to make petitioner aware of his right to counsel and of the consequences of any statement he might make to police. Gresham read the warnings aloud, as petitioner read along with him. Petitioner initialed each of the five warnings, and signed the waiver form. Petitioner then gave a lengthy statement to police officers concerning the Jackson murder; petitioner's statement described in detail the role of each of the Vice Lords— including himself—in the murder of James Jackson.

Later that day, petitioner confessed involvement in the murder for a second time. This confession came in an interview with Assistant State's Attorney (ASA) George Smith. At the outset of the interview, Smith reviewed with petitioner the *Miranda* waiver he had previously signed, and petitioner confirmed that he had signed the waiver and understood his rights. Smith went through the waiver procedure once again: reading petitioner his rights, having petitioner initial each one, and sign a waiver form. In addition, Smith informed petitioner that he was a lawyer working with the police investigating the Jackson case. Petitioner then gave another inculpatory statement concerning the crime.

■ ■ ■

There can be no doubt that petitioner had the right to have the assistance of counsel at his postindictment interviews with law enforcement authorities. Our cases make it plain that the Sixth Amendment guarantees this right to criminal defendants. . . .

Petitioner, however, at no time sought to exercise his right to have counsel present. The fact that petitioner's Sixth Amendment right came into existence with his indictment, *i.e.*, that he had such a right at the time of his questioning, does not distinguish him from the preindictment interrogatee whose right to counsel is in existence and available for his exercise while he is questioned. Had petitioner indicated he wanted the assistance of counsel, the authorities' interview with him would have stopped, and further questioning would have been forbidden (unless petitioner called for such a meeting). This was our holding in *Michigan v. Jackson* [(1986)], which applied *Edwards* [*v. Arizona* (1981)] to the Sixth Amendment context. We observe that the analysis in *Jackson* is rendered wholly unnecessary if petitioner's position is correct: under petitioner's theory, the officers in *Jackson* would have been completely barred from approaching the accused in that case unless he called for them. Our decision in *Jackson*, however, turned on the fact that the accused "ha[d] asked for the help of a lawyer" in dealing with the police.

At bottom, petitioner's theory cannot be squared with our rationale in *Edwards*, the case he relies on for support. *Edwards* rested on the view that once "an accused . . . ha[s] expressed his desire to deal with the police only through counsel" he should "not [be] subject to further interrogation by the authorities until counsel has been made available to him, unless the accused himself initiates further communication." Preserving the integrity of an accused's choice to communicate with police only through counsel is the essence of *Edwards* and its progeny—not barring an accused from making an *initial* election as to whether he will face the State's officers during questioning with the aid of counsel, or go it alone. If an accused "knowingly and intelligently" pursues the latter course, we see no reason why the uncounseled statements he then makes must be excluded at his trial.

■   ■   ■

Petitioner's principal and more substantial claim is that questioning him without counsel present violated the Sixth Amendment because he did not validly waive his right to have counsel present during the interviews. Since it is clear that after the *Miranda* warnings were given to petitioner, he not only voluntarily answered questions without claiming his right to silence or his right to have a lawyer present to advise him but also executed a written waiver of his right to counsel during questioning, the specific issue posed here is whether this waiver was a "knowing and intelligent" waiver of his Sixth Amendment right.

■   ■   ■

First, the *Miranda* warnings given petitioner made him aware of his right to have counsel present during the questioning. By telling petitioner that he had a right to consult with an attorney, to have a lawyer present while he was questioned, and even to have a lawyer appointed for him if he could not afford to retain one on his own, Officer Gresham and ASA Smith conveyed to petitioner the sum and substance of the rights that the Sixth Amendment provided him. "Indeed, it seems self-evident that one who is told he" has such rights to counsel "is in a curious posture to later complain" that his waiver of these rights was unknowing.

Second, the *Miranda* warnings also served to make petitioner aware of the consequences of a decision by him to waive his Sixth Amendment rights during postindictment questioning. Petitioner knew that any statement that he made could be used against him in subsequent criminal proceedings. This is the ultimate adverse consequence petitioner could have suffered by virtue of his choice to make uncounseled admissions to the authorities.

■ ■ ■

As a general matter, then, an accused who is admonished with the warnings prescribed by this Court in *Miranda*, has been sufficiently apprised of the nature of his Sixth Amendment rights, and of the consequences of abandoning those rights, so that his waiver on this basis will be considered a knowing and intelligent one. We feel that our conclusion in a recent Fifth Amendment case is equally apposite here: "Once it is determined that a suspect's decision not to rely on his rights was uncoerced, that he at all times knew he could stand mute and request a lawyer, and that he was aware of the State's intention to use his statements to secure a conviction, the analysis is complete and the waiver is valid as a matter of law."

■ ■ ■

We consequently reject petitioner's argument, which has some acceptance from courts and commentators, that since "the sixth amendment right [to counsel] is far superior to that of the fifth amendment right" and since "[t]he greater the right the greater the loss from a waiver of that right," waiver of an accused's Sixth Amendment right to counsel should be "more difficult" to effectuate than waiver of a suspect's Fifth Amendment rights. While our cases have recognized a "difference" between the Fifth Amendment and Sixth Amendment rights to counsel, and the "policies" behind these constitutional guarantees, we have never suggested that one right is "superior" or "greater" than the other, nor is there any support in our cases for the notion that because a Sixth Amendment right may be involved, it is more difficult to waive than the Fifth Amendment counterpart.

■ ■ ■

Applying this approach, it is our view that whatever warnings suffice for *Miranda*'s purposes will also be sufficient in the context of postindictment questioning. The State's decision to take an additional step and commence formal adversarial proceedings against the accused does not substantially increase the value of counsel to the accused at questioning, or expand the limited purpose that an attorney serves when the accused is questioned by authorities. With respect to this inquiry, we do not discern a substantial difference between the usefulness of a lawyer to a suspect during custodial interrogation, and his value to an accused at postindictment questioning.

■ ■ ■

Before confessing to the murder of James Jackson, petitioner was meticulously informed by authorities of his right to counsel, and of the consequences of any choice not to exercise that right. On two separate occasions, petitioner elected to forgo the assistance of counsel, and speak directly to officials concerning his role in the murder. Because we believe that petitioner's waiver of his Sixth Amendment rights was "knowing and intelligent," we find no error in the decision of the trial court to permit petitioner's confessions to be used against him. Consequently, the judgment of the Illinois Supreme Court is
Affirmed.

Justice BLACKMUN, dissenting.

I agree with most of what Justice Stevens says in his dissenting opinion, however, merely would hold that after formal adversary proceedings against a defendant have been commenced, the Sixth Amendment mandates that the defendant not be " 'subject to further interrogation by the authorities until counsel has been made available to him, unless the accused himself initiates further communication, exchanges, or conversations with the police.' " *Michigan v. Jackson*, quoting *Edwards v. Arizona*.

■ ■ ■

Justice STEVENS, with whom Justice BRENNAN and Justice MARSHALL join, dissenting.

The Court should not condone unethical forms of trial preparation by prosecutors or their investigators. In civil litigation it is improper for a lawyer to communicate with his or her adversary's client without either notice to opposing counsel or the permission of the court. An attempt to obtain evidence for use at trial by going behind the back of one's adversary would be not only a serious breach of professional ethics but also a manifestly unfair form of trial practice. In the criminal context, the same ethical rules apply and, in my opinion, notions of fairness that are at least as demanding should also be enforced.

After a jury has been empaneled and a criminal trial is in progress, it would obviously be improper for the prosecutor to conduct a private interview with the defendant for the purpose of obtaining evidence to be used against him at trial. By "private interview" I mean, of course, an interview initiated by the prosecutor, or his or her agents, without notice to the defendant's lawyer and without the permission of the court. Even if such an interview were to be commenced by giving the defendant the five items of legal advice that are mandated by *Miranda*, I have no doubt that this Court would promptly and unanimously condemn such a shabby practice. As our holding in *Michigan v. Jackson* suggests, such a practice would not simply constitute a serious ethical violation, but would rise to the level of an impairment of the Sixth Amendment right to counsel.

The question that this case raises, therefore, is at what point in the adversary process does it become impermissible for the prosecutor, or his or her agents, to conduct such private interviews with the opposing party? Several alternatives are conceivable: when the trial commences, when the defendant has actually met and accepted representation by his or her appointed counsel, when counsel is appointed, or when the adversary process commences. In my opinion, the Sixth Amendment right to counsel demands that a firm and unequivocal line be drawn at the point at which adversary proceedings commence.

In prior cases this Court has used strong language to emphasize the significance of the formal commencement of adversary proceedings.

■ ■ ■

Today, however, in reaching a decision similarly favorable to the interest in law enforcement unfettered by process concerns, the Court backs away from the significance previously attributed to the initiation of formal proceedings. In the majority's view, the purported waiver of counsel in this case is properly equated with that of an unindicted suspect.

■ ■ ■

It is well settled that there is a strong presumption against waiver of Sixth Amendment protections, see *Michigan v. Jackson*.

■ ■ ■

The majority premises its conclusion that *Miranda* warnings lay a sufficient basis for accepting a waiver of the right to counsel on the assumption that those warnings make clear to an accused "what a lawyer could 'do for him' during the postindictment questioning: namely, advise [him] to refrain from making any [incriminating] statements." Yet, this is surely a gross understatement of the disadvantage of proceeding without a lawyer and an understatement of what a defendant must understand to make a knowing waiver. The *Miranda* warnings do not, for example, inform the accused that a lawyer might examine the indictment for legal sufficiency before submitting his or her client to interrogation or that a lawyer is likely to be considerably more skillful at negotiating a plea bargain and that such negotiations may be most fruitful if initiated prior to any interrogation. Rather, the warnings do not even go so far as to explain to the accused the nature of the charges pending against him—advice that a court would insist upon before allowing a defendant to enter a guilty plea with or without the presence of an attorney. Without defining precisely the nature of the inquiry required to establish a valid waiver of the Sixth Amendment right to counsel, it must be conceded that at least minimal advice is necessary—the accused must be told of the "dangers and disadvantages of self-representation."

Yet, once it is conceded that certain advice is required and that after indictment the adversary relationship between the state and the accused has solidified, it inescapably follows that a prosecutor may not conduct private interviews with a charged defendant. As at least one Court of Appeals has recognized, there are ethical constraints that prevent a prosecutor from giving legal advice to an uncounseled adversary. Thus, neither the prosecutor nor his or her agents can ethically provide the unrepresented defendant with the kind of advice that should precede an evidence-gathering interview after formal proceedings have been commenced. Indeed, in my opinion even the *Miranda* warnings themselves are a species of legal advice that is improper when given by the prosecutor after indictment.

■ ■ ■

In sum, without a careful discussion of the pitfalls of proceeding without counsel, the Sixth Amendment right cannot properly be waived. An adversary party, moreover, cannot adequately provide such advice. As a result, once the right to counsel attaches and the adversary relationship between the state and the accused solidifies, a prosecutor cannot conduct a private interview with an accused party without "dilut[ing] the protection afforded by the right to counsel," *Maine v. Moulton* (1985). Although this ground alone is reason enough to never permit such private interviews, the rule also presents the added virtue of drawing a clear and easily identifiable line at the point between the investigatory and adversary stages of a criminal proceeding. Such clarity in definition of constitutional rules that govern criminal proceedings is important to the law enforcement profession as well as to the private citizen.

■ ■ ■

I therefore respectfully dissent.

Montejo v. Louisiana

556 U.S. 778 (2009)

SCALIA, J., delivered the opinion of the Court, in which ROBERTS, C.J., and KENNEDY, THOMAS, and ALITO, JJ., joined. ALITO, J., filed a concurring opinion, in which KENNEDY, J., joined. STEVENS, J., filed a dissenting opinion, in which SOUTER and GINSBURG, JJ., joined, and in which BREYER, J., joined, except for fn5. BREYER, J., filed a dissenting opinion.

We consider in this case the scope and continued viability of the rule announced by this Court in *Michigan v. Jackson* (1986), forbidding police to initiate interrogation of a criminal defendant once he has requested counsel at an arraignment or similar proceeding.

I

Petitioner Jesse Montejo was arrested on September 6, 2002, in connection with the robbery and murder of Lewis Ferrari, who had been found dead in his own home one day earlier. Suspicion quickly focused on Jerry Moore, a disgruntled former employee of Ferrari's dry cleaning business. Police sought to question Montejo, who was a known associate of Moore.

Montejo waived his rights under *Miranda v. Arizona* (1966), and was interrogated at the sheriff's office by police detectives through the late afternoon and evening of September 6 and the early morning of September 7. During the interrogation, Montejo repeatedly changed his account of the crime, at first claiming that he had only driven Moore to the victim's home, and ultimately admitting that he had shot and killed Ferrari in the course of a botched burglary. These police interrogations were videotaped.

On September 10, Montejo was brought before a judge for what is known in Louisiana as a "72-hour hearing"—a preliminary hearing required under state law. Although the proceedings were not transcribed, the minute record indicates what transpired: "The defendant being charged with First Degree Murder, Court ordered N[o] Bond set in this matter. Further, Court ordered the Office of Indigent Defender be appointed to represent the defendant."

Later that same day, two police detectives visited Montejo back at the prison and requested that he accompany them on an excursion to locate the murder weapon (which Montejo had earlier indicated he had thrown into a lake). After some back-and-forth, the substance of which remains in dispute, Montejo was again read his *Miranda* rights and agreed to go along; during the excursion, he wrote an inculpatory letter of apology to the victim's widow. Only upon their return did Montejo finally meet his court-appointed attorney, who was quite upset that the detectives had interrogated his client in his absence.

At trial, the letter of apology was admitted over defense objection. The jury convicted Montejo of first-degree murder, and he was sentenced to death.

The Louisiana Supreme Court affirmed the conviction and sentence. As relevant here, the court rejected Montejo's argument that under the rule of *Jackson*, the letter should have been suppressed. *Jackson* held that "if police initiate interrogation after a defendant's assertion, at an arraignment or similar proceeding, of his right to counsel, any waiver of the defendant's right to counsel for that police-initiated interrogation is invalid."

■ ■ ■

II

Montejo and his *amici* raise a number of pragmatic objections to the Louisiana Supreme Court's interpretation of *Jackson*. We agree that the approach taken below would lead either to an unworkable standard, or to arbitrary and anomalous distinctions between defendants in different States. Neither would be acceptable.

Under the rule adopted by the Louisiana Supreme Court, a criminal defendant must request counsel, or otherwise "assert" his Sixth Amendment right at the preliminary hearing, before the *Jackson* protections are triggered. If he does so, the police may not initiate further interrogation in the absence of counsel. But if the court on its own appoints counsel, with the defendant taking no affirmative action to invoke his right to counsel, then police are free to initiate further interrogations provided that they first obtain an otherwise valid waiver by the defendant of his right to have counsel present.

This rule would apply well enough in States that require the indigent defendant formally to request counsel before any appointment is made, which usually occurs after the court has informed him that he will receive counsel if he asks for it. That is how the system works in Michigan, for example, whose scheme produced the factual background for this Court's decision in *Michigan v. Jackson.* Jackson, like all other represented indigent defendants in the State, had requested counsel in accordance with the applicable state law.

But many States follow other practices. In some two dozen, the appointment of counsel is automatic upon a finding of indigency, and in a number of others, appointment can be made either upon the defendant's request or *sua sponte* by the court. Nothing in our *Jackson* opinion indicates whether we were then aware that not all States require that a defendant affirmatively request counsel before one is appointed; and of course we had no occasion there to decide how the rule we announced would apply to these other States.

The Louisiana Supreme Court's answer to that unresolved question is troublesome. The central distinction it draws—between defendants who "assert" their right to counsel and those who do not—is exceedingly hazy when applied to States that appoint counsel absent request from the defendant. How to categorize a defendant who merely asks, prior to appointment, whether he will be appointed counsel? Or who inquires, after the fact, whether he has been? What treatment for one who thanks the court after the appointment is made? And if the court asks a defendant whether he would object to appointment, will a quick shake of his head count as an assertion of his right?

To the extent that the Louisiana Supreme Court's rule also permits a defendant to trigger *Jackson* through the "acceptance" of counsel, that notion is even more mysterious: How does one affirmatively accept counsel appointed by court order? An indigent defendant has no right to choose his counsel, so it is hard to imagine what his "acceptance" would look like, beyond the passive silence that Montejo exhibited.

In practice, judicial application of the Louisiana rule in States that do not require a defendant to make a request for counsel could take either of two paths. Courts might ask on a case-by-case basis whether a defendant has somehow invoked his right to counsel, looking to his conduct at the preliminary hearing—his statements and gestures—and the totality of the circumstances. Or, courts might simply determine as a categorical matter that defendants in these States—over half of those in the Union—simply have no opportunity to assert their right to counsel at the hearing and are therefore out of luck.

Neither approach is desirable. The former would be particularly impractical in light of the fact that, as *amici* describe, preliminary hearings are often rushed, and are frequently not recorded or transcribed. The sheer volume of indigent defendants would render the monitoring of each particular defendant's reaction to the appointment of counsel almost impossible. And sometimes the defendant is not even present. Police who did not attend the hearing would have no way to know whether they could approach a particular defendant; and for a court to adjudicate that question *ex post* would be a fact-intensive and burdensome task, even if monitoring were possible and transcription available. Because "clarity of . . . command" and "certainty of . . . application" are crucial in rules that govern law enforcement, this would be an unfortunate way to proceed.

The second possible course fares no better, for it would achieve clarity and certainty only at the expense of introducing arbitrary distinctions: Defendants in States that automatically appoint counsel would have no opportunity to invoke their rights and trigger *Jackson*, while those in other States, effectively instructed by the court to request counsel, would be lucky winners. That sort of hollow formalism is out of place in a doctrine that purports to serve as a practical safeguard for defendants' rights.

■ ■ ■

It is worth emphasizing first what is *not* in dispute or at stake here. Under our precedents, once the adversary judicial process has been initiated, the Sixth Amendment guarantees a defendant the right to have counsel present at all "critical" stages of the criminal proceedings.

Our precedents also place beyond doubt that the Sixth Amendment right to counsel may be waived by a defendant, so long as relinquishment of the right is voluntary, knowing, and intelligent. *Patterson v. Illinois* (1988). The defendant may waive the right whether or not he is already represented by counsel; the decision to waive need not itself be counseled. And when a defendant is read his *Miranda* rights (which include the right to have counsel present during interrogation) and agrees to waive those rights, that typically does the trick, even though the *Miranda* rights purportedly have their source in the *Fifth* Amendment.

■ ■ ■

The *only* question raised by this case, and the only one addressed by the *Jackson* rule, is whether courts must *presume* that such a waiver is invalid under certain circumstances. We created such a presumption in *Jackson* by analogy to a similar prophylactic rule established to protect the Fifth Amendment based *Miranda* right to have counsel present at any custodial interrogation. *Edwards v. Arizona* (1981) decided that once "an accused has invoked his right to have counsel present during custodial interrogation . . . [he] is not subject to further interrogation by the authorities until counsel has been made available," unless he initiates the contact.

The *Edwards* rule is "designed to prevent police from badgering a defendant into waiving his previously asserted *Miranda* rights." It does this by presuming his postassertion statements to be involuntary, "even where the suspect executes a waiver and his statements would be considered voluntary under traditional standards." This prophylactic rule thus "protect[s] a suspect's voluntary choice not to speak outside his lawyer's presence."

Jackson represented a "wholesale importation of the *Edwards* rule into the Sixth Amendment." The *Jackson* Court decided that a request for counsel at an arraignment should be treated as an invocation of the Sixth Amendment right to counsel "at every critical stage of the prosecution," despite doubt that defendants "actually inten[d] their request for counsel to encompass representation during any further questioning," because doubts must be "resolved in favor of protecting the constitutional claim." Citing *Edwards*, the Court held that any subsequent waiver would thus be "insufficient to justify police-initiated interrogation." In other words, we presume such waivers involuntary "based on the supposition that suspects who assert their right to counsel are unlikely to waive that right voluntarily" in subsequent interactions with police.

■ ■ ■

With this understanding of what *Jackson* stands for and whence it came, it should be clear that Montejo's interpretation of that decision—that no *represented* defendant can ever be approached by the State and asked to consent to interrogation—is off the mark. When a court appoints counsel for an indigent defendant in the absence of any request on his part, there is no basis for a presumption that any subsequent waiver of the right to counsel will be involuntary. There is no "*initial* election" to exercise the right that must be preserved through a prophylactic rule against later waivers. No reason exists to assume that a defendant like Montejo, who has done *nothing at all* to express his intentions with respect to his Sixth Amendment rights, would not be perfectly amenable to speaking with the police without having counsel present. And no reason exists to prohibit the police from inquiring. *Edwards* and *Jackson* are meant to prevent police from badgering defendants into changing their minds about their rights, but a defendant who never asked for counsel has not yet made up his mind in the first instance.

The dissent's argument to the contrary rests on a flawed *a fortiori*: "If a defendant is entitled to protection from police-initiated interrogation under the Sixth Amendment when he merely *requests* a lawyer, he is even more obviously entitled to such protection when he has *secured* a lawyer." The question in *Jackson*, however, was not whether respondents were entitled to counsel (they unquestionably were), but "whether respondents validly waived their right to counsel," and even if it is reasonable to presume from a defendant's *request* for counsel that any subsequent waiver of the right was coerced, no such presumption can seriously be entertained when a lawyer was merely "secured" on the defendant's behalf, by the State itself, as a matter of course. Of course, reading the dissent's analysis, one would have no idea that Montejo executed any waiver at all.

In practice, Montejo's rule would prevent police-initiated interrogation entirely once the Sixth Amendment right attaches, at least in those States that appoint counsel promptly without request from the defendant. As the dissent in *Jackson* pointed out, with no expressed disagreement from the majority, the opinion "most assuredly [did] *not* hold that the *Edwards per se* rule prohibiting all police-initiated interrogations applies from the moment the defendant's Sixth Amendment right to counsel attaches, with or without a request for counsel by the defendant." That would have constituted a "shockingly dramatic restructuring of the balance this Court has traditionally struck between the rights of the defendant and those of the larger society."

Montejo's rule appears to have its theoretical roots in codes of legal ethics, not the Sixth Amendment. The American Bar Association's Model Rules of Professional Conduct (which nearly all States have adopted into law in whole or in part) mandate that "a lawyer shall not communicate about the subject of [a] representation with a party the lawyer knows to be represented by another lawyer in the matter, unless the lawyer has the consent of the other lawyer or is authorized to do so by law or a court order." But the Constitution does not codify the ABA's Model Rules, and does not make investigating police officers lawyers. Montejo's proposed rule is both broader and narrower than the Model Rule. Broader, because Montejo would apply it to all agents of the State, including the detectives who interrogated him, while the ethical rule governs only lawyers. And narrower, because he agrees that if a defendant initiates contact with the police, they may talk freely—whereas a lawyer could be sanctioned for interviewing a represented party even if that party "initiates" the communication and consents to the interview. Model Rule 4.2, Comment 3.

■ ■ ■

Montejo also points to descriptions of the *Jackson* holding in two later cases. In one, we noted that "analysis of the waiver issue changes" once a defendant "obtains or even requests counsel." But elsewhere in the same opinion, we explained that *Jackson* applies "after a defendant requests assistance of counsel," "when a suspect charged with a crime requests counsel outside the context of interrogation," and to "suspects who assert their right to counsel." The accuracy of the "obtains" language is thus questionable. Anyway, since *Harvey* held that evidence obtained in violation of the *Jackson* rule *could* be admitted to impeach the defendant's trial testimony, the Court's varying descriptions of when the rule was violated were dicta.

■ ■ ■

The upshot is that even on *Jackson*'s own terms, it would be completely unjustified to presume that a defendant's consent to police-initiated interrogation was involuntary or coerced simply because he had previously been appointed a lawyer.

So on the one hand, requiring an initial "invocation" of the right to counsel in order to trigger the *Jackson* presumption is consistent with the theory of that decision, but . . . would be unworkable in more than half the States of the Union. On the other hand, eliminating the invocation requirement would render the rule easy to apply but depart fundamentally from the *Jackson* rationale.

We do not think that *stare decisis* requires us to expand significantly the holding of a prior decision—fundamentally revising its theoretical basis in the process—in order to cure its practical deficiencies. To the contrary, the fact that a decision has proved "unworkable" is a traditional ground for overruling it.

■ ■ ■

Which brings us to the strength of *Jackson*'s reasoning. When this Court creates a prophylactic rule in order to protect a constitutional right, the relevant "reasoning" is the weighing of the rule's benefits against its costs. "The value of any prophylactic rule . . . must be assessed not only on the basis of what is gained, but also on the basis of what is lost." We think that the marginal benefits of *Jackson* (viz., the number of confessions obtained coercively that are suppressed by its bright-line rule and would otherwise have been admitted) are dwarfed by its substantial costs (viz., hindering "society's compelling interest in finding, convicting, and punishing those who violate the law.").

What does the *Jackson* rule actually achieve by way of preventing unconstitutional conduct? Recall that the purpose of the rule is to preclude the State from badgering defendants into waiving their previously asserted rights. The effect of this badgering might be to coerce a waiver, which would render the subsequent interrogation a violation of the Sixth Amendment. Even though involuntary waivers are invalid even apart from *Jackson*, mistakes are of course possible when courts conduct case-by-case voluntariness review. A bright-line rule like that adopted in *Jackson* ensures that no fruits of interrogations made possible by badgering-induced involuntary waivers are ever erroneously admitted at trial.

But without *Jackson*, how many would be? The answer is few if any. The principal reason is that the Court has already taken substantial other, overlapping measures toward the same end. Under *Miranda*'s prophylactic protection of the right against compelled self-incrimination, any suspect subject to custodial interrogation has the right to have a lawyer present if he so requests, and to be advised of that right. Under *Edwards*' prophylactic protection of the *Miranda* right, once such a defendant "has invoked his right to have counsel present," interrogation must stop. And under *Minnick*'s prophylactic protection of the *Edwards* right, no subsequent interrogation may take place until counsel is present, "whether or not the accused has consulted with his attorney."

These three layers of prophylaxis are sufficient. Under the *Miranda-Edwards-Minnick* line of cases (which is not in doubt), a defendant who does not want to speak to the police without counsel present need only say as much when he is first approached and given the *Miranda* warnings. At that point, not only must the immediate contact end, but "badgering" by later requests is prohibited. If that regime suffices to protect the integrity of "a suspect's voluntary choice not to speak outside his lawyer's presence" before his arraignment, it is hard to see why it would not also suffice to protect that same choice after arraignment, when Sixth Amendment rights have attached. And if so, then *Jackson* is simply superfluous.

■ ■ ■

Montejo also correctly observes that the *Miranda-Edwards* regime is narrower than *Jackson* in one respect: The former applies only in the context of custodial interrogation. If the defendant is not in custody then those decisions do not apply; nor do they govern other, noninterrogative types of interactions between the defendant and the State (like pretrial lineups). However, those uncovered situations are the *least* likely to pose a risk of coerced waivers. When a defendant is not in custody, he is in control, and need only shut his door or walk away to avoid police badgering. And noninterrogative interactions with the State do not involve the "inherently compelling pressures" that one might reasonably fear could lead to involuntary waivers.

Jackson was policy driven, and if that policy is being adequately served through other means, there is no reason to retain its rule. *Miranda* and the cases that elaborate upon it already guarantee not simply noncoercion in the traditional sense, but what Justice Harlan referred to as "voluntariness with a vengeance." There is no need to take *Jackson*'s further step of requiring voluntariness on stilts.

On the other side of the equation are the costs of adding the bright-line *Jackson* rule on top of *Edwards* and other extant protections. The principal cost of applying any exclusionary rule "is, of course, letting guilty and possibly dangerous criminals go free...." *Jackson* not only "operates to invalidate a confession given by the free choice of suspects who have received proper advice of their *Miranda* rights but waived them nonetheless," but also deters law enforcement officers from even trying to obtain voluntary confessions. The "ready ability to obtain uncoerced confessions is not an evil but an unmitigated good." Without these confessions, crimes go unsolved and criminals unpunished. These are not negligible costs, and in our view the *Jackson* Court gave them too short shrift.

Notwithstanding this calculus, Montejo and his *amici* urge the retention of *Jackson*. Their principal objection to its elimination is that the *Edwards* regime which remains will not provide an administrable rule. But this Court has praised *Edwards* precisely because it provides " 'clear and unequivocal' guidelines to the law enforcement profession." ... That concern is misguided. "We have in fact never held that a person can invoke his *Miranda* rights anticipatorily, in a context other than 'custodial interrogation'...." What matters for *Miranda* and *Edwards* is what happens when the defendant is approached for interrogation, and (if he consents) what happens during the interrogation—not what happened at any preliminary hearing.

In sum, when the marginal benefits of the *Jackson* rule are weighed against its substantial costs to the truth-seeking process and the criminal justice system, we readily conclude that the rule does not "pay its way," *United States v. Leon* (1984). *Michigan v. Jackson* should be and now is overruled.

■ ■ ■

Montejo understandably did not pursue an *Edwards* objection, because *Jackson* served as the Sixth Amendment analogy to *Edwards* and offered broader protections. Our decision today, overruling *Jackson*, changes the legal landscape and does so in part based on the protections already provided by *Edwards*. Thus we think that a remand is appropriate so that Montejo can pursue this alternative avenue for relief. Montejo may also seek on remand to press any claim he might have that his Sixth Amendment waiver was not knowing and voluntary, *e.g.*, his argument that the waiver was invalid because it was based on misrepresentations by police as to whether he had been appointed a lawyer. These matters have heightened importance in light of our opinion today.

We do not venture to resolve these issues ourselves, not only because we are a court of final review, "not of first view," but also because the relevant facts remain unclear. Montejo and the police gave inconsistent testimony about exactly what took place on the afternoon of September 10, 2002, and the Louisiana Supreme Court did not make an explicit credibility determination. Moreover, Montejo's testimony came not at the suppression hearing, but rather only at trial, and we are unsure whether under state law that testimony came too late to affect the propriety of the admission of the evidence. These matters are best left for resolution on remand.

This case is an exemplar of Justice Jackson's oft quoted warning that this Court "is forever adding new stories to the temples of constitutional law, and the temples have a way of collapsing when one story too many is added." We today remove *Michigan v. Jackson*'s fourth story of prophylaxis.

The judgment of the Louisiana Supreme Court is vacated, and the case is remanded for further proceedings not inconsistent with this opinion.

It is so ordered.

Justice ALITO, with whom Justice KENNEDY joins, concurring.

Earlier this Term, in *Arizona v. Gant* (2009), the Court overruled *New York v. Belton* (1981), even though that case had been on the books for 28 years, had not been undermined by subsequent decisions, had been recently reaffirmed and extended, had proven to be eminently workable (indeed, had been adopted for precisely that reason), and had engendered substantial law enforcement reliance. The Court took this step even though we were not asked to overrule *Belton* and this new rule is almost certain to lead to a host of problems.

Justice Scalia, who cast the deciding vote to overrule *Belton*, dismissed *stare decisis* concerns with the following observation: "[I]t seems to me ample reason that the precedent was badly reasoned and produces erroneous ... results." This narrow view of *stare decisis* provides the only principle on which the decision in *Gant* can be justified.

In light of *Gant*, the discussion of *stare decisis* in today's dissent is surprising. The dissent in the case at hand criticizes the Court for "[a]cting on its own" in reconsidering *Michigan v. Jackson* (opinion of Stevens, J.). But the same was true in *Gant*, and in this case, the Court gave the parties and interested *amici* the opportunity to submit supplemental briefs on the issue, a step not taken in *Gant*.

The dissent faults the Court for "cast[ing] aside the reliance interests of law enforcement," but in *Gant*, there were real and important law enforcement interests at stake. Even the Court conceded that the *Belton* rule had "been widely taught in police academies and that law enforcement officers ha[d] relied on the rule in conducting vehicle searches during the past 28 years." And whatever else might be said about *Belton*, it surely provided a bright-line rule.

■ ■ ■

The dissent, finally, invokes *Jackson*'s antiquity, stating that "the 23-year existence of a simple bright-line rule" should weigh in favor of its retention. But in *Gant*, the Court had no compunction about casting aside a 28-year-old bright-line rule. I can only assume that the dissent thinks that our constitutional precedents are like certain wines, which are most treasured when they are neither too young nor too old, and that *Jackson*, at 23, is in its prime, whereas *Belton*, at 28, had turned brownish and vinegary.

I agree with the dissent that *stare decisis* should promote " 'the evenhanded ... development of legal principles.' " The treatment of *stare decisis* in *Gant* fully supports the decision in the present case.

Justice STEVENS, with whom Justice SOUTER and Justice GINSBURG join, and with whom Justice BREYER joins, except for footnote 5, dissenting.

Today the Court properly concludes that the Louisiana Supreme Court's parsimonious reading of our decision in *Michigan v. Jackson* is indefensible. Yet the Court does not reverse. Rather, on its own initiative and without any evidence that the longstanding Sixth Amendment protections established in *Jackson* have caused any harm to the workings of the criminal justice system, the Court rejects *Jackson* outright on the ground that it is "untenable as a theoretical and doctrinal matter." That conclusion rests on a misinterpretation of *Jackson*'s rationale and a gross undervaluation of the rule of *stare decisis*. The police interrogation in this case clearly violated petitioner's Sixth Amendment right to counsel.

■ ■ ■

In *Jackson*, this Court considered whether the Sixth Amendment bars police from interrogating defendants who have requested the appointment of counsel at arraignment. Applying the presumption that such a request constitutes an invocation of the right to counsel "at every critical stage of the prosecution," we held that "a defendant who has been formally charged with a crime and who has requested appointment of counsel at his arraignment" cannot be subject to uncounseled interrogation unless he initiates "exchanges or conversations with the police."

In this case, petitioner Jesse Montejo contends that police violated his Sixth Amendment right to counsel by interrogating him following his "72-hour hearing" outside the presence of, and without prior notice to, his lawyer. The Louisiana Supreme Court rejected Montejo's claim. Relying on the fact that the defendants in *Jackson* had "requested" counsel at arraignment, the state court held that *Jackson*'s protections did not apply to Montejo because his counsel was appointed automatically; Montejo had not explicitly requested counsel or affirmatively accepted the counsel appointed to represent him before he submitted to police interrogation.

I agree with the majority's conclusion that the Louisiana Supreme Court's decision, if allowed to stand, "would lead either to an unworkable standard, or to arbitrary and anomalous distinctions between defendants in different States."

■ ■ ■

Our decision in *Jackson* involved two consolidated cases, both arising in the State of Michigan. Under Michigan law in effect at that time, when a defendant appeared for arraignment the court was required to inform him that counsel would be provided if he was financially needy *and he requested representation*. It was undisputed that the *Jackson* defendants made such a "request" at their arraignment: one by completing an affidavit of indigency, and the other by responding affirmatively to a question posed to him by the court. In neither case, however, was it clear that counsel had actually been appointed at the arraignment. Thus, the defendants' requests for counsel were significant as a matter of state law because they served as evidence that the appointment of counsel had been effectuated even in the absence of proof that defense counsel had actual notice of the appointments.

Unlike Michigan, Louisiana does not require a defendant to make a request in order to receive court-appointed counsel. Consequently, there is no reason to place constitutional significance on the fact that Montejo neither voiced a request for counsel nor affirmatively embraced that appointment *post hoc*. Certainly our decision in *Jackson* did not mandate such an odd rule. If a defendant is entitled to protection from police-initiated interrogation under the Sixth Amendment when he merely *requests* a lawyer, he is even more obviously entitled to such protection when he has *secured* a lawyer.... Once an attorney-client relationship has been established through the appointment or retention of counsel, as a matter of federal law the method by which the relationship was created is irrelevant: The existence of a valid attorney-client relationship provides a defendant with the full constitutional protection afforded by the Sixth Amendment.

Today the Court correctly concludes that the Louisiana Supreme Court's holding is "troublesome," "impractical," and "unsound." Instead of reversing the decision of the state court by simply answering the question on which we granted certiorari in a unanimous opinion, however, the majority has decided to change the law. Acting on its own initiative, the majority overrules *Jackson* to correct a "theoretical and doctrinal" problem of its own imagining. A more careful reading of *Jackson* and the Sixth Amendment cases upon which it relied reveals that the rule announced in *Jackson* protects a fundamental right that the Court now dishonors.

The majority's decision to overrule *Jackson* rests on its assumption that *Jackson*'s protective rule was intended to "prevent police from badgering defendants into changing their minds about their rights," just as the rule adopted in *Edwards v. Arizona* was designed to prevent police from coercing unindicted suspects into revoking their requests for counsel at interrogation. Operating on that limited understanding of the purpose behind *Jackson*'s protective rule, the Court concludes that *Jackson* provides no safeguard not already secured by this Court's Fifth Amendment jurisprudence.

The majority's analysis flagrantly misrepresents *Jackson*'s underlying rationale and the constitutional interests the decision sought to protect. While it is true that the rule adopted in *Jackson* was patterned after the rule in *Edwards*, the *Jackson* opinion does not even mention the anti-badgering considerations that provide the basis for the Court's decision today. Instead, *Jackson* relied primarily on cases discussing the broad protections guaranteed by the Sixth Amendment right to counsel—not its Fifth Amendment counterpart. *Jackson* emphasized that the purpose of the Sixth Amendment is to " 'protec[t] the unaided layman at critical confrontations with his adversary,' " by giving him " 'the right to rely on counsel as a "medium" between him[self] and the State.' " Underscoring that the commencement of criminal proceedings is a decisive event that transforms a suspect into an accused within the meaning of the Sixth Amendment, we concluded that arraigned defendants are entitled to "at least as much protection" during interrogation as the Fifth Amendment affords unindicted suspects. *Jackson* ("[T]he *difference* between the legal basis for the rule applied in *Edwards* and the Sixth Amendment claim asserted in these cases actually provides additional support for the application of the rule in these circumstances" (emphasis added)). Thus, although the rules adopted in *Edwards* and *Jackson* are similar, *Jackson* did not rely on the reasoning of *Edwards* but remained firmly rooted in the unique protections afforded to the attorney-client relationship by the Sixth Amendment.

Once *Jackson* is placed in its proper Sixth Amendment context, the majority's justifications for overruling the decision crumble. Ordinarily, this Court is hesitant to disturb past precedent and will do so only when a rule has proven "outdated, ill-founded, unworkable, or otherwise legitimately vulnerable to serious reconsideration." While *stare decisis* is not "an inexorable command," we adhere to it as "the preferred course because it promotes the evenhanded, predictable, and consistent development of legal principles, fosters reliance on judicial decisions, and contributes to the actual and perceived integrity of the judicial process."

Paying lip service to the rule of *stare decisis*, the majority acknowledges that the Court must consider many factors before taking the dramatic step of overruling a past decision. Specifically, the majority focuses on four considerations: the reasoning of the decision, the workability of the rule, the reliance interests at stake, and the antiquity of the precedent. The Court exaggerates the considerations favoring reversal, however, and gives short shrift to the valid considerations favoring retention of the *Jackson* rule.

First, and most central to the Court's decision to overrule *Jackson*, is its assertion that *Jackson*'s " 'reasoning' "—which the Court defines as "the weighing of the [protective] rule's benefits against its costs"—does not justify continued application of the rule it created. The balancing test the Court performs, however, depends entirely on its misunderstanding of *Jackson* as a rule designed to prevent police badgering, rather than a rule designed to safeguard a defendant's right to rely on the assistance of counsel.

Next, in order to reach the conclusion that the *Jackson* rule is unworkable, the Court reframes the relevant inquiry, asking not whether the *Jackson* rule as applied for the past quarter century has proved easily administrable, but instead whether the Louisiana Supreme Court's cramped interpretation of that rule is practically workable. The answer to that question, of course, is no. When framed more broadly, however, the evidence is overwhelming that *Jackson*'s simple, bright-line rule has done more to advance effective law enforcement than to undermine it.

■ ■ ■

Turning to the reliance interests at stake in the case, the Court rejects the interests of criminal defendants with the flippant observation that any who are knowledgeable enough to rely on *Jackson* are too savvy to need its protections, and casts aside the reliance interests of law enforcement on the ground that police and prosecutors remain free to employ the *Jackson* rule if it suits them. Again as a result of its mistaken understanding of the purpose behind *Jackson*'s protective rule, the Court fails to identify the real reliance interest at issue in this case: the public's interest in knowing that counsel, once secured, may be reasonably relied upon as a medium between the accused and the power of the State. That interest lies at the heart of the Sixth Amendment's guarantee, and is surely worthy of greater consideration than it is given by today's decision.

Finally, although the Court acknowledges that "antiquity" is a factor that counsels in favor of retaining precedent, it concludes that the fact *Jackson* is "only two decades old" cuts "in favor of abandoning" the rule it established. I would have thought that the 23-year existence of a simple bright-line rule would be a factor that cuts in the other direction.

Despite the fact that the rule established in *Jackson* remains relevant, well grounded in constitutional precedent, and easily administrable, the Court today rejects it *sua sponte*. Such a decision can only diminish the public's confidence in the reliability and fairness of our system of justice.[5]

■ ■ ■

The Court avoids confronting the serious Sixth Amendment concerns raised by the police interrogation in this case by assuming that Montejo validly waived his Sixth Amendment rights before submitting to interrogation. It does so by summarily concluding that "doctrines ensuring voluntariness of the Fifth Amendment waiver simultaneously ensure the voluntariness of the Sixth Amendment waiver"; thus, because Montejo was given *Miranda* warnings prior to interrogation, his waiver was presumptively valid. Ironically, while the Court faults *Jackson* for blurring the line between this Court's Fifth and Sixth Amendment jurisprudence, it commits the same error by assuming that the *Miranda* warnings given in this case, designed purely to safeguard the Fifth Amendment right against self-incrimination, were somehow adequate to protect Montejo's more robust Sixth Amendment right to counsel.

The majority's cursory treatment of the waiver question rests entirely on the dubious decision in *Patterson*, in which we addressed whether, by providing *Miranda* warnings, police had adequately advised an indicted but unrepresented defendant of his Sixth Amendment right to counsel. The majority held that "[a]s a general matter . . . an accused who is admonished with the warnings prescribed . . . in *Miranda* . . . has been sufficiently apprised of the nature of his Sixth Amendment rights, and of the consequences of abandoning those rights." The Court recognized, however, that "because the Sixth Amendment's protection of the attorney-client relationship . . . extends beyond *Miranda*'s protection of the Fifth Amendment right to counsel, . . . there will be cases

---

5. In his concurrence, Justice Alito assumes that my consideration of the rule of *stare decisis* in this case is at odds with the Court's recent rejection of his reliance on that doctrine in his dissent in *Arizona v. Gant*. While I agree that the reasoning in his dissent supports my position in this case, I do not agree with his characterization of our opinion in *Gant*. Contrary to his representation, the Court did not overrule our precedent in *New York v. Belton*. Rather, we affirmed the narrow interpretation of *Belton*'s holding adopted by the Arizona Supreme Court, rejecting the broader interpretation adopted by other lower courts that had been roundly criticized by judges and scholars alike. By contrast, in this case the Court flatly overrules *Jackson*—a rule that has drawn virtually no criticism—on its own initiative. The two cases are hardly comparable. If they were, and if Justice Alito meant what he said in *Gant*, I would expect him to join this opinion.

where a waiver which would be valid under *Miranda* will not suffice for Sixth Amendment purposes." This is such a case.

As I observed in *Patterson*, the conclusion that *Miranda* warnings ordinarily provide a sufficient basis for a knowing waiver of the right to counsel rests on the questionable assumption that those warnings make clear to defendants the assistance a lawyer can render during post-indictment interrogation. Because *Miranda* warnings do not hint at the ways in which a lawyer might assist her client during conversations with the police, I remain convinced that the warnings prescribed in *Miranda*, while sufficient to apprise a defendant of his Fifth Amendment right to remain silent, are inadequate to inform an unrepresented, indicted defendant of his Sixth Amendment right to have a lawyer present at all critical stages of a criminal prosecution. The inadequacy of those warnings is even more obvious in the case of a *represented* defendant. While it can be argued that informing an indicted but unrepresented defendant of his right to counsel at least alerts him to the fact that he is entitled to obtain something he does not already possess, providing that same warning to a defendant who has *already* secured counsel is more likely to confound than enlighten. By glibly assuming that the *Miranda* warnings given in this case were sufficient to ensure Montejo's waiver was both knowing and voluntary, the Court conveniently avoids any comment on the actual advice Montejo received, which did not adequately inform him of his relevant Sixth Amendment rights or alert him to the possible consequences of waiving those rights.

A defendant's decision to forgo counsel's assistance and speak openly with police is a momentous one. Given the high stakes of making such a choice and the potential value of counsel's advice and mediation at that critical stage of the criminal proceedings, it is imperative that a defendant possess "a full awareness of both the nature of the right being abandoned and the consequences of the decision to abandon it," before his waiver is deemed valid. Because the administration of *Miranda* warnings was insufficient to ensure Montejo understood the Sixth Amendment right he was being asked to surrender, the record in this case provides no basis for concluding that Montejo validly waived his right to counsel, even in the absence of *Jackson*'s enhanced protections.

The Court's decision to overrule *Jackson* is unwarranted. Not only does it rest on a flawed doctrinal premise, but the dubious benefits it hopes to achieve are far outweighed by the damage it does to the rule of law and the integrity of the Sixth Amendment right to counsel. Moreover, even apart from the protections afforded by *Jackson*, the police interrogation in this case violated Jesse Montejo's Sixth Amendment right to counsel.

I respectfully dissent.

Justice Breyer, dissenting.

I join Justice Stevens' dissent except for footnote 5. Although the principles of *stare decisis* are not inflexible, I believe they bind the Court here. I reached a similar conclusion in *Arizona v. Gant* and in several other recent cases.

3. Fruits Analysis and Exclusionary Rule

Fellers v. United States

540 U.S. 519 (2004)

O'CONNOR, J., delivered the opinion of the unanimous Court.

After a grand jury indicted petitioner John J. Fellers, police officers arrested him at his home. During the course of the arrest, petitioner made several inculpatory statements. He argued that the officers deliberately elicited these statements from him outside the presence of counsel, and that the admission at trial of the fruits of those statements therefore violated his Sixth Amendment right to counsel. Petitioner contends that in rejecting this argument, the Court of Appeals for the Eighth Circuit improperly held that the Sixth Amendment right to counsel was "not applicable" because "the officers did not interrogate [petitioner] at his home." We granted the petition for a writ of certiorari, and now reverse. . . .

On February 24, 2000, after a grand jury indicted petitioner for conspiracy to distribute methamphetamine, Lincoln Police Sergeant Michael Garnett and Lancaster County Deputy Sheriff Jeff Bliemeister went to petitioner's home in Lincoln, Nebraska, to arrest him. The officers knocked on petitioner's door and, when petitioner answered, identified themselves and asked if they could come in. Petitioner invited the officers into his living room.

The officers advised petitioner they had come to discuss his involvement in methamphetamine distribution. They informed petitioner that they had a federal warrant for his arrest and that a grand jury had indicted him for conspiracy to distribute methamphetamine. The officers told petitioner that the indictment referred to his involvement with certain individuals, four of whom they named. Petitioner then told the officers that he knew the four people and had used methamphetamine during his association with them.

After spending about 15 minutes in petitioner's home, the officers transported petitioner to the Lancaster County jail. There, the officers advised petitioner for the first time of his rights under *Miranda v. Arizona* (1966) and *Patterson v. Illinois* (1988). Petitioner and the two officers signed a *Miranda* waiver form, and petitioner then reiterated the inculpatory statements he had made earlier, admitted to having associated with other individuals implicated in the charged conspiracy, and admitted to having loaned money to one of them even though he suspected that she was involved in drug transactions.

Before trial, petitioner moved to suppress the inculpatory statements he made at his home and at the county jail. A Magistrate Judge conducted a hearing and recommended that the statements petitioner made at his home be suppressed because the officers had not informed petitioner of his *Miranda* rights. The Magistrate Judge found that petitioner made the statements in response to the officers' "implici[t] questions," noting that the officers had told petitioner that the purpose of their visit was to discuss his use and distribution of methamphetamine. The Magistrate Judge further recommended that portions of petitioner's jailhouse statement be suppressed as fruits of the prior failure to provide *Miranda* warnings.

The District Court suppressed the "unwarned" statements petitioner made at his house but admitted petitioner's jailhouse statements pursuant to *Oregon v. Elstad* (1985), concluding petitioner had knowingly and voluntarily waived his *Miranda* rights before making the statements.

Following a jury trial at which petitioner's jailhouse statements were admitted into evidence, petitioner was convicted of conspiring to possess with intent to distribute methamphetamine. Petitioner appealed, arguing that his jailhouse statements should have been suppressed as fruits of the statements obtained at his home in violation of the Sixth Amendment. The Court of Appeals affirmed. With respect to petitioner's argument that the officers' failure to administer *Miranda* warnings at his home violated his Sixth Amendment right to counsel under *Patterson*, the Court of Appeals stated: "*Patterson* is not applicable here . . . for the officers did not interrogate [petitioner] at his home." The Court of Appeals also concluded that the statements from the jail were properly admitted under the rule of *Elstad*. (" 'Though *Miranda* requires that the unwarned admission must be suppressed, the admissibility of any subsequent statement should turn in these circumstances solely on whether it is knowingly and voluntarily made' ".)

Judge Riley filed a concurring opinion. He concluded that during their conversation at petitioner's home, officers "deliberately elicited incriminating information" from petitioner. That "post-indictment conduct outside the presence of counsel," Judge Riley reasoned, violated petitioner's Sixth Amendment rights. Judge Riley nevertheless concurred in the judgment, concluding that the jailhouse statements were admissible under the rationale of *Elstad* in light of petitioner's knowing and voluntary waiver of his right to counsel.

The Sixth Amendment right to counsel is triggered "at or after the time that judicial proceedings have been initiated . . . 'whether by way of formal charge, preliminary hearing, indictment, information, or arraignment.' " We have held that an accused is denied "the basic protections" of the Sixth Amendment "when there [is] used against him at his trial evidence of his own incriminating words, which federal agents . . . deliberately elicited from him after he had been indicted and in the absence of his counsel." *Massiah v. United States* (1964); *Patterson* (holding that the Sixth Amendment does not bar postindictment questioning in the absence of counsel if a defendant waives the right to counsel).

We have consistently applied the deliberate-elicitation standard in subsequent Sixth Amendment cases, see *United States v. Henry* (1980) ("The question here is whether under the facts of this case a Government agent 'deliberately elicited' incriminating statements . . . within the meaning of *Massiah*").

■ ■ ■

The Court of Appeals erred in holding that the absence of an "interrogation" foreclosed petitioner's claim that the jailhouse statements should have been suppressed as fruits of the statements taken from petitioner at his home. First, there is no question that the officers in this case "deliberately elicited" information from petitioner. Indeed, the officers, upon arriving at petitioner's house, informed him that their purpose in coming was to discuss his involvement in the distribution of methamphetamine and his association with certain charged co-conspirators. Because the ensuing discussion took place after petitioner had been indicted, outside the presence of counsel, and in the absence of any waiver of petitioner's Sixth Amendment rights, the Court of Appeals erred in holding that the officers' actions did not violate the Sixth Amendment standards established in *Massiah* and its progeny.

Second, because of its erroneous determination that petitioner was not questioned in violation of Sixth Amendment standards, the Court of Appeals improperly conducted its "fruits" analysis under the Fifth Amendment. Specifically, it applied *Elstad*, to hold that the admissibility of the jailhouse statements turns solely on whether the statements were "'knowingly and voluntarily made.'" The Court of Appeals did not reach the question whether the Sixth Amendment requires suppression of petitioner's jailhouse statements on the ground that they were the fruits of previous questioning conducted in violation of the Sixth Amendment deliberate-elicitation standard. We have not had occasion to decide whether the rationale of *Elstad* applies when a suspect makes incriminating statements after a knowing and voluntary waiver of his right to counsel notwithstanding earlier police questioning in violation of Sixth Amendment standards. We therefore remand to the Court of Appeals to address this issue in the first instance.

Accordingly, the judgment of the Court of Appeals is reversed, and the case is remanded for further proceedings consistent with this opinion.

It is so ordered.

Kansas v. Ventris

556 U.S. 586 (2009)

SCALIA, J., delivered the opinion of the Court, in which ROBERTS, C.J., and KENNEDY, SOUTER, THOMAS, BREYER, and ALITO, JJ., joined. STEVENS, J., filed a dissenting opinion, in which GINSBURG, J., joined.

We address in this case the question whether a defendant's incriminating statement to a jailhouse informant, concededly elicited in violation of Sixth Amendment strictures, is admissible at trial to impeach the defendant's conflicting statement.

In the early hours of January 7, 2004, after two days of no sleep and some drug use, Rhonda Theel and respondent Donnie Ray Ventris reached an ill-conceived agreement to confront Ernest Hicks in his home. The couple testified that the aim of the visit was simply to investigate rumors that Hicks abused children, but the couple may have been inspired by the potential for financial gain: Theel had recently learned that Hicks carried large amounts of cash.

The encounter did not end well. One or both of the pair shot and killed Hicks with shots from a .38-caliber revolver, and the companions drove off in Hicks's truck with approximately $300 of his money and his cell phone. On receiving a tip from two friends of the couple who had helped transport them to Hicks's home, officers arrested Ventris and Theel and charged them with various crimes, chief among them murder and aggravated robbery. The State dropped the murder charge against Theel in exchange for her guilty plea to the robbery charge and her testimony identifying Ventris as the shooter.

Prior to trial, officers planted an informant in Ventris's holding cell, instructing him to "keep [his] ear open and listen" for incriminating statements. According to the informant, in response to his statement that Ventris appeared to have "something more serious weighing in on his mind," Ventris divulged that "[h]e'd shot this man in his head and in his chest" and taken "his keys, his wallet, about $350.00, and . . . a vehicle."

At trial, Ventris took the stand and blamed the robbery and shooting entirely on Theel. The government sought to call the informant, to testify to Ventris's prior contradictory statement; Ventris objected. The State conceded that there was "probably a violation" of Ventris's Sixth Amendment right to counsel but nonetheless argued that the statement was admissible for impeachment purposes because the violation "doesn't give the Defendant . . . a license to just get on the stand and lie." The trial court agreed and allowed the informant's testimony, but instructed the jury to "consider with caution" all testimony given in exchange for benefits from the State. The jury ultimately acquitted Ventris of felony murder and misdemeanor theft but returned a guilty verdict on the aggravated burglary and aggravated robbery counts.

The Kansas Supreme Court reversed the conviction, holding that "[o]nce a criminal prosecution has commenced, the defendant's statements made to an undercover informant surreptitiously acting as an agent for the State are not admissible at trial for any reason, including the impeachment of the defendant's testimony."

The Sixth Amendment, applied to the States through the Fourteenth Amendment, guarantees that "[i]n all criminal prosecutions, the accused shall . . . have the Assistance of Counsel for his defence." The core of this right has historically been, and remains today, "the opportunity for a defendant to consult with an attorney and to have him investigate the case and prepare a defense for trial." *Michigan v. Harvey* (1990). We have held, however, that the right extends to having counsel present at various pretrial "critical" interactions between the defendant and the State, *United States v. Wade* (1967), including the deliberate elicitation by law enforcement officers (and their agents) of statements pertaining to the charge, *Massiah v. United States* (1964). The State has conceded throughout these proceedings that Ventris's confession was taken in violation of *Massiah*'s dictates and was therefore not admissible in the prosecution's case in chief. Without affirming that this concession was necessary, see *Kuhlmann v. Wilson* (1986), we accept it as the law of the case. The only question we answer today is whether the State must bear the additional consequence of inability to counter Ventris's contradictory testimony by placing the informant on the stand.

Whether otherwise excluded evidence can be admitted for purposes of impeachment depends upon the nature of the constitutional guarantee that is violated. Sometimes that explicitly mandates exclusion from trial, and sometimes it does not. The Fifth Amendment guarantees that no person shall be compelled to give evidence against himself, and so is violated whenever a truly coerced confession is introduced at trial, whether by way of impeachment or otherwise. The Fourth Amendment, on the other hand, guarantees that no person shall be subjected to unreasonable searches or seizures, and says nothing about excluding their fruits from evidence; exclusion comes by way of deterrent sanction rather than to avoid violation of the substantive guarantee. Inadmissibility has not been automatic, therefore, but we have instead applied an exclusionary-rule balancing test. The same is true for violations of the Fifth and Sixth Amendment prophylactic rules forbidding certain pretrial police conduct. See *Harris v. New York* (1971).

Respondent argues that the Sixth Amendment's right to counsel is a "right an accused is to enjoy a[t] trial." The core of the right to counsel is indeed a trial right, ensuring that the prosecution's case is subjected to "the crucible of meaningful adversarial testing." But our opinions under the Sixth Amendment, as under the Fifth, have held that the right covers pretrial interrogations to ensure that police manipulation does not render counsel entirely impotent—depriving the defendant of " 'effective representation by counsel at the only stage when legal aid and advice would help him.' "

Our opinion in *Massiah*, to be sure, was equivocal on what precisely constituted the violation. It quoted various authorities indicating that the violation occurred at the moment of the postindictment interrogation because such questioning " 'contravenes the basic dictates of fairness in the conduct of criminal causes.' " But the opinion later suggested that the violation occurred only when the improperly obtained evidence was "used against [the defendant] at his trial." That question was irrelevant to the decision in *Massiah* in any event. Now that we are confronted with the question, we conclude that the *Massiah* right is a right to be free of uncounseled interrogation, and is infringed at the time of the interrogation. That, we think, is when the "Assistance of Counsel" is denied.

■ ■ ■

This case does not involve, therefore, the prevention of a constitutional violation, but rather the scope of the remedy for a violation that has already occurred. Our precedents make clear that the game of excluding tainted evidence for impeachment purposes is not worth the candle. The interests safeguarded by such exclusion are "outweighed by the need to prevent perjury and to assure the integrity of the trial process." "It is one thing to say that the Government cannot make an affirmative use of evidence unlawfully obtained.

It is quite another to say that the defendant can...provide himself with a shield against contradiction of his untruths." *Walder* [*v. United States* (1954)]. Once the defendant testifies in a way that contradicts prior statements, denying the prosecution use of "the traditional truth-testing devices of the adversary process" is a high price to pay for vindication of the right to counsel at the prior stage.

On the other side of the scale, preventing impeachment use of statements taken in violation of *Massiah* would add little appreciable deterrence. Officers have significant incentive to ensure that they and their informants comply with the Constitution's demands, since statements lawfully obtained can be used for all purposes rather than simply for impeachment. And the *ex ante* probability that evidence gained in violation of *Massiah* would be of use for impeachment is exceedingly small. An investigator would have to anticipate both that the defendant would choose to testify at trial (an unusual occurrence to begin with) *and* that he would testify inconsistently despite the admissibility of his prior statement for impeachment. Not likely to happen—or at least not likely enough to risk squandering the opportunity of using a properly obtained statement for the prosecution's case in chief.

In any event, even if "the officer may be said to have little to lose and perhaps something to gain by way of possibly uncovering impeachment material," we have multiple times rejected the argument that this "speculative possibility" can trump the costs of allowing perjurious statements to go unchallenged. *Oregon v. Hass* (1975). We have held in every other context that tainted evidence—evidence whose very introduction does not constitute the constitutional violation, but whose obtaining was constitutionally invalid—is admissible for impeachment.

We hold that the informant's testimony, concededly elicited in violation of the Sixth Amendment, was admissible to challenge Ventris's inconsistent testimony at trial. The judgment of the Kansas Supreme Court is reversed, and the case is remanded for further proceedings not inconsistent with this opinion.

It is so ordered.

Justice STEVENS, with whom Justice GINSBURG joins, dissenting.

In *Michigan v. Harvey* (1990), the Court held that a statement obtained from a defendant in violation of the Sixth Amendment could be used to impeach his testimony at trial. As I explained in a dissent joined by three other Members of the Court, that holding eroded the principle that "those who are entrusted with the power of government have the same duty to respect and obey the law as the ordinary citizen." It was my view then, as it is now, that "the Sixth Amendment is violated when the fruits of the State's impermissible encounter with the represented defendant are used for impeachment just as it is when the fruits are used in the prosecutor's case in chief."

In this case, the State has conceded that it violated the Sixth Amendment as interpreted in *Massiah v. United States*, when it used a jailhouse informant to elicit a statement from the defendant. No *Miranda* warnings were given to the defendant, nor was he otherwise alerted to the fact that he was speaking to a state agent. Even though the jury apparently did not credit the informant's testimony, the Kansas Supreme Court correctly concluded that the prosecution should not be allowed to exploit its pretrial constitutional violation during the trial itself. The Kansas Court's judgment should be affirmed.

This Court's contrary holding relies on the view that a defendant's pretrial right to counsel is merely "prophylactic" in nature. The majority argues that any violation of this prophylactic right occurs solely at the time the State subjects a counseled defendant to an uncounseled interrogation, not when the fruits of the encounter are used against the defendant at trial. This reasoning is deeply flawed.

The pretrial right to counsel is not ancillary to, or of lesser importance than, the right to rely on counsel at trial. The Sixth Amendment grants the right to counsel "[i]n all criminal prosecutions," and we have long recognized that the right applies in periods before trial commences. We have never endorsed the notion that the pretrial right to counsel stands at the periphery of the Sixth Amendment. To the contrary, we have explained that the pretrial period is "perhaps the most critical period of the proceedings" during which a defendant "requires the guiding hand of counsel." Placing the prophylactic label on a core Sixth Amendment right mischaracterizes the sweep of the constitutional guarantee.

Treating the State's actions in this case as a violation of a prophylactic right, the Court concludes that introducing the illegally obtained evidence at trial does not itself violate the Constitution. I strongly disagree. While the constitutional breach began at the time of interrogation, the State's use of that evidence at trial compounded the violation. The logic that compels the exclusion of the evidence during the State's case in chief extends to any attempt by the State to rely on the evidence, even for impeachment. The use of ill-gotten evidence during any phase of criminal prosecution does damage to the adversarial process—the fairness of which the Sixth Amendment was designed to protect. See *Strickland v. Washington* (1984); see also *Adams v. United States ex rel. McCann* (1942) ("[The] procedural devices rooted in experience were written into the Bill of Rights not as abstract rubrics in an elegant code but in order to assure fairness and justice before any person could be deprived of 'life, liberty, or property' ").

When counsel is excluded from a critical pretrial interaction between the defendant and the State, she may be unable to effectively counter the potentially devastating, and potentially false, evidence subsequently introduced at trial. Inexplicably, today's Court refuses to recognize that this is a constitutional harm. Yet in *Massiah*, the Court forcefully explained that a defendant is "denied the basic protections of the [Sixth Amendment] guarantee when there [is] used against him at his trial evidence of his own incriminating words" that were "deliberately elicited from him after he had been indicted and in the absence of counsel." Sadly, the majority has retreated from this robust understanding of the right to counsel.

Today's decision is lamentable not only because of its flawed underpinnings, but also because it is another occasion in which the Court has privileged the prosecution at the expense of the Constitution. Permitting the State to cut corners in criminal proceedings taxes the legitimacy of the entire criminal process. "The State's interest in truthseeking is congruent with the defendant's interest in representation by counsel, for it is an elementary premise of our system of criminal justice 'that partisan advocacy on both sides of a case will best promote the ultimate objective that the guilty be convicted and the innocent go free.'" Although the Court may not be concerned with the use of ill-gotten evidence in derogation of the right to counsel, I remain convinced that such shabby tactics are intolerable in all cases. I respectfully dissent.

CHAPTER 6

Eyewitness Identification

Introduction

Eyewitness identification, which results in the conviction of many innocent people, is the problematic police practice considered by the Warren Court through a trilogy of cases decided on the same day. *Wade* declares that the pretrial lineup is a critical stage for the attachment of the right to counsel because counsel is needed to observe the lineup in order to eliminate unfairness. *Wade* also discusses the ramifications of a witness's faulty pretrial identification when the witness testifies during the trial. This so-called fruits doctrine is discussed in Chapter 1. Using a due process analysis, *Stovall* and *Gilbert* suppress eyewitness identification that is unnecessarily suggestive. Subsequent Courts have cut back on these decisions. As you read the later cases, keep in mind the following language from *Wade*:

> "Since it appears that there is grave potential for prejudice, intentional or not, in the pretrial lineup, which may not be capable of reconstruction at trial, and since presence of counsel itself can often avert prejudice and assure a meaningful confrontation at trial, there can be little doubt that for Wade the postindictment lineup was a critical stage of the prosecution at which he was 'as much entitled to such aid [of counsel] as at the trial itself.'"

Kirby cut back on *Wade* by redefining the critical stage for the attachment of the right to counsel, holding that the right to counsel attaches only *after* there has been some sort of court involvement rather than when counsel would be *useful*. *Rothgery* further defines what is meant by court involvement. *Ash* declares that there would be no right to counsel even if there had been court involvement at a photo array.

Manson emphasizes that an unnecessarily suggestive identification can be overcome by the the ultimate reliability of the identification, in the due process analysis of *Stovall-Gilbert*. However, the final case, *Perry*, declares that in order for there to be unnecessarily suggestive analysis there must be some police activity.

A. WARREN COURT APPROACH

United States v. Wade

388 U.S. 218 (1967)

Brennan, J., delivered the opinion of the Court, in which Warren, C.J., Douglas and Fortas, JJ., joined (except as to Part I). White, J., wrote an opinion dissenting in part and concurring in part, in which Harlan and Stewart, JJ., joined. Black, J., wrote an opinion dissenting in part and concurring in part.

The question here is whether courtroom identifications of an accused at trial are to be excluded from evidence because the accused was exhibited to the witnesses before trial at a post-indictment lineup conducted for identification purposes without notice to and in the absence of the accused's appointed counsel.

The federally insured bank in Eustace, Texas, was robbed on September 21, 1964. A man with a small strip of tape on each side of his face entered the bank, pointed a pistol at the female cashier and the vice president, the only persons in the bank at the time, and forced them to fill a pillowcase with the bank's money. The man then drove away with an accomplice who had been waiting in a stolen car outside the bank. On March 23, 1965, an indictment was returned against respondent, Wade, and two others for conspiring to rob the bank, and against Wade and the accomplice for the robbery itself. Wade was arrested on April 2, and counsel was appointed to represent him on April 26. Fifteen days later an FBI agent, without notice to Wade's lawyer, arranged to have the two bank employees observe a lineup made up of Wade and five or six other prisoners and conducted in a courtroom of the local county courthouse. Each person in the line wore strips of tape such as allegedly worn by the robber and upon direction each said something like "put the money in the bag," the words allegedly uttered by the robber. Both bank employees identified Wade in the lineup as the bank robber.

At trial the two employees, when asked on direct examination if the robber was in the courtroom, pointed to Wade. The prior lineup identification was then elicited from both employees on cross-examination. . . .

I

■ ■ ■

We have no doubt that compelling the accused merely to exhibit his person for observation by a prosecution witness prior to trial involves no compulsion of the accused to give evidence having testimonial significance. It is compulsion of the accused to exhibit his physical characteristics, not compulsion to disclose any knowledge he might have. It is no different from compelling Schmerber to provide a blood sample or Holt to wear the blouse, and, as in those instances, is not within the cover of the privilege. Similarly, compelling Wade to speak within hearing distance of the witnesses, even to utter words purportedly uttered by the robber, was not compulsion to utter statements of a "testimonial" nature; he was required to use his voice as an identifying physical characteristic, not to speak his guilt. We held in *Schmerber* [*v. California* (1966)] that the distinction to be drawn under the Fifth Amendment privilege against self-incrimination is one between an accused's "communications" in whatever form, vocal or physical, and "compulsion which makes a suspect or accused the source of 'real or physical evidence,'" *Schmerber*. We recognized that "both federal and state courts have usually held that [the privilege] offers no protection against compulsion to submit to fingerprinting, photography, or measurements, to write or speak for identification, to appear in court, to stand, to assume a stance, to walk, or to make a particular gesture." None of these activities becomes testimonial within the scope of the privilege because required of the accused in a pretrial lineup.

■ ■ ■

II

The fact that the lineup involved no violation of Wade's privilege against self-incrimination does not, however, dispose of his contention that the courtroom identifications should have been excluded because the lineup was conducted without notice to and in the absence of his counsel. . . .

The Framers of the Bill of Rights envisaged a broader role for counsel than under the practice then prevailing in England of merely advising his client in "matters of law" and eschewing any responsibility for "matters of fact." The constitutions in at least 11 of the 13 States expressly or impliedly abolished this distinction. "Though the colonial provisions about counsel were in accord on few things, they agreed on the necessity of abolishing the facts-law distinction; the colonists appreciated that if a defendant were forced to stand alone against the state, his case was foredoomed." This background is reflected in the scope given by our decisions to the Sixth Amendment's guarantee to an accused of the assistance of counsel for his defense. When the Bill of Rights was adopted, there were no organized police forces as we know them today. The accused confronted the prosecutor and the witnesses against him, and the evidence was marshalled, largely at the trial itself. In contrast, today's law enforcement machinery involves critical confrontations of the accused by the prosecution at pretrial proceedings where the results might well settle the accused's fate and reduce the trial itself to a mere formality. In recognition of these realities of modern criminal prosecution, our cases have construed the Sixth Amendment guarantee to apply to "critical" stages of the proceedings. The guarantee reads: "In all criminal prosecutions, the accused shall enjoy the right to have the Assistance of Counsel *for his defence.*" (Emphasis supplied.) The plain wording of this guarantee thus encompasses counsel's assistance whenever necessary to assure a meaningful "defence."

■ ■ ■

In *Escobedo v. Illinois* (1964), we drew upon the rationale of *Hamilton* [*v. Alabama* (1961)] and *Massiah* [*v. United States* (1964)] in holding that the right to counsel was guaranteed at the point where the accused, prior to arraignment, was subjected to secret interrogation despite repeated requests to see his lawyer. We again noted the necessity of counsel's presence if the accused was to have a fair opportunity to present a defense at the trial itself:

> "The rule sought by the State here, however, would make the trial no more than an appeal from the interrogation; and the 'right to use counsel at the formal trial [would be] a very hollow thing [if], for all practical purposes, the conviction is already assured by pretrial examination.'...'One can imagine a cynical prosecutor saying: "Let them have the most illustrious counsel, now. They can't escape the noose. There is nothing that counsel can do for them at the trial."'"

■ ■ ■

III

The Government characterizes the lineup as a mere preparatory step in the gathering of the prosecution's evidence, not different—for Sixth Amendment purposes—from various other preparatory steps, such as systematized or scientific analyzing of the accused's fingerprints, blood sample, clothing, hair, and the like. We think there are differences which preclude such stages being characterized as critical stages at which the accused has the right to the presence of his counsel. Knowledge of the techniques of science and technology is sufficiently available, and the variables in techniques few enough, that the accused has the opportunity for a meaningful confrontation of the Government's case at trial through the ordinary processes of cross-examination of the Government's expert witnesses and the presentation of the evidence of his own experts. The denial of a right to have his counsel present at such analyses does not therefore violate the Sixth Amendment; they are not critical stages since there is minimal risk that his counsel's absence at such stages might derogate from his right to a fair trial.

IV

But the confrontation compelled by the State between the accused and the victim or witnesses to a crime to elicit identification evidence is peculiarly riddled with innumerable dangers and variable factors which might seriously, even crucially, derogate from a fair trial. The vagaries of eyewitness identification are well-known; the annals of criminal law are rife with instances of mistaken identification. Mr. Justice Frankfurter once said: "What is the worth of identification testimony even when uncontradicted? The identification of strangers is proverbially untrustworthy. The hazards of such testimony are established by a formidable number of instances in the records of English and American trials. These instances are recent—not due to the brutalities of ancient criminal procedure." The Case of Sacco and Vanzetti (1927). A major factor contributing to the high incidence of miscarriage of justice from mistaken identification has been the degree of suggestion inherent in the manner in which the prosecution presents the suspect to witnesses for pretrial identification. A commentator has observed that "[t]he influence of improper suggestion upon identifying witnesses probably accounts for more miscarriages of justice than any other single factor—perhaps it is responsible for more such errors than all other factors combined." Suggestion can be created intentionally or unintentionally in many subtle ways. And the dangers for the suspect are particularly grave when the witness' opportunity for observation was insubstantial, and thus his susceptibility to suggestion the greatest.

Moreover, "[i]t is a matter of common experience that, once a witness has picked out the accused at the line-up, he is not likely to go back on his word later on, so that in practice the issue of identity may (in the absence of other relevant evidence) for all practical purposes be determined there and then, before the trial."

The pretrial confrontation for purpose of identification may take the form of a lineup, also known as an "identification parade" or "showup," as in the present case, or presentation of the suspect alone to the witness, as in *Stovall v. Denno* [1967]]. It is obvious that risks of suggestion attend either form of confrontation and increase the dangers inhering in eyewitness identification. But as is the case with secret interrogations, there is serious difficulty in depicting what transpires at lineups and other forms of identification confrontations. "Privacy results in secrecy and this in turn results in a gap in our knowledge as to what in fact goes on." *Miranda v. Arizona* (1966). For the same reasons, the defense can seldom reconstruct the manner and mode of lineup identification for judge or jury at trial. Those participating in a lineup with the accused may often be police officers; in any event, the participants' names are rarely recorded or divulged at trial. The impediments to an objective observation are increased when the victim is the witness. Lineups are prevalent in rape and robbery prosecutions and present a particular hazard that a victim's understandable outrage may excite vengeful or spiteful motives. In any event, neither witnesses nor lineup participants are apt to be alert for conditions prejudicial to the suspect. And if they were, it would likely be of scant benefit to the suspect since neither witnesses nor lineup participants are likely to be schooled in the detection of suggestive influences. Improper influences may go undetected by a suspect, guilty or not, who experiences the emotional tension which we might expect in one being confronted with potential accusers. Even when he does observe abuse, if he has a criminal record he may be reluctant to take the stand and open up the admission of prior convictions. Moreover any protestations by the suspect of the fairness of the lineup made at trial are likely to be in vain; the jury's choice is between the accused's unsupported version and that of the police officers present. In short, the accused's inability effectively to reconstruct at trial any unfairness that occurred at the lineup may deprive him of his only opportunity meaningfully to attack the credibility of the witness' courtroom identification.

What facts have been disclosed in specific cases about the conduct of pretrial confrontations for identification illustrate both the potential for substantial prejudice to the accused at that stage and the need for its revelation at trial. A commentator provides some striking examples:

"In a Canadian case . . . the defendant had been picked out of a lineup of six men, of which he was the only Oriental. On other cases, a black-haired suspect was placed among a group of light-haired persons, tall suspects have been made to stand with short nonsuspects, and, in a case where the perpetrator of the crime was known to be a youth, a suspect under twenty was placed in a lineup with five other persons, all of whom were forty or over."

Similarly state reports, in the course of describing prior identifications admitted as evidence of guilt, reveal numerous instances of suggestive procedures, for example, that all in the lineup but the suspect were known to the identifying witness, that the other participants in a lineup were grossly dissimilar in appearance to the suspect, that only the suspect was required to wear distinctive clothing which the culprit allegedly wore, that the witness is told by the police that they have caught the culprit after which the defendant is brought before the witness alone or is viewed in jail, that the suspect is pointed out before or during a lineup, and that the participants in the lineup are asked to try on an article of clothing which fits only the suspect.

The potential for improper influence is illustrated by the circumstances, insofar as they appear, surrounding the prior identifications in the three cases we decide today. In the present case, the testimony of the identifying witnesses elicited on cross-examination revealed that those witnesses were taken to the courthouse and seated in the courtroom to await assembly of the lineup. The courtroom faced on a hallway observable to the witnesses through an open door. The cashier testified that she saw Wade "standing in the hall" within sight of an FBI agent. Five or six other prisoners later appeared in the hall. The vice president testified that he saw a person in the hall in the custody of the agent who "resembled the person that we identified as the one that had entered the bank."

The lineup in *Gilbert* [*v. California* (1967)] was conducted in an auditorium in which some 100 witnesses to several alleged state and federal robberies charged to Gilbert made wholesale identifications of Gilbert as the robber in each other's presence, a procedure said to be fraught with dangers of suggestion. And the vice of suggestion created by the identification in *Stovall* was the presentation to the witness of the suspect alone handcuffed to police officers. It is hard to imagine a situation more clearly conveying the suggestion to the witness that the one presented is believed guilty by the police. See Frankfurter, The Case of Sacco and Vanzetti. . . .

Insofar as the accused's conviction may rest on a courtroom identification in fact the fruit of a suspect pretrial identification which the accused is helpless to subject to effective scrutiny at trial, the accused is deprived of that right of cross-examination which is an essential safeguard to his right to confront the witnesses against him. . . . And even though cross-examination is a precious safeguard to a fair trial, it cannot be viewed as an absolute assurance of accuracy and reliability. Thus in the present context, where so many variables and pitfalls exist, the first line of defense must be the prevention of unfairness and the lessening of the hazards of eyewitness identification at the lineup itself. The trial which might determine the accused's fate may well not be that in the courtroom but that at the pretrial confrontation, with the State aligned against the accused, the witness the sole jury, and the accused unprotected against the overreaching, intentional or unintentional, and with little or no effective appeal from the judgment there rendered by the witness—"that's the man."

Since it appears that there is grave potential for prejudice, intentional or not, in the pretrial lineup, which may not be capable of reconstruction at trial, and since presence of counsel itself can often avert prejudice and assure a meaningful confrontation at trial, there can be little doubt that for Wade the postindictment lineup was a critical stage of the prosecution at which he was "as much entitled to such aid [of counsel] as at the trial itself." *Powell v. Alabama* (1932). Thus both Wade and his counsel should have been notified of the impending lineup, and counsel's presence should have been a requisite to conduct of the lineup, absent an "intelligent waiver." . . . No substantial countervailing policy considerations have been advanced against the requirement of the presence of counsel. Concern is expressed that the requirement will forestall prompt identifications and result in obstruction of the confrontations. As for the first, we note that in the two cases in which the right to counsel is today held to apply, counsel had already been appointed and no argument is made in either case that notice to counsel would have prejudicially delayed the confrontations. Moreover, we leave open the question whether the presence of substitute counsel might not suffice where notification and presence of the suspect's own counsel would result in prejudicial delay. And to refuse to recognize the right to counsel for fear that counsel will obstruct the course of justice is contrary to the basic assumptions upon which this Court has operated in Sixth Amendment cases. We rejected similar logic in *Miranda v. Arizona*, concerning presence of counsel during custodial interrogation:

> "[A]n attorney is merely exercising the good professional judgment he has been taught. This is not cause for considering the attorney a menace to law enforcement. He is merely carrying out what he is sworn to do under his oath—to protect to the extent of his ability the rights of his client. In fulfilling this responsibility the attorney plays a vital role in the administration of criminal justice under our Constitution."

In our view counsel can hardly impede legitimate law enforcement; on the contrary, for the reasons expressed, law enforcement may be assisted by preventing the infiltration of taint in the prosecution's identification evidence. That result cannot help the guilty avoid conviction but can only help assure that the right man has been brought to justice.

Legislative or other regulations, such as those of local police departments, which eliminate the risks of abuse and unintentional suggestion at lineup proceedings and the impediments to meaningful confrontation at trial may also remove the basis for regarding the stage as "critical." But neither Congress nor the federal authorities have seen fit to provide a solution. What we hold today "in no way creates a constitutional straitjacket which will handicap sound efforts at reform, nor is it intended to have this effect." *Miranda v. Arizona.*

V

We come now to the question whether the denial of Wade's motion to strike the courtroom identification by the bank witnesses at trial because of the absence of his counsel at the lineup required, as the Court of Appeals held, the grant of a new trial at which such evidence is to be excluded. We do not think this disposition can be justified without first giving the Government the opportunity to establish by clear and convincing evidence that the in-court identifications were based upon observations of the suspect other than the lineup identification. Where, as here, the admissibility of evidence of the lineup identification itself is not involved, a per se rule of exclusion of court-room identification would be unjustified. A rule limited solely to the exclusion of testimony concerning identification at the lineup itself, without regard to admissibility of the courtroom identification, would render the right to counsel an empty one. The lineup is most often used, as in the present case, to crystallize the witnesses' identification of the defendant for future reference. We have already noted that the lineup identification will have that effect. The State may then rest upon the witnesses' unequivocal courtroom identifications, and not mention the pretrial identification as part of the State's case at trial. Counsel is then in the predicament in which Wade's counsel found himself—realizing that possible unfairness at the lineup may be the sole means of attack upon the unequivocal courtroom identification, and having to probe in the dark in an attempt to discover and reveal unfairness, while bolstering the government witness' courtroom identification by bringing out and dwelling upon his prior identification. Since counsel's presence at the lineup would equip him to attack not only the lineup identification but the courtroom identification as well, limiting the impact of violation of the right to counsel to exclusion of evidence only of identification at the lineup itself disregards a critical element of that right.

We think it follows that the proper test to be applied in these situations is that quoted in *Wong Sun v. United States* (1963), "[W]hether, granting establishment of the primary illegality, the evidence to which instant objection is made has been come at by exploitation of that illegality or instead by means sufficiently distinguishable to be purged of the primary taint." Application of this test in the present context requires consideration of various factors; for example, the prior opportunity to observe the alleged criminal act, the existence of any discrepancy between any pre-lineup description and the defendant's actual description, any identification prior to lineup of another person, the identification by picture of the defendant prior to the lineup, failure to identify the defendant on a prior occasion, and the lapse of time between the alleged act and the lineup identification. It is also relevant to consider those facts which, *un/cor on record. & ID had independent basis*

despite the absence of counsel, are disclosed concerning the conduct of the lineup....

On the record now before us we cannot make the determination whether the in-court identifications had an independent origin. This was not an issue at trial, although there is some evidence relevant to a determination. That inquiry is most properly made in the District Court. We therefore think the appropriate procedure to be followed is to vacate the conviction pending a hearing to determine whether the in-court identifications had an independent source, or whether, in any event, the introduction of the evidence was harmless error, *Chapman v. California* (1967), and for the District Court to reinstate the conviction or order a new trial, as may be proper.

The judgment of the Court of Appeals is vacated and the case is remanded to that court with direction to enter a new judgment vacating the conviction and remanding the case to the District Court for further proceedings consistent with this opinion. It is so ordered.

Judgment of Court of Appeals vacated and case remanded with direction.

■ ■ ■

Justice BLACK, dissenting in part and concurring in part.

■ ■ ■

In rejecting Wade's claim that his privilege against self-incrimination was violated by compelling him to appear in the lineup wearing the tape and uttering the words given him by the police, the Court relies on the recent holding in *Schmerber v. California*. In that case the Court held that taking blood from a man's body against his will in order to convict him of a crime did not compel him to be a witness against himself. I dissented from that holding, and still dissent. The Court's reason for its holding was that the sample of Schmerber's blood taken in order to convict him of crime was neither "testimonial" nor "communicative" evidence. I think it was both. It seems quite plain to me that the Fifth Amendment's Self-incrimination Clause was designed to bar the Government from forcing any person to supply proof of his own crime, precisely what Schmerber was forced to do when he was forced to supply his blood. The Government simply took his blood against his will and over his counsel's protest for the purpose of convicting him of crime. So here, having Wade in its custody awaiting trial to see if he could or would be convicted of crime, the Government forced him to stand in a lineup, wear strips on his face, and speak certain words, in order to make it possible for government witnesses to identify him as a criminal. Had Wade been compelled to utter these or any other words in open court, it is plain that he would have been entitled to a new trial because of having been compelled to be a witness against himself. Being forced by the Government to help convict himself and to supply evidence against himself by talking outside the courtroom is equally violative of his constitutional right not to be compelled to be a witness against himself. Consequently, because of this violation of the Fifth Amendment, and not because of my own personal view that the Government's conduct was "unfair," "prejudicial," or "improper," I would prohibit the prosecution's use of lineup identification at trial.

■ ■ ■

I would reverse Wade's conviction without further ado had the prosecution at trial made use of his lineup identification either in place of courtroom identification or to bolster in a harmful manner crucial courtroom identification. But the prosecution here did neither of these things. After prosecution witnesses under oath identified Wade in the courtroom, it was the defense, and not the prosecution, which brought out the prior lineup identification. While stating that "a per se rule of exclusion of courtroom identification would be unjustified," the Court, nevertheless remands this case for "a hearing to determine whether the in-court identifications had an independent source," or were the tainted fruits of the invalidly conducted lineup. From this holding I dissent.

In the first place, even if this Court has power to establish such a rule of evidence, I think the rule fashioned by the Court is unsound. The "tainted fruit" determination required by the Court involves more than considerable difficulty. I think it is practically impossible. How is a witness capable of probing the recesses of his mind to draw a sharp line between a courtroom identification due exclusively to an earlier lineup and a courtroom identification due to memory not based on the lineup? What kind of "clear and convincing evidence" can the prosecution offer to prove upon what particular events memories resulting in an in-court identification rest? How long will trials be delayed while judges turn psychologists to probe the subconscious minds of witnesses? All these questions are posed but not answered by the Court's opinion. In my view, the Fifth and Sixth Amendments are satisfied if the prosecution is precluded from using lineup identification as either an alternative to or corroboration of courtroom identification. If the prosecution does neither and its witnesses under oath identify the defendant in the courtroom, then I can find no justification for stopping the trial in midstream to hold a lengthy "tainted fruit" hearing. The fact of and circumstances surrounding a prior lineup identification might be used by the defense to impeach the credibility of the in-court identifications, but not to exclude them completely.

■ ■ ■

Justice WHITE, whom Justice HARLAN and Justice STEWART join, dissenting in part and concurring in part.

The Court has again propounded a broad constitutional rule barring the use of a wide spectrum of relevant and probative evidence, solely because a step in its ascertainment or discovery occurs outside the presence of defense counsel. This was the approach of the Court in *Miranda v. Arizona*. I objected then to what I thought was an uncritical and doctrinaire approach without satisfactory factual foundation.

The Court's opinion is far-reaching. It proceeds first by creating a new per se rule of constitutional law: a criminal suspect cannot be subjected to a pretrial identification process in the absence of his counsel without violating the Sixth

Amendment. If he is, the State may buttress a later courtroom identification of the witness by any reference to the previous identification. Furthermore, the courtroom identification is not admissible at all unless the State can establish by clear and convincing proof that the testimony is not the fruit of the earlier identification made in the absence of defendant's counsel—admittedly a heavy burden for the State and probably an impossible one. To all intents and purposes, courtroom identifications are barred if pretrial identifications have occurred without counsel being present.

The rule applies to any lineup, to any other techniques employed to produce an identification and a fortiori to a face-to-face encounter between the witness and the suspect alone, regardless of when the identification occurs, in time or place, and whether before or after indictment or information. It matters not how well the witness knows the suspect, whether the witness is the suspect's mother, brother, or long-time associate, and no matter how long or well the witness observed the perpetrator at the scene of the crime. The kidnap victim who has lived for days with his abductor is in the same category as the witness who has had only a fleeting glimpse of the criminal. Neither may identify the suspect without defendant's counsel being present. The same strictures apply regardless of the number of other witnesses who positively identify the defendant and regardless of the corroborative evidence showing that it was the defendant who had committed the crime.

The premise for the Court's rule is not the general unreliability of eyewitness identifications nor the difficulties inherent in observation, recall, and recognition. The Court assumes a narrower evil as the basis for its rule—improper police suggestion which contributes to erroneous identifications. The Court apparently believes that improper police procedures are so widespread that a broad prophylactic rule must be laid down, requiring the presence of counsel at all pretrial identifications, in order to detect recurring instances of police misconduct. I do not share this pervasive distrust of all official investigations.

■ ■ ■

The Court goes beyond assuming that a great majority of the country's police departments are following improper practices at pretrial identifications. To find the lineup a "critical" stage of the proceeding and to exclude identifications made in the absence of counsel, the Court must also assume that police "suggestion," if it occurs at all, leads to erroneous rather than accurate identifications and that reprehensible police conduct will have an unavoidable and largely undiscoverable impact on the trial. This in turn assumes that there is now no adequate source from which defense counsel can learn about the circumstances of the pretrial identification in order to place before the jury all of the considerations which should enter into an appraisal of courtroom identification evidence. But these are treacherous and unsupported assumptions resting as they do on the notion that the defendant will not be aware, that the police and the witnesses will forget or prevaricate, that defense counsel will be unable to bring out the truth and that neither jury, judge, nor appellate court is a sufficient safeguard against unacceptable police conduct occurring at a pretrial identification procedure. I am unable to share the Court's view of the willingness of the police and the ordinary citizen witness to dissemble, either with respect to the identification of the defendant or with respect to the circumstances surrounding a pretrial identification.

There are several striking aspects to the Court's holding. First, the rule does not bar courtroom identifications where there have been no previous identifications in the presence of the police, although when identified in the courtroom, the defendant is known to be in custody and charged with the commission of a crime. Second, the Court seems to say that if suitable legislative standards were adopted for the conduct of pretrial identifications, thereby lessening the hazards in such confrontations, it would not insist on the presence of counsel. But if this is true, why does not the Court simply fashion what it deems to be constitutionally acceptable procedures for the authorities to follow? Certainly the Court is correct in suggesting that the new rule will be wholly inapplicable where police departments themselves have established suitable safeguards.

■ ■ ■

I share the Court's view that the criminal trial, at the very least, should aim at truthful fact-finding, including accurate eyewitness identifications. I doubt, however, on the basis of our present information, that the tragic mistakes which have occurred in criminal trials are as much the product of improper police conduct as they are the consequence of the difficulties inherent in eyewitness testimony and in resolving evidentiary conflicts by court or jury. I doubt that the Court's new rule will obviate these difficulties, or that the situation will be measurably improved by inserting defense counsel into the investigative processes of police departments everywhere.

■ ■ ■

I would not extend this system, at least as it presently operates, to police investigations and would not require counsel's presence at pretrial identification procedures. Counsel's interest is in not having his client placed at the scene of the crime, regardless of his whereabouts. Some counsel may advise their clients to refuse to make any movements or to speak any words in a lineup or even to appear in one. To that extent the impact on truthful fact-finding is quite obvious. Others will not only observe what occurs and develop possibility for later cross-examination but will hover over witnesses and begin their cross-examination then, menacing truthful fact-finding as thoroughly as the Court fears the police now do. Certainly there is an implicit invitation to counsel to suggest rules for the lineup and to manage and produce it as best he can. I therefore doubt that the Court's new rule, at least absent some clearly defined limits on counsel's role, will measurably contribute to more reliable pretrial identifications. My fears are that it will have precisely the opposite result. It may well produce fewer convictions, but that is hardly a proper measure of its long-run acceptability. In my view, the State is entitled to investigate and develop its case outside the presence of defense counsel. This includes the right to have private conversations with identification witnesses, just as defense counsel may have his own consultations with these and other witnesses without having the prosecutor present.

Whether today's judgment would be an acceptable exercise of supervisory power over federal courts is another question. But as a constitutional matter, the judgment in this case is erroneous and although I concur in Parts I and III of the Court's opinion I respectfully register this dissent.

Stovall v. Denno

388 U.S. 293 (1967)

BRENNAN, J., delivered the opinion of the Court, in which WARREN, C.J., CLARK, WHITE, HARLAN, and STEWART, JJ., joined. DOUGLAS and FORTAS, JJ., dissented in part. BLACK, J., dissented.

This federal habeas corpus proceeding attacks collaterally a state criminal conviction for the same alleged constitutional errors in the admission of allegedly tainted identification evidence that were before us on direct review of the convictions involved in *United States v. Wade* (1967) and *Gilbert v. California* (1967). This case therefore provides a vehicle for deciding the extent to which the rules announced in *Wade* and *Gilbert*—requiring the exclusion of identification evidence which is tainted by exhibiting the accused to identifying witnesses before trial in the absence of his counsel—are to be applied retroactively. A further question is whether in any event, on the facts of the particular confrontation involved in this case, petitioner was denied due process of law in violation of the Fourteenth Amendment.

Dr. Paul Behrendt was stabbed to death in the kitchen of his home in Garden City, Long Island, about midnight August 23, 1961. Dr. Behrendt's wife, also a physician, had followed her husband to the kitchen and jumped at the assailant. He knocked her to the floor and stabbed her 11 times. The police found a shirt on the kitchen floor and keys in a pocket which they traced to petitioner. They arrested him on the afternoon of August 24. An arraignment was promptly held but was postponed until petitioner could retain counsel.

Mrs. Behrendt was hospitalized for major surgery to save her life. The police, without affording petitioner time to retain counsel, arranged with her surgeon to permit them to bring petitioner to her hospital room about noon of August 25, the day after the surgery. Petitioner was handcuffed to one of five police officers who, with two members of the staff of the District Attorney, brought him to the hospital room. Petitioner was the only Negro in the room. Mrs. Behrendt identified him from her hospital bed after being asked by an officer whether he "was the man" and after petitioner repeated at the direction of an officer a "few words for voice identification." None of the witnesses could recall the words that were used. Mrs. Behrendt and the officers testified at the trial to her identification of the petitioner in the hospital room, and she also made an in-court identification of petitioner in the courtroom.

■ ■ ■

We hold that *Wade* and *Gilbert* affect only those cases and all future cases which involve confrontations for identification purposes conducted in the absence of counsel after this date. The rulings of *Wade* and *Gilbert* are therefore inapplicable in the present case. We think also that on the facts of this case petitioner was not deprived of due process of law in violation of the Fourteenth Amendment. The judgment of the Court of Appeals is, therefore, affirmed.

Our recent discussions of the retroactivity of the constitutional rules of criminal procedure make unnecessary any detailed treatment of that question here. *Linkletter v. Walker* (1965); *Tehan v. Shott* (1966); *Johnson v. New Jersey* (1966). "These cases establish the principle that in criminal litigation concerning constitutional claims, 'the Court may in the interest of justice make the rule prospective where the exigencies of the situation require such an application.'" The criteria guiding resolution of the question implicates (a) the purpose to be served by the new standards, (b) the extent of the reliance by law enforcement authorities on the old standards, and (c) the effect on the administration of justice of a retroactive application of the new standards. "[T]he retroactivity or nonretroactivity of a rule is not automatically determined by the provision of the Constitution on which the dictate is based. Each constitutional rule of criminal procedure has its own distinct functions, its own background of precedent, and its own impact on the administration of justice, and the way in which these factors combine must inevitably vary with the dictate involved."

Wade and *Gilbert* fashion exclusionary rules to deter law enforcement authorities from exhibiting an accused to witnesses before trial for identification purposes without notice to and in the absence of counsel. A conviction which rests on a mistaken identification is a gross miscarriage of justice. The *Wade* and *Gilbert* rules are aimed at minimizing that possibility by preventing the unfairness at the pretrial confrontation that experience has proved can occur and assuring meaningful examination of the identification witness' testimony at trial. Does it follow that the rules should be applied retroactively? We do not think so.

It is true that the right to the assistance of counsel has been applied retroactively at stages of the prosecution where denial of the right must almost invariably deny a fair trial, for example, at the trial itself, *Gideon v. Wainwright* (1963). "The basic purpose of a trial is the determination of truth, and it is self-evident that to deny a lawyer's help through the technical intricacies of a criminal trial or to deny a full opportunity to appeal a conviction because the accused is poor is to impede that purpose and to infect a criminal proceeding with the clear danger of convicting the innocent." Although the *Wade* and *Gilbert* rules also are aimed at avoiding unfairness at the trial by enhancing the reliability of the fact-finding process in the area of identification evidence, "the question whether a constitutional rule of criminal procedure does or does not enhance the reliability of the fact-finding process at trial is necessarily a matter of degree." The extent to which a condemned practice infects the integrity of the truth-determining process at trial is a "question of probabilities." Such probabilities must in turn be weighed against the prior justified reliance upon the old standards and the impact of retroactivity upon the administration of justice.

We have outlined in *Wade* the dangers and unfairness inherent in confrontations for identification. The possibility of unfairness at that point is great, both because of the manner in which confrontations are frequently conducted, and because of the likelihood that the accused will often be precluded from reconstructing what occurred and thereby from obtaining a full hearing on the identification issue at trial. The presence of counsel will significantly promote fairness at the confrontation and a full hearing at trial on the issue of identification. We have, therefore, concluded that the confrontation is a "critical stage," and that counsel is required at all confrontations. It must be recognized, however, that, unlike cases in which counsel is absent at trial or on appeal, it may confidently be assumed that confrontations for identification can be and often have been conducted in the absence of counsel with scrupulous fairness and without prejudice to the accused at trial. Therefore, while we feel that the exclusionary rules set forth in *Wade* and *Gilbert* are justified by the need to assure the integrity and reliability of our system of justice, they undoubtedly will affect cases in which no unfairness will be present. Of course, we should also assume there have been injustices in the past which could have been averted by having counsel present at the confrontation for identification, just as there are injustices when counsel is absent at trial. But the certainty and frequency with which we can say in the confrontation cases that no injustice occurred differs greatly enough from the cases involving absence of counsel at trial or on appeal to justify treating the situations as different in kind for the purpose of retroactive application, especially in light of the strong countervailing interests outlined below, and because it remains open to all persons to allege and prove, as Stovall attempts to do in this case, that the confrontation resulted in such unfairness that it infringed his right to due process of law.

■ ■ ■

The unusual force of the countervailing considerations strengthens our conclusion in favor of prospective application. The law enforcement officials of the Federal Government and of all 50 States have heretofore proceeded on the premise that the Constitution did not require the presence of counsel at pretrial confrontations for identification.

■ ■ ■

We turn now to the question whether petitioner, although not entitled to the application of *Wade* and *Gilbert* to his case, is entitled to relief on his claim that in any event the confrontation conducted in this case was so unnecessarily suggestive and conducive to irreparable mistaken identification that he was denied due process of law. This is a recognized ground of attack upon a conviction independent of any right to counsel claim. The practice of showing suspects singly to persons for the purpose of identification, and not as part of a lineup, has been widely condemned. However, a claimed violation of due process of law in the conduct of a confrontation depends on the totality of the circumstances surrounding it, and the record in the present case reveals that the showing of Stovall to Mrs. Behrendt in an immediate hospital confrontation was imperative.

> "Here was the only person in the world who could possibly exonerate Stovall. Her words, and only her words, 'He is not the man' could have resulted in freedom for Stovall. The hospital was not far distant from the courthouse and jail. No one knew how long Mrs. Behrendt might live. Faced with the responsibility of identifying the attacker, with the need for immediate action and with the knowledge that Mrs. Behrendt could not visit the jail, the police followed the only feasible procedure and took Stovall to the hospital room. Under these circumstances, the usual police station line-up, which Stovall now argues he should have had, was out of the question."

The judgment of the Court of Appeals is affirmed. It is so ordered.
Affirmed.

Gilbert v. California

388 U.S. 263 (1967)

BRENNAN, J., delivered the opinion of the Court, in which DOUGLAS and MARSHALL, JJ., join and WARREN, C.J., BLACK, WHITE, FORTAS, HARLAN, and STEWART, JJ., concur in part and dissent in part.

This case was argued with *United States v. Wade* (1967) and presents the same alleged constitutional error in the admission in evidence of in-court identification there considered.

The following description comes from the Ninth Circuit Court of Appeals decision in Gilbert v. United States *(1967):*

"The lineup occurred on March 26, 1964, after Gilbert had been indicted and had obtained counsel. It was held in an auditorium used for that purpose by the Los Angeles police. Some ten to thirteen prisoners were placed on a lighted stage. The witnesses were assembled in a darkened portion of the room, facing the stage and separated from it by a screen. They could see the prisoners but could not be seen by them. State and federal officers were also present and one of them acted as 'moderator' of the proceedings.

Each man in the lineup was identified by number, but not by name. Each man was required to step forward into a marked circle, to turn, presenting both profiles as well as a face and back view, to walk, to put on or take off certain articles of clothing. When a man's number was called and he was directed to step into the circle, he was asked certain questions: where he was picked up, whether he owned a car, whether, when arrested, he was armed, where he lived. Each was also asked to repeat certain phrases, both in a loud and in a soft voice, phrases that witnesses to the crimes had heard the robbers use: 'Freeze, this is a stickup; this is a holdup; empty your cash drawer; this is a heist; don't anybody move.'

Either while the men were on the stage, or after they were taken from it, it is not clear which, the assembled witnesses were asked if there were any that they would like to see again, and told that if they had doubts, now was the time to resolve them. Several gave the numbers of men they wanted to see, including Gilbert's. While the other prisoners were no longer present, Gilbert and 2 or 3 others were again put through a similar procedure. Some of the witnesses asked that a particular prisoner say a particular phrase, or walk a particular way. After the lineup, the witnesses talked to each other; it is not clear that they did so during the lineup. They did, however, in each other's presence, call out the numbers of men they could identify."

THE HANDWRITING EXEMPLARS

Petitioner was arrested in Philadelphia by an FBI agent and refused to answer questions. . . . He later did answer questions of another agent about some Philadelphia robberies in which the robber used a handwritten note demanding that money be handed over to him, and during that interrogation gave the agent the handwriting exemplars. . . .

The taking of the exemplars did not violate petitioner's Fifth Amendment privilege against self-incrimination. The privilege reaches only compulsion of "an accused's communications, whatever form they might take, and the compulsion of responses which are also communications, for example, compliance with a subpoena to produce one's papers," and not "compulsion which makes a suspect or accused the source of 'real or physical evidence'. . . ." *Schmerber v. California* (1967). One's voice and handwriting are, of course, means of communication. It by no means follows, however, that every compulsion of an accused to use his voice or write compels a communication within the cover of the privilege. A mere handwriting exemplar, in contrast to the content of what is written, like the voice or body itself, is an identifying physical characteristic outside its protection. . . .

THE IN-COURT AND LINEUP IDENTIFICATIONS

Three eyewitnesses to the Alhambra crimes who identified Gilbert at the guilt stage of the trial had observed him at a lineup conducted without notice to his counsel in a Los Angeles auditorium 16 days after his indictment and after appointment of counsel. The manager of the apartment house in which incriminating evidence was found, and in which Gilbert allegedly resided, identified Gilbert in the courtroom and also testified, in substance, to her prior lineup identification on examination by the State. Eight witnesses who identified him in the courtroom at the penalty stage were not eyewitnesses to the Alhambra crimes but to other robberies allegedly committed by him. In addition to their in-court identifications, these witnesses also testified that they identified Gilbert at the same lineup.

The line-up was on a stage behind bright lights which prevented those in the line from seeing the audience. Upwards of 100 persons were in the audience, each an eyewitness to one of the several robberies charged to Gilbert. The record is otherwise virtually silent as to what occurred at the lineup.

The admission of the in-court identifications without first determining that they were not tainted by the illegal lineup but were of independent origin was constitutional error. *United States v. Wade* (1967). We there held that a post-indictment pretrial lineup at which the accused is exhibited to identifying witnesses is a critical stage of the criminal prosecution; that police conduct of such a lineup without notice to and in the absence of his counsel denies the accused his Sixth Amendment right to counsel and calls in question the admissibility at trial of the in-court identifications of the accused by witnesses who attended the lineup. However, as in *Wade*, the record does not permit an informed judgment whether the in-court identifications at the two stages of the trial had an independent source. Gilbert is therefore entitled only to a vacation of his conviction pending the holding of such proceedings as the California Supreme Court may deem appropriate to afford the State the opportunity to establish that the in-court identifications had an independent source, or that their introduction in evidence was in any event harmless error. . . .

The judgment of the California Supreme Court and the conviction are vacated, and the case is remanded to that court for further proceedings not inconsistent with this opinion. It is so ordered.

Judgment and conviction vacated and case remanded with directions.

B. SIXTH AMENDMENT—ATTACHMENT OF RIGHT TO COUNSEL

Kirby v. Illinois

406 U.S. 682 (1972)

STEWART, J., announced the Court's judgment and delivered an opinion in which BURGER, C.J., and BLACKMUN and REHNQUIST, JJ., joined. POWELL, J., filed a statement concurring in the result. . . . BRENNAN, J., filed a dissenting opinion, in which DOUGLAS and MARSHALL, JJ., joined. WHITE, J., filed a dissenting statement.

■ ■ ■

On February 21, 1968, a man named Willie Shard reported to the Chicago police that the previous day two men had robbed him on a Chicago street of a wallet containing, among other things, traveler's checks and a Social Security card. On February 22, two police officers stopped the petitioner and a companion, Ralph Bean, on West Madison Street in Chicago. When asked for identification, the petitioner produced a wallet that contained three traveler's checks and a Social Security card, all bearing the name of Willie Shard. Papers with Shard's name on them were also found in Bean's possession. When asked to explain his possession of Shard's property, the petitioner first said that the traveler's checks were "play money," and then told the officers that he had won them in a crap game. The officers then arrested the petitioner and Bean and took them to a police station.

Only after arriving at the police station, and checking the records there, did the arresting officers learn of the Shard robbery. A police car was then dispatched to Shard's place of employment, where it picked up Shard and brought him to the police station. Immediately upon entering the room in the police station where the petitioner and Bean were seated at a table, Shard positively identified them as the men who had robbed him two days earlier. No lawyer was present in the room, and neither the petitioner nor Bean had asked for legal assistance, or been advised of any right to the presence of counsel.

More than six weeks later, the petitioner and Bean were indicted for the robbery of Willie Shard. Upon arraignment, counsel was appointed to represent them, and they pleaded not guilty. A pretrial motion to suppress Shard's identification testimony was denied, and at the trial Shard testified as a witness for the prosecution. In his testimony he described his identification of the two men at the police station on February 22, and identified them again in the courtroom as the men who had robbed him on February 20. He was cross-examined at length regarding the circumstances of his identification of the two defendants. The jury found both defendants guilty, and the petitioner's conviction was affirmed on appeal. The Illinois appellate court held that the admission of Shard's testimony was not error, relying upon an earlier decision of the Illinois Supreme Court, holding that the *Wade-Gilbert* per se exclusionary rule is not applicable to preindictment confrontations. We granted certiorari, limited to this question. . . .

In a line of constitutional cases in this Court stemming back to the Court's landmark opinion in *Powell v. Alabama* (1932), it has been firmly established that a person's Sixth and Fourteenth Amendment right to counsel attaches only at or after the time that adversary judicial proceedings have been initiated against him. . . .

The only seeming deviation from this long line of constitutional decisions was *Escobedo v. Illinois* (1964). But *Escobedo* is not apposite here for two distinct reasons. First, the Court in retrospect perceived that the "prime purpose" of *Escobedo* was not to vindicate the constitutional right to counsel as such, but, like *Miranda* [v. *Arizona* (1966)], "to guarantee full effectuation of the privilege against self-incrimination. . . ." Secondly, and perhaps even more important for purely practical purposes, the Court has limited the holding of *Escobedo* to its own facts. . . .

The initiation of judicial criminal proceedings is far from a mere formalism. It is the starting point of our whole system of adversary criminal justice. For it is only then that the government has committed itself to prosecute, and only then that the adverse positions of government and defendant have solidified. It is then that a defendant finds himself faced with the prosecutorial forces of organized society, and immersed in the intricacies of substantive and procedural criminal law. It is this point, therefore, that marks the commencement of the "criminal prosecutions" to which alone the explicit guarantees of the Sixth Amendment are applicable.

In this case we are asked to import into a routine police investigation an absolute constitutional guarantee historically and rationally applicable only after the onset of formal prosecutorial proceedings. We decline to do so. Less than a year after [*United States v.*] *Wade* [(1967)] and *Gilbert* [*v. California* (1967)] were decided, the Court explained the rule of those decisions as follows: "The rationale of those cases was that an accused is entitled to counsel at any 'critical stage of the prosecution,' and that a post-indictment lineup is such a 'critical stage.'" We decline to depart from that rationale today by imposing a per se exclusionary rule upon testimony concerning an identification that took place long before the commencement of any prosecution whatever.

What has been said is not to suggest that there may not be occasions during the course of a criminal investigation when the police do abuse identification procedures. Such abuses are not beyond the reach of the Constitution. As the Court pointed out in *Wade* itself, it is always necessary to "scrutinize any pretrial confrontation . . .". The Due Process Clause of the Fifth and Fourteenth Amendments forbids a lineup that is unnecessarily suggestive and conducive to irreparable mistaken identification. When a person has not been formally charged with a criminal offense, *Stovall* [*v. Denno* (1967)] strikes the appropriate constitutional balance between the right of a suspect to be protected from prejudicial procedures and the interest of society in the prompt and purposeful investigation of an unsolved crime.

The judgment is affirmed.

Justice BRENNAN, with whom Justice DOUGLAS and Justice MARSHALL join, dissenting.

. . . This analysis led to the Court's formulation of the controlling principle for pretrial confrontations:

> "In sum, the principle of *Powell v. Alabama* and succeeding cases requires that we scrutinize any pretrial confrontation of the accused to determine whether the presence of his counsel is necessary to preserve the defendant's basic right to a fair trial as affected by his right meaningfully to cross-examine the witnesses against him and to have effective assistance of counsel at the trial itself. It calls upon us to analyze whether potential substantial prejudice to defendant's rights inheres in the particular confrontation and the ability of counsel to help avoid that prejudice."

It was that constitutional principle that the Court applied in *Wade* to pretrial confrontations for identification purposes. The Court first met the Government's contention that a confrontation for identification is "a mere preparatory step in the gathering of the prosecution's evidence," much like the scientific examination of fingerprints and blood samples. The Court responded that in the latter instances "the accused has the opportunity for a meaningful confrontation of the Government's case at trial through the ordinary processes of cross-examination of the Government's expert witnesses and the presentation of the evidence of his own experts." The accused thus has no right to have counsel present at such examinations: "they are not critical stages since there is minimal risk that his counsel's absence at such stages might derogate from his right to a fair trial."

In contrast, the Court said, "the confrontation compelled by the State between the accused and the victim or witnesses to a crime to elicit identification evidence is peculiarly riddled with innumerable dangers and variable factors which might seriously, even crucially, derogate from a fair trial." Most importantly, "the accused's inability effectively to reconstruct at trial any unfairness that occurred at the lineup may deprive him of his only opportunity meaningfully to attack the credibility of the witness' courtroom identification."

■ ■ ■

And even though cross-examination is a precious safeguard to a fair trial, it cannot be viewed as an absolute assurance of accuracy and reliability. Thus in the present context, where so many variables and pitfalls exist, the first line of defense must be the prevention of unfairness and the lessening of the hazards of eyewitness identification at the lineup itself. The trial which might determine the accused's fate may well not be that in the courtroom but that at the pretrial confrontation, with the State aligned against the accused, the witness the sole jury, and the accused unprotected against the overreaching, intentional or unintentional, and with little or no effective appeal from the judgment there rendered by the witness—"that's the man."

The Court then applied that conclusion to the specific facts of the case. "Since it appears that there is grave potential for prejudice, intentional or not, in the pretrial lineup, which may not be capable of reconstruction at trial, and since presence of counsel itself can often avert prejudice and assure a meaningful confrontation at trial, there can be little doubt that for *Wade* the post-indictment lineup was a critical stage of the prosecution at which he was 'as much entitled to such aid [of counsel] . . . as at the trial itself.'"

While it should go without saying, it appears necessary, in view of the plurality opinion today, to re-emphasize that *Wade* did not require the presence of counsel at pretrial confrontations for identification purposes simply on the basis of an abstract consideration of the words "criminal prosecutions" in the Sixth Amendment. Counsel is required at those confrontations because "the dangers inherent in eyewitness identification and the suggestibility inherent in the context of the pretrial identification" mean that protection must be afforded to the "most basic right [of] a criminal defendant—his right to a fair trial at which the witnesses against him might be meaningfully cross-examined." . . .

In view of *Wade*, it is plain, and the plurality today does not attempt to dispute it, that there inhere in a confrontation for identification conducted after arrest the identical hazards to a fair trial that inhere in such a confrontation conducted "after the onset of formal prosecutorial proceedings." The plurality apparently considers an arrest, which for present purposes we must assume to be based upon probable cause, to be nothing more than part of "a routine police investigation," and thus not "the starting point of our whole system of adversary criminal justice." An arrest, according to the plurality, does not face the accused "with the prosecutorial forces of organized society," nor immerse him "in the intricacies of substantive and procedural criminal law." Those consequences ensue, says the plurality, only with "[t]he initiation of judicial criminal proceedings," "[f]or it is only then that the government has committed itself to prosecute, and only then that the adverse positions of government and defendant have solidified." If these propositions do not amount to "mere formalism," it is difficult to know how to characterize them. An arrest evidences the belief of the police that the perpetrator of a crime has been caught. A post-arrest confrontation for identification is not "a mere preparatory step in the gathering of the prosecution's evidence." A primary, and frequently sole, purpose of the confrontation for identification at that stage is to accumulate proof to buttress the conclusion of the police that they have the offender in hand. The plurality offers no reason, and I can think of none, for concluding that a post-arrest confrontation for identification, unlike a post-charge confrontation, is not among those "critical confrontations of the accused by the prosecution at pretrial proceedings where the results might well settle the accused's fate and reduce the trial itself to a mere formality."

■ ■ ■

The highly suggestive form of confrontation employed in this case underscores the point. This showup was particularly fraught with the peril of mistaken identification. In the setting of a police station squad room where all present except petitioner and Bean were police officers, the danger was quite real that Shard's understandable resentment might lead him too readily to agree with the police that the pair under arrest, and the only persons exhibited to him, were indeed the robbers. "It is hard to imagine a situation more clearly conveying the suggestion to the witness that the one presented is believed guilty by the police." The State had no case without Shard's identification testimony, and safeguards against that consequence were therefore of critical importance. Shard's testimony itself demonstrates the necessity for such safeguards. On direct examination, Shard identified petitioner and Bean not as the alleged robbers on trial in the courtroom, but as the pair he saw at the police station. His testimony thus lends strong support to the observation, quoted by the Court in *Wade*, that "[i]t is a matter of common experience that, once a witness has picked out the accused at the line-up, he is not likely to go back on his word later on, so that in practice the issue of identity may (in the absence of other relevant evidence) for all practical purposes be determined there and then, before the trial."

■ ■ ■

The plurality might also have discovered a different "rationale" for *Wade* and *Gilbert* had it examined *Stovall v. Denno*, decided the same day. In *Stovall*, the confrontation for identification took place one day after the accused's arrest. Although the accused was first brought to an arraignment, it "was postponed until [he] could retain counsel." Hence, in the plurality's terms today, the confrontation was held "before the commencement of any prosecution."

■ ■ ■

Wade and *Gilbert*, of course, happened to involve post-indictment confrontations. Yet even a cursory perusal of the opinions in those cases reveals that nothing at all turned upon that particular circumstance. In short, it is fair to conclude that rather than "declin[ing] to depart from [the] rationale" of *Wade* and *Gilbert*, the plurality today, albeit purporting to be engaged in "principled constitutional adjudication," refuses even to recognize that "rationale."

■ ■ ■

Rothgery v. Gillespie County, Texas

554 U.S. 191 (2008)

SOUTER, J., delivered the opinion of the Court, in which ROBERTS, C.J., STEVENS, SCALIA, KENNEDY, GINSBURG, BREYER, and ALITO, JJ., joined. THOMAS, J., filed a dissenting opinion.

This Court has held that the right to counsel guaranteed by the Sixth Amendment applies at the first appearance before a judicial officer at which a defendant is told of the formal accusation against him and restrictions are imposed on his liberty. The question here is whether attachment of the right also requires that a public prosecutor (as distinct from a police officer) be aware of that initial proceeding or involved in its conduct. We hold that it does not.

■ ■ ■

The Sixth Amendment right of the "accused" to assistance of counsel in "all criminal prosecutions" is limited by its terms: "it does not attach until a prosecution is commenced." We have, for purposes of the right to counsel, pegged commencement to "'the initiation of adversary judicial criminal proceedings—whether by way of formal charge, preliminary hearing, indictment, information, or arraignment.'" The rule is not "mere formalism," but a recognition of the point at which "the government has committed itself to prosecute," "the adverse positions of government and defendant have solidified," and the accused "finds himself faced with the prosecutorial forces of organized society, and immersed in the intricacies of substantive and procedural criminal law." The issue is whether Texas's article 15.17 hearing marks

Issue

that point, with the consequent state obligation to appoint counsel within a reasonable time once a request for assistance is made.

■ ■ ■

Our holding is narrow. We do not decide whether the 6-month delay in appointment of counsel resulted in prejudice to Rothgery's Sixth Amendment rights, and have no occasion to consider what standards should apply in deciding this. We merely reaffirm what we have held before and what an overwhelming majority of American jurisdictions understand in practice: a criminal defendant's initial appearance before a judicial officer, where he learns the charge against him and his liberty is subject to restriction, marks the start of adversary judicial proceedings that trigger attachment of the Sixth Amendment right to counsel. Because the Fifth Circuit came to a different conclusion on this threshold issue, its judgment is vacated, and the case is remanded for further proceedings consistent with this opinion.

It is so ordered.

■ ■ ■

Justice THOMAS, dissenting.

The Court holds today—for the first time after plenary consideration of the question—that a criminal prosecution begins, and that the Sixth Amendment right to counsel therefore attaches, when an individual who has been placed under arrest makes an initial appearance before a magistrate for a probable-cause determination and the setting of bail. Because the Court's holding is not supported by the original meaning of the Sixth Amendment or any reasonable interpretation of our precedents, I respectfully dissent.

The Sixth Amendment provides that "[i]n all criminal prosecutions, the accused shall enjoy the right . . . to have the Assistance of Counsel for his defence." The text of the Sixth Amendment thus makes clear that the right to counsel arises only upon initiation of a "criminal prosecutio[n]." For that reason, the Court has repeatedly stressed that the Sixth Amendment right to counsel "does not attach until a prosecution is commenced." *McNeil v. Wisconsin* (1991); see also *United States v. Gouveia* (1984) ("[T]he literal language of the Amendment . . . requires the existence of both a 'criminal prosecutio[n]' and an 'accused'?"). Echoing this refrain, the Court today reiterates that "[t]he Sixth Amendment right of the 'accused' to assistance of counsel in 'all criminal prosecutions' is limited by its terms."

Given the Court's repeated insistence that the right to counsel is textually limited to "criminal prosecutions," one would expect the Court's jurisprudence in this area to be grounded in an understanding of what those words meant when the Sixth Amendment was adopted. Inexplicably, however, neither today's decision nor any of the other numerous decisions in which the Court has construed the right to counsel have attempted to discern the original meaning of "criminal prosecutio[n]." I think it appropriate to examine what a "criminal prosecutio[n]" would have been understood to entail by those who adopted the Sixth Amendment. . . .

Kirby [*v. Illinois* (1972)] gave five examples of events that initiate "adversary judicial criminal proceedings": formal charge, preliminary hearing, indictment, information, and arraignment. None of these supports the result the Court reaches today. I will apply them *seriatim.* No indictment or information had been filed when petitioner appeared before the magistrate. Nor was there any other formal charge. Although the plurality in *Kirby* did not define "formal charge," there is no reason to believe it would have included an affidavit of probable cause in that category. None of the cases on which it relied stood for that proposition....

■ ■ ■

United States v. Ash

413 U.S. 300 (1973)

BLACKMUN, J., delivered the opinion of the Court, in which BURGER, C.J., POWELL, WHITE, and REHNQUIST, JJ., joined. STEWART, J., filed an opinion concurring in the judgment. BRENNAN, J., filed a dissenting opinion, in which DOUGLAS and MARSHALL, JJ., joined.

In this case the Court is called upon to decide whether the Sixth Amendment grants an accused the right to have counsel present whenever the Government conducts a post-indictment photographic display, containing a picture of the accused, for the purpose of allowing a witness to attempt an identification of the offender. The United States Court of Appeals for the District of Columbia Circuit, sitting en banc, held, by a 5-to-4 vote, that the accused possesses this right to counsel. The court's holding is inconsistent with decisions of the courts of appeals of nine other circuits. We granted certiorari to resolve the conflict and to decide this important constitutional question. We reverse and remand.

On the morning of August 26, 1965, a man with a stocking mask entered a bank in Washington, D.C., and began waving a pistol. He ordered an employee to hang up the telephone and instructed all others present not to move. Seconds later a second man, also wearing a stocking mask, entered the bank, scooped up money from tellers' drawers into a bag, and left. The gunman followed, and both men escaped through an alley. The robbery lasted three or four minutes.

A Government informer, Clarence McFarland, told authorities that he had discussed the robbery with Charles J. Ash, Jr., the respondent here. Acting on this information, an FBI agent, in February 1966, showed five black-and-white mug shots of Negro males of generally the same age, height, and weight, one of which was of Ash, to four witnesses. All four made uncertain identifications of Ash's picture. At this time Ash was not in custody and had not been charged. On April 1, 1966, an indictment was returned charging Ash and a codefendant, John L. Bailey, in five counts related to this bank robbery.

■ ■ ■

Trial was finally set for May 1968, almost three years after the crime. In preparing for trial, the prosecutor decided to use a photographic display to determine whether the witnesses he planned to call would be able to make in-court identifications. Shortly before the trial, an FBI agent and the prosecutor showed five color photographs to the four witnesses who previously had tentatively identified the black-and-white photograph of Ash. Three of the witnesses selected the picture of Ash, but one was unable to make any selection. None of the witnesses selected the picture of Bailey which was in the group. This post-indictment identification provides the basis for respondent Ash's claim that he was denied the right to counsel at a "critical stage" of the prosecution.

■ ■ ■

This historical background suggests that the core purpose of the counsel guarantee was to assure "Assistance" at trial, when the accused was confronted with both the intricacies of the law and the advocacy of the public prosecutor. Later developments have led this Court to recognize that "Assistance" would be less than meaningful if it were limited to the formal trial itself.

This extension of the right to counsel to events before trial has resulted from changing patterns of criminal procedure and investigation that have tended to generate pretrial events that might appropriately be considered to be parts of the trial itself. At these newly emerging and significant events, the accused was confronted, just as at trial, by the procedural system, or by his expert adversary, or by both. In [United States v.] Wade [(1967)], the Court explained the process of expanding the counsel guarantee to these confrontations:

> "When the Bill of Rights was adopted, there were no organized police forces as we know them today. The accused confronted the prosecutor and the witnesses against him, and the evidence was marshalled, largely at the trial itself. In contrast, today's law enforcement machinery involves critical confrontations of the accused by the prosecution at pretrial proceedings where the results might well settle the accused's fate and reduce the trial itself to a mere formality. In recognition of these realities of modern criminal prosecution, our cases have construed the Sixth Amendment guarantee to apply to 'critical' stages of the proceedings."

The Court consistently has applied a historical interpretation of the guarantee, and has expanded the constitutional right to counsel only when new contexts appear presenting the same dangers that gave birth initially to the right itself.

■ ■ ■

> "The trial which might determine the accused's fate may well not be that in the courtroom but that at the pretrial confrontation, with the State aligned against the accused, the witness the sole jury, and the accused unprotected against the overreaching, intentional or unintentional, and with little or no effective appeal from the judgment there rendered by the witness—'that's the man.'" Wade.

Throughout this expansion of the counsel guarantee to trial-like confrontations, the function of the lawyer has remained essentially the same as his function at trial. In all cases considered by the Court, counsel has continued to act as a spokesman for, or advisor to, the accused. The accused's right to the "Assistance of Counsel" has meant just that, namely, the right of the accused to have counsel acting as his assistant. In *Hamilton* [*v. Alabama* (1961)] and *White* [*v. Maryland* (1963)], for example, the Court envisioned the lawyer as advising the accused on available defenses in order to allow him to plead intelligently. In *Massiah* [*v. United States* (1964)] counsel could have advised his client on the benefits of the Fifth Amendment and could have sheltered him from the overreaching of the prosecution. In *Coleman* [*v. Alabama* (1970)] the skill of the lawyer in examining witnesses, probing for evidence, and making legal arguments was relied upon by the Court to demonstrate that, in the light of the purpose of the preliminary hearing under Alabama law, the accused required "Assistance" at that hearing.

The function of counsel in rendering "Assistance" continued at the lineup under consideration in *Wade* and its companion cases. Although the accused was not confronted there with legal questions, the lineup offered opportunities for prosecuting authorities to take advantage of the accused. Counsel was seen by the Court as being more sensitive to, and aware of, suggestive influences than the accused himself, and as better able to reconstruct the events at trial. Counsel present at lineup would be able to remove disabilities of the accused in precisely the same fashion that counsel compensated for the disabilities of the layman at trial.

■ ■ ■

This review of the history and expansion of the Sixth Amendment counsel guarantee demonstrates that the test utilized by the Court has called for examination of the event in order to determine whether the accused required aid in coping with legal problems or assistance in meeting his adversary. Against the background of this traditional test, we now consider the opinion of the Court of Appeals.

■ ■ ■

We conclude that the dangers of mistaken identification, mentioned in *Wade*, were removed from context by the Court of Appeals and were incorrectly utilized as a sufficient basis for requiring counsel. Although *Wade* did discuss possibilities for suggestion and the difficulty for reconstructing suggestivity, this discussion occurred only after the Court had concluded that the lineup constituted a trial-like confrontation, requiring the "Assistance of Counsel" to preserve the adversary process by compensating for advantages of the prosecuting authorities.

The above discussion of *Wade* has shown that the traditional Sixth Amendment test easily allowed extension of counsel to a lineup. The similarity to trial was apparent, and counsel was needed to render "Assistance" in counterbalancing any "overreaching" by the prosecution.

After the Court in *Wade* held that a lineup constituted a trial-like confrontation requiring counsel, a more difficult issue remained in the case for consideration. The same changes in law enforcement that led to lineups and pretrial hearings also generated other events at which the accused was confronted by the prosecution. The Government had argued in *Wade* that if counsel was required at a lineup, the same forceful considerations would mandate counsel at other preparatory steps in the "gathering of the prosecution's evidence," such as, for particular example, the taking of fingerprints or blood samples.

The Court concluded that there were differences. Rather than distinguishing these situations from the lineup in terms of the need for counsel to assure an equal confrontation at the time, the Court recognized that there were times when the subsequent trial would cure a one-sided confrontation between prosecuting authorities and the uncounseled defendant. In other words, such stages were not "critical." Referring to fingerprints, hair, clothing, and other blood samples, the Court explained:

> "Knowledge of the techniques of science and technology is sufficiently available, and the variables in techniques few enough, that the accused has the opportunity for a meaningful confrontation of the Government's case at trial through the ordinary processes of cross-examination of the Government's expert witnesses and the presentation of the evidence of his own experts."

The structure of *Wade*, viewed in light of the careful limitation of the Court's language to "confrontations," makes it clear that lack of scientific precision and inability to reconstruct an event are not the tests for requiring counsel in the first instance. These are, instead, the tests to determine whether confrontation with counsel at trial can serve as a substitute for counsel at the pretrial confrontation. If accurate reconstruction is possible, the risks inherent in any confrontation still remain, but the opportunity to cure defects at trial causes the confrontation to cease to be "critical." The opinion of the Court even indicated that changes in procedure might cause a lineup to cease to be a "critical" confrontation.

■ ■ ■

A substantial departure from the historical test would be necessary if the Sixth Amendment were interpreted to give Ash a right to counsel at the photographic identification in this case. Since the accused himself is not present at the time of the photographic display, and asserts no right to be present, no possibility arises that the accused might be misled by his lack of familiarity with the law or overpowered by his professional adversary. Similarly, the counsel guarantee would not be used to produce equality in a trial-like adversary confrontation. Rather, the guarantee was used by the Court of Appeals to produce confrontation at an event that previously was not analogous to an adversary trial.

Even if we were willing to view the counsel guarantee in broad terms as a generalized protection of the adversary process, we would be unwilling to go so far as to extend the right to a portion of the prosecutor's trial-preparation interviews with witnesses. Although photography is relatively new, the interviewing of witnesses before trial is a procedure that predates the Sixth Amendment. In England in the 16th and 17th centuries counsel regularly interviewed witnesses before trial. The traditional counterbalance in the American adversary system for these interviews arises from the equal ability of defense counsel to seek and interview witnesses himself.

That adversary mechanism remains as effective for a photographic display as for other parts of pretrial interviews. No greater limitations are placed on defense counsel in constructing displays, seeking witnesses, and conducting photographic identifications than those applicable to the prosecution. Selection of the picture of a person other than the accused, or the inability of a witness to make any selection, will be useful to the defense in precisely the same manner that the selection of a picture of the defendant would be useful to the prosecution. In this very case, for example, the initial tender of the photographic display was by Bailey's counsel, who sought to demonstrate that the witness had failed to make a photographic identification. Although we do not suggest that equality of access to photographs removes all potential for abuse, it does remove any inequality in the adversary process itself and thereby fully satisfies the historical spirit of the Sixth Amendment's counsel guarantee.

The argument has been advanced that requiring counsel might compel the police to observe more scientific procedures or might encourage them to utilize corporeal rather than photographic displays. This Court has recognized that improved procedures can minimize the dangers of suggestion. Commentators have also proposed more accurate techniques.

Pretrial photographic identifications, however, are hardly unique in offering possibilities for the actions of the prosecutor unfairly to prejudice the accused. Evidence favorable to the accused may be withheld; testimony of witnesses may be manipulated; the results of laboratory tests may be contrived. In many ways the prosecutor, by accident or by design, may improperly subvert the trial. The primary safeguard against abuses of this kind is the ethical responsibility of the prosecutor, who, as so often has been said, may "strike hard blows" but not "foul ones."

We are not persuaded that the risks inherent in the use of photographic displays are so pernicious that an extraordinary system of safeguards is required.

We hold, then, that the Sixth Amendment does not grant the right to counsel at photographic displays conducted by the Government for the purpose of allowing a witness to attempt an identification of the offender. This holding requires reversal of the judgment of the Court of Appeals. Although respondent Ash has urged us to examine this photographic display under the due process standard enunciated in *Simmons v. United States* (1968), the Court of Appeals, expressing the view that additional findings would be necessary, refused to decide the issue. We decline to consider this question on this record in the first instance. It remains open, of course, on the Court of Appeals' remand to the District Court.

Reversed and remanded.

Justice STEWART, concurring in the judgment.

■ ■ ■

A photographic identification is quite different from a lineup, for there are substantially fewer possibilities of impermissible suggestion when photographs are used, and those unfair influences can be readily reconstructed at trial. It is true that the defendant's photograph may be markedly different from the others displayed, but this unfairness can be demonstrated at trial from an actual comparison of the photographs used or from the witness' description of the display. Similarly, it is possible that the photographs could be arranged in a suggestive manner, or that by comment or gesture the prosecuting authorities might single out the defendant's picture. But these are the kinds of overt influence that a witness can easily recount and that would serve to impeach the identification testimony. In short, there are few possibilities for unfair suggestiveness—and those rather blatant and easily reconstructed. Accordingly, an accused would not be foreclosed from an effective cross-examination of an identification witness simply because his counsel was not present at the photographic display. For this reason, a photographic display cannot fairly be considered a "critical stage" of the prosecution.

■ ■ ■

Justice BRENNAN, with whom Justice DOUGLAS and Justice MARSHALL join, dissenting.

The Court holds today that a pretrial display of photographs to the witnesses of a crime for the purpose of identifying the accused, unlike a lineup, does not constitute a "critical stage" of the prosecution at which the accused is constitutionally entitled to the presence of counsel. In my view, today's decision is wholly unsupportable in terms of such considerations as logic, consistency, and, indeed, fairness. As a result, I must reluctantly conclude that today's decision marks simply another step towards the complete evisceration of the fundamental constitutional principles established by this Court, only six years ago, in *United States v. Wade*; *Gilbert v. California* [(1967)]; and *Stovall v. Denno*. I dissent.

■ ■ ■

In June 1967, this Court decided a trilogy of "lineup" cases which brought into sharp focus the problems of pretrial identification. See *United States v. Wade*; *Gilbert v. California*; *Stovall v. Denno*. In essence, those decisions held (1) that a pretrial lineup is a "critical stage" in the criminal process at which the accused is constitutionally entitled to the presence of counsel; (2) that evidence of an identification of the accused at such an uncounseled lineup is per se inadmissible; and (3) that evidence of a subsequent in-court identification of the accused is likewise inadmissible unless the Government can demonstrate by clear and convincing evidence that the in-court identification was based upon observations of the accused independent of the prior uncoun-seled lineup identification. The considerations relied upon by the Court in reaching these conclusions are clearly applicable to photographic as well as corporeal identifications. Those considerations bear repeating here in some detail, for they touch upon the very heart of our criminal justice system— the right of an accused to a fair trial, including the effective "Assistance of Counsel for his defence."

■ ■ ■

As the Court of Appeals recognized, "the dangers of mistaken identification . . . set forth in *Wade* are applicable in large measure to photo-graphic as well as corporeal identifications." To the extent that misidentifica-tion may be attributable to a witness' faulty memory or perception, or inadequate opportunity for detailed observation during the crime, the risks are obviously as great at a photographic display as at a lineup. But "[b]ecause of the inherent limitations of photography, which presents its subject in two dimensions rather than the three dimensions of reality, . . . a photographic identification, even when properly obtained, is clearly inferior to a properly obtained corporeal identification." Indeed, noting "the hazards of initial iden-tification by photograph," we have expressly recognized that "a corporeal identification . . . is normally more accurate" than a photographic identifica-tion. Thus, in this sense at least, the dangers of misidentification are even greater at a photographic display than at a lineup.

Moreover, as in the lineup situation, the possibilities for impermissible suggestion in the context of a photographic display are manifold. Such sugges-tion, intentional or unintentional, may derive from three possible sources. First, the photographs themselves might tend to suggest which of the pictures is that of the suspect. For example, differences in age, pose, or other physical characteristics of the persons represented, and variations in the mounting, background, lighting, or markings of the photographs all might have the effect of singling out the accused.

Second, impermissible suggestion may inhere in the manner in which the photographs are displayed to the witness. The danger of misidentification is, of course, "increased if the police display to the witness . . . the pictures of several persons among which the photograph of a single such individual recurs or is in some way emphasized." And, if the photographs are arranged in an asymme-trical pattern, or if they are displayed in a time sequence that tends to empha-size a particular photograph, "any identification of the photograph which stands out from the rest is no more reliable than an identification of a single photograph, exhibited alone."

Third, gestures or comments of the prosecutor at the time of the display may lead an otherwise uncertain witness to select the "correct" photograph. For example, the prosecutor might "indicate to the witness that [he has] other evidence that one of the persons pictured committed the crime," and might even point to a particular photograph and ask whether the person pictured "looks familiar." More subtly, the prosecutor's inflection, facial expressions, physical motions, and myriad other almost imperceptible means of communication might tend, intentionally or unintentionally, to compromise the witness' objectivity. Thus, as is the case with lineups, "[i]mproper photographic identification procedures, . . . by exerting a suggestive influence upon the witnesses, can often lead to an erroneous identification. . . ." And "[r]egardless of how the initial misidentification comes about, the witness thereafter is apt to retain in his memory the image of the photograph rather than of the person actually seen. . . ." As a result, "the issue of identity may [in the absence of other relevant evidence] for all practical purposes be determined there and then, before the trial."

Moreover, as with lineups, the defense can "seldom reconstruct" at trial the mode and manner of photographic identification. It is true, of course, that the photographs used at the pretrial display might be preserved for examination at trial. But "it may also be said that a photograph can preserve the record of a lineup; yet this does not justify a lineup without counsel." Indeed, in reality, preservation of the photographs affords little protection to the unrepresented accused. For, although retention of the photographs may mitigate the dangers of misidentification due to the suggestiveness of the photographs themselves, it cannot in any sense reveal to defense counsel the more subtle, and therefore more dangerous, suggestiveness that might derive from the manner in which the photographs were displayed or any accompanying comments or gestures. Moreover, the accused cannot rely upon the witnesses themselves to expose these latter sources of suggestion, for the witnesses are not "apt to be alert for conditions prejudicial to the suspect. And if they were, it would likely be of scant benefit to the suspect" since the witnesses are hardly "likely to be schooled in the detection of suggestive influences."

Finally, and unlike the lineup situation, the accused himself is not even present at the photographic identification, thereby reducing the likelihood that irregularities in the procedures will ever come to light. Indeed, in *Wade*, the Government itself observed:

> "When the defendant is present—as he is during a lineup—he may personally observe the circumstances, report them to his attorney, and (if he chooses to take the stand) testify about them at trial. . . . [I]n the absence of an accused, on the other hand, there is no one present to verify the fairness of the interview or to report any irregularities. If the prosecution were tempted to engage in 'sloppy or biased or fraudulent' conduct . . . , it would be far more likely to do so when the accused is absent than when he is himself being 'used.'"

Thus, the difficulties of reconstructing at trial an uncounseled photographic display are at least equal to, and possibly greater than, those involved in reconstructing an uncounseled lineup. And, as the Government argued in *Wade*, in terms of the need for counsel, "[t]here is no meaningful difference between a witness' pretrial identification from photographs and a similar identification made at a lineup." For in both situations, "the accused's inability effectively to reconstruct at trial any unfairness that occurred at the [pretrial identification] may deprive him of his only opportunity meaningfully to attack the credibility of the witness' courtroom identification."

Ironically, the Court does not seriously challenge the proposition that presence of counsel at a pretrial photographic display is essential to preserve the accused's right to a fair trial on the issue of identification. Rather, in what I can only characterize a triumph of form over substance, the Court seeks to justify its result by engrafting a wholly unprecedented—and wholly unsupportable—limitation on the Sixth Amendment right of "the accused . . . to have the Assistance of Counsel for his defence." Although apparently conceding that the right to counsel attaches, not only at the trial itself, but at all "critical stages" of the prosecution, the Court holds today that, in order to be deemed "critical," the particular "stage of the prosecution" under consideration must, at the very least, involve the physical "presence of the accused," at a "trial-like confrontation" with the Government, at which the accused requires the "guiding hand of counsel." According to the Court a pretrial photographic identification does not, of course, meet these criteria. . . .

The fundamental premise underlying all of this Court's decisions holding the right to counsel applicable at "critical" pretrial proceedings, is that a "stage" of the prosecution must be deemed "critical" for the purposes of the Sixth Amendment if it is one at which the presence of counsel is necessary "to protect the fairness of the trial itself." . . . Indeed, to exclude counsel from a pretrial proceeding at which his presence might be necessary to assure the fairness of the subsequent trial would, in practical effect, render the Sixth Amendment guarantee virtually meaningless, for it would "deny a defendant 'effective representation by counsel at the only stage when legal aid and advice would help him.'"

This established conception of the Sixth Amendment guarantee is, of course, in no sense dependent upon the physical "presence of the accused," at a "trial-like confrontation" with the Government, at which the accused requires the "guiding hand of counsel."

■ ■ ■

Thus, contrary to the suggestion of the Court, the conclusion in *Wade* that a pretrial lineup is a "critical stage" of the prosecution did not in any sense turn on the fact that a lineup involves the physical "presence of the accused" at a "trial-like confrontation" with the Government. And that conclusion most certainly did not turn on the notion that presence of counsel was necessary so that counsel could offer legal advice or "guidance" to the accused at the lineup. On the contrary, *Wade* envisioned counsel's function at the lineup to be primarily that of a trained observer, able to detect the existence of any suggestive influences and capable of understanding the legal implications of the events that transpire. Having witnessed the proceedings, counsel would then be in a position effectively to reconstruct at trial any unfairness that occurred at the lineup, thereby preserving the accused's fundamental right to a fair trial on the issue of identification.

There is something ironic about the Court's conclusion today that a pretrial lineup identification is a "critical stage" of the prosecution because counsel's presence can help to compensate for the accused's deficiencies as an observer, but that a pretrial photographic identification is not a "critical stage" of the prosecution because the accused is not able to observe at all. In my view, there simply is no meaningful difference, in terms of the need for attendance of counsel, between corporeal and photographic identifications. And applying established and well-reasoned Sixth Amendment principles, I can only conclude that a pretrial photographic display, like a pretrial lineup, is a "critical stage" of the prosecution at which the accused is constitutionally entitled to the presence of counsel.

C. DUE PROCESS

Manson v. Brathwaite

432 U.S. 98 (1977)

BLACKMUN, J., delivered the opinion of the Court, in which BURGER, C.J., STEVENS, REHNQUIST, STEWART, and WHITE, JJ., joined. MARSHALL, J., filed a dissenting opinion, in which BRENNAN, J., joined.

This case presents the issue as to whether the Due Process Clause of the Fourteenth Amendment compels the exclusion, in a state criminal trial, apart from any consideration of reliability, of pretrial identification evidence obtained by a police procedure that was both suggestive and unnecessary. This Court's decisions in *Stovall v. Denno* (1967) and *Neil v. Biggers* (1972) are particularly implicated.

Jimmy D. Glover, a full-time trooper of the Connecticut State Police, in 1970 was assigned to the Narcotics Division in an undercover capacity. On May 5 of that year, about 7:45 p.m., e.d.t., and while there was still daylight, Glover and Henry Alton Brown, an informant, went to an apartment building at 201 Westland, in Hartford, for the purpose of purchasing narcotics from "Dickie Boy" Cicero, a known narcotics dealer. Cicero, it was thought, lived on the third floor of that apartment building. Glover and Brown entered the building, observed by back-up Officers D'Onofrio and Gaffey, and proceeded by stairs to the third floor. Glover knocked at the door of one of the two apartments served by the stairway. The area was illuminated by natural light from a window in the third floor hallway. The door was opened 12 to 18 inches in response to the knock. Glover observed a man standing at the door and, behind him, a woman. Brown identified himself. Glover then asked for "two things" of narcotics. The man at the door held out his hand, and Glover gave him two $10 bills. The door closed. Soon the man returned and handed Glover two glassine bags. While the door was open, Glover stood within two feet of the person from whom he made the purchase and observed his face. Five to seven minutes elapsed from the time the door first opened until it closed the second time.

Glover and Brown then left the building. This was about eight minutes after their arrival. Glover drove to headquarters where he described the seller to D'Onofrio and Gaffey. Glover at that time did not know the identity of the seller. He described him as being "a colored man, approximately five feet eleven inches tall, dark complexion, black hair, short Afro style, and having high cheekbones, and of heavy build. He was wearing at the time blue pants and a plaid shirt." D'Onofrio, suspecting from this description that respondent might be the seller, obtained a photograph of respondent from the Records Division of the Hartford Police Department. He left it at Glover's office. D'Onofrio was not acquainted with respondent personally but did know him by sight and had seen him "[s]everal times" prior to May 5. Glover, when alone, viewed the photograph for the first time upon his return to headquarters on May 7; he identified the person shown as the one from whom he had purchased the narcotics.

The toxicological report on the contents of the glassine bags revealed the presence of heroin. The report was dated July 16, 1970.

Respondent was arrested on July 27 while visiting at the apartment of a Mrs. Ramsey on the third floor of 201 Westland. This was the apartment at which the narcotics sale had taken place on May 5.

Respondent was charged, in a two-count information, with possession and sale of heroin. At his trial in January1971, the photograph from which Glover had identified respondent was received in evidence without objection on the part of the defense. Glover also testified that, although he had not seen respondent in the eight months that had elapsed since the sale, "there [was] no doubt whatsoever" in his mind that the person shown on the photograph was respondent. Glover also made a positive in-court identification without objection.

■ ■ ■

No explanation was offered by the prosecution for the failure to utilize a photographic array or to conduct a lineup.

Stovall v. Denno, decided in 1967, concerned a petitioner who had been convicted in a New York court of murder. He was arrested the day following the crime and was taken by the police to a hospital where the victim's wife, also wounded in the assault, was a patient. After observing Stovall and hearing him speak, she identified him as the murderer. She later made an in-court identification. On federal habeas, Stovall claimed the identification testimony violated his Fifth, Sixth, and Fourteenth Amendment rights. The District Court dismissed the petition, and the Court of Appeals, en banc, affirmed. This Court also affirmed. On the identification issue, the Court reviewed the practice of showing a suspect singly for purposes of identification, and the claim that this was so unnecessarily suggestive and conducive to irreparable mistaken identification that it constituted a denial of due process of law. The Court noted that the practice "has been widely condemned," but it concluded that "a claimed violation of due process of law in the conduct of a confrontation depends on the totality of the circumstances surrounding it." Ibid. In that case, showing Stovall to the victim's spouse "was imperative." The Court then quoted the observations of the Court of Appeals, to the effect that the spouse was the only person who could possibly exonerate the accused; that the hospital was not far from the courthouse and jail; that no one knew how long she might live; that she was not able to visit the jail; and that taking Stovall to the hospital room was the only feasible procedure, and, under the circumstances, "'the usual police station line-up . . . was out of the question.'"

Neil v. Biggers, decided in 1972, concerned a respondent who had been convicted in a Tennessee court of rape, on evidence consisting in part of the victim's visual and voice identification of Biggers at a station-house showup seven months after the crime. The victim had been in her assailant's presence for some time and had directly observed him indoors and under a full moon outdoors. She testified that she had "no doubt" that Biggers was her assailant. She previously had given the police a description of the assailant. She had made no identification of others presented at previous showups, lineups, or through photographs. On federal habeas, the District Court held that the confrontation was so suggestive as to violate due process. The Court of Appeals affirmed. This Court reversed on that issue, and held that the evidence properly had been allowed to go to the jury. The Court reviewed *Stovall* and certain later cases where it had considered the scope of due process protection against the admission of evidence derived from suggestive identification procedures, namely *Simmons v. United States* (1968); *Foster v. California* (1969); and *Coleman v. Alabama* (1970). The Court concluded that general guidelines emerged from these cases "as to the relationship between suggestiveness and misidentification." The "admission of evidence of a showup without more does not violate due process." The Court expressed concern about the lapse of seven months between the crime and the confrontation and observed that this "would be a seriously negative factor in most cases." The "central question," however, was "whether under the 'totality of the circumstances' the identification was reliable even though the confrontation procedure was suggestive." Applying that test, the Court found "no substantial likelihood of misidentification. The evidence was properly allowed to go to the jury."

Biggers well might be seen to provide an unambiguous answer to the question before us: The admission of testimony concerning a suggestive and unnecessary identification procedure does not violate due process so long as the identification possesses sufficient aspects of reliability. In one passage, however, the Court observed that the challenged procedure occurred pre-*Stovall* and that a strict rule would make little sense with regard to a confrontation that preceded the Court's first indication that a suggestive procedure might lead to the exclusion of evidence. One perhaps might argue that, by implication, the Court suggested that a different rule could apply post-*Stovall*. The question before us, then, is simply whether the *Biggers* analysis applies to post-*Stovall* confrontations as well to those pre-*Stovall*.

In the present case the District Court observed that the "sole evidence tying Brathwaite to the possession and sale of the heroin consisted in his identifications by the police undercover agent, Jimmy Glover." On the constitutional issue, the court stated that the first inquiry was whether the police used an impermissibly suggestive procedure in obtaining the out-of-court identification. If so, the second inquiry is whether, under all the circumstances, that suggestive procedure gave rise to a substantial likelihood of irreparable misidentification. . . .

Petitioner at the outset acknowledges that "the procedure in the instant case was suggestive (because only one photograph was used) and unnecessary" (because there was no emergency or exigent circumstance). The respondent, in agreement with the Court of Appeals, proposes a per se rule of exclusion that he claims is dictated by the demands of the Fourteenth Amendment's guarantee of due process. He rightly observes that this is the first case in which this Court has had occasion to rule upon strictly post-*Stovall* out-of-court identification evidence of the challenged kind.

Since the decision in *Biggers*, the Courts of Appeals appear to have developed at least two approaches to such evidence. The first, or per se approach, employed by the Second Circuit in the present case, focuses on the procedures employed and requires exclusion of the out-of-court identification evidence, without regard to reliability, whenever it has been obtained through unnecessarily suggestive confrontation procedures. The justifications advanced are the elimination of evidence of uncertain reliability, deterrence of the police and prosecutors, and the stated "fair assurance against the awful risks of misidentification."

The second, or more lenient, approach is one that continues to rely on the totality of the circumstances. It permits the admission of the confrontation evidence if, despite the suggestive aspect, the out-of-court identification possesses certain features of reliability. Its adherents feel that the per se approach is not mandated by the Due Process Clause of the Fourteenth Amendment. This second approach, in contrast to the other, is ad hoc and serves to limit the societal costs imposed by a sanction that excludes relevant evidence from consideration and evaluation by the trier of fact.

■ ■ ■

There are, of course, several interests to be considered and taken into account. The driving force behind *United States v. Wade* (1967), *Gilbert v. California* (1967), and *Stovall*, all decided on the same day, was the Court's concern with the problems of eyewitness identification. Usually the witness must testify about an encounter with a total stranger under circumstances of emergency or emotional stress. The witness' recollection of the stranger can be distorted easily by the circumstances or by later actions of the police. Thus, *Wade* and its companion cases reflect the concern that the jury not hear eyewitness testimony unless that evidence has aspects of reliability. It must be observed that both approaches before us are responsive to this concern. The per se rule, however, goes too far since its application automatically and peremptorily, and without consideration of alleviating factors, keeps evidence from the jury that is reliable and relevant.

The second factor is deterrence. Although the per se approach has the more significant deterrent effect, the totality approach also has an influence on police behavior. The police will guard against unnecessarily suggestive procedures under the totality rule, as well as the per se one, for fear that their actions will lead to the exclusion of identifications as unreliable.

The third factor is the effect on the administration of justice. Here the per se approach suffers serious drawbacks. Since it denies the trier reliable evidence, it may result, on occasion, in the guilty going free. Also, because of its rigidity, the per se approach may make error by the trial judge more likely than the totality approach. And in those cases in which the admission of identification evidence is error under the per se approach but not under the totality approach—cases in which the identification is reliable despite an unnecessarily suggestive identification procedure—reversal is a Draconian sanction. Certainly, inflexible rules of exclusion that may frustrate rather than promote justice have not been viewed recently by this Court with unlimited enthusiasm.

■ ■ ■

The standard, after all, is that of fairness as required by the Due Process Clause of the Fourteenth Amendment. *Stovall*, with its reference to "the totality of the circumstances," and *Biggers*, with its continuing stress on the same totality, did not, singly or together, establish a strict exclusionary rule or new standard of due process.

■ ■ ■

We therefore conclude that reliability is the linchpin in determining the admissibility of identification testimony for both pre- and post-*Stovall* confrontations. The factors to be considered are set out in *Biggers*. These include the opportunity of the witness to view the criminal at the time of the crime, the witness' degree of attention, the accuracy of his prior description of the criminal, the level of certainty demonstrated at the confrontation, and the time between the crime and the confrontation. Against these factors is to be weighed the corrupting effect of the suggestive identification itself.

We turn, then, to the facts of this case and apply the analysis:

The opportunity to view. Glover testified that for two to three minutes he stood at the apartment door, within two feet of the respondent. The door opened twice, and each time the man stood at the door. The moments passed, the conversation took place, and payment was made. Glover looked directly at his vendor. It was near sunset, to be sure, but the sun had not yet set, so it was not dark or even dusk or twilight. Natural light from outside entered the hallway through a window. There was natural light, as well, from inside the apartment.

The degree of attention. Glover was not a casual or passing observer, as is so often the case with eyewitness identification. Trooper Glover was a trained police officer on duty—and specialized and dangerous duty—when he called at the third floor of 201 Westland in Hartford on May 5, 1970. Glover himself was a Negro and unlikely to perceive only general features of "hundreds of Hartford black males," as the Court of Appeals stated. It is true that Glover's duty was that of ferreting out narcotics offenders and that he would be expected in his work to produce results. But it is also true that, as a specially trained, assigned, and experienced officer, he could be expected to pay scrupulous attention to detail, for he knew that subsequently he would have to find and arrest his vendor. In addition, he knew that his claimed observations would be subject later to close scrutiny and examination at any trial.

The accuracy of the description. Glover's description was given to D'Onofrio within minutes after the transaction. It included the vendor's race, his height, his build, the color and style of his hair, and the high cheekbone facial feature. It also included clothing the vendor wore. No claim has been made that respondent did not possess the physical characteristics so described. D'Onofrio reacted positively at once. Two days later, when Glover was alone, he viewed the photograph D'Onofrio produced and identified its subject as the narcotics seller.

The witness' level of certainty. There is no dispute that the photograph in question was that of respondent. Glover, in response to a question whether the photograph was that of the person from whom he made the purchase, testified: "There is no question whatsoever." This positive assurance was repeated.

The time between the crime and the confrontation. Glover's description of his vendor was given to D'Onofrio within minutes of the crime. The photographic identification took place only two days later. We do not have here the passage of weeks or months between the crime and the viewing of the photograph.

These indicators of Glover's ability to make an accurate identification are hardly outweighed by the corrupting effect of the challenged identification itself. Although identifications arising from single-photograph displays may be viewed in general with suspicion, we find in the instant case little pressure on the witness to acquiesce in the suggestion that such a display entails. D'Onofrio had left the photograph at Glover's office and was not present when Glover first viewed it two days after the event. There thus was little urgency and Glover could view the photograph at his leisure. And since Glover examined the photograph alone, there was no coercive pressure to make an identification arising from the presence of another. The identification was made in circumstances allowing care and reflection.

Although it plays no part in our analysis, all this assurance as to the reliability of the identification is hardly undermined by the facts that respondent was arrested in the very apartment where the sale had taken place, and that he acknowledged his frequent visits to that apartment.

Surely, we cannot say that under all the circumstances of this case there is "a very substantial likelihood of irreparable misidentification." Short of that point, such evidence is for the jury to weigh. We are content to rely upon the good sense and judgment of American juries, for evidence with some element of untrustworthiness is customary grist for the jury mill. Juries are not so susceptible that they cannot measure intelligently the weight of identification testimony that has some questionable feature.

Of course, it would have been better had D'Onofrio presented Glover with a photographic array including "so far as practicable . . . a reasonable number of persons similar to any person then suspected whose likeness is included in the array." The use of that procedure would have enhanced the force of the identification at trial and would have avoided the risk that the evidence would be excluded as unreliable. But we are not disposed to view D'Onofrio's failure as one of constitutional dimension to be enforced by a rigorous and unbending exclusionary rule. The defect, if there be one, goes to weight and not to substance.

We conclude that the criteria laid down in *Biggers* are to be applied in determining the admissibility of evidence offered by the prosecution concerning a post-*Stovall* identification, and that those criteria are satisfactorily met and complied with here.

The judgment of the Court of Appeals is reversed.

Justice MARSHALL, with whom Justice BRENNAN joins, dissenting.

Today's decision can come as no surprise to those who have been watching the Court dismantle the protections against mistaken eyewitness testimony erected a decade ago in *United States v. Wade; Gilbert v. California;* and *Stovall v. Denno*. But it is still distressing to see the Court virtually ignore the teaching of experience embodied in those decisions and blindly uphold the conviction of a defendant who may well be innocent.

The magnitude of the Court's error can be seen by analyzing the cases in the *Wade* trilogy and the decisions following it. The foundation of the *Wade* trilogy was the Court's recognition of the "high incidence of miscarriage of justice" resulting from the admission of mistaken eyewitness identification evidence at criminal trials. *United States v. Wade.* Relying on numerous studies made over many years by such scholars as Professor Wigmore and Mr. Justice Frankfurter, the Court concluded that "[t]he vagaries of eyewitness identification are well-known; the annals of criminal law are rife with instances of mistaken identification." It is, of course, impossible to control one source of such errors—the faulty perceptions and unreliable memories of witnesses—except through vigorously contested trials conducted by diligent counsel and judges. The Court in the *Wade* cases acted, however, to minimize the more preventable threat posed to accurate identification by "the degree of suggestion inherent in the manner in which the prosecution presents the suspect to witnesses for pretrial identification."

The Court did so in *Wade* and *Gilbert v. California* by prohibiting the admission at trial of evidence of pretrial confrontations at which an accused was not represented by counsel. Further protection was afforded by holding that an in-court identification following an uncounseled lineup was allowable only if the prosecution could clearly and convincingly demonstrate that it was not tainted by the constitutional violation. Only in this way, the Court held, could confrontations fraught with the danger of misidentification be made fairer, and could Sixth Amendment rights to assistance of counsel and confrontation of witnesses at trial be effectively preserved. The crux of the *Wade* decisions, however, was the unusual threat to the truth-seeking process posed by the frequent untrustworthiness of eyewitness identification testimony. This, combined with the fact that juries unfortunately are often unduly receptive to such evidence, is the fundamental fact of judicial experience ignored by the Court today.

Stovall v. Denno, while holding that the *Wade* prophylactic rules were not retroactive, was decided at the same time and reflects the same concerns about the reliability of identification testimony. *Stovall* recognized that, regardless of Sixth Amendment principles, "the conduct of a confrontation" may be "so unnecessarily suggestive and conducive to irreparable mistaken identification" as to deny due process of law. The pretrial confrontation in *Stovall* was plainly suggestive, and evidence of it was introduced at trial along with the witness' in-court identification. The Court ruled that there had been no violation of due process, however, because the unusual necessity for the procedure outweighed the danger of suggestion.

Stovall thus established a due process right of criminal suspects to be free from confrontations that, under all the circumstances, are unnecessarily suggestive. The right was enforceable by exclusion at trial of evidence of the constitutionally invalid identification. Comparison with *Wade* and *Gilbert* confirms this interpretation. Where their Sixth Amendment holding did not apply, *Stovall* found an analogous Fourteenth Amendment right to a lineup conducted in a fundamentally fair manner. This interpretation is reinforced by the Court's statement that "a claimed violation of due process of law in the conduct of a confrontation depends on the totality of the circumstances surrounding it." Significantly, several years later, *Stovall* was viewed in precisely the same way, even as the Court limited *Wade* and *Gilbert* to post-indictment confrontations: "The Due Process Clause . . . forbids a lineup that is unnecessarily suggestive and conducive to irreparable mistaken identification."

The development of due process protections against mistaken identification evidence, begun in *Stovall*, was continued in *Simmons v. United States*. There, the Court developed a different rule to deal with the admission of in-court identification testimony that the accused claimed had been fatally tainted by a previous suggestive confrontation. In *Simmons*, the exclusionary effect of *Stovall* had already been accomplished, since the prosecution made no use of the suggestive confrontation. *Simmons*, therefore, did not deal with the constitutionality of the pretrial identification procedure. The only question was the impact of the Due Process Clause on an in-court identification that was not itself unnecessarily suggestive. *Simmons* held that due process was violated by the later identification if the pretrial procedure had been "so impermissibly suggestive as to give rise to a very substantial likelihood of irreparable misidentification." This test focused, not on the necessity for the challenged pretrial procedure, but on the degree of suggestiveness that it entailed. In applying this test, the Court understandably considered the circumstances surrounding the witnesses' initial opportunity to view the crime. Finding that any suggestion in the pretrial confrontation had not affected the fairness of the in-court identification, *Simmons* rejected petitioner's due process attack on his conviction.

Again, comparison with the *Wade* cases is instructive. The inquiry mandated by *Simmons* is similar to the independent-source test used in *Wade* where an in-court identification is sought following an uncounseled lineup. In both cases, the issue is whether the witness is identifying the defendant solely on the basis of his memory of events at the time of the crime, or whether he is merely remembering the person he picked out in a pretrial procedure. Accordingly, in both situations, the relevant inquiry includes factors bearing on the accuracy of the witness' identification, including his opportunity to view the crime.

Thus, *Stovall* and *Simmons* established two different due process tests for two very different situations. Where the prosecution sought to use evidence of a questionable pretrial identification, *Stovall* required its exclusion, because due process had been violated by the confrontation, unless the necessity for the unduly suggestive procedure outweighed its potential for generating an irreparably mistaken identification. The *Simmons* test, on the other hand, was directed to ascertaining due process violations in the introduction of in-court identification testimony that the defendant claimed was tainted by pretrial procedures. In the latter situation, a court could consider the reliability of the identification under all the circumstances.

■ ■ ■

The Court inexplicably seemed to erase the distinction between *Stovall* and *Simmons* situations in *Neil v. Biggers*. In *Biggers* there was a pretrial confrontation that was clearly both suggestive and unnecessary. Evidence of this, together with an in-court identification, was admitted at trial. *Biggers* was, in short, a case plainly cast in the *Stovall* mold. Yet the Court, without explanation or apparent recognition of the distinction, applied the *Simmons* test. The Court stated: "[T]he primary evil to be avoided is 'a very substantial likelihood of irreparable misidentification.' *Simmons v. United States*. It is the likelihood of misidentification which violates a defendant's right to due process...." While this statement accurately describes the lesson of *Simmons*, it plainly ignores the teaching of *Stovall* and *Foster* that an unnecessarily suggestive pretrial confrontation itself violates due process.

■ ■ ■

Apparently, the Court does not consider *Biggers* controlling in this case. I entirely agree, since I believe that *Biggers* was wrongly decided. The Court, however, concludes that *Biggers* is distinguishable because it, like the identification decisions that preceded it, involved a pre-*Stovall* confrontation, and because a paragraph in *Biggers* itself seems to distinguish between pre- and post-*Stovall* confrontations. Accordingly, in determining the admissibility of the post-*Stovall* identification in this case, the Court considers two alternatives, a per se exclusionary rule and a totality-of-the circumstances approach. The Court weighs three factors in deciding that the totality approach, which is essentially the test used in *Biggers*, should be applied. In my view, the Court wrongly evaluates the impact of these factors.

First, the Court acknowledges that one of the factors, deterrence of police use of unnecessarily suggestive identification procedures, favors the per se rule. Indeed, it does so heavily, for such a rule would make it unquestionably clear to the police they must never use a suggestive procedure when a fairer alternative is available. I have no doubt that conduct would quickly conform to the rule.

Second, the Court gives passing consideration to the dangers of eyewitness identification recognized in the *Wade* trilogy. It concludes, however, that the grave risk of error does not justify adoption of the per se approach because that would too often result in exclusion of relevant evidence. In my view, this conclusion totally ignores the lessons of *Wade*. The dangers of mistaken identification are, as *Stovall* held, simply too great to permit unnecessarily suggestive identifications. Neither *Biggers* nor the Court's opinion today points to any contrary empirical evidence. Studies since *Wade* have only reinforced the validity of its assessment of the dangers of identification testimony. While the Court is "content to rely on the good sense and judgment of American juries," the impetus for *Stovall* and *Wade* was repeated miscarriages of justice resulting from juries' willingness to credit inaccurate eyewitness testimony.

Finally, the Court errs in its assessment of the relative impact of the two approaches on the administration of justice. The Court relies most heavily on this factor, finding that "reversal is a Draconian sanction" in cases where the identification is reliable despite an unnecessarily suggestive procedure used to obtain it. Relying on little more than a strong distaste for "inflexible rules of exclusion," the Court rejects the per se test. In so doing, the Court disregards two significant distinctions between the per se rule advocated in this case and the exclusionary remedies for certain other constitutional violations.

First, the per se rule here is not "inflexible." Where evidence is suppressed, for example, as the fruit of an unlawful search, it may well be forever lost to the prosecution. Identification evidence, however, can by its very nature be readily and effectively reproduced. The in-court identification, permitted under *Wade* and *Simmons* if it has a source independent of an uncounseled or suggestive procedure, is one example. Similarly, when a prosecuting attorney learns that there has been a suggestive confrontation, he can easily arrange another lineup conducted under scrupulously fair conditions. Since the same factors are evaluated in applying both the Court's totality test and the *Wade-Simmons* independent-source inquiry, any identification which is "reliable" under the Court's test will support admission of evidence concerning such a fairly conducted lineup. The evidence of an additional, properly conducted confrontation will be more persuasive to a jury, thereby increasing the chance of a justified conviction where a reliable identification was tainted by a suggestive confrontation. At the same time, however, the effect of an unnecessarily suggestive identification which has no value whatsoever in the law enforcement process will be completely eliminated.

Second, other exclusionary rules have been criticized for preventing jury consideration of relevant and usually reliable evidence in order to serve interests unrelated to guilt or innocence, such as discouraging illegal searches or denial of counsel. Suggestively obtained eyewitness testimony is excluded, in contrast, precisely because of its unreliability and concomitant irrelevance. Its exclusion both protects the integrity of the truth-seeking function of the trial and discourages police use of needlessly inaccurate and ineffective investigatory methods. . . .

For these reasons, I conclude that adoption of the per se rule would enhance, rather than detract from, the effective administration of justice. In my view, the Court's totality test will allow seriously unreliable and misleading evidence to be put before juries. Equally important, it will allow dangerous criminals to remain on the streets while citizens assume that police action has given them protection. According to my calculus, all three of the factors upon which the Court relies point to acceptance of the per se approach.

Even more disturbing than the Court's reliance on the totality test, however, is the analysis it uses, which suggests a reinterpretation of the concept of due process of law in criminal cases. The decision suggests that due process violations in identification procedures may not be measured by whether the government employed procedures violating standards of fundamental fairness. By relying on the probable accuracy of a challenged identification, instead of the necessity for its use, the Court seems to be ascertaining whether the defendant was probably guilty. Until today, I had thought that "Equal justice under law" meant that the existence of constitutional violations did not depend on the race, sex, religion, nationality, or likely guilt of the accused. The Due Process Clause requires adherence to the same high standard of fundamental fairness in dealing with every criminal defendant, whatever his personal characteristics and irrespective of the strength of the State's case against him. Strong evidence that the defendant is guilty should be relevant only to the determination whether an error of constitutional magnitude was nevertheless harmless beyond a reasonable doubt. By importing the question of guilt into the initial determination of whether there was a constitutional violation, the apparent effect of the Court's decision is to undermine the protection afforded by the Due Process Clause. "It is therefore important to note that the state courts remain free, in interpreting state constitutions, to guard against the evil clearly identified by this case."

■ ■ ■

The use of a single picture (or the display of a single live suspect, for that matter) is a grave error, of course, because it dramatically suggests to the witness that the person shown must be the culprit. Why else would the police choose the person? And it is deeply ingrained in human nature to agree with the expressed opinions of others—particularly others who should be more knowledgeable—when making a difficult decision. In this case, moreover, the pressure was not limited to that inherent in the display of a single photograph. Glover, the identifying witness, was a state police officer on special assignment. He knew that D'Onofrio, an experienced Hartford narcotics detective, presumably familiar with local drug operations, believed respondent to be the seller. There was at work, then, both loyalty to another police officer and deference to a better-informed colleague. Finally, of course, there was Glover's knowledge that without an identification and arrest, government funds used to buy heroin had been wasted.

The Court discounts this overwhelming evidence of suggestiveness, however. It reasons that because D'Onofrio was not present when Glover viewed the photograph, there was "little pressure on the witness to acquiesce in the suggestion." That conclusion blinks psychological reality. There is no doubt in my mind that even in D'Onofrio's absence, a clear and powerful message was telegraphed to Glover as he looked at respondent's photograph. He was emphatically told that "this is the man," and he responded by identifying respondent then and at trial "whether or not he was in fact 'the man.'"

I must conclude that this record presents compelling evidence that there was "a very substantial likelihood of misidentification" of respondent Brathwaite. The suggestive display of respondent's photograph to the witness Glover likely erased any independent memory that Glover had retained of the seller from his barely adequate opportunity to observe the criminal.

Perry v. New Hampshire

132 S. Ct. 716 (2012)

Ginsburg, J. delivered the opinion of the Court, in which Roberts, C.J., and Scalia, Kennedy, Thomas, Breyer, Alito, and Kagan, JJ., joined. Thomas, J., filed a concurring opinion. Sotomayor, J., filed a dissenting opinion.

In our system of justice, fair trial for persons charged with criminal offenses is secured by the Sixth Amendment, which guarantees to defendants the right to counsel, compulsory process to obtain defense witnesses, and the opportunity to cross-examine witnesses for the prosecution. Those safeguards apart, admission of evidence in state trials is ordinarily governed by state law, and the reliability of relevant testimony typically falls within the province of the jury to determine. This Court has recognized, in addition, a due process check on the admission of eyewitness identification, applicable when the police have arranged suggestive circumstances leading the witness to identify a particular person as the perpetrator of a crime.

■ ■ ■

We have not extended pretrial screening for reliability to cases in which the suggestive circumstances were not arranged by law enforcement officers. Petitioner requests that we do so because of the grave risk that mistaken identification will yield a miscarriage of justice. Our decisions, however, turn on the presence of state action and aim to deter police from rigging identification procedures, for example, at a lineup, showup, or photograph array. When no improper law enforcement activity is involved, we hold, it suffices to test reliability through the rights and opportunities generally designed for that purpose, notably, the presence of counsel at postindictment lineups, vigorous cross-examination, protective rules of evidence, and jury instructions on both the fallibility of eyewitness identification and the requirement that guilt be proved beyond a reasonable doubt.

I

A

Around 3 a.m. on August 15, 2008, Joffre Ullon called the Nashua, New Hampshire, Police Department and reported that an African-American male was trying to break into cars parked in the lot of Ullon's apartment building. Officer Nicole Clay responded to the call. Upon arriving at the parking lot, Clay heard what "sounded like a metal bat hitting the ground." She then saw petitioner Barion Perry standing between two cars. Perry walked toward Clay, holding two car-stereo amplifiers in his hands. A metal bat lay on the ground behind him. Clay asked Perry where the amplifiers came from. "[I] found them on the ground," Perry responded.

Meanwhile, Ullon's wife, Nubia Blandon, woke her neighbor, Alex Clavijo, and told him she had just seen someone break into his car. Clavijo immediately went downstairs to the parking lot to inspect the car. He first observed that one of the rear windows had been shattered. On further inspection, he discovered that the speakers and amplifiers from his car stereo were missing, as were his bat and wrench. Clavijo then approached Clay and told her about Blandon's alert and his own subsequent observations.

By this time, another officer had arrived at the scene. Clay asked Perry to stay in the parking lot with that officer, while she and Clavijo went to talk to Blandon. Clay and Clavijo then entered the apartment building and took the stairs to the fourth floor, where Blandon's and Clavijo's apartments were located. They met Blandon in the hallway just outside the open door to her apartment.

Asked to describe what she had seen, Blandon stated that, around 2:30 a.m., she saw from her kitchen window a tall, African-American man roaming the parking lot and looking into cars. Eventually, the man circled Clavijo's car, opened the trunk, and removed a large box.

Clay asked Blandon for a more specific description of the man. Blandon pointed to her kitchen window and said the person she saw breaking into Clavijo's car was standing in the parking lot, next to the police officer. Perry's arrest followed this identification.

About a month later, the police showed Blandon a photographic array that included a picture of Perry and asked her to point out the man who had broken into Clavijo's car. Blandon was unable to identify Perry.

B

Perry was charged in New Hampshire state court with one count of theft by unauthorized taking and one count of criminal mischief. Before trial, he moved to suppress Blandon's identification on the ground that admitting it at trial would violate due process. Blandon witnessed what amounted to a one-person showup in the parking lot, Perry asserted, which all but guaranteed that she would identify him as the culprit.

The New Hampshire Superior Court denied the motion. To determine whether due process prohibits the introduction of an out-of-court identification at trial, the Superior Court said, this Court's decisions instruct a two-step inquiry. First, the trial court must decide whether the police used an unnecessarily suggestive identification procedure. If they did, the court must next consider whether the improper identification procedure so tainted the resulting identification as to render it unreliable and therefore inadmissible. (citing *Neil v. Biggers* (1972) and *Manson v. Brathwaite* (1977)).

Perry's challenge, the Superior Court concluded, failed at step one: Blandon's identification of Perry on the night of the crime did not result from an unnecessarily suggestive procedure "manufacture[d] . . . by the police." . . .

At the ensuing trial, Blandon and Clay testified to Blandon's out-of-court identification. The jury found Perry guilty of theft and not guilty of criminal mischief.

On appeal, Perry repeated his challenge to the admissibility of Blandon's out-of-court identification. The trial court erred, Perry contended, in requiring an initial showing that the police arranged the suggestive identification procedure. Suggestive circumstances alone, Perry argued, suffice to trigger the reliability of the resulting identification before allowing presentation of the evidence to the jury.

The New Hampshire Supreme Court rejected Perry's argument and affirmed his conviction. Only where the police employ suggestive identification techniques, that court held, does the Due Process Clause require a trial court to assess the reliability of identification evidence before permitting a just to consider it.

We granted certiorari to resolve a division of opinion on the question whether the Due Process Clause requires a trial judge to conduct a preliminary assessment of the reliability of an eyewitness identification made under suggestive circumstances not arranged by the police.

II

A

The Constitution, our decisions indicate, protects a defendant against a conviction based on evidence of questionable reliability, not by prohibiting introduction of the evidence, but by affording the defendant means to persuade the jury that the evidence should be discounted as unworthy of credit. Constitutional safeguards available to defendants to counter the State's evidence include the Sixth Amendment rights to counsel, *Gideon v. Wainwright* (1963); compulsory process, *Taylor v. Illinois* (1988); and confrontation plus cross-examination of witnesses, *Delaware v. Fensterer* (1985) (*per curiam*). Apart from these guarantees, we have recognized, state and federal statutes and rules ordinarily govern the admissibility of evidence, and juries are assigned the task of determining the reliability of the evidence presented at trial. See *Kansas v. Ventris* (2009) ("Our legal system . . . is built on the premise that it is the province of the jury to weigh the credibility of competing witnesses."). Only when evidence "is so extremely unfair that its admission violates fundamental conceptions of justice," *Dowling v. United States* (1990), have we imposed a constraint tied to the Due Process Clause. See, *e.g.*, *Napue v. Illinois* (1959) (Due process prohibits the State's "knowin[g] use [of] false evidence," because such use violates "any concept of ordered liberty.").

Contending that the Due Process Clause is implicated here, Perry relies on a series of decisions involving police-arranged identification procedures. In *Stovall v. Denno* (1967), first of those decisions, a witness identified the defendant as her assailant after police officers brought the defendant to the witness' hospital room. At the time the witness made the identification, the defendant—the only African-American in the room—was handcuffed and surrounded by police officers. Although the police-arranged showup was undeniably suggestive, the Court held that no due process violation occurred. Crucial to the Court's decision was the procedure's necessity: The witness was the only person who could identify or exonerate the defendant; the witness could not leave her hospital room; and it was uncertain whether she would live to identify the defendant in more neutral circumstances.

A year later, in *Simmons v. United States* (1968), the Court addressed a due process challenge to police use of a photographic array. When a witness identifies the defendant in a police-organized photo lineup, the Court ruled, the identification should be suppressed only where "the photographic identification procedure was so [unnecessarily] suggestive as to give rise to a very substantial likelihood of irreparable misidentification." Satisfied that the photo array used by Federal Bureau of Investigation agents in Simmons was both necessary and unlikely to have led to a mistaken identification, the Court rejected the defendant's due process challenge to admission of the identification. In contrast, the Court held in *Foster v. California* (1969) that due process required the exclusion of an eyewitness identification obtained through police-arranged procedures that "made it all but inevitable that [the witness] would identify [the defendant]."

Synthesizing previous decisions, we set forth in *Neil v. Biggers*, and reiterated in *Manson v. Brathwaite*, the approach appropriately used to determine whether the Due Process Clause requires suppression of an eyewitness identification tainted by police arrangement. The Court emphasized, first, that due process concerns arise only when law enforcement officers use an identification procedure that is both suggestive and unnecessary. Even when the police use such a procedure, the Court next said, suppression of the resulting identification is not the inevitable consequence.

A rule requiring automatic exclusion, the Court reasoned, would "g[o] too far," for it would "kee[p] evidence from the jury that is reliable and relevant," and "may result, on occasion, in the guilty going free." *Brathwaite* (when an "identification is reliable despite an unnecessarily suggestive [police] identification procedure," automatic exclusion "is a Draconian sanction," one "that may frustrate rather than promote justice").

Instead of mandating a *per se* exclusionary rule, the Court held that the Due Process Clause requires courts to assess, on a case-by-case basis, whether improper police conduct created a "substantial likelihood of misidentification." "[R]eliability [of the eyewitness identification] is the linchpin" of that evaluation, the Court stated in *Brathwaite*. Where the "indicators of [a witness'] ability to make an accurate identification" are "outweighed by the corrupting effect" of law enforcement suggestion, the identification should be suppressed. Otherwise, the evidence (if admissible in all other respects) should be submitted to the jury.

Applying this "totality of the circumstances" approach, the Court held in *Biggers* that law enforcement's use of an unnecessarily suggestive showup did not require suppression of the victim's identification of her assailant. Notwithstanding the improper procedure, the victim's identification was reliable: She saw her assailant for a considerable period of time under adequate light, provided police with a detailed description of her attacker long before the showup, and had "no doubt" that the defendant was the person she had seen. Similarly, the Court concluded in *Brathwaite* that police use of an unnecessarily suggestive photo array did not require exclusion of the resulting identification. The witness, an undercover police officer, viewed the defendant in good light for several minutes, provided a thorough description of the suspect, and was certain of his identification. Hence, the "indicators of [the witness'] ability to make an accurate identification [were] hardly outweighed by the corrupting effect of the challenged identification."

B

Perry concedes that, in contrast to every case in the *Stovall* line, law enforcement officials did not arrange the suggestive circumstances surrounding Blandon's identification. He contends, however, that it was mere happenstance that each of the *Stovall* cases involved improper police action. The rationale underlying our decisions, Perry asserts, supports a rule requiring trial judges to prescreen eyewitness evidence for reliability any time an identification is made under suggestive circumstances. We disagree.

Perry's argument depends, in large part, on the Court's statement in *Brathwaite* that "reliability is the linchpin in determining the admissibility of identification testimony." If reliability is the linchpin of admissibility under the Due Process Clause, Perry maintains, it should make no difference whether law enforcement was responsible for creating the suggestive circumstances that marred the identification.

Perry has removed our statement in *Brathwaite* from its mooring, and thereby attributes to the statement a meaning a fair reading of our opinion does not bear. As just explained, the *Brathwaite* Court's reference to reliability appears in a portion of the opinion concerning the appropriate remedy *when the police use an unnecessarily suggestive identification procedure*. The Court adopted a judicial screen for reliability as a course preferable to a *per se* rule requiring exclusion of identification evidence whenever law enforcement officers employ an improper procedure. The due process check for reliability, *Brathwaite* made plain, comes into play only after the defendant establishes improper police conduct. The very purpose of the check, the Court noted, was to avoid depriving the jury of identification evidence that is reliable, *notwithstanding* improper police conduct.

Perry's contention that improper police action was not essential to the reliability check *Brathwaite* required is echoed by the dissent. Both ignore a key premise of the *Brathwaite* decision: A primary aim of excluding identification evidence obtained under unnecessarily suggestive circumstances, the Court said, is to deter law enforcement use of improper lineups, showups, and photo arrays in the first place. . . .

Coleman v. Alabama (1970), another decision in the *Stovall* line, similarly shows that the Court has linked the due process check, not to suspicion of eyewitness testimony generally, but only to improper police arrangement of the circumstances surrounding an identification. The defendants in *Coleman* contended that a witness' in-court identifications violated due process, because a pretrial stationhouse lineup was "so unduly prejudicial and conducive to irreparable misidentification as fatally to taint [the later identifications]." The Court rejected this argument. No due process violation occurred, the plurality explained, because nothing "the police said or did prompted [the witness'] virtually spontaneous identification of [the defendants]." True, Coleman was the only person in the lineup wearing a hat, the plurality noted, but "nothing in the record show[ed] that he was required to do so." See also *Colorado v. Connelly* (1986) (Where the "crucial element of police overreaching" is missing, the admissibility of an allegedly unreliable confession is "a matter to be governed by the evidentiary laws of the forum, . . . and not by the Due Process Clause.").

■ ■ ■

C

In urging a broadly applicable due process check on eyewitness identifications, Perry maintains that eyewitness identifications are a uniquely unreliable form of evidence. We do not doubt either the importance or the fallibility of eyewitness identifications. Indeed, in recognizing that defendants have a constitutional right to counsel at postindictment police lineups, we observed that "the annals of criminal law are rife with instances of mistaken identification." [*United States v.*] *Wade* [(1967)].

We have concluded in other contexts, however, that the potential unreliability of a type of evidence does not alone render its introduction at the defendant's trial fundamentally unfair. *Ventris* (declining to "craft a broa[d] exclusionary rule for uncorroborated statements obtained [from jailhouse snitches]," even though "rewarded informant testimony" may be inherently untrustworthy); . . . We reach a similar conclusion here:

The fallibility of eyewitness evidence does not, without the taint of improper state conduct, warrant a due process rule requiring a trial court to screen such evidence for reliability before allowing the jury to assess its creditworthiness.

Our unwillingness to enlarge the domain of due process as Perry and the dissent urge rests, in large part, on our recognition that the jury, not the judge, traditionally determines the reliability of evidence. We also take account of other safeguards built into our adversary system that caution juries against placing undue weight on eyewitness testimony of questionable reliability. These protections include the defendant's Sixth Amendment right to confront the eyewitness.... Another is the defendant's right to the effective assistance of an attorney, who can expose the flaws in the eyewitness' testimony during cross-examination and focus the jury's attention on the fallibility of such testimony during opening and closing arguments. Eyewitness-specific jury instructions, which many federal and state courts have adopted, likewise warn the jury to take care in appraising identification evidence. See ... *Ventris* (citing jury instructions that informed jurors about the unreliability of uncorroborated jailhouse-informant testimony as a reason to resist a ban on such testimony)....

State and federal rules of evidence, moreover, permit trial judges to exclude relevant evidence if its probative value is substantially outweighed by its prejudicial impact or potential for misleading the jury....

Many of the safeguards just noted were at work at Perry's trial. During her opening statement, Perry's court-appointed attorney cautioned the jury about the vulnerability of Blandon's identification.... While cross-examining Blandon and Officer Clay, Perry's attorney constantly brought up the weaknesses of Blandon's identification....

After closing arguments, the trial court read the jury a lengthy instruction on identification testimony and the factors the jury should consider when evaluating it. The court also instructed the jury that the defendant's guilt must be proved beyond a reasonable doubt, and specifically cautioned that "one of the things the State must prove [beyond a reasonable doubt] is the identification of the defendant as the person who committed the offense."

Given the safeguards generally applicable in criminal trials, protections availed of by the defense in Perry's case, we hold that the introduction of Blandon's eyewitness testimony, without a preliminary judicial assessment of its reliability, did not render Perry's trial fundamentally unfair.

For the foregoing reasons, we agree with the New Hampshire courts' appraisal of our decisions. See supra, at 4-5. Finding no convincing reason to alter our precedent, we hold that the Due Process Clause does not require a preliminary judicial inquiry into the reliability of an eyewitness identification when the identification was not procured under unnecessarily suggestive circumstances arranged by law enforcement. Accordingly, the judgment of the New Hampshire Supreme court is

Affirmed.

Justice THOMAS, concurring.

The Court correctly concludes that its precedents establish a due process right to the pretrial exclusion of an unreliable eyewitness identification only if the identification results from police suggestion. I therefore join its opinion. I write separately because I would not extend *Stovall v. Denno* and its progeny even if the reasoning of those opinions applied to this case. The *Stovall* line of cases is premised on a "substantive due process" right to "fundamental fairness." . . . In my view, those cases are wrongly decided because the Fourteenth Amendment's Due Process Clause is not a "secret repository of substantive guarantees against 'unfairness'" . . . . Accordingly, I would limit the Court's suggestive eyewitness identification cases to the precise circumstances that they involved.

Justice SOTOMAYOR, dissenting.

■ ■ ■

I

The "driving force" behind *United States v. Wade, Gilbert v. California* (1967), and *Stovall v. Denno* was "the Court's concern with the problems of eyewitness identification"—specifically, "the concern that the jury not hear eyewitness testimony unless that evidence has aspects of reliability." *Manson v. Brathwaite.* We have pointed to the "'formidable'" number of "miscarriage[s] of justice from mistaken identification" in the annals of criminal law. We have warned of the "vagaries" and "'proverbially untrustworthy'" nature of eyewitness identifications. And we have singled out a "major factor contributing" to that proverbial unreliability: "the suggestibility inherent in the context of the pretrial identification."

Our precedents make no distinction between intentional and unintentional suggestion. To the contrary, they explicitly state that "[s]uggestion can be created intentionally or unintentionally in many subtle ways." Rather than equate suggestive conduct with misconduct, we specifically have disavowed the assumption that suggestive influences may only be "the result of police procedures intentionally designed to prejudice an accused." [*Wade*] (describing lack of lineup regulations addressing "risks of abuse and unintentional suggestion"). "Persons who conduct the identification procedure may suggest, intentionally or unintentionally, that they expect the witness to identify the accused." *Moore v. Illinois* (1977). The implication is that even police acting with the best of intentions can inadvertently signal "'that's the man.'" *Wade*; see also *Kirby v. Illinois* (1972) ("[I]t is always necessary to 'scrutinize any pretrial confrontation . . .'").

In *Wade* itself, we noted that the "potential for improper influence [in pretrial confrontations] is illustrated by the circumstances . . . [i]n the present case." We then highlighted not the lineup procedure, but rather a preprocedure encounter: The two witnesses who later identified Wade in the lineup had seen Wade outside while "await[ing] assembly of the lineup." Wade had been standing in the hallway, which happened to be "observable to the witnesses through an open door." One witness saw Wade "within sight of an FBI agent"; the other saw him "in the custody of the agent." In underscoring the hazards of these circumstances, we made no mention of whether the encounter had been arranged; indeed, the facts suggest that it was not.

More generally, our precedents focus not on the act of suggestion, but on suggestion's "corrupting effect" on reliability. *Brathwaite*. Eyewitness evidence derived from suggestive circumstances, we have explained, is uniquely resistant to the ordinary tests of the adversary process. An eyewitness who has made an identification often becomes convinced of its accuracy. *"Regardless of how the initial misidentification comes about,* the witness thereafter is apt to retain in his memory the image of the photograph rather than of the person actually seen, reducing the trustworthiness of subsequent . . . courtroom identification." *Simmons v. United States* (emphasis added); see also *Wade* (witness is "not likely" to recant). Suggestion bolsters that confidence.

At trial, an eyewitness' artificially inflated confidence in an identification's accuracy complicates the jury's task of assessing witness credibility and reliability. It also impairs the defendant's ability to attack the eyewitness' credibility. *Stovall*. That in turn jeopardizes the defendant's basic right to subject his accuser to meaningful cross-examination. ("[C]ross-examination . . . cannot be viewed as an absolute assurance of accuracy and reliability . . . where so many variables and pitfalls exist"). The end result of suggestion, whether intentional or unintentional, is to fortify testimony bearing directly on guilt that juries find extremely convincing and are hesitant to discredit. ("[A]t pretrial proceedings . . . the results might well settle the accused's fate and reduce the trial itself to a mere formality"); *Gilbert* ("[T]he witness' testimony of his lineup identification will enhance the impact of his in-court identification on the jury").

Consistent with our focus on reliability, we have declined to adopt a *per se* rule excluding all suggestive identifications. Instead, "reliability is the linchpin" in deciding admissibility. *Brathwaite*. We have explained that a suggestive identification procedure "does not in itself intrude upon a constitutionally protected interest." [S]ee . . . *Neil v. Biggers* (rejecting the proposition that "unnecessary suggestiveness alone requires the exclusion of evidence"). . . .

To protect that evidentiary interest, we have applied a two-step inquiry: First, the defendant has the burden of showing that the eyewitness identification was derived through "impermissibly suggestive" means. *Simmons*. Second, if the defendant meets that burden, courts consider whether the identification was reliable under the totality of the circumstances. That step entails considering the witness' opportunity to view the perpetrator, degree of attention, accuracy of description, level of certainty, and the time between the crime and pretrial confrontation, then weighing such factors against the "corrupting effect of the suggestive identification." *Brathwaite*. Most identifications will be admissible. The standard of "fairness as required by the Due Process Clause," however, demands that a subset of the most unreliable identifications—those carrying a "'very substantial likelihood of . . . misidentification'"—will be excluded.

II

A

The majority today creates a novel and significant limitation on our long-standing rule: Eyewitness identifications so impermissibly suggestive that they pose a very substantial likelihood of an unreliable identification will be deemed inadmissible at trial only if the suggestive circumstances were "police-arranged." Absent "improper police arrangement," "improper police conduct," or "rigging," the majority holds, our two-step inquiry does not even "com[e] into play." I cannot agree.

The majority does not simply hold that an eyewitness identification must be the product of police action to trigger our ordinary two-step inquiry. Rather, the majority maintains that the suggestive circumstances giving rise to the identification must be "police-arranged," "police rigg[ed]," "police-designed," or "police-organized." Those terms connote a degree of intentional orchestration or manipulation. . . . The majority categorically exempts all eyewitness identifications derived from suggestive circumstances that were not police-manipulated—however suggestive, and however unreliable—from our due process check. The majority thus appears to graft a mens rea requirement onto our existing rule.

As this case illustrates, police intent is now paramount. As the Court acknowledges, Perry alleges an "accidental showup." He was the only African-American at the scene of the crime standing next to a police officer. For the majority, the fact that the police did not intend that showup, even if they inadvertently caused it in the course of a police procedure, ends the inquiry. The police were questioning the eyewitness, Blandon, about the perpetrator's identity, and were intentionally detaining Perry in the parking lot—but had not intended for Blandon to identify the perpetrator from her window. Presumably, in the majority's view, had the police asked Blandon to move to the window to identify the perpetrator, that could have made all the difference.

I note, however, that the majority leaves what is required by its arrangement-focused inquiry less than clear. In parts, the opinion suggests that the police must arrange an identification "procedure," regardless of whether they "inten[d] the arranged procedure to be suggestive." Elsewhere, it indicates that the police must arrange the "suggestive circumstances" that lead the witness to identify the accused. Still elsewhere it refers to "improper" police conduct, connoting bad faith. Does police "arrangement" relate to the procedure, the suggestiveness, or both? If it relates to the procedure, do suggestive preprocedure encounters no longer raise the same concerns? If the police need not "inten[d] the arranged procedure to be suggestive," what makes the police action "improper"? And does that mean that good-faith, unintentional police suggestiveness in a police-arranged lineup can be "impermissibly suggestive"? If no, the majority runs headlong into *Wade*. If yes, on what basis—if not deterrence—does it distinguish unintentional police suggestiveness in an accidental confrontation?

The arrangement-focused inquiry will sow needless confusion. If the police had called Perry and Blandon to the police station for interviews, and

Blandon saw Perry being questioned, would that be sufficiently "improper police arrangement"? If Perry had voluntarily come to the police station, would that change the result? Today's opinion renders the applicability of our ordinary inquiry contingent on a murky line-drawing exercise. Whereas our two-step inquiry focuses on overall reliability—and could account for the spontaneity of the witness' identification and degree of police manipulation under the totality of the circumstances—today's opinion forecloses that assessment by establishing a new and inflexible step zero.

B

The majority regards its limitation on our two-step rule as compelled by precedent. Its chief rationale, is that none of our prior cases involved situations where the police "did not arrange the suggestive circumstances." That is not necessarily true, given the seemingly unintentional encounter highlighted in Wade. But even if it were true, it is unsurprising. The vast majority of eyewitness identifications that the State uses in criminal prosecutions are obtained in lineup, showup, and photograph displays arranged by the police. Our precedents reflect that practical reality.

It is also beside the point. Our due process concerns were not predicated on the source of suggestiveness. Rather, "[i]t is the likelihood of misidentification which violates a defendant's right to due process," Biggers. . . . Accordingly, whether the police have created the suggestive circumstances intentionally or inadvertently, the resulting identification raises the same due process concerns. It is no more or less likely to misidentify the perpetrator. It is no more or less powerful to the jury. And the defendant is no more or less equipped to challenge the identification through cross-examination or prejudiced at trial. The arrangement-focused inquiry thus untethers our doctrine from the very "'evidentiary interest'" it was designed to protect, inviting arbitrary results.

Indeed, it is the majority's approach that lies in tension with our precedents. Whereas we previously disclaimed the crabbed view of suggestiveness as "the result of police procedures intentionally designed to prejudice an accused," Wade, the majority's focus on police rigging and improper conduct will revive it. Whereas our precedents were sensitive to intentional and unintentional suggestiveness alike, today's decision narrows our concern to intentionally orchestrated suggestive confrontations. We once described the "primary evil to be avoided" as the likelihood of misidentification. Biggers. Today's decision, however, means that even if that primary evil is at its apex, we need not avoid it at all so long as the suggestive circumstances do not stem from improper police arrangement.

C

The majority gives several additional reasons for why applying our due process rule beyond improperly police-arranged circumstances is unwarranted. In my view, none withstands close inspection.

First, the majority insists that our precedents "aim to deter police from rigging identification procedures," so our rule should be limited to applications that advance that "primary aim" and "key premise." That mischaracterizes our cases. We discussed deterrence in *Brathwaite* because Brathwaite challenged our two-step inquiry as lacking deterrence value. Brathwaite argued that deterrence demanded a *per se* rule excluding all suggestive identifications. He said that our rule, which probes the reliability of suggestive identifications under the totality of the circumstances, "cannot be expected to have a significant deterrent impact."

We rebutted Brathwaite's criticism in language the majority now wrenches from context: Upon summarizing Brathwaite's argument, we acknowledged "several interests to be considered." We then compared the two rules under each interest: First, we noted the "driving force" behind *Wade* and its companion cases—"the concern that the jury not hear eyewitness testimony unless that evidence has aspects of reliability"—and found both approaches "responsive to this concern," but the *per se* rule to go "too far" in suppressing reliable evidence. We noted a "second factor"—deterrence—conceding that the *per se* rule had "more significant deterrent effect," but noting that our rule "also has an influence on police behavior." Finally, we noted a "third factor"—"the effect on the administration of justice"—describing the *per se* rule as having serious drawbacks on this front. That was no list of "primary aim[s]." Nor was it a ringing endorsement of the primacy of deterrence. We simply underscored, in responding to Brathwaite, that our rule was not without deterrence benefits. To the contrary, we clarified that deterrence was a subsidiary concern to reliability, the "driving force" of our doctrine. It is a stretch to claim that our rule cannot apply wherever "[t]his deterrence rationale is inapposite."

Second, the majority states that *Coleman v. Alabama* held that "[n]o due process violation occurred . . . because nothing 'the police said or did prompted'" the identification and shows that our rule is linked "only to improper police arrangement." That misreads the decision. In *Coleman*, the petitioners challenged a witness' in-court identification of them at trial on grounds that it had been tainted by a suggestive pretrial lineup. We held that no due process violation occurred because the in-court identification appeared to be "entirely based upon observations at the time of the assault and not at all induced by the conduct of the lineup," and thus could not be said to stem from an identification procedure "'so impermissibly suggestive as to give rise to a very substantial likelihood of irreparable misidentification.'" We then dismissed each of the asserted suggestive influences as having had no bearing on the identification at all: The petitioners claimed that the police intimated to the witness that his attackers were in the lineup; we found the record "devoid of evidence that anything the police said or did" induced the identification. The petitioners claimed that they alone were made to say certain words; we found that the witness identified petitioners before either said anything. One petitioner claimed he was singled out to wear a hat; we found that the witness' identification "d[id] not appear . . . based on the fact that he remembered that [the attacker] had worn a hat." Thus, far from indicating that improper police conduct is a prerequisite, *Coleman* merely held that there had been no influence on the witness. In fact, in concluding that the lineup was not "'so impermissibly suggestive as to give rise to a very substantial likelihood of irreparable misidentification,'" *Coleman* indicates that the two-step inquiry is not truncated at the threshold by the absence of police misconduct.

Third, the majority emphasizes that we should rely on the jury to determine the reliability of evidence. But our cases are rooted in the assumption that eyewitness identifications upend the ordinary expectation that it is "the province of the jury to weigh the credibility of competing witnesses." *Kansas v. Ventris*. As noted, jurors find eyewitness evidence unusually powerful and their ability to assess credibility is hindered by a witness' false confidence in the accuracy of his or her identification. That disability in no way depends on the intent behind the suggestive circumstances.

■ ■ ■

Fourth, the majority suggests that applying our rule beyond police-arranged suggestive circumstances would entail a heavy practical burden, requiring courts to engage in "preliminary judicial inquiry" into "most, if not all, eyewitness identifications." But that is inaccurate. The burden of showing "impermissibly suggestive" circumstances is the defendant's, so the objection falls to the defendant to raise. And as is implicit in the majority's reassurance that Perry may resort to the rules of evidence in lieu of our due process precedents, trial courts will be entertaining defendants' objections, pretrial or at trial, to unreliable eyewitness evidence in any event. The relevant question, then, is what the standard of admissibility governing such objections should be. I see no reason to water down the standard for an equally suggestive and unreliable identification simply because the suggestive confrontation was unplanned.

■ ■ ■

Finally, the majority questions how to "rationally distinguish suggestiveness from other factors bearing on the reliability of eyewitness evidence," such as "poor vision" or a prior "grudge," and more broadly, how to distinguish eyewitness evidence from other kinds of arguably unreliable evidence. Our precedents, however, did just that. We emphasized the "'formidable number of instances in the records of English and American trials'" of "miscarriage[s] of justice from mistaken identification." *Wade*. We then observed that "'the influence of improper suggestion upon identifying witnesses probably accounts for more miscarriages of justice than any other single factor.'" Moreover, the majority points to no other type of evidence that shares the rare confluence of characteristics that makes eyewitness evidence a unique threat to the fairness of trial. Jailhouse informants, cf., unreliable as they may be, are not similarly resistant to the traditional tools of the adversarial process and, if anything, are met with particular skepticism by juries.

It would be one thing if the passage of time had cast doubt on the empirical premises of our precedents. But just the opposite has happened. A vast body of scientific literature has reinforced every concern our precedents articulated nearly a half-century ago, though it merits barely a parenthetical mention in the majority opinion. Over the past three decades, more than two thousand studies related to eyewitness identification have been published. One state supreme court recently appointed a special master to conduct an exhaustive survey of the current state of the scientific evidence and concluded that "[t]he research...is not only extensive," but "it represents the 'gold standard in terms of the applicability of social science research to law.'" *State v. Henderson*, 208 N.J. 208 (2011). "Experimental methods and findings have been tested and retested, subjected to scientific scrutiny through peer-reviewed journals, evaluated through the lens of meta-analyses, and replicated at times in real-world settings." *Ibid.*; see also Schmechel, O'Toole, Easterly, & Loftus, Beyond the Ken? Testing Jurors' Understanding of Eyewitness Reliability Evidence, 46 Jurimetrics 177, 180 (2006) (noting "nearly unanimous consensus among researchers about the [eyewitness reliability] field's core findings").

The empirical evidence demonstrates that eyewitness misidentification is "'the single greatest cause of wrongful convictions in this country.'" Researchers have found that a staggering 76% of the first 250 convictions overturned due to DNA evidence since 1989 involved eyewitness misidentification. Study after study demonstrates that eyewitness recollections are highly susceptible to distortion by postevent information or social cues; that jurors routinely overestimate the accuracy of eyewitness identifications; that jurors place the greatest weight on eyewitness confidence in assessing identifications even though confidence is a poor gauge of accuracy; and that suggestiveness can stem from sources beyond police-orchestrated procedures. The majority today nevertheless adopts an artificially narrow conception of the dangers of suggestive identifications at a time when our concerns should have deepened.

III

There are many reasons why Perry's particular situation might not violate due process. The trial court found that the circumstances surrounding Blandon's identification did not rise to an impermissibly suggestive level. It is not at all clear, moreover, that there was a very substantial likelihood of misidentification, given Blandon's lack of equivocation on the scene, the short time between crime and confrontation, and the "fairly well lit" parking lot. The New Hampshire Supreme Court, however, never made findings on either point and, under the majority's decision today, never will.

The Court's opinion today renders the defendant's due process protection contingent on whether the suggestive circumstances giving rise to the eyewitness identification stem from improper police arrangement. That view lies in tension with our precedents' more holistic conception of the dangers of suggestion and is untethered from the evidentiary interest the due process right protects. In my view, the ordinary two-step inquiry should apply, whether the police created the suggestive circumstances intentionally or inadvertently. Because the New Hampshire Supreme Court truncated its inquiry at the threshold, I would vacate the judgment and remand for a proper analysis. I respectfully dissent.